guide to
GOLF
courses

 **Lifestyle
Guides**

Produced by AA Publishing
Maps prepared by the Cartographic Department of
The Automobile Association
Maps © The Automobile Association 2000
Directory generated by the AA Establishment
Database, Information Research, AA Hotel Services
Design by Nautilus Design UK Ltd, Basingstoke,
Hampshire

The Automobile Association would like to thank
the following photographers and libraries for their
assistance in preparation of this book:

Front Cover: Allsport UK Ltd/Craig Jones
Back Cover (a): Allsport UK Ltd/Andrew Redington
Back Cover (b): Allsport UK Ltd/Harry How
Page 8: Lady golfers, New Forest GC & Sandown
GC,1913. Courtesy of Hampshire Rose Books

The remaining photographs are held in the
Association's own library (AA PHOTOLIBRARY) and
were taken by the following photographers;
AA PHOTOLIBRARY 7; ADRIAN BAKER 313; PETE
BENNET 9a; JIM CARNIE 3b; STEVE DAY 9b, 11;
MICHAEL DIGGIN 417; KEN PATERSON 5b;
MICHAEL SHORT 3a; RONNIE WEIR 2; HARRY
WILLIAMS 389

Advertisement Sales
Telephone Karen Weeks 01256 491545

Typeset/Repro by Avonset, 11 Kelso Place, Bath

Printed in Italy by Rotolito Lombarda SpA

The contents of this book are believed correct at
the time of printing. Nevertheless, the Publisher
cannot be held responsible for any errors or
omissions or for changes in the details given in this
guide or for the consequences of any reliance on
the information provided in the same. We have
tried to ensure accuracy in this guide but things do
change and we would be grateful if readers would
advise us of any inaccuracies they may encounter.

A CIP catalogue record for this book is available
from the British Library

Published by AA Publishing, which is a trading
name of Automobile Association Developments
Limited whose registered office is Norfolk House,
Priestley Road, Basingstoke,
Hampshire RG24 9NY

Registered number 1878835.

ISBN 0 7495 2526 6

How to Use the Guide

General Information

The AA Guide to Golf Courses aims to provide useful information about a large number of courses across Britain and Ireland. Entries include the contact details for each course, a brief description of the type of course and details of green fees, leisure, club or catering facilities. AA recommended accommodation follows the golf course entry.

Arranging to visit a golf course

The guide includes information on special requirements such as advance notice, handicap certificates or letters of introduction. It is always a good idea to check this with courses in advance as details in the directory, particularly green fees, may change during the currency of the guide.

Key to Symbols and Abbreviations

A number of symbols and abbreviations may appear under the **Facilities** heading for each entry as follows:

☎	Telephone number	⛳	Clubs for hire
IR£	Irish Punts (Republic only, the exchange rate between Punts and pounds sterling is liable to fluctuate)	🏌	Motorised cart/trolley for hire
		🚜	Buggies for hire
⊗	Lunch	🏌	Trolley for hire
⅏	Dinner	ℓ	Driving range
🍴	Bar snacks	★	AA star classification for hotels
☕	Tea/coffee	✿	AA Rosette Award (applicable to championship course entries)
☲	Bar open midday and evenings		
🛏	accommodation at club	◆	AA Guest house classification
⬡	Changing rooms	B	AA Branded group hotels
🏪	Well-stocked shop	TH	Town House hotel

Finding a golf course in the directory

The directory is arranged in countries. England, Northern Ireland and the Republic of Ireland list golf courses alphabetically by town within each county. Scotland and Wales list golf courses alphabetically by town within regions. The counties comprising these regions are listed below the region heading. The index at the back of the book lists golf course names.

AA Hotels with special arrangements for golf are listed at the back of the guide. Arrangements may include reduced green fees, preferential tee times or golfing packages.

Map References and Directions

The 16 page atlas at the back of the book has a black dot and town name marking the location of towns with golf courses listed in the guide. Map references are shown alongside the town headings throughout the guide. These include the map page number and National Grid reference. The grid references for the Republic of Ireland are unique to this atlas. Brief directions for each course appear under the heading **Location** in each entry. It is advisable to contact the course for full directions if you are unsure of the exact location.

Highlighted Courses

Green boxes in the guide highlight selected courses considered to be of particular merit or interest. These may include historic clubs, particularly testing or enjoyable courses or those in holiday areas popular with visiting golfers. The selection cannot be either exhaustive or totally objective and these courses do not represent any formal category on quality or other grounds. Major Championship Courses are shown with a full page entry which includes a selection of AA recommended restaurants as well as hotels.

Entries in Bold Italics

We make every effort to obtain current information from golf clubs however in some cases we have been unable to verify details with the club. In this case the course name is shown in bold italics and you are strongly advised to check any details with the club in advance of your visit.

Telephone Codes

The area telephone codes shown for the Republic of Ireland apply only within the Republic. The area telephone codes shown for Great Britain and Northern Ireland do not apply when dialling from

Accommodation

transferable if an establishment changes hands. The Hotel Guide and Bed & Breakfast Guide, published annually by the AA, give further details of AA recognised establishments and the classification schemes. A summary of the star classification for hotels is shown on page 6.

Quality Percentage Score and Red Star Hotels

The quality percentage score is an additional assessment made by AA hotel inspectors. This assessment of quality covers everything the hotel has to offer, including hospitality. The quality percentage score appears in red after the star

the Republic of Ireland. Check your telephone directory for details.

Golf course entries in the guide are followed by details of a nearby AA recognised hotel. In some cases the hotel will be in the grounds of the golf course. Most of the recommended hotels fall within the two, three and four star classifications. Where there is no nearby AA recognised hotel AA Guest accommodation is recommended with a diamond classification from 1 to five diamonds.

AA Classification and Inspection

The AA inspects and classifies hotels and guest accommodation under quality standards agreed between the AA, English Tourism Council and RAC. Hotels receive a star classification from one to five stars and Guest accommodation establishments receive between one and five diamonds. AA recognised establishments pay an annual fee, this varies according to the classification level and the number of bedrooms. The establishment receives an unannounced inspection visit from a qualified AA inspector who recommends the appropriate classification. Return visits are made to check that standards are maintained and the classification is not

classification in the guide and allows a comparison between hotels with the same number of stars. A three star hotel with a score of 79% therefore compares favourably with a three star hotel with a score of 65%. To gain AA recognition a hotel must score a minimum of 50%, while hotels scoring over 80% generally qualify for AA Red Star Awards. Red Star Awards are the highest accolade awarded by the AA to hotels and the stars are shown in red in the guide. No percentage score is shown for red star hotels.

Club Accommodation at golf courses

Where courses offer club accommodation the bed symbol appears under club facilities in the entry. This is listed as an option for readers wishing to stay at the course, however, unless the club accommodation has an AA star classification, the only AA recommended accommodation is the hotel or guest house which follows each entry.

AA Star Classification

Quality standards you can expect from an AA recognised hotel

All hotels recognised by the AA should have the highest standards of cleanliness, proper records of booking, give prompt and professional service to guests, assist with luggage on request, accept and deliver messages, provide a designated area for breakfast and dinner with drinks available in a bar or lounge, provide an early morning call on request, good quality furniture and fittings, adequate heating and lighting and proper maintenance. A guide to some of the general expectations for each star classification is as follows:

What you can expect from a one star hotel ★

Polite, courteous staff providing a relatively informal yet competent style of service, available during the day and evening to receive guests. At least one designated eating area open to residents for breakfast and dinner. Last orders for dinner no earlier than 6.30pm, a reasonable choice of hot and cold dishes and a short range of wines available. Television in lounge or bedroom. Majority of rooms en suite, bath or shower room available at all times.

What you can expect from a two star hotel ★ ★

Smartly and professionally presented management and staff providing competent, often informal service, available throughout the day and evening to greet guests. At least one restaurant or dining room open to residents for breakfast and dinner. Last orders for dinner no earlier than 7pm, a choice of substantial hot and cold dishes and a short range of wines available. Television in bedrooms. En suite or private bath or shower and WC.

What you can expect from a three star hotel ★ ★ ★

Management and staff smartly and professionally presented and usually uniformed. Technical and social skills of a good standard in responding to requests. A dedicated receptionist on duty, clear direction to rooms and some explanation of hotel facilities. At least one restaurant or dining room open to residents and non-residents for breakfast and dinner whenever the hotel is open. A wide selection of drinks served in a bar or lounge, available to residents and their guest throughout the day and evening. Last orders for dinner no earlier than 8pm, full dinner service provided. Remote control television, direct dial telephone. En suite bath or shower and WC.

What you can expect from a four star hotel ★ ★ ★ ★

A formal, professional staffing structure with smartly presented, uniformed staff, anticipating and responding to your needs or requests. Usually spacious, well appointed public areas. Bedrooms offering superior quality and comfort than at three star. A strong emphasis on food and beverages and a serious approach to cuisine. Reception staffed 24 hours per day by well-trained staff. Express checkout facilities where appropriate. Porterage available on request and readily provided by uniformed staff. Night porter available. Newspapers can be ordered and delivered to your room, additional services and concierge as appropriate to the style and location of the hotel. At least one restaurant open to residents and non-residents for all meals seven days per week. Drinks available to residents and their guests throughout the day and evening, table service available. Last orders for dinner no earlier than 9pm, an extensive choice of hot and cold dishes and comprehensive list of wines. Remote control television, direct dial telephone, a range of high quality toiletries. En suite bath with fixed overhead shower, WC.

What you can expect from a five star hotel ★ ★ ★ ★ ★

Flawless guest services, professional, attentive staff, technical and social skills of the highest order. Spacious and luxurious accommodation and public areas with a range of extra facilities. As a minimum, first-time guests shown to their bedroom. Multilingual service consistent with the needs of the hotel's normal clientele. Guest accounts well explained and presented. Porterage offered and provided by uniformed staff. Luggage handling on arrival and departure. Doorman or means of greeting guests at the hotel entrance, full concierge service. At least one restaurant open to residents and non-residents for all meals seven days per week. Staff showing knowledge of food and wine. A wide selection of drinks, including cocktails, available in a bar or lounge, table service provided. Last orders for dinner no earlier than 10pm. High quality menu and wine list properly reflecting and complementing the style of cooking and providing exceptional quality. Evening turn-down service. Remote control television, direct dial telephone at bedside and desk, a range of luxury toiletries, bath sheets and robes. En suite bath with fixed overhead shower, WC.

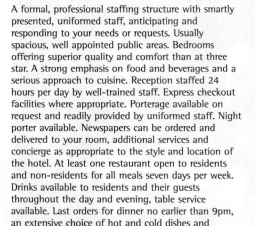

The Changing Scene
of Ladies Golf

By Elisabeth Borrow

Ladies' societies and groups are now a firmly established scene in the golfing world. They love the challenge of new venues and now have the independence, transport and financial ability to play far and wide.

Ladies were playing golf in organised groups well before 1900. The Ladies Golf Union and the Irish Ladies' Golf Union were both founded in 1893. The Scottish and Welsh Ladies' Golf Associations were both established in 1904. The LGU ran ladies golf in England until 1952, when England formed its own association. Today the LGU numbers 2,697 affiliated clubs, and approximately 237,500 ladies are members of their home country associations. The Womens' Professional Golf Association was formed in 1978. There are now 38 ladies holding the post of club professional, as well as a further 35 lady golf teachers and 22 trainees, and many more playing on the professional tour.

In the south of England, ladies on the Isle of Wight formed themselves into an association in 1897. There were at least twelve clubs on the Island before the turn of the century. Queen Victoria was in residence with her court at Osborne House and officers of the Royal Household Artillery were also stationed on the Island. The Needles golf course (now amalgamated with Freshwater Bay) listed 45 lady members in 1897 and Lord Tennyson was a patron. Osborne, a parkland 9-hole course with magnificent sea views, was laid out beside Queen Victoria's house and

boasts a washing pit for her Indian elephants. Shanklin & Sandown is an undulating 18-hole course with carries over heather and water and has a very demanding par 3 5th hole. Five other Island courses exist today.

At first shorter courses were built for ladies. It was thought that they could not possibly hit more than a short shot followed by a putt, and it was considered unseemly for ladies to lift a club above shoulder height! Despite the restrictions of dress that included long skirts to the ground, high starched collars, and wide brimmed hats tied on securely with muslin; lady golfers became more numerous and began to tackle the longer courses. Ladies inter County golf matches started in England in 1900. In 1902 the Kent County team hired a railway carriage saloon from Paddington to take them on a tour which took in Paignton in Devon, Penarth in Glamorganshire and Stroud in Gloucestershire. The same year Surrey were no less adventurous clocking up 23 county matches covering all corners of England.

Some of the early ladies' courses survive today. Sunningdale Ladies is a tremendous test of golf for anyone, with many par 3s. It also offers an open mixed foursomes competition (booked in advance) on the first Sunday in each month. Another of the very few independent ladies' clubs is Formby Ladies in Lancashire. This course is 18 holes and requires much course management and accuracy - and bunker play, should you fail the other tests.

Even 40 years ago ladies had to contend with more than just the hazards on the golf course. One lady remembers the thrill and honour of being invited to play in her first club match. As her husband used the one car they owned to drive to work, she set off for the golf club by boarding the local bus. The other passengers were quite bemused to see a heavily pregnant lady struggling up the aisle wrestling with a small assortment of golf clubs hanging out of a pencil bag.

In the 1980's a group of ladies from Corhampton set out by coach to play at Marlborough on the Wiltshire downs. On arrival they discovered a sprinkling of snow on the ground and mist encompassing them as they gazed out from the windows of the circular clubhouse. Undeterred they set off to play eighteen holes, followed by a very enjoyable lunch at which the Men's Captain appeared to find out where all the laughter was coming from. He was so amazed to see a society of lady golfers that he promptly put up a trophy to be played for annually between the two clubs' ladies sections.

A good opportunity to play competitive golf is afforded by joining Ladies' County Golf Associations. In Hampshire, Stoneham is extremely challenging, though not overlong, for ladies. The parkland course has holes undulating over ditches and ravines with heather to catch wayward shots and greens to envy. Blackmoor, Liphook and North Hants are more level with pine, silver birch and heather. The latter two host prestigious open ladies 36-hole scratch events.

There are many fine courses in the New Forest. Burley, among the heath and holly trees, is a 9-hole delight and the greens remain good despite the grazing horses and cattle. Bramshaw has two courses; The Forest, the oldest course in Hampshire, is criss-crossed by streams, and the fallen acorns are devoured by families of pigs in the autumn. The Manor is lusher and more manicured with cattle grids to keep out the ponies. At the entrance to Brokenhurst Manor be sure to look left and right to catch a glimpse of the herd of deer with the white stag. The par 3s are testing, mostly over ponds, streams or ravines, and the 184-yard uphill 10th hole with a two tier green is a challenge for any lady.

The Isle of Purbeck must, on a clear sunny day, be one of the most beautiful courses in England with sea views all round. A journey to Bournemouth entails a little trip across Poole Harbour on the chainlink car ferry which is great fun. Queens Park, Parkstone, Ferndown and Broadstone nearby are all much admired, and Knighton Heath has a lady professional. Many clubs have undergone major refits of their changing rooms over recent years. At Rowlands Castle the ladies rooms were refurbished using their own expertise in interior design. Another club with a fine suite of ladies' rooms is Goodwood in Sussex. The views overlooking Chichester and the sea beyond are breathtaking. The greens have many subtle slopes but the locals give a tip that the borrows 'come from the trundle', the hill overlooking the famous racecourse nearby. The oldest ladies course in Hampshire and only links is Hayling Ladies. A visit there entails another trip over the water though this time via a bridge.

Ladies' societies and groups are now a firmly established scene in the golfing world. They love the challenge of new venues and now have the independence, transport and financial ability to play far and wide. Quite unlike the expectations of the early days, that the first ladies' championship would be the last, and that ladies could not cope with the severe strain of competition, the game is now enjoyed throughout the land by all golfers - women and men.

Liz Borrow started golf at the age of 6 encouraged by her parents who were both single figure golfers. After marriage and three children she resumed golf in Hampshire and was Club Captain, joined the County Committee and became County Captain during the period when Hampshire Ladies were at the top in England. She enjoys golf throughout Great Britain especially in the English Seniors scene. She recently co-authored a book entitled "One Hundred Years of Hampshire Ladies' Golf", for details e-mail golfbook@hampshirerosebooks.fsnet.co.uk

AA Rosette Awards

How the AA assesses restaurants for Rosette Awards

The AA's rosette award scheme was the first nation-wide scheme for assessing the quality of food served by restaurants and hotels. The rosette scheme is an award scheme, not a classification scheme and although there is necessarily an element of subjectivity when it comes to assessing taste, we aim for a consistent approach to our awards throughout the UK. It is important, however, to remember that many places serve enjoyable food but do not qualify for an AA award.

Our awards are made solely on the basis of a meal visit or visits by one or more of our hotel and restaurant inspectors who have an unrivalled breadth and depth of experience in assessing quality. They award rosettes annually on a rising scale of one to five.

So what makes a restaurant worthy of a Rosette Award?

For our inspectors the top and bottom line is the food. The taste of the food is what counts for them, and whether the dish successfully delivers to the diner what the menu promises. A restaurant is only as good as its worst meal. Although presentation and competent service should be appropriate to the style of the restaurant and the quality of the food, they cannot affect the rosette assessment as such, either up or down.

The following summaries attempt to explain what our inspectors look for, but are intended only as guidelines. The AA is constantly reviewing its award criteria and competition usually results in an all-round improvement in standards, so it becomes increasingly difficult for restaurants to reach award level.

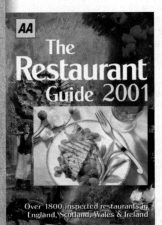

AA
The Restaurant Guide 2001
Over 1800 inspected restaurants in England, Scotland, Wales & Ireland

One rosette ❀

At the simplest level, one rosette, the chef should display a mastery of basic techniques and be able to produce dishes of sound quality and clarity of flavours, using good, fresh ingredients

Two rosettes ❀ ❀

To gain two rosettes, the chef must show greater technical skill, more consistency and judgement in combining and balancing ingredients and a clear ambition to achieve high standards. Inspectors will look for evidence of innovation to test the dedication of the kitchen brigade, and the use of seasonal ingredients sourced from quality suppliers.

Three rosettes ❀ ❀ ❀

This award takes a restaurant into the big league, and, in a typical year, fewer than 10 per cent of restaurants in our scheme achieve this distinction. Expectations of the kitchen are high, and inspectors find little room for inconsistencies. Exact technique, flair and imagination will come through in every dish, and balance and depth of flavour are all-important.

Four rosettes ❀ ❀ ❀ ❀

This is an exciting award because, at this level, not only should all technical skills be exemplary, but there should also be daring ideas, and they must work. There is no room for disappointment. Flavours should be accurate and vibrant.

Five rosettes ❀ ❀ ❀ ❀ ❀

This award is the ultimate awarded only when the cooking is at the pinnacle of achievement. Technique should be of such perfection that flavours, combinations and textures show a faultless sense of balance, giving each dish an extra dimension. The sort of cooking that never falters and always strives to give diners a truly memorable taste experience.

Further details of all restaurants with AA rosette awards can be found in The Restaurant Guide published annually by the AA and available from bookshops.

England

ENGLAND

BEDFORDSHIRE

ASPLEY GUISE   Map 04 SP93

Aspley Guise & Woburn Sands West Hill MK17 8DX
☎ 01908 583596 Fax 01908 583596 (Secretary)
A fine undulating course in expansive heathland
interspersed with many attractive clumps of gorse,
broom and bracken. Some well-established silver birch
are a feature. The 7th, 8th and 9th are really tough holes
to complete the first half.
18 holes, 6079yds, Par 71, SSS 70, Course record 67.
Club membership 560.
Visitors   with member only at weekends.
Societies   Wed & Fri normally booked 6 mths ahead.
Green Fees £35 per day; £23 per round.
Prof   David Marsden
Designer   Sandy Herd
Facilities   ⊗ ⅧI by prior arrangement ⅃ ♨ ♀ ♣ ⌂
                    🐾 ♂
Location   2m W of M1 junc 13

Hotel   ★★★ 66% Moore Place Hotel, The
                    Square, ASPLEY GUISE
                    ☎ 01908 282000
                    39 ➪ ⋒ Annexe 15 ➪ ⋒

BEDFORD   Map 04 TL04

Bedford Great Denham Golf Village MK40 4BF
☎ 01234 320022 Fax 01234 320023
American styled course with 89 bunkers, 8 large water
features and large contoured greens. Built on sand and gravel
the course is open all year round.
18 holes, 6471yds, Par 72, SSS 72.
Club membership 600.
Visitors   contact in advance, limited weekends.
Societies   telephone for details.
Green Fees £20 per round (£28 weekends and bank
                    holidays).
Cards   ▭ ▬ ▬ ▩ ▨
Prof   Jermiah Richardson
Designer   David Pottage
Facilities   ⊗ ⅧI ⅃ ♨ ♀ ♣ ⌂ ⅌ 🐾 ⚒ ♂ ⚐
Location   2.5m W of Bedford off A428

Hotel   ★★★ 74% Woodlands Manor Hotel, Green Ln,
                    Clapham, BEDFORD ☎ 01234 363281
                    30 ➪ ⋒ Annexe 3 ➪ ⋒

Bedford & County Green Ln, Clapham MK41 6ET
☎ 01234 352617 Fax 01234 357195
A mature parkland course established in 1912 with views
over Bedford and surrounding countryside. Beware of the
brook that discreetly meanders through the 7th, 10th, 11th
and 15th holes. The testing par 4 15th is one of the most
challenging holes in the area.
18 holes, 6347yds, Par 70, SSS 70.
Club membership 600.
Visitors   handicap certificate required, weekends with
                    member only.

Societies   welcome Mon,Tue,Thu & Fri, telephone in
                    advance.
Green Fees £30 per day; £24 per round.
Prof   R Tattersall
Facilities   ⊗ ⅧI by prior arrangement ⅃ ♨ ♀ ♣ ⌂ ♂
Location   2m N off A6

Hotel   ★★★ 74% Woodlands Manor Hotel, Green Ln,
                    Clapham, BEDFORD ☎ 01234 363281
                    30 ➪ ⋒ Annexe 3 ➪ ⋒

Bedfordshire Bromham Rd, Biddenham MK40 4AF
☎ 01234 261669 Fax 01234 261669
An attractive and easy walking parkland course with plenty
of trees providing a problem for 'off-line' golfers.
18 holes, 6305yds, Par 70, SSS 70, Course record 63.
Club membership 700.
Visitors   may not play at weekends except with member.
Societies   must telephone in advance/confirm in writing.
Green Fees not confirmed.
Prof   Peter Saunders
Facilities   ♣ ⌂ 🐾 ♂
Location   1m W on A428

Hotel   ★★★ 74% Woodlands Manor Hotel, Green Ln,
                    Clapham, BEDFORD ☎ 01234 363281
                    30 ➪ ⋒ Annexe 3 ➪ ⋒

Mowsbury Cleat Hill, Kimbolton Rd MK41 8DQ
☎ 01234 771041 & 216374 (prof)
Parkland municipal course in rural surroundings. Long and
testing 14-bay driving range and squash facilities.
18 holes, 6451yds, Par 72, SSS 71, Course record 66.
Club membership 550.
Visitors   no restrictions.
Societies   apply in writing.
Green Fees £9 per round (£12 weekends and bank holidays).
Prof   Malcolm Summers
Designer   Hawtree
Facilities   ⊗ ⅧI by prior arrangement ⅃ ♨ ♀ ♣
                    ⌂ ⅌ ♂ ⚐
& Leisure   squash.
Location   2m N of town centre on B660

Hotel   ★★★ 74% Woodlands Manor Hotel, Green Ln,
                    Clapham, BEDFORD ☎ 01234 363281
                    30 ➪ ⋒ Annexe 3 ➪ ⋒

CHALGRAVE   Map 04 TL02

Chalgrave Manor Dunstable Rd LU5 6JN
☎ 01525 876556 Fax 01525 876556
Undulating course constructed in 1994 offering a good test of
golf for all standards of golfer. Feature holes include the
short 10th (150 yards) that requires an accurate shot across
water to a splendid sloping green, and the Par 4 11th which
incorporates an elevated tee, a ditch, several bunkers, a pond
and perilously close out of bounds.
18 holes, 6382yds, Par 72, SSS 70, Course record 69.
Club membership 450.
Visitors   welcome, dress code smart casual, after 11am at
                    weekends.
Societies   apply in writing or telephone, in advance.
Green Fees £15 per round (£20 weekends).
Prof   Terry Bunyan
Designer   M Palmer
Facilities   ⊗ ⅃ ♨ ♀ ♣ ⌂ 🐾 ♂ ⚐
Location   From M1 junct 12 take A5120 through   ▶

Toddington, entrance about 1m out, well signposted

Hotel ★★★ 68% Old Palace Lodge Hotel, Church St, DUNSTABLE ☎ 01582 662201 68 ⇄ ♠

COLMWORTH
Map 04 TL15

Colmworth & North Bedfordshire New Rd MK44 2NU
☎ 01234 378181 Fax 01234 376235
An easy walking course with well-bunkered greens, opened in 1991. The course is often windy and plays longer than the yardage suggests. Water comes into play on 3 holes.
18 holes, 6435yds, Par 72, SSS 71, Course record 71.
Club membership 200.

Visitors advisable to contact in advance, may only play at weekends after 9.30am.
Societies telephone in advance.
Green Fees not confirmed.
Prof M Fields/S Bonham/S Richardson
Designer John Glasgow
Facilities ⊗ ⅲ by prior arrangement ⓑ ♥ ♀ ♨ ♐ ♙ ⇄ ♣ ♂ ♪
& Leisure fishing, par 3 course, snooker room.
Location 7m NE of Bedford, off B660

Hotel ★★★ 72% The Barns Hotel, Cardington Rd, BEDFORD ☎ 01234 270044 48 ⇄ ♠

DUNSTABLE
Map 04 TL02

Dunstable Downs Whipsnade Rd LU6 2NB
☎ 01582 604472 Fax 01582 478700
A fine downland course set on two levels with far-reaching views and frequent sightings of graceful gliders. The 9th hole is one of the best short holes in the country. There is a modernised clubhouse.
18 holes, 6251yds, Par 70, SSS 70, Course record 64.
Club membership 600.
Visitors welcome Mon,Tue and Fri, weekends with member only. Handicap certificate required.
Societies apply in advance.
Green Fees £35 per day; £22.50 per round.
Prof Michael Weldon
Designer James Braid
Facilities ⊗ ⓑ ♥ ♀ ♨ ⇄ ♣ ♂
Location 2m S off B4541

Hotel ★★★ 68% Old Palace Lodge Hotel, Church St, DUNSTABLE ☎ 01582 662201 68 ⇄ ♠

Griffin Chaul End Rd, Caddington LU1 4AX
☎ 01582 415573 Fax 01582 415314
A challenging 18-hole course with ponds and lakes.
18 holes, 6240yds, Par 71, SSS 70.
Club membership 510.
Visitors welcome Mon-Fri & after 2pm weekends no need to book.
Societies welcome midweek book by telephone.
Green Fees £12.50 per 18 holes Mon-Thu (£15 Fri, £17.50 weekends & bank holidays).
Facilities ⊗ ⓑ ♥ ♀ ♨ ♣
Location Off A505 Luton/Dunstable

Hotel ★★★ 68% Old Palace Lodge Hotel, Church St, DUNSTABLE ☎ 01582 662201 68 ⇄ ♠

LEIGHTON BUZZARD
Map 04 SP92

Leighton Buzzard Plantation Rd LU7 7JF
☎ 01525 244800 (Office) & 244805 (Club)
Fax 01525 244801
Parkland course with easy walking. The 17th and 18th holes are challenging tree-lined finishing holes with tight fairways. 11th par 3 is signature hole.
18 holes, 6101yds, Par 71, SSS 70, Course record 66.
Club membership 700.
Visitors may play yellow tees, may not play Tue (Ladies Day). May only play with member weekends and bank holidays. Handicap certificate required unless playing with member.
Societies prior booking required.
Green Fees £30 per day; £24 per round.
Prof Lee Scarbrow
Facilities ⊗ ⅲ ⓑ ♥ ♀ ♨ ♣ ♐ ♙ ⇄ ♂
Location 1.5m N of town centre off A4146

Hotel ★★★ 68% Old Palace Lodge Hotel, Church St, DUNSTABLE ☎ 01582 662201 68 ⇄ ♠

LOWER STONDON
Map 04 TL13

Mount Pleasant Station Rd SG16 6JL ☎ 01462 850999
A 9-hole course which, when played over 18 totals some 6003 yards. The course is undulating meadowland with mature hedges and trees and also 10,000 new trees. Two small ponds are crossed and there is a significant ditch in play on several holes. The 5,11 and 14th holes are all 400yds and play long into the prevailing West wind. Visitors consider the greens some of the best conditioned in the area and with good drainage the course rarely has to close.
9 holes, 6003yds, Par 70, SSS 69, Course record 71.
Club membership 300.
Visitors no restrictions, can book 2 days in advance, booking advisable weekends & evenings May-Sep.
Societies telephone or apply in writing.
Green Fees 18 holes £12, 9 holes £7 (£16/£9 weekends & bank holidays).
Cards ⬛ ⬛ ⬛ ⬛ ⬛ ⬛
Prof Mike Roberts
Designer Derek Young
Facilities ⓑ ♥ ♀ ♨ ♣ ♐ ♙ ⇄ ♂
Location 0.75m W of A600, 4m N of Hitchin

▶

Hotel   ★★★ 79% Flitwick Manor Hotel, Church Rd,
FLITWICK
☎ 0500 636943 (Central Res) Fax 01773 88032
1 17 ⇄ ↾*

LUTON   Map 04 TL02

South Beds Warden Hill LU2 7AE
☎ 01582 591500 Fax 01582 495381
18 and 9 hole downland courses, slightly undulating.
*Galley Course: 18 holes, 6389yds, Par 71, SSS 71, Course
record 64.*
Warden Course: 9 holes, 2424yds, Par 32, SSS 32.
Club membership 1000.
Visitors   must contact in advance and have a handicap
certificate.
Societies   telephone for details.
Green Fees   telephone shop for fees - 01582 591209.
Prof   Eddie Cogle
Designer   1892
Facilities   ⊗ ⅃ ⅃ ▼ ♀ ⅍ 🏠 ♂
Location   2m N of Luton on A6

Hotel   ★★★ 56% The Chiltern, Waller Av, LUTON
☎ 01582 575911 91 ⇄ ↾*

Stockwood Park London Rd LU1 4LX ☎ 01582 413704
Well laid out municipal parkland course with established
trees and several challenging holes.
18 holes, 6049yds, Par 69, SSS 69, Course record 67.
Club membership 800.
Visitors   no restrictions.
Societies   Mon, Tue & Thu only, telephone for
application.
Green Fees   not confirmed.
Prof   Glyn McCarthy
Facilities   ⊗ ⅂ ⅃ ⅃ ▼ ♀ ⅍ 🏠 ♂ ↾
Location   1m S

Hotel   ★★★ 56% The Chiltern, Waller Av, LUTON
☎ 01582 575911 91 ⇄ ↾*

MILLBROOK   Map 04 TL03

Lyshott Heath Millbrook Village MK45 2JB
☎ 01525 840252 Fax 01525 406249
Long parkland course, on rolling countryside high above the
Bedfordshire plains. Laid out on well-drained sandy soil with
many fairways lined with silver birch, pine and larch.
18 holes, 7100yds, Par 74, SSS 73, Course record 69.
Club membership 550.
Visitors   must contact in advance, may not play after
11am on Thu or after 12.30am at weekends.
Societies   telephone for details.
Green Fees   not confirmed.
Prof   David Armor
Designer   William Sutherland
Facilities   ⊗ ⅂ ⅃ ⅃ ▼ ♀ ⅍ 🏠 ♂
Location   E side of village off A507

Hotel   ★★★ 79% Flitwick Manor Hotel, Church Rd,
FLITWICK ☎ 0500 636943 (Central Res)
Fax 01773 880321 17 ⇄ ↾*

PAVENHAM   Map 04 SP95

Pavenham Park MK43 7PE
☎ 01234 822202 Fax 01234 826602
Mature, undulating parkland course with fast contoured
greens.
18 holes, 6400yds, Par 72, SSS 71, Course record 63.
Club membership 790.
Visitors   welcome weekdays, weekends as members
guests only.
Societies   telephone in advance.
Green Fees   £20.
Cards   🖭 📇 🖭 📇 💳
Prof   Zac Thompson
Designer   Zac Thompson
Facilities   ⊗ ⅃ ⅃ ▼ ♀ ⅍ 🏠 ♂ ↾ 🏌 ♂
Location   1.5m from A6, N of Bedford

Hotel   ★★★ 74% Woodlands Manor Hotel, Green Ln,
Clapham, BEDFORD ☎ 01234 363281
30 ⇄ ↾* Annexe 3 ⇄ ↾*

SANDY   Map 04 TL14

John O'Gaunt Sutton Park SG19 2LY
☎ 01767 260360 Fax 01767 262834
Two magnificent parkland courses - John O'Gaunt and
Carthagena - covering a gently undulating and tree-lined
terrain. The John O'Gaunt course makes the most of
numerous natural features, notably a river which crosses the
fairways of four holes. The Carthagena course has larger
greens, longer tees and from the back tees is a challenging
course. Fine clubhouse.
*John O'Gaunt Course: 18 holes, 6513yds, Par 71, SSS 71,
Course record 64.*
Carthagena Course: 18 holes, 5869yds, Par 69, SSS 69.
Club membership 1500.
Visitors   must contact in advance.
Societies   must pre-book.
Green Fees   not confirmed.
Prof   Peter Round
Designer   John O'Gaunt/Others
Facilities   ⊗ ⅂ ⅃ ⅃ ▼ ♀ ⅍ 🏠 ♂ 🏌 ♂
Location   3m NE of Biggleswade on B1040

Hotel   ★★ 63% Abbotsley Golf Hotel & Country
Club, Potton Rd, Eynesbury Hardwicke, ST
NEOTS ☎ 01480 474000 17 ⇄ ↾*

SHEFFORD   Map 04 TL13

Beadlow Manor Hotel & Golf & Country Club
SG17 5PH ☎ 01525 860800 Fax 01525 861345
A 36-hole golf and leisure complex. The Baroness Manhattan
and the Baron Manhattan golf courses are undulating with
water hazards on numerous holes. These are good
challenging courses for both the beginner and low handicap
player.
*Baroness Course: 18 holes, 6072yds, Par 71, SSS 69, Course
record 67.*
*Baron Course: 18 holes, 6619yds, Par 73, SSS 72, Course
record 67.*
Club membership 300.
Visitors   book in advance & must adhere to dress code.
Societies   apply in writing or telephone in advance.

Green Fees Baroness: £16 (£23 weekends); Baron: £13 (£18 weekends).
Cards 🔲 🔲 🔲 🔲 🔲 🔲
Prof Geraint Dixon
Facilities ⊗ 🏶 🏌 🍴 ♀ 🏖 🍽 ⛳ 🏇 ❀ 🚗 ♿ ⚐
& Leisure sauna, solarium, gymnasium.
Location (on A507)

Hotel ★★ 66% Stratton House Hotel, London Rd, BIGGLESWADE ☎ 01767 312442   31 🛏 📞

TILSWORTH   Map 04 SP92

Tilsworth Dunstable Rd LU7 9PU
☎ 01525 210721/2 Fax 01525 210465
An undulating 18 hole parkland course with a 30-bay floodlit driving range.
18 holes, 5306yds, Par 69, SSS 66, Course record 66.
Club membership 400.
Visitors may book up to 7 days in advance. May not play before 10am Sundays.
Societies welcome weekdays, apply in advance.
Green Fees £10 per 18 holes; £6.50 per 9 holes (£12/£7.50 weekends).
Cards 🔲 🔲 🔲 🔲 🔲
Prof Nick Webb
Facilities ⊗ 🏶 🏌 🍴 ♀ 🏖 🍽 ⛳ ❀ 🚗 ♿ ⚐
Location 0.5m NE off A5, N of Dunstable

Hotel ★★★ 68% Old Palace Lodge Hotel, Church St, DUNSTABLE ☎ 01582 662201   68 🛏 📞

WHIPSNADE   Map 04 TL01

Whipsnade Park Studham Ln, Dagnall HP4 1RH
☎ 01442 842330 Fax 01442 842090
Parkland course situated on downs overlooking the Chilterns adjoining Whipsnade Zoo. Easy walking, good views.
18 holes, 6800yds, Par 73, SSS 72, Course record 66.
Club membership 600.
Visitors welcome weekdays, with member only at weekends. Must contact in advance.
Societies by prior arrangement.
Green Fees £35 per day; £25 per round.
Cards 🔲 🔲 🔲
Prof Michael Lewendon
Facilities ⊗ 🏶 🏌 🍴 ♀ 🏖 🍽 ⛳ ❀ 🚗 ⚐
Location 1m E off B4506 between villages of Dagnall & Studham

Hotel ★★★ 68% Old Palace Lodge Hotel, Church St, DUNSTABLE ☎ 01582 662201   68 🛏 📞

WYBOSTON   Map 04 TL15

Wyboston Lakes MK44 3AL
☎ 01480 223004 Fax 01480 407330
Parkland course, with narrow fairways, small greens, set around four lakes and a river which provide the biggest challenge on this very scenic course.

> Entries with a green background
> identify courses considered to be
> particularly interesting

18 holes, 5955yds, Par 70, SSS 69, Course record 65.
Club membership 300.
Visitors a booking system is in operation at weekends, book no more than 8 days in advance.

Societies telephone in advance.
Green Fees £12.50 per 18 holes (£16.50 weekends).
Cards 🔲 🔲
Prof Paul Ashwell
Designer N Oakden
Facilities ⊗ 🏶 🏌 🍴 ♀ 🏖 🍽 ⛳ 🏇 ❀ 🚗 ♿ ⚐
& Leisure fishing, sauna, solarium, gymnasium, watersports.
Location 1m S of St Neots off A1/A428

Hotel ★★★ 74% Woodlands Manor Hotel, Green Ln, Clapham, BEDFORD ☎ 01234 363281   30 🛏 📞 Annexe 3 🛏 📞

BERKSHIRE

ASCOT   Map 04 SU96

Berkshire Swinley Rd SL5 8AY ☎ 01344 621496
Two heathland courses with splendid tree-lined fairways.
Red Course: 18 holes, 6369yds, Par 72, SSS 71.
Blue Course: 18 holes, 6260yds, Par 71, SSS 71.
Club membership 1000.
Visitors weekdays only on application to secretary.
Societies applications in writing only.
Green Fees not confirmed.
Prof P Anderson
Designer H Fowler
Facilities ⊗ 🏌 🍴 ♀ 🏖 🍽 ⛳ 🏇 ❀ 🚗 ⚐
Location 2.5m NW of M3 jct 3 on A332

Hotel ★★★★ 62% The Berystede, Bagshot Rd, Sunninghill, ASCOT ☎ 0870 400 8111 90 🛏 📞

Lavender Park Swinley Rd SL5 8BD ☎ 01344 893344
Public parkland course, ideal for the short game featuring challenging narrow fairways. Driving range with 9-hole par 3 course, floodlit until 22.00 hrs.
9 holes, 1102yds, Par 27, SSS 28.
Visitors no restrictions.
Societies welcome, notice preferred.
Green Fees £3.50 per 9 holes (£5 per 9 holes weekends & bank holidays).

▶

Cards	
Prof	David Johnson/Andy Piper
Facilities	🛒 🍴 ♀ 🏠 ⛳ ℓ
& Leisure	snooker.
Location	3.5m SW of Ascot, on A332

Hotel	★★★★ 62% The Berystede, Bagshot Rd, Sunninghill, ASCOT ☎ 0870 400 8111 90 ⇋ 🅿

Mill Ride Mill Ride SL5 8LT
☎ 01344 886777 Fax 01344 886820
Opened for play in 1991, this 18-hole course combines links and parkland styles. The holes require as much thinking as playing.
18 holes, 6752yds, Par 72, SSS 72, Course record 64.
Club membership 400.

Visitors	must contact in advance, limited access at weekends.
Societies	apply in advance.
Green Fees	not confirmed.
Prof	Terry Wild
Designer	Donald Steel
Facilities	⊗ 🎿 🛒 🍴 ♀ 🏠 ⛳ 🐾 ℓ
& Leisure	sauna.
Location	2m W of Ascot

Hotel	★★★★ 62% The Berystede, Bagshot Rd, Sunninghill, ASCOT ☎ 0870 400 8111 90 ⇋ 🅿

Royal Ascot Winkfield Rd SL5 7LJ
☎ 01344 625175 Fax 01344 872330
Heathland course inside Ascot racecourse and exposed to weather.
18 holes, 5716yds, Par 68, SSS 68, Course record 65.
Club membership 620.

Visitors	must be guest of member or contact secretary in advance. Not weekends.
Societies	telephone for provisional booking.
Green Fees	not confirmed.
Prof	Alistair White
Designer	J H Taylor
Facilities	🛒 🏠 ℓ
Location	0.5m N on A330

Hotel	★★★★ 62% The Berystede, Bagshot Rd, Sunninghill, ASCOT ☎ 0870 400 8111 90 ⇋ 🅿

Swinley Forest Coronation Rd SL5 9LE
☎ 01344 874979 (Secretary) Fax 01344 874733
An attractive and immaculate course of heather and pine situated in the heart of Swinley Forest. The 17th is as good a short hole as will be found, with a bunkered plateau green and the 12th hole is one of the most challenging par 4's.
18 holes, 6100yds, Par 69, SSS 70, Course record 62.
Club membership 325.

Visitors	on introduction of a member or by invitation only.
Societies	must contact in writing.
Green Fees	£70.
Prof	R C Parker
Designer	Harry Colt
Facilities	⊗ 🛒 🍴 ♀ 🏠 ⛳ 🐾 🏌 ℓ
Location	1.5m S, off A330

Hotel	★★★★ 62% The Berystede, Bagshot Rd, Sunninghill, ASCOT ☎ 0870 400 8111 90 ⇋ 🅿

BINFIELD   Map 04 SU87

Blue Mountain Golf Centre Wood Ln RG42 4EX
☎ 01344 300200 Fax 01344 360960
An 18-hole Pay and Play course with many testing holes with water hazards. Greens are large, undulating and strategically placed bunkers provide a fair challenge.
18 holes, 6097yds, Par 70, SSS 70, Course record 61.
Club membership 1250.

Visitors	tee times bookable in advance by phoning 01344 300220,
Societies	must contact in advance.
Green Fees	£18 per 18 holes Mon-Thu, £20 Fri, £24 weekends.
Cards	
Prof	Iain Looms
Facilities	⊗ 🎿 🛒 🍴 ♀ 🏠 ⛳ 🐾 🏌 ℓ ℓ
Location	2m from junct 10 of the M4

Hotel	★★★★ 76% Coppid Beech, John Nike Way, BRACKNELL ☎ 01344 303333 205 ⇋ 🅿

CHADDLEWORTH   Map 04 SU47

West Berkshire RG20 7DU
☎ 01488 638574 & 638851 Fax 01488 638781
Challenging and interesting downland course with testing 627yds 5th hole, one of the longest par 5's in southern England. Bunkers are well placed from tees and around the greens to catch any wayward shots.
18 holes, 7001yds, Par 73, SSS 74.
Club membership 650.

Visitors	must contact in advance, may play weekends pm only.
Societies	telephone in advance.
Green Fees	£35 per day; £25 per round (£35 weekends pm only).
Cards	
Prof	Paul Simpson
Designer	Robin Stagg
Facilities	⊗ 🛒 🍴 ♀ 🏠 ⛳ 🏌 ℓ ℓ
Location	1m S of village off A338

▶

Hotel   ★★★ 64% The Chequers, Oxford St,
NEWBURY ☎ 01635 38000
45 ⇆ ⋔ Annexe 11 ⇆ ⋔

COOKHAM   Map 04 SU88

Winter Hill Grange Ln SL6 9RP
☎ 01628 527613 (Secretary)
Parkland course set in a curve of the Thames with wonderful views across the river to Cliveden.
18 holes, 6408yds, Par 72, SSS 71, Course record 63.
Club membership 850.
Visitors   not permitted weekends.
Societies   welcome Wed & Fri, telephone initially.
Green Fees not confirmed.
Prof   Mark Booth
Designer   Charles Lawrie
Facilities   ⊗ ⓑ 🛢 ♀ ♒ 🍴 ♂ 🥂 ⓣ
Location   1m NW off B4447

Hotel   ★★★★ 73% The Compleat Angler, Marlow
Bridge, MARLOW ☎ 0870 400 8100 65 ⇆ ⋔

CROWTHORNE   Map 04 SU86

East Berkshire Ravenswood Ave RG45 6BD
☎ 01344 772041 Fax 01344 777378
An attractive heathland course with an abundance of heather and pine trees. Walking is easy and the greens are exceptionally good. Some fairways become tight where the heather encroaches on the line of play. The course is testing and demands great accuracy.
18 holes, 6344yds, Par 69, SSS 70.
Club membership 766.
Visitors   must contact in advance and have a
handicap certificate; must play with
member at weekends & bank holidays.
Societies   telephone for availability.
Green Fees not confirmed.
Prof   Arthur Roe
Designer   P Paxton
Facilities   ⊗ ⍟ by prior arrangement ⓑ 🛢 ♀ ♒
🏠 🍴 ♂
Location   W side of town centre off B3348

Hotel   ★★★★★ 72% Pennyhill Park Hotel &
Country Club, London Rd, BAGSHOT
☎ 01276 471774
31 ⇆ ⋔ Annexe 92 ⇆ ⋔

DATCHET   Map 04 SU97

Datchet Buccleuch Rd SL3 9BP
☎ 01753 543887 & 541872 Fax 01753 541872
Meadowland course, easy walking.
9 holes, 5978yds, Par 70, SSS 69, Course record 63.
Club membership 430.
Visitors   may play weekdays before 3pm.
Societies   Tue only. (Other times by prior arrangement)
Green Fees not confirmed.
Facilities   ⊗ ⍟ ⓑ 🛢 ♀ ♒ 🏠 ♂
Location   NW side of Datchet off B470

Hotel   ★★★ 67% The Castle Hotel, High St,
WINDSOR ☎ 0870 400 8300 111 ⇆ ⋔

MAIDENHEAD   Map 04 SU88

Bird Hills Drift Rd, Hawthorn Hill SL6 3ST
☎ 01628 771030 Fax 01628 631023
A gently undulating course with easy walking and many water hazards. Some challenging holes are the Par 5 6th dogleg, Par 3 9th surrounded by water and bunkers, and the 16th which is a long uphill Par 4 and a two-tier green.
18 holes, 6176yds, Par 72, SSS 69, Course record 65.
Club membership 400.

Visitors   to book ring 7 days in advance.
Societies   write or telephone in advance.
Green Fees not confirmed.
Cards   🟰 💳 💳 💳 🟢
Prof   Nick Slimming
Facilities   ⊗ ⍟ ⓑ 🛢 ♀ ♒ 🏠 🍴 ♂ ⓣ
Location   4m SW of Bray on A330

Hotel   ★★★ 73% Stirrups Country House, Maidens
Green, BRACKNELL ☎ 01344 882284
29 ⇆ ⋔

Maidenhead Shoppenhangers Rd SL6 2PZ
☎ 01628 624693 Fax 01628 624693
A pleasant parkland course on level ground with easy walking to good greens. Perhaps a little short but there are many natural features and some first-rate short holes.
18 holes, 6364yds, Par 70, SSS 70.
Club membership 650.
Visitors   may not play after noon on Fri or at
weekends. Must contact in advance and
have a handicap certificate.
Societies   must contact in writing.
Green Fees not confirmed.
Prof   Steve Geary
Designer   Alex Simpson
Facilities   ⊗ ⍟ ⓑ 🛢 ♀ ♒ 🏠 🍴 ♂
Location   S side of town centre off A308

Hotel   ★★★★ Fredrick's Hotel, Shoppenhangers
Rd, MAIDENHEAD
☎ 01628 581000   37 ⇆ ⋔

Temple Henley Rd, Hurley SL6 5LH
☎ 01628 824795 Fax 01628 828119
An open parkland course offering extensive views over the Thames Valley. Firm, relatively fast greens, natural slopes and subtle contours provide a challenging test to golfers of all abilities. Excellent drainage assures play during inclement weather.
▶

18 holes, 6232yds, Par 70, SSS 70, Course record 63.
Club membership 480.

Visitors	must contact in advance, limited weekend access.
Societies	apply in writing for formal bookings.
Green Fees	£50 per day; £30 per round (£55/£35 weekends & bank holidays).
Cards	🃏 💳 💳
Prof	James Whiteley
Designer	Willie Park (Jnr)
Facilities	⊗ 🏠 🍴 ♀ 🖥 ☂ ✎ 🏌 ♣ 𝄞
Location	Exit M4 jct 8/9 take A404M then A4130,or M40 exit jct 4 take A404 then A4130,signposted Henley
Hotel	★★★★ 73% The Compleat Angler, Marlow Bridge, MARLOW ☎ 0870 400 8100 65 ⇔ 🐾

NEWBURY   Map 04 SU46

Donnington Valley Old Oxford Rd, Donnington RG14 3AG
☎ 01635 568142 Fax 01635 568141
Undulating, testing course with mature trees and elevated greens, some protected by water.
18 holes, 6353yds, Par 71, SSS 71.
Club membership 520.

Visitors	booking system up to 7 days in advance, members have priority weekends.
Societies	write or telephone in advance.
Green Fees	not confirmed.
Prof	Edward Lainchbury
Designer	Mike Smith
Facilities	⊗ 🏠 🍴 ♀ 🖥 ☂ ✎ 🏌 🏠 ✈ ♣ 𝄞
Location	2m N of Newbury
Hotel	★★★★ 76% Donnington Valley Hotel & Golf Course, Old Oxford Rd, Donnington, NEWBURY ☎ 01635 551199 58 ⇔ 🐾

Newbury & Crookham Bury's Bank Rd, Greenham RG19 8BZ ☎ 01635 40035 Fax 01635 40045
A well-laid out, attractive course running mostly through woodland, and giving more of a challenge than its length suggests.
18 holes, 5940yds, Par 69, SSS 68.
Club membership 800.

Visitors	must play with member on weekends & bank holidays. Handicap certificate required.
Societies	must contact in advance.
Green Fees	£30 per day; £20 per round.
Prof	David Harris

Facilities	⊗ 🍴 🏠 ♀ 🖥 ☂ 🏠 𝄞
Location	2m SE off A34
Hotel	★★★ 64% The Chequers, Oxford St, NEWBURY ☎ 01635 38000 45 ⇔ 🐾 Annexe 11 ⇔ 🐾

READING   Map 04 SU77

Calcot Park Bath Rd, Calcot RG31 7RN
☎ 0118 942 7124 Fax 0118 945 3373
A delightfully sporting, slightly undulating parkland course just outside the town. Hazards include streams, a lake and many trees. The 6th is the longest, 507 yard par 5, with the tee-shot hit downhill over cross-bunkers to a well-guarded green, the 7th (162 yards) is played over the lake to an elevated green and the 13th (194 yards) requires a big carry over a gully to a plateau green.
18 holes, 6283yds, Par 70, SSS 70, Course record 63.
Club membership 750.

Visitors	must have handicap certificate or letter of introduction from club. May play weekdays only, excluding bank holidays.
Societies	must apply in writing.
Green Fees	£36 per day/round.
Prof	Ian Campbell
Designer	H S Colt
Facilities & Leisure	⊗ 🍴 🏠 ♀ 🖥 ☂ 🏠 ✈ 𝄞 fishing.
Location	1.5m from M4 junct 12 on A4 towards Reading
Hotel	★★★ 76% The Copper Inn Hotel & Restaurant, PANGBOURNE ☎ 0118 984 2244 14 ⇔ 🐾 Annexe 8 ⇔ 🐾

Hennerton Crazies Hill Rd, Wargrave RG10 8LT
☎ 0118 940 1000 Fax 0118 940 1042
Overlooking the Thames Valley, this Par 68 course has many existing natural features and a good number of hazards such as bunkers, mature trees and two small lakes. The most memorable hole is probably the 7th which is a par 3, 183 yards crossing a sharp valley to the green from which there are spectacular views of the course.
9 holes, 5460yds, Par 68, SSS 67, Course record 66.
Club membership 450.

Visitors	book 48 hours in advance, play weekends after 10am.
Societies	telephone or write for information.
Green Fees	£10 per 9 holes (£14 weekends & bank holidays); £15 per 18 holes (£18 weekends & bank holidays).
Cards	💳 💳 💳 💳 💳
Prof	William Farrow
Designer	Col D Beard
Facilities	⊗ 🏠 ♀ 🖥 ☂ 🏠 ✈ 𝄞
Location	Follow signs from A321 Wargrave High Street
Hotel	★★★ 71% Red Lion Hotel, Hart St, HENLEY-ON-THAMES ☎ 01491 572161 27 ⇔ 🐾

> Where to stay, where to eat?
> Visit the AA internet site
> www.theaa.co.uk

Sunningdale

Sunningdale, *Berkshire* ☎ 01344 621681 Fax 01344 624154 Map 04 SU96

Visitors may not play Fri, Sat, Sun or public holidays. Must contact in advance, and have a handicap certificate and letter of introduction

Societies Tue, Wed, Thu by arrangement

Green Fees Old Course £110 per round; New Course £78 (Day ticket for both courses £135)

Facilities ⊗ ⓛ ⍰ ♀ ⚲ ☎ ⚐ 𝄞
Professional (Keith Maxwell)

Location Ridgemount Rd, Sunningdale, Ascot SL5 9RR (1m S of Sunningdale, off A30)

Holes/Par/Course record 36 holes.
Old Course: 18 holes, 6308 yds, Par 70, SSS 70
New Course: 18 holes, 6443 yds, Par 71, SSS 72

WHERE TO STAY AND EAT NEARBY

Hotels

ASCOT

★★★★⊛ 68% The Royal Berkshire, London Rd, Sunninghill.
☎ 01344 623322. 63 ⇌ 🐾

★★★★ 62% The Berystede, Bagshot Rd, Sunninghill. ☎ 0870 400 8111.
90 (89 ⇌ 🐾 1 🐾)

★★ 74% Highclere, 19 Kings Rd, Sunninghill. ☎ 01344 625220. 11 🐾

★★ 66% Brockenhurst, Brockenhurst Rd. ☎ 01344 621912. 11 (10 ⇌ 1 🐾)
Annexe 4 (1 ⇌ 3 🐾)

BAGSHOT

★★★★★ ⊛ ⊛ ⊛ 72% Pennyhill Park, London Rd. ☎ 01276 471774.
31 ⇌ 🐾 Annexe 92 ⇌ 🐾

Restaurant

BRAY

⊛ ⊛ ⊛ ⊛ Waterside Inn, Ferry Rd.
☎ 01628 620691.

The Old Course, founded in 1900, was designed by Willie Park. It is a classic course at just 6308 yards long, with gorse and pine trees, silver birch, heather and immaculate turf. The new course is no less a challenge, created by HS Holt in 1922 it is 6443 yards. There is a long wait for anyone wishing to become a member of this prestigious club, it's location within easy reach of London is an attraction in itself. Visitors playing two rounds will be asked to alternate onto the other course in the afternoon. Short rounds may be played by finishing at the 10th or 13th green on the Old Course, and the 10th or 11th green on the New Course. On Monday one course is designated the two ball course until 3.00pm, check when booking a tee time.

Championship Course

19

Mapledurham Chazey Heath, Mapledurham RG4 7UD
☎ 0118 946 3353 Fax 0118 946 3363
18-hole course designed by Bob Sandow. Flanked by
hedgerows and mature woods, it is testing for players of all
levels.
*18 holes, 5750yds, Par 69, SSS 68, Course record 66 or 57
holes.*
Club membership 340.

Visitors	dress code and advanced booking required.
Societies	must contact in advance.
Green Fees	not confirmed.
Cards	🖃 🖃 🖃 🗐
Prof	Symon O'Keefe
Designer	Bob Sandow
Facilities	⊗ 🕪 🕪 🎱 🗗 🍴 ✧
Location	On A4074 to Oxford
Hotel	★★★★ 59% Holiday Inn, Caversham Bridge,
	Richfield Av, READING
	☎ 0118 925 9988 111 ⇌ 🗨

Reading 17 Kidmore End Rd, Emmer Green RG4 8SG
☎ 0118 947 2909 (Manager) Fax 0118 946 4468
Pleasant tree-lined parkland course, part hilly and part flat
with interesting views and several challenging par 3's.
18 holes, 6212yds, Par 70, SSS 70, Course record 67.
Club membership 585.

Visitors	contact the professional. Welcome weekdays,
	with member only Fridays & weekends.
Societies	apply by telephone.
Green Fees	£30 per day.
Cards	🖃
Prof	Scott Fotheringham
Designer	James Braid
Facilities	⊗ 🕪 🕪 🎱 🗗 ✧
& Leisure	indoor nets.
Location	2m N off B481
Hotel	★★★ 64% Royal County Hotel, 4-8 Duke St,
	READING ☎ 0118 958 3455 52 ⇌ 🗨

SINDLESHAM
Map 04 SU76

Bearwood Mole Rd RG41 5DB ☎ 0118 976 0060
Flat parkland course with one water hazard, the 40 acre lake
which features on the challenging 6th and 7th holes. Also
driving range.
9 holes, 5610yds, Par 70, SSS 68, Course record 66.
Club membership 500.

Visitors	welcome weekdays and weekend afternoons
	(contact in advance for pm weekend bookings)
Societies	apply in writing.

Green Fees	£18 per 18 holes; £12 per 9 holes.
Cards	🖃 🖃 🖃 🗐 🖃 🗐
Prof	Bayley Tustin
Designer	Barry Tustin
Facilities	⊗ 🕪 🕪 🎱 🗗 ✧ 🍴
Location	1m SW on B3030
Hotel	★★★★ 64% Reading Moat House, Mill Ln,
	Sindlesham, WOKINGHAM
	☎ 0118 949 9988 100 ⇌ 🗨

SONNING
Map 04 SU77

Sonning Duffield Rd RG4 6GJ
☎ 0118 969 3332 Fax 0118 944 8409
A quality parkland course and the scene of many county
championships. Wide fairways, not overbunkered, and
very good greens. Holes of changing character through
wooded belts.
18 holes, 6366yds, Par 70, SSS 70, Course record 65.
Club membership 750.

Visitors	weekdays only. Handicap certificate or
	proof of membership of another club
	required.
Societies	must apply in writing. Wed only.
Green Fees	£35 per day (£25 after 10.30am).
Prof	R McDougall
Designer	Hawtree
Facilities	⊗ 🕪 by prior arrangement 🕪 🎱 🗗
	🗗 ✧
Location	1m S off A4
Hotel	★★★ 76% The French Horn, SONNING
	ON THAMES ☎ 0118 969 2204
	12 ⇌ 🗨 Annexe 8 ⇌ 🗨

STREATLEY
Map 04 SU58

Goring & Streatley RG8 9QA
☎ 01491 873229 Fax 01491 875224
A parkland/moorland course that requires 'negotiating'.
Four well-known first holes lead up to the heights of the
5th tee, to which there is a 300ft climb. Wide fairways,
not overbunkered, with nice rewards on the way home
down the last few holes. A delightful course that
commands magnificent views of the Ridgeway and the
River Thames.
18 holes, 6320yds, Par 71, SSS 70, Course record 65.
Club membership 740.

Visitors	must contact in advance, with member only
	at weekends. Handicap certificate required.
Societies	telephone in advance.
Green Fees	£35 per day; £25 per round.
Cards	🖃 🗐
Prof	Jason Hadland
Designer	Tom Morris
Facilities	⊗ 🕪 🕪 🎱 🗗 🗗 ✧
Location	N of village off A417
Hotel	★★★★ 69% The Swan Diplomat Hotel,
	High St, STREATLEY ☎ 01491 878800
	46 ⇌ 🗨

> ### Looking for a driving range?
> ### See the index at the back of the guide

SUNNINGDALE   Map 04 SU96

SUNNINGDALE See page 19

Sunningdale Ladies Cross Rd SL5 9RX ☎ 01344 620507
A short 18-hole course with a typical Surrey heathland
layout. A very tight course, making for a challenging game.
18 holes, 3616yds, Par 60, SSS 60, Course record 51.
Club membership 350.
Visitors   telephone in advance.
Societies   Ladies societies only.
Green Fees   not confirmed.
Facilities   ⊗ 🏌 🛒 ♀ ⚐ ✐
& Leisure   Practice net.
Location   1m S off A30

Hotel   ★★★★ 62% The Berystede, Bagshot Rd,
                   Sunninghill, ASCOT ☎ 0870 400 8111
                   90 ⇔ ♟

WOKINGHAM   Map 04 SU86

Downshire Easthampstead Park RG40 3DH
☎ 01344 302030 Fax 01344 301020
Beautiful municipal parkland course with mature trees.
Water hazards come into play on the 14th and 18th holes,
and especially on the short 7th, a testing downhill 169 yards
over the lake. Pleasant easy walking. Challenging holes: 7th
(par 4), 15th (par 4), 16th (par 3).
18 holes, 6416yds, Par 73, SSS 71.
Club membership 1000.
Visitors   must book six days in advance by telephone or
                   seven days in person, weekend times available.
Societies   must telephone in advance.
Green Fees   not confirmed.
Prof   Wayne Owers
Facilities   ⊗ 🏌 🛒 ♀ ⚐ 🍴 ⚒ ✈ ✐ ✐
& Leisure   9 hole pitch & putt.
Location   3m SW of Bracknell

Hotel   ★★★★ 76% Coppid Beech, John Nike Way,
                   BRACKNELL ☎ 01344 303333 205 ⇔ ♟

Sand Martins Finchampstead Rd RG40 3RQ
☎ 0118 977 0265 Fax 0118 977 0282
Two different 9-hole loops: the front nine is mostly tree-lined
with ponds and the back nine is similar to a links course.
18 holes, 6212yds, Par 70, SSS 70, Course record 65.
Club membership 800.

Visitors   must telephone in advance. Restricted Thu, with
                   member only at weekends.

Societies   prior arrangement by telephone.
Green Fees   £30.
Cards   ⚏ ⚏ ⚏ ⚏ ⚏
Prof   Andrew Hall
Designer   Edward Fox
Facilities   ⊗ 🏌 🛒 🛒 ♀ ⚐ 🍴 ⚒ ✈ ✐ ✐
Location   1m S of Wokingham

Hotel   ★★★★ 64% Reading Moat House, Mill Ln,
                   Sindlesham, WOKINGHAM
                   ☎ 0118 949 9988 100 ⇔ ♟

BRISTOL

BRISTOL   Map 03 ST57

Bristol and Clifton Beggar Bush Ln, Failand BS8 3TH
☎ 01275 393474 Fax 01275 394611
A downland course with splendid turf and fine tree-lined
fairways. The 222-yard (par 3) 13th with the green well
below, and the par 4 16th, with its second shot across an
old quarry, are outstanding. There are splendid views
over the Bristol Channel towards Wales.
18 holes, 6316yds, Par 70, SSS 70, Course record 65.
Club membership 950.
Visitors   must have a handicap certificate. Weekends
                   restricted.
Societies   telephone to enquire.
Green Fees   £32 per day (£35 weekends).
Cards   ⚏
Prof   Peter Mawson
Facilities   ⊗ 🏌 🛒 🛒 ♀ ⚐ 🍴 ⚒ ✈ ✐ ✐
Location   4m W on B3129 off A369

Hotel   ★★★ 70% Redwood Lodge Hotel, Beggar
                   Bush Ln, Failand, BRISTOL
                   ☎ 01275 393901 112 ⇔ ♟

Filton Golf Course Ln, Filton BS34 7QS
☎ 0117 969 4169 Fax 0117 931 4359
Challenging parkland course situated on high ground in a
pleasant suburb to the north of the city. Extensive views can
be enjoyed from the course, especially from the second tee
and the clubhouse, where on a clear day the Cotswold Hills
and the Brecon Beacons can be seen. Good par 4 testing hole
'dog-leg' 383 yds.
18 holes, 6318yds, Par 70, SSS 70, Course record 63.
Club membership 776.
Visitors   advisable to contact in advance for availability,
                   may not play at weekends unless with member.
                   Must have a handicap certificate.
Societies   apply in writing/phone for details.
Green Fees   £25 per day; £20 per round.
Prof   J C N Lumb
Facilities   ⊗ 🏌 🛒 🛒 ♀ ⚐ 🍴 ⚒ ✐
Location   5m NW off A38

Hotel   ★★★ 69% Posthouse Bristol, Filton Rd,
                   Hambrook, BRISTOL ☎ 0870 400 9014
                   198 ⇔ ♟

Henbury Henbury Hill, Westbury-on-Trym BS10 7QB
☎ 0117 950 0044 & 950 2121 (Prof)
Fax 0117 959 1928
A parkland course tree-lined and on two levels. The
River Trym comes into play on the 7th drop-hole with its
green set just over the stream. The last nine holes have
the beautiful Blaise Castle woods for company.
18 holes, 6039yds, Par 70, SSS 70, Course record 65.
Club membership 760.
Visitors   handicap certificate required, with member
                only at weekends. Advisable to contact in
                advance for availability.
Societies   apply in writing or telephone well in
                advance. Tue & Fri only.
Green Fees   not confirmed.
Prof   Nick Riley
Facilities   ⊗ ⅷ by prior arrangement ⓑ ⓦ ♀ ♨
                🏠 ⛳ ♂
Location   3m NW of city centre on B4055 off A4018

Hotel   ★★★ 63% Henbury Lodge Hotel, Station
                Rd, Henbury, BRISTOL
                ☎ 0117 950 2615 12 ⇋ ♠ Annexe 9 ⇋ ♠

Knowle West Town Ln, Brislington BS4 5DF
☎ 0117 977 0660 Fax 0117 972 0615
A parkland course with nice turf. The first five holes
climb up and down hill but the remainder are on a more
even plane.
18 holes, 6016yds, Par 69, SSS 69, Course record 61.
Club membership 700.
Visitors   must have handicap certificate, must
                telephone professional 0117 977 9193 for
                weekends.
Societies   Thu only, apply in writing.
Green Fees   not confirmed.
Prof   Gordon Brand Snr
Designer   Hawtree/J H Taylor
Facilities   ⊗ ⓑ ⓦ ♀ ♨ 🏠 ⛳ ♞ ♂
Location   3m SE of city centre off A37

Hotel   ★★★ 76% Hunstrete House Hotel,
                HUNSTRETE ☎ 01761 490490 23 ⇋ ♠

Mangotsfield Carsons Rd, Mangotsfield BS17 3LW
☎ 0117 956 5501
An easy hilly parkland course. Caravan site.
18 holes, 5337yds, Par 68, SSS 66, Course record 61.
Club membership 400.
Visitors   no restrictions.
Societies   bookings in advance to Craig Trewin.
Green Fees   not confirmed.
Prof   Craig Trewin
Designer   John Day
Facilities   ⊗ ⓑ ⓦ ♀ ♨ 🏠 ⛳ ♞ ♂
& Leisure   sauna.
Location   6m NE of city centre off B4465

Hotel   ★★★ 69% Posthouse Bristol, Filton Rd,
                Hambrook, BRISTOL ☎ 0870 400 9014
                198 ⇋ ♠

Entries with a green background
identify courses considered to be
particularly interesting

Shirehampton Park Park Hill, Shirehampton BS11 0UL
☎ 0117 982 3059 & 9822083 Fax 0117 982 2083
A lovely parkland course with views across the Avon Gorge.
18 holes, 5430yds, Par 67, SSS 66.
Club membership 600.
Visitors   with member only at weekends. Must have a
                handicap certificate.
Societies   weekdays (book through Secretary)
Green Fees   £30 per day; £20 per round (weekdays).
Prof   Brent Ellis
Facilities   ⊗ ⅷ by prior arrangement ⓑ ⓦ ♀ ♨ 🏠 ⛳ ♂
Location   2m E of junct 18 M5 on B4054

Hotel   ★★★ 70% Redwood Lodge Hotel, Beggar
                Bush Ln, Failand, BRISTOL ☎ 01275 393901
                112 ⇋ ♠

Woodlands Woodlands Ln, Almondsbury BS12 4JZ
☎ 01454 619319 Fax 01454 619397
Situated on the edge of the Severn Valley, bordered by
Hortham Brook and Shepherds Wood this interesting
parkland course, features five testing par 3's set around the
course's five lakes, notably the 206 yd 5th hole which
extends over water.
18 holes, 6068yds, Par 69, SSS 67.
Club membership 101.
Visitors   no restrictions.
Societies   telephone in advance.
Green Fees   not confirmed.
Designer   Cliff Chapman
Facilities   ⊗ ⓑ ⓦ ♀ ♨ 🏠 ⛳ ♞ ♂
& Leisure   fishing.
Location   N of Bristol off A38

Hotel   ★★★ 69% Posthouse Bristol, Filton Rd,
                Hambrook, BRISTOL ☎ 0870 400 9014
                198 ⇋ ♠

BUCKINGHAMSHIRE

AYLESBURY   Map 04 SP81

Aylesbury Golf Centre Hulcott Ln, Bierton HP22 5GA
☎ 01296 393644
A parkland course with magnificent views to the Chiltern
Hills. A good test of golf with out of bounds coming into
play on 9 of the holes, also a number of water hazards and
bunkers.
18 holes, 5965yds, Par 71, SSS 69.
Club membership 200.
Visitors   no restrictions, but booking advisable.
Societies   telephone for details.
Green Fees   £10 per round (£12 weekends & bank holidays).
Cards   ▭ ▭
Prof   Mitch Kierstenson
Designer   T S Benwell
Facilities   ♀ ♨ 🏠 ⛳ ♂ ♝
Location   1m N of Aylesbury on A418

Hotel   ★★★ 69% Posthouse Aylesbury, Aston
                Clinton Rd, AYLESBURY
                ☎ 0870 400 9002 94 ⇋ ♠

Aylesbury Park Oxford Rd HP17 8QQ
☎ 01296 399196 Fax 01296 336830
Parkland course with mature trees, located just south-west of Aylesbury.
18 holes, 6148yds, Par 70, SSS 69, Course record 69.
Club membership 340.

Visitors	may book up to 1 week in advance.
Societies	telephone for Society Pack
Green Fees	£12.50 per round (£18.50 weekends).
Cards	
Prof	David Boot
Designer	H Hawtree
Facilities	
Location	0.5m SW of Aylesbury, on the A418

Hotel	★★★ 69% Posthouse Aylesbury, Aston Clinton Rd, AYLESBURY ☎ 0870 400 9002 94

Ellesborough Butlers Cross HP17 0TZ
☎ 01296 622114 Fax 01296 622114
Once part of the property of Chequers, and under the shadow of the famous monument at the Wendover end of the Chilterns. A downland course, it is rather hilly with most holes enhanced by far-ranging views over the Aylesbury countryside.
18 holes, 6360yds, Par 71, SSS 71, Course record 64.
Club membership 700.

Visitors	welcome on weekdays, handicap certificate required.
Societies	Wed & Thu only, by prior arrangement with General Manager.
Green Fees	£40 per day; £25 per round.
Prof	Mark Squire
Designer	James Braid
Facilities	
Location	1m E of Ellesborough on B4010

Beaconsfield Seer Green HP9 2UR
☎ 01494 676545 Fax 01494 681148
An interesting and, at times, testing tree-lined and parkland course which frequently plays longer than appears on the card! Each hole differs to a considerable degree and here lies the charm. Walking is easy, except perhaps to the 6th and 8th. Well bunkered.
18 holes, 6493yds, Par 72, SSS 71, Course record 63.
Club membership 850.

Visitors	must contact in advance and have a handicap certificate. May not play weekends.
Societies	phone for details
Green Fees	£48 per day; £35 per round.
Prof	Michael Brothers
Designer	H S Colt
Facilities	
Location	2m E,S of Seer Green

Hotel	★★★★ 67% Bellhouse Hotel, Oxford Rd, BEACONSFIELD ☎ 01753 887211 136

Windmill Hill Tattenhoe Ln MK3 7RB
☎ 01908 631113 & 366457 (Sec) Fax 01908 630034
Long, open-parkland course, the first championship course designed by Henry Cotton, opened in 1972. Proprietary Pay & Play. No winter greens.
18 holes, 6720yds, Par 73, SSS 72, Course record 68.
Club membership 400.

Visitors	booking system in operation up to 7 days in advance.
Societies	packages available, contact for details.
Green Fees	£10.75 per 18 holes (£14.50 weekends).
Cards	
Prof	Colin Clingan
Designer	Henry Cotton
Facilities	
& Leisure	pool tables.
Location	W side of town centre on A421

Hotel	★★★ 66% Posthouse Milton Keynes, 500 Saxon Gate West, MILTON KEYNES ☎ 0870 400 9057 150

Buckingham Tingewick Rd MK18 4AE
☎ 01280 815566 Fax 01280 821812
Undulating parkland course with a stream and river affecting 8 holes.
18 holes, 6082yds, Par 70, SSS 69, Course record 67.
Club membership 690.

Visitors	welcome Mon-Fri, with member only at weekends.
Societies	by prior arrangement.
Green Fees	not confirmed.
Prof	Tom Gates
Facilities	
Location	1.5m W on A421

Hotel	★★★ 66% Buckingham Four Pillars Hotel, Buckingham Ring Rd South, BUCKINGHAM ☎ 01280 822622 70

AA Hotels that have special
arrangements with golf courses are listed at
the back of the guide

BURNHAM
Map 04 SU98

Burnham Beeches Green Ln SL1 8EG
☎ 01628 661448 Fax 01628 668968
A wooded parkland course on the edge of the historic
Burnham Beeches Forests with a good variety of holes.
18 holes, 6449yds, Par 70, SSS 71.
Club membership 670.
Visitors	must contact in advance. May play on weekdays only. Handicap certificate required.
Societies	welcome Apr-Oct, write or telephone for information.
Green Fees	£48 per day; £32 per round.
Prof	Ronnie Bolton
Facilities	⊗ ⅷ by prior arrangement ⓑ ☕ ♀ ⚘ 🏠 ⛳ ⚒ ⚒ ∅
Location	0.5m NE of Burnham
Hotel	★★★ 68% Burnham Beeches, Grove Rd, BURNHAM ☎ 01628 429955 82 ⇄ ⚑

Lambourne Dropmore Rd SL1 8NF
☎ 01628 666755 Fax 01628 663301
A championship standard 18-hole parkland course.
Undulating terrain with many trees and several lakes, notably
on the tricky 7th hole which has a tightly guarded green
reached via a shot over a lake. Seven par 4's over 400yds
with six picturesque lakes, excellent drainage and full
irrigation.
18 holes, 6771yds, Par 72, SSS 73, Course record 67.
Club membership 740.
Visitors	must contact in advance & have a handicap certificate. May not play at weekends.
Green Fees	£36 (£45 weekends).
Cards	🖃 ▬ 🖃 🖃 🖃 ∅
Prof	David Hart
Designer	Donald Steel
Facilities & Leisure	⊗ ⅷ ⓑ ☕ ♀ ⚘ 🏠 ⛳ ⚒ ⚒ ∅ sauna.
Location	Access via M4 junct 7 towards Burnham or M40 junct 2 towards Slough/Burnham
Hotel	★★★ 68% Burnham Beeches, Grove Rd, BURNHAM ☎ 01628 429955 82 ⇄ ⚑

CHALFONT ST GILES
Map 04 SU99

Harewood Downs Cokes Ln HP8 4TA
☎ 01494 762308 Fax 01494 766869
A testing undulating parkland course with sloping greens and
plenty of trees.
18 holes, 5958yds, Par 69, SSS 69, Course record 64.
Visitors	must contact in advance.
Societies	apply in writing or telephone.
Green Fees	£25 per day/round (£33 weekends & bank holidays).
Cards	🖃 🖃
Prof	G C Morris
Facilities	⊗ ⅷ by prior arrangement ⓑ ☕ ♀ ⚘ 🏠 ⚒ ⚒ ∅
Location	2m E of Amersham on A413
Hotel	★★★★ 67% Bellhouse Hotel, Oxford Rd, BEACONSFIELD ☎ 01753 887211 136 ⇄ ⚑

Oakland Park Threehouseholds HP8 4LW
☎ 01494 876293 Fax 01494 874692
Parkland with mature trees, hedgerows and water features,
designed to respect the natural features of the land and lakes
whilst providing a good challenge for players at all levels.
18 holes, 5246yds, Par 67, SSS 66.
Club membership 750.
Visitors	weekdays only.
Societies	Mon, Wed & Fri. Must apply in writing.
Green Fees	£20 per round.
Cards	🖃 ▬ 🖃 🖃 ∅
Prof	Allistair Thatcher
Designer	Johnathan Gaunt
Facilities	⊗ ⅷ by prior arrangement ⓑ ☕ ♀ ⚘ 🏠 ⛳ ⚒ ⚒ ∅
Location	3m N of M40 junct 3
Hotel	★★★★ 67% Bellhouse Hotel, Oxford Rd, BEACONSFIELD ☎ 01753 887211 136 ⇄ ⚑

CHARTRIDGE
Map 04 SP90

Chartridge Park HP5 2TF ☎ 01494 791772
A family run, easy walking parkland course set high in the
beautiful Chiltern Hills, affording breathtaking views.
18 holes, 5516yds, Par 69, SSS 67, Course record 65.
Club membership 700.
Visitors	may not play before 10.30am weekends.
Societies	must telephone in advance.
Green Fees	not confirmed.
Cards	🖃 ▬ 🖃 🖃 ∅
Prof	Peter Gibbins
Designer	John Jacobs
Facilities	⊗ ⅷ ⓑ ☕ ♀ ⚘ 🏠 ⛳ ⚒ ⚒ ∅
Location	3m NW of Chesham
Hotel	★★★ 66% The Crown, High St, AMERSHAM ☎ 0870 400 8103 19 ⇄ ⚑ Annexe 18 ⇄ ⚑

CHESHAM
Map 04 SP90

Chesham & Ley Hill Ley Hill Common HP5 1UZ
☎ 01494 784541 Fax 01494 785506
Wooded parkland course on hilltop with easy walking.
9 holes, 5296yds, Par 66, SSS 65, Course record 62.
Club membership 400.
Visitors	may play Mon & Thu all day, Wed after noon, Fri up to 4pm.
Societies	subject to approval, Thu only.
Green Fees	£13 per round.
Facilities	⊗ ⅷ ⓑ ☕ ♀ ⚘
Location	2m E of Chesham
Hotel	★★★ 66% The Crown, High St, AMERSHAM ☎ 0870 400 8103 19 ⇄ ⚑ Annexe 18 ⇄ ⚑

DENHAM
Map 04 TQ08

Buckinghamshire Denham Court Dr UB9 5BG
☎ 01895 835777 Fax 01895 835210
A John Jacobs designed championship-standard course.
Visitors only welcome as guests of members to this beautiful
course in 269 acres of lovely grounds including mature trees,
five lakes and two rivers. The testing 7th hole requires a ▶

185 yd carry over a stream, followed by a second shot over a river to a green guarded by a lake.
18 holes, 6880yds, Par 72, SSS 73, Course record 70.
Club membership 600.

Visitors	contact 48 hours in advance, with member only or introduced by member. Weekdays only.
Societies	must contact in advance.
Green Fees	£70 per 18 holes (£80 weekends & bank holidays).
Cards	☰ ■ ☰ ☰ ▨
Prof	John O'Leary
Designer	John Jacobs
Facilities	⊗ ⍥ ⅃ ▱ ☕ ♀ ♨ ☖ ⛳ ⚲ ⚐
Location	Just beyond junct 1 on M40
Hotel	★★★★ 67% Bellhouse Hotel, Oxford Rd, BEACONSFIELD ☎ 01753 887211 136 ⇆ ▮

Denham Tilehouse Ln UB9 5DE
☎ 01895 832022 Fax 01895 835340
A beautifully maintained parkland/heathland course, home of many county champions. Slightly hilly and calling for good judgement of distance in the wooded areas.
18 holes, 6462yds, Par 70, SSS 71, Course record 66.
Club membership 790.

Visitors	must contact in advance & have handicap certificate. Must play with member Fri-Sun.
Societies	Tue-Thu. Must book in advance.
Green Fees	£58 per day; £40 per round.
Prof	Stuart Campbell
Designer	H S Colt
Facilities	⊗ ▱ ☕ ♀ ♨ ☖ ⛳ ⚲
Location	0.5m N of North Orbital Road, 2m from Uxbridge
Hotel	★★★★ 67% Bellhouse Hotel, BEACONSFIELD ☎ 01753 887211 136 ⇆ ▮

FLACKWELL HEATH   Map 04 SU89

Flackwell Heath Treadaway Rd, High Wycombe HP10 9PE
☎ 01628 520929 Fax 01628 530040
Open sloping heath and tree-lined course on hills overlooking Loudwater and the M40. Some good challenging par 3's and several testing small greens.
18 holes, 6211yds, Par 71, SSS 70, Course record 65.
Club membership 800.

Visitors	with member only at weekends. Must contact in advance and hold a handicap certificate.
Societies	Wed & Thu only, by prior booking.
Green Fees	£36 per day; £24 per round.
Cards	☰ ■ ☰ ▨ ☰ ▨ ▨
Prof	Paul Watson
Facilities	⊗ ⍥ ⅃ ▱ ☕ ♀ ♨ ☖ ⚲
Location	NE side of town centre
Hotel	★★★★ 67% Bellhouse Hotel, Oxford Rd, BEACONSFIELD ☎ 01753 887211 136 ⇆ ▮

GERRARDS CROSS   Map 04 TQ08

Gerrards Cross Chalfont Park SL9 0QA
☎ 01753 278500 Fax 01753 883593
A wooded parkland course which has been modernised in recent years and is now a very pleasant circuit with

infinite variety. The best part lies on the plateau above the clubhouse where there are some testing holes.
18 holes, 6295yds, Par 69, SSS 70, Course record 64.
Club membership 773.

Visitors	must contact professional in advance, a handicap certificate is required, may not play Tuesday, weekends or public holidays.
Societies	booking well in advance necessary, handicap certicates required, packages to suit.
Green Fees	£46 per day; £33 per 18 holes.
Cards	☰ ☰ ▨
Prof	Matthew Barr
Designer	Bill Pedlar
Facilities	⊗ ⍥ by prior arrangement ▱ ☕ ♀ ♨ ☖ ⚲
Location	NE side of town centre off A413
Hotel	★★★★ 67% Bellhouse Hotel, Oxford Rd, BEACONSFIELD ☎ 01753 887211 136 ⇆ ▮

HALTON   Map 04 SP81

Chiltern Forest Aston Hill HP22 5NQ
☎ 01296 631267 Fax 01296 631267
This very hilly wooded parkland course is on two levels. It is a true test of skill to the low handicap golfer, as well as being a fair challenge to higher handicap golfers. The surrounding woodland makes the course very scenic.
18 holes, 5765yds, Par 70, SSS 70, Course record 69.
Club membership 650.

Visitors	welcome weekdays, must play with member at weekends.
Societies	contact in advance for booking form.
Green Fees	£25 per day; £20 per round.
Cards	☰ ☰ ☰ ▨ ▨
Prof	A Lavers
Facilities	⊗ ⍥ by prior arrangement ▱ ☕ ♀ ♨ ☖ ⚲
Location	1m NE off A4011
Hotel	★★★ 63% Rose & Crown Hotel & Restaurant, High St, TRING ☎ 01442 824071 27 ⇆ ▮

HIGH WYCOMBE   Map 04 SU89

Hazlemere Golf & Country Club Penn Rd, Hazlemere HP15 7LR ☎ 01494 714722 Fax 01494 713914
Undulating parkland course in beautiful countryside with water hazards in play on some holes. Two long par 5s and a fine par 4 closing hole.
18 holes, 5873yds, Par 70, SSS 68, Course record 62.
Club membership 700.

Visitors	weekdays all day. Weekends by prior arrangement through Pro. shop telephone 01494 718298.
Societies	by prior telephone arrangement.
Green Fees	not confirmed.
Cards	☰ ☰ ▨
Prof	Alistair McKay/Paul Harrison
Designer	Terry Murray
Facilities	⊗ ⅃ ☕ ♀ ♨ ☖ ⛳ ⚲ ⚐
Location	2m NE, A404 towards Amersham

Hotel   ★★★ 66% The Crown, High St,
AMERSHAM ☎ 0870 400 8103
19 ⇉ ⋒ Annexe 18 ⇉ ⋒

IVER   Map 04 TQ08

Iver Hollow Hill Ln, Langley Park Rd SL0 0JJ
☎ 01753 655615 Fax 01753 654225
Fairly flat, pay and play parkland course with challenging par
5s, plenty of hazards - water and ditches - and strong
crosswinds to contend with.
9 holes, 6288yds, Par 72, SSS 72, Course record 66.
Club membership 250.
Visitors   competitions at weekends, telephone to pre book
                  tee times.
Societies   telephone in advance.
Green Fees not confirmed.
Cards   ▱ ▱ ▱ ▱
Prof   Karl Teschner
Facilities   ⊗ ∭ by prior arrangement ▱ ▱ ♀ ⚎
                  ▱ ⊤ ⌀ ⋔
Location   1.5m SW off B470

Hotel   ★★★★ 68% Slough/Windsor Marriott, Ditton
Rd, Langley, SLOUGH ☎ 01753 544244
380 ⇉ ⋒

Richings Park Golf & Country Club North Park SL0 9DL
☎ 01753 655370 Fax 01753 655409
Set amongst mature trees and attractive lakes, this testing par
70 parkland course provides a suitable challenge to golfers of
all abilities. Well irrigated greens and abundant wildlife.
There is an academy course with 5 short holes and teaching
facilities on the driving range.
18 holes, 6144yds, Par 70, SSS 69.
Club membership 620.
Visitors   welcome but may not play until after 12 noon at
                  weekends.
Societies   apply in writing or telephone.
Green Fees not confirmed.
Cards   ▱ ▱ ▱ ▱ ▱
Prof   Seab Kelly
Designer   Alan Higgins
Facilities   ⊗ ∭ ▱ ▱ ♀ ⚎ ▱ ⊤ ⟍ ⚞ ⌀ ⋔
& Leisure   5 hole academy course.
Location   Junct 5 on M4, A4 towards Heathrow, left at
                  lights, Sutton Lane, right at next lights North
                  Park

Hotel   ★★★ 68% Courtyard by Marriott
Slough/Windsor, Church St, SLOUGH
☎ 01753 551551 148 ⇉ ⋒

Thorney Park Thorney Mill Rd SL0 9AL
☎ 01895 422095 Fax 01895 431307
Thorney Park is a 9 hole parkland course, which will test
both the beginner and established golfer. Fairway irrigation
ensures lush green fairways and smooth putting surfaces.
Many interesting holes including the testing par 4 ninth
which needs a long drive to the waters edge and a well hit
iron onto the bunker guarded green.
9 holes, 2834yds, Par 34, SSS 33.
Club membership 180.
Visitors   must telephone in advance.
Societies   must telephone in advance.
Green Fees £12 per 18 holes; £7.50 per 9 holes (£15/£9
                  weekends & bank holidays).

Cards   ▱ ▱ ▱ ▱ ▱
Prof   Andrew Killing
Facilities   ⊗ ▱ ▱ ♀ ⚎ ▱ ⊤ ⌀ ⋔
Location   From M4 junct 5 left onto A4. Left into Sutton
                  Lane and right for Thorney Mill Road

Hotel   ★★★★ 68% Slough/Windsor Marriott, Ditton
Rd, Langley, SLOUGH ☎ 01753 544244
380 ⇉ ⋒

LITTLE CHALFONT   Map 04 SU99

Little Chalfont Lodge Ln HP8 4AJ
☎ 01494 764877 Fax 01494 762860
Gently undulating parkland course surrounded by mature
trees.
9 holes, 5852yds, Par 68, SSS 68, Course record 66.
Club membership 300.
Visitors   no restrictions, please phone to ensure there are
                  no competitions in progress. Must contact for
                  weekend play.
Societies   please telephone in advance.
Green Fees not confirmed.
Cards   ▱ ▱ ▱ ▱ ▱
Prof   M Dunne
Facilities   ⊗ ∭ by prior arrangement ▱ ▱ ♀ ⚎ ▱ ⊤ ⌀
& Leisure   one motorised cart for hire by arrangement.
Location   Between Little Chalfont & Chorleywood

Hotel   ★★★ 66% The Crown, High St,
AMERSHAM ☎ 0870 400 8103
19 ⇉ ⋒ Annexe 18 ⇉ ⋒

LOUDWATER   Map 04 SU89

Wycombe Heights Golf Centre Rayners Ave HP10 9SW
☎ 01494 816686 Fax 01494 816728
Opened in 1991 and designed by the John Jacobs
Partnership. The golf centre includes a 24-bay driving range.
18 holes, 6253yds, Par 70, SSS 72, Course record 64.
Club membership 750.
Visitors   booking advisable 6 days in advance.
Societies   telephone in advance & confirm in writing.
Green Fees £7.95 (£15.95 weekends & bank holidays).
Cards   ▱ ▱ ▱ ▱ ▱ ▱
Prof   Adam Bishop
Designer   John Jacobs
Facilities   ⊗ ∭ ▱ ▱ ♀ ⚎ ▱ ⊤ ⟍ ⚞ ⌀ ⋔

Hotel   ★★★ 66% Posthouse High Wycombe, Handy
Cross, HIGH WYCOMBE
☎ 0870 400 9042 106 ⇉ ⋒

MARLOW   Map 04 SU88

Harleyford Harleyford Estate, Henley Rd SL7 2SP
☎ 01628 402300 Fax 01628 478434
Set in 160 acres, this Donald Steel designed course, founded
in 1996, makes the most of the natural rolling contours of the
beautiful parkland of the historic Harleyford Estate. A
challenging course to golfers of all handicaps. Stunning
views across the Thames Valley.
18 holes, 6653yds, Par 72, SSS 72, Course record 72.
Club membership 800.
Visitors   soft spikes only. Must contact in advance and
                  have a handicap certificate.

                                                        ▶

Societies handicap cert required, Tel 01628 402344 Groups co-ordinator.
Green Fees £40 per round (£60 weekends & bank holidays).
Cards
Prof Alasdair Barr
Designer Donald Steel
Facilities ⊗ ⅏ ⅃ ⊾ ♥ ♀ ⅄ 🏠 ⛳ 🏌 ↘ ⚒ ♂ ⚘
Location S side A4156 Marlow/Henley road, close to A404 Marlow bypass linking junct 4 M40/junct 8/9 M4

Hotel ★★★★ 75% Danesfield House, Henley Rd, MARLOW-ON-THAMES ☎ 01628 891010 87 ⇆ 🛏

MENTMORE — Map 04 SP91

Mentmore Golf & Country Club LU7 0UA
☎ 01296 662020 Fax 01296 662592
Two 18-hole courses - Rosebery and Rothschild - set within the wooded estate grounds of Mentmore Towers. Gently rolling parkland course with mature trees and lakes and two interesting feature holes; the long par 5 (606 yds) 9th on the Rosebery course with fine views of the Chilterns and the par 4 (340yd) 14th on the Rothschild course, in front of the Towers.
Rosebery Course: 18 holes, 6777yds, Par 72, SSS 72, Course record 68.
Rothschild Course: 18 holes, 6700yds, Par 72, SSS 72.
Club membership 1100.
Visitors must contact in advance, may not play weekends before 11am.
Societies by prior arrangement.
Green Fees not confirmed.
Cards
Prof Pip Elson
Designer Bob Sandow
Facilities ⊗ ⅏ ⅃ ⊾ ♥ ♀ ⅄ 🏠 ⛳ 🏌 ↘ ⚒ ♂ ⚘
& Leisure hard tennis courts, heated indoor swimming pool, fishing, sauna, gymnasium.
Location 4m S of Leighton Buzzard

MILTON KEYNES — Map 04 SP83

Abbey Hill Monks Way, Two Mile Ash MK8 8AA
☎ 01908 562408
Undulating municipal course within the new city. Tight fairways and well-placed bunkers. Stream comes into play on five holes. Also Par 3 course.
18 holes, 6122yds, Par 71, SSS 69, Course record 71.
Club membership 500.
Visitors no restrictions.
Societies must telephone (01908) 562408 in advance.
Green Fees not confirmed.
Cards
Prof Keith Bond
Facilities ⊗ ⅏ ⅃ ⊾ ♥ ♀ ⅄ 🏠 ⛳ 🏌 ↘ ⚒ ♂ ⚘
Location 2m W of new town centre off A5

Hotel ★★★ 64% Quality Hotel & Suites Milton Keynes, Monks Way, Two Mile Ash, MILTON KEYNES ☎ 01908 561666 88 ⇆ 🛏

Three Locks Great Brickhill MK17 9BH
☎ 01525 270470 & 270050 Fax 01525 270470
Parkland course offering a challenge to beginners and experienced golfers, with water coming into play on ten holes. Magnificent views.

18 holes, 6036yds, Par 71, SSS 68, Course record 69.
Club membership 300.
Visitors telephone 01525 270050 to book tee times.
Societies write or telephone for details.
Green Fees £15 per round (£17 weekends).
Cards
Prof G Harding
Facilities ⊗ ⅏ ♀ ⊾ 🏠 ⛳ 🏌 ↘ ⚒ ♂
& Leisure fishing.
Location A4146 between Leighton Buzzard/Bletchley

Hotel ★★★ 66% Posthouse Milton Keynes, 500 Saxon Gate West, MILTON KEYNES ☎ 0870 400 9057 150 ⇆ 🛏

PRINCES RISBOROUGH — Map 04 SP80

Whiteleaf Upper Icknield Way, Whiteleaf HP27 0LY
☎ 01844 274058 Fax 01844 275551
Short, hilly and tricky 9-hole parkland course, requiring great accuracy, set high in the Chilterns with beautiful views.
9 holes, 5391yds, Par 66, SSS 66, Course record 64.
Club membership 400.
Visitors advisable to contact in advance, with member only at weekends.
Societies on Thu only, must contact the secretary in advance.
Green Fees £25 per day; £18 per round.
Prof Ken Ward
Facilities ⊗ ⅏ by prior arrangement ⊾ ♥ ♀ ⅄ 🏠 ⛳ ♂
Location 1m NE off A4010

Hotel ★★ 63% Rose & Crown Hotel, Wycombe Rd, SAUNDERTON ☎ 01844 345299 15 ⇆ 🛏

STOKE POGES — Map 04 SU98

Farnham Park Park Rd SL2 4PJ
☎ 01753 643332 & 647065 Fax 01753 643332 & 647065
Fine, public parkland course in pleasing setting.
18 holes, 6172yds, Par 71, SSS 70, Course record 68.
Club membership 600.
Visitors telephone in advance for tee times.
Societies apply in writing.
Green Fees £10 per round (£13.50 weekends & bank holidays).
Cards
Prof Paul Warner
Designer Hawtree
Facilities ⊗ ⊾ ♥ ♀ ⅄ 🏠 ⛳ ♂
Location W side of village off B416

Hotel ★★★★ 68% Slough/Windsor Marriott, Ditton Rd, Langley, SLOUGH ☎ 01753 544244 380 ⇆ 🛏

Stoke Poges Stoke Park, Park Rd SL2 4PG
☎ 01753 717171 Fax 01753 717181
Judgement of the distance from the tee is all important on this first-class parkland course. Fairways are wide and the challenge seemingly innocuous. The 7th hole being the model for the well known 12th hole at Augusta. Stoke Poges is a 27 hole course and is considered the best traditional course in the British Isles.
Course 1: 18 holes, 6721yds, Par 71, SSS 72.
Course 2: 18 holes, 6551yds, Par 72, SSS 73.

Course 3: 18 holes, 6318yds, Par 71, SSS 70.
Club membership 750.

Visitors	must contact in advance.
Societies	telephone in advance.
Green Fees	on application.
Cards	🟦 ⬛ 🟦 🟦 📶
Prof	David Woodward
Designer	Harry Shapland Colt
Facilities	⊗ ⅲ 🏌 💺 ♀ 🏔 🏠 ⛳ 🏁 🛒 ⛳ (
& Leisure	hard and grass tennis courts, fishing.
Location	Turn off A4 at Slough into Stoke Poges Lane B416, club is 1.5m on left
Hotel	★★★★ 68% Slough/Windsor Marriott, Ditton Rd, Langley, SLOUGH ☎ 01753 544244 380 🛏 🐾

See advertisement in prelims

WAVENDON

Map 04 SP93

Wavendon Golf Centre Lower End Rd MK17 8DA
☎ 01908 281811 Fax 01908 281257
Pleasant parkland course set within mature oak and lime trees and incorporating several small lakes as water hazards. Easy walking.
18 holes, 5540yds, Par 68, SSS 68.
Club membership 300.

Visitors	booking advised.
Societies	must contact in advance by telephone.
Green Fees	not confirmed.
Cards	🟦 ⬛ 🟦 🟦 📶
Prof	Greg Iron
Designer	J Drake/N Elmer
Facilities	⊗ ⅲ 🏌 💺 ♀ 🏔 🏠 ⛳ 🛒 ⛳ (
Location	Just off A421
Hotel	★★★ 66% Moore Place Hotel, The Square, ASPLEY GUISE ☎ 01908 282000 39 🛏 🐾 Annexe 15 🛏 🐾

WESTON TURVILLE

Map 04 SP81

Weston Turville Golf & Squash Club New Rd HP22 5QT
☎ 01296 424084 Fax 01296 395376
Parkland course situated at the foot of the Chiltern Hills and providing an excellent challenge for the accomplished golfer, yet not too daunting for the higher handicap player. Flat easy walking with water hazards and many interesting holes, notably the testing dog-leg 5th (418yds).
18 holes, 6008yds, Par 69, SSS 69, Course record 68.
Club membership 600.

Visitors	no restrictions.
Societies	must contact in advance.
Green Fees	£25 per day; £20 per round (£25 weekends).
Cards	🟦 🟦 📶
Prof	Gary George
Facilities	⊗ 🏌 💺 ♀ 🏔 🏠 ⛳ 🏁 🛒 ⛳
& Leisure	squash.
Location	2m SE of Aylesbury, off A41

WEXHAM STREET

Map 04 SU98

Wexham Park SL3 6ND
☎ 01753 663271 Fax 01753 663318
Gently undulating parkland course. Three courses. One 18 hole, one challenging 9 hole and another 9 hole suitable for beginners.
Blue: 18 holes, 5346yds, Par 68, SSS 66.
Red: 9 holes, 2727yds, Par 68, SSS 67.
Green: 9 holes, 2219yds, Par 64, SSS 62.
Club membership 850.

Visitors	no restrictions
Societies	must contact in advance.
Green Fees	not confirmed.
Cards	🟦 🟦 📶
Prof	John Kennedy
Designer	E Lawrence/D Morgan
Facilities	⊗ 🏌 💺 ♀ 🏔 🏠 ⛳ 🛒 ⛳ (
Location	0.5m S
Hotel	★★★★ 68% Slough/Windsor Marriott, Ditton Rd, Langley, SLOUGH ☎ 01753 544244 380 🛏 🐾

WING

Map 04 SP82

Aylesbury Vale Stewkley Rd LU7 0UJ
☎ 01525 240196 Fax 01525 240848
The course set in quiet countryside is gently undulating. There are five ponds to add interest, notably on the par 4 420 yd 13th - unlucky for some - where the second shot is all downhill with an inviting pond spanning the approach to the green. In addition there is a 10-bay driving range and practice putting green.
18 holes, 6612yds, Par 72, SSS 72, Course record 68.
Club membership 545.

Visitors	must adhere to dress regulations. Must contact in advance.
Societies	telephone to book in advance.
Green Fees	£16 per day; £12 per 18 holes; £6 per 9 holes (£28/£21/£11 weekends & bank holidays).
Cards	🟦 🟦
Prof	Chris Skeet
Designer	D Wright
Facilities	⊗ ⅲ by prior arrangement 🏌 💺 ♀ 🏔 🏠 ⛳ 🛒 ⛳ (
Location	2m NW of Leighton Buzzard on unclassified Stewkley road, between Wing/Stewkley

---

AA Hotels that have special arrangements with golf courses are listed at the back of the guide

---

CAMBRIDGESHIRE

BAR HILL   Map 05 TL36

Cambridgeshire Moat House Moat House Hotel, Bar
Hill CB3 8EU
☎ 01954 780098 & 249971 Fax 01954 780010
Mature undulating parkland course with tree-lined
fairways, easy walking.
18 holes, 6734yds, Par 72, SSS 72, Course record 68.
Club membership 600.

Visitors	must book in advance.
Societies	must telephone in advance.
Green Fees	£20 per round (£30 weekends & bank holidays).
Cards	〰 ■ ■ ⬚ 🃏 🔄 ▨
Prof	Paul Simpson
Facilities	⊗ ⅏ ⬧ ■ ⬤ ♀ ♨ 🏠 🍸 🏑 🐎 ⚘
& Leisure	hard tennis courts, heated indoor swimming pool, sauna, solarium, gymnasium.
Location	5m NW of Cambridge

Hotel   ★★★ 66% Cambridgeshire Moat House,
BAR HILL ☎ 01954 249988 134 ⇆ ⌷

BRAMPTON   Map 04 TL27

Brampton Park Buckden Rd PE18 8NF
☎ 01480 434700 Fax 01480 411145
Set in truly attractive countryside, bounded by the River
Great Ouse and bisected by the River Lane. Great variety
with mature trees, lakes and water hazards. One of the most
difficult holes is the 4th, a Par 3 island green, 175 yards in
length.
18 holes, 6300yds, Par 71, SSS 72, Course record 64.
Club membership 650.

Visitors	must contact in advance.
Societies	apply in advance.
Green Fees	£25 per day/round (£35 weekends & bank holidays).
Cards	〰 ■
Prof	Alisdair Currie
Designer	Simon Gidman
Facilities	⊗ ⬧ ■ ⬤ ♀ ♨ 🏠 🐎 ⚘
Location	Follow signs from A1 or A14 to RAF Brampton

Hotel   ★★★ 75% The Old Bridge Hotel, 1 High St,
HUNTINGDON ☎ 01480 452681   24 ⇆ ⌷

CAMBRIDGE   Map 05 TL45

Gog Magog Shelford Bottom CB2 4AB
☎ 01223 247626 Fax 01223 414990
Situated just outside the centre of the university town,
Gog Magog, established in 1901, is known as the nursery
of Cambridge undergraduate golf. The courses are on
high ground, and it is said that if you stand on the highest
point and could see far enough to the east the next
highest ground would be the Ural Mountains! The
courses are open but there are enough trees and other
hazards to provide plenty of problems. Views from the
high parts are superb. The nature of the ground ensures
good winter golf. The area has been designated a Site of
Special Scientific Interest (SSSI).

*Old Course: 18 holes, 6400yds, Par 70, SSS 70, Course
record 60.*
Wandlebury: 18 holes, 6735yds, Par 72, SSS 72.
Club membership 1280.

Visitors	Must contact in advance. Mon-Fri only.
Societies	Tue & Thu by reservation.
Green Fees	not confirmed.
Prof	Ian Bamborough
Designer	Hawtree Ltd
Facilities	⊗ ⅏ ⬧ ■ ⬤ ♀ ♨ 🏠 🍸 🏑 ⚘ ⌷
Location	3m SE on A1307

Hotel   ★★★ 70% Gonville Hotel, Gonville Place,
CAMBRIDGE
☎ 01223 366611 & 221111
Fax 01223 315470   64 ⇆ ⌷

ELY   Map 05 TL58

Ely City 107 Cambridge Rd CB7 4HX
☎ 01353 662751 (Office) Fax 01353 668636
Parkland course slightly undulating with water hazards
formed by lakes and natural dykes. Demanding par 4 5th hole
(467yds), often into a headwind, and a testing par 3 2nd hole
(160yds) played over 2 ponds Magnificent views of
Cathedral. Lee Trevino is the professional record holder.
18 holes, 6627yds, Par 72, SSS 72, Course record 66.
Club membership 850.

Visitors	advisable to contact the club in advance.
Societies	Tue to Fri, advisable to contact club well in advance.
Green Fees	£28 per day (£34 weekends & bank holidays).
Prof	Andrew George
Designer	Sir Henry Cotton
Facilities	⊗ ⅏ ⬧ ■ ⬤ ♀ ♨ 🏠 🍸 ⚘
& Leisure	snooker.
Location	S of city on A10

Hotel   ★★ 60% The Nyton Hotel, 7 Barton Rd, ELY
☎ 01353 662459   10 ⇆ ⌷

GIRTON   Map 05 TL46

Girton Dodford Ln CB3 0QE
☎ 01223 276169 Fax 01223 277150
Flat, open parkland course with many trees and ditches.
Easy walking.
18 holes, 6085yds, Par 69, SSS 69, Course record 66.
Club membership 800.

Visitors	with member only at weekends. Contact professional in advance (01223 276991).
Societies	apply writing.
Green Fees	£20 per round.
Prof	Scott Thomson
Designer	Allan Gow
Facilities	⊗ ⅏ ⬧ ■ ⬤ ♀ ♨ 🏠 🍸 ⚘
Location	NW side of village

Hotel   ★★★ 68% Posthouse Cambridge,
Lakeview, Bridge Rd, Impington,
CAMBRIDGE ☎ 08703 400 9015
165 ⇆ ⌷

Looking for a driving range?
See the index at the back of the guide

HEMINGFORD ABBOTS
Map 04 TL27

Hemingford Abbots Cambridge Rd PE18 9HQ
☎ 01480 495000 & 493900 Fax 01480 4960000
Interesting 9-hole course featuring a par 5 dog-leg 4th with a testing tapering fairway, two ponds at the entrance to the 8th green and an island green on the 9th.
9 holes, 5468yds, Par 68, SSS 68, Course record 69.
Club membership 170.

Visitors	advisable to phone in advance, particularly for weekends.
Societies	advise in writing or telephone.
Green Fees	not confirmed.
Prof	Craig Watson
Designer	Ray Paton
Facilities	⊗ ⍢ ⓺ ⓛ ⓨ ♨ ⓐ ⓣ ✐ ↾
Location	A14 Hemingford Abbots turning

Hotel ★★★ 75% The Old Bridge Hotel, 1 High St, HUNTINGDON ☎ 01480 452681 24 ⇄ ↾

LONGSTANTON
Map 05 TL36

Cambridge Station Rd CB4 5DR ☎ 01954 789388
An undulating parkland course with bunkers and ponds.
18 holes, 6736yds, Par 72, SSS 73.
Club membership 300.

Visitors	must contact in advance.
Societies	must telephone in advance.
Green Fees	£9 per round (£12 weekends).
Cards	▭ ▭ ▭ ▭ ▭
Prof	Geoff Huggett
Facilities	⊗ ⓺ ⓛ ⓨ ♨ ⓣ ↾ ➘ ↾ ✐ ↾
& Leisure	fishing.

Hotel ★★★ 66% Cambridgeshire Moat House, BAR HILL ☎ 01954 249988 134 ⇄ ↾

MARCH
Map 05 TL49

March Frogs Abbey, Grange Rd PE15 0YH
☎ 01354 652364 Fax 01354 652364
Nine-hole parkland course with a particularly challenging par 3 9th hole, with out of bounds on the right and high hedges to the right.
9 holes, 6204yds, Par 70, SSS 70, Course record 65.
Club membership 413.

Visitors	contact in advance, with member only at weekends.
Societies	must contact in advance.
Green Fees	£16.50 per day.
Cards	▭ ▭ ▭
Prof	Phillip Dimmock
Facilities	⊗ by prior arrangement ⍢ by prior arrangement ⓺ by prior arrangement ⓨ ♨ ⓐ ✐
Location	0.5m off A141, March bypass

Hotel ★★ 64% Olde Griffin Hotel, High St, MARCH ☎ 01354 652517 20rm (19 ⇄ ↾)

> AA Hotels that have special arrangements with golf courses are listed at the back of the guide

PETERBOROUGH
Map 04 TL19

Elton Furze Bullock Rd, Haddon PE7 3TT
☎ 01832 280189 & 280614 (Pro shop) Fax 01832 280299
Wooded parkland 18-hole course in lovely surroundings.
18 holes, 6289yds, Par 70, SSS 70, Course record 67.
Club membership 620.

Visitors	welcome, preferably Mon-Thu, weekends only with prior permission (phone in advance).
Societies	by prior arrangement telephone for details.
Green Fees	£30 per day; £22 per round (£32 per round weekends).
Prof	Frank Kiddie
Designer	Roger Fitton
Facilities	⊗ ⍢ ⓺ ⓛ ⓨ ♨ ⓐ ♨ ✐ ↾
Location	4m SW of Peterborough, off A605

Hotel ★★★★ 68% Swallow Hotel, Peterborough Business Park, Lynchwood, PETERBOROUGH ☎ 01733 371111 163 ⇄ ↾

Orton Meadows Ham Ln, Orton Waterville PE2 5UU
☎ 01733 237478 Fax 01733 332774
Pretty public parkland course set within the Nene Valley Country Park with large lakes and water hazards. Challenging 3rd hole (480yards from white tee) incorporating lots of water and 'out of bounds' areas. Also 12-hole pitch and putt course.
18 holes, 5269yds, Par 67, SSS 68, Course record 69.
Club membership 650.

Visitors	phone for reservations 7 days in advance.
Societies	apply in advance.
Green Fees	£10.50 per round (£13.50 weekends & bank holidays).
Cards	▭ ▭ ▭ ▭ ▭
Prof	Jason Mitchell
Designer	D & R Fitton
Facilities	⊗ ⍢ ⓺ ⓛ ⓨ ♨ ⓐ ♨ ↾ ⇄ ✐
& Leisure	12 hole pitch & putt.
Location	3m W of town on A605

Hotel ★★★ 66% Orton Hall Hotel, Orton Longueville, PETERBOROUGH ☎ 01733 391111 65 ⇄ ↾

Peterborough Milton Milton Ferry PE6 7AG
☎ 01733 380489 Fax 01733 380489
Designed by James Braid, this well-bunkered parkland course is set in the grounds of the Milton Estate, many of the holes being played in full view of Milton Hall. Challenging holes are the difficult dog-leg 10th and 15th. Easy walking.
18 holes, 6479yds, Par 71, SSS 72, Course record 62.
Club membership 800.

Visitors	must contact in advance. Handicap certificate required.
Societies	bookings in writing to secretary.
Green Fees	£35 per day; £25 per round (£35 per round weekends).
Prof	Michael Gallagher
Designer	James Braid
Facilities	⊗ ⍢ ⓺ ⓛ ⓨ ♨ ⓐ ✐ ↾
Location	2m W of Peterborough on A47

Hotel ★★★ 66% Butterfly Hotel, Thorpe Meadows, Longthorpe Parkway, PETERBOROUGH ☎ 01733 64240 70 ⇄ ↾

Thorpe Wood Thorpe Wood, Nene Parkway PE3 6SE
☎ 01733 267701 Fax 01733 332774
Gently undulating, parkland course designed by Peter Alliss
and Dave Thomas. Challenging holes include the 5th, the
longest hole usually played with prevailing wind and the
14th, entailing a difficult approach shot over water to a two-
tier green.
18 holes, 7086yds, Par 73, SSS 74, Course record 68.
Club membership 750.
Visitors   phone for reservations 7 days in advance.
Societies   must telephone in advance, society bookings
                taken up to year ahead.
Green Fees £10.50 per round (£13.50 weekends & bank
                holidays).
Cards   🃏 💳 💳 💳 🃏
Prof   Dennis & Roger Fitton
Designer   Peter Allis/Dave Thomas
Facilities ⊗ ⏐ ⓑ ⬛ ♀ ⚘ 🖭 ⏱ ♂
Location   3m W of city centre on A47

Hotel   ★★★ 67% Peterborough Moat House, Thorpe
                Wood, PETERBOROUGH
                ☎ 01733 289988 133 ➿ ⋔

PIDLEY   Map 05 TL37

Lakeside Lodge Fen Rd PE17 3DD
☎ 01487 740540 Fax 01487 740852
A well designed, spacious course incorporating eight lakes,
12,000 trees and a modern clubhouse. The 9th and 18th holes
both finish dramatically alongside a lake in front of the
clubhouse. Also 9-hole Par 3 and 25-bay driving range. The
Manor provides an interesting contrast with its undulating
fairways and angular greens.
*Lodge Course: 18 holes, 6821yds, Par 72, SSS 73, Course
record 72.*
The Manor: 9 holes, 2601yds, Par 68.
Club membership 850.
Visitors   no restrictions.
Societies   must telephone in advance.
Green Fees £11 (£17 weekends).
Prof   Scott Waterman
Designer   A W Headley
Facilities ⊗ ⏐ ⓑ ⬛ ♀ ⚘ 🖭 ⏱ ⇖ ♂ ⏱ ♂
& Leisure   fishing, ten pin bowling, smart golf simulator.

Hotel   ★★★ 67% Slepe Hall Hotel, Ramsey Rd, ST
                IVES ☎ 01480 463122 16 ➿ ⋔

RAMSEY   Map 04 TL28

Old Nene Golf & Country Club Muchwood Ln, Bodsey
PE17 1XQ ☎ 01487 813519 & 815622
A flat well-drained course with water hazards. There are
excellent greens and there are many challenging holes across
water in either a head wind or cross wind.
9 holes, 5605yds, Par 68, SSS 68, Course record 66.
Club membership 170.
Visitors   book in advance especially evenings &
                weekends. Dress code must be adhered to.
Societies   arrange in advance with Secretary.
Green Fees £15 per day; £10 per 18 holes; £7 per 9 holes
                (£15/£9 weekends & bank holidays).
Prof   Roland Tinsdal
Designer   R Edrich

Facilities ⊗ ⏐ ⓑ ⬛ ♀ ⚘ 🖭 ⏱ ⇖ 🚲 ♂ ⏱
& Leisure   fishing, practice area.
Location   0.75m N of Ramsey towards Ramsey Mereside

Hotel   ★★★ 75% The Old Bridge Hotel, 1 High St,
                HUNTINGDON ☎ 01480 452681 24 ➿ ⋔

Ramsey 4 Abbey Ter PE17 1DD
☎ 01487 812600 Fax 01487 815746
Flat, parkland course with water hazards and well irrigated
greens, mature tees and fairways, assuring a good surface
whatever the conditions. It gives the impression of wide open
spaces, but the wayward ball is soon punished.
18 holes, 5830yds, Par 71, SSS 68, Course record 65.
Club membership 750.
Visitors   contact professional in advance 01487 813022,
                may only play with member at weekends &
                bank holidays.
Societies   apply in writing.
Green Fees £25 per day/round.
Prof   Stuart Scott
Designer   J Hamilton Stutt
Facilities ⊗ by prior arrangement ⏐ by prior arrangement
                ⓑ ⬛ ♀ ⚘ 🖭 ⏱ ♂
& Leisure   snooker tables, bowls rinks.
Location   12m SE of Peterborough on B1040

Hotel   ★★★ 75% The Old Bridge Hotel, 1 High St,
                HUNTINGDON ☎ 01480 452681 24 ➿ ⋔

ST IVES   Map 05 TL37

St Ives (Cambs) Westwood Rd PE17 4RS
☎ 01480 468392 Fax 01480 468392
Picturesque parkland course.
9 holes, 6100yds, Par 70, SSS 69, Course record 68.
Club membership 500.
Visitors   may not play weekends.
Societies   welcome Wed & Fri.
Green Fees not confirmed.
Prof   Darren Glasby
Facilities ⊗ ⏐ ⓑ ⬛ ♀ ⚘ 🖭 ⏱ ♂
Location   W side of town centre off A1123

Hotel   ★★★ 67% Slepe Hall Hotel, Ramsey Rd, ST
                IVES ☎ 01480 463122 16 ➿ ⋔

ST NEOTS   Map 04 TL16

Abbotsley Golf & Squash Club Eynesbury Hardwicke
PE19 4XN ☎ 01480 474000 & 215153 Fax 01480 403280
Two courses - main Abbotsley course featuring mature
parkland with tree-lined fairways, plenty of water hazards
and a particularly testing par 3 2nd hole - the 'Mousehole'.
Cromwell course is less demanding with tricky driving holes
and sloping greens. Courses surround moated country house
and hotel. Residential golf schools 30 weeks of the year plus
floodlit, covered driving range, par 3 course and grass
practice area..
*Abbotsley Course: 18 holes, 6311yds, Par 73, SSS 72,
Course record 69.*
Cromwell Course: 18 holes, 6087yds, Par 70, SSS 69.
Club membership 550.
Visitors   welcome all times. Necessary to book
                weekends.
Societies   prior booking essential.

▶

Green Fees Abbotsley: Apr-Oct £19 (£25 weekends)
Cromwell: £9 (£15 weekends).
Cards ▭▭ ▭▭ ▭▭ 🖸
Prof Denise Hastings
Designer D Young/V Saunders
Facilities ⊗ ⫴ ⬛ ♿ ⬛ ♀ ⚐ ☖ 🏳 🏌 🛒 ♣ ✆ ⚷
& Leisure squash, gymnasium, 9 hole par 3 course.
Location 2m SE off B1046

Hotel ★★ 63% Abbotsley Golf Hotel & Country
Club, Potton Rd, Eynesbury Hardwicke, ST
NEOTS ☎ 01480 474000 17 ⇋ 🐾

St Neots Crosshall Rd PE19 4AE ☎ 01480 472363
Undulating and very picturesque parkland course with lake
and water hazards and exceptional greens, close to the Kym
and Great Ouse rivers. Easy, level walking.
18 holes, 6074yds, Par 69, SSS 69, Course record 64.
Club membership 630.
Visitors must book in advance. with member only at
weekends.
Societies must contact in advance.
Green Fees £35 per day; £25 per round.
Prof Graham Bithrey
Designer H Vardon
Facilities ⊗ ⫴ ⬛ ♿ ⬛ ♀ ⚐ ☖ 🏳 🛒 ♣ ✆
Location Just off the A1 with the jct B1048 heading into
St Neots

Hotel ★★ 63% Abbotsley Golf Hotel & Country
Club, Potton Rd, Eynesbury Hardwicke, ST
NEOTS ☎ 01480 474000 17 ⇋ 🐾

THORNEY
Map 04 TF20

Thorney English Drove, Thorney PE6 0TJ
☎ 01733 270570 Fax 01733 270842
The 18-hole Fen course is ideal for the beginner, while the
Lakes course has a challenging links-style layout with eight
holes around water.
*Fen Course: 18 holes, 6104yds, Par 70, SSS 69, Course
record 66.*
*Lakes Course: 18 holes, 6402yds, Par 71, SSS 70, Course
record 65.*
Club membership 400.
Visitors book in advance for Fen course, limited
weekend play Lakes course.
Societies contact in advance.
Green Fees Fen Course: £6.75 per round (£8.75 weekends).
Lakes Course: £18.50 per day; £11 per round
(£28/£17.50 weekends).
Prof Mark Templeman
Designer A Dow
Facilities ⊗ ⫴ ⬛ ♿ ⬛ ♀ ⚐ ☖ 🏳 🛒 ♣ ✆ ⚷
Location Off A47, 7m NE of Peterborough

Hotel ★★★ 66% Butterfly Hotel, Thorpe Meadows,
Longthorpe Parkway, PETERBOROUGH
☎ 01733 64240 70 ⇋ 🐾

TOFT
Map 05 TL35

Cambridge Meridian Comberton Rd CB3 7RY
☎ 01223 264700 Fax 01223 264701
Set in 207 acres to a Peter Allis/Clive Clark design with
sweeping fairways, lakes and well bunkered greens. The 4th
hole has bunker complexes, a sharp dog-leg and a river with

the green heavily guarded by bunkers. The 9th and 10th holes
challenge the golfer with river crossings.
18 holes, 6651yds, Par 73, SSS 72, Course record 72.
Club membership 600.
Visitors must contact in advance.
Societies telephone for provisional booking
Green Fees £14 per round (£18 weekends).
Cards ▭▭ ▭▭
Prof Michael Clemons
Designer Peter Alliss/Clive Clark
Facilities ⬛ ♿ ⬛ ♀ ⚐ ☖ 🏳 🛒 ♣ ✆
Location 3m W of Cambridge, on B1046

Hotel ★★ 63% Abbotsley Golf Hotel & Country
Club, Potton Rd, Eynesbury Hardwicke, ST
NEOTS ☎ 01480 474000 17 ⇋ 🐾

CHESHIRE

ALDERLEY EDGE
Map 07 SJ87

Alderley Edge Brook Ln SK9 7RU ☎ 01625 585583
Well-wooded, undulating pastureland course. A stream
crosses 7 of the 9 holes.
9 holes, 5823yds, Par 68, SSS 68, Course record 62.
Club membership 400.
Visitors by arrangement on Thu.
Societies Thu only, apply in writing or telephone.
Green Fees £20 per round; (£25 weekends).
Prof Peter Bowring
Facilities ⊗ ⫴ ⬛ ♿ ⬛ ♀ ⚐ ☖ ✆
Location 1m NW on B5085

Hotel ★★★ 71% Alderley Edge Hotel, Macclesfield
Rd, ALDERLEY EDGE ☎ 01625 583033
46 ⇋ 🐾

ALSAGER
Map 07 SJ75

Alsager Golf & Country Club Audley Rd ST7 2UR
☎ 01270 875700 Fax 01270 882207
An 18-hole parkland course situated in rolling Cheshire
countryside and offering a challenge to all golfers whatever
their standard. Clubhouse is well appointed with good
facilities and a friendly atmosphere.
18 holes, 6225yds, Par 70, SSS 70, Course record 68.
Club membership 640.
Visitors must contact in advance, may not play Fri
afternoon, can only play with member at
weekends.
Societies must contact in advance.
Green Fees not confirmed.
Prof Richard Brown
Facilities ⊗ ⫴ ⬛ ♿ ⬛ ♀ ⚐ ☖ ✆
Location 2m NE of M6 junct 16

Hotel ★★★ 73% Manor House Hotel, Audley Rd,
ALSAGER ☎ 01270 884000 57 ⇋ 🐾

Where to stay, where to eat?
Visit the AA internet site
www.theaa.co.uk

CHESTER
Map 07 SJ46

Carden Park Hotel Carden Park CH3 9DQ
☎ 01829 731000 Fax 01829 731032
A superb golf resort set in 750 acres of beautiful Cheshire
countryside. Facilities include the mature parkland Cheshire
Course, the Nicklaus Course, the 9 hole par 3 Azalea Course,
Europe's first Jack Nicklaus Residential Golf School and a
luxurious clubhouse.
Cheshire: 18 holes, 6891yds, Par 72, SSS 71,
Course record 69.
Nicklaus: 18 holes, 6302yds, Par 72, SSS 72.
Club membership 250.

Visitors	must contact in advance, handicap certificate required for the Nicklaus Course. To help maintain the highest quality metal spikes cannot be worn.
Societies	contact for details, tel: 01829 731594.
Green Fees	Cheshire: £40 per round; Nicklaus: £60 per round.
Cards	🚗 ▬▬ 💳 📇 🔲
Prof	Simon Edwards
Facilities	⊗ ⫼ 🍴 🏌 🍺 ♀ 🏖 🏠 ⛳ 🚩 🐎 ➰ 👤
& Leisure	hard tennis courts, heated indoor swimming pool, sauna, solarium, gymnasium, residential golf school, snooker room, dance studio.
Location	Off A534
Hotel	★★★★ 72% De Vere Carden Park Hotel Golf Resort & Spa, Carden Park, BROXTON ☎ 01829 731000 115 ⇌ ⟟ Annexe 77 ⇌ ⟟

Chester Curzon Park CH4 8AR
☎ 01244 677760 Fax 01244 676667
Meadowland course on two levels contained within a loop of
the River Dee. The car park overlooks the racecourse across
the river.
18 holes, 6508yds, Par 72, SSS 71, Course record 66.
Club membership 820.

Visitors	must contact in advance.
Societies	must telephone or write in advance.
Green Fees	£25 per day (£30 weekends).
Prof	George Parton
Facilities	⊗ ⫼ 🍴 🏌 🍺 ♀ 🏖 🏠 🔲 ➰
Location	1m W of city centre
Hotel	★★★★ 67% Chester Moat House, Trinity St, CHESTER ☎ 01244 899988 160 ⇌ ⟟

> Entries with a green background
> identify courses considered to be
> particularly interesting

Eaton Guy Ln, Waverton CH3 7PH
☎ 01244 335885 & 335826 Fax 01244 335782
A parkland course with a liberal covering of both mature
trees and new planting enhanced by natural water hazards.
18 holes, 6562yds, Par 72, SSS 71, Course record 69.
Club membership 550.

Visitors	must contact in advance particularly for weekends.
Societies	must contact in advance. May not play weekends or Wednesdays.
Green Fees	not confirmed.
Cards	▬
Prof	Neil Dunroe
Designer	Donald Steel
Facilities	⊗ ⫼ 🍴 🏌 🍺 ♀ 🏖 🏠 🚩 🐎 ➰
Location	3m SE of Chester off A41
Hotel	★★★★★ 78% The Chester Grosvenor Hotel, Eastgate, CHESTER ☎ 01244 324024 85 ⇌ ⟟

Upton-by-Chester Upton Ln, Upton-by-Chester CH2 1EE
☎ 01244 381183 Fax 01244 376955
Pleasant, tree-lined, parkland course. Not easy for low-
handicap players to score well. Testing holes are 2nd (par 4),
14th (par 4) and 15th (par 3).
18 holes, 5808yds, Par 69, SSS 68, Course record 63.
Club membership 800.

Visitors	must contact in advance.
Societies	apply in writing.
Green Fees	£25 per day. £30 per round weekends & bank holidays.
Prof	P A Gardner
Facilities	⊗ ⫼ 🍴 🏌 🍺 ♀ 🏖 🏠 🐎 ➰
Location	N side off A5116
Hotel	★★★★ 66% Mollington Banastre Hotel, Parkgate Rd, CHESTER ☎ 01244 851471 63 ⇌

Vicars Cross Tarvin Rd, Great Barrow CH3 7HN
☎ 01244 335174 Fax 01244 335686
Tree-lined parkland course, with undulating terrain.
18 holes, 6365yds, Par 72, SSS 70, Course record 64.
Club membership 750.

Visitors	advisable to contact in advance, visitors may not play competition days or Wed.
Societies	Tue & Thu only. Must book in advance.
Green Fees	£25 per day.
Prof	J A Forsythe
Designer	J Richardson

▶

Facilities ⊗ ≋ ᕦ ♥ ♀ ⚐ 🏠 ⚒
Location 4m E on A51

Hotel ★★★ 68% Rowton Hall Country House Hotel, Whitchurch Rd, Rowton, CHESTER ☎ 01244 335262 42 ⇄ ⟰

CONGLETON   Map 07 SJ86

Astbury Peel Ln, Astbury CW12 4RE
☎ 01260 279139 Fax 01260 279139
Parkland course in open countryside, bisected by a canal. The testing 12th hole involves a long carry over a tree-filled ravine. Large practice area.
18 holes, 6296yds, Par 71, SSS 70, Course record 61.
Club membership 720.
Visitors must be a member of a recognised golf club and possess official handicap. May only play weekdays Apr-Nov.
Societies contact for details.
Green Fees £30 per round.
Prof Ashley Salt
Facilities ⊗ ᕦ ♥ ♀ ⚐ 🏠 ⚒
Location 1.5m S between A34 and A527

Hotel ★★★ 61% Lion & Swan Hotel, Swan Bank, CONGLETON ☎ 01260 273115 21 ⇄ ⟰

Congleton Biddulph Rd CW12 3LZ ☎ 01260 273540
Superbly-manicured parkland course with views over three counties from the balcony of the clubhouse.
9 holes, 5103yds, Par 68, SSS 65.
Club membership 400.
Visitors may not play during competitions. Must contact in advance.
Societies must apply in writing to Secretary.
Green Fees £21 per round (£31 weekends).
Prof John Colclough
Facilities ᕦ ♥ by prior arrangement ♀ ⚐ 🏠
Location 1.5m SE on A527

Hotel ★★★ 61% Lion & Swan Hotel, Swan Bank, CONGLETON ☎ 01260 273115 21 ⇄ ⟰

CREWE   Map 07 SJ75

Crewe Fields Rd, Haslington CW1 5TB
☎ 01270 584099 Fax 01270 584099
Undulating parkland course.
18 holes, 6424yds, Par 71, SSS 71, Course record 66.
Club membership 674.
Visitors may not play at weekends, contact professional for details.
Societies Tue only, prior arrangement with the secretary.
Green Fees Summer: £27 per day; £22 after 1pm Winter: £15 per day.
Prof Mike Booker
Facilities ⊗ ≋ by prior arrangement ᕦ ♥ ♀ ⚐ 🏠 ⚒
Location 2.25m NE off A534

Hotel ★★★ 64% Hunters Lodge Hotel, Sydney Rd, Sydney, CREWE ☎ 01270 583440 47 ⇄ ⟰

Queen's Park Queen's Park Dr CW2 7SB
☎ 01270 666724 Fax 01270 569902
A short but testing municipal course, the 9 holes are highlighted by the tight dogleg 4th holes and 450yard Par 4

7th hole. There is a testing Par 4 on finishing hole with a bomb crater on left and outerbounds on the right.
9 holes, 4920yds, Par 68, SSS 64, Course record 67.
Club membership 400.
Visitors booking for weekends, cannot play Wed or Sun before 10.30am.
Societies must book at least 2 weeks in advance.
Green Fees not confirmed.
Cards 💳 💳 💳 💳 💳 💳 💳
Prof David Evanson
Facilities ⊗ ᕦ ♥ ♀ ⚐ 🏠 ⚒
& Leisure hard tennis courts, bowling green.
Location Located behind Queen's Park. Well signposted

Hotel ★★★ 64% Hunters Lodge Hotel, Sydney Rd, Sydney, CREWE ☎ 01270 583440 47 ⇄ ⟰

DELAMERE   Map 07 SJ56

Delamere Forest Station Rd CW8 2JE
☎ 01606 883264 (Office) 883307 (Pro)
Fax 01606 883800 (Sec)
Played mostly on undulating open heath there is great charm in the way this course drops down into the occasional pine sheltered valley. Six of the first testing nine hole are between 420 and 455 yards in length.
18 holes, 6328yds, Par 72, SSS 70, Course record 63.
Club membership 500.

Visitors must contact in advance.
Societies apply in writing or by telephone.
Green Fees not confirmed.
Prof Ellis B Jones
Designer H Fowler
Facilities ⊗ ≋ by prior arrangement ᕦ ♥ ♀ ⚐ 🏠 ⚒
Location 1.5m NE, off B5152

Hotel ★★★ Nunsmere Hall Country House Hotel, Tarporley Rd, SANDIWAY ☎ 01606 889100 37 ⇄ ⟰

DISLEY   Map 07 SJ98

Disley Stanley Hall Ln SK12 2JX
☎ 01663 762071 & 764001 (Sec) Fax 01663 762678
Straddling a hilltop site above Lyme Park, this undulating parkland/moorland course affords good views and requires accuracy of approach to almost all the greens which lie on either a ledge or plateau. Testing holes are the 3rd and 4th.
18 holes, 6015yds, Par 71, SSS 69, Course record 63.
Club membership 658.

▶

Visitors	contact in advance, may not normally play at weekends.
Societies	by prior arrangement.
Green Fees	£25.
Prof	Andrew Esplin
Facilities	⊗ ⁜ ⅃ ♥ ♀ ♋ 🖰 ⏱ ⎘
Location	NW side of village off A6

Hotel	★★★ 64% County Hotel Bramhall, Bramhall Ln South, BRAMHALL ☎ 0161 455 9988 65 ⇄ 🐾

ELLESMERE PORT   Map 07 SJ47

Ellesmere Port Chester Rd, Childer Thornton CH66 1QF
☎ 0151 339 7689 Fax 0151 339 7689
Municipal parkland course that is easy walking, with natural hazards of woods, brook and ponds.
18 holes, 6432yds, Par 71, SSS 70.
Club membership 300.

Visitors	must book with professional & send a deposit.
Societies	by arrangement with professional.
Green Fees	£6.90 (£8 weekends).
Cards	🖻 💳 🅿 🖻 📇 🗗
Prof	Tony Roberts
Designer	Cotton, Pennick & Lawrie
Facilities	⊗ ⁜ ⅃ ♥ ♀ ♋ 🖰 ⏱ ⎘
& Leisure	squash.
Location	NW side of town centre on A41

Hotel	★★★ 65% Quality Hotel Chester, Welsh Road/Berwick Rd, Little Sutton, WIRRAL ☎ 0151 339 5121 53 ⇄ 🐾

FRODSHAM   Map 07 SJ57

Frodsham Simons Ln WA6 6HE
☎ 01928 732159 Fax 01928 734070
Undulating parkland course with pleasant views from all parts. Emphasis on accuracy over the whole course, the long and difficult par 5 18th necessitating a drive across water to the green. Crossed by two footpaths so extreme care needed.
18 holes, 6298yds, Par 70, SSS 70, Course record 67.
Club membership 600.

Visitors	must contact in advance. May not play at weekends.
Societies	telephone for bookings.
Green Fees	£30 per round.
Cards	🖻 💳 🖻 📇 🗗
Prof	Graham Tonge
Designer	John Day
Facilities	⊗ ⁜ ⅃ ♥ ♀ ♋ 🖰 ⏱ ⎘
& Leisure	snooker.
Location	1.5m SW

Hotel	★★★ 67% Forest Hills Hotel & Leisure Complex, Bellemonte Rd, Overton Hill, FRODSHAM ☎ 01928 735255 57 ⇄ 🐾

HELSBY   Map 07 SJ47

Helsby Towers Ln WA6 0JB
☎ 01928 722021 Fax 01928 725384
Parkland course with several tree plantations and natural pits as water hazards. Total of 41 bunkers.
18 holes, 6221yds, Par 70, SSS 70, Course record 69.
Club membership 590.

Visitors	must contact in advance. Weekends and bank holidays with member only.
Societies	Tue & Thu. Booking through Hon Secretary.
Green Fees	£34 per day; £25 per round.
Prof	Matthew Jones
Designer	James Braid (part)
Facilities	⊗ ⁜ ⅃ ♥ ♀ ♋ 🖰 ⏱ ⎘
Location	1m S off A56

Hotel	★★★★★ 78% The Chester Grosvenor Hotel, Eastgate, CHESTER ☎ 01244 324024 85 ⇄ 🐾

KNUTSFORD   Map 07 SJ77

Heyrose Budworth Rd, Tabley WA16 0HZ
☎ 01565 733664 Fax 01565 734267
An 18-hole course in wooded and gently undulating terrain. The par 3 16th (237yds), bounded by a small river in a wooded valley, is an interesting and testing hole - one of the toughest par 3s in Cheshire. Several water hazards. Both the course and the comfortable clubhouse have attractive views.
18 holes, 6515yds, Par 73, SSS 71, Course record 66.
Club membership 600.

Visitors	not before 3.30pm Sat, ladies priority Wed and seniors priority Thu am.
Societies	must contact in advance.
Green Fees	£19 per 18 holes (£24 weekends & bank holidays).
Cards	🖻 💳
Prof	Colin Iddon
Designer	C N Bridge
Facilities	⊗ ⁜ by prior arrangement ⅃ ♥ ♀ ♋ 🖰 ⎘
Location	1.5m from junc 19 on M6

Hotel	★★★★ 66% Cottons Hotel, Manchester Rd, KNUTSFORD ☎ 01565 650333 99 ⇄ 🐾

Knutsford Mereheath Ln WA16 6HS ☎ 01565 633355
Parkland course set in a beautiful old deer park. It demands some precise iron play.
9 holes, 6288yds, Par 70, SSS 70.
Club membership 230.

Visitors	restricted Wed and weekends. Must contact in advance.
Societies	Thursday only by prior arrangement.
Green Fees	£25 (£30 weekends & bank holidays).
Prof	A Gillies
Facilities	⅃ ♥ ♀ ♋ ⎘
Location	N side of town centre off A50

Hotel	★★★★ 66% Cottons Hotel, Manchester Rd, KNUTSFORD ☎ 01565 650333 99 ⇄ 🐾

Mere Golf & Country Club Chester Rd, Mere
WA16 6LJ ☎ 01565 830155 Fax 01565 830713
A gracious parkland championship course designed by James Braid in the Cheshire sand belt, with several holes close to a lake. The round has a tight finish with four testing holes.
18 holes, 6817yds, Par 71, SSS 73, Course record 64.
Club membership 540.

Visitors	by prior arrangement only, not able to play Wed, Fri, Sat & Sun.
Societies	Mon,Tue & Thu only by prior arrangement.
Green Fees	not confirmed.

▶

Cards	▒▒ ▨▨ ▨▨ ▨ ▧▧ ▨
Prof	Peter Eyre
Designer	James Braid
Facilities	⊗ 〗⌂ ﹗﹗♀⚐🏠 ⌇🚣 ♂ ↑
& Leisure	hard tennis courts, heated indoor swimming pool, squash, fishing, sauna, solarium, gymnasium.
Location	1m E of junc 19 of M6
Hotel	★★★★ 66% Cottons Hotel, Manchester Rd, KNUTSFORD ☎ 01565 650333 99 ⇥ ⌁

Peover Plumley Moor Rd, Lower Peover WA16 9SE
☎ 01565 723337 Fax 01565 723311
Tees and greens have been positioned to maximise the benefits of the natural contours of the land. An excellent mix of holes varying in design and character with many doglegs and water hazards including a river which three of the fairways cross, including the first.
18 holes, 6702yds, Par 72, SSS 72, Course record 69.
Club membership 450.

Visitors	dress code must be observed.
Societies	apply in writing/telephone in advance
Green Fees	£18 weekdays (£23 weekends & bank holidays).
Cards	▒▒ ▨▨ ▧▧ ▨
Prof	Bobby Young
Designer	P A Naylor
Facilities	⊗ 〗⌂ ﹗♀⚐🏠 ⌇🚣 ♂
Location	M6 junct19/A556 onto Plumley Moor Rd
Hotel	★★ 74% The Longview Hotel & Restaurant, 55 Manchester Rd, KNUTSFORD ☎ 01565 632119 13 ⇥ ⌁ Annexe 10 ⇥ ⌁

LYMM   Map 07 SJ68

Lymm Whitbarrow Rd WA13 9AN
☎ 01925 752177 & 755020 Fax 01925 755020
First ten holes are gently undulating with the Manchester Ship Canal running alongside the 9th hole. The remaining holes are comparatively flat.
18 holes, 6304yds, Par 71, SSS 70.
Club membership 650.

Visitors	may not play at weekends except with member.
Societies	Wed only, must contact in advance.
Green Fees	not confirmed.
Prof	Steve McCarthy
Facilities	⚐🏠 ♂
Location	0.5m N off A6144

Hotel	★★ 74% Rockfield Hotel, Alexandra Rd, Grappenhall, WARRINGTON ☎ 01925 262898 6 ⇥ ⌁ Annexe 6 ⇥ ⌁

MACCLESFIELD   Map 07 SJ97

Macclesfield The Hollins SK11 7EA
☎ 01625 615845 (Secretary) Fax 01625 260061
Hillside heathland course situated on the edge of the Pennines with excellent views across the Cheshire Plain. A pleasant course providing a good test for players of all abilities.
18 holes, 5769yds, Par 70, SSS 68, Course record 66.
Club membership 620.

Visitors	apply in advance and have a handicap certificate.
Societies	telephone initially.
Green Fees	not confirmed.
Prof	Tony Taylor
Designer	Hawtree & Son
Facilities	⊗ 〗⌂ ﹗♀⚐🏠 ⌇🚣 ♂
Location	SE side of town centre off A523
Hotel	★★★ 67% Belgrade Hotel & Restaurant, Jackson Ln, Kerridge, Bollington, MACCLESFIELD ☎ 01625 573246 54 ⇥ ⌁

Shrigley Hall Hotel Shrigley Park, Pott Shrigley SK10 5SB
☎ 01625 575757 Fax 01625 575437
Parkland course set in 262-acre estate with breathtaking views over the Peak District and Cheshire Plain. Designed by Donald Steel, this championship standard course provides a real sporting challenge while the magnificent hotel provides a wealth of sporting facilities as well as accommodation and food.
18 holes, 6281yds, Par 71, SSS 71, Course record 68.
Club membership 500.

Visitors	must contact in advance by telephone.
Societies	contact in advance.
Green Fees	£36 (£41 weekends & bank holidays).
Cards	▒▒ ▨▨ ▨
Prof	Tony Stevens
Designer	Donald Steel
Facilities	⊗ 〗⌂ ﹗♀⚐🏠 ⌇🚣 ♂
& Leisure	hard tennis courts, heated indoor swimming pool, fishing, sauna, solarium, gymnasium.
Hotel	★★★★ 63% Shrigley Hall Hotel Golf & Country Club, Shrigley Park, Pott Shrigley, MACCLESFIELD ☎ 01625 575757 150 ⇥ ⌁

Tytherington Dorchester Way, Tytherington SK10 2JP
☎ 01625 434562 Fax 01625 430882
Modern championship course in beautiful, mature
parkland setting with numerous water features. Testing
holes, notably the signature 12th hole (par 5), played
from an elevated tee with adjacent snaking ditch and a
lake guarding the green. Headquarters of the Women's
European Tour and venue of the WPGET English Open
and County matches. Country club facilities.
18 holes, 6750yds, Par 72, SSS 74.
Club membership 3100.

Visitors	advisable to contact in advance and be of handicap standard.
Societies	weekdays only by prior arrangement.
Green Fees	not confirmed.
Cards	
Prof	Gordon McLeod
Designer	Dave Thomas/Patrick Dawson
Facilities	⊗ ℐℿ ℒ 🅱 ♀ ♨ 🏠 ℸ ♦ 🛪 ♂ ₤
Location	1m N of Macclesfield off A523
Hotel	★★★★ 63% Shrigley Hall Hotel Golf & Country Club, Shrigley Park, Pott Shrigley, MACCLESFIELD ☎ 01625 575757 150 ⇌ ⌂

NANTWICH
Map 07 SJ65

Reaseheath Reaseheath College CW5 6DF
☎ 01270 625131
The course at Reaseheath is attached to Reaseheath College,
which is one of the major centres of greenkeeper training in
the UK. It is a short 9-hole which can only be played with a
member.
9 holes, 1882yds, Par 62, SSS 58.
Club membership 350.

Visitors	with member only.
Societies	by prior arrangement, apply in writing.
Green Fees	£6 per 18 holes.
Designer	D Mortram
Facilities	⊗ by prior arrangement ℐℿ by prior arrangement
Location	1.5m NE of Nantwich, off A51

OSCROFT
Map 07 SJ56

Pryors Hayes Willington Rd CH3 8NL
☎ 01829 741250 & 740140 Fax 01829 749077
Picturesque 18-hole parkland course set in the heart of
Cheshire. Gently undulating fairways demand accurate
drives, and numerous trees and water hazards make the
course a challenging test of golf.
18 holes, 6054yds, Par 69, SSS 69.
Club membership 530.

Visitors	no restrictions.
Societies	apply for application form.
Green Fees	£20 per round (£25 weekends). Reductions in winter.
Cards	
Prof	Martin Redrup
Designer	John Day
Facilities	⊗ ℐℿ ℒ 🅱 ♀ ♨ 🏠 ♦ 🛪 ♂
Location	Between A54 & A51 roads, approx 6m E of Chester, village of Oscroft near Tarvin
Hotel	★★★ 62% Blossoms Hotel, St John St, CHESTER ☎ 0870 400 8108 64 ⇌ ⌂

POYNTON
Map 07 SJ98

Davenport Worth Hall, Middlewood Rd SK12 1TS
☎ 01625 876951 Fax 01625 877489
Undulating parkland course. Extensive view over Cheshire
Plain from elevated 5th tee. Testing 17th hole, par 4.
18 holes, 6027yds, Par 69, SSS 69, Course record 64.
Club membership 700.

Visitors	contact professional in advance, 01625 858387. May not play Wed or Sat.
Societies	Tue and Thu only. Must apply in advance.
Green Fees	£27 (£32 weekends & bank holidays).
Prof	Gary Norcott
Facilities	⊗ ℐℿ ℒ 🅱 ♀ ♨ 🏠 ♂
& Leisure	snooker.
Location	1m E off A523
Hotel	★★★ 64% County Hotel Bramhall, Bramhall Ln South, BRAMHALL ☎ 0161 455 9988 65 ⇌ ⌂

PRESTBURY
Map 07 SJ97

Prestbury Macclesfield Rd SK10 4BJ
☎ 01625 828241 Fax 01625 828241
Undulating parkland course, with many plateau greens.
The 9th hole has a challenging uphill 3-tier green and the
17th is over a valley. Host to county and inter-county
championships.
18 holes, 6359yds, Par 71, SSS 71, Course record 64.
Club membership 702.

Visitors	must contact in advance and have an introduction from own club, with member only at weekends.
Societies	apply in writing, Thu only.
Green Fees	£40 per day.
Cards	
Prof	Nick Summerfield
Designer	Harry S Colt
Facilities	⊗ ℐℿ ℒ 🅱 ♀ ♨ 🏠 ℸ ♂ ₤
Location	S side of village off A538
Hotel	★★★★ 67% Mottram Hall Hotel, Wilmslow Rd, Mottram St Andrew, Prestbury, ☎ 01625 828135 132 ⇌ ⌂

AA Hotels that have special
arrangements with golf courses are listed at
the back of the guide

RUNCORN
Map 07 SJ58

Runcorn Clifton Rd WA7 4SU
☎ 01928 574214 Fax 01928 574214
Parkland course with tree-lined fairways and easy walking.
Fine views over Mersey and Weaver valleys. Testing holes:
7th par 5; 14th par 5; 17th par 4.
18 holes, 6048yds, Par 69, SSS 69, Course record 63.
Club membership 570.
Visitors weekends restricted to playing with member
only, Tuesday Ladies Day.
Societies telephone in advance.
Green Fees £20 per day.
Prof A Franklin
Facilities ⊗ ∭ by prior arrangement 🏋 🍺 ♀ 🏌 🏠 ♂
Location 1.25m S of Runcorn Station

Hotel ★★★ 66% Posthouse Warrington/Runcorn,
Wood Ln, Beechwood, RUNCORN
☎ 0870 400 9070 135 ⇋ ℝ

SANDBACH
Map 07 SJ76

Malkins Bank Betchton Rd, Malkins Bank CW11 4XN
☎ 01270 765931 Fax 01270 764730
Parkland course. Tight 13th hole with stream running
through.
18 holes, 6071yds, Par 70, SSS 69, Course record 65.
Club membership 500.
Visitors no restrictions. Advisable to book in advance.
Societies apply for booking form to course professional
Green Fees not confirmed.
Prof David Wheeler
Designer Hawtree
Facilities ⊗ ∭ 🏋 🍺 ♀ 🏌 🏠 ⛳ ♂
Location 1.5m SE off A533

Hotel ★★ 60% Saxon Cross Hotel, Holmes Chapel
Rd, SANDBACH ☎ 01270 763281 52 ⇋ ℝ

SANDIWAY
Map 07 SJ67

Sandiway Chester Rd CW8 2DJ
☎ 01606 883247 (Secretary) Fax 01606 888548
Delightful undulating wood and heathland course with
long hills up to the 8th, 16th and 17th holes. Many dog-
legged and tree-lined holes give opportunities for the
deliberate fade or draw.
18 holes, 6404yds, Par 70, SSS 72, Course record 67.
Club membership 700.
Visitors book through secretary, members have
reserved tees 8.30-9.30 and 12.30-1.30
(11.30-12.30 winter). Handicap certificate
required
Societies book in advance through
Secretary/Manager.
Green Fees not confirmed.
Prof William Laird
Designer Ted Ray
Facilities ⊗ ∭ 🏋 🍺 ♀ 🏌 🏠 ⛳ ♂
Location 2m W of Northwich on A556

Hotel ★★ 66% Wincham Hall, Hall Ln,
Wincham, NORTHWICH ☎ 01606 43453
10rm(9 ⇋ ℝ)

TARPORLEY
Map 07 SJ56

Portal Golf & Country Club Cobbler's Cross Ln CW6 0DJ
☎ 01829 733933 Fax 01829 733928
Opened in 1991, there are two 18-hole courses here -
Championship and Premier - one 9-hole course - Arderne and
the largest indoor golf academy in Britain. They are set in
mature, wooded parkland. There are fine views over the
Cheshire Plain and numerous water hazards. The
Championship 14th is just a short iron through trees, but its
green is virtually an island surrounded by water.
*Championship Course: 18 holes, 7037yds, Par 73, SSS 74,
Course record 64.*
*Premier Course: 18 holes, 6508yds, Par 71, SSS 72, Course
record 64.*
Arderne Course: 9 holes, 1724yds, Par 30.
Club membership 300.

Visitors must contact in advance.
Societies must pre-book.
Green Fees not confirmed.
Cards 💳 💳 🗋
Prof Mike Slater/Adrian Hill
Designer Donald Steel
Facilities ⊗ ∭ 🏋 🍺 ♀ 🏌 🏠 ⛳ 🏓 🛶 ♂ ℂ
& Leisure hard tennis courts, indoor golf academy.
Location Off A49

Hotel ★★★ 62% The Wild Boar, Whitchurch Rd,
Beeston, TARPORLEY ☎ 01829 260309
37 ⇋ ℝ

WARRINGTON
Map 07 SJ68

Birchwood Kelvin Close, Science Park North, Birchwood
WA3 7PB
☎ 01925 818819 (Club) & 816574 (Pro) Fax 01925 822403
Very testing parkland course with many natural water
hazards and the prevailing wind creating a problem on each
hole. The 11th hole is particularly challenging.
*Pilgrims: 18 holes, 6727yds, Par 71, SSS 73, Course
record 66.*
Progress: 18 holes, 6359yds, Par 71, SSS 72.
*Mayflower (ladies course): 18 holes, 5849yds, Par 74,
SSS 74.*
Club membership 745.
Visitors advisable to check with the professional to
determine if course is fully booked.
Societies Mon, Wed & Thu. Apply in writing, or
telephone.
Green Fees £26 per day; £20 per round (£34 per day
weekends & bank holidays).
Cards 💳 💳

▶

Prof	Paul McEwan
Designer	T J A Macauley
Facilities	⊗ ⅲ 🛏 🍽 ♀ 🛋 🖂 ✐
& Leisure	sauna.
Location	Junct 11 on M62, follow signs for Science Park North, 2m from the junct

| Hotel | ★★★ 66% Posthouse Haydock, Lodge Ln, HAYDOCK ☎ 0870 400 9039 138 ⇄ ☏ |

Leigh Kenyon Hall, Broseley Ln, Culcheth WA3 4BG
☎ 01925 762943 (Secretary) Fax 01925 765097
A pleasant, well-wooded parkland course. Any discrepancy in length is compensated by the wide variety of golf offered here. The course is well maintained and there is a comfortable clubhouse.
18 holes, 5853yds, Par 69, SSS 68, Course record 64.
Club membership 550.

Visitors	contact professional for details.
Societies	Mon (ex bank holidays) & Tue, apply by telephone.
Green Fees	not confirmed.
Prof	Andrew Baguley
Designer	James Braid
Facilities	⊗ ⅲ 🛏 🍽 ♀ 🛋 🖂 ✐
Location	5m NE off A579

| Hotel | ★★★ 69% Fir Grove Hotel, Knutsford Old Rd, WARRINGTON ☎ 01925 267471 40 ⇄ ☏ |

Poulton Park Dig Ln, Cinnamon Brow, Padgate WA2 0SH
☎ 01925 822802 Fax 01925 822802
Tight, flat parkland course with good greens and many trees. A straight drive off each tee is important. The 4/13th has a fairway curving to the left with water and out-of-bounds on left and trees on right.
9 holes, 4978mtrs, Par 68, SSS 66, Course record 66.
Club membership 350.

Visitors	midweek only. Contact professional for details 01925 825220.
Societies	apply in advance.
Green Fees	£15 (£19 weekends).
Prof	Andrew Matthews
Facilities	⊗ ⅲ 🛏 🍽 ♀ 🛋 🖂
Location	3m from Warrington on A574

| Hotel | ★★★ 69% Fir Grove Hotel, Knutsford Old Rd, WARRINGTON ☎ 01925 267471 40 ⇄ ☏ |

Walton Hall Warrington Rd, Higher Walton WA4 5LU
☎ 01925 263061 (bookings)
A quiet, wooded, municipal parkland course on Walton Hall estate.
18 holes, 6801yds, Par 72, SSS 73, Course record 70.
Club membership 250.

Visitors	must book 6 days in advance.
Societies	must contact in writing.
Green Fees	not confirmed.
Prof	John Jackson
Facilities	⊗ ⅲ 🛏 🍽 ♀ 🛋 🖂 ⚑ ✐
Location	2m from junct 11 of M56

| Hotel | ★★★ 69% Fir Grove Hotel, Knutsford Old Rd, WARRINGTON ☎ 01925 267471 40 ⇄ ☏ |

Warrington Hill Warren, London Rd, Appleton WA4 5HR
☎ 01925 261775 (Secretary) Fax 01925 265933
Meadowland, with varied terrain and natural hazards. Major work has recently been carried out on both the clubhouse and the course to ensure high standards. The course is a constant challenge with ponds, trees and bunkers threatening the errant shot!
18 holes, 6305yds, Par 72, SSS 70, Course record 61.
Club membership 840.

Visitors	contact in advance.
Societies	by prior arrangement with Secretary.
Green Fees	£27 per day (£32 weekends & bank holidays).
Prof	Reay Mackay
Designer	James Braid
Facilities	⊗ ⅲ 🛏 🍽 ♀ 🛋 🖂 ⚑ ✐
Location	1.5m N of junct 10 of M56 on A49

| Hotel | ★★ 74% Rockfield Hotel, Alexandra Rd, Grappenhall, WARRINGTON ☎ 01925 262898 6 ⇄ ☏ Annexe 6 ⇄ ☏ |

WIDNES Map 07 SJ58

St Michael Jubilee Dundalk Rd WA8 8BS
☎ 0151 424 6230 Fax 0151 495 2124
Municipal parkland course dominated by the 'Stewards Brook'. It is divided into two sections which are split by the main road and joined by an underpass.
18 holes, 5925yds, Par 69, SSS 67.

Visitors	welcome.
Societies	must contact in writing.
Green Fees	not confirmed.
Prof	Darren Chapman
Facilities	⊗ 🛏 🍽 ♀ 🛋 🖂 ⚑
Location	W side of town centre off A562

| Hotel | ★★★ 64% Everglades Park Hotel, Derby Rd, WIDNES ☎ 0151 495 2040 65 ⇄ ☏ |

Widnes Highfield Rd WA8 7DT
☎ 0151 424 2440 Fax 0151 495 2849
Parkland course, easy walking.
18 holes, 5719yds, Par 69, SSS 68.

Visitors	may play after 9am & after 4pm on competition days. Must contact in advance.
Societies	must contact the secretary in writing.
Green Fees	not confirmed.
Prof	J O'Brien
Facilities	⊗ ⅲ 🛏 🍽 ♀ 🛋 🖂

| Hotel | ★★★ 64% Everglades Park Hotel, Derby Rd, WIDNES ☎ 0151 495 2040 65 ⇄ ☏ |

WILMSLOW — Map 07 SJ88

Mottram Hall Wilmslow Rd, Mottram St Andrew
SK10 4QT ☎ 01625 828135 Fax 01625 828950
Championship standard course with flat meadowland on the front nine and undulating woodland on the back with well guarded greens. The course is unusual as each half opens and closes with Par 5's. The hotel offers many leisure facilities.
18 holes, 7006yds, Par 72, SSS 74, Course record 65.
Club membership 500.
Visitors must contact in advance. Cannot play before 11am Sat/Sun. Handicap certificate required.
Societies must contact in advance.
Green Fees £39 per round (£44 weekends).
Cards ▬ ▬ ▬ ▬ ▬ ▬
Prof Tim Rastall
Designer Dave Thomas
Facilities ⊗ ╟ ╚ ♥ ☲ ⚐ ♈ ☒ ↘ ♣ ✆ ↾
& Leisure hard tennis courts, heated indoor swimming pool, squash, sauna, solarium, gymnasium, practice bunker & chipping green.
Location On A538 between Wilmslow and Preston

Hotel ★★★★ 67% Mottram Hall Hotel, Wilmslow Rd, Mottram St Andrew, Prestbury, ☎ 01625 828135 132 ⇋ ☞

Styal Station Rd, Styal SK9 4JN
☎ 01625 531359 Fax 01625 530063
Well designed flat parkland course with testing bunkers and water hazards. Boasts the longest hole in Cheshire!
18 holes, 6301yds, Par 71, SSS 70.
Club membership 700.
Visitors contact to reserve tee time.
Societies telephone in advance.
Green Fees not confirmed.
Prof Simon Forrest
Designer Tony Holmes
Facilities ⊗ ╟ ╚ ♥ ☲ ⚐ ♈ ☒ ↘ ♣ ✆ ↾
Location M56 junct 5, 5min drive from Wilmslow

Hotel ★★★★ 65% Belfry House Hotel, Stanley Rd, HANDFORTH ☎ 0161 437 0511 80 ⇋ ☞

Wilmslow Great Warford, Mobberley WA16 7AY
☎ 01565 872148 Fax 01565 872172
A fine parkland championship course, of middle length, fair to all classes of player and almost in perfect condition.
18 holes, 6607yds, Par 72, SSS 72, Course record 62.
Club membership 800.
Visitors must contact in advance.
Societies Tue & Thu only application in writing.
Green Fees £50 per day; £40 per round (£60/£50 weekends & bank holidays).
Prof John Nowicki
Facilities ⊗ ╟ ╚ ♥ ☲ ⚐ ♈ ✆ ↾
Location 2m SW off B5058

Hotel ★★★ 71% Alderley Edge Hotel, Macclesfield Rd, ALDERLEY EDGE ☎ 01625 583033 46 ⇋ ☞

Looking for a driving range?
See the index at the back of the guide

WINSFORD — Map 07 SJ66

Knights Grange Grange Ln CW7 2PT ☎ 01606 552780
Attractive, well maintained municipal parkland course with water hazards. Within a large recreation complex including a public house and childrens' play area.
9 holes, 2719yds, Par 33, SSS 68.
Visitors 24 hr booking system for weekly play, after 10am Wed for weekend bookings.
Societies apply in writing.
Green Fees not confirmed.
Prof Graham Moore
Facilities ☲ ☒ ⚐ ♈ ✆
& Leisure hard and grass tennis courts.
Location N side of town off A54

Hotel ★★ 66% Wincham Hall, Hall Ln, Wincham, NORTHWICH ☎ 01606 43453 10rm (9 ⇋ ☞)

WINWICK

Alder Root Alder Root Ln WA2 8R2
☎ 01925 291919 Fax 01925 291919
A woodland course, flat in nature but with many undulations. Several holes have water hazards. One of the most testing nine hole courses in the north west.
9 holes, 5837yds, Par 69, SSS 68, Course record 67.
Club membership 400.
Visitors telephone for details of dress code.
Societies must telephone in advance.
Green Fees £12 per 18 holes (£14 weekends).
Cards ▬ ▬
Prof C McKevitt
Designer Mr Lander/Mr Millington
Facilities ⊗ ╚ ♥ ☲ ⚐ ☒ ↘ ♣ ✆
Location From M62 junct 9 take A49 N for 800mtrs then left at lights and 1st right into Alder Root Lane

Hotel ★★ 63% Paddington House Hotel, 514 Old Manchester Rd, WARRINGTON ☎ 01925 816767 37 ⇋ ☞

CORNWALL & ISLES OF SCILLY

BODMIN — Map 02 SX06

Lanhydrock Lostwithiel Rd, Lanhydrock PL30 5AQ
☎ 01208 73600 Fax 01208 77325
An acclaimed parkland/moorland course adjacent to the National Trust property Lanhydrock house. Nestling in a picturesque wooded valley of oak and birch, this undulating course provides an exciting and enjoyable challenge to all abilities with discreet use of water and bunkers.
18 holes, 6100yds, Par 70, SSS 70, Course record 66.
Club membership 400.
Visitors no restrictions.
Societies please telephone in advance.
Green Fees £28 per round.
Cards ▬ ▬ ▬ ▬ ▬
Prof Jason Broadway
Designer Hamilton Stutt

▶

Facilities ⊗ ⫫ ⛳ ♥ ♀ ⚲ 🏠 ⚐ 🏨 ❦ ♣ ⚲ ↑
Location 1m S of Bodmin from B3268

Hotel ★★★ 64% Restormel Lodge Hotel, Hillside Gardens, LOSTWITHIEL
☎ 01208 872223   21 ⇋ ♣ Annexe 12 ⇋

BUDE   Map 02 SS20

Bude & North Cornwall Burn View EX23 8DA
☎ 01288 352006 Fax 01288 356855
Seaside links course with natural sand bunkers, superb greens and breathtaking views. Club established in 1893.
18 holes, 6205yds, Par 71, SSS 70.
Club membership 1000.
Visitors book by telephone 6 days in advance for starting time - or before 6 days with a deposit.
Societies apply in writing or by telephone/fax.
Green Fees £20 per round; £8 per additional round (£25 weekends & bank holidays).
Prof John Yeo
Facilities ⊗ ⫫ ⛳ ♥ ♀ ⚲ 🏠 ⚲
Location N side of town

Hotel ★★ 61% Camelot Hotel, Downs View, BUDE
☎ 01288 352361   24 ⇋ ♣

BUDOCK VEAN   Map 02 SW73

Budock Vean Golf & Country House Hotel
Mawnan Smith TR11 5LG
☎ 01326 250288 (Hotel) & 252102 (shop)
Fax 01326 250892
Set in 65 acres of mature grounds with a private foreshore to the Helford River, this 18 tee undulating parkland course has a tough par 4 5th hole (456yds) which dog-legs at halfway around an oak tree. The 16th hole measures 572 yds, par 5.
9 holes, 5227yds, Par 68, SSS 65, Course record 61.
Club membership 140.
Visitors must contact in advance.
Societies apply in writing or telephone in advance.
Green Fees £16 per round (£20 Sun & bank holidays).
Cards ⬜ 🟦 🟥 🟦 🟢
Prof Tony Ramsden
Designer James Braid
Facilities ⊗ ⫫ ⛳ ♥ ♀ ⚲ 🏠 ⚐ 🏨 ❦ ♣ ⚲
& Leisure hard tennis courts, heated indoor swimming pool.
Location 1.5m SW

Hotel ★★★★ 73% Budock Vean Golf & Country House Hotel, MAWNAN SMITH
☎ 01326 252100 & Freephone 0800 833927
Fax 01326 250892   58 ⇋ ♣

CAMBORNE   Map 02 SW64

Tehidy Park TR14 0HH
☎ 01209 842208 Fax 01209 843680
A well-maintained parkland course providing good holiday golf.
18 holes, 6241yds, Par 72, SSS 71, Course record 62.
Club membership 850.
Visitors must contact in advance and have a handicap certificate.
Societies telephone followed by letter.
Green Fees £25 per day (£30 weekends).
Prof James Dumbreck
Facilities ⊗ ⫫ ⛳ ♥ ♀ ⚲ 🏠 ❦ ⚲
Location On Portreath/Pool road, 2m S of Camborne

Hotel ★★★ 65% Penventon Hotel, REDRUTH
☎ 01209 203000   50 ⇋ ♣

CAMELFORD   Map 02 SX18

Bowood Park Lanteglos PL32 9RF
☎ 01840 213017 Fax 01840 212622
A testing parkland course situated in Bowood Park, formerly the largest deer park in Cornwall. The first nine holes are designed around rolling hills; the back nine being played through the River Allen Valley. Plenty of wildlife, water and trees.
18 holes, 6692yds, Par 72, SSS 72.
Club membership 300.

Visitors booking system in operation
Societies contact for details.
Green Fees not confirmed.
Cards ⬜ 🟦 🟥 🟦 🟢
Prof Richard Jenkins
Designer Sandow
Facilities ⊗ ⫫ ⛳ ♥ ♀ ⚲ 🏠 ⚐ 🏨 ❦ ♣ ⚲ ↑
Location Through Camelford, 0.5m turn right Tintagel/Boscastle B3266, 1st left at garage

▶

> AA Hotels that have special arrangements with golf courses are listed at the back of the guide

Hotel ★★♨ 78% Trebrea Lodge, Trenale,
TINTAGEL ☎ 01840 770410
6 ⇄ ╟ Annexe 1 ⇄ ╟

CARLYON BAY
Map 02 SX05

Carlyon Bay Hotel Sea Rd PL25 3RD
☎ 01726 814250
Championship-length, cliff-top course moving into
parkland. Magnificent views surpassed only by the
quality of the course. The 230-yard (par 3) 18th with
railway and road out-of-bounds, holds the player's
interest to the end.
18 holes, 6549yds, Par 72, SSS 71, Course record 66.
Club membership 500.
Visitors   must contact in advance.
Societies   must contact in advance.
Green Fees   £28-£35 per round depending on season.
Cards   ⚏ ▨ ▨ ▨
Prof   Mark Rowe
Facilities   ⊗ ⫴ ╚ ♥ ♀ ♨ ⌂ ⫫ ⫯ ⤸ ⤳ ⚌
& Leisure   hard tennis courts, outdoor and indoor
                 heated swimming pools, sauna, solarium, 9
                 hole approach course.

Hotel ★★★★ 74% Carlyon Bay Hotel, Sea Rd,
Carlyon Bay, ST AUSTELL
☎ 01726 812304 73 ⇄ ╟
See advertisement on inside back cover

CONSTANTINE BAY
Map 02 SW87

Trevose PL28 8JB
☎ 01841 520208 Fax 01841 521057
Well known links course with early holes close to the sea
on excellent springy turf. A championship course
affording varying degrees of difficulty appealing to both
the professional and higher handicap player. It is a good
test with well-positioned bunkers, a meandering
stream, and the wind playing a decisive role in
preventing low scoring. Self-catering accommodation is
available at the club.
Championship Course: 18 holes, 6461yds, Par 71, SSS
71, Course record 66.
Club membership 1500.
Visitors   subject to reservations, handicap certificate
                 required for championship course.
                 Advisable to contact in advance.
Societies   telephone or write to the secretary.
Green Fees   £25-£36 per day.
Cards   ⚏ ▨ ▨ ▨ ▨
Prof   Gary Alliss

Designer H S Colt
Facilities ⊗ ⫴ by prior arrangement ╚ ♥ ♀ ♨ ⌂
& Leisure hard tennis courts, heated outdoor
              swimming pool, 2 x 9 hole courses, snooker
              & games room.
Location N of Constantine Bay, off B3276

Hotel ★★★ 77% Treglos Hotel,
CONSTANTINE BAY
☎ 01841 520727 44 ⇄ ╟

FALMOUTH
Map 02 SW83

Falmouth Swanpool Rd TR11 5BQ
☎ 01326 311262 & 314296 Fax 01326 317783
Seaside/parkland course with outstanding coastal views.
Sufficiently bunkered to punish any inaccurate shots. Five
acres of practice grounds.
18 holes, 5937yds, Par 71, SSS 70.
Club membership 500.

Visitors   please book for tee time.
Societies   must contact in advance.
Green Fees   £26 per day; £20 per round.
Cards   ⚏ ▨ ▨ ▨ ▨
Prof   Bryan Patterson
Facilities   ⊗ ⫴ ╚ ♥ ♀ ♨ ⌂ ⫫ ⫯ ⤳ ⚌ ⚍ ⌿
Location   SW side of town centre

Hotel ★★★★ 70% Royal Duchy Hotel, Cliff Rd,
FALMOUTH ☎ 01326 313042 43 ⇄ ╟

Where to stay, where to eat?
Visit the AA internet site
www.theaa.co.uk

43

HOLYWELL BAY   Map 02 SW75

Holywell Bay TR8 5PW
☎ 01637 830095 Fax 01637 831000
Holywell Golf Club is situated beside a family fun park with many amenities. The course is an 18 hole Par 3 with excellent sea views. Fresh Atlantic winds make the course hard to play and there are several tricky holes, particularly the 18th over the trout pond. The site also has an excellent 18 hole Pitch & Putt course for the whole family.
18 holes, 2784yds, Par 61, Course record 58.
Club membership 100.

Visitors	no restrictions.
Societies	telephone in advance.
Green Fees	£8 per round.
Designer	Hartley
Facilities	⊗ ⅷ ⅃ ⓐ ☂ ✆
& Leisure	hard tennis courts, heated outdoor swimming pool, fishing.
Location	Off A3075 Newquay/Perranporth road

Hotel   ★★★ 70% Barrowfield Hotel, Hilgrove Rd, NEWQUAY ☎ 01637 878878 81 ⇆ ♠ Annexe 2 ⇆ ♠

LAUNCESTON   Map 02 SX38

Launceston St Stephens PL15 8HF
☎ 01566 773442 Fax 01566 777506
Undulating parkland course with views over Tamar Valley to Dartmoor and Bodmin Moor. Dominated by the 'The Hill' up which the 8th and 11th fairways rise, and on which the 8th, 9th, 11th and 12th greens sit.
18 holes, 6407yds, Par 70, SSS 71, Course record 65.
Club membership 800.

Visitors	must contact in advance, may not play weekends Apr-Oct.
Societies	telephone in first instance.
Green Fees	not confirmed.
Prof	John Tozer
Facilities	⅀ ☂ ⓐ ☂ ✆
Location	NW side of town centre on B3254

Hotel   ★★ 64% Eagle House, Castle St, LAUNCESTON ☎ 01566 772036 14 ⇆ ♠

Trethorne Kennards House PL15 8QE
☎ 01566 86324 Fax 01566 86903
Rolling parkland course with well maintained fairways and computer irrigated greens. Plenty of trees and natural water hazards make this well respected course a good challenge.

18 holes, 6432yds, Par 71, SSS 71.
Club membership 630.

Visitors	must contact in advance.
Societies	write or telephone Colin Willis.
Green Fees	£25 per day; £22 per round.
Cards	▦ ▦ ▦ ◪ ◪
Prof	Mark Boundy
Designer	Frank Frayne
Facilities	⊗ ⅷ ⅃ ☂ ⅀ ☂ ⓐ ☂ ✎ ⛳ ✆ ☂
Location	Just off the A30, 3m W of Launceston, on junct with the A395 (Camelford)

Hotel   ★★ 75% Penhallow Manor Hotel, ALTARNUN ☎ 01566 86206 6 ⇆ ♠

LELANT   Map 02 SW53

West Cornwall TR26 3DZ
☎ 01736 753401 & 753177 Fax 01736 753401
A seaside links with sandhills and lovely turf adjacent to the Hayle estuary and St Ives Bay. A real test of the player's skill, especially 'Calamity Corner' starting at the 5th on the lower land by the River Hayle. A small (3 hole) course is available for practice.
18 holes, 5884yds, Par 69, SSS 69, Course record 63.
Club membership 748.

Visitors	must prove handicap certificate, be a member of a club affiliated to the EGU, advisable to contact in advance.
Societies	must apply in writing.
Green Fees	£25 per day (£30 weekends & bank holidays).
Prof	Paul Atherton
Designer	Reverend Tyack
Facilities	⊗ ⅷ ⅃ ☂ ⅀ ☂ ⓐ ☂ ✆
& Leisure	snooker.
Location	N side of village off A3074

Hotel   ★★ Pedn-Olva Hotel, The Warren, ST IVES ☎ 01736 796222 28 ⇆ ♠ Annexe 7rm (4 ⇆ ♠)

LOOE   Map 02 SX25

Looe Widegates PL13 1PX
☎ 01503 240239 Fax 01503 240864
Designed by Harry Vardon in 1935, this downland/parkland course commands panoramic views over south-east Cornwall and the coast. Easy walking.
18 holes, 5940yds, Par 70, SSS 68, Course record 64.
Club membership 600.

▶

Visitors	handicap certificate preferred, booking in advance recommended, no limitations subject to availability.
Societies	telephone in advance, booking to be confirmed in writing.
Green Fees	not confirmed.
Cards	▨ ▨ ▨ ▨
Prof	Alistair Macdonald
Designer	Harry Vardon
Facilities & Leisure	⊗ ⅏ � ♟ ♀ ♐ ♙ ⚑ ⛳ ⛏ ♣ practice nets.
Location	3.5m NE off B3253

Hotel ★★★ 65% Hannafore Point Hotel, Marine Dr, West Looe, LOOE ☎ 01503 263273 37 ⇆ 🏌

LOSTWITHIEL

Map 02 SX15

Lostwithiel Hotel, Golf & Country Club Lower Polscoe
PL22 0HQ ☎ 01208 873550 Fax 01208 87479
An undulating, parkland course with water hazards.
Overlooked by Restormel Castle and the River Fowey flows
alongside the course. Driving range.
18 holes, 5984yds, Par 72, SSS 71, Course record 67.
Club membership 500.

Visitors	must contact in advance.
Societies	contact in advance.
Green Fees	not confirmed.
Cards	▨ ▨ ▨ ▨ ▨ ▨
Prof	Tony Nash
Designer	S Wood

Facilities & Leisure	⊗ ⅏ ▮ ♟ ♀ ♐ ♙ ⚑ ⛳ ⛏ ♣ ⛳ hard tennis courts, heated indoor swimming pool, fishing, gymnasium.
Location	1m outside Lostwithiel off A390
Hotel	★★★ 64% Lostwithiel Hotel Golf & Country Club, Lower Polscoe, LOSTWITHIEL ☎ 01208 873550 19 ⇆ 🏌

MAWGAN PORTH

Map 02 SW86

Merlin TR8 4DN ☎ 01841 540222 Fax 01841 541031
A heathland course. The most challenging hole is the Par 5
12th with out of bounds along the lefthand side.
18 holes, 5227yds, Par 67, SSS 67.
Club membership 350.

Visitors	no restrictions, except during club competitions.
Societies	telephone in advance.

▶

GOLFING BREAKS
IN DEVON AND CORNWALL
MARINE AND HOTEL LEISURE

Golf and Relaxation.
Three hotels along South-West Coast.
All AA★★★
Superb seaviews.
Excellent Golf.

BERRY HEAD HOTEL, BRIXHAM, DEVON
Nestles at the water's edge, near
picturesque harbour. Astounding
views of Torbay.

COURSES: Churston, Torquay, Dartmouth,
Looe, Lahydrock, St. Enodoc, Mullion,
Tehiddy Park.

HANNAFORE POINT HOTEL, LOOE,
CORNWALL. Overlooking Looe estuary,
close to fishing port. Panoramic views
of Cornish coastline.

Mix-and-match your Accommodation
to suit your choice of Golfing Venues
Two nights from £115 pp DBB
including one round of golf each day.

POLURRIAN HOTEL, MULLION, CORNWALL
On the lizard, cliffside setting, views
across Mount's Bay, overlooking
sandy cove.

BOOKINGS and ENQUIRIES — 0800-698-3733

Green Fees £12 per day.
Cards
Designer   Ross Oliver
Facilities ⊗ 》≡ ┗ ▆ ♉ ♈ 🏠 🍴 ➤ ♣ ♂ 🍸
Location   On the coast rd Newquay/Padstow. After
            Mawgan Porth follow signs for St Eval, golf
            course on right

Hotel   ★★ 67% Tredragon Hotel, MAWGAN
            PORTH ☎ 01637 860213 26 ⇄ 🐾

MAWNAN SMITH   Map 02 SW72

See **Budock Vean**

MULLION   Map 02 SW61

Mullion Cury TR12 7BP ☎ 01326 240685
Founded in 1895, a clifftop and links course with
panoramic views over Mounts Bay. A steep downhill
slope on 6th and the 10th descends to the beach with a
deep ravine alongside the green. Most southerly course
in the British Isles.
18 holes, 6037yds, Par 70, SSS 70.
Club membership 654.
Visitors   preferable to contact in advance, restricted
             during club competitions.
Societies   must contact in advance.
Green Fees   £20 per day/round (£25 weekends).
Prof   Phil Blundell
Designer   W Sich
Facilities   ⊗ 》≡ ┗ ▆ ♉ ♈ 🏠 🍴 ♣ ♂
& Leisure   golf academy.
Location   1.5m NW of Mullion, off A3083

Hotel   ★★★ 71% Polurrian Hotel, MULLION
             ☎ 01326 240421 39 ⇄ 🐾

NEWQUAY   Map 02 SW86

Newquay Tower Rd TR7 1LT
☎ 01637 874354 & 872091 Fax 01637 874066
Gently undulating seaside course running parallel to the
beach and open to wind. Breathtaking views.
18 holes, 6140yds, Par 69, SSS 69, Course record 63.
Club membership 700.
Visitors   please telephone in advance.
Societies   apply in writing or telephone.
Green Fees   not confirmed.
Cards   ▬ ▬ ▬
Prof   Andrew J Cullen
Designer   H Colt
Facilities   ⊗ 》≡ ┗ ▆ ♉ ♈ 🏠 🍴 ♂
& Leisure   hard tennis courts.
Location   W side of town

Hotel   ★★★ 69% Hotel Bristol, Narrowcliff,
             NEWQUAY ☎ 01637 875181 74 ⇄ 🐾

Treloy TR8 4JN ☎ 01637 878554 Fax 01637 871710
An executive course constructed in 1991 to American
specifications with large contoured and mounded greens.
Offers an interesting round for all categories of player.
9 holes, 2143yds, Par 32, SSS 31, Course record 63.

Visitors   no restrictions.
Societies   telephone in advance.
Green Fees   £12.50 per 18 holes, £8 per 9 holes.
Cards   ▬ ▬ ▬
Designer   M R M Sandow
Facilities   ┗ ▆ ♉ ♈ 🏠 🍴 ♣ ♂
Location   On A3059 Newquay to St Columb Major Road

Hotel   ★★ 71% Whipsiderry Hotel, Trevelgue Rd,
             Porth, NEWQUAY ☎ 01637 874777
             24rm (5 ⇄14 🐾)

PADSTOW   Map 02 SW97

See **Constantine Bay**

PERRANPORTH   Map 02 SW75

Perranporth Budnick Hill TR6 0AB
☎ 01872 573701 Fax 01872 573701
There are three testing par 5 holes on the links course (2nd,
5th, 11th) and a fine view over Perranporth Beach from all
holes.
18 holes, 6288yds, Par 72, SSS 72, Course record 62.
Club membership 832.
Visitors   no reserved tee times.
Societies   by prior arrangement.
Green Fees   £25 per day (£30 weekends).
Cards   ▬ ▬
Prof   D Michell
Designer   James Braid
Facilities   ⊗ 》≡ ┗ ▆ ♉ ♈ 🏠 🍴 ♣ ♂
Location   0.75m NE on B3285

Hotel   ★★ 63% Beach Dunes Hotel, Ramoth Way,
             Reen Sands, PERRANPORTH
             ☎ 01872 572263 6rm (5 ⇄ 🐾) Annexe 3 ⇄ 🐾

PRAA SANDS   Map 02 SW52

Praa Sands Germoe Cross Roads TR20 9TQ
☎ 01736 763445 Fax 01736 763399
A beautiful parkland course, overlooking Mount's Bay with
outstanding sea views from every tee and green.
9 holes, 4122yds, Par 62, SSS 60, Course record 59.
Club membership 220.

Visitors   restricted Sun 8-12.30pm, no need to phone.
Societies   telephone in advance for details.
Green Fees   not confirmed.
Designer   R Hamilton

Facilities ⊗ ⑂ ⅃ ┗ ▬ ♀ ♨ ☎ ⛳ ♂
& Leisure pool, darts.
Location A394 midway between Penzance/Helston

Hotel ★★ 78% Nansloe Manor Hotel, Meneage Rd, HELSTON ☎ 01326 574691 7rm(6 ⇆ ♠)

ROCK
Map 02 SW97

St Enodoc PL27 6LD
☎ 01208 863216 Fax 01208 862976
Classic links course with huge sand hills and rolling fairways. James Braid laid out the original 18 holes in 1907 and changes were made in 1922 and 1935. On the Church, the 10th is the toughest par 4 on the course and on the 6th is a truly enormous sand hill known as the Himalayas. The Holywell is not as exacting as the Church, it is less demanding on stamina but still a real test of skill for golfers of any handicap.
Church Course: 18 holes, 6243yds, Par 69, SSS 70, Course record 64.
Holywell Course: 18 holes, 4103yds, Par 63, SSS 61.
Club membership 1500.
Visitors may not play on bank holidays. Must have a handicap certificate of 24 or below for Church Course. Must contact in advance.
Societies must contact in writing.
Green Fees not confirmed.
Prof Nick Williams
Designer James Braid
Facilities ⊗ ⑂ ⅃ ┗ ▬ ♀ ♨ ☎ ♂ ⚑ ♠ ⛳ ♂
Location W side of village

Hotel ★★ 69% Cornish Cottage Hotel & Restaurant, New Polzeath, POLZEATH ☎ 01208 862213 13 ⇆ ♠

ST AUSTELL
Map 02 SX05

See advertisement on inside back cover
Porthpean Porthpean PL26 6AY ☎ 01726 64613
A picturesque 18 hole course, the outward holes are in a pleasant parkland setting whilst the return holes command spectacular views over St Austell Bay.
18 holes, 5209yds, Par 67, SSS 67.
Club membership 300.
Visitors no restrictions
Societies telephone in advance.
Green Fees £12.50 per day/round.
Cards ▭ ▭ ▭ ▭
Facilities ⊗ ┗ ▬ ♀ ♨ ☎ ♂ ⛳ ♂
Location 1.5m from St Austell by-pass

Hotel ★★ 70% The Pier House, Harbour Front, Charlestown, ST AUSTELL ☎ 01726 67955 26 ⇆ ♠

St Austell Tregongeeves Ln PL26 7DS
☎ 01726 72649 Fax 01726 71978
Very interesting inland parkland course designed by James Braid and offering glorious views of the surrounding countryside. Undulating, well-covered with tree plantations and well-bunkered. Notable holes are 8th (par 4) and 16th (par 3).
18 holes, 6089yds, Par 69, SSS 69, Course record 64.
Club membership 700.

Visitors advisable to contact in advance, weekend play is limited. Must be a member of a recognised golf club and hold a handicap certificate.
Societies must apply in writing.
Green Fees £20 (£22 weekends).
Prof Tony Pitts
Facilities ⊗ ┗ ▬ ♀ ♨ ☎ ♂ ♂
Location 1m W of St Austell on A390

Hotel ★★★ 61% Porth Avallen Hotel, Sea Rd, Carlyon Bay, ST AUSTELL ☎ 01726 812802 24 ⇆ ♠

ST IVES
Map 02 SW54

Tregenna Castle Hotel, Golf & Country Club TR26 2DE
☎ 01736 797381 Fax 01736 796066
Parkland course surrounding a castellated hotel and overlooking St Ives Bay and harbour.
18 holes, 3260yds, Par 60, SSS 58.
Club membership 140.
Visitors no booking needed. Dress code in operation.
Societies telephone for details.
Green Fees not confirmed.
Cards ▭ ▭
Designer Abercrombie
Facilities ⊗ ⑂ ⅃ ┗ ▬ ♀ ☎ ♂ ⚑ ♂
& Leisure hard tennis courts, outdoor and indoor heated swimming pools, squash, sauna, solarium, gymnasium.
Location From A30 Penzance road turn off just past Hayle onto A3074

Hotel ★★★ 73% Carbis Bay Hotel, Carbis Bay, ST IVES ☎ 01736 795311 30 ⇆ ♠

ST JUST (NEAR LAND'S END)
Map 02 SW33

Cape Cornwall Golf & Country Club Cape Cornwall
TR19 7NL ☎ 01736 788611 Fax 01736 788611
Coastal parkland, walled course. The walls are an integral part of the course. Country club facilities.
18 holes, 5650yds, Par 70, SSS 68, Course record 69.
Club membership 630.
Visitors may not play before 11.30am at weekends.
Societies must contact in advance.
Green Fees not confirmed.
Cards ▭ ▭ ▭
Prof Paul Atherton
Designer Bob Hamilton

▶

Facilities ⊗ ⊾ ♥ ♀ ⚲ 🏠 ⛳ 🛏 🚉 ♿
& Leisure heated indoor swimming pool, sauna, solarium, gymnasium.
Location 1m W of St Just

Hotel ★★★⚽⚽ 65% Higher Faugan Hotel, Newlyn, PENZANCE ☎ 01736 362076   11 ⇄ 📻

ST MELLION   Map 02 SX36

ST MELLION See page 49

ST MINVER   Map 02 SW97

Roserrow Golf & Country Club Roserrow PL27 6QT
☎ 01208 863000 Fax 01208 863002
Challenging par 72 course in an undulating wooded valley.
Stunning views over the Cornish countryside and out to
Hayle Bay. Accommodation and numerous facilities on site.
18 holes, 6551yds, Par 72, SSS 72.
Club membership 400.

Visitors by arrangement weekdays or weekends, must pre book tee times.
Societies apply in writing or telephone in advance.
Green Fees £32 per day, £25 per round. Nov-Mar £17 per round/day.
Cards 💳 💳 💳 💳
Prof Andrew Cullen
Facilities ⊗ 🏮 ⊾ ♥ ♀ ⚲ 🏠 ⛳ 🛏 🏌 🚉 ♿ ⅃
& Leisure hard tennis courts, heated indoor swimming pool, sauna, gymnasium, bowling green, croquet lawn.
Location Between Wadebridge and Polzeath off the B3314

Hotel ★★ 65% The Molesworth Arms Hotel, Molesworth St, WADEBRIDGE
☎ 01208 812055 16rm (14 ⇄ 📻)

SALTASH   Map 02 SX45

China Fleet Country Club PL12 6LJ
☎ 01752 848668 Fax 01752 848456
A parkland course with river views. The 14th tee shot has to
carry a lake of approximately 150yards.
18 holes, 6551yds, Par 72, SSS 72, Course record 69.
Club membership 550.
Visitors may play anytime and can book up to 7 days in advance.
Societies telephone 01752 854657 for provisional booking.
Green Fees £25 (£30 weekends).
Cards 💳 💳 💳 💳 💳
Prof Robert Moore
Designer Hawtree
Facilities ⊗ 🏮 ⊾ ♥ ♀ ⚲ 🏠 ⛳ 🛏 🚉 ♿ ⅃
& Leisure hard tennis courts, heated indoor swimming pool, squash, sauna, solarium, gymnasium.
Location 1m from the Tamar Bridge

Hotel L Travelodge, Callington Rd, Carkeel, SALTASH
☎ Central Res 0800 850950 Fax 01752 849028
31 ⇄ 📻

TORPOINT   Map 02 SX45

Whitsand Bay Hotel Golf & Country Club Portwrinkle
PL11 3BU ☎ 01503 230276 Fax 01503 230329
Testing seaside course laid-out on cliffs overlooking
Whitsand Bay. Easy walking after 1st hole. The par 3 (3rd)
hole is acknowledged as one of the most attractive holes in
Cornwall.
18 holes, 5998yds, Par 69, SSS 68, Course record 62.
Club membership 400.
Visitors visitors welcome.
Societies must contact in advance.
Green Fees £20 (£22 weekends).
Cards 💳 💳 💳 💳 💳
Prof Stephen Poole
Designer Fernie
Facilities ⊗ 🏮 ⊾ ♥ ♀ ⚲ 🏠 ⛳ 🛏 🏌 🚉 ♿
& Leisure heated indoor swimming pool, sauna, solarium, gymnasium.
Location 5m W off B3247

Hotel ★ 71% Whitsand Bay Hotel, Golf & Country Club, Portwrinkle, TORPOINT
☎ 01503 230276 39rm(37 ⇄ 📻)

St Mellion Hotel

St Mellion, *Cornwall* ☎ 01579 351351   Fax 01579 350537   Map 02 SX36

e-mail: stay@st-mellion.co.uk

Described by Jack Nicklaus as 'One of the finest galleried golf courses in the world', the Nicklaus Course at St Mellion offers a unique and challenging experience. The Old Course, designed by H. J. Stutt is a gentler complement but no less spectacular. To give you an extra edge the resident Professionals offer a range of personalised tuition including club fitting and swing analysis.

St Mellion is not just about playing golf, the complex caters for weekend breaks, family holidays, weddings and corporate events, conferences and banqueting. For those seeking a more relaxing experience, Aero at St Mellion provides superb leisure facilities including a state of the art gym, Skin Care and Spa Centre, sauna and pool. St Mellion is easily accessed by road, rail or sea and even by helicopter with its own landing facilities.

Visitors telephone in advance 01579 352002

Societies apply in writing or telephone in advance

Green Fees not confirmed

Facilities ⊗ 🏌 🛒 ⛳ 🥤 ⛱ 🏠 🏳 🐾 🛒 🚗 ✎ ⚑ Professional (David Moon)

Leisure tennis, swimming, sauna, solarium, gymnasium

Location Saltash PL12 6SD (0.5m NW off A388)

Holes/Par/Course record 36 holes. Nicklaus Course: 18 holes, 6651 yds, Par 72, SSS 72, Course record 63 The Old Course: 18 holes, 5742 yds, Par 68, SSS 68

WHERE TO STAY NEARBY

Hotels
ST MELLION

★★★ 🏵 71% St Mellion International ☎ 01579 351351. Annexe 39 🛏 ⚐

LISKEARD

★★ 🏵 🏵 🏵 ⚬⚬ Well House, St Keyne ☎ 01579 342001. 9 🛏 ⚐

★★ 64% Lord Eliot, Castle St. ☎ 01579 342717. 15 (2 🛏 ⚐ 2 🛏 10 ⚐)

Championship Course

TRURO   Map 02 SW84

Killiow Park Kea TR3 6AG
☎ 01872 270246 & 240915 Fax 01872 240915
Picturesque parkland course with mature oaks and woodland and five holes played across or around water hazards. Floodlit, all-weather driving range and practice facilities.
18 holes, 3829yds, Par 61.
Club membership 500.
Visitors	must telephone in advance to check on course availability.
Societies	apply in writing/telephone, limited catering facilities at present.
Green Fees	£13.50 per round.
Designer	Ross Oliver
Facilities	⚑♀♨🛋🕴🏌⛳
Location	3m SW of Truro, off A39

Hotel	★★★ 72% Alverton Manor, Tregolls Rd, TRURO ☎ 01872 276633 34 🛏 🐾

Truro Treliske TR1 3LG
☎ 01872 278684 (manager) & 272640 (club)
Fax 01872 278684
Picturesque and gently undulating parkland course with small greens requiring accurate play. Lovely views over the cathedral city of Truro and the surrounding countryside.
18 holes, 5306yds, Par 66, SSS 66, Course record 60.
Club membership 900.
Visitors	must have handicap certificate, advisable to ring for availability although casual fees welcome.
Societies	telephone for details.
Green Fees	£20 per day (£25 weekends & bank holidays).
Prof	Nigel Bicknell
Designer	Colt, Alison & Morrison
Facilities	⊗🍴🍺🛋♀♨🛋🕴⛳
Location	1.5m W on A390 towards Redruth, adjacent to Treliske Hospital

Hotel	★★★ 72% Alverton Manor, Tregolls Rd, TRURO ☎ 01872 276633 34 🛏 🐾

WADEBRIDGE   Map 02 SW97

St Kew St Kew Highway PL30 3EF
☎ 01208 841500 Fax 01208 841500
An interesting, well-laid out 9-hole parkland course with 6 holes with water and 15 bunkers. In a picturesque setting there are 10 par 4s and 8 par 3s. No handicap certificate required but some experience of the game is essential. 9 extra tees have now been provided allowing a different teeing area for the back nine.
18 holes, 4543yds, Par 64, SSS 62, Course record 63.
Club membership 240.
Visitors	no restrictions. Start time system in operation allowing prebooking.
Societies	apply in writing, telephone or fax
Green Fees	not confirmed.
Prof	Nick Rogers
Designer	David Derry
Facilities	⊗🛋🍺♀♨🛋🕴🏌🏑⛳🕴
& Leisure	fishing.
Location	2m N, main A39

Hotel	★★ 65% The Molesworth Arms Hotel, Molesworth St, WADEBRIDGE ☎ 01208 812055 16rm (14 🛏 🐾)

CUMBRIA

ALSTON   Map 12 NY74

Alston Moor The Hermitage, Middleton in Teesdale Rd CA9 3DB ☎ 01434 381675 Fax 01434 381354
Parkland and Fell, in process of upgrading to full 18 holes, stunning views of the North Pennines.
10 holes, 5518yds, Par 68, SSS 66, Course record 67.
Club membership 170.
Visitors	usually turn up and play but for weekends telephone secretary for information and availability.
Societies	telephone or write in advance.
Green Fees	£9 per day (£11 weekends & bank holidays).
Facilities	⊗🛋⚑♀♨
Location	1 S of Alston on B6277

Hotel	★★ 68% Lowbyer Manor Country House Hotel, ALSTON ☎ 01434 381230 8 🛏 🐾 Annexe 4 🛏

APPLEBY-IN-WESTMORLAND   Map 12 NY62

Appleby Brackenber Moor CA16 6LP
☎ 017683 51432
This remotely situated heather and moorland course offers interesting golf with the rewarding bonus of several long par-4 holes that will be remembered. There are superb views of the Pennines and the Lakeland hills.

18 holes, 5901yds, Par 68, SSS 68, Course record 63.
Club membership 800.
Visitors	phone for details. May not play before 3pm weekends/competition days.
Societies	must contact in advance by letter.
Green Fees	£16 per day (£20 per day weekend & bank holidays).
Prof	Paul Jenkinson
Designer	Willie Fernie
Facilities	⊗🍴🛋⚑♀♨🛋🕴🏌🏑⛳
Location	2m E of Appleby 0.5m off A66

Hotel	★★★♨ 77% Appleby Manor Country House Hotel, Roman Rd, APPLEBY-IN-WESTMORLAND ☎ 017683 51571 23 🛏 🐾 Annexe 7 🛏 🐾

ASKAM-IN-FURNESS   Map 07 SD27

Dunnerholme Duddon Rd LA16 7AW
☎ 01229 462675 & 465095 Fax 01229 462675
Unique 10-hole (18 tee) links course with view of the Cumbrian mountains and a stream running through.
10 holes, 6154yds, Par 72, SSS 70.
Club membership 400.
Visitors	restricted times on Sun.
Societies	apply in writing to the secretary.
Green Fees	not confirmed.
Facilities	⚑♀♨
Location	1m N on A595

▶

| Hotel | ★★ 60% Lisdoonie Hotel, 307/309 Abbey Rd, BARROW-IN-FURNESS ☎ 01229 827312 12 ⌨ ⋔ |

BARROW-IN-FURNESS   Map 07 SD26

Barrow Rakesmoor Ln, Hawcoat LA14 4QB
☎ 01229 825444 & 832121 (Prof) Fax 01229 832121
Pleasant course laid out on two levels on meadowland with
extensive views of the nearby Lakeland fells. Upper level is
affected by easterly winds.
18 holes, 6184yds, Par 71, SSS 70, Course record 66.
Club membership 700.

Visitors	must be a member of a recognised golf club or hold a handicap certificate, advisable to contact the professional regarding tee time.
Societies	small groups ring professional for details, groups over 12 apply to the secretary in advance.
Green Fees	£20 per day/round.
Prof	Jim McLeod
Facilities	⊗ 〗Ⅲ by prior arrangement Ⅼᴡ ♀ ⅄ ⌂ ⅋ ⌀
Location	2m from Barrow off A590

| Hotel | ★★ 60% Lisdoonie Hotel, 307/309 Abbey Rd, BARROW-IN-FURNESS ☎ 01229 827312 12 ⌨ ⋔ |

Furness Central Dr LA14 3LN ☎ 01229 471232
Links golf with a fairly flat first half but a much sterner
second nine played across subtle sloping ground. There are
good views of the Lakes, North Wales and the Isle of Man.
18 holes, 6363yds, Par 71, SSS 71, Course record 65.
Club membership 630.

Visitors	must contact the secretary in advance.
Societies	apply in writing, must be member of recognised club with handicap certificate.
Green Fees	£17 per day.
Facilities	⊗ 〗Ⅲ Ⅼ ᴡ ♀ ⅄ ⌂ ⌀
Location	1.75 W of town centre off A590 to Walney Island

| Hotel | ★★ 60% Lisdoonie Hotel, 307/309 Abbey Rd, BARROW-IN-FURNESS ☎ 01229 827312 12 ⌨ ⋔ |

BOWNESS-ON-WINDERMERE   Map 07 SD49

Windermere Clearbarrow LA23 3NB
☎ 015394 43123 Fax 015394 43123
Enjoyable holiday golf on a short, slightly hilly but
sporting course in this delightful area of the Lake District
National Park, with superb views of the mountains as the
backcloth to the lake and the course.
18 holes, 5122yds, Par 67, SSS 65, Course record 58.
Club membership 1043.

Visitors	contact pro shop 7 days before day of play, 10-12 & 2-4.30 or before 9am by arrangement.
Societies	by arrangement contact the secretary.
Green Fees	not confirmed.
Cards	▬▬ ▣▬ ▣▬
Prof	W S M Rooke
Designer	G Lowe
Facilities & Leisure	⊗ 〗Ⅲ Ⅼ ᴡ ♀ ⅄ ⌂ ⅋ ⅋ ⌀ snooker.
Location	B5284 1.5m from Bowness

| Hotel | ★★★ 68% Wild Boar Hotel, Crook, WINDERMERE ☎ 015394 45225 36 ⌨ ⋔ *See advertisement on page 55.* |

BRAMPTON   Map 12 NY56

Brampton Talkin Tarn CA8 1HN
☎ 016977 2255 & 2000 Fax 016877 41487
Challenging golf across glorious rolling fell country
demanding solid driving and many long second shots. A
number of particularly fine holes, the pick of which may
arguably be, the 3rd and 11th. The course offers
unrivalled panoramic views from its hilly position.
18 holes, 6407yds, Par 72, SSS 71, Course record 64.
Club membership 800.

Visitors	visitors intending to play at weekends are recommended to telephone in advance.
Societies	apply in writing to M Ogilvie (Hon Commercial Sec), 3 Warwick St, Carlisle, Cumbria CA3 8QW or telephone 01228 401996.
Green Fees	£22 per day/round (£28 weekends & bank holidays).
Prof	Stewart Wilkinson
Designer	James Braid
Facilities & Leisure	⊗ 〗Ⅲ Ⅼ ᴡ ♀ ⅄ ⌂ ⅋ ⌀ games room.
Location	1.5m SE of Brampton on B6413

| Hotel | ★★ 65% The Tarn End House Hotel, Talkin Tarn, BRAMPTON ☎ 016977 2340 7 ⌨ ⋔ *See advertisement on page 52.* |

CARLISLE   Map 11 NY35

Carlisle Aglionby CA4 8AG
☎ 01228 513029 Fax 01228 513303
Majestic looking parkland course with great appeal. A
complete but not too severe test of golf, with fine turf,
natural hazards, a stream and many beautiful trees. A
qualifying course for the Open Championship.
18 holes, 6278yds, Par 71, SSS 70, Course record 63.
Club membership 800.

Visitors	may not play before 9am and between 12-1.30 and when tee is reserved. Very limited play Sunday and with member only Saturday and Tuesday.
Societies	Mon, Wed & Fri, contact in advance for details.
Green Fees	£40 per day; £25 per round (Sun £60/£40).
Prof	Martin Heggie
Designer	Mackenzie Ross
Facilities	⊗ �🏌 ⅃ 🏋 ♀ 🛆 🏠 🚅 ✔
Location	On A69 0.5m E of M6 junc 43

Hotel	★★★ 71% Crown Hotel, Wetheral, CARLISLE ☎ 01228 561888 49 ⇋ ♠ Annexe 2 ⇋ ♠

Stony Holme Municipal St Aidans Rd CA1 1LS
☎ 01228 625511
Municipal parkland course, bounded on three sides by the
River Eden.
18 holes, 5783yds, Par 69, SSS 68, Course record 68.
Club membership 350.

Visitors	advance booking recommended at weekends.
Societies	must telephone pro shop 01228 34856 in advance.
Green Fees	not confirmed.
Prof	S Ling
Facilities	⊗ �🏌 ⅃ 🏋 ♀ 🛆 🏠 🍴 🚅 ✔
Location	2m W of M6 (junct 43) and A69

Hotel	★★★ 67% Posthouse Carlisle, Parkhouse Rd, CARLISLE ☎ 0870 400 9018 127 ⇋ ♠

COCKERMOUTH   Map 11 NY13

Cockermouth Embleton CA13 9SG
☎ 017687 76223 & 76941 Fax 017687 76941
Fell-land course, fenced, with exceptional views and a hard
climb on the 3rd and 11th holes. Testing holes: 10th and 16th
(rearranged by James Braid).
18 holes, 5496yds, Par 69, SSS 67, Course record 62.
Club membership 600.

Visitors	restricted Wed, Sat & Sun.
Societies	apply in writing to the secretary.
Green Fees	£15 per day/round (£20 weekends & bank holidays).
Designer	J Braid
Facilities	⊗ �🏌 by prior arrangement ⅃ 🏋 ♀ 🛆 ✔
Location	3m E off A66

Hotel	★★★ 71% The Trout Hotel, Crown St, COCKERMOUTH ☎ 01900 823591 30 ⇋ ♠

CROSBY-ON-EDEN   Map 12 NY45

Eden CA6 4RA
☎ 01228 573003 & 573013 Fax 01228 818435
Open, championship-length parkland course following the
River Eden. A large number of water hazards, including the
river on certain holes, demands acuracy, as do the well
designed raised greens. Flood-lit driving range and excellent
clubhouse facilities.
18 holes, 6410yds, Par 72, SSS 72, Course record 64.
Club membership 500.

Visitors	must contact in advance.
Societies	telephone to check availability.
Green Fees	£22 (£27 weekends & bank holidays).
Cards	🗖 🗖 🗖 🗖
Prof	Steve Harrison
Facilities	⊗ ⅶ ┗ ➊ ♀ ♨ ➋ ⚑ ⚌ ₹
& Leisure	hard tennis courts.
Location	5m from M6 junc 44,on A689 towards Brampton & Newcastle-Upon-Tyne
Hotel	★★★✦✦ 77% Crosby Lodge Country House Hotel, High Crosby, Crosby-on-Eden, CARLISLE ☎ 01228 573618 9 ⇆ 🐾 Annexe 2 ⇆ 🐾

GRANGE-OVER-SANDS   Map 07 SD47

Grange Fell Fell Rd LA11 6HB
☎ 015395 32536 Fax 015395 35357
Hillside course with magnificent views over Morecambe
Bay and the surrounding Lakeland mountains.
9 holes, 5278yds, Par 70, SSS 66, Course record 65.
Club membership 400.

Visitors	may normally play Mon-Sat.
Green Fees	£12 per day (£18 weekends & bank holidays).
Facilities	➊ ♀ ♨
Location	1m W on Grange-Over-Sands/Cartmel
Hotel	★★★ 69% Netherwood Hotel, Lindale Rd, GRANGE-OVER-SANDS ☎ 015395 32552 28 ⇆ 🐾

Grange-over-Sands Meathop Rd LA11 6QX
☎ 015395 33180 or 33754 Fax 015395 33754
Interesting parkland course with well sited tree plantations,
ditches and water features. The four par 3s are considered to
be some of the best in the area.
18 holes, 5958yds, Par 70, SSS 69, Course record 68.
Club membership 650.

Visitors	must be a member of Golf Club or recognised Golf Society, advisable to contact in advance for play at weekends.
Societies	apply in writing.
Green Fees	£25 per day; £20 per round (£30/£25 weekends & bank holidays).
Prof	Steve Sumner-Roberts
Designer	Mackenzie (part)
Facilities	⊗ ⅶ ┗ ➊ ♀ ♨ ➋ ⚑ ⚌
Location	NE of town centre off B5277
Hotel	★★★ 64% Graythwaite Manor Hotel, Fernhill Rd, GRANGE-OVER-SANDS ☎ 015395 32001 & 33755 Fax 015395 35549 21 ⇆ 🐾

KENDAL   Map 07 SD59

Carus Green Burneside Rd LA9 6EB
☎ 01539 721097 Fax 01539 721097
Bounded by the Kent and Sprint rivers (brought into play on 5
holes), this flat course enjoys open views to the Lakeland Fells.
18 holes, 5691yds, Par 70, SSS 68.
Club membership 400.

Visitors	no restrictions except during Club competitions at weekend, check by phone.
Societies	telephone for details.
Green Fees	not confirmed.
Designer	W Adamson
Facilities	♀ ♨ ➋ ⚑ ⚌
Hotel	★★ 64% Garden House Hotel, Fowl-ing Ln, KENDAL ☎ 01539 731131 11 ⇆ 🐾

Kendal The Heights LA9 4PQ ☎ 01539 723499
Elevated parkland/fell course affording breathtaking views of
Lakeland fells and surrounding district.
18 holes, 5765yds, Par 70, SSS 67, Course record 60.
Club membership 737.

Visitors	must have a handicap certificate, weekends subject to availability. Telephone to reserve tee-off time.
Societies	must contact in advance.
Green Fees	not confirmed.
Prof	to be appointed
Facilities	⊗ ⅶ ┗ ➊ ♀ ♨ ➋ ⚑ ⚌
Location	1m W of town centre
Hotel	★★ 64% Garden House Hotel, Fowl-ing Ln, KENDAL ☎ 01539 731131 11 ⇆ 🐾

KESWICK   Map 11 NY22

Keswick Threlkeld Hall CA12 4SX
☎ 017687 79324 Fax 017687 79861
Varied fell and tree-lined course with commanding views of
Lakeland scenery.
18 holes, 6225yds, Par 71, SSS 72, Course record 67.
Club membership 866.

Visitors	booking up to 7 days in advance 017687 79010. Restricted on competition days.
Societies	apply in writing to secretary.
Green Fees	£20 per day (£25 weekends & bank holidays).
Prof	Craig Hamilton
Designer	Eric Brown
Facilities	⊗ ⅶ ┗ ➊ ♀ ♨ ➋ ⚑ ⚌
& Leisure	fishing.

Location	4m E of Keswick, off A66

Hotel	★★★★ 56% Keswick Country House Hotel, Station Rd, KESWICK ☎ 017687 72020 74 ⇥ ☞

KIRKBY LONSDALE   Map 07 SD67

Kirkby Lonsdale Scaleber Ln, Barbon LA6 2LJ
☎ 015242 76365
Parkland course on the east bank of the River Lune and crossed by Barbon Beck. Mainly following the lie of the land, the gently undulating course uses the beck to provide water hazards.
18 holes, 6472yds, Par 72, SSS 71, Course record 68.
Club membership 600.

Visitors	restricted on Sunday, must telephone in advance or call in at pro shop.
Societies	apply in writing for society package.
Green Fees	not confirmed.
Prof	Chris Barrett
Designer	Bill Squires
Facilities	⊗ 洲 ╚ ☑ ♀ ⚖ 🏠 ☍ ⌀
Location	3m NE of Kirkby Lonsdale on A683

Hotel	★★ 69% Pheasant Inn, CASTERTON ☎ 015242 71230 11 ⇥ ☞

MARYPORT   Map 11 NY03

Maryport Bankend CA15 6PA ☎ 01900 812605
A tight seaside links course exposed to Solway breezes. Fine views across Solway Firth. Course comprises 9 holes links and 9 holes parkland and small streams can be hazardous on several holes.
18 holes, 6088yds, Par 70, SSS 69, Course record 65.
Club membership 400.

Visitors	contact club in advance. Dress code must be observed.
Societies	must apply in writing.
Green Fees	not confirmed.
Facilities	⊗ 洲 ╚ ☑ ♀ ⚖ 🏠
Location	1m N on B5300

Hotel	★★ 64% Broughton Craggs Hotel, Great Broughton, COCKERMOUTH ☎ 01900 824400 14 ⇥ ☞

PENRITH   Map 12 NY53

Penrith Salkeld Rd CA11 8SG
☎ 01768 891919 Fax 01768 891919
A beautiful and well-balanced course, always changing direction, and demanding good length from the tee. It is set on rolling moorland with occasional pine trees and some fine views.
18 holes, 6047yds, Par 69, SSS 69, Course record 63.
Club membership 850.

Visitors	contact in advance. Handicap certificate required.
Societies	telephone in advance.
Green Fees	£25 per day; £20 per round (£30/£25 weekends).
Prof	Garry Key
Facilities	⊗ 洲 ╚ ☑ ♀ ⚖ 🏠 ☍ ⌀ ⌀
Location	0.75m N off A6

Hotel	★★ 66% Brantwood Country Hotel, Stainton, PENRITH ☎ 01768 862748 6 ☞ Annexe 5 ⇥ ☞

ST BEES   Map 11 NX91

St Bees CA27 0EJ ☎ 01946 824300
Links course, down hill and dale, with sea views.
9 holes, 5082yds, Par 64, SSS 65.
Club membership 275.

Visitors	no restrictions.
Green Fees	not confirmed.
Location	0.5m W of village off B5345

Hotel	★★★ 76% Ennerdale Country House Hotel, CLEATOR ☎ 01946 813907 30 ⇥ ☞

SEASCALE   Map 06 NY00

Seascale The Banks yA20 1QL
☎ 019467 28202 Fax 019467 28202
A tough links requiring length and control. The natural terrain is used to give a variety of holes and considerable character. Undulating greens add to the challenge. Fine views over the Western Fells, the Irish Sea and Isle of Man.
18 holes, 6416yds, Par 71, SSS 71, Course record 65.
Club membership 650.

Visitors	no restrictions, but advisable to contact for tee reservation times.
Societies	telephone to make provisional booking.
Green Fees	£26 per day; £21 per round (£31/£26 weekends & bank holidays).
Prof	Craig Hamilton
Designer	Willie Campbell
Facilities	⊗ 洲 ╚ ☑ ♀ ⚖ 🏠 ☍ ⌀ ⌀ ⌀
Location	NW side of village off B5344

Hotel	★★ 71% Westlakes Hotel, GOSFORTH ☎ 019467 25221 9 ⇥ ☞

SEDBERGH   Map 07 SD69

Sedbergh Catholes, Abbot Holme LA10 5SS
☎ 015396 21551 (Club) & 20993 (Sec)
A tree-lined grassland course with superb scenery in the Yorkshire Dales National Park. Feature hole is the par 3 2nd (110yds) where the River Dee separates the tee from the green.
9 holes, 5624yds, Par 70, SSS 68, Course record 66.
Club membership 250.

Visitors	must book to play on weekends & bank holidays.
Societies	must contact in advance.
Green Fees	not confirmed.
Designer	W G Squires
Facilities	⊗ 洲 ╚ ☑ ♀ ⚖ 🏠 ☍ ⌀
Location	1m S off A683, 5m junct 37 M6

Hotel	★★ 64% Garden House Hotel, Fowl-ing Ln, KENDAL ☎ 01539 731131 11 ⇥ ☞

Looking for a driving range?
See the index at the back of the guide

SILECROFT
Map 06 SD18

Silecroft LA18 4AG ☎ 01229 774250
Seaside links course parallel to the coast of the Irish Sea.
Often windy. Easy walking. Spectacular views inland of
Lakeland hills.
9 holes, 5877yds, Par 68, SSS 68, Course record 66.
Club membership 300.
Visitors	may be restricted competition days & bank holidays
Societies	must contact in writing.
Green Fees	£15 per day.
Facilities	♥ ♀ ⚘
Location	3m W of Millom

SILLOTH
Map 11 NY15

Silloth on Solway The Clubhouse CA7 4BL
☎ 016973 31304 & 32404 Fax 016973 31782
Billowing dunes, narrow fairways, heather and gorse and
the constant subtle problems of tactics and judgement
make these superb links on the Solway an exhilarating
and searching test. The 13th is a good long hole. Superb
views.
18 holes, 6614yds, Par 72, SSS 73, Course record 65.
Club membership 700.
Visitors	must contact in advance.
Societies	telephone for times available.
Green Fees	£25 per day (£32 per round weekends).
Prof	J Graham
Designer	David Grant/Willie Park Jnr
Facilities	⊗ ⍟ ⮕ ♥ ♀ ⚘ 🏠 ✐
Location	S side of village off B5300
Hotel	★ 62% Golf Hotel, Criffel St, SILLOTH ☎ 016973 31438 22 ⇆ ⟆

ULVERSTON
Map 07 SD27

Ulverston Bardsea Park LA12 9QJ
☎ 01229 582824 Fax 01229 588910
Inland golf with many medium length holes on
undulating parkland. The 17th is a testing par 4.
Overlooking Morecambe Bay the course offers extensive
views to the Lakeland Fells.
18 holes, 6201yds, Par 71, SSS 70, Course record 64.
Club membership 750.
Visitors	must contact in advance, be a member of an accredited golf club with a handicap certificate. May not play on Sat, competition days & restricted on Tue-Ladies day.
Societies	by arrangement in writing.
Green Fees	Apr-Oct: £30 per day; £25 per round (£35/£30 weekends & bank holidays) Nov-Mar: £18 per day; £14 per round (£22/£18 weekends & bank holidays).
Prof	M R Smith
Designer	A Herd/H S Colt (1923)
Facilities	⊗ ⍟ ⮕ ♥ ♀ ⚘ 🏠 ⛏ ✐
Location	2m S off A5087
Hotel	★★★ 65% Whitewater Hotel, The Lakeland Village, NEWBY BRIDGE ☎ 015395 31133 35 ⇆ ⟆

WINDERMERE

See **Bowness-on-Windermere**

WORKINGTON
Map 11 NY02

Workington Branthwaite Rd CA14 4SS
☎ 01900 67828 Fax 01900 607123
Meadowland course, undulating, with natural hazards created
by stream and trees. Good views of Solway Firth and
Lakeland Hills. 10th, 13th and 15th holes are particularly
testing.
18 holes, 6217yds, Par 72, SSS 70, Course record 65.
Club membership 735.
Visitors	advisable to contact pro for weekday, weekends are generally very busy & Tue is Ladies Day. No vistors before 9.30am.
Societies	booking required for over 8 people.
Green Fees	£20 per day (£25 weekends & bank holidays).
Prof	Aidrian Drabble
Designer	James Braid
Facilities	⊗ ⍟ ⮕ ♥ ♀ ⚘ 🏠 ⛏ ✐
& Leisure	snooker table.
Location	1.75m E off A596
Hotel	★★★ 78% Washington Central Hotel, Washington St, WORKINGTON ☎ 01900 65772 46 ⇆ ⟆

DERBYSHIRE

ALFRETON   Map 08 SK45

Alfreton Wingfield Rd, Oakerthorpe DE55 7LH
☎ 01773 832070
A small parkland course with tight fairways and many
natural hazards.
11 holes, 5393yds, Par 67, SSS 66, Course record 67.
Club membership 300.
Visitors   must contact in advance.
Societies   apply in writing or telephone in advance.
Green Fees £22 per day Mon-Fri.
Prof   Julian Mellor
Facilities   ⌚♥♀⛄🏠
Location   1m W on A615

Hotel   ★★★★ 67% Swallow Hotel, Carter Ln East,
                  SOUTH NORMANTON ☎ 01773 812000
                  160 ⇔ ⛳

ASHBOURNE   Map 07 SK14

Ashbourne Wyaston Rd DE6 1NB
☎ 01335 342078 Fax 01335 347937
With fine views over surrounding countryside, the course
uses natural contours and water features.
18 holes, 6402yds, Par 72, SSS 72.
Club membership 650.
Visitors   must contact professional in advance, may not
                  play on competition days. With member only at
                  weekends.
Societies   telephone in advance.
Green Fees £20 per round (£30 per round weekends & bank
                  holidays).
Cards   💳💳💳💳💳
Prof   Andrew Smith
Designer   D Hemstock
Facilities   ⊗⌚♥♀⛄🏠
Location   Off Wyaston Road

Hotel   ★★★♨ 75% Callow Hall, Mappleton Rd,
                  ASHBOURNE ☎ 01335 300900 16 ⇔ ⛳

BAKEWELL   Map 08 SK26

Bakewell Station Rd DE45 1GB ☎ 01629 812307
Parkland course, hilly, with plenty of natural hazards to test
the golfer. Magnificent views across the Wye Valley.
9 holes, 5240yds, Par 68, SSS 66.
Club membership 325.
Visitors   limited at weekends due to competitions,
                  generally available mid week but occasional
                  matches/competitions.
Societies   apply in writing.
Green Fees £15 per day (£20 weekends & bank holidays).
Facilities   ⊗⌚♥♀⛄
Location   E side of town off A6

Hotel   ★★♨ 73% Croft Country House Hotel, Great
                  Longstone, BAKEWELL ☎ 01629 640278
                  9 ⇔ ⛳

BAMFORD   Map 08 SK28

Sickleholme Saltergate Ln S33 0BN
☎ 01433 651306 Fax 01433 659498
Undulating downland course in the lovely Peak District, with
rivers and ravines and spectacular scenery.
18 holes, 6064yds, Par 69, SSS 69, Course record 62.
Club membership 700.
Visitors   must contact in advance, restricted weekends.
Societies   telephone in advance.
Green Fees £28 per day (£32 weekends).
Prof   P H Taylor
Facilities   ⊗⌚♥♀⛄🏠
Location   0.75m S on A6013

Hotel   ★★ 69% Yorkshire Bridge Inn, Ashopton Rd,
                  Hope Valley, BAMFORD
                  ☎ 01433 651361 14 ⇔ ⛳

BREADSALL   Map 08 SK33

Marriot Breadsall Priory Hotel & Country Club Moor
Rd, Morley DE7 6DL ☎ 01332 832235 Fax 01332 833509
Set in 200 acres of mature parkland, the Priory Course is
built on the site of a 13th-century priory. Full use has been
made of natural features and fine old trees. In contrast the
Moorland Course, designed by Donald Steel and built by
Brian Piersen, features Derbyshire stone walls and open
moors heavily affected by winds. Open when most other
clubs are closed in winter.
*Priory Course: 18 holes, 6100yds, Par 72, SSS 69, Course
record 63.*
Moorland Course: 18 holes, 6028yds, Par 70, SSS 69.
Club membership 900.

Visitors   must contact in advance, 10 day booking
                  service.
Societies   telephone in advance.
Green Fees seasonal from £25-£36 per round.
Prof   Darren Steels
Designer   D Steel
Facilities   ⊗⌚♥♀⛄🏠🏌🏇🏀
& Leisure   hard tennis courts, heated indoor swimming
                  pool, sauna, solarium, gymnasium.
Location   0.75m W

Hotel   ★★★★ 62% Marriott Breadsall Priory
                  Hotel/Country Club, Moor Rd, MORLEY
                  ☎ 01332 832235 12 ⇔ ⛳ Annexe 100 ⇔ ⛳

BUXTON   Map 07 SK07

Buxton & High Peak Townend, Waterswallows Rd
SK17 7EN ☎ 01298 23453
Bracing, well-drained meadowland course; the highest in
Derbyshire. Challenging course where wind direction is a
major factor on some holes; others require blind shots to
sloping greens.
18 holes, 5966yds, Par 69, SSS 69, Course record 65.
Club membership 670.
Visitors   contact Mrs S Arnfield.
Societies   apply in writing to Mrs S Arnfield.
Green Fees   not confirmed.
Prof   Gary Brown
Designer   J Morris
Facilities   ⊗ ℍ ┗ ■ ♀ 👌 🖻 ⛳ 🚜 ♂ ⚑
Location   1m NE off A6

Hotel   ★★★ 67% Palace Hotel, Palace Rd, BUXTON
                  ☎ 01298 22001 122 ⇉ 🐾

Cavendish Gadley Ln SK17 6XD
☎ 01298 79708 Fax 01298 79708
This parkland/moorland course with its comfortable
clubhouse nestles below the rising hills. Generally open
to the prevailing west wind, it is noted for its excellent
surfaced greens which contain many deceptive subtleties.
Designed by Dr Alastair McKenzie, good holes include
the 8th, 9th and 18th.
18 holes, 5721yds, Par 68, SSS 68, Course record 61.
Club membership 650.
Visitors   must contact in advance, weekends are
                  restricted by competitions. Ladies day
                  Thursday
Societies   telephone professional on 01298 25052.
Green Fees   £26 per round (£35 weekends).
Cards   ▬ 🃏
Prof   Paul Hunstone
Designer   Dr Mackenzie
Facilities   ⊗ ℍ by prior arrangement ┗ ■ ♀ 👌
                  🖻 ⛳ ♂ ⚑
Location   0.75m W of town centre off A53

Hotel   ★★★ 75% Best Western Lee Wood Hotel,
                  The Park, BUXTON ☎ 01298 23002
                  35 ⇉ 🐾 Annexe 5 ⇉ 🐾

CHAPEL-EN-LE-FRITH   Map 07 SK08

Chapel-en-le-Frith The Cockyard, Manchester Rd SK23 9UH
☎ 01298 812118 & 813943 (sec) Fax 01298 814990
Scenic parkland course, with testing holes at the 14th (par 4)
and 18th (517 yds), par 5. Good views.
18 holes, 6054yds, Par 70, SSS 69, Course record 67.
Club membership 676.
Visitors   must contact professional or secretary in
                  advance.
Societies   apply in advance to Secretary.
Green Fees   £22 per day (£30 weekends & bank holidays).
Prof   David J Cullen
Facilities   ⊗ ℍ ┗ ■ ♀ 👌 🖻 ⛳ ♂
Location   On B5470

Hotel   ★★★ 75% Best Western Lee Wood Hotel, The
                  Park, BUXTON ☎ 01298 23002
                  35 ⇉ 🐾 Annexe 5 ⇉ 🐾

CHESTERFIELD   Map 08 SK37

Chesterfield Walton S42 7LA
☎ 01246 279256 Fax 01246 276622
A varied and interesting, undulating parkland course with
trees picturesquely adding to the holes and the outlook alike.
Stream hazard on back nine. Views over four counties.
18 holes, 6326yds, Par 71, SSS 70, Course record 65.
Club membership 600.
Visitors   must contact in advance and must play with
                  member at weekends and bank holidays. A
                  handicap certificate is generally required.
Societies   apply in writing.
Green Fees   £35 per day; £26 per round.
Prof   Mike McLean
Facilities   ⊗ ┗ ■ ♀ 👌 🖻 ♂
Location   2m SW off A632

Hotel   ★★ 67% Abbeydale Hotel, Cross St,
                  CHESTERFIELD ☎ 01246 277849
                  12rm(11 ⇉ 🐾)

Grassmoor Golf Centre North Wingfield Rd, Grassmoor
S42 5EA ☎ 01246 856044 Fax 01246 853486
An 18-hole heathland course with interesting and challenging
water features. 26-bay floodlit driving range, practice
bunkers and putting area.
18 holes, 5723yds, Par 69, SSS 69, Course record 67.
Club membership 420.
Visitors   contact Manager in advance. Smart dress code.
Societies   telephone Manager in advance.
Green Fees   £10 per round (£12 weekends).
Cards   ▬ ▬ 🃏
Prof   Gary Hagues
Designer   Hawtree
Facilities   ⊗ ℍ ┗ ■ ♀ 👌 🖻 ⛳ ♂ ⚑
Location   Between Chesterfield & Grassmoor, off B6038

Hotel   ★★ 67% Abbeydale Hotel, Cross St,
                  CHESTERFIELD ☎ 01246 277849
                  12rm (11 ⇉ 🐾)

Stanedge Walton Hay Farm, Stonedge, Ashover S45 0LW
☎ 01246 566156
Moorland course in hilly situation open to strong winds.
Some tricky short holes with narrow fairways, so accuracy is
paramount. Magnificent views over four counties. Extended
course now open.
9 holes, 5786yds, Par 69, SSS 68, Course record 68.
Club membership 310.
Visitors   with member only Sat & Sun, and may not play
                  after 2pm weekdays.
Societies   apply in writing.
Green Fees   £15 per round (18 holes).
Facilities   ■ ♀ 👌
Location   5m SW off B5057 nr Red Lion public house

Hotel   ★★ 67% Abbeydale Hotel, Cross St,
                  CHESTERFIELD ☎ 01246 277849
                  12rm (11 ⇉ 🐾)

AA Hotels that have special
arrangements with golf courses are listed at
the back of the guide

Tapton Park Municipal Tapton Park, Tapton S41 0EQ
☎ 01246 239500
Municipal parkland course with some fairly hard walking.
The 620 yd (par 5) 5th is a testing hole.
Tapton Main: 18 holes, 6013yds, Par 71, SSS 69.
Dobbin Clough: 9 holes, 2613yds, Par 34.
Club membership 750.
Visitors   must contact in advance. No caddies allowed.
Societies   apply in writing.
Green Fees £5.80 per 18 holes; £3.20 per 9 holes
          (£7.50/£4.20 weekends).
Prof   Fraser Scott
Facilities   ♀⚐☎⛳
Location   0.5m E of Chesterfield Station

Hotel   ★★ 67% Abbeydale Hotel, Cross St,
          CHESTERFIELD ☎ 01246 277849
          12rm (11 ⇋ ℟)

CODNOR   Map 08 SK44

Ormonde Fields Golf & Country Club Nottingham Rd
DE5 9RG ☎ 01773 570043 (Secretary) & 742987 (Pro)
Fax 01773 742987
Parkland course with undulating fairways and natural
hazards. There is a practice area.
18 holes, 6502yds, Par 71, SSS 72, Course record 68.
Club membership 500.
Visitors   must contact in advance.
Societies   telephone in advance.
Green Fees not confirmed.
Prof   Peter Buttifant
Designer   W Hawtree
Facilities   ⊗℠℡⚐♀⚐☎⛳
Location   1m SE on A610

Hotel   ★★★ 70% Makeney Hall Country House
          Hotel, Makeney, Milford, BELPER
          ☎ 01332 842999   27 ⇋ ℟ Annexe 18 ⇋ ℟

DERBY   Map 08 SK33

Allestree Park Allestree Hall, Duffield Rd, Allestree
DE22 2EU ☎ 01332 550616 Fax 01332 541195
Public course, picturesque and undulating set in 300 acre
park with views across Derbyshire.
18 holes, 5806yds, Par 68, SSS 68.
Visitors   start times may be booked in advance by
          telephone, visitors welcome any day.
Societies   apply in writing or by telephone in advance.
Green Fees not confirmed.
Cards   ▭▭ ▥▥ ▨▨ ▧▧ ▦
Prof   John Siddons
Facilities   ⊗℠℡⚐♨♀⚐☎⛳
& Leisure   fishing.
Location   N of Derby, from A38 take A6 towards north,
          course in 1.5m on left

Hotel   ★★★★ 62% Marriott Breadsall Priory
          Hotel/Country Club, Moor Rd, MORLEY
          ☎ 01332 832235   12 ⇋ ℟ Annexe 100 ⇋ ℟

Mickleover Uttoxeter Rd, Mickleover DE3 5AD
☎ 01332 518662 Fax 01332 512092
Undulating parkland course in pleasant setting, affording
splendid country views. Some attractive par 3s and a number
of elevated greens.

18 holes, 5702yds, Par 68, SSS 68, Course record 64.
Club membership 800.
Visitors   must contact Professional in advance.
Societies   apply in writing.
Green Fees £22 per day/round (£25 weekends).
Prof   Tim Coxon
Designer   J Pennink
Facilities   ⊗℠℡⚐♀⚐☎⛳⛳
Location   3m W off A516/B5020

Hotel   ★★★★ 74% Mickleover Court Hotel, Etwall
          Rd, Mickleover, DERBY ☎ 0500 636943
          99 ⇋ ℟

Sinfin Wilmore Rd, Sinfin DE24 9HD
☎ 01332 766462 Fax 01332 769004
Municipal parkland course with tree lined fairways an
excellent test of golf. Generally a flat course it is suitable for
golfers of all ages.
18 holes, 6163yds, Par 70, SSS 69.
Visitors   starting time must be booked in advance by
          telephone, visitors welcome any day.
Societies   apply in writing or by telephone in advance.
Green Fees not confirmed.
Cards   ▭▭ ▥▥ ▨▨ ▧▧ ▦
Prof   Steven Lamb
Facilities   ⊗℠℡⚐♀⚐☎⛳⛳
Location   3.5m S of city centre

Hotel   ★★★ 63% International Hotel, 288 Burton Rd,
          DERBY ☎ 01332 369321
          41 ⇋ ℟ Annexe 21 ⇋ ℟

DRONFIELD   Map 08 SK37

Hallowes Hallowes Ln S18 1UR
☎ 01246 411196 Fax 01246 411196
Attractive moorland/parkland course set in the Derbyshire
hills. Several testing par 4's and splendid views.
18 holes, 6342yds, Par 71, SSS 71, Course record 64.
Club membership 630.
Visitors   may only play with member at weekends. Must
          contact in advance.
Societies   contact in advance, various packages.
Green Fees £35 per day; £30 per round.
Prof   Philip Dunn
Facilities   ⊗℠℡⚐♀⚐☎⛳
& Leisure   snooker.
Location   S side of town

Hotel   ★★ 66% Chantry Hotel, Church St,
          DRONFIELD ☎ 01246 413014 7 ⇋ ℟

DUFFIELD   Map 08 SK34

Chevin Golf Ln DE56 4EE
☎ 01332 841864 Fax 01332 841864
A mixture of parkland and moorland, this course is rather
hilly which makes for some hard walking, but with most
rewarding views of the surrounding countryside. The 8th
hole, aptly named "Tribulation", requires an accurate tee
shot, and is one of the most difficult holes in the country.
18 holes, 6057yds, Par 69, SSS 69, Course record 64.
Club membership 750.
Visitors   not before 9.30am or off first tee between 12.30
          and 2pm. Proof of handicap required.
Societies   contact in advance.

▶

Green Fees £27.50 per round/day.
Prof Willie Bird
Facilities ⊗ ⊞ ⓛ ⓗ ⓨ ⚲ ⓣ ⓥ ∅
Location N side of town off A6

Hotel ★★★ 70% Makeney Hall Country House Hotel, Makeney, Milford, BELPER
☎ 01332 842999 27 ⇄ ⓡ Annexe 18 ⇄ ⓡ

GLOSSOP
Map 07 SK09

Glossop and District Hurst Ln, off Sheffield Rd SK13 7PU
☎ 01457 865247
Moorland course in good position, excellent natural hazards. Difficult closing hole (9th & 18th).
11 holes, 5800yds, Par 68, SSS 68.
Club membership 250.
Visitors may not play on bank holidays or Sat (Apr-Nov).
Societies must apply in writing to professional.
Green Fees not confirmed.
Prof Daniel Marsh
Facilities ⊗ ⊞ ⓛ ⓗ ⓨ ⓐ ∅
Location 1m E off A57

Hotel ★★ 69% York House Hotel, York Place, Richmond St, ASHTON-UNDER-LYNE
☎ 0161 330 9000 24 ⇄ ⓡ Annexe 10 ⇄ ⓡ

HORSLEY
Map 08 SK34

Horsley Lodge Smalley Mill Rd DE21 5BL
☎ 01332 780838 Fax 01332 781118
This lush meadowland course is set in 100 acres of Derbyshire countryside, has some challenging holes. Also Par 3 course and floodlit driving range. USGA world class greens designed by former World Champion Peter McEvoy.
18 holes, 6400yds, Par 72, SSS 71, Course record 72.
Club membership 650.
Visitors must contact professional in advance and have handicap. May not play weekends before noon.
Societies must telephone in advance.
Green Fees £28.
Cards ▦ ▦ ▦ ▦ ▦ ▦
Prof Paul Kent
Designer Bill White
Facilities ⓐ ⓖ ⓣ ⓥ ⓦ ⚲ ∅ ⓡ
& Leisure fishing, sauna, solarium.
Location 4m NE of Derby, off A38 at Belper then follow tourist signs

Hotel ★★★★ 62% Marriott Breadsall Priory Hotel/Country Club, Moor Rd, MORLEY
☎ 01332 832235 12 ⇄ ⓡ Annexe 100 ⇄ ⓡ

KEDLESTON
Map 08 SK34

Kedleston Park DE22 5JD
☎ 01332 840035 Fax 01332 840035
The course is laid out in flat mature parkland with fine trees and background views of historic Kedleston Hall (National Trust). Many testing holes are included in each nine and there is an excellent modern clubhouse.
18 holes, 6675yds, Par 72, SSS 72.
Club membership 847.

Visitors must contact in advance. With member only at weekends.
Societies weekdays only, apply in writing.
Green Fees £30 per round (£40 weekends).
Prof David J Russell
Designer James Braid
Facilities ⊗ ⊞ ⓛ ⓗ ⓨ ⚲ ⓐ ⓣ ⓥ ⓦ ∅
& Leisure sauna.
Location Signposted Kedleston Hall from A38

Hotel ★★★ 63% International Hotel, 288 Burton Rd, DERBY ☎ 01332 369321
41 ⇄ ⓡ Annexe 21 ⇄ ⓡ

MATLOCK
Map 08 SK36

Matlock Chesterfield Rd, Matlock Moor DE4 5LZ
☎ 01629 582191
Moorland course with fine views of the beautiful Peak District.
18 holes, 5996yds, Par 70, SSS 69, Course record 63.
Club membership 700.
Visitors with member only weekends & bank holidays. Members only weekdays 12.30-1.30pm.
Societies prior arrangement with Secretary.
Green Fees £30 per day; £25 per round.
Prof M A Whithorn
Designer Tom Williamson
Facilities ⊗ by prior arrangement ⊞ by prior arrangement ⓛ ⓗ ⓨ ⚲ ⓐ ∅
Location 1.5m NE of Matlock on A632

Hotel ★★★ 65% New Bath Hotel, New Bath Rd, MATLOCK ☎ 0870 400 8119 55 ⇄ ⓡ

MICKLEOVER
Map 08 SK33

Pastures Social Centre, Hospital Ln DE3 5DQ
☎ 01332 521074
Challenging course laid-out on undulating meadowland with good views across the Trent valley. Numerous yesying Par 3s.
9 holes, 5095yds, Par 64, SSS 65, Course record 67.
Club membership 320.
Visitors must be accompanied by a member, may not play on Sun & between noon-4pm Sat. Handicap certificate required.
Societies Mon & Tue, must contact in advance.
Green Fees £8 per round; £15 per 18 holes.
Designer J F Pennik
Facilities ⓛ ⓗ ⓨ evenings ⚲ ⓐ
Location 1m SW off A516

Hotel ★★★ 63% International Hotel, 288 Burton Rd, DERBY ☎ 01332 369321
41 ⇄ ⓡ Annexe 21 ⇄ ⓡ

MORLEY
Map 08 SK34

Morley Hayes Main Rd DE7 6DG
☎ 01332 780480 Fax 01332 781094
Peaceful pay and play course set in a splendid valley and incorporating charming water features and woodland. Floodlit driving range. Challenging 9 hole short course (Tower Course).
Manor Course: 18 holes, 6726yds, Par 72, SSS 72.
Tower Course: 9 holes, 1614yds, Par 30.

▶

Visitors	welcome.
Societies	booking essential telephone for details.
Green Fees	Manor course: £17.50 per 18 holes (£22.50 weekends & bank holidays) Tower course: £8 (£10 weekends & Bank holidays).
Cards	〰️ ▪️▪️ 〰️ 🅿️ 〰️ 〰️
Prof	Mark Whithorn
Facilities	⊗ 〰️ 🏌️ 🍴 ♀ 👥 🏠 🚩 🛒 ✂ ⛳
Location	A608
Hotel	★★★★ 62% Marriott Breadsall Priory Hotel/Country Club, Moor Rd, MORLEY ☎ 01332 832235 12 🛏️ 🏳️ Annexe 100 🛏️ 🏳️

NEW MILLS   Map 07 SK08

New Mills Shaw Marsh SK12 4QE ☎ 01663 743485
Moorland course with panoramic views and first-class
greens.
9 holes, 5633yds, Par 68, SSS 67.
Club membership 365.

Visitors	telephone in advance, cannot play during competitions.
Societies	must contact secretary or professional in advance.
Green Fees	not confirmed.
Prof	Stephen James
Facilities	⊗ 〰️ 🏌️ 🍴 ♀ 👥 🏠 🚩 🛒 ⛳
Location	0.5m N off B6101
Hotel	★★ 70% Springfield Hotel, Station Rd, MARPLE ☎ 0161 449 0721 7 🛏️ 🏳️

RENISHAW   Map 08 SK47

Renishaw Park Club House, Mill Ln S21 3UZ
☎ 01246 432044 & 435484
Part parkland and part meadowland with easy walking.
18 holes, 6262yds, Par 71, SSS 70, Course record 65.
Club membership 750.

Visitors	must contact in advance. Visitors not allowed on competition days.
Societies	by arrangement.
Green Fees	£34 per day; £24.50 per round (£38.50 per day/round weekends & bank holidays).
Prof	John Oates
Designer	Sir George Sitwell
Facilities	⊗ 🏌️ 🍴 ♀ 👥 🏠 ⛳
Location	1.5m W of junct 30 M1
Hotel	★★★ 62% Sitwell Arms Hotel, Station Rd, RENISHAW ☎ 01246 435226 30 🛏️ 🏳️

RISLEY   Map 08 SK43

Maywood Rushy Ln DE72 3ST ☎ 0115 939 2306
Wooded parkland course with numerous water hazards.
18 holes, 6424yds, Par 72, SSS 71, Course record 70.
Club membership 450.

Visitors	advisable to contact in advance during summer, may not play during competitions. Standard dress code applies.
Societies	by prior arrangement.
Green Fees	not confirmed.
Prof	Colin Henderson
Designer	P Moon

Facilities	🏌️ ♀ 🍴 👥 🏠 ⛳
Location	Near junct 25 on M1
Hotel	★★★ 70% Risley Hall Hotel, Derby Rd, RISLEY ☎ 01159 399000 16 🛏️ 🏳️

SHIRLAND   Map 08 SK45

Shirland Lower Delves DE55 6AU ☎ 01773 834935
Rolling parkland and tree-lined course with extensive views
of Derbyshire countryside.
18 holes, 6072yds, Par 71, SSS 70, Course record 70.
Club membership 600.

Visitors	contact professional in advance.
Societies	contact Professional.
Green Fees	£17 per round (£22 weekends).
Prof	Neville Hallam
Facilities	⊗ 〰️ 🏌️ 🍴 ♀ 👥 🏠 🚩 ⛳
Location	S side of village off A61
Hotel	★★★★ 67% Swallow Hotel, Carter Ln East, SOUTH NORMANTON ☎ 01773 812000 160 🛏️ 🏳️

STANTON-BY-DALE   Map 08 SK43

Erewash Valley DE7 4QR
☎ 0115 932 3258 Fax 0115 932 2984
Parkland/meadowland course overlooking valley and M1.
Unique 4th and 5th in Victorian quarry bottom: 5th-testing
par 3.
18 holes, 6557yds, Par 72, SSS 71, Course record 67.
Club membership 750.

Visitors	no restrictions except when club events in progress.
Societies	contact in advance.
Green Fees	£29.50 per day; £24.50 per round (£29.50 weekends).
Prof	M J Ronan
Designer	Hawtree
Facilities	⊗ 〰️ by prior arrangement 🏌️ 🍴 ♀ 👥 🏠 🚩 🛒 ⛳
Location	1m W, 2m from junct 25 on M1
Hotel	★★★ 70% Risley Hall Hotel, Derby Rd, RISLEY ☎ 01159 399000 16 🛏️ 🏳️

UNSTONE   Map 08 SK37

Birch Hall Sheffield Rd S18 4DB
☎ 01246 291979 Fax 01246 412912
Very testing woodland/moorland course demanding respect
and a good straight game if one is to walk away with a
respectable card. Sloping fairways gather wayward drives
into thick gorse and deep ditches. Signature holes are the
tough 6th and scenic 13th, the latter begs a big-hitter to go
for a shot to the green.
18 holes, 6379yds, Par 73, SSS 71, Course record 72.
Club membership 320.

Visitors	welcome at all times except before noon at weekends, midweek medals held regularly telephone for details. Advisable to telephone in advance at all times
Societies	apply in writing to secretary or telephone course.
Green Fees	not confirmed.

Prof	Pete Ball
Designer	D Tucker
Facilities	⊗ 爪 ⬛ 💪 ♀ ⚲
Location	Turn off A61 between Sheffield and Chesterfield, outskirts of Unstone village

Hotel ★★ 66% Chantry Hotel, Church St, DRONFIELD ☎ 01246 413014 7 ⇆ 🏌

DEVON

AXMOUTH
Map 03 SY29

Axe Cliff Squires Ln EX12 4AB
☎ 01297 21754 & 24371 Fax 01297 24371
Undulating links course with coastal views.
18 holes, 6000yds, Par 70, SSS 70, Course record 70.
Club membership 400.
Visitors	must contact in advance.
Societies	must contact in advance.
Green Fees	£20 per day (£22 weekends).
Prof	Mark Dack
Facilities	⊗ 爪 ⬛ 💪 ♀ ⚲ 🏌 ⚌
Location	0.75m S on B3172

Hotel ★★ 77% Swallows Eaves, COLYFORD ☎ 01297 553184 8 ⇆ 🏌

BIGBURY-ON-SEA
Map 03 SX64

Bigbury TQ7 4BB
☎ 01548 810557 (Secretary) 810412 (Pro Shop)
Fax 01548 810207
Clifftop, heathland course with easy walking. Exposed to winds, but with fine views over the sea and River Avon. 7th hole particularly tricky.
18 holes, 6048yds, Par 70, SSS 69, Course record 65.
Club membership 850.
Visitors	must have handicap certificate. Must contact in advance.
Societies	must apply in writing.
Green Fees	£25 (£30 weekends).
Prof	Simon Lloyd
Designer	J H Taylor
Facilities	⊗ 爪 by prior arrangement 💪 ⬛ ♀ ⚲ 🏌 ⚌ ⚲
Location	1m S on B3392 between Bigbury and Bigbury-on-Sea

Hotel ★★★★ 72% Thurlestone Hotel, THURLESTONE ☎ 01548 560382 64 ⇆ 🏌

BLACKAWTON
Map 03 SX85

Dartmouth Golf & Country Club TQ9 7DE
☎ 01803 712686 & 712650 Fax 01803 712628
The 9-hole Club course and the 18-hole Championship course are both worth a visit and not just for the beautiful views. The Championship is one of the most challenging courses in the West Country with a 4th hole visitors will always remember.

Championship Course: 18 holes, 6663yds, Par 72, SSS 72.
Club Course: 9 holes, 5166yds, Par 66, SSS 65.
Club membership 800.
Visitors	must contact in advance, visitors welcome subject to availability.
Societies	telephone in advance.
Green Fees	not confirmed.
Cards	💳 ▬ ▬ ▬ 🏧
Prof	Steve Dougan
Designer	Jeremy Pern
Facilities	⊗ 爪 💪 ⬛ ♀ ⚲ 🏌 🏌 ⚌ ⚲ 🏌
& Leisure	heated indoor swimming pool, sauna, solarium, gymnasium.
Location	On A3122 Totnes/Dartmouth road

Hotel ★★★ 67% Stoke Lodge Hotel, Stoke Fleming, DARTMOUTH ☎ 01803 770523 25 ⇆ 🏌

BUDLEIGH SALTERTON
Map 03 SY08

East Devon North View Rd EX9 6DQ
☎ 01395 443370 Fax 01395 445547
An interesting course with downland turf, much heather and gorse, and superb views over the bay. The early holes climb to the cliff edge. The downhill 17th has a heather section in the fairway, leaving a good second to the green.
18 holes, 6239yds, Par 70, SSS 70, Course record 64.
Club membership 850.
Visitors	advisable to contact in advance, no visitors before 10am. Visitors must be member of a recognised club and must produce proof of handicap.
Societies	must contact in advance.
Green Fees	£35 per day; £27 per round (£42/£35 weekends & bank holidays).
Cards	💳 ▬ 🏧
Prof	Trevor Underwood
Facilities	⊗ 爪 💪 ⬛ ♀ ⚲ 🏌 🏌 ⚲
Location	W side of town centre

Hotel ★★★ 62% The Imperial, The Esplanade, EXMOUTH ☎ 01395 274761 57 ⇆ 🏌

CHITTLEHAMHOLT
Map 03 SS62

Highbullen Hotel EX37 9HD
☎ 01769 540561 Fax 01769 540492
Mature parkland course with water hazards and outstanding scenic views to Exmoor and Dartmoor. Excellent facilities offered by the hotel.
18 holes, 5755yds, Par 68, SSS 67.
Club membership 100.
Visitors	to book tee time telephone 01769 540530 daytime, 01769 540561 evenings.
Societies	must contact in advance.
Green Fees	not confirmed.
Prof	Paul Weston
Designer	M Neil/ J Hamilton
Facilities	⚲ 🏌 🏌 ⚌ ⚲ 🏌 ⚌ ⚲
& Leisure	hard tennis courts, outdoor and indoor heated swimming pools, squash, fishing, sauna, solarium, gymnasium.
Location	0.5m S of village

Hotel ★★★🏌 69% Highbullen Hotel, CHITTLEHAMHOLT ☎ 01769 540561 12 ⇆ Annexe 25 ⇆ 🏌

CHRISTOW
Map 03 SX88

Teign Valley EX6 7PA
☎ 01647 253026 Fax 01647 253026
A scenically spectacular 18 hole course set beside the River
Teign in the Dartmoor National Park. Offering a good
challenge to both low and high handicap golfers, it features
two lakeside holes, rolling fairways and fine views.
18 holes, 5913yds, Par 70, SSS 68.
Club membership 300.

Visitors	no restrictions, but need to book by telephone.
Societies	write or telephone for bookings.
Green Fees	not confirmed.
Prof	Richard Stephenson
Designer	P Nicholson
Facilities	⊗ ⅏ ⅃ ▙ ♥ ♀ ♨ 🖻 ⫪ ⊁ ☵ ⊘
Location	Take Teignvalley exit off A38, Exeter/Plymouth Expressway and follow GC signs up valley on B3193

Hotel ★★★★ 67% Manor House Hotel,
MORETONHAMPSTEAD
☎ 01647 440355 90 ⇌ 🏮

CHULMLEIGH
Map 03 SS61

Chulmleigh Leigh Rd EX18 7BL
☎ 01769 580519 Fax 01769 580519
Situated in a scenic area with views to distant Dartmoor, this
undulating meadowland course offers a good test for the
most experienced golfer and is enjoyable for newcomers to
the game. Short 18 hole summer course with a tricky 1st
hole; in winter the course is changed to 9 holes and made
longer for players to extend their game.
Summer Short Course: 18 holes, 1450yds, Par 54, SSS 54,
Course record 49.
Winter Course: 9 holes, 2310yds, Par 54, SSS 54.
Club membership 77.

Visitors	welcome anytime.
Societies	telephone in advance.
Green Fees	£11 per day; £9 per 36 holes; £6.50 per 18 holes.
Designer	John Goodban
Facilities	⅃ ▙ ♥ ♀ ♨ 🖻 ⫪ ☵ ⊘
Location	SW side of village just off A377

Hotel ★★★ 78% Northcote Manor, BURRINGTON
☎ 01769 560501 11 ⇌ 🏮

Where to stay, where to eat?
Visit the AA internet site
www.theaa.co.uk

CHURSTON FERRERS
Map 03 SX95

Churston Dartmouth Rd TQ5 0LA
☎ 01803 842751 & 842218 Fax 01803 845738
A cliff-top downland course with splendid views over
Brixham harbour and Tor Bay. There is some gorse with
a wooded area inland. A variety of shot is called for,
with particularly testing holes at the 3rd, 9th and 15th, all
par 4. Conference facilities and a well equipped shop are
also available.
18 holes, 6219yds, Par 70, SSS 70, Course record 64.
Club membership 700.

Visitors	must telephone in advance and be a member of recognised golf club with a handicap certificate.
Societies	apply in writing or telephone.
Green Fees	not confirmed.
Cards	💳
Prof	Neil Holman
Facilities	⊗ ⅏ ⅃ ▙ ♥ ♀ ♨ 🖻 ⫪ ⊘
Location	NW side of village on A379

Hotel ★★ 65% Dainton Hotel, 95 Dartmouth Rd,
Three Beaches, Goodrington, PAIGNTON
☎ 01803 550067 11 ⇌ 🏮

CREDITON
Map 03 SS80

Downes Crediton Hookway EX17 3PT
☎ 01363 773025 & 774464 Fax 01363 775060
Parkland course with water features. Flat front nine. Hilly
and wooded back nine.
18 holes, 5951yds, Par 70, SSS 69.
Club membership 700.

Visitors	handicap certificate required, must contact in advance, restricted at weekends.
Societies	must contact in advance.
Green Fees	£22 per round (£25 weekends).
Prof	Howard Finch
Facilities	⊗ ⅏ ⅃ ▙ ♥ ♀ ♨ 🖻 ⫪ ⊘
Location	1.5m SE off A377

Hotel ★★★ 73% Barton Cross Hotel & Restaurant,
Huxham, Stoke Canon, EXETER
☎ 01392 841245 9 ⇌ 🏮

CULLOMPTON
Map 03 ST00

Padbrook Park EX15 1RU
☎ 01884 38286 Fax 01884 34359
A 9-hole, 18 tee parkland course with many water and
woodland hazards and spectacular views. The dog-leg 2nd
and pulpit 7th are of particular challenge to golfers of all
standards.
9 holes, 6108yds, Par 70, SSS 70, Course record 67.
Club membership 250.

Visitors	welcome at all times, tee must be reserved by telephoning in advance.
Societies	apply in writing or telephone.
Green Fees	£12 per 18 holes, £8 per 9 holes (£16/£10 weekends).
Cards	💳 💳
Prof	Stewart Adwick
Designer	Bob Sandow

Facilities & Leisure ⊗ 🛏 📶 💺 🍷 🏌 🏡 ⛳ ✏ fishing, gymnasium, indoor bowling centre, health suite.

Location Southern edge of Cullompton on B3181

Hotel ★★★ 65% The Tiverton Hotel, Blundells Rd, TIVERTON ☎ 01884 256120 74 ⇔ 🝙

DAWLISH WARREN   Map 03 SX97

Warren EX7 0NF
☎ 01626 862255 & 864002 Fax 01626 888005
Typical flat, genuine links course lying on spit between sea and Exe estuary. Picturesque scenery, a few trees but much gorse. Testing in windy conditions. The 7th hole provides the opportunity to go for the green across a bay on the estuary.
18 holes, 5965yds, Par 69, SSS 69.
Club membership 600.
Visitors must contact in advance & have handicap certificate.
Societies prior arrangement essential.
Green Fees £21.50 per day (£24.50 weekends & bank holidays).
Prof Darren Prowse
Facilities ⊗ 📶 🛏 💺 🍷 ⛳ 🏡 ✏
Location E side of village

Hotel ★★★ 68% Langstone Cliff Hotel, Dawlish Warren, DAWLISH ☎ 01626 868000 64 ⇔ 🝙 Annexe 4 ⇔ 🝙

DOWN ST MARY   Map 03 SS70

Waterbridge EX17 5LG ☎ 01363 85111
A testing course of 9-holes set in a gently sloping valley. The Par of 32 will not be easily gained with 1 par 5, 3 par 4's and 5 par 3's, although the course record holder has Par 29! The 3rd hole which is a raised green is surrounded by water and the 4th (439 yards) is demanding for beginners.
9 holes, 3910yds, Par 64, SSS 64.
Visitors no restrictions.
Societies no restrictions.
Green Fees £10 per 18 holes; £6 per 9 holes (£12/£7 weekends & bank holidays).
Prof David Ridyard
Designer D Taylor
Facilities 💺 🏌 ✏
Location From Exeter on A377 towards Barnstaple

Hotel ★★★ 78% Northcote Manor, BURRINGTON ☎ 01769 560501 11 ⇔ 🝙

EXETER   Map 03 SX99

Exeter Golf & Country Club Topsham Rd, Countess Wear EX2 7AE ☎ 01392 874139 Fax 01392 874914
A sheltered parkland course with some very old trees and known as the flattest course in Devon. 15th & 17th are testing par 4 holes. Small, well guarded greens.
18 holes, 6008yds, Par 69, SSS 69, Course record 62.
Club membership 800.
Visitors welcome but may not play during match or competitions, very busy pre booking needed up to 1 week in advance. Must have handicap certificate. Ring starter in advance.

Societies welcome Thu only, booking available by telephone to manager tel 01392 874139.
Green Fees £28 per day.
Cards ▭▭ ▭▭ 🟢
Prof Mike Rowett
Designer J Braid
Facilities ⊗ 📶 🛏 💺 🍷 ⛳ 🏡 ✏
& Leisure hard tennis courts, heated indoor plus outdoor swimming pool, squash, sauna, solarium, gymnasium.
Location SE side of city centre off A379

Hotel L Travel Inn, 398 Topsham Rd, EXETER ☎ 01392 875441 44 ⇔ 🝙

Woodbury Park Woodbury Castle, Woodbury EX5 1JJ
☎ 01395 233382 Fax 01395 233384
Two courses set in the lovely wooded parkland of Woodbury Castle.
Oaks: 18 holes, 6870yds, Par 72, SSS 72, Course record 66.
Acorn: 9 holes, 3000yds, Par 35, SSS 70, Course record 64.
Club membership 750.
Visitors welcome, please reserve tee times in advance.
Societies contact in advance.
Green Fees not confirmed.
Prof Alan Richards
Designer J Hamilton-Stutt
Facilities ⊗ 📶 🛏 💺 🍷 ⛳ 🏡 🏌 🏟 ⛳ 🛶 ✏ ⛏
& Leisure hard tennis courts, heated indoor swimming pool, squash, fishing, sauna, gymnasium.
See advertisement on page 64.

Hotel ★★ 65% Ebford House Hotel, Exmouth Rd, EBFORD ☎ 01392 877658 16 ⇔ 🝙

HIGH BICKINGTON   Map 02 SS52

Libbaton EX37 9BS
☎ 01769 560269 & 560167 Fax 01769 560342
Parkland course on undulating land with no steep slopes. Floodlit driving range.
18 holes, 6494yds, Par 73, SSS 72, Course record 72.
Club membership 500.
Visitors book in advance. No jeans, trainers or collarless shirts.
Societies telephone to book in advance.
Green Fees not confirmed.
Cards ▭▭ ▭▭
Designer H Col Badham
Facilities ⊗ 📶 🛏 💺 🍷 ⛳ 🏡 🏌 🛶 ⛳ ✏ ⛏
& Leisure fishing.

Hotel ★★★👥 69% Highbullen Hotel, CHITTLEHAMHOLT ☎ 01769 540561 12 ⇔ Annexe 25 ⇔ 🝙

HOLSWORTHY   Map 02 SS30

Holsworthy Killatree EX22 6LP
☎ 01409 253177 Fax 01409 253177
Pleasant parkland course with gentle slopes and numerous trees.
18 holes, 6100yds, Par 70, SSS 69, Course record 64.
Club membership 600.
Visitors may not play Sun am.
Societies by arrangement with secretary or professional.
Green Fees £18.
Cards ▭▭ ▭▭ ▭▭
Prof Graham Webb

▶

Facilities ⊗ 〗 🛏 ☕ ⚑ ♀ ⚒ 🏠 ⚐ ⚒
Location 1.5m W on A3072

Hotel ★★★ 70% Falcon Hotel, Breakwater Rd,
BUDE ☎ 01288 352005 26 ⇆ 🐾

HONITON   Map 03 ST10

Honiton Middlehills EX14 9TR
☎ 01404 44422 & 42943 Fax 01404 46383
Level parkland course on a plateau 850ft above sea level.
Easy walking and good views. The 4th hole is a testing par 3.
The club was founded in 1896.
18 holes, 5902yds, Par 69, SSS 68.
Club membership 800.
Visitors must contact in advance.
Societies society bookings on Thursdays.
Green Fees £22 per day (£27 weekends & bank holidays).
Prof Adrian Cave
Facilities ⊗ 〗 🛏 ☕ ⚑ ♀ ⚒ 🏠 ⚐ ⚒
Location 1.25m SE of Honiton

Hotel ★★ 71% Home Farm Hotel & Restaurant,
Wilmington, HONITON
☎ 01404 831278 & 831246 Fax 01404 831411
6 ⇆ Annexe 7 ⇆ 🐾

ILFRACOMBE   Map 02 SS54

Ilfracombe Hele Bay EX34 9RT
☎ 01271 862176 Fax 01271 867731
A sporting, clifftop, heathland course with views over the
Bristol Channel and moors from every tee and green.

18 holes, 5893yds, Par 69, SSS 69, Course record 66.
Club membership 642.
Visitors recommended to make tee reservation prior to
visit, member only 12-2 daily and before 10am
on weekends.
Societies telephone in advance.
Green Fees not confirmed.
Prof Mark Davies
Designer T K Weir
Facilities ⊗ 〗 🛏 ☕ ⚑ ♀ ⚒ 🏠 ⚐ ⚒
Location 1.5m E off A399

Hotel ★★ 71% Elmfield Hotel, Torrs Park,
ILFRACOMBE ☎ 01271 863377
11 ⇆ 🐾 Annexe 2 ⇆ 🐾

IPPLEPEN   Map 03 SX86

Dainton Park Totnes Rd, Ipplepen TQ12 5TN
☎ 01803 815000 Fax 01803 815009
A challenging parkland type course in typical Devon
countryside, with gentle contours, tree-lined fairways and
raised tees. Water hazards make the two opening holes
particularly testing. The 8th, a dramatic 180yard drop hole
totally surrounded by sand, is one of four tough Par 3's on
the course. It is advisable to book start times.
18 holes, 6207yds, Par 71, SSS 70, Course record 70.
Club membership 600.
Visitors prior booking by phone advisable to guarantee
start time.
Societies must contact in advance.
Green Fees £16 per round (£18 weekends).
Cards 💳 💳 💳

▶

Prof	Martin Tyson
Designer	Adrian Stiff
Facilities	⊗)Ⅲ Ⅲ Ⅲ Ⅲ Ⅾ Ⅾ Ⅾ Ⅾ
& Leisure	solarium, gymnasium.
Location	2m S of Newton Abbot on A381

Hotel	★★★ 60% Old Church House Inn, Torbryan, IPPLEPEN ☎ 01803 812372 12 ⇋ 🐾

IVYBRIDGE   Map 02 SX65

Dinnaton Sporting & Country Club Blachford Rd
PL21 9HU ☎ 01752 892512 & 892452 Fax 01752 698334
Challenging 9-hole moorland course overlooking the South
Hams. With 5 par 4 and 4 par 3 holes, three lakes and tight
fairways; excellent for improving the short game. Floodlit
practice area.
9 holes, 4089yds, Par 64, SSS 60.
Club membership 275.

Visitors	no restrictions.
Societies	telephone in advance.
Green Fees	not confirmed.
Prof	David Ridyard
Designer	Cotton & Pink
Facilities	⊗)Ⅲ ⅢⅢⅢ ⅢⅢⅢ
& Leisure	hard tennis courts, heated indoor swimming pool, squash, sauna, solarium, gymnasium.
Location	Leave A38 at Ivybridge junct and continue towards town centre. At first rdbt follow signs for club

Hotel	★★ 74% Glazebrook House Hotel & Restaurant, SOUTH BRENT ☎ 01364 73322 11 ⇋ 🐾

MORETONHAMPSTEAD   Map 03 SX78

Manor House Hotel TQ13 8RE
☎ 01647 440998 Fax 01647 440961
This enjoyable parkland course has enough hazards to
make any golfer think. Most hazards are natural such as
the Rivers Bowden and Bovey which meander through
the first eight holes.
18 holes, 6016yds, Par 69, SSS 69, Course record 63.
Club membership 120.

Visitors	must contact in advance and pre-arrange starting times.
Societies	must telephone for reservation in advance.
Green Fees	£30 per day; £25 per round (£37/£32 weekends).
Cards	▭ 💳 💳 📇
Prof	Richard Lewis
Designer	J Abercrombie
Facilities	⊗)Ⅲ ⅢⅢⅢⅢⅢⅢⅢⅢⅢ
& Leisure	hard tennis courts, fishing, Par 3 course, snooker.
Location	3m W of Moretonhampstead, off B3212

Hotel	★★★★ 67% Manor House Hotel, MORETONHAMPSTEAD ☎ 01647 440355 90 ⇋ 🐾

Entries with a green background
identify courses considered to be
particularly interesting

MORTEHOE   Map 02 SS44

Mortehoe & Woolacombe EX34 7EH
☎ 01271 870225 & 870745 (Sec)
Attached to a camping and caravan site, this 9-hole course
has 2 par 3s and 7 par 4s. The gently sloping clifftop course
has spectacular views across Morte Bay.
9 holes, 4690yds, Par 66, SSS 63, Course record 66.
Club membership 245.

Visitors	no restrictions.
Societies	must telephone or write in advance.
Green Fees	£12 per 18 holes; £7 per 9 holes.
Designer	D Hoare
Facilities	⊗)Ⅲ ⅢⅢⅢ ⅢⅢⅢ
& Leisure	heated indoor swimming pool, indoor bowls, skittles, table tennis, pool table.
Location	0.25m before Mortehoe on station road

Hotel	★★★ 74% Watersmeet Hotel, Mortehoe, WOOLACOMBE ☎ 01271 870333 23 ⇋ 🐾

NEWTON ABBOT   Map 03 SX87

Newton Abbot (Stover) Bovey Rd TQ12 6QQ
☎ 01626 352460 (Secretary) Fax 01626 330210
Wooded parkland course with a stream coming into play on
eight holes. Fairly flat.
18 holes, 5862yds, Par 69, SSS 68, Course record 63.
Club membership 800.

Visitors	must have proof of membership of recognised club or current handicap certificate. Advised to contact in advance.
Societies	by arrangement on Thu only.
Green Fees	£24 per day.
Cards	▭ 💳 💳 📇
Prof	Malcolm Craig
Designer	James Braid
Facilities	⊗)Ⅲ ⅢⅢⅢ ⅢⅢⅢ
Location	3m N on A382

Hotel	★★ 65% Queens Hotel, Queen St, NEWTON ABBOT ☎ 01626 363133 & 354106 Fax 01626 364922 22rm (20 ⇋ 🐾)

OKEHAMPTON   Map 02 SX59

Ashbury Higher Maddaford EX20 4NL
☎ 01837 55453 Fax 01837 55468
A parkland style courses with natural undulations and
hazards. Set in 235 acres of Devon countryside with 137
bunkers and 18 lakes, the course comprises a loop of 9 holes
played as 18 holes. Each hole has a purpose built alternative
green so that greens can be changed in adverse weather.
Ashbury Beeches: 18 holes, 5109yds, Par 67, SSS 65.
Ashbury Willows: 18 holes, 5365yds, Par 69, SSS 66.
Ashbury Pines: 18 holes, 5540yds, Par 68, SSS 67.
Oakwood: 18 holes, 5343yds, Par 68, SSS 66.
Club membership 170.

Visitors	must contact in advance.
Green Fees	£14 per day (£18 weekends).
Cards	▭ 💳 💳 📇
Prof	Reg Cade
Designer	David Fensom

Facilities ⊗ 🛏 ♨ ♀ ⚲ 🏠 ⛳ 🍴 ➘ ⛳ ✂ ⚑
& Leisure hard tennis courts, heated indoor swimming pool, sauna, solarium, Indoor bowls, Snooker.
Location Off A386 Okehampton-Holsworthy

Hotel ★★ 65% Ashbury Hotel, Higher Maddaford, Southcott, OKEHAMPTON
☎ 01837 55453 26 ➪ ⚑ Annexe 29 ➪ ⚑

Okehampton Tors Rd EX20 1EF
☎ 01837 52113 Fax 01837 52734
A good combination of moorland, woodland and river make this one of the prettiest, yet testing courses in Devon.
18 holes, 5243yds, Par 68, SSS 67, Course record 66.
Club membership 600.
Visitors advance booking recommended, limited times available at weekends. Saturdays by prior arrangement only
Societies by prior arrangement.
Green Fees £20 per day.
Prof Simon Jefferies
Designer J F Taylor
Facilities ♀ ⚲ 🏠 ⛳ ✂ ⚑
Location 1m S off A30

Hotel ★★ 67% Oxenham Arms, SOUTH ZEAL
☎ 01837 840244 & 840577 Fax 01837 840791
8rm (7 ➪ ⚑)

Map 02 SX45

Elfordleigh Colebrook, Plympton PL7 5EB
☎ 01752 336428 (hotel) & 348425 (golf shop)
Fax 01752 344581
Charming, saucer-shaped parkland course with alternate tees for 18 holes. Tree-lined fairways and three lakes. Fairly hard walking.
9 holes, 5664yds, Par 68, SSS 67, Course record 66.
Club membership 600.
Visitors must contact in advance and hold a handicap certificate.
Societies by arrangement.
Green Fees £15 per day (£20 weekends & bank holidays).
Cards 🟦 🟥 🟨 🟩 🟪 🟫
Prof Ross Troake
Designer J H Taylor
Facilities ⊗ ⚒ 🛏 ♨ ♀ ⚲ 🏠 ⛳ 🍴 ⛳ ✂ ⚑
& Leisure hard tennis courts, heated outdoor swimming pool, squash, gymnasium, golf tuition breaks.
Location 2m NE off A374

Staddon Heights Plymstock PL9 9SP
☎ 01752 402475 Fax 01752 401998
Seaside course affording spectacular views across Plymouth Sound, Dartmoor and Bodmin Moor. Testing holes include the par 3 17th with its green cut into a hillside and the par 4 14th across a road. Easy walking.
18 holes, 5869yds, Par 68, SSS 70, Course record 66.
Club membership 750.
Visitors must have handicap certificate and contact the pro or secretary in advance.
Societies apply by telephone in advance.
Green Fees not confirmed.
Prof Ian Marshall
Designer Hamilton Stutt
Facilities ⊗ ⚒ 🛏 ♨ ♀ ⚲ 🏠 ⛳ 🍴 ✂
& Leisure snooker.
Location 5m SW of city centre

Hotel ★★★ 66% Posthouse Plymouth, Cliff Rd, The Hoe, PLYMOUTH ☎ 0870 400 9064
106 ➪ ⚑

Map 02 SS43

Saunton EX33 1LG
☎ 01271 812436 Fax 01271 814241
Two traditional championship links courses. Windy, with natural hazards.
East Course: 18 holes, 6373yds, Par 71, SSS 71, Course record 65.
West Course: 18 holes, 6138yds, Par 71, SSS 70, Course record 67.
Club membership 1350.

Visitors prior booking recommended and must have handicap certificate.
Societies must apply in advance, handicap certificates required. ▶

Green Fees	£60 per day; £40 per round (£75/£50 weekends & bank holidays).
Cards	
Prof	A T MacKenzie
Designer	F Pennick
Facilities	⊗ ⅷ ⅙ ♥ ♀ ⚐ ⚑ ⚒ ♂
Location	S side of village off B3231

| Hotel | ★★★★ 70% Saunton Sands Hotel, SAUNTON ☎ 01271 890212 92 ⇔ ⚑ |
| Additional hotel | ★★ 69% Kittiwell House Hotel & Restaurant, St Mary's Rd, CROYDE ☎ 01271 890247 Fax 01271 890460 12 ⇔ ⚑ |

SIDMOUTH
Map 03 SY18

Sidmouth Cotmaton Rd, Peak Hill EX10 8SX
☎ 01395 513451 & 516407 Fax 01395 514661
Situated on the side of Peak Hill, offering beautiful coastal views. Club founded in 1889.
18 holes, 5100yds, Par 66, SSS 65, Course record 59. Club membership 700.
Visitors	by prior arrangement.
Societies	by prior arrangement with the secretary.
Green Fees	£20 per day/round.
Prof	Gaele Tapper
Designer	J H Taylor
Facilities	⊗ ⅷ ⅙ ♥ ♀ ⚐ ⚑ ♂
Location	W side of town centre

| Hotel | ★★★★ 72% Victoria Hotel, Esplanade, SIDMOUTH ☎ 01395 512651 61 ⇔ ⚑ |

SOUTH BRENT
Map 03 SX66

Wrangaton (S Devon) Golf Links Rd, Wrangaton TQ10 9HJ ☎ 01364 73229 Fax 01364 73229
Unique 18 hole course with 9 holes on moorland and 9 holes on parkland. The course lies within Dartmoor National Park. Spectacular views towards sea and rugged terrain. Natural fairways and hazards include bracken, sheep and ponies.
18 holes, 6083yds, Par 70, SSS 69, Course record 66. Club membership 600.
Visitors	contact in advance.
Societies	write or telephone.
Green Fees	£18.
Cards	
Prof	Adrian Whitehead
Designer	D M A Steel
Facilities	⊗ ⅷ ⅙ ♥ ♀ ⚐ ⚑ ⚒ ♂
Location	2.25 m SW off A38

| Hotel | ★★ 74% Glazebrook House Hotel & Restaurant, SOUTH BRENT ☎ 01364 73322 11 ⇔ ⚑ |

SPARKWELL
Map 02 SX55

Welbeck Manor & Sparkwell Golf Course Blacklands PL7 5DF ☎ 01752 837219 Fax 01752 837219
A mature parkland course with several challenging holes, it features fairway and greenside bunkers, mature trees and streams. The house on the site, now the hotel, was built by Isambard Kingdom Brunel. Several holes commemorate his famous works - the 6th being The Great Western. This is a very challenging Par 5 tee is out of bounds all the way up the left.
9 holes, 2886yds, Par 68, SSS 68, Course record 68. Club membership 200.
Visitors	no restrictions
Societies	telephone in advance.
Green Fees	not confirmed.
Cards	
Designer	John Gabb
Facilities	⊗ ⅷ ⅙ ♥ ♀ ⚐ ⚑ ⚒ ♂
Location	1m N of A38 Plymouth/Ivybridge road

| Hotel | ★★★ 65% Boringdon Hall, Colebrook, Plympton, PLYMOUTH ☎ 01752 344455 41 ⇔ ⚑ |

TAVISTOCK
Map 02 SX47

Hurdwick Tavistock Hamlets PL19 8PZ ☎ 01822 612746
An executive parkland course with many bunkers and fine views. Executive golf originated in America and the concept is that a round should take no longer than 3 hours whilst offering solid challenge.
18 holes, 5200yds, Par 68, SSS 67. Club membership 180.
Visitors	no restrictions.
Societies	must contact in advance.
Green Fees	£14 per day.
Designer	Hawtree
Facilities	⊗ ⅙ ♥ ♀ ⚐ ⚑ ⚒ ♂
Location	1m N of Tavistock

| Hotel | ★★★ 65% Bedford Hotel, Plymouth Rd, TAVISTOCK ☎ 01822 613221 30 ⇔ ⚑ |

Tavistock Down Rd PL19 9AQ
☎ 01822 612344 Fax 01822 612344
Set on Whitchurch Down in south-west Dartmoor with easy walking and magnificent views over rolling countryside into Cornwall. Downland turf with some heather, and interesting holes on undulating ground.
18 holes, 6250yds, Par 70, SSS 70, Course record 64. Club membership 700.
Visitors	advisable to contact in advance.
Societies	by arrangement with secretary.
Green Fees	£22 per day/round (£28 weekends).
Prof	D Rehaag
Designer	H Fowler
Facilities	⊗ ⅷ ⅙ ♥ ♀ ⚐ ⚑ ♂
Location	1m SE of town centre, on Whitchurch Down
Hotel	★★★ 65% Bedford Hotel, Plymouth Rd, TAVISTOCK ☎ 01822 613221 30 ⇔ ⚑

TEDBURN ST MARY   Map 03 SX89

Fingle Glen EX6 6AF ☎ 01647 61817
9-hole course containing six par 4's and three par 3's set in
52 acres of rolling countryside. Testing 4th, 5th and 9th
holes. 12-bay floodlit driving range.
9 holes, 4818yds, Par 66, SSS 63, Course record 63.
Club membership 400.
Visitors   must contact in advance.
Societies   write or telephone in advance.
Green Fees   not confirmed.
Prof   Stephen Gould
Designer   Bill Pilz
Facilities   ⊗ ⅏ ⅃ ▆ ♀ ♨ ☕ ☂ ⚲ ⚸ ⚑
Location   5m W of Exeter, off A30

Hotel   ★★★ 65% Lord Haldon Hotel, Dunchideock,
            EXETER ☎ 01392 832483   19 ⇔ ⏃

TEIGNMOUTH   Map 03 SX97

Teignmouth Haldon Moor TQ14 9NY
☎ 01626 777070 Fax 01626 777070
This fairly flat heathland course is high up with a fine
panoramic views of sea, moors and river valley. Good
springy turf with some heather and an interesting layout
makes for very enjoyable holiday golf. Designed by Dr
Alister MacKenzie, the world famous architect who also
designed Augusta GC USA.
18 holes, 6200yds, Par 71, SSS 70, Course record 65.
Club membership 900.
Visitors   handicap certificate required, groups must
                  contact in advance, restricted tee off times
                  at weekends.
Societies   Tue & Thu only, telephone in advance and
                  confirm in writing.
Green Fees   £25 per round; £30 per 36 holes (£30 per
                  round weekends).
Prof   Peter Ward
Designer   Dr Alister Mackenzie
Facilities   ⊗ ⅏ ⅃ ▆ ♀ ♨ ☕ ☂ ⚸
Location   2m NW off B3192

Hotel   ★★ 70% Ness House Hotel, Marine Dr,
            Shaldon, TEIGNMOUTH
            ☎ 01626 873480 7 ⇔ ⏃ Annexe 5 ⇔ ⏃

THURLESTONE   Map 03 SX64

Thurlestone TQ7 3NZ
☎ 01548 560405 Fax 01548 562149
Situated on the edge of the cliffs with typical downland turf
and good greens. The course, after an interesting opening
hole, rises to higher land with fine seaviews, and finishes
with an excellent 502-yard downhill hole to the clubhouse.
18 holes, 6340yds, Par 71, SSS 70, Course record 65.
Club membership 770.
Visitors   must contact in advance & have handicap
                  certificate from a recognised club.
Green Fees   not confirmed.
Prof   Peter Laugher
Designer   Harry S Colt
Facilities   ⊗ ⅃ ▆ ♀ ♨ ☕ ☂ ⚸
& Leisure   hard and grass tennis courts.
Location   S side of village

Hotel   ★★★★ 72% Thurlestone Hotel,
            THURLESTONE ☎ 01548 560382
            64 ⇔ ⏃

TIVERTON   Map 03 SS91

Tiverton Post Hill EX16 4NE ☎ 01884 252187
A parkland course where the many different species of tree
are a feature and where the lush pastures ensure some of
the finest fairways in the south-west. There are a number of
interesting holes which visitors will find a real challenge.
18 holes, 6236yds, Par 71, SSS 71, Course record 65.
Club membership 725.
Visitors   must have a current handicap certificate.
Societies   apply in writing or telephone.
Green Fees   £24 per day; £20 per round (£35/£30
                  weekends).
Prof   David Sheppard
Designer   Braid
Facilities   ⊗ ⅏ by prior arrangement ⅃ ▆ ♀ ♨
                  ☕ ⚸

Hotel   ★★ 76% Bark House Hotel, Oakford
            Bridge, BAMPTON ☎ 01398 351236
            5rm (2 ⇔ 2 ⏃)

TORQUAY   Map 03 SX96

Torquay 30 Petitor Rd, St Marychurch TQ1 4QF
☎ 01803 314591 Fax 01803 316116
Unusual combination of cliff and parkland golf, with
wonderful views over the sea and Dartmoor.
18 holes, 6175yds, Par 69, SSS 70, Course record 65.
Club membership 700.
Visitors   must contact in advance.
Societies   must apply in writing.
Green Fees   £24-£28.
Prof   Martin Ruth
Facilities   ⊗ ⅏ ⅃ ▆ ♀ ♨ ☕ ☂ ⚲ ⚸ ⚑
Location   1.25m N

Hotel   ★★ 60% Norcliffe Hotel, 7 Babbacombe
            Downs Rd, Babbacombe, TORQUAY
            ☎ 01803 328456   27 ⇔ ⏃

TORRINGTON (GREAT)   Map 02 SS41

Torrington Weare Trees, Great Torrington EX38 7EZ
☎ 01805 622229
Attractive and challenging 9 hole course. Free draining to
allow play all year round. Excellent greens and outstanding
views.
9 holes, 4423yds, Par 64, SSS 62, Course record 58.
Club membership 420.
Visitors   must contact in advance. May not play Tues,
                  Wed, Sat, Sun or bank holidays before noon.
Societies   by arrangement.
Green Fees   £12 per day.
Facilities   ⊗ ⅃ ▆ ♀ ♨ ☕ ⚲ ⚸
Location   1m W of Torringdon

Hotel   ★★★ 65% Royal Hotel, Barnstaple St,
            BIDEFORD ☎ 01237 472005   31 ⇔ ⏃

UPOTTERY
Map 03 ST20

Otter Valley Golf Centre
☎ 01404 861266, Fax 01404 861266 (5m NW of Honiton off A30, on Upottery Rd)
This Golf School set in beautiful Devon countryside was established in 1989. There are practice facilities with driving range, approach green, chipping green with bunkers and 8 practice holes. Weekend and 5 day courses are available and there is self catering accommodation, telephone for details. All coaching is given personally by Andrew Thompson P.G.A.

WESTWARD HO!
Map 02 SS42

Royal North Devon Golf Links Rd EX39 1HD
☎ 01237 473817 Fax 01237 423456
Oldest links course in England with traditional links features and a museum in the clubhouse.
18 holes, 6644yds, Par 71, SSS 72, Course record 68.
Club membership 1150.

Visitors	advisable to telephone and book tee time, handicap certificate preferred or letter of introduction from club.
Societies	apply in writing or telephone.
Green Fees	£36 per day; £30 per round (£40/£36 weekends & bank holidays).
Cards	🌐 💳
Prof	Richard Herring
Designer	Old Tom Morris
Facilities	⊗ ⅷ ╠ 🍺 ♀ 🛆 🏠 ⛊ ⚐
& Leisure	museum of Golf Memorabilia, snooker.
Location	N side of village off B3236

Guest house	♦♦♦ Culloden House Hotel, Fosketh Hill, WESTWARD HO! ☎ 01237 479421 9rm (2 ⇄5 🐾)

WOOLSERY
Map 02 SS32

Hartland Forest Woolsery EX39 5RA
☎ 01237 431442 Fax 01237 431734
Exceptionally varied course with many water hazards.
18 holes, 6015yds, Par 71, SSS 69.
Club membership 240.

Visitors	no restrictions.
Societies	telephone in advance or apply in writing.
Green Fees	£30 per day; £20 per round.
Cards	🌐 💳
Designer	A Cartwright
Facilities	⊗ by prior arrangement ⅷ ╠ 🍺 ♀ 🛆 ⛊ 🏠 🛆 ⚐
& Leisure	hard tennis courts, heated indoor swimming pool, fishing, sauna, solarium.
Location	1.7m E of A39

Hotel	★★★ 73% Penhaven Country House, PARKHAM ☎ 01237 451388 & 451711 Fax 01237 451878 12 ⇄ 🐾

YELVERTON
Map 02 SX56

Yelverton Golf Links Rd PL20 6BN
☎ 01822 852824 Fax 01822 852824
An excellent course on Dartmoor with plenty of gorse and heather. Tight lies in the fairways, fast greens and challenging hazards. Boasts 3 of the best holes in Devon (12th, 13th & 16th). Outstanding views.
18 holes, 6363yds, Par 71, SSS 72, Course record 67.
Club membership 650.

Visitors	must have handicap certificate and subject to availability, contact in advance.
Societies	must be booked in advance, by telephone initially.
Green Fees	£30 per day (£40 weekends & bank holidays).
Prof	Tim McSherry
Designer	Herbert Fowler
Facilities	⊗ ⅷ by prior arrangement ╠ 🍺 ♀ 🛆 🏠 ⛊ ⚐
& Leisure	snooker.
Location	1m S of Yelverton, off A386

Hotel	★★★ 71% Moorland Links Hotel, YELVERTON ☎ 01822 852245 45 ⇄ 🐾

DORSET

BEAMINSTER
Map 03 ST40

Chedington Court South Perrott DT8 3HU
☎ 01935 891413 Fax 01935 891217
This beautiful 18 hole parkland course is set on the Dorset-Somerset borders with mature trees and interesting water hazards.
18 holes, 5924yds, Par 70, SSS 70, Course record 71.
Club membership 400.

Visitors	must book tee time in advance at weekends.
Societies	apply in writing or telephone.
Green Fees	£16 per round/day (£20 weekends).
Cards	〓〓〓〓
Prof	S Ritchie
Designer	David Hemstock
Facilities	⊗ ⅲ ⅼ Ⅼ ⅬⅬⅬⅬⅬⅬⅬⅬ
Location	5m NE of Beaminster on A356 Dorchester-Crewkerne

Hotel	★★★ 71% Bridge House Hotel, 3 Prout Bridge, BEAMINSTER ☎ 01308 862200 9 ⇆ ⅬⅬ Annexe 5 ⇆ ⅬⅬ

BELCHALWELL
Map 03 ST70

Dorset Heights DT11 0EG
☎ 01258 861386 Fax 01258 860900
Set in an area of outstanding natural beauty, rich in wildlife, which provides a picturesque backdrop to this stimulating, undulating course. Modern clubhouse with magnificent views.
18 holes, 6138yds, Par 70, SSS 70, Course record 74.
Club membership 270.

Visitors	must contact in advance, dress restrictions.
Societies	must telephone in advance.
Green Fees	not confirmed.
Cards	〓〓〓〓
Prof	Andy Stuart
Designer	David Astill
Facilities	⊗ ⅼ ⅬⅬⅬⅬⅬⅬⅬⅬⅬ

Hotel	★★★ 67% Crown Hotel, West St, BLANDFORD FORUM ☎ 01258 456626 32 ⇆ ⅬⅬ

BERE REGIS
Map 03 SY89

East Dorset BH20 7NT
☎ 01929 472244 Fax 01929 471294
Lakeland is a long 18-hole parkland course with natural water features. The Woodland is a second 9-hole, 18-tee course set amongst trees and rhododendrons. Floodlit 22-bay driving range, golf shop.
Lakeland Course: 18 holes, 6580yds, Par 72, SSS 73, Course record 66.
Woodland Course: 9 holes, 4887yards, Par 66, SSS 64.
Club membership 550.

Visitors	must book in advance and handicap certificate required for Lakeland course.
Societies	apply in advance.
Green Fees	Lakeland: £35 per day; £30 per round (£40/£35 weekends). Woodland: £23 per day; £21 per round (£25/£23 weekends).

Cards	〓〓〓〓
Prof	Derwynne Honan
Designer	Martin Hawtree
Facilities	⊗ ⅲ ⅼ ⅬⅬⅬⅬⅬⅬⅬⅬⅬⅬⅬⅬ
Location	5m from Bere Regis on Wool Road

Hotel	★★ 69% Kemps Country House Hotel, East Stoke, WAREHAM ☎ 01929 462563 5rm(4 ⇆ ⅬⅬ) Annexe 10 ⇆ ⅬⅬ

BLANDFORD FORUM
Map 03 ST80

Ashley Wood Wimborne Rd DT11 9HN
☎ 01258 452253 Fax 01258 450190
Undulating and well drained downland course with superb views over the Tarrant and Stour Valleys.
18 holes, 6276yds, Par 70, SSS 70, Course record 65.
Club membership 700.

Visitors	phone in advance. Handicap certificate required weekends unless with member.
Societies	apply to Secretary.
Green Fees	not confrmed.
Prof	Spencer Taylor
Designer	P Tallack
Facilities	⊗ ⅲ ⅼ ⅬⅬⅬⅬⅬⅬⅬⅬ
Location	2m E on B3082

Hotel	★★★ 67% Crown Hotel, West St, BLANDFORD FORUM ☎ 01258 456626 32 ⇆ ⅬⅬ

BOURNEMOUTH
Map 04 SZ09

Bournemouth & Meyrick Central Dr, Meyrick Park
BH2 6LH ☎ 01202 292425
Picturesque muncipal parkland course founded in 1890.
18 holes, 5852yds, Par 70, SSS 69, Course record 64.
Club membership 500.

Visitors	advance booking is essential.
Societies	telephone in advance.
Green Fees	not confirmed.
Prof	Lee Thompson
Facilities	ⅬⅬⅬⅬⅬ
& Leisure	squash.

Hotel	★★★ 64% Burley Court Hotel, Bath Rd, BOURNEMOUTH ☎ 01202 552824 & 556704 Fax 01202 298514 38 ⇆ ⅬⅬ

Knighton Heath Francis Av, West Howe BH11 8NX
☎ 01202 572633 Fax 01202 590774
Undulating heathland course on high ground inland from Poole.
18 holes, 6084yds, Par 70, SSS 69.
Club membership 700.
Visitors may not play weekend. Phone for availability.
Societies must book in advance.
Green Fees not confirmed.
Prof Jane Miles
Facilities ⊗ ⫫ ⅃ ⅃ ⚑ ⚐ ♨
Location N side of Poole, junct of A348/A3409 signposted at rdbt

Hotel ★★ Beechleas Hotel, 17 Poole Rd, WIMBORNE MINSTER ☎ 01202 841684 5 ⇌ ↿ Annexe 4 ⇌ ↿

Queen's Park Queens Park Dr West BH8 9BY
☎ 01202 396198 & 302611 Fax 01202 302611
Undulating parkland course of pine and heather, with narrow, tree-lined fairways. Public course played over by 'Boscombe Golf Club' and 'Bournemouth Artisans Golf Club'.
18 holes, 6305yds, Par 72, SSS 70, Course record 69.
Visitors Thu (ladies day)
Societies must contact in advance.
Green Fees not confirmed.
Cards ▭▭ ▭▭
Prof Richard Hill
Facilities ⊗ ⫫ ⅃ ⅃ ⚑ ♨ ♨
Location 2m NE of town centre off A338

Hotel ★★★ 70% Queens Hotel, Meyrick Rd, East Cliff, BOURNEMOUTH ☎ 01202 554415 113 ⇌ ↿

BRIDPORT Map 03 SY49

Bridport & West Dorset East Cliff, West Bay DT6 4EP
☎ 01308 421491 & 421095 Fax 01308 421095
Seaside links course on the top of the east cliff, with fine views over Lyme Bay and surrounding countryside. A popular feature is the pretty and deceptive 14th hole, its sunken green lying 90 feet below the tee and guarded by natural hazards and bunkers.
18 holes, 6488yds, Par 73, SSS 71.
Club membership 600.
Visitors must contact in advance.
Societies must contact in writing in advance.
Green Fees £22 per day (£16 after 12 noon, £10 after 5pm).
Prof David Parsons
Designer Hawtree
Facilities ⊗ ⅃ ⅃ ⅃ ⚑ ♨
& Leisure pitch & putt (holiday season).
Location 2m S of Bridport

Hotel ★★★ 58% Haddon House Hotel, West Bay, BRIDPORT ☎ 01308 423626 & 425323 Fax 01308 427348 12 ⇌ ↿

BROADSTONE Map 04 SZ09

Broadstone (Dorset) Wentworth Dr BH18 8DQ
☎ 01202 692595 Fax 01202 692595
Undulating and demanding heathland course with the 2nd, 7th, 13th and 16th being particularly challenging holes.
18 holes, 6315yds, Par 70, SSS 70, Course record 66.
Club membership 700.
Visitors restricted at weekends & bank holidays. Must contact in advance.
Societies contact in advance.
Green Fees £26 per round (£40 weekends).
Prof Nigel Tokely
Designer Colt/Dunn
Facilities ⊗ ⫫ ⅃ ⅃ ⅃ ⚑ ♨ ♨
Location N side of village off B3074

Hotel ★★★ 57% King's Head Hotel, The Square, WIMBORNE ☎ 01202 880101 27 ⇌ ↿

CHRISTCHURCH Map 04 SZ19

Dudmoor Farm Dudmoor Farm Rd, Off Fairmile Rd BH23 6AQ ☎ 01202 473826 Fax 01202 480207
A testing par 3 & 4 woodland course in an area of outstanding natural beauty.
9 holes, 1428mtrs, Par 31.
Visitors no restrictions.
Societies telephone in advance.
Green Fees £6 per 18 holes.
Facilities ⅃ ⅃ ♨ ⌑
& Leisure squash, fishing.
Location Located on a private road off B3073 Christchurch to Hurn road

Hotel ★★★ 74% Waterford Lodge Hotel, 87 Bure Ln, Friars Cliff, Mudeford, CHRISTCHURCH ☎ 01425 272948 & 278801 Fax 01425 279130 18 ⇌

Iford Bridge Barrack Rd BH23 2BA ☎ 01202 473817
Parkland course with the River Stour running through. Driving range.
9 holes, 2165yds, Par 34, SSS 32.
Club membership 350.
Visitors must contact in advance.
Societies must contact in advance.
Green Fees not confirmed.
Prof Peter Troth
Facilities ⅃ ⅃ ⅃ ⚑ ♨ ♨ ⌑
& Leisure hard and grass tennis courts.
Location W side of town centre on A35

Hotel ★★★ 74% Waterford Lodge Hotel, 87 Bure Ln, Friars Cliff, Mudeford, CHRISTCHURCH ☎ 01425 272948 & 278801 Fax 01425 279130 18 ⇌

Entries with a green background identify courses considered to be particularly interesting

Where to stay, where to eat?
Visit the AA internet site
www.theaa.co.uk

DORCHESTER — Map 03 SY69

Came Down Came Down DT2 8NR
☎ 01305 813494 (manager) & 812670 (pro)
Fax 01305 813494
Scene of the West of England Championships on several occasions, this fine course lies on a high plateau commanding glorious views over Portland. Three par 5 holes add interest to a round. The turf is of the springy, downland type.
18 holes, 6244yds, Par 70, SSS 71.
Club membership 750.
Visitors	advisable to phone in advance, must have handicap certificate. May play after 9am weekdays & after noon Sun.
Societies	by arrangement on Wed only.
Green Fees	£24 per day (£28 weekends & bank holidays).
Prof	David Holmes
Designer	J H Taylor
Facilities	⊗ ⽊ ⓑ ♥ ♀ ⚘ 🏠 ⛳ 🏌 ✓
Location	2m S off A354

Guest house	◆◆◆◆◆ Yalbury Cottage Hotel & Restaurant, Lower Bockhampton, DORCHESTER ☎ 01305 262382 8 ⇥ 🅟

FERNDOWN — Map 04 SU00

Dudsbury Christchurch Rd BH22 8ST
☎ 01202 593499 Fax 01202 594555
Set in 150 acres of beautiful Dorset countryside rolling down to the River Stour. Wide variety of interesting and challenging hazards, notably water which comes into play on 14 holes.
Championship Course: 18 holes, 6904yds, Par 71, SSS 73.
Club membership 700.
Visitors	welcome by arrangement with secretary or golf professional.
Societies	telephone in advance.
Green Fees	£30 per round (£35 weekends & bank holidays).
Cards	▬ ■ ▬ 🅢
Prof	Mark Thomas
Designer	Donald Steel
Facilities	⊗ ⽊ ⓑ ♥ ♀ ⚘ 🏠 ⛳ ↘ 🏌 ✓ 𝄢
& Leisure	fishing, 6 Hole Par 3 Academy Course.
Location	3m N of Bournemouth on B3073, between Parley and Longham

Hotel	★★★★ 69% The Dormy, New Rd, FERNDOWN ☎ 01202 872121 115 ⇥ 🅟

Ferndown 119 Golf Links Rd BH22 8BU
☎ 01202 874602 Fax 01202 873926
Fairways are gently undulating amongst heather, gorse and pine trees giving the course a most attractive appearance. There are a number of dog-leg holes, and, on a clear day, there are views across to the Isle of Wight.
Championship Course: 18 holes, 6452yds, Par 71, SSS 71, Course record 65.
Presidents Course: 9 holes, 5604yds, Par 70, SSS 68, Course record 65.
Club membership 700.
Visitors	must contact in advance & have handicap certificate, no visitors on Thursdays except on Presidents course, numbers restricted at weekends.
Societies	welcome Tue & Fri only, telephone in advance.
Green Fees	not confirmed.
Prof	Iain Parker
Designer	Harold Hilton
Facilities	⊗ ⽊ ⓑ ♥ ♀ ⚘ 🏠 ⛳ 🏌 ✓
Location	S side of town centre off A347

Hotel	★★★★ 69% The Dormy, New Rd, FERNDOWN ☎ 01202 872121 115 ⇥ 🅟

Ferndown Forest Forest Links Rd BH22 9QE
☎ 01202 876096 Fax 01202 894095
Flat parkland course dotted with mature oak trees, several interesting water features, and some tight fairways.
18 holes, 5068yds, Par 67, SSS 65.
Club membership 400.
Visitors	advisable to contact in advance.
Societies	apply in writing.
Green Fees	£10 per 18 holes (£12 weekends).
Cards	▬ ■ ▬ 🅢
Designer	Guy Hunt/Richard Graham
Facilities	⊗ ⽊ ⓑ ♥ ♀ ⚘ 🏠 ⛳ 🏌 ✓ 𝄢
Location	From London M3 then A31, end of dual carriageway Dolmans Crossing rdbt right exit Forest Links Rd

Hotel	★★ 59% Coach House Inn, 579 Winborne Rd East, Tricketts Cross, FERNDOWN ☎ 01202 861222 Annexe 44 ⇥

HALSTOCK — Map 03 ST50

Halstock Common Ln BA22 9SF
☎ 01935 891689 Fax 01935 891839
Halstock is a short tight course, but presents an interesting challenge to players of all abilities. The terrain is gently undulating in places and there are plenty of trees and water hazards.
18 holes, 4481yds, Par 66, SSS 63, Course record 63.
Club membership 200.
Visitors	must telephone in advance. Restricted until 10.30am on Sundays.
Societies	telephone in advance.
Green Fees	not confirmed.
Cards	▬ ■ ▬ 🅢
Facilities	♥ ♀ ⚘ 🏠 ⛳ ✓ 𝄢
Location	6m S of Yeovil

▶

Hotel   ★★★♨♨ Summer Lodge, EVERSHOT
☎ 01935 83424 11 ⇋ ↿ Annexe 6 ⇋ ↿

HIGHCLIFFE   Map 04 SZ29

Highcliffe Castle 107 Lymington Rd BH23 4LA
☎ 01425 272210 Fax 01425 272210
Picturesque parkland course with easy walking.
18 holes, 4776yds, Par 64, SSS 63, Course record 58.
Club membership 500.
Visitors	must have handicap certificate and be a member of recognised club. Telephone in advance.
Societies	write or telephone in advance.
Green Fees	£25.50 per day (£35.50 weekends & bank holidays 9.30am-noon); £15.50 any day after 4pm.
Facilities	⊗ ⅊ ▱ ♀ ⅄
Location	SW side of town on A337

Hotel   ★★★ 74% Waterford Lodge Hotel, 87 Bure
Ln, Friars Cliff, Mudeford, CHRISTCHURCH
☎ 01425 272948 & 278801 Fax 01425 279130
18 ⇋

HURN   Map 04 SZ19

Parley Parley Green Ln BH23 6BB
☎ 01202 591600 & 593131
Flat parkland course with few hazards and only one par 5.
Friendly atmosphere.
9 holes, 4584yds, Par 66, SSS 64, Course record 69.
Club membership 238.
Visitors	good standard of dress expected.
Societies	write or telephone.
Green Fees	£5 per 9 holes (£5.50 weekends).
Prof	Ken Gilhespy/Chris Brook
Designer	P Goodfellow
Facilities	⊗ ⅏ ⅊ ▱ ♀ ⅄ ☞ ♂ ⅂
Location	Opposite Bournemouth airport

Hotel   ★★ 68% Fisherman's Haunt Hotel, Sailsbury
Rd, Winkton, CHRISTCHURCH
☎ 01202 477283 & 484071 Fax 01202 478883
4 ⇋ ↿ Annexe 14 ⇋ ↿

LYME REGIS   Map 03 SY39

Lyme Regis Timber Hill DT7 3HQ ☎ 01297 442963
Undulating cliff-top course with magnificent views of
Golden Cap and Lyme Bay.
18 holes, 6283yds, Par 71, SSS 70, Course record 67.
Club membership 575.
Visitors	must contact in advance & have handicap certificate or be a member of recognised golf club. No play on Thu & Sun mornings.
Societies	Tue, Wed & Fri; must contact in writing.
Green Fees	not confirmed.
Prof	Andrew Black
Designer	Donald Steel
Facilities	⅄ ☞ ♂
Location	1.5m N on A3052

Hotel   ★★★ 70% Alexandra Hotel, Pound St, LYME
REGIS ☎ 01297 442010 27rm (26 ⇋ ↿)

POOLE   Map 04 SZ09

Parkstone Links Rd, Parkstone BH14 9QS
☎ 01202 707138 Fax 01202 796027
Very scenic heathland course with views of Poole Bay.
Club founded in 1910.
18 holes, 6250yds, Par 72, SSS 70, Course record 63.
Club membership 700.
Visitors	must contact in advance and have handicap certificate.
Societies	apply in writing/telephone in advance.
Green Fees	£50 per day; £35 per round (£60/£45 weekends & bank holidays).
Prof	Andy Peach
Designer	Willie Park Jnr
Facilities	⊗ ⅏ ⅊ ▱ ♀ ⅄ ☞ ♂ ⅂
Location	E side of town centre off A35

Hotel   ★★★ 80% Salterns Hotel, 38 Salterns
Way, Lilliput, POOLE
☎ 01202 707321   20 ⇋ ↿

SHERBORNE   Map 03 ST61

Sherborne Higher Clatcombe DT9 4RN
☎ 01935 814431 Fax 01935 814218
A sporting course of first-class fairways with far-
reaching views over the lovely Blackmore Vale and the
Vale of Sparkford. Parkland in character, the course has
many well-placed bunkers. The dog-leg 2nd calls for an
accurately placed tee shot, and another testing hole is the
7th, a 194-yard, par 3. There is a practice area.   ▶

18 holes, 5882yds, Par 70, SSS 68, Course record 63.
Club membership 600.

Visitors	must contact in advance & have handicap certificate.
Societies	prior booking only (Tue & Wed only).
Green Fees	£25 per day; £20 per round (£30/£25 weekends).
Prof	Stewart Wright
Designer	James Braid (part)
Facilities	⊗ ⫙ ⬚ ⬛ ♀ ⅄ 🛍 ∅
Location	2m N off B3145

Hotel	★★★ 63% The Sherborne Hotel, Horsecastles Ln, SHERBORNE ☎ 01935 813191 59 ⇋ ⋔

SLEPE
Map 03 SY99

Bulbury Woods Bulbury Ln BH16 6HR
☎ 01929 459574 Fax 01929 459000
Parkland course amidst ancient woodland, with a mixture of American and traditional style greens and extensive views over the Purbecks and Poole Harbour.
18 holes, 6065yds, Par 72, SSS 70.
Club membership 700.

Visitors	visitors may book 2 days in advance and subject to availability.
Societies	must contact in advance.
Green Fees	£18 (£24 weekends).
Cards	▭ ▭ 🖃
Facilities	⅄ 🛍 ⬚ ❧ 🛒 ∅
Location	A35 Poole to Dorchester, 3m from Poole centre

Hotel	★★★⚘ Priory Hotel, Church Green, WAREHAM ☎ 01929 551666 15 ⇋ ⋔ Annexe 4 ⇋ ⋔

STURMINSTER MARSHALL
Map 03 ST90

Sturminster Marshall Moor Ln BH21 4AH
☎ 01258 858444 Fax 01258 858262
Privately owned club with pay & play facilities set in beautiful Dorset countryside. Played off 18 different tees the course is ideal for golfers of all standards.
9 holes, 4882yds, Par 68, SSS 64.
Club membership 350.

Visitors	no restrictions.
Societies	must contact in advance.
Green Fees	not confirmed.
Cards	▭ ▭
Prof	Graham Howell
Designer	John Sharkey/David Holdsworth
Facilities	⊗ ⫙ ⬚ ⬛ ♀ ⅄ 🛍 🍴 🛒 ∅
Location	On A350. Signposted from village

Hotel	★★★ 67% Crown Hotel, West St, BLANDFORD FORUM ☎ 01258 456626 32 ⇋ ⋔

SWANAGE
Map 04 SZ07

Isle of Purbeck BH19 3AB
☎ 01929 450361 & 450354 Fax 01929 450501
A heathland course sited on the Purbeck Hills with grand views across Swanage, the Channel and Poole Harbour.

Holes of note include the 5th, 8th, 14th, 15th, and 16th where trees, gorse and heather assert themselves. The very attractive clubhouse is built of the local stone.
Purbeck Course: 18 holes, 6295yds, Par 70, SSS 71, Course record 66.
Dene Course: 9 holes, 4014yds, Par 60.
Club membership 500.

Visitors	advisable to telephone.
Societies	must contact in advance.
Green Fees	not confirmed.
Cards	▭ ▭ ▭ 🖃
Prof	Ian Brake
Designer	H Colt
Facilities	⊗ ⫙ by prior arrangement ⅄ ⬛ ♀ ⅄ 🛍 🍴 ❧ 🛒 ∅
Location	2.5m N on B3351

Hotel	★★★ 67% The Pines Hotel, Burlington Rd, SWANAGE ☎ 01929 425211 49 ⇋ ⋔

VERWOOD
Map 04 SU00

Crane Valley BH31 7LE
☎ 01202 814088 Fax 01202 813407
Two secluded parkland courses set amid rolling Dorset countryside and mature woodland - a 9-hole Pay and Play and an 18-hole Valley course for golfers holding a handicap certificate.The 6th nestles in the bend of the River Crane and there are 4 long Par 5's ranging from 499 to 545 yards.
Valley: 18 holes, 6445yds, Par 72, SSS 71, Course record 66.
Woodland: 9 holes, Par 66, SSS 60.
Club membership 700.

Visitors	must have handicap certificate for Valley course. Woodland course is pay and play.
Societies	telephone in advance.
Green Fees	not confirmed.
Cards	▭ ▭
Prof	Paul Cannings
Designer	Donald Steel
Facilities	⊗ ⫙ ⬚ ⬛ ♀ ⅄ 🛍 🍴 🛒 ❧ 🛒 ∅ ⨖
Location	6m W of Ringwood on B3081

Hotel	★★★★ 69% The Dormy, New Rd, FERNDOWN ☎ 01202 872121 115 ⇋ ⋔

Entries with a green background
identify courses considered to be
particularly interesting

WAREHAM   Map 03 SY98

Wareham Sandford Rd BH20 4DH
☎ 01929 554147 & 554156 Fax 01929 554147
At the entrance to the Purbecks with splendid views over
Poole Harbour and Wareham Forest. A mixture of undulating
parkland and heathland fairways. A challenge for golfers of
all abilities.
18 holes, 5753yds, Par 69, SSS 68, Course record 66.
Club membership 500.
Visitors   must contact the club in advance and hold a
handicap certificate. Must be accompanied by a
member at weekends & bank holidays.
Societies   weekdays only. Must contact in advance.
Green Fees £25 per day; £20 per round.
Facilities ⊗ ⅷ by prior arrangement ⓑ ♠ ♀ ⚘ ⚌
Location Adjacent to A351, nr Wareham railway station

Hotel   ★★★ 71% Springfield Country Hotel &
Leisure Club, Grange Rd, WAREHAM
☎ 01929 552177 48 ⇄ ⋔

WEYMOUTH   Map 03 SY67

Weymouth Links Rd DT4 0PF
☎ 01305 773981 (Secretary) & 773997 (Prof)
Fax 01305 788029
Seaside parkland course. The 5th is played off an elevated tee
over copse.
18 holes, 5981yds, Par 70, SSS 69, Course record 63.
Club membership 750.
Visitors   advisable to contact in advance.
Societies apply in writing/telephone
Green Fees £24 per day (£30 weekends & bank holidays).
Prof   Des Lochrie
Designer James Braid
Facilities ⊗ ⅷ ⓑ ♠ ♀ ⚘ ⓐ ⚌ ⚌
Location N side of town centre off B3157

Hotel   ★★★ 61% Hotel Rex, 29 The Esplanade,
WEYMOUTH ☎ 01305 760400 31 ⇄ ⋔

WIMBORNE   Map 03 SZ09

Canford Magna Knighton Ln BH21 2AS
☎ 01202 592552 Fax 01202 592550
Lying in 350 acres of Dorset countryside, the Canford Magna
Golf Club provides 45 holes of challenging golf for the
discerning player. The 18 hole Parkland and Riverside
courses are quite different and, for the short game, the new
9 hole Knighton course demands the same level of playing

skill. For those wishing to improve their handicap, the Golf
Academy offers a covered driving range, pitching greens, a
chipping green and bunkers, together with a 6 hole par 3
academy course.
*Parkland: 18 holes, 6495yds, Par 71, SSS 71, Course
record 66.*
*Riverside: 18 holes, 6214yds, Par 70, SSS 70, Course
record 68.*
Knighton: 9 holes, 1377yds, Par 27, Course record 26.
Club membership 1000.
Visitors   are advised to contact in advance.
Societies must telephone in advance.
Green Fees Parkland: £20 per round (£23 weekends).
Knighton & Riverside: £16 per round (£19
weekends).
Prof   Martyn Thompson
Designer Howard Swan
Facilities ⊗ ⅷ ⓑ ♠ ♀ ⚘ ⓐ ⚌ ⚌ ⚌ ⚘ ⚌
& Leisure Golf lessons.
Location On A341

Hotel   ★★★ 57% King's Head Hotel, The Square,
WIMBORNE ☎ 01202 880101 27 ⇄ ⋔

BARNARD CASTLE   Map 12 NZ01

Barnard Castle Harmire Rd DL12 8QN
☎ 01833 638355 & 631980 Fax 01833 638355
Perched high on the steep bank of the River Tees, the
extensive remains of Barnard Castle with its splendid
round tower dates back to the 12th and 13th centuries.
The parkland course is flat and lies in open coutryside.
18 holes, 6406yds, Par 73, SSS 71, Course record 66.
Club membership 650.
Visitors   must contact in advance, restricted at
weekends. Handicap certificate required.
Societies apply in writing.
Green Fees £18 per round (£25 weekends & bank
holidays).
Prof   Darren Pearce
Designer A Watson
Facilities ⊗ ⅷ ⓑ ♠ ♀ ⚘ ⓐ ⚌ ⚌
Location 1m N of town centre on B6278

Hotel   ★★ 78% Rose & Crown Hotel,
ROMALDKIRK ☎ 01833 650213
7 ⇄ ⋔ Annexe 5 ⇄ ⋔

BEAMISH   Map 12 NZ25

Beamish Park DH9 0RH
☎ 0191 370 1382 Fax 0191 370 2937
Parkland course. Designed by Henry Cotton and W
Woodend.
18 holes, 6204yds, Par 71, SSS 70, Course record 64.
Club membership 630.
Visitors   must contact in advance and may only play
weekdays.
Societies telephone in advance.
Green Fees £20 per day; £16 per round.

▶

Prof	Chris Cole
Designer	H Cotton
Facilities	⊗)⫙ ⫿ 👜 💺 🛎 ⛳
Location	1m NW off A693

Hotel	★★★ 67% Beamish Park Hotel, Beamish Burn Rd, MARLEY HILL ☎ 01207 230666 47 ⇄ 🐾

BILLINGHAM   Map 08 NZ42

Billingham Sandy Ln TS22 5NA
☎ 01642 533816 & 554494 Fax 01642 533816
Parkland course on edge of urban-rural district, with hard walking and water hazards.
18 holes, 6404yds, Par 73, SSS 71, Course record 63.
Club membership 1050.

Visitors	contact professional in advance on 01642 557060 a handicap certificate may be requested.
Societies	apply in writing to Secretary/Manager.
Green Fees	£20 per day (£33 weekends).
Prof	Michael Ure
Designer	F Pennick
Facilities	⊗)⫙ ⫿ 👜 💺 🛎 ⛳
Location	1m W of town centre E of A19

Hotel	★★★ 70% Parkmore Hotel, 636 Yarm Rd, Eaglescliffe, STOCKTON-ON-TEES ☎ 01642 786815 55 ⇄ 🐾

BISHOP AUCKLAND   Map 08 NZ22

Bishop Auckland High Plains, Durham Rd DL14 8DL
☎ 01388 663648 & 661618 (pro) Fax 01388 607005
A rather hilly parkland course with many well-established trees offering a challenging round. A small ravine adds interest to several holes including the short 7th, from a raised tee to a green surrounded by a stream, gorse and bushes. Pleasant views down the Wear Valley and over the residence of the Bishop of Durham.
18 holes, 6420yds, Par 72, SSS 71, Course record 64.
Club membership 950.

Visitors	parties must contact in advance. Handicap certificate advisable. Dress rules apply.
Societies	weekdays only; must contact in advance.
Green Fees	£26 per day; £22 per round (£28 per round weekends).
Cards	💳 💳 💳 💳 💳
Prof	David Skiffington
Designer	James Kay
Facilities	⊗)⫙ ⫿ 👜 💺 🛎 ⛳ 🍴
& Leisure	snooker.
Location	1m NE on A689

Hotel	★★★ 69% Swallow Eden Arms Hotel, RUSHYFORD ☎ 01388 720541 45 ⇄ 🐾

BURNOPFIELD   Map 12 NZ15

Hobson Municipal Hobson NE16 6BZ
☎ 01207 271605 Fax 01207 271069
Meadowland course with very easy walking.
18 holes, 6403yds, Par 69, SSS 68, Course record 65.
Club membership 700.

Visitors	must book in advance at weekends.
Societies	must contact in advance.

Green Fees	£15 (£18 weekends).
Cards	💳 💳 💳
Prof	Jack Ord
Facilities	⊗)⫙ ⫿ 👜 💺 🛎 ⛳
& Leisure	snooker.
Location	0.75m S on A692

Hotel	★★★ 67% Swallow Hotel, High West St, GATESHEAD ☎ 0191 477 1105 103 ⇄ 🐾

CHESTER-LE-STREET   Map 12 NZ25

Chester-le-Street Lumley Park DH3 4NS
☎ 0191 388 3218 (Secretary) Fax 0191 388 1220
Parkland course in castle grounds, good views, easy walking.
18 holes, 6437yds, Par 71, SSS 71, Course record 71.
Club membership 650.

Visitors	must contact in advance and have an introduction from own club or handicap certificate.
Societies	must apply in writing.
Green Fees	£20 per day (£25 weekends & bank holidays).
Prof	David Fletcher
Designer	J H Taylor
Facilities	💺 🛎 ⛳
Location	0.5m E off B1284

Hotel	★★★ 70% Ramside Hall Hotel, Carrville, DURHAM ☎ 0191 386 5282 80 ⇄ 🐾

Roseberry Grange Grange Villa DH2 3NF
☎ 0191 370 0670 Fax 0191 370 0660
Testing holes on this parkland course include the uphill par 3 12th (147yds) and the par 4 8th (438yds) with a ditch crossing the fairway.
18 holes, 5628yds, Par 70, SSS 69.
Club membership 550.

Visitors	after 11.30am Sun & 10.30am Sat in summer, pay and play Mon-Fri.
Societies	booking form available on request.
Green Fees	not confirmed.
Cards	💳 💳 💳 💳
Prof	Alan Hartley
Facilities	⊗)⫙ ⫿ 👜 💺 🛎 ⛳ 🍴

Hotel	★★★ 65% George Washington Golf & Country Club, Stone Cellar Rd, District 12, High Usworth, WASHINGTON ☎ 0191 402 9988 103 ⇄ 🐾

CONSETT   Map 12 NZ15

Consett & District Elmfield Rd DH8 5NN
☎ 01207 502186 Fax 01207 505060
Undulating parkland/moorland course with views across the Derwent Valley to the Cheviot Hills.
18 holes, 6023yds, Par 71, SSS 69, Course record 63.
Club membership 900.

Visitors	advised to contact Professional in advance on 01207 580210.
Societies	apply in writing.
Green Fees	£18 per day (£26 weekends).
Prof	Craig Dilley
Facilities	⊗)⫙ ⫿ 👜 💺 🛎
& Leisure	snooker room.
Location	N side of town on A691

▶

Hotel   ★★ 68% Lord Crewe Arms Hotel,
BLANCHLAND ☎ 01434 675251
9 ⇄ ♠ Annexe 10 ⇄ ♠

CROOK   Map 12 NZ13

Crook Low Jobs Hill DL15 9AA
☎ 01388 762429 & 767926
Meadowland/parkland course in elevated position with
natural hazards, varied holes and terrain. Panoramic views
over Durham and Cleveland Hills.
18 holes, 6102yds, Par 70, SSS 69, Course record 64.
Club membership 550.
Visitors   must contact Secretary for weekend play,
limited availability.
Societies   apply in writing to Secretary.
Green Fees £18 per day; £16 per round (£25 per round Sun).
Facilities   ⊗ ⊪ ⅃ ♣ ♀ ⚲
Location   0.5m E off A690

Hotel   ★★ 66% Kensington Hall Hotel, Kensington
Ter, WILLINGTON ☎ 01388 745071
10 ⇄ ♠

DARLINGTON   Map 08 NZ21

Blackwell Grange Briar Close, Blackwell DL3 8QX
☎ 01325 464458 Fax 01325 464458
Pleasant parkland course with good views, easy walking.
18 holes, 5621yds, Par 68, SSS 67, Course record 63.
Club membership 1020.
Visitors   restricted Wed & weekends.
Societies   welcome weekdays except Wed (Ladies Day).
Green Fees £25 per day; £20 per round (£30 weekends &
bank holidays).
Prof   Ralph Givens
Designer   F Pennink
Facilities   ⊗ ⊪ ⅃ ♣ ♀ ⚲ 🏠 ⛳ ⚲
Location   1m SW off A66, turn into Blackwell, signposted

Hotel   ★★★ 67% Blackwell Grange, Blackwell
Grange, DARLINGTON
☎ 01325 509955 99 ⇄ ♠ Annexe 11 ⇄ ♠

Darlington Haughton Grange DL1 3JD
☎ 01325 355324 Fax 01325 488126
Fairly flat parkland course with tree-lined fairways, and large
first-class greens.
18 holes, 6271yds, Par 71, SSS 70, Course record 64.
Club membership 850.
Visitors   may not play weekends unless accompanied by
member.
Societies   by prior arrangement with the Secretary but not
at weekends.
Green Fees not confirmed.
Prof   Mark Rogers
Designer   McKenzie (part)
Facilities   ⊗ ⊪ ⅃ ♣ ♀ ⚲ 🏠 ⛳ ⚲
Location   N side of town centre off A1150

Hotel   ★★★🏾 68% Headlam Hall Hotel, Headlam,
Gainford, DARLINGTON
☎ 01325 730238 19 ⇄ ♠ Annexe 17 ⇄ ♠

Hall Garth Golf & Country Club Hotel Coatham
Mundeville DL1 3LU ☎ 01325 320246 Fax 01325 310083
A 6900yard course with mature trees and Victorian deer
folly. The challenging 165 yard Par 3 3rd requires teeing
over water, whilst the 500 yard Par 5 6th hole features the
picturesque River Swale running alongside the fairway and
the green.
9 holes, 6621yds, Par 72, SSS 72.
Visitors   advisable to book 1 week in advance.
Societies   prior booking by telephone.
Green Fees £12.50 per 18 holes.
Cards   💳 💳 💳 💳 💳 💳 💳
Designer   Brian Moore
Facilities   ⊗ ⊪ ⅃ ♣ ♀ ⚲ 🏠 ⛳ ⚲
& Leisure   heated indoor swimming pool, sauna, solarium,
gymnasium.
Location   0.5m from A1(M), junct 59 off A167

Hotel   ★★★ 74% Hall Garth Golf and Country Club
Hotel, Coatham Mundeville, DARLINGTON
☎ 01325 300400 30 ⇄ ♠ Annexe 11 ⇄ ♠

Stressholme Snipe Ln DL2 2SA
☎ 01325 461002 Fax 01325 351826
Picturesque municipal parkland course, long but wide, with
98 bunkers and a par 3 hole played over a river.
18 holes, 6229yds, Par 70, SSS 69, Course record 64.
Club membership 650.
Visitors   must book 8 days in advance.
Societies   apply to the steward or professional.
Green Fees £9.50 per 18 holes (£11.50 weekends & bank
holidays).
Cards   💳 💳 💳 💳 💳 💳
Prof   Mark Watkins
Facilities   ⊗ ⊪ ⅃ ♀ ⚲ 🏠 ⛳ ⚲ ♣
Location   SW side of town centre on A67

Hotel   ★★★ 67% Blackwell Grange, Blackwell
Grange, DARLINGTON
☎ 01325 509955 99 ⇄ ♠ Annexe 11 ⇄ ♠

DURHAM   Map 12 NZ24

Brancepeth Castle Brancepeth Village DH7 8EA
☎ 0191 378 0075 Fax 0191 3783835
Parkland course overlooked at the 9th hole by beautiful
Brancepeth Castle.
18 holes, 6234yds, Par 70, SSS 70, Course record 64.
Club membership 780.
Visitors   must contact in advance, restricted weekends.
Societies   must contact in advance.
Green Fees not confirmed.
Cards   💳 💳 💳
Prof   David Howdon
Designer   H S Holt
Facilities   ⊗ ⊪ ⅃ ♣ ♀ ⚲ 🏠 ⛳ ⚲
Location   4m from Durham A690 towards Crook, left at
xrds in Brancepath, left turn at Castle
Gates,400yds

Hotel   ★★★★ 72% Swallow Royal County Hotel,
Old Elvet, DURHAM ☎ 0191 386 6821
151 ⇄ ♠

Durham City Littleburn, Langley Moor DH7 8HL
☎ 0191 378 0806 & 378 0029 Fax 0191 378 4265
Undulating parkland course bordered on several holes by the
River Browney.
18 holes, 6321yds, Par 71, SSS 70, Course record 67.
Club membership 750.
Visitors   restricted on competition days.
Societies   apply in writing or telephone the club
                   professional on 0191 378 0029
Green Fees   not confirmed.
Prof   Steve Corbally
Designer   C Stanton
Facilities   ⊗ ⫘ ⬧ ⬛ ♀ ⚬ 🖻 🖴 ✐
& Leisure   practice bunker & driving nets.
Location   2m W of Durham City, turn left off A690 into
                   Littleburn Ind Est

Hotel   ★★★ 69% Swallow Three Tuns Hotel, New
                   Elvet, DURHAM ☎ 0191 386 4326 50 ⇔ �ች

Mount Oswald South Rd DH1 3TQ
☎ 0191 386 7527 Fax 0191 386 0975
Flat, wooded parkland course with a Georgian clubhouse and
good views of Durham cathedral on the back nine.
18 holes, 6101yds, Par 71, SSS 69.
Club membership 120.
Visitors   must contact in advance for weekends but may
                   not play before 10am on Sun.
Societies   must telephone in advance.
Green Fees   £11 per round Mon-Thu; (£12.50 Fri-Sun &
                   bank holidays). Prices under review.
Cards   ⬛⬛ ⬛⬛ ⬛⬛ ⬛ 🔄 🗐
Facilities   ⊗ ⫘ ⬧ ⬛ ♀ ⚬ 🖴 ✐
Location   On A177, 1m SW of city centre

Hotel   ★★★ 70% Ramside Hall Hotel, Carrville,
                   DURHAM ☎ 0191 386 5282 80 ⇔ 🌭

Ramside Hall Carrville DH1 1TD
☎ 0191 386 9514 Fax 0191 386 9519
Three recently constructed 9-hole parkland courses - Princes,
Bishops, Cathedral - with 14 lakes and panoramic views
surrounding an impressive hotel. Excellent golf academy and
driving range.
Princes: 9 holes, 3235yds, Par 36, SSS 36.
Bishops: 9 holes, 3285yds, Par 36.
Cathedral: 9 holes, 2874yds, Par 34.
Club membership 400.
Visitors   open at all times subject to tee availability.
Societies   telephone in advance.
Green Fees   not confirmed.
Cards   ⬛⬛ ⬛⬛ ⬛⬛ ⬛ 🔄 🗐
Prof   Robert Lister
Designer   Johnathan Gaunt
Facilities   ⊗ ⫘ ⬧ ⬛ ♀ ⚬ ☝ 🖻 🐦 🖴 ✐ (
Location   500m from A1/A690 interchange

Hotel   ★★★ 70% Ramside Hall Hotel, Carrville,
                   DURHAM ☎ 0191 386 5282 80 ⇔ 🌭

EAGLESCLIFFE   Map 08 NZ41

Eaglescliffe and District Yarm Rd TS16 0DQ
☎ 01642 780098 Fax 01642 780238
This hilly course offers both pleasant and interesting golf
to all classes of player. It lies in a delightful setting on a

rolling plateau, shelving to the River Tees. There are fine
views to the Cleveland Hills.
18 holes, 6275yds, Par 72, SSS 70, Course record 63.
Club membership 700.
Visitors   restricted Tue, Thu, Fri & weekends.
Societies   must contact in advance, apply to secretary
                   on 01642 780238
Green Fees   £35 per day, £20 (£50/25 weekends & bank
                   holidays).
Prof   Paul Bradley
Designer   J Braid/H Cotton
Facilities   ⊗ ⫘ ⬧ ⬛ ♀ ⚬ 🖻 🖴 ✐
Location   E side of village off A135

Hotel   ★★★★ 61% Swallow Hotel, John Walker
                   Square, STOCKTON-ON-TEES
                   ☎ 01642 679721 0800 7317549
                   Fax 01642 601714 125 ⇔ 🌭

HARTLEPOOL   Map 08 NZ53

Castle Eden & Peterlee Castle Eden TS27 4SS
☎ 01429 836510
Beautiful parkland course alongside a nature reserve. Hard
walking but trees provide wind shelter.
18 holes, 6262yds, Par 70, SSS 70, Course record 65.
Club membership 750.
Visitors   with member only during 12-1.30pm & 4-
                   6.30pm. Must contact in advance.
Societies   must contact in advance tel: 01429 836510.
Green Fees   £22 per day/round.
Prof   Graham J Laidlaw
Designer   Henry Cotton
Facilities   ⊗ ⫘ ⬧ ⬛ ♀ ⚬ 🖻 🐦 🖴 ✐
& Leisure   snooker.
Location   2m S of Peterlee on B1281 off A19

Hotel   ★★ 69% Hardwicke Hall Manor Hotel,
                   Hesleden, PETERLEE ☎ 01429 836326
                   15 ⇔ 🌭

Hartlepool Hart Warren TS24 9QF
☎ 01429 274398 Fax 01429 274129
A seaside course, half links, overlooking the North Sea.
A good test and equally enjoyable to all handicap
players. The 10th, par 4, demands a precise second shot
over a ridge and between sand dunes to a green down
near the edge of the beach, alongside which several holes
are played.
18 holes, 6215yds, Par 70, SSS 70, Course record 62.
Club membership 700.
Visitors   with member only on Sun.
Societies   must apply in writing in advance.
Green Fees   £25 per day (£35 weekends).
Prof   Malcolm E Cole
Designer   Partly Braid
Facilities   ⊗ ⫘ ⬧ ⬛ ♀ ⚬ 🖻 🐦 ✐
Location   N of Hartlepool, off A1086

Hotel   ★★ 65% Ryedale Moor, 3 Beaconsfield St,
                   Headland, HARTLEPOOL
                   ☎ 01429 231436 16 ⇔ 🌭

MIDDLETON ST GEORGE   Map 08 NZ31

Dinsdale Spa Neasham Rd DL2 1DW
☎ 01325 332297 Fax 01325 332297
A mainly flat, parkland course on high land above the
River Tees with views of the Cleveland Hills. Water
hazards in front 10th tee and green, the prevailing west
wind affects the later holes. There is a practice area by
the clubhouse.
18 holes, 6090yds, Par 71, SSS 69, Course record 65.
Club membership 870.

Visitors	welcome Mon & Wed-Fri, contact for further details.
Societies	bookings through office, no weekends or Tue. Apply in writing or telephone.
Green Fees	not confirmed.
Prof	Neil Metcalfe
Facilities	⊗ ⅲ ⓑ ♥ ♀ ⚘ 🖨 ✐
Location	1.5m SW
Hotel	★★★ 62% The St George, Middleton St George, Darlington, TEES-SIDE AIRPORT ☎ 01325 332631 59 ⇌ ⋒

NEWTON AYCLIFFE   Map 08 NZ22

Oakleaf School Aycliffe Ln DL5 4EF ☎ 01325 310820
A parkland course in a country setting.
18 holes, 5732yds, Par 69, SSS 70.
Club membership 165.

Visitors	dress code enforced and must contact in advance for weekends.
Societies	apply in writing.
Green Fees	not confirmed.
Facilities	ⓑ ♥ ♀ ⚘ 🖨 ✐ ⓕ
& Leisure	squash.
Location	6m N of Darlington, off A6072
Hotel	★★★★ 71% Redworth Hall Hotel & Country Club, REDWORTH ☎ 01388 772442 100 ⇌ ⋒

Woodham Golf & Country Club Burnhill Way DL5 4PN
☎ 01325 320574 (Office) 315257 (Pro Shop)
Fax 01325 315254
Beautiful parkland course offering golfers a full and varied
challenge with plenty of trees, numerous lakes and
meandering streams.
18 holes, 6771yds, Par 73, SSS 72, Course record 68.
Club membership 694.

Visitors	must book 1 week in advance for weekends.
Societies	telephone or write in advance.
Green Fees	£15 per round (£24 weekends & bank holidays).
Cards	💳 💳 💳 💳
Prof	Ernie Wilson
Designer	James Hamilton Stutt
Facilities	⊗ ⅲ ⓑ ♥ ♀ ⚘ 🖨 ⌖ ❧ 🛒 ✐
Location	Off A167
Hotel	★★★ 69% Swallow Eden Arms Hotel, RUSHYFORD ☎ 01388 720541 45 ⇌ ⋒

> Looking for a driving range?
> See the index at the back of the guide

SEAHAM   Map 12 NZ44

Seaham Dawdon SR7 7RD
☎ 0191 581 2354 & 581 1268 (Sec)
Heathland links course with several holes affected by strong
prevailing winds.
18 holes, 6017yds, Par 70, SSS 69, Course record 64.
Club membership 600.

Visitors	contact professional at all times, with member only weekends until 3.30pm.
Societies	must apply in advance.
Green Fees	£18 per day; (£23 per round weekends).
Prof	Glyn Jones
Facilities	⊗ by prior arrangement ⅲ by prior arrangement ⓑ ♥ ♀ ⚘ 🖨 ⌖ ✐
Location	3m E of A19, exit for Seaham
Hotel	★★★★ 67% Swallow Hotel, Queen's Pde, Seaburn, SUNDERLAND ☎ 0191 529 2041 98 ⇌ ⋒

SEATON CAREW   Map 08 NZ52

Seaton Carew Tees Rd TS25 1DE
☎ 01429 261040 & 266249
A championship links course taking full advantage of its
dunes, bents, whins and gorse. Renowned for its par 4
(17th); just enough fairway for an accurate drive
followed by another precise shot to a pear-shaped,
sloping green that is severely trapped.
The Old Course: 18 holes, 6604yds, Par 72, SSS 72.
Brabazon Course: 18 holes, 6849yds, Par 73, SSS 73.
Club membership 650.

Visitors	restricted until after 10am at weekends & bank holidays.
Societies	must apply in writing.
Green Fees	£30 per day (£40 weekends & bank holidays).
Prof	W Hector
Designer	McKenzie
Facilities	⊗ ⅲ ⓑ ♥ ♀ ⚘ 🖨 ❧ 🛒 ✐
Location	SE side of village off A178
Hotel	★★ 65% Ryedale Moor, 3 Beaconsfield St, Headland, HARTLEPOOL ☎ 01429 231436 16 ⇌ ⋒

SEDGEFIELD   Map 08 NZ32

Knotty Hill Golf Centre TS21 2BB
☎ 01740 620320 Fax 01740 622227
The 18-hole Princes course is set in rolling parkland with
many holes routed through shallow valleys. Several holes are
set wholly or partially within woodland and water hazards
abound. Bishops Course is a developing 18-hole course with
varied water features on attractive terrain. Several holes are
routed through mature woodland.
Princes Course (A+B): 18 holes, 6577yds, Par 72, SSS 71.
Bishops Course (C+D): 18 holes, 5915yds, Par 70, SSS 71.

Visitors	must telephone in advance for tee reservations.
Societies	package available on request.
Green Fees	Mon-Fri:£24 per 36 holes, £20 per 27 holes, £12 per 18 holes, £8 per 9 holes.
Designer	C Stanton

▶

Facilities
& Leisure indoor golf academy, target golf.
Location 1m N of Sedgefield on A177, 2m from junct 60 on A1(M)

Hotel ★★★ 65% Hardwick Hall Hotel, SEDGEFIELD ☎ 01740 620253 17 🛏 🐾

STANLEY
Map 12 NZ15

South Moor The Middles, Craghead DH9 6AG
☎ 01207 232848 Fax 01207 284616
Moorland course with natural hazards designed by Dr Alistair McKenzie in 1926 and remains one the most challenging of its type in north east England. Out of bounds features on 11 holes from the tee and the testing par 5 12th hole is uphill and usually against a strong headwind.
18 holes, 6445yds, Par 72, SSS 71, Course record 66.
Club membership 650.
Visitors welcome except sundays, must contact in advance. Handicap certificate required.
Societies apply in writing to Secretary.
Green Fees £22 per day; £15 per round (£26 per day/round weekends).
Prof Shaun Cowell
Designer Dr Alistair Mackenzie
Facilities ⊗ ℳ ㊑ ♥ ♀ △ 🖢 🥄 🥅 ♂
Location 1.5m SE on B6313

Hotel ★★★ 67% Beamish Park Hotel, Beamish Burn Rd, MARLEY HILL ☎ 01207 230666 47 🛏 🐾

STOCKTON-ON-TEES
Map 08 NZ41

Norton Norton TS20 1SU
☎ 01642 676385 Fax 01642 608467
An interesting parkland course with long drives from the 7th and 17th tees. Several water hazards.
18 holes, 5855yds, Par 70.
Visitors no visiting party tee times booked on weekends.
Societies apply in advance.
Green Fees £10 per round.
Cards 🔲 🔳 🔳 🔳 🖸
Designer T Harper
Facilities ⊗ ℳ ㊑ ♥ ♀ ♂
& Leisure bowling green.
Location At Norton 2m N off A19

Hotel ★★★ 70% Parkmore Hotel, 636 Yarm Rd, Eaglescliffe, STOCKTON-ON-TEES ☎ 01642 786815 55 🛏 🐾

Teesside Acklam Rd, Thornaby TS17 7JS
☎ 01642 616516 & 673822 (pro) Fax 01642 676252
Flat parkland course, easy walking.
18 holes, 6535yds, Par 72, SSS 71, Course record 64.
Club membership 700.
Visitors with member only weekdays after 4.30pm, weekends after 11am.
Societies must contact in writing.
Green Fees £26 per day.
Prof Ken Hall
Designer Makepiece & Dr Somerville
Facilities ⊗ ℳ ㊑ ♥ ♀ △ 🖢 ♂
Location 1.5m SE on A1130, off A19 at Mandale interchange

Hotel ★★★ 66% Posthouse Teesside, low Ln, Stainton Village, Thornaby, STOCKTON-ON-TEES ☎ 0870 400 9081 136 🛏 🐾

ABRIDGE
Map 05 TQ49

Abridge Golf and Country Club Epping Ln, Stapleford Tawney RM4 1ST
☎ 01708 688396 Fax 01708 688550
A parkland course with easy walking. The quick drying course is by no means easy to play. This has been the venue of several professional tournaments. Abridge is a Golf and Country Club and has all the attendant facilities.
18 holes, 6692yds, Par 72, SSS 72, Course record 67.
Club membership 650.
Visitors must have current handicap certificate, contact in advance. Play with member only at weekends.
Societies telephone in advance.
Green Fees not confirmed.
Prof Stuart Layton
Designer Henry Cotton
Facilities ⊗ ㊑ ♥ ♀ △ 🖢 🥄 🥅 ♂ 🥃
& Leisure heated outdoor swimming pool, sauna.
Location 1.75m NE

Hotel ★★★ 62% Posthouse Epping, High Rd, Bell Common, EPPING ☎ 0870 400 9027 Annexe 79 🛏 🐾

BASILDON
Map 05 TQ78

Basildon Clay Hill Ln, Kingswood SS16 5JP
☎ 01268 533297 Fax 01268 533849
Undulating municipal parkland course. Testing 13th hole (par 4).
18 holes, 6236yds, Par 72, SSS 70.
Club membership 350.
Visitors contact professional in advance 01268 533532.
Societies may contact for details.
Green Fees £9 per round (£15 weekends & bank holidays).
Prof M Oliver
Designer A Cotton
Facilities ⊗ ℳ ㊑ ♥ ♀ △ 🖢 🥅 ♂
Location 1m S off A176

Hotel ★★★ 64% Posthouse Basildon, Cranes Farm Rd, BASILDON ☎ 0870 400 9003 149 🛏 🐾

BENFLEET
Map 05 TQ78

Boyce Hill Vicarage Hill, South Benfleet SS7 1PD
☎ 01268 793625 & 752565 Fax 01268 750497
Hilly parkland course with good views.
18 holes, 5983yds, Par 68, SSS 68, Course record 61.
Club membership 700.
Visitors must have a handicap certificate, must contact 24hrs in advance, may not play at weekends. ▶

Societies	Thu only, book well in advance by telephone.
Green Fees	£25 per round.
Prof	Graham Burroughs
Designer	James Braid
Facilities	⊗ ⅏ 🍴 🍺 ♀ ⚐ 🛒 ⚒ ♂
Location	0.75m NE of Benfleet Station

Hotel	★★★ 64% Posthouse Basildon, Cranes Farm Rd, BASILDON ☎ 0870 400 9003 149 🛏 ✆

BILLERICAY   Map 05 TQ69

The Burstead Tye Common Rd, Little Burstead CM12 9SS
☎ 01277 631171 Fax 01277 632766
The Burstead is an attractive parkland course set amidst some of the most attractive countryside in south Essex. It is an excellent test of golf to players of all standards with the greens showing maturity beyond their years. Challenging holes include the Par 4 16th hole which at 348yds requires an accurate tee shot to leave a second shot played over a lake protecting an attractive contoured green. The 18th is the longest hole on the course.
18 holes, 6275yds, Par 71, SSS 70, Course record 67.
Club membership 900.

Visitors	must have handicap certificate and may only play weekdays.
Societies	apply in writing and/or telephone for reservation.
Green Fees	not confirmed.
Cards	🗾 🗾 🗾
Prof	Keith Bridges
Designer	Patrick Tallack
Facilities	⊗ ⅏ 🍴 🍺 ♀ ⚐ 🛒 🛒 ♂

Hotel	★★★ 67% Chichester Hotel, Old London Rd, Wickford, BASILDON ☎ 01268 560555 2 🛏 ✆ Annexe 32 🛏 ✆

Stock Brook Golf & Country Club Queens Park Av, Stock CM12 0SP ☎ 01277 653616 & 650400 Fax 01277 633063
Set in 250 acres of picturesque countryside the 27 holes comprise three undulating 9's, offering the challenge of water on a large number of holes. Any combination can be played, but the Stock and Brook courses make the 18-hole, 6750 yard championship course. There are extensive clubhouse facilities.
Stock & Brook Courses: 18 holes, 6728yds, Par 72, SSS 72, Course record 66.
Manor Course: 9 holes, 2997yds, Par 35.
Club membership 750.

Visitors	handicap certificate required, must contact 24hrs in advance.
Societies	apply in writing or telephone.

Green Fees	not confirmed.
Prof	Kevin Merry
Designer	Martin Gillet
Facilities	⊗ ⅏ 🍴 🍺 ♀ ⚐ ⚒ ♂ ℓ
& Leisure	hard tennis courts, heated outdoor swimming pool, sauna, gymnasium, Bowls.

Hotel	★★★ 66% The Heybridge Hotel, Roman Rd, INGATESTONE ☎ 01277 355355 22 🛏 ✆

BRAINTREE   Map 05 TL72

Braintree Kings Ln, Stisted CM7 8DA
☎ 01376 346079 Fax 01376 334117
Parkland course with many unique mature trees. Good par 3s with the 14th -'Devils Lair'-regarded as one of the best in the county.
18 holes, 6174yds, Par 70, SSS 69, Course record 65.
Club membership 750.

Visitors	weekdays only, contact the pro shop in advance 01376 343465.
Societies	society days Wed & Thu early booking advised.
Green Fees	£31.50 per day; £21 per round.
Prof	Tony Parcell
Designer	Hawtree
Facilities	♀ ⚐ ⚒ ♂ ℓ
Location	1m E, off A120

Hotel	★★★ 61% White Hart Hotel, Bocking End, BRAINTREE ☎ 01376 321401 31 🛏 ✆

Towerlands Panfield Rd CM7 5BJ
☎ 01376 326802 Fax 01376 552487
Undulating, grassland course. Driving range and sports hall.
9 holes, 2749yds, Par 34, SSS 66.
Club membership 300.

Visitors	must not play before 12.30pm weekends or before 5pm Wed. Correct dress at all times. Must contact in advance.
Societies	must contact in advance by telephone.
Green Fees	not confirmed.
Cards	🗾 🗾 🗾 🗾 🗾
Designer	G Shiels
Facilities	⊗ ⅏ 🍴 🍺 ♀ ⚐ ⚒ ♂ ℓ
& Leisure	squash, gymnasium.
Location	On B1053

Hotel	★★★ 61% White Hart Hotel, Bocking End, BRAINTREE ☎ 01376 321401 31 🛏 ✆

BRENTWOOD   Map 05 TQ59

Bentley Ongar Rd CM15 9SS
☎ 01277 373179 Fax 01277 375097
Parkland course with water hazards.
18 holes, 6709yds, Par 72, SSS 72.
Club membership 600.

Visitors	should contact in advance, may not play at weekends.
Societies	must write or telephone in advance.
Green Fees	prices not confirmed.
Cards	🗾 🗾
Prof	Nick Garrett
Designer	Alec Swann
Facilities	⊗ ⅏ by prior arrangement 🍴 🍺 ♀ ⚐ ♂
Location	3m NW on A128

▶

Hotel ★★★ 69% Posthouse Brentwood, Brook St, BRENTWOOD ☎ 0870 400 9012 145 ⇨ ☜

Hartswood King George's Playing Fields, Ingrave Rd CM14 5AE ☎ 01277 218850
Municipal parkland course, easy walking.
18 holes, 5648yds, Par 70, SSS 69, Course record 64.
Club membership 500.
Visitors pre-booking usually essential am.
Societies weekdays only, must contact in advance.
Green Fees £9.20 (£12.50 weekends & bank holidays).
Cards
Prof Stephen Cole
Facilities ⊗ ⌇ ⅃ ⋤ ⋓ ⚲ ⋀ ▱ ⚑ ⚘
Location 0.75m SE on A128

Hotel ★★★ 69% Posthouse Brentwood, Brook St, BRENTWOOD ☎ 0870 400 9012 145 ⇨ ☜

Warley Park Magpie Ln, Little Warley CM13 3DX ☎ 01277 224891 Fax 01277 200679
Parkland course with reasonable walking. Numerous water hazards. There is also a golf-practice ground.
1st & 2nd: 18 holes, 5967yds, Par 69, SSS 68, Course record 67.
1st & 3rd: 18 holes, 6232yds, Par 71, SSS 69, Course record 65.
2nd & 3rd: 18 holes, 6223yds, Par 70, SSS 69, Course record 70.
Club membership 800.
Visitors must have handicap certificate and contact in advance. May not play at weekends.
Societies telephone in advance for provisional booking.
Green Fees £35 per day; £26 per round.
Prof Jason Groat
Designer Reg Plumbridge
Facilities ⊗ ⋤ ⋓ ⚲ ⋀ ▱ ⚘ ⚑
Location 0.5m N off junct 29 of M25/A127

Hotel ★★★ 69% Posthouse Brentwood, Brook St, BRENTWOOD ☎ 0870 400 9012 145 ⇨ ☜

Weald Park Coxtie Green Rd, South Weald CM14 5RJ ☎ 01277 375101 Fax 01277 374888
Tranquil parkland course with many mature oak trees, lakes, ponds and plentiful wildlife. The undulating terrain and the numerous hedges and ponds make this par 71 course a fair test of golf for all abilities.
18 holes, 6612yds, Par 71, SSS 70, Course record 65.
Club membership 570.
Visitors telephone booking preferable, no weekday restrictions
Societies apply in writing or telephone for package.
Green Fees £20 per round (£25 weekends).
Cards
Prof Ian Parker
Designer Reg Plumbridge
Facilities ⊗ ⌇ ⋤ ⋓ ⚲ ⋀ ▱ ⚘
Location 3m from M25

Hotel ★★★★ 70% Marygreen Manor, London Rd, BRENTWOOD ☎ 01277 225252 3 ⇨ ☜ Annexe 40 ⇨ ☜

BULPHAN Map 05 TQ68

Langdon Hills Golf Centre Lower Dunton Rd RM14 3TY ☎ 01268 548444 Fax 01268 490084
Well situated with the Langdon Hills on one side and dramatic views across London on the other, the Centre offers an interchangeable 27 hole course, a floodlit 22-bay driving range and three academy holes.
Langdon Course: 9 holes, 3132yds, Par 35, SSS 71.
Horndon Course: 9 holes, 3054yds, Par 36, SSS 70.
Bulpman Course: 9 holes, 3054yds, Par 36, SSS 70.
Club membership 600.
Visitors preference given to members on weekend mornings.
Societies apply in writing or telephone.
Green Fees not confirmed.
Prof Terry Moncur
Designer Howard Swan
Facilities ⊗ ⌇ ⋤ ⋓ ⚲ ⋀ ▱ ⚑ ⋈ ⚘ ⋘ ⚘ ⚐
Location Between A13 & A127 N of A128 S of Basildon

Hotel ★★★★ 70% Marygreen Manor, London Rd, BRENTWOOD ☎ 01277 225252 3 ⇨ ☜ Annexe 40 ⇨ ☜

BURNHAM-ON-CROUCH Map 05 TQ99

Burnham-on-Crouch Ferry Rd, Creeksea CM0 8PQ ☎ 01621 782282 Fax 01621 784489
Undulating meadowland riverside course, easy walking.
18 holes, 6056yds, Par 70, SSS 69, Course record 66.
Club membership 586.
Visitors welcome weekdays. Must play with member at weekends.
Societies apply in writing or telephone.
Green Fees £24 per day/round.
Cards
Designer Swan
Facilities ⊗ ⌇ ⋤ ⋓ ⚲ ⋀ ▱ ⚘ ⋈ ⚘
Location 1.25m W off B1010

CANEWDON Map 05 TQ99

Ballards Gore Gore Rd SS4 2DA ☎ 01702 258917 Fax 01702 258571
A parkland course with several lakes.
18 holes, 6874yds, Par 73, SSS 73, Course record 69.
Club membership 500.
Visitors must contact in advance.
Societies weekdays only, apply in advance.
Green Fees £25 per day; £20 per round.
Cards
Prof Richard Emery
Designer D T J Caton
Facilities ⊗ ⋤ ⋓ ⚲ ⋀ ▱ ⚘ ⚘
Location 2m NE of Rochford

Hotel ★★★ 68% Hotel Renouf, Bradley Way, ROCHFORD ☎ 01702 541334 24 ⇨ ☜

CANVEY ISLAND Map 05 TQ78

Castle Point Somnes Av SS8 9FG ☎ 01268 696298 (Secretary) & 510830 (Pro)
A flat seaside links and part parkland course with water

▶

hazards on 13 holes and views of the estuary and Hadleigh Castle. Always a test for any golfer when the wind starts to blow.
18 holes, 6176yds, Par 71, SSS 69, Course record 69.
Club membership 275.
Visitors must book for weekends.
Societies phone or write for details.
Green Fees not confirmed.
Prof Michael Utteridge
Facilities ⊗ ⓑ 🖳 🍴 🎒 🛅 🤵 🏌 ♂ ℓ
Location SE of Basildon, A130 to Canvey Island

Hotel ★★★ 67% Chichester Hotel, Old London Rd, Wickford, BASILDON ☎ 01268 560555
2 ⇔ ⎈ Annexe 32 ⇔ ⎈

CHELMSFORD Map 05 TL70

Channels Belstead Farm Ln, Little Waltham CM3 3PT
☎ 01245 440005 Fax 01245 442032
The Channels course is built on land from reclaimed gravel pits, 18 very exciting holes with plenty of lakes providing an excellent test of golf. Belsteads a nine hole course is mainly flat but has 3 holes where water has to be negotiated.
Channels Course: 18 holes, 6300yds, Par 71, SSS 71, Course record 67.
Belsteads: 9 holes, 2467yds, Par 34, SSS 32.
Club membership 650.
Visitors Channels Course; must contact in advance and may only play with member at weekends. Belsteads Course; available anytime.
Societies telephone starter on 01245 443311.
Green Fees Channels: £25 per round. Belsteads: £18 per 18 holes; £12 per 9 holes (£20/£14 weekends).
Cards 💳
Prof Ian Sinclair
Designer Cotton & Swan
Facilities ⊗ ⓜ ⓑ 🖳 🍴 🎒 🛅 🤵 🏌 ♂ ℓ
& Leisure fishing.
Location 2m NE on A130

Hotel ★★★ 68% County Hotel, Rainsford Rd, CHELMSFORD ☎ 01245 491911
28 ⇔ ⎈ Annexe 8 ⇔ ⎈

Chelmsford Widford Rd CM2 9AP
☎ 01245 256483 Fax 01245 256483
An undulating parkland course, hilly in parts, with 3 holes in woods and four difficult par 4's. From the reconstructed clubhouse there are fine views over the course and the wooded hills beyond.
18 holes, 5981yds, Par 68, SSS 69, Course record 65.
Club membership 650.
Visitors must contact in advance. Society days Wed/Thu, Ladies Day Tue. With member only at weekends.
Societies must contact in advance.
Green Fees £35 per round.
Prof Mark Welch
Designer Tom Dunn
Facilities ⊗ by prior arrangement ⓑ 🖳 🍴 🎒 🛅 🤵 🏌 ♂
Location 1.5m S of town centre off A12

Hotel ★★★ 69% Pontlands Park Country Hotel, West Hanningfield Rd, Great Baddow, CHELMSFORD ☎ 01245 476444
17 ⇔ ⎈

CHIGWELL Map 05 TQ49

Chigwell High Rd IG7 5BH ☎ 020 8500 2059
Fax 020 8501 3410
A course of high quality, mixing meadowland with parkland. For those who believe 'all Essex is flat' the undulating nature of Chigwell will be a refreshing surprise. The greens are excellent and the fairways tight with mature trees.
18 holes, 6279yds, Par 71, SSS 70, Course record 66.
Club membership 670.
Visitors must contact in advance & have handicap certificate, but must be accompanied by member at weekends.
Societies recognised societies welcome by prior arrangement.
Green Fees not confirmed.
Prof Ray Beard
Designer Hawtree/Taylor
Facilities ⊗ ⓜ by prior arrangement ⓑ 🖳 🍴 🎒 ♂
Location 0.5m S on A113

Hotel ★★★ 63% Roebuck Hotel, North End, BUCKHURST HILL ☎ 020 8505 4636
28 ⇔ ⎈

CHIGWELL ROW Map 05 TQ49

Hainault Forest Romford Rd, Chigwell Row IG7 4QW
☎ 020 8500 2131 Fax 020 8501 5196
Club playing over Borough of Redbridge public courses; hilly parkland subject to wind. Two courses, driving range.
No 1 Course: 18 holes, 5687yds, Par 70, SSS 67, Course record 65.
No 2 Course: 18 holes, 6238yds, Par 71, SSS 71.
Club membership 600.
Visitors no restrictions.
Societies must contact in writing.
Green Fees not confirmed.
Prof Chris Hope
Designer Taylor & Hawtree
Facilities ⊗ ⓑ 🖳 🍴 🎒 🛅 🤵 🏌 ♂
Location 0.5m S on A1112

Hotel ★★★ 66% County Hotel Epping Forest, Oak Hill, WOODFORD GREEN ☎ 020 8787 9988
99 ⇔ ⎈

CLACTON-ON-SEA Map 05 TM11

Clacton West Rd CO15 1AJ
☎ 01255 421919 Fax 01255 424602
Windy, seaside course.
18 holes, 6494yds, Par 71, SSS 69.
Club membership 650.
Visitors must contact in advance.
Societies must contact in writing.
Green Fees not confirmed.
Prof S J Levermore

▶

Facilities ⚐🏠🖳🖲✐

Location 1.25m SW of town centre

Hotel ★★ 71% Maplin Hotel, Esplanade, FRINTON-ON-SEA ☎ 01255 673832 11rm (10 ⇔ 🅿)

COLCHESTER   Map 05 TL92

Birch Grove Layer Rd, Kingsford CO2 0HS
☎ 01206 734276
A pretty, undulating course surrounded by woodland - small but challenging with excellent greens. Challenging 6th hole cut through woodland with water hazards and out of bounds.
9 holes, 4532yds, Par 66, SSS 63.
Club membership 250.
Visitors restricted Sun mornings.
Societies apply in writing or telephone.
Green Fees £16 per day; £12 per 18 holes; £9 per 9 holes.
Facilities ⊗🎯🖳🍸⚐🏠✐
Location 2.5m S on B1026

Hotel ★★★ 72% George Hotel, 116 High St, COLCHESTER ☎ 01206 578494 47 ⇔ 🅿

Colchester Braiswick CO4 5AU
☎ 01206 853396 Fax 01206 852698
A fairly flat, yet scenic, parkland course with tree-lined fairways and small copses. Mainly level walking.
18 holes, 6307yds, Par 70, SSS 70, Course record 64.
Club membership 700.
Visitors by prior arrangement.
Societies apply in writing or by telephone, Mon, Thu & Fri only.
Green Fees please contact for details.
Prof Mark Angel
Designer James Braid
Facilities ⊗🖳🍸⚐🏠✐ℓ
Location 1.5m NW of town centre on B1508

Hotel ★★★ 72% George Hotel, 116 High St, COLCHESTER ☎ 01206 578494 47 ⇔ 🅿

Colchester & Lexden Golf Centre Bakers Ln CD3 4AU
☎ 01206 843333 Fax 01206 854775
New 18-hole course within easy reach of the town centre. Also a 9-hole pitch and putt course, and a floodlit driving range.
18 holes, 5500yds, Par 67.
Club membership 500.
Visitors welcome.
Societies telephone for details.
Green Fees not confirmed.
Cards ▭▭ ▩ ▩ ▩
Prof Phil Grice
Designer J Johnson
Facilities ⊗🎯🖳🍸⚐🏠🖲✐ℓ
& Leisure 9 hole par 3.
Location Adjacent to A12. Take Colchester Central from A12 and then follow tourist signs

---

Hotel ★★★ 68% Marks Tey Hotel, London Rd, Marks Tey, COLCHESTER ☎ 01206 210001 110 ⇔ 🅿

Stoke-by-Nayland Keepers Ln, Leavenheath CO6 4PZ
☎ 01206 262836 Fax 01206 263356
Two undulating courses (Gainsborough and Constable) situated in Dedham Vale. Some water hazards and hedges. On Gainsborough the 10th (par 4) takes 2 shots over a lake; very testing par 3 at 11th.
Gainsborough Course: 18 holes, 6581yds, Par 72, SSS 71, Course record 68.
Constable Course: 18 holes, 6544yds, Par 72, SSS 71, Course record 66.
Club membership 1360.
Visitors write or telephone for details.
Societies write or telephone for brochures and booking forms.
Green Fees £25 per round Mon-Fri.
Cards ▭▭ ▩
Prof Kevin Lovelock
Facilities ⊗🖳🍸⚐🏠🖳🖲🖳ℓ
& Leisure fishing.
Location 1.5m NW of Stoke-by-Nayland on B1068

Hotel ★★★🏆 Maison Talbooth, Stratford Rd, DEDHAM ☎ 01206 322367 10 ⇔ 🅿

EARLS COLNE   Map 05 TL82

Colne Valley Station Rd CO6 2LT
☎ 01787 224233 Fax 01787 224126
An 18-hole course along the valley of the River Colne.
18 holes, 6301yds, Par 70, SSS 70, Course record 68.
Club membership 600.
Visitors only after 10.30am at weekends, must dress correctly, no sharing of clubs. Must contact in advance.
Societies apply in writing, minimum of 12 persons.
Green Fees £18.
Cards ▭▭ ▩ ▩ ▩ ▩
Prof James Taylor
Designer Howard Swan
Facilities ⊗🖳🍸⚐🏠✐
& Leisure sauna.
Location Off A604

Hotel ★★★ 68% Marks Tey Hotel, London Rd, Marks Tey, COLCHESTER ☎ 01206 210001 110 ⇔ 🅿

Essex Golf & Country Club CO6 2NS
☎ 01787 224466 Fax 01787 224410
Created on the site of a World War II airfield, this challenging course contains 12 lakes. Also 9-hole course as well as a variety of leisure facilities.
County Course: 18 holes, 6907yds, Par 73, SSS 73, Course record 67.
Garden Course: 9 holes, 2190yds, Par 34, SSS 34.
Club membership 600.
Visitors contact golf reception for bookings up to 1 week in advance.
Societies apply in writing to the Functions Manager.
Green Fees Country Course £20 per round (£25 weekends & bank holidays); Garden Course £15 per 18 holes, £10 per 9 holes.
Prof Mark Spooner
Designer Reg Plumbridge
Facilities ⊗🎯🖳🍸⚐🏠🖲🖳🖳🖲✐ℓ
& Leisure hard tennis courts, heated indoor swimming pool, fishing, sauna, solarium, gymnasium.

▶

| Location | Off the A120 onto the B1024 |
| Hotel | ★★★ 68% Marks Tey Hotel, London Rd, Marks Tey, COLCHESTER ☎ 01206 210001 110 ⇆ ❦ |

EPPING   Map 05 TL40

Nazeing Middle St, Nazeing EN9 2LW
☎ 01992 893798 Fax 01992 893882
Parkland course built with American sand based greens and tees and five strategically placed lakes. One of the most notable holes is the difficult par 3 13th with out of bounds and a large lake coming into play.
18 holes, 6598yds, Par 72, SSS 71, Course record 68.
Club membership 400.

Visitors	not compulsory to contact except for weekends when pm only available.
Societies	prior arrangement required in writing.
Green Fees	£20 Tue-Fri; £16 Mon (£28 weekends after 12.30pm).
Cards	💳 💳 💳 💳 💳
Prof	Robert Green
Designer	M Gillete
Facilities	⊗ ⫼ ﹖ ♿ ☕ ♣ 🚵 🛺 ∅ ℓ
Location	Just outside Waltham Abbey
Hotel	★★★ 65% Harlow Moat House, Southern Way, HARLOW ☎ 01279 829988 119 ⇆ ❦

FRINTON-ON-SEA   Map 05 TM22

Frinton 1 The Esplanade CO13 9EP
☎ 01255 674618 Fax 01255 674618
Deceptive, flat seaside links course providing fast, firm and undulating greens that will test the best putters and tidal ditches that cross many of the fairways, requiring careful placement of shots. Its open character means that every shot has to be evaluated with both wind strength and direction in mind. Easy walking.
Long Course: 18 holes, 6265yds, Par 71, SSS 70, Course record 64.
Short Course: 9 holes, 1367yds, Par 58.
Club membership 850.

Visitors	must contact in advance.
Societies	by arrangement, apply in writing to the secretary, Wed, Thu and some Fri.
Green Fees	£26, cheaper rate during Nov-Mar.
Prof	Peter Taggart
Designer	Willy Park Jnr
Facilities	⊗ ⫼ by prior arrangement ♿ ♣ ﹖ ☕ ☕ ♣ 🚵 ∅
Location	SW side of town centre
Hotel	★★ 71% Maplin Hotel, Esplanade, FRINTON-ON-SEA ☎ 01255 673832 11rm (10 ⇆ ❦)

GOSFIELD   Map 05 TL72

Gosfield Lake The Manor House, Hall Dr CO9 1SE
☎ 01787 474747 Fax 01787 476044
Parkland course with bunkers, lakes and water hazards. Designed by Sir Henry Cotton/Mr Howard Swan. Also 9-hole course; ideal for beginners and improvers.
Lakes Course: 18 holes, 6615yds, Par 72, SSS 72.

Meadows Course: 9 holes, 4180yds, Par 66, SSS 63.
Club membership 650.

Visitors	Lakes Course: must contact in advance, handicap certificate required, Sat & Sun from noon only. Meadows Course: restricted during competitions, handicap certificate not required, advisable to contact.
Societies	welcome Mon-Fri by arrangement, telephone or write.
Green Fees	not confirmed.
Prof	Richard Wheeler
Designer	Henry Cotton/Howard Swan
Facilities & Leisure	⊗ ⫼ ♿ ♣ ﹖ ☕ ☕ ♣ 🚵 ∅ sauna.
Location	1m W of Gosfield off B1017
Hotel	★★★ 61% White Hart Hotel, Bocking End, BRAINTREE ☎ 01376 321401 31 ⇆ ❦

HARLOW   Map 05 TL40

Canons Brook Elizabeth Way CM19 5BE
☎ 01279 421482 Fax 01279 626393
Challenging parkland course designed by Henry Cotton. Accuracy is the key requiring straight driving from the tees, especially on the par 5 11th to fly a gap with out of bounds left and right before setting up the shot to the green.
18 holes, 6800yds, Par 73, SSS 72, Course record 65.
Club membership 850.

Visitors	may not play at weekends.
Societies	welcome Mon, Wed and Fri, must book in advance by telephone.
Green Fees	not confirmed.
Prof	Alan McGinn
Designer	Henry Cotton
Facilities	♣ ☕ ﹖ 🚵 ∅
Location	3m NW of junct 7 on M11
Hotel	★★★ 73% Swallow Churchgate Hotel, Churchgate St Village, Old Harlow, HARLOW ☎ 01279 420246 85 ⇆ ❦

North Weald Rayley Ln, North Weald CM16 6AR
☎ 01992 522118 Fax 01992 522881
Although only opened in November 1995, the blend of lakes and meadowland give this testing course an air of maturity.
18 holes, 6311yds, Par 71, SSS 70, Course record 66.
Club membership 500.

Visitors	must contact in advance, limited at weekends.
Societies	contact in advance.
Green Fees	£20 per round (£27.50 weekends).
Cards	💳
Prof	Michael Janes
Designer	David Williams
Facilities & Leisure	⊗ ♿ ♣ ﹖ ☕ ☕ ♣ 🚵 ∅ ℓ gymnasium.
Location	M11 exit 7,off A414 towards Chipping Ongar & Chelmsford
Hotel	★★★ 65% Harlow Moat House, Southern Way, HARLOW ☎ 01279 829988 119 ⇆ ❦

HARWICH   Map 05 TM23

Harwich & Dovercourt Station Rd, Parkeston CO12 4NZ
☎ 01255 503616 Fax 01255 503323
Flat parkland course with easy walking.

▶

9 holes, 5900yds, Par 70, SSS 69, Course record 58.
Club membership 420.

Visitors visitors with handicap certificate may play by prior arrangement, with member only at weekends.
Societies prior arrangement essential.
Green Fees £17 per 18 holes; £8.50 per 9 holes.
Facilities ⊗ ⊤Ⅲ 🏪 💺 ♀ ⚑ 🏠 🛒
Location Off A120 near Ferry Terminal

Hotel ★★ 71% The Pier at Harwich, The Quay, HARWICH ☎ 01255 241212 6 🛏 Annexe 7 🛏 🐾

INGRAVE   Map 05 TQ69

Thorndon Park CM13 3RH
☎ 01277 811666 Fax 01277 810645
Among the best of the Essex courses with a fine purpose-built clubhouse and a lake. The springy turf is easy on the feet. Many young trees now replace the famous old oaks that were such a feature of this course.
18 holes, 6492yds, Par 71, SSS 71.
Club membership 670.
Visitors must contact in advance, at weekends with member only.
Societies welcome Tue and Fri but must apply in writing.
Green Fees £50 per day; £35 per round.
Prof Brian White
Designer Colt/Alison
Facilities ⊗ 🏪 💺 ♀ ⚑ 🏠 🛒 🐾 ⚘
Location W side of village off A128

Hotel ★★★ 69% Posthouse Brentwood, Brook St, BRENTWOOD ☎ 0870 400 9012 145 🛏 🐾

LOUGHTON   Map 05 TQ49

High Beech Wellington Hill IG10 4AH ☎ 020 8508 7323
Short 9-hole course set in Epping Forest.
9 holes, 1477, Par 27, Course record 25.
Visitors welcome.
Green Fees not confirmed.
Prof Clark Baker
Facilities 🏠 🐾 ⚘
Location Close to M25 Waltham Abbey junct

Loughton Clays Ln, Debden Green IG10 2RZ
☎ 020 8502 2923
Hilly 9-hole parkland course on the edge of Epping Forest.
9 holes, 4652yds, Par 66, SSS 63, Course record 65.
Club membership 180.
Visitors must contact in advance.
Societies telephone in advance.
Green Fees not confirmed.
Prof Richard Layton
Facilities 🏪 💺 ♀ ⚑ 🏠 🐾 ⚘
Location 1.5m SE of Theydon Bois

Hotel ★★★ 62% Posthouse Epping, High Rd, Bell Common, EPPING ☎ 0870 400 9027 Annexe 79 🛏 🐾

MALDON   Map 05 TL80

Forrester Park Beckingham Rd, Great Totham CM9 8EA
☎ 01621 891406 Fax 01621 891406
Tight, undulating parkland course with tree-lined fairways and good views over the Blackwater estuary. Easy walking. Attractive 16th-century clubhouse.
18 holes, 6073yds, Par 71, SSS 69, Course record 69.
Club membership 1000.
Visitors must contact in advance but may not play before noon weekends & bank holidays.
Societies must apply in advance.
Green Fees not confirmed.
Cards 🖭 📠
Prof Gary Pike
Designer T R Forrester-Muir
Facilities ⊗ 🏪 💺 ♀ ⚑ 🏠 🛒 ⚘ ⚑
& Leisure hard tennis courts.
Location 3m NE of Maldon off B1022

Hotel ★★★ 69% Pontlands Park Country Hotel, West Hanningfield Rd, Great Baddow, CHELMSFORD ☎ 01245 476444 17 🛏 🐾

Maldon Beeleigh, Langford CM9 6LL ☎ 01621 853212
Flat, parkland course in a triangle of land bounded by the River Chelmer, the Blackwater Canal and an old railway embankment. Alternate tees on 2nd nine holes. Testing par 3 14th (166yds) demanding particular accuracy to narrow green guarded by bunkers and large trees.
9 holes, 6253yds, Par 71, SSS 70, Course record 71.
Club membership 380.
Visitors telephone to check availability, may only play with member at weekends. Handicap certificate required.
Societies intially telephone then confirm in writing.
Green Fees not confirmed.
Designer Thompson of Felixstowe
Facilities ⊗ ⊤Ⅲ by prior arrangement 🏪 💺 ♀ ⚑ 🏠
Location 1m NW off B1019

Hotel ★★★ 69% Pontlands Park Country Hotel, West Hanningfield Rd, Great Baddow, CHELMSFORD ☎ 01245 476444 17 🛏 🐾

ORSETT   Map 05 TQ68

Orsett Brentwood Rd RM16 3DS
☎ 01375 891352 Fax 01375 892471
A very good test of golf - this heathland course with its sandy soil is quick drying and provides easy walking. Close to the Thames estuary it is seldom calm and the main hazards are the prevailing wind and thick gorse. Any slight deviation can be exaggerated by the wind and a lost ball in the gorse results. The clubhouse has been modernised to very high standards.
18 holes, 6614yds, Par 72, SSS 72, Course record 68.
Club membership 750.
Visitors weekdays only. Must contact in advance and have a handicap certificate.
Societies must contact in advance.
Green Fees £40 per day; £27.50 per round.
Prof Paul Joiner
Designer James Braid
Facilities ⊗ ⊤Ⅲ 🏪 💺 ♀ ⚑ 🏠 🛒 🛒 ⚘
& Leisure coaching.
Location At junct of A13 off A128   ▶

| Hotel | ★★★ 64% Posthouse Basildon, Cranes Farm Rd, BASILDON ☎ 0870 400 9003 149 ⇌ ☞ |

Facilities ⊗ ⫴ ⬄ ♨ ♀ ⛳ 🛏 ⛷ 🚲 ⛴ ⛏
Location NW side of town centre off B184

| Hotel | ★★ 67% The Crown House, GREAT CHESTERFORD ☎ 01799 530515 8 ⇌ ☞ Annexe 10 ⇌ ☞ |

PURLEIGH   Map 05 TL80

Three Rivers Stow Rd, Cold Norton CM3 6RR
☎ 01621 828631 Fax 01621 828060
Set in landscaped wooded parkland, Kings Course is fully matured with 18-holes, affording good valley views over the Crouch, Blackwater and Roach rivers that give the club its name. With ponds and dog-legs among the challenges is ideal for beginners and seasoned golfers who have the opportunity to improve their short game. The Jubilee Course offers an alternative in both style and challenge.
Kings Course: 18 holes, 6296yds, Par 72, SSS 70.
Jubilee Course: 18 holes, 4583yds, Par 64, SSS 63.
Club membership 800.
Visitors   telephone before visit.
Societies   apply in writing or telephone.
Green Fees   Kings: £20 (£30 weekends); Jubilee £10.
Cards   ▭▭ ▭ ▭ ▭ ▭ ▭
Prof   Pat O'Connor
Designer   Hawtree
Facilities   ⊗ ⫴ ⬄ ♨ ♀ ⛳ 🛏 ⛏ 🏹 ⛷ 🚲 ⛴ ⛏
& Leisure   hard tennis courts, video swing analysis centre.
Location   2.5m from South Woodham Ferrers

| Hotel | ★★★ 69% Pontlands Park Country Hotel, West Hanningfield Rd, Great Baddow, CHELMSFORD ☎ 01245 476444 17 ⇌ ☞ |

ROCHFORD   Map 05 TQ89

Rochford Hundred Hall Rd SS4 1NW
☎ 01702 544302 Fax 01702 541343
Parkland course with ponds and ditches as natural hazards.
18 holes, 6292yds, Par 72, SSS 70, Course record 64.
Club membership 800.
Visitors   must have handicap certificate. Visitors may not play Tue morning (Ladies) or Sun without a member.
Societies   must contact in writing.
Green Fees   not confirmed.
Prof   Graham Hill
Designer   James Braid
Facilities   ⊗ ⬄ ♀ ♨ ⛳ 🛏 ⛴ ⛏
Location   W on B1013

| Hotel | ★★★ 68% Hotel Renouf, Bradley Way, ROCHFORD ☎ 01702 541334 24 ⇌ ☞ |

SAFFRON WALDEN   Map 05 TL53

Saffron Walden Windmill Hill CB10 1BX
☎ 01799 522786 Fax 01799 522786
Undulating parkland course, beautiful views.
18 holes, 6606yds, Par 72, SSS 72, Course record 63.
Club membership 950.
Visitors   must contact in advance and have a handicap certificate. With member only at weekends.
Societies   must contact in advance.
Green Fees   £30 per day/round.
Cards   ▭
Prof   Philip Davis

SOUTHEND-ON-SEA   Map 05 TQ88

Belfairs Eastwood Rd North, Leigh on Sea SS9 4LR
☎ 01702 525345 & 520202
Municipal parkland course run by the Borough Council. Tight second half through thick woods, easy walking.
18 holes, 5840yds, Par 70, SSS 68, Course record 68.
Club membership 350.
Visitors   contact for booking, correct dress code must be adhered to.
Societies   contact 01702 520202
Green Fees   £10.40 (£15.80 weekends).
Prof   Martin Foreman
Designer   H S Colt
Facilities   ⊗ ⫴ ⬄ ♀ ♨ ⛳ 🛏 ⛏ ⛏
& Leisure   hard tennis courts, 9 hole pitch & putt.
Location   Off A127

| Hotel | ★★ 70% Balmoral Hotel, 34 Valkyrie Rd, Westcliffe-on-Sea, SOUTHEND-ON-SEA ☎ 01702 342947 29 ⇌ ☞ |

Thorpe Hall Thorpe Hall Av, Thorpe Bay SS1 3AT
☎ 01702 582205
Parkland course with narrow fairways where placement rather than length is essential.
18 holes, 6286yds, Par 71, SSS 71, Course record 64.
Club membership 995.
Visitors   must contact in advance, with member only weekends & bank holidays.
Societies   apply in writing, only a certain number a year.
Green Fees   not confirmed.
Cards   ▭ ▭
Prof   Bill McColl
Facilities   ⊗ ⫴ ⬄ ♀ ♨ ⛳ 🛏 ⛏ ⛏ ⛷ ⛴
& Leisure   squash, sauna, snooker room.
Location   2m E off A13

| Hotel | ★★ 70% Balmoral Hotel, 34 Valkyrie Rd, Westcliffe-on-Sea, SOUTHEND-ON-SEA ☎ 01702 342947 29 ⇌ ☞ |

SOUTH OCKENDON   Map 05 TQ58

Belhus Park Belhus Park RM15 4QR
☎ 01708 854260 Fax 01708 851952
A well established 18 hole course set in beautiful parkland.
18 holes, 5589yds, Par 69, SSS 68, Course record 67.
Club membership 200.
Visitors   no restrictions. Must have proper golf shoes and shirts to be worn at all times. Booking advisable at weekends.
Societies   contact in writing or telephone
Green Fees   £9.50 (£14 weekends).
Prof   Gary Lunn
Designer   Capability Brown
Facilities   ⊗ ⫴ ⬄ ♀ ♨ ⛳ 🛏 ⛏ ⛴ ⛏
& Leisure   heated indoor swimming pool, solarium, gymnasium.

▶

Location	Off the B1335, follow brown tourist signs to course

Hotel	★★★ 69% Lakeside Moat House, High Rd, North Stifford, GRAYS ☎ 01708 719988 97 ⇋ ➤

Top Meadow Fen Ln, North Ockendon RM14 3PR
☎ 01708 852239
Set in the Essex countryside with a panoramic view of the area. Some holes are very difficult with the variable wind directions, especially 1st, 6th, 7th and 13th.
18 holes, 6348yds, Par 72, SSS 71, Course record 68.
Club membership 600.

Visitors	welcome Mon-Fri.
Societies	telephone in advance.
Green Fees	£12 per round inc breakfast.
Cards	〰️
Prof	Paul King/Kevin Smith
Designer	Burns/Stock
Facilities	⊗ ∭ ⓑ ┗ ♀ ♨ 🏠 ⌷ ✦ ➤ 🚜 ⌀ ⓣ
& Leisure	fishing.
Location	Junct 29 off M25, A127 towards Southend, B186 towards Ockendon, Fen Lane

Hotel	L Travelodge, EAST HORNDON ☎ 01277 810819 22 ⇋ ➤

STANFORD-LE-HOPE   Map 05 TQ68

St Clere's Hall London Rd SS17 0LX
☎ 01375 361565 Fax 01375 361565
All year round golf with views of the Thames, with several challenging par 3's, notably the 223 yard 13th.
18 holes, 6474yds, Par 72, SSS 71, Course record 71.
Club membership 460.

Visitors	welcome after 9.30am Mon-Fri, and 10am Sat & Sun. Telephone for times.
Societies	welcome Mon, Tue and Thu, telephone for details.
Green Fees	£15-£25 per day (£20-£35weekends).
Prof	David Wood
Facilities	⊗ ⓑ ┗ ♀ ♨ 🏠 ✦ 🚜 ⌀ ⓣ
Location	5m from M25 E of London on A13, take Stanford turn off in direction Linford, St Clere on the left

Hotel	★★★ 69% Lakeside Moat House, High Rd, North Stifford, GRAYS ☎ 01708 719988 97 ⇋ ➤

STAPLEFORD ABBOTTS   Map 05 TQ59

Stapleford Abbotts Horsemanside, Tysea Hill RM4 1JU
☎ 01708 381108 Fax 01708 386345
Abbotts course, provides a challenging test for players of all abilities as mature trees, large greenside bunkers and many lakes are all brought into play. The Priors course with its links-type layout gives a fresh challenge on each hole.
Abbotts Course: 18 holes, 6501yds, Par 72, SSS 71.
Priors Course: 18 holes, 5735yds, Par 70, SSS 69.
Friars Course: 9 holes, 1140yds, Par 27, SSS 27.
Club membership 800.

Visitors	Abbotts Course midweek only. Priors and Friars, 7 days per week. Advisable to telephone starter on 01277 373344 for Priors and 01277 381108 for Abbotts and Friars.

Societies	must be pre booked.
Green Fees	not confirmed.
Cards	〰️
Prof	Dominic Eagle
Designer	Henry Cotton/Howard Swan
Facilities	⊗ ∭ ⓑ ┗ ♀ ♨ 🏠 ⌷ ✦ 🚜 ⌀
& Leisure	sauna.
Location	1m E of Stapleford Abbotts, off B175

Hotel	★★★★ 70% Marygreen Manor, London Rd, BRENTWOOD ☎ 01277 225252 3 ⇋ ➤ Annexe 40 ⇋ ➤

STOCK   Map 05 TQ69

Crondon Park Stock Rd CM4 9DP
☎ 01277 841115 Fax 01277 841356
Undulating parkland course with many water hazards.
18 holes, 6585yards, Par 72, SSS 71, Course record 66.
Club membership 700.

Visitors	may play at weekends after mid-day.
Societies	telephone in advance.
Green Fees	not confirmed.
Cards	〰️
Prof	Paul Barham/Freddie Sunderland
Designer	Mr M Gillet
Facilities	⊗ ∭ ⓑ ┗ ♀ ♨ 🏠 🚜 ⌀ ⓣ
Location	On B1007, off A12

Hotel	★★★ 66% The Heybridge Hotel, Roman Rd, INGATESTONE ☎ 01277 355355 22 ⇋ ➤

THEYDON BOIS   Map 05 TQ49

Theydon Bois Theydon Rd CM16 4EH
☎ 01992 812460 & 813054 Fax 01992 813054
The course was originally nine-holes built into Epping Forest. It was later extended to 18-holes which were well-planned and well-bunkered but in keeping with the 'forest' tradition. The old nine in the Forest are short and have two bunkers between them, but even so a wayward shot can be among the trees. The autumn colours here are truly magnificent.
18 holes, 5480yds, Par 68, SSS 68, Course record 64.
Club membership 600.

Visitors	may not play Wed, Thu, Sat & Sun mornings, ring 01992 812460 in advance to be sure tee is available.
Societies	book through the secretary.
Green Fees	£25 per round.
Prof	R Hall
Designer	James Braid
Facilities	⊗ ∭ ⓑ ┗ ♀ ♨ 🏠 ⌷ ⌀
Location	2m from junct 26 on M25

Hotel	★★★ 62% Posthouse Epping, High Rd, Bell Common, EPPING ☎ 0870 400 9027 Annexe 79 ⇋ ➤

AA Hotels that have special arrangements with golf courses are listed at the back of the guide

TOLLESHUNT KNIGHTS   Map 05 TL91

Five Lakes Hotel Golf & Country Club Colchester Rd
CM9 8HX ☎ 01621 868888
Two 18-hole courses. The Links is a seaside course with a
number of greenside ponds and strategically placed bunkers,
while the Lakes is a championship course with large water
features and mounding between fairways.
*Links Course: 18 holes, 6250yds, Par 71, SSS 70,
Course record 67.*
*Lakes Course: 18 holes, 6767yds, Par 72, SSS 72,
Course record 63. Club membership 600.*

Visitors	must contact in advance.
Societies	must contact in advance.
Green Fees	not confirmed.
Cards	▭▬▬▬🄳 ▭▬
Prof	Gary Carter
Designer	Lakes Neil Cole
Facilities	⊗ ⅷ ⬥ ♫ ♀ ⚲ 🝆 🛱 ✈ ⅋ ♦
& Leisure	hard tennis courts, heated indoor swimming pool, squash, sauna, solarium, gymnasium, putting green.
Location	1.75m NE on B1026

Hotel	★★★★ 72% Five Lakes Hotel, Golf & Country Club, Colchester Rd, TOLLESHUNT KNIGHTS ☎ 01621 868888 114 ⇌ ♠

TOOT HILL   Map 05 TL50

Toot Hill School Rd CM5 9PU
☎ 01277 365523 Fax 01277 364509
Pleasant course with several water hazards and sand greens.
*18 holes, 6053yds, Par 70, SSS 69, Course record 65.
Club membership 400.*

FIVE LAKES
Hotel, Golf, Country Club & Spa

Two 18 hole courses.
The Lakes is a modern PGA championship course featuring
water on 8 of the last 10 holes. The Links is a seaside course
with a number of strategically placed bunkers.
The Hotel offers an excellent range of sporting and leisure
facilities including indoor heated swimming pool, sauna
and gym. For the more energetic tennis and squash.

Colchester Road, Tolleshunt Knights,
Maldon, Essex. CM9 8HX
Tel: 01621 868888 Fax: 01621 869696
E-mail enquiries@fivelakes.co.uk
Web http://www.fivelakes.co.uk

Visitors	welcome by prior arrangement, handicap certificate may be required.
Societies	Tue & Thu contact in advance.
Green Fees	£25 per round.
Prof	Mark Bishop
Designer	Martin Gillett
Facilities	⊗ ⅷ ⬥ ♫ ♀ ⚲ 🝆 🛱 ✈ ⅋ ♦
Location	7m SE of Harlow, off A414

Hotel	★★★ 62% Posthouse Epping, High Rd, Bell Common, EPPING ☎ 0870 400 9027 Annexe 79 ⇌ ♠

WITHAM   Map 05 TL81

Benton Hall Wickham Hill CM8 3LH
☎ 01376 502454 Fax 01376 521050
Set in rolling countryside surrounded by dense woodland,
this challenging course provides a severe test even to the best
golfers. The River Blackwater dominates the front nine and
natural lakes come into play on five other holes.
*18 holes, 6574yds, Par 72, SSS 72, Course record 64.
Club membership 470.*

Visitors	visitors can book 6 days in advance
Societies	telephone in advance.
Green Fees	not confirmed.
Cards	▭▬▬▬🄳 ▭▬
Prof	John Hudson/Peter McBride
Designer	Alan Walker/Charles Cox
Facilities	⊗ ⅷ ⬥ ♫ ♀ ⚲ 🝆 🛱 ✈ ⅋ ♦
Location	Witham turn off on A12, signposted

Hotel	★★★ 61% White Hart Hotel, Bocking End, BRAINTREE ☎ 01376 321401 31 ⇌ ♠

Braxted Park Braxted Park Estate CM8 3EN
☎ 01376 572372 Fax 01621 892840
A Pay and Play course in ancient parkland, surrounded by
lakes and extremely pretty countryside. Suitable for
beginners and experienced players.
9 holes, 2940yds, Par 35, SSS 34. Club membership 83.

Visitors	welcome weekdays from 7.30am onwards.
Societies	telephone to arrange.
Green Fees	not confirmed.
Prof	Tony Parcell
Designer	Sir Allen Clark
Facilities	⬥ ♀ ⚲ 🛱 🝆 ✈
& Leisure	fishing
Location	2m from A12 near Kelvedon/Witham, at Gt Braxted

Hotel	★★★ 61% White Hart Hotel, Bocking End, BRAINTREE ☎ 01376 321401 31 ⇌ ♠

WOODHAM WALTER   Map 05 TL80

Bunsay Downs Little Baddow Rd CM9 6RU
☎ 01245 222648 Fax 01245 223989
Attractive 9-hole public course, challenging for all abilities.
Also Par 3 course.
*9 holes, 2932yds, Par 70, SSS 68.
Badgers: 9 holes, 1319yds, Par 54. Club membership 400.*

Visitors	no restrictions.
Societies	Mon-Fri only. Must contact in advance.
Green Fees	£10 per 18 holes (12.50 weekends).
Cards	▭▬ ▭▬
Prof	Mickey Walker/Henry Roblin

▶

Designer John Durham
Facilities
Location 2m signposted from Danbury on A414

Hotel ★★★ 68% County Hotel, Rainsford Rd, CHELMSFORD ☎ 01245 491911 28 Annexe 8

Warren CM9 6RW ☎ 01245 223258 Fax 01245 223989
Attractive parkland course with natural hazards and good views.
18 holes, 6229yds, Par 70, SSS 70, Course record 65.
Club membership 765.
Visitors contact in advance, weekend pm only, Wed pm only.
Societies arrange by telephone, confirm in writing, weekdays ex Wed.
Green Fees not confirmed.
Prof Mickey Walker
Facilities by prior arrangement
Location 0.5m SW

Hotel ★★★ 68% County Hotel, Rainsford Rd, CHELMSFORD ☎ 01245 491911 28 Annexe 8

GLOUCESTERSHIRE

CHELTENHAM Map 03 SO92

Cotswold Hills Ullenwood GL53 9QT
☎ 01242 515264 Fax 01242 515263/4
A gently undulating course with open aspects and views of the Cotswolds.
18 holes, 6889yds, Par 71, SSS 74, Course record 67.
Club membership 750.
Visitors telephone in advance, handicap certificate preferred.
Societies must apply in writing or telephone.
Green Fees £30 per day: £25 per round (£36/£30 weekends).
Cards
Prof Norman Allen
Designer M D Little
Facilities
Location 3m SE on A435 and A436

Hotel ★★★ 68% Posthouse Gloucester, Crest Way, Barnwood, GLOUCESTER ☎ 0870 400 9034 122

Lilley Brook Cirencester Rd, Charlton Kings GL53 8EG
☎ 01242 526785 Fax 01242 256880
Undulating parkland course. Magnificent views over Cheltenham and surrounding coutryside.
18 holes, 6212yds, Par 69, SSS 70, Course record 61.
Club membership 800.
Visitors advisable to enquire of availability. Handicap certificate required.
Societies apply in writing.
Green Fees not confirmed.
Cards
Prof Forbes Hadden
Designer Mackenzie
Facilities
Location 2m S of Cheltenham on A435

Hotel ★★★★ 67% Cheltenham Park Hotel, Cirencester Rd, Charlton Kings, CHELTENHAM ☎ 01242 222021 144

Shipton Shipton Oliffe, Andoverford GL54 4HT
☎ 01242 890237 Fax 01242 820336
Deceptive, easy walking course situated in the heart of the Cotswolds giving a fair challenge and panoramic views.
9 holes, 2516yds, Par 34, Course record 33.
Visitors pay & play course no bookings taken.
Societies welcome.
Green Fees £6 per 9 holes (£7 weekends & bank holidays).
Facilities
Location On A436, south of junct with A40

Hotel ★★★ 64% Rising Sun Hotel, CLEEVE HILL ☎ 01242 676281 24

CHIPPING SODBURY Map 03 ST78

Chipping Sodbury BS37 6PU
☎ 01454 319042 Fax 01454 319042
Parkland courses of championship proportions. The old course may be seen from the large opening tee by the clubhouse at the top of the hill. Two huge drainage dykes cut through the course and form a distinctive hazard on eleven holes.

THE
CHELTENHAM PARK
· HOTEL ·

A Golfing Paradise with seven golf courses all within easy driving distance.
The luxury 4 star Cheltenham Park Hotel adjacent to the Lilley Brook Golf Course in the heart of the Cotswolds is certainly hard to beat for a Golfing Break.
Recently extended the Cheltenham Park Hotel is an attractive Georgian Manor House situated in its own colourful gardens two miles south of the fashionable spa town of Cheltenham.
The Egon Ronay recommended Lakeside Restaurant, Lilley Brook Bar and many bedrooms enjoy views over the gardens to the rolling hills of the golf course beyond.
During your stay you can enjoy complimentary use of our Leisure Club which includes a 15 metre indoor swimming pool, spa bath, steam room, sauna, cardio vascular and resistance gymnasiums.
Cirencester Road, Charlton Kings, Cheltenham, Gloucestershire GL53 8EA
Tel: 01242 222021 Fax: 01242 254880
E-mail: cheltenhampark@paramount-hotels.co.uk

New Course: 18 holes, 6912yds, Par 73, SSS 73, Course record 65.
Old Course: 9 holes, 6184yds, Par 70, SSS 69.
Club membership 800.

Visitors	no restriction on Old Course, must have a handicap certificate and may only play until after noon at weekends on New Course.
Societies	must contact in writing.
Green Fees	not confirmed.
Prof	Mike Watts
Designer	Hawtree
Facilities	⊗ ⊞ ⓑ ♥ ♀ ♨ 🏠 ☂ ⚑ 🛒 ⚬
Location	0.5m N

Hotel	★★ 70% Compass Inn, TORMARTON ☎ 01454 218242 & 218577 Fax 01454 218741 26 ⇔ ☞

CIRENCESTER
Map 04 SP00

Cirencester Cheltenham Rd, Bagendon GL7 7BH
☎ 01285 653939 Fax 01285 650665
Undulating open Cotswold course with excellent views.
18 holes, 6055yds, Par 70, SSS 69, Course record 65.
Club membership 800.

Visitors	restricted availability at weekends, contact professional shop in advance on 01285 656124.
Societies	telephone Secretary/Manager.
Green Fees	£25 per round/day (£30 per round/day weekends & bank holidays).
Prof	Peter Garratt
Designer	J Braid
Facilities	⊗ ⊞ ⓑ ♥ ♀ ♨ 🏠 ⚑ 🛒 ⚬ ☂
& Leisure	par 3 academy course.
Location	2m N of Cirencester on A435

Hotel	★★★ 68% Stratton House Hotel, Gloucester Rd, CIRENCESTER ☎ 01285 651761 41 ⇔ ☞

CLEEVE HILL
Map 03 SO92

Cleeve Hill GL52 3PW ☎ 01242 672025
Undulating and open heathland course affected by crosswinds.
18 holes, 6411yds, Par 72, SSS 71, Course record 69.
Club membership 450.

Visitors	bookings taken 7 days in advance. Limited play weekends.
Societies	telephone in advance.
Green Fees	not confirmed.
Prof	Dave Finch
Facilities	⊗ ⊞ ⓑ ♥ ♀ ♨ 🏠 ⚑ ⚬
Location	1m NE on B4632

Hotel	★★★ 64% Rising Sun Hotel, CLEEVE HILL ☎ 01242 676281 24 ⇔ ☞

COLEFORD
Map 03 SO51

Forest Hills Mile End Rd GL16 7BY
☎ 01594 810620 Fax 01594 810623
A parkland course on a plateau with panoramic views of Coleford and Forest of Dean. Some testing holes with the par-5 13th hole sitting tight on a water hazard, and the

challenging 18th with 2nd shot over large pond to a green protected by another pond and bunker - all in front of the clubhouse.
18 holes, 6740yds, Par 68, SSS 68, Course record 64.
Club membership 350.

Visitors	no restrictions.
Societies	contact in advance.
Green Fees	not confirmed.
Cards	🖸 🖸 🖸
Prof	Richard Ballard
Designer	A Stiff
Facilities	⊗ ⊞ ⓑ ♥ ♀ ♨ 🏠 ⚑ ☂ 🛒 ⚬ ☂
Hotel	★★★ 71% The Speech House, COLEFORD ☎ 01594 822607 15 ⇔ ☞ Annexe 16 (9 ☞)

Forest of Dean Golf Club & Bells Hotel Lords Hill
GL16 8BE ☎ 01594 832583 Fax 01594 832584
Established in 1973 and now matured into an extremely pleasant parkland course. Well bunkered with light rough, a few blind tee shots and water in play on several holes.
18 holes, 6033yds, Par 70, SSS 69.
Club membership 450.

Visitors	are required to book tee-off times.
Societies	must telephone in advance.
Green Fees	£16 per round (£18 weekends).
Cards	🖸 🖸 🖸 🖸 🖸
Prof	John Hansel
Designer	John Day
Facilities	⊗ ⊞ ⓑ ♥ ♀ ♨ 🏠 ⚑ ☂ 🛒 ⚬
& Leisure	hard tennis courts, bowling green.
Location	0.25m from Coleford town centre on B4431 Coleford to Parkend road

Hotel	★★★ 71% The Speech House, COLEFORD ☎ 01594 822607 15 ⇔ ☞ Annexe 16 (9 ☞)

DURSLEY
Map 03 ST79

Stinchcombe Hill Stinchcombe Hill GL11 6AQ
☎ 01453 542015 Fax 01453 549545
High on the hill with splendid views of the Cotswolds, the River Severn and the Welsh hills. A downland course with good turf, some trees and an interesting variety of greens. Protected greens make this a challenging course in windy conditions.
18 holes, 5734yds, Par 68, SSS 68, Course record 63.
Club membership 550.

Visitors	restricted at weekends. Must contact professional in advance 01453 543878.
Societies	must apply in advance.
Green Fees	£20 per 18 holes in summer (£25 weekends); £13 per 18 holes in winter (£25 weekends).
Prof	Paul Bushell
Designer	Arthur Hoare
Facilities	⊗ ⊞ ⓑ ♥ ♀ ♨ 🏠 ⚬
Location	1m W off A4135

Hotel	★★★ 66% Prince Of Wales Hotel, Berkeley Rd, BERKELEY ☎ 01453 810474 43 ⇔ ☞

Entries with a green background identify courses considered to be particularly interesting

GLOUCESTER   Map 03 SO81

Brickhampton Court Cheltenham Rd, Churchdown
GL2 9QF ☎ 01452 859444 Fax 01452 859333
27 holes, including the county's first intermediate course
(9-hole par 31) for the new and developing golfer, set in
undulating parkland. The Spa course offers a good golfing
challenge, featuring lakes, streams and well placed bunkers.
Spa: 18 holes, 6449yds, Par 71, SSS 71.
Glevum: 9 holes, 1859yds, Par 31.
Club membership 700.

Visitors	advance booking recommended, recognised golfing attire to be worn and evidence of golfing ability preferred.
Societies	contact for information and booking form.
Green Fees	Spa: £25 per day; £16 per round (£30/£22.50 weekends). Glevum: £10 per 18 holes; £6.50 per 9 holes (£12/£8 weekends).
Prof	Bruce Wilson
Designer	Simon Gidman
Facilities	⊗ ⅲ ᴛ ⓑ ♥ ♀ ᴧ ☐ ➔ ♣ ⚷ ᛖ
Location	Junct 11 M5, A40 towards Gloucester, at Elmbridge Court rdbt B4063 signed Churchdown, approx 2m

Hotel	★★★ 63% Hatherley Manor Hotel, Down Hatherley Ln, GLOUCESTER ☎ 01452 730217 56 ⇆ ♞

Jarvis Gloucester Hotel & Country Club Matson Ln,
Robinswood Hill GL4 6EA ☎ 01452 411331
Undulating, wooded course, built around a hill with
superb views over Gloucester and the Cotswolds. The
12th is a drive straight up a hill, nicknamed 'Coronary
Hill'.
18 holes, 6170yds, Par 70, SSS 69, Course record 65.
Club membership 600.

Visitors	can book up to 7 days in advance.
Societies	telephone in advance.
Green Fees	£19.50 (£25.50 weekends).
Cards	⬛ ⬛ 𝖵𝖨𝖲𝖠 ⬛ 🅖
Prof	Peter Darnell
Facilities & Leisure	⊗ ⅲ ᴛ ⓑ ♥ ♀ ᴧ ☐ ➔ ♣ ⚷ ᛖ hard tennis courts, heated indoor swimming pool, squash, sauna, solarium, gymnasium.
Location	2.5m SE of Gloucester, off B4073

Hotel	★★★ 69% Hatton Court, Upton Hill, Upton St Leonards, GLOUCESTER ☎ 01452 617412 17 ⇆ ♞ Annexe 28 ⇆ ♞

Rodway Hill Newent Rd, Highnam GL2 8DN
☎ 01452 384222
A challenging 18-hole course with superb panoramic views.
Testing front 5 holes and the par 3 13th and par 5 16th being
affected by strong crosswinds off the River Severn.
18 holes, 6070yds, Par 70, SSS 69, Course record 71.
Club membership 400.

Visitors	no restrictions.
Societies	telephone in advance.
Green Fees	not confirmed.
Cards	⬛ ⬛ 𝖵𝖨𝖲𝖠 🅖
Prof	Tony Grubb
Designer	John Gabb

Facilities	⊗ ⅲ ᴛ ⓑ ♥ ♀ ᴧ ☐ ➔ ♣ ⚷
Location	2m outside Gloucester on B4215

Hotel	★★★ 63% Hatherley Manor Hotel, Down Hatherley Ln, GLOUCESTER ☎ 01452 730217 56 ⇆ ♞

LYDNEY   Map 03 SO60

Lydney Lakeside Av GL15 5QA ☎ 01594 842614
Flat parkland/meadowland course with prevailing wind along
fairways.
9 holes, 5298yds, Par 66, SSS 66, Course record 63.
Club membership 350.

Visitors	with member only at weekends & bank holidays.
Societies	apply in writing to the Secretary.
Green Fees	not confirmed.
Facilities	ᴧ
Location	SE side of town centre

Hotel	★★★ 71% The Speech House, COLEFORD ☎ 01594 822607 15 ⇆ ♞ Annexe 16 (9 ♞)

MINCHINHAMPTON   Map 03 SO80

Minchinhampton (New Course) New Course GL6 9BE
☎ 01453 833866 Fax 01453 833860
The Cherington course is set in undulating upland. Large
contoured greens, pot bunkers, and, at times, a stiff breeze
present a very fair test of skill. The Avening course has a
variety of holes including water on the 10th and 13th.
Avening: 18 holes, 6279yds, Par 70, SSS 70,
Course record 65.
Cherington: 18 holes, 6320yds, Par 71, SSS 70.
Club membership 1200.

Visitors	must contact in advance.
Societies	must contact by telephone.
Green Fees	not confirmed.
Prof	Chris Steele
Designer	Hawtree & Son
Facilities	⊗ ⅲ ᴛ ⓑ ♥ ♀ ᴧ ☐ ➔ ♣ ⚷ ᛖ
Location	2m SE

Hotel	★★★ 69% Burleigh Court, Minchinhampton, STROUD ☎ 01453 883804 11 ⇆ ♞ Annexe 7 ⇆ ♞

Minchinhampton (Old Course) Old Course GL6 9AQ
☎ 01453 832642 & 836382
An open grassland course 600 feet above sea level. The
numerous humps and hollows around the greens tests the
golfer's ability to play a variety of shots - often in difficult
windy conditions. Panoramic Cotswold views.
18 holes, 6019yds, Par 71, SSS 69.
Club membership 700.

Visitors	must contact in advance.
Societies	must contact in advance.
Green Fees	£12 per day (£15 weekends & bank holidays).
Cards	⬛ ⬛ 𝖵𝖨𝖲𝖠 ⬛ 🅖
Facilities	ᴧ ☐
Location	1m NW

Hotel	★★★ 69% Burleigh Court, Minchinhampton, STROUD ☎ 01453 883804 11 ⇆ ♞ Annexe 7 ⇆ ♞

NAUNTON
Map 04 SP12

Naunton Downs GL54 3AE
☎ 01451 850090 Fax 01451 850091
Naunton Downs course plays over beautiful Cotswold
countryside. A valley running through the course is one of
the main features, creating 1 par 3 hole that crosses over it.
The prevailing wind adds extra challenge to the par 5's
(which play into the wind), combined with small undulating
greens.
18 holes, 6078yds, Par 71, SSS 70, Course record 67.
Club membership 900.
Visitors　　must contact in advance.
Societies　　telephone for details.
Green Fees　not confirmed.
Prof　　　　Martin Seddon
Designer　　J Pott
Facilities　　⊗ ℿ ⌺ ▼ ♀ ♨ ➳ ⛳ ➳ ⚐
& Leisure　　hard tennis courts.
Location　　B4068 Stow/Cheltenham

Hotel　　★★★ Lords of the Manor, UPPER
SLAUGHTER ☎ 01451 820243　27 ⇆ ♙

PAINSWICK
Map 03 SO80

Painswick GL6 6TL ☎ 01452 812180
Downland course set on Cotswold Hills at Painswick
Beacon, with fine views. Short course more than
compensated by natural hazards and tight fairways.
18 holes, 4895yds, Par 67, SSS 65, Course record 61.
Club membership 480.
Visitors　　member only on Sat pm & Sun.
Societies　　must apply in advance.
Green Fees　£20 per day; £15 per round.
Cards　　　⚏ ▆▆ 🖭 ⚏
Facilities　　⊗ ℿ ⌺ ▼ ♀ ♨ ➳ ⛳ ⚐
Location　　1m N on A46

Hotel　　★★★ 78% Painswick Hotel, Kemps Ln,
PAINSWICK ☎ 01452 812160　19 ⇆ ♙

TEWKESBURY
Map 03 SO83

Stakis Puckrup Hall Hotel Puckrup GL20 6EL
☎ 01684 296200 & 217591 (golf shop) Fax 01684 850788
Set in 140 acres of undulating parkland with lakes, existing
trees and marvellous views of the Malvern hills. There are
water hazards at the 5th and a cluster of bunkers on the long
14th before the challenging tee shot across the water to the
par-3 18th.
18 holes, 6189yds, Par 70, SSS 70, Course record 63.
Club membership 500.

Visitors　　must be a regular golfer familiar with rules and
etiquette, must book a tee time, may book up to
5 days in advance.
Societies　　telephone in advance.
Green Fees　£25 per round (£30 weekends).
Cards　　　⚏ ▆ ▆▆ 🖭 ⚏ ⚏
Prof　　　　Kevin Pickett
Designer　　Simon Gidman
Facilities　　⊗ ℿ ⌺ ▼ ♀ ♨ ➳ ⛳ ➳ ⚐
& Leisure　　heated indoor swimming pool, sauna, solarium,
gymnasium.
Location　　4m N, on main A38

Hotel　　★★★ 66% Old Schoolhouse Hotel & Restaurant,
SEVERN STOKE ☎ 01905 371368
& 371464 Fax 01905 37159113 ⇆ ♙

Tewkesbury Park Hotel Golf & Country Club
Lincoln Green Ln GL20 7DN
☎ 01684 295405 Fax 01684 292386
A parkland course overlooking the Abbey and rivers
Avon and Severn. The par 3, 5th is an exciting hole
calling for accurate distance judgment. The hotel and
country club offer many sports and club facilities
including a well equipped gym with cardio theatre.
18 holes, 6533yds, Par 73, SSS 72, Course record 66.
Club membership 650.

Visitors　　must book in advance via pro shop/hotel
reservations.
Societies　　telephone initially.
Green Fees　not confirmed.
Cards　　　⚏ ▆ ▆▆ 🖭 ⚏
Prof　　　　Robert Taylor
Designer　　Frank Pennick
Facilities　　⊗ ℿ ⌺ ▼ ♀ ♨ ➳ ⛳ ➳ ⚐ ⚐ ⚐
& Leisure　　hard tennis courts, heated indoor swimming
pool, squash, sauna, solarium, gymnasium,
6 hole par 3 pitch & putt.
Location　　1m SW off A38

Hotel　　★★★ 68% Tewkesbury Park Hotel Golf &
Country Club, Lincoln Green Ln,
TEWKESBURY ☎ 01684 295405　78 ⇆ ♙

THORNBURY
Map 03 ST69

Thornbury Golf Centre Bristol Rd BS35 3XL
☎ 01454 281144 Fax 01454 281177
Two 18 hole pay & play courses designed by Hawtree and
set in undulating terrain with extensive views towards the
Severn estuary. The Low 18 is a Par 3 with holes ranging ▶

from 80 to 207 yards and is ideal for beginners. The High course puts to test the more experienced golfer. Excellent 25 bay floodlit driving range.
High Course: 18 holes, 6154yds, Par 71, SSS 69, Course record 70.
Low Course: 18 holes, 2195yds, Par 54, SSS 54.
Club membership 484.

Visitors	welcome at all times, telephone to reserve.
Societies	apply in writing.
Green Fees	£24 per day; £15 per round; £9.50 per 9 holes (£28/£18/£10.50 weekends & bank holidays).
Cards	🖸 💳 🖸 🖸
Prof	Simon Hubbard
Designer	Hawtree
Facilities	⊗ 🏋 ⬛ 💺 ♀ ♨ 🖶 ☂ 🛒 ➷ 🏌 ♐ ✝
Location	Off A38
Hotel	★★ 67% Thornbury Golf Lodge, Bristol Rd, THORNBURY ☎ 01454 281144 11 ⇄ 🐾

WESTONBIRT   Map 03 ST88

Westonbirt Westonbirt School GL8 8QG ☎ 01666 880242
A parkland course with good views.
9 holes, 4504yds, Par 64, SSS 64.
Club membership 150.

Visitors	no restrictions.
Societies	no reserved tees.
Green Fees	not confirmed.
Facilities	🖶
Location	E side of village off A433
Hotel	★★★ 70% Hare & Hounds Hotel, Westonbirt, TETBURY ☎ 01666 880233 24 ⇄ 🐾 Annexe 7 ⇄ 🐾

WICK   Map 03 ST77

Tracy Park Tracy Park, Bath Rd BS30 5RN
☎ 0117 937 2251 Fax 0117 937 4288
Two 18 hole championship courses on the south-western escarpment of the Cotswolds, affording fine views. Both courses present a challenge to all levels of player, with water playing a part on a number of occasions. The clubhouse dates back to 1600 and is a building of great beauty and elegance, set in the 221 acre estate of this golf and country club.
Crown Course: 18 holes, 6443yds, Par 70, SSS 70.
Cromwell Course: 18 holes, 6011yds, Par 70, SSS 70.
Club membership 900.

Visitors	no restrictions.
Societies	must telephone/write to Robert Ford or Tim Thompson Green
Green Fees	£24 per day; £18 per round (£30/£24 weekends).
Cards	🖸 💳 🖸 🖸
Prof	Tim Thompson Green
Designer	Grant Aitken
Facilities & Leisure	⊗ 🏋 🗄 ⬛ 💺 ♀ ♨ 🖶 ☂ 🛒 ➷ 🏌 ♐ ✝ hard tennis courts, squash.
Location	S side of village off A420
Hotel	★★★ The Queensberry Hotel, Russel St, BATH ☎ 01225 447928 29 ⇄ 🐾

WOTTON-UNDER-EDGE   Map 03 ST79

Cotswold Edge Upper Rushmire GL12 7PT
☎ 01453 844167 Fax 01453 845120
Meadowland course situated in a quiet Cotswold valley with magnificent views. First half flat and open, second half more varied.
18 holes, 6170yds, Par 71, SSS 71.
Club membership 800.

Visitors	preferable to contact in advance, at weekends may only play with member.
Societies	must contact in writing or telephone in advance.
Green Fees	£15 (£20 weekends).
Prof	David Gosling
Facilities	⊗ 🗄 ⬛ 💺 ♀ ♨ 🖶 ☂ 🏌 ♐
Location	N of town on B4058 Wotton-Tetbury road
Hotel	★★ 70% Egypt Mill Hotel, NAILSWORTH ☎ 01453 833449 8 ⇄ 🐾 Annexe 10 ⇄ 🐾

GREATER LONDON

Those courses which fall within the confines of the London Postal District area (ie have London postcodes - W1, SW1 etc) are listed under the county heading of **London** in the gazetteer (see page 175).

GREATER LONDON

ADDINGTON
Map 05 TQ36

The Addington 205 Shirley Church Rd CR0 5AB
☎ 020 8777 1055
Designed by Abercromby, the famous golf course architect, and not altered since. Thought and skill are required at every hole.
18 holes, 6242yds, Par 71, SSS 71, Course record 66.

Visitors	may not play weekends. Must belong to recognised club.
Societies	weekdays only, telephone for prior arrangement.
Green Fees	£35 per day weekdays only.
Designer	Abercromby
Facilities	⊗ ♨ ♀ ♨ ℰ

Hotel	★★★★ 69% Selsdon Park Hotel, Addington Rd, Sanderstead, CROYDON ☎ 020 8657 8811 204 ⇔ ↖

Addington Court Featherbed Ln CR0 9AA
☎ 020 8657 0281 (booking) & 8651 5270 (admin)
Fax 020 8651 0282
Challenging, well-drained courses designed by F. Hawtree. Two 18-hole courses, 9-hole course and an 18 hole Par 3 course designed to suit all standards.
Championship Course: 18 holes, 5577yds, Par 68, SSS 67, Course record 60.
Falconwood: 18 holes, 5472yds, Par 68, SSS 67.
9 Hole: 9 holes, 1804yds, Par 31.
Club membership 350.

Visitors	no restrictions. Advisable to phone in advance to play on Championship Course.
Societies	must telephone in advance.
Green Fees	Championship: £14.75 per round (£18 weekends). Falconwood: £12.75 per round (£16 weekends). 9 hole £8 (£9 weekends).
Cards	▨▨ ▨▨ ▨▨
Prof	Russ Critcher
Designer	Hawtree Snr
Facilities	⊗ ♨ ♨ ♀ ♨ ℰ ℱ ♞ ♨ ℰ ℓ
Location	1m S off A2022

Hotel	★★★★ 69% Selsdon Park Hotel, Addington Rd, Sanderstead, CROYDON ☎ 020 8657 8811 204 ⇔ ↖

Addington Palace Addington Park, Gravel Hill CR0 5BB
☎ 020 8654 3061 Fax 020 8655 3632
Hard-walking parkland course, with two (par 4) testing holes (2nd and 10th).
18 holes, 6286yds, Par 71, SSS 71, Course record 63.
Club membership 700.

Visitors	telephone in advance, must play with member at weekends & bank holidays.
Societies	Tue, Wed & Fri only, telephone in advance.
Green Fees	£30 per day.
Prof	Roger Williams
Designer	J H Taylor
Facilities	⊗ ♨ ♨ ♀ ♨ ℰ ℓ
Location	0.5m SW on A212

Hotel	★★★★ 69% Selsdon Park Hotel, Addington Rd, Sanderstead, CROYDON ☎ 020 8657 8811 204 ⇔ ↖

BARNEHURST
Map 05 TQ57

Barnehurst Mayplace Rd East DA7 6JU
☎ 01322 523746 Fax 01322 554612
Public parkland course with well matured greens. Easy walking.
9 holes, 5320yds, Par 66, SSS 66.
Club membership 300.

Visitors	restricted Tue, Thu, Sat (pm) & Sun.
Societies	by arrangement.
Green Fees	not confirmed.
Facilities	⊗ ♨ ♨ ♀ ♨ ℱ ℓ
Location	0.75m NW of Crayford off A2000

Hotel	★★★ 65% Posthouse Bexley, Black Prince Interchange, Southwold Rd, BEXLEY ☎ 0870 400 9006 105 ⇔ ↖

BARNET
Map 04 TQ29

Arkley Rowley Green Rd EN5 3HL
☎ 020 8449 0394 Fax 020 8440 5214
Wooded parkland course situated on highest spot in Hertfordshire with fine views.
9 holes, 6117yds, Par 69, SSS 69.
Club membership 450.

Visitors	may play weekdays only (ex Tue).
Societies	must contact in advance.
Green Fees	£22 per day/round.
Prof	Martin Porter
Designer	Braid
Facilities	⊗ ♨ ♨ ♀ ♨ ℰ ℓ
Location	Off A1 at Arkley sign

Hotel	★★★ 72% Edgwarebury Hotel, Barnet Ln, ELSTREE ☎ 020 8953 8227 47 ⇔ ↖

Dyrham Park Country Club Galley Ln EN5 4RA
☎ 020 8440 3361 Fax 020 8441 9836
Parkland course.
18 holes, 6369yds, Par 71, SSS 70, Course record 65.
Club membership 1200.

Visitors	must be guest of member.
Societies	Wed only, must book in advance.
Green Fees	not confirmed.
Prof	Bill Large

▶

Facilities ⊗ ✗ ⅃ 🏌 ♀ (all day) ⚐ ☂ ⚑ 🏌 ♂
& Leisure hard tennis courts, heated outdoor swimming pool, fishing, caddies available.
Location 3m NW off A1081

Hotel ★★★ 65% Posthouse South Mimms, SOUTH MIMMS ☎ 0870 400 9072 143 ⇆ ☍

Old Fold Manor Old Fold Ln, Hadley Green EN5 4QN ☎ 020 8440 9185 Fax 020 8441 4863
Heathland course, good test of golf.
18 holes, 6466yds, Par 71, SSS 71, Course record 66.
Club membership 520.
Visitors with member only weekends & bank holidays.
Societies must apply in writing.
Green Fees £27 per day; £20 per 18 holes;.
Prof to be appointed
Facilities ⊗ ✗ ⅃ 🏌 ♀ ⚐ ☂ ⚑ ♂
& Leisure snooker.
Location Off A1000 between Barnet/Potters Bar

Hotel ★★★★♨ 71% West Lodge Park Hotel, Cockfosters Rd, HADLEY WOOD ☎ 020 8216 3900 46 ⇆ ☍ Annexe 9 ⇆ ☍

BECKENHAM Map 05 TQ36

Beckenham Place Park The Mansion, Beckenham Place Park BR3 2BP ☎ 020 8650 2292 Fax 020 8663 1201
Picturesque course in the grounds of a public park. The course varies from open to tight surroundings with the back nine providing a challenge for both the novice and low handicapper. A water-filled ditch comes into play on several holes.
18 holes, 5722yds, Par 68, SSS 68.
Visitors booked tee times operate contact for details.
Societies apply in writing or telephone for Society pack.
Green Fees not confirmed.
Cards 🪪 🪪 🪪 🪪 🪪
Prof Huw Davis-Thomas
Facilities ⊗ ⅃ 🏌 ♀ ⚐ ☂ ⚑ ♂
& Leisure hard tennis courts.
Location Main Catford/Beckenham road, just off A21

Hotel ★★★ 70% Bromley Court Hotel, Bromley Hill, BROMLEY ☎ 020 8464 5011 115 ⇆ ☍

Langley Park Barnfield Wood Rd BR3 6SZ ☎ 020 8658 6849 Fax 020 8658 6310
This is a pleasant, but difficult, well-wooded, parkland course with natural hazards including a lake at the 18th hole.
18 holes, 6488yds, Par 69, SSS 71, Course record 65.
Club membership 700.
Visitors must contact in advance and may not play weekends.
Societies Wed & Thu only, telephone to book.
Green Fees not confirmed.
Prof Colin Staff
Designer J H Taylor
Facilities ⊗ ✗ ⅃ 🏌 ♀ ⚐ ☂ ⚑ ♂
Location 0.5 N on B2015

Hotel ★★★ 70% Bromley Court Hotel, Bromley Hill, BROMLEY ☎ 020 8464 5011 115 ⇆ ☍

BEXLEYHEATH Map 05 TQ47

Bexleyheath Mount Rd DA6 8JS ☎ 020 8303 6951
Undulating course.
9 holes, 5162yds, Par 66, SSS 66, Course record 65.
Club membership 330.
Visitors must contact Secretary in advance, may not play weekends.
Societies telephone in advance.
Green Fees £20 per round.
Facilities ⊗ ✗ ⅃ 🏌 ♀ ⚐
Location 1m SW

Hotel ★★★ 65% Posthouse Bexley, Black Prince Interchange, Southwold Rd, BEXLEY ☎ 0870 400 9006 105 ⇆ ☍

BIGGIN HILL Map 05 TQ45

Cherry Lodge Jail Ln TN16 3AX ☎ 01959 572250 & 572989 Fax 01959 540672
Undulating parkland course set 600 feet above sea level with panoramic views of the surrounding Kent countryside. An enjoyable test of golf for all standards. The 14th is 434 yards across a valley and uphill, requiring two good shots to reach the green.
18 holes, 6652yds, Par 72, SSS 73, Course record 69.
Club membership 700.
Visitors must contact in advance but may not play at weekends.
Societies must telephone in advance.
Green Fees not confirmed.
Prof Nigel Child
Designer John Day
Facilities ⊗ ✗ ⅃ 🏌 ♀ ⚐ ☂ ⚑ 🏌 ♂
Location 1m E

Hotel ★★★ 68% Kings Arms Hotel, Market Square, WESTERHAM ☎ 01959 562990 17 ⇆ ☍

BROMLEY Map 05 TQ46

Bromley Magpie Hall Ln BR2 8JF ☎ 020 8462 7014 Fax 020 8462 6916
Flat course, ideal for beginners.
9 holes, 2745yds, Par 70, SSS 67.
Visitors no restrictions.
Societies apply in writing.
Green Fees not confirmed.
Cards 🪪 🪪 🪪 🪪 🪪
Prof Alan Hodgson
Facilities ☂ ⚑ ♂
Location 2m SE off A21

Hotel ★★★ 70% Bromley Court Hotel, Bromley Hill, BROMLEY ☎ 020 8464 5011 115 ⇆ ☍

Shortlands Meadow Rd, Shortlands BR2 0PB ☎ 020 8460 8828 Fax 020 8460 8828
Easy walking parkland course with a brook as a natural hazard.
9 holes, 5261yds, Par 65, SSS 66, Course record 59.
Club membership 410.
Visitors must be guest of member.
Societies must contact in advance.
Green Fees £10 per day.

▶

Prof	John Murray
Facilities	⊗ ⏝ by prior arrangement 🛍 🍴 🏆 ⛳ 🏩 ✐
Location	0.75m W off A222

Hotel ★★★ 70% Bromley Court Hotel, Bromley Hill, BROMLEY ☎ 020 8464 5011 115 ⇋ 🐾

> **Sundridge Park** Garden Rd BR1 3NE
> ☎ 020 8460 0278 Fax 020 8289 3050
> The East course is longer than the West but many think the shorter of the two courses is the more difficult. The East is surrounded by trees while the West is more hilly, with good views. Both are certainly a good test of golf.
> *East Course: 18 holes, 6516yds, Par 71, SSS 71, Course record 63.*
> *West Course: 18 holes, 6019yds, Par 69, SSS 69, Course record 65.*
> *Club membership 1200.*
>
> | | |
> |---|---|
> | **Visitors** | may only play on weekdays. Must contact in advance and must have a handicap certificate. No advance booking necessary. |
> | **Societies** | must contact well in advance. |
> | **Green Fees** | £45 per day. |
> | **Prof** | Bob Cameron |
> | **Designer** | Willie Park |
> | **Facilities** | ⊗ ⏝ 🛍 🍴 🏆 ⛳ 🏩 ✐ |
> | **Location** | N side of town centre off A2212 |
>
> ---
>
> **Hotel** ★★★ 70% Bromley Court Hotel, Bromley Hill, BROMLEY ☎ 020 8464 5011 115 ⇋ 🐾

CARSHALTON — Map 04 TQ26

Oaks Sports Centre Woodmansterne Rd SM5 4AN
☎ 020 8643 8363 Fax 020 8770 7303
Public parkland course with floodlit, covered driving range.
18 Holes: 18 holes, 6025yds, Par 70, SSS 69, Course record 65.
The Oaks: 9 holes, 1443yds, Par 28, SSS 28.
Club membership 864.

Visitors	no restrictions weekdays. May not play mornings at weekends.
Societies	must apply in writing.
Green Fees	18 Hole: £13.50 (£16 weekends). The Oaks: £6.40 (£8 weekends).
Prof	Horley/Russell/Pilkington
Facilities	🛍 🍴 🏆 ⛳ 🏩 ✐ 🏹 ✐
& Leisure	squash.
Location	0.5m S on B278

Hotel ★★★ 65% Posthouse Croydon, Purley Way, CROYDON ☎ 0870 400 9022 83 ⇋ 🐾

CHESSINGTON — Map 04 TQ16

Chessington Garrison Ln KT9 2LW
☎ 020 8391 0948 Fax 020 8397 2068
Tree-lined parkland course designed by Patrick Tallack.
9 holes, 1400yds, Par 27, SSS 28.
Club membership 100.

Visitors	must book 7.30am-noon weekends only.
Societies	must telephone 1 month in advance.
Green Fees	not confirmed.
Designer	Patrick Tallack
Facilities	⊗ ⏝ 🛍 🍴 🏆 ⛳ 🏩 🏹 ✐ 🍷
Location	Opposite Chessington South Station nr Zoo

Hotel ★★ 64% Haven Hotel, Portsmouth Rd, ESHER ☎ 020 8398 0023 16 ⇋ 🐾 Annexe 4 ⇋ 🐾

CHISLEHURST — Map 05 TQ47

Chislehurst Camden Park Rd BR7 5HJ
☎ 020 8467 2782 Fax 020 8295 0974
Pleasantly wooded undulating parkland/heathland course. Magnificent clubhouse with historical associations.
18 holes, 5106yds, Par 66, SSS 65, Course record 61.
Club membership 800.

Visitors	with member only weekends.
Societies	weekdays only.
Green Fees	£25 per round/day.
Prof	Mark Lawrence
Designer	Park
Facilities	⊗ ⏝ by prior arrangement 🛍 🍴 🏆 ⛳ 🏩 🏹 ✐
Hotel	★★★ 70% Bromley Court Hotel, Bromley Hill, BROMLEY ☎ 020 8464 5011 115 ⇋ 🐾

COULSDON — Map 04 TQ25

Coulsdon Manor Hotel Coulsdon Court Rd CR5 2LL
☎ 020 8668 0414 Fax 020 8668 3118
Set in its own 140 acres of landscaped parkland.
18 holes, 6037yds, Par 70, SSS 68.

Visitors	must telephone up to 5 days in advance.
Societies	by arrangement.
Green Fees	not confirmed.
Cards	▨ ■ ■ ▨ 🔁 ▨ 🔁
Prof	David Copsey
Designer	Harry Colt
Facilities	⊗ ⏝ 🛍 🍴 🏆 ⛳ 🏩 🏹 🏒 🛺 ✐
& Leisure	hard tennis courts, squash, sauna, solarium, gymnasium.
Location	0.75m E off A23 on B2030

Hotel ★★★★ 77% Coulsdon Manor, Coulsdon Court Rd, Coulsdon, CROYDON ☎ 020 8668 0414 35 ⇋ 🐾

See advertisement on page 98

Woodcote Park Meadow Hill, Bridle Way CR5 2QQ
☎ 020 8668 2788 Fax 020 8668 2788
Slightly undulating parkland course.
18 holes, 6669yds, Par 71, SSS 72, Course record 66.
Club membership 650.

▶

Visitors handicap certificate required, contact professional for details. Visitors may not play weekends.
Societies must contact Secretary in advance.
Green Fees £40 per day; £30 per round.
Prof I Golding
Facilities ⌂ 🏠 ✓
Location 1m N of town centre off A237

Hotel ★★★ 65% Posthouse Croydon, Purley Way, CROYDON ☎ 0870 400 9022 83 ⇆ 🐾

CROYDON   Map 04 TQ36

Croham Hurst Croham Rd CR2 7HJ
☎ 020 8657 5581 Fax 020 8657 3229
Parkland course with tree-lined fairways and bounded by wooded hills. Easy walking.
18 holes, 6290yds, Par 70, SSS 70.
Club membership 800.

Visitors must contact in advance & have handicap certificate. With member only weekends & bank holidays.
Societies must book 1 year in advance.
Green Fees £37 per round/day.
Cards 🖃 💳
Prof Eric Stillwell
Designer Hawtree
Facilities ⊗ 🍴 ▬ ♀ ⌂ 🏠 🐾 ✓
Location 1.5m SE, between South Croydon and Selsdon on B269

Hotel ★★★★ 69% Selsdon Park Hotel, Addington Rd, Sanderstead, CROYDON ☎ 020 8657 8811 204 ⇆ 🐾

Selsdon Park Addington Rd, Sanderstead CR2 8YA
☎ 020 8657 8811 Fax 020 8651 6171
Parkland course. Full use of hotel's sporting facilities by residents.
18 holes, 6473yds, Par 73, SSS 71, Course record 63.
Visitors welcome, booking advisable, booking 1 week in advance for weekends.
Societies telephone in advance.
Green Fees not confirmed.
Cards 🖃 💳 💳 💳 🖃 ▤
Prof Malcolm Churchill
Designer J H Taylor
Facilities ⊗ 🍴 ▬ ♀ ⌂ 🏠 🐾 ✓ 🏏 🎯 ⛏ ✓ ⚑
& Leisure hard and grass tennis courts, outdoor and indoor heated swimming pools, squash, sauna, solarium, gymnasium.
Location 3m S on A2022

Hotel ★★★★ 69% Selsdon Park Hotel, Addington Rd, Sanderstead, CROYDON ☎ 020 8657 8811 204 ⇆ 🐾

Shirley Park 194 Addiscombe Rd CR0 7LB
☎ 020 8654 1143 Fax 020 8654 6733
This parkland course lies amid fine woodland with good views of Shirley Hills. The more testing holes come in the middle section of the course. The remarkable 7th hole calls for a 187-yard iron or wood shot diagonally across a narrow valley to a shelved green set right-handed into a ridge. The 13th hole, 160yds, is considered to be one of the finest short holes in the county.
18 holes, 6210yds, Par 71, SSS 70, Course record 66.
Club membership 600.
Visitors should contact in advance. With member only at weekends.
Societies by arrangement.
Green Fees £30 per day/round weekdays.
Prof Wraith Grant   ▶

Facilities ⊗ 🎿 🏌 💺 ⚲ ⛳ 🏠 ⛵ 🏌
& Leisure snooker.
Location E side of town centre on A232

Hotel ★★★★ 69% Selsdon Park Hotel,
Addington Rd, Sanderstead, CROYDON
☎ 020 8657 8811 204 ⇆ 🏳

DOWNE   Map 05 TQ46

High Elms High Elms Rd BR6 7JL
☎ 01689 853232 & 858175 bookings Fax 01689 856326
Municipal parkland course. Very tight 13th, 221 yds (par 3).
18 holes, 6210yds, Par 71, SSS 70, Course record 68.
Club membership 450.
Visitors no restrictions.
Societies telephone to book. Tel 01689 861813.
Green Fees not confirmed.
Cards 🟦 🟥 🟩 🟦 🟥
Prof Peter Remy
Designer Hawthorn
Facilities ⊗ 🎿 🏌 💺 ⚲ ⛳ 🏠 ⛵ 🏌 🏌
Location 2m E of A21

Hotel ★★★ 70% Bromley Court Hotel, Bromley
Hill, BROMLEY ☎ 020 8464 5011 115 ⇆ 🏳

West Kent West Hill BR6 7JJ
☎ 01689 851323 Fax 01689 858693
Partly hilly downland course.
18 holes, 6399yds, Par 70, SSS 70.
Club membership 700.
Visitors with member only at weekends. Must contact in
advance.
Societies must apply in writing.
Green Fees £40 per day; £30 per round.
Prof Roger Fidler
Designer W Fowler & J Abercrombie
Facilities ⊗ 🎿 by prior arrangement 🏌 💺 ⚲ 🏠 🏌
Location 0.75m SW

Hotel ★★★ 70% Bromley Court Hotel, Bromley
Hill, BROMLEY ☎ 020 8464 5011 115 ⇆ 🏳

ENFIELD   Map 04 TQ39

Crews Hill Cattlegate Rd, Crews Hill EN2 8AZ
☎ 020 8363 6674 Fax 020 8364 5641
Parkland course in country surroundings.
18 holes, 6250yds, Par 70, SSS 70, Course record 65.
Club membership 600.

Visitors all day Mon, 7-9.30am Tue-Fri and after 2pm
Wed & Fri, must play with member at
weekends. Handicap certificate required.
Societies Wed-Fri; must apply in writing.
Green Fees £34 per day; £23 per round.
Prof Neil Wichelow
Designer Harry Colt
Facilities ⊗ 🎿 🏌 💺 ⚲ ⛳ 🏠 ⛵ 🏌 🏌
Location 3m NW off A1005

Hotel ★★ 71% Oak Lodge Hotel, 80 Village Rd,
Bush Hill Park, ENFIELD ☎ 020 8360 7082
7 ⇆ 🏳

Enfield Old Park Rd South EN2 7DA
☎ 020 8363 3970 Fax 020 8342 0381
Parkland course. Salmons Brook crosses 7 holes.
18 holes, 6154yds, Par 72, SSS 70, Course record 61.
Club membership 700.
Visitors must contact the Professional in advance.
Societies must contact the secretary in advance.
Green Fees £25 per round.
Cards 🟦 🟥 🟩 🟦 🟥
Prof Lee Fickling
Designer James Braid
Facilities ⊗ 🎿 🏌 💺 ⚲ ⛳ 🏠 🏌
Location M25 jnct 24, A1005 to Enfield to rdbt with
church on left, right down Slades Hill, 1st left to
end

Hotel ★★ 71% Oak Lodge Hotel, 80 Village Rd,
Bush Hill Park, ENFIELD ☎ 020 8360 7082
7 ⇆ 🏳

Whitewebbs Park Whitewebbs Ln EN2 9JN
☎ 020 8363 4454
Gently undulating wooded parkland course with an attractive
brook running through four holes.
18 holes, 5782yds, Par 68, SSS 68, Course record 61.
Club membership 190.
Visitors can play all times, can book in advance
Societies must apply in writing or by phone to Course
Manager.
Green Fees £12 per round (£15 weekends).
Cards 🟦 🟥 🟩 🟦 🟥
Prof Peter Garlick
Facilities ⊗ 🎿 🏌 💺 ⚲ ⛳ 🏠 ⛵ 🏌
Location N side of town centre

Hotel ★★ 71% Oak Lodge Hotel, 80 Village Rd,
Bush Hill Park, ENFIELD ☎ 020 8360 7082
7 ⇆ 🏳

GREENFORD   Map 04 TQ18

C & L Golf & Country Club Westend Rd, Northolt
UB5 6RD ☎ 020 8845 5662
Parkland course.
18 holes, 4438yds, Par 64, SSS 63.
Club membership 150.
Visitors welcome, but may not play Sun mornings.
Societies contact for details.
Green Fees not confirmed.
Prof Richard Kelly
Designer Patrick Tallack
Facilities ⊗ 🎿 🏌 💺 ⚲ 🏌
& Leisure hard tennis courts, outdoor swimming pool,
squash, sauna, solarium, gymnasium.

▶

Location   Junct Westend Road/A40

Hotel   ★★★ 69% The Bridge Hotel, Western Av, GREENFORD ☎ 020 8566 6246 68 ⇔ ♠

Ealing Perivale Ln UB6 8SS
☎ 020 8997 0937 Fax 020 8998 0756
Flat, parkland course relying on natural hazards; trees, tight fairways, and the River Brent which affects 9 holes.
18 holes, 6216yds, Par 70, SSS 70, Course record 64.
Club membership 600.
Visitors   Mon-Fri only on application to pro shop.
Societies   Mon, Wed & Thu only by arrangement
Green Fees £30.
Prof   Ian Parsons
Designer   H S Colt
Facilities   ⊗ ▥ by prior arrangement ♣ ♥ ♀ ⚐ ↖ 🖪 🏌 ⛟ ⛳
Location   Off A40 travelling W from London

Hotel   ★★★ 69% The Bridge Hotel, Western Av, GREENFORD ☎ 020 8566 6246 68 ⇔ ♠

Horsenden Hill Whitton Av, Woodland Rise UB6 0RD
☎ 020 8902 4555
A well-kept, tree-lined short course.
9 holes, 1632yds, Par 28, SSS 28.
Club membership 135.
Visitors   no restrictions.
Societies   telephone for details.
Green Fees not confirmed.
Prof   Simon Hoffman
Facilities   ⊗ ▥ ♣ ♥ ♀ ⚐ 🖪 🏌 ⛳
Location   3m NE on A4090

Hotel   ★★★ 69% The Bridge Hotel, Western Av, GREENFORD ☎ 020 8566 6246 68 ⇔ ♠

Lime Trees Park Ruislip Rd, Northolt UB5 6QZ
☎ 020 8842 0442
Parkland course.
9 holes, 5836yds, Par 71, SSS 69.
Club membership 300.
Visitors   no restrictions, but advisable to book for weekends.
Societies   contact for details.
Green Fees not confirmed.
Prof   Ian Godleman
Facilities   ⊗ ♣ ♥ ♀ ⚐ 🖪 🏌 ⛳ ⛳
Location   300yds off A40 at Polish War Memorial/A4180 towards Hayes

Hotel   ★★★ 69% The Bridge Hotel, Western Av, GREENFORD ☎ 020 8566 6246 68 ⇔ ♠

Perivale Park Stockdove Way UB6 8TJ ☎ 020 8575 7116
Parkland course.
9 holes, 2667yds, Par 68, SSS 67.
Club membership 250.
Visitors   no restrictions.
Societies   one weeks notice required.
Green Fees £5.50 per 9 holes (£8.25 weekends & bank holidays).
Cards   ▭▬ ▭ ▬ ▭ ▨ 🖭
Prof   Peter Bryant
Facilities   ⚐ 🖪 🏌 ⛳
Location   E side of town centre, off A40

Hotel   ★★★ 67% Cumberland Hotel, 1 St Johns Rd, HARROW ☎ 020 8863 4111
31 ⇔ ♠ Annexe 53 ⇔ ♠

HADLEY WOOD   Map 04 TQ29

Hadley Wood Beech Hill EN4 0JJ
☎ 020 8449 4328 & 4486 Fax 020 8364 8633
A parkland course on the northwest edge of London. The gently undulating fairways have a friendly width inviting the player to open his shoulders, though the thick rough can be very punishing to the unwary. The course is pleasantly wooded and there are some admirable views.
18 holes, 6457yds, Par 72, SSS 71, Course record 67.
Club membership 600.
Visitors   handicap certificate required, may not play Tue mornings & Sat. Must contact in advance.
Societies   must contact in advance.
Green Fees on application.
Prof   Peter Jones
Designer   Alistair Mackenzie
Facilities   ⊗ by prior arrangement ▥ by prior arrangement ♣ ♥ ♀ ⚐ 🖪 🏌 ⛳ ⛳
Location   E side of village

Hotel   ★★★★♨ 71% West Lodge Park Hotel, Cockfosters Rd, HADLEY WOOD ☎ 020 8216 3900 46 ⇔ ♠ Annexe 9 ⇔ ♠

HAMPTON   Map 04 TQ17

Fulwell Wellington Rd, Hampton Hill TW12 1JY
☎ 020 8977 3844 & 020 8977 2733 Fax 020 8977 7732
Championship-length parkland course with easy walking. The 575-yd, 17th, is notable.
18 holes, 6544yds, Par 71, SSS 71.
Club membership 750.
Visitors   may not play Tue & weekends. Must contact in advance and have a handicap certificate.
Societies   must apply in writing.
Green Fees not confirmed.
Prof   Nigel Turner
Facilities   ⚐ 🖪 🏌 ⛟ ⛳
Location   1.5m N on A311

Hotel   ★★★ 69% Richmond Hill, Richmond Hill, RICHMOND UPON THAMES ☎ 020 8940 2247 & 940 5466 Fax 020 8940 5424 138 ⇔ ♠

HAMPTON WICK   Map 04 TQ16

Home Park KT1 4AD
☎ 020 8977 2423 Fax 020 8977 4414
Flat, parkland course with easy walking.
18 holes, 6584yds, Par 71, SSS 71.
Club membership 550.
Visitors   welcome all week subject to club competitions.
Societies   apply in writing.
Green Fees £22 per round (£25 weekends & bank holidays).
Prof   Len Roberts
Facilities   ⊗ ♣ ♥ ♀ ⚐ 🖪 ⛳
Location   Off A308 on W side of Kingston Bridge

▶

Hotel ★★★ 69% Richmond Hill, Richmond Hill, RICHMOND UPON THAMES
☎ 020 8940 2247 & 940 5466
Fax 020 8940 5424 138 ⇥ ♠

HILLINGDON
Map 04 TQ08

Hillingdon 18 Dorset Way UB10 0JR
☎ 01895 233956 & 239810 Fax 01895 233956
Parkland course west of London, with gentle undulations.
9 holes, 5490yds, Par 68, SSS 67.
Club membership 370.

Visitors	must contact in advance. May not play Thu, weekends, or bank holidays. Handicap certificate required.
Societies	must apply in writing.
Green Fees	£15 per 18 holes.
Prof	Phil Smith
Facilities	⊗ ⓑ ♥ ♀ ⚘ 🖩 ♂
Location	W side of town off A4020

Hotel ★★★ 70% Novotel, Junction 4 M4, Cherry Ln, WEST DRAYTON ☎ 01895 431431
178 ⇥ ♠

HOUNSLOW
Map 04 TQ17

Airlinks Southall Ln TW5 9PE ☎ 020 8561 1418
Meadowland/parkland course designed by P. Allis and D. Thomas.
18 holes, 6000yds, Par 71, SSS 69.
Club membership 500.

Visitors	welcome all times.
Societies	must apply in writing.
Green Fees	not confirmed.
Cards	▬ ▬ ▬ ▬ ▣
Prof	Tony Martin
Designer	P Alliss/D Thomas
Facilities	⊗ ⍦ ⓑ ♥ ♀ ⚘ 🖩 ♈ ⚒ ♂ ♩
& Leisure	Sports centre.
Location	W of Hounslow off M4 junc 3

Hotel ★★★ 65% Master Robert Hotel, Great West Rd, HOUNSLOW ☎ 020 8570 6261 94 ⇥ ♠

Hounslow Heath Municipal Staines Rd TW4 5DS
☎ 020 8570 5271
Heathland course in a conservation area, planted with an attractive variety of trees. The 15th hole lies between the fork of two rivers.
18 holes, 5901yds, Par 69, SSS 68, Course record 62.
Club membership 300.

Visitors	pay & play, bookings taken for weekends & bank holidays seven days in advance.
Societies	must telephone and confirm at least 14 days in advance.
Green Fees	not confirmed.
Prof	Joe Smith
Designer	Fraser M Middleton
Facilities	⊗ ⍦ ⓑ ♥ ⚘ 🖩 ♈ ♂
Location	On A315 towards Bedfont

Hotel ★★★★ 67% Forte Crest Heathrow, Sipson Rd, WEST DRAYTON ☎ 020 8759 2323
610 ⇥ ♠

ILFORD
Map 05 TQ48

Ilford Wanstead Park Rd IG1 3TR
☎ 020 8554 2930 Fax 020 8554 0822
Fairly flat parkland course with the River Roding running through it. The river borders four holes, and is crossed by three holes. Whilst not a relatively long course, the small greens, and many holes requiring brains rather than brawn, provide a challenging test to all ranges of golfer.
18 holes, 5299yds, Par 67, SSS 66, Course record 61.
Club membership 500.

Visitors	must contact in advance, book with pro on 020 8554 0094.
Societies	telephone for provisional date and booking form.
Green Fees	£20 per day; £16 per round (£19 per round weekends).
Cards	▬ ▬ ▬ ▣ ▣
Prof	S Dowsett
Designer	Whitehead
Facilities	⊗ ♥ ♀ ⚘ 🖩 ♂
Location	NW side of town centre off A12

Hotel ★★★ 66% County Hotel Epping Forest, Oak Hill, WOODFORD GREEN ☎ 020 8787 9988
99 ⇥ ♠

ISLEWORTH
Map 04 TQ17

Wyke Green Syon Ln TW7 5PT
☎ 020 8847 0685 (Prof) & 8560 8777 (Sec)
Fax 020 8569 8392
Fairly flat parkland course.
18 holes, 6211yds, Par 69, SSS 70, Course record 64.
Club membership 650.

Visitors	may not play before 3pm weekends and bank holidays, must have a handicap certificate or equivalent.
Societies	must apply in writing or telephone in advance.
Green Fees	£30 per day; £28 per round.
Prof	Neil Smith
Designer	Hawtree
Facilities	⊗ ⍦ ⓑ ♥ ♀ ⚘ 🖩 ♈ ♨ ⚒ ♂
Location	0.5m N on B454 off A4 at Gillette Corner

Hotel ★★★ 65% Master Robert Hotel, Great West Rd, HOUNSLOW ☎ 020 8570 6261 94 ⇥ ♠

KINGSTON UPON THAMES
Map 04 TQ16

Coombe Hill Golf Club Dr, Coombe Ln West KT2 7DF
☎ 020 8336 7600 Fax 020 8336 7601
A splendid course in wooded terrain. The undulations and trees make it an especially interesting course of great charm. And there is a lovely display of rhododendrons in May and June.
18 holes, 6293yds, Par 71, SSS 71, Course record 67.
Club membership 600.

Visitors	must contact in advance. With member only at weekends.
Societies	must book in advance.
Green Fees	£80 per 36 holes; £60 per 18 holes.
Cards	▬
Prof	Craig Defoy
Designer	J F Abercromby

▶

Facilities ⊗ ◼ ◼ ◼ ◼ ◼ ◼ ◼ ◼
& Leisure sauna.
Location 1.75m E on A238

Hotel ★★★ 70% Kingston Lodge Hotel, Kingston Hill, KINGSTON UPON THAMES ☎ 0870 400 8115 64

Coombe Wood George Rd, Kingston Hill KT2 7NS
☎ 020 8942 0388 Fax 020 8942 5665
Mature parkland course with seven varied and challenging par 3's.
18 holes, 5299yds, Par 66, SSS 66, Course record 61.
Club membership 660.
Visitors must play with member at weekends.
Societies Wed, Thu & Fri; must contact in advance.
Green Fees £35 per day; £23 per round (£15 after 5pm).
Cards
Prof David Butler
Designer Tom Williamson
Facilities by prior arrangement
Location 1.25m NE on A308

Hotel ★★★ 70% Kingston Lodge Hotel, Kingston Hill, KINGSTON UPON THAMES ☎ 0870 400 8115 64

Mitcham — Map 04 TQ26

Mitcham Carshalton Rd CR4 4HN
☎ 020 8648 4280 Fax 020 8647 4197
A wooded heathland course on a gravel base.
18 holes, 5935yds, Par 69, SSS 68, Course record 65.
Club membership 500.
Visitors must telephone & book in advance, restricted play at weekends.
Societies must phone in advance.
Green Fees not confirmed.
Prof Jeff Godfrey
Designer T Scott/T Morris
Facilities
Location 1m S

Hotel ★★★ 65% Posthouse Croydon, Purley Way, CROYDON ☎ 0870 400 9022 83

New Malden — Map 04 TQ26

Malden Traps Ln KT3 4RS
☎ 020 8942 0654 Fax 020 8336 2219
Parkland course with the hazard of the Beverley Brook which affects 4 holes (3rd, 7th, 8th and 12th).
18 holes, 6295yds, Par 71, SSS 70.
Club membership 800.
Visitors restricted weekends and bank holidays. Advisable to telephone.
Societies must apply in writing.
Green Fees not confirmed.
Prof Robert Hunter
Facilities
Location N side of town centre off B283

Hotel ★★★ 70% Kingston Lodge Hotel, Kingston Hill, KINGSTON UPON THAMES ☎ 0870 400 8115 64

Northwood — Map 04 TQ09

Haste Hill The Drive HA6 1HN
☎ 01923 822877 & 829808 Fax 01923 824683
Parkland course with stream running through. Excellent views.
18 holes, 5787yds, Par 68, SSS 68, Course record 67.
Club membership 250.

Visitors advised to book in advance 01923 825224
Societies must apply in advance.
Green Fees £12.50 per round (£17.50 weekends).
Cards
Prof Cameron Smilie
Facilities by prior arrangement
Location 0.5m S off A404

Hotel ★★★ 67% Quality Harrow Hotel, Roxborough Bridge, 12-22 Pinner Rd, HARROW ☎ 020 8427 3435 53 Annexe 23

Northwood Rickmansworth Rd HA6 2QW
☎ 01923 821384 Fax 01923 840150
A very old club to which, it is said, golfers used to drive from London by horse-carriage. They would find their golf interesting as present-day players do. The course is relatively flat although there are some undulations, and trees and whins add not only to the beauty of the course but also to the test of golf.
18 holes, 6553yds, Par 71, SSS 71, Course record 67.
Club membership 650.
Visitors must contact in advance. May not play weekends.
Societies must apply in writing.
Green Fees not confirmed.
Prof C J Holdsworth
Facilities
Location On main A404

Hotel ★★★ 67% Quality Harrow Hotel, Roxborough Bridge, 12-22 Pinner Rd, HARROW ☎ 020 8427 3435 53 Annexe 23

Sandy Lodge Sandy Lodge Ln HA6 2JD
☎ 01923 825429 Fax 01923 824319
A links-type, very sandy, heathland course.
18 holes, 6347yds, Par 71, SSS 71, Course record 64.
Club membership 780.
Visitors must contact in advance, may not play at weekends. Handicap certificate required. ▶

Societies   must telephone in advance.
Green Fees   not confirmed.
Prof   Jeff Pinsent
Designer   H Vardon
Facilities   ⊗ ⅷ ⅊ 🍴 🍺 ♀ 🛇 🏠 🦬 ⚑ ♥
Location   N side of town centre off A4125

Hotel   ★★★ 64% The White House, Upton Rd,
             WATFORD ☎ 01923 237316
             60 ⇔ ♥ Annexe 26 ⇔ ♥

ORPINGTON   Map 05 TQ46

Chelsfield Lakes Golf Centre Court Rd BR6 9BX
☎ 01689 896266 Fax 01689 824577
A downland course but some holes are played through the
orchards which used to occupy the site. The 9th and 18th
holes are separated by a hazardous lake.
18 holes, 6077yds, Par 71, SSS 69, Course record 64.
Warren: 9 holes, 1188yds, Par 27.
Club membership 438.
Visitors   must book in advance.
Societies   telephone in advance.
Green Fees   not confirmed.
Cards   ⬛ ⬛ ⬛ ▨ 🅖
Prof   N Lee/B Hodkin
Designer   M Sandow
Facilities   ⊗ ⅷ ⅊ 🍴 🍺 ♀ 🛇 🏠 ⚑ ♥
Location   Exit M25 junct 4, on A224 Court Rd

Hotel   ★★★ 70% Bromley Court Hotel, Bromley
             Hill, BROMLEY ☎ 020 8464 5011 115 ⇔ ♥

Cray Valley Sandy Ln, St Paul's Cray BR5 3HY
☎ 01689 837909 & 871490 Fax 01689 891428
An easy walking open parkland course comprising an 18 hole
par70 and a 9 hole par32. Challenging for all standards of
golfers.
18 hole: 18 holes, 5669yds, Par 70, SSS 67.
9 holes: 9 holes, 2140yds, Par 32.
Club membership 1000.
Visitors   no restrictions, may book up to 7 days in
             advance.
Societies   by arrangement.
Green Fees   £15 per 18 holes; £7.50 per 9 holes (£20/£10
             weekends).
Cards   ⬛ ⬛ ⬛ ▨ 🅖
Prof   Andy Langdon
Facilities   ⊗ ⅷ ⅊ 🍴 🍺 ♀ 🛇 🏠 🦬 ⚑ ♥
Location   1m off A20, Critley's Corner junction

Hotel   ★★★ 70% Bromley Court Hotel, Bromley
             Hill, BROMLEY ☎ 020 8464 5011 115 ⇔ ♥

Lullingstone Park Parkgate Rd, Chelsfield BR6 7PX
☎ 01959 533793 & 533794 Fax 01959 533795
Popular 27-hole public course set in 690 acres of undulating
parkland. Championship length 18-holes, plus 9-hole course
and a further 9-hole pitch and putt.
*Main Course: 18 holes, 6778yds, Par 72, SSS 72, Course
record 71.*
9 hole course: 9 holes, 2432yds, Par 33, SSS 31.
Club membership 400.
Visitors   telephone for details.
Societies   must telephone in advance.
Green Fees   not confirmed.

Cards   ⬛ ⬛ ⬛ ▨ 🅖
Prof   Mark Watt
Facilities   ⊗ ⅷ ⅊ 🍴 🍺 ♀ 🛇 🏠 ⚑ ♥
Location   Leave M25 junct 4 and take Well Hill turn

Hotel   ★★★ 70% Bromley Court Hotel, Bromley
             Hill, BROMLEY ☎ 020 8464 5011 115 ⇔ ♥

Ruxley Park Golf Centre Sandy Ln, St Paul's Cray
BR5 3HY ☎ 01689 871490 Fax 01689 891428
Undulating parkland course with public, floodlit driving
range. Difficult 6th hole, par 4. Easy walking and good
views.
18 holes, 5703yds, Par 70, SSS 68, Course record 63.
Club membership 1000.
Visitors   may book 7 days in advance and regular dress
             code expected.
Societies   telephone for details 01689 839677.
Green Fees   not confirmed.
Cards   ⬛ ⬛ ⬛ ▨ 🅖
Prof   Andy Langdon
Facilities   ⊗ ⅷ ⅊ 🍴 🍺 ♀ 🛇 🏠 🦬 ⚑ ♥
Location   2m NE on A223

Hotel   ★★★ 70% Bromley Court Hotel, Bromley
             Hill, BROMLEY ☎ 020 8464 5011 115 ⇔ ♥

PINNER   Map 04 TQ18

Grims Dyke Oxhey Ln, Hatch End HA5 4AL
☎ 020 8428 4539 Fax 020 8421 5494
Pleasant, undulating parkland course.
18 holes, 5600yds, Par 69, SSS 67, Course record 61.
Club membership 580.
Visitors   must contact in advance, may not play
             weekends.
Societies   by arrangement, booked in advance.
Green Fees   not confirmed.
Prof   John Rule
Designer   Braid
Facilities   ⊗ ⅷ ⅊ 🍴 🍺 ♀ 🛇 🏠 ⚑ ♥
Location   3m N of Harrow on A4008

Hotel   ★★★ 67% Cumberland Hotel, 1 St Johns Rd,
             HARROW ☎ 020 8863 4111
             ⇔ ♥ Annexe 53 ⇔ ♥

Pinner Hill Southview Rd, Pinner Hill HA5 3YA
☎ 020 8866 0963 Fax 020 8868 4817
A hilly, wooded parkland course.
18 holes, 6086yds, Par 71, SSS 69.
Club membership 710.
Visitors   are required to have handicap certificate on
             Mon, Tue & Fri. Public days Wed & Thu.
             Contact in advance.
Societies   Mon, Tue & Fri only, by arrangement.
Green Fees   £25 per day (£32 Sundays & bank holidays);
             £12 per round.
Prof   Mark Grieve
Designer   J H Taylor
Facilities   ⊗ ⅷ ⅊ 🍴 🍺 ♀ 🛇 🏠 ⚑ ♥
Location   2m NW off A404

Hotel   ★★★ 67% Quality Harrow Hotel, Roxborough
             Bridge, 12-22 Pinner Rd, HARROW
             ☎ 020 8427 3435 53 ⇔ ♥ Annexe 23 ⇔ ♥

PURLEY   Map 05 TQ36

Purley Downs 106 Purley Downs Rd CR2 0RB
☎ 020 8657 8347 Fax 020 8651 5044
Hilly downland course which is a good test for golfers.
18 holes, 6262yds, Par 70, SSS 70, Course record 64.
Club membership 650.

Visitors	must contact in advance & play on weekends only with member.
Societies	must contact in advance.
Green Fees	£35 per day; £25 per round.
Prof	Graham Wilson
Designer	J Taylor/H S Colt
Facilities	⊗ ⓑ ☕ ♀ ♣ 🖚 🛒 🏌
Location	E side of town centre off A235

Hotel   ★★★ 65% Posthouse Croydon, Purley Way, CROYDON ☎ 0870 400 9022 83 ⇔ ⌖

RICHMOND UPON THAMES   Map 04 TQ17

Richmond Sudbrook Park, Petersham TW10 7AS
☎ 020 8940 4351 8332 7914
A beautiful and historic wooded, parkland course on the edge of Richmond Park, with six par-3 holes. The 4th is often described as the best short hole in the south of England. Low scores are uncommon because cunningly sited trees call for great accuracy. The clubhouse is one of the most distinguished small Georgian mansions in England.
18 holes, 6007yds, Par 70, SSS 69.
Club membership 700.

Visitors	may not play weekends.
Societies	must apply in writing.
Green Fees	£45 per day; £27 per round weekdays.
Cards	🖃 ■ 🖃 🖃 🖃
Prof	Nick Job
Facilities	⊗ ⓂⓂ ⓑ ☕ ♀ ♣ 🖚 🏌 🛒 ⌖
Location	1.5m S off A307

Hotel   ★★★ 69% Richmond Hill, Richmond Hill, RICHMOND UPON THAMES
☎ 020 8940 2247 & 940 5466
Fax 020 8940 5424 138 ⇔ ⌖

Royal Mid-Surrey Old Deer Park TW9 2SB
☎ 020 8940 1894 Fax 020 8332 2957
A long playing parkland course. The flat fairways are cleverly bunkered. The 18th provides an exceptionally good par 4 finish with a huge bunker before the green to catch the not quite perfect long second.
Outer Course: 18 holes, 6343yds, Par 69, SSS 70, Course record 62.
Inner Course: 18 holes, 5544yds, Par 68, SSS 67.
Club membership 1250.

Visitors	may not play at weekends. Must contact in advance and bring a handicap certificate.
Societies	must apply in writing.
Green Fees	£43 per day winter; £65 per day summer.
Prof	David Talbot
Designer	J H Taylor
Facilities	⊗ ☕ ♀ ♣ 🖚 🏌 🛒 🛒 🏌
& Leisure	snooker.
Location	0.5m N of Richmond upon Thames off A316

Hotel   ★★★ 69% Richmond Hill, Richmond Hill, RICHMOND UPON THAMES
☎ 020 8940 2247 & 940 5466
Fax 020 8940 5424 138 ⇔ ⌖

ROMFORD   Map 05 TQ58

Maylands Golf Club & Country Park Colchester Rd, Harold Park RM3 0AZ
☎ 01708 346466 Fax 01708 373080
Picturesque undulating parkland course.
18 holes, 6361yds, Par 71, SSS 70, Course record 65.
Club membership 700.

Visitors	handicap certificate required.
Societies	Mon, Wed & Fri only, by arrangement.
Green Fees	£30 per day; £20 per round (£40/£30 weekends & bank holidays).
Prof	J Hopkin/T Wheals
Designer	H S Colt
Facilities	⊗ ⓂⓂ ⓑ ☕ ♀ ♣ 🖚 🏌 🛒 🏌
Location	Junct 28 off M25, 0.5m down A12 towards London, club on right hand side

Hotel   ★★★ 69% Posthouse Brentwood, Brook St, BRENTWOOD ☎ 0870 400 9012 145 ⇔ ⌖

Risebridge Golf Centre Risebridge Chase, Lower Bedfords Rd RM1 4DG ☎ 01708 741429 Fax 01708 741429
A well matured parkland golf course, with many challenging holes especially the long 12th, the Par 4 13th and Par 5 14th with water and a two tiered green.
18 holes, 6000yds, Par 71, SSS 70, Course record 66.
Club membership 300.

Visitors	no restrictions.
Societies	must telephone in advance.
Green Fees	£10.50 per round (£13.50 weekends).
Prof	Paul Jennings
Designer	Hawtree
Facilities	⊗ ⓂⓂ ☕ ♀ ♣ 🖚 🏌 🛒 ⌖
& Leisure	pitch & putt.
Location	Between Colier Row and Harold Hill

Hotel   ★★★ 69% Posthouse Brentwood, Brook St, BRENTWOOD ☎ 0870 400 9012 145 ⇔ ⌖

Romford Heath Dr, Gidea Park RM2 5QB
☎ 01708 740986 Fax 01708 752157
A many-bunkered parkland course with easy walking. It is said there are as many bunkers as there are days in the year. The ground is quick drying making a good course for winter play when other courses might be too wet.
18 holes, 6410yds, Par 72, SSS 70, Course record 64.
Club membership 693.

Visitors	with member only weekends & bank holidays. Must contact in advance & have handicap certificate.
Societies	must telephone in advance.
Green Fees	£35 per day; £25 per round.
Prof	Harry Flatman
Designer	H Colt
Facilities	⊗ ⓂⓂ by prior arrangement ⓑ ☕ ♀ ♣ 🖚 🏌
Location	1m NE on A118

▶

Hotel	★★★ 69% Posthouse Brentwood, Brook St, BRENTWOOD ☎ 0870 400 9012 145 ⇄ 🕏

RUISLIP   Map 04 TQ08

Ruislip Ickenham Rd HA4 7DQ
☎ 01895 638081 & 638835 Fax 01895 635780
Municipal parkland course. Many trees.
18 holes, 5700yds, Par 69, SSS 68, Course record 65.
Club membership 300.

Visitors	telephone in advance.
Societies	must contact in advance.
Green Fees	£17.50 per round.
Cards	💳 💳 💳 💳 💳 💳 💳
Prof	Paul Glozier
Designer	Sand Herd
Facilities	⊗ ⊓ ⓛ ⓛ ⚑ ⚑ ⚑ ⚑ ⚑ ⚑ ⚑
Location	0.5m SW on B466
Hotel	★★★ 67% Quality Harrow Hotel, Roxborough Bridge, 12-22 Pinner Rd, HARROW ☎ 020 8427 3435 53 ⇄ 🕏 Annexe 23 ⇄ 🕏

SIDCUP   Map 05 TQ47

Sidcup 7 Hurst Rd DA15 9AE ☎ 020 8300 2150
Easy walking parkland course with natural water hazards.
9 holes, 5722yds, Par 68, SSS 68.
Club membership 370.

Visitors	contact in advance and may not play weekends.
Societies	must contact in advance.
Green Fees	£18 per round.
Designer	James Braid
Facilities	⚑ ⚑
Location	N side of town centre off A222
Hotel	★★★★ 69% Swallow Hotel, 1 Broadway, BEXLEYHEATH ☎ 020 8298 1000 142 ⇄ 🕏

SOUTHALL   Map 04 TQ17

West Middlesex Greenford Rd UB1 3EE
☎ 020 8574 3450 Fax 020 8574 2383
Gently undulating parkland course.
18 holes, 6242yds, Par 69, SSS 69, Course record 64.
Club membership 700.

Visitors	must contact in advance and may not play at weekends.
Societies	must apply in advance.

Green Fees	on request.
Prof	I P Harris
Facilities	⊗ ⊓ ⓛ ⓛ ⓛ ⚑ ⚑ ⚑
& Leisure	squash.
Location	W side of town centre on A4127 off A4020
Hotel	★★★ 65% Master Robert Hotel, Great West Rd, HOUNSLOW ☎ 020 8570 6261 94 ⇄ 🕏

STANMORE   Map 04 TQ19

Stanmore 29 Gordon Av HA7 2RL ☎ 020 8954 2599
North London parkland course.
18 holes, 5860yds, Par 68, SSS 68, Course record 61.
Club membership 560.

Visitors	may not play weekends. Contact professional 0181 954 2646.
Societies	phone in advance for booking sheet.
Green Fees	not confirmed.
Prof	V Law
Facilities	⊗ ⓛ ⓛ ⚑ ⚑ ⚑ ⚑
Location	S side of town centre, between Stanmore & Belmont
Hotel	★★★ 67% Quality Harrow Hotel, Roxborough Bridge, 12-22 Pinner Rd, HARROW ☎ 020 8427 3435 53 ⇄ 🕏 Annexe 23 ⇄ 🕏

SURBITON   Map 04 TQ16

Surbiton Woodstock Ln KT9 1UG
☎ 020 8398 3101 (Secretary & 8398 6619 (Pro) Fax 020 83 39 0992
Parkland course with easy walking.
18 holes, 6055yds, Par 70, SSS 69, Course record 63.
Club membership 700.

Visitors	must call in advance, handicap certificate required. With member only at weekends & bank holidays. No visitors Tue am (Ladies Day).
Societies	Mon & Fri only. Apply year in advance.
Green Fees	summer: £30 per round; winter: £25.
Prof	Paul Milton
Designer	Tom Dunn
Facilities	⊗ ⓛ ⓛ ⚑ ⚑ ⚑ ⚑
Location	2m S off A3, take A309 from Hook junct of A3, turn left into Woodstock Lane
Hotel	★★ 64% Haven Hotel, Portsmouth Rd, ESHER ☎ 020 8398 0023 16 ⇄ 🕏 Annexe 4 ⇄ 🕏

TWICKENHAM   Map 04 TQ17

Strawberry Hill Wellesley Rd, Strawberry Hill TW2 5SD
☎ 020 8894 0165
Parkland course with easy walking.
9 holes, 4762yds, Par 64, SSS 62, Course record 59.
Club membership 300.

Visitors	must contact in advance, with member only at weekends.
Societies	must apply in writing.
Green Fees	not confirmed.
Prof	Peter Buchan
Designer	J H Taylor
Facilities	⊗ ⓛ ⓛ ⚑ ⚑ ⚑
Location	S side of town centre off A311

▶

Hotel   ★★★ 69% Richmond Hill, Richmond Hill,
RICHMOND UPON THAMES
☎ 020 8940 2247 & 940 5466
Fax 020 8940 5424 138 ⇆ ✿

Twickenham Staines Rd TW2 5JD
☎ 020 8783 1748 & 1698 Fax 020 8941 9134
Interesting tree lined parkland course with water feature.
9 holes, 3180yds, Par 36, SSS 69.

Visitors	must book in advance for weekends & bank holidays.
Societies	apply in advance
Green Fees	£7 per 9 holes.
Cards	▭ ▬ ▬ ▭ ▨ ▨
Prof	Suzy Watt
Facilities	⊗ ☷ ♥ ♀ 🏠 ⌐ ⌗ ⌐
& Leisure	putting green.
Location	2m W on A305

Hotel   ★★★ 69% Richmond Hill, Richmond Hill,
RICHMOND UPON THAMES
☎ 020 8940 2247 & 940 5466
Fax 020 8940 5424 138 ⇆ ✿

UPMINSTER   Map 05 TQ58

Upminster 114 Hall Ln RM14 1AU
☎ 01708 222788 (Secretary) 220000 (Pro)
Fax 01708 222788
The meandering River Ingrebourne features on several holes
of this partly undulating parkland course situated on one side
of the river valley. It provides a challenge for golfers of all
abilities. The clubhouse is a beautiful Grade II listed
building.
18 holes, 6076yds, Par 69, SSS 69, Course record 66.
Club membership 1000.

Visitors	contact in advance, may not play at weekends.
Societies	telephone initially.
Green Fees	not confirmed.
Prof	Neil Carr
Designer	W G Key
Facilities	⊗ ☷ ☷ ♥ ♀ 🏠 ⌐
Location	2m W from A127 junct with M25

Hotel   ★★★ 69% Posthouse Brentwood, Brook St,
BRENTWOOD ☎ 0870 400 9012 145 ⇆ ✿

UXBRIDGE   Map 04 TQ08

Stockley Park Stockley Park UB11 1AQ
☎ 020 8813 5700 (8561 6339 tee times) Fax 020 8813 5655
Hilly and challenging parkland championship course
designed by Trent Jones in 1993 and situated within two
miles of Heathrow Airport.
18 holes, 6548yds, Par 72, SSS 71.

Visitors	6 day in advance reservation facility.
Societies	please telephone for details.
Green Fees	£24 per round; £13 per 9 holes (£34/£18 weekends).
Cards	▭ ▬ ▬ ▨ ▨
Prof	Alex Knox
Designer	Robert Trent Jones Snr
Facilities	⊗ ☷ ♥ ♀ 🏠 ⌐
Location	2m N of junct4 M4

Hotel   ★★★★ 75% Crowne Plaza London -
Heathrow, Stockley Rd, WEST DRAYTON
☎ 01895 445555 458 ⇆ ✿

Uxbridge The Drive, Harefield Place UB10 8AQ
☎ 01895 237287 Fax 01895 813539
Municipal parkland course, undulating and tricky.
18 holes, 5750yds, Par 68, SSS 68, Course record 66.
Club membership 400.

Visitors	no restrictions.
Societies	by arrangement.
Green Fees	not confirmed.
Cards	▭ ▬ ▨ ▨
Prof	Phil Howard
Facilities	⊗ ☷ ☷ ♥ ♀ ☷ 🏠 ⌐ ☷ ☷ ⌐
Location	2m N off B467

Hotel   ★★★★ 75% Crowne Plaza London -
Heathrow, Stockley Rd, WEST DRAYTON
☎ 01895 445555 458 ⇆ ✿

WEMBLEY   Map 04 TQ18

Sudbury Bridgewater Rd HA0 1AL
☎ 020 8902 3713 Fax 020 8903 2966
Undulating parkland course very near centre of London.
18 holes, 6282yds, Par 69, SSS 70.
Club membership 650.

Visitors	must have handicap certificate. With member only at weekends.
Societies	must apply in writing.
Green Fees	not confirmed.
Prof	Neil Jordan
Designer	Colt
Facilities	⊗ ☷ ☷ ♥ ♀ 🏠 ☷ ☷ ⌐
Location	SW side of town centre on A4090

Hotel   ★★★ 69% The Bridge Hotel, Western Av,
GREENFORD ☎ 020 8566 6246 68 ⇆ ✿

WEST DRAYTON   Map 04 TQ07

Heathpark Stockley Rd UB7 9NA
☎ 01895 444232 Fax 01895 444232
Fairly large, testing, hilly par 4 course suitable both for
beginners and scratch players.
9 holes, 2032yds, Par 64, Course record 50.
Club membership 80.

Visitors	may not play before 11.15am weekends. Restricted play on club competition days. Telephone for details.
Societies	by arrangement.

▶

Green Fees £7 per round (£8 weekends & bank holidays).
Cards
Designer Niel Coles
Facilities ⊗ ℍ by prior arrangement ⓑ ☕ ♀ ⚂
🏨 ⛢ 🛄 ✓
& Leisure heated indoor swimming pool, sauna, solarium, gymnasium.
Location 1m SE off A408 via junct 4 on M4

Hotel ★★★★ 75% Crowne Plaza London - Heathrow, Stockley Rd, WEST DRAYTON
🏨 01895 445555 458 ⇄ ⛳

WOODFORD GREEN   Map 05 TQ49

Woodford Sunset Av IG8 0ST
🏨 020 8504 3330 & 8504 0553 Fax 020 8559 0504
Forest land course on the edge of Epping Forest. Views over the Lea Valley to the London skyline.
9 holes, 5806yds, Par 70, SSS 68, Course record 66.
Club membership 420.
Visitors advisable to contact in advance. May not play Sat or Sun afternoon.
Societies telephone for details.
Green Fees not confirmed.
Prof Ashley Johns
Designer Tom Dunn
Facilities ⊗ ☕ ♀ ⚂ 🏨
Location NW side of town centre off A104

Hotel ★★★ 66% County Hotel Epping Forest, Oak Hill, WOODFORD GREEN
🏨 020 8787 9988 99 ⇄ ⛳

GREATER MANCHESTER

ALTRINCHAM   Map 07 SJ78

Altrincham Stockport Rd WA15 7LP 🏨 0161 928 0761
Municipal parkland course with easy walking, water on many holes, rolling contours and many trees. Driving range in grounds.
18 holes, 6162yds, Par 71, SSS 69.
Club membership 350.
Visitors must book in advance via course office.
Societies by prior arrangement.
Green Fees not confirmed.
Cards
Prof Scott Partington
Facilities ⚂ 🏨 ⛢ ✓ ⛳
Location 0.75 E of Altrincham on A560

Hotel ★★★ 65% Cresta Court Hotel, Church St, ALTRINCHAM 🏨 0161 927 7272 138 ⇄ ⛳

Dunham Forest Oldfield Ln WA14 4TY
🏨 0161 928 2605 Fax 0161 929 8975
Attractive parkland course cut through magnificent beech woods.
18 holes, 6636yds, Par 72, SSS 72.
Club membership 680.
Visitors by prior arrangement. May not play weekends & bank holidays.

Societies apply in writing or telephone in advance.
Green Fees £40 per round; £45 per 27 holes (£45 per round weekends).
Cards
Prof Ian Wrigley
Designer Dave Thomas
Facilities ⊗ ℍ by prior arrangement ⓑ ☕ ♀ ⚂
🏨 ⛢ 🛄 🏌 ✓
& Leisure hard tennis courts, squash.
Location 1.5m W off A56

Hotel ★★★ 67% Quality Hotel Altrincham, Langham Rd, Bowdon, ALTRINCHAM
🏨 0161 928 7121 89 ⇄ ⛳

Ringway Hale Mount, Hale Barns WA15 8SW
🏨 0161 980 8432 (pro) & 0161 904 9609
Parkland course, with interesting natural hazards. Easy walking, good views.
18 holes, 6494yds, Par 71, SSS 71, Course record 67.
Club membership 700.
Visitors must have handicap certificate, may not play before 9.30am or between 1-2pm, play restricted Tue, Fri & Sat.
Societies Thu only May-Sep.
Green Fees £35 per round (£45 weekends and bank holidays).
Cards
Prof Nick Ryan
Designer Colt
Facilities ⊗ ℍ ⓑ ☕ ♀ ⚂ 🏨 ⛢ ✓
Location M56 junct 6, take A538 signposted Hale & Altrincham

Hotel ★★★ 65% Cresta Court Hotel, Church St, ALTRINCHAM 🏨 0161 927 7272 138 ⇄ ⛳

ASHTON-IN-MAKERFIELD   Map 07 SJ59

Ashton-in-Makerfield Garswood Park, Liverpool Rd WN4 0YT 🏨 01942 727267 & 719330
Well-wooded parkland course. Easy walking.
18 holes, 6250yds, Par 70, SSS 70.
Club membership 800.
Visitors with member only weekends & bank holidays. No visitors Wed.
Societies apply in writing.
Green Fees £28 per round.
Prof Peter Allan
Facilities ⊗ ℍ ⓑ ☕ ♀ ⚂ 🏨 ⛢ ✓
Location 0.5m W of M6 (junc 24) on A58

Hotel ★★★ 66% Posthouse Haydock, Lodge Ln, HAYDOCK 🏨 0870 400 9039 138 ⇄ ⛳

ASHTON-UNDER-LYNE   Map 07 SJ99

Ashton-under-Lyne Gorsey Way, Higher Hurst OL6 9HT
🏨 0161 330 1537 Fax 0161 330 1537
A testing, varied moorland course, with large greens. Easy walking. Three new holes have improved the course.
18 holes, 6209yds, Par 70, SSS 70, Course record 67.
Club membership 550.
Visitors must contact in advance, with member only weekends & bank holidays.
Societies apply in advance.
Green Fees not confirmed.

▶

Prof Colin Boyle
Facilities
Location N off B6194

Hotel ★★ 69% York House Hotel, York Place, Richmond St, ASHTON-UNDER-LYNE ☎ 0161 330 9000 24 ⇆ ⬧ Annexe 10 ⇆ ⬧

Dukinfield Lyne Edge, Yew Tree Ln SK16 5DF
☎ 0161 338 2340
Recently extended, tricky hillside course with several difficult Par 3s and a very long par 5.
18 holes, 5303yds, Par 67, SSS 66.
Club membership 400.
Visitors may not play on Wed afternoons & must play with member at weekends, advisable to contact in advance.
Societies apply in writing or telephone.
Green Fees not confirmed.
Prof Jason Peel
Facilities ⊗ 〣 ⮇ ⬧ ♟ ⚲ 🏠 ✍
Location S off B6175

Hotel ★★ 69% York House Hotel, York Place, Richmond St, ASHTON-UNDER-LYNE ☎ 0161 330 9000 24 ⇆ ⬧ Annexe 10 ⇆ ⬧

BOLTON   Map 07 SD70

Bolton Lostock Park, Chorley New Rd BL6 4AJ
☎ 01204 843067 & 843278 Fax 01204 843067
This well maintained heathland course is always a pleasure to visit. The 12th hole should be treated with respect and so too should the final four holes which have ruined many a card.
18 holes, 6237yds, Par 70, SSS 70, Course record 64.
Club membership 612.

Visitors not able to play Tue before 2.30pm or on competition days or before 10am and between 12-2pm.
Societies write or telephone in advance, not accepted Tue, Sat or Sun.
Green Fees £36 per day; £30 per round (£40/£33 weekends & bank holidays).
Prof R Longworth
Facilities ⊗ 〣 ⮇ ⬧ ♟ ⚲ 🏠 ✍
Location 3m W of Bolton, on A673

Hotel ★★★ 59% Posthouse Bolton, Beaumont Rd, BOLTON ☎ 08704 400 9011 101 ⇆ ⬧

Breightmet Red Bridge, Ainsworth BL2 5PA
☎ 01204 527381
Long parkland course.
9 holes, 6416yds, Par 72, SSS 71, Course record 68.
Club membership 350.
Visitors may not play Wed or weekends.
Societies welcome Mon, Tue, Thu & Fri only, apply in advance in writing.
Green Fees £15 (£18 weekends & bank holidays).
Facilities ⊗ 〣 ⮇ ⬧ ♟ ⚲
Location E side of town centre off A58

Hotel ★★★ 59% Posthouse Bolton, Beaumont Rd, BOLTON ☎ 08704 400 9011 101 ⇆ ⬧

Deane Broadford Rd, Deane BL3 4NS
☎ 01204 61944 (Professional) Fax 01204 651808
Undulating parkland course with small ravines on approaches to some holes.
18 holes, 5652yds, Par 68, SSS 67, Course record 64.
Club membership 470.
Visitors must be a member of a golf club or member's guest. Restricted weekends.
Societies must telephone in advance and confirm in writing.
Green Fees £20 per day (£25 weekends).
Prof David Martindale
Facilities ⊗ 〣 ⮇ ⬧ ♟ ⚲ 🏠 ✍
Location 1m from exit 5 on M61 towards Bolton

Hotel ★★★ 59% Posthouse Bolton, Beaumont Rd, BOLTON ☎ 08704 400 9011 101 ⇆ ⬧

Dunscar Longworth Ln, Bromley Cross BL7 9QY
☎ 01204 303321
A scenic moorland course with panoramic views. A warm friendly club.
18 holes, 6085yds, Par 71, SSS 69, Course record 65.
Club membership 600.
Visitors must telephone 01204 592992 in advance and have a handicap certificate.
Societies must apply in writing.
Green Fees £20 per round (£30 weekends & bank holidays).
Prof Gary Treadgold
Facilities ⊗ 〣 ⮇ ⬧ ♟ ⚲ 🏠 ✍
Location 2m N off A666

Hotel ★★★ 59% Posthouse Bolton, Beaumont Rd, BOLTON ☎ 08704 400 9011 101 ⇆ ⬧

Great Lever & Farnworth Plodder Ln, Farnworth BL4 0LQ
☎ 01204 656137 Fax 01204 656137
Downland course with easy walking.
18 holes, 6064yds, Par 70, SSS 69, Course record 67.
Club membership 600.
Visitors must contact in advance, weekend by prior arrangement.
Societies must contact in advance.
Green Fees not confirmed.
Prof Tony Howarth
Facilities ⊗ 〣 ⮇ ⬧ ♟ ⚲ 🏠 ⬎ ✍
Location 1m junct 4 M61

Hotel ★★★ 59% Posthouse Bolton, Beaumont Rd, BOLTON ☎ 08704 400 9011 101 ⇆ ⬧

Harwood Springfield, Roading Brook Rd, Harwood
BL2 4JD ☎ 01204 522878 & 524233 (Sec)
Mainly flat parkland course.
18 holes, 5778yds, Par 70, SSS 69.
Club membership 584.
Visitors	must be members of a golf club and hold a current handicap certificate. May not play at weekends.
Societies	contact the Secretary by telephone or in writing.
Green Fees	£20 per round.
Prof	A Rogers
Facilities	⊗ ⅷ ⅃ ☕ ♟ ⚐ 🏌
Location	2.5m NE off B6196

Hotel   ★★★ 59% Posthouse Bolton, Beaumont Rd,
BOLTON ☎ 08704 400 9011 101 ⇆ ♞

Old Links Chorley Old Rd, Montserrat BL1 5SU
☎ 01204 842307 Fax 01204 842307 ext 25
Championship moorland course.
18 holes, 6406yds, Par 72, SSS 72.
Club membership 600.
Visitors	must contact in advance and may only play weekends with member.
Societies	apply by letter or telephone.
Green Fees	not confirmed.
Prof	Paul Horridge
Designer	Dr Alistair MacKenzie
Facilities	⊗ ⅷ ⅃ ☕ ♟ ⚐ 🏌 ✎
Location	NW of town centre on B6226

Hotel   ★★★ 59% Posthouse Bolton, Beaumont Rd,
BOLTON ☎ 08704 400 9011 101 ⇆ ♞

Regent Park Links Rd, Chorley New Rd BL2 9XX
☎ 01204 844170
Parkland course.
18 holes, 6130yds, Par 70, SSS 69, Course record 67.
Club membership 200.
Visitors	must book 6 days in advance.
Societies	must telephone 01204 495421 in advance.
Green Fees	not confirmed.
Cards	💳
Prof	P A Wells
Facilities	⊗ ⅷ ⅃ ☕ ♟ ⚐ 🏌 🏌 ✎
Location	3.5m W off A673

Hotel   ★★★ 59% Posthouse Bolton, Beaumont Rd,
BOLTON ☎ 08704 400 9011 101 ⇆ ♞

BRAMHALL   Map 07 SJ88

Bramall Park 20 Manor Rd SK7 3LY
☎ 0161 485 3119 & 7101 (secretary) Fax 0161 485 7101
Well-wooded parkland course with splendid views of the
Pennines.
18 holes, 6043yds, Par 70, SSS 69.
Club membership 600.
Visitors	must contact in advance.
Societies	apply in writing.
Green Fees	not confirmed.
Prof	M Proffitt
Facilities	⊗ ⅷ ⅃ ☕ ♟ ⚐ 🏌 ✎
Location	NW side of town centre off B5149

Hotel   ★★★ 64% County Hotel Bramhall, Bramhall
Ln South, BRAMHALL ☎ 0161 455 9988
65 ⇆ ♞

Bramhall Ladythorn Rd SK7 2EY
☎ 0161 439 6092 Fax 0161 439 0264
Undulating parkland course, easy walking.
18 holes, 6340yds, Par 70, SSS 70.
Club membership 700.
Visitors	must contact in advance.
Societies	apply in writing.
Green Fees	£28 per round (£35 weekends & bank holidays).
Prof	Richard Green
Facilities	⊗ ⅃ ☕ ♟ ⚐ 🏌 🏌
Location	E side of town centre off A5102

Hotel   ★★★ 64% County Hotel Bramhall, Bramhall
Ln South, BRAMHALL ☎ 0161 455 9988
65 ⇆ ♞

BROMLEY CROSS   Map 07 SD71

Turton Wood End Farm, Chapeltown Rd BL7 9QH
☎ 01204 852235
Moorland course with panoramic views. A wide variety of
holes which challenge any golfer's technique.
18 holes, 6159yds, Par 70, SSS 70, Course record 70.
Club membership 450.
Visitors	avoid 11.30-2pm Wed Ladies day. Sat tee available after last competition. Restricted Sun.
Societies	must contact in writing.
Green Fees	£18 per day (£22 per round weekends & bank holidays).
Designer	Alex Herd
Facilities	⊗ ⅷ by prior arrangement ⅃ ☕ ♟ ⚐
Location	3m N on A666

Hotel   ★★★ 59% Posthouse Bolton, Beaumont Rd,
BOLTON ☎ 08704 400 9011 101 ⇆ ♞

BURY   Map 07 SD81

Bury Unsworth Hall, Blackford Bridge, Manchester Rd
BL9 9TJ ☎ 0161 766 4897 Fax 0161 796 3480
Moorland course, difficult in part. Tight and good test of
golf.
18 holes, 5961yds, Par 69, SSS 69, Course record 64.
Club membership 650.
Visitors	may not normally play at weekends. Must contact in advance.
Societies	telephone 0161 766 4897.
Green Fees	not confirmed.
Designer	Mackenzie
Facilities	⊗ ⅷ ⅃ ☕ ♟ ⚐ 🏌 ✎
Location	2m S on A56

Hotel   ★★★ 65% Bolholt Country Park Hotel,
Walshaw Rd, BURY ☎ 0161 762 4000
66 ⇆ ♞

Lowes Park Hilltop, Lowes Rd BL9 6SU
☎ 0161 764 1231 Fax 0161 763 9503
Moorland course, with easy walking. Exposed outlook with
good views.
9 holes, 6009yds, Par 70, SSS 69, Course record 65.
Club membership 400.

▶

Visitors may not play Wed & Sat, by appointment Sun. Must contact in advance.
Societies apply in writing.
Green Fees not confirmed.
Facilities ⊗ ⅲ ᴸ ♥ ♀ ⅄
Location N side of town centre off A56

Hotel ★★★ 65% Bolholt Country Park Hotel, Walshaw Rd, BURY ☎ 0161 762 4000 66 ⊸ ⋔

Walmersley Garretts Close, Walmersley BL9 6TE
☎ 0161 764 1429 & 0161 764 7770 Fax 01706 827618
Moorland hillside course, with wide fairways, large greens and extensive views. Testing holes: 2nd (484 yds) par 5; 5th par 4 with severe dogleg and various hazards.
18 holes, 5341yds, Par 69, SSS 67.
Club membership 475.
Visitors welcome by arrangement with secretary. May only play with member at weekend,
Societies must apply in writing.
Green Fees £20 per day.
Prof S Crake
Designer S Marnoch
Facilities ⊗ ⅲ ᴸ ♥ ♀ ⅄ ⌂
Location 2m N off A56

CHEADLE
Map 07 SJ88

Cheadle Cheadle Rd SK8 1HW ☎ 0161 491 4452
Parkland course with hazards on every hole, from sand bunkers and copses to a stream across six of the fairways.
9 holes, 5006yds, Par 64, SSS 65.
Club membership 425.
Visitors may not play Tue & Sat, & restricted Sun. Must contact in advance and have a handicap certificate and be member of a bona-fide golf club.
Societies apply in writing to secretary
Green Fees not confirmed.
Prof S Booth
Designer T Renouf
Facilities ⊗ ⅲ ᴸ ♥ ♀ ⅄ ⌂ ⌀
Location S side of village off A5149

Hotel ★★ 67% The Wycliffe Hotel, 74 Edgeley Rd, Edgeley, STOCKPORT ☎ 0161 477 5395 20 ⊸ ⋔

DENTON
Map 07 SJ99

Denton Manchester Rd M34 2GG ☎ 0161 336 3218
Easy, flat parkland course with brook running through.
Notable hole is one called 'Death and Glory'.
18 holes, 6541yds, Par 72, SSS 71, Course record 66.
Club membership 585.
Visitors must contact in advance & may not play summer weekends.
Societies apply in advance.
Green Fees not confirmed.
Prof M Hollingworth
Designer R McCauley
Facilities ᴸ ♥ ♀ ⅄ ⌂ ⌀
Location 1.5m W on A57

Hotel ★★ 69% York House Hotel, York Place, Richmond St, ASHTON-UNDER-LYNE
☎ 0161 330 9000 24 ⊸ ⋔ Annexe 10 ⊸ ⋔

FAILSWORTH
Map 07 SD80

Brookdale Medlock Rd M35 9WQ
☎ 0161 681 4534 Fax 0161 681 4534
Undulating parkland course, with river crossed 5 times in play. Hard walking.
18 holes, 5841yds, Par 68, SSS 68, Course record 64.
Club membership 600.
Visitors advisable to contact in advance. May only play as guest of member at weekends.
Societies must contact in advance.
Green Fees not confirmed.
Prof Tony Cuppello
Facilities ⊗ ⅲ by prior arrangement ᴸ ♥ ♀ ⅄ ⌂ ⌀
Location N side of Manchester

Hotel ★★ 69% York House Hotel, York Place, Richmond St, ASHTON-UNDER-LYNE
☎ 0161 330 9000 24 ⊸ ⋔ Annexe 10 ⊸ ⋔

FLIXTON
Map 07 SJ79

William Wroe Municipal Pennybridge Ln, Flixton Rd M41 5DX ☎ 0161 748 8680
Parkland course, with easy walking.
18 holes, 4395yds, Par 68, SSS 65.
Visitors must book in advance.
Societies contact for details.
Green Fees not confirmed.
Prof Scott Partington
Facilities ⅄ ⌂ ⋔
Location E side of village off B5158

Hotel ★★★ 60% Trafford Hall Hotel, 23 Talbot Rd, Old Trafford, MANCHESTER
☎ 0161 848 7791 31 ⊸ ⋔ Annexe 3 ⊸ ⋔

GATLEY
Map 07 SJ88

Gatley Waterfall Farm, Styal Rd, Heald Green SK8 3TW
☎ 0161 437 2091
Parkland course. Moderately testing.
9 holes, 5934yds, Par 68, SSS 68.
Visitors may not play Tue & Sat. With member only weekends. Handicap certificate required.
Societies apply in writing.
Green Fees not confirmed.
Prof Simon Reeves
Facilities ⊗ ⅲ ᴸ ♥ ♀ ⅄ ⌂
Location S side of village off B5166

Hotel ★★★★ 65% Belfry House Hotel, Stanley Rd, HANDFORTH ☎ 0161 437 0511 80 ⊸ ⋔

HALE
Map 07 SJ78

Hale Rappax Rd WA15 0NU ☎ 0161 980 4225
Beautiful, undulating parkland course, with the River Bollin winding round fairways.
9 holes, 5780yds, Par 70, SSS 68, Course record 65.
Club membership 300.

▶

Visitors may not play before 4.30pm Thu; with member only weekends.
Societies apply in writing
Green Fees not confirmed.
Prof Mike Grantham
Facilities ⊗ ⅏ by prior arrangement ⤵ ♥ ♀ 👤 🖼
Location Off Bankhall Lane close to Altrincham Priory Hospital

Hotel ★★★ 67% Quality Hotel Altrincham, Langham Rd, Bowdon, ALTRINCHAM ☎ 0161 928 7121 89 ⇆ ♞

HAZEL GROVE   Map 07 SJ98

Hazel Grove Buxton Rd SK7 6LU ☎ 0161 483 3978
Testing parkland course with tricky greens and water hazards coming into play on several holes.
18 holes, 6310yds, Par 71, SSS 71, Course record 62.
Club membership 600.
Visitors must contact in advance tel: 0161 483 7272.
Societies must apply in writing, Thu & Fri only.
Green Fees £30 per day (£35 weekends & bank holidays).
Prof M E Hill
Facilities ⊗ ⅏ ⤵ ♥ ♀ 👤 🖼 ♉ ♂
Location 1m E off A6

Hotel ★★★ 64% County Hotel Bramhall, Bramhall Ln South, BRAMHALL ☎ 0161 455 9988 65 ⇆ ♞

HINDLEY   Map 07 SD60

Hindley Hall Hall Ln WN2 2SQ
☎ 01942 255131 Fax 01942 253871
Parkland course with mostly easy walking.
18 holes, 5913yds, Par 69, SSS 68, Course record 64.
Club membership 430.
Visitors must contact in advance, may not play on weekend competition days.
Societies apply in advance to Secretary
Green Fees £20 (£27 weekends).
Prof Neil Brazell
Facilities ⊗ ⅏ ⤵ ♥ ♀ 👤 🖼 ♂
Location 1m N off A58

Hotel ★★★ 65% Quality Hotel Wigan, Riverway, WIGAN ☎ 01942 826888 88 ⇆ ♞

HYDE   Map 07 SJ99

Werneth Low Werneth Low Rd, Gee Cross SK14 3AF
☎ 0161 368 2503 Fax 0161 320 0053
Hard walking but good views from this moorland course. Exposed to wind.
11 holes, 6113yds, Par 70, SSS 70, Course record 69.
Club membership 375.
Visitors may not play Tue mornings, Thu afternoons or Sun and by prior arrangement on Sat.
Societies must contact in at least 14 days in advance.
Green Fees not confirmed.
Cards 💳 💳 💳 💳 💳
Prof Tony Bacchus
Facilities ⊗ ⅏ ⤵ ♥ ♀ 👤 🖼 ♂
Location 2m S of town centre

Hotel ★★ 77% Wind in the Willows Hotel, Derbyshire Level, Sheffield Rd, GLOSSOP ☎ 01457 868001 12 ⇆ ♞

KEARSLEY   Map 07 SD70

Manor Moss Ln BL4 8SF
☎ 01204 701027 Fax 01204 796914
Parkland course with water features. Treelined fairways including evergreen and deciduous trees. Suitable for players of all levels.
18 holes, 5010yds, Par 66, SSS 64, Course record 65.
Club membership 500.
Visitors book in advance. Must observe dress code.
Societies contact in advance for details.
Green Fees £5 Mon-Thu, £6.50 Fri (£10 weekends & bank holidays, £8.50 after noon).
Cards 💳 💳 💳 💳
Designer Jeff Yates
Facilities ⊗ ⅏ ⤵ ♥ ♀ 👤 🖼 ♉ ♂
& Leisure fishing.
Location Off A666, Manchester Rd

Hotel ★★★ 66% Novotel, Worsley Brow, WORSLEY ☎ 0161 799 3535 119 ⇆ ♞

LITTLEBOROUGH   Map 07 SD91

Whittaker Whittaker Ln OL15 0LH ☎ 01706 378310
Moorland 9-hole course with outstanding views of Hollingworth Lake Countryside Park and the Pennine Hills.
9 holes, 5632yds, Par 68, SSS 67, Course record 61.
Club membership 210.
Visitors welcome except for Tue pm and Sun.
Societies apply to Secretary.
Green Fees not confirmed.
Facilities ♀ 👤
Location 1.5m out of Littleborough off A58

Hotel ★★★★ 64% Norton Grange Hotel, Manchester Rd, Castleton, ROCHDALE ☎ 01706 630788 51 ⇆ ♞

MANCHESTER   Map 07 SJ89

Blackley Victoria Ave East, Blackley M9 7HW
☎ 0161 643 2980 & 654 7770 Fax 0161 653 8300
Parkland course. Course crossed by footpath.
18 holes, 6237yds, Par 70, SSS 70.
Club membership 800.
Visitors with member only Thu, weekends and bank holidays.
Societies apply in advance.
Green Fees £24 per day.
Prof Craig Gould
Facilities ⊗ ⅏ ⤵ ♥ ♀ 👤 🖼 ♉ ♂
Location 4m N of city centre, on Rochdale Rd

Hotel ★★★ 74% Malmaison Hotel, Gore St, Piccadilly, MANCHESTER ☎ 0161 278 1000 112 ⇆ ♞

Where to stay, where to eat?
Visit the AA internet site
www.theaa.co.uk

Chorlton-cum-Hardy Barlow Hall, Barlow Hall Rd,
Chorlton-cum-Hardy M21 7JJ
☎ 0161 881 5830 Fax 0161 881 4532
Meadowland course with trees, stream and several ditches.
18 holes, 5980yds, Par 70, SSS 69, Course record 64.
Club membership 802.
Visitors handicap certificate required.
Societies on Thu & Fri only by prior booking.
Green Fees £25 per day (£30 weekends & bank holidays).
Prof David Valentine
Facilities ⊗ ⅲ ⅃ 🍺 ♀ ♨ 🏠 ♋ ✐
Location 4m S of Manchester A5103/A5145

Hotel ★★ 63% Willow Bank Hotel, 340-342
Wilmslow Rd, Fallowfield, MANCHESTER
☎ 0161 224 0461 116 ⇌ ♟

Davyhulme Park Gleneagles Rd, Davyhulme M41 8SA
☎ 0161 748 2260 Fax 0161 747 4067
Parkland course.
18 holes, 6237yds, Par 72, SSS 70, Course record 67.
Club membership 680.
Visitors may play Mon, Tue & Thu.
Societies telephone in advance.
Green Fees not confirmed.
Prof Dean Butler
Facilities ⊗ ⅃ 🍺 ♀ ♨ 🏠 ✐
& Leisure snooker.
Location 8m S adj to Trafford General Hospital

Hotel ★★★ 60% Trafford Hall Hotel, 23 Talbot Rd,
Old Trafford, MANCHESTER
☎ 0161 848 7791 31 ⇌ ♟ Annexe 3 ⇌ ♟

Didsbury Ford Ln, Northenden M22 4NQ
☎ 0161 998 9278 Fax 0161 998 9278
Parkland course.
18 holes, 6273yds, Par 70, SSS 70, Course record 63.
Club membership 750.
Visitors advised to check dates/times with manager or
professional.
Societies Thu & Fri, must contact in advance.
Green Fees £26 per day (£30 weekends).
Cards 💳 💳
Prof Peter Barber
Facilities ⊗ ⅲ ⅃ 🍺 ♀ ♨ 🏠 ♋ ♨ ✐
Location 6m S of city centre off A5145

Hotel ★★★ 64% Posthouse Manchester, Palatine Rd,
Northenden, MANCHESTER
☎ 0870 400 9056 190 ⇌ ♟

Fairfield "Boothdale", Booth Rd, Audenshaw M34 5GA
☎ 0161 370 1641 & 370 2292
Parkland course set around a reservoir. Course demands
particularly accurate placing of shots.
18 holes, 4956yds, Par 68, SSS 66, Course record 65.
Club membership 450.
Visitors may not play mornings at weekends & may be
restricted on Wed & Thu.
Societies prior booking through Secretary.
Green Fees £18 per round (£23 weekends & bank holidays).
Prof Stephen Pownell
Facilities ⊗ ⅲ ⅃ 🍺 ♀ ♨ 🏠 ✐
Location 5m E of Manchester, off A635

Hotel ★★ 69% York House Hotel, York Place,
Richmond St, ASHTON-UNDER-LYNE
☎ 0161 330 9000 24 ⇌ ♟ Annexe10 ⇌ ♟

Marriott Manchester Hotel & Country Club Worsley
Park, Worsley M28 2QT
☎ 0161 975 2043 Fax 0161 975 2058
Set in 200 acres of parkland with a range of tee positions, 8
lakes and 70 strategically placed bunkers and providing an
exciting challenge to golfers of all abilities, very often
requiring brains rather than brawn to make a successful score
18 holes, 6611yds, Par 71, SSS 72.
Club membership 400.

Visitors must have a handicap certificate. Must contact
in advance.
Societies weekdays only. Telephone in advance.
Green Fees £60 per day; £40 per round (£70/£50 weekends
& bank holidays).
Prof David Screeton
Designer Ross McMurray
Facilities ⊗ ⅲ ⅃ 🍺 ♀ ♨ 🏠 ♋ 🥘 ♨ ✐
& Leisure heated indoor swimming pool, sauna, solarium,
gymnasium.

Hotel ★★★★ 67% Marriott Manchester Hotel &
Country Club, Worsley Park, Worsley,
MANCHESTER ☎ 0161 975 2000 159 ⇌ ♟

Northenden Palatine Rd, Northenden M22 4FR
☎ 0161 998 4738 Fax 0161 998 5592
Parkland course surrounded by the River Mersey.
18 holes, 6503yds, Par 72, SSS 71, Course record 64.
Club membership 800.
Visitors must contact in advance.
Societies Tue & Fri only, apply in advance to Secretary.
Green Fees £27 per day (£30 weekends & bank holidays).
Prof P A Scott
Designer Renouf
Facilities ⊗ ⅲ ⅃ 🍺 ♀ ♨ 🏠 ✐
Location 6.5m S of city centre on B1567 off A5103

Hotel ★★★ 64% Posthouse Manchester, Palatine Rd,
Northenden, MANCHESTER
☎ 0870 400 9056 190 ⇌ ♟

Withington 243 Palatine Rd, West Didsbury M20 2UE
☎ 0161 445 9544 Fax 0161 445 5210
Flat parkland course bordering the river Mersey. Easy
walking with an extremely tough finish.
18 holes, 6410yds, Par 71, SSS 71.
Club membership 600.
Visitors welcome except Thu, must contact in advance,
restricted at weekends.

Societies telephone in advance, welcome except Thu, Sat & Sun.
Green Fees not confirmed.
Prof R J Ling
Facilities ⊗ ⅷ ┗ ☕ ♀ 🛆 🏕 ✔
Location 4m SW of city centre off B5167

Hotel ★★★ 64% Posthouse Manchester, Palatine Rd, Northenden, MANCHESTER
☎ 0870 400 9056 190 ⇌ ✦

Worsley Stableford Av, Worsley M30 8AP
☎ 0161 789 4202 Fax 0161 789 3200
Well-wooded parkland course.
18 holes, 6252yds, Par 71, SSS 70, Course record 65.
Club membership 600.
Visitors must contact professional in advance restricted during club competitions.
Societies apply in advance.
Green Fees £30 per day (£35 weekends).
Cards 💳 💳
Prof Ceri Cousins
Designer James Braid
Facilities ⊗ ⅷ ┗ ☕ ♀ 🛆 🏕 ✔ ✔
& Leisure snooker.
Location 6.5m NW of city centre off A572

Hotel ★★★ 66% Novotel, Worsley Brow,
WORSLEY ☎ 0161 799 3535 119 ⇌ ✦

MELLOR
Map 07 SJ98

Mellor & Townscliffe Gibb Ln, Tarden SK6 5NA
☎ 0161 427 2208 (secretary) & 427 5759 (pro)
Scenic parkland and moorland course, undulating with some hard walking. Good views. Testing 200 yd, 9th hole, par 3.
18 holes, 5925yds, Par 70, SSS 69.
Club membership 650.
Visitors with member only weekends & bank holidays.
Societies apply by letter.
Green Fees £20 per day.
Prof Gary R Broadley
Facilities ⊗ ⅷ ┗ ☕ ♀ 🛆 🏕 ✔
Location 7m SE of Stockport off A626

Hotel ★★ 70% Springfield Hotel, Station Rd,
MARPLE ☎ 0161 449 0721 7 ⇌ ✦

MIDDLETON
Map 07 SD80

Manchester Hopwood Cottage, Rochdale Rd M24 2QP
☎ 0161 643 3202 Fax 0161 643 9174
Moorland golf of unique character over a spaciously laid out course with generous fairways sweeping along to large greens. A wide variety of holes will challenge the golfer's technique, particularly the testing last three holes.
18 holes, 6519yds, Par 72, SSS 70, Course record 65.
Club membership 650.
Visitors must contact in advance, limited play weekends and Wed.
Societies telephone in advance.
Green Fees £40 per day; £30 per round.
Cards 💳 💳 💳
Prof Brian Connor
Designer Shapland Colt

Facilities ⊗ ⅷ ┗ ☕ ♀ 🛆 🏕 🛥 ✔ ✔
Location 2.5m N off A664. M62 junct 20

Hotel ★★★★ 64% Norton Grange Hotel, Manchester Rd, Castleton, ROCHDALE
☎ 01706 630788 51 ⇌ ✦

North Manchester Rhodes House, Manchester Old Rd M24 4PE ☎ 0161 643 9033 Fax 0161 643 7775
A long, tight heathland course with natural water hazards. Excellent views of the Yorkshire Wolds.
18 holes, 6527yds, Par 72, SSS 72, Course record 66.
Club membership 750.
Visitors contact Pro Shop on 0161 643 7094 for availability.
Societies telephone in advance.
Green Fees not confirmed.
Prof Jason Peel
Designer J Braid
Facilities ⊗ ⅷ ┗ ☕ ♀ 🛆 🏕 ✔
Location W side of town centre off A576

Hotel ★★★ 68% Avant Hotel, Windsor Rd, Manchester St, OLDHAM
☎ 0500 636943 (Central Res)
Fax 01773 880321 103 ⇌ ✦

MILNROW
Map 07 SD91

Tunshill Kiln Ln OL16 3TS ☎ 01706 342095
Testing moorland course, particularly 7th and 15th (par 5's).
9 holes, 5743yds, Par 70, SSS 68, Course record 64.
Club membership 275.
Visitors must contact in advance, restricted weekends & evenings.
Societies apply in writing.
Green Fees £15 per day/round.
Facilities 🛆
Location 1m NE M62 exit junc 21 off B6225

Hotel ★★★★ 64% Norton Grange Hotel, Manchester Rd, Castleton, ROCHDALE
☎ 01706 630788 51 ⇌ ✦

OLDHAM
Map 07 SD90

Crompton & Royton Highbarn OL2 6RW
☎ 0161 624 0986 Fax 0161 624 0986
Undulating moorland course.
18 holes, 6214yds, Par 70, SSS 70, Course record 65.
Club membership 500.
Visitors must contact in advance and may not play Tue or Sat, limited play Sun pm and Wed.
Societies apply in advance
Green Fees not confirmed.
Prof David Melling
Facilities ⊗ ⅷ ┗ ☕ ♀ 🛆 🏕 ✔
Location 0.5m NE of Royton

Hotel ★★★ 68% Avant Hotel, Windsor Rd, Manchester St, OLDHAM
☎ 0500 636943 (Central Res)
Fax 01773 880321 103 ⇌ ✦

Oldham Lees New Rd OL4 5PN ☎ 0161 624 4986
Moorland course, with hard walking.
18 holes, 5122yds, Par 66, SSS 65, Course record 62.
Club membership 370.
Visitors   no restrictions.
Societies   must contact in advance.
Green Fees £18 (£24 weekends & bank holidays).
Prof   C Atkinson
Facilities ⊗ ⅏ ⅃ ♣ ♀ ♨ ☎ ✓
Location   2.5m E off A669

Hotel   ★★ 69% York House Hotel, York Place,
Richmond St, ASHTON-UNDER-LYNE
☎ 0161 330 9000 24 ⇆ ⋔ Annexe 10 ⇆ ⋔

Werneth Green Ln, Garden Suburb OL8 3AZ
☎ 0161 624 1190
Semi-moorland course, with a deep gulley and stream
crossing eight fairways. Testing hole: 3rd (par 3).
18 holes, 5363yds, Par 68, SSS 66, Course record 63.
Club membership 460.
Visitors   may not play on Tue or Thu and weekends.
Must contact in advance.
Societies   must contact in advance.
Green Fees £18 per day.
Prof   Roy Penney
Designer   Sandy Herd
Facilities ⊗ ⅏ ⅃ ♣ ♀ ♨ ☎ ✓
Location   S side of town centre off A627

Hotel   ★★ 69% York House Hotel, York Place,
Richmond St, ASHTON-UNDER-LYNE
☎ 0161 330 9000 24 ⇆ ⋔ Annexe 10 ⇆ ⋔

PRESTWICH   Map 07 SD80

Heaton Park Municipal Heaton Park, Middleton Rd M25
2SW ☎ 0161 654 9899 Fax 0161 653 2003
A parkland style course in historic Heaton Park with rolling
hills and lakes, boasting some spectacular holes. A good test
of skill for golfers of all abilities.
18 holes, 5815yds, Par 70, SSS 70.
Club membership 190.
Visitors   restricted to club members only between 8-10am
Sat & Sun.
Societies   apply in writing or by telephone to Matthew
Riley
Green Fees not confirmed.
Cards   ▭ ▭
Prof   Dennis Durnian
Designer   J H Taylor
Facilities ⊗ ⅏ ⅃ ♣ ♀ ♨ ☎ ⋔ ✓ ⌘
Location   N of Manchester near junct 18 of M62

Hotel   ★★★★ 63% Bolton Moat House, 1 Higher
Bridge St, BOLTON
☎ 01204 879988 128 ⇆ ⋔

Prestwich Hilton Ln M25 9XB
☎ 0161 773 1404 Fax 0161 772 0700
Parkland course, near to Manchester city centre. A testing
course with small greens.
18 holes, 4806yds, Par 64, SSS 63, Course record 60.
Club membership 565.
Visitors   handicap certificate, weekdays by arrangement.
Restricted at weekends, ladies day Tue.
Societies   apply in writing or telephone.

Green Fees £20 per day (£20 per round weekends).
Prof   Simon Wakefield
Facilities ⊗ ⅏ ⅃ ♣ ♀ ♨ ☎ ⋔ ✓
Location   N side of town centre on A6044

Hotel   ★★★ 66% Novotel, Worsley Brow,
WORSLEY ☎ 0161 799 3535 119 ⇆ ⋔

ROCHDALE   Map 07 SD81

Castle Hawk Chadwick Ln, Castleton OL11 3BY
☎ 01706 640841 Fax 01706 860587
Two parkland courses, with challenging par 3s, and a driving
range.
*New Course: 9 holes, 2699yds, Par 34, SSS 34, Course
record 30.*
Old Course: 18 holes, 3276yds, Par 55, SSS 55.
Club membership 220.
Visitors   no restrictions.
Societies   must contact in advance.
Green Fees £7 per day (£10 weekends).
Cards   ▭ ▭ ▭ ▭ ▭ ▭
Prof   Frank Accleton
Designer   T Wilson
Facilities ⊗ ⅏ ⅃ ♣ ♀ ♨ ☎ ⋔ ✓ ⌘
Location   S of Rochdale, nr junc 20 (M62)

Hotel   ★★★★ 64% Norton Grange Hotel, Manchester
Rd, Castleton, ROCHDALE
☎ 01706 630788 51 ⇆ ⋔

Rochdale Edenfield Rd OL11 5YR
☎ 01706 643818 Fax 01706 861113
Parkland course with enjoyable golf and easy walking.
18 holes, 6050yds, Par 71, SSS 69, Course record 65.
Club membership 750.
Visitors   must telephone in advance.
Societies   apply in writing or telephone
Green Fees £30 per day/round, reductions in winter.
Cards   ▭ ▭ ▭ ▭ ▭
Prof   Andrew Laverty
Designer   George Lowe
Facilities ⊗ ⅏ ⅃ ♣ ♀ ♨ ☎ ⋔ ✓
Location   1.75m W on A680

Hotel   ★★★★ 64% Norton Grange Hotel, Manchester
Rd, Castleton, ROCHDALE
☎ 01706 630788 51 ⇆ ⋔

Springfield Park Springfield Park, Bolton Rd OL11 4RE
☎ 01706 56401 (weekend only)
Parkland-moorland course situated in a valley. The River
Roch adds an extra hazard to the course.
18 holes, 5237yds, Par 67, SSS 66, Course record 64.
Club membership 300.
Visitors   must contact professional in advance.
Societies   telephone in advance.
Green Fees not confirmed.
Prof   David Wills
Facilities ☎ ⋔
Location   1.5m SW off A58

Hotel   ★★★★ 64% Norton Grange Hotel, Manchester
Rd, Castleton, ROCHDALE
☎ 01706 630788 51 ⇆ ⋔

ROMILEY

Map 07 SJ99

Romiley Goose House Green SK6 4LJ
☎ 0161 430 2392 Fax 0161 430 7258
Semi-parkland course on the edge of the Derbyshire Hills,
providing a good test of golf with a number of outstanding
holes, notably the 6th, 9th, 14th and 16th. The latter enjoys
magnificent views from the tee.
18 holes, 6454yds, Par 70, SSS 71, Course record 66.
Club membership 700.
Visitors	are advised to contact in advance, may not play Thu or Sat before 4pm.
Societies	Tue & Wed, must book in advance.
Green Fees	not confirmed.
Prof	Gary Butler
Facilities	⊗ ℳ by prior arrangement ﹅ ♥ ⚑ 🏠 𝄢
Location	E side of town centre off B6104

Hotel ★★ 67% The Wycliffe Hotel, 74 Edgeley Rd,
Edgeley, STOCKPORT
☎ 0161 477 5395 20 ⇥ ↖

SALE

Map 07 SJ79

Ashton on Mersey Church Ln M33 5QQ
☎ 0161 976 4390 & 962 3727 Fax 0161 976 4390
Parkland course with easy walking alongside the River
Mersey.
9 holes, 6146yds, Par 71, SSS 69, Course record 66.
Club membership 485.
Visitors	with member only Sun & bank holidays, not Sat or Tue.
Societies	Thu only. Apply in writing.
Green Fees	not confirmed.
Prof	Mike Williams
Facilities	⊗ ℳ ﹅ ♥ ⚑ 🏠 𝄢
& Leisure	sauna.
Location	1m W of M60 (M63) junc 7, off Glebelands Road

Hotel ★★★ 65% Cresta Court Hotel, Church St,
ALTRINCHAM
☎ 0161 927 7272 138 ⇥ ↖

Sale Golf Rd M33 2XU
☎ 0161 973 1638 (Gen Man) Fax 0161 962 4217
Tree-lined parkland course. Feature holes are the 13th -
Watery Gap - and the par 3 (117yd) 17th.
18 holes, 6352yds, Par 71, SSS 70.
Club membership 700.
Visitors	contact professional in advance.
Societies	apply by letter.
Green Fees	not confirmed.
Prof	Mike Stewart
Facilities	🏠 🏠 𝄢
Location	0.5m from M60 J6, NW side of town centre off A6144

Hotel ★★★ 65% Cresta Court Hotel, Church St,
ALTRINCHAM
☎ 0161 927 7272 138 ⇥ ↖

SHEVINGTON

Map 07 SD50

Gathurst 62 Miles Ln WN6 8EW
☎ 01257 255235 (Secretary) & 254909 (Pro)
Testing parkland course, slightly hilly.
18 holes, 6016yds, Par 70, SSS 69, Course record 64.
Club membership 575.
Visitors	may play anytime except competition days.
Societies	welcome Mon, Tue, Thu & Fri. Apply in writing to Secretary.
Green Fees	not confirmed.
Prof	Rob Eastwood
Designer	N Pearson
Facilities	⊗ ℳ ﹅ ♥ ⚑ 🏠 𝄢
Location	W side of village B5375 off junc 27 of M6

Hotel ★★★ 65% Wigan/Standish Moat House,
Almond Brook Rd, Standish, WIGAN
☎ 01257 499988 124 ⇥ ↖

STALYBRIDGE

Map 07 SJ99

Stamford Oakfield House, Huddersfield Rd SK15 3PY
☎ 01457 832126 & 834829
Undulating moorland course.
18 holes, 5701yds, Par 70, SSS 68, Course record 62.
Club membership 600.
Visitors	limited play at weekends.
Societies	apply in writing or telephone 0161 633 5721
Green Fees	£20 (25 weekends).
Facilities	⊗ ℳ ﹅ ♥ ⚑ 🏠 𝄢
Location	2m NE off A635

Hotel ★★ 69% York House Hotel, York Place,
Richmond St, ASHTON-UNDER-LYNE
☎ 0161 330 9000 24 ⇥ ↖ Annexe 10 ⇥ ↖

STANDISH

Map 07 SD51

Standish Court Rectory Ln WN6 0XD
☎ 01257 425777 Fax 01257 425888
Undulating 18 hole parkland course, not overly long but
provides a good test for all level of players. Front nine more
open with room for errors, back nine very scenic through
woodland, a number of tight driving holes. Greens in
excellent condition.
18 holes, 5625yds, Par 68, SSS 66.
Club membership 375.
Visitors	can play anytime, phone in advance for tee time, standard golfing dress required.
Societies	telephone in advance.
Green Fees	£12 (£15 weekends).
Cards	〰 ▭ ▩ ▨ 🔾
Prof	J Kershaw
Designer	P Dawson
Facilities	⊗ ℳ ﹅ ♥ ⚑ 🏠 ⚒ 𝄢 𝄐
Location	Off M6 junct 27, just through traffic lights in Standish village

Hotel ★★★★ 64% Kilhey Court Hotel, Chorley Rd,
Standish, WIGAN ☎ 01257 472100 62 ⇥ ↖

STOCKPORT   Map 07 SJ89

Heaton Moor Heaton Mersey SK4 3NX ☎ 0161 432 0846
Parkland course, easy walking.
18 holes, 5968, Par 70, SSS 69, Course record 66.
Club membership 400.
Visitors   restricted Tue, bank holidays & Sat (summer).
Societies   apply in writing.
Green Fees not confirmed.
Prof   Simon Marsh
Facilities ⊗ ⏃ ⓛ 🖤 ♀ ♨ 🏠 ⛳ ♂
Location   N of town centre off B5169

Hotel   ★★ 67% Saxon Holme Hotel, 230 Wellington
                Rd, STOCKPORT ☎ 0161 432 2335 33 ➡ ↟

Houldsworth Houldsworth Park, Reddish SK5 6BN
☎ 0161 442 9611 & 0161 442 1712 Fax 0161 442 1712
Flat parkland course, tree-lined and with water hazards.
Testing holes 9th (par 5) and 13th (par 5).
18 holes, 6209yds, Par 71, SSS 70.
Club membership 680.
Visitors   may not play weekends & bank holidays unless
                by prior arrangement with professional.
Societies   by prior arrangement, telephone Secretary.
Green Fees £20 per round (£25 weekends).
Prof   David Naylor
Designer   Dave Thomas
Facilities ⊗ ⏃ ⓛ 🖤 ♀ ♨ 🏠 ⛳ ♂
Location   4m SE of city centre off A6

Hotel   ★★ 63% Willow Bank Hotel, 340-342
                Wilmslow Rd, Fallowfield, MANCHESTER
                ☎ 0161 224 0461 116 ➡ ↟

Marple Barnsfold Rd, Hawk Green, Marple SK6 7EL
☎ 0161 427 2311 Fax 0161 427 1125
Parkland course.
18 holes, 5552yds, Par 68, SSS 67, Course record 66.
Club membership 640.
Visitors   restricted Thu afternoon & weekend competition
                days.
Societies   apply in writing to professional.
Green Fees £20 per day (£30 weekends & bank holidays).
Prof   David Myers
Facilities ⊗ ⏃ ⓛ 🖤 ♀ ♨ 🏠 ♂
Location   S side of town centre

Hotel   ★★ 70% Springfield Hotel, Station Rd,
                MARPLE ☎ 0161 449 0721 7 ➡ ↟

Reddish Vale Southcliffe Rd, Reddish SK5 7EE
☎ 0161 480 2359 Fax 0161 477 8242
Undulating heathland course designed by Dr. A Mackenzie
and situated in the River Tame valley.
18 holes, 6100yds, Par 69, SSS 69, Course record 64.
Club membership 550.
Visitors   must play with member at weekends. No
                societies at weekends.
Societies   must contact in writing.
Green Fees not confirmed.
Prof   Bob Freeman
Designer   Dr A Mackenzie
Facilities ⊗ ⓛ 🖤 ♀ 🏠 ⛳ ♂
Location   1.5m N off Sandy Lane

Hotel   ★★ 67% The Wycliffe Hotel, 74 Edgeley Rd,
                Edgeley, STOCKPORT
                ☎ 0161 477 5395 20 ➡ ↟

Stockport Offerton Rd, Offerton SK2 5HL
☎ 0161 427 8369 (Secretary) & 427 2421 (Pro)
Fax 0161 449 8293
A beautifully situated course in wide open countryside with
views of the Cheshire and Derbyshire hills. It is not too long
but requires that the player plays all the shots, to excellent
greens. Demanding holes include the dog-leg 3rd, 12th, and
18th and the 460 yard opening hole is among the toughest in
Cheshire.
18 holes, 6326yds, Par 71, SSS 71, Course record 66.
Club membership 500.
Visitors   must contact professional in advance, limited
                play weekends.
Societies   Wed & Thu only, apply in writing to Secretary.
Green Fees £45 per day; £35 per round (£55/£45 weekends).
Prof   Mike Peel
Designer   P Barrie/A Herd
Facilities ⊗ ⏃ ⓛ 🖤 ♀ ♨ 🏠 ⛳ ♂
Location   4m SE on A627

Hotel   ★★ 70% Springfield Hotel, Station Rd,
                MARPLE ☎ 0161 449 0721 7 ➡ ↟

SWINTON   Map 07 SD70

Swinton Park East Lancashire Rd M27 5LX
☎ 0161 794 0861 Fax 0161 281 0698
One of Lancashire's longest inland courses.
18 holes, 6726yds, Par 73, SSS 72, Course record 66.
Club membership 600.
Visitors   may not play weekends or Thu. Must
                contact in advance and have handicap
                certificate.
Societies   apply by letter.
Green Fees not confirmed.
Prof   James Wilson
Designer   James Braid
Facilities ⊗ ⏃ ⓛ 🖤 ♀ ♨ 🏠 ♂
Location   1m W off A580

Hotel   ★★★ 66% Novotel, Worsley Brow,
                WORSLEY ☎ 0161 799 3535 119 ➡ ↟

UPPERMILL   Map 07 SD90

Saddleworth Mountain Ash OL3 6LT
☎ 01457 873653 Fax 01457 820647
Moorland course, with superb views of Pennines.
18 holes, 5976yds, Par 71, SSS 69, Course record 61.
Club membership 800.
Visitors   must contact in advance, restricted at weekends.
Societies   contact in advance.
Green Fees £23 per day (£30 weekends & bank holidays).
Prof   Robert Johnson
Designer   George Lowe/Dr McKenzie
Facilities ⊗ ⏃ ⓛ 🖤 ♀ ♨ 🏠 ⛳ ↟ 🏌 ♂
Location   E side of town centre off A670

Hotel   ★★★ 70% Hotel Smokies Park, Ashton Rd,
                Bardsley, OLDHAM
                ☎ 0161 785 5000 73 ➡ ↟

URMSTON   Map 07 SJ79

Flixton Church Rd, Flixton M41 6EP
☎ 0161 748 2116 Fax 0161 748 2116
Meadowland course bounded by River Mersey.
9 holes, 6410yds, Par 71, SSS 71.
Club membership 430.
Visitors	contact professional in advance, with member only weekends & bank holidays.
Societies	apply in writing.
Green Fees	£16 per day.
Prof	Daniel Procter
Facilities	⊗ ⍟ by prior arrangement ⓑ ♥ ♀ ♣ ☕ 🏌
Location	S side of town centre on B5213

Hotel ★★★★ 66% Copthorne Manchester, Clippers Quay, Salford Quays, MANCHESTER
☎ 0161 873 7321 166 ⇆ ♞

WALKDEN   Map 07 SD70

Brackley Municipal M38 9TR ☎ 0161 790 6076
Mostly flat course.
9 holes, 3003yds, Par 35, SSS 69.
Visitors	no restrictions.
Green Fees	not confirmed.
Facilities	☕
Location	2m NW on A6

Hotel ★★★ 66% Novotel, Worsley Brow, WORSLEY
☎ 0161 799 3535 119 ⇆ ♞

WESTHOUGHTON   Map 07 SD60

Westhoughton Long Island, School St BL5 2BR
☎ 01942 811085 & 608958 Fax 01942 608958
Compact downland course.
9 holes, 2886yds, Par 70, SSS 68, Course record 64.
Club membership 280.
Visitors	with member only at weekends.
Societies	telephone in advance or apply in writing.
Green Fees	£16 per day.
Prof	Jason Seed
Facilities	⊗ ⍟ ⓑ ♥ ♀ ♣ ☕
Location	0.5m NW off A58

Hotel ★★★ 59% Posthouse Bolton, Beaumont Rd, BOLTON ☎ 08704 400 9011 101 ⇆ ♞

WHITEFIELD   Map 07 SD80

Stand The Dales, Ashbourne Grove M45 7NL
☎ 0161 766 3197 Fax 0161 796 3234
A semi-parkland course with five moorland holes. A fine test of golf with a very demanding finish.
18 holes, 6411yds, Par 72, SSS 71, Course record 66.
Club membership 500.
Visitors	must contact professional in advance.
Societies	Wed & Fri, apply by telephone.
Green Fees	not confirmed.
Prof	Mark Dance
Designer	G Lowe/A Herd
Facilities	⊗ ⍟ ⓑ ♥ ♀ ♣ ☕ 🏌 🏌
Location	1m W off A667

Hotel ★★★ 65% Bolholt Country Park Hotel, Walshaw Rd, BURY
☎ 0161 762 4000 66 ⇆ ♞

Whitefield Higher Ln M45 7EZ
☎ 0161 351 2700 Fax 0161 351 2712
Fine sporting parkland course with well-watered greens.
18 holes, 6045yds, Par 69, SSS 69, Course record 64.
Club membership 540.
Visitors	play restricted Tue & Sun. Booking essential weekends and bank holidays, contact the proffesional shop on 0161 7663096.
Societies	must contact in advance.
Green Fees	not confirmed.
Cards	⊟ ■ ▦ ▨ ▦ ▧ 🝛
Prof	Paul Reeves
Facilities	⊗ ⍟ ⓑ ♥ ♀ ♣ ☕ 🏌 🏌 🏌
& Leisure	hard tennis courts, snooker room.
Location	N side of town centre on A665

Hotel ★★★ 74% Malmaison Hotel, Gore St, Piccadilly, MANCHESTER
☎ 0161 278 1000 112 ⇆ ♞

WIGAN   Map 07 SD50

Haigh Hall Haigh Country Park, Aspull WN2 1PE
☎ 01942 831107
Municipal parkland course, with hard walking, and a canal forms the west boundary. Adjacent to 'Haigh Country Park' with many facilities.
18 holes, 6423yds, Par 70, SSS 71, Course record 65.
Club membership 250.
Visitors	must contact professional in advance.
Societies	apply in writing to professional.
Green Fees	not confirmed.
Prof	Ian Lee
Designer	Frank Pennink
Facilities	ⓑ ♥ ♣ ☕ 🏌 🏌
Location	2m NE off B5238

Hotel ★★ 63% Bel-Air Hotel, 236 Wigan Ln, WIGAN ☎ 01942 241410 11 ⇆ ♞

Wigan Arley Hall, Haigh WN1 2UH ☎ 01257 421360
Among the best of Lancashire's 9-hole courses. The fine old clubhouse is the original Arley Hall, and is surrounded by a 12th century moat.
9 holes, 6036yds, Par 70, SSS 69.
Club membership 200.
Visitors	must contact in advance. May not play Tue or Sat.
Societies	apply by telephone.
Green Fees	£25 per day.
Facilities	⊗ ⍟ ⓑ ♥ ♀ ♣
Location	3m NE off B5238

Hotel ★★★ 65% Wigan/Standish Moat House, Almond Brook Rd, Standish, WIGAN
☎ 01257 499988 124 ⇆ ♞

WOODFORD   Map 07 SJ88

Avro Old Hall Ln SK7 1QR ☎ 0161 439 2709
An attractive, tight and challenging 9-hole course.
9 holes, 5735yds, Par 69, SSS 68.
Club membership 400.

▶

Visitors	restricted weekends and competition days. not able to take societies.
Green Fees	not confirmed.
Facilities	♥ ᗄ
Location	W side of village on A5102

| Hotel | ★★★ 64% County Hotel Bramhall, Bramhall Ln South, BRAMHALL ☎ 0161 455 9988 65 ⇌ 🐾 |

WORSLEY   Map 07 SD70

Ellesmere Old Clough Ln M28 7HZ
☎ 0161 799 0554 (office) & 790 8591 (pro)
Parkland course with natural hazards. Testing holes: 3rd (par 5), 9th (par 3), 15th (par 5). Hard walking.
18 holes, 6248yds, Par 70, SSS 70, Course record 67.
Club membership 700.

Visitors	welcome except club competition days & bank holidays.
Societies	apply in advance.
Green Fees	£25 per day; £19 per round (£26 per round weekends).
Prof	Terry Morley
Facilities	⊗ ㎜ 🐾 ♥ ♀ ᗄ 🏠 ⌀
Location	N side of village off A580

| Hotel | ★★★ 66% Novotel, Worsley Brow, WORSLEY ☎ 0161 799 3535 119 ⇌ 🐾 |

HAMPSHIRE

ALDERSHOT   Map 04 SU85

Army Laffans Rd GU11 2HF
☎ 01252 337272 Fax 01252 337562
The second oldest course in Hampshire. Picturesque heathland course with three par 3's, over 200 yds.
18 holes, 6550yds, Par 71, SSS 71, Course record 67.
Club membership 825.

Visitors	may not play weekends.
Societies	apply in writing.
Green Fees	£25 per round.
Prof	Graham Cowley
Facilities	⊗ ㎜ 🐾 ♥ ♀ ᗄ 🏠 ⌀
Location	1.5m N of town centre off A323/A325

| Hotel | ★★★ 69% Potters International Hotel, 1 Fleet Rd, ALDERSHOT ☎ 01252 344000 97 ⇌ 🐾 |

ALRESFORD   Map 04 SU53

Alresford Cheriton Rd, Tichborne Down SO24 0PN
☎ 01962 733746 Fax 01962 736040
A testing downland course on well drained chalk. Expanded to 18 holes, incorporating the original 12, but changing direction of play to give two starting points and two closing greens near clubhouse.
18 holes, 5905yds, Par 69, SSS 68, Course record 63.
Club membership 750.

Visitors	must contact in advance.
Societies	must telephone in advance.
Green Fees	not confirmed.
Prof	Malcolm Scott
Designer	Scott Webb Young
Facilities	⊗ ㎜ 🐾 ♥ ♀ ᗄ 🏠 🐾 ⌀
Location	1m S on B3046

| Hotel | ★★ 63% Swan Hotel, 11 West St, ALRESFORD ☎ 01962 732302 & 734427 Fax 01962 735274 11rm(3 ⇌7 🐾) Annexe 12 ⇌ 🐾 |

ALTON   Map 04 SU73

Alton Old Odiham Rd GU34 4BU
☎ 01420 82042 & 86518
Undulating meadowland course.
9 holes, 5744yds, Par 68, SSS 68, Course record 52.
Club membership 350.

Visitors	must contact in advance and must have a handicap certificate to play at weekends.
Societies	must contact in advance.
Green Fees	not confirmed.
Prof	Paul Brown
Designer	James Braid
Facilities	⊗ ㎜ 🐾 ♥ ♀ ᗄ 🏠 ⌀
Location	2m N of Alton off B3349 at Golden Pot

| Hotel | ★★★ 67% Alton House Hotel, Normandy St, ALTON ☎ 01420 80033 39 ⇌ 🐾 |

Worldham Park Cakers Ln, East Worldham GU34 3BF
☎ 01420 543151 Fax 01420 84124
The course is in a picturesque woodland setting with an abundance of challenging holes (doglegs, water and sand).
18 holes, 5800yds, Par 71, SSS 68.
Club membership 500.

Visitors	are advised to book in advance at weekends.
Societies	Mon-Fri only. Must contact in advance.
Green Fees	not confirmed.
Cards	🔳 🔳 🔳 🔳 🔳
Prof	Jon Le Roux
Designer	F J Whidborne
Facilities	⊗ ㎜ 🐾 ♥ ♀ ᗄ 🏠 🐾 ➹ ⌀ ⌀
Location	B3004, 2mins from Alton

| Hotel | ★★★ 66% Alton Grange Hotel, London Rd, ALTON ☎ 01420 86565 26 ⇌ 🐾 Annexe 4 ⇌ 🐾 |

AMPFIELD   Map 04 SU42

Ampfield Par Three Winchester Rd SO51 9BQ
☎ 01794 368480
Pretty parkland course designed by Henry Cotton in 1963. Well-bunkered greens.
18 holes, 2478yds, Par 54, SSS 53, Course record 49.
Club membership 470.

Visitors	must contact in advance & have a handicap certificate to play at weekends & bank holidays, recognised golfshoes must be worn.
Societies	must contact in advance.
Green Fees	not confirmed.
Prof	Richard Benfield
Designer	Henry Cotton
Facilities	⊗ ㎜ 🐾 ♥ ♀ ᗄ 🏠 🐾 ⌀
Location	4m NE of Romsey on A31

▶

ENGLAND

Hotel ★★★ 67% Potters Heron Hotel, Winchester Rd, Ampfield, ROMSEY
☎ 023 80266611 54 🛏 📠

ANDOVER
Map 04 SU34

Andover 51 Winchester Rd SP10 2EF
☎ 01264 358040 Fax 01264 358040
Undulating downland course combining a good test of golf for all abilities with breathtaking views across Hampshire countryside. Well guarded greens and a notable par 3, 9th (225yds) with the tee perched on top of a hill, 100ft above the green.
9 holes, 6096yds, Par 70, SSS 69, Course record 66.
Club membership 450.
Visitors must contact professional in advance tel: 01264 324151.
Societies Mon-Wed only. Must contact in advance.
Green Fees not confirmed.
Prof D Lawrence
Designer J H Taylor
Facilities ⊗ 🏅 🏌 ♀ 🏃 📠 ✓
Location 0.5m S on A3057

Hotel ★★★ 63% Quality Hotel Andover, Micheldever Rd, ANDOVER
☎ 01264 369111 9 🛏 📠 Annexe 26 🛏 📠

ASHLEY HEATH
Map 04 SU10

Moors Valley Moors Valley Country Park, Horton Rd BH24 2ET ☎ 01425 479776 Fax 01425 472057
This municipal course is set in the beautiful surroundings of a country park. It offers a test for all standards. It is gently undulating, with water hazards on six holes.
18 holes, 6200yds, Par 72, SSS 70.
Club membership 250.
Visitors must contact in advance.
Societies telephone for availability.
Green Fees £11.50 per 18 holes (£14 weekends).
Cards 🖃 🖃 🖃 🖃 🖃
Prof Michael Torrens
Designer Hawtree & Son
Facilities 🏃 📠 ✓ ♀ 🍴
Location Signposted from A31 Ashley Heath roundabout

Hotel ★★★ 64% St Leonards Hotel, Ringwood Rd (A31), ST LEONARDS
☎ 01425 471220 34 🛏 📠

BARTON-ON-SEA
Map 04 SZ29

Barton-on-Sea Milford Rd BH25 5PP
☎ 01425 615308 Fax 01425 621457
Though not strictly a links course, it is situated on a coastal cliff with views over the Solent to the Isle of Wight. With 27 holes (three loops of nine), sea breezes often add to the test.
Becton-Needles: 18 holes, 6521yds, Par 72, SSS 71, Course record 65.
Needles-Stroller: 18 holes, 6521yds, Par 72, SSS 71.
Stroller-Becton: 18 holes, 6296yds, Par 72, SSS 70.
Club membership 940.
Visitors must contact in advance and have a handicap certificate.
Societies must telephone in advance.

Green Fees £30 per day (£35 weekends & bank holidays).
Prof Peter Rodgers
Designer Hamilton Stutt
Facilities & Leisure ⊗ 🏅 🏌 ♀ 🏃 📠 ✓ �̶ ✓ snooker.
Location B3058 SE side of town

Hotel ★★★★★ ♨ Chewton Glen Hotel, Christchurch Rd, NEW MILTON
☎ 01425 275341 52 🛏 📠 Annexe 2 🛏 📠

BASINGSTOKE
Map 04 SU65

Basingstoke Kempshott Park RG23 7LL
☎ 01256 465990 Fax 01256 331793
A well-maintained parkland course with wide and inviting fairways. You are inclined to expect longer drives than are actually achieved - partly on account of the trees. There are many two-hundred-year-old beech trees, since the course was built on an old deer park.
18 holes, 6350yds, Par 70, SSS 70, Course record 66.
Club membership 700.
Visitors must contact in advance and play Mon-Fri only (ex bank holidays).
Societies must contact in advance.
Green Fees £38 per day; £28 per round.
Cards 🖃 🖃 🖃 🖃
Prof Guy Shoesmith
Designer James Braid
Facilities ⊗ 🏛 🏅 🏌 ♀ 🏃 📠 ✓ 🚛 ✓
Location 3.5m SW on A30 M3 exit 7

Hotel ★★★ 63% Posthouse Basingstoke, Grove Rd, BASINGSTOKE
☎ 0870 400 9004 84 🛏 📠

Dummer Dummer RG25 2AR
☎ 01256 397888 Fax 01256 397889
Designed by Peter Alliss/Clive Clark, this course is set in 180 acres of countryside with panoramic views. It provides a challenge for all playing categories and is open all year round. All facilities, including the clubhouse have recently been enhanced.
18 holes, 6385yds, Par 72, SSS 70, Course record 64.
Club membership 650.

Visitors must contact in advance, adhere to dress code, handicap required, limited at weekends.
Societies contact in advance.
Green Fees £27 per round (£30 weekends & bank holidays).

▶

119

Cards　　≡≡ ☰☰ ≡≡ ☒☒ 〇
Prof　　　Andrew Fannon & Anthony Weir
Designer　Peter Allis
Facilities　☒ 〿 ⅓ ⬛ ♀ ⛩ 🏠 ⛳ 🚗 🏌 ⌇ ⌐
& Leisure　sauna, golf school.
Location　Off junc 7 of M3 towards Dummer village

Hotel　　★★★ 70% Basingstoke Country Hotel, Scures
　　　　　Hill, Nately Scures, Hook, BASINGSTOKE
　　　　　☎ 01256 764161 100 ⇔ 🐾

Weybrook Park Rooksdown Ln RG24 9NT
☎ 01256 320347 Fax 01256 812973
A course designed to be enjoyable for all standards of player.
Easy walking with fablous views.
18 holes, 6468yds, Par 71, SSS 71.
Club membership 600.
Visitors　　telephone for availability.
Societies　　telephone in advance for availability and
　　　　　　confirm in writing.
Green Fees　£25.50 per day; £18.50 per round
　　　　　　(£30.50/£23.50 weekends).
Prof　　　　Anthony Dillon
Facilities　☒ 〿 ⅓ ⬛ ♀ ⛩ 🏠 🏌 🚗 ⌇
Location　　2m W of town centre, entrance via A339

Hotel　　★★★ 62% Ringway Hotel, Popley Way,
　　　　　Aldermaston Roundabout, Ringway North
　　　　　(A339), BASINGSTOKE
　　　　　☎ 01256 796700 128 ⇔ 🐾

BORDON   Map 04 SU73

Blackmoor Firgrove Rd, Whitehill GU35 9EH
☎ 01420 472775 Fax 01420 487666
A first-class moorland course with a great variety of
holes. Fine greens and wide pine tree-lined fairways are
a distinguishing feature. The ground is mainly flat and
walking easy.
18 holes, 6164yds, Par 69, SSS 69, Course record 64.
Club membership 750.
Visitors　　must contact in advance, must have
　　　　　　handicap certificate and may not play at
　　　　　　weekends.
Societies　　must telephone in advance.
Green Fees　£45 per 36 holes; £33 per 18 holes.
Prof　　　　Stephen Clay
Designer　　H S Colt
Facilities　☒ 〿 ⅓ ⬛ ♀ ⛩ 🏠 🚗 ⌇
Location　　Travelling S on A325, 6m beyond Farnham,
　　　　　　pass through Whitehill and turn right at
　　　　　　crossroads

Hotel　　★★★ 67% Alton House Hotel, Normandy
　　　　　St, ALTON ☎ 01420 80033 39 ⇔ 🐾

BOTLEY   Map 04 SU51

Botley Park Hotel, Golf & Country Club Winchester Rd,
Boorley Green SO32 2UA
☎ 01489 780888 Fax 01489 789242
Pleasantly undulating course with water hazards. Driving
range and country club facilities.
18 holes, 6341yds, Par 70, SSS 70, Course record 67.
Club membership 1500.

Visitors　　must play with member at weekends. Must
　　　　　　contact in advance & have handicap certificate.
Societies　　contact in advance.
Green Fees　£30 per round.
Cards　　　≡≡ ☰☰ ≡≡ ☒☒ 〇
Prof　　　　Tim Barter
Designer　　Ewan Murray
Facilities　☒ 〿 ⅓ ⬛ ♀ ⛩ 🏠 ⛳ 🏟 🚗 ⌇ ⌐
& Leisure　hard tennis courts, heated indoor swimming
　　　　　　pool, squash, sauna, solarium, gymnasium,
　　　　　　beauty spa with 3 treatment rooms, relaxation
　　　　　　room.
Location　　1m NW of Botley on B3354

Hotel　　★★★★ 69% Botley Park Hotel Golf &
　　　　　Country Club, Winchester Rd, Boorley Green,
　　　　　BOTLEY ☎ 01489 780888 100 ⇔ 🐾

BROCKENHURST   Map 04 SU20

Brokenhurst Manor Sway Rd SO42 7SG
☎ 01590 623332 (Secretary) Fax 01590 624140
An attractive woodland/heathland course set at the edge
of the New Forest, with the unusual feature of three
loops of six holes each to complete the round.
Fascinating holes include the short 5th and 12th, and the
4th and 17th, both dog-legged. A stream also features on
seven of the holes.
18 holes, 6222yds, Par 70, SSS 70, Course record 63.
Club membership 850.
Visitors　　must contact in advance, numbers limited.
　　　　　　Must have a handicap certificate.
Societies　　Thu only, apply in writing.　　　　　　▶

Green Fees £45 per day; £35 per round (£60/£45 weekends & bank holidays).
Cards ▭ ▭ ▢
Prof Bruce Parker
Designer H S Colt
Facilities ⊗ ⅲ ⅃ ▆ ♥ ♀ ⅄ 🏠 ∅
Location 1m S on B3055

Hotel ★★★ 69% Balmer Lawn Hotel, Lyndhurst Rd, BROCKENHURST ☎ 01590 623116 55 ⇌ ℟

Additional hotel ★★ 67% Watersplash Hotel, The Rise, BROCKENHURST ☎ 01590 622344 Fax 01590 624047 23 ⇌ ℟

BURLEY   Map 04 SU20

Burley Cott Ln BH24 4BB
☎ 01425 402431 & 403737 Fax 01425 402431
Undulating heather and gorseland. The 7th requires an accurately placed tee shot to obtain par 4. Played off different tees on second nine.
9 holes, 6149yds, Par 71, SSS 69, Course record 68.
Club membership 520.
Visitors must contact in advance & preferably have a handicap certificate or be a member of a recognised golf club. May not play before 4pm Sat.
Societies telephone in advance, parties up to 14 only.
Green Fees not confirmed.
Facilities ▆ ⅄ ∅
Location E side of village

Hotel ★★★ 63% Moorhill House, BURLEY ☎ 01425 403285 24 ⇌ ℟

CORHAMPTON   Map 04 SU62

Corhampton Sheep's Pond Ln SO32 3LP ☎ 01489 877279
Free draining downland course situated in the heart of the picturesque Meon Valley.
18 holes, 6444yds, Par 71, SSS 71.
Club membership 800.
Visitors weekdays only and must contact in advance.
Societies Mon & Thu only, contact in writing or telephone.
Green Fees not confirmed.
Prof Ian Roper
Facilities ⊗ ⅃ ▆ ⅄ 🏠 ♥ ⏚ ∅
Location 1m W of Corhampton, off B3035

Hotel ★★ 73% Old House Hotel, The Square, WICKHAM ☎ 01329 833049 9 ⇌ ℟

CRONDALL   Map 04 SU74

Oak Park Heath Ln GU10 5PB
☎ 01252 850850 Fax 01252 850851
Village: Gently undulating parkland course overlooking pretty village. 16-bay floodlit driving range, practice green and practice bunker. Woodland: Undulating on holes 10 to 13. Panoramic views, mature trees, very challenging.

Woodland: *18 holes, 6352yds, Par 70, SSS 70.*
Village: *9 holes, 3279yds, Par 36.*
Club membership 500.
Visitors no restrictions, all tee times are bookable in advance.
Societies must telephone in advance.
Green Fees Woodland: £20 per round (£28 weekends & bank holidays). Village: £10 per round (£12 weekends & bank holidays). Prices under review.
Prof Gary Murton
Designer Patrick Dawson
Facilities ⊗ ⅲ ⅃ ▆ ♥ ♀ ⅄ 🏠 ♥ ♦ ⏚ ∅ ℓ
& Leisure gymnasium, steam room.
Location 0.5m E of village off A287 Farnham-Odiham

Hotel ★★★♣ 61% Farnham House Hotel, Alton Rd, FARNHAM ☎ 01252 716908 25 ⇌ ℟

DENMEAD   Map 04 SU61

Furzeley Furzeley Rd PO7 6TX
☎ 023 92231180 Fax 023 92230921
A well laid parkland course with many features including several strategically placed lakes which provide a good test set in beautiful scenery. Straight hitting and club selection on the short holes is the key to manufacturing a low score.
18 holes, 4363yds, Par 62, SSS 61, Course record 56.
Club membership 4000.
Visitors may book 2 days in advance.
Societies must telephone in advance and confirm in writing.
Green Fees £10 per 18 holes; £5.80 per 9 holes (£11.50/£6.30 weekends).
Prof Derek Brown
Designer Mark Sale/Robert Brown
Facilities ⊗ ⅲ ▆ ♥ ♀ ⅄ 🏠 ♥ ∅
Location From Waterlooville take Hambledon Road NW and follow golf course signs

Hotel ★★ 63% The Bear Hotel, East St, HAVANT ☎ 023 92486501 42 ⇌ ℟

DIBDEN   Map 04 SU40

Dibden Main Rd SO45 5TB ☎ 023 80207508
Municipal parkland course with views over Southampton Water. A pond guards the green at the par 5, 3rd hole. Twenty-bay driving range.
Course 1: 18 holes, 5931yds, Par 70, SSS 69, Course record 64.
Course 2: 9 holes, 1520yds, Par 29.
Club membership 600.
Visitors must book in advance for 18 hole course. 9 hole is pay & play.
Societies must contact in advance.
Green Fees not confirmed.
Prof Paul Smith & John Slade
Designer Hamilton Stutt
Facilities ⊗ ⅲ ⅃ ▆ ♥ ♀ ⅄ 🏠 ♥ ∅ ℓ
Location 2m NW of Dibden Purlieu, off A326 to Hythe

Hotel ★★★ 64% Forest Lodge Hotel, Pikes Hill, Romsey Rd, LYNDHURST ☎ 023 80283677 28 ⇌ ℟

EASTLEIGH   Map 04 SU41

Fleming Park Magpie Ln SO50 9LS ☎ 023 80612797
Parkland course with stream-'Monks Brook'-running through.
18 holes, 4436yds, Par 65, SSS 62, Course record 62.
Club membership 300.
Visitors   must contact in advance, no restrictions.
Societies   must contact in advance.
Green Fees   £7.50 per 18 holes; £4.75 per 9 holes
                  (£11.10/£7.55 weekends & bank holidays).
Prof   Chris Strickett
Designer   David Miller
Facilities   ⊗ ⅢⅬ 🍴 ♀ 🛋 🏠 🏌 🛒 ⚐
Location   E side of town centre

Hotel   ★★★ 64% Posthouse Eastleigh/Southampton,
                  Leigh Rd, EASTLEIGH
                  ☎ 0870 400 9075 116 ⇋ 🐾

EAST WELLOW   Map 04 SU32

Wellow Ryedown Ln SO51 6BD
☎ 01794 323833 & 322872 Fax 01794 323832
Three 9-hole courses set in 217 acres of parkland
surrounding Embley Park, former home of Florence
Nightingale.
Ryedown & Embley: 18 holes, 5966yds, Par 70, SSS 69.
Embley & Blackwater: 18 holes, 6295yds, Par 72, SSS 70.
Blackwater & Ryedown: 18 holes, 5819yds, Par 70, SSS 68.
Club membership 600.
Visitors   advisable to contact in advance weekdays only.
Societies   apply in writing or telephone, Mon-Fri not bank
                  holidays.
Green Fees   £20 per day; £16 per 18 holes.
Prof   Neil Bratley
Designer   W Wiltshire
Facilities   ⊗ ⅢⅬ 🍴 ♀ 🛋 🏠 🦅 🛒 ⚐
Location   Exit2 of M27, then A36 to Salisbury then 1m
                  right

Hotel   ★★★ 58% The White Horse, Market Place,
                  ROMSEY ☎ 0870 400 8123 33 ⇋ 🐾

FAREHAM   Map 04 SU50

Cams Hall Cams Hall Estate PO16 8UP
☎ 01329 827222 Fax 01329 827111
Two Peter Alliss/Clive Clark designed golf courses. The
Creek Course is coastal and has salt and fresh water lakes
and the fairways are lined with undulating hills. The Park
Course is designed in the grounds of Cams Hall.
*Creek Course: 18 holes, 6244yds, Par 71, SSS 70, Course
record 69.*
Park Course: 9 holes, 3247yds, Par 36, SSS 36.
Club membership 950.
Visitors   must contact in advance, tee times available any
                  time.
Societies   telephone for details and society golf day pack.
Green Fees   £34 per day, £20 per 18 holes (£40/27.50
                  weekends & bank holidays).
Prof   Jason Neve
Designer   Peter Alliss
Facilities   ⊗ ⅢⅬ 🍴 ♀ 🛋 🏠 🏌 🦅 🛒 ⚐
& Leisure   sauna.
Location   M27 exit 11 to A27

Hotel   ★★★ 62% Lysses House Hotel, 51 High St,
                  FAREHAM ☎ 01329 822622 21 ⇋ 🐾

FARNBOROUGH   Map 04 SU85

Southwood Ively Rd, Cove GU14 0LJ
☎ 01252 548700 Fax 01252 515855
Municipal parkland course with stream running through.
18 holes, 5738yds, Par 69, SSS 68, Course record 61.
Club membership 650.
Visitors   must book in advance.
Societies   must contact in advance.
Green Fees   £14 per 18 holes (£16.50 weekends).
Cards   💳 📇 💳 📇 📇 🄶
Prof   Bob Hammond
Designer   Hawtree & Son
Facilities   🛋 🏠 🦅 🛒 🏌 ⚐
Location   0.5m W

Hotel   ★★★ 67% Posthouse Farnborough, Lynchford
                  Rd, FARNBOROUGH
                  ☎ 0870 400 9029 143 ⇋ 🐾

FLEET   Map 04 SU85

North Hants Minley Rd GU13 8RE
☎ 01252 616443 Fax 01252 811627
Picturesque tree-lined course with much heather and
gorse close to the fairways. A comparatively easy par-4
first hole may lull the golfer into a false sense of
security, only to be rudely awakened at the testing holes
which follow. The ground is rather undulating and,
though not tiring, does offer some excellent 'blind'
shots, and more than a few surprises in judging distance.
18 holes, 6257yds, Par 69, SSS 70, Course record 65.
Club membership 600.

Visitors   must contact at least 48 hours in advance.
                  Must play with member at weekends.
Societies   Tue & Wed only. Subject to pre-booking.
Green Fees   not confirmed.
Prof   Steve Porter
Designer   James Braid
Facilities   ⊗ ⅢⅬ 🍴 ♀ 🛋 🏠 ⚐
Location   0.25m N of Fleet station on B3013

Hotel   ★★★ 62% Lismoyne Hotel, Church Rd,
                  FLEET ☎ 01252 628555 44 ⇋ 🐾

Looking for a driving range?
See the index at the back of the guide

Historically one of only 3 original houses in Fleet the Lismoyne, dates from the 1880s and still retains the elegant charm of a grand private house. Refurbished during the autumn of 1997 the Hampshire restaurant and well stocked Wellington bar provide a haven of relaxation, with fine food, excellent wines and quality service seldom available these days. A 5 minute walk takes you to the heart of the town where shopping is a delight. Ideally situated for the surrounding countryside with a wealth of natural history, including Fleet pond one of England's largest fresh water nature reserves.

**Church Road, Fleet,
Hants GU13 8NA
Tel: +44 (0) 1252 628555
Fax: +44 (0) 1252 811761**

GOSPORT

Map 04 SZ69

Gosport & Stokes Bay Off Fort Rd, Haslar PO12 2AT
☎ 023 92527941 Fax 023 92527941
A testing links course overlooking the Solent, with plenty of gorse and short rough. Changing winds.
9 holes, 5999yds, Par 70, SSS 69, Course record 65.
Club membership 499.
Visitors may not play Sun and Thu.
Societies must contact in writing.
Green Fees £20 per day; £15 per 18 holes.
Facilities ⊗ ⅷ ᕋ ᕬ ♀ ᕤ ᒣ ♐ ♂
Location A32 S from Fareham, E on Fort rd to Haslar

Hotel ★★★ 60% Belle Vue Hotel, 39 Marine Pde East, LEE-ON-THE-SOLENT
☎ 023 92550258 24 ⇆ ♞ Annexe 3 ⇆ ♞

HARTLEY WINTNEY

Map 04 SU75

Hartley Wintney London Rd RG27 8PT
☎ 01252 844211 (Sec) & 843779 (Prof) Fax 01252 844211
Easy walking, parkland course in pleasant countryside.
Played off different tees on back nine, with testing par 4s at 4th and 13th.
9 holes, 6096yds, Par 70, SSS 69, Course record 63.
Club membership 475.
Visitors must contact in advance, restricted at weekends.
Societies Tue & Thu only by prior arrangement.
Green Fees £20 per round (£25 weekends). Prices under review.
Cards ▭▭ ▭▭

Prof Martin Smith
Facilities ⊗ ⅷ ᕋ ᕬ ♀ ᕤ ᒣ ♐ ♂
Location NE side of village on A30

Hotel ★★★ 62% Lismoyne Hotel, Church Rd, FLEET ☎ 01252 628555 44 ⇆ ♞

HAYLING ISLAND

Map 04 SU70

Hayling Links Ln PO11 0BX
☎ 023 92464446 Fax 023 92464446
A delightful links course among the dunes offering fine sea-scapes and views across to the Isle of Wight.
Varying sea breezes and sometimes strong winds ensure that the course seldom plays the same two days running.
Testing holes at the 12th and 13th, both par 4. Club selection is important.
18 holes, 6531yds, Par 71, SSS 71, Course record 65.
Club membership 800.
Visitors must contact in advance and have a handicap certificate, no jeans, denims or collarless shirts allowed.
Societies welcome Tue & Wed, or half days Mon & Thu, apply in writing or telephone.
Green Fees £38 per day; £30 per round (£50/£40 weekends).
Prof Raymond Gadd
Designer Taylor 1905, Simpson 1933
Facilities ⊗ ⅷ by prior arrangement ᕋ ᕬ ᕤ ᒣ ♐ ♂
Location SW side of island at West Town

Hotel ★★★ 63% Posthouse Havant, Northney Rd, HAYLING ISLAND
☎ 0870 400 9038 92 ⇔ ⦗

KINGSCLERE
Map 04 SU55

Sandford Springs Wolverton RG26 5RT
☎ 01635 296800 & 296808 (Pro Shop)
Fax 01635 296801
The course has unique variety in beautiful surroundings and offers three distinctive loops of 9 holes. There are water hazards, woodlands and gradients to negotiate, providing a challenge for all playing categories.
The Park: 9 holes, 2963yds, Par 34.
The Lakes: 9 holes, 3042yds, Par 35.
The Wood: 9 holes, 3180yds, Par 36.
Club membership 650.
Visitors must contact in advance. Restricted at weekends.
Societies must contact in advance.
Green Fees not confirmed.
Cards ⬛ ⬛ ⬛ 🖂
Prof Gary Edmunds/Kim Brake
Designer Hawtree & Son
Facilities ⊗ ⧎ ⬛ ⬛ ♀ ⨇ ⬛ 🏴 🛺 ⨍
Location On A339 between Basingstoke and Newbury

Hotel ★★★ 64% The Chequers, Oxford St, NEWBURY ☎ 01635 38000
45 ⇔ ⦗ Annexe 11 ⇔ ⦗

KINGSLEY
Map 04 SU73

Dean Farm GU35 9NG ☎ 01420 489478 & 472313
Undulating downland course.
9 holes, 1500yds, Par 29.
Visitors no restrictions. Course closed Mon until 1pm.
Societies must contact in writing.
Green Fees £4.50 per 9 holes.
Facilities ♀ 🏴
& Leisure hard tennis courts.
Location W side of village off B3004

Hotel ★★★ 66% Alton Grange Hotel, London Rd, ALTON
☎ 01420 86565 26 ⇔ ⦗ Annexe 4 ⇔ ⦗

LECKFORD
Map 04 SU33

Leckford SO20 6JG ☎ 01264 810320
A testing downland course with good views.
9 holes, 6444yds, Par 70, SSS 71.
Club membership 200.
Green Fees not confirmed.
Facilities ⨇
Location 1m SW off A3057

Hotel ★★★ 63% Grosvenor Hotel, High St, STOCKBRIDGE ☎ 01264 810606 25 ⇔ ⦗

Looking for a driving range?
See the index at the back of the guide

LEE-ON-THE-SOLENT
Map 04 SU50

Lee-on-Solent Brune Ln PO13 9PB
☎ 023 92551170 Fax 023 92554233
A modest parkland/heathland course, yet a testing one. The five short holes always demand a high standard of play and the 13th is rated one of the best in the country. The last 6 holes are amongst the most difficult in Hampshire.
18 holes, 5933yds, Par 69, SSS 69, Course record 64.
Club membership 750.
Visitors may not play before 9am or after 2.30pm on weekends. Handicap certificate required.
Societies must contact in advance.
Green Fees £30 per day/round.
Cards ⬛ ⬛ ⬛ 🖂
Prof John Richardson
Facilities ⊗ ⧎ ⬛ ⬛ ♀ ⨇ ⬛ 🏴 ⨍ ⦗
Location 1m N off B3385

Hotel ★★★ 60% Belle Vue Hotel, 39 Marine Pde East, LEE-ON-THE-SOLENT
☎ 023 92550258 24 ⇔ ⦗ Annexe 3 ⇔ ⦗

LIPHOOK
Map 04 SU83

Liphook Wheatsheaf Enclosure GU30 7EH
☎ 01428 723271 & 723785 Fax 01428 724853
Heathland course with easy walking and fine views.
18 holes, 6167yds, Par 70, SSS 69, Course record 67.
Club membership 800.
Visitors must contact in advance; may not play Tue, competition days etc.
Societies Wed-Fri only. Must contact in advance.
Green Fees not confirmed.
Prof Ian Large
Designer A C Croome
Facilities ⊗ ⬛ ⬛ ♀ ⨇ ⬛ 🏴 ⨍
Location 1m S on B2030 (old A3)

Hotel ★★★★ 71% Lythe Hill Hotel, Petworth Rd, HASLEMERE ☎ 01428 651251 41 ⇔ ⦗

Old Thorns Hotel, Golf & Country Club Griggs Green GU30 7PE ☎ 01428 724555 Fax 01428 725036
A challenging 18-hole championship-standard course designed around magnificent oaks, beeches, Scots pine and lakes.
18 holes, 6581yds, Par 72, SSS 71, Course record 69.
Club membership 220.
Visitors subject to availability.
Societies must telephone in advance.
Green Fees £40 per day; £35 per round (£50/£40 weekends).
Cards ⬛ ⬛ ⬛ ⬛ 🖂
Prof Alan Bott
Designer Peter Alliss/Dave Thomas
Facilities ⊗ ⧎ ⬛ ⬛ ♀ ⨇ ⬛ 🏴 🛺 🛺 ⨍ ⦗
& Leisure hard tennis courts, heated indoor swimming pool, sauna, solarium, gymnasium.
Location Leave A3 at Griggs Green, S of Liphook, signposted 'Old Thorns'

Hotel ★★★ 73% Old Thorns Hotel, Golf & Country Club, Longmoor Rd, Griggs Green, LIPHOOK ☎ 01428 724555
28 ⇔ ⦗ Annexe 4 ⦗

LYNDHURST   Map 04 SU20

Bramshaw Brook SO43 7HE
☎ 023 80813433 Fax 023 80813958
Two 18-hole courses. The Manor Course is landscaped parkland with excellent greens, and features mature trees and streams. The Forest course is set amidst beautiful open forest. Easy walking. The Bell Inn Hotel, attached to the club, provides fine accommodation just a wedge shot from the first tee, and reserved tee times for its guests.
Manor Course: 18 holes, 6517yds, Par 71, SSS 71, Course record 65.
Forest Course: 18 holes, 5774yds, Par 69, SSS 68, Course record 65.
Club membership 950.

Visitors	limited availability weekends and bank holidays unless accompanied by member or resident of Bell Inn.
Societies	apply in writing or telephone in advance.
Green Fees	£44 per day; Manor: £30 per round; Forest: £25 per round.
Cards	🔲 🔲 🔲 🔲 🔲
Prof	Clive Bonner
Facilities	⊗ 🍽 🏌 ♀ 🏐 🛒 ⛳ 🥅 🏹 🎯 ✔
& Leisure	golfing rates at Bell Inn.
Location	On B3079 1m W of M27 junc 1
Hotel	★★★ 66% Bell Inn, BROOK ☎ 023 8081 2214 25 ⇄ 🦶

New Forest Southampton Rd SO43 7BU
☎ 023 80282752 Fax 023 80282484
This picturesque heathland course is laid out in a typical stretch of the New Forest on high ground a little above the village of Lyndhurst. Natural hazards include the inevitable forest ponies. The first two holes are somewhat teasing, as is the 485-yard (par 5) 9th. Walking is easy.
18 holes, 5742yds, Par 69, SSS 68.
Club membership 700.

Visitors	must contact in advance.
Societies	must contact in advance.
Green Fees	not confirmed.
Prof	Danny Harris
Facilities	⊗ 🍽 by prior arrangement 🏐 🍺 ♀ 🛒 💼 ✔
Location	0.5m NE off A35
Hotel	★★★ 69% Crown Hotel, High St, LYNDHURST ☎ 023 80282922 39 ⇄ 🦶

NEW MILTON   Map 04 SZ29

Chewton Glen Hotel Christchurch Rd BH25 6QS
☎ 01425 275341 Fax 01425 272310
A 9-hole, Par 3 course with the hotel grounds plus a practice area. ONLY open to residents of the hotel or as a guest of a member of the club.
9 holes, 854yds, Par 27.
Club membership 150.

▶

Visitors	non residents must play with member.
Societies	must contact in advance.
Green Fees	not confirmed.
Cards	[card symbols]
Facilities	[facility symbols]
& Leisure	hard tennis courts, outdoor and indoor heated swimming pools, sauna, gymnasium.
Hotel	★★★★★🏆 Chewton Glen Hotel, Christchurch Rd, NEW MILTON ☎ 01425 275341 52 🛏 🐾 Annexe 2 🛏 🐾

OVERTON   Map 04 SU54

Test Valley Micheldever Rd RG25 3DS
☎ 01256 771737 Fax 01256 770916
A downland course with excellent drainage, fine year-round greens and prominent water and bunker features. On undulating terrain with lovely views over the Hampshire countryside. Has hosted the Hampshire Open and the PGA Lombard Trophy.
18 holes, 6811yds, Par 72, SSS 73, Course record 66.
Club membership 500.

Visitors	must phone in advance. Must play after 11am weekends & bank holidays.
Societies	apply in writing or telephone in advance.
Green Fees	£25 per day; £17 per round (£34/£23 weekends).
Cards	[card symbols]
Prof	Alastair Briggs
Designer	Don Wright
Facilities	[facility symbols]
Location	1.5m N of a303 on road to Overton
Hotel	★★★ 69% The Hampshire Centrecourt Hotel, Centre Dr, Chineham, BASINGSTOKE ☎ 01256 816664 50 🛏 🐾

OWER   Map 04 SU31

Paultons Golf Centre Old Salisbury Rd SO51 6AN
☎ 023 80813992
A Pay and Play 18-hole course built within the original Paultons parkland which was laid out by 'Capability' Brown. There is also a 9-hole academy course, ideal for beginners or players wishing to improve their short games as well as a 20-bay floodlit driving range.
18 holes, 6238yds, Par 71, SSS 70, Course record 72.
Academy: 9 holes, 1324yds, Par 27, SSS 27, Course record 24.
Club membership 500.

Visitors	pay & play.
Societies	telephone for details.
Green Fees	not confirmed.
Prof	John Cave & Heath Teschner
Designer	J R Smith
Facilities	[facility symbols]
Hotel	★★★ 69% Bartley Lodge, Lyndhurst Rd, CADNAM ☎ 023 80812248 31 🛏 🐾

PETERSFIELD   Map 04 SU72

Petersfield (New Course) Tankerdale Ln, Liss GU33 7QY
☎ 01730 895165 (office) & 895216 (pro)
Fax 01730 894713
Gently undulating course with mature trees and hedgerows. All the advantages of a course recently built to USGA specifications.
18 holes, 6387yds, Par 72, SSS 71.
Club membership 725.

Visitors	start times required.
Societies	booking forms and deposit required.
Green Fees	£25 per round (£30 weekends & bank holidays).
Prof	Greg Hughes
Facilities	[facility symbols]
Location	Off the A3 (M), between the Liss/Petersfield exits southbound
Hotel	★★★ 77% Spread Eagle Hotel and Health Spa, South St, MIDHURST ☎ 01730 816911 35 🛏 🐾 Annexe 4 🐾

Petersfield (Old Course) Sussex Rd GU31 4EJ
☎ 01730 895165 Fax 01730 894713
9 hole parkland course on level ground in an area of outstanding natural beauty. Numerous trees and water features. Part of Petersfield Golf Club although 1.5m away from the 18 hole New Course.
9 holes, 3005yds, Par 72, SSS 69.

Visitors	starting times required, pay & play at all times.
Societies	booking form must be completed & deposit paid.
Green Fees	not confirmed.
Prof	Greg Hughes
Facilities	[facility symbols]
Location	Off Sussex Road , B214
Hotel	★★★ 77% Spread Eagle Hotel and Health Spa, South St, MIDHURST ☎ 01730 816911 35 🛏 🐾 Annexe 4 🐾

PORTSMOUTH & SOUTHSEA   Map 04 SU60

Great Salterns Public Course Burrfields Rd PO3 5HH
☎ 023 92664549 Fax 023 92650525
Easy walking, seaside course with open fairways and testing shots onto well-guarded, small greens. Testing 13th hole, par 4, requiring 130yd shot across a lake.
18 holes, 5575yds, Par 70, SSS 67, Course record 64.
Club membership 700.

Visitors	book up to 1 week in advance.
Societies	must contact in advance.
Green Fees	£10.30 per round (£12.50 weekends).
Cards	[card symbols]
Prof	Terry Healy
Facilities	[facility symbols]
Location	NE of town centre on A2030
Hotel	★★★ 65% Innlodge Hotel, Burrfields Rd, PORTSMOUTH ☎ 023 92650510 73 🛏 🐾

Southsea The Clubhouse, Burrfields Rd PO3 5JJ
☎ 023 92664549 Fax 023 92668667
Municipal, meadowland course.
18 holes, 5800yds, Par 71, SSS 68, Course record 64.
Club membership 435.

Visitors	no restrictions. Booking advisable.
Societies	must contact in advance.
Green Fees	£11 per round (£13 weekends & bank holidays).
Prof	Terry Healy
Facilities	[facility symbols]
Location	0.5m off M27
Hotel	★★★ 65% Innlodge Hotel, Burrfields Rd, PORTSMOUTH ☎ 023 92650510 73 🛏 🐾

ROMSEY   Map 04 SU32

Dunwood Manor Danes Rd, Awbridge SO51 0GF
☎ 01794 340549 Fax 01794 34215
Undulating parkland course with fine views. Fine holes
running through mature woodland.
18 holes, 5767yds, Par 69, SSS 68, Course record 65.
Club membership 620.

Visitors	always welcome advisable to contact in advance; essential for weekends after 11am.
Societies	must contact in advance.
Green Fees	£30 per day; £22 per round (£30 per round weekendsafter 11am).
Prof	Heath Teschner
Facilities	⊗ ⅲ ⅃ 🛆 🍺 ♀ ♨ 🏠 ⚑ 🏌 🛺 ♣
Location	4m W off A27

Hotel   ★★★ 66% Bell Inn, BROOK
☎ 023 8081 2214 25 ⇆ 🐾

Romsey Romsey Rd, Nursling SO16 0XW
☎ 023 80734637 Fax 023 80741036
Parkland/woodland course with narrow tree-lined fairways.
Six holes are undulating, rest are sloping. There are superb
views over the Test valley.
18 holes, 5851yds, Par 69, SSS 68.
Club membership 900.

Visitors	welcome Mon-Fri, must play with member weekends and bank holidays.
Societies	Mon, Tue & Thu, must contact in advance.
Green Fees	not confirmed.
Prof	Mark Desmond
Facilities	⊗ ⅲ ⅃ 🛆 🍺 ♀ ♨ 🏠 🏌
Location	3m S on A3057

Hotel   ★★★ 58% The White Horse, Market Place,
ROMSEY ☎ 0870 400 8123 33 ⇆ 🐾

ROTHERWICK   Map 04 SU75

Tylney Park RG27 9AY
☎ 01256 762079 Fax 01256 763079
Parkland course. Practice area.
18 holes, 6109yds, Par 70, SSS 69, Course record 67.
Club membership 730.

Visitors	must be with member at weekends or have a handicap certificate.
Societies	must apply by phone in advance.
Green Fees	£23 per day/round (£30 per weekends).
Cards	🖩 ▬ 📇 💳
Prof	Chris de Bruin
Designer	W Wiltshire
Facilities	⊗ ⅲ by prior arrangement 🛆 🍺 ♀ ♨ 🏠 ⚑ 🏌 🛺 ♣
Location	0.5m SW of Rotherwick, 2m NW of Hook, 2.5m from M3 junct 5 via Newnham

Hotel   ★★★★🏌 Tylney Hall Hotel, Tylney Hall,
ROTHERWICK ☎ 01256 764881
35 ⇆ 🐾 Annexe 75 ⇆ 🐾

> AA Hotels that have special
> arrangements with golf courses are listed at
> the back of the guide

ROWLANDS CASTLE   Map 04 SU71

Rowlands Castle 31 Links Ln PO9 6AE
☎ 023 92412784 Fax 023 92413649
Reasonably dry in winter, the flat parkland course is a
testing one with a number of tricky dog-legs and bunkers
much in evidence. The Par 4 13th is a signature hole
necessitating a drive to a narrow fairway and a second
shot to a two-tiered green. The 7th, at 522yds, is the
longest hole on the course and leads to a well-guarded
armchair green.
18 holes, 6612yds, Par 72, SSS 72, Course record 69.
Club membership 800.

Visitors	may not play Sat; must contact in advance and hold a handicap certificate.
Societies	Tue & Thu only; must contact in writing.
Green Fees	£30 per day (£32 weekends).
Prof	Peter Klepacz
Designer	Colt
Facilities	⊗ ⅲ ⅃ 🛆 🍺 ♀ ♨ 🏠 🏌 🛺 ♣
Location	W side of village off B2149

Hotel   ★★★ 68% Brookfield Hotel, Havant Rd,
EMSWORTH
☎ 01243 373363 & 376383 Fax 01243 376
342 40 ⇆ 🐾

SHEDFIELD   Map 04 SU51

Marriott Meon Valley Hotel & Country Club Sandy Ln
SO32 2HQ ☎ 01329 833455 Fax 01329 834411
It has been said that a golf course architect is as good as
the ground on which he has to work. Here Hamilton Stutt
had magnificent terrain at his disposal and a very good
and lovely parkland course is the result. There are three
holes over water. The hotel provides many sports
facilities. The Championship Meon Course plays host to
the Phillips PFA Golf Classic in 1998 and 1999, a true
testament to the challenge it offers.
Meon Course: 18 holes, 6520yds, Par 71, SSS 71,
Course record 66.
Valley Course: 9 holes, 2721yds, Par 35, SSS 33.
Club membership 910.

Visitors	may book up to seven days in advance, not available at weekends and bank holidays.
Societies	telephone in advance, written confirmation.
Green Fees	not confirmed.
Cards	🖩 ▬ 📇 💳 📇 🖩 💳
Prof	Jason O'Malley
Designer	Hamilton Stutt

▶

Facilities & Leisure	⊗ ⛤ ⮃ ☕ ♀ ⚲ 🏠 🚶 🏌 🛥 ✎ 🏌
	hard tennis courts, heated indoor swimming pool, sauna, solarium, gymnasium, health & beauty salon, spa bath, aerobics studio.
Location	Off A334 between Botley and Wickham. Access via junct 7 M27
Hotel	★★★★ 70% Marriott Meon Valley Hotel & Country Club, Sandy Ln, SHEDFIELD ☎ 01329 833455 113 ⇄ 🏌

SOUTHAMPTON   Map 04 SU41

Chilworth Main Rd, Chilworth SO16 7JP
☎ 023 80740544
A course with two loops of nine holes, with a booking system to allow undisturbed play. The front nine are fairly long and undulating and include water hazards. The back nine are tighter and quite a challenge.
Manor Golf Course: 18 holes, 5740yds, Par 69, SSS 69, Course record 68.
Club membership 600.

Visitors	no restrictions.
Societies	telephone in advance and complete booking form, various packages available.
Green Fees	£12 per round (£15 weekends).
Cards	💳 💳 💳 💳 💳 💳
Designer	J Garner
Facilities	⊗ ⛤ by prior arrangement ⮃ ☕ ♀ ⚲ 🏠 🏌 🏌
Location	A27 between Chilworth and Romsey
Hotel	★★★ 61% Highfield House, Highfield Ln, Portswood, SOUTHAMPTON ☎ 023 80359955 66 ⇄ 🏌

Southampton Golf Course Rd, Bassett SO16 7AY
☎ 023 80760478 & 80760546 (booking) Fax 023 80760472
This beautiful municipal parkland course always ensures a good game, fast in summer, slow in winter. Three par 4's over 450 yds.
18 holes, 6103yds, Par 69, SSS 70.
9 holes, 2395yds, Par 33.

Visitors	18 hole course: min 2 players (3 weekends and bank holidays) booking advisable but not always necessary. 9 hole course: 1-4 players per tee
Societies	welcome, book up to 1yr in advance.
Green Fees	18 hole course: £9.30 (£12.70 weekends & bank holidays); 9 hole course: £4.20 per round (£6 weekends & bank holidays).
Prof	John Waring
Designer	Hockley/A P Taylor
Facilities	⊗ ⛤ ⮃ ☕ ♀ ⚲ 🏠 🏌 🏌
Location	4m N of city centre off A33
Hotel	★★ 63% The Star Hotel & Restaurant, 26 High St, SOUTHAMPTON ☎ 023 80339939 43rm (37 ⇄ 🏌)

Stoneham Monks Wood Close, Bassett SO16 3TT
☎ 023 80769272 Fax 023 80766320
A hilly, heather course with sand or peat sub-soil; the fairways are separated by belts of woodland and heather to present a varied terrain. The interesting 4th is a difficult par 4 and the fine 11th has cross-bunkers about 150 yards from the tee.

18 holes, 6310yds, Par 72, SSS 70, Course record 63.
Club membership 800.

Visitors	advisable to contact in advance, handicap certificate required.
Societies	Mon, Thu & Fri only. Must telephone in advance or apply in writing.
Green Fees	not confirmed.
Prof	Ian Young
Designer	Willie Park
Facilities	⊗ ⛤ ⮃ ☕ ♀ ⚲ 🏠 🏌 🏌
Location	4m N of city centre off A27
Hotel	★★★ 61% Highfield House, Highfield Ln, Portswood, SOUTHAMPTON ☎ 023 80359955 66 ⇄ 🏌

SOUTHWICK   Map 04 SU60

Southwick Park Naval Recreation Centre Pinsley Dr PO17 6EL ☎ 023 92380131 Fax 023 92210289
Set in 100 acres of parkland.
18 holes, 5992yds, Par 69, SSS 69, Course record 64.
Club membership 700.

Visitors	contact in advance, welcome weekends after 2pm
Societies	Tue only, telephone in advance.
Green Fees	£18 per day; £10.20 per round (£12 weekends) reductions in winter.
Prof	John Green
Designer	C Lawrie
Facilities	⊗ ⛤ by prior arrangement ⮃ ☕ ♀ ⚲ 🏠 🏌 🏌
Location	0.5m SE off B2177
Hotel	★★ 73% Old House Hotel, The Square, WICKHAM ☎ 01329 833049 9 ⇄ 🏌

TADLEY   Map 04 SU66

Bishopswood Bishopswood Ln RG26 4AT
☎ 0118 9812200 Fax 0118 9408606
Wooded course, fairly tight, with stream and natural water hazards.
9 holes, 6474yds, Par 72, SSS 71, Course record 66.
Club membership 485.

Visitors	must contact in advance. No play weekends or bank holidays.
Societies	must contact by telephone.
Green Fees	£10 per 9 holes; £15 per 18 holes.
Cards	💳 💳
Prof	Steve Ward
Designer	M W Phillips/G Blake
Facilities	⊗ ⛤ ⮃ ☕ ♀ ⚲ 🏠 🏌 🏌
Location	6m N of Basingstoke off the A340
Hotel	★★★ 74% Romans Country House Hotel, Little London Rd, SILCHESTER ☎ 0118 970 0421 11 ⇄ 🏌 Annexe 14 ⇄ 🏌

WATERLOOVILLE   Map 04 SU60

Portsmouth Crookhorn Ln, Purbrook PO7 5QL
☎ 023 92372210 Fax 023 92200766
Hilly, challenging course with good views of Portsmouth Harbour. Rarely free from the wind and the picturesque 6th, 17th and 18th holes can test the best.
18 holes, 6139yds, Par 69, SSS 70, Course record 64.
Club membership 700.

▶

Visitors	must book in advance.
Societies	must book in advance, in writing or by telephone.
Green Fees	£10.30 per round; 7.40 per 9 holes (£12.50 weekends).
Cards	💳 💳 💳 💳 💳
Prof	Jason Banting
Designer	Hawtree
Facilities	⊗ ⅢⅢ ⅃ ♥ ♀ ⚓ 🏠 ⛳ ✐
Location	2m S, off A3
Hotel	★★ 63% The Bear Hotel, East St, HAVANT ☎ 023 92486501 42 ⇆ 🏧

Waterlooville Cherry Tree Av, Cowplain PO8 8AP
☎ 023 92263388 Fax 023 92347513
Parkland course, easy walking. Challenging course with 5 par 5's over 500 yards and featuring 4 ponds and a stream running through.
18 holes, 6602yds, Par 72, SSS 72, Course record 64.
Club membership 800.

Visitors	must contact in advance & may only play on weekdays. Handicap certificate required.
Societies	Thu only; apply by letter or telephone.
Green Fees	£30 per day; £25 per round.
Prof	John Hay
Designer	Henry Cotton
Facilities	⊗ ⅃ ♥ ♀ ⚓ 🏠 ✐
Location	NE side of town centre off A3
Hotel	★★★ 63% Posthouse Havant, Northney Rd, HAYLING ISLAND ☎ 0870 400 9038 92 ⇆ 🏧

WINCHESTER   Map 04 SU42

Hockley Twyford SO21 1PL
☎ 01962 713165 Fax 01962 713612
High downland course with good views.
18 holes, 6336yds, Par 71, SSS 70, Course record 64.
Club membership 750.

Visitors	are advised to phone in advance. Restricted times at weekends. Handicap certificate required.
Societies	must telephone in advance and confirm in writing with deposit.
Green Fees	£38 per day; £30 per round (£40 weekends & bank holidays).
Prof	Terry Lane
Designer	James Braid
Facilities	⊗ ⅢⅢ ⅃ ♥ ♀ ⚓ 🏠 ✐
Location	Jct 11 M3, follow sign to Twyford
Hotel	★★★★ 62% The Wessex, Paternoster Row, WINCHESTER ☎ 0870 400 8126 94 ⇆ 🏧

Royal Winchester Sarum Rd SO22 5QE
☎ 01962 852462 Fax 01962 865048
The Royal Winchester course is a sporting downland course centred on a rolling valley, so the course is hilly in places. Royal Winchester must be included in any list of notable clubs, because of its age (it dates from 1888) and also because the club was involved in one of the very first professional matches.
18 holes, 6204yds, Par 71, SSS 70, Course record 65.
Club membership 800.

Visitors	must play with member at weekends. Must contact in advance and have a handicap certificate.
Societies	must contact in writing or by telephone.
Green Fees	£38 per day; £30 per round.
Cards	💳
Prof	Steven Hunter
Designer	J H Taylor
Facilities	⊗ ⅢⅢ ⅃ ♥ ♀ ⚓ 🏠 ✐
Location	1.5m W off A3090
Hotel	★★★★🏌🏌 73% Lainston House Hotel, Sparsholt, WINCHESTER ☎ 01962 863588 38 ⇆ 🏧

South Winchester Romsey Rd SO22 5QW
☎ 01962 877800 Fax 01962 877900
This Dave Thomas designed course incorporates downland, meadows and seven lakes. Home of the Hampshire PGA and the venue for European Ladies Tour Pro-Ams.
18 holes, 7086yds, Par 72, SSS 74, Course record 68.
Club membership 750.

Visitors	guests only by arrangement.
Societies	must contact in advance.
Green Fees	by appointment.
Cards	💳 💳 💳 💳 💳
Prof	Richard Adams
Designer	Dave Thomas
Facilities	⊗ ⅢⅢ ⅃ ♥ ♀ ⚓ 🏠 ⛳ 🏌 ⚓ ✐ 🏌
Location	On A3090 Romsey road
Hotel	★★★ 70% Royal Hotel, Saint Peter St, WINCHESTER ☎ 01962 840840 75 ⇆ 🏧

HEREFORDSHIRE

HEREFORD   Map 03 SO53

Belmont Lodge Belmont HR2 9SA
☎ 01432 352666 Fax 01432 358090
Parkland course designed in two loops of nine. The first nine take the higher ground, offering magnificent views over Herefordshire. The second nine run alongside the river Wye with five holes in play against the river.
18 holes, 6511yds, Par 72, SSS 71, Course record 66.
Club membership 450.

Visitors advised to contact in advance at weekends. Tel: 01432 352666 or 352717.
Societies must telephone in advance.
Green Fees £18 per round (£25 weekends). Winter reductions.
Cards
Prof Mike Welsh
Designer Bob Sandow
Facilities ⊗ ⵊ 🛈 ▙ � ♨ 🏌 ☻ ✦ ⛏ ⚷
& Leisure hard tennis courts, fishing, snooker room.
Location 2m S off A465

Hotel ★★★ 62% Belmont Lodge & Golf Course, Belmont, HEREFORD ☎ 01432 352666 30 ⇄ ⟝

Burghill Valley Tillington Rd, Burghill HR4 7RW ☎ 01432 760456 Fax 01432 761654
The course is situated in typically beautiful Herefordshire countryside. The walking is easy on gently rolling fairways with a background of hills and woods and in the distance, the Welsh mountains. Some holes are played through mature cider orchards and there are two lakes to negotiate. A fair but interesting test for players of all abilities.
18 holes, 6239yds, Par 71, SSS 70, Course record 69.
Club membership 700.
Visitors contact in advance.
Societies apply in writing or telephone in advance.
Green Fees not confirmed.
Cards ▀ 🛈 ◼ 🄌
Prof Nigel Clarke
Designer M Barnett
Facilities ▙ P ☻ 🏌 ✦ ⛏ ⚷
Location 4m NW of Hereford

Hotel ★★★ 63% The Green Dragon, Broad St, HEREFORD ☎ 0870 400 8113 83 ⇄ ⟝

Hereford Municipal Hereford Leisure Centre, Holmer Rd HR4 9UD ☎ 01432 344376 Fax 01432 266281
This municipal parkland course is more challenging than first appearance. The well-drained greens are open all year round with good drainage for excellent winter golf.
9 holes, 3060yds, Par 35, SSS 69.
Club membership 195.
Visitors restrictions on race days.
Societies telephone in advance.
Green Fees £6.50 18 holes, £4.25 9 holes (£8/£5.25 weekends).
Cards ▀ 🛈 ◼ 🄌
Prof Gary Morgan
Designer J Leek
Facilities ⊗ ⵊ 🛈 ▙ ▙ P ♨ ☻ ✦ ⚷
& Leisure squash, gymnasium.
Location Adjacent to race course & leisure centre

Hotel ★★ 63% The Merton Hotel & Governors Restaurant, 28 Commercial Rd, HEREFORD ☎ 01432 265925 19 ⇄ ⟝

KINGTON   Map 03 SO25

Kington Bradnor Hill HR5 3RE ☎ 01544 230340 & 231320
The highest 18-hole course in England, with magnificent views over seven counties. A natural heathland course with easy walking on mountain turf cropped by sheep. There is bracken to catch any really bad shots but no sand traps.

---

18 holes, 5980yds, Par 70, SSS 68, Course record 63.
Club membership 640.
Visitors contact the professional.
Societies must book in advance through the Hon Secretary.
Green Fees not confirmed.
Prof Dean Oliver
Designer Major Hutchison
Facilities ⊗ ⵊ 🛈 ▙ ▙ P ♨ ☻ ✦ ⚷ ⛏
Location 0.5m N of Kington, off B4355

Hotel ★★★ 65% Talbot Hotel, West St, LEOMINSTER ☎ 01568 616347 20 ⇄ ⟝

LEOMINSTER   Map 03 SO45

Leominster Ford Bridge HR6 0LE ☎ 01568 611402 (Prof) & 610055 (Sec/Mngr) Fax 01568 610055
On undulating parkland with the lower holes running alongside the River Lugg and others on the higher part of the course affording fine panoramic views over the surrounding countryside.
18 holes, 6026yds, Par 70, SSS 69.
Club membership 550.
Visitors must contact in advance.
Societies must telephone in advance.
Green Fees Tue-Fri: £22 per day; £17 per round; Mon after 9.30am :£15 per day; £8 per round (£28/£23 weekends & bank holidays).
Prof Andrew Ferriday
Designer Bob Sandow   ▶

Facilities & Leisure	⊗ ⵊ 🏌 ♟ ♟ ↄ 🏕 ⚑ 𝄢
	fishing.
Location	3m S of Leominster on A49. Clearly signposted from Leominster by-pass
Hotel	★★ 60% Royal Oak Hotel, South St, LEOMINSTER ☎ 01568 612610 17 ⇆ ↳ Annexe 1 ⇆ ↳
Additional hotel	★★★ 65% Talbot Hotel, West St, LEOMINSTER ☎ 01568 616347 Fax 01568 614880 20 ⇆ ↳

ROSS-ON-WYE
Map 03 SO62

Ross-on-Wye Two Park, Gorsley HR9 7UT
☎ 01989 720267 Fax 01989 720212
The undulating, parkland course has been cut out of a silver birch forest; the fairways being well-screened from each other. The fairways are tight, the greens good and the bunkers have been re-structured.
18 holes, 6451yds, Par 72, SSS 73, Course record 68.
Club membership 760.

Visitors	must contact professional in advance 01989 720439.
Societies	must telephone in advance.
Green Fees	£32 per round.
Cards	🃏 ▬ ▬ 🃏 🌐
Prof	Nick Catchpole
Facilities	⊗ ⵊ 🏌 ♟ ♟ ↄ 🏕 𝄢 𝄢
Location	On B4221 N side of M50 junc 3

Hotel	★★★ 77% Pengethley Manor, Pengethley Park, ROSS-ON-WYE ☎ 01989 730211 11 ⇆ ↳ Annexe 14 ⇆ ↳

South Herefordshire Twin Lakes HR9 7UA
☎ 01989 780535 Fax 01989 740611
A parkland course of over 180 acres with fine views. The landscape has enabled the architect to design 18 individual and varied holes and golfers have a chance to use every club in the bag. Free draining soil provides year round play.
Twin Lakes: 18 holes, 6672yds, Par 71, SSS 72, Course record 71.
Club membership 300.

Green Fees	£15 weekdays (£20 weekends).
Designer	John Day
Facilities	⊗ ⵊ 🏌 ♟ ♟ ↄ 🏕 ⚑ 𝄢 𝄢
Hotel	★★★⚘ 68% Pencraig Court Hotel, Pencraig, ROSS-ON-WYE ☎ 01989 770306 11 ⇆

UPPER SAPEY
Map 03 SO66

Sapey WR6 6XT
☎ 01886 853288 & 853567 Fax 01886 853485
Parkland course with views of the Malvern Hills. Trees, lakes and water hazards. Not too strenuous a walk.
18 holes, 5935yds, Par 69, SSS 68, Course record 63.
Club membership 520.

Visitors	must contact in advance.
Societies	must contact in advance.
Green Fees	not confirmed.
Prof	Chris Knowles
Designer	R McMurray
Facilities	⊗ ⵊ 🏌 ♟ ♟ ↄ 🏕 ⚑ ⚑ 𝄢 𝄢
Location	B4203 Bromyard/Stourport Rd
Hotel	★★★ 78% The Elms, Stockton Rd, ABBERLEY ☎ 01299 896666 16 ⇆ ↳

WORMSLEY
Map 03 SO44

Herefordshire Ravens Causeway HR4 8LY
☎ 01432 830219 & 830465 (pro) Fax 01432 830095
Undulating parkland course with expansive views.
18 holes, 6036yds, Par 70, SSS 69, Course record 61.
Club membership 800.

Visitors	must contact in advance, possibility of weekend play if no competitions are taking place.
Societies	must apply in advance.
Green Fees	£25 per day; £19 per round (£30/£22 weekends & bank holidays).
Cards	🃏 ▬ 🃏 🌐
Prof	David Hemming
Designer	James Braid
Facilities	⊗ ⵊ 🏌 ♟ ♟ ↄ 🏕 ⚑ ⚑ 𝄢
Location	E side of village
Hotel	★★★ 63% The Green Dragon, Broad St, HEREFORD ☎ 0870 400 8113 83 ⇆ ↳

ALDBURY
Map 04 SP91

Stocks Hotel Golf & Country Club Stocks Rd HP23 5RX
☎ 01442 851341 Fax 01442 851253
An 18-hole parkland course is one of the many facilities at this country club.
Stocks Golf & Country Club: 18 holes, 6804yds, Par 72, SSS 73, Course record 65.
Club membership 350.

Visitors	must contact in advance and have a handicap certificate. May not play before 12pm at weekends.
Societies	must contact well in advance.
Green Fees	£25 per round (£30 weekends).
Cards	🃏 ▬ 🃏
Prof	Peter Lane
Designer	Mike Billcliffe
Facilities	⊗ ⵊ 🏌 ♟ ♟ ↄ 🏕 ⚑ 🍴 ⚑ ⚑ 𝄢
& Leisure	hard tennis courts, heated outdoor swimming pool, sauna, solarium.
Location	2m from A41 at Tring

▶

Hotel ★★★★ 65% Pendley Manor, Cow Ln, TRING
☎ 01442 891891 71 ⇆ ⋒

ALDENHAM   Map 04 TQ19

Aldenham Golf and Country Club Church Ln WD2 8AL
☎ 01923 853929 Fax 01923 858472
Undulating parkland course with many specimen trees.
Beautiful views across countryside.
Old Course: 18 holes, 6480yds, Par 70, SSS 71.
White Course: 9 holes, 2350yds, Par 33, SSS 33.
Club membership 550.
Visitors   Old Course restricted weekends before noon.
           White Course no restrictions.
Societies   must contact in advance.
Green Fees Old Course: £24 per day (£32 weekends & bank
           holidays). White Course:£10 (£12 weekends).
Cards   ⚏ ⚏ ⚏ ⚏ ⚏
Prof   Tim Dunstan
Facilities ⊗ ⅲ ⅃ ▆ ⚑ ⚲ 🏠 ⚐ ⚒ ⚒ ✓
Location   W side of village

Hotel ★★★ 64% Watford Moat House, 30-40 St
Albans Rd, WATFORD
☎ 01923 429988 90 ⇆ ⋒

BERKHAMSTED   Map 04 SP90

Berkhamsted The Common HP4 2QB
☎ 01442 865832 Fax 01442 863730
There are no sand bunkers on this Championship
heathland course but this does not make it any easier to
play. The natural hazards will test the skill of the most
able players, with a particularly testing hole at the 11th,
568 yards, par 5. Fine Greens, long carries and heather
and gorse. The clubhouse is very comfortable.
18 holes, 6605yds, Par 71, SSS 72, Course record 65.
Club membership 700.
Visitors   must contact in advance.
Societies   must contact in advance.
Green Fees £38 per day; £28 per round (£38 weekends).
Prof   Basil Proudfoot
Designer   Colt/Braid
Facilities ⊗ ⅲ ⅃ ▆ ⚑ ⚲ 🏠 ✓
Location   1.5m E

Hotel ★★★★ 65% Pendley Manor, Cow Ln,
TRING ☎ 01442 891891 71 ⇆ ⋒

BISHOP'S STORTFORD   Map 05 TL42

Bishop's Stortford Dunmow Rd CM23 5HP
☎ 01279 654715 Fax 01279 655215
Well established parkland course, fairly flat, but undulating,
with easy walking.
18 holes, 6404yds, Par 71, SSS 71, Course record 66.
Club membership 900.
Visitors   must have a valid handicap certificate, must play
           with member at weekends. Ladies day Wed.
Societies   must contact in writing.
Green Fees £35 per day; £31 per 27 holes; £27 per 18 holes.
Cards   ⚏ ⚏ ⚏ ⚏ ⚏
Designer   James Braid

Facilities ⊗ ⅲ ⅃ ▆ ⚑ ⚲ 🏠 ⚐ ⚒ ✓
& Leisure snooker tables.
Location   0.5m W of M11 junc 8 on A1250

Hotel ★★★★ 67% Down Hall Country House Hotel,
Hatfield Heath, BISHOP'S STORTFORD
☎ 01279 731441 103 ⇆ ⋒

Great Hadham Golf & Country Club Great Hadham Rd,
Much Hadham SG10 6JE
☎ 01279 843558 Fax 01279 842122
An undulating open meadowland/links course offering
excellent country views and a challenge with its ever present
breeze.
18 holes, 6854yds, Par 72, SSS 73, Course record 67.
Club membership 700.
Visitors   welcome all times except am Mon, Wed, Sat &
           Sun.
Societies   by advance booking in writing.
Green Fees £18 per round (£25 per round weekends & bank
           holidays).
Cards   ⚏ ⚏ ⚏
Prof   Kevin Lunt
Designer   Iain Roberts
Facilities ⊗ ⅲ ⅃ ▆ ⚑ ⚲ 🏠 ⚐ ✓ ⚷
& Leisure sauna, solarium, gymnasium, health club.
Location   On the B1004, 3m SW of Bishop's Stortford

Hotel ★★★★ 67% Down Hall Country House Hotel,
Hatfield Heath, BISHOP'S STORTFORD
☎ 01279 731441 103 ⇆ ⋒

BRICKENDON   Map 05 TL30

Brickendon Grange SG13 8PD
☎ 01992 511258 Fax 01992 511411
Undulating parkland course with some fine par 4's. 17th hole
reputed to be best in the county.
18 holes, 6395yds, Par 71, SSS 70, Course record 66.
Club membership 680.
Visitors   must have handicap certificate. With member
           only at weekends & bank holidays.
Societies   by arrangement.
Green Fees £38 per day; £28 per round.
Prof   Graham Tippett
Designer   C K Cotton
Facilities ⊗ ⅲ ⅃ ▆ ⚑ ⚲ 🏠 ⚐ ⚒ ✓
Location   W side of village

Hotel ★★★ 66% The White Horse, Hertingfordbury,
HERTFORD ☎ 0870 400 8114 42 ⇆ ⋒

BROOKMANS PARK
Map 04 TL20

Brookmans Park Golf Club Rd AL9 7AT
☎ 01707 652487 Fax 01707 661851
Brookman's Park is an undulating parkland course, with several cleverly constructed holes. But it is a fair course, although it can play long. The 11th, par 3, is a testing hole which plays across a lake.
18 holes, 6460yds, Par 71, SSS 71, Course record 66.
Club membership 750.

Visitors	must contact professional in advance 01707 652468 and have a handicap certificate; must play with member at weekends & bank holidays.
Societies	must telephone or write in advance.
Green Fees	not confirmed.
Prof	Ian Jelley
Designer	Hawtree/Taylor
Facilities	⊗ ℿ ⅃ ▄ ♀ ♨ 🛈 ⚐ 🛒 🏌
Location	N side of village off A1000
Hotel	★★★ 65% Posthouse South Mimms, SOUTH MIMMS ☎ 0870 400 9072 143 ⇄ 🏌

BUNTINGFORD
Map 05 TL32

East Herts Hamels Park SG9 9NA
☎ 01920 821922 (Pro)
An attractive undulating parkland course with magnificent specimen trees.
18 holes, 6456yds, Par 71, SSS 71.
Club membership 750.

Visitors	must contact in advance & have handicap certificate, but may not play on Wed & weekends.
Societies	apply in writing.
Green Fees	£35 per day/round.
Prof	S Bryan
Facilities	⊗ ⅃ ▄ ♀ ♨ 🛈 ⚐ 🏌 🛒
Location	1m N of Puckeridge off A10
Hotel	★★★ 64% Novotel, Knebworth Park, STEVENAGE ☎ 01438 742299 100 ⇄ 🏌

BUSHEY
Map 04 TQ19

Bushey Golf & Country Club High St WD2 1BJ
☎ 020 8950 2283 Fax 020 8386 1181
Undulating parkland with challenging 2nd and 9th holes. The latter has a sweeping dolgleg left, playing to a green in front of the club house. For the rather too enthusiatic golfer, Bushey offers its own physiotherapist!
9 holes, 6120yds, Par 70, SSS 69, Course record 67.
Club membership 411.

Visitors	must contact in advance.
Societies	apply in writing or by telephone.
Green Fees	not confirmed.
Cards	▭ 🗓
Prof	Michael Lovegrove
Facilities	⊗ ℿ ⅃ ▄ ♀ ♨ 🛈 ⚐ 🏌 🛒 🛈
& Leisure	sauna, solarium, gymnasium.
Hotel	★★★ 72% Edgwarebury Hotel, Barnet Ln, ELSTREE ☎ 020 8953 8227 47 ⇄ 🏌

Bushey Hall Bushey Hall Dr WD2 2EP
☎ 01923 225802 & 222253 Fax 01923 229759
Tree lined parkland course.
18 holes, 6099yds, Par 70, SSS 69.
Club membership 500.

Visitors	may book 7 days in advance.
Societies	must contact in writing.
Green Fees	not confirmed.
Cards	▭ ▭ 🗓 🗓
Prof	Ken Wickham
Designer	Clouston
Facilities	⊗ ℿ ⅃ ▄ ♀ ♨ 🛈 ⚐ 🏌 🛒
Location	1.5m NW on A4008
Hotel	★★★ 64% Watford Moat House, 30-40 St Albans Rd, WATFORD ☎ 01923 429988 90 ⇄ 🏌

Hartsbourne Golf & Country Club Hartsbourne Ave WD2 1JW ☎ 020 8950 1133
Parkland course with good views.
18 holes, 6305yds, Par 71, SSS 70, Course record 62.
Club membership 750.

Visitors	must be guest of a member.
Societies	phone for details.
Green Fees	not confirmed.
Prof	Geoff Hunt
Facilities	⊗ ℿ ⅃ ▄ ♀ ♨ 🛈 ⚐ 🏌 🛒 🛈 🛈
Location	5m SE of Watford
Hotel	★★★ 64% Watford Moat House, 30-40 St Albans Rd, WATFORD ☎ 01923 429988 90 ⇄ 🏌

CHESHUNT
Map 05 TL30

Cheshunt Cheshunt Park, Park Ln EN7 6QD
☎ 01992 624009
Municipal parkland course, well-bunkered with ponds, easy walking.
18 holes, 6613yds, Par 71, SSS 71.
Club membership 350.

Visitors	must book Tee-times through Reception. Must contact in advance.
Societies	must apply in writing.
Green Fees	not confirmed.
Cards	▭ ▭ ▭ 🗓 🗓
Prof	Andy Traynor
Designer	P Wawtry
Facilities	⊗ ℿ ⅃ ▄ ♀ ♨ 🛈 ⚐ 🛒 🏌
Location	1.5m NW off B156

▶

Hotel ★★★★ 65% Cheshunt Marriott Hotel, Halfhide Ln, Turnford, BROXBOURNE ☎ 01992 451245 143 ⇔ ☞

CHORLEYWOOD
Map 04 TQ09

Chorleywood Common Rd WD3 5LN
☎ 01923 282009 Fax 01923 286739
Very attractive mix of woodland and heathland with natural hazards and good views.
9 holes, 5712yds, Par 68, SSS 67.
Club membership 300.
Visitors must contact in advance, restricted weekends & Tues.
Societies initial contact by telephone.
Green Fees £16 per day (£20 weekends & bank holidays).
Facilities ⊗ ⟩Ⅲ by prior arrangement �iℰ 💺 ♀ 🛆
Location E side of village off A404

Hotel ★★★ 69% The Bedford Arms Chenies, CHENIES ☎ 01923 283301 10 ⇔ ☞

ELSTREE
Map 04 TQ19

Elstree Watling St WD6 3AA
☎ 020 8953 6115 Fax 020 8207 6390
Parkland course.
18 holes, 6556yds, Par 73, SSS 72.
Club membership 650.
Visitors advisable to contact in advance, no restrictions weekdays, may not play until after 2pm weekends unless tee time available day prior.
Societies telephone in advance.
Green Fees £20 (£25 after midday weekends & bank holidays).
Cards 🃏🃏
Prof Marc Warwick
Designer Donald Steel
Facilities ⊗ ▾ 💺 ♀ 🛆 🏠 ⛳ 🛺 ℰ ℓ
Location A5183 between Radlett and Elstree

Hotel ★★★ 72% Edgwarebury Hotel, Barnet Ln, ELSTREE ☎ 020 8953 8227 47 ⇔ ☞

ESSENDON
Map 04 TL20

Hatfield London Country Club Bedwell Park AL9 6JA
☎ 01707 642624 Fax 01707 646187
Parkland course with many varied hazards, including ponds, a stream and a ditch. 19th-century manor clubhouse. 9-hole pitch and putt.
18 holes, 6880yds, Par 72, SSS 72.
Club membership 250.
Visitors must contact in advance.
Societies must contact in advance.
Green Fees not confirmed.
Cards 🃏🃏🃏🃏🃏
Prof Norman Greer
Designer Fred Hawtry
Facilities ⊗ ⟩Ⅲ 💺 💺 ♀ 🛆 🏠 ⛳ 🛺 ℰ
& Leisure hard tennis courts, pitch & putt.
Location On B158 1m S

Hotel ★★★ 64% Quality Hotel Hatfield, Roehyde Way, HATFIELD ☎ 01707 275701 76 ⇔ ☞

GRAVELEY
Map 04 TL22

Chesfield Downs Jack's Hill SG4 7EQ
☎ 01462 482929 Fax 01462 482930
A revolutionary golf course with the emphasis on facilities for the entire family. Its undulating, open downland course has an inland links feel. There is a 25-bay floodlit, covered driving range, a 9-hole Par 3 and many other facilities.
18 holes, 6648yds, Par 71, SSS 72.
Club membership 500.
Visitors no restrictions.
Societies must telephone in advance.
Green Fees not confirmed.
Prof Jane Fernley
Designer J Gaunt
Facilities ⊗ ⟩Ⅲ by prior arrangement ▾ 💺 ♀ 🛆 🏠 ⛳ 🛺 🛺 ℰ ℓ
& Leisure par3 9 hole course.
Location Jct 8 of A1, B197 to Graveley

Hotel ★★★ 59% Hotel Ibis, Danestrete, STEVENAGE ☎ 01438 779955 98 ⇔ ☞

HARPENDEN
Map 04 TL11

Aldwickbury Park Piggottshill Ln AL5 1AB
☎ 01582 760112 Fax 01582 760113
Attractive parkland course with large areas of mature woodland and good views across the Lee Valley.
18 holes, 6352yds, Par 71, SSS 70, Course record 66.
Club membership 700.
Visitors telephone in advance.
Societies telephone for brochure, various packages available.
Green Fees Park: £22 (£25 weekends).
Cards 🃏🃏🃏🃏
Prof Simon Plumb
Designer Ken Brown/Martin Gillett
Facilities ⊗ ⟩Ⅲ 💺 💺 ♀ 🛆 🏠 ⛳ 🛺 🛺 ℰ
Location Located just off Wheathampstead Road, between Harpenden/Wheathampstead, 10mins from junct 9 of M1

Hotel ★★★ 69% Harpenden House, 18 Southdown Rd, HARPENDEN ☎ 01582 449955 17 ⇔ ☞ Annexe 36 ⇔ ☞

Harpenden Hammonds End, Redbourn Ln AL5 2AX
☎ 01582 712580 Fax 01582 712725
Gently undulating parkland course, easy walking.
18 holes, 6381yds, Par 70, SSS 70, Course record 67.
Club membership 800.
Visitors must contact in advance. May not play Thu & weekends.
Societies must apply in writing.
Green Fees not confirmed.
Cards 🃏🃏🃏🃏
Prof Peter Cherry
Designer Hawtree & Taylor
Facilities ⊗ ⟩Ⅲ 💺 💺 ♀ 🛆 🏠 ⛳ ℰ ℓ
Location 1m S on B487

Hotel ★★★ 69% Harpenden House, 18 Southdown Rd, HARPENDEN ☎ 01582 449955 17 ⇔ ☞ Annexe 36 ⇔ ☞

Harpenden Common Cravells Rd, East Common AL5 1BL
☎ 01582 715959 Fax 01582 715959
Flat, easy walking, good greens, typical common course.
18 holes, 6214yds, Par 70, SSS 70, Course record 67.
Club membership 710.

Visitors	must contact in advance.
Societies	Thu & Fri only. Must apply in writing.
Green Fees	£30 per day; £25 per round.
Prof	Danny Fitzsimmons
Designer	K Brown
Facilities	⊗ ⏶ ⮂ ⬛ ♀ ⛳ ☕ ⚐ ♟ ♂
Location	1m S on A1081

Hotel ★★★ 73% Glen Eagle Hotel, 1 Luton Rd,
HARPENDEN ☎ 01582 760271 60 ⇄ ♞

HEMEL HEMPSTEAD   Map 04 TL00

Boxmoor 18 Box Ln, Boxmoor HP3 0DJ
☎ 01442 242434
Challenging, very hilly, moorland course with sloping
fairways divided by trees. Fine views. Testing holes: 3rd (par
3), 4th (par 4).
9 holes, 4812yds, Par 64, SSS 63, Course record 62.
Club membership 280.

Visitors	may not play on Sun & bank holidays. Restricted some Sat.
Societies	must contact in advance.
Green Fees	£15 per round.
Facilities	⮂ ⬛ ♀ ⬟
Location	2m SW on B4505

Hotel ★★ 72% The Two Brewers, The Common,
CHIPPERFIELD ☎ 01923 265266 20 ⇄ ♞

Little Hay Box Ln, Bovingdon HP3 0DQ ☎ 01442 833798
Semi-parkland, inland links.
18 holes, 6678yds, Par 72, SSS 72.

Visitors	advisable to contact in advance.
Societies	telephone for details.
Green Fees	not confirmed.
Cards	▭ ▭ ▦ ▧
Prof	D Johnson/M Campbell
Designer	Hawtree
Facilities	⊗ ⏶ ⮂ ⬛ ♀ ⬟ ☕ ⚐ ♟ ♂ ♟
Location	1.5m SW on B4505 off A41

Hotel ★★★ 66% Posthouse Hemel Hempstead,
Breakspear Way, HEMEL HEMPSTEAD
☎ 0870 400 9041 145 ⇄ ♞

Shendish Manor London Rd, Apsley HP3 0AA
☎ 01442 251806 Fax 01442 230683
A hilly course with plenty of trees and good greens. A tough
course for any golfer.
18 holes, 5660yds, Par 70, SSS 67.
Club membership 100.

Visitors	no restrictions but advisable to book in advance
Societies	must contact in advance.
Green Fees	not confirmed.
Cards	▭ ▭
Prof	Murray White
Designer	D Steel
Facilities	⊗ ⏶ by prior arrangement ⮂ ⬛ ♀ ⬟ ☕ ⚐ ♟ ♂
& Leisure	sauna, solarium, gymnasium.
Location	Just off A4251

Hotel ★★★★ 65% Pendley Manor, Cow Ln, TRING
☎ 01442 891891 71 ⇄ ♞

KNEBWORTH   Map 04 TL22

Knebworth Deards End Ln SG3 6NL
☎ 01438 812752 Fax 01438 815216
Parkland course, easy walking.
18 holes, 6492yds, Par 71, SSS 71, Course record 66.
Club membership 900.

Visitors	must have handicap certificate , but must play with member at weekends.
Societies	Mon, Tue & Thu. Must contact in advance.
Green Fees	£30 per day/round.
Cards	▭ ▭ ▦ ▧
Prof	Garry Parker
Designer	W Park (Jun)
Facilities	⊗ ⏶ by prior arrangement ⮂ ⬛ ♀ ⬟ ☕ ⚐ ♂
Location	N side of village off B197

Hotel ★★★ 61% Posthouse Stevenage, Old London
Rd, Broadwater, STEVENAGE
☎ 0870 400 9076 54 ⇄ ♞

LETCHWORTH   Map 04 TL23

Letchworth Letchworth Ln SG6 3NQ
☎ 01462 683203 Fax 01462 484567
Planned more than 50 years ago by Harry Vardon, this
adventurous, parkland course is set in a peaceful corner
of 'Norman' England. To its variety of natural and
artificial hazards is added an unpredictable wind.
18 holes, 6181yds, Par 70, SSS 69, Course record 65.
Club membership 750.

Visitors	with member only at weekends. Must contact in advance and have a handicap certificate.
Societies	Wed, Thu & Fri only, must telephone in advance.
Green Fees	£38 per day; £27 per round (£25/£15 Mon).
Prof	S Allen
Designer	Harry Vardon
Facilities	⊗ ⏶ ⮂ ⬛ ♀ ⬟ ☕ ♟ ♂
Location	S side of town centre off A505

Hotel ★★★ 62% Cromwell Hotel, High St, Old
Town, STEVENAGE
☎ 01438 779954 57 ⇄ ♞

LITTLE GADDESDEN   Map 04 SP91

Ashridge HP4 1LY
☎ 01442 842244 Fax 01442 843770
Good parkland course, challenging but fair. Good clubhouse
facilities.
18 holes, 6547yds, Par 72, SSS 71, Course record 63.
Club membership 720.

Visitors	must contact in advance , be a member of a recognised club & have handicap certificate, may not play weekends & bank holidays.
Societies	must apply in writing and complete booking form.
Green Fees	on application.
Prof	Andrew Ainsworth

▶

Designer	Sir G Campbell/C Hutchinson/N Hutchinson
Facilities	⊗ 🏌 🍴 ♀ 🛒 🏠 🚩 ✎
Location	5m N of Berkhamsted on the B4506

| Hotel | ★★★ 69% Harpenden House, 18 Southdown Rd, HARPENDEN ☎ 01582 449955 17 ⇄ 🐾 Annexe 36 ⇄ 🐾 |

MUCH HADHAM   Map 05 TL41

Much Hadham Little Hadham Rd SG10 6HD
☎ 01279 843253 Fax 01920 468686
Naturally undulating course with good views extending to
Canary Wharf in London on a clear day.
18 holes, 6516yds, Par 71, Course record 71.
Visitors	no restrictions.
Societies	telephone in advance.
Green Fees	not confirmed.
Designer	Martin Gillett
Facilities	🏌 🍴 ♀ 🛒 🏠
Location	1.5m S of A120 fom Little Hadham traffic lights

| Hotel | ★★★ 62% Roebuck Hotel, Baldock St, WARE ☎ 01920 409955 50 ⇄ 🐾 |

POTTERS BAR   Map 04 TL20

Potters Bar Darkes Ln EN6 1DE
☎ 01707 652020 Fax 01707 655051
Undulating parkland course with water in play on many
holes.
18 holes, 6279yds, Par 71, SSS 70.
Club membership 650.
Visitors	with member only at weekends, Ladies Day Wed morning.
Societies	Mon-Fri & Wed (pm only) by arrangement with Secretary.
Green Fees	not confirmed.
Prof	Gary A'Ris
Designer	James Braid
Facilities	⊗ 🏌 🍴 ♀ 🛒 🏠 🚩 🐎 🛒 ✎
Location	1m N of M25 junct 24

| Hotel | ★★★ 65% Posthouse South Mimms, SOUTH MIMMS ☎ 0870 400 9072 143 ⇄ 🐾 |

RADLETT   Map 04 TL10

Porters Park Shenley Hill WD7 7AZ
☎ 01923 854127 Fax 01923 855475
A splendid, undulating parkland course with fine trees
and lush grass. The holes are all different and interesting
- on many accuracy of shot to the green is of paramount
importance.
18 holes, 6313yds, Par 70, SSS 70, Course record 64.
Club membership 1000.
Visitors	must book 24hrs in advance. With member only weekends.
Societies	Wed & Thu only, must apply in writing.
Green Fees	£30.50 per 18 holes.
Prof	David Gleeson
Designer	Braid
Facilities	⊗ 🏌 🍴 ♀ 🛒 🏠 🚩 ✎ ✐
Location	NE side of village off A5183

| Hotel | ★★★ 65% Posthouse South Mimms, SOUTH MIMMS ☎ 0870 400 9072 143 ⇄ 🐾 |

REDBOURN   Map 04 TL11

Redbourn Kinsbourne Green Ln AL3 7QA
☎ 01582 793493 Fax 01582 794362
Testing parkland course (Five par 4's over 400 yds). Also 9-
hole par 3 course.
*Ver Course: 18 holes, 6506yds, Par 70, SSS 71, Course
record 67.*
Kingsbourne Course: 9 holes, 1361yds, Par 27.
Club membership 750.
Visitors	must contact up to 3 days in advance for Ver Course. No restrictions for Par 3.
Societies	must telephone in advance.
Green Fees	£20 (£30 weekends).
Cards	💳 💳 💳 💳 💳
Prof	Stephen Hunter
Facilities	⊗ 🍴 🏌 🍴 ♀ 🛒 🏠 🚩 🐎 🛒 ✎ ✐
Location	1m N off A5183

| Hotel | ★★★ 69% Harpenden House, 18 Southdown Rd, HARPENDEN ☎ 01582 449955 17 ⇄ 🐾 Annexe 36 ⇄ 🐾 |

RICKMANSWORTH   Map 04 TQ09

Moor Park WD3 1QN
☎ 01923 773146 Fax 01923 777109
Two parkland courses - High Course is challenging and
wil test the best golfer and West Course demands a high
degree of accuracy.
*High Golf Course: 18 holes, 6713yds, Par 72, SSS 72,
Course record 63.*
*West Golf Course: 18 holes, 5815yds, Par 69, SSS 68,
Course record 62.*
Club membership 1700.
Visitors	must contact in advance but may not play at weekends, bank holidays or before 1pm on Tue & Thu.
Societies	must contact in advance.
Green Fees	High: £50 per round. West: £30 per round. Prices under review.
Prof	Lawrence Farmer
Designer	H S Colt
Facilities	⊗ 🍴 by prior arrangement 🏌 🍴 ♀ 🛒 🏠 🚩 🐎 🛒 ✎ ✐
& Leisure	hard and grass tennis courts, snooker.
Location	Off A404 to Northwood

| Hotel | ★★★ 64% Watford Moat House, 30-40 St Albans Rd, WATFORD ☎ 01923 429988 90 ⇄ 🐾 |

Rickmansworth Public Course Moor Ln WD3 1QL
☎ 01923 775278
Undulating, municipal parkland course.
18 holes, 4469yds, Par 63, SSS 62.
Club membership 240.
Visitors	must contact the club in advance, 7 day booking.
Societies	must contact in advance.
Green Fees	not confirmed.
Cards	💳 💳 💳 💳
Prof	Alan Dobbins
Designer	Colt
Facilities	⊗ 🍴 🏌 🍴 ♀ 🛒 🏠 🚩 🐎 🛒 ✎
Location	2m S of town off A4145

Hotel ★★★ 64% Watford Moat House, 30-40 St Albans Rd, WATFORD ☎ 01923 429988 90 🛏 🄿

ROYSTON Map 05 TL34

Barkway Park Nuthampstead Rd, Barkway SG8 8EN
☎ 01763 849070 & 848215
An undulating course criss-crossed by ditches which come into play on several holes. The challenging par 3 7th features a long, narrow green with out of bounds close to the right edge of the green.
18 holes, 6997yds, Par 74, SSS 74.
Club membership 310.
Visitors must contact in advance, telephone for tee times.
Societies apply for booking form.
Green Fees £10 per round (£15 weekends & bank holidays).
Cards 🖃 🖃 🖃 🖃
Prof Jamie Bates
Designer Vivien Saunders
Facilities ⊗ 🖢 🖤 ♀ 🏖 🍴 🕭 ⚸
Location Off B1368 from A10

Hotel ★★★ 72% Duxford Lodge Hotel, Ickleton Rd, DUXFORD ☎ 01223 836444 11 🛏 🄿 Annexe 4 🛏 🄿

Heydon Grange Golf & Country Club Heydon SG8 7NS
☎ 01763 208988 Fax 01763 208926
Three 9-hole parkland courses - the Essex, Cambridgeshire and Hertfordshire - situated in gently rolling countryside. Courses are playable all year round.
Essex: 9 holes, 3138yds, Par 36, SSS 35, Course record 67.
Cambridgeshire: 9 holes, 3323yds, Par 36, SSS 36.
Hertfordshire: 9 holes, 3180yds, Par 36, SSS 36.
Club membership 250.
Visitors must contact to book tee times, welcome all times weekends included.
Societies telephone in advance for booking form.
Green Fees not confirmed.
Cards 🖃 🖃 🖃 🖃 🖃 🖃 🖃
Prof Stuart Smith
Designer Cameron Sinclair
Facilities ⊗ 🎢 🖢 🖤 ♀ 🏖 🍴 🕭 ⚸ ↿
Location A505 between Royston/Duxford, off junct 10 on M11

Hotel ★★★ 72% Duxford Lodge Hotel, Ickleton Rd, DUXFORD ☎ 01223 836444 11 🛏 🄿 Annexe 4 🛏 🄿

Kingsway Cambridge Rd, Melbourn SG8 6EY
☎ 01763 262727 Fax 01763 263298
Short and deceptively tricky 9-hole course providing a good test for both beginners and experienced golfers. Out of bounds and strategically placed bunkers come into play on several holes, in particular the tough par 3 7th.
9 holes, 2455yds, Par 33, SSS 32.
Club membership 150.
Visitors welcome.
Societies telephone for details.
Green Fees £5 per round (£7 weekends).
Prof Denise Hastings/Mark Sturgess
Facilities 🖤 ♀ 🏖 🍴 🕭 ⚸ ↿
& Leisure crazy golf.
Location Off the A10

Hotel ★★★ 72% Duxford Lodge Hotel, Ickleton Rd, DUXFORD ☎ 01223 836444 11 🛏 🄿 Annexe 4 🛏 🄿

Royston Baldock Rd SG8 5BG
☎ 01763 242696 Fax 01763 242696
Heathland course on undulating terrain and fine fairways. The 8th, 10th and 15th are the most notable holes on this all weather course.
18 holes, 6052yds, Par 70, SSS 70, Course record 65.
Club membership 850.
Visitors Mon-Fri only subject to availability. Must contact in advance.
Societies by arrangement Mon-Fri.
Green Fees £30 per day; £25 per round.
Cards 🖃 🖃
Prof Sean Clark
Designer Harry Vardon
Facilities ⊗ 🎢 🖢 🖤 ♀ 🏖 🍴 🕭 ⚸
Location 0.5m W of town centre

Hotel ★★★ 72% Duxford Lodge Hotel, Ickleton Rd, DUXFORD ☎ 01223 836444 11 🛏 🄿 Annexe 4 🛏 🄿

ST ALBANS Map 04 TL10

Abbey View Westminster Lodge Leisure Ctr, Hollywell Hill AL1 2DL ☎ 01727 868227 Fax 01727 863017
Abbey View is a public golf course designed for beginners, but is sufficiently challenging for experienced golfers who only have time for a short game. There is a resident professional for assistance and lessons.
9 holes, 1383yds, Par 29.
Visitors welcome but no sharing clubs, suitable footwear & wide wheel trolleys.
Societies telephone or write in advance.
Green Fees not confirmed.
Prof Ian Goosey
Facilities ⊗ 🎢 🖤 🏖 🍴 🕭 ⚸
& Leisure hard and grass tennis courts, heated indoor swimming pool, sauna, solarium, gymnasium.
Location Centre of St Albans, off Holywell hill

Hotel ★★ 68% Lake Hotel, 234 London Rd, ST ALBANS ☎ 01727 840904 43 🛏 🄿

Batchwood Hall Batchwood Dr AL3 5XA
☎ 01727 844250 Fax 01727 858506
Municipal parkland course designed by J H Taylor and opened in 1935.
18 holes, 6487yds, Par 71, SSS 71.
Club membership 200.
Visitors must contact in advance, in person.
Societies must contact in advance.
Green Fees not confirmed.
Cards 🖃 🖃 🖃
Prof Mark Flitton
Facilities ⊗ 🎢 🖢 🖤 ♀ 🏖 🍴 🕭 ⚸
& Leisure hard tennis courts, squash, solarium, gymnasium.
Location 1m NW off A5183

Hotel ★★★ 76% St Michael's Manor, Fishpool St, ST ALBANS ☎ 01727 864444 23 🛏 🄿

Verulam London Rd AL1 1JG
☎ 01727 853327 Fax 01727 812201
Easy walking parkland course with fourteen holes having
out-of-bounds. Water affects the 12th, 13th and 14th holes.
Samuel Ryder was Captain here in 1927 when he began the
now celebrated Ryder Cup Competition.
18 holes, 6448yds, Par 72, SSS 71, Course record 67.
Club membership 700.

Visitors	must contact pro shop in advance. With member only at weekends.
Societies	must contact advance.
Green Fees	Mon: £25 per day, £15 per round. Tue-Fri: £35/£25.
Prof	Nick Burch
Designer	Braid
Facilities	⊗ ℳ by prior arrangement ⬛ ☕ ♀ ♨ 🏠 ⚐ ♂
Location	1m from junc 22 of M25 off A1081

Hotel   ★★★★ 74% Sopwell House Hotel & Country
Club, Cottonmill Ln, Sopwell, ST ALBANS
☎ 01727 864477 122 ⬅ ☎ Annexe 16 ⬅ ☎

SAWBRIDGEWORTH   Map 05 TL41

Manor of Groves Golf & Country Club High Wych
CM21 0LA ☎ 01279 722333 Fax 01279 726972
The course is set out over 150 acres of established parkland and
rolling countryside and is a true test of golf for the club golfer.
18 holes, 6280yds, Par 71, SSS 70, Course record 65.
Club membership 450.

Visitors	telephone bookings preferred, restrictions on Tue, Thu and weekends.
Societies	Mon-Fri by prior arrangement, telephone in advance.
Green Fees	£20 per round (£25 weekends)..
Cards	〰 ⬛ 〓 🔁 📶 🟢
Prof	Craig Laurence
Designer	S Sharer
Facilities	⊗ ℳ ⬛ ☕ ♀ 🏠 ⚐ 🛏 ♂ 🚲 ♂
& Leisure	hard tennis courts, outdoor swimming pool, gymnasium.
Location	1.5m on west side of town

Hotel   ★★★ 73% Swallow Churchgate Hotel,
Churchgate St Village, Old Harlow, HARLOW
☎ 01279 420246   85 ⬅ ☎

STANSTEAD ABBOTS   Map 05 TL31

Briggens House Hotel Briggens Park, Stanstead Rd
SG12 8LD ☎ 01279 793742 Fax 01279 793685
An attractive 9-hole course set in the grounds of a 80 acres of
countryside.
9 holes, 2793yds, Par 36, SSS 69, Course record 31.
Club membership 230.

Visitors	may not play Thu 5-6pm and Sun am. No jeans. Must have own clubs and golf shoes (hire available).
Societies	must contact in advance.
Green Fees	£14 per 18 holes (£17 weekends & bank holidays).
Cards	〰 ⬛ 〓 💳 📶 🟢
Prof	Alan McGinn
Facilities	⊗ ℳ ⬛ ☕ ♀ 🏠 ⚐ 🛏 🚲 ♂
& Leisure	hard tennis courts, heated outdoor swimming pool, fishing.
Location	Off Stanstead road A414

Hotel   ★★★★ 60% Briggens House Hotel, Stanstead
Rd, STANSTEAD ABBOTTS
☎ 01279 829955   54 ⬅ ☎

STEVENAGE   Map 04 TL22

Stevenage Golf Centre Aston Ln SG2 7EL
☎ 01438 880424 & 880223 Fax 01438 880040
Municipal course designed by John Jacobs, with natural
water hazards and some wooded areas.
18 holes, 6451yds, Par 72, SSS 71.
Club membership 600.

Visitors	no restrictions.
Societies	must contact 1 week in advance. Deposit required.
Green Fees	not confirmed.
Cards	〰 ⬛ 〓 🔁 📶 🟢
Prof	Steve Barker
Designer	John Jacobs
Facilities	⊗ ℳ ⬛ ☕ ♀ 🏠 ⚐ 🛏 🚲 ♂ ♂
& Leisure	par3 course.
Location	4m SE off B5169

Hotel   ★★★ 61% Posthouse Stevenage, Old London
Rd, Broadwater, STEVENAGE
☎ 0870 400 9076 54 ⬅ ☎

WARE   Map 05 TL31

Chadwell Springs Hertford Rd SG12 9LE
☎ 01920 461447
Quick drying moorland course on high plateau subject to
wind. The first two holes are par 5 and notable.
9 holes, 6418yds, Par 72, SSS 71, Course record 68.
Club membership 650.

Visitors	with member only at weekends.
Societies	bookings accepted, Mon, Wed & Fri only.
Green Fees	not confirmed.
Cards	〰 ⬛ 〓
Prof	Mark Wall
Facilities	⊗ ℳ ⬛ ☕ ♀ 🏠 ♂
Location	0.75m W on A119

Hotel   ★★★ 62% Roebuck Hotel, Baldock St,
WARE ☎ 01920 409955   50 ⬅ ☎

MARRIOTT HANBURY MANOR
GOLF AND COUNTRY CLUB   See page 139

Whitehill Dane End SG12 0JS
☎ 01920 438495 Fax 01920 438891
Undulating course providing a good test for both the average
golfer and the low handicapper. Several lakes in challenging
positions.
18 holes, 6618yds, Par 72, SSS 72.
Club membership 600.

Visitors	handicap certificate must be produced or competence test taken (free), appropriate clothing must be worn.
Societies	telephone or write for booking form.
Green Fees	£25 per day; £19.50 per round (£22.50 per round weekends).
Cards	〰 〓 📶 🟢
Prof	David Ling
Facilities	⊗ ℳ ⬛ ☕ ♀ 🏠 ⚐ 🛏 🚲 ♂ ♂

Marriott Hanbury Manor

Ware, *Hertfordshire*   ☎ **01920 487722**   Fax **01920 487692**   Map **05 TL31**

This PGA European Tour venue has played host to many major championships, most recently it has been a regular venue for the English Open. Golf clinics, tuition, swing analysis and corporate events are available, complemented by the extensive leisure facilities.

The superb parkland course was first built around the family home in 1890, the original Harry Vardon course has since been sympathetically redesigned by Jack Nicklaus II to create something unforgettable. Its cleverly sited trees and several picturesque water features offer a true challenge to anyone who enjoys their golf. The Par 4 13th hole is an interesting dog-leg which requires a mid iron second shot over a lake to a well guarded two tiered green, being stroke index two it could make or break your score.

Visitors with handicap certificate, members guests and hotel residents welcome. Must contact in advance

Societies must be booked in advance. Mon-Wed only

Green Fees £75 per round as hotel guest

Facilities ⊗ ╫ ▣ ▆ ♀ ♣ ⊟ ↑ ↘ ♨ ♪ ♩ Professional (Peter Blaze)

Leisure tennis, swimming, sauna, solarium, gymnasium

Location Ware SG12 0SD (adjacent to A10. From N just past sign for Thunderidge)

Holes/Par/Course record 18 holes, 6622 yds, Par 72, SSS 72, Course record 61

WHERE TO STAY AND EAT NEARBY

Hotel
WARE

★★★★★ ❀ ❀ ❀ 78% Marriott Hanbury Manor Hotel & Country Club
☎ 01920 487722. 69 ⇆ ♙
Annexe 27 ⇆ ♙

Championship Course

Hotel   ★★★ 62% Roebuck Hotel, Baldock St,
WARE ☎ 01920 409955 50 ⇌ ♟

WATFORD   Map 04 TQ19

West Herts Cassiobury Park WD1 7SL
☎ 01923 236484 Fax 01923 222300
Another of the many clubs that were inaugurated in the
1890's when the game of golf was being given a
tremendous boost by the the performances of the first
star professionals, Braid, Vardon and Taylor. The West
Herts course is close to Watford but its tree-lined setting
is beautiful and tranquil. Set out on a plateau the course
is exceedingly dry. It also has a very severe finish with
the 17th, a hole of 378 yards, the toughest on the course.
The last hole measures over 480 yards.
18 holes, 6400yds, Par 72, SSS 71, Course record 66.
Club membership 700.
Visitors   must contact in advance.
Societies   must telephone in advance and confirm in
                  writing.
Green Fees £25 per round (£30 weekends).
Prof   Charles Gough
Designer   Tom Morris
Facilities   ⊗ 〗 ╚ ■ ♀ ♧ ♙ ⛳ ↖ ♥ ♠ ♂
& Leisure   indoor teaching facility.
Location   W side of town centre off A412

Hotel   ★★★ 64% Watford Moat House, 30-40 St
Albans Rd, WATFORD
☎ 01923 429988 90 ⇌ ♟

WELWYN GARDEN CITY   Map 04 TL21

Mill Green Gypsy Ln AL6 4TY
☎ 01707 276900 & 270542 (Pro shop) Fax 01707 276898
The course plays over the second 9 holes around the lakes
and sweeps back through the woods. The first 9 holes are
subject to the prevailing winds. The par 3 9-hole gives a
good test for improving the short game.
18 holes, 6615yds, Par 72, SSS 72, Course record 64.
Club membership 700.
Visitors   must contact in advance by telephone. 7 day
                  booking arrangement.
Societies   apply in writing for details.
Green Fees Mon: £15 per round Tues-Fri: £19 per round
                  (£25 weekends).
Cards   ⬜ ▬ ▬ ▬ ▧ ▨
Prof   Alan Hall
Designer   Alliss & Clark
Facilities   ⊗ 〗 ╚ ■ ♀ ♧ ♙ ⛳ ↖ ♥ ♠ ♂ ♢
& Leisure   9 hole par 3 course..
Location   Exit 4 of A1(M), A414 to Mill Green

Hotel   ★★★ 64% Quality Hotel Welwyn, The Link,
WELWYN ☎ 01438 716911 96 ⇌ ♟

Panshanger Golf & Squash Complex Old Herns Ln
AL7 2ED ☎ 01707 333350 & 333312 Fax 01707 390010
Picturesque, mature course overlooking Mimram Valley.
18 holes, 6347yds, Par 72, SSS 70, Course record 65.
Club membership 400.
Visitors   advisable to book 1 week in advance by
                  telephone. Dress code in force.
Societies   telephone for details.
Green Fees £13 per round (£18 weekends & bank holidays).

Cards   ⬜ ▬ ▬ ▬ ▧ ▨
Prof   Bryan Lewis/Mick Corlass
Designer   Peter Kirkham
Facilities   ⊗ ╚ ■ ♀ ♧ ♙ ⛳ ↖ ♥ ♠ ♂
& Leisure   squash, 9 hole Par 3 course.
Location   N side of town centre signposted off B1000

Hotel   ★★★ 64% Quality Hotel Welwyn, The Link,
WELWYN ☎ 01438 716911 96 ⇌ ♟

Welwyn Garden City Mannicotts, High Oaks Rd AL8 7BP
☎ 01707 325243 Fax 01707 393213
Undulating parkland course with a ravine. A former course
record holder is Nick Faldo.
18 holes, 6074yds, Par 70, SSS 69, Course record 63.
Club membership 975.
Visitors   must contact in advance but may not play Sun
                  am.
Societies   must contact in advance.
Green Fees £30 per day; £25 per round (£30 per round
                  weekends).
Cards   ⬜ ▬ ▬ ▧ ▨
Prof   Richard May
Facilities   ⊗ 〗 ╚ ■ ♀ ♧ ♙ ⛳ ♥ ♠ ♂
Location   W side of city, exit 6 off A1

Hotel   ★★★ 64% Quality Hotel Welwyn, The Link,
WELWYN ☎ 01438 716911 96 ⇌ ♟

WHEATHAMPSTEAD   Map 04 TL11

Mid Herts Lamer Ln, Gustard Wood AL4 8RS
☎ 01582 832242 Fax 01582 834834
Commonland, wooded with heather and gorse-lined
fairways.
18 holes, 6060yds, Par 69, SSS 69.
Club membership 760.
Visitors   may not play Tue, Wed afternoons & weekends.
Societies   must contact in writing/telephone
Green Fees £35 per day; £25 per round.
Facilities   ⊗ ╚ ■ ♀ ♧ ♥ ♠ ♂
Location   1m N on B651

Hotel   ★★★ 69% Harpenden House, 18 Southdown
Rd, HARPENDEN ☎ 01582 449955
17 ⇌ ♟ Annexe 36 ⇌ ♟

KENT

ADDINGTON   Map 05 TQ65

West Malling London Rd ME19 5AR
☎ 01732 844785 Fax 01732 844795
Two 18-hole parkland courses.
Spitfire Course: 18 holes, 6142yds, Par 70, SSS 70, Course
record 67.
Hurricane Course: 18 holes, 6281yds, Par 70, SSS 70,
Course record 69.
Visitors   must contact in advance, may not play weekends
                  until 2pm.
Societies   prior booking required.
Green Fees £35 per day; £25 per round (£35 per round after
                  noon weekends & bank holidays).   ▶

Prof	Duncan Lambert
Designer	Max Falkner
Facilities	⊗ ♨ ♭ ♟ ♀ ♨ ➟ ♣ ⚐ ✆
& Leisure	gymnasium.
Location	1m S off A20
Hotel	★★★ 63% Larkfield Priory Hotel, London Rd, Larkfield, MAIDSTONE ☎ 01732 846858 52 ⇄ ♠

ASH   Map 05 TQ66

The London South Ash Manor Estate TN15 7EN
☎ 01474 879899 Fax 01474 879912
Visitors may only play the courses at LGC as guests of members or prospective members by invitation.The courses, the Heritage and the International were designed by Jack Nicklaus: both include a number of lakes, generous fairways framed with native grasses and many challenging holes. A state-of-the-art drainage system ensures continuous play.
Heritage Course: 18 holes, 7208yds, Par 72, SSS 74, Course record 68.
International Course: 18 holes, 7005yds, Par 72, SSS 74, Course record 66.
Club membership 600.

Visitors	guest of member & prospective members invited by the membership office only.
Societies	must write in advance
Green Fees	Guest of member. Heritage: £50 per round; International £40 per round (£60/£45 weekends).
Prof	Gavin Ryan
Designer	Jack Nicklaus
Facilities	⊗ ♨ ♭ ♟ ♀ ♨ ⚐ ♣ ➟ ♣ ⚐ ✆
& Leisure	sauna.
Location	A20, 2m from Brands Hatch
Hotel	★★★ 63% Larkfield Priory Hotel, London Rd, Larkfield, MAIDSTONE ☎ 01732 846858 52 ⇄ ♠

ASHFORD   Map 05 TR04

Ashford Sandyhurst Ln TN25 4NT
☎ 01233 622655 Fax 01233 622655
Parkland course with good views and easy walking. Narrow fairways and tightly bunkered greens ensure a challenging game.
18 holes, 6263yds, Par 71, SSS 70, Course record 65.
Club membership 650.

Visitors	must contact in advance & have handicap certificate.
Societies	Tue & Thu only, by arrangement.
Green Fees	£32 per day; £22 per round (£30 weekends and bank holidays).
Cards	💳
Prof	Hugh Sherman
Designer	Cotton
Facilities	⊗ ♨ by prior arrangement ♭ ♟ ♀ ♨ ⚐ ✆
Location	1.5m NW off A20
Hotel	★★★★ 62% Ashford International, Simone Weil Av, ASHFORD ☎ 01233 219988 200 ⇄ ♠

Homelands Bettergolf Centre Ashford Rd, Kingsnorth
TN26 1NJ ☎ 01233 661620 Fax 01233 720553
Challenging 9-hole course designed by Donald Steel to provide a stern test for experienced golfers and for others to develop their game. With 4 par 3s and 5 par 4s it demands accuracy rather than length. Floodlit driving range.
9 holes, 2205yds, Par 32, SSS 31.
Club membership 200.

Visitors	no restrictions, but booking essential for weekend and summer evenings.
Societies	prior arrangements are essential.
Green Fees	£11 per 18 holes; £7 per 9 holes (£14/£10 weekends).
Cards	💳 💳 💳
Prof	Tony Bowers
Designer	Donald Steel
Facilities	♭ ♟ ♀ ♨ ⚐ ♣ ➟ ♣ ⚐ ✆
Location	Take exit 10 off M20, follow A2070, course signposted from 2nd rdbt to Kingsnorth
Hotel	★★★ 64% Pilgrims Rest Hotel, Canterbury Rd, Kennington, ASHFORD ☎ 01233 636863 34 ⇄ ♠

BARHAM   Map 05 TR25

Broome Park The Broome Park Estate CT4 6QX
☎ 01227 830728 Fax 01227 832591
Championship standard parkland course in a valley, with a 350-year-old mansion clubhouse.
18 holes, 6610yds, Par 72, SSS 72, Course record 66.
Club membership 700.

Visitors	advisable to contact in advance, must have handicap certificate, but may not play Sat/Sun mornings.
Societies	Mon-Fri and Sat-Sun after 1pm, apply in writing or by telephone.
Green Fees	not confirmed.
Cards	💳 💳 💳 💳
Prof	Tienne Britz
Designer	Donald Steel
Facilities	⊗ ♨ ♭ ♟ ♀ ♨ ⚐ ♣ ➟ ♣ ⚐ ✆
& Leisure	hard tennis courts, sauna, solarium.
Location	1.5m SE on A260
Hotel	★★★ 62% The Chaucer, Ivy Ln, CANTERBURY ☎ 0870 400 8106 42 ⇄ ♠

BEARSTED   Map 05 TQ85

Bearsted Ware St ME14 4PQ
☎ 01622 738198 Fax 01622 738198
Parkland course with fine views of the North Downs.
18 holes, 6437yds, Par 72, SSS 71.
Club membership 780.

Visitors	must have handicap certificate and may not play weekends unless with member. Must contact in advance.
Societies	write for reservation forms.
Green Fees	£36 per day; £27 per round.
Prof	Tim Simpson
Facilities	⊗ ♨ ♭ ♟ ♀ ♨ ⚐ ✆
Location	2.5m E of Maidstone off A20
Hotel	★★★★ 70% Marriott Tudor Park Hotel & Country Club, Ashford Rd, Bearsted, MAIDSTONE ☎ 01622 734334 118 ⇄ ♠

BIDDENDEN　　　　　　　　　Map 05 TQ83

Chart Hills Weeks Ln TN27 8JX
☎ 01580 292222 Fax 01580 292233
Created by Nick Faldo, this huge course of grand design measures 7,000 yards from the back tees. Facilities include a David Leadbetter Golf Academy.
18 holes, 7119yds, Par 72, SSS 74, Course record 66.
Club membership 380.

Visitors	welcome Sun-Fri, contact for details.
Societies	telephone for details.
Green Fees	on application.
Cards	
Prof	Danny French
Designer	Nick Faldo
Facilities	
& Leisure	sauna, solarium, gymnasium.
Location	1m N of Biddenden off A274

Hotel　★★♨ Kennel Holt Hotel, Goudhurst Rd, CRANBROOK ☎ 01580 712032　10

BOROUGH GREEN　　　　　　Map 05 TQ65

Wrotham Heath Seven Mile Ln TN15 8QZ
☎ 01732 884800 Fax 01732 887370
Heathland woodland course with magnificent views of North Downs.
18 holes, 5954yds, Par 70, SSS 69.
Club membership 550.

Visitors	must contact in advance, weekends with member only.
Societies	Thu & Fri only, by arrangement.
Green Fees	£25 per round.
Cards	
Prof	Harry Dearden
Designer	Donald Steel (part)
Facilities	
Location	2.25m E on B2016

Hotel　★★★ 66% Posthouse Maidstone/Sevenoaks, London Rd, Wrotham Heath, WROTHAM ☎ 0870 400 9054 106

BRENCHLEY　　　　　　　　Map 05 TQ64

Moatlands Watermans Ln TN12 6ND
☎ 01892 724400 Fax 01892 723300
A rolling parkland course with dramatic views over the Weald of Kent. The challenging holes are the Par 4 8th with its tough dogleg, the 10th where there is a wooded copse

with a Victorian bath-house to be avoided and the 14th where the approach to the green is guarded by oak trees.
18 holes, 6693yds, Par 72, SSS 72, Course record 63.
Club membership 620.

Visitors	must book in advance.
Societies	apply in writing or telephone.
Green Fees	£29 per round (£39 weekends).
Cards	
Prof	Simon Wood
Designer	H Sugio
Facilities	
& Leisure	hard tennis courts, heated indoor swimming pool, sauna, gymnasium.
Location	3m N of Brenchley off B2160

Hotel　★★ 64% Russell Hotel, 80 London Rd, TUNBRIDGE WELLS ☎ 01892 544833　19 Annexe 5

BROADSTAIRS　　　　　　　Map 05 TR36

North Foreland Convent Rd, Kingsgate CT10 3PU
☎ 01843 862140 Fax 01843 862663
A picturesque course situated where the Thames Estuary widens towards the sea. North Foreland always seems to have a breath of tradition of golf's earlier days about it. Perhaps the ghost of one of its earlier professionals, the famous Abe Mitchell, still haunts the lovely turf of the fairways. Walking is easy and the wind is deceptive. The 8th and 17th, both par 4, are testing holes. There is also an 18 hole approach and putting course.
18 holes, 6430yds, Par 71, SSS 71, Course record 65.
Club membership 1100.

Visitors	for Main course required to book in advance & have handicap certificate. May play afternoons only Mon and Tue, weekends restricted and no visitors Sun morning. Northcliffe course has no restrictions.
Societies	Wed & Fri only, by arrangement.
Green Fees	£40 per day; £30 per round (£40 per round weekends).
Cards	
Prof	Neil Hansen
Designer	Fowler & Simpson
Facilities	
& Leisure	hard tennis courts.
Location	1.5m N off B2052

Hotel　★★★ 61% Royal Albion Hotel, Albion St, BROADSTAIRS ☎ 01843 868071　19

CANTERBURY　　　　　　　Map 05 TR15

Canterbury Scotland Hills, Littlebourne Rd CT1 1TW
☎ 01227 453532 Fax 01227 784277
Undulating parkland course, densely wooded in places, with elevated tees and challenging drives on several holes.
18 holes, 6249yds, Par 70, SSS 70, Course record 64.
Club membership 650.

Visitors	restricted times on weekends & bank holidays. Must have a handicap certificate.
Societies	by arrangement.
Green Fees	£36 per day, £27 per round; (£36 per day weekends & bank holidays).
Prof	Paul Everard

▶

Designer Harry Colt
Facilities ⊗ ⁘ by prior arrangement 🏌 🍺 🏆 🏊 🏧 ⛳
Location 1.5m E on A257

Hotel ★★★ 62% The Chaucer, Ivy Ln,
CANTERBURY ☎ 0870 400 8106 42 ⇄ 🐾

CHART SUTTON   Map 05 TQ84

The Ridge Chartway St, East Sutton ME17 3DL
☎ 01622 844382
This flat parkland course was designed by Patrick Dawson
around mature orchards to challenge all levels of player. The
par 5, 18th has two lakes to negotiate.
18 holes, 6254yds, Par 71, SSS 70, Course record 68.
Club membership 650.
Visitors weekdays only, must have handicap certificate.
Societies Tue & Thu, by arrangement.
Green Fees not confirmed.
Prof Tim Milford
Designer Tyton Design
Facilities ⊗ ⁘ 🏌 🍺 🏆 🏊 🏧 ⛳ 🛒 ⛳
& Leisure solarium, gymnasium.
Location 5m S of Bearsted, off A274

Hotel ★★★★ 70% Marriott Tudor Park Hotel &
Country Club, Ashford Rd, Bearsted,
MAIDSTONE ☎ 01622 734334 118 ⇄ 🐾

CRANBROOK   Map 05 TQ73

Executive Golf Club at Cranbrook Golford Rd TN17 4AL
☎ 01580 712833 Fax 01580 714274
Scenic, parkland course with easy terrain, backed by
Hemstead Forest and close to Sissinghurst Castle (1m) and
Bodiam Castle (6m). The course has been transformed over
recent years with the introduction of over 5,000 mature pine
trees. Keeping the ball straight is paramount, a challenging
test of golf for all levels.
18 holes, 6305yds, Par 70, SSS 71.
Visitors welcome weekdays after 8.30 am. weekends
after 11.30 am. Tee reservations may be booked
up to 1 calendar month in advance.
Societies minimum of 12. Write or telephone to book.
Green Fees not confirmed.
Designer Commander J Harris
Facilities ⊗ ⁘ 🏌 🍺 🏆 🏊 🏧 ⛳ ⛳
Location 2m E

Hotel ★★⚓ Kennel Holt Hotel, Goudhurst Rd,
CRANBROOK ☎ 01580 712032 10 ⇄ 🐾

DARTFORD   Map 05 TQ57

Birchwood Park Birchwood Rd, Wilmington DA2 7HJ
☎ 01322 662038 & 660554 Fax 01322 667283
The main course offers highly challenging play and will test
golfers of all abilities. Beginners and those requiring a quick
game or golfers wishing to improve their short game will
appreciate the Orchard course where holes range from 96 to
258yards.
18 holes, 6364yds, Par 71, SSS 70, Course record 64.
Orchard: 9 holes, 1349yds, Par 29.
Club membership 500.
Visitors must contact in advance for Main Course.
Societies telephone for details.

Green Fees Main Course: £15.50 per round (£20 weekends).
Orchard: £4.40 per round (£5.50 weekends).
Cards 🔲 🔲 🔲 🔲 🔲
Designer Howard Swann
Facilities ⊗ ⁘ 🏌 🍺 🏆 🏊 🏧 ⛳ 🛒 ⛳ ⛳
& Leisure sauna, solarium, gymnasium.
Location B258 between Dartford & Swanley

Hotel ★★★★ 69% Swallow Hotel, 1 Broadway,
BEXLEYHEATH ☎ 020 8298 1000 142 ⇄ 🐾

Dartford Upper Heath Ln, Dartford Heath DA1 2TN
☎ 01322 226455
Heathland course.
18 holes, 5914yds, Par 69, SSS 69, Course record 63.
Club membership 700.
Visitors may not play at weekends. Must have a
handicap certificate.
Societies Mon & Fri only by prior arrangement with
Secretary.
Green Fees £30 per 2 rounds; £21 per round.
Prof John Gregory
Designer James Braid
Facilities ⊗ ⁘ 🏌 🍺 🏆 🏊 🏧 ⛳

Hotel ★★★ 65% Posthouse Bexley, Black Prince
Interchange, Southwold Rd, BEXLEY
☎ 0870 400 9006 105 ⇄ 🐾

DEAL   Map 05 TR35

Royal Cinque Ports Golf Rd CT14 6RF
☎ 01304 374007 Fax 01304 379530
Famous championship seaside links, windy but with easy
walking. Outward nine is generally considered the easier,
inward nine is longer and includes the renowned 16th,
perhaps the most difficult hole. On a fine day there are
wonderful views across the Channel.
18 holes, 6785yds, Par 72, SSS 72.
Club membership 850.
Visitors restricted Wed mornings, weekends & bank
holidays. Must contact in advance and have
a handicap certificate. Men max 18
handicap; Ladies max 28 handicap.
Societies must contact in advance.
Green Fees £60 per day/round.
Cards 🔲 🔲 🔲
Prof Andrew Reynolds
Designer James Braid
Facilities ⊗ ⁘ by prior arrangement
🏌 🍺 🏆 🏊 🏧 ⛳ 🛒 ⛳ ⛳
Location Along seafront at N end of Deal

▶

| Hotel | ★★★ 66% Dunkerleys Hotel & Restaurant, 19 Beach St, DEAL ☎ 01304 375016 16 ⇆ ⋔ |

EDENBRIDGE   Map 05 TQ44

Edenbridge Golf & Country Club
Crouch House Rd TN8 5LQ
☎ 01732 865097 & 867381 Fax 01732 867029
Parkland course with water on many holes, quiet with excellent views of rural Kent.
Old Course: 18 holes, 6646yds, Par 73, SSS 72.
Skeynes Course: 18 holes, 5605yds, Par 67, SSS 68.
Club membership 750.
Visitors must contact in advance for Old Course. All tee times bookable 7 days in advance.
Societies contact in advance.
Green Fees Old Course: £20 (£27.50 weekends); New Course: £12 (£16 weekends).
Cards 🗋 💳 💳 💳 💳
Prof Stephen Bryan
Facilities ⊗ ⅍ ⅃ ▨ ♀ ♨ 🛍 ⋔ ♠ 🛒 𝄐 ⟨
& Leisure hard tennis courts, gymnasium.
Location 0.75m W of town centre, signposted 'Golf Course'

| Hotel | ★★★✦✦ Gravetye Manor Hotel, EAST GRINSTEAD ☎ 01342 810567 18 ⇆ ⋔ |

Sweetwoods Park Cowden TN8 7JN
☎ 01342 850729 (Pro shop) & 850942 (Secretary)
Fax 01342 850866
An undulating and mature parkland course with fast greens, testing water hazards and fine views across the Weald from four holes. A good challenge off the back tees. Signature holes include the 2nd, 4th and 14th.
18 holes, 6512yds, Par 71, SSS 71, Course record 67.
Club membership 800.
Visitors no restrictions.
Societies Mon-Fri after 9am, contact for details.
Green Fees not confirmed.
Cards 🗋 💳 💳
Prof Bob Wynn/Ben Clover
Designer P Strand
Facilities ⊗ ⅍ ⅃ ▨ ♀ ♨ 🛍 🛒 𝄐 ⟨
Location 5m E of East Grinstead on the A264

| Hotel | ★★★ 64% Woodbury House Hotel, Lewes Rd, EAST GRINSTEAD ☎ 01342 313657 14 ⇆ ⋔ |

EYNSFORD   Map 05 TQ56

Austin Lodge Upper Austin Lodge Rd DA4 0HU
☎ 01322 863000 Fax 01322 862406
A well drained course designed to lie naturally in three secluded valleys in rolling countryside. Over 7000 yds from the medal tees. Practice ground, nets and a putting green add to the features.
18 holes, 6600yds, Par 73, SSS 71, Course record 68.
Club membership 600.
Visitors must contact in advance, may not play until after 1pm on weekends.
Societies telephone for bookings.

Green Fees £18 per 18 holes Mon-Wed, £20 Thu-Fri (£25 weekends & bank holidays).
Cards 🗋 💳 💳 💳 💳
Prof Paul Edwards
Designer P Bevan
Facilities ⊗ ⅍ ⅃ ▨ ♀ ♨ 🛍 ⋔ ♠ 🛒 𝄐 ⟨
Location 6m S of Dartford

| Hotel | ★★★ 67% Brandshatch Place, Fawkham, BRANDS HATCH ☎ 01474 872239 29 ⇆ ⋔ Annexe 12 ⇆ ⋔ |

FAVERSHAM   Map 05 TR06

Boughton Brickfield Ln ME13 9AJ
☎ 01227 752277 Fax 01227 752361
Rolling parkland/downland course set in 160 acres of Kent countryside, providing a good test of golf, even for the more accomplished players.
18 holes, 6452yds, Par 72, SSS 71, Course record 70.
Club membership 325.
Visitors booking by telephone advisable.
Societies telephone for details.
Green Fees not confirmed.
Cards 🗋 💳 💳 💳
Prof Trevor Dungate
Designer P Sparks
Facilities ⊗ ⅍ ⅃ ▨ ♀ ♨ 🛍 ⋔ ♠ 🛒 𝄐 ⟨
Location Off junct 7 of M2 - Brenley Corner

| Hotel | ★★★★✦✦ 78% Eastwell Manor, Eastwell Park, Boughton Lees, ASHFORD ☎ 01233 213000 23 ⇆ ⋔ Annexe 39 ⇆ ⋔ |

Faversham Belmont Park ME13 0HB
☎ 01795 890561 Fax 01795 890760
A beautiful inland course laid out over part of a large estate with pheasants walking the fairways quite tamely. Play follows two heavily wooded valleys but the trees affect only the loose shots going out of bounds. Fine views.
18 holes, 6030yds, Par 70, SSS 69, Course record 63.
Club membership 800.
Visitors must have handicap certificate. With member only at weekends. Contacting the club in advance is advisable.
Societies must contact in advance.
Green Fees £35 per day; £30 per round.
Prof Stuart Rokes
Facilities ⊗ ⅍ ⅃ ▨ ♀ ♨ 🛍 ♠ 🛒 𝄐
Location 3.5m S

| Hotel | ★★★★✦✦ 78% Eastwell Manor, Eastwell Park, Boughton Lees, ASHFORD ☎ 01233 213000 23 ⇆ ⋔ Annexe 39 ⇆ ⋔ |

FOLKESTONE   Map 05 TR23

Etchinghill Canterbury Rd, Etchinghill CT18 8FA
☎ 01303 863863 Fax 01303 863210
A varied course incorporating parkland on the outward 9 holes and an interesting downland landscape with many challenging holes on the back 9.
18 holes, 6121yds, Par 70, SSS 69, Course record 67.
Club membership 600.   ▶

Visitors   advisable to reserve tee time in advance.
Societies   telephone or write, packages available.
Green Fees   not confirmed.
Prof   Chris Hodgson
Designer   John Sturdy
Facilities   ⊗ ⅏ ﹟ 🍴 ♀ 🏌 🏠 ⛱ ⚒ ∅ ⊺
& Leisure   9 hole par3.
Location   N of M20, access from junct 11 or 12

Hotel   ★★★ 70% Clifton Hotel, The Leas, FOLKESTONE ☎ 01303 851231 80 ⇥ 🛏

GILLINGHAM Map 05 TQ76

Gillingham Woodlands Rd ME7 2AP
☎ 01634 853017 (office) & 855862 (pro)
Fax 01634 574749
Parkland course.
18 holes, 5557yds, Par 69, SSS 67, Course record 64.
Club membership 800.
Visitors   contact in advance, weekends only with member, must have handicap certificate.
Societies   must apply in writing.
Green Fees   not confirmed.
Prof   Barry Coomber
Designer   James Braid
Facilities   ⊗ ⅏ ﹟ 🍴 ♀ 🏌 🏠 ⛱ ∅ ⊺
Location   1.5m SE on A2

Hotel   ★★★ 65% Posthouse Rochester, Maidstone Rd, ROCHESTER
☎ 0870 400 9069 145 ⇥ 🛏

GRAVESEND Map 05 TQ67

Mid Kent Singlewell Rd DA11 7RB
☎ 01474 568035 Fax 01474 564218
A well-maintained downland course with some easy walking and some excellent greens. The first hole is short, but nonetheless a real challenge. The slightest hook and the ball is out of bounds or lost.
18 holes, 6199yds, Par 69, SSS 69, Course record 60.
Club membership 900.
Visitors   must contact in advance & have handicap certificate. May not play weekends.
Societies   Tue only, apply in writing.
Green Fees   £20 per round.
Prof   Mark Foreman
Designer   Frank Pennick
Facilities   ⊗ ⅏ ﹟ 🍴 ♀ 🏌 🏠 ⛱ ∅
Location   S side of town centre off A227

Hotel   ★★★ 60% Overcliffe Hotel, 15-16 The Overcliffe, GRAVESEND
☎ 01474 322131 19 🛏 Annexe 10 ⇥ 🛏

Southern Valley Thong Ln, Shorne DA12 4LF
☎ 01474 568568 Fax 01474 360366
All year playing conditions on a course landscaped with gorse, bracken and thorn and designed to enhance the views across the Thames Estuary. The course features undulating greens, large trees and rolling fairways with both the 9th and 18th holes located close to the clubhouse.
18 holes, 6500yds, Par 71, SSS 72.
Club membership 450.
Visitors   no restrictions.
Societies   must telephone in advance.
Green Fees   £13.50 per round (£17.50 weekends).
Cards   ≈ 💳 💳 💳 🖼
Prof   Tony Blackburn
Facilities   ⊗ ⅏ ﹟ 🍴 ♀ 🏌 🏠 ⛱ ⚒ ∅
Location   From A2 junct 4 at top of slip-road turn left into Thong Lane and continue for 1m

Hotel   ★★★ 60% Overcliffe Hotel, 15-16 The Overcliffe, GRAVESEND
☎ 01474 322131 19 🛏 Annexe 10 ⇥ 🛏

HALSTEAD Map 05 TQ46

Broke Hill Sevenoaks Rd TN14 7HR
☎ 01959 533225 Fax 01959 532680
Testing downland course featuring 80 bunkers, strategically placed water hazards and good views.
18 holes, 6454yds, Par 72, SSS 71, Course record 69.
Club membership 650.
Visitors   weekdays only. Must book in advance.
Societies   telephone for details.
Green Fees   £35.
Cards   ≈ 💳 💳 💳 💳 🖼
Prof   Chris West
Designer   David Williams
Facilities   ⊗ ⅏ ﹟ 🍴 ♀ 🏌 🏠 ⛱ 🏌 ⚒ ∅
& Leisure   sauna.
Location   Off junct 4 of M25, opposite Knockholt railway station

Hotel   ★★★ 68% Kings Arms Hotel, Market Square, WESTERHAM
☎ 01959 562990 17 ⇥ 🛏

HAWKHURST Map 05 TQ73

Hawkhurst High St TN18 4JS
☎ 01580 754074 & 752396 Fax 01580 754074
Undulating parkland course.
9 holes, 5751yds, Par 70, SSS 68, Course record 69.
Club membership 508.
Visitors   may play weekdays, weekends after 12 noon subject to availability.
Societies   must apply in advance.
Green Fees   £24 per day; £18 per round (£20 per round weekends).
Prof   Tony Collins
Designer   W A Baldock

▶

Facilities ⊗ ⅏ by prior arrangement
🄻 🖤 ♀ 🛇 🏠 ⛳ 🛒 ✧

& Leisure squash.

Location W side of village off A268

Hotel ★★★ 70% Tudor Court Hotel, Rye Rd,
HAWKHURST ☎ 01580 752312 18 ⇔ 🏴

HEADCORN   Map 05 TQ84

Weald of Kent Maidstone Rd TN27 9PT
☎ 01622 891671 Fax 01622 891793
Enjoying delightful views over the Weald of Kent, this pay
and play course features a range of natural hazards, including
lakes, trees, ditches and undulating fairways. A good test to
golfers of every standard.
18 holes, 6240yds, Par 70, SSS 70, Course record 64.
Club membership 450.

Visitors can book 3 days in advance, smart casual dress
no jeans.
Societies apply in writing or by telephone.
Green Fees not confirmed.
Cards 🌐 💳 💳 🔗 🄸
Designer John Millen
Facilities ⊗ ⅏ 🄻 🖤 ♀ 🛇 🏠 ⛳ 🛒 🛒 ✧
Location Through Leeds village take A274 towards
Headcorn, golf course on left

Hotel ★★★★ 70% Marriott Tudor Park Hotel &
Country Club, Ashford Rd, Bearsted,
MAIDSTONE ☎ 01622 734334 118 ⇔ 🏴

HERNE BAY   Map 05 TR16

Herne Bay Eddington CT6 7PG ☎ 01227 374727
Parkland course with bracing air.
18 holes, 5567yds, Par 68, SSS 68.
Club membership 500.

Visitors may not play mornings at weekends.
Societies apply in advance.
Green Fees not confirmed.
Prof S Dordoy
Designer James Braid
Facilities ♀ 🛇 🏠 ⛳ ✧
Location On A299 at Herne Bay/Canterbury junct

Hotel ★★★ 67% Falstaff Hotel, St Dunstans St,
Westgate, CANTERBURY
☎ 01227 462138 26 ⇔ 🏴 Annexe 22 ⇔ 🏴

HEVER   Map 05 TQ44

Hever Edenbridge TN8 7NG
☎ 01732 700771 Fax 01732 700775
This 27-hole parkland course is set in 250 acres with water
hazards and outstanding holes like the Par 3 12th which is
similar to the 12th at Augusta.
27 holes, 7002yds, Par 72, SSS 75, Course record 69.
Club membership 620.

Visitors must book tee times Mon-Fri.
Societies telephone for details.
Green Fees not confirmed.
Cards 🌐 💳 💳 🄸
Prof Richard Tinworth
Designer Dr Nicholas

Facilities ⊗ ⅏ 🄻 🖤 ♀ 🛇 🏠 ⛳ 🛒 🛒 ✧ ✦
& Leisure hard tennis courts, heated indoor swimming
pool, fishing, sauna, solarium, gymnasium.
Location 10mins from M25

Hotel ★★★ 76% The Spa Hotel, Mount Ephraim,
TUNBRIDGE WELLS
☎ 01892 520331 74 ⇔

HILDENBOROUGH   Map 05 TQ54

Nizels Nizels Ln TN11 9LU
☎ 01732 838926 (Bookings) Fax 01732 833764
Woodland course with many mature trees, wildlife and lakes
that come into play on several holes. The 2nd hole is a 553yd
Par 5, the green being guarded by bunkers hidden by a range
of hillocks. The Par 4 7th has water on both sides of the
fairway and a pitch over water to the green. The 10th is
539yd Par 5 with a sharp dogleg to the right, followed by a
very narrow entry between trees for the 2nd shot.
18 holes, 6408yds, Par 72, SSS 71, Course record 66.
Club membership 650.

Visitors telephone professional shop for tee reservation
01732 838926 at least 4 days in advance.
Societies weekdays only, telephone initially.
Green Fees not confirmed.
Cards 🌐 💳 💳 🔗 🄸
Prof Sue Hodge
Designer Donaldson/Edwards Partnership
Facilities ⊗ ⅏ 🄻 🖤 ♀ 🛇 🏠 ⛳ 🛒 🛒 ✧
Location Off B245

Hotel ★★★ 64% Rose & Crown Hotel, 125 High St,
TONBRIDGE ☎ 01732 357966 48 ⇔ 🏴

HOO   Map 05 TQ77

Deangate Ridge Dux Court Rd ME3 8RZ
☎ 01634 251180 Fax 01634 250537
Parkland, municipal course designed by Fred Hawtree. 18-
hole pitch and putt.
18 holes, 6300yds, Par 71, SSS 70, Course record 65.
Club membership 500.

Visitors no restrictions.
Societies please telephone 01634 255370.
Green Fees not confirmed.
Cards 🌐 💳 💳 🔗 🄸
Prof Richard Fox
Facilities ⊗ ⅏ 🄻 🖤 ♀ 🛇 🏠 ⛳ 🛒 ✧ ✦
& Leisure hard tennis courts.
Location 4m NE of Rochester off A228

▶

| Hotel | ★★★ 65% Posthouse Rochester, Maidstone Rd, ROCHESTER ☎ 0870 400 9069 145 ⇆ ↾ |

HYTHE Map 05 TR13

Hythe Imperial Princes Pde CT21 6AE
☎ 01303 267441 Fax 01303 264610
A 9-hole 18 tee links course bounded by the Royal Military Canal and the English Channel. Although the course is relatively flat, its aspect offers an interesting and challenging round to a wide range of golfers
9 holes, 5560yds, Par 68, SSS 66, Course record 62.
Club membership 300.

Visitors	course closed some Sun until 11am for competitions.
Societies	must apply in writing.
Green Fees	£10 per day (£15 weekends).
Prof	Gordon Ritchie
Facilities	⊗ ⋔ ♿ ▆ ♀ ♨ 🖶 ⛳ 🏌 ➷ ⚷
& Leisure	hard and grass tennis courts, heated indoor swimming pool, squash, sauna, solarium, gymnasium, croquet, snooker, hair & beauty salon.
Location	SE side of town

| Hotel | ★★★★ 76% The Hythe Imperial Hotel, Princes Pde, HYTHE ☎ 01303 267441 100 ⇆ ↾ |
| Additional hotel | ★★★ 74% Stade Court, West Pde, HYTHE ☎ 01303 268263 Fax 01303 261803 42 ⇆ ↾ |

Sene Valley Sene CT18 8BL
☎ 01303 268513 (Manager) & 268514 (Pro) Fax 01303 237513
A two-level downland course which provides interesting golf over an undulating landscape with sea views.
18 holes, 6196yds, Par 71, SSS 70, Course record 61.
Club membership 600.

Visitors	must contact professional in advance.
Societies	telephone in advance.
Green Fees	contact professional.
Cards	▬ ▬
Prof	Nick Watson
Designer	Henry Cotton
Facilities	⊗ ⋔ ♿ ▆ ♀ ♨ 🖶 ⚷ ♘
Location	1m NE off B2065

| Hotel | ★★★★ 76% The Hythe Imperial Hotel, Princes Pde, HYTHE ☎ 01303 267441 100 ⇆ ↾ |

KINGSDOWN Map 05 TR34

Walmer & Kingsdown The Leas CT14 8EP
☎ 01304 373256 & 363017 Fax 01304 382336
This course near Deal has through the years been overshadowed by its neighbours at Deal and Sandwich, yet it is a testing circuit with many undulations. The course is famous as being the one on which, in 1964, Assistant Professional, Roger Game became the first golfer in Britain to hole out in one at two successive holes; the 7th and 8th. The course is situated on top of the cliffs, with fine views.
18 holes, 6444yds, Par 72, SSS 71, Course record 66.
Club membership 680.

Visitors	must contact in advance. Not before 9.30am weekdays and noon weekends & bank holidays.
Societies	apply in advance.
Green Fees	£30 per day; £25 per round (£30 per round weekends).
Prof	Matthew Paget
Designer	James Braid
Facilities	⊗ ⋔ ♿ ▆ ♀ ♨ 🖶 ⛳ ➷ ⚷
Location	1.5m E of Ringwould off A258 Dover-Deal road

| Hotel | ★★★ Posthouse Dover, Singledge Ln, Whitfield, DOVER ☎ 0870 400 9024 68 ⇆ ↾ |

LAMBERHURST Map 05 TQ63

Lamberhurst Church Rd TN3 8DT
☎ 01892 890591 Fax 01892 891140
Parkland course crossing river twice. Fine views.
18 holes, 6345yds, Par 72, SSS 70, Course record 65.
Club membership 700.

Visitors	may only play after noon weekends unless with member, handicap certificate required.
Societies	Tue, Wed & Thu only from Apr-Oct, by arrangement
Green Fees	£33 per day; £22 per round (£36 weekends). Prices under review.
Cards	▬ ▬ ▬ 🟦
Prof	Brian Impett
Facilities	⊗ ⋔ by prior arrangement ▆ ♀ ♨ 🖶 ⛳ ➷ ⚷
Location	N side of village on B2162

| Hotel | ★★★ 76% The Spa Hotel, Mount Ephraim, TUNBRIDGE WELLS ☎ 01892 520331 74 ⇆ |

LITTLESTONE Map 05 TR02

Littlestone St Andrew's Rd TN28 8RB
☎ 01797 363355 Fax 01797 362740
Located in the Romney Marshes, this flattish seaside links course calls for every variety of shot. The 8th, 15th, 16th and 17th are regarded as classics by international golfers. Allowance for wind must always be made. Extensive practice area.
18 holes, 6471yds, Par 71, SSS 72, Course record 67.
Club membership 550.

Visitors	must contact in advance, no visitors before 3pm weekends and bank holidays.
Societies	must apply in advance.
Green Fees	not confirmed.
Cards	▬ ▬ ▬ 🟦
Prof	Stephen Watkins
Designer	Laidlaw Purves
Facilities	⊗ ⋔ ♿ ▆ ♀ ♨ 🖶 ⛳ ➷ ⚷
& Leisure	hard tennis courts.
Location	1m from New Romney off Littlestone road B2070

| Hotel | ★★★★ 76% The Hythe Imperial Hotel, Princes Pde, HYTHE ☎ 01303 267441 100 ⇆ ↾ |

Romney Warren St Andrews Rd TN28 8RB
☎ 01797 362231 Fax 01797 362740
A links style course, normally very dry. Flat providing easy walking and play challenged by sea breezes.
18 holes, 5126yds, Par 67, SSS 65, Course record 69.
Club membership 300.
Visitors   contact professional in advance.
Societies   contact in advance.
Green Fees £13 per round (£18 weekends & bank holidays).
Cards   ▨▨ ▨▨ ▨▨ ▨
Prof   Stephen Watkins
Facilities   ⊗ ⅲ ▨ ▨ ♀ ☖ ☖ ⚐ ⚲ ➘ ⚒ ⚬
Location   N side of Littlestone

Hotel   ★★★★ 76% The Hythe Imperial Hotel, Princes Pde, HYTHE
☎ 01303 267441 100 ⇆ 🏻

LYDD   Map 05 TR02

Lydd Romney Rd TN29 9LS
☎ 01797 320808 Fax 01797 321482
A links-type course offering some interesting challenges, including a number of eye-catching water hazards, wide fairways and plenty of semi-rough. A good test for experienced golfers and appealing to the complete novice.
18 holes, 6517yds, Par 71, Course record 65.
Club membership 415.
Visitors   contact in advance on 01797 321201.
Societies   telephone in advance.
Green Fees not confirmed.
Cards   ▨▨ ▨▨
Prof   Andrew Jones
Designer   Mike Smith
Facilities   ⊗ ⅲ ▨ ▨ ♀ ☖ ☖ ⚐ ⚲ ➘ ⚒ ⚬ ⚑
Location   B2075

Hotel   ★★★ 61% The George, High St, RYE
☎ 01797 222114 22 ⇆ 🏻

MAIDSTONE   Map 05 TQ75

Cobtree Manor Park Chatham Rd, Sandling ME14 3AZ
☎ 01622 753276 Fax 01634 262003
An undulating parkland course with some water hazards.
18 holes, 5611yds, Par 69, SSS 69, Course record 66.
Club membership 500.
Visitors   no restrictions but advisable to telephone in advance.
Societies   Mon-Fri only, by arrangement tel: 01622 751881.
Green Fees not confirmed.
Prof   Paul Foston
Facilities   ☖ ⚐ ⚲ ➘ ⚬
Location   On A229 0.25m N of M20 junc 6

Hotel   ★★★ 66% Russell Hotel, 136 Boxley Rd, MAIDSTONE ☎ 01622 692221 42 ⇆ 🏻

Leeds Castle Ashford Rd ME17 1PL
☎ 01622 767828 Fax 01622 735616
Situated around Leeds Castle, this is one of the most picturesque courses in Britain. Re-designed in the 1980s by Neil Coles, it is a challenging 9-hole course with the added hazard of the Castle moat.
9 holes, 2681yds, Par 33, SSS 33, Course record 30.

Visitors   bookings taken from 6 days in advance.
Societies   must telephone in advance.
Green Fees £18.50 per 18 holes, £11 per 9 holes (£26/£13 weekends). Green fees include admission to castle and gardens..
Cards   ▨▨ ▨▨ ▨
Prof   Stephen Purves
Designer   Neil Coles
Facilities   ⊗ ⅲ ▨ ▨ ☖ ☖ ⚐ ⚲ ⚬
Location   On A20 towards Lenham, 4m E of Maidstone via M20 junct 8

Hotel   ★★★★ 70% Marriott Tudor Park Hotel & Country Club, Ashford Rd, Bearsted, MAIDSTONE ☎ 01622 734334 118 ⇆ 🏻

Marriott Tudor Park Hotel & Country Club Ashford Rd, Bearsted ME14 4NQ ☎ 01622 734334 Fax 01622 735360
The course is set in a 220 acre former deerpark with the pleasant undulating Kent countyside as a backdrop. The natural features of the land have been incorporated into this picturesque course to form a challenge for those of both high and intermediate standard. The Par 5 14th is particularly interesting. It can alter your score dramatically should you gamble with a drive to a narrow fairway. This hole has to be carefully thoughout from tee to green depending on the wind direction.
18 holes, 6041yds, Par 70, SSS 69, Course record 64.
Club membership 725.

Visitors   may not play Sat & Sun before noon. Contact pro shop 01622 739412 for bookings.
Societies   please call the Golf Manager.
Green Fees £25 (£35 weekends and bank holidays).
Cards   ▨▨ ▨▨ ▨▨ ▨ ▨▨ ▨▨ ▨
Prof   Nick McNally
Designer   Donald Steel

▶

Royal St George's

Sandwich, *Kent*

☎ **01304 613090** Fax **01304 611245** Map **05 TR35**

This long-established 18-hole championship links course has been the host venue for the Open Championship on 12 occasions, and will be again in 2003. It has been the host venue for the Amateur Championship on 12 occasions, most recently in 1997.

The course itself is the truest links you might find in England, designed by Dr Laidlaw Purves in 1887. Close to the sea, overlooking Pegwell Bay, any kind of wind can make this man-size test even tougher. The sweeping rough at the 1st can be daunting, as can the bunkers and the huge sandhills. Off-sea breezes can become incredible gales and it is possible to find the course virtually unplayable.

Championship Course

Facilities ⊗ 〄 🏋 ☕ 💺 ♀ 🛋 🏠 🍴 🏌 🛥 ⚙
& Leisure hard tennis courts, heated indoor swimming
pool, sauna, solarium, gymnasium, steam room
& jacuzzi, golf academy.
Location On A20, 1.25m W of M20 junct 8

Hotel ★★★★ 70% Marriott Tudor Park Hotel &
Country Club, Ashford Rd, Bearsted,
MAIDSTONE ☎ 01622 734334 118 ⇆ 🐾

RAMSGATE   Map 05 TR36

St Augustine's Cottington Rd, Cliffsend CT12 5JN
☎ 01843 590333 Fax 01843 590444
A comfortably flat course in this famous bracing
Championship area of Kent. Neither as long nor as
difficult as its lordly neighbours, St Augustine's will
nonetheless extend most golfers. Dykes run across the
course.
18 holes, 5197yds, Par 69, SSS 65, Course record 61.
Club membership 670.
Visitors must contact in advance.
Societies must contact in advance.
Green Fees not confirmed.
Prof Derek Scott
Designer Tom Vardon
Facilities ⊗ 〄 🏋 ☕ 💺 ♀ 🛋 🛥 ⚙
Location Off A256 Ramsgate/Sandwich

Hotel ★★★ 66% San Clu Hotel, Victoria Pde,
East Cliff, RAMSGATE
☎ 01843 592345 44 ⇆ 🐾

ROCHESTER   Map 05 TQ76

Rochester & Cobham Park Park Pale ME2 3UL
☎ 01474 823411 Fax 01474 824446
A first-rate course of challenging dimensions in
undulating parkland. All holes differ and each requires
accurate drive placing to derive the best advantage. The
clubhouse and course are situated a quarter of a mile
from the western end of the M2.
18 holes, 6596yds, Par 71, SSS 72, Course record 67.
Club membership 720.
Visitors must contact in advance & have handicap
certificate. No visitors weekends.
Societies apply in advance.
Green Fees £40 per day; £30 per round.
Prof Iain Higgins
Designer Donald Steel
Facilities ⊗ 〄 🏋 ☕ 💺 ♀ 🛋 🏠 🍴 🛥 ⚙ ⚐
Location 2.5m W on A2

Hotel ★★★★ 77% Bridgewood Manor Hotel,
Bridgewood Roundabout, Walderslade
Woods, CHATHAM
☎ 01634 201333 100 ⇆ 🐾

SANDWICH   Map 05 TR35

Prince's Prince's Dr, Sandwich Bay CT13 9QB
☎ 01304 611118 Fax 01304 612000
With 27 championship holes, Prince's Golf Club enjoys
a world wide reputation as a traditional links of the finest
quality and is a venue that provides all that is best in

modern links golf. The purpose built clubhouse, located
at the centre of the three loops of nine, can seat 200
diners and offers panoramic views over Sandwich Bay
and the course.
Dunes: 9 holes, 3343yds, Par 36, SSS 36.
Himalayas: 9 holes, 3321yds, Par 35, SSS 35.
Shore: 9 holes, 3455yds, Par 36, SSS 36.
Club membership 250.
Visitors available all week, must contact in advance.
Societies welcome all week, please contact in
advance.
Green Fees £36-£55 per 27 holes; £30-£45 per 18 holes
(£44-£65/£35-£55 weekends).
Cards 💳 💳 💳 💳 💳
Prof Derek Barbour
Designer (1951 Sir Guy Campbell & J S F Morrison)
Facilities ⊗ 〄 🏋 ☕ 💺 ♀ 🛋 🏠 🍴 🏌 🛥 ⚙ ⚐
& Leisure snooker.
Location 2m E via toll road, follow signs from
Sandwich

Hotel ★★★ 66% San Clu Hotel, Victoria Pde,
East Cliff, RAMSGATE
☎ 01843 592345 44 ⇆ 🐾

SANDWICH See page 149

SEVENOAKS   Map 05 TQ55

Knole Park Seal Hollow Rd TN15 0HJ
☎ 01732 452150 Fax 01732 463159
The course is set in a majestic park with many fine trees
and deer running loose. It has a wiry turf seemingly
impervious to rain. Certainly a pleasure to play on.
Excellent views of Knole House and the North Downs.
Outstanding greens.
18 holes, 6266yds, Par 70, SSS 70, Course record 62.
Club membership 800.
Visitors must have a handicap certificate and contact
the secretary in advance, may not play at
weekends or bank holidays.
Societies telephone initially.
Green Fees £46 per 36 holes; £35 per 18 holes.
Prof Phil Sykes
Designer J A Abercromby
Facilities ⊗ 〄 🏋 ☕ 💺 ♀ 🛋 🏠 🍴 ⚙
& Leisure squash.
Location SE side of town centre off B2019

Hotel ★★★ 67% Donnington Manor, London
Rd, Dunton Green, SEVENOAKS
☎ 01732 462681 62 ⇆ 🐾

SHEERNESS   Map 05 TQ97

Sheerness Power Station Rd ME12 3AE
☎ 01795 662585 Fax 01795 668100
Semi-links, marshland course, few bunkers, but many ditches
and water hazards.
18 holes, 6460yds, Par 72, SSS 71, Course record 66.
Club membership 750.
Visitors with member only at weekends.
Societies weekdays only, book in advance.
Green Fees £25 per day; £18 per round.   ▶

Prof	L Stanford
Facilities	⊗ ⵜ by prior arrangement ዄ ♥ ♀ ♨ 📠 ✦
Location	1.5m E off A249

Hotel	★★★★ 77% Bridgewood Manor Hotel, Bridgewood Roundabout, Walderslade Woods, CHATHAM ☎ 01634 201333 100 ⇆ ☏

SHOREHAM — Map 05 TQ56

Darenth Valley Station Rd TN14 7SA
☎ 01959 522944 & 522922 Fax 01959 525089
Easy walking parkland course in beautiful valley. Testing 12th hole, par 4.
18 holes, 6327yds, Par 72, SSS 71, Course record 64.

Visitors	must book in advance.
Societies	contact in advance.
Green Fees	£15 per round (£20 weekends & bank holidays).
Cards	🖃 🖃 🖃 🖃
Prof	David J Copsey
Facilities	⊗ ⵜ by prior arrangement ዄ ♥ ♀ ♨ 📠 ⵀ ✦
& Leisure	fishing.
Location	1m E on A225

Hotel	★★★ 67% Donnington Manor, London Rd, Dunton Green, SEVENOAKS ☎ 01732 462681 62 ⇆ ☏

SITTINGBOURNE — Map 05 TQ96

The Oast Golf Centre Church Rd, Tonge ME9 9AR
☎ 01795 473527
A Par 3 Approach course of 9 holes with 18 tees augmented by a 17-bay floodlit driving range and a putting green.
9 holes, 1664yds, Par 54, SSS 54.

Visitors	no restrictions.
Societies	telephone in advance.
Green Fees	£6.50 per 18 holes; £4.50 per 9 holes.
Prof	D Chambers
Designer	D Chambers
Facilities	ዄ ♥ ♀ 📠 ⵀ ✦ ⵏ
Location	2m NE, A2 between Bapchild/Teynham

Hotel	★★★★ 77% Bridgewood Manor Hotel, Bridgewood Roundabout, Walderslade Woods, CHATHAM ☎ 01634 201333 100 ⇆ ☏

Sittingbourne & Milton Regis Wormdale, Newington ME9 7PX ☎ 01795 842261 Fax 01795 844117
A downland course with pleasant vistas. There are a few uphill climbs, but the course is far from difficult. The new back nine holes are very testing.
18 holes, 6291yds, Par 71, SSS 70, Course record 63.
Club membership 670.

Visitors	by prior arrangement or letter of introduction. Must contact in advance, may not play at weekends.
Societies	Tue & Thu, apply in advance.
Green Fees	£35 per 36 holes; £22 per 18 holes.
Prof	John Hearn
Designer	Donald Steel
Facilities	⊗ ⵜ ዄ ♥ ♀ ♨ 📠 ⵀ 🛪 ✦
Location	Turn off Chestnut Street (old A249) at Danaway

Hotel	★★★★ 77% Bridgewood Manor Hotel, Bridgewood Roundabout, Walderslade Woods, CHATHAM ☎ 01634 201333 100 ⇆ ☏

Upchurch River Valley Golf Centre Oak Ln, Upchurch
ME9 7AY ☎ 01634 379592 Fax 01634 387784
Undulating parkland course set in picturesque countryside. Testing water hazards on several holes. Excellent winter course. The 9-hole course is ideal for beginners and for those keen to sharpen up their short game.
18 holes, 6237yds, Par 70, SSS 70.
Club membership 421.

Visitors	can play anytime, book for weekend 5 days in advance, weekdays 2 days in advance.
Societies	telephone 01634 360626 for details.
Green Fees	not confirmed.
Cards	🖃 🖃 🖃 🖃
Prof	Roger Cornwell
Designer	David Smart
Facilities	⊗ ⵜ ዄ ♥ ♀ ♨ 📠 🛪 🛪 ✦ ⵏ
& Leisure	heated outdoor swimming pool.
Location	A2 between Rainham and Newington

Hotel	★★★ 66% Russell Hotel, 136 Boxley Rd, MAIDSTONE ☎ 01622 692221 42 ⇆ ☏

SNODLAND — Map 05 TQ76

Oastpark Malling Rd ME6 5LG
☎ 01634 242661 Fax 01634 240744
A challenging parkland course for golfers of all abilities. The course has water hazards, orchards and views across the Valley of Dean.
18 holes, 6173yds, Par 69, SSS 69, Course record 71.
Club membership 300.

Visitors	may book 7 days in advance.
Societies	early booking with deposits required.
Green Fees	£10 per 18 holes; £7 per 9 holes (£14/£8 weekends)
Cards	🖃 🖃 🖃 🖃
Prof	Nathan French
Designer	J D Banks
Facilities	⊗ ⵜ ዄ ♥ ♀ ♨ 📠 ✦ ⵏ
Location	Access via junct 4 on M20

Hotel	★★★ 63% Larkfield Priory Hotel, London Rd, Larkfield, MAIDSTONE ☎ 01732 846858 52 ⇆ ☏

TENTERDEN — Map 05 TQ83

Tenterden Woodchurch Rd TN30 7DR
☎ 01580 763987 (sec) & 762409 (shop) Fax 01580 763987
Set in tranquil undulating parkland with beautiful views, the course is challenging with several difficult holes.
18 holes, 6071yds, Par 70, SSS 69, Course record 61.
Club membership 600.

Visitors	contact secretary. May only play with member weekends and bank holidays. Handicap certificate required.
Societies	contact secretary, full details on request.
Green Fees	£22 per day.
Cards	🖃 🖃 🖃
Prof	Kyle Kelsall
Facilities	⊗ ⵜ ዄ ♥ ♀ ♨ 📠 🛪 🛪 ✦
Location	0.75m E on B2067

Hotel	★★♨ Kennel Holt Hotel, Goudhurst Rd, CRANBROOK ☎ 01580 712032 10 ⇆ ☏

TONBRIDGE   Map 05 TQ54

Poultwood Higham Ln TN11 9QR
☎ 01732 364039 Fax 01732 353781
There are two public 'pay and play' parkland courses in an idyllic woodland setting. The courses are ecologically designed, over predominantly flat land offering challenging hazzards and interesting playing conditions for all standards of golfer.
Course 1: 18 holes, 5569yds, Par 68, SSS 67 or 9 holes, 1281yds, Par 28.
Course 2: 9 holes, 1218yds, Par 28, SSS 28.

Visitors	non registered golfers may book up to 2 days in advance for 18 hole course, or take available tee times, pay and play system on 9 hole.
Societies	apply in advance to the clubhouse manager tel 01732 366180.
Green Fees	£14 per 18 holes (£16.50 weekends).
Cards	〓 〓 〓 〓 〓
Prof	Chris Miller
Facilities	⊗ ⊪ ⅃ ♥ ♀ ♨ ⚐ ☏ ✐
& Leisure	squash.
Location	Off A227, 3m N of Tonbridge

Hotel	★★★ 64% Rose & Crown Hotel, 125 High St, TONBRIDGE ☎ 01732 357966 48 ⇋ ☏

TUNBRIDGE WELLS (ROYAL)   Map 05 TQ53

Nevill Benhall Mill Rd TN2 5JW
☎ 01892 525818 Fax 01892 517861
Just within Sussex, the county boundary with Kent runs along the northern perimeter of the course. Open undulating ground, well-wooded with some heather and gorse for the first half. The second nine holes slope away from the clubhouse to a valley where a narrow stream hazards two holes.
18 holes, 6349yds, Par 71, SSS 70, Course record 64.
Club membership 900.

Visitors	must contact 48 hours in advance, handicap certificate required, permission from secretary for weekends play.
Societies	must apply in writing one month in advance.
Green Fees	not confirmed.
Prof	Paul Huggett
Designer	Henry Cotton
Facilities	⊗ ⊪ ⅃ ♥ ♀ ♨ ⚐ ☏ 🛒 ✐
Location	S of Tunbridge Wells, off forest road

Hotel	★★★ 76% The Spa Hotel, Mount Ephraim, TUNBRIDGE WELLS ☎ 01892 520331 74 ⇋

Tunbridge Wells Langton Rd TN4 8XH
☎ 01892 523034 Fax 01892 536918
Somewhat hilly, well-bunkered parkland course with lake; trees form natural hazards.
9 holes, 4725yds, Par 65, SSS 62, Course record 59.
Club membership 450.

Visitors	must contact in advance, limited availability weekends.
Societies	weekdays, apply in advance.
Green Fees	£25 per day; £15 per 18 holes; £10 per 9 holes (£25 per 18 holes; £15 per 9 holes weekends).
Cards	〓 〓 〓 〓

Prof	Mike Barton
Facilities	⊗ ⊪ by prior arrangement ⅃ ♥ ♀ ♨ ⚐ ☏ ✐
Location	1m W on A264

Hotel	★★★ 76% The Spa Hotel, Mount Ephraim, TUNBRIDGE WELLS ☎ 01892 520331 74 ⇋

WESTERHAM   Map 05 TQ45

Parkwood Chestnut Av, Tatsfield TN16 2EG
☎ 01959 577744 & 577177 (pro-shop) Fax 01959 572702
Situated in an area of natural beauty, flanked by an ancient woodland with superb views across Kent and Surrey. An undulating course, tree lined and with some interesting water features. Playable in all weather conditions.
18 holes, 6835yds, Par 72, SSS 72, Course record 66.
Club membership 500.

Visitors	telephone in advance. May not play bank holidays.
Societies	apply in writing/telephone in advance.
Green Fees	£30 per day, £20 per round (£40/£30 weekends).
Cards	〓 〓 〓
Prof	Nick Terry
Facilities	⊗ ⊪ ⅃ ♥ ♀ ♨ ⚐ 🛒 🛒 ✐
Location	A25 onto B2024 Croydon Rd which becomes Clarks Lane. At Church Hill junct join Chestnut Av

Hotel	★★★ 68% Kings Arms Hotel, Market Square, WESTERHAM ☎ 01959 562990 17 ⇋ ☏

Westerham Valence Park, Brasted Rd TN16 1LJ
☎ 01959 567100 Fax 01959 567101
Originally completely wooded forestry land with thousands of mature pines. The storms of 1987 created natural fairways and the mature landscape makes the course both demanding and spectacular. New clubhouse with first class facilities and magnificent views.
18 holes, 6272yds, Par 72, SSS 72.
Club membership 700.

Visitors	welcome but may not play Sat & Sun am.
Societies	telephone events office for details.
Green Fees	£40 per day; £25 per round (£34 weekends).
Cards	〓 〓 〓 〓
Prof	Ewan Campbell
Designer	D Williams
Facilities	⊗ ⊪ by prior arrangement ⅃ ♥ ♀ ♨ ⚐ 🛒 ✐ ☏
Location	A25 between Westerham and Brasted

Hotel	★★★ 68% Kings Arms Hotel, Market Square, WESTERHAM ☎ 01959 562990 17 ⇋ ☏

WESTGATE ON SEA   Map 05 TR37

Westgate and Birchington 176 Canterbury Rd CT8 8LT
☎ 01843 831115
A fine blend of inland and seaside holes which provide a good test of the golfer despite the apparently simple appearance of the course.
18 holes, 4926yds, Par 64, SSS 64, Course record 60.
Club membership 320.

Visitors	Mon-Sat after 10am, Sun and bank holidays after 11am, must contact in advance & have handicap certificate, restricted at weekends.

▶

Societies must contact the secretary.
Green Fees £12 per day (£15 weekends & bank holidays).
Prof Roger Game
Facilities 🏌 🍴 ♀ 🏊 🏠 ✍
Location E side of town centre off A28

Hotel ★★★ 61% Royal Albion Hotel, Albion St,
BROADSTAIRS ☎ 01843 868071 19 ⇄ ♠

WEST KINGSDOWN
Map 05 TQ56

Woodlands Manor Woodlands TN15 6AB
☎ 01959 523806 & 524161
Interesting, challenging & undulating parkland course with
testing 1st, 9th and 15th holes. Set in a designated area of
outstanding natural beauty.
18 holes, 6100yds, Par 69, SSS 68, Course record 64.
Club membership 650.
Visitors welcome, at weekends by arrangement.
Societies apply in advance.
Green Fees not confirmed.
Cards 💳 💳 💳 💳 💳
Prof Philip Womack
Designer Lyons/Coles
Facilities ⊗ ╫ 🏌 🍴 ♀ 🏊 🏠 🛒 ❦ 🛥 ✍ ♭
& Leisure hard tennis courts.
Location 2m S off A20

Hotel ★★★ 66% Posthouse Maidstone/Sevenoaks,
London Rd, Wrotham Heath, WROTHAM
☎ 0870 400 9054 106 ⇄ ♠

WHITSTABLE
Map 05 TR16

Chestfield (Whitstable) 103 Chestfield Rd CT5 3LU
☎ 01227 794411 & 792243 Fax 01227 794454
Gently undulating parkland course with sea views. The Par 3
3rd is generally played into the wind and the Par 4th has a
difficult lefthand dogleg.
18 holes, 6200yds, Par 70, SSS 70.
Club membership 650.
Visitors contact for times.
Societies must apply in writing/telephone.
Green Fees £30 per day; £22 per round (£25 weekends).
Prof John Brotherton
Designer D Steel/James Braid
Facilities ⊗ ╫ 🏌 🍴 ♀ 🏊 🏠 ❦ 🛥 ✍
Location 0.5m S by Chestfield Railway Station

Hotel ★★★ 62% The Chaucer, Ivy Ln,
CANTERBURY ☎ 0870 400 8106 42 ⇄ ♠

Whitstable & Seasalter Collingwood Rd CT5 1EB
☎ 01227 272020 Fax 01227 280822
Links course.
9 holes, 5357yds, Par 66, SSS 63, Course record 62.
Club membership 300.
Visitors must contact in advance. Weekend play by prior
arrangement.
Green Fees not confirmed.
Facilities 🏌 🍴 ♀ 🏊
Location W side of town centre off B2205

Hotel ★★★ 62% The Chaucer, Ivy Ln,
CANTERBURY ☎ 0870 400 8106 42 ⇄ ♠

ACCRINGTON
Map 07 SD72

Accrington & District Devon Av, Oswaldtwistle BB5 4LS
☎ 01254 381614 Fax 01254 381614
Moorland course with pleasant views of the Pennines and
surrounding areas.
18 holes, 6044yds, Par 70, SSS 69, Course record 63.
Club membership 600.
Visitors must contact in advance.
Societies contact in advance.
Green Fees £20 (£25 weekends & bank holidays).
Reductions in winter.
Prof Bill Harling
Designer J Braid
Facilities ♀ 🏊 🏠 🛒 ❦ 🛥 ✍ ♭
Location Mid way between Accrington & Blackburn

Hotel ★★★★ 62% Dunkenhalgh Hotel, Blackburn
Rd, Clayton-le-Moors, ACCRINGTON
☎ 01254 398021 37 ⇄ ♠ Annexe 42 ⇄ ♠

Baxenden & District Top o' th' Meadow, Baxenden BB5
2EA ☎ 01254 234555
Moorland course with a long par 3 to start.
9 holes, 5740yds, Par 70, SSS 68, Course record 67.
Club membership 340.
Visitors may not play Sat, Sun and bank holidays except
with member.
Societies must contact in advance.
Green Fees not confirmed.
Facilities ⊗ ╫ 🏌 🍴 ♀ 🏊
Location 1.5m SE off A680

Hotel ★★★★ 62% Dunkenhalgh Hotel, Blackburn
Rd, Clayton-le-Moors, ACCRINGTON
☎ 01254 398021 37 ⇄ ♠ Annexe 42 ⇄ ♠

Green Haworth Green Haworth BB5 3SL
☎ 01254 237580 Fax 01254 396176
Moorland course dominated by quarries and difficult in
windy conditions.
9 holes, 5556yds, Par 68, SSS 67, Course record 65.
Club membership 320.
Visitors may not play Sun, Mar-Oct.
Societies apply in writing. Weekdays only before 5pm. Or
contact secretary on above telephone number.
Green Fees not confirmed.
Facilities ⊗ ╫ 🏌 🍴 ♀ 🏊
Location 2m S off A680

Hotel ★★★ 63% County Hotel Blackburn, Preston
New Rd, BLACKBURN
☎ 01254 899988 101 ⇄ ♠

BACUP
Map 07 SD82

Bacup Maden Rd OL13 8HY
☎ 01706 873170 & 877726 Fax 01706 877726
Moorland course, predominantly flat except climbs to 1st and
10th holes.
9 holes, 6008yds, Par 70, SSS 69.
Club membership 350.

▶

Visitors	no restrictions. Club competitions in season on Sat & some Sun, advisable to contact in advance.
Societies	must contact in writing.
Green Fees	not confirmed.
Facilities	♿
Location	W side of town off A671

| Hotel | ★★ 60% Comfort Inn, Keirby Walk, BURNLEY ☎ 01282 427611 50 ⇄ ♟ |

BARNOLDSWICK   Map 07 SD84

Ghyll Skipton Rd BB18 6JH ☎ 01282 842466
Excellent, parkland course with outstanding views, especially from the 8th tee where you can see the Three Peaks. Testing 8th hole is an uphill par 4. 11 holes in total 9 in Yorkshire and 2 in Lancashire.
9 holes, 5790yds, Par 68, SSS 66, Course record 62.
Club membership 345.

Visitors	may not play Tue, Fri after 4.30pm & Sun.
Societies	must contact in writing.
Green Fees	£14 per day (£18 weekends).
Facilities	⊗ ☕ ♿
Location	1m NE on B6252

| Hotel | ★★★ 67% Stirk House Hotel, GISBURN ☎ 01200 445581 40 ⇄ ♟ Annexe 10 ⇄ ♟ |

BLACKBURN   Map 07 SD62

Blackburn Beardwood Brow BB2 7AX
☎ 01254 51122 Fax 01254 665578
Parkland course on a high plateau with stream and hills. Superb views of Lancashire coast and the Pennines.
18 holes, 6144yds, Par 71, SSS 70.
Club membership 550.

Visitors	must contact professional in advance.
Societies	must contact in advance.
Green Fees	not confirmed.
Prof	Alan Rodwell
Facilities	⊗ ⊪ ⅃ ☕ ♀ ♿ 🏠 ♟ ♂
Location	1.25m NW of town centre off A677

| Hotel | ★★★ 63% County Hotel Blackburn, Preston New Rd, BLACKBURN ☎ 01254 899988 101 ⇄ ♟ |

BLACKPOOL   Map 07 SD33

Blackpool North Shore Devonshire Rd FY2 0RD
☎ 01253 352054 Fax 01253 591240
Undulating parkland course.
18 holes, 6432yds, Par 71, SSS 71, Course record 63.
Club membership 900.

Visitors	may not play Thu & Sat. Advisable to contact in advance.
Societies	must contact in advance.
Green Fees	£30 (£35 weekends).
Prof	Brendan Ward
Facilities	⊗ ⊪ ⅃ ☕ ♀ ♿ 🏠 ♟ ♂
Location	On A587 N of town centre

| Hotel | ★★ 66% Brabyns Hotel, 1-3 Shaftesbury Av, North Shore, BLACKPOOL ☎ 01253 354263 22 ⇄ ♟ Annexe 3 ⇄ ♟ |

De Vere Blackpool (Herons Reach) East Park Blackpool FY3 8LL ☎ 01253 766156 & 838866 Fax 01253 798800
The course was designed by Peter Alliss and Clive Clarke. There are 10 man-made lakes and several existing ponds. Built to a links design, well mounded but fairly easy walking. Water comes into play on 9 holes, better players can go for the carry or shorter hitters can take the safe route. The course provides an excellent and interesting challenge for golfers of all standards.
18 holes, 6628yds, Par 72, SSS 71, Course record 64.
Club membership 450.

Visitors	may book up to 2 weeks in advance tel 01253 766156, (hotel guest/visiting society no limit to how far in advance bookings can be made). Handicap essential, etiquette and dress rules must be adhered to
Societies	telephone or write to golf sales office 01253 838866.
Green Fees	£35 per round (£40 weekends).
Cards	💳 ▬ ▬ 💳 💳
Prof	Dominik Naughton
Designer	Peter Alliss/Clive Clark
Facilities	⊗ ⊪ ⅃ ☕ ♀ ♿ 🏠 ♟ ♂ ⛳ 🛒 ♂ ♟
& Leisure	hard tennis courts, heated indoor swimming pool, squash, sauna, solarium, gymnasium.
Location	Off A587 adjacent to Stanley Park & Zoo

| Hotel | ★★★★ 64% De Vere Hotel, East Park Dr, BLACKPOOL ☎ 01253 838866 164 ⇄ ♟ |

Stanley Park Municipal North Park Dr FY3 8LS
☎ 01253 397916 Fax 01253 397916
The golf course, situated in Stanley Park is municipal. The golf club (Blackpool Park) is private but golfers may use the clubhouse facilities if playing the course. An abundance of grassy pits, ponds and open dykes.
18 holes, 6087yds, Par 70, SSS 69, Course record 64.
Club membership 600.

Visitors	must apply to Mrs A Hirst, Town Hall, Talbot Square, Blackpool.
Societies	must apply in writing to Mrs A Hirst, Blackpool Borough Council, Town Hall, Talbot Square, Blackpool.
Green Fees	not confirmed.
Prof	Brian Purdie
Designer	Mckenzie
Facilities	⊗ ⊪ ⅃ ☕ ♀ ♿ 🏠 ♟ ♂
Location	1m E of Blackpool Tower

| Hotel | ★★★ 60% Savoy Hotel, Queens Promenade, North Shore, BLACKPOOL ☎ 01253 352561 131 ⇄ ♟ |

ENGLAND

LANCASHIRE

BURNLEY — Map 07 SD83

Burnley Glen View BB11 3RW
☎ 01282 421045 & 451281 Fax 01282 451281
Moorland course with hilly surrounds.
18 holes, 5911yds, Par 69, SSS 69, Course record 64.
Club membership 750.
Visitors must contact in advance. May not play on Saturdays.
Societies must apply in writing.
Green Fees £20 per day (£25 weekends & bank holidays).
Prof William Tye
Facilities ⊗ ⅢⅬ ▯ ♀ ♁ 🛅 ✆
Location 1.5m S off A646

Hotel ★★ 60% Comfort Inn, Keirby Walk, BURNLEY ☎ 01282 427611 50 ⇔ 🖚

Towneley Towneley Park, Todmorden Rd BB11 3ED
☎ 01282 438473
Parkland course, with other sporting facilities.
18 holes, 5811yds, Par 70, SSS 68, Course record 67.
Club membership 290.
Visitors must contact in advance.
Societies must contact in advance in writing.
Green Fees not confirmed.
Cards ▭ ▬ ▭
Facilities ⊗ Ⅼ ▯ ♀ ♁ 🛅 ⌁ ✆
Location 1m SE of town centre on A671

Hotel ★★★ 73% Oaks Hotel, Colne Rd, Reedley, BURNLEY ☎ 01282 414141 50 ⇔ 🖚

CHORLEY — Map 07 SD51

Charnock Richard Preston Rd, Charnock Richard PR7 5LE
☎ 01257 470707 Fax 01257 794343
Flat parkland course with plenty of Americanised water hazards. Signature hole the 6th Par 5 with an island green.
18 holes, 6234yds, Par 71, SSS 70, Course record 68.
Club membership 550.
Visitors strict full dress code, members time 8.30-9.30pm and 12.00-1.00pm weekdays, telephone for weekend play.
Societies contact club secretary in writing.
Green Fees £15 per round (£20 weekends).
Cards ▭ ▬ ▭ ▭
Designer Chris Court
Facilities ♀ ♁ 🛅 ♦ ♨ ✆
Location On the main A49, 0.25m from Camelot Theme Park

Hotel ★★★ 69% Park Hall Hotel, Park Hall Rd, Charnock Richard, CHORLEY ☎ 01257 452090 54 ⇔ 🖚 Annexe 84 ⇔ 🖚

Chorley Hall o' th' Hill, Heath Charnock PR6 9HX
☎ 01257 480263 Fax 01257 480722
A splendid moorland course with plenty of fresh air. The well-sited clubhouse affords some good views of the Lancashire coast and of Angelzarke, a local beauty spot. Beware of the short 3rd hole with its menacing out-of-bounds.
18 holes, 6307yds, Par 71, SSS 70, Course record 63.
Club membership 550.
Visitors must contact in advance and may not play weekends or bank holidays.

Societies must contact in advance. Tue-Fri only.
Green Fees not confirmed.
Prof Gavin Mutch
Designer J A Steer
Facilities ⊗ by prior arrangement
Ⅼ ▯ ♀ ♁ 🛅 ♨ ✆
Location 2.5m SE on A673

Hotel ★★★ 66% Pines Hotel, Clayton le Woods, CHORLEY ☎ 01772 338551 37 ⇔ 🖚

Duxbury Jubilee Park Duxbury Hall Rd PR7 4AS
☎ 01257 265380 & 241634
Municipal parkland course.
18 holes, 6390yds, Par 71, SSS 70.
Club membership 250.
Visitors must contact 6 days in advance via Pro shop.
Societies must contact in advance by letter.
Green Fees not confirmed.
Prof S Middelman
Designer Hawtree & Sons
Facilities ♁ 🛅 ⌁ ✆
Location 2.5m S off A6

Hotel L Welcome Lodge, Welcome Break, Charnock Richard - M6, Mill Ln, CHORLEY ☎ 01257 791746 100 ⇔ 🖚

Shaw Hill Hotel Golf & Country Club Preston Rd, Whittle-Le-Woods PR6 7PP
☎ 01257 269221 Fax 01257 261223
A fine course designed by one of Europe's most prominent golf architects and offering a considerable challenge as well as tranquillity and scenic charm. Seven lakes guard par 5 and long par 4 holes.
18 holes, 6252yds, Par 72, SSS 70, Course record 65.
Club membership 500.
Visitors must contact in advance, denims and trainers not allowed on course or in clubhouse.
Societies must telephone in advance.
Green Fees £30 per 18 holes (£40 Fri-Sun & bank holidays).
Cards ▭ ▬ ▭ ▭ ▭ ▭
Prof David Clark
Facilities ♁ 🛅 ⌁ ⌂ ♦ ♨ ✆
& Leisure heated indoor swimming pool, sauna, solarium, gymnasium.
Location On A6 1.5m N

Hotel ★★★ 70% Shaw Hill Hotel Golf & Country Club, Preston Rd, Whittle-le-Woods, CHORLEY ☎ 01257 269221 26 ⇔ 🖚 Annexe 4 ⇔ 🖚

CLITHEROE — Map 07 SD74

Clitheroe Whalley Rd, Pendleton BB7 1PP
☎ 01200 422292 Fax 01200 422292
One of the best inland courses in the country. Clitheroe is a parkland-type course with water hazards and good scenic views, particularly on towards Longridge, and Pendle Hill.
18 holes, 6326yds, Par 71, SSS 71, Course record 67.
Club membership 750. ▶

Visitors	must contact in advance.
Societies	must contact in advance.
Green Fees	£33 per day (£39 weekends & bank holidays).
Prof	John Twissell
Designer	James Braid
Facilities	⊗ ⊫ ⅃ ⬛ ♀ ♨ 🏠 ⚐ ♂ ♙
Location	2m S of Clitheroe on Whalley Road
Hotel	★★ 68% Shireburn Arms Hotel, Whalley Rd, Hurst Green, CLITHEROE ☎ 01254 826518 18 ⇆ ♞

COLNE   Map 07 SD84

Colne Law Farm, Skipton Old Rd BB8 7EB
☎ 01282 863391
Moorland course with scenic surroundings.
9 holes, 5961yds, Par 70, SSS 69, Course record 63.
Club membership 356.

Visitors	restricted Thu. Must contact in advance.
Societies	must contact in advance.
Green Fees	£16 per day (£20 weekends).
Facilities	⊗ ⊫ ⅃ ⬛ ♀ ♨
Location	1m E off A56
Hotel	★★★ 67% Stirk House Hotel, GISBURN ☎ 01200 445581 40 ⇆ ♞ Annexe 10 ⇆ ♞

DARWEN   Map 07 SD62

Darwen Winter Hill BB3 0LB
☎ 01254 701287 (club) & 776370 (pro) Fax 01254 773833
First 9 holes on parkland, the second 9 on moorland.
18 holes, 5863yds, Par 69, SSS 68, Course record 63.
Club membership 600.

Visitors	may not play on Tue or Sat.
Societies	must contact in advance.
Green Fees	£30 per day; £20 per round (£30 Sun).
Prof	Wayne Lennon
Facilities	⊗ ⊫ ⅃ ⬛ ♀ ♨ 🏠
Location	1m NW
Hotel	★★★ 66% Whitehall Hotel, Springbank, Whitehall, DARWEN ☎ 01254 701595 17 ⇆ ♞

FLEETWOOD   Map 07 SD34

Fleetwood Princes Way FY7 8AF
☎ 01253 873661 & 773573 Fax 01253 773573
Championship length, flat seaside links where the player must always be alert to changes of direction or strength of the wind.
18 holes, 6723yds, Par 72, SSS 72.
Club membership 600.

Visitors	may not play on competition days or Tue.
Societies	must contact in advance. A deposit of £5 per player is required.
Green Fees	not confirmed.
Prof	S McLaughlin
Designer	J A Steer
Facilities	⊗ ⊫ ⅃ ⬛ ♀ ♨ 🏠 ⚐ ♂
Location	W side of town centre

Hotel	★★ 66% Brabyns Hotel, 1-3 Shaftesbury Av, North Shore, BLACKPOOL ☎ 01253 354263 22 ⇆ ♞ Annexe 3 ⇆ ♞

GARSTANG   Map 07 SD44

Garstang Country Hotel & Golf Club Garstang Rd, Bowgreave PR3 1YE ☎ 01995 600100 Fax 01995 600950
Fairly flat parkland course following the contours of the Rivers Wyre and Calder and providing a steady test of ability, especially over the longer back nine. Exceptional drainage makes the course playable all year round.
18 holes, 6050yds, Par 68, SSS 68.

Visitors	tee times bookable 6 days in advance.
Societies	telephone for availability and confirm in writing.
Green Fees	£13 per round (£15 weekends & bank holidays).
Cards	💳 💳 💳 💳 💳
Prof	Robert Head
Designer	Richard Bradbeer
Facilities	⊗ ⊫ ⅃ ⬛ ♀ ♨ 🏠 ⚐ ♂ ♙
Location	Situated on B6430 1m S of Garstang

GREAT HARWOOD   Map 07 SD73

Great Harwood Harwood Bar, Whalley Rd BB6 7TE
☎ 01254 884391
Flat parkland course with fine views of the Pendle region.
9 holes, 6411yds, Par 73, SSS 71, Course record 68.
Club membership 320.

Visitors	must contact in advance.
Societies	welcome mid-week only, apply in writing.
Green Fees	not confirmed.
Facilities	⊗ ⊫ ⅃ ⬛ ♀ ♨
Location	E side of town centre on A680
Hotel	★★★★ 62% Dunkenhalgh Hotel, Blackburn Rd, Clayton-le-Moors, ACCRINGTON ☎ 01254 398021 37 ⇆ ♞ Annexe 42 ⇆ ♞

HASLINGDEN   Map 07 SD72

Rossendale Ewood Ln Head BB4 6LH
☎ 01706 831339 & 213616 (Pro) Fax 01706 228669
Testing meadowland course, mainly flat, situated on a plateau with panoramic views.
18 holes, 6293yds, Par 72, Course record 64.
Club membership 700.

Visitors	must contact in advance. Must play with member on Sat.
Societies	must telephone in advance & confirm in writing.
Green Fees	not confirmed.
Prof	Stephen Nicholls
Facilities	⊗ ⊫ ⅃ ⬛ ♀ (ex Mon) ♨ 🏠 ♂
Location	0.5m S off A56
Hotel	★★★ 63% County Hotel Blackburn, Preston New Rd, BLACKBURN ☎ 01254 899988 101 ⇆ ♞

Where to stay, where to eat?
Visit the AA internet site
www.theaa.co.uk

Heysham   Map 07 SD46

Heysham Trumacar Park, Middleton Rd LA3 3JH
☎ 01524 851011 Fax 01524 853030
Seaside parkland course, partly wooded. The 15th is a 459
yard Par 4 hole nearly always played into the prevailing
south west wind.
18 holes, 6266yds, Par 69, SSS 70, Course record 64.
Club membership 1100.

Visitors	book in advance via the professional, restricted at weekends.
Societies	must contact in advance.
Green Fees	£25 per day; £20 per round (£30 weekends & bank holidays).
Prof	Ryan Done
Designer	Alex Herd
Facilities	⊗ ⍟ ⅃ ⓛ ♥ ⌁ ♨ ⌂ ∂
Location	0.75m S off A589

Hotel   ★ *57%* Clarendon Hotel, Marine Rd West,
West End Promenade, MORECAMBE
☎ 01524 410180 31rm (28 ⇆ ⋔)

Knott End-on-Sea   Map 07 SD34

Knott End Wyreside FY6 0AA
☎ 01253 810576 Fax 01253 813446
Pleasant, undulating parkland course on banks of River
Wyre. Open to sea breezes.
18 holes, 5789yds, Par 69, SSS 68, Course record 63.
Club membership 500.

Visitors	book via professional up to 7 days in advance.
Societies	must contact in advance.
Green Fees	£22 per round (£25 weekends).
Prof	Paul Walker
Designer	Braid
Facilities	⊗ ⍟ ⅃ ⓛ ♥ ⌁ ♨ ⌂ ∂
Location	W side of village off B5377

Hotel   ★★ *66%* Brabyns Hotel, 1-3 Shaftesbury Av,
North Shore, BLACKPOOL
☎ 01253 354263 22 ⇆ ⋔ Annexe 3 ⇆ ⋔

Lancaster   Map 07 SD46

Lancaster Golf Club Ashton Hall, Ashton-with-
Stodday LA2 0AJ ☎ 01524 751247 Fax 01524 752742
This course is unusual for parkland golf as it is exposed
to the winds coming off the Irish Sea. It is situated on the
Lune estuary and has some natural hazards and easy
walking. There are however several fine holes among
woods near the old clubhouse.
18 holes, 6282yds, Par 71, SSS 71, Course record 66.
Club membership 925.

Visitors	must play with member or resident weekends. Must contact in advance and have a handicap certificate.
Societies	Mon-Fri only. Must contact in advance. Handicap certificate required.
Green Fees	£32 per day.
Cards	▭ ▬ ▥ ▧
Prof	David Sutcliffe
Designer	James Braid
Facilities	⊗ ⍟ ⅃ ⓛ ♥ ⌁ ♨ ⌂ ∂
Location	3m S on A588

Hotel   ★★★★ *67%* Lancaster House Hotel,
Green Ln, Ellel, LANCASTER
☎ 01524 844822 80 ⇆ ⋔

Lansil Caton Rd LA1 3PE ☎ 01524 61233
Challenging parkland course.
9 holes, 5608yds, Par 70, SSS 67, Course record 68.
Club membership 375.

Visitors	may not play before 1pm on Sun.
Societies	weekdays only; must contact in writing.
Green Fees	not confirmed.
Facilities	⌁
Location	N side of town centre on A683

Hotel   ★★★ *67%* Posthouse Lancaster, Waterside
Park, Caton Rd, LANCASTER
☎ 0870 400 9047 157 ⇆ ⋔

Langho   Map 07 SD73

Mytton Fold Hotel & Golf Complex Whalley Rd BB6 8AB
☎ 01254 240662 & 245392 (pro shop) Fax 01254 248119
The course has panoramic views across the Ribble Valley
and Pendle Hill. Tight fairways and water hazards are
designed to make this a challenging course for any golfer.
18 holes, 6082yds, Par 72, SSS 69, Course record 69.
Club membership 350.

Visitors	weekends restricted must contact in advance.
Societies	telephone in advance.
Green Fees	£14 per day (£16 weekends & bank holidays).
Cards	▭ ▬ ▥ ▧ ▤
Prof	Gary P Coope
Designer	Frank Hargreaves
Facilities	⊗ ⍟ ⅃ ⓛ ♥ ⌁ ♨ ⌂ ⋔ ➤ ♨ ∂
Location	On A59 between Langho and Whalley

Hotel   ★★★ *71%* Northcote Manor, Northcote Rd,
LANGHO ☎ 01254 240555 14 ⇆ ⋔

Leyland   Map 07 SD52

Leyland Wigan Rd PR5 2UD
☎ 01772 436457 Fax 01772 436457
Parkland course, fairly flat and usually breezy.
18 holes, 6123yds, Par 69, SSS 70, Course record 64.
Club membership 650.

Visitors	must contact in advance. Welcome weekdays, with member only at weekends.
Societies	must contact in advance.
Green Fees	£25.
Prof	Colin Burgess
Facilities	⊗ ⍟ ⅃ ⓛ ♥ ⌁ ♨ ⌂ ∂ ⌁
Location	E side of town centre on A49

Hotel   ★★★ *66%* Pines Hotel, Clayton le Woods,
CHORLEY ☎ 01772 338551 37 ⇆ ⋔

Longridge   Map 07 SD63

Longridge Fell Barn, Jeffrey Hill PR3 2TU
☎ 01772 783291 Fax 01772 783022
One of the oldest clubs in England. A moorland course with
panoramic views of the Ribble Valley, Trough of Bowland,
The Fylde and Welsh Mountains.
18 holes, 5975yds, Par 70, SSS 69, Course record 65.
Club membership 700.

▶

Visitors   welcome. Must contact in advance. May not
                  play at weekends Jul-Aug.
Societies   welcome by prior arrangement.
Green Fees   not confirmed.
Prof   Stephen Taylor
Facilities   ⊗ ⫴ ⤧ ▙ ⚐ ♀ ⚎ 🛄 ⌀
Location   8m NE of Preston off B6243

Hotel   ★★ 68% Shireburn Arms Hotel, Whalley Rd,
                  Hurst Green, CLITHEROE
                  ☎ 01254 826518   18 ⇆ ͡

LYTHAM ST ANNES   Map 07 SD32

Fairhaven Lytham Hall Park, Ansdell FY8 4JU
☎ 01253 736741 (Secretary) 736976 (Pro)
A flat, but interesting parkland links course of good standard.
There are natural hazards as well as numerous bunkers and
players need to produce particularly accurate second shots.
18 holes, 6883yds, Par 74, SSS 73, Course record 66.
Club membership 750.
Visitors   telephone professional in advance.
Societies   must contact in advance.
Green Fees   not confirmed.
Prof   Brian Plucknett
Designer   J A Steer
Facilities   ⊗ ⫴ ⤧ ▙ ⚐ ♀ ⚎ 🛄 ⌀
Location   E side of town centre off B5261

Hotel   ★★★ 64% Bedford Hotel, 307-311 Clifton Dr
                  South, LYTHAM ST ANNES
                  ☎ 01253 724636   36 ⇆ ͡

Lytham Green Drive Ballam Rd FY8 4LE
☎ 01253 737390 Fax 01253 731350
Pleasant parkland course, ideal for holidaymakers.
18 holes, 6163yds, Par 70, SSS 69, Course record 64.
Club membership 740.
Visitors   must contact in advance. May not play at
                  weekends.
Societies   must apply in writing.
Green Fees   not confirmed.
Prof   Andrew Lancaster
Designer   Steer
Facilities   ⊗ ⫴ ⤧ ▙ ⚐ ♀ ⚎ 🛄 ⌀
Location   E side of town centre off B5259

Hotel   ★★★★ 64% Clifton Arms, West Beach,
                  Lytham, LYTHAM ST ANNES
                  ☎ 01253 739898   44 ⇆ ͡

LYTHAM ST ANNES See page 159

St Annes Old Links Highbury Rd FY8 2LD
☎ 01253 723597 Fax 01253 781506
Seaside links, qualifying course for Open Championship;
compact and of very high standard, particularly greens.
Windy, very long 5th, 17th and 18th holes. Famous hole: 9th
(171 yds), par 3. Excellent club facilities.
18 holes, 6616yds, Par 72, SSS 72.
Club membership 950.
Visitors   may not play on Sat or before 9.15am &
                  between noon-2pm weekdays. Sundays by prior
                  arrangement only. Handicap certificate
                  requested.
Societies   must contact in advance.

Green Fees   £38 per day/round (£50 weekends and bank
                  holidays).
Prof   G Hardiman
Designer   George Lowe
Facilities   ⊗ ⫴ ⤧ ▙ ⚐ ♀ ⚎ 🛄 ⌀
Location   N side of town centre

Hotel   ★★★ 64% Bedford Hotel, 307-311 Clifton Dr
                  South, LYTHAM ST ANNES
                  ☎ 01253 724636   36 ⇆ ͡

MORECAMBE   Map 07 SD46

Morecambe Bare LA4 6AJ
☎ 01524 412841 Fax 01524 412841
Holiday golf at its most enjoyable. The well-maintained,
wind-affected seaside parkland course is not long but full
of character. Even so the panoramic views across
Morecambe Bay and to the Lake District and Pennines
make concentration difficult. The 4th is a testing hole.
18 holes, 5770yds, Par 67, SSS 69, Course record 69.
Club membership 850.
Visitors   may play from yellow tees, must contact in
                  advance.
Societies   must contact in advance.
Green Fees   £28 per day; £23 per round (£33/£28
                  weekends).
Prof   Simon Fletcher
Designer   Dr Alister Mackenzie
Facilities   ⊗ ⫴ ⤧ ▙ ⚐ ♀ ⚎ 🛄 ⌀
Location   N side of town centre on A5105

Hotel   ★★★ 64% Elms Hotel, Bare Village,
                  MORECAMBE
                  ☎ 01524 411501   40 ⇆ ͡

NELSON   Map 07 SD83

Marsden Park Townhouse Rd BB9 8DG
☎ 01282 661912
A semi-parkland course offering panoramic views of
surrounding countryside, set in the foothills of Pendle
Marsden Park, a testing 18 holes for golfers of all abilities.
18 holes, 5813yds, Par 70, SSS 68, Course record 66.
Club membership 298.
Visitors   welcome at any time, advised to book in
                  advance at weekends.
Societies   Must contact in writing.
Green Fees   £8.50 per 18 holes; £6.50 per 9 holes (£11.50
                  weekends & bank holidays).
Cards   ⊡ ■ ▦ 🗎
Prof   Martin Ross
Facilities   ⊗ ⫴ ⤧ ▙ ♀ ⚎ 🛄 🏌 ⌀
Location   E side of town centre off A56

Hotel   ★★★ 73% Oaks Hotel, Colne Rd, Reedley,
                  BURNLEY ☎ 01282 414141   50 ⇆ ͡

Nelson King's Causeway, Brierfield BB9 0EU
☎ 01282 611834 & 617000 Fax 01282 606226
Moorland course, usually windy, with good views. Testing
8th hole, par 4.
18 holes, 5967yds, Par 70, SSS 69, Course record 63.
Club membership 500.
Visitors   must telephone 01282 617000 in advance, may
                  not play before 9.30am or between 12.30-
                  1.30pm.   ▶

Royal Lytham & St Annes

Lytham St Annes, *Lancs* ☎ 01253 724206 | Fax 01253 780946 | Map 07 SD32

Visitors Mon & Thu (unless guest at Dormy House). Must contact in advance and have a handicap certificate

Societies must apply to Secretary (large groups Mon & Thu only)

Green Fees £90 per round (includes lunch)

Facilities ⊗ ⋈ ⓛ 🍽 ⓨ ⚲ 📷 ♂ ⟊

Location Links Gate, Lytham FY8 3LQ (0.5m E of St Annes town)

Holes/Par/Course record 18 holes, 6334 yds, Par 71, SSS 71

WHERE TO STAY AND EAT NEARBY

Hotels

★★★★64% Clifton Arms, West Beach, Lytham. ☎ 01253 739898. 48 ⇆ ⓘ

★★★67% Chadwick, South Promenade. ☎ 01253 720061. 75 ⇆ ⓘ

★★★64% Bedford, 307-311 Clifton Drive South. ☎ 01253 724636. 36 (14 ⓘ 22 ⇆ ⓘ)

★★68% Glendower, North Promenade. ☎ 01253 723241. 60 (40 ⇆ ⓘ 20 ⓘ)

★★68% Lindum Hotel, 63-67 South Promenade. ☎ 01253 721534. 76 (10 ⇆ ⓘ 50 ⇆ 16 ⓘ)

Restaurant

LYTHAM ST ANNES

🍽 Q Brasserie, 5 Henry St. ☎ 01253 733124

Founded in 1886, this huge links course can be difficult, especially in windy conditions. Unusually for a championship course it starts with a par 3, the nearby railway line and red-brick houses create distractions which only add to the challenge.

The course has hosted many Open Championships with some memorable victories, amateur Bobby Jones famously won here in 1926; Bob Charles of New Zealand became the only left-hander to win the title and in 1969 Tony Jacklin helped to revive British golf with his win here.

Championship Course

Societies	must contact in advance.
Green Fees	£25 per day (£30 weekends & bank holidays).
Prof	Nigel Sumner
Designer	Dr Mackenzie
Facilities	⊗ ⅢⅢ ⤶ ■ ⬤ ♀ ♨ 🏠 ⚸
Location	Take A682 to Brierfield, left at traffic lights into Halifax Road which becomes Kings Causeway

Hotel   ★★★ 73%   Oaks Hotel, Colne Rd, Reedley, BURNLEY ☎ 01282 414141   50 ⇆ ☛

ORMSKIRK   Map 07 SD40

Hurlston Hall Hurlston Ln, Southport Rd, Scarisbrick L40 8HB
☎ 01704 840400 & 841120 (pro shop) Fax 01704 841404
Designed by Donald Steel, this gently undulating course offers fine views across the Pennines and Bowland Fells. With generous fairways, large tees and greens, two streams and seven lakes, it provides a good test of golf for players of all standards. Luxurious colonial-style clubhouse.
18 holes, 6746yds, Par 72, SSS 72, Course record 66.
Club membership 600.

Visitors	welcome, but may be asked for handicap certificate or letter of introduction from own club. Preferable to book in advance.
Societies	registered Golf Societies and others approved by club, write or telephone for details.
Green Fees	Summer: £27.50 (£33 weekends and bank holidays); Winter: £21 (£26 weekends and bank holidays).
Cards	🖃 🖃 🖃 🖃 🖃 🖃
Prof	Jon Esclapez
Designer	Donald Steel
Facilities	⊗ ⅢⅢ ⤶ ■ ⬤ ♀ ♨ 🏠 ⌁ ⚐ ⚒ ⚸ ⚐
& Leisure	fishing.
Location	Situated 6m from Southport and 2m from Ormskirk along A570

Hotel   ★★★ 67%   Beaufort Hotel, High Ln, Burscough, ORMSKIRK ☎ 01704 892655   20 ⇆ ☛

Ormskirk Cranes Ln, Lathom L40 5UJ
☎ 01695 572227 Fax 01695 572227
A pleasantly secluded, fairly flat, parkland course with much heath and silver birch. Accuracy from the tees will provide an interesting variety of second shots.
18 holes, 6358yds, Par 70, SSS 71, Course record 63.
Club membership 300.

Visitors	restricted Sat.
Societies	must telephone or contact in writing.
Green Fees	not confirmed.
Prof	Jack Hammond
Facilities	♨ 🏠 ⚸
Location	1.5m NE

Hotel   ★★★ 67%   Beaufort Hotel, High Ln, Burscough, ORMSKIRK ☎ 01704 892655   20 ⇆ ☛

Entries with a green background identify courses considered to be particularly interesting

PLEASINGTON   Map 07 SD62

Pleasington BB2 5JF
☎ 01254 202177 Fax 01254 201028
Plunging and rising across lovely parkland and heathland turf this course tests judgement of distance through the air to greens of widely differing levels. The 11th and 4th are testing holes.
18 holes, 6417yds, Par 71, SSS 71.
Club membership 700.

Visitors	may play Mon & Wed-Fri only.
Societies	must contact in advance.
Green Fees	£40 per day; £35 per round.
Prof	Ged Furey
Facilities	⊗ ⅢⅢ ⤶ ■ ⬤ ♀ ♨ 🏠 ⚸
Location	J3 off M65 follow sign for Blackburn

Hotel   ★★★ 63%   County Hotel Blackburn, Preston New Rd, BLACKBURN ☎ 01254 899988 101 ⇆ ☛

POULTON-LE-FYLDE   Map 07 SD33

Poulton-le-Fylde Breck Rd FY6 7HJ
☎ 01253 892444 Fax 01253 892444
Municipal parkland course, with easy walking.
12 holes, 4454yds, Par 71, SSS 68.
Club membership 200.

Visitors	no restrictions.
Societies	contact in advance by telephone or in writing.
Green Fees	£18 per day; £10 per round.
Cards	🖃 ⚐
Prof	Lewis Ware
Designer	E Astbury
Facilities	⊗ ⤶ ■ ⬤ ♀ ♨ 🏠 ⌁ ⚸ ⚐
& Leisure	heated indoor swimming pool.
Location	N side of town

Hotel   ★★ 66%   Brabyns Hotel, 1-3 Shaftesbury Av, North Shore, BLACKPOOL ☎ 01253 354263   22 ⇆ ☛ Annexe 3 ⇆ ☛

PRESTON   Map 07 SD52

Ashton & Lea Tudor Av, Lea PR4 0XA
☎ 01772 726480 & 735282 Fax 01772 735762
Fairly flat parkland course with pond and streams, offering pleasant walks and some testing holes for golfers of all standards.
18 holes, 6370yds, Par 71, SSS 70, Course record 65.
Club membership 650.

Visitors	must contact professional on 01772 720374 or secretary on 01772 735282.
Societies	must contact in writing or by telephone.
Green Fees	£23 per round (£25 weekends).
Prof	M Greenough
Designer	J Steer
Facilities	⊗ ⅢⅢ ⤶ ■ ⬤ ♀ ♨ 🏠 ⚸
Location	3m W of Preston on A5085

Hotel   ★★★ 59%   Posthouse Preston, Ringway, PRESTON ☎ 0870 400 9066 119 ⇆ ☛

Fishwick Hall Glenluce Dr, Farringdon Park PR1 5TD
☎ 01772 798300 & 795870 Fax 01772 704600
Meadowland course overlooking River Ribble. Natural
hazards.
18 holes, 6045yds, Par 70, SSS 69, Course record 66.
Club membership 750.
Visitors advisable to contact in advance.
Societies must contact in advance.
Green Fees £26 per day (£31 weekends & bank holidays).
Prof Nick Paranomos
Facilities ⊗ ⅷ ﹗ ▙ ♥ ♀ ♨ ⌂ ✐
Hotel ★★★ 59% Posthouse Preston, Ringway,
PRESTON ☎ 0870 400 9066 119 ⇆ ☛

Ingol Tanterton Hall Rd, Ingol PR2 7BY
☎ 01772 734556 Fax 01772 729815
Long, high course with natural water hazards set in 250 acres
of beautiful parkland.
18 holes, 6294yds, Par 72, SSS 70, Course record 68.
Club membership 700.
Visitors must contact booking office in advance.
Societies must contact.
Green Fees Apr-Sep £20 per round (£25 weekends), Oct-
Mar £15 per round (£20 weekends).
Cards ▭ ▬ ▧ 🗓
Prof Mark Bradley
Designer Henry Cotton
Facilities ⊗ ▙ ♥ ♀ ♨ ⌂ ⏚ ✐
& Leisure squash.
Location 2m NW junc 32 of M55 off B5411

Hotel ★★★ 59% Posthouse Preston, Ringway,
PRESTON ☎ 0870 400 9066 119 ⇆ ☛

Penwortham Blundell Ln, Penwortham PR1 0AX
☎ 01772 744630 Fax 01772 744630
A progressive golf club set close to the banks of the
River Ribble. The course has tree-lined fairways,
excellent greens, and provides easy walking. Testing
holes include the 178-yd, par 3 third, the 480-yd, par 5
sixth, and the 398-yd par 4 sixteenth.
18 holes, 6056yds, Par 69, SSS 69.
Club membership 975.
Visitors must contact in advance; restricted Tue &
Sat.
Societies must apply in writing.
Green Fees £28 per day (£32 weekends & bank
holidays); £24 per round.
Cards ▭ ■ ▬ ▤ ▧ 🗓
Facilities ⊗ ⅷ ▙ ♥ ♀ ♨ ⌂ ✐
Location 1.5m W of town centre off A59

Hotel ★★★★ 63% Tickled Trout, Preston New
Rd, Samlesbury, PRESTON
☎ 01772 877671 72 ⇆ ☛

Preston Fulwood Hall Ln, Fulwood PR2 8DD
☎ 01772 700011 Fax 01772 794234
Pleasant inland golf at this course set in very agreeable
parkland. There is a well-balanced selection of holes,
undulating amongst groups of trees, and not requiring great
length.
18 holes, 6312yds, Par 71, SSS 71.
Club membership 800.

Visitors may play midweek only. Must contact in
advance and have a handicap certificate.
Societies must contact in writing/telephone.
Green Fees £32 per day; £27 per round.
Prof Andrew Greenbank
Designer James Braid
Facilities ⊗ ⅷ ▙ ♥ ♀ ♨ ⌂ ✐
Location N side of town centre

Hotel ★★★★ 67% Preston Marriott, Garstang Rd,
Broughton, PRESTON
☎ 01772 864087 150 ⇆ ☛

RISHTON   Map 07 SD73

Rishton Eachill Links, Hawthorn Dr BB1 4HG
☎ 01254 884442 Fax 01254 601205
Undulating moorland course.
9 holes, 6097yds, Par 70, SSS 69, Course record 68.
Club membership 270.
Visitors must play with member on weekends and bank
holidays.
Societies must contact in writing.
Green Fees not confirmed.
Facilities ⊗ ⅷ ▙ ♥ ♀ by arrangement ♨
Location S side of town off A678

Hotel ★★★★ 62% Dunkenhalgh Hotel, Blackburn
Rd, Clayton-le-Moors, ACCRINGTON
☎ 01254 398021 37 ⇆ ☛ Annexe 42 ⇆ ☛

SILVERDALE   Map 07 SD47

Silverdale Redbridge Ln LA5 0SP
☎ 01524 701300 Fax 01524 702074
Difficult heathland course with rock outcrops. Excellent
views.
12 holes, 5463yds, Par 69, SSS 67.
Club membership 500.
Visitors telephone to confirm availability.
Societies must contact in writing.
Green Fees not confirmed.
Facilities ⊗ ⅷ by prior arrangement ▙ ♥ ♀ ♨ ⌂ ✐
Location Opposite Silverdale Station

Hotel ★ 66% Royal Station Hotel, Market St,
CARNFORTH ☎ 01524 732033 & 733636
Fax 01524 720267 13 ⇆ ☛

UPHOLLAND   Map 07 SD50

Beacon Park Beacon Ln WN8 7RU
☎ 01695 622700 Fax 01695 633066
Undulating/hilly parkland course, designed by Donald Steel,
with magnificent view of the Welsh hills. Twenty-four-bay
floodlit driving range open 9am-9pm in summer.
18 holes, 6000yds, Par 72, SSS 69, Course record 68.
Club membership 200.
Visitors may book 6 days in advance.
Societies must contact in advance.
Green Fees not confirmed.
Prof Ray Peters
Designer Donald Steel
Facilities ⊗ ⅷ ▙ by prior arrangement
♥ ♀ ♨ ⌂ ✐ ✦
Location S of Ashurst Beacon Hill

▶

Hotel   ★★★ 67% Beaufort Hotel, High Ln,
Burscough, ORMSKIRK
☎ 01704 892655 20 ⇥ ⌂

Dean Wood Lafford Ln WN8 0QZ
☎ 01695 622219 Fax 01695 622245
This parkland course has a varied terrain - flat front nine,
undulating back nine. Beware the par 4, 11th and 17th
holes, which has ruined many a card. If there were a
prize for the best maintained course in Lancashire, Dean
Wood would be a strong contender.
18 holes, 6179yds, Par 71, SSS 71, Course record 66.
Club membership 800.
Visitors   must play with member Tue, Wed.
Societies   must contact in advance.
Green Fees £30 per day (£35 weekends).
Prof   Stuart Danchin
Designer James Braid
Facilities ⊗ ⅏ ⮾ ⮿ ♥ ⚲ ⚗ ⌂ ⛳ ⚘
Location 1m from junct 26 of M6

WHALLEY   Map 07 SD73

Whalley Long Leese Barn, Clerk Hill Rd BB7 9DR
☎ 01254 822236
Parkland course near Pendle Hill, overlooking the Ribble
Valley. Superb views. Ninth hole over pond.
9 holes, 6258yds, Par 72, SSS 70, Course record 69.
Club membership 400.
Visitors   must telephone 01254 824766 in advance.
Societies   must apply in writing.
Green Fees £16 per day (£20 weekends & bank holidays).
Prof   H Smith
Facilities ⊗ ⅏ ⮾ ⮿ ♥ ⚲ ⌂ ⚘
Location 1m SE off A671

Hotel   ★★★★ 64% Clarion Hotel & Suites Foxfields,
Whalley Rd, Billington, CLITHEROE
☎ 01254 822556 44 ⇥ ⌂

WHITWORTH   Map 07 SD81

Lobden Lobden Moor OL12 8XJ
☎ 01706 343228 Fax 01706 343228
Moorland course, with hard walking. Windy.
9 holes, 5697yds, Par 70, SSS 68, Course record 66.
Club membership 250.
Visitors   must contact in advance. May not play Sat.
Societies   must apply in writing to Secretary.
Green Fees not confirmed.
Facilities ⊗ ⅏ ⮾ ⮿ ♥ ⚲
Location E side of town centre off A671

Hotel   ★★★★ 64% Norton Grange Hotel, Manchester
Rd, Castleton, ROCHDALE
☎ 01706 630788 51 ⇥ ⌂

AA Hotels that have special
arrangements with golf courses are listed at
the back of the guide

WILPSHIRE   Map 07 SD63

Wilpshire Whalley Rd BB1 9LF
☎ 01254 248260 Fax 01254 248260
Parkland/moorland course with varied and interesting holes.
Magnificent views of Ribble Valley, the coast and the
Yorkshire Dales.
18 holes, 5971yds, Par 69, SSS 69, Course record 68.
Club membership 500.
Visitors   must contact in advance.
Societies   must contact by telephone and confirm in
writing.
Green Fees £25.50 (£30.50 weekends & bank holidays).
Cards   ▭ ▬
Prof   Walter Slaven
Designer James Braid
Facilities ⊗ ⅏ ⮾ ⮿ ♥ ⚲ ⌂ ⛳ ⚘
Location 2m NE of Blackburn, on A666 towards
Clitheroe

Hotel   ★★★ 63% County Hotel Blackburn, Preston
New Rd, BLACKBURN
☎ 01254 899988 101 ⇥ ⌂

LEICESTERSHIRE

ASHBY-DE-LA-ZOUCH   Map 08 SK31

Willesley Park Measham Rd LE65 2PF
☎ 01530 414596 Fax 01530 414596
Undulating heathland and parkland course with quick
draining sandy sub-soil.
18 holes, 6304yds, Par 70, SSS 70, Course record 64.
Club membership 600.
Visitors   must contact in advance. Restricted weekends.
Handicap certificate required.
Societies   Wed-Fri only. Must apply in writing.
Green Fees not confirmed.
Prof   C J Hancock
Designer J Braid
Facilities ⊗ ⅏ ⮾ ⮿ ♥ ⚲ ⌂ ⚲ ⚘
Location SW side of town centre on A453

Hotel   ★★ 66% Kegworth Hotel, Packington Hill,
KEGWORTH ☎ 01509 672427 60 ⇥ ⌂

BIRSTALL   Map 04 SK50

Birstall Station Rd LE4 3BB
☎ 0116 267 4322 Fax 0116 267 4322
Parkland course with trees, shrubs, ponds and ditches.
18 holes, 6222yds, Par 70, SSS 70.
Club membership 650.
Visitors   with member only weekends; may not play Tue,
Wed & Fri after 9am.
Societies   apply in writing.
Green Fees £30 per day; £25 per round.
Prof   David Clark
Facilities ⊗ ⅏ ⮾ ⮿ ♥ ⚲ ⌂ ⚘
Location 3m N of Leicester on A6

▶

Hotel ★★ 65% Red Cow, Hinckley Rd, Leicester Forest East, LEICESTER ☎ 0116 238 7878 31 ⇥ ⋔

BOTCHESTON
Map 04 SK40

Forest Hill Markfield Ln LE9 9FJ
☎ 01455 824800 Fax 01455 828522
Parkland course with many trees, four Par 4s, but no steep gradients.
18 holes, 6039yds, Par 72, SSS 69.
Club membership 450.
Visitors must contact in advance for weekends.
Societies Mon-Fri, must telephone in advance.
Green Fees not confirmed.
Prof Philip Harness
Facilities ⊗ ⋔ ⓑ ♥ ♀ ≜ 🖴 ⛳ ♂ ⓛ
Hotel ★★★ 63% Field Head Hotel, Markfield Ln, MARKFIELD ☎ 01530 245454 28 ⇥ ⋔

COSBY
Map 04 SP59

Cosby Chapel Ln, Broughton Rd LE9 1RG
☎ 0116 286 4759 Fax 0116 286 4484
Undulating parkland course with a number of tricky, tight driving holes.
18 holes, 6410yds, Par 71, SSS 71, Course record 68.
Club membership 750.
Visitors welcome weekdays before 4pm. May not play at weekends. Recommended to telephone in advance. Handicap certificate required.
Societies book with secretary.
Green Fees £26 per day; £18 per round.
Prof Martin Wing
Designer Hawtree
Facilities ⊗ ⋔ by prior arrangement ⓑ ♥ ♀ ≜ 🖴 ⛳ ⓛ
Location S side of village

Hotel ★★★ 68% Posthouse Leicester, Braunstone Ln East, LEICESTER ☎ 0870 400 9051 172 ⇥ ⋔

EAST GOSCOTE
Map 08 SK61

Beedles Lake 170 Broome Ln LE7 3WQ
☎ 0116 260 6759
Fairly flat parkland course, founded in 1992, with an adjoining lake and well maintained greens.
18 holes, 6625yds, Par 72, SSS 72, Course record 71.
Club membership 400.
Visitors telephone booking required for weekends.
Societies welcome Mon-Fri
Green Fees £10 (£13 weekends & bank holidays).
Prof Sean Byrne
Designer D Tucker
Facilities ♀ ≜ 🖴 ⛳ ⓛ
& Leisure fishing.
Location Off A46, just N of Leicester through village of Ratcliffe on the Wreake

Hotel ★★★ 60% Rothley Court, Westfield Ln, ROTHLEY ☎ 0116 237 4141 13 ⇥ ⋔ Annexe 21 ⇥ ⋔

ENDERBY
Map 04 SP59

Enderby Mill Ln LE9 5HL
☎ 0116 284 9388 Fax 0116 284 9388
A gently undulating 9-hole course at which beginners are especially welcome. The longest hole is the 2nd at 407 yards and there are 5 Par 3's.
9 holes, 2750yds, Par 36, SSS 36.
Club membership 150.
Visitors no restrictions.
Societies must telephone in advance.
Green Fees £5.95 (£7.95 weekends).
Prof Chris D'Araujo
Designer David Lowe
Facilities ⊗ ⋔ ⓑ ♥ ♀ ≜ 🖴 ⛳ ♂ ⓛ
& Leisure heated indoor swimming pool, squash, sauna, solarium, gymnasium.
Location 2m S, M1 junct21 on Narborough road. Right turn off roundabout at Foxhunter pub, 0.5m on left

Hotel ★★ 65% Charnwood Hotel, 48 Leicester Rd, Narborough, LEICESTER ☎ 0116 286 2218 20 ⇥ ⋔

HINCKLEY
Map 04 SP49

Hinckley Leicester Rd LE10 3DR
☎ 01455 615124 & 615014 Fax 01455 890841
Rolling parkland with lake features, and lined fairways.
18 holes, 6517yds, Par 71, SSS 71, Course record 65.
Club membership 1000.
Visitors with member only weekends and bank holidays. Must contact in advance and have a handicap certificate.
Societies must contact in advance.
Green Fees not confirmed.
Cards 🌑 ■ ■ ■ 🌑 🌑 🌑
Prof Richard Jones
Facilities ⊗ ⋔ ⓑ ♥ ♀ ≜ 🖴 ♖ ⛳ ⓛ
Location 1.5m NE on B4668

Hotel ★★★ 62% Weston Hall, Weston Ln, Weston in Arden, Bulkington, NUNEATON ☎ 024 76312989 40 ⇥ ⋔

KETTON
Map 04 SK90

Luffenham Heath PE9 3UU
☎ 01780 720205 Fax 01780 722146
This undulating heathland course with low bushes, much gorse and many trees, lies in a conservation area for flora and fauna. From the higher part of the course there is a magnificent view across the Chater Valley.
18 holes, 6273yds, Par 70, SSS 70, Course record 64.
Club membership 550.
Visitors must contact in advance.
Societies write or telephone in advance.
Green Fees not confirmed.
Cards 🌑
Prof Ian Burnett
Designer James Braid
Facilities ⊗ ⋔ by prior arrangement ⓑ ♥ ♀ ≜ 🖴 ⛳ ⓛ
Location 1.5m SW of Ketton by Fosters Railway Bridge on A6121 ▶

| Hotel | ★★★ 75% The George of Stamford, 71 St Martins, STAMFORD ☎ 01780 750750 & 750700 (Res) Fax 01780 750701 47 ⇋ 🐾 |

KIBWORTH   Map 04 SP69

Kibworth Weir Rd, Beauchamp LE8 0LP
☎ 0116 279 2301 Fax 0116 279 6434
Parkland course with easy walking. A brook affects a number of fairways
18 holes, 6333yds, Par 71, SSS 70, Course record 65.
Club membership 700.
Visitors must contact in advance. With member only weekends.
Societies must contact in advance.
Green Fees £30 per day; £23 per round.
Prof Bob Larratt
Facilities ⊗ ℳ 🐾 ⬛ ♀ ⚐ 🏠 🛈 ∅ ℓ
Location S side of village off A6

Hotel ★★★ 72% Three Swans Hotel, 21 High St, MARKET HARBOROUGH
☎ 01858 466644 18 ⇋ 🐾 Annexe 31 ⇋ 🐾

KIRBY MUXLOE   Map 04 SK50

Kirby Muxloe Station Rd LE9 2EP
☎ 0116 239 3457 Fax 0116 239 3457
Pleasant parkland course with a lake in front of the 17th green and a short 18th.
18 holes, 6351yds, Par 70, SSS 70, Course record 65.
Club membership 870.
Visitors must contact in advance and a handicap certificate is required. No visitors on Tue or at weekends.
Societies must contact in advance.
Green Fees £30 per day; £25 per round.
Prof Bruce Whipham
Facilities ⊗ ℳ 🐾 ⬛ ♀ ⚐ 🏠 🛈 ∅ ℓ
Location S side of village off B5380

Hotel ★★★ 68% Posthouse Leicester, Braunstone Ln East, LEICESTER
☎ 0870 400 9051 172 ⇋ 🐾

LEICESTER   Map 04 SK50

Humberstone Heights Gypsy Ln LE5 0TB
☎ 0116 276 3680 & 299 5570 (Pro Shop Fax 0116 2995569
Municipal parkland course with 9 hole pitch and putt and 30 bay driving range.
18 holes, 6343yds, Par 70, SSS 70, Course record 66.
Club membership 400.
Visitors must telephone in advance at weekends.
Societies must telephone in advance.
Green Fees not confirmed.
Prof Phil Highfield
Designer Hawtry & Sons
Facilities ⊗ ℳ by prior arrangement 🐾 ⬛ ♀ ⚐ 🏠 🛈 🖑 🛒 ∅ ℓ
Location 2.5m NE of city centre

Hotel ★★★ 72% Belmont House Hotel, De Montfort St, LEICESTER
☎ 0116 254 4773 75rm (74 ⇋ 🐾)

Leicestershire Evington Ln LE5 6DJ
☎ 0116 273 8825 Fax 0116 273 1900
Pleasantly undulating parkland course.
18 holes, 6326yds, Par 68, SSS 70, Course record 63.
Club membership 800.
Visitors must contact in advance. May not play Sat. Must hold a handicap certificate.
Societies must contact in advance.
Green Fees on request.
Prof Darren Jones
Designer Hawtree
Facilities ⊗ ℳ 🐾 ⬛ ♀ ⚐ 🏠 ∅
Location 2m E of city off A6030

Hotel ★★★ 68% Hermitage Hotel, Wigston Rd, Oadby, LEICESTER
☎ 0116 256 9955 57 ⇋ 🐾

Western Scudamore Rd, Braunstone Frith LE3 1UQ
☎ 0116 299 5566 Fax 0116 299 5568
Pleasant, undulating parkland course with open aspect fairways in two loops of nine holes.Not too difficult but a good test of golf off the back tees.
18 holes, 6518yds, Par 72, SSS 71.
Club membership 400.
Visitors must contact in advance.
Societies must contact the professional in advance.
Green Fees not confirmed.
Cards 🌐 💳 💳 📇 💳
Prof Dave Butler
Facilities ⊗ ℳ 🐾 ⬛ ♀ ⚐ 🏠 🛈 ∅ ℓ
Location 1.5m W of city centre off A47

Hotel ★★★ 68% Posthouse Leicester, Braunstone Ln East, LEICESTER
☎ 0870 400 9051 172 ⇋ 🐾

LOUGHBOROUGH   Map 08 SK51

Longcliffe Snell's Nook Ln, Nanpantan LE11 3YA
☎ 01509 239129 Fax 01509 231286
A re-designed course of natural heathland with outcrops of granite forming natural hazards especially on the 1st and 15th. The course is heavily wooded and has much bracken and gorse. There are a number of tight fairways and one blind hole.
18 holes, 6625yds, Par 72, SSS 72.
Club membership 660.
Visitors must contact in advance. With member only at weekends.
Societies telephone for availability, handicap certificate required.
Green Fees not confirmed.
Prof Ian D Bailey
Designer Williamson
Facilities ⊗ ℳ 🐾 ⬛ ♀ ⚐ 🏠 ∅
Location 3m SW off B5350

Hotel ★★★ 64% Quality Hotel, New Ashby Rd, LOUGHBOROUGH
☎ 01509 211800 94 ⇋ 🐾

Looking for a driving range?
See the index at the back of the guide

LUTTERWORTH   Map 04 SP58

Kilworth Springs South Kilworth Rd, North Kilworth
LE17 6HJ ☎ 01858 575082 & 575974 Fax 01858 575078
An 18-hole course of two loops of 9: the front 9 are links
style while the back 9 are in parkland with 4 lakes. On a
windy day it is a very challenging course and the 6th hole is
well deserving of its nickname 'the Devil's Toenail'.
18 holes, 6543yds, Par 72, SSS 71, Course record 66.
Club membership 800.

Visitors	welcome subject to availability. May only play after 12am at weekends.
Societies	contact in advance.
Green Fees	£17 (£21 weekends).
Cards	💳 💳 💳 💳 💳
Prof	Anders Mankert
Designer	Ray Baldwin
Facilities	⊗ ⏫ ⓑ ▆ ♀ ⚲ 🏠 🏌 ♂ 𝄞
Location	4m E of M1 junc 20, A4304 to Mkt Harborough

Lutterworth Rugby Rd LE17 4HN
☎ 01455 552532 Fax 01455 553586
Hilly course with River Swift running through.
18 holes, 6226yds, Par 70, SSS 70.
Club membership 700.

Visitors	must play with member at weekends.
Societies	must contact in advance.
Green Fees	not confirmed.
Prof	Roland Tisdall
Facilities	⊗ ⏫ ⓑ ▆ ♀ ⚲ 🏠 🏌 ♐ 𝄞 ⏰
Location	0.5m S on A426

MARKET HARBOROUGH   Map 04 SP78

Market Harborough Oxendon Rd LE16 8NF
☎ 01858 463684 Fax 01858 432906
A parkland course situated close to the town. There are wide-
ranging views over the surrounding countryside. Lakes a
feature on 4 holes; challenging last 3 holes.
18 holes, 6070yds, Par 70, SSS 69, Course record 63.
Club membership 600.

Visitors	must play with member at weekends.
Societies	must apply in writing.
Green Fees	£20 per round.
Prof	Frazer Baxter
Designer	H Swan
Facilities	⊗ ⏫ ⓑ ▆ ♀ ⚲ 🏠 𝄞
Location	1m S on A508

Hotel	★★★ 72% Three Swans Hotel, 21 High St, MARKET HARBOROUGH ☎ 01858 466644 18 🛏 🅿 Annexe 31 🛏 🅿

Stoke Albany Ashley Rd, Stoke Albany LE16 8PL
☎ 01858 535208 Fax 01858 535505
Parkland course in the picturesque Welland Valley.
Affording good views, the course should appeal to the mid-
handicap golfer, and provide an interesting test to the more
experienced player.
18 holes, 6132yds, Par 71, SSS 69.
Club membership 400.

Visitors	welcome at all times.
Societies	please telephone secretary.
Green Fees	not confirmed.
Prof	Adrian Clifford
Designer	Hawtree

Facilities	⊗ ⏫ ⓑ ▆ ♀ ⚲ 🏠 𝄞
Location	Located N off A427 Market Harborough/Corby Road, follow Stoke Albany 500m towards Ashley village

Hotel	★★★ 72% Three Swans Hotel, 21 High St, MARKET HARBOROUGH ☎ 01858 466644 18 🛏 🅿 Annexe 31 🛏 🅿

MELTON MOWBRAY   Map 08 SK71

Melton Mowbray Waltham Rd, Thorpe Arnold LE14 4SD
☎ 01664 562118 Fax 01664 562118
Downland but flat course providing easy walking.
18 holes, 6222yds, Par 70, SSS 70.
Club membership 650.

Visitors	must contact professional on 01664 569629.
Societies	must contact in advance.
Green Fees	£20 per round (£23 weekends).
Prof	James Hetherington
Facilities	⊗ by prior arrangement ⏫ by prior arrangement ⓑ ▆ ♀ ⚲ 🏠 🏌 𝄞
Location	2m NE of Melton Mowbray on A607

Hotel	★★★ 67% Sysonby Knoll Hotel, Asfordby Rd, MELTON MOWBRAY ☎ 01664 563563 23 🛏 🅿 Annexe 1 🛏 🅿

OADBY   Map 04 SK60

Glen Gorse Glen Rd LE2 4RF
☎ 0116 271 4159 Fax 0116 271 4159
Fairly flat 18-hole parkland course with some strategically
placed mature trees, new saplings and ponds affecting play
on 6 holes. Ridge and furrow is a feature of 5 holes.
18 holes, 6648yds, Par 72, SSS 72, Course record 67.
Club membership 600.

Visitors	must contact in advance. Must play with member at weekends.
Societies	must telephone secretary in advance.
Green Fees	£28.50 per day; £24 per round.
Prof	Dominic Fitzpatrick
Facilities & Leisure	⊗ ⏫ ⓑ ▆ ♀ ⚲ 🏠 𝄞 snooker.
Location	On A6 trunk road between Oadby/Great Glen

Hotel	★★★ 68% Hermitage Hotel, Wigston Rd, Oadby, LEICESTER ☎ 0116 256 9955 57 🛏 🅿

Oadby Leicester Rd LE2 4AJ
☎ 0116 270 9052
Municipal parkland course.
18 holes, 6376yds, Par 72, SSS 70, Course record 60.
Club membership 500.

Visitors	no restrictions.
Societies	by arrangement contact pro shop.
Green Fees	not confirmed.
Prof	Alan Kershaw
Facilities	⊗ ⓑ ▆ ♀ ⚲ 🏠 🏌 𝄞
Location	West of Oadby, off A6

Hotel	★★★ 68% Hermitage Hotel, Wigston Rd, Oadby, LEICESTER ☎ 0116 256 9955 57 🛏 🅿

ROTHLEY

Map 08 SK51

Rothley Park Westfield Ln LE7 7LH
☎ 0116 230 2809 Fax 0116 230 2809
Parkland course in picturesque situation.
18 holes, 6477yds, Par 71, SSS 71, Course record 67.
Club membership 600.

Visitors	must contact professional on 0116 230 3023. Weekends and bank holidays with member only.
Societies	apply in writing to secretary.
Green Fees	£30 per day; £25 per round.
Prof	Andrew Collins
Facilities	⊗ ⅏ ⅃ ⊒ ♀ ♨ ⌂ ⌁ ∢
Location	Off A6 N of Leicester
Hotel	★★★ 60% Rothley Court, Westfield Ln, ROTHLEY ☎ 0116 237 4141 13 ⇄ ↾ Annexe 21 ⇄ ↾

SCRAPTOFT

Map 04 SK60

Scraptoft Beeby Rd LE7 9SJ
☎ 0116 241 8863 Fax 0116 241 8863
Pleasant, inland country course.
18 holes, 6166yds, Par 70, SSS 70.
Club membership 650.

Visitors	with member only weekends. Handicap certificate required.
Societies	apply in writing.
Green Fees	£25 per day; £20 per round.
Prof	Simon Wood
Facilities	⊗ ⅏ ⅃ ⊒ ♀ ♨ ⌂ ∢ ∢
Location	1m NE
Hotel	★★★ 68% Hermitage Hotel, Wigston Rd, Oadby, LEICESTER ☎ 0116 256 9955 57 ⇄ ↾

SEAGRAVE

Map 08 SK61

Park Hill Park Hill LE12 7NG
☎ 01509 815454 & 815775 (pro) Fax 01509 816062
A rolling parkland course with tree lined fairways and views over Charnwood Forest. The opening hole is 420yards with a forced water carry 100yards short of the green. The 10th is a 610 yard Par 5 against the prevailing wind. The closing hole is a challenging Par 5 with water protecting both sides of the green.
18 holes, 7219yds, Par 73, SSS 75, Course record 71.
Club membership 500.

Visitors	must contact in advance.
Societies	apply in advance.
Green Fees	£20 (£24 weekends & bank holidays).
Cards	⬚ ⬛ ⬚
Prof	David C Mee
Facilities	⊗ ⅏ ⅃ ⊒ ♀ ♨ ⌂ ∢ ∢
Location	6m N of Leicester on A46, follow signs to Seagrave
Hotel	★★★ 64% Quality Hotel, New Ashby Rd, LOUGHBOROUGH ☎ 01509 211800 94 ⇄ ↾

ULLESTHORPE

Map 04 SP58

Ullesthorpe Frolesworth Rd LE17 5BZ
☎ 01455 209023 Fax 01455 202537
Set in 130 acres of parkland surrounding a 17th-century manor house, this championship length course can be very demanding and offers a challenge to both beginners and professionals. Excellent leisure facilities. Water plays a part on 3 holes.
18 holes, 6650yds, Par 72, SSS 72, Course record 67.
Club membership 650.

Visitors	must contact in advance. With member only Sat, no play on Sun.
Societies	contact well in advance.
Green Fees	£30 per day; £18 per round.
Cards	⬚ ⬛ ⬚ ⬚ ⬚ ⬚
Prof	David Bowring
Facilities	⊗ ⅏ ⅃ ⊒ ♀ ♨ ⌂ ⌁ ∢ ⌂ ∢ ∢ ∢
& Leisure	hard tennis courts, heated indoor swimming pool, sauna, solarium, gymnasium.
Location	0.5m N off B577
Hotel	★★★ 67% Ullesthorpe Court Country Hotel & Golf Club, Frolesworth Rd, ULLESTHORPE ☎ 01455 209023 38 ⇄ ↾

WHETSTONE

Map 04 SP59

Whetstone Cambridge Rd, Cosby LE9 1SJ
☎ 0116 286 1424 Fax 0116 286 1424
Easy to walk, parkland course where accuracy rather than length is required.
18 holes, 5795yds, Par 68, SSS 68, Course record 63.
Club membership 500.

Visitors	must contact in advance, limited times at weekends.
Societies	must contact in advance.
Green Fees	£15 (£16 weekends & bank holidays).
Cards	⬚ ⬛ ⬚ ⬚ ⬚ ⬚
Prof	David Raitt
Designer	E Calloway
Facilities	⊗ ⅏ ⅃ ⊒ ♀ ♨ ⌂ ⌁ ∢ ∢ ∢
Location	1m S of village
Hotel	★★★ 66% Time Out Hotel & Leisure, Enderby Rd, Blaby, LEICESTER ☎ 0116 278 7898 48 ⇄ ↾

WILSON
Map 08 SK42

Breedon Priory Green Ln DE73 1AT
☎ 01332 863081
A relatively short and forgiving course set in undulating countryside with magnificent views from several holes.
18 holes, 5530yds, Par 70, SSS 67, Course record 67.
Club membership 779.

Visitors	may play any time if tee available, must book for weekends.
Societies	apply in writing or telephone for booking form.
Green Fees	not confirmed.
Prof	Ben Hill
Designer	David Snell
Facilities	⬛🍴♀🏖🏠🔨⚒
Location	4m W of A42/M1 junct 24

Hotel ★★★ 69% The Priest House on the River, Kings Mills, CASTLE DONINGTON ☎ 01332 810649 25 ⇔ Annexe 20 ⇔

WOODHOUSE EAVES
Map 08 SK51

Charnwood Forest Breakback Ln LE12 8TA
☎ 01509 890259 Fax 01509 890925
Hilly heathland course with hard walking, but no bunkers.
9 holes, 5960yds, Par 69, SSS 69, Course record 64.
Club membership 210.

Visitors	must contact in advance.
Societies	Wed & Thu only. Must contact in advance. Mon & Fri by special arrangement.
Green Fees	£15 per 18 holes (£25 weekends & bank holidays).
Designer	James Braid
Facilities	⊗⬛🍴♀🏖
Location	3m from junct 22 or 23 of M1

Hotel ★★★★ 70% Quorn Country Hotel, Charnwood House, 66 Leicester Rd, QUORN ☎ 01509 415050 23 ⇔

Lingdale Joe Moore's Ln LE12 8TF
☎ 01509 890703
Parkland course located in Charnwood Forest with some hard walking at some holes. The par 3, (3rd) and par 5, (8th) are testing holes. Several holes have water hazards.
18 holes, 6545yds, Par 71, SSS 71, Course record 68.
Club membership 610.

Visitors	must telephone professional in advance for weekend play.
Societies	must contact in advance.
Green Fees	not confirmed.
Prof	Peter Sellears
Designer	David Tucker
Facilities	⊗🏵⬛🍴♀🏖🏠⚒
Location	1.5m S off B5330

Hotel ★★★★ 70% Quorn Country Hotel, Charnwood House, 66 Leicester Rd, QUORN ☎ 01509 415050 23 ⇔

AA Hotels that have special arrangements with golf courses are listed at the back of the guide

BELTON
Map 08 SK93

Belton Woods Hotel NG32 2LN
☎ 01476 593200 Fax 01476 574547
Two challenging 18-hole courses, a 9-hole Par 3 and a driving range. The Lakes Course has 13 lakes, while The Woodside boasts the third longest hole in Europe at 613 yards. Many leisure facilities.
The Lakes Course: 18 holes, 6781yds, Par 72, SSS 72, Course record 68.
The Woodside Course: 18 holes, 6605yds, Par 73, SSS 73.
Spitfire Course: 9 holes, 1116yds, Par 27, SSS 27.
Club membership 600.

Visitors	book tee times in advance with exception of the Spitfire. Dress code ie. no jeans and spike shoes must be worn.
Societies	welcome all week, reservations to be made by telephone or letter.
Green Fees	not confirmed.
Prof	Steve Sayers
Facilities & Leisure	⊗🏵⬛🍴♀🏖🏠⚒🏓🎱⚒ hard tennis courts, heated indoor swimming pool, squash, sauna, solarium, gymnasium, beauty salon, quad biking, archery, go-karting.
Location	On A607, 2m N of Grantham

Hotel ★★★★ 73% Belton Woods Hotel, BELTON ☎ 01476 593200 136 ⇔

BLANKNEY
Map 08 TF06

Blankney LN4 3AZ
☎ 01526 320263 Fax 01526 322521
Open parkland course with mature trees; fairly flat.
18 holes, 6634yds, Par 72, SSS 73, Course record 69.
Club membership 700.

Visitors	must contact in advance, may not play Wed mornings, restricted at weekends.
Societies	not Wed mornings, booking required.
Green Fees	£30 per day; £20 per round (£35/£30 weekends & bank holidays).
Prof	Graham Bradley
Designer	C Sinclair
Facilities & Leisure	⊗🏵⬛🍴♀🏖🏠⚒🏓⚒ snooker.
Location	10m SW on B1188

Hotel ★★★ 65% Moor Lodge Hotel, Sleaford Rd, BRANSTON ☎ 01522 791366 24 ⇔

BOSTON
Map 08 TF34

Boston Cowbridge, Horncastle Rd PE22 7EL
☎ 01205 350589 Fax 01205 350589
Parkland course many water hazards in play on ten holes.
18 holes, 6490yds, Par 72, SSS 71, Course record 69.
Club membership 650.

Visitors	evidence of handicap may be requested, contact in advance for tee time.
Societies	apply in writing.
Green Fees	£24 per day; £18 per round (£30/£24 weekends & bank holidays).
Prof	Terry Squires

▶

Facilities ⊗ ⅢⅢ 🏌 ♣ ♀ ⌂ ☎ ♌
Location 2m N of Boston on B1183

Hotel ★★★ 59% New England, 49 Wide Bargate, BOSTON ☎ 0500 636943 (Central Res) Fax 01773 880321 25 ⇄ ♞

Kirton Holme Holme Rd, Kirton Holme PE20 1SY
☎ 01205 290669
A young parkland course designed for mid to high handicappers. It is flat but has 2500 young trees, two natural water course plus water hazards. The 2nd is a challenging, 386yard Par 4 dogleg.
9 holes, 5778yds, Par 70, SSS 68, Course record 71.
Club membership 350.
Visitors no restrictions but booking advisable for weekends & summer evenings.
Societies by prior arrangement.
Green Fees £8 per day; £4.50 per 9 holes (£9/£5.50 weekends & bank holidays).
Designer D W Welberry
Facilities ⊗ ⅢⅢ by prior arrangement 🏌 ♣ ♀ ⌂ ☎ ♌
Location 4m W of Boston off A52

Hotel ★★ 67% Comfort Inn, Donnington Rd, Bicker Bar, BOSTON ☎ 01205 820118 55 ⇄ ♞

BOURNE
Map 08 TF02

Toft Hotel Toft PE10 0JT
☎ 01778 590614 Fax 01778 590264
Parkland course on the verge of the Lincoln Edge. Includes lake and uses contours of the hills to full effect.
18 holes, 6486yds, Par 72, SSS 71, Course record 63.
Club membership 450.

Visitors advisable to book for weekends.
Societies apply in advance by telephone.
Green Fees £25 per day; £20 per round (£35/£25 weekends).
Cards
Prof Mark Jackson
Designer Roger Fitton
Facilities ⊗ ⅢⅢ 🏌 ♣ ♀ ⌂ ☎ ♌ ⛳ ♞ ♣ ♌ ♟
Location On A6121 Bourne/Stamford road

Hotel ★★ 68% Black Horse Inn, Grimsthorpe, BOURNE ☎ 01778 591247 6 ⇄ ♞

Where to stay, where to eat?
Visit the AA internet site
www.theaa.co.uk

CLEETHORPES
Map 08 TA30

Cleethorpes Kings Rd DN35 0PN ☎ 01472 814060
Flat meadowland seaside course intersected by large dykes.
18 holes, 6349yds, Par 70, SSS 69, Course record 64.
Club membership 710.
Visitors restricted Wed afternoons, handicap certificate preferred, must be a member of a golf club.
Societies Tue,Thu or Fri only. Must contact in advance.
Green Fees £20 weekdays (£25 weekends).
Prof Paul Davies
Designer Harry Vardon
Facilities ⊗ ⅢⅢ 🏌 ♣ ♀ ⌂ ☎ ♌
Location 1.5m S off A1031

Hotel ★★★ 70% Kingsway Hotel, Kingsway, CLEETHORPES ☎ 01472 601122 50 ⇄ ♞

Tetney Station Rd, Tetney DN36 5HY
☎ 01472 211644 & 811344 Fax 01472 211644
18-hole parkland course set at the foot of the Lincolnshire Wolds. Noted for its challenging water features.
18 holes, 6100yds, Par 71, SSS 69, Course record 65.
Club membership 450.
Visitors contact in advance.
Societies apply in writing.
Green Fees £10 per 18 holes.
Cards
Prof Jason Abrams
Designer J S Grant
Facilities ⊗ ⅢⅢ 🏌 ♣ ♀ ⌂ ☎ ♌ ♞ ♣ ♌ ♟
Location 1m off A16 Louth/Grimsby road

Hotel ★★★ 70% Kingsway Hotel, Kingsway, CLEETHORPES ☎ 01472 601122 50 ⇄ ♞

CROWLE
Map 08 SE71

Hirst Priory DN17 4BU ☎ 01724 711619
Traditional flat parkland course. Generous sized greens with discreet use of water and bunkers.
18 holes, 6283yds, Par 71, SSS 70.
Club membership 380.
Visitors no restrictions.
Societies may only play at weekends after 11am.
Green Fees £20 per day, £13.75 per round (£26/£17.50 weekends).
Prof Gavin Keeley
Designer David Barter
Facilities ⊗ ⅢⅢ 🏌 ♣ ♀ ⌂ ☎ ♌ ♞ ♣ ♌
Hotel ★★ 70% Belmont Hotel, Horsefair Green, THORNE ☎ 01405 812320 23 ⇄ ♞

ELSHAM
Map 08 TA01

Elsham Barton Rd DN20 0LS
☎ 01652 680291(Sec) 680432(Pro) Fax 01652 680308
Parkland course in country surroundings. Easy walking. Totally secluded. Large modern clubhouse.
18 holes, 6402yds, Par 71, SSS 71, Course record 67.
Club membership 650.
Visitors with member only weekends & bank holidays. Preferable to contact in advance.
Societies must apply in writing.
Green Fees Summer: £25 per round; Winter: from £18 per round.
▶

Prof	Stuart Brewer
Facilities	⊗ ⑂ 🏌 💼 ♀ ⛳ 🏠 🍴 🚜 ♐
Location	2m SW of Brigg on B1206

Hotel	★★★ 66% Wortley House Hotel, Rowland Rd, SCUNTHORPE ☎ 01724 842223 38 🛏 🕮

GAINSBOROUGH   Map 08 SK88

Gainsborough Thonock DN21 1PZ
☎ 01427 613088 Fax 01427 810172
Thonock Park course, founded in 1894 is an attractive parkland course with many deciduous trees. Karsten Lakes course is a championship course designed by Neil Coles. Set in rolling countryside the lakes and well bunkered greens provide a true test of golf. Floodlit driving range.
Thonock Park: 18 holes, 6266yds, Par 72, SSS 70, Course record 63.
Karsten Lakes: 18 holes, 6721yds, Par 72, SSS 72, Course record 65.
Club membership 600.

Visitors	Thonock Park: welcome weekdays. Ladies Day Thu morning. Karsten Lakes: welcome 7 days, advance booking available.
Societies	must telephone in advance.
Green Fees	not confirmed.
Cards	💳 💳 💳 💳 💳
Prof	Stephen Cooper
Designer	Neil Coles
Facilities	⊗ ⑂ 🏌 💼 ♀ ⛳ 🏠 🍴 ♐ 🚜 ♐ 🏌
Location	1m N off A159. Signposted off A631

Hotel	★★★ 64% West Retford Hotel, 24 North Rd, RETFORD ☎ 01777 706333 Annexe 62 🛏 🕮

GEDNEY HILL   Map 08 TF31

Gedney Hill West Drove PE12 0NT
☎ 01406 330922 Fax 01406 330323
Flat parkland course similar to a links course. Made testing by Fen winds and small greens. Also a 10-bay driving range.
18 holes, 5493yds, Par 70, SSS 66, Course record 67.
Club membership 300.

Visitors	no restrictions.
Societies	telephone in advance.
Green Fees	£6.25 (£10.50 weekends).
Cards	💳 💳 💳 💳 💳
Prof	David Hutton
Designer	Monkwise Ltd
Facilities	⊗ ⑂ 🏌 💼 ♀ ⛳ 🏠 🍴 ♐ 🚜 ♐ 🏌
& Leisure	bowling green, snooker room, pool table.
Location	5m SE of Spalding

Hotel	★★ 63% Rose & Crown Hotel, Market Place, WISBECH ☎ 01945 589800 20 🛏 🕮

GRANTHAM   Map 08 SK93

Belton Park Belton Ln, Londonthorpe Rd NG31 9SH
☎ 01476 567399 Fax 01476 592078
Three 9-hole courses set in classic mature parkland of Lord Brownlow's country seat, Belton House. Gently undulating with streams, ponds, plenty of trees and beautiful scenery, including a deer park. Famous holes: 5th, 12th, 16th and 18th. Combine any of the three courses for a testing 18-hole round.

Brownlow: 18 holes, 6420yds, Par 71, SSS 71, Course record 65.
Ancaster: 18 holes, 6305yds, Par 70, SSS 70.
Belmont: 18 holes, 6075yds, Par 69, SSS 69.
Club membership 850.

Visitors	contact professional for suitable tee times. No green fees on Tuesday before 3pm.
Societies	apply in advance.
Green Fees	£32 per day, £26 per round (£38/32 weekends).
Prof	Brian McKee
Designer	Williamson/Allis
Facilities	⊗ ⑂ 🏌 💼 ♀ ⛳ 🏠 🍴 ♐ 🏌
Location	1.5m NE of Grantham

Hotel	★★★ 67% Kings Hotel, North Pde, GRANTHAM ☎ 01476 590800 21 🛏 🕮

Sudbrook Moor Charity St, Carlton Scroop NG32 3AT
☎ 01400 250796 Fax 01400 250796
A testing 9-hole parkland/meadowland course in a picturesque valley setting with easy walking.
9 holes, 4811yds, Par 66, SSS 64, Course record 69.

Visitors	telephone in advance.
Green Fees	Summer: £6 per day (£9 weekends); Winter: £5 per day (£7 weekends).
Prof	Tim Hutton
Designer	Tim Hutton
Facilities	⛳ 🏠 🍴 🏌
Location	6m NE of Grantham on A607

Hotel	★★★ 67% Kings Hotel, North Pde, GRANTHAM ☎ 01476 590800 21 🛏 🕮

GRIMSBY   Map 08 TA21

Grimsby Littlecoates Rd DN34 4LU
☎ 01472 342630 Fax 01472 342630
Undulating parkland course.
18 holes, 6098yds, Par 70, SSS 69, Course record 66.
Club membership 730.

Visitors	contact in advance.
Societies	by prior arrangement with secretary.
Green Fees	£28 per day; £22 per round (£28 weekends).
Prof	Richard Smith
Designer	Colt
Facilities	⊗ ⑂ 🏌 💼 ♀ ⛳ 🏠 🍴 ♐ 🚜 ♐
Location	1m from A180 & 1m from A46

Hotel	★★★ 63% Humber Royal, Littlecoates Rd, GRIMSBY ☎ 01472 350311 52 🛏 🕮

HORNCASTLE   Map 08 TF26

Horncastle West Ashby LN9 5PP ☎ 01507 526800
Parkland course with many water hazards and bunkers; very challenging. There is a 25-bay floodlit driving range.
18 holes, 5717yds, Par 70, SSS 70, Course record 71.
Club membership 200.

Visitors	dress code must be adhered to, welcome anytime, may contact in advance.
Societies	apply in writing or telephone in advance.
Green Fees	£20 per day; £15 per round.
Cards	💳
Prof	E C Wright
Designer	E C Wright
Facilities	⊗ ⑂ 🏌 💼 ♀ ⛳ 🏠 🍴 🏌
& Leisure	fishing.

▶

The Admiral Rodney Hotel is situated in the Market Town of Horncastle, well known for its many Antique Shops, and has a reputation for friendliness. All bedrooms are en-suite, and the hotel benefits from a full refurbishment. The splendid furnishings and unique decor of the Courtyard Restaurant provides a delightful setting for dinner and the popular Rodney Bar, with it's 'Nautical Theme' serves a selection of Real Ales.

SPECIAL GOLFING BREAKS AVAILABLE WITH LOUTH AND HORNCASTLE GOLF CLUB

AA
★ ★

North Street, Horncastle, Lincoln LN9 5DX
Telephone: 01507 523131   Fax: 01507 523104
10 minutes drive from Woodhall Spa's Famous Courses

Location	Off A158 Lincoln/Skegness road at Edlington, off A153 at West Ashby

Hotel	★★ 71% Admiral Rodney Hotel, North St, HORNCASTLE ☎ 01507 523131 31 ⇌ ♟

IMMINGHAM   Map 08 TA11

Immingham St Andrews Ln, off Church Ln DN40 2EU
☎ 01469 575298 Fax 01469 577636
An excellent, flat parkland course noted for its numerous dykes which come into play on most holes.
18 holes, 6215yds, Par 71, SSS 70, Course record 69.
Club membership 700.

Visitors	telephone in advance.
Societies	telephone (am) to arrange date.
Green Fees	£23 per day; £16 per round (£23 per day/round weekends).
Prof	Nick Harding
Designer	Hawtree & Son
Facilities	⊗ ⊪ by prior arrangement ⓑ ♥ ♀ ⌂ 🏠 ⚐ ✐
Location	7m NW off Grimsby

Hotel	★★ 65% Old Chapel Hotel & Restaurant, 50 Station Rd, Habrough, IMMINGHAM ☎ 01469 572377 14 ⇌ ♟

LACEBY   Map 08 TA20

Manor Barton St, Laceby Manort DN37 7EA
☎ 01472 873468 Fax 01472 276706
The first nine holes played as a parkland course, all the fairways lined with young trees. The second nine are mainly open fairways. The 18th hole green is surrounded by water.
18 holes, 6354yds, Par 71, SSS 70.
Club membership 550.

Visitors	booked tee system at all times, visitors may book 6 days in advance.
Societies	telephone in advance.
Green Fees	£15 per 18 holes. Prices under review.
Cards	▭ ▭ ▭ ▭
Prof	Paul Rushworth
Facilities	⊗ ⊪ by prior arrangement ⓑ ♥ ♀ ⌂ 🏠 🚃 ✐
& Leisure	fishing.
Location	A18 Barton St - Laceby/Louth

Hotel	★★★ 63% Humber Royal, Littlecoates Rd, GRIMSBY ☎ 01472 350311 52 ⇌ ♟

LINCOLN   Map 08 SK97

Canwick Park Canwick Park, Washingborough Rd LN4 1EF ☎ 01522 522166 & 542912
Parkland course with views of Lincoln Cathedral. Testing 5th hole (200 yd par 3).
18 holes, 6160yds, Par 70, SSS 69, Course record 65.
Club membership 650.

Visitors	with member only Sat also Sun before 3pm.
Societies	weekdays only by prior arrangement in writing.
Green Fees	£16/£20 weekdays (£20/£25 weeknds).
Prof	S Williamson
Designer	Hawtree & Sons
Facilities	⊗ ⊪ ⓑ ♥ ♀ ⌂ 🏠 ⚐ ✒ 🚃 ✐
Location	1m E of Lincoln

Hotel	★★★ 65% Posthouse Lincoln, Eastgate, LINCOLN ☎ 0870 400 9052 70 ⇌ ♟

Carholme Carholme Rd LN1 1SE
☎ 01522 523725 Fax 01522 533733
Parkland course where prevailing west winds can add interest. Good views. 1st hole out of bounds left and right of fairway, pond in front of bunkered green at 5th, lateral water hazards across several fairways.
18 holes, 6243yds, Par 71, SSS 70, Course record 69.
Club membership 625.

Visitors	must contact in advance. Weekends may not play before 2.30pm.
Societies	apply in writing.
Green Fees	£15 per round.
Prof	Richard Hunter
Facilities	⊗ ⊪ by prior arrangement ⓑ ♥ ♀ ⌂ 🏠 ⚐ ✐
Location	1m W of city centre on A57

Hotel	★★★★ 59% The White Hart, Bailgate, LINCOLN ☎ 0870 400 8117 48 ⇌ ♟

LOUTH   Map 08 TF38

Louth Crowtree Ln LN11 9LJ
☎ 01507 603681 Fax 01507 603681
Undulating parkland course, fine views in an area of
outstanding natural beauty.
18 holes, 6424yds, Par 72, SSS 71, Course record 64.
Club membership 700.
Visitors   must contact in advance to make sure tee is not
       reserved for competition.
Societies   a booking form will be sent on request.
Green Fees not confirmed.
Prof   A Blundell
Facilities   ⊗ ℹ 🏌 💺 🍴 🍸 ♣ 🏡 🛈 🏌 🐾 🚣 🖊
& Leisure squash.
Location   W side of Louth between A157/A153

Hotel   ★★★ 69% Beaumont Hotel, 66 Victoria Rd,
       LOUTH ☎ 01507 605005   16 ⇆ ↾

MARKET RASEN   Map 08 TF18

Market Rasen & District Legsby Rd LN8 3DZ
☎ 01673 842319
Picturesque, well-wooded heathland course, easy walking,
breezy with becks forming natural hazards. Good views of
Lincolnshire Wolds.
18 holes, 6045yds, Par 70, SSS 69, Course record 66.
Club membership 600.
Visitors   must play with member at weekends and must
       contact in advance.
Societies   Tue & Fri only; must contact in advance.
Green Fees £25 per day; £18 per round.
Prof   A M Chester
Facilities   ⊗ ℹ 🏌 💺 🍴 🍸 🏡 🖊
Location   1m E, off A46

Hotel   ★★★ 69% Beaumont Hotel, 66 Victoria Rd,
       LOUTH ☎ 01507 605005   16 ⇆ ↾

Market Rasen Race Course (Golf Course) Legsby Rd
LN8 3EA ☎ 01673 843434 Fax 01673 844532
This is a public course set within the bounds of Market Rasen
race course - the entire racing area is out of bounds. The
longest hole is the 4th at 454yards with the race course
providing a hazard over the whole length of the drive.
9 holes, 2532yds, Par 32.

Visitors   closed racedays apart from evening meetings
       when open until noon.
Societies   telephone in advance to arrange.
Green Fees not confirmed.
Designer   Edward Stenton

Facilities   ⊓
Location   2m E of Market Rasen

Hotel   ★★★ 69% Beaumont Hotel, 66 Victoria Rd,
       LOUTH ☎ 01507 605005   16 ⇆ ↾

NORMANBY   Map 08 SE81

Normanby Hall Normanby Park DN15 9HU
☎ 01724 720226 (Pro shop) 853212 (Secretary)
Well maintained course set in secluded mature parkland. A
challenge to golfers of all abilities.
18 holes, 6561yds, Par 71, SSS 71, Course record 66.
Club membership 850.
Visitors   book in advance by contacting professional.
Societies   must contact in advance: Rachael Lennox,
       01724 297860.
Green Fees £19 per day; £11.85 per round (£13.50 per round
       weekends & bank holidays).
Cards   🌑 🚍 💳 🔲 🕯
Prof   Christopher Mann
Designer   Hawtree & Son
Facilities   ⊗ ℹ 🏌 💺 🍴 🍸 🏡 🖊 ♣ 🐾 🚣 🖊
& Leisure free hire of handigolf buggies for disabled.
Location   3m N of Scunthorpe adj to Normanby Hall on
       B1130

Hotel   ★★★ 67% Royal Hotel, Doncaster Rd,
       SCUNTHORPE ☎ 0500 636943 (Central Res)
       Fax 01773 880321   33 ⇆ ↾

SCUNTHORPE   Map 08 SE81

Ashby Decoy Burringham Rd DN17 2AB
☎ 01724 866561 Fax 01724 271708
Pleasant, flat parkland course to satisfy all tastes, yet test the
experienced golfer.
18 holes, 6281yds, Par 71, SSS 71, Course record 66.
Club membership 650.
Visitors   may not play Tue, weekends or bank holidays.
       Handicap certificate required.
Societies   apply in advance.
Green Fees £24 per day; £18 per round.
Prof   A Miller
Facilities   ⊗ ℹ 🏌 💺 🍴 🍸 🏡 🐾 🚣 🖊
Location   2.5m SW on B1450 near Asda Superstore

Hotel   ★★★ 67% Royal Hotel, Doncaster Rd,
       SCUNTHORPE ☎ 0500 636943 (Central Res)
       Fax 01773 880321   33 ⇆ ↾

Forest Pines - Briggate Lodge Inn Hotel Ermine St,
Broughton DN20 0AQ
☎ 01652 650770 & 650756 Fax 01652 650495
Set in 185 acres of mature parkland and open heathland and
constructed in a similar design to that of Wentworth or
Sunningdale, Forest Pines offers three challenging 9-hole
courses - Forest, Pines and Beeches. Any combination can be
played. Facilities include a 17-bay driving range and a
spacious clubhouse.
Forest Course: 9 holes, 3291yds, Par 36, SSS 36.
Pines Course: 9 holes, 3591yds, Par 37, SSS 37.
Beeches: 9 holes, 3102yds, Par 35, SSS 35.
Club membership 330.
Visitors   must contact in advance.
Societies   telephone in advance.
Green Fees £35 per day; £30 per round.   ▶

Forest Pines Golf Club

Cards	▭ ▭ ▭ ▭ ▭ ▭ ▭
Prof	David Edwards
Designer	John Morgan
Facilities & Leisure	⊗ ⅲ ⅃ ♨ 🏌 🍴 🎯 ⚑ 🛒 ♂ (heated indoor swimming pool, sauna, solarium, gymnasium.
Location	200yds from junct 4 M180
Hotel	★★★ 74% Forest Pines Hotel, Ermine St, Broughton, SCUNTHORPE ☎ 01652 650770 86 🛏 ᴿ

Holme Hall Holme Ln, Bottesford DN16 3RF
☎ 01724 862078 Fax 01724 862078
Heathland course with sandy subsoil. Easy walking.
18 holes, 6404yds, Par 71, SSS 71, Course record 65.
Club membership 724.

Visitors	must play with member at weekends & bank holidays. Must contact in advance.
Societies	must contact in advance.
Green Fees	not confirmed.
Prof	Richard McKiernan
Facilities	⊗ ⅲ ⅃ ♨ 🍴 🎯 ⚑ 🛒 ♂
Location	3m SE
Hotel	★★★ 67% Royal Hotel, Doncaster Rd, SCUNTHORPE ☎ 0500 636943 (Central Res) Fax 01773 880321 33 🛏 ᴿ

Kingsway Kingsway DN15 7ER ☎ 01724 840945
Parkland course with many par 3's.
9 holes, 1915yds, Par 29, Course record 28.

Visitors	no restrictions.
Green Fees	not confirmed.
Prof	Chris Mann
Facilities	♨ 🎯 ♂
Location	W side of town centre off A18
Hotel	★★★ 67% Royal Hotel, Doncaster Rd, SCUNTHORPE ☎ 0500 636943 (Central Res) Fax 01773 880321 33 🛏 ᴿ

SKEGNESS

Map 09 TF56

North Shore Hotel & Golf Club North Shore Rd PE25 1DN
☎ 01754 763298 Fax 01754 761902
A half-links, half-parkland course designed by James Braid
in 1910. Easy walking and good sea views.
18 holes, 6200yds, Par 71, SSS 71, Course record 67.
Club membership 450.

Visitors	tee times must be booked if possible.
Societies	write or telephone in advance.
Green Fees	not confirmed.
Prof	J Cornelius
Designer	James Braid
Facilities & Leisure	⊗ ⅲ ⅃ ♨ 🍴 🎯 ⚑ 🛒 ♂ snooker.
Location	1m N of town centre off A52
Hotel	★★ 65% North Shore Hotel & Golf Course, North Shore Rd, SKEGNESS ☎ 01754 763298 30 🛏 ᴿ Annexe 3 🛏 ᴿ

Seacroft Drummond Rd, Seacroft PE25 3AU
☎ 01754 763020 Fax 01754 763020
A championship seaside links traditionally laid out with
tight undulations and hogsback fairways. Adjacent to
'Gibraltar Point Nature Reserve'.
18 holes, 6479yds, Par 71, SSS 71, Course record 66.
Club membership 590.

Visitors	must be a member of an affiliated golf club.
Societies	contact in advance.
Green Fees	£35 per day; £25 per round (£40/£30 weekends & bank holidays).
Prof	Robin Lawie
Designer	Tom Dunn/Willie Fernie
Facilities	⊗ ⅲ ⅃ ♨ 🍴 🎯 ⚑ 🛒 ♂
Location	S side of town centre
Hotel	★★★ 63% Crown Hotel, Drummond Rd, Seacroft, SKEGNESS ☎ 01754 610760 27 🛏 ᴿ

> Entries with a green background
> identify courses considered to be
> particularly interesting

Woodhall Spa

The Championship Course at Woodhall Spa, now known as The Hotchkin, is arguably the best inland course in Britain. Golf has been played here for over 100 years and the Hotchkin has hosted most of the top national and international amateur events.

The English Golf Union acquired Woodhall Spa in 1995 to create a centre of excellence. A second course, The Bracken, has been built together with extensive practice facilities including one of Europe's finest short game practice areas. The English Golf Union actively encourages visitors throughout the year to The National Golf Centre to experience these facilities and to enjoy the unique ambience. The Academy aims to coach players of all standards with a special driving range and indoor school with computer/video equipment.

Visitors must be a member of a golf club affiliated to the appropriate Golf Union. Handicap certificate must be produced

Societies must apply by telephone initially

Green Fees not confirmed

Facilities ⊗ ⅷ ⅃ ☕ ⚲ ⚐ ⚑
⚑ ♟ ⚑ Professional (C. C. Elliot)

Location The Broadway LN10 6PU (NE side of village off B1191)

Holes/Par/Course record 18 holes, 6921 yds, Par 73, SSS 73, Course record 68

WHERE TO STAY AND EAT NEARBY

Hotels
WOODHALL SPA

★★★67% Petwood Hotel, Stixwould Rd. ☎ 01526 352411. 50 ⇌ 🐾

★★★63% Golf Hotel, The Broadway. ☎ 01526 353535. 50 (36 ⇌ 🐾 14 🐾)

★★60% Eagle Lodge, The Broadway. ☎ 01526 353231. 23 (15 ⇌ 🐾 7 🐾)

Restaurant
HORNCASTLE

🌼 🌼 Magpies, 71-75 East St. ☎ 01507 527004.

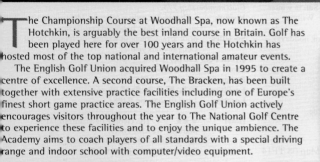

Championship Course

SLEAFORD Map 08 TF04

Sleaford Willoughby Rd, South Rauceby NG34 8PL
☎ 01529 488273 Fax 01529 488326
Inland links-type course, moderately wooded and fairly flat.
18 holes, 6443yds, Par 72, SSS 71, Course record 64.
Club membership 630.
Visitors   contact in advance, may not play Sun in winter.
Societies   telephone enquiry to professional. Written confirmation required.
Green Fees £22 per day (£36 weekends & bank holidays); £16 per round.
Prof   James Wilson
Designer   T Williamson
Facilities   ⊗ ℿ ㄴ ☕ ♀ ⚐ 🏠 🚂 ∅
Location   2m W of Sleaford, off A153

Hotel   ★★★ 67% Kings Hotel, North Pde, GRANTHAM
☎ 01476 590800 21 ⇄ ℟

SOUTH KYME Map 08 TF14

South Kyme Skinners Ln LN4 4AT
☎ 01526 861113 Fax 01526 861113
A challenging fenland course described as an 'Inland links' with water hazards, trees and fairway hazards.
18 holes, 6568yds, Par 72, SSS 71, Course record 67.
Club membership 370.
Visitors   advisable to telephone in advance for course availability.
Societies   telephone for booking form.
Green Fees £14 per round (£16 weekends).
Cards   ▭▭ ▥▦
Prof   Peter Chamberlain
Facilities   ⊗ ℿ ㄴ ☕ ♀ ⚐ 🏠 🚂 ∅
Location   Off B1395 in South Kyme village

Hotel   L Travelodge, Holdingham, SLEAFORD
☎ 01529 414752 40 ⇄ ℟

SPALDING Map 08 TF22

Spalding Surfleet PE11 4EA
☎ 01775 680988 (office) & 680474 (pro)
Fax 01775 680988
A pretty, well laid-out course in a fenland area. The River Glen runs beside the 1st, 2nd and 4th holes, and ponds and lakes are very much in play on the 9th, 10th and 11th holes. Challenging holes include the river dominated 2nd and the 10th which involves a tight drive and dog-leg left to reach a raised three-tier green.
18 holes, 6478yds, Par 72, SSS 71, Course record 62.
Club membership 750.
Visitors   must contact in advance. Handicap certificate required.
Societies   write to the secretary, Societies on Thu all day and Tue pm.
Green Fees £25 per day (£30 weekends & bank holidays); £20 per round.
Prof   John Spencer
Designer   Price/Spencer/Ward
Facilities   ⊗ ℿ ㄴ ☕ ♀ ⚐ 🏠 🚂 ∅
Location   4m N of Spalding adjacent to A16

Hotel   ★★ 65% Cley Hall Hotel, 22 High St, SPALDING
☎ 01775 725157 4 ⇄ ℟ Annexe 8 ⇄ ℟

STAMFORD Map 08 TF00

Burghley Park St Martins PE9 3JX
☎ 01780 762100 & 753789 Fax 01780 753789
Open parkland course with superb greens, many trees, ponds and bunkers. Situated in the grounds of Burghley House.
18 holes, 6236yds, Par 70, SSS 70, Course record 64.
Club membership 775.
Visitors   with member only weekends. Must contact in advance & have handicap certificate.
Societies   prior arrangement in writing, preferably by 1st Dec previous year.
Green Fees £22 per day.
Prof   Glenn Davies
Designer   Rev J Day (1938)
Facilities   ⊗ ㄴ ☕ ♀ ⚐ 🏠 🚩 🚂 ∅
Location   1m S of town on B1081

Hotel   ★★★ 75% The George of Stamford, 71 St Martins, STAMFORD
☎ 01780 750750 & 750700 (Res)
Fax 01780 750701 47 ⇄ ℟

STOKE ROCHFORD Map 08 SK92

Stoke Rochford NG33 5EW ☎ 01476 530275
Parkland course designed by C. Turner and extended in 1936 to 18 holes by Major Hotchkin.
18 holes, 6252yds, Par 70, SSS 70, Course record 65.
Club membership 525.
Visitors   must contact in advance, restricted to 9am weekdays, 10.30am weekends & bank holidays.
Societies   contact one year in advance, in writing.
Green Fees not confirmed.
Prof   Angus Dow
Designer   Major Hotchkin
Facilities   ㄴ 🏠 🚩 🚂 ∅
Location   Off A1 5m S of Grantham

Hotel   ★★★ 67% Kings Hotel, North Pde, GRANTHAM
☎ 01476 590800 21 ⇄ ℟

SUTTON BRIDGE Map 09 TF42

Sutton Bridge New Rd PE12 9RQ
☎ 01406 350323
Parkland course built around Victorian dock basin, near river Nene.
9 holes, 5724yds, Par 70, SSS 68.
Club membership 350.
Visitors   may not play competition days, weekends & bank holidays, must contact in advance. Must have handicap certificate.
Societies   write or telephone in advance.
Green Fees £19 per day/round.
Prof   D Woolley
Facilities   ⊗ ℿ ㄴ ☕ ♀ ⚐ 🏠 🚩 ∅
Location   E side of village off A17

Hotel   ★★★ 64% The Duke's Head, Tuesday Market Place, KING'S LYNN
☎ 01553 774996 71 ⇄ ℟

SUTTON ON SEA
Map 09 TF58

Sandilands Roman Bank LN12 2RJ
☎ 01507 441432 Fax 01507 441617
Flat links course on the sea shore.
18 holes, 5995yds, Par 70, SSS 69.
Club membership 200.
Visitors   no restrictions.
Societies   telephone in advance.
Green Fees £18 per day; £12 per round (£18 per round weekends & bank holidays).
Cards   ▨
Facilities   ⊗ ⅷ ⅙ ♣ ♀ ♨ ↑ 🐴 🏌 ⚒ ⚘
& Leisure   grass tennis courts, gymnasium.
Location   1.5m S off A52

Hotel   ★★★ 66% Grange & Links Hotel, Sea Ln, Sandilands, MABLETHORPE
☎ 01507 441334 23 ⇆ ℝ

TORKSEY
Map 08 SK87

Lincoln LN1 2EG ☎ 01427 718721 Fax 01427 718721
A mature testing inland course on near ideal golfing terrain.
18 holes, 6438yds, Par 71, SSS 71, Course record 67.
Club membership 700.
Visitors   welcome on non event days.
Societies   apply in writing or telephone.
Green Fees not confirmed.
Prof   Ashley Carter
Facilities   ⊗ ⅷ ⅙ ♣ ♀ ♨ 🏌 ⚘ ⚒
Location   NE side of village, off A156 midway between Lincoln & Gainsborough

Hotel   ★★★★ 59% The White Hart, Bailgate, LINCOLN ☎ 0870 400 8117 48 ⇆ ℝ

Millfield Laughterton LN1 2LB
☎ 01427 718255 Fax 01427 718473
This golf complex offers a range of facilities to suit every golfer. The Millfield is designed to suit the more experienced golfer and follows the natural contours of the landscape. The Grenville Green is designed for more casual golfers and the Par 3 is suitable for beginners, family games or for warm-up and practice play.
The Millfield: 18 holes, 6004yds, Par 72, SSS 69, Course record 68.
The Grenville Green: 18 holes, 4485yds, Par 65.
Visitors   Millfield: shoes must be worn, no jeans etc. Grenville Green no restrictions. Par 3 9 hole no restrictions.
Societies   telephone in advance.
Green Fees Millfield: £10 per day. Grenville Green 18 hole: £5 per day.
Prof   Richard Hunter
Designer   C W Watson
Facilities   ⊗ ⅙ ♣ ♀ ♨ 🏌 🐴 🏌 ⚒ ⚘ ↑
& Leisure   grass tennis courts.
Location   On A1133 1m N of A57

Hotel   ★★★★ 59% The White Hart, Bailgate, LINCOLN ☎ 0870 400 8117 48 ⇆ ℝ

Looking for a driving range?
See the index at the back of the guide

WOODHALL SPA
Map 08 TF16

Hotel   ★★★ 67% Petwood Hotel, Stixwould Rd, WOODHALL SPA
☎ 01526 352411 47 ⇆ ℝ

WOODHALL SPA See page 173

WOODTHORPE
Map 09 TF48

Woodthorpe Hall LN13 0DD
☎ 01507 450000 Fax 01507 450000
Parkland course.
18 holes, 5140yds, Par 67, SSS 65, Course record 68.
Club membership 300.
Visitors   contact in advance for weekends.
Societies   Mon-Fri, apply to the secretary at least one month prior to visit.
Green Fees £10 per day.
Facilities   ⊗ ⅷ ⅙ ♣ ♀ ♨
& Leisure   fishing.
Location   3m NNW of Alford on B1373

Hotel   ★★★ 66% Grange & Links Hotel, Sea Ln, Sandilands, MABLETHORPE
☎ 01507 441334 23 ⇆ ℝ

LONDON

Courses within the London Postal District area (ie those that have London Postcodes - W1, SW1 etc) are listed here in postal district order commencing East then North, South and West. Courses outside the London Postal area, but within Greater London are to be found listed under the county of **Greater London** in the gazetteer (see page 95).

LONDON

E4 CHINGFORD

Royal Epping Forest Forest Approach, Chingford E4 7AZ
☎ 020 8529 2195 Fax 020 8559 4664
Woodland course. 'Red' garments must be worn.
18 holes, 6342yds, Par 71, SSS 70.
Club membership 400.
▶

Visitors	booking system in operation.
Societies	must contact secretary in advance.
Green Fees	£10.40 weekdays (£14.25 weekends).
Prof	J Francis
Facilities	🏠⛳🏌
Location	300 yds S of Chingford station

Hotel	★★★ 66% County Hotel Epping Forest, Oak Hill, WOODFORD GREEN ☎ 020 8787 9988 99 ⇥ 🐾

West Essex Bury Rd, Sewardstonebury, Chingford E4 7QL
☎ 020 8529 7558 Fax 020 8524 7870
Testing parkland course within Epping Forest. Notable holes are 8th (par 5), 16th (par 4), 18th (par 5).
18 holes, 6289yds, Par 71, SSS 70.
Club membership 645.

Visitors	must have handicap certificate but may not play on Tue morning, Thu afternoon & weekends.
Societies	must contact in advance.
Green Fees	£35 per day; £28 per round.
Cards	💳
Prof	Robert Joyce
Designer	James Braid
Facilities	⊗🍴🏠⛳🏌🛒🅿🚶 🐾🏌
Location	1.5m N of Chingford station. Access via M25 junct 26

Hotel	★★★ 63% Roebuck Hotel, North End, BUCKHURST HILL ☎ 020 8505 4636 28 ⇥ 🐾

E11 Leytonstone & Wanstead

Wanstead Overton Dr, Wanstead E11 2LW
☎ 020 8989 3938 Fax 020 8532 9138
A flat, picturesque parkland course with many trees and shrubs and providing easy walking. The par 3, 16th, involves driving across a lake.
18 holes, 6004yds, Par 69, SSS 69, Course record 62.
Club membership 600.

Visitors	must contact in advance and may only play Mon, Tue & Fri.
Societies	by prior arrangement.
Green Fees	£28 per day.
Prof	David Hawkins
Designer	James Braid
Facilities	⊗🍴🏠⛳🏌🛒🅿🏌
& Leisure	fishing.
Location	From central London A12 NE to Wanstead

Hotel	★★★ 66% County Hotel Epping Forest, Oak Hill, WOODFORD GREEN ☎ 020 8787 9988 99 ⇥ 🐾

N2 East Finchley

Hampstead Winnington Rd N2 0TU
☎ 020 8455 0203 Fax 020 8731 6194
Undulating parkland course with many mature trees.
18 holes, 5822yds, Par 68, SSS 68, Course record 64.
Club membership 526.

Visitors	restricted Tue and weekends. Contact Professional in advance on 0181 455 7089.
Societies	small societies by prior arrangement.
Green Fees	not confirmed.
Prof	Peter Brown

Designer	Tom Dunn
Facilities	⊗🏠⛳🏌🛒🅿🏌
Location	Off Hampstead Lane

Hotel	★★★ 64% Posthouse Hampstead, 215 Haverstock Hill, LONDON ☎ 0870 400 9037 140 ⇥ 🐾

N6 Highgate

Highgate Denewood Rd N6 4AH
☎ 020 8340 5467 Fax 020 8348 9152
Parkland course.
18 holes, 5985yds, Par 69, SSS 69, Course record 66.
Club membership 800.

Visitors	may not play Wed & weekends.
Societies	by arrangement.
Green Fees	£30 per round.
Prof	Robin Turner
Facilities	🛒🅿🏌🏌
Hotel	★★★★ 68% London Marriott Hotel Regents Park, 128 King Henry's Rd, LONDON ☎ 020 7722 7711 303 ⇥ 🐾

N9 Lower Edmonton

Lee Valley Leisure Lee Valley Leisure Centre, Meridian Way, Edmonton N9 0AS ☎ 020 8803 3611
Tricky municipal parkland course with some narrow fairways and the River Lea providing a natural hazard.
18 holes, 4902yds, Par 66, SSS 64, Course record 66.
Club membership 200.

Visitors	may telephone for advance bookings.
Societies	must telephone in advance.
Green Fees	not confirmed.
Prof	R Gerken
Facilities	🏠⛳ by prior arrangement ⛳🛒🅿🏌🏌🏌
& Leisure	heated indoor swimming pool, squash, sauna, solarium, gymnasium.
Hotel	★★ 71% Oak Lodge Hotel, 80 Village Rd, Bush Hill Park, ENFIELD ☎ 020 8360 7082 7 ⇥ 🐾

N14 Southgate

Trent Park Bramley Rd, Oakwood N14 4UW
☎ 020 8366 7432
Parkland course set in 150 acres of green belt area. Seven holes played across Merryhills brook. Testing holes are 2nd (423 yds) over brook, 190 yds from the tee, and up to plateau green; 7th (463 yds) dog-leg, over brook, par 4.
18 holes, 6085yds, Par 70, SSS 69, Course record 68.
Club membership 1200.

Visitors	must contact 7 days in advance.
Societies	must telephone in advance.
Green Fees	not confirmed.
Prof	Mike Plumbridge
Designer	D McGibbon
Facilities	⊗🍴🏠⛳🏌🛒🅿🏌🏌🏌
Location	Opposite Oakwood underground station

Hotel	★★★★♨ 71% West Lodge Park Hotel, Cockfosters Rd, HADLEY WOOD ☎ 020 8216 3900 46 ⇥ 🐾 Annexe 9 ⇥ 🐾

N20 WHETSTONE

North Middlesex The Manor House, Friern Barnet Ln, Whetstone N20 0NL
☎ 020 8445 1604 & 020 8445 3060 Fax 020 8445 5023
Short parkland course renowned for its tricky greens.
18 holes, 5625yds, Par 69, SSS 67, Course record 64.
Club membership 580.
Visitors advisable to contact in advance, contact professional shop. May not play at weekends
Societies bookings in advance, winter offers & summer packages by prior arrangement.
Green Fees £22 per round.
Prof Steve Roberts
Designer Willie Park Jnr
Facilities ⊗ ⊪ ৬ ▼ ♀ ﹟ 🏠 ♈ 🐾 ♂
Hotel ★★★ 72% Edgwarebury Hotel, Barnet Ln, ELSTREE ☎ 020 8953 8227 47 ⇔ ☞

South Herts Links Dr, Totteridge N20 8QU
☎ 020 8445 2035 Fax 020 8445 7569
An open undulating parkland course officially in Hertfordshire, but now in a London postal area. It is, perhaps, most famous for the fact that two of the greatest of all British professionals, Harry Vardon and Dai Rees, CBE were professionals at the club. The course is testing, over rolling fairways, especially in the prevailing south-west wind.
18 holes, 6432yds, Par 72, SSS 71, Course record 63.
Club membership 850.
Visitors must be members of recognised golf club & have handicap certificate of 24 or less. May not play at weekends.
Societies Wed-Fri only, must apply in writing.
Green Fees not confirmed.
Prof Bobby Mitchell
Designer Harry Vardon
Facilities ﹟ 🏠 ♈ 🐾 ♂
Location 2m E of A1 at Apex Corner

Hotel ★★★ 65% Posthouse South Mimms, SOUTH MIMMS ☎ 0870 400 9072 143 ⇔ ☞

N21 WINCHMORE HILL

Bush Hill Park Bush Hill, Winchmore Hill N21 2BU
☎ 020 8360 5738 Fax 020 8360 5583
Pleasant parkland course surrounded by trees. Contains a large number of both fairway sandtraps and green side bunkers. Undulating, but not too harsh.
18 holes, 5809yds, Par 70, SSS 68.
Club membership 700.
Visitors may not play Wed mornings or weekends & bank holidays. Handicap certificate required.
Societies by arrangement.
Green Fees £35 per day; £25 per round.
Prof Adrian Andrews
Facilities ﹟ 🏠 ♂
Location 1m S of Enfield

Hotel ★★ 71% Oak Lodge Hotel, 80 Village Rd, Bush Hill Park, ENFIELD ☎ 020 8360 7082 7 ⇔ ☞

N22 WOOD GREEN

Muswell Hill Rhodes Av, Wood Green N22 4UT
☎ 020 8888 1764 Fax 020 8889 9380
Narrow parkland course featuring numerous water hazards.
18 holes, 6438yds, Par 71, SSS 71, Course record 65.
Club membership 560.
Visitors must contact in advance, restricted weekends.
Societies apply in writing or telephone.
Green Fees £33 per day; £23 per round.
Prof David Wilton
Facilities ⊗ ⊪ ৬ ▼ ♀ ﹟ 🏠 ♈ 🐾 ♂
Location Off N Circular Rd at Bounds Green

Hotel ★★★ 68% Raglan Hall Hotel, 8-12 Queens Ave, Muswell Hill, LONDON ☎ 020 8883 9836 46 ⇔ ☞

NW4 HENDON   Map 04 TQ28

The Metro Golf Centre Barnet Copthall Sports Centre, Gt North Way NW4 1PF
☎ 020 8202 1202 Fax 020 8203 1203
Located just seven miles from London's West End, the Metro Golf Centre represents a new generation of golf facility dedicated to the development of all standards of golfer. Facilities include a 48 bay two-tiered driving range, a testing 9-hole par 3 course with water hazards, pot bunkers and postage stamp greens, a short game practice area, and a Golf Academy offering unique teaching methods.
9 holes, 898yds, Par 27, SSS 27, Course record 24.
Club membership 500.
Visitors welcome any time between 8am-10pm all week for lessons, to play on the course or use driving range.
Societies telephone in advance.
Green Fees not confirmed.
Cards 💳 💳 💳 💳 💳
Prof Barney Puttick
Designer Cousells
Facilities ⊗ ⊪ ৬ ▼ ♀ 🏠 ♈ ♂ ⚑
Location Just off A41 and A1 at junct 2 of the M1, within the Barnet Copthall Sporting Complex

Hotel ★★★★ 68% London Marriott Hotel Regents Park, 128 King Henry's Rd, LONDON ☎ 020 7722 7711 303 ⇔ ☞

NW7 MILL HILL

Finchley Nether Court, Frith Ln, Mill Hill NW7 1PU
☎ 020 8346 2436 & 8346 5086 Fax 020 8343 4205
Easy walking on wooded parkland course.
18 holes, 6411yds, Par 72, SSS 71.
Club membership 500.
Visitors must contact in advance.
Societies must apply in writing.
Green Fees £30 per day, £24 per round (£36/30 weekend pm).
Cards 💳 💳 💳 💳 💳
Prof David Brown
Designer James Braid
Facilities ⊗ ⊪ by prior arrangement ৬ ▼ ♀ ﹟ 🏠 ♈ 🐾 ♂
Location Near Mill Hill East Tube Station

▶

Finchley Golf Club

Hotel ★★★ 72% Edgwarebury Hotel, Barnet Ln, ELSTREE ☎ 020 8953 8227 47 ⇄ ♞

Hendon Ashley Walk, Devonshire Rd, Mill Hill NW7 1DG
☎ 020 8346 6023 Fax 020 8343 1974
Easy walking, parkland course with a good variety of trees, and providing testing golf.
18 holes, 6266yds, Par 70, SSS 70.
Club membership 540.
Visitors must contact in advance. Restricted weekends & bank holidays.
Societies Tue-Fri. Must contact in advance.
Green Fees £35 per day; £28 per round (£35 weekends & bank holidays).
Cards 💳 💳 💳 💳 💳
Prof Matt Deal
Designer H S Colt
Facilities ⊗ 🏌 🍴 ♀ 🏌 🏠 🚩 ♂
Location 10 mins from junc 2 of M1 southbound

Hotel ★★★ 72% Edgwarebury Hotel, Barnet Ln, ELSTREE ☎ 020 8953 8227 47 ⇄ ♞

Mill Hill 100 Barnet Way, Mill Hill NW7 3AL
☎ 020 8959 2339 Fax 020 8906 0731
Undulating parkland course with tree and shrub lined fairways, water features strongly on holes 2,10 and 17.
18 holes, 6247yds, Par 70, SSS 70, Course record 65.
Club membership 550.

Visitors restricted weekends & bank holidays. Must contact in advance.
Societies must contact in advance.
Green Fees not confirmed.
Prof David Beal
Designer J F Abercrombie/H S Colt
Facilities ⊗ 🏌 by prior arrangement
🏌 🍴 ♀ 🏠 🚩 ♂
Location On A1 S bound carriageway

Hotel ★★★ 72% Edgwarebury Hotel, Barnet Ln, ELSTREE ☎ 020 8953 8227 47 ⇄ ♞

SE9 ELTHAM

Eltham Warren Bexley Rd, Eltham SE9 2PE
☎ 020 8850 4477 & 8850 1166
Parkland course with narrow fairways and small greens. The course is bounded by the A210 on one side and Eltham Park on the other.
9 holes, 5840yds, Par 69, SSS 68, Course record 66.
Club membership 440.
Visitors may not play at weekends. Must contact in advance and have a handicap certificate.
Societies Thu only. Must book in advance. Deposit required.
Green Fees £25 per day.
Prof Gary Brett
Designer James Braid
Facilities ⊗ 🏌 🍴 ♀ 🏠 ♂
& Leisure snooker.
Location 0.5m from Eltham station on A210

Hotel ★★★ 70% Bromley Court Hotel, Bromley Hill, BROMLEY ☎ 020 8464 5011 115 ⇄ ♞

Royal Blackheath Court Rd SE9 5AF
☎ 020 8850 1795 Fax 020 8859 0150
A pleasant, parkland course of great character as befits the antiquity of the Club; the clubhouse dates from the 17th century. Many great trees survive and there are two ponds. The 18th requires a pitch to the green over a thick clipped hedge, which also crosses the front of the 1st tee.
18 holes, 6219yds, Par 70, SSS 70.
Club membership 720.
Visitors must contact in advance but may play mid-week only, handicap certificate is required.
Societies must apply in writing.
Green Fees £45 per day; £35 per round.
Cards 💳 💳 💳 💳
Prof Ian McGregor
Designer James Braid
Facilities ⊗ 🏌 🏌 🍴 ♀ 🏠 🏠 🚩 🏌 🚜 ♂
Location From M25 junct 3 take A20 towards London. Turn right at 2nd traffic lights to club 500yds on right

Hotel ★★★ 70% Bromley Court Hotel, Bromley Hill, BROMLEY
☎ 020 8464 5011 115 ⇄ ♞

SE18 WOOLWICH

Shooters Hill Eaglesfield Rd, Shooters Hill SE18 3DA
☎ 020 8854 6368 Fax 020 8854 0469
Hilly and wooded parkland course with good view and natural hazards.
18 holes, 5721 yds, Par 69, SSS 68, Course record 63.
Club membership 900.
Visitors must have handicap certificate and be a member of a recognised golf club but may not play at weekends, unless with member.
Societies Tue & Thu only, by arrangement.
Green Fees £27 per day; £22 per round.

▶

Prof	David Brotherton
Designer	Willie Park
Facilities	⊗ �ⅢⅢ ☇ ♘ ♟ ⚘ ☎ ✎
Location	Shooters Hill Rd from Blackheath

Hotel ★★★ 65% Posthouse Bexley, Black Prince
Interchange, Southwold Rd, BEXLEY
☎ 0870 400 9006 105 ⇥ ☏

SE21 DULWICH

Dulwich & Sydenham Hill Grange Ln,
College Rd SE21 7LH
☎ 020 8693 3961 & 8693 8491 Fax 020 8693 2481
Parkland course overlooking London. Hilly with narrow
fairways.
18 holes, 6008yds, Par 69, SSS 69, Course record 63.
Club membership 850.

Visitors	must contact in advance and have a handicap certificate. May not play weekends or bank holidays.
Societies	must telephone in advance & confirm in writing.
Green Fees	£35 per day; £25 per round.
Prof	David Baillie
Designer	H Colt
Facilities	⊗ ♘ ♟ ☇ ♟ ☎ ♞ ⚘ ✎
Hotel	★★★ 70% Bromley Court Hotel, Bromley Hill, BROMLEY ☎ 020 8464 5011 115 ⇥ ☏

SE22 EAST DULWICH

Aquarius Marmora Rd, Honor Oak, Off Forest Hill Rd
SE22 0RY ☎ 020 8693 1626
Course laid-out on two levels around and over covered
reservoir; hazards include vents and bollards.
9 holes, 5246yds, Par 66, SSS 66, Course record 66.
Club membership 350.

Visitors	must be accompanied by member and have a handicap certificate.
Green Fees	not confirmed.
Prof	Frederick Private
Facilities	♘ ♟ ☇ ♟ ☎
Hotel	★★★ 70% Bromley Court Hotel, Bromley Hill, BROMLEY ☎ 020 8464 5011 115 ⇥ ☏

SE28 WOOLWICH

Riverside Summerton Way, Thamesmead SE28 8PP
☎ 020 8310 7975
A delightful undulating course with a mix of mature trees,
new trees and water hazards. The 4th hole is a challenging
515yards down a narrow fairway.
9 holes, 5462yds, Par 70, SSS 66.
Club membership 150.

Visitors	no restrictions.
Societies	book by telephone or in writing.
Green Fees	not confirmed.
Cards	⚌ 🆎 ☰☰☰ ⚏ 🆐
Prof	Mark Nicholls
Designer	Heffernan
Facilities	⊗ ⅢⅢ ♟ ☇ ♟ ☎ ♞ ✎
Location	Off A2 near Woolwich ferry
Hotel	★★ 64% Bardon Lodge Hotel, 15-17 Stratheden Rd, LONDON ☎ 020 8853 7000 32 ⇥ ☏

SW15 PUTNEY

Richmond Park Roehampton Gate, Priory Ln SW15 5JR
☎ 020 8876 1795 Fax 020 8878 1354
Two public parkland courses.
Princes Course: 18 holes, 5868yds, Par 69, SSS 68,
Course record 64.
Dukes Course: 18 holes, 6036yds, Par 69, SSS 68.

Visitors	must contact in advance or pay and play.
Societies	must contact in advance.
Green Fees	not confirmed.
Cards	⚌ ▦ ☰☰☰ ⚏ 🆐
Prof	Stuart Hill & David Bown
Designer	Fred Hawtree
Facilities	☇ ☎ ♞ ♟ ☎ ✎ ☏
Location	Inside Richmond Park Roehampton gate
Hotel	★★★ 69% Richmond Hill, Richmond Hill, RICHMOND UPON THAMES ☎ 020 8940 2247 & 940 5466 Fax 020 8940 5424 138 ⇥ ☏

SW18 WANDSORTH

Central London Golf Centre Burntwood Ln, Wandsworth
SW17 0AT ☎ 020 8871 2468 Fax 020 8874 7447
Attractive flat parkland course in the middle of London. The
longest drive is the 430 yard 3rd to one of the course's
superb greens. Well placed bunkers trap the careless shot and
the course rewards the accurate player.
9 holes, 2277yds, Par 62, SSS 62.
Club membership 200.

Visitors	must book tee-times for weekends.
Societies	telephone or write to the manager.
Green Fees	£14 for 18 holes, £8 for 9 holes (£17/£10 weeknds).
Cards	⚌ ☰☰☰ ⚏ 🆐
Prof	Jeremy Robson
Designer	Patrick Tallock
Facilities	⊗ ♘ ♟ ☇ ♟ ☎ ♞ ✎ ☏
& Leisure	putting green, practice area.
Location	Between Garatt Lane and Trinity Road
Hotel	★★★★ 77% Cannizaro House, West Side, Wimbledon Common, LONDON ☎ 020 8879 1464 45 ⇥ ☏

SW19 WIMBLEDON

Royal Wimbledon 29 Camp Rd SW19 4UW
☎ 020 8946 2125 Fax 020 8944 8652
A club steeped in the history of the game, it is also of
great age, dating back to 1865. Of sand and heather like
so many of the Surrey courses its 12th hole (par 4) is
rated as the best on the course.
18 holes, 6300yds, Par 70, SSS 70, Course record 66.
Club membership 1050.

Visitors	must be guests of current club member or contact club in advance, weekdays only. Maximum handicap 18 and must be member of recognised club.
Societies	welcome Wed-Thu. Must apply in writing.
Green Fees	£55 per round.
Prof	Hugh Boyle
Designer	H Colt

▶

Facilities	⊗ by prior arrangement 🖢 🍽 ⅌ ☂
	🏠 ⛳
Hotel	★★★★ 77% Cannizaro House, West Side,
	Wimbledon Common, LONDON
	☎ 020 8879 1464 45 ⇆ ℞

Wimbledon Common 19 Camp Rd SW19 4UW
☎ 020 8946 0294 (Pro shop) 8946 7571 (Sec)
Fax 020 8947 8697
Quick-drying course on Wimbledon Common. Well wooded, with tight fairways, challenging short holes but no bunkers.The course is also played over by London Scottish Golf Club. All players must wear plain red upper garments.
18 holes, 5438yds, Par 68, SSS 66, Course record 63.
Club membership 265.
Visitors   with member only at weekends.
Societies   must telephone in advance, confirm in writing. £25 deposit.
Green Fees £22 per day; £15 per round (£15/£10 Mon).
Prof   J S Jukes
Designer   Tom & Willie Dunn
Facilities   ⊗ ⅲ 🖢 🍽 ⅌ ☂ 🏠 ⛳
& Leisure   snooker room..
Location   0.5m N of Wimbledon Village

Hotel   ★★★★ 77% Cannizaro House, West Side,
                    Wimbledon Common, LONDON
                    ☎ 020 8879 1464 45 ⇆ ℞

Wimbledon Park Home Park Rd, Wimbledon SW19 7HR
☎ 020 8946 1250 Fax 020 8944 8688
Easy walking on parkland course. Sheltered lake provides hazard on 3 holes.
18 holes, 5465yds, Par 66, SSS 66.
Club membership 700.
Visitors   restricted weekends & bank holidays. Must contact in advance and have handicap certificate or letter of introduction.
Societies   must apply in writing.
Green Fees not confirmed.
Prof   Dean Wingrove
Designer   Willie Park Jnr
Facilities   ⊗ ⅲ 🖢 🍽 ⅌ ☂ 🏠 ⛳
Location   400 yds from Wimbledon Park Station

Hotel   ★★★ 69% Richmond Hill, Richmond Hill,
                    RICHMOND UPON THAMES
                    ☎ 020 8940 2247 & 940 5466
                    Fax 020 8940 5424 138 ⇆ ℞

W7 HANWELL

Brent Valley 138 Church Rd, Hanwell W7 3BE
☎ 020 8567 1287
Municipal parkland course with easy walking. The River Brent winds through the course.
18 holes, 5426yds, Par 67, SSS 66.
Club membership 350.
Visitors   no restrictions.
Societies   one month's notice required.
Green Fees not confirmed.
Cards   💳 💳 💳 💳 🔲
Prof   Peter Bryant
Facilities   ⊗ 🖢 🍽 ⅌ ☂ 🏠 ⛳
Hotel   ★★★ 65% Master Robert Hotel, Great West
                    Rd, HOUNSLOW ☎ 020 8570 6261 94 ⇆ ℞

BEBINGTON   Map 07 SJ38

Brackenwood Brackenwood Golf Course,
Bracken Ln CH63 2LY ☎ 0151 608 3093
Municipal parkland course with easy walking, a very testing but fair course in a fine rural setting, usually in very good condition.
18 holes, 6285yds, Par 70, SSS 70, Course record 66.
Club membership 320.
Visitors   must book for weekends one week in advance.
Societies   must telephone in advance.
Green Fees £7.50.
Prof   Ken Lamb
Facilities   🖢 🍽 🏠 ⛳
Location   0.75m N of M53 junc 4 on B5151

Hotel   ★★★ 70% Thornton Hall Hotel, Neston Rd,
                    THORNTON HOUGH
                    ☎ 0151 336 3938 5 ⇆ ℞ Annexe 58 ⇆ ℞

BIRKENHEAD   Map 07 SJ38

Arrowe Park Woodchurch L49 5LW
☎ 0151 677 1527
Pleasant municipal parkland course.
18 holes, 6435yds, Par 72, SSS 71, Course record 66.
Club membership 220.
Visitors   no restrictions, Booking at weekends 1wk in advance.
Societies   must telephone in advance.
Green Fees not confirmed.
Prof   Colin Disbury
Facilities   ⊗ ⅲ 🖢 🍽 ⅌ 🏠 ⛳
& Leisure   tennis courts, pitch & putt.
Location   1m from M53 junc 3 on A551

Hotel   ★★★ 69% Bowler Hat Hotel, 2 Talbot Rd,
                    Prenton, BIRKENHEAD
                    ☎ 0151 652 4931 32 ⇆ ℞

Prenton Golf Links Rd, Prenton CH42 8LW
☎ 0151 608 1053 Fax 0151 609 1580
Parkland course with easy walking and views of the Welsh Hills.
18 holes, 6429yds, Par 71, SSS 71.
Club membership 610.
Visitors   no restrictions.
Societies   must telephone in advance and confirm in writing.
Green Fees £30 per day (£35 weekends & bank holidays).
Prof   Robin Thompson
Designer   James Braid
Facilities   ⊗ ⅲ 🖢 🍽 ⅌ ☂ 🏠 ⛳
Location   M53 junct 3 off A552 towards Birkenhead

Hotel   ★★ 65% Riverhill Hotel, Talbot Rd, Prenton,
                    BIRKENHEAD ☎ 0151 653 3773 14 ⇆ ℞

Wirral Ladies 93 Bidston Rd, Oxton CH43 6TS
☎ 0151 652 1255 Fax 0151 653 4323
Heathland course with heather and birch.
18 holes, 4948yds, Par 69, SSS 69.
Club membership 430.

▶

Visitors	may not play before 11am weekends or over Christmas and Easter holidays.
Societies	must telephone in advance. Weekdays only.
Green Fees	£25.50 per round.
Prof	Angus Law
Facilities	⊗ 🔥 🍴 ♀ 🏌 🏠 ✓
Location	W side of town centre on B5151
Hotel	★★★ 69% Bowler Hat Hotel, 2 Talbot Rd, Prenton, BIRKENHEAD ☎ 0151 652 4931 32 🛏 ♠

BLUNDELLSANDS   Map 07 SJ39

West Lancashire Hall Rd West L23 8SZ
☎ 0151 924 1076 Fax 0151 931 4448
Challenging, traditional links with sandy subsoil overlooking the Mersey Estuary. The course provides excellent golf throughout the year. The four short holes are very fine.
18 holes, 6763yds, Par 72, SSS 73, Course record 66.
Club membership 650.

Visitors	must have a handicap certificate. May not play before 9.30am Mon-Fri and on competition days and weekends only after 3.30pm.
Societies	must contact in advance.
Green Fees	£55 per day; £45 per round (£60 per 18 holes weekends).
Prof	Tim Hastings
Designer	C K Cotton
Facilities	⊗ 🏛 🔥 🍴 ♀ 🏌 🏠 ✓
Location	N side of village
Hotel	★★★ 64% The Blundellsands Hotel, Blundellsands Rd West, BLUNDELLSANDS ☎ 0151 924 6515 30 🛏 ♠

BOOTLE   Map 07 SJ39

Bootle 2 Dunnings Bridge Rd L30 2PP
☎ 0151 928 6196
Municipal seaside course, with prevailing north-westerly wind. Testing holes: 5th (200 yds) par 3; 7th (415 yds) par 4.
18 holes, 6362yds, Par 70, SSS 70, Course record 64.
Club membership 380.

Visitors	must contact Golf Shop on 0151 928 1371 not between 9-9.45am Sat and 7.45-12 Sun.
Societies	must apply in writing.
Green Fees	not confirmed.
Prof	Alan Bradshaw
Facilities	⊗ 🏛 🔥 🍴 ♀ 🍸 ✓
Location	2m NE on A5036
Hotel	★★★ 64% The Blundellsands Hotel, Blundellsands Rd West, BLUNDELLSANDS ☎ 0151 924 6515 30 🛏 ♠

BROMBOROUGH   Map 07 SJ38

Bromborough Raby Hall Rd L63 0NW
☎ 0151 334 2155 Fax 0151 334 0303
Parkland course.
18 holes, 6650yds, Par 72, SSS 73, Course record 67.
Club membership 800.

Visitors	are advised to contact professional on 0151 334 4499 in advance.
Societies	normal society day Wed ; must apply in advance.
Green Fees	not confirmed.
Prof	Geoff Berry
Designer	J Hassall
Facilities	⊗ 🏛 🔥 🍴 ♀ 🏌 🏠 🍸 ✓
Location	0.5m W of Station
Hotel	L Travel Inn, High St, Bromborough Cross, BROMBOROUGH ☎ 0151 334 2917 31 🛏 ♠

CALDY   Map 07 SJ28

Caldy Links Hey Rd L48 1NB
☎ 0151 625 5660 Fax 0151 6257394
A parkland course situated on the estuary of the River Dee with many of the fairways running parallel to the river. Of Championship length, the course offers excellent golf all year, but is subject to variable winds that noticeably alter the day to day playing of each hole. There are excellent views of North Wales and Snowdonia.
18 holes, 6668yds, Par 72, SSS 73, Course record 68.
Club membership 800.

Visitors	may play on weekdays only by prior arrangement.
Societies	must telephone in advance.
Green Fees	£42 per day, £38 per round after 2pm.
Cards	💳 💳
Prof	K Jones
Designer	J Braid
Facilities	⊗ 🏛 🔥 🍴 ♀ 🏌 🏠 🍸 ⛳ ✓
Location	SE side of village, from Caldy rdbt on A540 follow signs to Caldy and golf club
Hotel	★★★ 70% Thornton Hall Hotel, Neston Rd, THORNTON HOUGH ☎ 0151 336 3938 5 🛏 ♠ Annexe 58 🛏 ♠

EASTHAM   Map 07 SJ38

Eastham Lodge 117 Ferry Rd CH62 0AP
☎ 0151 327 3003 Fax 0151 327 3003
A parkland course with many mature trees, recently upgraded to 18 holes.
18 holes, 5706yds, Par 68, SSS 68.
Club membership 800.

Visitors	advisable to telephone in advance to check availability, tel 0151 327 3008 professionals shop, start times available up to 2 weeks in advance, with member only at weekends.
Societies	welcome Tue. Must apply in writing.
Green Fees	£22 per day/round.
Prof	R Boobyer
Designer	Hawtree/D Hemstock
Facilities	⊗ 🏛 🔥 🍴 ♀ 🏌 🏠 ✓
Location	1.5m N
Hotel	L Travel Inn, High St, Bromborough Cross, BROMBOROUGH ☎ 0151 334 2917 31 🛏 ♠

FORMBY   Map 07 SD30

Formby Golf Rd L37 1LQ
☎ 01704 872164 Fax 01704 833028
Championship seaside links through sandhills and partly
through pine trees. Partly sheltered from the wind by
high dunes it features firm, springy turf, fast seaside
greens and natural sandy bunkers. Well drained it plays
well throughout the year.
18 holes, 6701yds, Par 72, SSS 72, Course record 65.
Club membership 700.

Visitors	must contact in advance, very limited on Sat & Wed.
Societies	must contact well in advance.
Green Fees	£60 per day/round.
Cards	🔲 VISA
Prof	Gary Butler
Designer	Park/Colt
Facilities	⊗ ⊪ ⊾ ☕ ♀ 🏌 🖾 🏐 🛒 ∂
Location	N side of town
Hotel	★★★ 64% The Blundellsands Hotel, Blundellsands Rd West, BLUNDELLSANDS ☎ 0151 924 6515 30 ⇥ 🐾

Formby Ladies Golf Rd L37 1YH
☎ 01704 873493 Fax 01704 873493
Seaside links - one of the few independent ladies clubs in the
country. The course has contrasting hard-hitting holes in flat
country and tricky holes in sandhills and woods.
18 holes, 5374yds, Par 71, SSS 71, Course record 60.
Club membership 570.

Visitors	must contact in advance and may not play Thu or 11am Sat & Sun.
Societies	must apply in advance. Handicap certificate required.
Green Fees	£30 per day (£35 weekends).
Prof	Gary Butler
Facilities	⊗ ⊾ ☕ ♀ 🏌 🖾 ∂
Location	N side of town
Hotel	★★★ 64% The Blundellsands Hotel, Blundellsands Rd West, BLUNDELLSANDS ☎ 0151 924 6515 30 ⇥ 🐾

HESWALL   Map 07 SJ28

Heswall Cottage Ln CH60 8PB
☎ 0151 342 1237 Fax 0151 342 1237
A pleasant parkland course in soft undulating country
over-looking the estuary of the River Dee. There are
excellent views of the Welsh hills and coastline, and a
good test of golf. The clubhouse is modern and well-
appointed with good facilities.
18 holes, 6492yds, Par 72, SSS 72, Course record 62.
Club membership 940.

Visitors	must contact in advance.
Societies	must apply in advance.
Green Fees	£35 per day (£40 weekends).
Prof	Alan Thompson
Facilities	⊗ ⊪ ⊾ ☕ ♀ 🏌 🖾 ∂
Location	1m S off A540

Hotel	★★★ 70% Thornton Hall Hotel, Neston Rd, THORNTON HOUGH ☎ 0151 336 3938 5 ⇥ 🐾 Annexe 58 ⇥ 🐾

HOYLAKE   Map 07 SJ28

Hoylake Carr Ln, Municipal Links CH47 4BG
☎ 0151 632 2956
Flat, generally windy semi-links course. Tricky fairways,
with some very deep bunkers.
18 holes, 6313yds, Par 70, SSS 70, Course record 67.
Club membership 303.

Visitors	tee times booked with professional, weekend bookings one week in advance
Societies	must telephone 0151 632 4883 club steward or 0151 632 2956 club professional.
Green Fees	£7.50 per round.
Cards	🔲 ■ 🔲 🔲
Prof	Simon Hooton
Designer	James Braid
Facilities	⊗ ⊪ ⊾ ☕ ♀ 🏌 🖾 🏐 🛒 ∂
Location	SW side of town off A540
Hotel	★★★ 65% Leasowe Castle Hotel, Leasowe Rd, MORETON ☎ 0151 606 9191 47 ⇥ 🐾

Royal Liverpool Meols Dr CH47 4AL
☎ 0151 632 3101 & 632 3102 Fax 0151 632 6737
A world famous, windswept seaside links course, venue
for ten Open Championships and 17 Amateur
Championships.
18 holes, 6219yds, Par 72, SSS 71.
Club membership 650.

Visitors	must contact in advance & have a handicap certificate. Restricted before 9.30am & between 1-2pm. No play Thu am (ladies day). Limited play weekends (pm only).
Societies	must contact in advance.
Green Fees	£45-£65 per round.
Cards	🔲 ■ 🔲 🔲 🔲 🔲
Prof	John Heggarty
Designer	R Chambers/G Morris
Facilities	⊗ ⊪ by prior arrangement ⊾ ☕ ♀ 🏌 🖾 🏐 ∂ 🐾
Location	SW side of town on A540
Hotel	★★★ 65% Leasowe Castle Hotel, Leasowe Rd, MORETON ☎ 0151 606 9191 47 ⇥ 🐾

HUYTON   Map 07 SJ49

Bowring Bowring Park, Roby Rd L36 4HD
☎ 0151 489 1901
Flat parkland course.
18 holes, 5651yds, Par 70.
Club membership 200.

Visitors	no restrictions.
Green Fees	not confirmed.
Facilities	⊾ ☕ 🖾
Location	On A5080 adjacent M62 junc 5
Hotel	★ 62% Rockland Hotel, View Rd, RAINHILL ☎ 0151 426 4603 11rm(9 ⇥ 1 🐾)

Huyton & Prescot Hurst Park, Huyton Ln L36 1UA
☎ 0151 489 3948 Fax 0151 489 0797
An easy walking, parkland course providing excellent golf.
18 holes, 5779yds, Par 68, SSS 68, Course record 65.
Club membership 700.

Visitors	must contact in advance and be arranged with secretary,
Societies	must apply in writing.
Green Fees	not confirmed.
Prof	Gerry Bond
Facilities	⊗ ∭ ⓛ ▆ ♀ ♙ ☕ ⌀
Location	1.5m NE off B5199

Hotel	★ 62% Rockland Hotel, View Rd, RAINHILL ☎ 0151 426 4603 11rm(9 ⇆1 🐾)

LIVERPOOL   Map 07 SJ39

Allerton Park Allerton Manor Golf Estate,
Allerton Rd L18 3JT ☎ 0151 428 1046
Parkland course.
18 holes, 5459yds, Par 67, SSS 67.

Visitors	must book with professional in advance.
Societies	by prior arrangement with professional.
Green Fees	not confirmed.
Prof	Barry Large
Facilities	☕ ⑂ ⌀
Location	5.5m SE of city centre off A562 and B5180

Hotel	★★★ 63% The Royal Hotel, Marine Ter, Waterloo, LIVERPOOL ☎ 0151 928 2332 25 ⇆ 🐾

The Childwall Naylors Rd, Gateacre L27 2YB
☎ 0151 487 0654 Fax 0151 487 0882
Parkland golf is played here over a testing course, where
accuracy from the tee is well-rewarded. The course is
very popular with visiting societies for the clubhouse has
many amenities. Course designed by James Braid.
18 holes, 6425yds, Par 72, SSS 71, Course record 66.
Club membership 650.

Visitors	must contact in advance.
Societies	must apply in writing.
Green Fees	£26 per day (£35 weekends & bank holidays).
Prof	Nigel M Parr
Designer	James Braid
Facilities	⊗ ∭ ⓛ ▆ ♀ ♙ ☕ ⑂ ⌀ ℓ
Location	7m E of city centre off B5178

Hotel	★ 62% Rockland Hotel, View Rd, RAINHILL ☎ 0151 426 4603 11rm (9 ⇆1 🐾)

Kirkby-Liverpool Municipal Ingoe Ln, Kirkby L32 4SS
☎ 0151 546 5435
Flat, easy course.
18 holes, 6704yds, Par 72, SSS 72, Course record 68.
Club membership 150.

Societies	must contact 1 week in advance.
Green Fees	not confirmed.
Prof	Dave Weston
Facilities	⊗ ∭ ⓛ ▆ ♀ ♙ ☕ ⑂ ⌀
Location	7.5m NE of city centre on A506

Hotel	★★★★ 59% Liverpool Moat House Hotel, Paradise St, LIVERPOOL ☎ 0151 471 9988 263 ⇆ 🐾

Lee Park Childwall Valley Rd L27 3YA
☎ 0151 487 3882 Fax 0151 487 3882
Flat parkland course with ponds in places and plenty of trees.
18 holes, 6095yds, Par 72, SSS 69.
Club membership 600.

Visitors	must dress acceptably. Must contact in advance.
Societies	must contact in advance.
Green Fees	not confirmed.
Designer	G Cotton
Facilities	⊗ ∭ ⓛ ▆ ♀ ♙ ⌀
Location	7m E of city centre off B5178

Hotel	★★★★ 59% Liverpool Moat House Hotel, Paradise St, LIVERPOOL ☎ 0151 471 9988 263 ⇆ 🐾

West Derby Yew Tree Ln, West Derby L12 9HQ
☎ 0151 254 1034 Fax 0151 259 0505
A parkland course always in first-class condition, and so
giving easy walking. The fairways are well-wooded.
Care must be taken on the first nine holes to avoid the
brook which guards many of the greens. A modern well-
designed clubhouse with many amenities, overlooks the
course.
18 holes, 6277yds, Par 72, SSS 70, Course record 65.
Club membership 550.

Visitors	may not play before 9.30am. May not play weekends and bank holidays.
Societies	may not play on Sat, Sun & bank holidays; must contact in advance.
Green Fees	£26 per round (£36 weekends).
Prof	Andrew Witherup
Facilities	⊗ ∭ ⓛ ▆ ♀ ♙ ☕ ⑂ ⌀
Location	4.5m E of city centre off A57

Hotel	★★★ 63% The Royal Hotel, Marine Ter, Waterloo, LIVERPOOL ☎ 0151 928 2332 25 ⇆ 🐾

Woolton Speke Rd, Woolton L25 7TZ
☎ 0151 486 2298 Fax 0151 486 1664
Parkland course providing a good round of golf for all
standards.
18 holes, 5717yds, Par 69, SSS 68.
Club membership 700.

Visitors	must contact in advance. Restricted at weekends.
Societies	must contact in advance.
Green Fees	not confirmed.
Prof	Alan Gibson
Facilities	⊗ ∭ ⓛ ▆ ♀ ♙ ☕ 🐾 ⛳
Location	7m SE of city centre off A562

Hotel	★★★ 63% The Royal Hotel, Marine Ter, Waterloo, LIVERPOOL ☎ 0151 928 2332 25 ⇆ 🐾

Where to stay, where to eat?
Visit the AA internet site
www.theaa.co.uk

NEWTON-LE-WILLOWS — Map 07 SJ59

Haydock Park Newton Ln WA12 0HX
☎ 01925 228525 Fax 01925 228525
A well-wooded parkland course, close to the well-known racecourse, and always in excellent condition. The pleasant undulating fairways offer some very interesting golf and the 6th, 9th, 11th and 13th holes are particularly testing. The clubhouse is very comfortable.
18 holes, 6043yds, Par 70, SSS 69, Course record 65.
Club membership 560.
Visitors welcome weekdays except Tue, with member only weekends & bank holidays. Must contact in advance.
Societies must contact in advance.
Green Fees £27 per day/round.
Prof Peter Kenwright
Designer James Braid
Facilities ⊗ 洲 區 ➤ ♀ ♨ 愈 ✔
Location 0.75m NE off A49

Hotel ★★★ 66% Posthouse Haydock, Lodge Ln, HAYDOCK ☎ 0870 400 9039 138 ⇌ 📡

RAINHILL — Map 07 SJ49

Blundells Hill Blundells Ln L35 6NA
☎ 01744 24892 Fax 01744 28861
Parkland course, with free-draining sandy soil, which allows play throughout the winter.
18 holes, 6256yds, Par 71, SSS 70.
Club membership 600.
Visitors may not play off white tees.
Societies telephone for prices and availability.
Green Fees £30 per day (£30-£40 weekends & bank holidays); £25 per round.
Cards 💳
Prof Richard Burbidge
Designer Steve Marnoch
Facilities ⊗ 洲 區 ➤ ♀ ♨ 愈 ➤ ✔ (
Location 3 mins from junct 7 (eastbound M62)

Hotel ★ 62% Rockland Hotel, View Rd, RAINHILL ☎ 0151 426 4603 11rm (9 ⇌1 📡)

Eccleston Park Rainhill Rd L35 4PG
☎ 0151 493 0033 Fax 0151 493 0044
A tough parkland course designed to test all golfing abilities. Strategically placed water features, bunkers and mounding enhance the beauty and difficulty of this manicured course.
18 holes, 6495yds, Par 70.
Club membership 500.
Visitors booking 7 days in advance.
Societies telephone in advance.
Green Fees not confirmed.
Cards 💳
Prof Richard Stockdale
Facilities ⊗ 洲 區 ➤ ♀ ♨ 愈 ✔
Hotel ★ 62% Rockland Hotel, View Rd, RAINHILL ☎ 0151 426 4603 11rm (9 ⇌1 📡)

> Looking for a driving range?
> See the index at the back of the guide

ST HELENS — Map 07 SJ59

Grange Park Prescot Rd WA10 3AD
☎ 01744 26318 Fax 01744 26318
A course of Championship length set in pleasant country surroundings - playing the course it is hard to believe that industrial St Helens lies so close at hand. The course is a fine test of golf and there are many attractive holes liable to challenge all grades. The course has recently undergone a programme of modernisation.
18 holes, 6446yds, Par 72, SSS 71, Course record 65.
Club membership 730.
Visitors welcome except tuesdays, weekends by prior arrangement. Advisable to contact professional in advance (01744 28785)
Societies apply in writing
Green Fees £26 (£33 weekends).
Prof Paul Roberts
Designer James Braid
Facilities ⊗ 洲 區 ➤ ♀ ♨ 愈 ✔
Location 1.5m SW on A58

Hotel ★★ 65% Kirkfield Hotel, 2/4 Church St, NEWTON LE WILLOWS ☎ 01925 228196 15 ⇌ 📡

Houghwood Golf Billinge Hill, Crank Rd, Crank WA11 8RL ☎ 01744 894444 Fax 01744 894754
In a perfect setting Houghwood has magnificent panoramic views over Lancashire plain and Welsh Hills. With large USGA greens this undulating course is a superb test of golf for all abilities.
18 holes, 6202yds, Par 70, SSS 69, Course record 68.
Club membership 700.
Visitors no restrictions but dress code must be adhered to.
Societies telephone enquiries welcome, deposit secures booking.
Green Fees £14.50 per round (£17.50 weekends and bank holidays).
Cards 💳
Prof Paul Dickenson
Designer Neville Pearsons
Facilities ⊗ 洲 區 ➤ ♀ ♨ 愈 ➤ ➤ ✔
& Leisure indoor golf simulator.
Location From M6 junct 23 follow A580 to A571 to Billinge

Hotel ★★★ 66% Posthouse Haydock, Lodge Ln, HAYDOCK ☎ 0870 400 9039 138 ⇌ 📡

Sherdley Park Sherdley Rd WA9 5DE
☎ 01744 813149
Fairly hilly course with ponds in places.
18 holes, 5941yds, Par 70, SSS 69.
Club membership 160.
Visitors no restrictions.
Green Fees not confirmed.
Facilities ♨ 愈 ⊺
Location 2m S off A570

Hotel ★★ 65% Kirkfield Hotel, 2/4 Church St, NEWTON LE WILLOWS ☎ 01925 228196 15 ⇌ 📡

The Royal Birkdale

Southport, *Merseyside* ☎ 01704 567920 Fax 01704 562327 Map 07 SD31

Visitors must apply in advance

Societies must contact in advance and have a handicap certificate. Not Sat, and restricted on Sun

Green Fees contact secretary's office

Facilities ⊗ ⋔ ⓛ ☐ ⓨ ⚒ ☐ ⛨ ✓ Professional (Richard Bradbeer)

Location Waterloo Rd, Birkdale, Southport PR8 2LX (1.75m S of town centre on A565)

Holes/Par/Course record 18 holes, 6726 yds, Par 72, SSS 73, Course record 65

WHERE TO STAY AND EAT NEARBY

Hotels
SOUTHPORT

★★★ ⚜ 68% Royal Clifton, Promenade. ☎ 01704 533771. 106 (100 ⇌ ⛨ 6 ⋒)

★★★ 68% Stutelea Hotel & Leisure Club, Alexandra Rd. ☎ 01704 544220. 20 ⇌ ⋒

★★★ 67% Scarisbrick, Lord St. ☎ 01704 543000. 90 (89 ⇌ ⋒ 1 ⋒)

★★ 68% Balmoral Lodge, 41 Queens Rd. ☎ 01704 544298. 15 ⇌ ⋒

Restaurant
WRIGHTINGTON

⚜ High Moor Inn, Highmoor Ln (jct 27 off M6, take B5239). ☎ 01257 252364

The Royal Birkdale is considered by many to be the ultimate championship venue having hosted every major event in the game including eight Open Championships, two Ryder Cup matches, the Walker Cup, the Curtis Cup and many major amateur events. The Ryder Cup match played here in September 1969 was perhaps the most memorable as for the first time ever a Ryder Cup match was halved. Tony Jacklin's final putt on the 18th green was conceded by Jack Nicklaus to half their game and the match; an unforgettable gesture of sportsmanship.

The club was founded in 1889 by eight golfing enthusiasts who rented a piece of land for a nine hole golf course. In 1897 some 230 acres of sandhills was leased and it is here that the present course stands. The links have been fine-tuned over the years to keep up with developments in equipment, course design and talent, and to provide a severe but fair test. All the greens were re-designed and completely rebuilt between the 1991 and 1998 Open Championships.

Championship Course

185

SOUTHPORT Map 07 SD31

The Hesketh Cockle Dick's Ln, off Cambridge Rd
PR9 9QQ ☎ 01704 536897 Fax 01704 539250
The Hesketh is the oldest of the six clubs in Southport, founded in 1885. Used as a final qualifying course for the Open Championship.
18 holes, 6572yds, Par 72, SSS 72, Course record 67.
Club membership 600.
Visitors	welcome, with handicap certificate, at all time other than Tues am (Ladies) and 12.30-2pm daily. Must contact in advance.
Societies	please contact Martyn G Senior in advance.
Green Fees	£50 per day; £38 per round.
Prof	John Donoghue
Designer	J F Morris
Facilities	⊗ Ⅷℕℙᴉₐ⅌
Location	1m NE of town centre off A565

Hotel ★★★ 68% Stutelea Hotel & Leisure Club, Alexandra Rd, SOUTHPORT ☎ 01704 544220 20 ⇌ ⏴

Hillside Hastings Rd, Hillside PR8 2LU
☎ 01704 567169 Fax 01704 563192
Championship links course with natural hazards open to strong wind.
18 holes, 6850yds, Par 72, SSS 74, Course record 66.
Club membership 700.
Visitors	welcome except Sat, restricted on Sun & Tue (Ladies Day), must contact in advance through secretary.
Societies	must apply to secretary in advance.
Green Fees	£60 per day; £45 per round.
Prof	Brian Seddon
Designer	Hawtree
Facilities	⊗ Ⅷℕℙᴉₐ⅌
Location	3m S of town centre on A565

Hotel ★★★ 68% Royal Clifton Hotel, Promenade, SOUTHPORT ☎ 01704 533771 106 ⇌ ⏴

SOUTHPORT See page 185

Southport & Ainsdale Bradshaws Ln, Ainsdale
PR8 3LG ☎ 01704 578000 Fax 01704 570896
'S and A', as it is known in the North is another of the fine Championship courses for which this part of the country is famed. This Club has staged many important events and offers golf of the highest order.
18 holes, 6603yds, Par 72, SSS 73, Course record 62.
Club membership 815.
Visitors	welcome except Thu, Sat & Sun am & bank holidays. Must contact club in advance & have handicap certificate.
Societies	must apply in advance.
Green Fees	£50 per day; £40 per round (£50 weekends).
Cards	🟦🟦🟦🟦
Prof	M Houghton
Designer	James Braid
Facilities	⊗ Ⅷℕℙᴉₐ⅌
Location	3m S off A565

Hotel ★★★ 68% Royal Clifton Hotel, Promenade, SOUTHPORT ☎ 01704 533771 106 ⇌ ⏴

Southport Municipal Park Rd West PR9 0JR
☎ 01704 535286
Municipal seaside links course. Played over by Southport Municipal, Alt and Park golf clubs.
18 holes, 6400yds, Par 70, SSS 69, Course record 67.
Club membership 750.
Visitors	no restrictions.
Societies	must telephone 6 days in advance.
Green Fees	not confirmed.
Cards	🟦🟦🟦
Prof	Bill Fletcher
Facilities	⊗ ℕℙᴉₐ⅌
Location	N side of town centre off A565

Hotel ★★★ 68% Royal Clifton Hotel, Promenade, SOUTHPORT ☎ 01704 533771 106 ⇌ ⏴

Southport Old Links Moss Ln, Churchtown PR9 7QS
☎ 01704 228207 Fax 01704 505353
Seaside course with tree-lined fairways and easy walking. One of the oldest courses in Southport, Henry Vardon won the 'Leeds Cup' here in 1922.
9 holes, 6244yds, Par 72, SSS 71, Course record 68.
Club membership 450.
Visitors	advisable to contact in advance.
Societies	apply in writing.
Green Fees	not confirmed.
Facilities	⊗ Ⅷℕℙᴉₐ
Location	NW side of town centre off A5267

Hotel ★★ 67% Bold Hotel, 585 Lord St, SOUTHPORT ☎ 01704 532578 23rm (9 ⇌11 ⏴)

WALLASEY Map 07 SJ29

Bidston Bidston Link Rd L44 2HR ☎ 0151 638 3412
Parkland course, with westerly winds.
18 holes, 6140yds, Par 70, SSS 71, Course record 66.
Club membership 650.
Visitors	must contact in advance, restricted weekends.
Societies	must apply in writing.
Green Fees	not confirmed.
Prof	J Law
Facilities	⊗ ℕℙᴉₐ
Location	0.5m W of M53 junc 1 entrance off A551

Hotel ★★★ 65% Leasowe Castle Hotel, Leasowe Rd, MORETON ☎ 0151 606 9191 47 ⇌ ⏴

Leasowe Moreton CH46 3RD
☎ 0151 677 5852 Fax 0151 677 5852
Rather flat, semi-links, seaside course.
18 holes, 6227yds, Par 71, SSS 71.
Club membership 637.
Visitors	telephone professional (0151 678 5460). Handicap certificate required. Not Sat play and not before noon on Sun.
Societies	contact in advance.
Green Fees	£23.50 per day (£30 Sunday).
Cards	🟦🟦🟦🟦
Prof	Andrew Ayres

▶

Designer   John Ball Jnr
Facilities   ⊗ ⅏ ⓛ ⬛ ♀ ⚲ 📠 ⛳ ∅
Location   2m W on A551

Hotel   ★★★ 65% Leasowe Castle Hotel, Leasowe Rd,
         MORETON ☎ 0151 606 9191 47 ⇄ 🐾

Wallasey Bayswater Rd L45 8LA
☎ 0151 691 1024 Fax 0151 638 8988
A well-established sporting links, adjacent to the Irish
Sea, with huge sandhills and many classic holes where
the player's skills are often combined with good fortune.
Large, firm greens and fine views but not for the faint-
hearted.
18 holes, 6607yds, Par 72.
Club membership 605.
Visitors   must contact one month in advance.
Societies   must apply in writing or telephone.
Green Fees   not confirmed.
Cards   🖃
Prof   Mike Adams
Designer   Tom Morris
Facilities   ⊗ ⓛ ⬛ ♀ 📠 ⛳ ∅
Location   N side of town centre off A554

Hotel   ★★ 72% Grove House Hotel, Grove Rd,
         WALLASEY
         ☎ 0151 639 3947 & 0151 630 4558 Fax 01
         51 639 0028 14 ⇄ 🐾

Warren Grove Rd CH45 0JA ☎ 0151 639 8323
Short, undulating links course with first-class greens and
prevailing winds off the sea.
9 holes, 5854yds, Par 72, SSS 68.
Club membership 150.
Visitors   welcome except Sun 7-11am.
Green Fees   £6.40 per 18 holes; £3.20 per 9 holes.
Prof   Steve Konrad
Facilities   📠 ⛳ ∅
Location   N side of town centre off A554

Hotel   ★★★ 65% Leasowe Castle Hotel, Leasowe Rd,
         MORETON ☎ 0151 606 9191 47 ⇄ 🐾

NORFOLK

BARNHAM BROOM   Map 05 TG00

Barnham Broom Hotel, Golf, Conference, Leisure
Honingham Rd NR9 4DD
☎ 01603 759393 hotel 759552 golf shop
Fax 01603 758224
Valley course meanders through the River Yare Valley,
parkland and mature trees. Hill course has wide
fairways, heavily guarded greens and spectacular views.
Valley Course: 18 holes, 6603yds, Par 72, SSS 72.
Hill Course: 18 holes, 6495yds, Par 71, SSS 71.
Club membership 500.
Visitors   must contact in advance.
Societies   must contact in advance.
Green Fees   Hill Course: £20; Valley Course: £25.

AA   **AA**
                    ★ ★ ★

BARNHAM BROOM

GOLF • CONFERENCE • LEISURE

Situated in the river Yare valley the hotel has 52
en-suite bedrooms (fully refurbished April 2000),
two 18 hole golf courses, practice facilities, Flints
Restaurant, Sports Bar & Cafe with 6ft satellite TV
screen, Valley Bar, lounge, fitness centre with
indoor swimming pool, steam room, sauna, spa,
squash & tennis courts, hair & beauty salons,
conference & banqueting facilities and ample free
parking. Barnham Broom is home of the **Peter
Ballingall Golf School**, two, three and four day
residential courses and individual tuition is
available. *VISITORS WELCOME..*

**GOLF AND LEISURE BREAKS,
CORPORATE & SOCIETY DAYS AVAILABLE.**
Host: Richard Bond _ General Manager
For further information and brochure call
01603 759393

*Access: From London and South via A11; from Midlands and North
via A47, 8 miles south-west of Norwich.*

Norwich • Norfolk • NR9 4DD
**Tel: (01603) 759393   Fax: (01603) 758224
email: enquiry@barnhambroomhotel.co.uk
www.barnham-broom.co.uk**

Prof   P Ballingall
Designer   Frank Pennink
Facilities ⊗ ⅏ ⓛ ⬛ ♀ ⚲ 📠 ⛳ 🛒 ⛏ ∅ ∤
& Leisure   hard tennis courts, heated indoor swimming
            pool, squash, sauna, solarium, gymnasium,
            Indoor golf simulator with video analysis,
            workshop for club repairs.
Location   1m N, S of A47

Hotel   ★★★ 70% Barnham Broom Hotel,
         BARNHAM BROOM
         ☎ 01603 759393 52 ⇄ 🐾

BAWBURGH   Map 05 TG10

Bawburgh Glen Lodge, Marlingford Rd NR9 3LU
☎ 01603 740404 Fax 01603 740403
Undulating course, mixture of parkland & heathland.
Excellent 18th hole to finish.
18 holes, 5959yds, Par 70, SSS 69.
Club membership 700.
Visitors   must contact in advance, limited play at
             weekends.
Societies   must contact in advance.
Green Fees   £20 per round (£25 weekends).
Cards   ⚏ ▦ ▦
Prof   Chris Potter
Designer   Shaun Manser
Facilities   ⊗ ⓛ ⬛ ♀ ⚲ 📠 🛒 ⛏ ∅ ∤
Location   S of Royal Norfolk Showground, on A47

▶

187

Hotel   ★★★ 72% Park Farm Hotel, HETHERSETT
☎ 01603 810264 6 ⇄ ♟ Annexe 30 ⇄ ♟

BRANCASTER   Map 09 TF74

Royal West Norfolk PE31 8AX
☎ 01485 210223 Fax 01485 210087
If you want to see what golf courses were like years ago, then go to the Royal West Norfolk where tradition exudes from both clubhouse and course. Close by the sea, the links are laid out in the grand manner and are characterised by sleepered greens, superb cross-bunkering and salt marshes.
18 holes, 6428yds, Par 71, SSS 71, Course record 66.
Club membership 740.
Visitors	must contact well in advance. Restrictions at weekends and in Aug.
Societies	must contact Secretary in advance.
Green Fees	£50 per day (£60 weekends). Reduced winter rate.
Cards	⬜ 💳
Prof	S Rayner
Designer	Holcombe-Ingleby
Facilities	⊗ ⅲ ⅼ ⅼ 💺 ♀ △ 🏠 🛒 ✐
Location	7m E of Hunstanton. In Brancaster village turn N at the beach/Broad Lane junct with A149 for 1m

Hotel   ★★ 72% Titchwell Manor Hotel,
TITCHWELL ☎ 01485 210221
11rm(7 ⇄ ♟) Annexe 4 ⇄ ♟

CROMER   Map 09 TG24

Royal Cromer 145 Overstrand Rd NR27 0JH
☎ 01263 512884 Fax 01263 512884
Seaside course set out on cliff edge, hilly and subject to wind. Challenging upland course with spectacular views out to sea and overlooking town. Strong sea breezes affect the clifftop holes, the most famous being the 14th (the Lighthouse).
18 holes, 6508yds, Par 72, SSS 72, Course record 67.
Club membership 650.
Visitors	must contact in advance & have handicap certificate. Restricted at weekends.
Societies	must contact in advance.
Green Fees	£35 per day (£40 weekends & bank holidays). Winter £25 (£30 weekends & bank holidays).
Prof	Robin Page
Designer	J H Taylor
Facilities	⊗ ⅲ ⅼ ⅼ 💺 ♀ △ 🏠 🛒 ✐
Location	1m E on B1159

Hotel   ★★ 66% Red Lion, Brook St, CROMER
☎ 01263 514964 12 ⇄ ♟

DENVER   Map 05 TF60

Ryston Park PE38 0HH
☎ 01366 382133 Fax 01366 383834
Parkland course.
9 holes, 6310yds, Par 70, SSS 70, Course record 66.
Club membership 330.

Visitors	must contact in advance. May not play weekends or bank holidays.
Societies	must apply in writing.
Green Fees	not confirmed.
Designer	James Braid
Facilities	⊗ ⅲ ⅼ ⅼ 💺 ♀ △ 🏠 ✐
Location	0.5m S on A10

Hotel   ★★ 69% Castle Hotel, High St, DOWNHAM
MARKET ☎ 01366 384311 12 ⇄ ♟

DEREHAM   Map 09 TF91

Dereham Quebec Rd NR19 2DS
☎ 01362 695900 & 695904 Fax 01362 695904
Parkland course.
9 holes, 6225yds, Par 71, SSS 70, Course record 64.
Club membership 400.
Visitors	must contact in advance and have a handicap certificate; must play with member at weekends.
Societies	must apply in writing.
Green Fees	not confirmed.
Prof	Robert Curtis
Facilities	⊗ ⅲ ⅼ ⅼ ♀ △ 🏠 ✐
Location	N side of town centre off B1110

Hotel   ★★★ 70% Barnham Broom Hotel,
BARNHAM BROOM
☎ 01603 759393 52 ⇄ ♟

The Norfolk Golf & Country Club Hingham Rd,
Reymerston NR9 4QQ
☎ 01362 850297 Fax 01362 850614
The course meanders through more than 200 acres of rolling Norfolk countryside, including ancient ditches, hedging and woodland. Large greens are built to USGA specification.
18 holes, 6609yds, Par 72, SSS 72, Course record 69.
Club membership 400.
Visitors	contact Golf reception for advance bookings.
Societies	apply in writing to the Society Organiser.
Green Fees	£20 per round (£24 weekends).
Cards	⬜ ▬ 💳 💳 🉐
Prof	Tony Varney
Facilities	⊗ ⅲ ⅼ ⅼ 💺 ♀ △ 🏠 🛒 ⛳ 🛒 ✐ ℓ
& Leisure	heated indoor swimming pool, sauna, solarium, gymnasium, pitch & putt.
Location	12m W of Norwich, off B1135

Hotel   ★★★ 70% Barnham Broom Hotel,
BARNHAM BROOM
☎ 01603 759393 52 ⇄ ♟

DISS   Map 05 TM18

Diss Stuston IP22 3JB ☎ 01379 641025 Fax 01379 641025
Commonland course with natural hazards.
18 holes, 6238yds, Par 73, SSS 70.
Club membership 750.
Visitors	must contact in advance but may not play weekends & bank holidays.
Societies	by arrangement.
Green Fees	not confirmed.
Prof	N J Taylor
Facilities	⊗ ⅲ ⅼ ⅼ 💺 ♀ △ 🏠 🛒 ⛳ ✐
Location	1.5m SE on B1118

Hotel ★★★ 70% Cornwallis Arms, BROME
☎ 01379 870326 11 ⇆ 🏠 Annexe 5 ⇆ 🏠

FAKENHAM   Map 09 TF92

Fakenham Gallow Sports Centre, The Race Course
N21 7NY ☎ 01328 863534
A well-wooded 9-hole course.
9 holes, 6174yds, Par 71, SSS 70, Course record 65.
Club membership 460.

Visitors	any time with member, restricted until after noon weekends and bank holidays.
Societies	apply in writing or telephone.
Green Fees	not confirmed.
Prof	Colin Williams
Facilities	⊗ 🕳 ♿ 🍽 ♀ ♣ 📷 🏌
& Leisure	hard tennis courts, squash.

Hotel ★★ 66% Crown Hotel, Market Place,
FAKENHAM ☎ 01328 851418 12 ⇆ 🏠

GORLESTON-ON-SEA   Map 05 TG50

Gorleston Warren Rd NR31 6JT
☎ 01493 661911 & 662103 Fax 01493 661911
Cliff top course, the most easterly in the British Isles.
18 holes, 6391yds, Par 71, SSS 71, Course record 68.
Club membership 860.

Visitors	advisable to contact in advance, must have handicap. Dress code in operation.
Societies	must apply in writing.
Green Fees	£21 per day (£25 weekends).
Prof	Nick Brown
Designer	J H Taylor
Facilities	⊗ 🕳 ♿ 🍽 ♀ ♣ 📷 ⛳ 🏌
Location	S side of town centre

Hotel ★★★ 73% Cliff Hotel, Gorleston, GREAT
YARMOUTH ☎ 01493 662179 39 ⇆ 🏠

GREAT YARMOUTH   Map 05 TG50

Caldecott Hall Golf & Leisure Caldecott Hall, Beccles Rd,
Fritton NR31 9EY ☎ 01493 488488 Fax 01493 488561
Facilities at Caldecott Hall include an 18-hole course with
testing dog-leg fairways, a short par 3 9-hole course, a
floodlit driving range, and good practising areas.
Club membership 500.

Societies	arrangements in advance.
Prof	Mark Snazell
Facilities	⊗ 🕳 ♿ 🍽 ♀ ♣ 📷 ⛳ 🚣 ⛵ 🏌 ⛳
& Leisure	equestrian centre with tuition and 400 acres of woodland hacking.

Location On the A143 Beccles/Gt Yarmouth road at
Fritton

Hotel ★★★ 73% Cliff Hotel, Gorleston, GREAT
YARMOUTH ☎ 01493 662179 39 ⇆ 🏠

Great Yarmouth & Caister Beach House, Caister-on-
Sea NR30 5TD ☎ 01493 728699
This great old club, which celebrated its centenary in
1982, has played its part in the development of the game.
It is a fine old-fashioned links where not many golfers
have bettered the SSS in competitions. The 468-yard 8th
(par 4), is a testing hole and the 7th is an extremely fine
short hole. A feature of the course is a number of
sleepered bunkers, a line of 4 bisecting the 4th.
18 holes, 6330yds, Par 70, SSS 70, Course record 66.
Club membership 720.

Visitors	must contact in advance. Restricted weekends.
Societies	must apply in writing or telephone.
Green Fees	£27 per day (£30 weekends & bank holidays).
Prof	James Hill
Designer	H Colt
Facilities	⊗ 🕳 ♿ 🍽 ♀ ♣ 📷 🏌
Location	0.5m N off A149

Hotel ★★★ 66% Imperial Hotel, North Dr,
GREAT YARMOUTH
☎ 01493 851113 39 ⇆ 🏠

HUNSTANTON   Map 09 TF64

Hunstanton Golf Course Rd PE36 6JQ
☎ 01485 532811 Fax 01485 532319
A championship links course set among some of the
most natural golfing country in East Anglia. Keep out of
the numerous bunkers and master the fast greens to play
to your handicap - then you only have the wind to
contend with! Good playing conditions all year round.
18 holes, 6735yds, Par 72, SSS 72, Course record 65.
Club membership 675.

Visitors	must contact in advance and be a club member with current handicap certificate. Restricted at weekends & may not play bank holiday weekends. Play in two ball format ie singles or foursomes.
Societies	apply in advance.
Green Fees	£35-£50 per day (£45-£60 weekends).
Prof	John Carter
Designer	James Braid
Facilities	⊗ 🕳 by prior arrangement ♿ 🍽 ♀ ♣ 📷 ⛳ 🚣 🏌
Location	Off A149 in Old Hunstanton Village signposted

Hotel ★★ 72% Caley Hall Motel, Old
Hunstanton Rd, HUNSTANTON
☎ 01485 533486 Annexe 33 ⇆

KING'S LYNN   Map 09 TF62

Eagles 39 School Rd, Tilney All Saints PE34 4RS
☎ 01553 827147 Fax 01553 829777
Parkland course with plenty of water hazards and bunkers.
Also Par-3 course and floodlit, covered driving range. ▶

9 holes, 4284yds, Par 64, SSS 61, Course record 64.
Club membership 200.
Visitors   no restrictions.
Societies   must apply in writing.
Green Fees   £14.50 per 18 holes, £7.25 per 9 holes
                   (£16.50/£8.25 weekends & bank holidays).
Cards   ⊞ ▦ ▦ ▦ ▦
Prof   Nigel Pickerell
Designer   D W Horn
Facilities   ⊗ ⬥ ⬥ ▼ ♀ ⏛ 🛍 ⚲ ⚑
& Leisure   hard tennis courts, Par 3 course.
Location   Off A47 at roundabout to Tilney All Saints
                   between Kings Lynn and Wisbech

Hotel   ★★★ 64% The Duke's Head, Tuesday Market
                   Place, KING'S LYNN
                   ☎ 01553 774996 71 ⇄ 🏮

King's Lynn Castle Rising PE31 6BD ☎ 01553 631654
Challenging, wooded parkland course.
18 holes, 6609yds, Par 72, SSS 72.
Club membership 1000.
Visitors   must contact in advance.
Societies   must contact in advance.
Green Fees   not confirmed.
Prof   Chris Hanlon
Designer   Thomas & Allis
Facilities   ⊗ ⫿ ⬥ ▼ ♀ ⏛ 🛍 ⚑ ⚲
Location   4m NE off A149

Hotel   ★★★ 64% The Duke's Head, Tuesday Market
                   Place, KING'S LYNN
                   ☎ 01553 774996 71 ⇄ 🏮

MATTISHALL   Map 09 TG01

Mattishall South Green NR20 3JZ ☎ 01362 850111
Mattishall has the distinction of having the longest hole in
Norfolk at a very demanding 625yds.
9 holes, 3300mtrs, Par 72, SSS 69.
Club membership 120.
Visitors   no restrictions.
Societies   welcome.
Green Fees   £8 per 9 holes; £12 per 18 holes.
Designer   B Todd
Facilities   ▼ ♀ ⏛ ⚑ ⚲
Location   0.75m S of Mattishall Church

Hotel   ★★★ 70% Barnham Broom Hotel,
                   BARNHAM BROOM ☎ 01603 759393
                   52 ⇄ 🏮

MIDDLETON   Map 09 TF61

Middleton Hall Hall Orchards PE32 1RH
☎ 01553 841800 Fax 01553 841800
The setting is one of natural undulations, and mature
specimen trees, offering a most attractive environment for the
game of golf. The architecturally designed course provides a
challenge for the competent golfer, there is also a covered
floodlit driving range and practice putting green.
18 holes, 6004yds, Par 71, SSS 69.
Club membership 600.
Visitors   no restrictions.
Societies   must contact in advance.
Green Fees   £28 per day; £22 per round (£34/£28 weekends).
Cards   ▦ ▦ ▦ ▦ ▦ ▦ ▦

Prof   David Edwards
Designer   D Scott
Facilities   ⊗ ⫿ ⬥ ▼ ♀ ⏛ 🛍 ⚲ ⚑
Location   4m from King's Lynn off A47

Hotel   ★★★ 66% Butterfly Hotel, Beveridge Way,
                   Hardwick Narrows, KING'S LYNN
                   ☎ 01553 771707 50 ⇄ 🏮

MUNDESLEY   Map 09 TG33

Mundesley Links Rd NR11 8ES
☎ 01263 720279 & 720095 Fax 01263 720279
Parkland course, undulating with panoramic views, short but
competitive. One mile from the sea.
9 holes, 5377yds, Par 68, SSS 66, Course record 64.
Club membership 450.
Visitors   restricted Wed & weekends, also Tue 4-6pm,
                   dress regulations, no sharing clubs, golf shoes
                   must be worn, prior booking preferred.
Societies   must contact one month in advance.
Green Fees   £20 per day; £18 per round; £12 per 9 holes
                   (£25 per round weekends).
Prof   T G Symmons
Facilities   ⊗ ⫿ by prior arrangement ⬥ ▼ ♀ ⏛ 🛍 ⚲ ⚑
Location   W side of village off B1159

Hotel   ★★ 66% Red Lion, Brook St, CROMER
                   ☎ 01263 514964 12 ⇄ 🏮

NORWICH   Map 05 TG20

Costessey Park Old Costessey NR8 5AL
☎ 01603 746333 & 747085 Fax 01603 746185
The course lies in the gently contoured Two River valley,
providing players with a number of holes that bring the river
and man-made lakes into play.
18 holes, 5820yds, Par 71, SSS 68, Course record 68.
Club membership 600.
Visitors   may not play competition days, prior booking
                   required for weekends.
Societies   welcome by prior arrangement.
Green Fees   not confirmed.
Cards   ▦ ▦ ▦ ▦
Prof   Simon Cook
Facilities   ⊗ ⫿ ⬥ ▼ ♀ ⏛ 🛍 ⚑ ⚲ ⚲ ⚲

Hotel   ★★★ 66% Quality Hotel, 2 Barnard Rd,
                   Bowthorpe, NORWICH
                   ☎ 01603 741161 80 ⇄ 🏮

De Vere Dunston Hall Hotel Ipswich Rd NR14 8PQ
☎ 01508 470444 Fax 01508 470689
Parkland course with water features at many holes. Varied
and challenging woodland setting. Floodlit driving range.
18 holes, 6300yds, Par 71, SSS 70, Course record 70.
Visitors   must book in advance.
Societies   apply in writing or telephone for details.
Green Fees   £25 per round weekdays (£30 weekends).
Cards   ▦ ▦ ▦ ▦ ▦ ▦ ▦
Prof   Peter Briggs
Designer   M Shaw
Facilities   ⊗ ⫿ ⬥ ▼ ♀ ⏛ 🛍 ⚑ ⚲ ⚲ ⚑
& Leisure   hard tennis courts, heated indoor swimming
                   pool, sauna, solarium, gymnasium.
Location   On A140

Hotel ★★★★ 65% De Vere Dunston Hall, Ipswich Rd, Dunston, NORWICH
☎ 01508 470444 72 🛏 🟊

Eaton Newmarket Rd NR4 6SF
☎ 01603 451686 & 452881 Fax 01603 451686
An undulating, tree-lined parkland course with excellent trees. Easy opening par 5 followed by an intimidating par 3 that is well bunkered with deep rough on both sides. The challenging 17th hole is uphill to a small hidden green and always needs more club than expected.
18 holes, 6114yds, Par 70, SSS 69, Course record 64.
Club membership 800.

Visitors	restricted before 11.30am weekends. Advised to contact in advance.
Societies	must contact in advance.
Green Fees	£30 (£40 weekends).
Prof	Mark Allen
Facilities	⊗ ℳ ⅃ ⌶ 🍴 ♀ ⚲ 🏌 🛍 ⚑
Location	1.5m SW of city centre off A11

Hotel ★★★ 72% Park Farm Hotel, HETHERSETT
☎ 01603 810264 6 🛏 🟊 Annexe 30 🛏 🟊

Royal Norwich Drayton High Rd, Hellesdon NR6 5AH
☎ 01603 429928 & 408459 (Pro) Fax 01603 417945
Undulating mature parkland course complimented with gorse. Largely unchanged since the alterations carried out by James Braid in 1924. A challenging test of golf.
18 holes, 6506yds, Par 72, SSS 72, Course record 65.
Club membership 700.

Visitors	must contact in advance. Restricted weekends & bank holidays.
Societies	must contact in advance.
Green Fees	£30 per day (£36 weekends & bank holidays).
Prof	Dean Futter
Designer	James Braid
Facilities	⊗ ℳ by prior arrangement ⅃ ⌶ 🍴 ♀ ⚲ 🏌 🛍 ⚑
Location	2.5m NW of city centre on A1067

Hotel ★★★ 66% Quality Hotel, 2 Barnard Rd, Bowthorpe, NORWICH
☎ 01603 741161 80 🛏 🟊

Sprowston Park Wroxham Rd NR7 8RP
☎ 01603 410657 Fax 01603 788884
Set in 100 acres of parkland. A very tight course, so accuracy is required for good golf. The facilities include a 27-bay driving range, a practice area and tuition from a team of professionals.
18 holes, 5843yds, Par 70, SSS 68, Course record 63.
Club membership 660.

Visitors	no restrictions.
Societies	must contact in advance.
Green Fees	£17 (£23 weekends & bank holidays).
Cards	🖻 🖴 🖮 🖵 🖷 🖸 🖹
Prof	Guy D Ireson
Facilities	⊗ ℳ ⅃ ⌶ 🍴 ♀ ⚲ 🏌 🛍 ⚑
Location	4m NE from city centre on A1151

Hotel ★★★★ 74% Sprowston Manor, Sprowston Park, Wroxham Rd, Sprowston, NORWICH
☎ 01603 410871 94 🛏 🟊

Wensum Valley Hotel, Golf & Country Club Beech Av, Taverham NR8 6HP ☎ 01603 261012 Fax 01603 261664
An undulating, picturesque golf course situated on the side of a valley. The greens in particular are very undulating and always give the average golfer a testing time. The 12th hole from a raised tee provides a blind and windy tee shot and a very sloping green.
Valley Course: 18 holes, 6172yds, Par 71, SSS 69, Course record 67.
Wensum Course: 9 holes, 5812yds, Par 70, SSS 68.
Club membership 900.

Visitors	no restrictions but advisable to book tee times at weekends.
Societies	apply in writing or by telephone.
Green Fees	£18 per day.
Cards	🖻 🖴 🖮 🖷 🖸 🖹
Prof	Peter Whittle
Designer	B Todd
Facilities	⊗ ℳ ⅃ ⌶ 🍴 ♀ ⚲ 🏌 🛍 🚣 ⚑
& Leisure	heated indoor swimming pool, fishing, sauna, solarium, gymnasium.
Location	5m N of Norwich

Hotel ★★★ 67% Swallow Nelson Hotel, Prince of Wales Rd, NORWICH
☎ 01603 760260 132 🛏 🟊

SHERINGHAM   Map 09 TG14

Sheringham Weybourne Rd NR26 8HG
☎ 01263 823488 & 822038 Fax 01263 825189
Splendid cliff-top links with gorse, good 'seaside turf' and plenty of space. Straight driving is essential for a low score. The course is close to the shore and can be very windswept, but offers magnificent views.
18 holes, 6495yds, Par 70, SSS 71, Course record 65.
Club membership 680.

Visitors	must contact in advance & have handicap certificate. Restricted weekends.
Societies	must apply in writing.

Green Fees £39 per day (£44 weekends & bank holidays).
Prof M W Jubb
Designer Tom Dunn
Facilities ⊗ ⅢⅢ ᴸ ♥ ♀ ⏚ 📶 ♒
Location W side of town centre on A149

Hotel ★★ 70% Beaumaris Hotel, South St, SHERINGHAM
☎ 01263 822370 21 ⇆ ⸙

SWAFFHAM
Map 05 TF80

Swaffham Cley Rd PE37 8AE ☎ 01760 721611
Heathland course and designated wildlife site.
9 holes, 6252yds, Par 72, SSS 70.
Club membership 400.
Visitors must contact in advance. With member only at weekends & not before mid day.
Societies must contact in advance.
Green Fees not confirmed.
Prof Peter Field
Facilities ⊗ ⅢⅢ ᴸ ♥ ♀ ⏚ 📶 ♒
Location 1.5m SW

Hotel ★★★ 65% George Hotel, Station Rd, SWAFFHAM ☎ 01760 721238 27 ⇆ ⸙

THETFORD
Map 05 TL88

Feltwell Thor Ave, Feltwell IP26 4AY ☎ 01842 827644
In spite of being an inland links, this 9-hole course is still open and windy.
9 holes, 6256yds, Par 70, SSS 70, Course record 68.
Club membership 400.
Visitors dress restriction, no jeans,tracksuits or collarless shirts, golf shoes to be worn.
Societies apply in writing or telephone in advance.
Green Fees Summer: £15 per day, £12 after 4pm (£24/£16 weekends). Winter: £15 per day, £7 after 2pm (£24/£10 weekends).
Cards 🖃 🖃
Prof Peter Field
Facilities ⊗ ⅢⅢ ᴸ ♥ ♀ (closed Mon) ⏚ ⸙ ♒
Location On B1112

Hotel ★★ 65% The Thomas Paine Hotel, White Hart St, THETFORD ☎ 01842 755631 13 ⇆ ⸙

Thetford Brandon Rd IP24 3NE
☎ 01842 752169 Fax 01842 766212
This is a course with a good pedigree. It was laid-out by a fine golfer, C.H. Mayo, later altered by James Braid and then again altered by another famous course designer, Mackenzie Ross. It is a testing heathland course with a particularly stiff finish.
18 holes, 6879yds, Par 72, SSS 73, Course record 66.
Club membership 850.
Visitors pre booking advisable, may not play weekends or bank holidays except with member. Handicap certificate required.
Societies must contact in advance, Wed-Fri only.
Green Fees not confirmed.
Prof Gary Kitley
Designer James Braid

Facilities ⊗ ⅢⅢ ᴸ ♥ ♀ ⏚ ⸙ 📶 ♒
Location 2m W of Thetford on B1107

Hotel ★★ 65% The Thomas Paine Hotel, White Hart St, THETFORD
☎ 01842 755631 13 ⇆ ⸙

WATTON
Map 05 TF90

Richmond Park Saham Rd IP25 6EA
☎ 01953 881803 Fax 01953 881817
Compact parkland course with mature and young trees. These together with the Little Wissey river and other water hazards create an interesting but not daunting challenge.
18 holes, 6289yds, Par 71, SSS 70, Course record 69.
Club membership 600.
Visitors not before 10.30am weekends & bank holidays.
Societies must contact in advance.
Green Fees £24 per day; £12 per round (£24 per day/round weekends & bank holidays).
Cards 🖃 🖃 🖃 🖃 🖃
Prof Alan Hemsley
Designer D Jessup/D Scott
Facilities ⊗ ⅢⅢ ᴸ ♥ ♀ ⏚ 📶 ⸙ ♒ ⸙ ⸙
& Leisure gymnasium.
Location 500yds NW of town centre

Hotel ★★★ 65% George Hotel, Station Rd, SWAFFHAM ☎ 01760 721238 27 ⇆ ⸙

WESTON LONGVILLE
Map 09 TG11

Weston Park NR9 5JW
☎ 01603 872363 Fax 01603 873040
Testing course set in 200 acres of mature parkland with specimen trees.
18 holes, 6603yds, Par 72, SSS 72, Course record 69.
Club membership 400.

Visitors must telephone for tee times on 01603 872998.
Societies must telephone for prices and tee times.
Green Fees £27 per round (£32 weekends).
Cards 🖃 🖃
Prof Michael Few
Facilities ⊗ ᴸ ♥ ♀ ⏚ ⸙ 🛒 ⸙ ♒
& Leisure hard tennis courts.
Location Off the A1067 Norwich/Fakenham road, 9m NW of Norwich

Hotel ★★★ 66% Quality Hotel, 2 Barnard Rd, Bowthorpe, NORWICH
☎ 01603 741161 80 ⇆ ⸙

WEST RUNTON
Map 09 TG14

Links Country Park Hotel & Golf Club NR27 9QH
☎ 01263 838215 Fax 01263 838264
Parkland course 500 yds from the sea, with superb views
overlooking West Runton. The hotel offers extensive leisure
facilities.
9 holes, 4842yds, Par 66, SSS 64.
Club membership 250.

Visitors	restrictions weekends.
Societies	must telephone in advance.
Green Fees	not confirmed.
Cards	🖃 🖃 🖃 🖃 🖃
Prof	Lee Patterson
Designer	J.H Taylor
Facilities	⊗ ⅲ ⅉ ♥ ♀ ⚲ 🖭 ⛳ ❦ 🦽 ♂
& Leisure	hard tennis courts, heated indoor swimming pool, sauna, solarium.
Location	S side of village off A149

Hotel	★★ 70% Beaumaris Hotel, South St, SHERINGHAM ☎ 01263 822370 21 ⇔ ♠

NORTHAMPTONSHIRE

CHACOMBE
Map 04 SP44

Cherwell Edge OX17 2EN
☎ 01295 711591 Fax 01295 712404
Parkland course. The front nine is short and tight with mature
trees. The back nine is longer and more open.
18 holes, 5947yds, Par 70, SSS 68, Course record 64.
Club membership 500.

Visitors	no restrictions but golf shoes to be worn (can be hired) and tidy appearance expected.
Societies	must apply in advance.
Green Fees	£12 (£16 weekends).
Cards	🖃 🖃 🖃 🖃 🖃
Prof	Joe Kingston
Designer	R Davies
Facilities	⊗ ⅲ ⅉ ♥ ♀ ⚲ 🖭 ⛳ ❦ 🦽 ♂ ♂
Location	Exit M40 junct 11, 0.5m S off B4525

Hotel	★★★ 68% Whately Hall, Banbury Cross, BANBURY ☎ 0870 400 8104 72 ⇔ ♠

COLD ASHBY
Map 04 SP67

Cold Ashby Stanford Rd NN6 6EP
☎ 01604 740548 Fax 01604 740548
Undulating parkland course, nicely matured, with superb
views. The 27 holes consist of three loops of nine which can
be interlinked with each other. All three loops have their own
challenge and any combination of two loops will give an
excellent course. The start of the Elkington loop offers 5
holes of scenic beauty and testing golf and the 3rd on the
Winwick loop is a 200-yard par 3 from a magnificent
plateau tee.
*Ashby-Elkington: 18 holes, 6308yds, Par 72, SSS 70, Course
record 69.*
*Winwick-Ashby: 18 holes, 6004yds, Par 70, SSS 69, Course
record 66.*
*Elkington-Winwick: 18 holes, 6250yds, Par 70, SSS 70,
Course record 69.*
Club membership 700.

Visitors	start time must be reserved at weekends.
Societies	must contact in advance.
Green Fees	£22 per day; £14 per 18 holes (£16 weekends).
Prof	Shane Rose
Designer	David Croxton
Facilities	⊗ ⅲ ⅉ ♥ ♀ ⚲ 🖭 ⛳ ❦ ♂
Location	Close to junct 1 A14 & junct 18 M1 midway between Rugby, Leicester & Northampton

Hotel	★★★ 66% Posthouse Northampton/Rugby, CRICK ☎ 0870 400 9059 88 ⇔ ♠

COLLINGTREE
Map 04 SP75

Collingtree Park Windingbrook Ln NN4 0XN
☎ 01604 700000 Fax 01604 702600
Superb 18-hole resort course designed by former U.S.
and British Open champion Johnny Miller. Stunning
island green at the 18th hole. The Golf Academy
includes a driving range, practice holes, indoor video
teaching room.
18 holes, 6776yds, Par 72, SSS 72, Course record 66.

Visitors	must contact in advance & have handicap certificate.
Societies	contact in advance.
Green Fees	£17.50 (£23 weekends & bank holidays).
Cards	🖃 🖃 🖃 🖃 🖃 🖃
Prof	Geoff Pook/Henry Bareham
Designer	Johnny Miller
Facilities	⊗ ⅲ by prior arrangement ⅉ ♥ ♀ ⚲ 🖭 ⛳ 🦽 ♂ ♂
& Leisure	fishing.
Location	M1-junc 15 on A508 to Northampton

| Hotel | ★★★★ 67% Swallow Hotel, Eagle Dr, NORTHAMPTON ☎ 01604 768700 120 ⇋ ℝ |

CORBY

Map 04 SP88

Corby Public Stamford Rd, Weldon NN17 3JH
☎ 01536 260756 Fax 01536 260756
Municipal course laid out on made-up quarry ground and open to prevailing wind. Wet in winter. Played over by Priors Hall Club.
18 holes, 6677yds, Par 72, SSS 72.
Club membership 600.
Visitors are advised to book in advance.
Societies must contact in advance.
Green Fees £9.35 per 18 holes; £5.25 per 9 holes (£12.10/£6.90 weekends).
Prof Jeff Bradbrook
Designer F Hawtree
Facilities ⊗ ⅏ ⅃ ⅃ ⅃ ⅃ ⅃ ⅃ ⅃ ⅃
Location 4m NE on A43

| Hotel | ★★★ 67% The Talbot, New St, OUNDLE ☎ 01832 273621 39 ⇋ ℝ |

DAVENTRY

Map 04 SP56

Daventry & District Norton Rd NN11 5LS
☎ 01327 702829
A hilly course with hard walking.
9 holes, 5812yds, Par 69, SSS 68, Course record 68.
Club membership 310.
Visitors restricted Sun mornings & weekends (Oct-Mar).
Societies contact the club secretary.
Green Fees £10 per round (£15 weekends & bank holidays).
Facilities ⅃ ⅃ ⅃ ⅃
Location 0.5m NE

| Hotel | ★★★★ 60% Hanover International Hotel & Club Daventry, Sedgemoor Way, off Ashby Rd, DAVENTRY ☎ 01327 301777 138 ⇋ ℝ |

FARTHINGSTONE

Map 04 SP65

Farthingstone Hotel & Golf Course NN12 8AH
☎ 01327 361533 & 361291 Fax 01327 361645
A mature and challenging course set in picturesque countryside.
18 holes, 6299yds, Par 70, SSS 70, Course record 68.
Club membership 500.
Visitors must contact in advance.
Societies must contact in advance.

Green Fees not confirmed.
Cards ▭ ▭ ▭ ▭ ▭
Prof Austin Curtis
Designer Don Donaldson
Facilities ⊗ ⅏ ⅃ ⅃ ⅃ ⅃ ⅃ ⅃ ⅃ ⅃
& Leisure squash, Snooker, Pool table, Indoor practice bay.
Location 1m W

| Hotel | ★★ 64% Globe Hotel, High St, WEEDON ☎ 01327 340336 15 ⇋ ℝ Annexe 3 ⇋ ℝ |

HELLIDON

Map 04 SP55

Hellidon Lakes Hotel & Country Club NN11 6GG
☎ 01327 262550 Fax 01327 262559
Spectacular parkland course designed by David Snell.
18 holes, 6691yds, Par 72, SSS 72.
Club membership 500.
Visitors 18 hole course; must contact in advance & have handicap certificate at weekends. 9 hole; open to beginners.
Societies must telephone in advance.
Green Fees £15 per 18 holes (£25 weekends & bank holidays).
Cards ▭ ▭ ▭ ▭ ▭
Prof Gary Wills
Designer D Snell
Facilities ⊗ ⅏ ⅃ ⅃ ⅃ ⅃ ⅃ ⅃ ⅃ ⅃
& Leisure hard tennis courts, heated indoor swimming pool, fishing, solarium, gymnasium, golf simulator, ten pin bowling.
Location 0.5m off A361 between Daventry & Banbury

| Hotel | ★★★★ 69% Hellidon Lakes Hotel & Country Club, HELLIDON ☎ 01327 262550 51 ⇋ ℝ |

KETTERING

Map 04 SP87

Kettering Headlands NN15 6XA
☎ 01536 511104 Fax 01536 511104
A very pleasant, mainly flat meadowland course with easy walking.
18 holes, 6081yds, Par 69, SSS 69, Course record 64.
Club membership 700.
Visitors welcome but with member only weekends & bank holidays.
Societies Wed & Fri only, apply in writing.
Green Fees £24 per day.
Prof Kevin Theobald
Designer Tom Morris
Facilities ⊗ ⅏ ⅃ ⅃ ⅃ ⅃ ⅃ ⅃
Location S side of town centre ▶

Hotel ★★★★ 72% Kettering Park Hotel, Kettering Parkway, **KETTERING**
☎ 01536 416666 119 ⇥ ♠

NORTHAMPTON
Map 04 SP76

Brampton Heath Sandy Ln, Church Brampton NN6 8AX
☎ 01604 843939 Fax 01604 843885
Appealing to both the novice and experienced golfer, this beautiful, well drained heathland course affords panoramic views over Northampton.
18 holes, 6366yds, Par 71, SSS 70, Course record 69.
Club membership 500.
Visitors advisable to book especially for weekends, may book up to 8 days in advance.
Societies write or telephone for details.
Green Fees not confirmed.
Cards ▭ ▭ ▭ ▭ ▭
Prof Richard Hudson
Designer D Snell
Facilities ⊗ ⊪ ㄴ ♥ ♀ ☆ 🏠 ☂ ♦ 🏌 ♣ ⚕ ╰
& Leisure short course par 3.
Location Signposted off old A50 Kingsthorpe to Welford road, 2m N of Kingsthorpe

Hotel ★★★ 71% Lime Trees Hotel, 8 Langham Place, Barrack Rd, **NORTHAMPTON**
☎ 01604 632188 27 ⇥ ♠

Delapre Golf Complex Eagle Dr, Nene Valley Way NN4 7DU ☎ 01604 764036 Fax 01604 706378
Rolling parkland course, part of municipal golf complex, which includes two 9-hole, par 3 courses, pitch-and-putt and 40 bay floodlit driving-range.
Main Course: 18 holes, 6269yds, Par 70, SSS 70, Course record 66.
Hardingstone Course: 9 holes, 2109yds, Par 32, SSS 32.
Club membership 900.
Visitors no restrictions but advance booking advised for weekends.
Societies must book and pay full green fees 2 weeks in advance.
Green Fees £9.50 per 18 holes; £6.50 per 9 holes (£13/£8 weekends & bank holidays).
Prof John Corby
Designer John Jacobs/John Corby
Facilities ⊗ ⊪ ㄴ ♥ ♀ ☆ 🏠 ☂ ⚕ ╰
Location 2m SE

Hotel ★★★ 64% Quality Hotel Northampton, Ashley Way, Weston Favell, **NORTHAMPTON**
☎ 01604 739955 31 ⇥ ♠ Annexe 35 ⇥ ♠

Kingsthorpe Kingsley Rd NN2 7BU
☎ 01604 710610 Fax 01604 710610
A compact, undulating parkland course set within the town boundary. Not a long course but testing enough to attract a competitive membership that boasts several County players.
18 holes, 5918yds, Par 69, SSS 69, Course record 63.
Club membership 600.
Visitors must contact in advance and have handicap certificate. With member only weekends.
Societies must contact in advance.
Green Fees £25 per day.
Prof Paul Armstrong
Designer Mr Alison
Facilities ⊗ ⊪ ㄴ ♀ ☆ 🏠 ⚕

Location N side of town centre on A5095 between the Racecourse and Kingsthorpe

Hotel ★★★ 64% Quality Hotel Northampton, Ashley Way, Weston Favell, **NORTHAMPTON**
☎ 01604 739955 31 ⇥ ♠ Annexe 35 ⇥ ♠

Northampton Harlestone NN7 4EF
☎ 01604 845155 Fax 01604 820262
Parkland course with water in play on three holes.
18 holes, 6615yds, Par 72, SSS 72, Course record 67.
Club membership 750.
Visitors must contact in advance and have handicap certificate. With member only at weekends, no visitors on Wed.
Societies must contact in advance.
Green Fees not confirmed.
Cards ▭ ▭ ▭ ▭ ▭
Prof Kevin Dickens
Designer Sinclair Steel
Facilities ⊗ ⊪ ㄴ ♥ ♀ ☆ 🏠 ⚕
Location NW of town centre on A428

Hotel ★★★ 67% Northampton Moat House, Silver St, **NORTHAMPTON**
☎ 01604 739988 145 ⇥ ♠

Northamptonshire County Golf Ln, Church Brampton NN6 8AZ ☎ 01604 843025 Fax 01604 843025
A fine, traditional championship golf course situated on undulating heathland with areas of gorse, heather and extensive coniferous and deciduous woodland. A river and a railway line pass through the course.
18 holes, 6508yds, Par 70, SSS 71, Course record 65.
Club membership 750.
Visitors restricted weekends. May not play on bank holidays. Must contact in advance and have a handicap certificate.
Societies Wed/Thu only, must contact in advance.
Green Fees £40 per day/round.
Prof Tim Rouse
Designer H S Colt
Facilities ♀ ☆ 🏠 ☂ ⚕ ╰
Location 5m NW of Northampton, off A50

Hotel ★★★ 64% Quality Hotel Northampton, Ashley Way, Weston Favell, **NORTHAMPTON**
☎ 01604 739955 31 ⇥ ♠ Annexe 35 ⇥ ♠

Overstone Park Billing Ln NN6 0AP
☎ 01604 647666 Fax 01604 642635
A testing parkland course, gently undulating within panoramic views of local stately home. Excellent drainage and fine greens make the course great all year round. Water comes into play on three holes.
18 holes, 6602yds, Par 72, SSS 72, Course record 69.
Club membership 500.
Visitors contact in advance, only after 2pm at weekends.
Societies write or telephone.
Green Fees Apr-Sep £30 per round.
Cards ▭ ▭ ▭ ▭ ▭
Prof Brain Mudge
Designer Donald Steel
Facilities ⊗ ⊪ ㄴ ♥ ♀ ☆ 🏠 ☂ 🏌 ♣ ⚕
& Leisure hard tennis courts, heated indoor swimming pool, fishing, sauna, solarium, gymnasium.
Location Exit M1 junct15, follow A45 to Billing Aquadrone turn off, course is 2m on Gt Billing Way ▶

Hotel ★★★ 71% Lime Trees Hotel, 8 Langham Place, Barrack Rd, NORTHAMPTON ☎ 01604 632188 27

OUNDLE — Map 04 TL08

Oundle Benefield Rd PE8 4EZ
☎ 01832 273267 (Gen Manager) Fax 01832 273267
Undulating parkland course, shortish but difficult. A small brook affects some of the approaches to the greens.
18 holes, 6235yds, Par 72, SSS 70, Course record 68.
Club membership 600.

Visitors may not play Tue (Ladies Day) or before 10.30am weekends unless with member.
Societies must apply in advance.
Green Fees £22.50 per day (£35.50 weekends).
Prof Richard Keys
Facilities ⊗
Location 1m W on A427

Hotel ★★★ 67% The Talbot, New St, OUNDLE ☎ 01832 273621 39

STAVERTON — Map 04 SP56

Staverton Park NN11 6JT ☎ 01327 302000
Open course, fairly testing with good views.
18 holes, 6661yds, Par 71, SSS 72, Course record 65.
Club membership 300.

Visitors restricted weekends. Must contact in advance. Handicap certificates preferred.
Societies must contact in advance.
Green Fees not confirmed.
Prof Richard Mudge
Designer Cmdr John Harris
Facilities ⊗
& Leisure sauna, gymnasium.
Location 0.75m NE of Staverton on A425

Hotel ★★★★ 60% Hanover International Hotel & Club Daventry, Sedgemoor Way, off Ashby Rd, DAVENTRY ☎ 01327 301777 138

WELLINGBOROUGH — Map 04 SP86

Rushden Kimbolton Rd, Chelveston NN9 6AN
☎ 01933 418511
Parkland course with brook running through the middle.
10 holes, 6335yds, Par 71, SSS 70, Course record 68.
Club membership 400.

Visitors may not play Wed afternoon. With member only weekends.
Societies must apply in writing.
Green Fees not confirmed.
Facilities ⊗
Location 2m E of Higham Ferrers on Kimbolton Rd

Hotel ★★★ 65% Hind Hotel, Sheep St, WELLINGBOROUGH ☎ 0500 636943 (Central Res) Fax 01773 880321 34

Wellingborough Great Harrowden Hall NN9 5AD
☎ 01933 677234 Fax 01933 679379
An undulating parkland course with many trees. The 514-yd, 14th is a testing hole. The clubhouse is a stately home.
18 holes, 6617yds, Par 72, SSS 72, Course record 68.
Club membership 820.

Visitors may not play at weekends & bank holidays or Tue between 10am and 2.30pm.
Societies must apply in writing.
Green Fees £35 per day; £25 per round (subject to change).
Prof David Clifford
Designer Hawtree
Facilities ⊗
& Leisure outdoor swimming pool.
Location 2m N on A509

Hotel ★★★ 65% Hind Hotel, Sheep St, WELLINGBOROUGH ☎ 0500 636943 (Central Res) Fax 01773 880321 34

WHITTLEBURY — Map 04 SP64

Whittlebury Park Golf & Country Club NN12 8XW
☎ 01327 858092 Fax 01327 858009
The 36 holes incorporate three loops of tournament-standard nines plus a short course. The 1905 Course is a reconstruction of the original parkland course built at the turn of the century, the Royal Whittlewood is a lakeland course playing around copses and the Grand Prix, next to Silverstone Motor Racing circuit has a strong links feel playing over gently undulating grassland with challenging lake features.
Grand Prix: 9 holes, 3339yds, Par 36, SSS 36.
Royal Whittlewood: 9 holes, 3323yds, Par 36, SSS 36.
1905: 9 holes, 3256yds, Par 36, SSS 36.
Club membership 400.

Visitors must contact in advance.
Societies telephone 01327 858092 in advance.
Green Fees not confirmed.
Designer Cameron Sinclair
Facilities ⊗
Location A413 Buckingham Road

Hotel ★★★ 66% Buckingham Four Pillars Hotel, Buckingham Ring Rd South, BUCKINGHAM ☎ 01280 822622 70

NORTHUMBERLAND

ALLENDALE — Map 12 NY85

Allendale High Studdon, Allenheads Rd NE47 9DH
☎ 01434 683926 & 683623 Fax 01434 683668
Challenging and hilly parkland course set 1000 feet above sea level with superb views of Allendale. New club house.
18 holes, 4541yds, Par 66, SSS 62, Course record 69.
Club membership 270.

Visitors may not play Aug bank holiday until after 3pm.
Societies must apply in writing to Secretary.
Green Fees not confirmed.
Facilities
Location 1.5m S on B6295

Hotel ★★★ 68% Beaumont Hotel, Beaumont St, HEXHAM ☎ 01434 602331 25

ALNMOUTH   Map 12 NU21

Alnmouth Foxton Hall NE66 3BE
☎ 01665 830231 Fax 01665 830922
Coastal course with pleasant views.
18 holes, 6429yds, Par 69, SSS 69, Course record 64.
Club membership 800.
Visitors	may not play Wed, Fri, weekends & bank holidays. Must contact in advance.
Societies	Mon, Tue or Thu only.
Green Fees	£29 per day.
Cards	🟰 ▬ ▬ 🟰
Designer	H S Colt
Facilities	⊗ �🍴 🄑 🛒 ♀ ♨ 🏠 ⛳ 🏒 🏑 🏌 🚲 ⚷
& Leisure	snooker.
Location	1m NE. 4m E of Alnwick

Hotel ★★★ 60% White Swan Hotel, Bondgate Within, ALNWICK ☎ 01665 602109 58 ⇥ 🐾

Alnmouth Village Marine Rd NE66 2RZ
☎ 01665 830370 Fax 01665 602096
Seaside course with part coastal view.
9 holes, 6090yds, Par 70, SSS 70, Course record 63.
Club membership 480.
Visitors	may not play before 11am on competition days.
Societies	must contact in advance.
Green Fees	£15 (£20 weekends & bank holidays).
Facilities	⊗ �🍴 🄑 🛒 ♀ ♨
Location	E side of village

Hotel ★★★ 60% White Swan Hotel, Bondgate Within, ALNWICK ☎ 01665 602109 58 ⇥ 🐾

ALNWICK   Map 12 NU11

Alnwick Swansfield Park NE66 2AB
☎ 01665 602632
Parkland course offering a fair test of golfing skills.
18 holes, 6284yds, Par 70, SSS 70, Course record 66.
Club membership 550.
Visitors	some restrictions on competition days.
Societies	must contact secretary in advance.
Green Fees	£20 per day; £15 per round (£25/£20 weekends & bank holidays).
Designer	Rochester
Facilities	⊗ ⍟ by prior arrangement 🄑 🛒 ♀ ♨ ⚷
Location	S side of town

Hotel ★★★ 60% White Swan Hotel, Bondgate Within, ALNWICK ☎ 01665 602109 58 ⇥ 🐾

BAMBURGH   Map 12 NU13

Bamburgh Castle The Club House, 40 The Wynding NE69 7DE ☎ 01668 214378 (club) & 214321 (sec)
Superb coastal course with excellent greens that are both fast and true, natural hazards of heather and whin bushes abound. Magnificent views of Farne Islands, Holy Island, Lindisfarne Castle, Bamburgh Castle and Cheviot Hils.
18 holes, 5621yds, Par 68, SSS 67, Course record 64.
Club membership 735.

must contact in advance. Restricted weekends, bank holidays and competition days.
Societies	apply in writing. Weekdays & Sun only.
Green Fees	£30 per day/round (£35 per day; £30 per round weekends & bank holidays).
Designer	George Rochester
Facilities	⊗ ⍟ 🄑 🛒 ♀ ♨ 🏠 ⚷
Location	6m E of A1 via B1341 or B1342

Hotel ★★ 65% Lord Crewe Arms, Front St, BAMBURGH ☎ 01668 214243 12rm (11 ⇥ 🐾)

BEDLINGTON   Map 12 NZ28

Bedlingtonshire Acorn Bank NE22 6AA ☎ 01670 822087
Meadowland/parkland course with easy walking. Under certain conditions the wind can be a distinct hazard.
18 holes, 6813mtrs, Par 73, SSS 73, Course record 68.
Club membership 960.
Visitors	must contact in advance.
Societies	must apply in writing.
Green Fees	not confirmed.
Prof	Marcus Webb
Designer	Frank Pennink
Facilities	⊗ ⍟ 🄑 🛒 ♀ ♨ 🏠 🏒 ⚷
Location	1m SW on A1068

Hotel ★★★★ 63% Holiday Inn, Great North Rd, SEATON BURN ☎ 0191 201 9988 150 ⇥ 🐾

BELFORD   Map 12 NU13

Belford South Rd NE70 7DP
☎ 01668 213433 Fax 01668 213919
An east coast parkland course. Crosswinds affect the 4th but the compensation is spectacular views over Holy Island.
9 holes, 3152yds, Par 72, SSS 70, Course record 72.
Club membership 200.
Visitors	no restrictions.
Societies	must contact in advance.
Green Fees	£14 per 18 holes; £10 per 9 holes (£17/£11 weekends and bank holidays).
Designer	Nigel Williams
Facilities	⊗ ⍟ 🄑 🛒 ♀ ♨ 🏠 🏒 🏑 ⚷ 🍴
Location	Off A1, midway between Alnwick & Berwick on Tweed

Hotel ★★★ 68% Blue Bell Hotel, Market Place, BELFORD ☎ 01668 213543 17 ⇥ 🐾

BELLINGHAM   Map 12 NY88

Bellingham Boggle Hole NE48 2DT
☎ 01434 220530 (Secretary) Fax 01434 220160
This highly regarded 18-hole golf course is situated between Hadrian's Wall and the Scottish Border. A rolling parkland course with many natural hazards. There is a mixture of testing par threes, long par fives and tricky par fours.
18 holes, 6093yds, Par 70, SSS 70, Course record 70.
Club membership 550.
Visitors	welcome all week, advisable to contact in advance as starting sheet in operation.
Societies	must contact in advance.

▶

Green Fees £20 per day (£25 weekends & bank holidays).
Designer E Johnson/I Wilson
Facilities ⊗ ⫴ ⌶ ⬛ ♀ ⌳ 🛒 ⚷ ⎰
Location N side of village on B6320

Hotel ★★ 68% Riverdale Hall Hotel,
BELLINGHAM ☎ 01434 220254 20 � ⭗

BERWICK-UPON-TWEED   Map 12 NT95

> **Berwick-upon-Tweed (Goswick)** Goswick TD15 2RW
> ☎ 01289 387256
> Natural seaside links course, with undulating fairways,
> elevated tees and good greens.
> *18 holes, 6465yds, Par 72, SSS 71, Course record 69.*
> *Club membership 600.*
> **Visitors** must contact in advance for weekends,
> advisable at other times.
> **Societies** must telephone in advance (apply in writing
> Apr-Sep).
> **Green Fees** not confirmed.
> **Prof** Paul Terras
> **Designer** James Braid
> **Facilities** ⊗ ⫴ ⌶ ⬛ ♀ ⌳ 🏠 ⛳ 🏌 🛒 ⚷ ⎰
> **Location** 6m S off A1
>
> **Hotel** ★★★ 68% Blue Bell Hotel, Market Place,
> BELFORD ☎ 01668 213543 17 � ⭗

Magdalene Fields Magdalene Fields TD15 1NE
☎ 01289 306384 & 306130 Fax 01289 306384
Seaside course with natural hazards formed by sea bays. All
holes open to winds. Testing 8th hole over bay (par 3).
18 holes, 6407yds, Par 72, SSS 71, Course record 65.
Club membership 400.
Visitors must contact in advance for weekend play.
Societies must contact in advance.
Green Fees not confirmed.
Designer Willie Park
Facilities ⊗ ⫴ ⌶ ⬛ ♀ ⌳ 🏠 🛒 ⚷
Location 0.5m on E side of town centre

Hotel ★★★⚑⚑ 68% Tillmouth Park Hotel,
CORNHILL-ON-TWEED
☎ 01890 882255 12 � ⭗ Annexe 2 � ⭗

BLYTH   Map 12 NZ38

Blyth New Delaval, Newsham NE24 4DB
☎ 01670 540110 (sec) & 356514 (pro) Fax 01670 540134
Course built over old colliery. Parkland with water hazards.
18 holes, 6456yds, Par 72, SSS 71, Course record 65.
Club membership 820.

Visitors with member only after 3pm & at weekends.
Must contact in advance.
Societies apply in writing/telephone.
Green Fees £21 per day; £18 per round.
Prof Andrew Brown
Designer Hamilton Stutt
Facilities ⊗ ⫴ by prior arrangement ⌶ ⬛ ♀ ⌳ 🏠 ⚷
Location 6m N of Whitley Bay

Hotel ★★★ 63% Windsor Hotel, South Pde,
WHITLEY BAY ☎ 0191 251 8888 63 � ⭗

CRAMLINGTON   Map 12 NZ27

Arcot Hall NE23 7QP
☎ 0191 236 2794 Fax 0191 217 0370
A wooded parkland course, reasonably flat.
18 holes, 6380yds, Par 70, SSS 70, Course record 65.
Club membership 695.
Visitors must contact in advance. May not play
weekends.
Societies must contact in advance.
Green Fees £26 per day (weekdays only).
Prof Graham Cant
Designer James Braid
Facilities ⊗ ⫴ ⌶ ⬛ ♀ ⌳ 🏠 🛒 ⚷
Location 2m SW off A1

Hotel ★★★★ 63% Holiday Inn, Great North Rd,
SEATON BURN
☎ 0191 201 9988 150 � ⭗

EMBLETON   Map 12 NU22

Dunstanburgh Castle NE66 3XQ
☎ 01665 576562 Fax 01665 576562
Rolling links designed by James Braid, adjacent to the
beautiful Embleton Bay. Historic Dunstansburgh Castle is at
one end of the course and a National Trust lake and bird
sanctuary at the other. Superb views.
18 holes, 6298yds, Par 70, SSS 69, Course record 69.
Club membership 394.
Visitors advisable to contact in advance at weekends and
holiday periods.
Societies must contact in advance.
Green Fees £16 per day (£26 per day; £20 per round
weekends & bank holidays).
Designer James Braid
Facilities ⊗ ⫴ ⌶ ⬛ ♀ ⌳ 🏠 🛒 ⚷
Location 7m NE of Alnwick off A1

Hotel ★★ 68% Beach House Hotel, Sea Front,
SEAHOUSES ☎ 01665 720337 14 � ⭗

GREENHEAD   Map 12 NY66

Haltwhistle Walend Farm CA6 7HN
☎ 016977 47367 & 01434 344000 (sec) Fax 01434 344311
Interesting course with panoramic views of Northumberland National Park. The 515yard Par 5 14th hole is a real test of golf skill, played from the highest point of the course through an undulating fairway to a viciously sloping green. The 188yard Par 3 now the 1st hole, played uphill, is particularly difficult playing into the prevailing west wind.
18 holes, 5522yds, Par 69, SSS 67, Course record 70.
Club membership 391.

Visitors	no visitors Sun mornings.
Societies	apply in writing to: Hon Secretary, John Gilbertson, Parkhead Farmhouse, Bardon Mill, Northumberland NE47 7JS.
Green Fees	£12 per day (£15 weekends).
Facilities	⊗ ⊞ ৳ ☕ ♀ ⚒
Location	N on A69 past Haltwhistle on Gilsland Road
Hotel	★★★🏖 Farlam Hall Hotel, Hallbankgate, BRAMPTON ☎ 016977 46234 11 ⇌ 🐾 Annexe 1 ⇌ 🐾

HEXHAM   Map 12 NY96

De Vere Slaley Hall, Golf Resort & Spa Slaley NE47 0BY
☎ 01434 673350 (hotel) & 673154 (pro) Fax 01434 673152
Measuring 7073yds from the championship tees, this Dave Thomas designed course incorporates forest, parkland and moorland with an abundance of lakes and streams. The challenging par 4 9th (452yds) is played over water through a narrow avenue of towering trees and dense rhododendrons. An official PGA European Tour venue and hosts the COMPAQ European Grand Prix. The Priestman course designed by PGA Chairman, Neil Coles is of equal length and standard as the Hunting course. Opened in spring 1999 the Priestman is situated in 280 acres on the western side of the estate, giving panoramic views over the Tyne Valley.
Hunting Course: 18 holes, 7073yds, Par 72, SSS 74, Course record 65.
Priestman Course: 18 holes, 7010yds, Par 72, SSS 74.
Club membership 350.

Visitors	must contact in advance, times subject to availability.
Societies	apply in writing to bookings co-ordinator, small groups 8 or less may book through pro shop.
Green Fees	Hunting Course: £55 per round; Priestman Course: £45 per round.
Cards	💳 💳 💳 💳 💳 💳
Prof	Mark Stancer
Designer	Dave Thomas/Neil Coles
Facilities & Leisure	⊗ ⊞ ৳ ☕ ♀ ⚒ 🏠 ⛳ ⛺ 🏹 ⚒ ₹ ✝ heated indoor swimming pool, fishing, sauna, solarium, gymnasium.
Location	8m S of Hexham off A68
Hotel	★★★★ 71% De Vere Slaley Hall, Slaley, HEXHAM ☎ 01434 673350 139 ⇌ 🐾

Hexham Spital Park NE46 3RZ
☎ 01434 603072 Fax 01434 601865
A very pretty well drained parkland course with interesting natural contours. Exquisite views from parts of the course, of the Tyne valley below. As good a parkland course as any in the North of England.

---

18 holes, 6000yds, Par 70, SSS 68, Course record 64.
Club membership 700.

Visitors	advance booking advisable.
Societies	welcome weekdays, contact in advance.
Green Fees	not confirmed.
Cards	💳 💳 💳 💳 💳 💳
Prof	Martin Forster
Facilities & Leisure	⊗ ⊞ ৳ ☕ ♀ ⚒ 🏠 ⛳ ⚒ squash.
Location	1m NW on B6531
Hotel	★★★ 68% Beaumont Hotel, Beaumont St, HEXHAM ☎ 01434 602331 25 ⇌ 🐾

LONGHORSLEY   Map 12 NZ19

Linden Hall NE65 8XF
☎ 01670 788050 Fax 01670 788544
Set within the picturesque Linden Hall Estate, with views of the Cheviot Hills and the Northumberland coast, this newly established course features mature woodland and several burns and lakes.
18 holes, 6809yds, Par 72, SSS 73.
Club membership 240.

Visitors	must book in advance.
Societies	must be of reasonable standard of play, observe dress code & etiquette, preferably have handicap certificate.
Green Fees	not confirmed.
Cards	💳 💳 💳 💳
Prof	David Curry
Designer	Jonathan Gaunt

▶

Facilities & Leisure	⊗ ⫴ ⬛ ♨ ☡ ⛳ ☕ ⛤ ➘ 🛒 ⚷ 𝄢
	hard tennis courts, heated indoor swimming pool, sauna, solarium, gymnasium, ballooning, croquet, clay pigeon shooting, quad bikes.
Location	From A1 N/S take A697 to Coldstream, approx 4m to Longhorsley, Linden Hall 0.5m past village
Hotel	★★★★⛴ 65% Linden Hall Hotel, Health Spa & Golf Course, LONGHORSLEY ☎ 01670 516611 50 ⇆ 𝄢

MATFEN   Map 12 NZ07

Matfen Hall NE20 0RH
☎ 01661 886400 Fax 01661 886055
An 18-hole parkland course set in beautiful countryside with many natural and man-made hazards. Also a challenging 9-hole par 3 course and a driving range.
18 holes, 6609yds, Par 73, SSS 72, Course record 67.
Club membership 500.
Visitors contact in advance, restricted on weekends between 8-10am.
Societies telephone for details.
Green Fees £35 per day; £25 per round (£40/£30 weekends).
Cards ▭▭ ▬ ▭ ▭ ▭ ▭ ▭
Prof John Harrison
Facilities ⊗ ⫴ ⬛ ♨ ☡ ⛳ ☕ ⛤ ➘ 🛒 ⚷ 𝄢
& Leisure beauty salon.
Location Just off B6318 Military road 15m W of Newcastle

Hotel ★★ 66% Angel Inn, Main St, CORBRIDGE ☎ 01434 632119 5 ⇆ 𝄢

MORPETH   Map 12 NZ28

Morpeth The Clubhouse NE61 2BT
☎ 01670 504942 Fax 01670 504918
Parkland course with views of the Cheviots. Venue for 2000 County Match Play Championship.
18 holes, 6206yds, Par 71, SSS 69, Course record 65.
Club membership 700.
Visitors restricted weekends & bank holidays. Must contact in advance and have a handicap certificate.
Societies apply in writing.
Green Fees £25 per day; £20 per round (£25 per round weekends; £30 per round bank holidays).
Prof Martin Jackson
Designer Harry Vardon
Facilities ⊗ ⫴ ⬛ ♨ ☡ ⛳ ☕ ⛤ ➘ ⚷
Location S side of town centre on A197

Hotel ★★★★⛴ 65% Linden Hall Hotel, Health Spa & Golf Course, LONGHORSLEY ☎ 01670 516611 50 ⇆ 𝄢

NEWBIGGIN-BY-THE-SEA   Map 12 NZ38

Newbiggin-by-the-Sea Prospect Place NE64 6DW
☎ 01670 817344 Fax 01670 520236
Seaside-links course.
18 holes, 6452yds, Par 72, SSS 71, Course record 65.
Club membership 570.
Visitors must contact professional on arrival and may not play before 10am.

Societies	must apply in writing.
Green Fees	not confirmed.
Prof	Marcus Webb
Facilities	⊗ ⫴ ⬛ ♨ ☡ ⛳ ☕ ⛤ ⚷
& Leisure	snooker.
Location	N side of town

Hotel ★★★★⛴ 65% Linden Hall Hotel, Health Spa & Golf Course, LONGHORSLEY ☎ 01670 516611 50 ⇆ 𝄢

PONTELAND   Map 12 NZ17

Ponteland 53 Bell Villas NE20 9BD
☎ 01661 822689 Fax 01661 860077
Open parkland course offering testing golf and good views.
18 holes, 6524yds, Par 72, SSS 71, Course record 66.
Club membership 720.
Visitors with member only Fri, weekends & bank holidays.
Societies welcome Tue & Thu only. Must contact in advance.
Green Fees £25 per day.
Cards ▭▭▭
Prof Alan Robson-Crosby
Designer Harry Fernie
Facilities ⊗ ⫴ ⬛ ♨ ☡ ⛳ ☕ ⛤ ⚷
Location 0.5m E on A696

Hotel ★★★ 66% Novotel, Ponteland Rd, Kenton, NEWCASTLE UPON TYNE ☎ 0191 214 0303 126 ⇆ 𝄢

PRUDHOE   Map 12 NZ06

Prudhoe Eastwood Park NE42 5DX
☎ 01661 832466 Fax 01661 830710
Parkland course with natural hazards and easy walking along undulating fairways.
18 holes, 5812yds, Par 69, SSS 68, Course record 60.
Club membership 700.
Visitors must contact in advance. Weekends after 4.30pm
Societies must contact in writing.
Green Fees not confirmed.
Prof John Crawford
Facilities ⊗ ⫴ ⬛ ♨ ☡ ⛳ ☕
Location E side of town centre off A695

Hotel ★★★ 69% Gibside Arms Hotel, Front St, WHICKHAM ☎ 0191 488 9292 45 ⇆ 𝄢

ROTHBURY   Map 12 NU00

Rothbury Old Race Course NE65 7TR
☎ 01669 620718 & 621271
Very flat parkland course alongside the River Coquet.
9 holes, 5681yds, Par 68, SSS 67, Course record 65.
Club membership 350.
Visitors may play at weekends by arrangement only.
Societies Must contact secretary in advance.
Green Fees £11 per day (£16 weekends & bank holidays).
Designer J Radcliffe
Facilities ⬛ ♨ ☡ ⛳ ☕
Location SW side of town off B6342

▶

Hotel   ★★★ 60%   White Swan Hotel, Bondgate Within, ALNWICK
☎ 01665 602109   58 ⇔ ↾

SEAHOUSES   Map 12 NU23

Seahouses Beadnell Rd NE68 7XT
☎ 01665 720794 Fax 01665 721994
Typical links course with many hazards, including the famous 10th, 'Logans Loch', water hole.
18 holes, 5516yds, Par 67, SSS 67, Course record 63.
Club membership 750.
Visitors   must contact in advance.
Societies   must contact in advance. May not play Sun.
Green Fees £18 per day (£25 weekends & bank holidays).
Facilities   ⊗ ⑈ 🟊 ➤ ♀ ♨ ⊘
Location   S side of village on B1340

Hotel   ★★ 68%   Bamburgh Castle Hotel, SEAHOUSES
☎ 01665 720283   20 ⇔ ↾

STOCKSFIELD   Map 12 NZ06

Stocksfield New Ridley Rd NE43 7RE
☎ 01661 843041 Fax 01661 843046
Challenging course: parkland (9 holes), woodland (9 holes). Some elevated greens and water hazards.
18 holes, 5978yds, Par 70, SSS 70, Course record 63.
Club membership 550.
Visitors   welcome except Wed am & Sat until 4pm, unless accompanied by a member.
Societies   must contact in advance.
Green Fees £30 per day; £25 per round (£30 weekends & bank holidays).
Prof   David Mather
Designer   Pennick
Facilities   ⊗ ⑈ by prior arrangement ➤ 🟊 ♀ ♨ 🏠 ↾ ⊘
& Leisure   snooker.
Location   2.5m SE off A695

Hotel   ★★★ 68%   Beaumont Hotel, Beaumont St, HEXHAM ☎ 01434 602331   25 ⇔ ↾

SWARLAND   Map 12 NU10

Swarland Hall Coast View NE65 9JG
☎ 01670 787010
Parkland course set in mature woodland. There are seven Par 4 holes in excess of 400 yards.
18 holes, 6628yds, Par 72, SSS 72.
Club membership 400.
Visitors   restricted on competition days. Advisable to contact in advance.
Societies   apply in advance.
Green Fees £14 per round (£18 weekends & bank holidays).
Prof   David Fletcher/Linzi Hardy
Facilities   ⊗ ⑈ ➤ 🟊 ♀ ♨ 🏠 ↾ ⚲ ♨ ⊘
Location   Approx 1m W of A1

Hotel   ★★★★♨ 65%   Linden Hall Hotel, Health Spa & Golf Course, LONGHORSLEY
☎ 01670 516611   50 ⇔ ↾

WARKWORTH   Map 12 NU20

Warkworth The Links NE65 0SW ☎ 01665 711596
Seaside links course, with good views and alternative tees for the back nine.
9 holes, 5870yds, Par 70, SSS 68, Course record 66.
Club membership 470.
Visitors   welcome except Tue & Sat.
Societies   must contact in advance.
Green Fees not confirmed.
Designer   T Morris
Facilities   ⊗ ➤ 🟊 ♀ ♨
Location   0.5m E of village off A1068

Hotel   ★★★ 60%   White Swan Hotel, Bondgate Within, ALNWICK
☎ 01665 602109   58 ⇔ ↾

WOOLER   Map 12 NT92

Wooler Dod Law, Doddington NE71 6EA
☎ 01668 282135
Hilltop, moorland course with spectacular views over the Glendale valley. Nine greens played from 18 tees. A very challenging course when windy with one Par 5 of 580 yards. The course is much under used during the week so is always available.
9 holes, 6358yds, Par 72, SSS 70, Course record 72.
Club membership 300.
Visitors   normally no restrictions.
Societies   by prior arrangement with secretary.
Green Fees not confirmed.
Facilities   ⊗ ➤ 🟊 ♨ ⚲ ♨ ⊘
Location   At Doddington on B6525 Wooler/Berwick Rd

Hotel   ★★★ 68%   Blue Bell Hotel, Market Place, BELFORD ☎ 01668 213543   17 ⇔ ↾

NOTTINGHAMSHIRE

CALVERTON   Map 08 SK64

Ramsdale Park Golf Centre Oxton Rd NG14 6NU
☎ 0115 965 5600 Fax 0115 965 4105
The High course is a challenging and comprehensive test for any standard of golf. A relatively flat front nine is followed by an undulating back nine that is renowned as one of the best 9 holes of golf in the county. The Low course is an 18 hole Par 3 course gaining a reputation as one of the best in the country. Hole lengths vary from 100 to 207yds.
High Course: 18 holes, 6546yds, Par 71, SSS 71, Course record 70.
Low Course: 18 holes, 2844yds, Par 54.
Club membership 400.
Visitors   may book up to 7 days in advance.
Societies   welcome midweek, apply in writing or telephone.
Green Fees Low Course: £7.70 (weekends £8.20); High Course: £14.50 (weekends £17).
Cards   ▭▭ ▭▭ ▰◥ 🟢
Prof   Robert Macey
Designer   Hawtree

▶

Facilities ⊗ ⅏ ⌂ 🍷 ♀ 🏖 🏠 ⛳ 🏌 🚃 ⚗ ♗
Location 8m NE of Nottingham, off B6386

Hotel ★★★ 64% Westminster Hotel, 312 Mansfield Rd, Carrington, NOTTINGHAM
☎ 0115 955 5000 72 ⇔ ⛏

Springwater Moor Ln NG14 6FZ ☎ 0115 965 2129
This attractive golf course, set in rolling countryside close to Nottingham, offers an interesting and challenging game of golf to players of all handicaps, as well as fine views over the Trent Valley.
18 holes, 6224yds, Par 71, SSS 70.
Visitors 5 day advance booking by telephone, booking available all week subject to competitions and Society/Corporate reservations.
Societies apply in writing or telephone for Society Pack.
Green Fees not confirmed.
Prof Paul Wharmsby
Designer Neil Footitty/Paul Wharmsby
Facilities ⊗ ⅏ ⌂ 🍷 ♀ 🏖 🏠 🏌 ⚗ ♗
& Leisure short game academy.
Location 300yds on the left from the turning to Calverton off A6097

Hotel ★★★ 64% Westminster Hotel, 312 Mansfield Rd, Carrington, NOTTINGHAM
☎ 0115 955 5000 72 ⇔ ⛏

EAST LEAKE   Map 08 SK52

Rushcliffe Stocking Ln LE12 5RL
☎ 01509 852959 Fax 01509 852688
Hilly, tree-lined and picturesque parkland course.
18 holes, 6013yds, Par 70, SSS 69, Course record 63.
Club membership 700.
Visitors welcome but may not play Tue and restricted weekends & bank holidays 9.30-11am & 3-4.30pm.
Societies must apply in advance.
Green Fees not confirmed.
Prof Chris Hall
Facilities ⊗ ⅏ ⌂ 🍷 ♀ 🏠 ⚗
Location 1m N

Hotel ★★★ 72% Yew Lodge Hotel & Conference Centre, Packington Hill, KEGWORTH
☎ 01509 672518 64 ⇔ ⛏

HUCKNALL   Map 08 SK54

Leen Valley Golf Centre Wigwam Ln NG15 7TA
☎ 0115 964 5020 Fax 0115 964 2724
An interesting and challenging parkland course, featuring several lakes, the River Leen and the Baker Brook. Suitable for all standards of golfers.
18 holes, 6233yds, Par 72, SSS 70.
Club membership 750.
Visitors tee times can be booked in advance and are advisable for Fri, Sat & Sun.
Societies by arrangement.
Green Fees £9.50 per 18 holes (£13.50 weekends).
Cards 💳 💳 💳 💳 💳
Prof John Lines
Designer Tom Hodgetts
Facilities ⊗ ⅏ ⌂ 🍷 ♀ 🏖 🏠 ⛳ 🏌 🚃 ⚗

Location 0.5m from Hucknall Town Centre, follow signs for railway station and turn right into Wigwam Lane

Hotel ★★★ 65% Bestwood Lodge, Bestwood Country Park, Arnold, NOTTINGHAM
☎ 0115 920 3011 40 ⇔ ⛏

KEYWORTH   Map 08 SK63

Stanton on the Wolds Golf Rd, Stanton-on-the-Wolds NG12 5BH
☎ 0115 937 4885 & 937 2044 Fax 0115 937 4885
Parkland course, fairly flat with stream running through four holes.
18 holes, 6437yds, Par 73, SSS 71, Course record 67.
Club membership 705.
Visitors must contact in advance. Must play with member at weekends and may not play Tue.
Societies must apply in writing.
Green Fees £22 per round.
Prof Nick Hernon
Designer Tom Williamson
Facilities ⊗ ⅏ by prior arrangement ⌂ 🍷 ♀ 🏖 🏠 ⚗
Location E side of village

Hotel ★★ 65% Rufford Hotel, 53 Melton Rd, West Bridgford, NOTTINGHAM
☎ 0115 981 4202 34 ⇔ ⛏

KIRKBY IN ASHFIELD   Map 08 SK55

Notts Derby Rd NG17 7QR
☎ 01623 753225 Fax 01623 753655
Undulating heathland Championship course.
18 holes, 7030yds, Par 72, SSS 74, Course record 64.
Club membership 500.
Visitors must contact in advance & have handicap certificate. With member only weekends & bank holidays.
Societies must apply in advance.
Green Fees £65 per day; £45 per round.
Prof Alasdair Thomas
Designer Willie Park
Facilities ⊗ ⅏ ⌂ 🍷 ♀ 🏖 🏠 ⛳ 🏌 🚃 ⚗ ♗
Location 1.5m SE off A611

Hotel ★★★★ 67% Swallow Hotel, Carter Ln East, SOUTH NORMANTON
☎ 01773 812000 160 ⇔ ⛏

LONG EATON   Map 08 SK43

Trent Lock Golf Centre Lock Ln, Sawley NG10 2FY
☎ 0115 946 4398 Fax 0115 946 1183
Main course has two par 5, five par 3 and eleven par 4 holes, plus water features and three holes adjacent to the river. A challenging test of golf. A 24 bay floodlit golf range is available.
Main Course: 18 holes, 5717yds, Par 69, SSS 68, Course record 73.
9 hole: 9 holes, 2911yds, Par 36.
Club membership 500.
Visitors no restriction Mon-Fri am but booking system 12pm Fri-closing Sun. May play 9 hole course at any time.

▶

Societies apply in writing or telephone in advance.
Green Fees 18 hole course £10 (£12 weekends). 9 hole £5.
Cards ⬚ ⬚ ⬚ ⬚ ⬚ ⬚
Prof M Taylor
Designer E McCausland
Facilities ⊗ 川 ⅃ ♭ ⬛ ♀ ⬿ 🏠 ◐ ⬿ ◐ ┃
Hotel ★★★ 65% Novotel, Bostock Ln, LONG EATON ☎ 0115 946 5111 108 ⇆ ⫽

MANSFIELD   Map 08 SK56

Sherwood Forest Eakring Rd NG18 3EW
☎ 01623 626689 Fax 01623 420412
As the name suggests, the Forest is the main feature of this natural heathland course with its heather, silver birch and pine trees. The homeward nine holes are particularly testing. The 11th to the 14th are notable par 4 holes on this well-bunkered course designed by the great James Braid.
18 holes, 6698yds, Par 71, SSS 73, Course record 64.
Club membership 750.
Visitors weekdays only by prior arrangement with the Secretary.
Societies by arrangement with the Secretary.
Green Fees £55 per day; £40 per round.
Prof Ken Hall
Designer W S Colt/James Braid
Facilities ⊗ 川 ⅃ ♭ ⬛ ♀ ⬿ 🏠 ◐
& Leisure snooker.
Location E of Mansfield

Hotel ★★ 66% Pine Lodge Hotel, 281-283 Nottingham Rd, MANSFIELD ☎ 01623 622308 20 ⇆ ⫽

MANSFIELD WOODHOUSE   Map 08 SK56

Mansfield Woodhouse Leeming Ln North NG19 9EU
☎ 01623 623521
Easy walking on heathland.
9 holes, 2446yds, Par 68, SSS 64.
Club membership 130.
Visitors no restrictions.
Societies must contact by telephone.
Green Fees not confirmed.
Prof Leslie Highfield
Designer A Highfield & F Horfman
Facilities ⊗ 川 ⅃ ♭ ⬛ ♀ 🏠 ⫽
Location N side of town centre off A60

Hotel ★★ 66% Pine Lodge Hotel, 281-283 Nottingham Rd, MANSFIELD ☎ 01623 622308 20 ⇆ ⫽

NEWARK-ON-TRENT   Map 08 SK75

Newark Coddington NG24 2QX
☎ 01636 626282 Fax 01636 626497
Wooded, parkland course in secluded situation with easy walking.
18 holes, 6457yds, Par 71, SSS 71, Course record 66.
Club membership 600.
Visitors must contact in advance and have handicap certificate. May not play Tue (Ladies Day) or weekends.
Societies must contact in advance.

Green Fees £28 per 36 holes; £23 per 18 holes (£28 weekends).
Prof P A Lockley
Designer T Williamson
Facilities ⊗ 川 ⅃ ♭ ⬛ ♀ ⬿ 🏠 ⫽
& Leisure snooker.
Location 4m E on A17

Hotel ★★ 71% Grange Hotel, 73 London Rd, NEWARK ☎ 01636 703399 10 ⇆ ⫽ Annexe 5 ⇆ ⫽

NOTTINGHAM   Map 08 SK53

Beeston Fields Old Dr, Wollaton Rd, Beeston NG9 3DD
☎ 0115 925 7062 Fax 0115 925 4280
Parkland course with sandy subsoil and wide, tree-lined fairways. The par 3, 14th has elevated tee and small bunker-guarded green.
18 holes, 6402yds, Par 71, SSS 71, Course record 64.
Club membership 800.
Visitors must contact professional on 0115 922 0872 for availability.
Societies must apply in advance.
Green Fees £36 per 36 holes; £26 per round.
Prof Alun Wardle
Designer Tom Williamson
Facilities ⊗ 川 ⅃ ♭ ⬛ ♀ ⬿ 🏠 ⫽ ◐
Location 400mtrs SW off A52 Nottingham/Derby road

Hotel ★★★ 67% Posthouse Nottingham/Derby, Bostocks Ln, SANDIACRE ☎ 0870 400 9062 93 ⇆ ⫽

Bramcote Hills Thoresby Rd, off Derby Rd, Bramcote NG9 3EP ☎ 0115 928 1880
A Pay and Play, 18-hole Par 3 course, a great challenge.
18 holes, 1500yds, Par 54.
Visitors no restrictions.
Societies telephone in advance.
Green Fees £6.30 per round (£6.80 weekends & bank holidays).
Facilities ⫽
Location Off A52 Derby rd

Hotel ★★★ 65% Posthouse Nottingham City, St James's St, NOTTINGHAM ☎ 0870 400 9061 130 ⇆ ⫽

Bulwell Forest Hucknall Rd, Bulwell NG6 9LQ
☎ 0115 977 0576
Municipal heathland course with many natural hazards. Very tight fairways and subject to wind.
18 holes, 5606yds, Par 68, SSS 67, Course record 62.
Club membership 350.
Visitors restricted weekends. Must contact in advance.
Societies must apply in advance.
Green Fees £16 per day; £11 per round.
Cards ⬚ ⬚ ⬚ ⬚ ⬚ ⬚
Prof Lee Rawlings
Facilities ⊗ 川 by prior arrangement ♭ ⬛ ♀ ⬿ 🏠 ⫽ ◐
& Leisure hard tennis courts.
Location 3m from junct 26 on M1. 4m NW of city centre on A611

Hotel ★★★ 64% Nottingham Moat House, Mansfield Rd, NOTTINGHAM ☎ 0115 935 9988 172 ⇆ ⫽

Chilwell Manor Meadow Ln, Chilwell NG9 5AE
☎ 0115 925 8958 Fax 0115 922 0575
Flat parkland course.
18 holes, 6379yds, Par 70, SSS 70, Course record 66.
Club membership 750.

Visitors	with member only weekends. Must contact in advance and have a handicap certificate.
Societies	welcome Mon, must apply in advance.
Green Fees	£18 per round (£20 weekends).
Prof	Paul Wilson
Designer	Tom Williamson
Facilities	⊗ �🏍 🖺 ▆ ♀ 🛆 🖻 𝒪
Location	4m SW on A6005

Hotel   ★★ 64% Europa Hotel, 20-22 Derby Rd, LONG EATON ☎ 0115 972 8481 15 ➡ 🏌

Edwalton Municipal Wellin Ln, Edwalton NG12 4AS
☎ 0115 923 4775
Gently sloping, 9-hole parkland course. Also 9-hole Par 3
and large practice ground.
9 holes, 3336yds, Par 72, SSS 72, Course record 71.
Club membership 900.

Visitors	booking system in operation.
Societies	prior booking necessary.
Green Fees	not confirmed.
Cards	🟰 ■ 🟰 📧 ⑨
Prof	John Staples
Facilities	⊗ 🖺 ▆ ♀ 🛆 🖻 𝒪
Location	S of Nottingham, off A606

Hotel   ★★ 65% Rufford Hotel, 53 Melton Rd, West Bridgford, NOTTINGHAM ☎ 0115 981 4202 34 ➡ 🏌

Mapperley Central Av, Plains Rd, Mapperley NG3 5RH
☎ 0115 955 6672 Fax 0115 955 6673
Hilly meadowland course but with easy walking.
18 holes, 6303yds, Par 71, SSS 70, Course record 68.
Club membership 650.

Visitors	must contact in advance. May not play Tue or Sat.
Societies	must telephone in advance.
Green Fees	£20 per day; £15 per round (£25/£20 weekends & bank holidays).
Prof	Malcolm Allen
Designer	John Mason
Facilities	⊗ �🏍 🖺 ▆ ♀ 🛆 🖻 𝒪
Location	3m NE of city centre off B684

Hotel   ★★★ 65% Posthouse Nottingham City, St James's St, NOTTINGHAM ☎ 0870 400 9061 130 ➡ 🏌

Nottingham City Lawton Dr, Bulwell NG6 8BL
☎ 0115 927 6916 & 927 2767 Fax 0115 927 6916
A pleasant municipal parkland course on the city outskirts.
18 holes, 6218yds, Par 69, SSS 70, Course record 65.
Club membership 425.

Visitors	restricted Sat 7am-3pm. Contact Professional in advance.
Societies	welcome, contact professional.
Green Fees	on request.
Cards	🟰 ■
Prof	Cyril Jepson
Designer	H Braid
Facilities	⊗ �🏍 🖺 ▆ ♀ 🛆 🖻 𝒪

Location	4m NW of city centre off A6002
Hotel	★★★ 64% Nottingham Moat House, Mansfield Rd, NOTTINGHAM ☎ 0115 935 9988 172 ➡ 🏌

Wollaton Park Limetree Av, Wollaton Park NG8 1BT
☎ 0115 978 7574 Fax 0115 978 7574
A pleasant, fairly level course set in a park close to the
centre of Nottingham, with red and fallow deer herds.
The fairways are tree-lined. The 502-yd dog-leg 15th is a
notable hole. The stately home - Wollaton Hall - is
situated in the park.
18 holes, 6445yds, Par 71, SSS 71, Course record 64.
Club membership 700.

Visitors	may not play Wed or competition days.
Societies	must apply in advance.
Green Fees	not confirmed.
Prof	John Lower
Designer	W Williamson
Facilities	⊗ ⃟ 🖺 ▆ ♀ 🛆 🖻 𝒪
Location	2.5m W of city centre off A52

Hotel   ★★★ 58% Swans Hotel & Restaurant, 84-90 Radcliffe Rd, West Bridgford, NOTTINGHAM ☎ 0115 981 4042 30 ➡ 🏌

OLLERTON   Map 08 SK66

Rufford Park Golf Centre Rufford Ln, Rufford NG22 9DG
☎ 01623 825253 Fax 01623 825254
Rufford Park is noted for its pictuesque 18 holes with its
especially challenging Par 3's. From the unique 173yard Par
3 17th over water to the riverside 596yard 13th, the course
offers everything the golfer needs from beginner to
professional.
18 holes, 6173yds, Par 70, SSS 69, Course record 67.
Club membership 650.

Visitors	are advised to book in advance. Unable to play weekend mornings.
Societies	society packages on request, need to be booked in advance.
Green Fees	£14 per round (£18 weekends).
Cards	🟰 ■ 🟰 📧 ⑨
Prof	John Vaughan/James Thompson
Designer	David Hemstock
Facilities	⊗ ⃟ 🖺 ▆ ♀ 🛆 🖻 ⃗ 🌳 𝒪 ⟊
Location	S Of Ollerton off A614. Take the 'Rufford Mill' turn

Hotel   ★★★ 68% Clumber Park Hotel, Clumber Park, WORKSOP ☎ 01623 835333   48 ➡ 🏌

OXTON   Map 08 SK65

Oakmere Park Oaks Ln NG25 0RH
☎ 0115 965 3545 Fax 0115 965 5628
Set in rolling parkland in the heart of picturesque Robin
Hood country. The par 4 (16th) and par 5 (1st) are notable.
Twenty-bay floodlit driving range.
Admirals: 18 holes, 6617yds, Par 72, SSS 72.
Commanders: 9 holes, 6407yds, Par 72, SSS 71.
Club membership 450.

Visitors	correct golf attire required, please book for weekends.

▶

Societies   please apply in writing or telephone.
Green Fees   Admirals: £18 per round (£24 weekends).
       Commanders: £10 per 18 holes (£14 weekends).
Cards
Prof   Daryl St-John Jones
Designer   Frank Pennick
Facilities
Location   1m NW off A6097

Hotel   ★★★ 64% Westminster Hotel, 312 Mansfield Rd, Carrington, NOTTINGHAM
    ☎ 0115 955 5000 72

RADCLIFFE-ON-TRENT   Map 08 SK63

Cotgrave Place Golf & Country Club Main Rd, Stragglethorpe NG12 3HB
☎ 0115 933 3344 Fax 0115 933 4567
The course now offers 36 holes of championship golf. The front nine of the Open Course are placed around a beautiful lake, man made ponds and the Grantham Canal. The back nine is set in magnificent parkland with mature trees and wide fairways. Masters has an opening nine set amongst hedgerows and coppices. The huge greens with their interesting shapes are a particularly challenging test of nerve. The par 5, 17th hole is one of the toughest in the country.
Open course: 18 holes, 6303yds, Par 71, SSS 70.
Masters course: 18 holes, 5887yds, Par 69, SSS 68.
Club membership 650.
Visitors   must contact, can book 1 week in advance.
Societies   telephone in advance.
Green Fees £16 per round (£20-£25 weekends).
Cards
Prof   Robert Smith
Facilities
Location   Off A52, 6 miles from Nottingham

Hotel   ★★♣♣ 70% Langar Hall, LANGAR
    ☎ 01949 860559   10

Radcliffe-on-Trent Dewberry Ln, Cropwell Rd NG12 2JH
☎ 0115 933 3000 Fax 0115 911 6991
Fairly flat, parkland course with three good finishing holes: 16th (427 yds) par 4; 17th (180 yds) through spinney, par 3; 18th (331 yds) dog-leg par 4. Excellent views.
18 holes, 6381yds, Par 70, SSS 71, Course record 64.
Club membership 670.
Visitors   must contact in advance for play on Wed only.
Societies   welcome Wed. Must contact in advance.
Green Fees £23 per day (£28 weekends).
Prof   Robert Ellis
Designer   Tom Williamson
Facilities
Location   Take the A52 to Nottingham, turn L at 2nd set of traffic lights, 400yds on left

Hotel   ★★★ 58% Swans Hotel & Restaurant, 84-90 Radcliffe Rd, West Bridgford, NOTTINGHAM
    ☎ 0115 981 4042 30

RETFORD   Map 08 SK78

Retford Brecks Rd, Ordsall DN22 7UA
☎ 01777 860682 (Secretary) & 703733 (Pro)
Fax 01777 710412
A wooded, parkland course.
18 holes, 6409yds, Par 72, SSS 72, Course record 67.
Club membership 700.

Visitors   advisable to contact in advance, with member only at weekends and holidays.
Societies   apply in writing or telephone. Not welcome Tue morning or bank holidays, limited availability weekends.
Green Fees not confirmed.
Prof   Craig Morris
Designer   Tom Williamson
Facilities
Location   1.5m S A620, between Worksop & Gainsborough

Hotel   ★★★ 64% West Retford Hotel, 24 North Rd, RETFORD ☎ 01777 706333 Annexe 62

RUDDINGTON   Map 08 SK53

Ruddington Grange Wilford Rd NG11 6NB
☎ 0115 984 6141
Undulating parkland course with water hazards on 12 holes.
18 holes, 6543yds, Par 72, SSS 72, Course record 69.
Club membership 650.
Visitors   a handicap certificate is required, tee time must be booked in advance. Play may be restricted Sat & Wed mornings.
Societies   must contact in advance.
Green Fees £16 per round (£23.50 weekends).
Prof   Robert Simpson
Designer   E MacAusland
Facilities
Location   5m S of Nottingham, A60 to Ruddington

Hotel   ★★★ 58% Swans Hotel & Restaurant, 84-90 Radcliffe Rd, West Bridgford, NOTTINGHAM
    ☎ 0115 981 4042 30

SERLBY   Map 08 SK68

Serlby Park DN10 6BA
☎ 01777 818268 Fax 01302 536336
Parkland course.
11 holes, 5325yds, Par 66, SSS 66, Course record 63.
Club membership 250.
Visitors   must be introduced by and play with member.
Societies   apply in writing before 31 Dec for following year.
Green Fees not confirmed.
Designer   Galway
Facilities
Location   E side of village off A638

Hotel   ★★★ 69% Charnwood Hotel, Sheffield Rd, BLYTH ☎ 01909 591610   34

SUTTON IN ASHFIELD   Map 08 SK45

Coxmoor Coxmoor Rd NG17 5LF
☎ 01623 557359 Fax 01623 557359
Undulating moorland/heathland course with easy walking and excellent views. The clubhouse is traditional with a well-equipped games room. The course lies adjacent to Forestry Commission land over which there are several footpaths and extensive views.
18 holes, 6571yds, Par 73, SSS 72, Course record 65.
Club membership 700.

▶

Visitors	must play with member weekends & bank holidays. Must contact in advance.
Societies	must apply in advance.
Green Fees	£35 per 18 holes; £45 per 27/36 holes.
Prof	David Ridley
Facilities	⊗ ⅢⅬ ⬛ ♀ ⚲ 🏠 ♂
& Leisure	snooker.
Location	2m SE off A611. 4m from junct 27 on M1

Hotel	★★★★ 67% Swallow Hotel, Carter Ln East, SOUTH NORMANTON ☎ 01773 812000 160 ⇄ ♠

WORKSOP   Map 08 SK57

Bondhay Golf & Country Club Bondhay Ln, Whitwell S80 3EH ☎ 01909 723608 Fax 01909 720226
The wind usually plays quite an active role in making this pleasantly undulating course testing. Signatures holes are the 10th which requires a 2nd shot over water into a basin of trees; the 11th comes back over the same expanse of water and requires a mid to short iron to a long, narrow green; the 18th is a Par 5 with a lake right in lay up distance - the dilemma is whether to lay up short or go for the carry. The par 3's are generally island like in design, requiring accuracy to avoid the protective bunker features.
Devonshire Course: 18 holes, 6705yds, Par 72, SSS 71, Course record 67.
Family Course: 9 holes, 1118yds, Par 27, Course record 24.
Club membership 400.

Visitors	must contact in advance.
Societies	must telephone in advance.
Green Fees	Summer: £15 per round (£20 weekends) Winter: £12.50 per round (£17.50 weekends).
Cards	💳
Prof	Michael Ramsden
Designer	Donald Steel
Facilities	⊗ ⅢⅬ ⬛ ♀ ⚲ 🏠 🏹 ⚓ ♂ ⚑
& Leisure	fishing.
Location	5m W of Worksop, off A619

Hotel	★★★ 62% Sitwell Arms Hotel, Station Rd, RENISHAW ☎ 01246 435226 30 ⇄ ♠

Kilton Forest Blyth Rd S81 0TL ☎ 01909 486563
Slightly undulating, parkland course on the north edge of Sherwood Forest. Includes three ponds. Excellent conditions all the year round.
18 holes, 6424yds, Par 72, SSS 71, Course record 69.
Club membership 320.

Visitors	must contact in advance. May not play at weekends before 10am.
Societies	must contact in advance.
Green Fees	contact professional.
Prof	Stuart Betteridge
Facilities	⊗ ⅢⅬ ⬛ ♀ ⚲ 🏠 🏹 ⚓ ♂
& Leisure	bowling.
Location	1m NE of town centre on B6045

Hotel	★★★ 65% Lion Hotel, 112 Bridge St, WORKSOP ☎ 01909 477925 32 ⇄ ♠

> Entries with a green background
> identify courses considered to be
> particularly interesting

Lindrick Lindrick Common S81 8BH
☎ 01909 475282 Fax 01909 488685
Heathland course with some trees and masses of gorse.
18 holes, 6486yds, Par 71, SSS 72, Course record 65.
Club membership 490.

Visitors	must contact in advance. Restricted Tue & weekends. Handicap certificate required.
Societies	welcome except Tue (am) & weekends by prior arrangement with the Secretary.
Green Fees	not confirmed.
Prof	John R King
Facilities	⊗ ⅢⅬ ⬛ ♀ ⚲ 🏠 ♂
& Leisure	buggies for disabled only.
Location	4m NW on A57

Hotel	★★★ 65% Lion Hotel, 112 Bridge St, WORKSOP ☎ 01909 477925 32 ⇄ ♠

Worksop Windmill Ln S80 2SQ
☎ 01909 472696 & 477731 Fax 01909 477731
Adjacent to Clumber Park this course has a heathland-type terrain, with gorse, broom, oak and birch trees. Fast, true greens, dry all year round.
18 holes, 6660yds, Par 72, SSS 73.
Club membership 600.

Visitors	by arrangement with professional tel: 01909 477732.
Societies	must apply in advance.
Green Fees	£35 per day; £26 per round (£35 per round weekends).
Prof	C Weatherhead
Facilities	⊗ ⅢⅬ ⬛ ♀ ⚲ 🏠 ♂
Location	Off A57 Ringroad, B6034 to Edwinstowe

Hotel	★★★ 68% Clumber Park Hotel, Clumber Park, WORKSOP ☎ 01623 835333 48 ⇄ ♠

OXFORDSHIRE

ABINGDON   Map 04 SU49

Drayton Park Steventon Rd, Drayton Village OX14 4LA
☎ 01235 550607 (Pro Shop) & 528989 (Secretary) Fax 012 35 525731
Set in the heart of the Oxfordshire countryside, an 18-hole parkland course designed by Hawtree. Five lakes and sand based greens.
18 holes, 5500yds, Par 67, SSS 67.
Club membership 500.

Visitors	may phone to book, must have golf shoes, no jeans or tracksuits.
Societies	contact in advance.
Green Fees	£25 per day; £14 per round (£17 per round weekends & bank holidays).
Prof	Martin Morbey
Designer	Hawtree
Facilities	⊗ ⅢⅬ ⬛ ♀ ⚲ 🏠 🏹 ⚓ ♂ ⚑
& Leisure	9 hole par 3 course.
Location	Between Oxford & Newbury,off A34 at Didcot

Hotel	★★★ 66% The Upper Reaches, Thames St, ABINGDON ☎ 0870 400 8101 31 ⇄ ♠

BANBURY
Map 04 SP44

Rye Hill Milcombe OX15 4RU
☎ 01295 721818 Fax 01295 720089
Well drained course features wide fairways, large undulating greens, water hazards on the 10th, and fine views of the surrounding countryside.
18 holes, 6919yds, Par 72, SSS 73, Course record 71.
Club membership 400.
Visitors must book in advance, especially at weekends. May not play Sat before 11am.
Societies telephone for details of Packages available.
Green Fees £25 per day; £14 per round (£30/£17 weekends and bank holidays).
Cards 〓 〓 〓 〓 〓
Prof Tony Pennock
Facilities ⊗ ⓑ ♥ ♀ ♣ ☎ ⛳ ♣ ♣ ♂
& Leisure fishing.
Location Junct 11 M40. A361 towards Chipping Norton, signed 1m out of Bloxham

Hotel ★★★ 70% Banbury House, Oxford Rd, BANBURY ☎ 01295 259361 63 ⇔ ♠

BURFORD
Map 04 SP21

Burford Swindon Rd OX18 4JG
☎ 01993 822583 Fax 01993 822801
Parkland with mature, treelined fairways and high quality greens.
18 holes, 6414yds, Par 71, SSS 71, Course record 64.
Club membership 830.
Visitors must contact in advance. May not play weekends.
Societies apply in writing.
Green Fees not confirmed.
Prof Michael Ridge
Designer John H Turner
Facilities ⊗ ⫴ by prior arrangement ⓑ ♥ ♀ ♣ ☎ ⛳ ♂
Location 0.5m S off A361

Hotel ★★ 65% Golden Pheasant Hotel, 91 High St, BURFORD ☎ 01993 823223 12rm (11 ⇔ ♠)

CHESTERTON
Map 04 SP52

Chesterton Golf & Country Club OX6 8TE
☎ 01869 242023
Laid out over one-time farmland. Well-bunkered, and water hazards increase the difficulty of the course.
18 holes, 6229yds, Par 71, SSS 70, Course record 68.
Club membership 400.
Visitors may pre-book upto 4 days ahead.
Societies must contact in advance.
Green Fees not confirmed.
Prof J Wilkshire
Designer R Stagg
Facilities ⓑ ♥ ♀ ♣ ☎ ♂
& Leisure Snooker.
Location 0.5m W off A4095, 1m E of B430 at Weston-on-the-Green

Hotel ★★ 68% Jersey Arms Hotel, MIDDLETON STONEY ☎ 01869 343234 & 343505 Fax 01869 343565 6 ⇔ Annexe 10 ⇔

CHIPPING NORTON
Map 04 SP32

Chipping Norton Southcombe OX7 5QH
☎ 01608 642383 Fax 01608 645422
Pleasant downland course open to winds.
18 holes, 6241yds, Par 71, SSS 70, Course record 62.
Club membership 900.
Visitors with member only at weekends & bank holidays.
Societies telephone in advance.
Green Fees £25 per day/round.
Prof Derek Craik
Facilities ⊗ ⫴ ⓑ ♥ ♀ ♣ ☎ ⛳ ♣ ♣ ♂
Location 1.5m E on A44

Lyneham Lyneham OX7 6QQ
☎ 01993 831841 Fax 01993 831775
Lyneham was designed to use the natural features. It is set in 170 acres on the fringe of the Costwolds and blends superbly with its surroundings. Lakes and streams enhance the challenge of the course with water coming into play on 8 of the 18 holes. All greens are sand based, built to USGA specification.
18 holes, 6669yds, Par 72, SSS 72, Course record 67.
Club membership 725.
Visitors must contact in advance.
Societies apply in advance.
Green Fees not confirmed.
Prof Richard Jefferies
Designer D G Carpenter
Facilities ⊗ ⫴ ⓑ ♥ ♀ ♣ ☎ ⛳ ♣ ♣ ♂ ♪
Location Off A361, between Burford/Chipping Norton

Hotel ★★ 66% Shaven Crown Hotel, SHIPTON-UNDER-WYCHWOOD ☎ 01993 830330 9rm (8 ⇔ ♠)

DIDCOT
Map 04 SU59

Hadden Hill Wallingford Rd OX11 9BJ
☎ 01235 510410 Fax 01235 510410
A challenging course on undulating terrain with excellent drainage so visitors can be sure of playing no matter what the weather conditions have been. Two loops of nine holes.
18 holes, 6563yds, Par 71, SSS 71, Course record 65.
Club membership 400.
Visitors telephone to book tee times.
Societies telephone to arrange times & dates & receive booking form.
Green Fees £14 per 18 holes; £8.50 per 9 holes (£18.50/£9.50 weekends).
Cards 〓 〓 〓 〓 〓
Prof Adrian Waters
Designer Michael V Morley
Facilities ⊗ ⫴ ⓑ ♥ ♀ ♣ ☎ ⛳ ♣ ♣ ♂ ♪
Location On A4130 1m E of Didcot

Hotel ★★★ 65% Abingdon Four Pillars Hotel, Marcham Rd, ABINGDON ☎ 01235 553456 62 ⇔ ♠

> AA Hotels that have special arrangements with golf courses are listed at the back of the guide

FARINGDON — Map 04 SU29

Carswell Carswell Home Farm, Carswell SN7 8PU
☎ 01367 870422 Fax 01367 870592
An attractive course set in undulating wooded countryside
close to Faringdon. Mature trees, five lakes and well placed
bunkers add interest to the course. Floodlit driving range.
18 holes, 6133yds, Par 72, SSS 70.

Visitors	book in advance to avoid dissapointment.
Societies	on weekdays only telephone to check availability, deposit required,
Green Fees	not confirmed.
Prof	Geoff Robbins
Facilities	⊗ ℳ ㄥ ♥ ♀ ♨ 🖻 🏌 🚶
& Leisure	sauna, gymnasium.
Location	Just off the A420 between Oxford and Swindon

Hotel ★★★ 73% Sudbury House Hotel &
Conference Centre, London St, FARINGDON
☎ 01367 241272 49 ⇄ 🐾

FRILFORD — Map 04 SU49

Frilford Heath OX13 5NW
☎ 01865 390864 Fax 01865 390823
54 holes in three distinctive layouts of significantly
differing character. The Green course is a fully mature
heathland course of some 6000 yards. The Red course is
of championship length at 6800 yards with a parkland
flavour and a marked degree of challenge. The Blue
course is of modern design, and at 6728 yards, it
incorporates water hazards and large shallow sand traps.
Red Course: 18 holes, 6884yds, Par 73, SSS 73, Course record 68.
Green Course: 18 holes, 6006yds, Par 69, SSS 69.
Blue Course: 18 holes, 6728yds, Par 72, SSS 72.
Club membership 1300.

Visitors	contact in advance. Handicap certificates required.
Societies	apply in advance.
Green Fees	£45 per day (£60 weekends).
Prof	Derek Craik
Designer	J Taylor/D Cotton/S Gidman
Facilities	⊗ ℳ ㄥ ♥ ♀ ♨ 🖻 🏌 🚶
Location	3m W of Abingdon off A338 Oxford-Wantage road

Hotel ★★★ 65% Abingdon Four Pillars Hotel,
Marcham Rd, ABINGDON
☎ 01235 553456 62 ⇄ 🐾

HENLEY-ON-THAMES — Map 04 SU78

Aspect Park Remenham Hill RG9 3EH
☎ 01491 577562 & 578306
Parkland course.
18 holes, 6643yds, Par 72, SSS 72.
Club membership 500.

Visitors	must contact in advance, suitable golf attire required on course, no jeans in the clubhouse.
Societies	must contact in advance.
Green Fees	not confirmed.
Prof	Terry Notley
Designer	Tim Winsland
Facilities	⊗ ℳ ㄥ ♥ ♀ ♨ 🖻 🏌 🚶

Hotel ★★★ 71% Red Lion Hotel, Hart St,
HENLEY-ON-THAMES
☎ 01491 572161 27 ⇄ 🐾

Badgemore Park RG9 4NR
☎ 01491 573667 Fax 01491 576899
Mature parkland course with easy walking. The 13th is a
very difficult par 3 hole played over a valley to a narrow
green and accuracy off the tee is essential.
18 holes, 6112yds, Par 69, SSS 69, Course record 65.
Club membership 600.

Visitors	contact professional shop on 01491 574175. Tuesday morning Ladies only, bookings to be made for all other times.
Societies	contact General Manager to book.
Green Fees	£20 (£30 weekends).
Cards	💳 💳 💳
Prof	Jonathan Dunn
Designer	Robert Sandow
Facilities	⊗ ℳ ㄥ ♥ ♀ ♨ 🖻 🏌 🚶
Location	From Henley take B290 to Rotherfield Greys Club, 1.5m on right

Hotel ★★★ 71% Red Lion Hotel, Hart St,
HENLEY-ON-THAMES
☎ 01491 572161 27 ⇄ 🐾

Henley Harpsden RG9 4HG
☎ 01491 575742 Fax 01491 412179
Undulating parkland course, with adjoining woodlands.
18 holes, 6329yds, Par 70, SSS 70, Course record 63.
Club membership 800.

Visitors	must contact in advance. Weekend only with a member.
Societies	Wed & Thu, apply in writing.
Green Fees	not confirmed.
Prof	Mark Howell
Designer	James Braid
Facilities	⊗ ℳ ㄥ ♥ ♀ ♨ 🖻
Location	1.25m S off A4155

Hotel ★★★ 71% Red Lion Hotel, Hart St,
HENLEY-ON-THAMES
☎ 01491 572161 27 ⇄ 🐾

HORTON-CUM-STUDLEY — Map 04 SP51

Studley Wood The Straight Mile OX33 1BF
☎ 01865 351122 & 351144 Fax 01865 351166
Woodland course set in a former deer park with twelve lakes
and specimen oak trees providing challenging natural hazards
on almost all the holes.
18 holes, 6811yds, Par 73, SSS 73, Course record 65.
Club membership 700.

Visitors	must play to handicap standard, tee times booked up to 4 days in advance.
Societies	contact secretary for details.
Green Fees	£25 per 18 holes (£35 weekend).
Cards	💳 💳 💳 💳
Prof	Tony Williams
Designer	Simon Gidman
Facilities	⊗ ℳ ㄥ ♥ ♀ ♨ 🖻 🏌 🚶
Location	4m from Oxford follow signs for Horton-cum-Studley from Headington rdbt on Oxford ringroad

Hotel ★★★⚓ 78% Studley Priory Hotel,
HORTON-CUM-STUDLEY
☎ 01865 351203 & 351254
Fax 01865 351613 18 ⇌ ⚑

KIRTLINGTON
Map 04 SP41

Kirtlington Lince Ln OX5 3JY
☎ 01869 351133 Fax 01869 351143
A three year old inland links type course with challenging greens.
18 holes, 6084yds, Par 70, SSS 69.
Club membership 300.
Visitors must book for weekends and advisable to book for weekdays. Must contact in advance.
Societies contact for Society packages.
Green Fees not confirmed.
Cards 💳
Prof Peter Hughes
Designer Graham Webster
Facilities ⊗ ⍬ ⌧ ⚑ ♀ ⚐ ⌂ ⍟ ⚑ ♦ ⚒ ♂ ⚵
Location On A4095 just outside village of Kirtlington

Hotel ★★★ 67% Weston Manor Hotel, WESTON-ON-THE-GREEN ☎ 01869 350621
16 ⇌ ⚑ Annexe 20 ⇌ ⚑

MILTON COMMON
Map 04 SP60

The Oxfordshire Rycote Ln OX9 2PU
☎ 01844 278300 Fax 01844 278003
Designed by Rees Jones, The Oxfordshire is considered to be one of the most exciting courses in the country. With four man-made lakes and 135 bunkers, it is a magnificent test of shot-making where almost every hole deserves special mention. Unfortunately it is only open to members and their guests.
18 holes, 7187yds, Par 72, SSS 76, Course record 64.
Club membership 750.
Visitors members guests only.
Green Fees £80 per round.
Cards 💳
Prof Neil Pike
Designer Rees Jones
Facilities ⚐ ⌂ ⍟ ♦ ⚒ ♂ ⚵
Location 1.5m from junct 7, M40 on A329

Hotel ★★★ 76% Spread Eagle Hotel,
Cornmarket, THAME
☎ 01844 213661 33 ⇌ ⚑

NUFFIELD
Map 04 SU68

Huntercombe RG9 5SL
☎ 01491 641207 Fax 01491 642060
This heathland/woodland course overlooks the Oxfordshire plain and has many attractive and interesting fairways and greens. Walking is easy after the 3rd hole which is a notable hole. The course is subject to wind and grass pot bunkers are interesting hazards.
18 holes, 6301yds, Par 70, SSS 70, Course record 63.
Club membership 800.
Visitors must contact in advance and have a handicap certificate.
Societies must contact in advance.
Green Fees not confirmed.

Prof John B Draycott
Designer Willy Park
Facilities ⚐ ⌂ ⚵
Location N off A423

Hotel ★★★ 64% Shillingford Bridge Hotel,
Shillingford, WALLINGFORD
☎ 01865 858567 34 ⇌ ⚑ Annexe 8 ⇌ ⚑

OXFORD
Map 04 SP50

North Oxford Banbury Rd OX2 8EZ
☎ 01865 554924 Fax 01865 515921
Gently undulating parkland course.
18 holes, 5736yds, Par 67, SSS 67, Course record 62.
Club membership 700.
Visitors at weekends & bank holidays may only play after 4pm.
Societies must contact in advance.
Green Fees £25 per day; £18 per round.
Prof Robert Harris
Facilities ⊗ ⍬ ⌧ ⚑ ♀ ⚐ ⌂ ⍟ ⚵
Location 3m N of city centre on A423

Hotel ★★★ 66% Oxford Moat House, Godstow Rd,
Wolvercote Roundabout, OXFORD
☎ 01865 489988 155 ⇌ ⚑

Southfield Hill Top Rd OX4 1PF
☎ 01865 242158 Fax 01865 242158
Home of the City, University and Ladies Clubs, and well-known to graduates throughout the world. A challenging course, in varied parkland setting, providing a real test for players.
18 holes, 6328yds, Par 70, SSS 70, Course record 61.
Club membership 850.
Visitors with member only at weekends.
Societies must apply in writing.
Green Fees £24 per day; £18 per round.
Cards 💳
Prof Tony Rees
Designer H S Colt
Facilities ⊗ ⍬ ⌧ ⚑ ♀ ⚐ ⌂ ⍟ ♦ ⚒ ⚵
Location 1.5m SE of city centre off B480

Hotel ★★★ 66% Eastgate Hotel, The High,
Merton St, OXFORD
☎ 0870 400 8201 64 ⇌ ⚑

SHRIVENHAM
Map 04 SU28

Shrivenham Park Penny Hooks SN6 8EX
☎ 01793 783853 Fax 01793 782999
An undulating course with excellent drainage, providing a good challenge for all standards of golfer.
18 holes, 5769yds, Par 69, SSS 69, Course record 64.
Club membership 350.
Visitors phone in advance.
Societies phone for details.
Green Fees £21 per day; £15 per 18 holes (£23/£17 weekends & bank holidays).
Cards 💳
Prof Jamie McArthur
Designer Gordon Cox

▶

Facilities	⊗ ⅷ ▮ ☟ ♀ ⚐ 🕭 🏌 ♿ ✐
Location	0.5m NE of town centre

| Hotel | ★★★ 73% Sudbury House Hotel & Conference Centre, London St, FARINGDON ☎ 01367 241272 49 ⇋ ﹇ |

TADMARTON   Map 04 SP33

Tadmarton Heath OX15 5HL
☎ 01608 737278 Fax 01608 730548
A mixture of heath and sandy land, the course, which is open to strong winds, incorporates the site of an old Roman encampment. The clubhouse is an old farm building with a 'holy well' from which the greens are watered. The 7th is a testing hole over water.
18 holes, 5917yds, Par 69, SSS 69, Course record 63.
Club membership 600.

Visitors	weekday by appointment, with member only at weekends.
Societies	by arrangement with club office.
Green Fees	£33 per day; £22 pm only (£35 per round weekends).
Prof	Tom Jones
Designer	Col Hutchinson
Facilities	⊗ ⅷ by prior arrangement ▮ ☟ ♀ ⚐ 🕭 🏌 ♿ ✐ (
& Leisure	fishing.
Location	1m SW of Lower Tadmarton off B4035, 4m from Banbury

| Hotel | ★★★ 70% Banbury House, Oxford Rd, BANBURY ☎ 01295 259361 63 ⇋ ﹇ |

WALLINGFORD   Map 04 SU68

Springs Hotel Wallingford Rd, North Stoke OX10 6BE
☎ 01491 827310 Fax 01491 827312
133 acres of park land, bordered by the river Thames, within which lie three lakes and challenging wetland areas. The course has traditional features like a double green and sleepered bunker with sleepered lake edges of the typical American design.
18 holes, 6470yds, Par 72, SSS 71.
Club membership 570.

Visitors	handicap certificate required. Must book in advance. Dress code must be adhered to.
Societies	
Green Fees	£35 per day, £24 per round (£45/£30 weekends).
Cards	▭ ▬ 💳 💳 ▦ ▩ 🗌
Prof	Leigh Atkins
Designer	Brian Hugget
Facilities	⊗ ⅷ ▮ ☟ ♀ ⚐ 🕭 🏌 🛒 ♿ ✐
& Leisure	heated outdoor swimming pool, fishing, sauna.

| Hotel | ★★★ 72% Springs Hotel, Wallingford Rd, North Stoke, WALLINGFORD ☎ 01491 836687 31 ⇋ ﹇ |

WATERSTOCK   Map 04 SP60

Waterstock Thame Rd OX33 1HT
☎ 01844 338093 Fax 01844 338036
A 6,500yard course designed by Donald Steel with USGA greens and tees fully computer irrigated. Four Par 3's facing North, South, East and West. A brook and hidden lake affect

six holes, with doglegs being 4th and 10th holes. Five Par 5's on the course, making it a challenge for players of all standards.
18 holes, 6535yds, Par 73, SSS 71, Course record 68.
Club membership 500.

Visitors	no restrictions.
Societies	apply in writing or telephone.
Green Fees	not confirmed.
Prof	Julian Goodman
Designer	Donald Steel
Facilities	⊗ ⅷ ▮ ☟ ♀ ⚐ 🕭 🏌 ♿ 🛒 ✐ (
& Leisure	fishing.
Location	On junc 8 of M40

| Hotel | ★★★ 76% Spread Eagle Hotel, Cornmarket, THAME ☎ 01844 213661 33 ⇋ ﹇ |

WITNEY   Map 04 SP31

Witney Lakes Downs Rd OX8 5SY
☎ 01993 893011 Fax 01993 778866
A lakeland style course with 5 large lakes coming into play on 8 holes. An excellent test of golf that will use every club in your bag.
18 holes, 6700yds, Par 71.
Club membership 400.

Visitors	may pre-book 5 days in advance.
Societies	telephone or write in advance.
Green Fees	not confirmed.
Designer	Simon Gidman
Facilities	♀ ⚐ 🕭 🏌 ♿ 🛒 ✐ (
& Leisure	heated indoor swimming pool, sauna, solarium, gymnasium.
Location	2m W of Witney town centre, off B4047 Witney/Burford road

| Hotel | ★★★ 70% Witney Four Pillars Hotel, Ducklington Ln, WITNEY ☎ 01993 779777 74 ⇋ ﹇ |

RUTLAND

GREAT CASTERTON   Map 08 TF00

Rutland County PE9 4AQ
☎ 01780 460330 Fax 01780 460437
Inland links-style course with gently rolling fairways, large tees and greens. Playable all year round due to good drainage.
18 holes, 6401yds, Par 71, SSS 71, Course record 64.
Club membership 600.

Visitors	must book in advance at the shop, tel 01780 460239.
Societies	contact office by phone, must be booked in advance.
Green Fees	£30 per day, £20 per round (£35/25 weekends).
Cards	▭ ▬ 💳 💳 ▦ ▩ 🗌
Prof	James Darroch
Designer	Cameron Sinclair
Facilities	⊗ ⅷ ▮ ☟ ♀ ⚐ 🕭 🏌 ♿ 🛒 ✐ (
Location	2m N of Stamford on A1

Hotel ★★ 67% The White Horse Inn, Main St,
EMPINGHAM ☎ 01780 460221 & 460521
Fax 01780 460521 4 ⇄ ↰ Annexe 9 ⇄ ↰

GREETHAM Map 08 SK91

Greetham Valley Wood Ln LE15 7NP
☎ 01780 460004 Fax 01780 460623
Set in 260 acres, including mature woodland, undulating
natural valley, and water hazards. The complex comprises
2x18 hole courses The Lakes and The Valley. A luxurious
clubhouse, 9 hole par 3, floodlit driving range and teaching
academy.
Lakes: 18 holes, 6779yds, Par 72, SSS 72, Course record 68.
Valley: 18 holes, 5595yds, Par 68, SSS 67.
Club membership 850.
Visitors must contact in advance.
Societies must contact in advance.
Green Fees £32 per day (£35 weekends); £24 per 18 holes
(£28 weekends).
Prof John Pengelly
Designer F E Hinch
Facilities ⊗ ⅏ ㄴ ▅ ♀ ⚲ ⌂ ⚑ ↾ ↳ ⚒ ⚙ ⚓
& Leisure bowls green.
Location Take the B668 Oakham road off the A1 and
follow signs to the course which are clearly
marked

Hotel ★★★ 72% Barnsdale Lodge Hotel, The
Avenue, Rutland Water, North Shore,
OAKHAM ☎ 01572 724678 45 ⇄ ↰

SHROPSHIRE

BRIDGNORTH Map 07 SO79

Bridgnorth Stanley Ln WV16 4SF
☎ 01746 763315 Fax 01746 761381
A pleasant course laid-out on parkland on the bank of the
River Severn.
18 holes, 6673yds, Par 73, SSS 73, Course record 65.
Club membership 725.
Visitors must contact in advance but may not play on
Wed. Restricted weekends.
Societies must contact in writing.
Green Fees £24 per round; £30 per 36 holes (£30/£36
weekends & bank holidays).
Prof Paul Hinton
Facilities ⊗ ⅏ ㄴ ▅ ♀ ⚲ ⌂ ↳ ⚙
& Leisure fishing.
Location 1m N off B4373, 0.5m from town centre

Hotel ★ 67% Croft Hotel, Saint Mary's St,
BRIDGNORTH
☎ 01746 762416 12rm (10 ⇄ ↰)

CHURCH STRETTON Map 07 SO49

Church Stretton Trevor Hill SY6 6JH
☎ 01694 722281 Fax 01694 722633
Hillside course designed by James Braid on the lower slopes
of the Long Mynd.
18 holes, 5020yds, Par 66, SSS 65, Course record 63.
Club membership 450.

Visitors Tee reserved for members Sat 9-10.30 & 1-2.30,
Sun prior to 10.30 & 1-2.30 (summer).
Societies must contact in advance.
Green Fees £14 per day/round (£20 weekends & bank
holidays).
Prof J Townsend
Designer James Braid
Facilities ⊗ ⅏ ㄴ ▅ ♀ ⚲ ⌂
Location W of the town. From Cardington Valley drive
up Trevor Hill, a steep, winding road

Hotel ★★ 69% Mynd House Hotel, Ludlow Rd,
Little Stretton, CHURCH STRETTON
☎ 01694 722212 7 ⇄ ↰

CLEOBURY MORTIMER Map 07 SO67

Cleobury Mortimer Wyre Common DY14 8HQ
☎ 01299 271112 Fax 01299 271628
Well designed 27-hole parkland course set in undulating
countryside with fine views from all holes, and offering an
interesting challenge to golfers of all abilities.
Foxes Run: 9 holes, 2980yds, Par 34, SSS 34.
Badgers Sett: 9 holes, 3271yds, Par 36, SSS 36.
Deer Park: 9 holes, 3167yds, Par 35, SSS 35.
Club membership 650.
Visitors advisable to book in advance, handicap
certificate may be required at weekends.
Societies write or telephone in advance.
Green Fees £18 per 18 holes (£21 weekends).
Cards ▭ ▭ ▭ ▭ ▭
Prof Graham Farr
Facilities ⊗ ⅏ ㄴ ▅ ♀ ⚲ ⌂ ↳ ⚙ ⚓
& Leisure fishing.
Location 10m W of Kidderminster on A4117 1m N of
Cleobury Mortimer, off B4201

Hotel ★★★ 71% Redfern Hotel, CLEOBURY
MORTIMER
☎ 01299 270395 5 ⇄ ↰ Annexe 6 ⇄ ↰

HIGHLEY Map 07 SO78

Severn Meadows WV16 6HZ ☎ 01746 862212
Picturesque course set alongside the River Severn and
providing a tight test of golf with much of the course
bordered by mature trees.
9 holes, 5258yds, Par 68, SSS 67.
Club membership 170.
Visitors booking advisable for weekends.
Societies advance booking necessary.
Green Fees not confirmed.
Facilities ⊗ ㄴ ▅ ♀ ⚲ ⌂
Hotel ★★★★ 66% Mill Hotel & Restaurant,
ALVELEY ☎ 01746 780437 21 ⇄ ↰

LILLESHALL Map 07 SJ71

Lilleshall Hall TF10 9AS ☎ 01952 603840
Heavily-wooded parkland course. Easy walking.
18 holes, 5906yds, Par 68, SSS 68.
Club membership 650.
Visitors must contact in advance and play with member
at weekends.
Societies must apply in writing by Dec for the following
year.
Green Fees not confirmed.

▶

Prof Nigel Bramall
Designer H S Colt
Facilities ⛳🏌♂
Location 3m SE

Hotel ★★ 68% White House Hotel, Wellington Rd, Muxton, TELFORD ☎ 01952 604276 & 603603 Fax 01952 670336 32 ⇥ ♠

LUDLOW   Map 07 SO57

Ludlow Bromfield SY8 2BT ☎ 01584 856285
A long-established heathland course in the middle of the racecourse. Very flat, quick drying, with broom and gorse-lined fairways.
18 holes, 6277yds, Par 70, SSS 70, Course record 65.
Club membership 700.
Visitors advisable to contact in advance.
Societies apply in advance.
Green Fees not confirmed.
Prof Russell Price
Facilities ⊗ ⅲ ⅂ ♥ ♀ ⛳ 🏌 🎯 ♂
Location 1m N of Ludlow, off A49

Hotel ★★★ 64% The Feathers at Ludlow, Bull Ring, LUDLOW ☎ 01584 875261 40 ⇥ ♠

MARKET DRAYTON   Map 07 SJ63

Market Drayton Sutton TF9 2HX
☎ 01630 652266 Fax 01630 652266
Parkland course in quiet, picturesque surroundings providing a good test of golf. Bungalow on course is made available for golfing holidays.
18 holes, 6290yds, Par 71, SSS 71, Course record 69.
Club membership 550.
Visitors may not play on Sun; must play with member on Sat. Must contact in advance.
Societies welcome Mon,Wed,Thu & Fri, must contact in advance.
Green Fees not confirmed.
Prof Russell Clewes
Facilities ⊗ ⅲ ⅂ ♥ ♀ ⛳ 🏌 ♂
Location 1m SW

Hotel ★★★⭐⭐ 72% Goldstone Hall, Goldstone, MARKET DRAYTON ☎ 01630 661202 & 661487 Fax 01630 661585 8 ⇥ ♠

MEOLE BRACE   Map 07 SJ41

Meole Brace SY2 6QQ ☎ 01743 364050
Pleasant municipal course.
9 holes, 5830yds, Par 68, SSS 68, Course record 66.
Club membership 300.
Visitors may not play Wed and must book in advance for weekends & bank holidays.
Societies must contact Mr R Wootton, Shrewsbury & Atcham Borough Council on 01743 231456.
Green Fees not confirmed.
Prof Ian Doran
Facilities 🏌 🎯 ♂
Location NE side of village off A49

Hotel ★★★ 66% The Lion, Wyle Cop, SHREWSBURY ☎ 01743 353107 59 ⇥ ♠

OSWESTRY   Map 07 SJ22

Mile End Mile End, Old Shrewsbury Rd SY11 4JE
☎ 01691 671246 Fax 01691 670580
A gently undulating parkland-type course boasting challenging holes for all standards of golfing ability. Longest hole is par 5 14th at 540yds. A number of water features need to be negotiated including two large ponds on the 3rd and 17th. The course is set in 140 acres, ensuring all holes are sufficiently isolated.
18 holes, 6194yds, Par 71, SSS 69, Course record 69.
Club membership 550.
Visitors welcome at all times please telephone in advance to check availability.
Societies must contact in advance, information available.
Green Fees £21 per day; £14 per round (£27/£18 weekends & bank holidays).
Prof Scott Carpenter
Designer Price/Gough
Facilities ⊗ ⅂ ♥ ♀ ⛳ 🏌 🎯 ♂ ♣
Location 1m SE of Oswestry, just off A5

Hotel ★★★ 68% Wynnstay Hotel, Church St, OSWESTRY ☎ 01691 655261 29 ⇥ ♠

Oswestry Aston Park SY11 4JJ
☎ 01691 610535 Fax 01691 610535
Parkland course laid-out on undulating ground.
18 holes, 6024yds, Par 70, SSS 69, Course record 62.
Club membership 960.
Visitors must contact in advance. Must have a handicap certificate or play with member.
Societies must contact in advance.
Green Fees £27 per day, £22 per round (£35/£30 weekends & bank holidays).
Prof David Skelton
Designer James Braid
Facilities ⊗ ⅲ ⅂ ♥ ♀ ⛳ 🏌 ♂
Location 2m SE on A5

Hotel ★★★ 68% Wynnstay Hotel, Church St, OSWESTRY ☎ 01691 655261 29 ⇥ ♠

PANT   Map 07 SJ22

Llanymynech SY10 8LB ☎ 01691 830983
Upland course on the site of an early Iron Age/Roman hillfort with far-reaching views. 15 holes in Wales 3 holes in England, drive off in Wales putt out in England on 4th hole.
18 holes, 6114yds, Par 70, SSS 69, Course record 65.
Club membership 700.
Visitors prior contact advisable, some weekends restricted.
Societies must contact Secretary.
Green Fees not confirmed.
Prof Andrew P Griffiths
Facilities ⊗ ⅲ ⅂ ♥ ♀ ⛳ 🏌 ♂
Location 6m S of Oswestry on A483. In village of Pant turn at Cross Guns Inn

Hotel ★★★ 68% Wynnstay Hotel, Church St, OSWESTRY ☎ 01691 655261 29 ⇥ ♠

SHIFNAL
Map 07 SJ70

Shifnal Decker Hill TF11 8QL
☎ 01952 460330 Fax 01952 460330
Well-wooded parkland course. Walking is easy and an
attractive country mansion serves as the clubhouse.
18 holes, 6468yds, Par 71, SSS 71, Course record 65.
Club membership 700.

Visitors	must contact in advance, may not play at weekends or on Thursdays.
Societies	must contact in advance.
Green Fees	£30 per 27/36 holes; £25 per 18 holes.
Cards	💳 💳 💳 💳 💳 💳
Prof	Justin Flanagan
Designer	Pennick
Facilities	⊗ ⫚ ᗏ ▼ ♀ ♙ 🏠 ✎
Location	1m N of Shifnal, off B4379

Hotel	★★★★ 63% Park House Hotel, Park St, SHIFNAL ☎ 01952 460128 38 🛏 🛋 Annexe 16 🛏 🛋

SHREWSBURY
Map 07 SJ41

Arscott Arscott, Pontesbury SY5 0XP
☎ 01743 860114 Fax 01743 860114
At 365 feet above sea level, the views from Arscott Golf
Club, of the hills of south Shropshire and Wales are superb.
Arscott is a new course, set in mature parkland with water
features and holes demanding all sorts of club choice. A
challenge to all golfers both high and low handicap.
18 holes, 6178yds, Par 70, SSS 69, Course record 68.
Club membership 480.

Visitors	most times available by prior arrangement.
Societies	apply in writing or telephone for tee reservation.
Green Fees	£22 per day; £16 per round (£25/£20 weekends).
Prof	Ian Doran
Designer	M Hamer
Facilities	⊗ ⫚ ᗏ ▼ ♀ ♙ 🏠 ✎
& Leisure	fishing.
Location	Off A488, S of Shrewsbury 3m from A5

Hotel	★★★ 66% The Lion, Wyle Cop, SHREWSBURY ☎ 01743 353107 59 🛏 🛋

Shrewsbury Condover SY5 7BL
☎ 01743 872976, 872977 (sec) & 873751 (pro)
Fax 01743 874647
Parkland course. First nine flat, second undulating with good
views of the Long Mynd Range. Several holes with water
features. Fast putting surfaces.
18 holes, 6300yds, Par 70, SSS 70.
Club membership 872.

Visitors	must contact in advance, weekend restrictions and have a handicap certificate.
Societies	must contact in writing.
Green Fees	£24 per day; £19 per round (£28/£23 weekends & bank holidays).
Prof	Peter Seal
Facilities	⊗ ⫚ ᗏ ▼ ♀ ♙ 🏠 ✎
Location	4m S off A49

Hotel	★★★ 68% Prince Rupert Hotel, Butcher Row, SHREWSBURY ☎ 01743 499955 69 🛏 🛋

TELFORD
Map 07 SJ60

The Shropshire Granville Park, Muxton TF2 8PQ
☎ 01952 677800 Fax 01952 677622
Designed by Martin Hawtree this 27 hole course
comprises 3 loops of 9. Each course has an abundance of
lakes and water hazards making club selection a vital part of
the round. Championship tees are available by pre-
arrangement for the low handicap player.
Blue: 9 holes, 3286yds, Par 35, SSS 35.
Silver: 9 holes, 3303yds, Par 36, SSS 36.
Gold: 9 holes, 3334yds, Par 36, SSS 36.
Club membership 400.

Visitors	recommended to book in advance.
Societies	must book in advance.
Green Fees	£17 per 18 holes; £8 per 9 holes (£24/£12.50 weekends).
Cards	💳 💳 💳 💳 💳 💳
Prof	Steve Marr
Designer	Martin Hawtree
Facilities	⊗ ⫚ ᗏ ▼ ♀ ♙ 🏠 ⚑ 🏐 🛒 ✎ 🏌
Location	From M54/A5 take B5060 towards Donnington. Take 3rd exit at Granville rdbt and continue

Hotel	★★★ 66% Telford Golf & Country Club, Great Hay Dr, Sutton Hill, TELFORD ☎ 01952 429977 96 🛏 🛋

Telford Golf & Country Club Great Hay Dr,
Sutton Heights TF7 4DT
☎ 01952 429977 Fax 01952 586602
Rolling parkland course with easy walking. Five lakes and
large sand traps are hazards to the fine greens.
18 holes, 6761yds, Par 72, SSS 72, Course record 66.
Club membership 450.

Visitors	must book in advance, be a competent golfer and abide by dress regulations.
Societies	must telephone advance 01952 429977
Green Fees	£25 per round.
Cards	💳 💳 💳 💳 💳 💳
Prof	Daniel Bateman
Designer	Harris/Griffiths
Facilities	⊗ ⫚ ᗏ ▼ ♀ ♙ 🏠 ⚑ 🏐 🛒 ✎ 🏌
& Leisure	heated indoor swimming pool, squash, sauna, solarium, gymnasium.
Location	4m S of town centre off A442

Hotel	★★★ 66% Telford Golf & Country Club, Great Hay Dr, Sutton Hill, TELFORD ☎ 01952 429977 96 🛏 🛋

WELLINGTON
Map 07 SJ61

Wrekin Ercall Woods, Golf Links Ln TF6 5BX
☎ 01952 244032 Fax 01952 252906
Downland course with some hard walking but
superb views.
18 holes, 5570yds, Par 67, SSS 66, Course record 64.
Club membership 675.

Visitors	must contact in advance. Limited weekends & bank holidays.
Societies	must apply in writing/telephone.
Green Fees	£28 per day; £20 per round (£28 weekends & bank holidays).
Prof	K Housden

▶

Wreckin Golf Club

Facilities ⊗ ⅷ ⅙ 🍴 ♀ ♨ 🏆 ✏

Location 1.25m S off B5061

Hotel ★★★★ 64% Buckatree Hall Hotel, The Wrekin, Wellington, TELFORD
☎ 01952 641821 60 ⇆ ♞

WESTON-UNDER-REDCASTLE
Map 07 SJ52

Hawkstone Park Hotel SY4 5UY
☎ 01939 200611 Fax 01939 200335
The Hawkstone Course plays through the English Heritage designated Grade I landscape of the historic park and follies providing a beautiful, tranquil yet dramatic back drop to a round of golf. The Windmill Course utilises many American style features and extensive water hazards and is a challenging alternative.
Hawkstone Course: 18 holes, 6491yds, Par 72, SSS 72.
Windmill Course: 18 holes, 6476yds, Par 72, SSS 72.
Academy Course: 6 holes, 741yds, Par 18.
Club membership 750.
Visitors must book and pay in advance.
Societies must contact in advance by telephone.
Green Fees not confirmed.
Cards 🌐 ▬ ▬ 💳 📶 💳
Prof Paul Brown & Paul Wesseling
Designer B Huggett
Facilities ⊗ ⅷ ⅙ 🍴 ♀ ♨ 🏆 🚰 🏌 ➣ 🏇 ✏ ♭
Location N side of village 0.75m E of A49

WHITCHURCH
Map 07 SJ54

Hill Valley Terrick Rd SY13 4JZ
☎ 01948 663584 & 667788 Fax 01948 665927
Two testing parkland courses ideally suited to the club and scratch golfer alike. The Emerald, cleverly designed by Peter Alliss and Dave Thomas, has fairways that thread their way through 160 acres of trees, lakes and streams to American-style greens trapped by sand and water. Shorter Sapphire with smaller greens requiring accurate approach shots.
Emerald: 18 holes, 6628yds, Par 73, SSS 72, Course record 64.
Sapphire: 18 holes, 4800yds, Par 66, SSS 64.
Club membership 600.
Visitors must contact in advance, deposit required.
Societies must contact in advance; a deposit will be required.
Green Fees Emerald: £14-£27.50 per round. Sapphire: £7-£12.50 per round.
Cards ▬ 💳 📶 💳

Prof A R Minshall & Clive Burgess
Designer Peter Alliss/Dave Thomas
Facilities ⊗ ⅷ ⅙ 🍴 ♀ ♨ 🏆 🚰 🏌 ➣ 🏇 ✏ ♭
& Leisure sauna, solarium, gymnasium.
Location 1m N. Follow signs from Bypass

Hotel ★★ 69% Crown Hotel & Restaurant, High St, NANTWICH
☎ 01270 625283 18 ⇆ ♞

WORFIELD
Map 07 SO79

Worfield Roughton WV15 5HE
☎ 01746 716372 Fax 01746 716302
This undulating course with good-sized greens, well placed bunkers and 3 lakes, rated highly in a golf magazine survey. All year round golf based on sandy soil.
18 holes, 6801yds, Par 73, SSS 73, Course record 68.
Club membership 500.
Visitors must contact in advance, weekends only after 2pm.
Societies contact in advance.
Green Fees £25 per day; £20 per 18 holes (£25 per 18 holes weekends after 2pm).
Cards ▬ ▬ 💳 📶 💳
Prof Steve Russell
Designer T Williams
Facilities ⊗ ⅷ ⅙ 🍴 ♀ ♨ 🏆 ➣ 🏇 ✏
Location 3m W of Bridgnorth, off A454

Hotel ★★★♣♣ Old Vicarage Hotel, WORFIELD
☎ 01746 716497 10 ⇆ ♞ Annexe 4 ⇆ ♞

SOMERSET

BACKWELL
Map 03 ST46

Tall Pines Cooks Bridle Path, Downside BS48 3DJ
☎ 01275 472076 Fax 01275 474869
Parkland course with views over the Bristol Channel.
18 holes, 6049yds, Par 70, SSS 69.
Club membership 500.
Visitors no green fees before 11am unless by prior arrangement. Must book in advance at weekends.
Societies prior arrangement by telephone for details.
Green Fees £16 per round.
Prof Alex Murray
Designer T Murray
Facilities ⊗ ⅷ ⅙ 🍴 ♀ ♨ 🏆 ➣ 🏇 ✏
Location Adjacent to Bristol Airport, 1m off A38

Hotel ★★★ 66% Beachlands Hotel, 17 Uphill Rd North, WESTON-SUPER-MARE
☎ 01934 621401 24 ⇆ ♞

AA Hotels that have special arrangements with golf courses are listed at the back of the guide

BATH   Map 03 ST76

Bath Sham Castle, North Rd BA2 6JG
☎ 01225 463834 Fax 01225 331027
Considered to be one of the finest courses in the west, this is
the site of Bath's oldest golf club. An interesting course
situated on high ground overlooking the city and with
splendid views over the surrounding countryside. The rocky
ground supports good quality turf and there are many good
holes. The 17th is a dog-leg right past, or over the corner of
an out-of-bounds wall, and thence on to an undulating green.
18 holes, 6438yds, Par 71, SSS 71, Course record 66.
Club membership 750.

Visitors	advisable to contact in advance. Handicap certificates required.
Societies	Wed & Fri by prior arrangement.
Green Fees	£30 per day; £25 per round (£35/£30 weekends & bank holidays).
Prof	Peter J Hancox
Designer	Colt & others
Facilities	⊗ ⍫ ⌸ ☕ 𝌆 △ 🏠 ⛳ ✐
Location	1.5m SE city centre off A36

Hotel ★★★ 70% The Francis, Queen Square,
BATH ☎ 0870 400 8223 94 🛏 🐾

Entry Hill BA2 5NA ☎ 01225 834248
9 holes, 2065yds, Par 33, SSS 30.
Club membership 300.

Visitors	advisable to book in advance, must wear golf shoes or training shoes.
Societies	bookings required in advance.
Green Fees	£8.25-£9.75 per 18 holes; £5.15-£6.20 per 9 holes.
Prof	Tim Tapley
Facilities	☕ △ 🏠 ⛳ ✐
Location	Off A367

Lansdown Lansdown BA1 9BT
☎ 01225 422138 Fax 01225 339252
A flat parkland course situated 800 feet above sea level,
providing a challenge to both low and high handicap golfers.
18 holes, 6316yds, Par 71, SSS 70, Course record 65.
Club membership 700.

Visitors	must contact in advance to ascertain availability and have a handicap certificate.
Societies	apply in writing or telephone in advance.
Green Fees	not confirmed.
Cards	〰 💳 💳 🌐 📱
Prof	Terry Mercer
Designer	C A Whitcombe
Facilities	⊗ ⍫ ⌸ ☕ 𝌆 △ 🏠 ✐ ƚ
Location	6m SW of exit 18 of M4

Hotel ★★★ 66% Pratt's Hotel, South Pde, BATH
☎ 01225 460441 46 🛏 🐾

BRIDGWATER   Map 03 ST23

Cannington Cannington College, Cannington TA5 2LS
☎ 01278 655050 Fax 01278 655055
Nine hole golf course with 18 tees of 'links-like' appearance,
designed by Martin Hawtree of Oxford. The 4th hole is a
challenging 464yard Par 4, slightly up hill and into the
prevailing wind.
9 holes, 6072yds, Par 68, SSS 70.
Club membership 200.

Visitors	pay & play anytime ex Wed evening.
Societies	apply in writing.
Green Fees	£8 per round; £12 per 18 holes (£10/£15 weekends & bank holidays).
Prof	Ron Macrow
Designer	Martin Hawtree
Facilities	△ 🏠 ⛳ ✐ ƚ
Location	4m NW of Bridgwater of A39

Hotel ★★ 66% Friarn Court Hotel, 37 St Mary St,
BRIDGWATER ☎ 01278 452859 16 🛏 🐾

BURNHAM-ON-SEA   Map 03 ST34

Brean Coast Rd, Brean Sands TA8 2QY
☎ 01278 752111 Fax 01278 752111
Level and open moorland course with water hazards.
Facilities of 'Brean Leisure Park' adjoining.
18 holes, 5715yds, Par 69, SSS 68, Course record 66.
Club membership 350.

Visitors	may not play on Sat & Sun before 11.30am. Book in advance through professional.
Societies	contact office or professional in advance.
Green Fees	£15 (£20 per round weekends).
Cards	〰 💳
Prof	David Haines
Facilities	⊗ ⍫ ⌸ ☕ 𝌆 △ 🏠 ⛳ 🛋 ↘ ⛵ ✐
& Leisure	heated indoor plus outdoor swimming pool, fishing, sauna.
Location	4m from junct 22 M5 on coast road

Hotel ★★♨ 68% Batch Country Hotel, Batch Ln,
LYMPSHAM ☎ 01934 750371 10 🛏 🐾

Burnham & Berrow St Christopher's Way TA8 2PE
☎ 01278 785760 Fax 01278 795440
Natural championship links course with panoramic
views of the Somerset hills sweeping across the famed
reed beds and the Bristol channel with the islands of
Steepholm and Flatholm against the background of the
Welsh coast line.
*Championship Course: 18 holes, 6606yds, Par 71, SSS
73, Course record 66.*
Channel Course: 9 holes, 6120yds, Par 70, SSS 69.
Club membership 900.

Visitors	must contact in advance & have handicap certificate (22 or under gentlemen, 30 or under ladies) to play on the Championship course.
Societies	telephone in advance.
Green Fees	Championship Course: £38 per day/round (£50 weekends & bank holidays); Channel Course £12 per day/round.
Prof	Mark Crowther-Smith ▶

| Facilities | ⊗ ⫼ ⬓ ⬛ ♀ ⚲ 🛍 ⛳ ⟿ ↘ ⌀ |
| Location | 1m N of town on B3140 |

| Hotel | ★★ 68% Woodlands Hotel, Hill Ln, BRENT KNOLL ☎ 01278 760232 8 ⇆ ⏏ |
| Additional hotel | ★★⚘ 68% Batch Country Hotel, Batch Ln, LYMPSHAM ☎ 01934 750371 Fax 01934 750501 10 ⇆ ⏏ |

CHARD   Map 03 ST30

Windwhistle Golf, Squash & Country Club Cricket St
Thomas TA20 4DG ☎ 01460 30231 Fax 01460 30055
Parkland course at 735 ft above sea level with outstanding
views over the Somerset Levels to the Bristol Channel and
South Wales.
*East/West Course: 18 holes, 5812yds, Par 71, SSS 68,
Course record 69.*
Club membership 600.

Visitors	must contact in advance.
Societies	by prior arrangement.
Green Fees	not confirmed.
Cards	⬚ ▤ ▦ ▨ ▦
Prof	Duncan Driver
Designer	Braid & Taylor
Facilities	⬓ ⬛ ♀ ⚲ 🛍 ⛳ ⌀
& Leisure	squash, driving range to open 1999.
Location	3m E of Chard on A30

| Hotel | ★★★ 66% Shrubbery Hotel, ILMINSTER ☎ 01460 52108 14 ⇆ ⏏ |

CLEVEDON   Map 03 ST47

Clevedon Castle Rd, Walton St Mary BS21 7AA
☎ 01275 874057 Fax 01275 341228
Situated on the cliff-top overlooking the Severn estuary
and with distant views of the Welsh coast. Excellent
parkland course in first-class condition overlooking the
Severn estuary. Magnificent scenery and some
tremendous 'drop' holes. Strong winds.
18 holes, 6117yds, Par 70, SSS 69, Course record 65.
Club membership 750.

Visitors	must contact in advance. No play Wed morning.
Societies	not bank holidays, telephone or apply in writing.
Green Fees	£25 (£40 per weekends & bank holidays).
Prof	Robert Scanlan
Designer	S Herd
Facilities	⊗ ⫼ ⬓ ⬛ ♀ ⚲ 🛍 ⛳ ⌀
Location	1m NE of town centre

| Hotel | ★★★ 65% Walton Park Hotel, Wellington Ter, CLEVEDON ☎ 01275 874253 40 ⇆ ⏏ |

CONGRESBURY   Map 03 ST46

Mendip Spring Honeyhall Ln BS49 5JT
☎ 01934 852322 Fax 01934 853021
Set in peaceful countryside with the Mendip Hills as a
backdrop, this 18-hole course includes lakes and numerous
water hazards covering some 12 acres of the course. The 12th
is an island green surrounded by water and there are long

drives on the 7th and 13th. The 9-hole Lakeside course is an
easy walking course, mainly par 4. Floodlit driving range.
*Brinsea Course: 18 holes, 6334yds, Par 71, SSS 70, Course
record 65.*
Lakeside: 9 holes, 4520yds, Par 68, SSS 68.
Club membership 445.

Visitors	must contact in advance for Brinsea course and handicap certificate required for weekends. Lakeside is play & pay anytime.
Societies	booking in advance by arrangement.
Green Fees	not confirmed.
Cards	⬚ ▤ ▦ ▨ ▦
Prof	John Blackburn & Robert Moss
Facilities	⊗ ⫼ ⬓ ⬛ ♀ ⚲ 🛍 ⛳ ↘ ⟿ ⌀ ⏏
Location	8m E of Weston-Super-Mare between A370 and A38

| Hotel | ★★★⚘ 73% Daneswood House Hotel, Cuck Hill, SHIPHAM ☎ 01934 843145 & 843945 Fax 01934 843824 9 ⇆ ⏏ Annexe 3 ⇆ ⏏ |

ENMORE   Map 03 ST23

Enmore Park TA5 2AN
☎ 01278 671481 & 671519 Fax 01278 671740
Hilly, parkland course with water features on foothills of
Quantocks. Wooded countryside and views of Quantocks and
Mendips. 1st and 10th are testing holes.
18 holes, 6406yds, Par 71, SSS 71, Course record 66.
Club membership 750.

Visitors	phone professional for details, must have handicap certificate for weekends.
Societies	must contact in advance.
Green Fees	£25 per day; £18 per round (£25 per round weekends).
Cards	⬚ ▤ ▦ ▨
Prof	Nigel Wixon
Designer	Hawtree
Facilities	⊗ ⫼ ⬓ ⬛ ♀ ⚲ 🛍 ⛳ ↘ ⟿ ⌀
Location	A39 to Minehead, at first set of lights turn left to Spaxton, then 1.5m to reservoir and turn left

| Hotel | ★★★ 73% Walnut Tree Hotel, North Petherton, BRIDGWATER ☎ 01278 662255 32 ⇆ |

FARRINGTON GURNEY   Map 03 ST65

Farrington Marsh Ln BS39 6TS
☎ 01761 241274 (office) & 241787 (pro)
Fax 01761 241274
USGA spec greens on both challenging 9 and 18 hole
courses. Newly completed 18 hole course with computerised
irrigation, six lakes, four tees per hole and excellent views.
Testing holes include the 12th (282yds) with the green set
behind a lake at the base of a 100ft drop, and the 17th which
is played between two lakes.
*Executive Course: 9 holes, 3022yds, Par 54, SSS 53, Course
record 54.*
*Main Course: 18 holes, 6316yds, Par 72, SSS 71, Course
record 66.*
Club membership 750.

| Visitors | must book starting times at weekends. |
| Societies | welcome except for weekends & bank holidays, telephone or write in advance. |

▶

Green Fees	Main course: £27.50 per day, £20 per round (£36/30 weekends & bank holidays); Executive course; £12 per day; £7 per 9 holes (£14/£9 weekends & bank holidays).
Prof	Peter Thompson
Designer	Peter Thompson
Facilities	⊗ ⍫ 👜 💪 ♀ 👥 🏠 🍴 ⛳ 🏌 ✎ ₤
& Leisure	sauna, video teaching studio.
Hotel	★★★ 70% Centurion Hotel, Charlton Ln, MIDSOMER NORTON ☎ 01761 417711 44 ⇄ ₨

FROME   Map 03 ST74

Frome Golf Centre Critchill Manor BA11 4LJ
☎ 01373 453410 Fax 01373 453410
Attractive parkland course, founded in 1993, situated in a picturesque valley just outside the town, complete with practice areas and a driving range.
18 holes, 4890yds, Par 66, SSS 64, Course record 62.
Club membership 330.

Visitors	no restrictions.
Societies	telephone in advance.
Green Fees	not confirmed.
Prof	Adrian Wright
Designer	R Flower
Facilities	⊗ 👜 💪 ♀ 👥 🏠 🍴 ✎ ₤
Location	A361 Frome/Shepton Mallet, at Nunney Catch rdbt through Nunney, course on left before Frome
Hotel	★★ 67% The George at Nunney, 11 Church St, NUNNEY ☎ 01373 836458 9rm (8 ⇄ ₨)

Orchardleigh BA11 2PH ☎ 01373 454200 & 454206 Fax 01373 454202
Originally designed by Ryder Cup golfer, Brian Huggett, as two returning nines through mature parkland. Five lakes bring water into play on seven holes.
18 holes, 6831yds, Par 72, SSS 73.
Club membership 500.

Visitors	no visitors before 11am at weekends.
Societies	apply in writing or telephone in advance.
Green Fees	not confirmed.
Cards	💳 💳 💳 💳
Prof	Peter Green/Steve Slinger
Designer	Brian Huggett
Facilities	⊗ ⍫ 👜 💪 ♀ 👥 🏠 🍴 ⛳ 🏌 ✎ ₤
& Leisure	fishing.
Location	1m W of Frome on the A362
Hotel	★★ 67% The George at Nunney, 11 Church St, NUNNEY ☎ 01373 836458 9rm (8 ⇄ ₨)

GURNEY SLADE   Map 03 ST64

Mendip BA3 4UT ☎ 01749 840570 Fax 01749 841439
Undulating downland course offering an interesting test of golf on superb fairways and extensive views over the surrounding countryside.
18 holes, 6383yds, Par 71, SSS 71, Course record 65.
Club membership 900.

Visitors	must contact in advance. Handicap certificates required for play at weekends and bank holidays.
Societies	by arrangement with secretary.

Green Fees	£26 per day; £21 per round (£31 weekends & bank holidays).
Prof	Ron Lee
Facilities	⊗ ⍫ 👜 💪 ♀ 👥 🏠 🍴 ⛳ ✎
Location	1.5m S off A37
Hotel	★★★ 70% Centurion Hotel, Charlton Ln, MIDSOMER NORTON ☎ 01761 417711 44 ⇄ ₨

KEYNSHAM   Map 03 ST66

Stockwood Vale Stockwood Ln BS31 2ER
☎ 0117 986 6505 Fax 0117 986 0509
Undulating and challenging public course in a beautiful setting with interesting well bunkered holes, in particular the beautiful and challenging 5th and 13th holes.
18 holes, 6031yds, Par 71, SSS 69.
Club membership 600.

Visitors	no restrictions, but must reserve a start time.
Societies	telephone in advance.
Green Fees	£15 per 18 holes (£17 weekends).
Cards	💳 💳 💳 💳
Prof	John Richards
Facilities	⊗ 👜 💪 ♀ 👥 🏠 ✎ ₤
Location	Off Hicks Gate on A4
Hotel	★★ 69% Chelwood House Hotel, CHELWOOD ☎ 01761 490730 12 ⇄ ₨

LANGPORT   Map 03 ST42

Long Sutton Long Sutton TA10 9JU
☎ 01458 241017 Fax 01458 241022
Gentle, undulating, Pay and Play course.
18 holes, 6367yds, Par 71, SSS 70, Course record 71.
Club membership 600.

Visitors	advisable to phone in advance.
Societies	telephone in advance.
Green Fees	not confirmed.
Cards	💳 💳 💳 💳
Prof	Michael Blackwell
Designer	Patrick Dawson
Facilities	⊗ ⍫ 👜 💪 ♀ 👥 🏠 🍴 ⛳ 🏌 ✎ ₤
Location	10m NW of Yeovil off A372
Hotel	★★★ 70% The Hollies, Bower Hinton, MARTOCK ☎ 01935 822232 Annexe 32 ⇄ ₨

LONG ASHTON   Map 03 ST57

Long Ashton The Clubhouse, Clarken Coombe BS41 9DW
☎ 01275 392316 Fax 01275 394395
Wooded parkland course with nice turf, wonderful views of Bristol and surrounding areas and a spacious practice area. Good testing holes, especially the back nine, in prevailing south-west winds. The short second hole (126yds) cut from an old quarry and played over a road can ruin many a card! Good drainage ensures pleasant winter golf.
18 holes, 6077yds, Par 70, SSS 70, Course record 66.
Club membership 700.

Visitors	recommended to telephone the professional.
Societies	must contact the secretary in advance.
Green Fees	not confirmed.
Prof	Denis Scanlan

▶

Designer   J H Taylor
Facilities   ⊗ ⛳ 🏌 ♀ ⛾ 🏌 ✧
Location   0.5m N on B3128

Hotel   ★★★ 70% Redwood Lodge Hotel, Beggar
Bush Ln, Failand, BRISTOL
☎ 01275 393901 112 ⇌ ☙

Woodspring Golf & Country Club Yanley Ln BS18 9LR
☎ 01275 394378 Fax 01275 394473
Set in 180 acres of undulating heathland featuring superb
natural water hazards, protected greens and a rising
landscape. Designed by Peter Alliss and Clive Clark and laid
out by Donald Steel, the course has three individual 9-hole
courses, the Avon, Severn & Brunel. The 9th hole on the
Brunel course is a feature hole here, with an elevated tee shot
over a natural gorge. In undulating hills south of Bristol, long
carries to tight fairways, elevated island tees and difficult
approaches to greens make the most of the 27 holes.
Avon Course: 9 holes, 2960yds, Par 35, SSS 34.
Brunel Course: 9 holes, 3320yds, Par 37, SSS 35.
Severn Course: 9 holes, 3267yds, Par 36, SSS 35.
Club membership 960.
Visitors   must contact in advance, weekends may be
limited to play after midday. Dress codes must
be adhered to.
Societies   must contact Kevin Pitts in advance.
Green Fees not confirmed.
Cards   [card symbols]
Prof   Nigel Beer
Designer   Clarke/Alliss/Steel
Facilities   ⊗ 川 ⛳ 🏌 ♀ ⛾ 🏌 ⛶ ✧ ❈
& Leisure   sauna.
Location   Off A38 Bridgewater Road

Hotel   ★★★ 70% Redwood Lodge Hotel, Beggar
Bush Ln, Failand, BRISTOL
☎ 01275 393901 112 ⇌ ☙

MIDSOMER NORTON   Map 03 ST65

Fosseway Country Club Charlton Ln BA3 4BD
☎ 01761 412214 Fax 01761 418357
Very attractive tree-lined parkland course, not demanding but
with lovely views towards the Mendip Hills.
9 holes, 4565yds, Par 67, SSS 61.
Club membership 250.
Visitors   may not play on Wed evenings, Sun mornings &
competitions days.
Societies   apply in writing or telephone.
Green Fees not confirmed.
Cards   [card symbols]
Designer   C K Cotton/F Pennink
Facilities   ⊗ 川 ⛳ 🏌 ♀ ⛾ 🏌 ⛶ ✧
& Leisure   heated indoor swimming pool, squash.
Location   SE of town centre off A367

Hotel   ★★★ 70% Centurion Hotel, Charlton Ln,
MIDSOMER NORTON
☎ 01761 417711 44 ⇌ ☙

MINEHEAD   Map 03 SS94

Minehead & West Somerset The Warren TA24 5SJ
☎ 01643 702057 Fax 01643 705095
Flat seaside links, very exposed to wind, with good turf
set on a shingle bank. The last five holes adjacent to the

---

beach are testing. The 215-yard 18th is wedged between
the beach and the club buildings and provides a good
finish.
18 holes, 6228yds, Par 71, SSS 71, Course record 65.
Club membership 620.
Visitors   must contact secretary in advance.
Societies   telephone in advance.
Green Fees £22 per day (£25 weekends & bank
holidays).
Prof   Ian Read
Facilities   ⊗ 川 ⛳ 🏌 ♀ ⛾ 🏌 ⛶ ❈ ✧
Location   E end of esplanade

Hotel   ★★ 76% Channel House Hotel, Church
Path, MINEHEAD
☎ 01643 703229 8 ⇌ ☙

SALTFORD   Map 03 ST66

Saltford Golf Club Ln BS31 3AA ☎ 01225 872043
Parkland course with easy walking and panoramic views
over the Avon Valley. The par 4, 2nd and 13th are notable.
18 holes, 6081yds, Par 71, SSS 71.
Club membership 800.
Visitors   must contact in advance & have handicap
certificate.
Societies   must telephone in advance.
Green Fees telephone for details.
Prof   Dudley Millinstead
Designer   Harry Vardon
Facilities   ⊗ 川 ⛳ 🏌 ♀ ⛾ 🏌 ⛶ ✧
Location   S side of village

Hotel   ★★★ 76% Hunstrete House Hotel,
HUNSTRETE ☎ 01761 490490 23 ⇌ ☙

SOMERTON   Map 03 ST42

Wheathill Wheathill TA11 7HG
☎ 01963 240667 Fax 01963 240230
A Par 68 parkland course with nice views in quiet
countryside. It is flat lying with the 13th hole along the river.
There is an Academy 4-hole course and a massive practice
area.
18 holes, 5362yds, Par 68, SSS 66.
Club membership 350.
Visitors   no restrictions.
Societies   telephone to arrange.
Green Fees not confirmed.
Prof   A England
Designer   J Pain
Facilities   ⊗ 川 ⛳ 🏌 ♀ ⛾ 🏌 ⛶ ❈ ✧
Location   5m E of Somerton off B3153

Hotel   ★★★ 62% Wessex Hotel, High St, STREET
☎ 01458 443383 50 ⇌ ☙

TAUNTON   Map 03 ST22

Oake Manor Oake TA4 1BA
☎ 01823 461993 Fax 01823 461995
A parkland/lakeland course situated in breathtaking Somerset
countryside with views of the Quantock, Blackdown and
Brendon Hills. Ten holes feature water hazards such as lakes,
cascades and a trout stream. The 15th hole (Par 5, 476yds) is

►

bounded by water all down the left with a carry over another
lake on to an island green. The course is challenging yet
great fun for all standards of golfer.
18 holes, 6109yds, Par 70, SSS 69.
Club membership 600.

Visitors	no restrictions but visitors must book start times in order to avoid disapointment.
Societies	contact Russell Gardner by telephone.
Green Fees	£17.50 per round (£22 weekends).
Cards	
Prof	Russell Gardner
Designer	Adrian Stiff
Facilities	⊗ ℿ ╚ ☐ ♀ ♨ ☎ ♍ ⌀ ♈
Location	Exit M5 junct 26, take A38 towards Taunton and follow signs to Oake

Hotel ★★★ 71% Rumwell Manor Hotel, Rumwell,
TAUNTON ☎ 01823 461902
10 ⇒ ☝ Annexe 10 ⇒ ☝

Taunton & Pickeridge Corfe TA3 7BY
☎ 01823 421537 Fax 01823 421742
Downland course with extensive views.
18 holes, 5927yds, Par 69, SSS 68, Course record 63.
Club membership 600.

Visitors	must have a handicap certificate
Societies	must telephone in advance.
Green Fees	£24 per day; £20 per round (£28 weekends).
Prof	Gary Milne
Facilities	⊗ ℿ ╚ ☐ ♀ ♨ ☎ ⌀
Location	4m S off B3170

Hotel ★★★ 75% The Mount Somerset Hotel,
Henlade, TAUNTON
☎ 01823 442500 11 ⇒ ☝

Taunton Vale Creech Heathfield TA3 5EY
☎ 01823 412220 Fax 01823 413583
An 18 hole and a 9 hole golf course in a parkland complex
occupying 156 acres in the Vale of Taunton. Complex
includes a floodlit driving range.
Charlton Course: 18 holes, 6167yds, Par 70, SSS 69, Course record 65.
Durston Course: 9 holes, 2004yds, Par 64, SSS 60.
Club membership 670.

Visitors	telephone booking essential. Must contact Professional on 01823 412880
Societies	must book in advance.
Green Fees	not confirmed.
Prof	Martin Keitch
Designer	John Payne
Facilities	⊗ ℿ ╚ ☐ ♀ ♨ ☎ ♍ ♈ ⌀ ♈
Location	Off A361 between juncts 24 & 25 on M5

Hotel ★★★ 75% The Mount Somerset Hotel,
Henlade, TAUNTON
☎ 01823 442500 11 ⇒ ☝

Vivary Park Municipal Fons George TA1 3JU
☎ 01823 333875
A parkland course, tight and narrow with ponds.
18 holes, 4620yds, Par 63, SSS 63, Course record 59.
Club membership 700.

Visitors	may play anytime except weekends before 9am, bookings can be made 8 days in advance.
Societies	apply in writing.
Green Fees	£8.50 per round.
Prof	Mike Steadman

Designer	W H Fowler
Facilities	⊗ ℿ ╚ ☐ ♀ ♨ ☎ ♍ ⌀
& Leisure	hard tennis courts.
Location	S side of town centre off A38

Hotel ★★ 61% Falcon Hotel, Henlade, TAUNTON
☎ 01823 442502 11 ⇒ ☝

WEDMORE Map 03 ST44

Isle of Wedmore Lineage BS28 4QT
☎ 01934 713649 (Office) 712452 (Pro) Fax 01934 713696
Gentle undulating course designed to maintain natural
environment. Existing woodland and hedgerow enhanced by
new planting. Magnificent panoramic views of Cheddar
Valley and Glastonbury Tor.
18 holes, 6006yds, Par 70, SSS 69, Course record 70.
Club membership 620.

Visitors	telephone professional in advance. Not before 9.30am weekends.
Societies	weekdays only, telephone in advance.
Green Fees	£18 per round (£22 weekends) evening ticket £9.
Cards	
Prof	Graham Coombe
Designer	Terry Murray
Facilities	⊗ ℿ ╚ ☐ ♀ ♨ ☎ ♍ ♈ ⌀
Location	Off B3139 between Wells & Burnham-on-Sea

Hotel ★★★ 69% Swan Hotel, Sadler St, WELLS
☎ 01749 678877 38 ⇒ ☝

WELLS Map 03 ST54

Wells (Somerset) East Horrington Rd BA5 3DS
☎ 01749 675005 Fax 01749 675005
Beautiful wooded course with wonderful views. The
prevailing SW wind complicates the 448-yd, 3rd.
18 holes, 6015yds, Par 70, SSS 69, Course record 66.
Club membership 700.

Visitors	must contact in advance & have handicap certificate weekends. Tee times restricted at weekends to after 9.30pm
Societies	must apply in advance.
Green Fees	£20 per round (£25 weekends).
Cards	
Prof	Adrian Bishop
Facilities	⊗ ℿ ╚ ☐ ♀ ♨ ☎ ♍ ♈ ⌀ ♈
Location	1.5m E off B3139

Hotel ★★★ 69% Swan Hotel, Sadler St, WELLS
☎ 01749 678877 38 ⇒ ☝

WESTON-SUPER-MARE Map 03 ST36

Weston-super-Mare Uphill Rd North BS23 4NQ
☎ 01934 626968 & 633360 Fax 01934 626968
A compact and interesting layout with the opening hole
adjacent to the beach. The sandy, links-type course is
slightly undulating and has beautifully maintained turf
and greens. The 15th is a testing 455-yard, par 4.
18 holes, 6300yds, Par 70, SSS 70, Course record 65.
Club membership 778.

Visitors	must have handicap certificate to play at weekends.
Societies	apply in writing or telephone. ▶

Green Fees not confirmed.
Prof Mike Laband
Designer T Dunne/Dr Mackenzie
Facilities ⊗ ⅲ ⅃ ⅃ ♈ ♉ ⅃ ⅃ ⅃
Location S side of town centre off A370

Hotel ★★★ 66% Beachlands Hotel, 17 Uphill Rd
North, WESTON-SUPER-MARE
☎ 01934 621401 24 ⇆ ⋔

Worlebury Monks Hill BS22 9SX
☎ 01934 625789 Fax 01934 621935
Situated on the ridge of Worlebury Hill, this seaside course
offers fairly easy walking and extensive views of the Severn
estuary and Wales.
18 holes, 5963yds, Par 70, SSS 69, Course record 66.
Club membership 590.
Visitors must be recognised golfers, handicap certificate
or proof of club membership may be required.
Societies apply in writing or telephone in advance.
Green Fees £20 per round (£30 weekends & bank holidays).
Prof Gary Marks
Designer H Vardon
Facilities ⊗ ⅲ ⅃ ⅃ ♈ ♉ ⅃ ⅃
Location 5m NE off A370

Hotel ★★★ 68% Commodore Hotel, Beach Rd, Sand
Bay, Kewstoke, WESTON-SUPER-MARE
☎ 01934 415778 12 ⇆ ⋔ Annexe 6 ⇆ ⋔

YEOVIL   Map 03 ST51

Yeovil Sherborne Rd BA21 5BW
☎ 01935 422965 Fax 01935 411283
On the Old Course the opener lies by the River Yeo
before the gentle climb to high downs with good views.
The outstanding 14th and 15th holes present a challenge,
being below the player with a deep railway cutting on
the left of the green. The 1st on the Newton Course is
played over the river which then leads to a challenging
but scenic golf course.
*Old Course: 18 holes, 6144yds, Par 72, SSS 70, Course
record 64.*
*Newton Course: 9 holes, 4891yds, Par 68, SSS 65,
Course record 65.*
Club membership 1000.
Visitors must contact in advance. Members only
before 9.30am and 12.30-2. Handicap
certificate required for Old Course.
Societies telephone in advance.
Green Fees Old Course: £30 per day; £25 per round
(£40/£30 weekends). Newton Course: £18
per day; £15 per round (£18 weekends).
Cards ▭ ▭ ▩ ⅃
Prof Geoff Kite
Designer Fowler & Allison
Facilities ⊗ ⅲ ⅃ ⅃ ♈ ♉ ⅃ ⅃ ⅃
Location 1m E on A30

Hotel ★★★ 72% Yeovil Court Hotel, West
Coker Rd, YEOVIL ☎ 01935 863746
15 ⇆ ⋔ Annexe 11 ⇆ ⋔

Looking for a driving range?
See the index at the back of the guide

BROCTON   Map 07 SJ91

Brocton Hall ST17 0TH
☎ 01785 661901 Fax 01785 661591
Parkland course with gentle slopes in places, easy walking.
18 holes, 6064yds, Par 69, SSS 69, Course record 66.
Club membership 665.
Visitors not competition days. Must contact in advance.
Societies must apply in advance.
Green Fees £33 per day (£40 weekends & bank holidays).
Prof R G Johnson
Designer Harry Vardon
Facilities ⊗ ⅲ ⅃ ⅃ ♈ ♉ ⅃ ⅃ ⅃ ⅃ ⅃
Location NW side of village off A34

Hotel ★★★ 65% Garth Hotel, Wolverhampton Rd,
Moss Pit, STAFFORD
☎ 01785 256124 60 ⇆ ⋔

BURTON-UPON-TRENT   Map 07 SK22

Branston Burton Rd, Branston DE14 3DP
☎ 01283 512211 Fax 01283 566984
Flat semi-parkland course, adjacent to River Trent, on
undulating ground with natural water hazards on 13 holes.
18 holes, 6647yds, Par 72, SSS 72, Course record 65.
Club membership 800.
Visitors may not play before noon or at weekends. Must
contact in advance.
Societies must telephone in advance.
Green Fees not confirmed.
Cards ▭ ▭ ▩ ▩ ⅃
Prof Jacob Sture
Designer G Ramshall
Facilities ⊗ ⅲ ⅃ ⅃ ♈ ♉ ⅃ ⅃ ⅃ ⅃ ⅃
& Leisure heated indoor swimming pool, sauna, solarium,
gymnasium.
Location 1.5m SW on A5121

Hotel ★★★ 68% Ye Olde Dog & Partridge Hotel,
High St, TUTBURY
☎ 01283 813030 6 ⇆ ⋔ Annexe 14 ⇆ ⋔

Burton-upon-Trent 43 Ashby Rd East DE15 0PS
☎ 01283 544551 Fax 01283 544551
Undulating parkland course with trees a major feature. There
are testing par 3s at 10th and 12th. The 18th has a lake on the
approach to the green.
18 holes, 6579yds, Par 71, SSS 71, Course record 63.
Club membership 650.
Visitors must contact in advance and have a handicap
certificate.
Societies must contact in advance.
Green Fees £34 per day; £27 per round (£36/£30 weekends
& bank holidays).
Prof Gary Stafford
Designer H S Colt
Facilities ⊗ ⅲ ⅃ ⅃ ♈ ♉ ⅃ ⅃ ⅃ ⅃
Location 3m E on A511

Guesthouse ♦♦♦ Edgecote Hotel, 179 Ashby Rd,
BURTON UPON TRENT
☎ 01283 568966 11rm (5 ⋔)

Craythorne Craythorne Rd, Stretton DE13 0AZ
☎ 01283 564329 Fax 01283 511908
A relatively short and challenging parkland course with tight fairways and views of the Trent Valley. Excellent greens. Suits all standards but particularly good for society players. The course is now settled and in good condition after major refurbishments.
18 holes, 5450yds, Par 68, SSS 67, Course record 66.
Club membership 500.

Visitors	must contact in advance.
Societies	apply in writing or telephone for details.
Green Fees	£20 per round (£25 per round weekends). Special winter rates.
Cards	▭▭ ▭▭
Prof	Steve Hadfield
Facilities	⊗ ⑪ ﮞ ♨ ♥ ♀ ♨ 🏠 ⛳ ⚲ ✎ ♪
Location	Off A38 through Stretton village

Guesthouse ◆◆◆◆Edgecote Hotel, 179 Ashby Rd, BURTON UPON TRENT
☎ 01283 568966 11rm(5 ♪)

Hoar Cross Hall Health Spa Golf Academy Hoar Cross DE13 8QS ☎ 01283 575671
Golf academy located in the grounds of a stately home, now a well appointed health spa resort and hotel. Driving range, bunker and practice areas.
.
Club membership 300.

Visitors	day guests & residents.
Societies	golfing societies that are resident only.
Green Fees	not confirmed.
Prof	Gary Prince
Designer	Geoffrey Collins
Facilities	⚲ 🏠 ⛳ ⚲ ✎
& Leisure	hard tennis courts, heated indoor swimming pool, sauna, solarium, gymnasium.

CANNOCK   Map 07 SJ91

Beau Desert Rugeley Rd, Hazelslade WS12 5PJ
☎ 01543 422626 Fax 01543 451137
Heathland course surrounded by a forest.
18 holes, 6310yds, Par 70, SSS 71, Course record 64.
Club membership 500.

Visitors	are advised to contact professional in advance.
Societies	must contact in advance.
Green Fees	£38 per day (£48 weekends & bank holidays).
Prof	Barrie Stevens
Designer	Herbert Fowler
Facilities	⊗ ⑪ ﮞ ♨ ♥ ♀ ♨ 🏠 ⛳ ⚲ ✎ ♪
Location	0.5m NE of village

Hotel   ★★★ 63% Roman Way Hotel, Watling St, Hatherton, CANNOCK
☎ 01543 572121   56 ➡ ♪

Cannock Park Stafford Rd WS11 2AL
☎ 01543 578850 Fax 01543 578850
Part of a large leisure centre, this parkland-type course plays alongside Cannock Chase. Good drainage, open all year.
18 holes, 5149yds, Par 67, SSS 65.
Club membership 250.

Visitors	must book in advance.
Societies	must contact in advance.
Green Fees	£8.50 weekdays (£9.50 weekends).
Prof	David Dunk
Designer	John Mainland

Facilities	⊗ ⑪ ﮞ ♨ ♥ ♀ ♨ 🏠 ⛳ ⚲ ✎
& Leisure	hard tennis courts, heated indoor swimming pool, sauna, solarium, gymnasium.
Location	0.5m N of town centre on A34

Hotel   ★★★ 63% Roman Way Hotel, Watling St, Hatherton, CANNOCK
☎ 01543 572121   56 ➡ ♪

ENVILLE   Map 07 SO88

Enville Highgate Common DY7 5BN
☎ 01384 872074 (Office) Fax 01384 873396
Easy walking on two fairly flat woodland/heathland courses - the 'Highgate' and the 'Lodge'.
Highgate Course: 18 holes, 6556yds, Par 72, SSS 72, Course record 65.
Lodge Course: 18 holes, 6290yds, Par 70, SSS 70.
Club membership 900.

Visitors	must play with member at weekends.
Societies	phone initially for details.
Green Fees	£40 per 36 holes; £30 per 18 holes.
Prof	Sean Power
Facilities	⊗ ⑪ ﮞ ♨ ♥ ♀ ♨ 🏠 ♪ ⚒
Location	From Stourbridge take A458 towards Bridgnorth, after 4.5m turn right. Golf club signposted

Hotel   ★★★★ 66% Mill Hotel & Restaurant, ALVELEY ☎ 01746 780437   21 ➡ ♪

GOLDENHILL   Map 07 SJ85

Goldenhill Mobberley Rd ST6 5SS
☎ 01782 234200 Fax 01782 234303
Rolling parkland course with water features on six of the back nine holes.
18 holes, 5957yds, Par 71, SSS 69.
Club membership 300.

Visitors	advisable to contact in advance.
Societies	must apply in writing or telephone.
Green Fees	Summer: £7.50 per round (£9 weekends). Winter £5 per round (£6 weekends).
Facilities	⊗ ⑪ ﮞ ♨ ♥ ♀ ♨ 🏠 ⛳ ⚲
Location	On A50, 4m N of Stoke

Hotel   ★★★ 73% Manor House Hotel, Audley Rd, ALSAGER ☎ 01270 884000   57 ➡ ♪

HIMLEY   Map 07 SO89

Himley Hall Golf Centre Log Cabin, Himley Hall Park DY3 4DF ☎ 01902 895207
Parkland course set in grounds of Himley Hall Park, with lovely views. Large practice area including a pitch-and-putt.
9 holes, 6215yds, Par 72, SSS 70, Course record 65.
Club membership 200.

Visitors	restricted weekends.
Green Fees	£5.80 per 9 holes; £8.50 per 18 holes.
Prof	Jeremy Nichols
Designer	A Baker
Facilities	⊗ ﮞ ♥ ♀ 🏠 ⚲
Location	0.5m E on B4176

Hotel   ★★★ 63% Himley Country Hotel, School Rd, HIMLEY ☎ 01902 896716   73 ➡ ♪

LEEK
Map 07 SJ95

Leek Birchall, Cheddleton Rd ST13 5RE
☎ 01538 384779 Fax 01538 384535
Undulating, challenging mainly parkland course, reputedly
one of the best in the area.
18 holes, 6218yds, Par 70, SSS 70, Course record 63.
Club membership 750.
Visitors	must contact Professional in advance.
Societies	must apply in advance.
Green Fees	£24 per day (£30 weekends & bank holidays).
Prof	Peter A Stubbs
Facilities	⊗ ∭ ⓑ ■ ♀ ⚲ 🏠 ⚘
Location	0.75m S on A520

Hotel	★★★ 69% George Hotel, Swan Square, Burslem, STOKE-ON-TRENT ☎ 01782 577544 39 ⇆ ⎧

Westwood (Leek) Newcastle Rd ST13 7AA
☎ 01538 398385 & 398897 (Prof) Fax 01538 382485
A challenging moorland/parkland course set in beautiful
open countryside with an undulating front nine. The back
nine is more open and longer with the River Churnet coming
into play on several holes.
18 holes, 6207yds, Par 70, SSS 69, Course record 66.
Club membership 700.
Visitors	must book in advance.
Societies	apply by phone or in writing.
Green Fees	not confirmed.
Prof	Neale Hyde
Facilities	⊗ ∭ ⓑ ■ ♀ ⚲ 🏠 ⚘ ⚘
Location	On A53, S of Leek

Hotel	★★★ 69% George Hotel, Swan Square, Burslem, STOKE-ON-TRENT ☎ 01782 577544 39 ⇆ ⎧

LICHFIELD
Map 07 SK10

Seedy Mill Elmhurst WS13 8HE
☎ 01543 417333 Fax 01543 418098
A 27 hole course in picturesque parkland scenery. Numerous
holes crossed by meandering mill streams. Undulating greens
defended by hazards lie in wait for the practised approach.
Well appointed clubhouse.
18 holes, 6308yds, Par 72, SSS 70, Course record 68.
Club membership 1200.
Visitors	must contact at least 3 days in advance, weekend time restrictions.
Societies	apply in writing or telephone.
Green Fees	£21 per 18 holes (£26 weekends).
Cards	▭▭ ▭▭ ▭▭ ▭ ▭
Prof	Mark Ashworth
Designer	Hawtree & Son
Facilities	⊗ ∭ ⓑ ■ ♀ ⚲ 🏠 ⚘ 🏌 ⚘ ⚘
Location	At Elmhurst, 2m N of Lichfield, off A515

Hotel	★★★ 66% Little Barrow Hotel, Beacon St, LICHFIELD ☎ 01543 414500 24 ⇆ ⎧

Whittington Heath Tamworth Rd WS14 9PW
☎ 01543 432317 Fax 01543 432317
18 magnificent holes winding their way through
heathland and trees, presenting a good test for the serious
golfer. Leaving the fairway can be severely punished. The

dog-legs are most tempting, inviting the golfer to chance
his arm. Local knowledge is a definite advantage. Clear
views of the famous three spires of Lichfield Cathedral.
18 holes, 6490yds, Par 70, SSS 71, Course record 64.
Club membership 660.
Visitors	must contact in advance. May not play at weekends. Handicap certificate required.
Societies	welcome Wed & Thu, must apply in writing.
Green Fees	£27 per 18 holes; £36 per 36 holes.
Cards	▭▭ ▭▭ ▭ ▭
Prof	Adrian Sadler
Designer	Colt
Facilities	⊗ ∭ ⓑ ■ ♀ ⚲ 🏠
Location	2.5m SE on A51 Lichfield-Tamworth road

Hotel	★★★ 66% Little Barrow Hotel, Beacon St, LICHFIELD ☎ 01543 414500 24 ⇆ ⎧

NEWCASTLE-UNDER-LYME
Map 07 SJ84

Keele Golf Club Newcastle Rd, Keele ST5 5AB
☎ 01782 627596
Open course on the side of a hill without maturing trees.
18 holes, 6396yds, Par 71, SSS 70, Course record 64.
Club membership 210.
Visitors	must contact in advance.
Societies	by prior arrangement to Newcastle-Under-Lyme Borough Council, Civic Offices, Merrial St, Newcastle-Under-Lyme, Staffs.
Green Fees	£7.20 per round (£8.75 weekends).
Prof	Colin Smith
Facilities	⊗ ∭ ⓑ ■ ♀ ⚲ 🏠 🏌 ⚘ ⚘
Location	2m W on A525

Hotel	★★★ Posthouse Stoke on Trent, Clayton Rd, NEWCASTLE-UNDER-LYME ☎ 0870 400 9077 119 ⇆ ⎧

Newcastle-Under-Lyme Whitmore Rd ST5 2QB
☎ 01782 617006
Parkland course.
18 holes, 6404yds, Par 72, SSS 71.
Club membership 600.
Visitors	must contact in advance. With member only weekends.
Societies	must contact in advance.
Green Fees	not confirmed.
Prof	Paul Symonds
Facilities	⊗ ∭ ⓑ ■ ♀ ⚲ 🏠 🏌 ⚘
Location	1m SW on A53

Hotel	★★ 63% Comfort Inn, Liverpool Rd, NEWCASTLE-UNDER-LYME ☎ 01782 717000 48 ⇆ ⎧ Annexe 24 ⇆ ⎧

Wolstanton Dimsdale Old Hall, Hassam Pde, Wolstanton
ST5 9DR ☎ 01782 622413 (Sec) & 616995
A challenging undulating suburban course incorporating 6
difficult Par 3 holes. The 6th hole (Par 3) is 233yds from the
Medal Tee.
18 holes, 5807yds, Par 68, SSS 68, Course record 63.
Club membership 700.
Visitors	must contact in advance. May not play Tue (Ladies Day). With member only at weekends & bank holidays.
Societies	must contact in advance.

Green Fees £21 per day/round.
Prof Simon Arnold
Facilities ⊗ ⅢⅢ ᗷ ▿ ♀ ⚲ 🏠 ✎
Location 1.5m from town centre. Turn off A34 at MacDonalds

Hotel ★★★ Posthouse Stoke on Trent, Clayton Rd, NEWCASTLE-UNDER-LYME
☎ 0870 400 9077 119 ➾ ⚑

ONNELEY
Map 07 SJ74

Onneley CW3 5QF ☎ 01782 750577
A tight, picturesque, hillside parkland course. An ideal test for the short game
9 holes, 5584yds, Par 70, SSS 67, Course record 67.
Club membership 410.
Visitors welcome except during competitions, but may not play on Sun and with member only Sat and bank holidays.
Societies packages available apply in writing to secretary.
Green Fees not confirmed.
Facilities ⊗ by prior arrangement ⅢⅢ by prior arrangement ᗷ ▿ ♀ ♨
Location 2m from Woore on A525

Hotel ★★ 69% Wheatsheaf Inn at Onneley, Barhill Rd, ONNELEY ☎ 01782 751581 6 ⚑

PATTINGHAM
Map 07 SO89

Patshull Park Hotel Golf & Country Club WV6 7HR
☎ 01902 700100 Fax 01902 700874
Picturesque course set in 280 acres of glorious Capability Brown landscaped parkland. Designed by John Jacobs, the course meanders alongside trout fishing lakes. Many leisure facilities.
18 holes, 6400yds, Par 72, SSS 71, Course record 63.
Club membership 330.

Visitors must contact in advance.
Societies must contact in advance.
Green Fees £25 per round (£30 weekends).
Cards 💳 💳 💳 💳 💳 💳
Prof Richard Bissell
Designer John Jacobs
Facilities ⊗ ⅢⅢ ᗷ ▿ ♀ ♨ 🏠 ♩ ➾ 🚗 ✎
& Leisure heated indoor swimming pool, fishing, sauna, solarium, gymnasium.
Location Off A464

Hotel ★★★ 66% Patshull Park Hotel Golf & Country Club, Patshull Park, PATTINGHAM
☎ 01902 700100 49 ➾ ⚑

PERTON
Map 07 SO89

Perton Park Wrottesley Park Rd WV6 7HL
☎ 01902 380103 & 380073 Fax 01902 380073
Challenging inland links style course set in the picturesque Staffordshire countryside.
18 holes, 6620yds, Par 72, SSS 72, Course record 61.
Club membership 500.
Visitors must book in advance.
Societies must telephone in advance.
Green Fees £12 per round (£18 weekends & bank holidays).
Cards 💳 💳
Prof Jeremy Harrold
Facilities ⊗ ⅢⅢ ᗷ ▿ ♀ ♨ 🏠 ♩ ♨ ✎ ⚲
& Leisure hard tennis courts, crown green bowls.
Location 6m W of Wolverhampton, off A454

Hotel ★★ 69% Ely House Hotel, 53 Tettenhall Rd, WOLVERHAMPTON
☎ 01902 311311 18 ➾ ⚑

STAFFORD
Map 07 SJ92

Stafford Castle Newport Rd ST16 1BP ☎ 01785 223821
Parkland type course built around Stafford Castle.
9 holes, 6382yds, Par 71, SSS 70, Course record 68.
Club membership 400.
Visitors must contact in advance. May not play Sun morning.
Societies must apply in writing or by telephone.
Green Fees £16 per day (£20 weekends).
Facilities ⊗ ⅢⅢ ᗷ ▿ ♀ ♨ 🏠
Location SW side of town centre off A518

Hotel ★★★ 65% Garth Hotel, Wolverhampton Rd, Moss Pit, STAFFORD
☎ 01785 256124 60 ➾ ⚑

STOKE-ON-TRENT
Map 07 SJ84

Burslem Wood Farm, High Ln, Tunstall ST6 7JT
☎ 01782 837006
On the outskirts of Tunstall, a moorland course with hard walking.
9 holes, 5354yds, Par 66, SSS 66, Course record 66.
Club membership 250.
Visitors except Sun & with member only Sat & bank holidays.
Societies must telephone in advance.
Green Fees not confirmed.
Facilities ⊗ ⅢⅢ ᗷ ▿ ♀ ♨
Location 4m N of city centre on B5049

Hotel ★★★ 69% George Hotel, Swan Square, Burslem, STOKE-ON-TRENT
☎ 01782 577544 39 ➾ ⚑

Greenway Hall Stanley Rd, Stockton Brook ST9 9LJ
☎ 01782 503158
Moorland course with fine views of the Pennines.
18 holes, 5678yds, Par 68, SSS 67.
Club membership 560.
Visitors may play weekdays only.
Societies must apply in writing.
Green Fees not confirmed.
Facilities ⊗ ⅢⅢ by prior arrangement ᗷ ▿ ♀ ♨ 🏠
Location 5m NE off A53

▶

Hotel ★★★ 69% George Hotel, Swan Square, Burslem, STOKE-ON-TRENT ☎ 01782 577544 39 ⇆ ♠

Trentham 14 Barlaston Old Rd, Trentham ST4 8HB ☎ 01782 658109 Fax 01782 644024
Parkland course. The par 3, 4th is a testing hole reached through a copse of trees.
18 holes, 6644yds, Par 72, SSS 72, Course record 67.
Club membership 600.
Visitors must contact in advance.
Societies must contact in advance.
Green Fees £30 per day (£40 weekends & bank holidays).
Cards ▨ ▧
Prof Sandy Wilson
Designer Colt & Alison
Facilities ⊗ ⅲ ⓛ ♥ ♀ ♨ 🛈 ⛳ ⚲ ♣ ♦
& Leisure squash.
Location 3m S off A5035

Hotel ★★★ 66% Haydon House Hotel, Haydon St, Basford, STOKE-ON-TRENT ☎ 01782 711311 17 ⇆ ♠ Annexe 6 ⇆ ♠

Trentham Park Trentham Park ST4 8AE ☎ 01782 658800 Fax 01782 658800
Fine woodland course. Set in established parkland with many challenging and interesting holes.
18 holes, 6425yds, Par 71, SSS 71, Course record 67.
Club membership 850.
Visitors must contact in advance.
Societies Wed & Fri, must apply in advance.
Green Fees £25 per day/round (£30 weekends).
Prof Brian Rimmer
Facilities ⊗ ⅲ ⓛ ♥ ♀ ♨ 🛈 ⛳ ⚲ ♦
Location Adjacent to Trentham Gardens, off A34 3m S of Newcastle-under-Lyme

Hotel ★★★ Posthouse Stoke on Trent, Clayton Rd, NEWCASTLE-UNDER-LYME ☎ 0870 400 9077 119 ⇆ ♠

STONE Map 07 SJ93

Barlaston Meaford Rd ST15 8UX ☎ 01782 372795 & 372867 Fax 01782 372867
Picturesque meadowland course designed by Peter Alliss.
18 holes, 5800yds, Par 69, SSS 68.
Club membership 650.
Visitors may not play before 10am or after 4pm Fridays, weekends and bank holidays.
Societies telephone or apply in writing.
Green Fees not confirmed.
Prof Ian Rogers
Designer Peter Alliss
Facilities ⊗ ⓛ ♥ ♀ ♨ 🛈 ♦
Hotel ★★★ 67% Stone House Hotel, Stafford Rd, STONE ☎ 01785 815531 50 ⇆ ♠

Izaak Walton Eccleshall Rd, Cold Norton ST15 0NS ☎ 01785 760900
A gently undulating meadowland course with streams and ponds as features.
18 holes, 6281yds, Par 72, SSS 72, Course record 72.
Club membership 400.
Visitors must contact in advance for weekends play.
Societies must telephone in advance.

Green Fees £16 (£20 weekends & bank holidays).
Prof Julie Brown
Facilities ⊗ ⅲ ⓛ ♥ ♀ ♨ 🛈 ⚲ ♦ ♣
Location On B5026 between Stone & Eccleshall

Hotel ★★★ 67% Stone House Hotel, Stafford Rd, STONE ☎ 01785 815531 50 ⇆ ♠

Stone Filleybrooks ST15 0NB ☎ 01785 813103
9-hole parkland course with easy walking and 18 different tees.
9 holes, 6299yds, Par 71, SSS 70, Course record 68.
Club membership 310.
Visitors with member only weekends & bank holidays.
Societies must apply in writing.
Green Fees not confirmed.
Facilities ⊗ ⅲ ⓛ ♥ ♀ ♨ ⚲ ♦
Location 0.5m W on A34

Hotel ★★★ 67% Stone House Hotel, Stafford Rd, STONE ☎ 01785 815531 50 ⇆ ♠

TAMWORTH Map 07 SK20

Drayton Park Drayton Park, Fazeley B78 3TN ☎ 01827 251139 Fax 01827 284035
Parkland course designed by James Braid. Club established since 1897.
18 holes, 6214yds, Par 71, SSS 71, Course record 62.
Club membership 450.
Visitors with member only weekends. Must book in advance (call either professional or secretary).
Societies must apply in writing.
Green Fees not confirmed.
Prof M W Passmore
Designer James Braid
Facilities ⊗ ⅲ ⓛ ♥ ♀ ♨ 🛈 ♦
Location 2m S on A4091, next to Drayton Manor Leisure Park

Hotel ★★★★ 74% The Belfry, WISHAW ☎ 01675 470301 324 ⇆ ♠

Tamworth Municipal Eagle Dr, Amington B77 4EG ☎ 01827 709303 Fax 01827 709304
First-class municipal, parkland course and a good test of golf.
18 holes, 6605yds, Par 73, SSS 72, Course record 63.
Club membership 600.
Visitors must book in advance at weekends.
Societies must contact in advance.
Green Fees £12.
Cards ▬
Prof Aynsley Hill
Designer Hawtree & Son
Facilities ⊗ ⅲ ⓛ ♥ ♀ ♨ 🛈 ⛳ ⚲ ♦ ♣
Location 2.5m E off B5000

Hotel ★★ 61% Angel Croft Hotel, Beacon St, LICHFIELD ☎ 01543 258737 10rm(3 ⇆ 5 ♠) Annexe 8 ⇆ ♠

UTTOXETER Map 07 SK03

Manor Leese Hill, Kingstone ST14 8QT ☎ 01889 563234 Fax 01889 563234
A short but tough course set in the heart of the Staffordshire countryside with fine views of the surrounding area.

18 holes, 6060yds, Par 71, SSS 69, Course record 67.
Club membership 400.
Visitors restricted at weekends.
Societies must telephone in advance.
Green Fees £12 (£20 weekends).
Cards ▭▭▭▭▭
Prof Sean Stiff
Facilities ⊗〗⌷🍴♟♨🏠🏌🍺🏌⛳♥
& Leisure fishing.
Location 2m from Uttoxeter on A518 towards Stafford

Hotel ★★ 65% Bank House Hotel, Church St,
UTTOXETER ☎ 01889 566922 14 🛏 ♠

Uttoxeter Wood Ln ST14 8JR
☎ 01889 564884 (Pro) & 566552 (Office)
Fax 01889 567501
Undulating, challenging course with spectacular views
adjacent to the racecourse.
18 holes, 5710yds, Par 70, SSS 69, Course record 66.
Club membership 900.
Visitors restricted weekends and competition days.
Advisable to check availability during peak
periods.
Societies must book in advance.
Green Fees £20 per day (£30 per 18 holes weekends & bank
holidays).
Prof Adam McCandless
Designer G Rothera
Facilities ⊗〗⌷🍴♟♨🏠🏌⛳
Location Close to A50, 0.5m beyond main entrance to
racecourse

Hotel ★★ 65% Bank House Hotel, Church St,
UTTOXETER ☎ 01889 566922 14 🛏 ♠

Weston
Map 07 SJ92

Ingestre Park ST18 0RE
☎ 01889 270845 Fax 01889 270845
Parkland course set in the grounds of Ingestre Hall, former
home of the Earl of Shrewsbury, with mature trees and
pleasant views.
18 holes, 6251yds, Par 70, SSS 70, Course record 67.
Club membership 750.
Visitors with member only weekends & bank holidays.
Must play before 3.30pm weekdays. Advance
booking preferred. Handicap certificate
required.
Societies must apply in advance.
Green Fees £28 per day; £23 per round.
Prof Danny Scullion
Designer Hawtree
Facilities ⊗〗⌷🍴♟♨🏠🏌🍺⛳
Location 2m SE off A51

Hotel ★★★ 66% Tillington Hall Hotel, Eccleshall
Rd, STAFFORD ☎ 01785 253531 90 🛏 ♠

Whiston
Map 07 SK04

Whiston Hall Whiston Hall ST10 2HZ ☎ 01538 266260
A challenging 18-hole course in scenic countryside,
incorporating many natural obstacles and providing a test for
all golfing abilities.
18 holes, 5742yds, Par 71, SSS 69, Course record 70.
Club membership 400.

Visitors reasonable dress on the course. Must telephone
in advance at weekends.
Societies phone for details.
Green Fees not confirmed.
Designer T Cooper
Facilities ⊗〗⌷🍴♟♨🏠⛳
& Leisure fishing, snooker.
Location Off A52, between Stoke-on-Trent and
Ashbourne

Hotel ★★★ 69% George Hotel, Swan Square,
Burslem, STOKE-ON-TRENT
☎ 01782 577544 39 🛏 ♠

Aldeburgh
Map 05 TM45

Aldeburgh Saxmundham Rd IP15 5PE
☎ 01728 452890 Fax 01728 452937
Fine heathland golf course providing a varied and
interesting challenge for the handicap golfer. Additional
9 hole course suitable for golfing holiday makers.
18 holes, 6330yds, Par 68, SSS 71, Course record 65.
River Course: 9 holes, 4228yds, Par 64, SSS 61, Course
record 62.
Club membership 850.
Visitors must contact in advance and have a
handicap certificate. 2 ball/foursomes only.

WENTWORTH
HOTEL ★★★
Aldeburgh, Suffolk
Tel: (01728) 452312 Fax: (01728) 454343
E-mail: wentworth.hotel@anglianet.co.uk
Website: www.wentworth-aldeburgh.com

The Hotel has the comfort and style of a Country House. Two
comfortable lounges, with open fires and antique furniture,
provide ample space to relax. Each individually decorated
bedroom, many with sea views, is equipped with a colour
television, radio, hairdryer and tea making facilities. The
Restaurant serves a variety of fresh produce whilst a light
lunch can be chosen from the Bar menu, eaten outside in the
sunken terrace garden. Aldeburgh is timeless and unhurried.
There are quality shops, two excellent golf courses within a
short distance from the Hotel, long walks and some of the best
birdwatching at Minsmere Bird reserve. Music and the Arts
can be heard at the Internationally famous Snape Malting
Concert hall. Lastly, there are miles of beach to sit upon and
watch the sea!

Societies   must contact in advance.
Green Fees   on request.
Prof   Keith Preston
Facilities   ⊗ 🄱 ⬛ ♀ 🛆 🖿 ✆ ⚑ ♂
Location   1m W of Aldeburgh on A1094

Hotel   ★★★ 72% Wentworth Hotel, Wentworth
                 Rd, ALDEBURGH ☎ 01728 452312
                 30rm(24 ⇆4 🏠) Annexe 7 ⇆ 🏠
                 See advertisement on page 225

BECCLES   Map 05 TM49

Beccles The Common NR34 9YN ☎ 01502 712244
Common course with gorse bushes, no water hazards or
bunkers.
9 holes, 2779yds, Par 68, SSS 67.
Club membership 175.
Visitors   must play with member on Sun.
Societies   must telephone in advance.
Green Fees   not confirmed.
Facilities   🄱 ⬛ ♀ 🛆 🖿 ✆ ♂
Location   NE side of town

Hotel   ★★★ 65% Hotel Hatfield, The Esplanade,
                 LOWESTOFT ☎ 01502 565337 33 ⇆ 🏠

BUNGAY   Map 05 TM38

Bungay & Waveney Valley Outney Common NR35 1DS
☎ 01986 892337 Fax 01986 892222
Heathland course partly comprising Neolithic stone
workings, easy walking.
18 holes, 6044yds, Par 69, SSS 69, Course record 64.
Club membership 730.
Visitors   should contact in advance. With member only
                 weekends & bank holidays.
Societies   must contact in advance.
Green Fees   not confirmed.
Prof   Nigel Whyte
Designer   James Braid
Facilities   ⊗ 🄱 ⬛ ♀ 🛆 🖿 ✆ ⚑ ♂
Location   0.5m NW on A143

Hotel   ★★★ 65% Hotel Hatfield, The Esplanade,
                 LOWESTOFT ☎ 01502 565337 33 ⇆ 🏠

BURY ST EDMUNDS   Map 05 TL86

Bury St Edmunds Tut Hill IP28 6LG
☎ 01284 755979 Fax 01284 763288
Undulating parkland course with easy walking and attractive
short holes, but quite long. 9 hole course made up of 5 Par
3's and 4x4..
18 holes, 6669yds, Par 72, SSS 72, Course record 68.
9 holes, 2217yds, Par 62, SSS 62.
Club membership 850.
Visitors   with member only at weekends for 18 hole
                 course and advance reservation needed
                 midweek.
Societies   must apply in writing.
Green Fees   18 hole course: £26 per day ; £24 per round. 9
                 hole course: £12 per 2 rounds (£14 weekends).
Cards   ⬛ ⬛ ⬛ ⬛ ⧉
Prof   Mark Jillings

Designer   Ted Ray
Facilities   ⊗ ⚒ by prior arrangement 🄱 ⬛ ♀ 🛆 🖿 ✆ ♂
Location   2m NW on B1106 off A14

Hotel   ★★★ 71% Angel Hotel, Angel Hill, BURY
                 ST EDMUNDS ☎ 01284 753926 66 ⇆ 🏠

The Suffolk Golf & Country Club Fornham St Genevieve
IP28 6JQ ☎ 01284 706777 Fax 01284 706721
A classic parkland course with the river Lark running
through it, which comes into play regularly.
The Genevieve Course: 18 holes, 6321yds, Par 72, SSS 71.
Club membership 600.
Visitors   contact Golf reception, bookings up to 1week in
                 advance.
Societies   apply inwriting to the General Manager.
Green Fees   not confirmed.
Cards   ⬛ ⬛ ⬛ ⧉
Prof   Steve Hall
Facilities   ⊗ ⚒ 🄱 ⬛ ♀ 🛆 🖿 ✆ 🛒 ⚑ ♂
& Leisure   heated indoor swimming pool, sauna, solarium,
                 gymnasium.
Location   Off the A14 onto the B1106 to Fornham

Hotel   ★★★⚓ 70% Ravenwood Hall Hotel,
                 Rougham, BURY ST EDMUNDS
                 ☎ 01359 270345 7 ⇆ Annexe 7 ⇆

CRETINGHAM   Map 05 TM26

Cretingham IP13 7BA
☎ 01728 685275 Fax 01728 685037
Parkland course.
9 holes, 4552yds, Par 66, SSS 64, Course record 61.
Club membership 350.
Visitors   booking required for weekends.
Societies   must contact in advance.
Green Fees   not confirmed.
Cards   ⬛ ⬛ ⧉
Prof   Colin Jenkins
Designer   J Austin
Facilities   ⊗ 🄱 ⬛ ♀ 🛆 🖿 ✆ 🛒 ♂ ♞
& Leisure   hard tennis courts, outdoor swimming pool,
                 pitch & putt.
Location   2m from A1120 at Earl Soham

Hotel   ★★ 65% Cedars Hotel, Needham Rd,
                 STOWMARKET ☎ 01449 612668 25 ⇆ 🏠

FELIXSTOWE   Map 05 TM33

Felixstowe Ferry Ferry Rd IP11 9RY
☎ 01394 286834 Fax 01394 273679
Seaside links course, pleasant views, easy walking. Testing
491-yd, 7th hole. 9 hole course now open.
Martello Course: 18 holes, 6272yds, Par 72, SSS 70.
Club membership 900.
Visitors   may not play weekends on Martello Course.
Societies   Tue, Wed & Fri.
Green Fees   not confirmed.
Prof   Ian MacPherson
Designer   Henry Cotton
Facilities   🛆 🖿 🛒 ♂
Location   NE side of town centre. Signposted from A14

Hotel   ★★ 70% Waverley Hotel, 2 Wolsey Gardens,
                 FELIXSTOWE ☎ 01394 282811 19 ⇆ 🏠

FLEMPTON
Map 05 TL86

Flempton IP28 6EQ ☎ 01284 728291
Breckland course.
9 holes, 6240yds, Par 70, SSS 70.
Club membership 300.
Visitors   must contact in advance and produce handicap
certificate. With member only weekends & bank
holidays.
Societies   limited to small societies - must apply in
writing.
Green Fees £30 per day; £25 per round.
Prof   Mark Jillings
Designer   J H Taylor
Facilities   ⊗ ⓑ ▼ ♀ ⚲ 🍴 ✆
Location   0.5m W on A1101

Hotel   ★★★ 69% The Priory Hotel, Tollgate, BURY
ST EDMUNDS ☎ 01284 766181
9 ⇆ ☏ Annexe 18 ⇆ ☏

HALESWORTH
Map 05 TM37

Halesworth Bramfield Rd IP19 9XA
☎ 01986 875567 Fax 01986 874565
A 27-hole professionally designed parkland complex of one
18 hole membership course and a 9 hole pay and play.
18 holes, 6580yds, Par 72, SSS 72, Course record 71.
9 holes, 2398yds, Par 33, SSS 33.
Club membership 700.
Visitors   visitors welcome at all times except for Sunday
before noon on the 18 hole course. Handicap
certificate required for 18 hole course.
Societies   telephone for booking form.
Green Fees not confirmed.
Prof   Richard Whyte
Designer   J W Johnson
Facilities   ⊗ 🏌 ⓑ ▼ ♀ ⚲ 🍴 ✆ ⚐
Location   0.75m S of town, signposted on left of A144
road to Bramfield

Hotel   ★★★ 71% Swan Hotel, Market Place,
SOUTHWOLD ☎ 01502 722186
26rm (25 ⇆ ☏) Annexe 17 ⇆ ☏

HAVERHILL
Map 05 TL64

Haverhill Coupals Rd CB9 7UW
☎ 01440 761951 Fax 01440 761951
An 18 hole course lying across two valleys in pleasant
parkland. The front nine with undulating fairways is
complimented by a saucer shaped back nine, bisected by the
River Stour, presenting a challenge to golfers of all
standards.
18 holes, 5898yds, Par 70, SSS 68, Course record 65.
Club membership 600.
Visitors   telephone to check for club competitions.
Societies   must contact in advance. Tue & Thu only.
Green Fees £23 per day; £20 per 18 holes (£28/£25
weekends & bank holidays).
Cards
Prof   Simon Mayfield
Designer   P Pilgrem
Facilities   ⊗ 🏌 ⓑ ▼ ♀ ⚲ 🍴 ⚐
Location   1m SE off A1017

Hotel   ★★ 70% Four Seasons Hotel, Walden Rd,
THAXTED ☎ 01371 830129 9rm (8 ⇆ ☏)

HINTLESHAM
Map 05 TM04

Hintlesham Hall IP8 3NS
☎ 01473 652761 Fax 01473 652750
Magnificent championship length course blending
harmoniously with the ancient parkland surrounding this
exclusive hotel. The 6630yd parkland course was
designed by Hawtree and Son, one of the oldest
established firms of golf course architects in the world.
The course is fair but challenging for low and high
handicappers alike. Hotel offers beautiful
accommodation, excellent cuisine and many facilities.
18 holes, 6638yds, Par 72, SSS 72, Course record 67.
Club membership 425.

Visitors   must contact 48 hours in advance.
Societies   must telephone in advance.
Green Fees not confirmed.
Cards
Prof   Alastair Spink
Designer   Hawtree & Sons
Facilities   ⊗ 🏌 ⓑ ▼ ♀ ⚲ 🍴 ⚐ ✆
& Leisure   hard tennis courts, heated outdoor
swimming pool, sauna, solarium,
gymnasium.
Location   In village on A1071

Hotel   ★★★★ Hintlesham Hall Hotel,
HINTLESHAM
☎ 01473 652334 & 652268
Fax 01473 652463 33 ⇆ ☏

IPSWICH
Map 05 TM14

Alnesbourne Priory Priory Park IP10 0JT
☎ 01473 727393 Fax 01473 278372
A fabulous outlook facing due south across the River Orwell
is one of the many good features of this course set in
woodland. All holes run among trees with some fairways
requiring straight shots. The 8th green is on saltings by the
river.
9 holes, 1700yds, Par 29.
Club membership 30.
Visitors   closed on Tuesday. Closed 6 Jan-28 Feb.
Societies   Tue only, telephone in advance.
Green Fees £10 (£11 Sat; £12 Sun & bank holidays).
Facilities   ⊗ 🏌 ⓑ ▼ ♀ ⚲ ⚐
Location   3m SE, off A14

Hotel ★★★ 69% Courtyard by Marriott Ipswich, The Havens, Ransomes Europark, IPSWICH ☎ 01473 272244 60 ⇌ ↣

Fynn Valley IP6 9JA ☎ 01473 785267 Fax 01473 785632
Undulating parkland course plus Par-3 nine-hole and driving range.
18 holes, 6373yds, Par 70, SSS 70, Course record 67.
Club membership 700.
Visitors members only Sun until noon.
Societies must apply in advance.
Green Fees £18 per 18 holes (£24 weekends & bank holidays).
Cards [card symbols]
Prof Kelvin Vince
Designer Tony Tyrrell
Facilities ⊗ ℑ ↳ ☕ ⚑ ♀ ⚐ 🛢 ↣ ⚘ ♂ ⚲
& Leisure Par 3 course.
Location 2m N of Ipswich on B1077

Hotel ★★★ 64% Novotel, Greyfriars Rd, IPSWICH ☎ 01473 232400 100 ⇌ ↣

Ipswich Purdis Heath IP3 8UQ
☎ 01473 728941 Fax 01473 715236
Many golfers are suprised when they hear that Ipswich has, at Purdis Heath, a first-class golf course. In some ways it resembles some of Surrey's better courses; a beautiful heathland/parkland course with two lakes and easy walking.
18 holes, 6405yds, Par 71, SSS 71, Course record 63 or 9 holes, 1930yds, Par 31, SSS 31.
Club membership 750.
Visitors must contact in advance & have a handicap certificate for 18 hole courses.
Societies must contact in advance.
Green Fees £40 per day; £25 per round (£43/£30 weekends & bank holidays).
Prof Stephen Whymark
Designer James Braid
Facilities ⊗ ℑ ↳ ☕ ⚑ ♀ ⚐ ⚲
Location E side of town centre off A1156

Hotel ★★★ 71% Marlborough Hotel, Henley Rd, IPSWICH ☎ 01473 257677 22 ⇌ ↣

Rushmere Rushmere Heath IP4 5QQ
☎ 01473 725648 Fax 01473 725648
Heathland course with gorse and prevailing winds. Testing 5th hole - dog leg, 419 yards (par 4).
18 holes, 6262yds, Par 70, SSS 70, Course record 66.
Club membership 770.
Visitors not before 2.30pm weekends & bank holidays. Must have a handicap certificate. Must contact in advance.
Societies weekdays (ex Wed) by arrangement.
Green Fees £25 per round.
Prof N T J McNeill
Facilities ⊗ ↳ ☕ ♀ ⚐ ⚲
Location Off A12 N of Ipswich. Signposted

Hotel ★★★ 71% Marlborough Hotel, Henley Rd, IPSWICH ☎ 01473 257677 22 ⇌ ↣

LOWESTOFT Map 05 TM59

Rookery Park Carlton Colville NR33 8HJ
☎ 01502 560380 Fax 01502 560380
Parkland course with a 9-hole, Par 3 adjacent.
18 holes, 6714yds, Par 72, SSS 72.
Club membership 1000.
Visitors must have handicap certificate.
Societies by arrangement.
Green Fees £30 per day (£35 weekends & bank holidays).
Prof Martin Elsworthy
Designer C D Lawrie
Facilities ⊗ ℑ ↳ ☕ ⚑ ♀ ⚐ 🛢 ↣ ⚲
Location 3.5m SW on A146

Hotel ★★★ 65% Hotel Hatfield, The Esplanade, LOWESTOFT ☎ 01502 565337 33 ⇌ ↣

NEWMARKET Map 05 TL66

Links Cambridge Rd CB8 0TG
☎ 01638 663000 Fax 01638 661476
Gently undulating parkland.
18 holes, 6574yds, Par 72, SSS 71, Course record 66.
Club membership 780.
Visitors must have handicap certificate, may not play Sun before 11.30am.
Societies telephone secretary in advance.
Green Fees not confirmed.
Prof John Sharkey
Designer Col. Hotchkin
Facilities ⊗ ℑ ↳ ☕ ⚑ ♀ ⚐ 🛢 ↣ ⚲
Location 1m SW on A1034

Hotel ★★★ 69% Heath Court Hotel, Moulton Rd, NEWMARKET ☎ 01638 667171 41 ⇌ ↣

NEWTON Map 05 TL94

Newton Green Newton Green CO10 0QN
☎ 01787 377217 & 377501
Flat, 18-hole course with lake.
18 holes, 5960yds, Par 69, SSS 68.
Club membership 640.
Visitors must contact in advance but may not play on Tue or Sat & Sun before 12.30.
Societies apply in advance.
Green Fees not confirmed.
Prof Tim Cooper
Facilities ⊗ ℑ ↳ ☕ ⚑ ♀ ⚐ 🛢 ↣ ⚲
Location W side of village on A134

Hotel ★★★ 67% The Bull, Hall St, LONG MELFORD ☎ 01787 378494 25 ⇌ ↣

RAYDON Map 05 TM03

Brett Vale Noakes Rd IP7 5LR
☎ 01473 310718 Fax 01473 312270
Brett Vale course takes you through a nature reserve and on lakeside walks, affording views over Dedham Vale. The excellent fairways demand an accurate tee and good approach shots. 1, 2, 3, 8, 10 and 15 are all affected by crosswinds, but once in the valley it is much more sheltered. Although only 5,797 yards the course is testing and interesting at all levels of golf.

18 holes, 5797yds, Par 70, SSS 69, Course record 65.
Club membership 550.

Visitors	must book tee times and wear appropriate clothing.
Societies	apply in writing or telephone.
Green Fees	£30 per day; £18 per round (£40/£25 weekends).
Cards	〓 〓 〓 〓 🅖
Prof	Robert Taylor
Designer	Howard Smith
Facilities	⊗ 〗 🍴 💺 ♀ 🛆 🏠 🐾 🚬 ✏
Location	B1070 at Raydon, 2m from A12
Hotel	★★★🏖 Maison Talbooth, Stratford Rd, DEDHAM ☎ 01206 322367 10 🛏 🏌

SOUTHWOLD
Map 05 TM57

Southwold The Common IP18 6TB
☎ 01502 723234 & 723248
Commonland course with 4-acre practice ground and panoramic views of the sea.
9 holes, 6052yds, Par 70, SSS 69, Course record 67.
Club membership 450.

Visitors	restricted on competition days (Ladies-Wed, Gents-Sun).
Societies	must contact in advance.
Green Fees	£18 per 18 holes; £10 per 9 holes (£20/£11 weekends & bank holidays).
Prof	Brian Allen
Facilities	⊗ 🍴 💺 ♀ 🛆 🏠 🐾 ✏
Location	From A12 - B1140 to Southwold
Hotel	★★★ 71% Swan Hotel, Market Place, SOUTHWOLD ☎ 01502 722186 26rm (25 🛏 🏌) Annexe 17 🛏 🏌

STOWMARKET
Map 05 TM05

Stowmarket Lower Rd, Onehouse IP14 3DA
☎ 01449 736473 Fax 01449 736826
Parkland course.
18 holes, 6107yds, Par 69, SSS 69, Course record 66.
Club membership 630.

Visitors	must contact in advance.
Societies	Thu or Fri, by arrangement.
Green Fees	£31 per day; £25 per round.
Prof	Duncan Burl
Facilities	⊗ 〗 🍴 💺 ♀ 🛆 🏠 🐾 🚬 ✏ 🍷
Location	2.5m SW off B1115
Hotel	★★ 65% Cedars Hotel, Needham Rd, STOWMARKET ☎ 01449 612668 25 🛏 🏌

THORPENESS
Map 05 TM45

Thorpeness Golf Club & Hotel IP16 4NH
☎ 01728 452176 Fax 01728 453868
The holes of this moorland course are pleasantly varied with several quite difficult par 4's. Natural hazards abound. The 15th, with its sharp left dog-leg, is one of the best holes. Designed by James Braid.
18 holes, 6271yds, Par 69, SSS 71, Course record 66.
Club membership 270.

Visitors	contact in advance.
Societies	telephone in advance, deposit required.
Green Fees	not confirmed.
Cards	〓 〓 〓 〓 🅖
Prof	Frank Hill
Designer	James Braid
Facilities & Leisure	⊗ 〗 🍴 💺 ♀ 🛆 🏠 🐾 🚬 ✏ hard tennis courts, snooker room.
Location	W side of village off B1353
Hotel	★★★ 73% White Lion Hotel Ltd, Market Cross Place, ALDEBURGH ☎ 01728 452720 38 🛏 🏌

WALDRINGFIELD
Map 05 TM24

Waldringfield Heath Newbourne Rd IP12 4PT
☎ 01473 736768 Fax 01473 736436
Easy walking heathland course with long drives on 1st and 13th (590yds) and some ponds.
18 holes, 6141yds, Par 71, SSS 69, Course record 67.
Club membership 630.

Visitors	welcome Mon-Fri, weekends & bank holidays after noon.
Societies	weekdays by arrangement.
Green Fees	not confirmed.
Prof	Robin Mann
Designer	Phillip Pilgrem
Facilities	⊗ 〗 🍴 💺 ♀ 🛆 🏠 🚬 ✏
Location	3m NE of Ipswich off old A12
Hotel	★★★🏖 75% Seckford Hall Hotel, WOODBRIDGE ☎ 01394 385678 22 🛏 🏌 Annexe 10 🛏 🏌

WOODBRIDGE
Map 05 TM24

Seckford Seckford Hall Rd, Great Bealings IP13 6NT
☎ 01394 388000 Fax 01394 382818
A challenging course interspersed with young tree plantations, numerous bunkers, water hazards and undulating fairways, providing a tough test for all levels of golfer. The testing 18th is almost completely surrounded by water.
18 holes, 5303yds, Par 68, SSS 66, Course record 65.
Club membership 400.

Visitors	telephone in advance for tee times.
Societies	telephone in advance. Computerised booking system.
Green Fees	£16 per 18 holes (£18.50 weekends).
Cards	〓 〓 🅳 〓 🅖
Prof	Simon Jay
Designer	J Johnson
Facilities & Leisure	⊗ 〗 🍴 💺 ♀ 🛆 🐾 🍷 heated indoor swimming pool, fishing, sauna, solarium, gymnasium.
Location	(3m W of Woodbridge, 0ff A12)
Hotel	★★★🏖 75% Seckford Hall Hotel, WOODBRIDGE ☎ 01394 385678 22 🛏 🏌 Annexe 10 🛏 🏌

> AA Hotels that have special arrangements with golf courses are listed at the back of the guide

Ufford Park Hotel Golf & Leisure Yarmouth Rd, Ufford IP12 1QW

☎ 01394 383555 & 382836 Fax 01394 383582

The 18-hole Par 71 course is set in ancient parkland has many natural features including 11 water hazards retained from the original parkland. Free draining making it playable all year. There is also an extensive hotel and leisure complex beside the course.

18 holes, 6325yds, Par 71, SSS 71, Course record 67.
Club membership 320.

Visitors	must book tee time from golf shop 01394 382836. Must adhere to dress code. Handicap certificates preferred but not essential.
Societies	telephone or fax in advance to book tee time.
Green Fees	£25 per day; £18 per round (£30/£22 weekends & bank holidays).
Cards	🖃 ■ ▦ 🖃 🖃 🖃 🖃
Prof	Stuart Robertson
Designer	Phil Pilgrim
Facilities	⊗ 𝔐 🝓 ▮ ♀ ⚘ 🏠 👕 🐎 🛒 🖫 ⟨
& Leisure	heated indoor swimming pool, fishing, sauna, solarium, gymnasium.
Location	Just off A12, on the B1438
Hotel	★★★ 70% Ufford Park Hotel Golf & Leisure, Yarmouth Rd, Ufford, WOODBRIDGE ☎ 01394 383555 42 ⇔ 🝓 Annexe 2 ⇔ 🝓

Woodbridge Bromeswell Heath IP12 2PF

☎ 01394 382038 Fax 01394 382392

A beautiful course, one of the best in East Anglia. It is situated on high ground and in different seasons present golfers with a great variety of colour. Some say that of the many good holes the 16th is the best.

18 holes, 6299yds, Par 70, SSS 70, Course record 64.
Forest Course: 9 holes, 3191yds, Par 35.
Club membership 900.

Visitors	Main Course: must contact in advance, handicap certificate required, with member only weekends. Forest Course: open all days and no handicap certificate required.
Societies	by prior telephone call or in writing.
Green Fees	Main Course: £32 per day/round. Forest Course: £16 per day/round.
Prof	Adrian Hubert
Designer	Davie Grant
Facilities	⊗ 𝔐 🝓 ▮ ♀ ⚘ 🏠 ⟨
Location	2.5m NE off A1152
Hotel	★★★🏊 75% Seckford Hall Hotel, WOODBRIDGE ☎ 01394 385678 22 ⇔ 🝓 Annexe 10 ⇔ 🝓

WORLINGTON
Map 05 TL67

Royal Worlington & Newmarket IP28 8SD

☎ 01638 712216 Fax 01638 717787

Inland 'links' course. Favourite 9-hole course of many golf writers.

9 holes, 3105yds, Par 35, SSS 70, Course record 67.
Club membership 325.

Visitors	with member only at weekends. Must contact in advance and have a handicap certificate.
Societies	must apply in writing.

Green Fees	not confirmed.
Prof	Malcolm Hawkins
Designer	Tom Dunn
Facilities	⊗ 🝓 ▮ ♀ ⚘ 🏠 👕 ⟨
Location	0.5m SE
Hotel	★★★ 71% Riverside Hotel, Mill St, MILDENHALL ☎ 01638 717274 17 ⇔ 🝓 Annexe 4 ⇔ 🝓

SURREY

ADDLESTONE
Map 04 TQ06

New Zealand Woodham Ln KT15 3QD

☎ 01932 345049 Fax 01932 342891

Heathland course set in trees and heather.

18 holes, 6012yds, Par 68, SSS 69, Course record 66.
Club membership 320.

Visitors	must contact in advance.
Societies	telephone initially.
Green Fees	available on application.
Prof	Vic Elvidge
Designer	Muir Fergusson/Simpson
Facilities	⊗ 🝓 ▮ ♀ ⚘ 🏠 👕 🐎 🛒 ⟨
Location	1.5m E of Woking
Hotel	★★★ 67% The Ship, Monument Green, WEYBRIDGE ☎ 01932 848364 39 ⇔ 🝓

ASHFORD
Map 04 TQ07

Ashford Manor Fordbridge Rd TW15 3RT

☎ 01784 424644 Fax 01784 424649

Tree lined parkland course, looks easy but is difficult.

18 holes, 6352yds, Par 70, SSS 70, Course record 64.
Club membership 700.

Visitors	advisable to telephone in advance, handicap certificate required, with member only at weekends but may not play competition days.
Societies	welcome weekdays, except Thu am, must contact in advance.
Green Fees	£35 per day, £30 per round (weekdays only).
Cards	🖃 🖃 🖃
Prof	Mike Finney
Facilities	⊗ 𝔐 🝓 ▮ ♀ ⚘ 🏠 ⟨
Location	2m E of Staines via A308 Staines by-pass
Hotel	★★★ 69% The Thames Lodge, Thames St, STAINES ☎ 0780 400 8121 79 ⇔ 🝓

BAGSHOT
Map 04 SU96

Pennyhill Park Hotel & Country Club London Rd GU19 5EU ☎ 01276 471774 Fax 01276 473217

A nine-hole course set in 11.4 acres of beautiful parkland. It is challenging to even the most experienced golfer.

9 holes, 2095yds, Par 32, SSS 32.
Club membership 100.

Visitors	prior booking must be made. telephone in advance.
Green Fees	not confirmed.
Cards	〰 💳 💳 💳 💳 💳
Facilities	⊗ ⁌ 🍴 🍺 ♀ ⚲ 📷 ⛳
& Leisure	hard tennis courts, heated outdoor swimming pool, fishing, gymnasium.
Location	Off A30 between Camberley and Bagshot
Hotel	★★★★★ 72% Pennyhill Park Hotel & Country Club, London Rd, BAGSHOT ☎ 01276 471774 31 ⇄ 🐾 Annexe 92 ⇄ 🐾

Windlesham Grove End GU19 5HY
☎ 01276 452220 Fax 01276 452290
A parkland course with many demanding Par 4 holes over 400 yards. Thoughtfully designed by Tommy Horton.
18 holes, 6650yds, Par 72, SSS 72, Course record 69.
Club membership 800.

Visitors	handicap certificate required, contact in advance.
Societies	apply in advance.
Green Fees	£25 per round (£35 weekends).
Cards	〰 💳 💳 💳
Prof	Lee Mucklow/Alan Barber
Designer	Tommy Horton
Facilities	⊗ ⁌ 🍺 ♀ ⚲ ⛳ 🛒 ⛳
Location	Junct of A30/A322
Hotel	★★★★★ 72% Pennyhill Park Hotel & Country Club, London Rd, BAGSHOT ☎ 01276 471774 31 ⇄ 🐾 Annexe 92 ⇄ 🐾

BANSTEAD
Map 04 TQ25

Banstead Downs Burdon Ln, Belmont, Sutton SM2 7DD
☎ 020 8642 2284 Fax 020 8642 5252
A natural downland course set on a site of botanic interest. A challenging 18 holes with narrow fairways and tight lies.
18 holes, 6194yds, Par 69, SSS 69, Course record 64.
Club membership 835.

Visitors	must book in advance and have handicap certificate or letter of introduction. With member only weekends.
Societies	Thu, by prior arrangement
Green Fees	not confirmed.
Prof	Robert Dickman
Designer	J H Taylor/James Braid
Facilities	⊗ ⁌ by prior arrangement ⁌ 🍺 ♀ ⚲ 📷 ⛳
Location	1.5m N on A217
Hotel	★★ 63% Thatched House Hotel, 135 Cheam Rd, Sutton ☎ 020 8642 3131 27rm (24 ⇄ 🐾) Annexe 5 ⇄ 🐾

Cuddington Banstead Rd SM7 1RD
☎ 020 8393 0952 Fax 020 8786 7025
Parkland course with easy walking and good views.
18 holes, 6436yds, Par 70, SSS 71, Course record 61.
Club membership 694.

Visitors	must contact in advance and have a handicap certificate or letter of introduction.
Societies	welcome Thu, must apply in advance.
Green Fees	not confirmed.
Prof	Mark Warner
Designer	H S Colt
Facilities	⊗ ⁌ 🍴 🍺 ♀ ⚲ 📷 ⛳ ⛳
Location	N of Banstead station on A2022
Hotel	★★ 63% Thatched House Hotel, 135 Cheam Rd, Sutton ☎ 020 8642 3131 27rm (24 ⇄ 🐾) Annexe 5 ⇄ 🐾

BRAMLEY
Map 04 TQ04

Bramley GU5 0AL ☎ 01483 892696 Fax 01483 894673
Parkland course, from the high ground picturesque views of the Wey Valley on one side and the Hog's Back. Full on course irrigation system with three reservoirs on the course.
18 holes, 5990yds, Par 69, SSS 69, Course record 63.
Club membership 850.

Visitors	may not play Tue am (Ladies Morning) and must play with member at weekends & bank holidays. Must contact secretary on 01483 892696.
Societies	must telephone the secretary in advance.
Green Fees	£34 per day; £28 per round.
Prof	Gary Peddie
Designer	James Braid
Facilities	⊗ ⁌ 🍴 🍺 ♀ ⚲ 📷 ⛳ 🛒 🛒 ⛳ 🍴
Location	3m S of Guildford on A281
Hotel	★★★ 69% Posthouse Guildford, Egerton Rd, GUILDFORD ☎ 0870 400 9036 162 ⇄ 🐾

BROOKWOOD
Map 04 SU95

West Hill Bagshot Rd GU24 0BH
☎ 01483 474365 Fax 01483 474252
Set in the Surrey landscape of heath, heather and tree lined fairways. An interesting and challenging course with subtle greens and a stream which affects play on seven holes. A premium on the well positioned drive.
18 holes, 6368yds, Par 69, SSS 70, Course record 62.
Club membership 500.

Visitors	must contact in advance & have handicap certificate, may not play weekends & bank holidays.
Societies	weekdays only (ex Wed). Telephone in advance.
Green Fees	£60 per day; £42.50 per round.
Prof	John A Clements
Designer	C Butchart/W Parke
Facilities	⊗ ⁌ by prior arrangement ⁌ 🍺 ♀ ⚲ 📷 ⛳ ⛳
Location	E side of village on A322
Hotel	★★★★★ 72% Pennyhill Park Hotel & Country Club, London Rd, BAGSHOT ☎ 01276 471774 31 ⇄ 🐾 Annexe 92 ⇄ 🐾

CAMBERLEY
Map 04 SU86

Camberley Heath Golf Dr GU15 1JG
☎ 01276 23258 Fax 01276 692505
One of the great 'heath and heather' courses so
frequently associated with Surrey. Several very good
short holes - especially the 8th. The 10th is a difficult
and interesting par 4, as also is the 17th, where the drive
must be held well to the left as perdition lurks on the
right. A fairway irrigation system has been installed.
18 holes, 6147yds, Par 72, SSS 70, Course record 65.
Club membership 600.

Visitors	may not play at weekends. Must contact in advance.
Societies	must apply in advance.
Green Fees	£58 per day; £38 per round.
Cards	
Prof	Glen Ralph
Designer	Harry S Colt
Facilities	⊗ ⅂₁ ♥ ♀ △ 🏠 ⚑ 🐾 🚜 ⚙ (
Location	1.25m SE of town centre off A325
Hotel	★★★★★ 72% Pennyhill Park Hotel & Country Club, London Rd, BAGSHOT ☎ 01276 471774 31 ⇋ ℟ Annexe 92 ⇋ ℟

Pine Ridge Old Bisley Rd, Frimley GU16 5NX
☎ 01276 675444 & 20770 Fax 01276 678837
Pay and play heathland course cut through a pine forest with
challenging par 3s, deceptively demanding par 4s and several
birdiable par 5s. Easy walking, but gently undulating. Good
corporate or society packages.
18 holes, 6458yds, Par 72, SSS 71, Course record 67.
Club membership 400.

Visitors	must pre book, no jeans or trainers.
Societies	apply in advance by writing/telephone, packages available to suit.
Green Fees	£20 per round (£25 weekends).
Cards	
Prof	Peter Sefton
Designer	Clive D Smith
Facilities	⊗ ⅏ ⅂₁ ♥ ♀ △ 🏠 ⚑ 🐾 🚜 ⚙ (
& Leisure	ten pin bowling.
Location	Just off B3015, near A30
Hotel	★★★ 69% Frimley Hall, Portsmouth Rd, CAMBERLEY ☎ 0870 400 8224 86 ⇋ ℟

CATERHAM
Map 05 TQ35

Happy Valley Rook Ln, Chaldon CR3 5AA
☎ 01883 344555 Fax 01883 344422
Opened in May 1999, this technically challenging course is
set in beautiful countryside and features fully irrigated greens
and fairways. It also has large practice areas.
18 holes, 6858yds, Par 72, SSS 73, Course record 73.
Club membership 750.

Visitors	may play weekdays only, and can book in advance.
Societies	apply in writing.
Green Fees	£25 Apr-Oct (£20 winter).
Cards	
Designer	David Williams
Facilities	⊗ ⅏ ⅂₁ ♥ ♀ △ 🏠 🐾 🚜 ⚙ (
& Leisure	indoor golf school.
Location	M25 junct 7/M23 junct 6/A22
Hotel	★★★★ 77% Coulsdon Manor, Coulsdon Court Rd, Coulsdon, CROYDON ☎ 020 8668 0414 35 ⇋ ℟

CHERTSEY
Map 04 TQ06

Laleham Laleham Reach KT16 8RP
☎ 01932 564211 Fax 01932 564448
Well-bunkered parkland/meadowland course.
18 holes, 6211yds, Par 70, SSS 70.
Club membership 600.

Visitors	members guests only at weekends.
Societies	must contact in writing/telephone.
Green Fees	£27 per day; £20 per round.
Prof	Hogan Stott
Facilities	⊗ ⅂₁ ♥ ♀ △ 🏠 ⚙
Location	M25 junct 11/A320 to Thorpe Park, at roundabout take exit to Penton Mauna and follow signs to club
Hotel	★★★ 69% The Thames Lodge, Thames St, STAINES ☎ 0780 400 8121 79 ⇋ ℟

CHIDDINGFOLD
Map 04 SU93

Chiddingfold Petworth Rd GU8 4SL
☎ 01428 685888 Fax 01428 685939
With panoramic views across the Surrey Downs, this
challenging course offers a unique combination of lakes,
mature woodland and wildlife.
18 holes, 5501yds, Par 70, SSS 67.
Club membership 325.

Visitors	telephone bookings up to one week in advance.
Societies	prior telephone booking required.
Green Fees	£10 Mon, except bank holidays; £15 Tue-Fri (£20 weekends).
Cards	
Prof	Paul Creamer
Designer	Johnathan Gaunt
Facilities	⊗ ⅏ ⅂₁ ♥ ♀ △ 🏠 ⚑ 🐾 🚜 ⚙ (
Location	A283
Hotel	★★★★ 71% Lythe Hill Hotel, Petworth Rd, HASLEMERE ☎ 01428 651251 41 ⇋ ℟

CHIPSTEAD
Map 04 TQ25

Chipstead How Ln CR5 3LN
☎ 01737 555781 Fax 01737 555404
Hilly parkland course, hard walking, good views. Testing 18th hole.
18 holes, 5491yds, Par 68, SSS 67, Course record 61.
Club membership 650.

Visitors	must contact in advance. May not play weekends or Tue mornings.
Societies	must apply in writing.
Green Fees	£25 per day; £20 per round.
Prof	Gary Torbett
Facilities	⊗ ⏸ ⅊ 🍺 ♀ 📐 🛄 📱 ➤ ♠ ✎ ✝
Location	0.5m N of village
Hotel	★★★★ 69% Selsdon Park Hotel, Addington Rd, Sanderstead, CROYDON ☎ 020 8657 8811 204 ⇔ 📮

CHOBHAM
Map 04 SU96

Chobham Chobham Rd, Knaphill GU21 2TZ
☎ 01276 855584 Fax 01276 855663
Designed by Peter Allis and Clive Clark, Chobham course sits among mature oaks and tree nurseries offering tree-lined fairways, together with six man-made lakes.
18 holes, 5959yds, Par 69, SSS 67, Course record 67.
Club membership 750.

Visitors	booking in advance essential.
Societies	by prior arrangement.
Green Fees	£35 (£40 weekends).
Cards	💳 💳 💳 💳 💳
Prof	Tim Coombes
Designer	Peter Alliss/Clive Clark
Facilities	⊗ ⏸ by prior arrangement 📐 🍺 ♀ 📐 🛄 ✎
Location	A3046 between Chobham and Knaphill
Hotel	★★★ 60% Falcon Hotel, 68 Farnborough Rd, FARNBOROUGH ☎ 01252 545378 30 ⇔ 📮

COBHAM
Map 04 TQ16

Silvermere Redhill Rd KT11 1EF
☎ 01932 866007 Fax 01932 868259
Parkland course with many very tight holes through woodland, 17th has 170-yd carry over the lake. 18th played to a new island green. Driving range.
18 holes, 6700yds, Par 73.
Club membership 740.

Visitors	may not play at weekends until 1pm. Must contact in advance.
Societies	must contact by telephone.
Green Fees	£20 (£30 weekends).
Cards	💳 💳 💳 💳 💳
Prof	Doug McClelland
Facilities	⊗ ⏸ 📐 🍺 ♀ 📐 🛄 📱 ✎ ✝
& Leisure	fishing.
Location	2.25m NW off A245
Hotel	★★★★ 62% Woodlands Park Hotel, Woodlands Ln, STOKE D'ABERNON ☎ 01372 843933 59 ⇔ 📮

CRANLEIGH
Map 04 TQ03

Fernfell Golf & Country Club Barhatch Ln GU6 7NG
☎ 01483 268855 Fax 01483 267251
Scenic woodland/parkland course at the base of the Surrey hills, easy walking. Clubhouse in 400-year-old barn.
18 holes, 5257yds, Par 68, SSS 67, Course record 64.
Club membership 1000.

Visitors	welcome weekdays except Thu am, for weekends contact professional shop in advance on 01483 277188
Societies	telephone in advance.
Green Fees	not confirmed.
Cards	💳 💳 💳 💳 💳
Prof	Trevor Longmuir
Facilities	⊗ ⏸ 📐 🍺 ♀ 📐 🛄 📱 ✎ ✝
& Leisure	hard tennis courts, heated indoor swimming pool, sauna, gymnasium.
Location	Off A281 Guildford to Horsham road, signposted Cranleigh
Hotel	★★★ 63% Gatton Manor Hotel Golf & Country Club, Standon Ln, OCKLEY ☎ 01306 627555 16 ⇔ 📮

Wildwood Country Club Horsham Rd, Alfold, Cranleigh GU6 8JE ☎ 01403 753255 Fax 01403 752005
Parkland with stands of old oaks dominating several holes, a stream fed by a natural spring winds through a series of lakes and ponds. The greens are smooth, undulating and large. The 5th and 16th are the most challenging holes.
18 holes, 6655yds, Par 72, SSS 73, Course record 65.
Club membership 400.

Visitors	welcome subject to availability & booking.
Societies	apply in writing or telephone for enquiries.
Green Fees	£20 (£30 weekends).
Cards	💳 💳 💳 💳 💳
Prof	Simon Andrews/Dean Mara
Designer	Hawtree & Sons
Facilities	⊗ ⏸ 📐 🍺 ♀ 📐 🛄 📱 ➤ ♠ ✎ ✝
& Leisure	fishing.
Location	Off A281, approx 9m S of Guildford
Hotel	★★★ 71% Random Hall Hotel, Stane St, Slinford, HORSHAM ☎ 01403 790558 15 ⇔ 📮

DORKING
Map 04 TQ14

Betchworth Park Reigate Rd RH4 1NZ ☎ 01306 882052
Parkland course, with hard walking on southern ridge of Boxhill.
18 holes, 6266yds, Par 69, SSS 70, Course record 64.
Club membership 725.

Visitors	weekend play Sun pm only. Must contact in advance.
Societies	apply in writing.
Green Fees	not confirmed.
Prof	Tocher
Designer	H Colt
Facilities	📐 🛄 📱 ✎
Location	1m E on A25
Hotel	★★★ 67% The White Horse, High St, DORKING ☎ 0870 400 8282 37 ⇔ 📮 Annexe 32 ⇔ 📮

Dorking Chart Park, Deepdene Av RH5 4BX
☎ 01306 886917
Undulating parkland course, easy slopes, wind-sheltered.
Testing holes: 5th 'Tom's Puddle' (par 4); 7th 'Rest and Be Thankful' (par 4); 9th 'Double Decker' (par 4).
9 holes, 5120yds, Par 66, SSS 65, Course record 62.
Club membership 408.

Visitors	may not play Wed am and with member only weekends & bank holidays. Contact in advance.
Societies	Tue & Thu, telephone in advance.
Green Fees	not confirmed.
Prof	Paul Napier
Designer	J Braid/Others
Facilities	🏌🏌🏌🏌🏌
Location	1m S on A24
Hotel	★★★★ 67% The Burford Bridge, Burford Bridge, Box Hill, DORKING ☎ 0870 400 8283 57 🛏🏌

EAST HORSLEY   Map 04 TQ05

Drift KT24 5HD ☎ 01483 284641 Fax 01483 284642
Woodland course with secluded fairways and picturesque setting. A challenging course that punishes the wayward shot.
18 holes, 6424yds, Par 73, SSS 72, Course record 68.
Club membership 760.

Visitors	book in advance to the pro shop, Mon-Fri only.
Societies	Mon-Fri, telephone in advance.
Green Fees	not confirmed.
Cards	🃏🃏🃏🃏🃏
Prof	Liam Greasley
Designer	Sandown
Facilities	🏌🏌🏌🏌🏌🏌🏌🏌🏌🏌
Location	1.5m N off B2039
Hotel	★★ 61% Bookham Grange Hotel, Little Bookham Common, Bookham, LEATHERHEAD ☎ 01372 452742 21 🛏🏌

EFFINGHAM   Map 04 TQ15

Effingham Guildford Rd KT24 5PZ
☎ 01372 452203 Fax 01372 459959
Easy-walking downland course laid out on 270-acres with tree-lined fairways. It is one of the longest of the Surrey courses with wide subtle greens that provide a provocative but by no means exhausting challenge. Fine views.
18 holes, 6524yds, Par 71, SSS 71, Course record 64.
Club membership 800.

Visitors	contact in advance. With member only weekends & bank holidays.
Societies	Wed, Thu & Fri only and must book in advance.
Green Fees	not confirmed.
Prof	Steve Hoatson
Designer	H S Colt
Facilities	🏌🏌🏌🏌🏌🏌🏌🏌🏌🏌
& Leisure	hard tennis courts.
Location	W side of village on A246
Hotel	★★ 61% Bookham Grange Hotel, Little Bookham Common, Bookham, LEATHERHEAD ☎ 01372 452742 21 🛏🏌

ENTON GREEN   Map 04 SU94

West Surrey GU8 5AF
☎ 01483 421275 Fax 01483 41519
A good parkland-type course in rolling, well-wooded setting. Some fairways are tight with straight driving at a premium. The 17th is a testing hole with a long hill walk.
18 holes, 6300yds, Par 71, SSS 70, Course record 65.
Club membership 600.

Visitors	must contact in advance and have a handicap certificate.
Societies	must apply in writing. All players to have a handicap.
Green Fees	not confirmed.
Prof	Alister Tawse
Designer	Herbert Fowler
Facilities	🏌🏌🏌🏌🏌🏌🏌
Location	S side of village
Hotel	★★★ 64% The Bush Hotel, The Borough, FARNHAM ☎ 0870 400 8225 83 🛏🏌

EPSOM   Map 04 TQ26

Epsom Longdown Ln South KT17 4JR
☎ 01372 721666 Fax 01372 817183
Traditional downland course with many mature trees and well watered greens.
18 holes, 5701yds, Par 69, SSS 68, Course record 62.
Club membership 800.

Visitors	available any day except Tue, Sat & Sun till 12.00 hrs.
Societies	telephone professional on 01372 741867.
Green Fees	£33 per day; £22 per round (£24 per round weekends).
Cards	🃏🃏🃏🃏🃏🃏
Prof	Ron Goudie
Designer	Willie Dunne
Facilities	🏌🏌🏌🏌🏌🏌🏌
Location	SE side of town centre on B288
Hotel	★★★★ 62% Woodlands Park Hotel, Woodlands Ln, STOKE D'ABERNON ☎ 01372 843933 59 🛏🏌

Horton Park Country Club Hook Rd KT19 8QG
☎ 020 8393 8400 & 8394 2626
Fax 020 8394 1369
Parkland course in picturesque surroundings within a country park with a natural lake. The course offers a challenge to all golfers with dog-legs, water hazards and the 10th at 160yds

with an island green. There is also a separate full length Par 3 9 hole course.
18 holes, 6257yds, Par 71.
Club membership 450.

Visitors must book for weekends, recommended booking for midweek. Dress code in force.
Societies must telephone in advance to play at weekends & bank holidays.
Green Fees not confirmed.
Cards ⬛⬛⬛⬛
Prof Jody September/Helen Omidiran
Designer Dr Peter Nicholson
Facilities ⊗ ⽱ ⽫ ⽭ ⽮ ⽯ ⽰ ⽱ ⽲ ⽳
Hotel ★★★★ 62% Woodlands Park Hotel, Woodlands Ln, STOKE D'ABERNON ☎ 01372 843933 59 ⇆ ➤

ESHER
Map 04 TQ16

Moore Place Portsmouth Rd KT10 9LN
☎ 01372 463533 Fax 01372 460274
Public course on attractive, undulating parkland laid out some 60 years ago by Harry Vardon. Examples of most of the trees that will survive in the UK are to be found on the course. Testing short holes at 2nd, 3rd and 9th.
9 holes, 2148yds, Par 32, SSS 30, Course record 25.
Club membership 300.
Visitors no restrictions.
Societies must contact in advance.
Green Fees not confirmed.
Prof David Allen
Designer Harry Vardon/David Allen
Facilities ⊗ ⽱ ⽫ ⽭ ⽮ ⽯ ⽰ ⽱
Location 0.5m from town centre on A307

Hotel ★★★ 67% The Ship, Monument Green, WEYBRIDGE ☎ 01932 848364 39 ⇆ ➤

Thames Ditton & Esher Portsmouth Rd KT10 9AL
☎ 020 8398 1551
Commonland course with public right of way across the course. Although the course is not long, accuracy is essential and wayward shots are normally punished.
18 holes, 5149yds, Par 66, SSS 65, Course record 63.
Club membership 250.
Visitors may not play on Sun mornings. Advisable to telephone for availability.
Societies must contact in advance.
Green Fees not confirmed.
Cards ⬛⬛⬛
Prof Mark Rodbard

Facilities ⊗ ⽱ by prior arrangement ⽭ ⽮ ⽯ ⽰ ⽱ ⽲
Location 1m NE on A307

Hotel ★★ 64% Haven Hotel, Portsmouth Rd, ESHER ☎ 020 8398 0023 16 ⇆ ➤ Annexe 4 ⇆ ➤

FARLEIGH
Map 05 TQ36

Farleigh Court Old Farleigh Rd CR6 9PX
☎ 0188362 7711 & 7733 Fax 0188362 7722
Members: 18 holes, 6414yds, Par 72, SSS 71.
Pay & Play: 9 holes, 6562yds, Par 72, SSS 71.
Club membership 450.
Visitors welcome on the Members Course and the Pay & Play Course.
Societies welcome, please and ask for Society Co ordinator.
Green Fees not confirmed.
Cards ⬛⬛⬛⬛
Prof Tom O'Keefe
Designer John Jacobs
Facilities ⊗ ⽱ ⽫ ⽭ ⽮ ⽯ ⽰ ⽱ ⽲ ⽳ ⽴
& Leisure sauna.
Location 1.5m from Selsdon

Hotel ★★★★ 69% Selsdon Park Hotel, Addington Rd, Sanderstead, CROYDON ☎ 020 8657 8811 204 ⇆ ➤

FARNHAM
Map 04 SU84

Blacknest Binsted GU34 4QL
☎ 01420 22888 Fax 01420 22001
Privately owned pay and play golf centre catering for all ages and levels of abilities. Facilities include a 15-bay driving range, gymnasium and a challenging 18-hole course featuring water on 14 holes.
18 holes, 6019yds, Par 69, SSS 69, Course record 65.
Club membership 450.
Visitors welcome at all times but should telephone for tee times especially weekends. No denims or collarless shirts.
Societies prior arrangements necessary telephone or write.
Green Fees £15 per round (£17-£20 weekends).
Cards ⬛⬛⬛⬛
Prof Ian Benson
Designer Mr Nicholson
Facilities ⊗ ⽱ by prior arrangement ⽭ ⽮ ⽯ ⽰ ⽱ ⽲ ⽳
& Leisure sauna, solarium, gymnasium.
Location 0.5m S of A31 at Bentley

Hotel ★★★♨ 61% Farnham House Hotel, Alton Rd, FARNHAM ☎ 01252 716908 25 ⇆ ➤

Farnham The Sands GU10 1PX
☎ 01252 782109 Fax 01252 781185
A mixture of meadowland and heath with quick drying sandy subsoil. Several of the earlier holes have interesting features, the finishing holes rather less.
18 holes, 6325yds, Par 72, SSS 70, Course record 66.
Club membership 700.
Visitors must contact in advance. Must be member of recognised club & have handicap certificate. With member only weekends. ▶

Societies	must apply in writing.
Green Fees	£37.50 per day; £30 per round.
Prof	Grahame Cowlishaw
Facilities	⊗ ⑭ ⓑ ⬛ ⓠ ⌂ 🏠 ✧
Location	3m E off A31
Hotel	★★★ 64% The Bush Hotel, The Borough, FARNHAM ☎ 0870 400 8225 83 ⇆ 🏌

Farnham Park Folly Hill, Farnham Park GU9 0AU
☎ 01252 715216
Pay & Play parkland course in Farnham Park.
9 holes, 1163yds, Par 27, SSS 50, Course record 50.

Visitors	pay and play everyday.
Societies	telephone in advance.
Green Fees	not confirmed.
Cards	💳 💳 💳 💳 💳
Prof	Peter Chapman
Designer	Henry Cotton
Facilities	⊗ ⑭ ⓑ ⬛ ⓠ 🏠 🏌
Location	N side of town centre on A287, adjacent to Farnham Castle
Hotel	★★★ 64% The Bush Hotel, The Borough, FARNHAM ☎ 0870 400 8225 83 ⇆ 🏌

GODALMING   Map 04 SU94

Broadwater Park Guildford Rd, Farncombe GU7 3BU
☎ 01483 429955 Fax 01483 429955
A Par-3 public course with floodlit driving range.
9 holes, 1287yds, Par 54, SSS 50.
Club membership 160.

Visitors	must book for weekends & bank holidays.
Societies	telephone in advance.
Green Fees	on request.
Cards	💳 💳 💳 💳 💳
Prof	Kevin D Milton
Designer	Kevin Milton
Facilities	ⓑ ⬛ ⓠ 🏠 ✧ ⌂
Location	4m SW of Guildford
Hotel	★★★ 78% The Angel Posting House and Livery, 91 High St, GUILDFORD ☎ 01483 564555 11 ⇆ 🏌

Hurtmore Hurtmore Rd, Hurtmore GU7 2RN
☎ 01483 426492 Fax 01483 426121
A Peter Alliss/Clive Clark Pay and Play course with seven lakes and 85 bunkers. The 15th hole is the longest at 537yds. Played mainly into the wind there are 10 bunkers to negotiate. The 3rd hole at 448yds stroke Index 1 is a real test. A dogleg right around a lake and 9 bunkers makes this hole worthy of its stroke index.
18 holes, 5514yds, Par 70, SSS 67, Course record 66.
Club membership 200.

Visitors	book by telephone up to 7 days in advance.
Societies	telephone in advance.
Green Fees	£12 per 18 holes (£16 weekends); £8.50 per 9 holes(£11 weekends).
Cards	💳 💳 💳 💳 💳
Prof	Maxine Burton
Designer	Peter Alliss/Clive Clark
Facilities	⊗ ⓑ ⬛ ⓠ ⌂ 🏠 🏌 ✧
Location	5m S of Guildford on the A3

Hotel	★★★ 78% The Angel Posting House and Livery, 91 High St, GUILDFORD ☎ 01483 564555 11 ⇆ 🏌

Shillinglee Park Chiddingfold GU8 4TA
☎ 01428 653237 & 708158 Fax 01428 644391
Manicured parkland course with many natural features including seven ponds. The 4th and 7th are the signature holes requiring tee shots and second shots over ponds, to well-guarded greens.
9 holes, 5032yds, Par 64, SSS 64, Course record 65.
Club membership 400.

Visitors	restricted Sat, Tue and Thu morning, advisable to book any other time.
Societies	apply for details.
Green Fees	not confirmed.
Cards	💳 💳 💳 💳 💳
Prof	David Parkinson
Designer	Roger Mace
Facilities	⊗ ⑭ by prior arrangement ⓑ ⬛ ⓠ ⌂ 🏠 🏌 🐾 🛒 ✧
Location	5m S of Godalming, off A283
Hotel	★★★★ 71% Lythe Hill Hotel, Petworth Rd, HASLEMERE ☎ 01428 651251 41 ⇆ 🏌

GUILDFORD   Map 04 SU94

Guildford High Path Rd, Merrow GU1 2HL
☎ 01483 563941 Fax 01483 453228
The course is on typical Surrey downland bordered by attractive woodlands. Situated on chalk, it is acknowledged to be one of the best all-weather courses in the area, and the oldest course in Surrey. The holes provide an interesting variety of play, an invigorating experience.
18 holes, 6090yds, Par 69, SSS 70, Course record 65.
Club membership 700.

Visitors	must contact in advance. With member only weekends & bank holidays.
Societies	welcome Mon-Fri. Must apply in advance.
Green Fees	£30 per round.
Prof	P G Hollington
Designer	J H Taylor/Hawtree
Facilities	⊗ ⑭ ⓑ ⬛ ⓠ ⌂ 🏠 🏌 🐾 ✧
& Leisure	practice nets & snooker.
Location	E side of town centre off A246
Hotel	★★★ 70% The Manor, Newlands Corner, GUILDFORD ☎ 01483 222624 45 ⇆ 🏌

Merrist Wood Coombe Ln, Worplesdon GU3 3PE
☎ 01483 884045 Fax 01483 884047
More parkland than heathland, Merrist Wood has a bit of everything. Water comes into play on five holes, the bunkering is fierce, the greens slope and the back nine has plenty of trees. Two holes stand out especially: the picturesque par 3 11th with a tee shot through the trees and the dastardly par 4 17th, including a 210yd carry over a lake and ditches either side of the green.
18 holes, 6600yds, Par 72, SSS 71, Course record 69.
Club membership 650.

Visitors	must contact in advance, at weekends only after 11am.
Societies	apply in writing.
Green Fees	£35 per round (£50 weekends).

Prof	Andrew Kirk
Designer	David Williams
Facilities	⊗ ⨅ 🄻 🄻 ♀ ⚘ 🏠 ♂ 🥂
Location	3m out of Guildford on A323 to Aldershot

Hotel ★★★ 78% The Angel Posting House and Livery, 91 High St, GUILDFORD ☎ 01483 564555 11 ⇌ ⏴

Milford Station Ln, Milford GU8 5HS
☎ 01483 419200 Fax 01483 419199
A Peter Alliss/Clive Clark designed course. The design has cleverly incorporated a demanding course within an existing woodland and meadow area.
18 holes, 5960yds, Par 69, SSS 68, Course record 64.
Club membership 750.

Visitors	must contact in advance, tee booking system, telephone 01483 416291 up to 1 week in advance. May not play weekends until 12 noon.
Societies	telephone in advance.
Green Fees	£19.50 per 18 holes (£25 weekends).
Cards	🖩 🖩 🖩 🖩 🖩
Prof	Nick English
Designer	Peter Allis
Facilities	⊗ ⨅ 🄻 🄻 ♀ ⚘ 🏠 ♂ 🥂 🛒 ⚘
Location	6m SW, leave A3 Milford then A3100 to Enton

Hotel ★★★ 78% The Angel Posting House and Livery, 91 High St, GUILDFORD ☎ 01483 564555 11 ⇌ ⏴

Roker Park Rokers Farm, Aldershot Rd GU3 3PB
☎ 01483 236677 Fax 01483 232324
A Pay and Play 9-hole parkland course. A challenging course with two Par 5 holes.
9 holes, 3037yds, Par 36, SSS 72.
Club membership 200.

Visitors	no restrictions, pay & play, phone for reservations.
Societies	prior arrangement with deposit at least 14 days before, minimum 12 persons.
Green Fees	£14 per 18 holes; £8 per 9 holes (£17/£9.50 weekends & bank holidays).
Prof	Kevin Warn
Designer	W V Roker
Facilities	⊗ 🄻 🄻 ♀ ⚘ 🏠 ♂ 🥂 🛒 ⚘
Location	A323, 3m from Guildford

Hotel ★★★ 78% The Angel Posting House and Livery, 91 High St, GUILDFORD ☎ 01483 564555 11 ⇌ ⏴

HINDHEAD Map 04 SU83

Hindhead Churt Rd GU26 6HX
☎ 01428 604614 Fax 01428 608508
An excellent example of a Surrey heath-and-heather course, and most picturesque. Players must be prepared for some hard walking. The first nine fairways follow narrow valleys requiring straight hitting; the second nine are much less restricted.
18 holes, 6356yds, Par 70, SSS 70, Course record 63.
Club membership 770.

Visitors	must contact in advance and have a handicap certificate.
Societies	Wed & Thu only, contact in advance

Green Fees	£47 per day; £36 per round (£57/£46 weekends & bank holidays).
Prof	Neil Ogilvy
Designer	J H Taylor
Facilities	⊗ ⨅ 🄻 🄻 ♀ ⚘ 🏠 ♂ 🥂 🛒 ⚘
Location	1.5m NW of Hindhead on A287

Hotel ★★★★ 71% Lythe Hill Hotel, Petworth Rd, HASLEMERE ☎ 01428 651251 41 ⇌ ⏴

KINGSWOOD Map 04 TQ25

Kingswood Sandy Ln KT20 6NE ☎ 01737 832188
Flat parkland course, easy walking.
18 holes, 6880yds, Par 72, SSS 73.
Club membership 700.

Visitors	must contact professional at least 24 hrs in advance. May not play weekend mornings.
Societies	must apply in advance.
Green Fees	£36 per round (£50 weekends).
Cards	🖩 🖩 🖩 🖩 🖩
Prof	James Dodds
Designer	James Braid
Facilities	⊗ ⨅ 🄻 🄻 ♀ ⚘ 🏠 ♂ 🥂 🛒 ⚘ 🥂
& Leisure	squash.
Location	0.5m S of village off A217

Hotel ★★★ 65% Reigate Manor Hotel, Reigate Hill, REIGATE ☎ 01737 240125 50 ⇌ ⏴

LEATHERHEAD Map 04 TQ15

Leatherhead Kingston Rd KT22 0EE
☎ 01372 843966 & 843956 Fax 01372 842241
Undulating parkland course with tree lined fairways and strategically placed bunkers. Easy walking.
18 holes, 6203yds, Par 71, SSS 70, Course record 67.
Club membership 630.

Visitors	telephone pro shop 01372 843956 up to 21 days in advance. May not play before 1pm weekends.
Societies	telephone in advance.
Green Fees	£35 per round (£45 weekends).
Cards	🖩 🖩 🖩 🖩 🖩
Prof	Simon Norman
Facilities	⊗ ⨅ 🄻 🄻 ♀ ⚘ 🏠 ♂ 🛒 ⚘
Location	0.25m from junct 9 of M25, on A243

Hotel ★★★★ 62% Woodlands Park Hotel, Woodlands Ln, STOKE D'ABERNON ☎ 01372 843933 59 ⇌ ⏴

Pachesham Park Golf Complex Oaklawn Rd KT22 0BT
☎ 01372 843453 Fax 01372 844076
A 9-hole undulating parkland course playing out over 18 holes at 5,618yds, starting with 5 shorter but tight holes followed by 4 longer more open but testing to finish.
9 holes, 2805yds, Par 70, SSS 67, Course record 67.
Club membership 300.

Visitors	book 2 days in advance by phone. May play weekends after 12.30pm.
Societies	apply in advance.
Green Fees	£15 per 18 holes; £9 per 9 holes (£18/£10 weekends & bank holidays).
Cards	🖩 🖩 🖩 🖩
Prof	Philip Taylor

▶

Designer Phil Taylor
Facilities ⊗ ℍ by prior arrangement
🝖 🍺 ⚲ ⚒ 🏠 ⛳ ♂ ℓ
Location On A244, 0.5m from M25 junct 9

Hotel ★★★★ 62% Woodlands Park Hotel,
Woodlands Ln, STOKE D'ABERNON
☎ 01372 843933 59 ⇥ 🐾

Tyrrells Wood The Drive KT22 8QP
☎ 01372 376025 Fax 01372 360836
Parkland course with easy walking.
18 holes, 6282yds, Par 71, SSS 70, Course record 65.
Club membership 700.
Visitors must contact in advance. Restricted weekends.
Societies must apply in advance.
Green Fees £34 per round.
Prof Max Taylor
Designer James Braid
Facilities ⊗ ℍ 🝖 🍺 ⚲ ⚒ 🏠 ⛳ ♂
Location 2m SE of town, off A24

Hotel ★★★★ 67% The Burford Bridge, Burford
Bridge, Box Hill, DORKING
☎ 0870 400 8283 57 ⇥ 🐾

LIMPSFIELD Map 05 TQ45

Limpsfield Chart Westerham Rd RH8 0SL
☎ 01883 723405
Tight heathland course set in National Trust land, well
wooded.
9 holes, 5718yds, Par 70, SSS 68, Course record 64.
Club membership 300.
Visitors with member only or by appointment weekends
& not before 3.30pm Thu (Ladies Day).
Societies must apply in advance.
Green Fees not confirmed.
Facilities ⊗ by prior arrangement ℍ by prior arrangement
🝖 🍺 ⚲ ⚒
& Leisure putting green, practice area.
Location 1m E on A25 from M25 junct 6

Hotel ★★★ 68% Kings Arms Hotel, Market Square,
WESTERHAM ☎ 01959 562990 17 ⇥ 🐾

LINGFIELD Map 05 TQ34

Lingfield Park Lingfield Rd, Racecourse Rd RH7 6PQ
☎ 01342 834602 Fax 01342 834602
Difficult and challenging, tree-lined parkland course set in
210 acres of beautiful Surrey countryside. Driving range.
18 holes, 6473yds, Par 71, SSS 72, Course record 69.
Club membership 700.
Visitors must be accompanied by member on Sat & Sun.
Advisable to telephone first.
Societies must telephone in advance.
Green Fees not confirmed.
Cards 💳 ▬ 💳 💳
Prof Christopher Morley
Facilities ⊗ ℍ 🝖 🍺 ⚲ ⚒ 🏠 ⛳ 🛒 ♂ ℓ
Location Entrance next to Lingfield race course

Hotel ★★★ 64% Woodbury House Hotel, Lewes Rd,
EAST GRINSTEAD
☎ 01342 313657 14 ⇥ 🐾

NEWDIGATE Map 04 TQ14

Rusper Rusper Rd RH5 5BX
☎ 01293 871871 (shop) & 871456 (office)
Fax 01293 871456
Course set in mature woodland. The opening two holes give
the golfer an encouraging start with the following holes
demanding accurate play through the trees. The 5th hole is a
challenging Par 5 from the back tee with a gentle dogleg
tempting the golfer to take a shortcut. Play is from two sets
of tees to 2 pin positions, giving the golfer alternative holes
on the second nine.
9 holes, 6218yds, Par 71, SSS 69, Course record 67.
Club membership 270.
Visitors welcome but telephone to reserve time, some
restrictions if competitions being played.
Societies telephone in advance for details.
Green Fees not confirmed.
Prof Janice Arnold
Designer A Blunden
Facilities ⊗ ℍ by prior arrangement 🝖 🍺 ⚲ ⚒ 🏠 ⛳
🛒 ♂ ℓ
Location Between Newdigate/Rusper, off A24

Hotel ★★★★ 67% The Burford Bridge, Burford
Bridge, Box Hill, DORKING
☎ 0870 400 8283 57 ⇥ 🐾

OCKLEY Map 04 TQ14

Gatton Manor Hotel Golf & Country Club Standon Ln
RH5 5PQ ☎ 01306 627555 Fax 01306 627713
Undulating parkland course through woods and over many
challenging water holes.
18 holes, 6629yds, Par 72, SSS 72, Course record 68.
Club membership 300.

Visitors may book up to 10 days in advance. Restricted
Sun (am). Tee times to be booked through
professional 01306 627557
Societies must apply in advance.
Green Fees Apr-Oct: £23 per round (£30 weekends); Nov-
Mar: £18 (£23 weekends).
Cards 💳 ▬ 💳 💳 💳 💳 💳
Prof Rae Sargent
Designer Henry Cotton
Facilities ⊗ ℍ 🝖 🍺 ⚲ ⚒ 🏠 ⛳ 🍴 🛒 ♂ ℓ
& Leisure grass tennis courts, fishing, sauna, solarium,
gymnasium.
Location 1.5m SW off A29

Hotel ★★★ 63% Gatton Manor Hotel Golf &
Country Club, Standon Ln, OCKLEY
☎ 01306 627555 16 ⇥ 🐾

OTTERSHAW
Map 04 TQ06

Foxhills Stonehill Rd KT16 0EL
☎ 01932 872050 Fax 01932 874762
A pair of parkland courses designed in the grand manner
and with American course-design in mind. One course is
tree-lined, the other, as well as trees, has massive
bunkers and artificial lakes which contribute to the
interest. Both courses offer testing golf and they finish
on the same long 'double green'. Par 3 'Manor' course
also available.
*The Bernard Hunt Course: 18 holes, 6734yds, Par 73,
SSS 72.*
Longcross Course: 18 holes, 6429yds, Par 72, SSS 71.
Manor Course: 9 holes, 2286yds, Par 27, SSS 27.

Visitors	contact sales office to reserve tee times. Restricted before noon weekends.
Societies	welcome Mon-Fri, must apply in advance.
Green Fees	£60 per round.
Prof	B Hunt/A Good/R Summerscales
Designer	F W Hawtree
Facilities	⊗ ⋔ ⓘ ⓛ ♀ ♨ 🏠 ⛳ 🏀 ➘ 🛶 ⚐ ⛵
& Leisure	hard tennis courts, outdoor and indoor heated swimming pools, squash, sauna, solarium, gymnasium.
Location	1m NW

Hotel ★★★ 65% The Crown Hotel, 7 London St,
CHERTSEY
☎ 01932 564657 Annexe 30 ⇥ ☞

PIRBRIGHT
Map 04 SU95

Goal Farm Gole Rd GU24 0PZ
☎ 01483 473183 & 473205
Beautiful lanscaped parkland 'Pay and Play' course with
excellent greens.
9 holes, 1273yds, Par 54, SSS 48.
Club membership 300.

Visitors	may not play on Sat before 4pm or Thu before 2pm.
Societies	telephone in advance.
Green Fees	not confirmed.
Designer	Bill Cox
Facilities	ⓛ ♀ ♨ 🏠 ⛳
Location	1.5m NW on B3012

Hotel ★★★ 67% Posthouse Farnborough, Lynchford
Rd, FARNBOROUGH
☎ 0870 400 9029 143 ⇥ ☞

PUTTENHAM
Map 04 SU94

Puttenham Heath Rd GU3 1AL
☎ 01483 810498 Fax 01483 810988
Picturesque tree-lined heathland course offering testing golf,
easy walking.
18 holes, 6211yds, Par 71, SSS 70.
Club membership 650.

Visitors	weekdays by prior arrangment tel: 01483 810498, with member only weekends & public holidays.
Societies	apply in advance to secretary.
Green Fees	£30 per day; £25 per round.
Prof	Gary Simmons

Facilities	⊗ ⋔ ⓘ ⓛ ♀ ♨ 🏠 ⚐
Location	1m SE on B3000

Hotel ★★★ 64% The Bush Hotel, The Borough,
FARNHAM ☎ 0870 400 8225 83 ⇥ ☞

REDHILL
Map 04 TQ25

Redhill & Reigate Clarence Rd, Pendelton Rd RH1 6LB
☎ 01737 240777 Fax 01737 242117
Flat well wooded parkland course.
18 holes, 5272yds, Par 68, SSS 66, Course record 65.
Club membership 600.

Visitors	may not play before 11am weekends or after 2pm Sun (Jun-Sep). Must contact in advance.
Societies	must apply in writing.
Green Fees	£15 (£25 weekends & bank holidays).
Cards	▬ ▬ 🔲 🔳 🔘
Prof	Warren Pike
Designer	James Braid
Facilities	⊗ ⓛ ♀ ♨ 🏠 ⛳ ⚐ ⛵
Location	1m S on A23

Hotel ★★★ 65% Reigate Manor Hotel, Reigate Hill,
REIGATE ☎ 01737 240125 50 ⇥ ☞

REIGATE
Map 04 TQ25

Reigate Heath Flanchford Rd RH2 8QR
☎ 01737 242610 & 226793 Fax 01737 226793
Gorse, heather, pine and birch trees abound on this popular
9-hole heathland course. Sandy soil gives all year round play
even in the wettest winters. Clubhouse enjoys panoramic
views of the North Downs and Leith Hill.
9 holes, 5658yds, Par 67, SSS 67, Course record 65.
Club membership 550.

Visitors	with member only weekends & bank holidays. Must contact in advance.
Societies	must apply in writing.
Green Fees	£30 per day; £15-£20 per round.
Prof	Barry Davies
Facilities	⊗ ⋔ by prior arrangement ⓛ ♀ ♨ 🏠 ⛵
Location	1.5m W off A25

Hotel ★★★ 65% Reigate Manor Hotel,
Reigate Hill, REIGATE
☎ 01737 240125 50 ⇥ ☞

Reigate Hill Gatton Bottom RH2 0TU
☎ 01737 645577 Fax 01737 642650
Championship standard course with fully irrigated tees and
greens. Feature holes include the 5th which is divided by four
bunkers and the par 5 14th involving a tricky second shot
across a lake. Very good short holes at 8th and 12th with
panoramic views from the tees.
18 holes, 6175yds, Par 72, SSS 70, Course record 75.
Club membership 550.

Visitors	must contact in advance to book tee time, may not play weekends until 12 noon.
Societies	welcome Mon-Fri but must book in advance.
Green Fees	£25 per round (£35 weekends & bank holidays after noon).
Cards	▬ ▬ 🔲 🔳 🔘 🔲
Prof	Martin Platts
Designer	David Williams
Facilities	⊗ ⓛ ♀ ♨ 🏠 ⛳ ➘ 🛶 ⚐ ⛵
Location	1m from junct 8 of M25

▶

Hotel ★★★ 65% Bridge House Hotel, Reigate Hill, REIGATE ☎ 01737 246801 & 244821 Fax 01737 223756 39 ⇄ ╟

SHEPPERTON   Map 04 TQ06

American Golf at Sunbury Charlton Ln TW17 8QA
☎ 01932 771414 Fax 01932 789300
27 holes of golf catering for all standards of golfer.
Sunbury Golf Course: 18 holes, 5103yds, Par 68, SSS 65, Course record 60.
Academy: 9 holes, 2444yds, Par 33, SSS 32.
Club membership 600.
Visitors no restrictions.
Societies advance booking necessary.
Green Fees £14 per 18 holes; £6 per 9 holes (£18/£8 weekends & bank holidays).
Cards ▭ ▬ ▭ ▭ ▭ ▭ ▭
Prof Alistair Hardaway
Facilities ⊗ ⅃ ▣ ♀ ⅄ 🏠 ⏱ 🏌 ⚘ ⏿
Location Off junct 1 of the M3

Hotel ★★★ 65% Shepperton Moat House Hotel, Felix Ln, SHEPPERTON ☎ 01932 899988 175 ⇄ ╟

SUTTON GREEN   Map 04 TQ05

Sutton Green New Ln GU4 7QT
☎ 01483 747898 Fax 01483 750289
Set in the Surrey countryside, a challenging course with many water features. Excellent year round conditions with fairway watering. Many testing holes with water surrounding greens and fairways, making accuracy a premium.
18 holes, 6350yds, Par 71, SSS 70, Course record 67.
Club membership 500.
Visitors must contact in advance.
Societies Mon-Fri. Must contact in advance.
Green Fees £30 (£40 weekends).
Cards ▭ ▬ ▭ ▭
Prof Tim Dawson
Designer David Walker/Laura Davies
Facilities ⊗ ⅏ ⅃ ▣ ♀ ⅄ 🏠 ⏱ 🏌 ⚘ ⏿
Location Off A320 between Woking & Guildford

Hotel ★★★★★ 72% Pennyhill Park Hotel & Country Club, London Rd, BAGSHOT ☎ 01276 471774 31 ⇄ ╟ Annexe 92 ⇄ ╟

TANDRIDGE   Map 05 TQ35

Tandridge RH8 9NQ
☎ 01883 712274 Fax 01883 730537
A parkland course with two loops of 9 holes from the clubhouse. The first 9 is relatively flat. The second 9 undulates and reveals several outstanding views of the North Downs and the South.
18 holes, 6250yds, Par 70, SSS 70, Course record 66.
Club membership 750.
Visitors must contact in advance. May play Mon, Wed, Thu
Societies Mon, Wed & Thu, apply in advance.
Green Fees £52 am round/all day; £40 pm round..
Prof Chris Evans
Designer H S Colt

Facilities ⊗ ⅃ ▣ ♀ ⅄ 🏠 ⏱ ⏿
Location 2m SE junc 6 M25, 1.5m E of Godstone on A25

Hotel ★★★★ 69% Nutfield Priory, Nutfield, REDHILL ☎ 01737 824400 60 ⇄ ╟

TILFORD   Map 04 SU84

Hankley Common GU10 2DD
☎ 01252 792493 Fax 01252 795699
A natural heathland course subject to wind. Greens are first rate. The 18th, a long par 4, is most challenging, the green being beyond a deep chasm which traps any but the perfect second shot. The 7th is a spectacular one-shotter.
18 holes, 6438yds, Par 71, SSS 71.
Club membership 700.
Visitors handicap certificate required, restricted to afternoons at weekends.
Societies apply in writing.
Green Fees £55 per day; £42 per round (£55 per round weekends & bank holidays).
Cards ▭ ▬ ▭ ▭ ▭ ▭
Prof Peter Stow
Facilities ⊗ ⅏ ⅃ ▣ ♀ ⅄ 🏠 ⏿
Location 0.75m SE

Hotel ★★★ 64% The Bush Hotel, The Borough, FARNHAM ☎ 0870 400 8225 83 ⇄ ╟

VIRGINIA WATER   Map 04 TQ06

VIRGINIA WATER See page 241.

WALTON-ON-THAMES   Map 04 TQ16

Burhill Burwood Rd KT12 4BL
☎ 01932 227345 Fax 01932 267159
A relatively short and easy parkland course with some truly magnificent trees. The 18th is a splendid par 4 requiring a well-placed drive and a long firm second. This course is always in immaculate condition.
18 holes, 6479yds, Par 70, SSS 71, Course record 65.
Club membership 1000.
Visitors may not play Fri-Sun unless introduced by member. Must contact in advance.
Societies apply in writing.
Green Fees £55 per day, £35 per round.
Prof Lee Johnson
Designer Willie Park
Facilities ⊗ ⅏ ⅃ ▣ ♀ ⅄ 🏠 ⏿
& Leisure squash.
Location 2m S

Hotel ★★★ 67% The Ship, Monument Green, WEYBRIDGE ☎ 01932 848364 39 ⇄ ╟

WALTON-ON-THE-HILL   Map 04 TQ25

WALTON-ON-THE-HILL See page 243.

Wentworth Club

Virginia Water, *Surrey*   ☎ 01344 842201   Fax 01344 842804   Map 04 TQ06

W entworth Club, the home of the Volvo PGA and Cisco World Match Play Championships, is a very special venue for any sporting, business or social occasion. The West Course (7047 yards) is familiar to millions of television viewers who have followed the championships here. There are two other 18-hole courses, The East Course (6188 yards) and The Edinburgh Course (7004 yards) as well as a 9-hole Par 3 executive course. The courses are Surrey heathland with woodland of pine, oak and birch trees.

The Club is renowned for its fine English food and the superb new Tennis and Health facility, which include a holistic Spa. The centre opened in January 1999 and has 13 outdoor tennis courts with 4 different playing surfaces, a 25m indoor pool and further extensive leisure facilities.

Visitors must contact in advance and have a handicap certificate (men max 24, ladies max 32). May not play weekends

Societies contact in advance in writing

Green Fees available on application — 🖼️ 🖼️ 🖼️ 🎨

Facilities ⊗ 🎿 🏌️ 💼 🏌️ 🍴 ⛳ 🏠 🎯 🏌️ 🚶 🏌️ 🏌️ Professional (David Rennie)

Leisure tennis, squash, swimming, sauna, solarium, gymnasium

Location Wentworth Drive GU25 4LS (main gate directly opposite turning for A329 on main A30)

Holes/Par/Course record 54 holes. West Course: 18 holes, 7047 yds, Par 73, SSS 74, Course record 63 East Course: 18 holes, 6198 yds, Par 68, SSS 70, Course record 62 Edinburgh: 18 holes, 6979 yds, Par 72, SSS 73, Course record 67

WHERE TO STAY AND EAT NEARBY

Hotels
ASCOT

★★★★ ⊕ 68% The Royal Berkshire, London Rd, Sunninghill. ☎ 01344 623322. 63 🛏️ 🐾

★★★★ 62% The Berystede, Bagshot Rd, Sunninghill. ☎ 0870 400 8111. 90 (89 🛏️ 🐾 1 🐾)

BAGSHOT

★★★★★ ⊕ ⊕ ⊕ 72% Pennyhill Park, London Rd. ☎ 01276 471774. 31 🛏️ 🐾 Annexe 92 🛏️ 🐾

EGHAM

★★★★ ⊕ ⊕ 73% Runnymede Hotel & Spa, Windsor Rd. ☎ 01784 436171. 180 🛏️ 🐾

Restaurant
BRAY

⊕ ⊕ ⊕ ⊕ Waterside Inn, Ferry Rd. ☎ 01628 620691

Championship Course

WEST BYFLEET   Map 04 TQ06

West Byfleet Sheerwater Rd KT14 6AA
☎ 01932 343433 Fax 01932 340667
An attractive course set against a background of
woodland and gorse. The 13th is the famous 'pond' shot
with a water hazard and two bunkers fronting the green.
No less than six holes of 420 yards or more.
18 holes, 6211yds, Par 70, SSS 70.
Club membership 600.
Visitors   must contact professional in advance, only
                 with member at weekends. Restricted Thu
                 (Ladies Day).
Societies   must apply in writing.
Green Fees   £38.50 per 36 holes; £30.50 per round.
Cards   ⚏ ⚏ ⚏ ⚏
Prof   David Regan
Designer   C S Butchart
Facilities   ⊗ ⏶ ⮤ 🍺 ♀ ⚲ 🖚 ⚑ ⚲ ∅
Location   W side of village on A245

Hotel   ★★★ 70% The Manor, Newlands Corner,
                 GUILDFORD ☎ 01483 222624 45 ⇋ ⬧

WEST CLANDON   Map 04 TQ05

Clandon Regis Epsom Rd GU4 7TT
☎ 01483 224888 Fax 01483 211781
High quality parkland course with challenging lake holes on
the back nine. European Tour specification tees and greens.
18 holes, 6412yds, Par 72, SSS 71.
Club membership 650.
Visitors   contact in advance. Afternoon only at weekends
                 & bank holidays.
Societies   telephone in advance.
Green Fees   £35 per 36 holes; £30 per 27 holes; £25 per 18
                 holes; £15 per 9 holes (£35 per 18 holes, £17.50
                 per 9 holes weekends).
Cards   ⚏ ⚏ ⚏ ⚏
Prof   Steve Lloyd
Designer   David Williams
Facilities   ⊗ ⏶ by prior arrangement
                 ⮤ 🍺 ♀ ⚲ 🖚 ∅ ⬧
& Leisure   sauna.
Location   From A246 Leatherhead direction

Hotel   ★★★ 70% The Manor, Newlands Corner,
                 GUILDFORD ☎ 01483 222624 45 ⇋ ⬧

WEST END   Map 04 SU96

Windlemere Windlesham Rd GU24 5LS
☎ 01276 858727
A parkland course, undulating in parts with natural water
hazards. There is also a floodlit driving range.
9 holes, 2673yds, Par 34, SSS 33, Course record 30.
Visitors   no restrictions.
Societies   advisable to contact in advance.
Green Fees   not confirmed.
Prof   David Thomas
Designer   Clive Smith
Facilities   ⊗ ⮤ 🍺 ♀ ⚲ 🖚 ∅ ⬧
Location   N side of village at junct of A319/A322

Hotel   ★★★★★ 72% Pennyhill Park Hotel &
                 Country Club, London Rd, BAGSHOT
                 ☎ 01276 471774 31 ⇋ ⬧ Annexe 92 ⇋ ⬧

WEYBRIDGE   Map 04 TQ06

St George's Hill Golf Club Rd, St George's Hill
KT13 0NL ☎ 01932 847758 Fax 01932 821564
Comparable and similar to Wentworth, a feature of this
course is the number of long and difficult par 4s. To
score well it is necessary to place the drive - and long
driving pays handsomely. Walking is hard on this
undulating, heavily wooded course with plentiful heather
and rhododendrons.
*Red & Blue: 18 holes, 6569yds, Par 70, SSS 71, Course
record 64.*
Green: 9 holes, 2869yds, Par 35.
Club membership 600.
Visitors   must contact in advance and have a
                 handicap certificate. Visitors may only play
                 Wed-Fri.
Societies   apply in writing
Green Fees   not confirmed.
Prof   A C Rattue
Designer   H S Colt
Facilities   ⊗ ⮤ 🍺 ♀ ⚲ 🖚 ⚑ ∅
Location   2m S off B374

Hotel   ★★★ 67% The Ship, Monument Green,
                 WEYBRIDGE ☎ 01932 848364 39 ⇋ ⬧

WOKING   Map 04 TQ05

Hoebridge Golf Centre Old Woking Rd GU22 8JH
☎ 01483 722611 Fax 01483 740369
Three public courses set in parkland on Surrey sand belt. 36-
bay floodlit driving range.
*Main Course: 18 holes, 6536yds, Par 72, SSS 71, Course
record 68.*
Shey Course: 9 holes, 2294yds, Par 33, SSS 31.
Maybury Course: 18 holes, 2230yds, Par 54, SSS 54.
Club membership 600.
Visitors   welcome every day, course and reservation desk
                 open dawn to dusk. Credit card reservations 6
                 days in advance.
Societies   Mon-Fri only, telephone in advance
Green Fees   Main course: £17 (£20 weekends).
Cards   ⚏ ⚏ ⚏ ⚏
Prof   Tim Powell
Designer   John Jacobs
Facilities   ⊗ ⏶ ⮤ 🍺 ♀ ⚲ 🖚 ⚑ 🖚 ∅ ⬧
& Leisure   snooker.
Location   On B382 Old Woking to West Byfleet road

Hotel   ★★★★★ 72% Pennyhill Park Hotel &
                 Country Club, London Rd, BAGSHOT
                 ☎ 01276 471774 31 ⇋ ⬧ Annexe 92 ⇋ ⬧

Pyrford Warren Ln, Pyrford GU22 8XR
☎ 01483 723555 Fax 01483 729777
This inland links style course was designed by Peter Alliss
and Clive Clark. Set between Surrey woodlands, the fairways
weave between 23 acres of water courses while the greens
and tees are connected by rustic bridges. The signature hole
is the Par 5 9th at 595 yards, with a dogleg and final
approach over water and a sand shelf.

Walton Heath

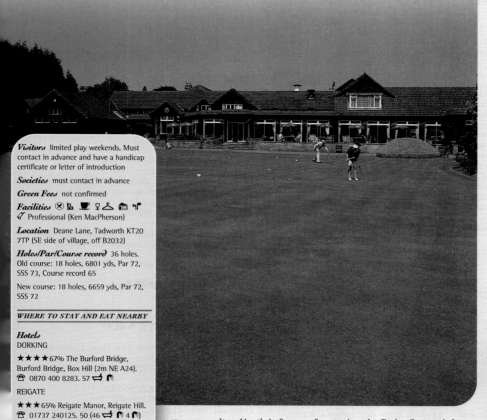

Visitors limited play weekends. Must contact in advance and have a handicap certificate or letter of introduction

Societies must contact in advance

Green Fees not confirmed

Facilities ⊗ 🏌 🍺 ♀ 🏌 🏠 ⛳
⛳ Professional (Ken MacPherson)

Location Deane Lane, Tadworth KT20 7TP (SE side of village, off B2032)

Holes/Par/Course record 36 holes. Old course: 18 holes, 6801 yds, Par 72, SSS 73, Course record 65

New course: 18 holes, 6659 yds, Par 72, SSS 72

WHERE TO STAY AND EAT NEARBY

Hotels

DORKING

★★★★67% The Burford Bridge, Burford Bridge, Box Hill (2m NE A24). ☎ 0870 400 8283. 57 ⇆ ⋔

REIGATE

★★★65% Reigate Manor, Reigate Hill. ☎ 01737 240125. 50 (46 ⇆ ⋔ 4 ⋔)

★★★ 🌼 65% Bridge House, Reigate Hill. ☎ 01737 246801. 39 (30 ⇆ ⋔ 9 ⋔)

STOKE D'ABERNON

★★★★ 🌼 67% Woodlands Park, Woodlands Ln. ☎ 01372 843933. 59 ⇆ ⋔

Restaurant

TADWORTH

🌼 Gemini, 28 Station Approach. ☎ 01737 812179

Walton Heath is famous for staging the Ryder Cup and the European Open Championships. Once owned by the News of the World Newspaper; MPs, Lords and members of the press would be invited down to Walton Heath by Sir Elmsley Carr, who was one of the first to employ a lady as Secretary and Manager of a well-known championship course.

The courses were designed in 1903 by Herbert Fowler, he used natural hollows and channels for drainage so the fairways dry out quickly. The Old Course is popular with visitors however the New Course is very challenging requiring subtle shots to get the ball near the hole. Straying from the fairway brings its punishment with gorse, bracken and heather to test the most patient golfer.

Championship Course

18 holes, 6230yds, Par 72, SSS 70, Course record 64.
Club membership 600.

Visitors	must book in advance.
Societies	must contact in advance.
Green Fees	£38 per 18 holes (£52 weekends).
Cards	▭ VISA ▭ ▭ 🔌
Prof	Richard Pilbury
Designer	Peter Allis & Clive Clark
Facilities	⊗ ❆ 🏐 🖤 ♀ 👥 🖤 🛄 ♂ 🏌
Location	Off A3 Ripley to Pyrford

Hotel ★★★★★ 72% Pennyhill Park Hotel &
Country Club, London Rd, BAGSHOT
☎ 01276 471774
31 ⇆ 🏌 Annexe 92 ⇆ 🏌

Traditions Pyrford Rd, Pyrford GU22 8UE
☎ 01932 350355 Fax 01932 350234
Situated in the heart of the Surrey countryside with a mature
setting which includes various woodland and water features.
A course with many challenges which can be enjoyed by
golfers of all levels and experience.
18 holes, 6304yds, Par 71, SSS 70, Course record 67.
Club membership 400.

Visitors	no restrictions.
Societies	telephone in advance.
Green Fees	£20 per 18 holes (£25 weekends).
Cards	▭ VISA ▭ ▭ 🔌
Prof	Darren Brewer
Designer	Peter Allis
Facilities	⊗ ❆ 🏐 🖤 ♀ 👥 🖤 🛄 👍 ♂
Location	Off A3 through Wisley village

Hotel ★★★★★ 72% Pennyhill Park Hotel &
Country Club, London Rd, BAGSHOT
☎ 01276 471774
31 ⇆ 🏌 Annexe 92 ⇆ 🏌

Woking Pond Rd, Hook Heath GU22 0JZ
☎ 01483 760053 Fax 01483 772441
An 18-hole course on Surrey heathland with few changes
from the original course designed in 1892 by Tom Dunn.
Bernard Darwin a past Captain and President has written
' the beauty of Woking is that there is something
distinctive about every hole...'.
18 holes, 6340yds, Par 70, SSS 70, Course record 65.
Club membership 550.

Visitors	must contact secretary at least 7 days prior to playing. No visitors weekends & bank holidays.
Societies	telephone intially then confrim in writing, normally 12 months notice.
Green Fees	not confirmed.
Prof	John Thorne
Designer	Tom Dunn
Facilities	⊗ ❆ 🏐 🖤 ♀ 👥 🖤 👍 ♂ 🏌
Location	W of town centre

Hotel ★★★★★ 72% Pennyhill Park Hotel &
Country Club, London Rd, BAGSHOT
☎ 01276 471774
31 ⇆ 🏌 Annexe 92 ⇆ 🏌

Looking for a driving range?
See the index at the back of the guide

Worplesdon Heath House Rd GU22 0RA
☎ 01483 472277
The scene of the celebrated mixed-foursomes
competition. Accurate driving is essential on this
heathland course. The short 10th across a lake from tee
to green is a notable hole, and the 18th provides a
wonderfully challenging par-4 finish.
18 holes, 6440yds, Par 71, SSS 71, Course record 64.
Club membership 590.

Visitors	must play with member at weekends & bank holidays. Must contact in advance and have a handicap certificate.
Societies	must contact in writing.
Green Fees	not confirmed.
Prof	J Christine
Facilities	⊗ 🏐 🖤 ♀ 👥 🖤 ♂
Location	6m N of Guildford, off A322

Hotel ★★★★★ 72% Pennyhill Park Hotel &
Country Club, London Rd, BAGSHOT
☎ 01276 471774
31 ⇆ 🏌 Annexe 92 ⇆ 🏌

WOLDINGHAM Map 05 TQ35

Duke's Dene Slines New Rd CR3 7HA
☎ 01883 653501 Fax 01883 653502
Located in Halliloo Valley and designed by the American
architect Bradford Benz, this pleasant course utilises all the
contours and features of the valley.
18 holes, 6393yds, Par 71, SSS 70.
Club membership 744.

Visitors	tee times should be booked in advance with pro shop. Weekends available after noon for visitors.
Societies	telephone to book.
Green Fees	not confirmed.
Cards	▭ ▭ ▭ ▭ 🔌
Prof	Paul Thornley
Designer	Bradford Benz
Facilities	⊗ ❆ by prior arrangement 🏐 🖤 ♀ 👥 🖤 🛄 👍 ♂

Hotel ★★★ 68% Kings Arms Hotel, Market Square,
WESTERHAM
☎ 01959 562990 17 ⇆ 🏌

North Downs Northdown Rd CR3 7AA
☎ 01883 652057 Fax 01883 652832
Downland course, 850 ft above sea-level, with several testing
holes and magnificent views.
18 holes, 5843yds, Par 69, SSS 68, Course record 66.
Club membership 700.

Visitors	must play with member at weekends and bank holidays. Must contact in advance.
Societies	must contact in writing.
Green Fees	not confirmed.
Prof	M Homewood
Designer	Pennink
Facilities	⊗ ❆ 🏐 🖤 ♀ 👥 🖤 ♂
Location	0.75m S

Hotel ★★★ 68% Kings Arms Hotel, Market Square,
WESTERHAM
☎ 01959 562990 17 ⇆ 🏌

SUSSEX, EAST

BEXHILL
Map 05 TQ70

Cooden Beach Cooden Sea Rd TN39 4TR
☎ 01424 842040 & 843938 (Pro Shop) Fax 01424 8420 40
The course is close by the sea, but is not real links in character. Despite that, it is dry and plays well throughout the year. There are some excellent holes such as the 4th, played to a built-up green, the short 12th, and three good holes to finish. There are added ponds which make the player think more about tee shots and shots to the green.
18 holes, 6470yds, Par 72, SSS 71, Course record 67.
Club membership 730.

Visitors	must have a handicap certificate. Restricted at weekends. Book in advance with professional 01424 843938.
Societies	must contact in advance by telephoning secretary.
Green Fees	£32 per day/round (£35 weekends & bank holidays).
Cards	
Prof	Jeffrey Sim
Designer	W Herbert Fowler
Facilities	⊗ 🄻 🛗 ♟ 🖫 🏠 ⛳ 🏌 ✆
Location	2m W on A259
Hotel	★★★ 73% Lansdowne Hotel, King Edward's Pde, EASTBOURNE ☎ 01323 725174 121 🛏 🐾

Highwoods Ellerslie Ln TN39 4LJ
☎ 01424 212625 Fax 01424 216866
Undulating course.
18 holes, 6218yds, Par 70, SSS 70.
Club membership 820.

Visitors	must play with member on Sun. Must contact in advance and have an introduction from own club. Handicap required.
Societies	advance notice advised.
Green Fees	£25 per round.
Prof	M Andrews
Designer	J H Taylor
Facilities	⊗ 🄻 🛗 🖫 ♟ 🏠 ✆
Location	1.5m NW
Hotel	★★★ 63% White Friars Hotel, Boreham St, HERSTMONCEUX ☎ 01323 832355 12 🛏 🐾 Annexe 8 🛏 🐾

BRIGHTON & HOVE
Map 04 TQ30

Brighton & Hove Devils Dyke Rd BN1 8YJ
☎ 01273 556482 Fax 01273 554247
Downland course with sea views. Famous drop hole par 3.
9 holes, 5704yds, Par 68, SSS 68, Course record 65.
Club membership 300.

Visitors	must contact in advance, restricted play Wed, Fri & weekends.
Societies	must contact secretary in advance.
Green Fees	£15 per 18 hole; £10 per 9 holes (£25/£15 weekends).
Cards	

Prof	Phil Bonsall
Designer	James Braid
Facilities	⊗ 🄻 🛗 🖫 ♟ 🏠 ⛳ 🏌 ✆
Location	4m NW
Hotel	★★ 63% St Catherines Lodge Hotel, Seafront, Kingsway, HOVE ☎ 01273 778181 50rm (40 🛏 🐾)

See advertisement on page 246

Dyke Devils Dyke, Dyke Rd BN1 8YJ
☎ 01273 857296 Fax 01273 857078
This downland course has some glorious views both towards the sea and inland. The best hole on the course is probably the 17th; it is one of those teasing short holes of just over 200 yards, and is played across a gully to a high green.
18 holes, 6611yds, Par 72, SSS 72, Course record 66.
Club membership 750.

Visitors	advisable to contact in advance. May not play before noon on Sun.
Societies	apply by telephone or in writing.
Green Fees	not confirmed.
Prof	Richard Arnold
Designer	Fred Hawtree
Facilities	⊗ 🄻 🛗 🖫 ♟ 🏠 ⛳ 🏌 ✆
Location	4m N of Brighton, between A23 & A27
Hotel	★★ 63% St Catherines Lodge Hotel, Seafront, Kingsway, HOVE ☎ 01273 778181 50rm (40 🛏 🐾)

East Brighton Roedean Rd BN2 5RA
☎ 01273 604838 Fax 01273 680277
Undulating downland course, overlooking the sea with extensive views.
18 holes, 6346yds, Par 72, SSS 70, Course record 62.
Club membership 650.

Visitors	contact in advance & may only play weekends after 11am.
Societies	must contact in advance, handicap certificate required.
Green Fees	£25 per round (£30 weekends & bank holidays).
Cards	
Prof	Mark Stuart-William
Designer	James Braid
Facilities	⊗ 🄻 🛗 🖫 ♟ 🏠 ⛳ 🏌 ✆
& Leisure	snooker tables.
Location	2m E of Palace Pier, overlooking marina
Hotel	★★★ 64% Quality Hotel Brighton, West St, BRIGHTON ☎ 01273 220033 138 🛏 🐾

Hollingbury Park Ditchling Rd BN1 7HS
☎ 01273 552010 (sec) & 500086 (res)
Municipal course in hilly situation on the Downs, overlooking the sea.
18 holes, 6500yds, Par 72, SSS 71, Course record 65.
Club membership 300.

Visitors	must contact in advance.
Societies	telephone the secretary for details.
Green Fees	not confirmed.
Prof	Graeme Crompton
Facilities	🖫 🏠 🏌 🐾 ✆
Location	2m N of town centre

▶

| Hotel | ★★★ 64% Quality Hotel Brighton, West St, BRIGHTON ☎ 01273 220033 138 ⇌ ℞ |

Waterhall Saddlescombe Rd BN1 8YN ☎ 01273 508658
Hilly downland course with hard walking and open to the wind. Private club playing over municipal course.
18 holes, 5773yds, Par 69, SSS 68, Course record 66.
Club membership 300.

Visitors	must contact in advance. Restricted tee times Sat and Sun am.
Societies	must contact the secretary in writing or telephone.
Green Fees	£19 per day; £12.50 per round (£16.50 per round weekends).
Prof	Paul Charman
Facilities	⊗ ℿ ﹗ ﹗ ♀ ⚲ 🍴 🏌
Location	2m NE from A27

| Hotel | ★★ 63% St Catherines Lodge Hotel, Seafront, Kingsway, HOVE ☎ 01273 778181 50rm (40 ⇌ ℞) |

West Hove Church Farm, Hangleton BN3 8AN
☎ 01273 419738 & 413494 (pro) Fax 01273 439988
A downland course designed by Hawtree & Sons.
18 holes, 6237yds, Par 70, SSS 70, Course record 69.
Club membership 625.

Visitors	tee times by arrangement.
Societies	by arrangement, telephone or write.
Green Fees	not confirmed.
Prof	Darren Cook
Designer	Hawtree & Sons
Facilities	⊗ ﹗ ﹗ ♀ ⚲ 🏌 ⛳
Location	Easy access from A27, N of Brighton

| Hotel | ★★ 63% St Catherines Lodge Hotel, Seafront, Kingsway, HOVE ☎ 01273 778181 50rm (40 ⇌ ℞) |

CROWBOROUGH
Map 05 TQ53

Crowborough Beacon Beacon Rd TN6 1UJ
☎ 01892 661511 Fax 01892 667339
Standing some 800 feet above sea level, this is a testing heathland course, with panoramic views of the South Downs, Eastbourne and even the sea on a clear day.
18 holes, 6279yds, Par 71, SSS 70, Course record 66.
Club membership 700.

Visitors	must contact in advance & have handicap certificate but may only play at weekends & bank holidays after 2.30pm.
Societies	telephone or apply in writing to secretary.
Green Fees	£40 per day; £25 per round (£30 per round weekends & bank holidays).

Prof	D C Newnham
Facilities	⊗ ℿ ﹗ ﹗ ♀ ⚲ 🍴 🏌
Location	1m SW on A26

| Hotel | ★★★ 76% The Spa Hotel, Mount Ephraim, TUNBRIDGE WELLS ☎ 01892 520331 74 ⇌ |

Dewlands Manor Cottage Hill, Rotherfield TN6 3JN
☎ 01892 852266 Fax 01892 853015
A beautifully kept meadowland course with water features.
9 holes, 3186yds, Par 36, SSS 70.

Visitors	must telephone in advance.
Societies	telephone for availability.
Green Fees	not confirmed.
Cards	💳 💳 💳 💳
Prof	Nick Godin
Designer	R M & N M Godin
Facilities	⊗ ﹗ ﹗ ♀ ⚲ 🍴 🏌 ⛳
& Leisure	indoor teaching facilities.
Location	0.5m S of Rotherfield

| Inn | ◆◆◆ Plough & Horses Inn, Walshes Rd, CROWBOROUGH ☎ 01892 652614 8 ⇌ ℞ |

DITCHLING
Map 05 TQ31

Mid Sussex Spatham Ln BN6 8XJ
☎ 01273 846567 Fax 01273 845767
Mature parkland course with many trees, water hazards, strategically placed bunkers and superbly contoured greens. The 14th hole, a spectacular par 5, demands accurate shotmaking to avoid the various hazards along its length.
18 holes, 6462yds, Par 71, SSS 71, Course record 65.
Club membership 600.

| Visitors | telephone in advance to book tee times. After 2pm at weekends in summer and after 12.30pm in winter. |
| Societies | advance booking required. ▶ |

Green Fees	£20 per round (£20 weekends after 1.30pm).
Cards	
Prof	Chris Connell
Designer	David Williams
Facilities	⊗ ⅏ ⅃ ⊾ ▦ ♀ ♨ ☎ ¶ ⚑ ⛳ ♣ ⚐
Location	1m E of Ditchling village
Hotel	★★★ 76% The Shelleys, High St, LEWES ☎ 01273 472361 19 ⇄ ⋔

EASTBOURNE
Map 05 TV69

Eastbourne Downs East Dean Rd BN20 8ES
☎ 01323 720827 Fax 01323 412506
This downland course has spectacular views over the South Downs and Channel. Situated in an area of outstanding natural beauty approximately 1 mile behind Beachy Head.
18 holes, 6601yds, Par 72, SSS 72, Course record 70.
Club membership 650.

Visitors	a handicap certificate is required for weekends. Visitors may not play before 9.15am weekdays and before 11am weekends except by arrangement.
Societies	contact secretary in advance for details.
Green Fees	£21 per day; £17 per round (£24/£21 weekends & bank holidays).
Prof	T Marshall
Designer	J H Taylor
Facilities	⊗ ⅏ ⅃ ⊾ ▦ ♀ ♨ ☎ ¶ ⚐
Location	0.5m W of town centre on A259
Hotel	★★★ 73% Lansdowne Hotel, King Edward's Pde, EASTBOURNE ☎ 01323 725174 121 ⇄ ⋔

Royal Eastbourne Paradise Dr BN20 8BP
☎ 01323 729738 Fax 01323 729738
A famous club which celebrated its centenary in 1987. The course plays longer than it measures. Testing holes are the 8th, a par 3 played to a high green and the 16th, a par 5 righthand dogleg.
Devonshire Course: 18 holes, 6107yds, Par 70, SSS 69, Course record 62.
Hartington Course: 9 holes, 2147yds, Par 64, SSS 61.
Club membership 800.

Visitors	must contact in advance, may not play weekends except by arrangement. Handicap certificate required for Devonshire course.
Societies	must apply in advance.
Green Fees	Devonshire: £22 (£27.50 weekends & bank holidays); Hartington: £14.
Prof	Richard Wooller
Designer	Arthur Mayhewe
Facilities	⊗ ⅏ by prior arrangement ⊾ ▦ ♀ ♨ ☎ ¶ ⚑ ♣ ⚐
Location	0.5m W of town centre
Hotel	★★★ 73% Lansdowne Hotel, King Edward's Pde, EASTBOURNE ☎ 01323 725174 121 ⇄ ⋔

Willingdon Southdown Rd, Willingdon BN20 9AA
☎ 01323 410981 Fax 01323 411510
Unique, hilly downland course set in oyster-shaped amphitheatre.
18 holes, 6118yds, Par 69, SSS 69.
Club membership 570.

Visitors	no restrictions.
Societies	apply in advance.
Green Fees	seasonal variations £14-£25 per day (£16-£28 weekends).
Prof	Troy Moore
Designer	J Taylor/Dr Mackenzie
Facilities	⊗ ⊾ ▦ ♀ ♨ ☎ ¶ ♣ ⚑ ⚐
Location	0.5m N of town centre off A22
Hotel	★★★ 61% Wish Tower Hotel, King Edward's Pde, EASTBOURNE ☎ 01323 722676 56 ⇄ ⋔

FOREST ROW
Map 05 TQ43

Ashdown Forest Golf Hotel Chapel Ln RH18 5BB
☎ 01342 824866 Fax 01342 824869
A natural undulating heathland and woodland course cut out of the Ashdown Forest. No sand bunkers, just equally testing heather dunes with the 14th hole regarded as the best. The hotel specialises in catering for golf breaks and societies.
West Course: 18 holes, 5606yds, Par 68, SSS 67.
Club membership 180.

Visitors	must contact in advance, bookings up to 6 days in advance. Prepayment required.
Societies	must telephone in advance.
Green Fees	£23 per day; £18 per round (£28/£23 weekends).
Cards	
Prof	Martyn Landsborough
Facilities	⊗ ⅏ ⅃ ⊾ ▦ ♀ ♨ ☎ ¶ ⚑ ⚐
Location	4m S of East Grinstead off A22 & B2110

Royal Ashdown Forest Chapel Ln RH18 5LR
☎ 01342 822018 Fax 01342 825211
Old Course on undulating heathland. No bunkers. Long
carries off the tees and magnificent views over the
Forest. Not a course for the high handicapper. West
Course on natural heathland. No bunkers.
*Old Course: 18 holes, 6477yds, Par 72, SSS 71, Course
record 67.*
West Course: 18 holes, 5606yds, Par 68, SSS 67.
Club membership 450.

Visitors	restricted weekends & Tue. Must have a handicap certificate on Old Course. No restrictions on West Course.
Societies	must contact in advance.
Green Fees	Old Course: £50 per day; £42 per round (£55 weekends & bank holidays). West Course: £23 per day; £18 per round (£28/£23 weekends).
Cards	🔲 💳
Prof	Martyn Landsborough
Facilities	⊗ ⓛ ⬛ 🍺 🍴 △ 🏠 🎯 🐾 🚃 ♂
Location	SE side of Forest Row village, off B2110

Hotel	★★★ 64% Woodbury House Hotel, Lewes Rd, EAST GRINSTEAD ☎ 01342 313657 14 ⇆ 🐾

HAILSHAM   Map 05 TQ50

Wellshurst Golf & Country Club North St, Hellingly
BN27 4EE ☎ 01435 813456 Fax 01435 812444
There are outstanding views of the South Downs and the
Weald Valley from this 18-hole, well-manicured, undulating
course. There are varied features and some water hazards. A
practice sand bunker, putting green and driving range are
available to improve your golf. The clubhouse and leisure
facilities are open to visitors.
18 holes, 5771yds, Par 70, SSS 68, Course record 64.
Club membership 320.

Visitors	no restrictions but advisable to book.
Societies	telephone in advance to book tee times.
Green Fees	£21 per day £16 per 18 holes (£26/20 weekends & bank holidays).
Cards	🔲 💳 🔲
Prof	Mark Jarvis
Designer	The Golf Corporation
Facilities	⊗ ⓛ ⬛ 🍺 🍴 △ 🏠 🎯 🐾 🚃 ♂
& Leisure	sauna, solarium, gymnasium, aerobics studio.
Location	2.5m N of Hailsham, on A267

Hotel	★★ 68% The Olde Forge Hotel & Restaurant, Magham Down, HAILSHAM ☎ 01323 842893 7rm (6 ⇆ 🐾)

HASTINGS & ST LEONARDS   Map 05 TQ80

Hastings Beauport Park Estate, St Leonards TN38 0TA
☎ 01424 852981
Played over Hastings Public Course. Undulating parkland
with stream and fine views.
18 holes, 6248yds, Par 71, SSS 70, Course record 70.
Club membership 400.

Visitors	no restrictions.
Societies	arrangement by telephone.
Green Fees	not confirmed.
Prof	Charles Giddins

Facilities	⊗ ⓛ ⬛ 🍺 🍴 △ 🏠 🎯 🐾 🚃 ♂
& Leisure	hard tennis courts, outdoor swimming pool.
Location	3m N of Hastings on A2100

Hotel	★★★ 69% Beauport Park Hotel, Battle Rd, HASTINGS ☎ 01424 851222 25 ⇆ 🐾

HEATHFIELD   Map 05 TQ52

Horam Park Chiddingly Rd, Horam TN21 0JJ
☎ 01435 813477 Fax 01435 813677
A pretty woodland course with lakes.
9 holes, 6237yds, Par 70, SSS 68, Course record 64.
Club membership 450.

Visitors	contact for tee times.
Societies	prior booking required.
Green Fees	£15 per 18 holes; £10 per 9 holes (£16/£10.50 weekends).
Cards	🔲 💳 🔲 🔲 💳
Prof	Giles Velvick
Designer	Glen Johnson
Facilities	⊗ ⓛ ⬛ 🍺 🍴 △ 🏠 🎯 🐾 🚃 ♂
& Leisure	pitch & putt.
Location	Off A267 Hailsham-Heathfield

Hotel	★★★ 68% Boship Farm Hotel, Lower Dicker, HAILSHAM ☎ 01323 844826 Annexe 47 ⇆ 🐾

Where to stay, where to eat?
Visit the AA internet site
www.theaa.co.uk

East Sussex National

e-mail esn@btinternet.com

ast Sussex National offers two huge courses ideal for big-hitting
professionals. The European Open has been staged here and it is
home to the European Headquarters of the David Leadbetter Golf
Academy, with indoor or outdoor video analysis. Bob Cupp designed the
courses using 'bent' grass from tee to green, resulting in an American-
style course to test everyone. The greens on both the East and West
courses are immaculately maintained, the West course is reserved for
members and their guests, but visitors are welcomed on the other
course.

The entrance seems daunting for first-time visitors unprepared for
the vast car park, huge red-brick clubhouse and suspended corridor
from the reception area through to the well-stocked professional's shop.

Visitors may only play West Course if
accompanied by member. Contact
Advance Reservations 01825 880231

Societies contact Advance Reservations
01825 880231

Green Fees £82 per round (includes
lunch)

Facilities ⊗ ⋔ ⊾ ♥ ♀ ⚘ 🏠
⚑ ⅂ ⚒ ♂ ♩ Professional (Phil
Lewin). Golf Academy

Leisure tennis, swimming, sauna,
solarium

Location Little Horsted TN22 5ES
(2m S of Uckfield on A22)

Holes/Par/Course record 36 holes.
East Course: 18 holes, 6046 yds, Par 72,
SSS 72, Course record 63
West Course: 18 holes, 6638 yds, Par 72,
SSS 72, Course record 64

WHERE TO STAY AND EAT NEARBY

Hotels
UCKFIELD

★★★★ ⊛ 70% Buxted Park Country
House Hotel, Buxted. ☎ 01825 732711.
44 ⇆ 🏷

★★★ ⊛ ⊛ ♨ 77% Horsted Place,
Little Horsted. ☎ 01825 750581.
17 ⇆ 🏷

HALLAND

★★★ 61% Halland Forge. ☎ 01825
840456. Annexe 20 (3 🏷 17 ⇆ 🏷)

NEWICK

★★★ ⊛ ⊛ 80% Newick Park Country
Estate ☎ 01825 723633. 13 (9 ⇆ 🏷 4 🏷)

HOLTYE   Map 05 TQ43

Holtye TN8 7ED
☎ 01342 850635 & 850576 Fax 01342 850576
Undulating forest/heathland course with tree-lined fairways
providing testing golf. Different tees on back nine.
9 holes, 5325yds, Par 66, SSS 66, Course record 62.
Club membership 430.
Visitors   may not play mornings Wed-Thu & weekends.
Societies   Tue & Fri by arrangement.
Green Fees £16 per 18 holes; £11 per 9 holes (£18/£12
                 weekends).
Prof   Kevin Hinton
Facilities   🏌 🍺 ♀ ♨ 🏡 ⛳
Location   4m E of East Grinstead and 6m W of Tunbridge
                 Wells on A264

Hotel   ★★★ 64% Woodbury House Hotel, Lewes Rd,
                 EAST GRINSTEAD
                 ☎ 01342 313657 14 ⇄ ♞

LEWES   Map 05 TQ41

Lewes Chapel Hill BN7 2BB ☎ 01273 483474 & 473245
Downland course. Fine views.
18 holes, 6220yds, Par 71, SSS 70, Course record 64.
Club membership 680.
Visitors   may not play at weekends before 2pm. Bookings
                 taken up to 7 days in advance.
Societies   must contact in advance.
Green Fees £30 per day; £20 per round (£30 per round
                 weekends & bank holidays after 2pm).
Prof   Paul Dobson
Designer   Jack Rowe
Facilities   ⊗ �🍴 by prior arrangement 🏌 🍺 ♀ ♨ 🏡 ⛳
                 ♨ ⛳
Location   E side of town centre

Hotel   ★★★ 65% White Hart Hotel, 55 High St,
                 LEWES ☎ 01273 476694
                 23rm (19 ⇄ ♞) Annexe 29 ⇄ ♞

NEWHAVEN   Map 05 TQ40

Peacehaven Brighton Rd BN9 9UH
☎ 01273 512571 & 514049 Fax 01273 512571
Downland course, sometimes windy. Testing holes: 1st (par
3), 4th (par 4), 9th (par 3), 10th (par 3), 18th (par 3).
Attractive views over the Sussex Downs, the River Ouse and
Newhaven Harbour.
9 holes, 5488yds, Par 70, SSS 67, Course record 65.
Club membership 270.
Visitors   may not play before 11am weekends.
Societies   telephone in advance.
Green Fees £12 per 18 holes; £9 per 9 holes (£18/£12
                 weekends).
Prof   Ian Pearson
Designer   James Braid
Facilities   🏌 🍺 ♀ ♨ 🏡 ⛳
Location   0.75m W of Newhaven on A259

Hotel   ★★★ 67% The Star Inn, ALFRISTON
                 ☎ 0870 400 8102 37 ⇄ ♞

RYE   Map 05 TQ92

Rye New Lydd Rd, Camber TN31 7QS
☎ 01797 225241 Fax 01797 225460
Unique links course with superb undulating greens set
amongst ridges of sand dunes alongside Rye Harbour.
Fine views over Romney Marsh and towards Fairlight
and Dungeness.
*Old Course: 18 holes, 6317yds, Par 68, SSS 71, Course
record 64.*
Jubilee Course: 9 holes, 3109yds, Par 71, SSS 70.
Club membership 1100.
Visitors   must be invited/introduced by a member.
Green Fees not confirmed.
Prof   Michael Lee
Designer   H S Colt
Facilities   ⊗ 🍺 ♀ ♨ 🏡 ⛳ 🏌 ⛳
Location   2.75m SE off A259

Hotel   ★★★ 61% The George, High St, RYE
                 ☎ 01797 222114 22 ⇄ ♞

SEAFORD   Map 05 TV49

Seaford Firle Rd, East Blatchington BN25 2JD
☎ 01323 892442 Fax 01323 89113
The great H. Taylor did not perhaps design as many
courses as his friend and rival, James Braid, but
Seaford's original design was Taylor's. It is a splendid
downland course with magnificent views and some fine
holes.
18 holes, 6551yds, Par 69, SSS 71.
Club membership 600.
Visitors   must contact in advance.
Societies   must contact in advance.
Green Fees not confirmed.
Cards   💳 💳 💳 🅿
Prof   David Mills
Designer   J H Taylor
Facilities   ⊗ 🍴 🏌 🍺 ♀ ♨ 🏡 🍴 🏌 ⛳ ♨
Location   Turn inland at war memorial off A259

Hotel   ★★★ 67% The Star Inn, ALFRISTON
                 ☎ 0870 400 8102 37 ⇄ ♞

Seaford Head Southdown Rd BN25 4JS
☎ 01323 890139 & 894843
A links type course situated on the cliff edge giving
exception views over the Seven Sisters and coastline. The
upper level is reached via a short hole with elevated green -
known as the 'Hell Hole' and the 18th Par 5 tee is on the
'Head' being 300 feet above sea level.
18 holes, 5848yds, Par 71, SSS 68, Course record 63.
Club membership 450.
Visitors   no restrictions.
Societies   write or telephone the Pro's shop.
Green Fees not confirmed.
Prof   Tony Lowles
Facilities   ⊗ 🍴 🏌 🍺 ♀ ♨ 🏡 ⛳ ⛳
Hotel   ★★★ 68% Deans Place, Seaford Rd,
                 ALFRISTON
                 ☎ 01323 870248 36 ⇄ ♞

SEDLESCOMBE — Map 05 TQ71

Sedlescombe Kent St TN33 0SD
☎ 01424 870898 Fax 01424 870855
Situated in the beautiful Sussex countryside. The natural water and tree line adds to the beauty as well as making it an enjoyable round of golf.
18 holes, 6359yds, Par 71, SSS 70, Course record 68.
Club membership 300.

Visitors	please telephone and reserve tee times.
Societies	please telephone to reserve tee times.
Green Fees	not confirmed.
Cards	▭ ▬ ▭ ▨ ▨
Prof	James Andrews
Facilities	⊗ ♿ ☕ ♟ △ ☎ ⛵ ▶ ♨ ✂ ↸
Location	A21, 4m N of Hastings

Hotel ★★★ 67% Brickwall Hotel, The Green, SEDLESCOMBE
☎ 01424 870253 26 ⇄ 🐾

TICEHURST — Map 05 TQ63

Dale Hill Hotel & Golf Club TN5 7DQ
☎ 01580 200112 Fax 01580 201249
Picturesque course with woodland, water and gently undulating fairways. Hotel and leisure centre within grounds.
Dale Hill: 18 holes, 6106yds, Par 70, SSS 69.
Ian Woosnam: 18 holes, 6512yds, Par 71, SSS 71.
Club membership 950.

Visitors	booking only 7 days in advance, may not play at weekends.
Societies	must contact in advance.
Green Fees	not confirmed.
Cards	▭ ▬ ▭ ▨ ▨
Prof	Andrew Good
Designer	Ian Woosnam
Facilities & Leisure	⊗ ♨ ♿ ☕ ♟ △ ☎ ⛵ ↸ ▶ ♨ ✂ heated indoor swimming pool, sauna, gymnasium.
Location	N side of village off B2087

Hotel ★★★★ 67% Dale Hill Hotel & Golf Club, TICEHURST
☎ 01580 200112 26 ⇄ 🐾

UCKFIELD — Map 05 TQ42

UCKFIELD See page 249.

Piltdown Piltdown TN22 3XB
☎ 01825 722033 Fax 01825 724192
Natural heathland course with much heather and gorse. No bunkers, easy walking, fine views.
18 holes, 6070yds, Par 68, SSS 69, Course record 67.
Club membership 400.

Visitors	must telephone pro shop in advance 01825 722389 and have a handicap certificate. Play on Tue, Thu and weekends is restricted.
Societies	must contact in writing.
Green Fees	£35 per day; £27.50 per round.
Prof	John Amos
Facilities	⊗ ♿ ☕ ♟ △ ☎ ⛵ ▶ ♨ ✂ ↸

Location Between Newick & Maresfield off A272, club signposted

Hotel ★★★ 61% Halland Forge Hotel & Restaurant, HALLAND
☎ 01825 840456 Annexe 20 ⇄ 🐾

SUSSEX, WEST

ANGMERING — Map 04 TQ00

Ham Manor BN16 4JE
☎ 01903 783288 Fax 01903 850886
Two miles from the sea, this parkland course has fine springy turf and provides an interesting test in two loops of nine holes each.
18 holes, 6267yds, Par 70, SSS 70, Course record 64.
Club membership 780.

Visitors	must have a handicap certificate. Telephone pro shop in advance 01903 783732.
Societies	telephone for details
Green Fees	not confirmed.
Prof	Simon Buckley
Designer	Harry Colt
Facilities	△ ☎ ✂
Location	Off A259

Hotel ★★★ 62% Chatsworth Hotel, Steyne, WORTHING ☎ 01903 236103 107 ⇄ 🐾

ARUNDEL — Map 04 TQ00

Avisford Park Yapton Ln, Walberton BN18 0LS
☎ 01243 554611 Fax 01243 555580
A 18 hole course enjoying a country hotel complex setting. The course opens with a real challenge as there is out of bounds water and tree hazards the whole length of this 414yard drive.
18 holes, 5703yds, Par 68, SSS 66.
Club membership 100.

Visitors	must contact in advance for weekend play.
Societies	apply in writing or telephone.
Green Fees	£12 (£15 weekends & bank holidays).
Cards	▭ ▬ ▭ ▨ ▨
Prof	Richard Beach
Facilities & Leisure	⊗ ♿ ☕ ♟ △ ☎ ⛵ ▶ ♨ ✂ hard tennis courts, outdoor and indoor heated swimming pools.
Location	Off A27, towards Yapton

Hotel ★★★ 67% Norfolk Arms Hotel, High St, ARUNDEL
☎ 01903 882101 21 ⇄ Annexe 13 ⇄

BOGNOR REGIS — Map 04 SZ99

Bognor Regis Downview Rd, Felpham PO22 8JD
☎ 01243 821929 (Secretary) Fax 01243 860719
This flattish, well tree lined, parkland course has more variety than is to be found on some other South Coast courses. The club is also known far and wide for its enterprise in creating a social atmosphere. The course is open to the prevailing wind and the river Rife and many water ditches need negotiation. ▶

18 holes, 6238yds, Par 70, SSS 70, Course record 64.
Club membership 700.

Visitors	handicap certificate required. Must contact in advance (pro shop 01243 865209).
Societies	phone initially.
Green Fees	£18 per round (£20 weekends & bank holidays).
Prof	Stephen Bassil
Designer	James Braid
Facilities	⊗ ⓑ 🏌 ♀ 🛆 🏠 ▾ 🎿 ✓
Location	0.5m N at Felpham traffic lights on A259
Hotel	★★ 69% Aldwick Hotel, Aldwick Rd, Aldwick, BOGNOR REGIS ☎ 01243 821945 20 ⇆ ☞

BURGESS HILL   Map 04 TQ31

Burgess Hill Cuckfield Rd RH15 8RE
☎ 01444 258585 Fax 247318
Opened May 1998, an academy course bordered by a
tributary of the River Adur. Facilities available for public use
include a floodlit driving range and a large sweeping putting
green.
9 holes, 1250yds, Par 27.

Visitors	None.
Societies	contact in advance.
Green Fees	£9 (9 holes).
Cards	🗖 🗖 🗖 🗖 🗖 🗖
Prof	Mark Collins
Designer	Donald Steel
Facilities	ⓑ 🏌 ♀ 🛆 🏠 ▾ 🎿 ✓ (
Location	N of town on B2036
Hotel	★★★⚑ 78% Ockenden Manor, Ockenden Ln, CUCKFIELD ☎ 01444 416111 22 ⇆ ☞

CHICHESTER   Map 04 SU80

Chichester Hunston Village PO20 6AX
☎ 01243 533833 Fax 01243 539922
Set amongst lush farmland, the Tower course has four lakes
which bring water into play on seven holes. Also the Florida-
style Cathedral and a 9-hole par 3 and a floodlit driving
range.
Tower Course: 18 holes, 6175yds, Par 72, SSS 69, Course
record 67.
Cathedral Course: 18 holes, 6461yds, Par 72, SSS 71,
Course record 65.
Club membership 600.

Visitors	a strict dress code is in operation. Must contact in advance. Tee reservations up to 7 days in advance on 01243 533833.
Societies	must contact in advance.
Green Fees	Tower; £15 (£20 weekend). Cathedral; £20 (£23 weekends).
Cards	🗖 🗖 🗖 🗖 🗖 🗖
Prof	John Slinger
Designer	Philip Saunders
Facilities	⊗ ⑴ ⓑ 🏌 ♀ 🛆 🏠 ▾ 🎿 ✓ (
& Leisure	mini golf and par 3 course..
Location	3m S of Chichester, on B2145 at Hunston
Hotel	★★★ 67% The Ship Hotel, North St, CHICHESTER ☎ 01243 778000 34 ⇆ ☞

COPTHORNE   Map 05 TQ33

Copthorne Borers Arms Rd RH10 3LL
☎ 01342 712033 & 712058 Fax 01342 717682
Despite it having been in existence since 1892, this club
remains one of the lesser known Sussex courses. It is
hard to know why because it is most attractive with
plenty of trees and much variety
18 holes, 6505yds, Par 71, SSS 71, Course record 67.
Club membership 550.

Visitors	advised to contact in advance, may not play weekends before 1pm.
Societies	must contact in advance.
Green Fees	not confirmed.
Prof	Joe Burrell
Designer	James Braid
Facilities	⊗ ⑴ ⓑ 🏌 ♀ 🛆 🏠 ✓
Location	E side of village junc 10 of M23 off A264
Hotel	★★★★ 70% Copthorne London Gatwick, Copthorne Way, COPTHORNE ☎ 01342 348800 & 348888 Fax 01342 348833 227 ⇆ ☞

Effingham Park The Copthorne Effingham Park, Hotel,
West Park Rd RH10 3EU ☎ 01342 716528 Fax 716039
Parkland course.
9 holes, 1769yds, Par 30, SSS 57, Course record 28.
Club membership 390.

Visitors	restricted at weekends before 11am and not after 4pm Tue, Apr-Oct.
Societies	Mon-Fri, and Sat/Sun after 1pm, must write/telephone in advance.
Green Fees	not confirmed.
Cards	🗖 🗖 🗖
Prof	Mark Root
Designer	Francisco Escario
Facilities	⊗ ⑴ ⓑ 🏌 ♀ 🛆 🏠 ▾ 🞻 ✓
& Leisure	hard tennis courts, heated indoor swimming pool, sauna, solarium, gymnasium.
Location	2m E on B2028
Hotel	★★★★ 64% Copthorne Effingham Park, West Park Rd, COPTHORNE ☎ 01342 714994 122 ⇆ ☞

> AA Hotels that have special
> arrangements with golf courses are listed at
> the back of the guide

CRAWLEY
Map 04 TQ23

Cottesmore Buchan Hill, Pease Pottage RH11 9AT
☎ 01293 528256 Fax 01293 522819
Founded in 1974, the Griffin Course is a fine test of golfing skill with fairways lined by silver birch, pine, oak and rhododendrons. 4 holes have lakes as hazards.
Griffin Course: 18 holes, 6248yds, Par 71, SSS 70, Course record 67.
Phoenix Course: 18 holes, 5482yds, Par 69, SSS 67.

Visitors	dress code applies. Advisable to contact in advance.
Societies	must telephone in advance.
Green Fees	Griffin: £19 per round (£25 weekends). Phoenix: £15 per round (£20 weekends).
Cards	[card symbols]
Prof	Calum J Callan
Designer	Michael J Rogerson
Facilities	⊗ ⏃ ╚ ♥ ♀ ⚲ 🏠 ⛳ 🖐 🛥 ✍
& Leisure	hard tennis courts, heated indoor swimming pool, sauna, solarium, gymnasium.
Location	3m SW 1m W of M23 junc 11
Hotel	★★★ Alexander House, East St, TURNERS HILL ☎ 01342 714914 15 ⇌ 🐾

Ifield Golf & Country Club Rusper Rd, Ifield RH11 0LN
☎ 01293 520222 Fax 01293 612973
Parkland course.
18 holes, 6330yds, Par 70, SSS 70, Course record 65.
Club membership 750.

Visitors	must contact professional in advance. Must be guest of member at weekends.
Societies	apply in advance.
Green Fees	£33 per day; £23 per round weekdays.
Prof	Jonathan Earl
Designer	Bernard Darwin
Facilities	⊗ ⏃ ╚ ♥ ♀ ⚲ 🏠 🖐 🛥 ✍
& Leisure	squash.
Location	1m W side of town centre off A23
Hotel	★★★ Alexander House, East St, TURNERS HILL ☎ 01342 714914 15 ⇌ 🐾

Tilgate Forest Golf Centre Titmus Dr RH10 5EU
☎ 01293 530103
Designed by former Ryder Cup players Neil Coles and Brian Huggett, the course has been carefully cut through a silver birch and pine forest. It is possibly one of th most beautiful public courses in the country. The 17th is a treacherous Par 5 demanding an uphill third shot to a green surrounded by rhododendrons.
18 holes, 6359yds, Par 72, SSS 69 or 9 holes, 1136yds, Par 27.

Visitors	may book up to 7 days in advance.
Societies	telephone in advance for details.
Green Fees	not confirmed.
Prof	Sean Trussell
Designer	Neil Coles/Brian Huggett
Facilities	⊗ ⏃ ╚ ♥ ♀ ⚲ 🏠 🖐 ✍ (
Hotel	★★★ Alexander House, East St, TURNERS HILL ☎ 01342 714914 15 ⇌ 🐾

> Entries with a green background identify courses considered to be particularly interesting

GOODWOOD
Map 04 SU80

Goodwood Kennel Hill PO18 0PN
☎ 01243 774968 Fax 01243 781741
Downland course designed by the master architect, James Braid. Many notable holes, particularly the finishing ones: 17 down an avenue of beech trees and 18 along in front of the terrace. Superb views of the downs and the coast.
18 holes, 6434yds, Par 72, SSS 71.
Club membership 930.

Visitors	must have handicap certificate
Societies	Wed & Thu, telephone secretary in advance.
Green Fees	£32 per day.
Prof	Keith MacDonald
Designer	J Braid
Facilities	⊗ ⏃ ╚ ♥ ♀ ⚲ 🏠 ⛳ 🖐 🛥 ✍
Location	3m NE of Chichester off A27
Hotel	★★★★ 69% Marriott Goodwood Park Hotel & Country Club, GOODWOOD ☎ 01243 775537 94 ⇌ 🐾

Marriott Goodwood Park Hotel & Country Club
PO18 0QB ☎ 01243 775537 Fax 01243 520120
A parkland course set within the 12,000 acre Goodwood estate.
18 holes, 6579yds, Par 72, SSS 71, Course record 66.
Club membership 700.

Visitors	must hold a current handicap certificate.
Societies	telephone or write.
Green Fees	£28 per round (£35 weekends & bank holidays).
Cards	[card symbols]
Prof	Adrian Wratting
Designer	Donald Steele
Facilities	⊗ ⏃ ╚ ♥ ♀ ⚲ 🏠 ⛳ 🖐 🛥 ✍ (
& Leisure	hard tennis courts, heated indoor swimming pool, sauna, solarium, gymnasium.
Location	3m N of Chichester, in the grounds of Goodwood House
Hotel	★★★★ 69% Marriott Goodwood Park Hotel & Country Club, GOODWOOD ☎ 01243 775537 94 ⇌ 🐾

HASSOCKS
Map 04 TQ31

Hassocks London Rd BN6 9NA
☎ 01273 846630 & 846990 Fax 01273 846070
Set against the backdrop of the South Downs, Hassocks is an 18 hole par 70 course designed and contoured to blend ▶

naturally with the surrounding countryside. A friendly and relaxed course, appealing to golfers of all ages and abilities.
18 holes, 5754yds, Par 70, SSS 68, Course record 70.
Club membership 350.

Visitors	phone Pro. Shop in advance.
Societies	apply in writing or telephone in advance.
Green Fees	£14.25 (£17.50 weekends).
Cards	▭ ▬ ▬ ▬ ▭
Prof	Charles Ledger
Designer	Paul Wright
Facilities	⊗)iii ⅃ ♥ ♀ ⅄ 🖝 ᵀ 🐾 ⚏ ⚐
Location	On the A273 between Burgess Hill and Hassocks
Hotel	★★★ 62% The Hickstead Hotel, Jobs Ln, Bolney, HICKSTEAD ☎ 01444 248023 50 ⇥ ♠

HAYWARDS HEATH   Map 05 TQ32

Haywards Heath High Beech Ln RH16 1SL
☎ 01444 414457 Fax 01444 458319
Pleasant parkland course with several challenging par 4s and 3s.
18 holes, 6216yds, Par 71, SSS 70, Course record 66.
Club membership 770.

Visitors	must have a handicap certificate. Must contact in advance.
Societies	Wed & Thu only by prior arrangement with the secretary.
Green Fees	£26 (£35 weekends).
Prof	Michael Henning
Facilities	⊗ ⅃ ♥ ♀ ⅄ 🖝 ⚏ ⚐
Location	1.25m N off B2028
Hotel	★★★★♣♣ 78% Ockenden Manor, Ockenden Ln, CUCKFIELD ☎ 01444 416111 22 ⇥ ♠

Paxhill Park East Mascalls Ln, Lindfield RH16 2QN
☎ 01444 484467 Fax 01444 482709
A relatively flat parkland course designed by Patrick Tallack. Water hazard on 5th, 13th and 14th holes.
18 holes, 6117yds, Par 70, SSS 69, Course record 67.
Club membership 430.

Visitors	welcome but may not play weekend and some weekday mornings.
Societies	must contact in advance.
Green Fees	£15 per round (£20 weekend & bank holidays).
Cards	▭ ▬ ▬ ▭
Prof	Paul Lyons
Designer	P Tallack
Facilities	⊗)iii by prior arrangement ♥ ♀ ⅄ 🖝 ᵀ ⚏ ⚐
& Leisure	snooker.
Hotel	★★★★♣♣ 78% Ockenden Manor, Ockenden Ln, CUCKFIELD ☎ 01444 416111 22 ⇥ ♠

HORSHAM   Map 04 TQ13

See also **Slinfold**

Horsham Worthing Rd RH13 7AX
☎ 01403 271525 Fax 01403 274528
A short but challenging course with six Par 4s and three Par 3s''s, two of which are played across water. Designed for

beginners and intermediates but also challenges better players with a standard scratch of six below par.
9 holes, 4122yds, Par 33, SSS 30, Course record 55.
Club membership 250.

Visitors	no restrictions other than not until after 11am on Sat.
Societies	apply in advance.
Green Fees	not confirmed.
Cards	▭ ▬ ▬ ▬ ▭
Prof	Neil Burke
Facilities	⊗ ♥ ♀ ⅄ 🖝 ᵀ ⚐ ⚏
& Leisure	gymnasium.
Location	Off A24 rdbt, between Horsham/Southwater, by garage on B2237
Hotel	★★ 67% Ye Olde King's Head Hotel, Carfax, HORSHAM ☎ 01403 253126 42rm(41 ⇥ ♠)

HURSTPIERPOINT   Map 04 TQ21

Singing Hills Albourne BN6 9EB
☎ 01273 835353 Fax 01273 835444
Three distinct nines (Lake, River & Valley) can be combined to make a truly varied game. Gently undulating fairways and spectacular waterholes make Singing Hills a test of accurate shotmaking. The opening 2 holes of the River nine have long drives, while the second hole on the Lake course is an Island green where the tee is also protected by two bunkers. The Valley Course demand long, accurate tee shots.
Lake: 9 holes, 3253yds, Par 35, SSS 35.
River: 9 holes, 2826yds, Par 34, SSS 35.
Valley: 9 holes, 3348yds, Par 36, SSS 35.
Club membership 390.

Visitors	no restrictions, but strict dress code observed.
Societies	apply in advance.
Green Fees	£18 per 18 holes (£26 weekends).
Prof	Wallace Street
Designer	M R M Sandow
Facilities	⊗)iii ♥ ♥ ♀ ⅄ 🖝 ᵀ ⚐ ⚏
Location	Off A23, on B2117
Hotel	★★★ 62% The Hickstead Hotel, Jobs Ln, Bolney, HICKSTEAD ☎ 01444 248023 50 ⇥ ♠

LITTLEHAMPTON   Map 04 TQ00

Littlehampton Rope Walk, West Beach BN17 5DL
☎ 01903 717170 Fax 726629
A delightful seaside links in an equally delightful setting - and the only links course in the area.
18 holes, 6244yds, Par 70, SSS 70, Course record 62.
Club membership 650.

Visitors	contact in advance & must have handicap certificate.
Societies	welcome weekdays.
Green Fees	not confirmed.
Prof	Guy McQuitty
Facilities	⊗ ♥ ♥ ♀ ⅄ 🖝 🚜 ⚐
Location	1m W off A259
Hotel	★★★ 76% Bailiffscourt Hotel, CLIMPING ☎ 01903 723511 9 ⇥ ♠ Annexe 22 ⇥ ♠

LOWER BEEDING
Map 04 TQ22

Brookfield RH13 6LY ☎ 01403 891191
An 8 hole practice course and a driving range, designed as an
executive course for beginners and those who find if difficult
to play a full 18 holes. It is very popular.
8 holes.

Visitors	no restrictions.
Societies	& groups apply in writing or telephone.
Green Fees	not confirmed.
Facilities	⊗ ⍟ 🕭 💺 ♀ 🖾
& Leisure	fishing.
Hotel	★★ 64% Brookfield Farm Hotel, Winterpit Ln, Lower Beeding, HORSHAM ☎ 01403 891191 19 ⇔ 🏿
Additional hotel	★★★★♨♨ South Lodge Hotel, Brighton Rd, LOWER BEEDING ☎ 01403 891711 Fax 01403 891766 39 ⇔

MANNINGS HEATH
Map 04 TQ22

Mannings Heath Fullers, Hammerpond Rd RH13 6PG
☎ 01403 210228 Fax 01403 270974
The course meanders up hill and down dale over
heathland with streams affecting 11 of the holes.
Wooded valleys protect the course from strong winds.
Famous holes at 12th (the 'Waterfall', par 3), 13th (the
'Valley', par 4).
*Waterfall: 18 holes, 6378yds, Par 71, SSS 70, Course
record 66.*
Kingfisher: 18 holes, 6217yds, Par 70, SSS 70.
Club membership 700.

Visitors	may book up to 7 days in advance.
Societies	must contact in advance.
Green Fees	not confirmed.
Cards	🖭 🖭 🖭 🖭 🖭 🖭 🖭
Prof	Clive Tucker
Designer	David Williams
Facilities	⊗ ⍟ 🕭 💺 ♀ 🖾 🖴 🌱 🐦 🏌 ⚷ ⚑
& Leisure	hard tennis courts, fishing, sauna, chipping practice area.
Location	M23 junct 11, take A281 from Horsham or Brighton. Club on N side of village
Hotel	★★★★♨♨ South Lodge Hotel, Brighton Rd, LOWER BEEDING ☎ 01403 891711 39 ⇔

MIDHURST
Map 04 SU82

Cowdray Park Petworth Rd GU29 0BB
☎ 01730 813599 Fax 01730 815900
Undulating parkland course with scenic views of surrounding
countryside, including Elizabethan ruins. The course is
situated in a National Park originally designed by Capability
Brown in the 18th century.
18 holes, 6212yds, Par 70, SSS 70, Course record 66.
Club membership 720.

Visitors	advised to contact in advance. Handicap certificate required.
Societies	apply in writing/telephone/e-mail/fax.
Green Fees	£25 (£35 weeeknds after 11.30am).
Prof	Richard Gough
Designer	Jack White
Facilities	⊗ ⍟ 🕭 💺 ♀ 🖴 🖾 🐦 🏌 ⚷
Location	1m E of Midhurst on A272

Hotel	★★★ 77% Spread Eagle Hotel and Health Spa, South St, MIDHURST ☎ 01730 816911 35 ⇔ 🏿 Annexe 4 🏿

PULBOROUGH
Map 04 TQ01

West Sussex Golf Club Ln, Wiggonholt RH20 2EN
☎ 01798 872563 Fax 01798 872033
Heathland course.
18 holes, 6221yds, Par 68, SSS 70, Course record 61.
Club membership 850.

Visitors	must contact in advance, may not play weekends except by prior agreement of the secretary.
Societies	Wed & Thu only, apply in writing.
Green Fees	£55 per day; £45 per round (£60/£50 weekends & bank holidays).
Prof	Tim Packham
Designer	Campbell/Hutcheson
Facilities	⊗ 🕭 💺 ♀ 🖴 🖾 🐦 🏌 ⚷ ⚑
Location	1.5m E off A283
Hotel	★★★ 65% Roundabout Hotel, Monkmead Ln, WEST CHILTINGTON ☎ 01798 813838 23 ⇔ 🏿

PYECOMBE
Map 04 TQ21

Pyecombe Clayton Hill BN45 7FF
☎ 01273 845372 Fax 01273 843338
Typical downland course on the inland side of the South
Downs. Picturesque with magnificent views. ▶

18 holes, 6278yds, Par 71, SSS 70, Course record 67.
Club membership 700.

Visitors	must contact in advance and may only play after 9.15am weekdays and after 2.15pm weekends
Societies	telephone secretary in advance.
Green Fees	£30 per day; £20 per round (£35/£30 weekends).
Prof	C R White
Facilities	⊗ ⑅ by prior arrangement 🝢 🝥 ♀ ⚲ 🝡 ⛾ ⚘
Location	E side of village on A273

Hotel	★★★ 64% Courtlands Hotel, 21-27 The Drive, HOVE ☎ 01273 731055 56 ⇌ ↟ Annexe 12 ⇌ ↟

SELSEY   Map 04 SZ89

Selsey Golf Links Ln PO20 9DR
☎ 01243 602203 Fax 01243 602722
Fairly difficult seaside course, exposed to wind and has natural ditches.
9 holes, 5834yds, Par 68, SSS 68, Course record 64.
Club membership 360.

Visitors	must contact in advance.
Societies	must contact in advance in writing
Green Fees	not confirmed.
Prof	Peter Grindley
Designer	J H Taylor
Facilities	⊗ ⑅ 🝢 🝥 ♀ ⚲ 🝡 ⚘
& Leisure	hard tennis courts.
Location	1m N off B2145

Hotel	★★★ 67% The Ship Hotel, North St, CHICHESTER ☎ 01243 778000 34 ⇌ ↟

SLINFOLD   Map 04 TQ13

Slinfold Park Golf & Country Club Stane St RH13 7RE
☎ 01403 791555 Fax 01403 791465
Slinfold course enjoys splendid views among mature trees. The 10th tee is spectacularly located on the centre of one of the two large landscaped lakes. The 166-yard 16th has water running in front of of the tee and everything sloping towards it!
Championship Course: 18 holes, 6407yds, Par 72, SSS 71, Course record 64.
Academy Course: 9 holes, 1315yds, Par 28.
Club membership 611.

Visitors	book 7 days in advance, restricted weekends and bank holidays.
Societies	advance booking required, weekends and bank holidays not available.
Green Fees	not confirmed.
Cards	▭ ▭ VISA ▭ ▭ 🟦

Prof	T Clingan
Designer	John Fortune
Facilities	⊗ ⑅ 🝢 🝥 ♀ ⚲ 🝡 ⛾ 🝣 ⚘ ⛾
Location	4m W on the A29

Hotel	★★★ 71% Random Hall Hotel, Stane St, Slinford, HORSHAM ☎ 01403 790558 15 ⇌ ↟

WEST CHILTINGTON   Map 04 TQ01

West Chiltington Broadford Bridge Rd RH20 2YA
☎ 01798 812115 (bookings) & 813574 Fax 01798 812631
The Main Course is situated on gently undulating, well-drained greens and offers panoramic views of the Sussex Downs. Three large double greens provide an interesting feature to this course. Also 9-hole short course and 13-bay driving range.
Windmill: 18 holes, 5888yds, Par 70, SSS 69, Course record 66 or 9 holes, 1360yds, Par 28.

Visitors	book tee times in advance.
Societies	by prior arrangement.
Green Fees	not confirmed.
Cards	▭ VISA 🟦
Prof	Barrie Aram
Designer	Brian Barnes
Facilities	⊗ ⑅ 🝢 🝥 ♀ ⚲ 🝡 ⛾ ⚘ ⛾
Location	On N side of village

Hotel	★★★ 65% Roundabout Hotel, Monkmead Ln, WEST CHILTINGTON ☎ 01798 813838 23 ⇌ ↟

WORTHING   Map 04 TQ10

Hill Barn Municipal Hill Barn Ln BN14 9QE
☎ 01903 237301
Downland course with views of both Isle of Wight and Brighton.
18 holes, 6224yds, Par 70, SSS 70.
Club membership 1000.

Visitors	no restrictions, but advisable to book tee times, 7 days in advance.
Societies	must telephone in advance.
Green Fees	£13.50 per round (£14.50 weekends).
Cards	▭ VISA CONNECT ▭ 🟦
Prof	S Blanshard
Designer	Fred Hawtree
Facilities	⊗ ⑅ 🝢 🝥 ♀ ⚲ 🝡 ⛾ 🝤 🝣 ⚘
Location	N side of town at junct of A24/A27

Hotel	★★★ 62% Chatsworth Hotel, Steyne, WORTHING ☎ 01903 236103 107 ⇌ ↟

Worthing Links Rd BN14 9QZ
☎ 01903 260801 Fax 01903 694664
The Upper Course, short and tricky with entrancing views, will provide good entertainment. 'Lower Course' is considered to be one of the best downland courses in the country.
Lower Course: 18 holes, 6530yds, Par 71, SSS 72, Course record 62.
Upper Course: 18 holes, 5243yds, Par 66, SSS 66.
Club membership 1200.

Visitors	advisable to contact in advance, not weekends during GMT.
Societies	contact in advance.
Green Fees	not confirmed.
Prof	Stephen Rolley
Designer	H S Colt
Facilities	⊗ �𝔐 ⮂ 🛈 ♀ ♁ ☎ ⛳ ⚒ ∅ ⌔
Location	N side of town centre off A27
Hotel	★★★ 71% Ardington Hotel, Steyne Gardens, WORTHING ☎ 01903 230451 45 ⇄ ⋔

TYNE & WEAR

BACKWORTH
Map 12 NZ37

Backworth The Hall NE27 0AH ☎ 0191 268 1048
Parkland course with easy walking, natural hazards and good scenery.
9 holes, 5930yds, Par 71, SSS 69, Course record 63.
Club membership 480.

Visitors	visitors may not play Tue (Ladies Day) & weekend mornings. Play limited Sat/Sun during Apr-Sep. Must contact in advance.
Societies	apply in writing to secretary.
Green Fees	£14 per round (£16 weekends & bank holidays).
Facilities	⊗ �𝔐 by prior arrangement ⮂ 🛈 ♀
& Leisure	bowling green.
Location	W side of town on B1322
Hotel	★★★★ 63% Holiday Inn, Great North Rd, SEATON BURN ☎ 0191 201 9988 150 ⇄ ⋔

BIRTLEY
Map 12 NZ25

Birtley Birtley Ln DH3 2LR ☎ 0191 410 2207
Parkland course.
9 holes, 5662yds, Par 67, SSS 67, Course record 63.
Club membership 270.

Visitors	must play with member at weekends & bank holidays.
Societies	apply in writing, must contact 1 month in advance in summer.
Green Fees	£12 per round. May only play with member weekends.
Facilities	🛈 ♀ ♁
Hotel	★★★ 67% Posthouse Washington, Emerson District 5, WASHINGTON ☎ 0870 400 9084 138 ⇄ ⋔

BOLDON
Map 12 NZ36

Boldon Dipe Ln, East Boldon NE36 0PQ
☎ 0191 536 5360 & 0191 536 4182 Fax 0191 537 2270
Parkland links course, easy walking, distant sea views.
18 holes, 6362yds, Par 72, SSS 70, Course record 67.
Club membership 700.

Visitors	may not play after 3.30pm at weekends & bank holidays.
Societies	must contact in advance.
Green Fees	not confirmed.
Designer	Harry Varden
Facilities & Leisure	⊗ ⯗ ⮂ 🛈 ♀ ♁ ☎ ⛳ ⚒ ∅ ⌔ snooker.
Location	S side of village off A184
Hotel	★★★ 68% Quality Hotel, Witney Way, Boldon, SUNDERLAND ☎ 0191 519 1999 82 ⇄ ⋔

CHOPWELL
Map 12 NZ15

Garesfield NE17 7AP
☎ 01207 561309 Fax 01207 561309
Undulating parkland course with good views and picturesque woodland surroundings.
18 holes, 6458yds, Par 72, SSS 71, Course record 68.
Club membership 746.

Visitors	weekends after 4.30pm only, unless with member. Must contact in advance. No visiting parties Mondays or Saturdays.
Societies	must contact secretary in advance.
Green Fees	£17 per day, £15 per round (midweek).
Prof	David Race
Designer	Harry Fernie
Facilities	⊗ ⯗ ⮂ 🛈 ♀ ♁ ☎ ⛳ ∅
Location	From A1 take A694 to Rowlands Gill. Turn right (signed Ryton) to High Spen. Turn left for Chopwell
Hotel	★★★ 61% Chasley Hotel, Newgate St, NEWCASTLE UPON TYNE ☎ 0191 232 5025 93 ⇄ ⋔

FELLING
Map 12 NZ26

Heworth Gingling Gate, Heworth NE10 8XY
☎ 0191 469 9832
Fairly flat, parkland course.
18 holes, 6437yds, Par 71, SSS 71.
Club membership 800.

Visitors	may not play Sat & before 10am Sun, Apr-Sep.
Societies	must apply in writing.
Green Fees	not confirmed.
Facilities	⊗ ⯗ ⮂ 🛈 ♀ ♁
Location	On A195, 0.5m NW of junc with A1(M)
Hotel	★★★ 67% Posthouse Washington, Emerson District 5, WASHINGTON ☎ 0870 400 9084 138 ⇄ ⋔

Where to stay, where to eat?
Visit the AA internet site
www.theaa.co.uk

GATESHEAD
Map 12 NZ26

Ravensworth Moss Heaps, Wrekenton NE9 7UU
☎ 0191 487 2843
Moorland/parkland course 600 ft above sea-level with fine views. Testing 13th hole (par 3).
18 holes, 5966yds, Par 69, SSS 69.
Club membership 600.
Visitors   apply in advance.
Societies   apply in writing to secretary.
Green Fees not confirmed.
Prof   Shaun Cowell
Designer   J W Fraser
Facilities   ⊗ by prior arrangement ⅏ by prior arrangement ⮞ ☕ 🏌 🏌 🍴 ♿
Location   3m SE off A6127

Hotel   ★★★ 67% Swallow Hotel, High West St, GATESHEAD ☎ 0191 477 1105 103 ⇆ 🐾

GOSFORTH
Map 12 NZ26

Gosforth Broadway East NE3 5ER ☎ 0191 285 3495
Parkland course with natural water hazards, easy walking.
18 holes, 6024yds, Par 69, SSS 68, Course record 65.
Club membership 500.
Visitors   must contact in advance. Restricted play on competition days.
Societies   telephone in advance.
Green Fees not confirmed.
Prof   G Garland
Facilities   ⊗ ⅏ ⮞ ☕ 🏌 🏌 🍴 ♿
Location   N side of town centre off A6125

Hotel   ★★★★ 74% Swallow Gosforth Park Hotel, High Gosforth Park, Gosforth, NEWCASTLE UPON TYNE ☎ 0191 236 4111 178 ⇆ 🐾

Parklands Gosforth Park Golfing Complex, High Gosforth Park NE3 5HQ ☎ 0191 236 4867 & 236 4480
Parklands course is set in pleasant parkland with challenging shots around and sometimes over attractive water hazards. The first 9 holes are easier but the second 9 test even the most experienced golfer.
18 holes, 6060yds, Par 71, SSS 69, Course record 66.
Club membership 750.
Visitors   a daily start sheet operates with bookings taken from 4.30pm the previous day during weekdays, and from 8am Fri & Sat for weekends.
Societies   by prior arrangement with club secretary.
Green Fees not confirmed.
Prof   Brian Rumney
Facilities   ⊗ ⅏ ⮞ ☕ 🏌 🏌 🍴 ♿ ♨
Location   3m N, at the end A1 Western by Pass

Hotel   ★★★★ 74% Swallow Gosforth Park Hotel, High Gosforth Park, Gosforth, NEWCASTLE UPON TYNE ☎ 0191 236 4111 178 ⇆ 🐾

HOUGHTON-LE-SPRING
Map 12 NZ35

Elemore Elemore Ln, Hetton-le-Hole DH5 0QB
☎ 0191 517 3061 Fax 0191 517 3054
Elemore course tests a players ability in all aspects of the game, with drives over water as well as wedges. The greens are firm all year round and there are well positioned bunkers.

18 holes, 5947yds, Par 69, Course record 68.
Club membership 100.
Visitors   no restrictions. Phone to avoid society days.
Societies   apply in writing, telephone enquiries welcome.
Green Fees £9 per 18 holes (£12 weekends).
Designer   J Gaunt
Facilities   ⊗ ⮞ ☕ 🏌 🏌 🍴 ♿ 🛺 ♨
Location   4m S of Houghton-Le-Spring on the A182

Hotel   ★★ 61% Chilton Lodge Country Pub & Motel, Black Boy Rd, Chilton Moor, Fencehouses, HOUGHTON-LE-SPRING ☎ 0191 385 2694 25 ⇆ 🐾

Houghton-le-Spring Copt Hill DH5 8LU
☎ 0191 584 1198 & 584 0048
Hilly, downland course with natural slope hazards.
18 holes, 6443yds, Par 72, SSS 71, Course record 64.
Club membership 600.
Visitors   may not play on Sun until 4pm.
Societies   must contact secretary in advance.
Green Fees not confirmed.
Prof   Kevin Gow
Facilities   ⊗ ⅏ ⮞ ☕ 🏌 🏌 🍴
Location   0.5m E on B1404

Hotel   ★★ 61% Chilton Lodge Country Pub & Motel, Black Boy Rd, Chilton Moor, Fencehouses, HOUGHTON-LE-SPRING ☎ 0191 385 2694 25 ⇆ 🐾

NEWCASTLE UPON TYNE
Map 12 NZ26

City of Newcastle Three Mile Bridge NE3 2DR
☎ 0191 285 1775 Fax 0191 2840700
A well-manicured parkland course in the Newcastle suburbs.
18 holes, 6528yds, Par 72, SSS 71, Course record 64.
Club membership 460.
Visitors   no restrictions but advisable to telephone first.
Societies   telephone in advance
Green Fees £24 per day (£28 weekends & bank holidays).
Prof   Steve McKenna
Designer   Harry Vardon
Facilities   ⊗ ⅏ ⮞ ☕ 🏌 🏌 🍴 ♿ ♨
Location   3m N on B1318

Hotel   ★★★ 64% The Caledonian Hotel, Newcastle, 64 Osborne Rd, Jesmond, NEWCASTLE UPON TYNE ☎ 0191 281 7881 89 ⇆ 🐾

Newcastle United Ponteland Rd, Cowgate NE5 3JW
☎ 0191 286 9998 Fax 0191 286 4323
Moorland course with natural hazards.
18 holes, 6617yds, Par 72, SSS 72, Course record 68.
Club membership 600.
Visitors   must play with member at weekends.
Societies   must contact in writing.
Green Fees not confirmed.
Facilities   ⊗ ⮞ ☕ 🏌 🏌 🍴 ♿ ♨
Location   1.25m NW of city centre off A6127

Hotel   ★★★ 63% Swallow Imperial Hotel, Jesmond Rd, NEWCASTLE UPON TYNE ☎ 0191 281 5511 122 ⇆ 🐾

Northumberland High Gosforth Park NE3 5HT
☎ 0191 236 2498 Fax 0191 236 2498
Many golf courses have been sited inside racecourses, although not so many survive today. One which does is the Northumberland Club's course at High Gosforth Park. Naturally the course is flat but there are plenty of mounds and other hazards to make it a fine test of golf. It should be said that not all the holes are within the confines of the racecourse, but both inside and out there are some good holes. This is a Championship course.
18 holes, 6629yds, Par 72, SSS 72, Course record 65.
Club membership 580.

Visitors	may not play at weekends or competition days. Must contact in advance.
Societies	must apply in writing.
Green Fees	£45 per day; £35 per round.
Designer	Colt/Braid
Facilities	⊗ ⁓ℍ ⅃ᴸ ♥ ♀ ♧ ⚘
Location	4m N of city centre off A1
Hotel	★★★★ 74% Swallow Gosforth Park Hotel, High Gosforth Park, Gosforth, NEWCASTLE UPON TYNE ☎ 0191 236 4111 178 ⇔ r

Westerhope Whorlton Grance, Westerhope NE5 1PP
☎ 0191 286 7636
Attractive parkland course with tree-lined fairways, and easy walking. Good open views towards the airport.
18 holes, 6444yds, Par 72, SSS 71, Course record 64.
Club membership 778.

Visitors	with member only at weekends. Must contact in advance.
Societies	must contact Secretary in advance.
Green Fees	not confirmed.
Prof	Nigel Brown
Facilities	⅃ᴸ ♧⚘ ⇘ ⚘
Location	4.5m NW of city centre off B6324
Hotel	★★★★ 74% Swallow Gosforth Park Hotel, High Gosforth Park, Gosforth, NEWCASTLE UPON TYNE ☎ 0191 236 4111 178 ⇔ r

RYTON   Map 12 NZ16

Ryton Clara Vale NE40 3TD
☎ 0191 413 3737 Fax 0191 413 1642
Parkland course.
18 holes, 5950yds, Par 70, SSS 69, Course record 67.
Club membership 600.

Visitors	with member only at weekends.
Societies	apply in advance.
Green Fees	£21 per day; £17 per round.
Facilities	⊗ ⁓ℍ ⅃ᴸ ♥ ♀ ♧
Location	NW side of town off A695
Hotel	★★★ 69% Gibside Arms Hotel, Front St, WHICKHAM ☎ 0191 488 9292 45 ⇔ r

Tyneside Westfield Ln NE40 3QE
☎ 0191 413 2742 Fax 0191 413 2742
Open parkland course, water hazard, hilly, practice area.
18 holes, 6042yds, Par 70, SSS 69, Course record 65.
Club membership 900.

Visitors	must contact in advance to play at weekends (after 3pm)
Societies	must apply in advance.
Green Fees	£25 per day; £20 per round.
Cards	▨▨▨ ▨▨
Prof	Malcolm Gunn
Designer	H S Colt
Facilities	⊗ ⁓ℍ ⅃ᴸ ♥ ♀ ♧ ⚘
Location	NW side of town off A695
Hotel	★★★ 69% Gibside Arms Hotel, Front St, WHICKHAM ☎ 0191 488 9292 45 ⇔ r

SOUTH SHIELDS   Map 12 NZ36

South Shields Cleadon Hills NE34 8EG ☎ 0191 456 8942
A slightly undulating downland course on a limestone base ensuring good conditions underfoot. Open to strong winds, the course is testing but fair. There are fine views of the coastline.
18 holes, 6264yds, Par 71, SSS 70, Course record 64.
Club membership 800.

Visitors	must contact in advance.
Societies	by arrangement.
Green Fees	not confirmed.
Prof	Gary Parsons
Designer	McKenzie-Braid
Facilities	⊗ ⁓ℍ ⅃ᴸ ♥ ♀ ♧ ⇘ ⚘
Location	SE side of town centre off A1300
Hotel	★★★ 64% Sea Hotel, Sea Rd, SOUTH SHIELDS ☎ 0191 427 0999 33 ⇔ r

Whitburn Lizard Ln NE34 7AF ☎ 0191 529 4944 (Sec) & 529 2144 (club) Fax 0191 529 4944
Parkland course.
18 holes, 5900yds, Par 69, SSS 68, Course record 64.
Club membership 650.

Visitors	restricted weekends & Tue. Contact professional in advance.
Societies	must apply in writing to secretary
Green Fees	£20 per day (£26 weekends & bank holidays).
Prof	David Stephenson
Designer	Colt, Alison & Morrison
Facilities	⊗ ⁓ℍ by prior arrangement ⅃ᴸ ♥ ♀ ♧ ⚘
Location	2.5m SE off A183
Hotel	★★★★ 67% Swallow Hotel, Queen's Pde, Seaburn, SUNDERLAND ☎ 0191 529 2041 98 ⇔ r

SUNDERLAND   Map 12 NZ35

Ryhope Leechmore Way, Ryhope SR2 0DH
☎ 0191 523 7333
A municipal course.
18 holes, 4601yds, Par 65, SSS 63.
Club membership 350.

Visitors	no restrictions.
Societies	apply in writing, telephone enquiries welcome.
Green Fees	not confirmed.
Facilities	♀ ♧ ⇘ ⚘
Location	3.5m S of city centre
Hotel	★★★★ 67% Swallow Hotel, Queen's Pde, Seaburn, SUNDERLAND ☎ 0191 529 2041 98 ⇔ r

Wearside Coxgreen SR4 9JT
☎ 0191 534 2518 Fax 0191 5342518
Open, undulating parkland course rolling down to the
River Wear and beneath the shadow of the famous
Penshaw Monument. Built on the lines of an Athenian
temple it is a well-known landmark. Two ravines cross
the course presenting a variety of challenging holes.
18 holes, 6373yds, Par 71, SSS 74, Course record 63.
Club membership 648.

Visitors	may not play before 9.30am, between 12.30-1.30 or after 4pm.
Societies	must apply in writing.
Green Fees	£20 per 36/27 holes; £16 per 18 holes (£22/£18 weekends).
Prof	Doug Brolls
Facilities	⊗ ⅏ ⓛ 🅱 ♀ ♨ 🛏 🏌
& Leisure	4 hole pqr 3 practice course.
Location	3.5m W off A183
Hotel	★★★★ 67% Swallow Hotel, Queen's Pde, Seaburn, SUNDERLAND ☎ 0191 529 2041 98 ⇆ ☏

TYNEMOUTH   Map 12 NZ36

Tynemouth Spital Dene NE30 2ER
☎ 0191 257 4578 Fax 0191 259 5193
Well-drained parkland course, easy walking.
18 holes, 6401yds, Par 70, SSS 71, Course record 64.
Club membership 824.

Visitors	must play with member weekends & bank holidays.
Societies	must contact in writing.
Green Fees	£21 per day; £16 per round.
Prof	J P McKenna
Designer	Willie Park
Facilities	⊗ ⅏ ⓛ 🅱 ♀ ♨ 🛏 🏌
Location	0.5m W
Hotel	★★★ 68% Grand Hotel, Grand Pde, TYNEMOUTH ☎ 0191 293 6666 40 ⇆ ☏ Annexe 5 ⇆ ☏

WALLSEND   Map 12 NZ26

Wallsend Rheydt Av, Bigges Main NE28 8SU
☎ 0191 262 1973
Parkland course.
18 holes, 6608yds, Par 72, SSS 72, Course record 66.
Club membership 670.

Visitors	may not play before 12.30pm weekends. Must book in advance.
Societies	must apply in writing.
Green Fees	£13 per round (£15 weekends).
Prof	Ken Phillips
Designer	A Snowball
Facilities	ⓛ 🅱 ♀ ♨ 🏆 🏌 ☏
Location	NW side of town centre off A193
Hotel	★★★ 63% Swallow Imperial Hotel, Jesmond Rd, NEWCASTLE UPON TYNE ☎ 0191 281 5511 122 ⇆ ☏

> Looking for a driving range?
> See the index at the back of the guide

WASHINGTON   Map 12 NZ25

George Washington Hotel Golf & Country Club Stone
Cellar Rd, High Usworth NE37 1PH
☎ 0191 402 9988 & 417 8346 Fax 0191 4151166
Championship-standard course. Also a 9-hole (par 3) course,
putting green and 21-bay floodlit driving range.
18 holes, 6604yds, Par 73, SSS 72, Course record 68.
Club membership 600.

Visitors	must contact in advance. May not play before 10am or between noon & 2pm at weekends.
Societies	book in advance.
Green Fees	£30 per day; £20 per round.
Cards	🖪 🖪 🖪 🖪
Prof	Warren Marshall
Designer	Eric Watson
Facilities	⊗ ⅏ ⓛ 🅱 ♀ ♨ 🛏 🏌 🏆 🚡 🏌 ☏
& Leisure	heated indoor swimming pool, squash, sauna, solarium, gymnasium, 9 hole par 3 course, golf tuition.
Location	From A195 signed Washington North take last exit on rdbt, then right at mini-rdbt
Hotel	★★★ 65% George Washington Golf & Country Club, Stone Cellar Rd, District 12, High Usworth, WASHINGTON ☎ 0191 402 9988 103 ⇆ ☏

WHICKHAM   Map 12 NZ26

Whickham Hollinside Park, Fellside Rd NE16 5BA
☎ 0191 488 1576 Fax 0191 488 1576
Undulating parkland course with attractive panoramic views.
18 holes, 5878yds, Par 68, SSS 68, Course record 61.
Club membership 660.

Visitors	must contact Professional in advance.
Societies	by arrangement.
Green Fees	£20 per day/round (£25 Sun).
Prof	Graeme Lisle
Facilities	⊗ ⅏ by prior arrangement 🅱 ♀ ♨ 🛏 🏌 ☏
Location	1.5m S
Hotel	★★★ 67% Swallow Hotel, High West St, GATESHEAD ☎ 0191 477 1105 103 ⇆ ☏

WHITLEY BAY   Map 12 NZ37

Whitley Bay Claremont Rd NE26 3UF
☎ 0191 252 0180 Fax 0191 297 0030
An 18-hole links type course, close to the sea, with a stream
running through the undulating terrain.
18 holes, 6579yds, Par 71, SSS 71, Course record 66.
Club membership 800.

Visitors	may not play Sat, telephone for Sun play. Advisable to contact in advance.
Societies	telephone initially.
Green Fees	£33 per day; £22 per round.
Prof	Gary Shipley
Facilities	⊗ ⅏ by prior arrangement 🅱 ♀ ♨ 🛏 🏌
Location	NW side of town centre off A1148
Hotel	★★★ 63% Windsor Hotel, South Pde, WHITLEY BAY ☎ 0191 251 8888 63 ⇆ ☏

WARWICKSHIRE

ATHERSTONE   Map 04 SP39

Atherstone The Outwoods, Coleshill Rd CV9 2RL
☎ 01827 713110 Fax 01827 715686
Scenic parkland course, established in 1894 and laid out on
hilly ground.
18 holes, 6006yds, Par 72, SSS 70, Course record 69.
Club membership 520.

Visitors	handicap certificate required. With member only weekends and bank holidays but not Sun. Also with holder of handicap certificate by permission of Club Secretary.
Societies	contact in advance.
Green Fees	£20 per day/round. With member only weekends.
Designer	Hawtree & Gaunt Mornoch
Facilities	⊗ 🍴 🏌 🍺 🏌 ⚒
Location	0.5m S on B4116

Hotel	★★ 75% Chapel House Hotel, Friar's Gate, ATHERSTONE ☎ 01827 718949 14 ⇄ 🐾

BIDFORD-ON-AVON   Map 04 SP15

Bidford Grange Stratford Rd B50 4LY
☎ 01789 490319 Fax 01789 778184
Designed by Howard Swan & Paul Tillman, this very long,
championship standard course is built to represent a links
course and is fully irrigated. There are water hazards on the
first 7 holes, and particularly challenging holes on the 16th
(223yds,par 3), 8th (600yds, par 5) and an uphill par 4 at the
13th.
18 holes, 7233yds, Par 72, SSS 74, Course record 66.
Club membership 200.

Visitors	no restrictions.
Societies	apply in writing or phone, minimum 12, maximum 36.
Green Fees	£12 per 18 holes (£15 weekends).
Cards	💳 💳 💳 💳
Facilities	🏌 🍺 🏌 ⚒ 🍴 🐾 ⚒
& Leisure	fishing, snooker & pool tables.
Location	4m W of Stratford upon Avon, B439

Hotel	★★★ 75% Salford Hall Hotel, ABBOT'S SALFORD ☎ 01386 871300 14 ⇄ 🐾 Annexe 19 ⇄ 🐾

BRANDON   Map 04 SP47

City of Coventry-Brandon Wood Brandon Ln, Wolston
CV8 3GQ ☎ 024 76543141 Fax 024 76545108
Municipal parkland course surrounded by fields and bounded
by River Avon on east side. Floodlit driving range.
18 holes, 6610yds, Par 72, SSS 71, Course record 68.
Club membership 500.

Visitors	telephone for details, advance booking recommended.
Societies	telephone secretary for details
Green Fees	£9.40 per round (£12.50 weekends & bank holidays).
Cards	💳 💳 💳 💳
Prof	Chris Gledhill

Facilities	⊗ 🍴 by prior arrangement 🏌 🍺 🏌 🍴 ⚒ 🐾 ⚒
Location	Off A45 southbound

Hotel	★★★ 64% The Brandon Hall, Main St, BRANDON ☎ 0870 400 8150 60 ⇄ 🐾

COLESHILL   Map 04 SP28

Maxstoke Park Castle Ln B46 2RD
☎ 01675 466743 Fax 01675 466743
Parkland course with easy walking. Numerous trees and a
lake form natural hazards.
18 holes, 6442yds, Par 71, SSS 71, Course record 64.
Club membership 720.

Visitors	with member only at weekends & bank holidays.
Societies	contact in advance.
Green Fees	£38 per day; £27.50 per 18 holes.
Prof	Neil McEwan
Facilities	⊗ 🍴 🏌 🍺 🏌 🍴 ⚒ 🐾 ⚒
Location	3m NE of Coleshill on B4114 turn right for Maxstoke then 1m on right

Hotel	★★★ 64% Coleshill Hotel, 152 High St, COLESHILL ☎ 01675 465527 15 ⇄ 🐾 Annexe 8 ⇄ 🐾

HENLEY-IN-ARDEN   Map 04 SP16

Henley Golf & Country Club Birmingham Rd B95 5QA
☎ 01564 793715 Fax 01564 795754
This improving course is maturing well and provides a good
golfing challenge for all handicaps. All facilities recently
upgraded.
18 holes, 6933yds, Par 73, SSS 73.
Club membership 675.

Visitors	may book up to 7 days in advance.
Societies	apply in writing or telephone in advance.
Green Fees	£25 per day; £20 per round (£30/£25 weekends).
Cards	💳 💳 💳 💳
Prof	Simon Edwin
Designer	N Selwyn Smith
Facilities	⊗ 🍴 🏌 🍺 🏌 🍴 ⚒ 🐾 ⚒
& Leisure	hard tennis courts.
Location	On the left hand side of the Birmingham road, just N of Henley-in-Arden

Hotel	★★★ 64% Quality Hotel, Pool Bank, Southcrest, REDDITCH ☎ 01527 541511 58 ⇄ 🐾

KENILWORTH   Map 04 SP27

Kenilworth Crewe Ln CV8 2EA
☎ 01926 858517 Fax 01926 864453
Parkland course in open hilly situation. Club founded in
1889.
18 holes, 6400yds, Par 73, SSS 71, Course record 62.
Club membership 755.

Visitors	must contact in advance.
Societies	apply in writing.
Green Fees	not confirmed.
Cards	💳 💳 💳 💳
Prof	Steve Yates
Designer	Hawtree

▶

Facilities ⊗ 🎍 ᴸᵇ 🍺 ♀ ♿ 🏠 ⛳ ⛵ ⛳ ₵
& Leisure Par 3 chipping green.
Location 0.5m NE

Hotel ★★ 68% Clarendon House Hotel, Old High St,
KENILWORTH ☎ 01926 857668 30 ⇌ ᴿ

LEA MARSTON   Map 04 SP29

Lea Marston Hotel & Leisure Complex Haunch Ln
B76 0BY ☎ 01675 470468 Fax 01675 470871
Par 3, 'pay-and-play' course, with water hazards, out of
bounds, and large bunkers. Golf driving range.
9 holes, 783yds, Par 27, SSS 27, Course record 46.
Club membership 150.
Visitors no restrictions.
Societies must telephone in advance.
Green Fees not confirmed.
Prof Andrew Stokes
Designer J R Blake
Facilities ⊗ 🎍 ᴸᵇ 🍺 ♀ 🏠 ⛳ 🚃 ₵
& Leisure hard tennis courts, heated indoor swimming
pool, sauna, solarium, gymnasium.
Hotel ★★★ 71% Lea Marston Hotel & Leisure
Complex, Haunch Ln, LEA MARSTON
☎ 01675 470468 83 ⇌ ᴿ

LEAMINGTON SPA   Map 04 SP36

Leamington & County Golf Ln, Whitnash CV31 2QA
☎ 01926 425961 Fax 01926 425961
Undulating parkland course with extensive views.
18 holes, 6488yds, Par 71, SSS 71, Course record 65.
Club membership 802.
Visitors must contact in advance.
Societies telephone in advance.
Green Fees £32 per day; £27 per round (£40 per round
weekends).
Prof Iain Grant
Designer H S Colt
Facilities ⊗ 🎍 ᴸᵇ 🍺 ♀ ♿ 🏠 ⛵ 🚃 ₵
& Leisure snooker.
Location S side of town centre

Hotel ★★★ 60% Manor House Hotel, Avenue Rd,
LEAMINGTON SPA
☎ 01926 423251 53 ⇌ ᴿ

Newbold Comyn Newbold Ter East CV32 4EW
☎ 01926 421157
Municipal parkland course with hilly front nine. The par 4,
9th is a 467-yd testing hole.
18 holes, 6315yds, Par 70, SSS 70, Course record 70.
Club membership 320.
Visitors no restrictions.
Societies apply to professional.
Green Fees not confirmed.
Prof Ricky Carvell
Facilities ⊗ 🎍 ᴸᵇ 🍺 ♀ ♿ 🏠 ⛳ ₵
& Leisure heated indoor swimming pool, gymnasium.
Location 0.75m E of town centre off B4099

Hotel ★★★ 60% Manor House Hotel, Avenue Rd,
LEAMINGTON SPA
☎ 01926 423251 53 ⇌ ᴿ

LEEK WOOTTON   Map 04 SP26

The Warwickshire CV35 7QT
☎ 01926 409409 Fax 01926 498911
This is an unusual championship standard course. Designed
by Karl Litten, the 36 holes are laid out as four
interchangeable loops of 9 holes to create six contrasting yet
superb courses in a parkland and woodland setting.
South East Course: 18 holes, 7000yds, Par 72, SSS 72,
Course record 68.
North West Course: 18 holes, 7421yds, Par 74, SSS 73,
Course record 70.
Club membership 880.

Visitors can book up to 7 days in advance.
Societies apply to sales office for details.
Green Fees £45 per round.
Cards 💳 💳 💳 💳 💳 💳
Prof Danny Peck
Designer Karl Litten
Facilities ⊗ 🎍 ᴸᵇ 🍺 ♀ ♿ 🏠 ⛳ ⛵ 🚃 ₵
Location 1m from Kenilworth on B4115

Hotel ★★★ 68% Chesford Grange Hotel,
Chesford Bridge, KENILWORTH
☎ 01926 859331 145 ⇌ ᴿ Annexe 9 ⇌ ᴿ

NUNEATON   Map 04 SP39

Nuneaton Golf Dr, Whitestone CV11 6QF
☎ 024 76347810 Fax 024 76327563
Undulating parkland and woodland course with Silver Birch
lining the fairways. Easy walking.
18 holes, 6429yds, Par 71, SSS 71.
Club membership 700.
Visitors must produce evidence of membership of a
recognised golf club or society, with member
only at weekends.
Societies apply in writing.
Green Fees £25 per round.
Prof Steven Bainbridge
Facilities ⊗ 🎍 ᴸᵇ 🍺 ♀ ♿ 🏠 🚃 ₵
Location 2m SE off B4114

Hotel ★★★ 62% Weston Hall, Weston Ln, Weston in
Arden, Bulkington, NUNEATON
☎ 024 76312989 40 ⇌ ᴿ

Oakridge Arley Ln, Ansley Village CV10 9PH
☎ 01676 541389 & 540542 Fax 01676 542709
There are a number of water hazards on the back nine which
add to the natural beauty of the countryside. The undulating
course is affected by winter cross winds on several holes. ▶

Overall it will certainly test golfing skills.
18 holes, 6242yds, Par 71, SSS 70.
Club membership 500.

Visitors contact in advance, with members only at weekends.
Societies apply in writing or telephone in advance.
Green Fees not confirmed.
Designer Algy Jayes
Facilities ⊗ ⅲ ♭ ♥ ♀ ♌ 🖼 ⛳ ⚲ ♨ ✧
Location 4m W

Hotel ★★★ 62% Weston Hall, Weston Ln, Weston in Arden, Bulkington, NUNEATON
☎ 024 76312989 40 ⇥ ♠

Purley Chase Pipers Ln, Ridge Ln CV10 0RB
☎ 024 76393118 Fax 024 76398015
Meadowland course with tricky water hazards on eight holes and undulating greens. 13-bay driving range.
18 holes, 6772yds, Par 72, SSS 72, Course record 67.
Club membership 750.

Visitors welcome weekends after 12 noon.
Societies telephone for provisional booking (Mon-Fri only).
Green Fees £15 per round (£25 weekends).
Cards ▭ ▭ ⑤
Prof Gary Carver
Facilities ⊗ ⅲ ♭ ♥ ♀ ♌ 🖼 ♠ ⚲ ✧ ♀
Location 2m NW off B4114

Hotel ★★★ 62% Weston Hall, Weston Ln, Weston in Arden, Bulkington, NUNEATON
☎ 024 76312989 40 ⇥ ♠

RUGBY
Map 04 SP57

Rugby Clifton Rd CV21 3RD
☎ 01788 542306 (Sec) 575134 (Pro) Fax 01788 542306
Parkland course with brook running through the middle and crossed by a viaduct.
18 holes, 5457yds, Par 68, SSS 67, Course record 62.
Club membership 700.

Visitors weekends & bank holidays with member only.
Societies apply in writing.
Green Fees £20 per day.
Prof Nat Summers
Facilities ⊗ ⅲ ♭ ♥ ♀ ♌ 🖼 ⛳ ♨ ✧
Location 1m NE on B5414

Hotel ★★★ 59% Grosvenor Hotel Rugby, Clifton Rd, RUGBY ☎ 01788 535686 26 ⇥ ♠

Whitefields Hotel Golf & Country Club Coventry Rd, Thurlaston CV23 9JR ☎ 01788 815555 Fax 01788 817777
Whitefields has superb natural drainage. There are many water features and the 13th has a stunnning dogleg 442yard Par 4 with a superb view across Draycote Water. The 16th is completely surrounded by water and is particularly difficult.
18 holes, 6223yds, Par 71, SSS 70, Course record 66.
Club membership 400.

Visitors advisable to book unless hotel guest, available 7 days, contact secretary on 01788 815555.
Societies contact secretary in advance.
Green Fees £25 weekdays (£32 weekends).
Cards ▭ ▭ ▭ 📧 ⑤
Prof not confirmed
Designer Reg Mason
Facilities ⊗ ⅲ ♭ ♥ ♀ ♌ 🖼 ⛳ ♨ ⚲ ♨ ✧ ♀

Location Junct of M45 where it meets the A45 Coventry road, near Dunchurch

Hotel ★★ 63% Whitefields Hotel Golf & Country Club, Coventry Rd, Thurlaston, RUGBY
☎ 01788 521800 & 522393
Fax 01788 521695 34 ⇥ ♠

STONELEIGH
Map 04 SP37

Stoneleigh Deer Park The Clubhouse, The Old Deer Park, Coventry Rd CV8 3DR
☎ 024 76639991 Fax 024 76511533
Parkland course in old deer park with many mature trees. The River Avon meanders through the course and comes into play on 4 holes. Also 9-hole course.
Tantara Course: 18 holes, 6023yds, Par 71, SSS 69.
Avon Course: 9 holes, 1251yds, Par 27.
Club membership 800.

Visitors must contact in advance, no visitors at weekends except by prior arrangement.
Societies by prior arrangement.
Green Fees not confirmed.
Prof Matt McGuire
Designer Ken Harrison
Facilities ⊗ ⅲ ♭ ♥ ♀ ♌ 🖼 ⛳ ⚲ ✧
Location 3m NE of Kenilworth

Hotel ★★★★ 63% De Montfort Hotel, The Square, KENILWORTH
☎ 01926 855944 104 ⇥ ♠

STRATFORD-UPON-AVON
Map 04 SP25

Stratford Oaks Bearley Rd, Snitterfield CV37 0EZ
☎ 01789 731980 Fax 01789 731981
American styled, level parkland course with some water features designed by Howard Swan.
18 holes, 6100yds, Par 71, SSS 69, Course record 66.
Club membership 655.

Visitors contact in advance.
Societies telephone in advance.
Green Fees £20 per round (£25 weekends).
Cards ▭ ▭ ▭ ⑤
Prof Andrew Dunbar
Designer H Swann
Facilities ⊗ ⅲ ♭ ♥ ♀ ♌ 🖼 ⛳ ✧ ♀
Location 4m N of Stratford-upon-Avon

Hotel ★★★★ 68% Stratford Manor, Warwick Rd, STRATFORD-UPON-AVON
☎ 01789 731173 103 ⇥ ♠

Stratford-upon-Avon Tiddington Rd CV37 7BA
☎ 01789 205749
Beautiful parkland course. The par 3, 16th is tricky and the par 5, 17th and 18th, provide a tough end.
18 holes, 6311yds, Par 72, SSS 70, Course record 64.
Club membership 750.
Visitors restricted on Wed.
Societies must telephone in advance.
Green Fees not confirmed.
Prof D Sutherland
Facilities ⊗ ⅷ Ⅼ ➍ ♀ ♨ 🛅 ↑ ⏚ ♂
Location 0.75m E on B4086

Hotel ★★★★ 65% The Alveston Manor, Clopton Bridge, STRATFORD-UPON-AVON ☎ 0870 400 8181 114 ⇔ ↑

Welcombe Hotel Warwick Rd CV37 0NR
☎ 01789 295252 Fax 01789 414666
Wooded parkland course of great character and boasting superb views of the River Avon, Stratford and the Cotswolds. Set within the hotel's 157-acre estate, it has two lakes and water features.
18 holes, 6274yds, Par 70, SSS 70, Course record 64.

Visitors must contact in advance.
Societies booking via Hotel.
Green Fees £40 per round (£50 weekends & bank holidays).
Cards ▭ ▨ 𝚅𝙸𝚂𝙰 ◎ ▨ ⓩ
Prof Carl Mason
Designer Thomas Macauley
Facilities ⊗ ⅷ Ⅼ ➍ ♀ ♨ 🛅 ↑ 🏂 🐎 ⏚ ♂ ⍢
& Leisure hard tennis courts, fishing, solarium, gymnasium, hairdresser, health & beauty salon, snooker.
Location 1.5m NE off A46

Hotel ★★★★ 74% Welcombe Hotel and Golf Course, Warwick Rd, STRATFORD-UPON-AVON ☎ 01789 295252 67 ⇔ ↑

TANWORTH-IN-ARDEN Map 07 SP17

Ladbrook Park Poolhead Ln B94 5ED
☎ 01564 742264 Fax 01564 742909
Parkland course lined with trees.
18 holes, 6427yds, Par 71, SSS 71, Course record 65.
Club membership 700.

Visitors welcome weekdays, with member at weekends. Must contact in advance & have handicap certificate.
Societies apply in advance.
Green Fees £40 for 36 holes, £32 per 28 holes, £25 per 18 holes.
Cards ▭ ▨ 𝚅𝙸𝚂𝙰 ⓩ
Prof Richard Mountford
Designer H S Colt
Facilities ⊗ ⅷ Ⅼ ➍ ♀ ♨ 🛅 ↑ ♂
Location 2.5m SE of M42 junct 3

Hotel ★★★♨♨ 78% Nuthurst Grange Country House Hotel, Nuthurst Grange Ln, HOCKLEY HEATH ☎ 01564 783972 15 ⇔ ↑

UPPER BRAILES Map 04 SP33

Brailes Sutton Ln, Lower Brailes OX15 5BB
☎ 01608 685336 Fax 01608 685205
Undulating meadowland on 130 acres of Cotswold countryside. Sutton brook passes through the course and is crossed 5 times. The Par 5 17th offers the most spectacular view of three counties from the tee. Challenging Par 3 short holes.
18 holes, 6311yds, Par 71, SSS 70, Course record 67.
Club membership 430.
Visitors advance telephone advisable to 01608 685633.
Societies telephone or write for information to the secretary.
Green Fees Apr-Oct: £27 per 27/36 holes; £18 per 18 holes (£36/£26 weekends & bank holidays) Nov-Mar: £22 per 27/36 holes; £15 per 18 holes (£25/£18 weekends & bank holidays).
Prof Steve Hutchinson
Designer B A Hull
Facilities ⊗ ⅷ Ⅼ ➍ ♀ ♨ 🛅 ↑ 🏂 🐎 ⏚ ♂
Location 4m E of Shipston-on-Stour, on B4035

Hotel ★★ 60% The Red Lion Hotel, Main St, Long Compton, SHIPSTON ON STOUR ☎ 01608 684221 5 ⇔ ↑

WARWICK Map 04 SP26

Warwick The Racecourse CV34 6HW
☎ 01926 494316
Parkland course with easy walking. Driving range with floodlit bays.
9 holes, 2682yds, Par 34, SSS 66, Course record 67.
Club membership 150.
Visitors must contact in advance. May not play Sun before 12.30pm
Societies contact in advance.
Green Fees £4.50 per 9 holes (£5 weekends).
Prof Phil Sharp
Designer D G Dunkley
Facilities ➍ ♀ ♨ 🛅 ↑ ♂ ⍢
Location W side of town centre

Hotel ★★ 65% Warwick Arms Hotel, 17 High St, WARWICK ☎ 01926 492759 35 ⇔ ↑

WEST MIDLANDS

ALDRIDGE
Map 07 SK00

Druids Heath Stonnall Rd WS9 8JZ
☎ 01922 455595 (Office) & 459523 (Prof)
Testing, undulating heathland course.
18 holes, 6659yds, Par 72, SSS 73.
Club membership 590.

Visitors	contact in advance recommended. Weekend play permitted after 2pm.
Societies	phone initially.
Green Fees	not confirmed.
Prof	Glenn Williams
Facilities	⊗ ⅲ ᴸ ☕ ♀ ⚑ ⚒ 🏌
& Leisure	snooker.
Location	NE side of town centre off A454

Hotel	★★★ 75% The Fairlawns at Aldridge, 178 Little Aston Rd, Aldridge, WALSALL
	☎ 01922 455122 46 ⇆ ᴿ

BIRMINGHAM
Map 07 SP08

Brandhall Heron Rd, Oldbury, Warley B68 8AQ
☎ 0121 552 2195
Municipal parkland course, easy walking, good hazards. Testing holes: 1st-502 yds (par 5); 10th-455 yds dog-leg (par 5).
18 holes, 5734yds, Par 70, SSS 68, Course record 66.

Visitors	restricted weekends. Telephone for tee times (access to clubhouse on payment of small entrance fee and subject to prior arrangement).
Societies	by arrangement, apply in writing
Green Fees	not confirmed.
Cards	🗪 🗪
Prof	Carl Yates
Facilities	⊗ ☕ ⚑ 🏌 ⚒
Location	5.5m W of Birmingham city centre off A4123

Hotel	★★★ 67% Posthouse Birmingham Great Barr, Chapel Ln, Great Barr, BIRMINGHAM
	☎ 0870 400 9009 192 ⇆ ᴿ

Cocks Moors Woods Alcester Rd South, Kings Heath
B14 4ER ☎ 0121 464 3584 Fax 0121 441 1305
Although quite short this tree-lined, parkland course has well maintained greens and offers a good test of golf.
18 holes, 5769yds, Par 69, SSS 68.
Club membership 400.

Visitors	no restrictions.
Societies	must contact in advance.
Green Fees	£9 per 18 holes; (£10 weekends).
Prof	Steve Ellis
Facilities	⊗ ⅲ ᴸ ☕ ♀ ⚑ ⚒ 🏌
& Leisure	heated indoor swimming pool, solarium, gymnasium.
Location	5m S of city centre on A435

Hotel	★★★ 64% Posthouse Birmingham City, Smallbrook Queensway, BIRMINGHAM
	☎ 0870 400 9008 251 ⇆ ᴿ

Edgbaston Church Rd, Edgbaston B15 3TB
☎ 0121 454 1736 Fax 0121 454 2395
Set in 144 acres of woodland, lake and parkland, two miles from the centre of Birmingham, this delightful course utilises the wealth of natural features to provide a series of testing and adventurous holes set in the traditional double loop that starts directly in front of the Clubhouse, an imposing Georgian mansion.
18 holes, 6106yds, Par 69, SSS 69, Course record 63.
Club membership 880.

Visitors	recommended to contact in advance through golf reservations, must have handicap certificate. Most weekends pm.
Societies	must apply in writing.
Green Fees	£35 per day (£50 weekends).
Prof	Jamie Cundy
Designer	H S Colt
Facilities	ᴸ ☕ ♀ ⚑ 🏌 ⚒
Location	2m S of city centre on B4217 off A38

Hotel	★★★ 64% Plough & Harrow, 135 Hagley Rd, EDGBASTON
	☎ 0121 454 4111 44 ⇆ ᴿ

Great Barr Chapel Ln, Great Barr B43 7BA
☎ 0121 357 5270
Parkland course with easy walking. Pleasant views of Barr Beacon National Park.
18 holes, 6523yds, Par 72, SSS 71, Course record 67.
Club membership 600.

Visitors	restricted at weekends.
Societies	must contact in writing.
Green Fees	not confirmed.
Prof	Richard Spragg
Facilities	⊗ ⅲ ᴸ ☕ ♀ ⚑ 🏌 ⚒
Location	6m N of city centre off A 34

Hotel	★★★ 67% Posthouse Birmingham Great Barr, Chapel Ln, Great Barr, BIRMINGHAM
	☎ 0870 400 9009 192 ⇆ ᴿ

Handsworth 11 Sunningdale Close, Handsworth Wood
B20 1NP ☎ 0121 554 0599 & 554 3387 Fax 0121 554 3387
Undulating parkland course with some tight fairways but subject to wind.
18 holes, 6267yds, Par 70, SSS 70, Course record 65.
Club membership 800.

Visitors	restricted weekends, bank holidays & Xmas. Must contact in advance and have a handicap certificate.
Societies	must contact in advance.
Green Fees	not confirmed.
Prof	Lee Bashford
Facilities	⊗ ⅲ ᴸ ☕ ♀ ⚑ ⚒
& Leisure	squash.
Location	3.5m NW of city centre off A4040

Hotel	★★★ 67% Birmingham/West Bromwich Moat House, Birmingham Rd, WEST BROMWICH
	☎ 0121 609 9988 168 ⇆ ᴿ

Harborne 40 Tennal Rd, Harborne B32 2JE
☎ 0121 427 3058
Parkland course in hilly situation, with brook running through.
18 holes, 6230yds, Par 70, SSS 70, Course record 65.
Club membership 655.

▶

Visitors must have handicap certificate, contact in advance, may not play weekends except with member, Ladies have priority Tue.
Societies Mon, Wed-Fri apply to secretary, by phone or letter.
Green Fees £35 per day; £30 per round.
Prof Alan Quarterman
Designer Harry Colt
Facilities ⊗ ⵝ ⬛ 💺 ♀ ⌂ ⛴ ⚷
Location 3.5 m SW of city centre off A4040

Hotel ★★★ 64% Plough & Harrow, 135 Hagley Rd, EDGBASTON
☎ 0121 454 4111 44 ⇄ 🐾

Harborne Church Farm Vicarage Rd, Harborne B17 0SN
☎ 0121 427 1204 Fax 0121 428 3126
Parkland course with water hazards and easy walking. Some holes might prove difficult.
9 holes, 4882yds, Par 66, SSS 64, Course record 62.
Club membership 200.
Visitors must contact in advance.
Societies must telephone in advance.
Green Fees contact for details.
Cards ▨ ▨ ▨ ▨ ▨ ▨
Prof Paul Johnson
Facilities ⊗ ⵝ ⬛ 💺 ⛴ ⌂ ⛴ ⚷
Location 3.5m SW of city centre off A4040

Hotel ★★★ 64% Plough & Harrow, 135 Hagley Rd, EDGBASTON
☎ 0121 454 4111 44 ⇄ 🐾

Hatchford Brook Coventry Rd, Sheldon B26 3PY
☎ 0121 743 9821 Fax 0121 743 3420
Fairly flat, municipal parkland course.
18 holes, 6155yds, Par 69, SSS 69.
Club membership 450.
Visitors are restricted early Sat & Sun.
Societies must contact in advance.
Green Fees £9 per round (£10 weekends).
Prof Mark Hampton
Facilities ⊗ ⬛ 💺 ⛴ ⌂ ⛴ ⚷
Location 6m E of city centre on A45

Hotel ★★★ 65% Posthouse Birmingham Airport, Coventry Rd, BIRMINGHAM
☎ 0870 400 9007 141 ⇄ 🐾

Hilltop Park Ln, Handsworth B21 8LJ
☎ 0121 554 4463
A good test of golf with interesting layout, undulating fairways and large greens, located in the Sandwell Valley conservation area.
18 holes, 6208yds, Par 71, SSS 70.
Club membership 400.
Visitors no restrictions but booking necessary.
Societies Mon-Fri, telephone Professional in advance.
Green Fees £9 per 18 holes; (£10 weekends).
Prof Kevin Highfield
Designer Hawtree
Facilities ⊗ ⵝ ⬛ 💺 ⛴ ⌂ ⛴ ⚷
Location On A41, 1m from junct 1 M5

Hotel ★★★ 67% Birmingham/West Bromwich Moat House, Birmingham Rd, WEST BROMWICH
☎ 0121 609 9988 168 ⇄ 🐾

Lickey Hills Rosehill, Rednal B45 8RR
☎ 0121 453 3159 Fax 0121 457 8779
Hilly municipal course overlooking the city.
18 holes, 5835yds, Par 68, SSS 68.
Club membership 300.
Visitors may not play between 9 & 10.30am weekends.
Societies must contact in advance.
Green Fees not confirmed.
Prof Joe Kelly
Facilities ⛴ ⌂ ⛴
& Leisure tennis courts.
Location 10m SW of city centre on B4096

Hotel ★★ 70% Norwood Hotel, 87-89 Bunbury Rd, Northfield, BIRMINGHAM
☎ 0121 411 2202 18 ⇄ 🐾

Moseley Springfield Rd, Kings Heath B14 7DX
☎ 0121 444 2115 Fax 0121 441 4662
Parkland course with a lake, pond and stream to provide natural hazards. The par-3, 4th goes through a cutting in woodland to a tree and garden-lined amphitheatre, and the par-4, 5th entails a drive over a lake to a dog-leg fairway.
18 holes, 6323yds, Par 70, SSS 70, Course record 64.
Club membership 600.
Visitors may only play by prior arrangement, weekdays excluding bank holidays.
Societies by prior arrangement.
Green Fees £37 per day.
Prof Gary Edge
Facilities ⊗ ⵝ ⬛ 💺 ♀ ⛴ ⌂ ⚷
Location 4m S of city centre on B4146 off A435

Hotel ★★ 70% Norwood Hotel, 87-89 Bunbury Rd, Northfield, BIRMINGHAM
☎ 0121 411 2202 18 ⇄ 🐾

North Worcestershire Frankley Beeches Rd, Northfield B31 5LP ☎ 0121 475 1047 Fax 0121 476 8681
Designed by James Braid and established in 1907, this is a mature parkland course. Tree plantations rather than heavy rough are the main hazards.
18 holes, 5959yds, Par 69, SSS 68, Course record 64.
Club membership 600.
Visitors by prior arrangement with professional. Must play with member at weekends. All visitors must have an official CONGU handicap.
Societies apply in advance in writing or by telephone to the professional tel: 0121 475 5721.
Green Fees not confirmed.
Prof Finley Clarke
Designer James Braid
Facilities ⛴ ⌂ ⛴ ⚷
Location 7m SW of Birmingham city centre, off A38

Hotel ★★ 70% Norwood Hotel, 87-89 Bunbury Rd, Northfield, BIRMINGHAM ☎ 0121 411 2202 18 ⇄ 🐾

Warley Woods The Pavilion, Lightswood Hill, Warley B67 5ED ☎ 0121 429 2440 Fax 0121 434 4430
Municipal parkland course in Warley Woods. New out of bounds areas and bunkers have tightened the course considerably with further improvement following tree planting.
9 holes, 5346yds, Par 68, SSS 66, Course record 64.
Club membership 200.

▶

Visitors must contact in advance. Linc card system for easier booking.
Societies booking advised, times very limited for large parties.
Green Fees £10 per round.
Cards ▭ ▭
Prof David Owen
Facilities ⊗ ⊞ ╠ ■ ♥ ⚑ ♞ ⚒
Location 4m W of city centre off A456

Hotel ★★★ 64% Plough & Harrow, 135 Hagley Rd, EDGBASTON ☎ 0121 454 4111 44 ⇆ ⋔

COVENTRY   Map 04 SP37

Ansty Golf Centre Brinklow Rd, Ansty CV7 9JH
☎ 024 76621341 Fax 024 76602671
18-hole Pay and Play course of two 9-hole loops. Membership competitions for handicaps. Driving range and putting green.
18 holes, 6079yds, Par 71, SSS 68, Course record 66.
Club membership 400.
Visitors no restrictions.
Societies welcome, telephone in advance.
Green Fees weekdays: £9 per 18 holes; £5 per 9 holes.
Cards ▭ ▭ ▭
Prof Craig Philips
Designer David Morgan
Facilities ⊗ ╠ ■ ♥ ⚑ ⚒ ♞ ⚒ ⚒
Location 3m from city centre via A4600

Hotel ★★★ 62% Novotel, Wilsons Ln, COVENTRY ☎ 024 76365000 98 ⇆ ⋔

Coventry St Martins Rd, Finham Park CV3 6RJ
☎ 024 76414152 Fax 024 76690131
The scene of several major professional events, this undulating parkland course has a great deal of quality. More than that, it usually plays its length, and thus scoring is never easy, as many professionals have found to their cost.
18 holes, 6601yds, Par 73, SSS 73, Course record 66.
Club membership 500.
Visitors must contact in advance. May not play at weekends and bank holidays.
Societies must apply in writing/telephone.
Green Fees £35 per day.
Cards ▭ ▭
Prof Philip Weaver
Designer Vardon Bros/Hawtree
Facilities ⊗ ⊞ ╠ ■ ♥ ⚑ ⚒
Location 3m S of city centre on B4133, 2m from jct of A45/A46

Hotel ★★★ 69% Hylands Hotel, Warwick Rd, COVENTRY ☎ 024 76501600 61 ⇆ ⋔

Coventry Hearsall Beechwood Av CV5 6DF
☎ 024 76713470 Fax 024 76691534
Parkland course with fairly easy walking. A brook provides an interesting hazard.
18 holes, 6005yds, Par 70, SSS 69.
Club membership 650.
Visitors with member only at weekends.
Societies apply in writing to secretary.
Green Fees £25 per day.

Prof Mike Tarn
Facilities ⊗ ⊞ ╠ ■ ♥ ⚑ ⚒ ♞ ⚒
Location 1.5m SW of city centre off A429

Hotel ★★★ 69% Hylands Hotel, Warwick Rd, COVENTRY ☎ 024 76501600 61 ⇆ ⋔

Windmill Village Hotel Golf & Leisure Club
Birmingham Rd, Allesley CV5 9AL
☎ 024 76404040 Fax 024 76404042
An attractive 18-hole course over rolling parkland with plenty of trees and two lakes that demand shots over open water. Four challenging Par 5 holes. Good leisure facilities.
18 holes, 5213yds, Par 70, SSS 67, Course record 66.
Club membership 600.
Visitors must contact in advance. Pre-payment required at peak times. May not play weekends 7-10am.
Societies telephone for booking form.
Green Fees not confirmed.
Cards ▭ ▭ ▭ ▭ ▭
Prof Robert Hunter
Designer Robert Hunter
Facilities ⊗ ⊞ ╠ ■ ♥ ⚑ ⚒ ⚑ ♞ ⚒ ⚒
& Leisure hard tennis courts, heated indoor swimming pool, fishing, sauna, solarium, gymnasium, beauty suite.
Location On A45 W of Coventry

Hotel ★★★ 73% Brooklands Grange Hotel & Restaurant, Holyhead Rd, COVENTRY ☎ 024 76601601 30 ⇆ ⋔

DUDLEY   Map 07 SO99

Dudley Turner's Hill, Rowley Regis, Warley B65 9DP
☎ 01384 233877 Fax 01384 233877
Fairly hilly parkland course.
18 holes, 5714yds, Par 69, SSS 68.
Club membership 550.
Visitors must contact in advance, may not play at weekends.
Societies must contact in advance.
Green Fees £25 per round/day.
Cards ▭ ▭ ▭
Prof Paul Taylor
Facilities ⊗ ⊞ ╠ ■ ♥ ⚑ ⚒
Location 2m S of town centre off B4171

Hotel ★★★ 63% Himley Country Hotel, School Rd, HIMLEY ☎ 01902 896716 73 ⇆ ⋔

Swindon Bridgnorth Rd, Swindon DY3 4PU
☎ 01902 897031 & 895226 Fax 01902 326219
Attractive undulating woodland/parkland course, with spectacular views.
Old Course: 18 holes, 6091yds, Par 71, SSS 69.
New Course: 9 holes, 1135yds, Par 27.
Club membership 700.
Visitors must contact in advance.
Societies must apply in writing.
Green Fees £18 per round (£27 weekends & bank holidays).
Prof Phil Lester
Facilities ⊗ ⊞ ╠ ■ ♥ ⚑ ⚒ ♞ ⚒ ⚒
& Leisure fishing.
Location On B4176, 3m from A449 at Himley

Hotel ★★★ 63% Himley Country Hotel, School Rd, HIMLEY ☎ 01902 896716 73 ⇆ ⋔

HALESOWEN   Map 07 SO98

Corngreaves Hall Corngreaves Rd B64 7NL
☎ 01384 567880
Mature course offering a good challenge to the best golfers with American specification greens and most holes holding a testing start. Magnificent views of the Clent Hills.
9 holes, 2800.
Visitors	at anytime by prior arrangement.
Societies	apply in writing in advance.
Green Fees	not confirmed.
Prof	S Joyce/C Yates
Facilities	⊗ 💺 ☂ ⚶
Hotel	★★ 64% Cedars Hotel, Mason Rd, KIDDERMINSTER ☎ 01562 515595 21 ⇄ ↾

Halesowen The Leasowes, Leasowes Ln B62 8QF
☎ 0121 501 3606 Fax 0121 501 3606
Parkland course in convenient position within the only Grade 1 listed park in the Midlands.
18 holes, 5754yds, Par 69, SSS 69, Course record 66.
Club membership 625.
Visitors	welcome weekdays, may only play weekends or bank holidays with member unless previously agreed.
Societies	must apply in writing.
Green Fees	£30 per day; £25 per round.
Prof	Jon Nicholas
Facilities	⊗ ℳ 🛅 💺 ♀ ⚲ 🏠 ☂ ⚶
Location	1m E junct 3 M5, Leasowes Lane off Manor Lane
Hotel	★★ 64% Cedars Hotel, Mason Rd, KIDDERMINSTER ☎ 01562 515595 21 ⇄ ↾

KNOWLE   Map 07 SP17

Copt Heath 1220 Warwick Rd B93 9LN
☎ 01564 772650 Fax 01564 771022
Flat parkland course designed by H. Vardon.
18 holes, 6517yds, Par 71, SSS 71, Course record 64.
Club membership 700.
Visitors	must contact in advance and possess official handicap certificate. May not play weekends & bank holidays.
Societies	must contact in advance.
Green Fees	£40 per day/round.
Prof	Brian J Barton
Designer	H Vardon
Facilities	⊗ ℳ 🛅 💺 ♀ ⚲ 🏠 ⚑ 🚃 ⚶ ↾
Location	On A4141, 0.50m S of junct 5 of M42
Hotel	★★★★ 64% Swallow St John's Hotel, 651 Warwick Rd, SOLIHULL ☎ 0121 711 3000 178 ⇄ ↾

MERIDEN   Map 04 SP28

MARRIOTT FOREST OF ARDEN HOTEL & COUNTRY CLUB See page 269.

North Warwickshire Hampton Ln CV7 7LL
☎ 01676 522259 Fax 01676 522915
Parkland course with easy walking.
9 holes, 6390yds, Par 72, SSS 71, Course record 65.
Club membership 425.
Visitors	must contact in advance. Must play with member at weekends.
Societies	must apply in writing to secretary.
Green Fees	£18 per round.
Prof	Andrew Bownes
Facilities	⊗ by prior arrangement 🛅 ♀ ⚲ 🏠 ⚶
Location	1m SW on B4102
Hotel	★★★ 74% Manor Hotel, Main Rd, MERIDEN ☎ 01676 522735 114 ⇄ ↾

Stonebridge Golf Centre Somers Rd CV7 7PL
☎ 01676 522442 Fax 01676 522447
The course is set in the beautiful landscape of the Packington estate, with mature shrubs and trees. Water features are incorporated to provide an excellent variety for a wide range of golfing abilities.
18 holes, 6240yds, Par 70, SSS 70, Course record 70.
Club membership 360.
Visitors	advisable to book in advance, booking up to 9 days in advance.
Societies	apply in writing or telephone in advance.
Green Fees	not confirmed.
Cards	🔲 🔲 🔲 🔲 🔲
Prof	Robert Grier
Designer	Mark Jones
Facilities	⊗ ℳ 🛅 💺 ♀ ⚲ 🏠 ⚑ 🚣 🚃 ⚶ ↾
& Leisure	fishing.
Hotel	★★★ 74% Manor Hotel, Main Rd, MERIDEN ☎ 01676 522735 114 ⇄ ↾

SEDGLEY   Map 07 SO99

Sedgley Golf Centre Sandyfields Rd DY3 3DL
☎ 01902 880503
Public Pay and Play course. Undulating contours and mature trees with extensive views over surrounding countryside.
9 holes, 3147yds, Par 72, SSS 70.
Club membership 150.
Visitors	booking advisable for weekends.
Societies	must contact in advance.
Green Fees	£7.50 per 18 holes; £5.50 per 9 holes (£8/£6 weekends & bank holidays).
Prof	Garry Mercer
Designer	W G Cox
Facilities	💺 ⚲ 🚣 🚃 ⚶ ↾
Location	0.5m from town centre off A463
Hotel	★★★ 63% Himley Country Hotel, School Rd, HIMLEY ☎ 01902 896716 73 ⇄ ↾

SOLIHULL   Map 07 SP17

Olton Mirfield Rd B91 1JH
☎ 0121 704 1936 & 0121 705 1083 Fax 0121 711 2010
Parkland course with prevailing southwest wind.
18 holes, 6265yds, Par 69, SSS 71, Course record 63.
Club membership 600.
Visitors	must contact in advance. No visitors at weekend.
Societies	apply in writing.
Green Fees	not confirmed.

▶

Marriott Forest of Arden

Meriden, *Warwickshire* ☎ 01676 522335 Fax 01676 523711 Map 04 SP28

Visitors ring to book in advance

Societies by arrangement

Green Fees Arden Course £50 per round (£60 weekends); Aylesford £35 per round (£40 weekends) — ▨▨ ▨▨ ▨ ▨
▨ ▨

Facilities ⊗ ⑩ 🍴 🍺 ♀ ⚒
🛄 🏌 🏌 🏌 ✦ 🏌 Professional (Kim Thomas)

Leisure tennis, swimming, fishing, sauna, solarium, gymnasium

Location Maxstoke Lane, Meriden CV7 7HR (1m SW of Meriden on B4102)

Holes/Par/Course record Arden Course: 18 holes, 6718 yds, Par 72, SSS 73, Course record 62
Aylesford Course: 18 holes, 6525 yds, Par 71, SSS 72

WHERE TO STAY AND EAT NEARBY

Hotels
MERIDEN

★★★★ ✿ 71% Marriott Forest of Arden Hotel & Country Club, Maxstoke Ln. ☎ 01676 522335. 214 ⇆ 🐾

★★★ ✿ ✿ 74% Manor Hotel, Main Rd. ☎ 01676 522735. 114 ⇆ 🐾

This is one of the finest golf destinations in the UK, with a range of facilities to impress every golfer. The jewel in the crown is the Arden course, one of the country's most spectacular challenges and host to a succession of international tournaments, including the British Masters and English Open.

The shorter Aylesford course offers a varied and enjoyable challenge which golfers of all abilities will find rewarding. Golf events are a speciality and there is a Golf Academy as well as extensive leisure facilities.

Championship Course

269

Prof	Mark Daubney
Designer	J H Taylor
Facilities	⊗ ⑂ ᵇ 🏌 ♀ ♨ 🍴 ⛳ ⚲
Location	Exit M42 junct 5 and take A41 for 1.5m

Hotel	★★★★ 64% Swallow St John's Hotel, 651 Warwick Rd, SOLIHULL ☎ 0121 711 3000 178 ⇥ 🐾

Robin Hood St Bernards Rd B92 7DJ
☎ 0121 706 0061 Fax 0121 706 0061
Pleasant parkland course with easy walking and open to good views.Tree lined fairways and varied holes, culminating in two excellent finishing holes. Modern clubhouse.
18 holes, 6635yds, Par 72, SSS 72, Course record 68.
Club membership 650.

Visitors	must contact in advance. With member only at weekends.
Societies	must contact in advance.
Green Fees	£35 per day; £29 per round.
Prof	Alan Harvey
Designer	H S Colt
Facilities	⊗ ⑂ ᵇ 🏌 ♀ ♨ 🍴 ⛳ ⚲
Location	2m W off B4025

Hotel	★★★★ 64% Swallow St John's Hotel, 651 Warwick Rd, SOLIHULL ☎ 0121 711 3000 178 ⇥ 🐾

Shirley Stratford Rd, Monkpath, Shirley B90 4EW
☎ 0121 744 6001 Fax 0121 745 8220
Fairly flat parkland course.
18 holes, 6510yds, Par 72, SSS 71.
Club membership 600.

Visitors	may not play bank holidays & with member only at weekends. Handicap certificate is required.
Societies	only on Thu, must contact in advance.
Green Fees	£25 per round.
Prof	S Bottrill
Facilities	⊗ ⑂ ᵇ 🏌 ♀ ♨ 🍴 ⚲
Location	3m SW off A34

Hotel	★★★ 66% Regency Hotel, Stratford Rd, Shirley, SOLIHULL ☎ 0121 745 6119 112 ⇥ 🐾

STOURBRIDGE   Map 07 SO98

Hagley Golf & Country Club Wassell Grove,
Hagley DY9 9JW ☎ 01562 883701 Fax 01562 887518
Undulating parkland course set beneath the Clent Hills; there are superb views. Testing 15th, par 5, 557 yards.
18 holes, 6353yds, Par 72, SSS 72, Course record 66.
Club membership 700.

Visitors	welcome weekdays but restricted Wed (Ladies Day) & with member only at weekends.
Societies	Mon-Fri only, must apply in writing.
Green Fees	£25 per day; £20 per round.
Prof	Iain Clark
Designer	Garratt & Co
Facilities	⊗ ⑂ ᵇ 🏌 ♀ ♨ 🍴 ⚲
& Leisure	squash.
Location	1m E of Hagley off A456. 2m from junct 3 on M5

Hotel	★★ 64% Cedars Hotel, Mason Rd, KIDDERMINSTER ☎ 01562 515595 21 ⇥ 🐾

Stourbridge Worcester Ln, Pedmore DY8 2RB
☎ 01384 395566 Fax 01384 444660
Parkland course.
18 holes, 6231yds, Par 70, SSS 69, Course record 67.
Club membership 857.

Visitors	contact secretary, no casual visitors weekends. Ladies day Wednesday.
Societies	must apply in writing.
Green Fees	£35 per day; £28 per round.
Prof	M Male
Facilities	⊗ ⑂ ᵇ 🏌 ♀ ♨ 🍴 ⚲
Location	2m from town centre

Hotel	★★ 64% Cedars Hotel, Mason Rd, KIDDERMINSTER ☎ 01562 515595 21 ⇥ 🐾

SUTTON COLDFIELD   Map 07 SP19

SUTTON COLDFIELD See page 271.

Boldmere Monmouth Dr B73 6JL
☎ 0121 354 3379 Fax 0121 355 4534
Established municipal course with 10 par 3s and a lake coming into play on the 16th and 18th holes.
18 holes, 4493yds, Par 63, SSS 62, Course record 57.
Club membership 300.

Visitors	must contact in advance.
Societies	midweek only, apply in writing.
Green Fees	not confirmed.
Prof	Trevor Short
Facilities	⊗ ᵇ 🏌 ♀ ♨ 🍴 ⚲
Location	Adjacent to Sutton Park

Hotel	★★★ 72% Moor Hall Hotel, Moor Hall Dr, Four Oaks, SUTTON COLDFIELD ☎ 0121 308 3751 75 ⇥ 🐾

Little Aston Streetly B74 3AN
☎ 0121 353 2942 Fax 0121 353 2942
Parkland course.
18 holes, 6670yds, Par 72, SSS 73, Course record 64.
Club membership 350.

Visitors	must contact in advance & may not play at weekends.
Societies	must apply in writing.
Green Fees	not confirmed.
Prof	John Anderson
Designer	H Vardon
Facilities	⊗ ⑂ 🏌 ♀ ♨ 🍴 ⚲
Location	3.5m NW of Sutton Coldfield off A454

Hotel	★★★ 72% Moor Hall Hotel, Moor Hall Dr, Four Oaks, SUTTON COLDFIELD ☎ 0121 308 3751 75 ⇥ 🐾

Moor Hall Moor Hall Dr B75 6LN
☎ 0121 308 6130 Fax 0121 308 6130
Parkland course. The 14th is a notable hole.
18 holes, 6249yds, Par 70, SSS 70.
Club membership 600.

Visitors	must contact in advance. With member only weekends & bank holidays.
Societies	must apply in writing.
Green Fees	£40 per day; £30 per round.

▶

The Belfry

Wishaw, *North Warwickshire* ☎ 01675 470301 Fax 01675 470178 Map 07 SP19

e-mail: enquiries@thebelfry.com

Visitors Handicap certificate is required for the Brabazon & PGA courses; 24 or better gentlemen, 32 or better ladies & juniors. Reservations 24 hrs in advance for non residents

Societies must telephone in advance

Green Fees Brabazon £90 per round, PGA £60, Derby £30 — ▭ ▭ ▭ ▭ ▭ ▭

Facilities ⊗ ⅏ ⌸ ♥ ♀ ⚲ 🏠 ⚐ ⤚ ⚐ ⚐ Professional (P. McGovern)

Leisure tennis, squash, swimming, sauna, solarium, gymnasium

Location Sutton Coldfield B76 9PR (exit junc 9 M42, 4m E)

Holes/Par/Course record Brabazon: 18 holes, 6724 yds, Par 72, SSS 71
Derby: 18 holes, 6009 yds, Par 69, SSS 69
PGA: 18 holes, 6639 yds, Par 71, SSS 70

WHERE TO STAY NEARBY

Hotels
WISHAW

★★★★@ @ 74% The Belfry, Lichfield Rd. ☎ 01675 470301. 324 ⇆ ↾

LEA MARSTON

★★★71% Lea Marston Hotel and Leisure Complex, Haunch Lane.
☎ 01675 470468. 83 (81 ⇆ ↾ 2 ↾)

SUTTON COLDFIELD

★★★★@ @ ≜≜ New Hall, Walmley Rd. ☎ 0121 378 2442. 60 ⇆ ↾

★★★64% Quality Hotel Sutton Court, 60-66 Lichfield Rd. ☎ 0870 6011160. 56 (49 ⇆ ↾ 7 ↾) Annexe 8 ↾

The Belfry is unique as the only venue to have staged the biggest golf event in the world, The Ryder Cup Matches, an unprecedented 3 times, with a 4th returning in 2001. The Brabazon is regarded throughout the world as a great championship course with some of the most demanding holes in golf; world famous holes like the 10th (Ballesteros' s Hole) and the 18th with its dangerous lakes and its amphitheatre around the final green. These remained intact during the £2.4million redevelopment in 1998 which made the course even more testing.

Alternatively, you can pit your wits against a new legend in the making, The PGA National Course, which has won plaudits from near and far. The Dave Thomas designed course has been used for professional competition and is already established as one of Britain's leading courses. For those who like their golf a little easier or like to get back into the swing gently, The Derby is ideal and can be played by golfers of any standard.

The Bel Air night club, The De Vere Club leisure centre and The Aqua Spa with its fire and ice bio-thermal treatments offer unique experiences away from the golf course.

Championship Course

Cards ⬜ ⬜
Prof Alan Partridge
Facilities ⊗ ⏵ ⓛ 🍺 ♀ ♨ 🛍 ⛳ ⚴
Location 2.5m N of town centre off A453

Hotel ★★★ 72% Moor Hall Hotel, Moor Hall Dr, Four Oaks, SUTTON COLDFIELD
☎ 0121 308 3751 75 ⇋ ⧉

Pype Hayes Eachel Hurst Rd, Walmley B76 1EP
☎ 0121 351 1014 Fax 0121 313 0206
Attractive, fairly flat course with excellent greens.
18 holes, 5927yds, Par 71, SSS 69.
Club membership 400.
Visitors phone professional in advance.
Societies contact professional in advance.
Green Fees £8.50.
Cards ⬜ ⬜ 🗓
Prof James Bayliss
Designer Bobby Jones
Facilities ⊗ ⏵ ⓛ 🍺 🛍 ⛳ ⚴
Location 2.5m S off B4148

Hotel ★★★ 65% Marston Farm Hotel, Bodymoor Heath, SUTTON COLDFIELD
☎ 01827 872133 37 ⇋ ⧉

Sutton Coldfield 110 Thornhill Rd, Streetly B74 3ER
☎ 0121 353 9633 Fax 0121 353 5503
A fine natural, all-weather, heathland course, with tight fairways, gorse, heather and trees. A good challenge for all standards of golfer.
18 holes, 6541yds, Par 72, SSS 71, Course record 65.
Club membership 600.
Visitors must contact in advance. Restricted at weekends and bank holidays.
Societies must apply in writing.
Green Fees not confirmed.
Prof Jerry Hayes
Designer D McKenzie
Facilities ⊗ ⏵ ⓛ 🍺 ♀ ♨ 🛍 ⚴
Location 3m NW on B4138

Hotel ★★★ 72% Moor Hall Hotel, Moor Hall Dr, Four Oaks, SUTTON COLDFIELD
☎ 0121 308 3751 75 ⇋ ⧉

Walmley Brooks Rd, Wylde Green B72 1HR
☎ 0121 373 0029 & 377 7272 Fax 0121 377 7272
Pleasant parkland course with many trees. The hazards are not difficult.
18 holes, 6585yds, Par 72, SSS 72, Course record 67.
Club membership 650.
Visitors must contact in advance. Weekends may only play as guest of member.
Societies must contact in advance.
Green Fees £35 per day; £30 per round.
Prof C J Wicketts
Facilities ⓛ 🍺 ♀ ♨ 🛍 ⛳ ⚴
Location 2m S off A5127

Hotel ★★★ 65% Marston Farm Hotel, Bodymoor Heath, SUTTON COLDFIELD
☎ 01827 872133 37 ⇋ ⧉

WALSALL Map 07 SP09

Bloxwich Stafford Rd, Bloxwich WS3 3PQ
☎ 01922 476593 Fax 01922 493449
Undulating parkland course with natural hazards and subject to strong north wind.
18 holes, 6273yds, Par 71, SSS 71, Course record 68.
Club membership 625.
Visitors may not play at weekends.
Societies must contact in advance.
Green Fees £30 per day; £25 per round.
Prof Richard J Dance
Facilities ⊗ ⏵ ⓛ 🍺 ♀ ♨ 🛍 ⚴
Location 3m N of town centre on A34

Hotel ★★★ 75% The Fairlawns at Aldridge, 178 Little Aston Rd, Aldridge, WALSALL
☎ 01922 455122 46 ⇋ ⧉

Calderfields Aldridge Rd WS4 2JS
☎ 01922 640540 Fax 01922 638787
Parkland course with lake.
18 holes, 6509yds, Par 73, SSS 71.
Club membership 526.
Visitors no restrictions.
Societies telephone 01922 632243 in advance.
Green Fees £18 per round.
Cards ⬜ ⬜ ⬜ 🗓
Prof David Williams
Designer Roy Winter
Facilities ⊗ ⏵ ⓛ 🍺 ♀ ♨ 🛍 ⛳ ⚓ 🚣 ⚴ ⚑
& Leisure fishing.
Location On A454

Hotel ★★★ 75% The Fairlawns at Aldridge, 178 Little Aston Rd, Aldridge, WALSALL
☎ 01922 455122 46 ⇋ ⧉

Walsall The Broadway WS1 3EY
☎ 01922 613512 Fax 01922 616460
Well-wooded parkland course with easy walking.
18 holes, 6300yds, Par 70, SSS 70, Course record 65.
Club membership 600.
Visitors must contact in advance. May not play weekends & bank holidays.
Societies must apply in writing.
Green Fees not confirmed.
Prof Richard Lambert
Designer McKenzie
Facilities ⊗ ⓛ 🍺 ♀ ♨ 🛍 ⚴
Location 1m S of town centre off A34

Hotel ★★★ 60% The Boundary Hotel, Birmingham Rd, WALSALL
☎ 01922 633555 94 ⇋ ⧉

WEST BROMWICH Map 07 SP09

Dartmouth Vale St B71 4DW
☎ 0121 588 2131 Fax 0121 588 2131
Meadowland course with undulating but easy walking. The 617 yd (par 5) first hole is something of a challenge.
9 holes, 6060yds, Par 71, SSS 71, Course record 66.
Club membership 350.
Visitors with member only at weekends. May not play bank holidays or medal weekends.
Societies must apply in writing/telephone.

▶

Green Fees not confirmed.
Prof Guy Dean
Facilities
Location E side of town centre off A4041

Hotel ★★★ 67% Birmingham/West Bromwich Moat House, Birmingham Rd, WEST BROMWICH
0121 609 9988 168

Sandwell Park Birmingham Rd B71 4JJ
0121 553 4637 Fax 0121 525 1651
Undulating wooded heathland course situated in the Sandwell Valley.
18 holes, 6468yds, Par 71, SSS 73, Course record 65.
Club membership 550.

Visitors must contact in advance. May not play at weekends.
Societies must contact in advance.
Green Fees £36 per 36 holes; £31 per 18 holes.
Prof Nigel Wylie
Designer H S Colt
Facilities
& Leisure practice chipping area/green.
Location On A41, 200yds from juct 1 of the M5

Hotel ★★★ 67% Birmingham/West Bromwich Moat House, Birmingham Rd, WEST BROMWICH
0121 609 9988 168

WOLVERHAMPTON Map 07 SO99

Oxley Park Stafford Rd, Bushbury WV10 6DE
01902 425892 Fax 01902 712241
Rolling parkland course with trees, bunkers and water hazards.
18 holes, 6226yds, Par 71, SSS 70, Course record 68.
Club membership 550.
Visitors must contact in advance.
Societies must contact in advance.
Green Fees £29 per day; £25 per round.
Prof Les Burlison
Designer H S Colt
Facilities
& Leisure snooker.
Location N of town centre off A449

Hotel ★★ 69% Ely House Hotel, 53 Tettenhall Rd, WOLVERHAMPTON
01902 311311 18

Penn Penn Common, Penn WV4 5JN 01902 341142
Heathland course just outside the town.
18 holes, 6462yds, Par 70, SSS 71, Course record 68.
Club membership 650.
Visitors must play with member at weekends.
Societies must contact in advance.
Green Fees £25 per day; £20 per round.
Prof A Briscoe
Facilities
Location SW side of town centre off A449

Hotel ★★★ 65% Quality Hotel Wolverhampton, Penn Rd, WOLVERHAMPTON
01902 429216 66 Annexe 26

South Staffordshire Danescourt Rd, Tettenhall WV6 9BQ
01902 751065 Fax 01902 741753
A parkland course.
18 holes, 6513yds, Par 71, SSS 71, Course record 67.
Club membership 500.
Visitors must contact in advance but may not play weekends & before 2pm Tue.
Societies must apply in writing.
Green Fees £40 per day; £34 per round.
Prof Mark Sparrow
Designer Harry Vardon
Facilities
Location 3m NW off A41

Hotel ★★ 69% Ely House Hotel, 53 Tettenhall Rd, WOLVERHAMPTON
01902 311311 18

Three Hammers Short Course Old Stafford Rd, Coven WV10 7PP 01902 790940
Well maintained short course designed by Henry Cotton and providing a unique challenge to golfers of all standards.
18 holes, 1438yds, Par 54, SSS 54, Course record 43.
Visitors no restrictions.
Societies contact for details.
Green Fees not confirmed.
Designer Henry Cotton
Facilities
Location On A449 N of junct 2 M54

Hotel ★★★ 63% Roman Way Hotel, Watling St, Hatherton, CANNOCK
01543 572121 56

Wergs Keepers Ln, Tettenhall WV6 8UA
01902 742225 Fax 01902 744748
Open parkland course with gently undulating fairways.
18 holes, 6949yds, Par 72, SSS 73.
Club membership 250.
Visitors are advised to contact in advance.
Societies must contact in advance.
Green Fees £15 per day; (£19 per round weekends & bank holidays).
Cards
Designer C W Moseley
Facilities by prior arrangement
Location From Wolverhampton take A41 towards Newport for 2.5m then R for 0.5m then R again

Hotel ★★ 69% Ely House Hotel, 53 Tettenhall Rd, WOLVERHAMPTON
01902 311311 18

COWES   Map 04 SZ49

Cowes Crossfield Av PO31 8HN
☎ 01983 292303 (secretary)
Fairly level, tight parkland course with difficult par 3s and
Solent views.
9 holes, 5934yds, Par 70, SSS 68, Course record 66.
Club membership 300.
Visitors   restricted Thu & Sun mornings.
Societies   Mon-Wed, must contact in advance.
Green Fees £15 per day (£18 weekends).
Designer   Hamilton-Stutt
Facilities ⊗ ℳ by prior arrangement ⬛ 💺 ♀ ⚲ ⛳ ⌀
Location   NW side of town, next to Cows High School

Hotel   ★★★ 66% New Holmwood Hotel,
                Queens Rd, Egypt Point, COWES
                ☎ 01983 292508 25 ⇄ 🐾

EAST COWES   Map 04 SZ59

Osborne Osborne House Estate PO32 6JX
☎ 01983 295421
Undulating parkland course in the grounds of Osborne
House. Quiet and peaceful situation.
9 holes, 6418yds, Par 70, SSS 70, Course record 71.
Club membership 450.
Visitors   may not play Tue before 1pm, weekends before
                noon & bank holidays before 11am.
Societies   telephone initially.
Green Fees £18 per day (£20 weekends & bank holidays).
Facilities ⊗ ℳ ⬛ 💺 ♀ ⚲ 🛍 ⛳ ⌀
Location   E side of town centre off A3021

Hotel   ★★★ 66% New Holmwood Hotel, Queens Rd,
                Egypt Point, COWES
                ☎ 01983 292508 25 ⇄ 🐾

FRESHWATER   Map 04 SZ38

Freshwater Bay Afton Down PO40 9TZ
☎ 01983 752955 Fax 01983 756704
A downland/seaside links with wide fairways and spectacular
coastal views of the Solent and Channel.
18 holes, 5725yds, Par 69, SSS 68.
Club membership 450.
Visitors   may play daily after 9.30 ex Thu & Sun (10.30).
Societies   apply to secretary.
Green Fees not confirmed.
Designer   J H Taylor
Facilities ⊗ ℳ ⬛ 💺 ♀ ⚲ ⛳ ⌀
Location   0.5m E of village off A3055

Hotel   ★★★ 66% Sentry Mead Hotel, Madeira Rd,
                TOTLAND BAY ☎ 01983 753212 14 ⇄ 🐾

NEWPORT   Map 04 SZ58

Newport St George's Down, Shide PO30 2JB
☎ 01983 525076
Downland course, fine views.
9 holes, 5710yds, Par 68, SSS 68.
Club membership 350.

Visitors   may not play Wed noon-3.30pm or before 3pm
                Sat & noon Sun.
Societies   contact Secretary in advance.
Green Fees £15 per round (£17 weekends & bank holidays).
Facilities ⬛ ♀ ⚲ 🛍 ⛳
Location   1.5m S off A3020

Hotel   ★★★ 66% New Holmwood Hotel, Queens Rd,
                Egypt Point, COWES
                ☎ 01983 292508 25 ⇄ 🐾

RYDE   Map 04 SZ59

Ryde Binstead Rd PO33 3NF
☎ 01983 614809 Fax 01983 567418
Downland course with wide views over the Solent.
9 holes, 5287yds, Par 66, SSS 66, Course record 65.
Club membership 500.
Visitors   may not play Wed afternoons, Sun mornings or
                before 10.30am Sat.
Societies   must contact in writing.
Green Fees £15 per day/round (£20 weekends & bank
                holidays).
Designer   Hamilton-Stutt
Facilities ⊗ ⬛ 💺 ♀ ⚲ 🛍 ⛳ ⌀
Location   1m W on A3054

Hotel   ★★ 70% Biskra Beach Hotel & Restaurant, 17
                Saint Thomas's St, RYDE
                ☎ 01983 567913 14 ⇄ 🐾

SANDOWN   Map 04 SZ58

Shanklin & Sandown The Fairway, Lake PO36 9PR
☎ 01983 403217 (office) & 404424 (pro) Fax 01983 40321
7 (office)/404424 (pro)
Heathland course with some hilly holes. Mostly sandy base
but some clay makes it generally playable all year.
18 holes, 6063yds, Par 70, SSS 69, Course record 64.
Club membership 640.
Visitors   must contact in advance & have handicap
                certificate. May not play before noon Sat or
                9.30am Sun.
Societies   apply in writing.
Green Fees £25 per day (£30 weekends & bank holidays).
Cards   💳 💳
Prof   Peter Hammond
Designer   Braid
Facilities ⊗ ℳ by prior arrangement ⬛ 💺 ♀ ⚲ 🛍 ⛳ ⌀
Location   From Sandown drive towards Shanklin past
                Heights Leisure Centre after 200yds R into
                Fairway for 1m

Hotel   ★★★ 62% Brunswick Hotel,
                Queens Rd, SHANKLIN
                ☎ 01983 863245 27 ⇄ 🐾 Annexe 5 ⇄ 🐾

VENTNOR   Map 04 SZ57

Ventnor Steephill Down Rd PO38 1BP
☎ 01983 853326
Downland course subject to wind. Fine seascapes.
12 holes, 5767yds, Par 70, SSS 68.
Club membership 297.
Visitors   may not play Fri noon-3pm or Sun mornings.
Societies   telephone initially.
Green Fees not confirmed.

Facilities ♨ 🍴 🏆 ⛳ ⛳ ⚐
Location 1m NW off B3327

Hotel ★★★★ 70% The Royal Hotel, Belgrave Rd,
VENTNOR ☎ 01983 852186 55 ⇔ ⁂

WILTSHIRE

BISHOPS CANNINGS Map 04 SU06

North Wilts SN10 2LP
☎ 01380 860627 Fax 01380 860877
High, downland course with fine views.
18 holes, 6322yds, Par 71, SSS 70, Course record 65.
Club membership 800.
Visitors welcome, a handicap certificate is required at weekends.
Societies must book in advance.
Green Fees £30 per day; £21 per round (£40/£24 weekends).
Cards ▭▭▭▭▭▭▭
Prof Graham Laing
Facilities ⊗ ⽶ ♨ 🍴 🏆 ⛳ 🏠 ⛳ ⚐ ⚑ ⚐
Location 2m NW

Hotel ★★★ 64% Bear Hotel, Market Place,
DEVIZES ☎ 01380 722444 24 ⇔ ⁂

CALNE Map 03 ST97

Bowood Golf & Country Club Derry Hill SN11 9PQ
☎ 01249 822228 Fax 01249 822218
Designed by Dave Thomas and set in a magnificent Grade I listed 'Capability Brown' park, this course provides a fine test for golfers and hosts the European Challenge Tour Championship. There are fine practice and teaching facilities and accommodation is available, along with conference facilities in the historic clubhouse.
18 holes, 6890yds, Par 72, SSS 73, Course record 63.
Club membership 500.

Visitors welcome except before noon on Sat and Sun. Advisable to book.
Societies booking by telephone.
Green Fees not confirmed.
Cards ▭▭▭▭▭▭▭
Prof Max Taylor
Designer Dave Thomas
Facilities ⊗ ⽶ by prior arrangement ♨ 🍴 🏆 ⛳ 🏠 ⛳ ⚐ ⚑ ⚐ ⚐
& Leisure Bowood House and Gardens.

Location M4 junct 17 off A4 between Chippenham & Calne

Hotel ★★ 68% Lansdowne Strand Hotel,
The Strand, CALNE
☎ 01249 812488 21 ⇔ ⁂ Annexe 5 ⇔ ⁂

CASTLE COMBE Map 03 ST87

Manor House SN14 7JW
☎ 01249 782982 Fax 01249 782992
Set in one of the finest locations in England, this 18-hole Peter Alliss/Clive Clark course was designed to marry neatly with the surrounding conservation area. Many mature trees have been used to great effect giving individuality and challenge to every shot. There are spectacular holes at the 17th & 18th with lakes and waterfalls making them memorable.
18 holes, 6286yds, Par 72, SSS 71.
Club membership 450.

Visitors must have a handicap certificate and must contact in advance.
Societies contact in advance.
Green Fees £40 per round (£50 weekends).
Cards ▭▭▭▭▭▭▭
Prof Chris Smith
Designer Peter Alliss/Clive Clark
Facilities ⊗ ⽶ ♨ 🍴 🏆 ⛳ 🏠 ⛳ ⚐ ⚑ ⚐ ⚐
& Leisure hard tennis courts, heated outdoor swimming pool, fishing, sauna, snooker.
Location On B4039, 5m NW of Chippenham

Hotel ★★★★ ♨♨ Manor House Hotel,
CASTLE COMBE
☎ 01249 782206 21 ⇔ ⁂ Annexe 24 ⇔ ⁂

CHAPMANSLADE Map 03 ST84

Thoulstone Park BA13 4AQ
☎ 01373 832825 Fax 01373 832821
A rolling parkland course with natural lakes and mature trees. Hole 7, stroke index 1 has a second shot over a large lake to the green so a straight drive is essential.
18 holes, 6161yds, Par 71, SSS 69.
Club membership 500.
Visitors restricted Sat & Sun mornings. Dress code applies.
Societies telephone in advance.
Green Fees not confirmed.
Prof Tony Isaac
Facilities ⊗ ♨ 🍴 🏆 ⛳ 🏠 ⛳ ⚐ ⚐ ⚐ ▶

Location On A36 between Bath/Warminster

Hotel ★★ 69% Woolpack Inn, BECKINGTON
☎ 01373 831244 12 ⇄ ▮

CHIPPENHAM Map 03 ST97

Chippenham Malmesbury Rd SN15 5LT
☎ 01249 652040 Fax 01249 446681
Easy walking on downland course. Testing holes at 1st and 15th.
18 holes, 5559yds, Par 69, SSS 67, Course record 64.
Club membership 650.
Visitors must contact in advance.
Societies must contact in writing.
Green Fees not confirmed.
Prof Bill Creamer
Facilities ⊗ ⫟ ⻑ ⻖ ⿕ ⒜ ⿋ ⛱ ⌀
Location M4 junct 17, 1m N of Chippenham beside A350

Hotel ★★★★🏖 Manor House Hotel,
CASTLE COMBE ☎ 01249 782206
21 ⇄ ▮ Annexe 24 ⇄ ▮

CRICKLADE Map 04 SU09

Cricklade Hotel & Country Club Common Hill SN6 6HA
☎ 01793 750751 Fax 01793 751767
A challenging 9-hole course with undulating greens and beautiful views. Par 3 6th (128yds) signature hole from an elevated tee to a green protected by a deep pot bunker.
9 holes, 1830yds, Par 62, SSS 57.
Club membership 170.
Visitors may not play weekends or bank holidays unless accompanied by a member. Must contact in advance.
Societies apply in writing.
Green Fees on application.
Cards ▭ ▬ ▬ ▧ ▨
Prof Ian Bolt
Designer Ian Bolt/Colin Smith
Facilities ⊗ ⫟ ⻑ ⻖ ⿕ ⒜ ⿋ ⛱ ⌀
& Leisure hard tennis courts, heated indoor swimming pool, solarium, gymnasium.
Location On the B4040 out of Cricklade, towards Malmesbury

Hotel ★★★ 67% Stanton House Hotel, The Avenue, Stanton Fitzwarren, SWINDON
☎ 01793 861777 86 ⇄ ▮

ERLESTOKE Map 03 ST95

Erlestoke Sands SN10 5UB
☎ 01380 831069 Fax 01380 831284
The course is set on the lower slopes of Salisbury Plain with distant views to the Cotswolds and Marlborough Downs. The 7th plunges from an elevated three-tiered tee, high in the woods, to a large green with a spectacular backdrop of a meandering river and hills. The course was built to suit every standard of golfer from the novice to the very low handicapper and its two tiers offer lakes and rolling downland.
18 holes, 6406yds, Par 73, SSS 71, Course record 69.
Club membership 706.

Visitors phone for tee booking in advance 01380 830300. Dress rules apply.
Societies must book in advance.
Green Fees £16 per 18 holes (£25 weekends & bank holidays).
Cards ▭ ▬ ▧ ▨
Prof Adrian Marsh
Designer Adrian Stiff
Facilities ⊗ ⫟ ⻑ ⻖ ⿕ ⒜ ⿋ ⛱ ⌀ ⌀
Location On B3098 Devizes/Westbury road

Hotel ★★★ 64% Bear Hotel, Market Place, DEVIZES ☎ 01380 722444 24 ⇄ ▮

GREAT DURNFORD Map 04 SU13

High Post SP4 6AT
☎ 01722 782356 Fax 01722 782674
An interesting downland course on Wiltshire chalk with good turf and splendid views over the southern area of Salisbury Plain. The par 3, 17th and the two-shot 18th require good judgement.
18 holes, 6305yds, Par 70, SSS 70, Course record 64.
Club membership 580.
Visitors a handicap certificate is required at weekends & bank holidays. Telephone professional in advance 01722 782219.
Societies apply by telephone to manager.
Green Fees not confirmed.
Prof Ian Welding
Facilities ⊗ ⫟ ⻑ ⻖ ⿕ ⒜ ⌀ ⌀
Location 1.75m SE on A345

Hotel ★★★ 68% Rose & Crown Hotel, Harnham Rd, Harnham, SALISBURY ☎ 01722 399955 28 ⇄ ▮

HIGHWORTH Map 04 SU29

Highworth Community Golf Centre Swindon Rd SN6 7SJ
☎ 01793 766014 Fax 01793 766014
Public downland course, situated in a high position affording good views of the Wiltshire Downs.
9 holes, 3120yds, Par 35, SSS 35, Course record 29.
Club membership 150.
Visitors no restrictions.
Societies advisable to contact in advance.
Green Fees not confirmed.
Prof Mark Toombs
Designer T Watt/ B Sandry/D Lang
Facilities ⻖ ⒜ ⛱ ⌀
Location Off A361 Swindon to Lechlade

Hotel ★★★ 73% Sudbury House Hotel & Conference Centre, London St, FARINGDON
☎ 01367 241272 49 ⇄ ▮

Wrag Barn Golf & Country Club Shrivenham Rd
SN6 7QQ ☎ 01793 861327 Fax 01793 861325
Listed in 'Golfs Best Top 100 UK Courses'. An outstanding course for golfers of all abilities.
18 holes, 6700yds, Par 72, SSS 71, Course record 65.
Club membership 600.
Visitors no restrictions but may not play before noon at weekends.
Societies contact in advance.
Green Fees £25 per round (£30 weekends).

Prof Barry Loughrey
Designer Hawtree
Facilities
Location On B4000 Shrivenham Road out of Highworth. Follow signs

Hotel ★★★ 67% Stanton House Hotel, The Avenue, Stanton Fitzwarren, SWINDON
☎ 01793 861777 86

KINGSDOWN Map 03 ST86

Kingsdown SN13 8BS
☎ 01225 742530 Fax 01225 743472
Fairly flat, open downland course with very sparse tree cover but surrounding wood.
18 holes, 6445yds, Par 72, SSS 71, Course record 64.
Club membership 650.
Visitors welcome except at weekends. Must contact in advance & have a handicap certificate.
Societies apply by letter.
Green Fees not confirmed.
Prof Andrew Butler
Facilities by prior arrangement
Location W side of village

Hotel ★★★★ Lucknam Park, COLERNE
☎ 01225 742777 23 Annexe 18

LANDFORD Map 04 SU21

Hamptworth Golf & Country Club Hamptworth Rd, Hamptworth SP5 2DU ☎ 01794 390155 Fax 01794 390022
Hamptworth enjoys ancient woodland and an abundance of wildlife in a beautiful setting on the edge of the New Forest. The 14th is one of its most challenging holes having a narrow fairway guarded by established forest oaks. The 2nd is a dogleg of 543yds and plays differently all year.
18 holes, 6516yds, Par 72, SSS 71, Course record 68.
Club membership 450.
Visitors telephone to check availability.
Societies write or telephone in advance.
Green Fees not confirmed.
Cards
Prof Phil Stevens
Designer Philip Sanders/Brian Pierson
Facilities
& Leisure gymnasium.
Location 1m NW, A36/B3079

Hotel ★★★ 69% Bartley Lodge, Lyndhurst Rd, CADNAM ☎ 023 80812248 31

MARLBOROUGH Map 04 SU16

Marlborough The Common SN8 1DU
☎ 01672 512147 Fax 01672 513164
Downland course with extensive views over the Og valley and Marlborough Downs.
18 holes, 6491yds, Par 72, SSS 71, Course record 61.
Club membership 900.
Visitors restricted at certain times; must have a handicap certificate at weekends. Must contact in advance.
Societies must contact in advance.
Green Fees £32 per day; £24 per round (£40/£30 weekends).
Cards
Prof S Amor
Facilities
Location N side of town centre on A346

Hotel ★★★ 61% The Castle & Ball, High St, MARLBOROUGH
☎ 01672 515201 34

OAKSEY Map 03 ST99

Oaksey Park Golf & Leisure SN16 9SB
☎ 01666 577995 Fax 01666 577174
A testing nine-hole parkland course set on the west side of the Cotswold Water Parks.
9 holes, 3100yds, Par 70, SSS 69, Course record 66.
Club membership 200.
Visitors no restrictions.
Societies telephone for details.
Green Fees not confirmed.
Cards
Designer Chapman & Warren
Facilities
& Leisure fishing, shooting, water sports, horse riding available.
Location On B road connecting A419 & A429, on outskirts of village of Oaksey. S of Cirencester

Hotel ★★★ 68% Stratton House Hotel, Gloucester Rd, CIRENCESTER
☎ 01285 651761 41

OGBOURNE ST GEORGE Map 04 SU27

Ogbourne Downs SN8 1TB
☎ 01672 841327 Fax 01672 841327
Downland turf and magnificent greens. Wind and slopes make this one of the most challenging courses in Wiltshire. Extensive views.
18 holes, 6353yds, Par 71, SSS 70, Course record 65.
Club membership 890.
Visitors phone in advance. Handicap certificate required.
Societies must apply for booking form in advance.
Green Fees £25 per round (£35 weekends).
Cards
Prof Colin Harraway
Designer J H Taylor
Facilities
Location N side of village on A346

Hotel ★★★ 74% Ivy House Hotel, High St, MARLBOROUGH
☎ 01672 515333 28

SALISBURY Map 04 SU12

Salisbury & South Wilts Netherhampton SP2 8PR
☎ 01722 742645 Fax 01722 742645
Gently undulating and well drained parkland courses in country setting with panoramic views of the cathedral and surrounding country. A 27 hole course played in various configurations.
Main Course: 18 holes, 6528yds, Par 71, SSS 71, Course record 61.
Bibury Course: 9 holes, 2738yds, Par 34.
Club membership 1150.

▶

Visitors	must telephone in advance.
Societies	telephone initially for infomation pack.
Green Fees	£25 per round; £9 per 9 holes (£40/£12 weekends & bank holidays).
Prof	John Cave/Geraldine Teschner
Designer	J H Taylor/S Gidman
Facilities	⊗ ⊪ ⓑ ⚑ ♀ 🏌 🛖 ⛽ ♂
Location	2m W on A3094

Hotel	★★★ 68% Rose & Crown Hotel, Harnham Rd, Harnham, SALISBURY ☎ 01722 399955 28 ⇄ ⮜

SWINDON   Map 04 SU18

Broome Manor Golf Complex Pipers Way SN3 1RG
☎ 01793 532403 Fax 01793 433255
Two courses and a 34-bay floodlit driving range. Parkland with water hazards, open fairways and short cut rough. Walking is easy on gentle slopes.
18 holes, 6283yds, Par 71, SSS 70, Course record 62.
Club membership 800.

Visitors	pre-booking advised for 18 hole course, payment of green fee is required at the time of booking by credit card.
Societies	must be prebooked.
Green Fees	£12.50 per round; £7.50 per 9 holes.
Cards	💳 💳 💳 💳 💳
Prof	Barry Sandry
Designer	Hawtree
Facilities	⊗ ⊪ ⓑ ⚑ ♀ 🏌 🛖 ⛽ ♂ ⛏
Location	1.75m SE of town centre off B4006

Hotel	★★★★ 65% Swindon Marriott, Pipers Way, SWINDON ☎ 01793 512121 153 ⇄ ⮜

TIDWORTH   Map 04 SU24

Tidworth Garrison Bulford Rd SP9 7AF
☎ 01980 842301 Fax 01980 842301
A breezy, dry downland course with lovely turf, fine trees and views over Salisbury Plain and the surrounding area. The 4th and 12th holes are notable. The 565-yard 14th, going down towards the clubhouse, gives the big hitter a chance to let fly.
18 holes, 6320yds, Par 70, SSS 70, Course record 62.
Club membership 800.

Visitors	must contact in advance, weekend & bank holiday bookings may not be made until Thursday prior.
Societies	Tue & Thu, bookings required 12-18 months in advance.
Green Fees	£25 per day/round.
Prof	Terry Gosden
Designer	Donald Steel
Facilities	⊗ ⊪ ⓑ ⚑ ♀ 🛖 ⛽ 🏌 ♂
Location	W side of village off A338

Hotel	★★★ 63% Quality Hotel Andover, Micheldever Rd, ANDOVER ☎ 01264 369111 9 ⇄ ⮜ Annexe 26 ⇄ ⮜

Where to stay, where to eat?
Visit the AA internet site
www.theaa.co.uk

TOLLARD ROYAL   Map 03 ST91

Rushmore Park Golf Club SP5 5QB
☎ 01725 516326 Fax 01725 516466
Peaceful and testing parkland course situated on Cranborne Chase with far-reaching views. An undulating course with avenues of trees and well drained greens.
18 holes, 5580yds, Par 71, SSS 67.
Club membership 350.

Visitors	Must book in advance. Strict dress code enforced.
Societies	welcome by appointment.
Green Fees	£19 per day; £14 per round (£26/£17 weekends).
Cards	💳 💳 💳 💳 💳
Prof	Sean McDonagh
Designer	Tony Crouch
Facilities	⊗ ⊪ by prior arrangement ⓑ ⚑ ♀ 🛖 🏌 ⛏ ⛽
Location	16m SW of Salisbury, entrance off the B3081 between Sixpenny Handley and Tollard Royal

Hotel	★★★ 72% Royal Chase Hotel, Royal Chase Roundabout, SHAFTESBURY ☎ 01747 853355 35 ⇄ ⮜

UPAVON   Map 04 SU15

Upavon Douglas Av SN9 6BQ
☎ 01980 630787 & 630281 Fax 01980 630787
Downland course set on sides of infamous valley, with some wind affecting play. Includes a par 5 of 602 yards and finishing hole of 170 yards across a ravine.
18 holes, 6407yds, Par 71, SSS 71, Course record 70.
Club membership 600.

Visitors	must contact in advance and may not play before noon at weekends.
Societies	telephone in advance.
Green Fees	£24 per day; £18 per round (£20 per round after noon only weekends).
Cards	💳 💳 💳 💳 💳
Prof	Richard Blake
Designer	Richard Blake
Facilities	⊗ ⊪ ⓑ ⚑ ♀ 🛖 🏌 ⛽ ♂
& Leisure	hard tennis courts.
Location	1.5m SE of Upavon on A342 Andover road

Hotel	★★★ 64% Bear Hotel, Market Place, DEVIZES ☎ 01380 722444 24 ⇄ ⮜

WARMINSTER   Map 03 ST84

West Wilts Elm Hill BA12 0AU
☎ 01985 213133 Fax 01985 219809
A hilltop course among the Wiltshire downs on downland turf. Free draining, short, but a very good test of accurate iron play. Excellent greens and clubhouse facilities.
18 holes, 5709yds, Par 70, SSS 68, Course record 62.
Club membership 650.

Visitors	must contact in advance. Handicap certificate required.
Societies	apply by letter.
Green Fees	£28 per day; £20 per round (£36 per day/round weekends & bank holidays).
Cards	💳 💳 💳 💳
Prof	Andrew Lamb

▶

Designer	J H Taylor
Facilities	⊗ ⅢⅢ 🏐 🍺 ♀ 🏌 🏐 ⛳ ✓
Location	N side of town centre off A350
Hotel	★★★★ 73% Bishopstrow House, WARMINSTER ☎ 01985 212312 31 ⇆ 🏌

WOOTTON BASSETT — Map 04 SU08

Brinkworth Longmans Farm, Brinkworth SN15 5DG
☎ 01666 510277
Fairly long and open course with ditches and water hazards on the 2nd and 18th holes. Several testing par 3s with crosswinds and three long and tricky par 5s, notably the 4th, 8th and 14th holes.
18 holes, 5884yds, Par 70, SSS 70.
Club membership 100.

Visitors	welcome any time no contact needed.
Societies	telephone in advance or apply in writing.
Green Fees	not confirmed.
Designer	Jullian Sheppard
Facilities	🏐 🍺 ♀ 🏐 ⛳ ✓
Location	Just off B4042 between Malmesbury/Wootton Bassett
Hotel	★★★ 74% Marsh Farm Hotel, Coped Hall, WOOTTON BASSETT ☎ 01793 848044 11 ⇆ 🏌 Annexe 27 ⇆ 🏌

Wiltshire Vastern SN4 7PB
☎ 01793 849999 Fax 01793 849988
A Peter Alliss/Clive Clark design set in rolling Wiltshire downland countryside. A number of lakes add a challenge for both low and high handicappers.
18 holes, 6522yds, Par 72, SSS 71.
Club membership 800.

Visitors	must contact in advance.
Societies	contact in advance.
Green Fees	£30 per day.
Cards	💳 💳 💳 💳 💳
Prof	Andy Gray
Designer	Peter Allis & Clive Clark
Facilities	⊗ ⅢⅢ 🏐 🍺 ♀ 🏐 ⛳ 🏌 🏐 🏐 ✓ ♪
Location	Leave M4 at junc 16, on A3102
Hotel	★★★ 74% Marsh Farm Hotel, Coped Hall, WOOTTON BASSETT ☎ 01793 848044 11 ⇆ 🏌 Annexe 27 ⇆ 🏌

WORCESTERSHIRE

ALVECHURCH — Map 07 SP07

Kings Norton Brockhill Ln, Weatheroak B48 7ED
☎ 01564 826706 & 826789 Fax 01564 826955
A 27 hole Championship venue, 18 hole course 7000yds par 72 plus 12 hole par 3 course. Parkland with water hazards.
Weatheroak: 18 holes, 6748yds, Par 72, SSS 72, Course record 65.

Brockhill: 18 holes, 6648yds, Par 72, SSS 72.
Wythall: 18 holes, 6612yds, Par 72, SSS 72.
Club membership 1000.

Visitors	must contact in advance. No visitors at weekends.
Societies	must telephone in advance.
Green Fees	£35 per day; £30 per 18 holes.
Cards	💳 💳 💳 💳 💳
Prof	Kevin Hayward
Designer	F Hawtree
Facilities	⊗ ⅢⅢ 🏐 🍺 ♀ 🏐 ⛳ 🏌 🏐 🏐 ✓
Location	M42 junct3, off A435
Hotel	★★★★ 69% Pine Lodge Hotel, Kidderminster Rd, BROMSGROVE ☎ 01527 576600 114 ⇆ 🏌

BEWDLEY — Map 07 SO77

Little Lakes Golf and Country Club Lye Head DY12 2UZ
☎ 01299 266385 Fax 01299 266178
A pleasant undulating parkland course extended to 18 holes. The course offers some pleasing views and several demanding holes.
18 holes, 5644yds, Par 69, SSS 68, Course record 63.
Club membership 400.

Visitors	advisable to telephone in advance.
Societies	must telephone in advance.
Green Fees	not confirmed.
Cards	💳 💳 💳 💳 💳
Prof	Mark A Laing
Designer	M Laing
Facilities	⊗ ⅢⅢ 🏐 🍺 ♀ 🏐 ⛳ 🏐 🏐 ✓
& Leisure	hard tennis courts, heated outdoor swimming pool, fishing.
Location	2.25m W off A456
Hotel	★★ 62% The George Hotel, Load St, BEWDLEY ☎ 01299 402117 11 ⇆ 🏌

Wharton Park Longbank DY12 2QW
☎ 01299 405222 & 405163 Fax 01299 405121
18-hole championship-standard course in 140 acres of countryside. Some long Par 5s eg the 9th (594yds) as well as superb par 3 holes at 3rd, 10th, 15th make this a very challenging course.
18 holes, 6603yds, Par 72, SSS 71, Course record 66.
Club membership 500.

Visitors	must contact in advance. May not play weekend mornings.
Societies	prior booking required.
Green Fees	not confirmed.
Cards	💳 💳 💳
Prof	Angus Hoare
Facilities	🏐 🍺 ♀ 🏐 ⛳ 🏐 🏐 ✓ ♪
Location	Off A456 Bewdley bypass
Hotel	★★ 62% The George Hotel, Load St, BEWDLEY ☎ 01299 402117 11 ⇆ 🏌

BISHAMPTON — Map 03 SO95

Vale Golf Club Hill Furze Rd WR10 2LZ
☎ 01386 462781 Fax 01386 462597
This course offers an American-style layout, with large greens, trees and bunkers and several water hazards. Its ▶

rolling fairways provide a testing round, as well as superb views of the Malvern Hills. Picturesque and peaceful. Also 9-hole course and 20-bay driving range.
International Course: 18 holes, 7114yds, Par 74, SSS 74, Course record 72.
Lenches Course: 9 holes, 2759yds, Par 35, SSS 34.
Club membership 650.
Visitors   booking up to one week in advance.
Societies   must apply in advance. May only play weekdays on 18 hole course.
Green Fees   not confirmed.
Cards   [icons]
Prof   Caroline Griffiths
Designer   Bob Sandon
Facilities   [icons]
& Leisure   fishing.
Location   Signposted off A4538

Hotel   ★★ 66% The Chequers Inn, Chequers Ln, FLADBURY ☎ 01386 860276 & 860527 Fax 01386 861286 8 [icons]

BLAKEDOWN   Map 07 SO87

Churchill and Blakedown Churchill Ln DY10 3NB
☎ 01562 700018 & 700200
Pleasant course on hilltop with extensive views.
9 holes, 6472yds, Par 72, SSS 71.
Club membership 380.
Visitors   with member only weekends & bank holidays. Handicap certificate required.
Societies   by arrangement through secretary.
Green Fees   £17.50 per round.
Facilities   [icons]
Location   W side of village off A456

Hotel   ★★★★ 67% Stone Manor Hotel, Stone, KIDDERMINSTER ☎ 01562 777555 52 [icons]

BRANSFORD   Map 03 SO75

Bank House Hotel Golf & Country Club WR6 5JD
☎ 01886 833551 Fax 01886 832461
The Pine Lakes course is designed as a 'Florida' style course with fairways weaving between water courses, 13 lakes and sculptured mounds with colouful plant displays. The 6,204yd course has doglegs, island greens and tight fairways to challenge all standards of player. The 10th, 16th and 18th (The Devil's Elbow) are particularly tricky.
18 holes, 6204yds, Par 72, SSS 71, Course record 65.
Club membership 380.

Societies   contact the golf secretary, all tee times must be booked in advance.
Green Fees £18 per 18 holes (£27 weekends).
Cards   [icons]
Prof   Craig George
Designer   Bob Sandow
Facilities   [icons]
& Leisure   outdoor swimming pool, sauna, solarium, gymnasium.
Location   3m S of Worcester, A4103

Hotel   ★★★ 68% Bank House Hotel Golf & Country Club, Hereford Rd, Bransford, WORCESTER ☎ 01886 833551 68 [icons]

BROADWAY   Map 04 SP03

Broadway Willersey Hill WR12 7LG
☎ 01386 853683 Fax 01386 858643
At the edge of the Cotswolds this downland course lies at an altitude of 900 ft above sea level, with extensive views. Natural contours and man made hazards mean that drives have to be placed, approaches carefully judged and the greens expertly read.
18 holes, 5970yds, Par 72, SSS 70, Course record 65.
Club membership 850.
Visitors   may not play Sat between Apr-Sep before 3pm. Restricted play Sun. Must contact in advance.
Societies   Wed-Fri, must contact in advance.
Green Fees £35 per day; £30 per round (£36 weekends & bank holidays).
Cards   [icons]
Prof   Martyn Freeman
Designer   James Braid
Facilities   [icons]
Location   1.5m E on A44

Hotel   ★★★ 74% Dormy House Hotel, Willersey Hill, BROADWAY ☎ 01386 852711 25 [icons] Annexe 23 [icon]

BROMSGROVE   Map 07 SO97

Blackwell Agmore Rd, Blackwell B60 1PY
☎ 0121 445 1994 Fax 0121 445 4911
Pleasantly undulating parkland with a variety of trees. Laid out in two 9-hole loops.
18 holes, 6230yds, Par 70, SSS 71, Course record 63.
Club membership 365.
Visitors   must contact in advance, must have handicap certificate, may not play at weekends,
Societies   must contact in advance.
Green Fees £50 per day.
Prof   Nigel Blake
Facilities   [icons]
Location   2m W of Alvechurch

Hotel   ★★★★ 69% Pine Lodge Hotel, Kidderminster Rd, BROMSGROVE ☎ 01527 576600 114 [icons]

Looking for a driving range?
See the index at the back of the guide

Bromsgrove Golf Centre Stratford Rd B60 1LD
☎ 01527 575886 Fax 01527 570964
Gently undulating parkland course with large contoured
greens, generous tee surfaces and superb views over
Worcestershire. Tricky par 3 16th across a lake. Also 41 bay
floodlit driving range, floodlit practice bunker and clubhouse
with conference facilities.
18 holes, 5880yds, Par 68, SSS 68.
Club membership 900.

Visitors	dress restriction, no T-shirts, jeans, tracksuits etc. 7 day booking facilities available.
Societies	packages available, apply in writing or telephone.
Green Fees	£13.50 per 18 holes; £8 per 9 holes (£17/£10.50 weekends & bank holidays).
Cards	🖃 💳 🖩 🗺
Prof	Graeme Long/James Stratham
Designer	Hawtree & Son
Facilities	⊗ 🏁 ᠘ 🍺 ♀ 👥 🏠 🥖 🛒 ⚁ 🛆
& Leisure	practice bunker.
Location	1m from Bromsgrove town centre at junct of A38/A448
Hotel	★★★★ 69% Pine Lodge Hotel, Kidderminster Rd, BROMSGROVE ☎ 01527 576600 114 ⇌ 🏕

DROITWICH

Droitwich Ford Ln WR9 0BQ
☎ 01905 774344 Fax 01905 797290
Undulating parkland course.
18 holes, 5976yds, Par 70, SSS 69, Course record 62.
Club membership 732.

Visitors	with member only weekends & bank holidays.
Societies	must apply by telephone and letter.
Green Fees	£26 per day/round.
Prof	C Thompson
Designer	J Braid/G Franks
Facilities	⊗ 🏁 ᠘ 🍺 ♀ 🛆 🏠 ⚁
& Leisure	snooker.
Location	Off A38 Droitwich to Bromsgrove road, midway between Droitwich and M5 junct 5
Hotel	★★★★ 67% Chateau Impney Hotel, DROITWICH SPA ☎ 01905 774411 67 ⇌ 🏕 Annexe 53 ⇌ 🏕

Gaudet Luce Middle Ln, Hadzor WR9 7DP
☎ 01905 796375 Fax 01905 797245
A challenging 18-hole course with two contrasting 9-hole
loops. The front nine are long and fairly open, the back nine

are tight and compact requiring good positional and approach
play. Water features on several holes.
18 holes, 5887yds, Par 70, SSS 68.
Club membership 360.

Visitors	welcome, advisable to telephone in advance, proper golfing attire required at all times.
Societies	telephone for details.
Green Fees	£14 per day; £17 per round weekends & bank holidays. Prices under review.
Cards	🖃 🖩 💳 🗺 🖩
Prof	Phil Lundy
Designer	1995
Facilities	᠘ 🍺 ♀ 🛆 🏠 ⚁ 🛆
& Leisure	indoor practice & teaching facility.
Location	M5 junct 5, left at Tagwell road into Middle Lane, 1st driveway on left to clubhouse
Hotel	★★★★ 67% Chateau Impney Hotel, DROITWICH SPA ☎ 01905 774411 67 ⇌ 🏕 Annexe 53 ⇌ 🏕

Ombersley Bishops Wood Rd, Lineholt, Ombersley
WR9 0LE ☎ 01905 620747 Fax 01905 620047
Undulating course in beautiful countryside high above the
edge of the Severn Valley. Covered driving range and putting
green.
18 holes, 6139yds, Par 72, SSS 69, Course record 67.
Club membership 750.

Visitors	suitable dress expected, no jeans, shirts must have a collar.
Societies	telephone in advance.
Green Fees	£16.80 per 18 holes (£22.25 weekends & bank holidays).
Cards	🖩
Prof	Graham Glenister
Designer	David Morgan
Facilities	⊗ 🏁 ᠘ 🍺 ♀ 🛆 🏠 🥖 🎣 🛒 ⚁ 🛆
Location	3m W of Droitwich, off A449. At Mitre Oak pub, take A4025 to Stourport, signposted 400yds on left
Hotel	★★★★ 65% Raven Hotel, Victoria Square, DROITWICH SPA ☎ 01905 772224 72 ⇌ 🏕

FLADBURY

Evesham Craycombe Links, Old Worcester Rd WR10 2QS
☎ 01386 860395
Parkland, heavily wooded, with the River Avon running
alongside 5th and 14th holes. Good views. Nine greens
played from eighteen different tees.
9 holes, 6415yds, Par 72, SSS 71, Course record 68.
Club membership 383.

Visitors	must contact in advance. With members only at weekends.
Societies	must apply by letter.
Green Fees	not confirmed.
Prof	Charles Haynes
Facilities	⊗ 🏁 ᠘ 🍺 ♀ 🛆 🏠 🥖 🎣 ⚁ 🛆
Location	0.75m N on A4538
Hotel	★★★ 71% The Evesham Hotel, Coopers Ln, Off Waterside, EVESHAM ☎ 01386 765566 & 0800 716969 (Res) Fax 01386 765443 39 ⇌ 🏕 Annexe 1 ⇌ 🏕

Hollywood Map 07 SP07

Gay Hill Hollywood Ln B47 5PP
☎ 0121 430 8544 & 474 6001 (pro) Fax 0121 436 7796
A meadowland course, some 7 miles from Birmingham.
18 holes, 6532yds, Par 72, SSS 71, Course record 64.
Club membership 740.
Visitors must contact in advance. No visitors at weekends or bank holidays
Societies telephone in advance.
Green Fees £28.50.
Prof Andrew Potter
Facilities ⊗ 𝕃 ☕ 🍸 ⛳ 🚗 ⛳ ✓
Location N side of village

Hotel ★★★ 66% Regency Hotel, Stratford Rd, Shirley, SOLIHULL
☎ 0121 745 6119 112 ⇌ ↱

Kidderminster Map 07 SO87

Habberley Low Trimpley DY11 5RG
☎ 01562 745756 Fax 01562 745756
Very hilly, wooded parkland course.
9 holes, 5481yds, Par 69, Course record 62.
Club membership 230.
Visitors may only play weekends with a member,
Societies telephone initially.
Green Fees £10 per round.
Facilities ⊗ 𝕄 𝕃 ☕ 🍸 ⛳
Location 2m NW of Kidderminster

Hotel ★★★★ 67% Stone Manor Hotel, Stone, KIDDERMINSTER
☎ 01562 777555 52 ⇌ ↱

Kidderminster Russell Rd DY10 3HT
☎ 01562 822303 Fax 01562 862041
Parkland course with natural hazards and some easy walking.
18 holes, 6405yds, Par 72, SSS 71, Course record 66.
Club membership 860.
Visitors with member only weekends & bank holidays. Must have a handicap certificate.
Societies Thu only, apply in advance.
Green Fees £40 per day; £30 per round.
Prof Nick Underwood
Facilities ⊗ 𝕄 𝕃 ☕ 🍸 ⛳ 🚗 ⛳ ✓
Location 0.5m SE of town centre, signposted off A449

Hotel ★★★★ 67% Stone Manor Hotel, Stone, KIDDERMINSTER
☎ 01562 777555 52 ⇌ ↱

Wyre Forest Zortech Av DY11 7EX
☎ 01299 822682 Fax 01299 879433
Making full use of the existing contours, this interesting and challenging course is bounded by woodland and gives extensive views over the surrounding area. Well drained fairways and greens.
18 holes, 5790yds, Par 70, SSS 68, Course record 68.
Club membership 397.
Visitors must telephone in advance.
Societies brochure on request, deposit secures date, write or telephone.
Green Fees £9 per 18 holes.
Cards [card symbols]
Prof Simon Price
Facilities ⊗ 𝕃 ☕ 🍸 ⛳ 🚗 ⛳ ✓
Location Approx half way between Kidderminster/Stourport, on the A451

Hotel ★★★★ 69% Stourport Manor, Hartlebury Rd, STOURPORT-ON-SEVERN
☎ 0500 636943 (Central Res)
Fax 01773 880321 68 ⇌ ↱

Malvern Wells Map 03 SO74

Worcestershire Wood Farm, Hanley Rd WR14 4PP
☎ 01684 575992 & 573905 Fax 01684 575992
Fairly easy walking on windy downland course with trees, ditches and other natural hazards. Outstanding views of Malvern Hills and Severn Valley. 17th hole (par 5) is approached over small lake.
18 holes, 6470yds, Par 71, SSS 71, Course record 65.
Club membership 770.
Visitors only after 10am at weekends or with a member. Must contact in advance. Handicap certificate required.
Societies Thu & Fri only, apply in writing.
Green Fees not confirmed.
Cards [card symbol]
Prof Richard Lewis
Designer Colt/Braid
Facilities ⊗ 𝕄 𝕃 ☕ 🍸 ⛳ 🚗 ✓
Location 2m S of Gt Malvern on B4209

Hotel ★★★ 73% The Cottage in the Wood Hotel, Holywell Rd, Malvern Wells, MALVERN
☎ 01684 575859 8 ⇌ ↱ Annexe 12 ⇌ ↱

Redditch Map 07 SP06

Abbey Hotel Golf & Country Club
Dagnell End Rd B98 7BD
☎ 01527 68006 (golf shop) & 63918 (reception)
Fax 01527 584112
Young parkland course with rolling fairways. A 'Site of Special Scientific Interest', the course includes two fishing lakes and is pleasant to play.
18 holes, 6561yds, Par 72, SSS 72.
Club membership 700.
Visitors must contact in advance.
Societies must apply in writing.
Green Fees £16 per round (£21 Fridays, weekends & bank holidays).
Prof S Edwards

▶

Facilities & Leisure ⊗ ▥ 🄻 ♨ ⚑ ♟ ⛴ ⛳ ♻ 🏌 ⛳ ♪ heated indoor swimming pool, fishing, sauna, solarium, gymnasium.

Location 1.25m N off A441 on B4101

Hotel ★★★ 69% The Abbey Hotel Golf & Country Club, Hither Green Ln, Dagnel End Rd, Bordesley, REDDITCH ☎ 01527 63918 38 ⇆ ♌

Pitcheroak Plymouth Rd B97 4PB
☎ 01527 541054 Fax 01527 65216
Woodland course, hilly in places.There is also a putting green and a practice ground.
9 holes, 4561yds, Par 65, SSS 62.
Club membership 200.
Visitors no restrictions.
Societies telephone to book.
Green Fees £7.85 per 18 holes; £6.05 per 9 holes (£9.10/£6.65 weekends).
Cards 🖸 🖸 🖸 🖸 🖸
Prof David Stewart
Facilities ⊗ ▥ 🄻 ♨ ⚑ ♟ ⛴ ⛳ ♪
Location SW side of town centre off A448

Hotel ★★★ 64% Quality Hotel, Pool Bank, Southcrest, REDDITCH ☎ 01527 541511 58 ⇆ ♌

Redditch Lower Grinsty, Green Ln, Callow Hill B97 5PJ
☎ 01527 543079 Fax 01527 543079
Parkland course, the hazards including woods, ditches and large ponds. The par 4, 14th is a testing hole.
18 holes, 6671yds, Par 72, SSS 72, Course record 68.
Club membership 650.
Visitors with member only weekends & bank holidays, no visitors on competition days, advisable to telephone in advance.
Societies telephone Secretary.
Green Fees £27.50.
Designer F Pennick
Facilities ⊗ ▥ 🄻 ♨ ⚑ ♟ ⛴ ⛳ 🏌 ⛳ ♪
Location 2m SW

Hotel ★★★ 64% Quality Hotel, Pool Bank, Southcrest, REDDITCH ☎ 01527 541511 58 ⇆ ♌

TENBURY WELLS

Map 07 SO56

Cadmore Lodge Hotel & Country Club St Michaels, Berrington Green WR15 8TQ
☎ 01584 810044 Fax 01584 810044

A picturesque 9-hole course in a brook valley. Challenging holes include the 1st and 6th over the lake, 8th over the valley and 9th over hedges.
9 holes, 5132yds, Par 68, SSS 65.
Club membership 200.

Visitors no restrictions but check availability.
Societies telephone in advance.
Green Fees not confirmed.
Cards 🖸 🖸 🖸 🖸 🖸 🖸
Facilities & Leisure ⊗ ▥ 🄻 ♨ ⚑ ♟ ⛴ ♪ hard tennis courts, heated indoor swimming pool, fishing, sauna, gymnasium, pool table.
Location From Tenbury take A4112 to Leominster, after approx 2m turn right for Berrington, 0.75 on left

Hotel ★★ 66% Cadmore Lodge Hotel & Country Club, Berrington Green, St Michaels, TENBURY WELLS ☎ 01584 810044 14 ⇆ ♌

WORCESTER

Map 03 SO85

Worcester Golf & Country Club Boughton Park WR2 4EZ
☎ 01905 422555 Fax 01905 749090
Fine parkland course with many trees, a lake, and views of the Malvern Hills.
18 holes, 6251yds, Par 70, SSS 70, Course record 67.
Club membership 1000.
Visitors must contact professional in advance. May not play at weekends.
Societies telephone in advance.
Green Fees not confirmed.
Prof Colin Colenso
Designer Dr A Mackenzie
Facilities ⊗ by prior arrangement ▥ by prior arrangement 🄻 ♨ ⚑ ♟ ⛴ ♪
& Leisure hard and grass tennis courts, squash.
Location 1.5m from city centre on A4103

Hotel ★★★ 61% The Gifford Hotel, High St, WORCESTER ☎ 01905 726262 103 ⇆ ♌

WYTHALL

Map 07 SP07

Fulford Heath Tanners Green Ln B47 6BH
☎ 01564 824758 Fax 01564 822629
A mature parkland course encompassing two classic par threes. The 11th, a mere 149 yards, shoots from an elevated tee through a channel of trees to a well protected green. The 16th, a 166 yard par 3, elevated green, demands a 140 yard carry over an imposing lake.
18 holes, 6179yds, Par 70, SSS 70, Course record 66.
Club membership 700.

▶

Visitors	with member only weekend & bank holidays. Handicap certificate required.
Societies	must apply in advance.
Green Fees	£35 per day.
Prof	David Down
Designer	Hawtree
Facilities	⊗ ⅢⓁ 🍴 ♀ ⚐ 🏌
Location	1m SE off A435

Hotel	★★★★ 64% Swallow St John's Hotel, 651 Warwick Rd, SOLIHULL ☎ 0121 711 3000 178 🛏

YORKSHIRE, EAST RIDING OF

AUGHTON   Map 08 SE73

Oaks Aughton Common YO42 4PW
☎ 01757 288577 & 288007 Fax 01757 289029
Built amongst mature woodland and six lakes in the picturesque Derwent Ings and further enhanced by thousands of specimen trees. Greens are built with substantial moulding.

.
Club membership 680.

Societies	may play weekdays. Telephone in advance.
Prof	Joe Townhill
Designer	Julian Covey
Facilities	⊗ ⅢⓁ 🍴 ♀ ⚐ 🏌
Location	1m N of Bubwith on B1228

Hotel	★★★ 75% The Parsonage Country House Hotel, York Rd, ESCRICK ☎ 01904 728111 12 🛏 Annexe 9 🛏

BEVERLEY   Map 08 TA03

Beverley & East Riding The Westwood HU17 8RG
☎ 01482 868757 Fax 01482 868757
Picturesque parkland course with some hard walking and natural hazards - trees and gorse bushes. Also cattle (spring to autumn); horse-riders are an occasional hazard in the early morning.
Westwood: 18 holes, 6127yds, Par 69, SSS 69, Course record 65.
Club membership 530.

Visitors	must contact in advance.
Societies	telephone 01482 868757, then written confirmation.
Green Fees	£17 per day; £13 per round (£22/£17 weekends & bank holidays).
Prof	Ian Mackie
Facilities	⊗ Ⓛ 🍴 ♀ ⚐ 🏌
Location	1m SW on B1230

Hotel	★★★ 67% Beverley Arms Hotel, North Bar Within, BEVERLEY ☎ 01482 869241 56 🛏

BRANDESBURTON   Map 08 TA14

Hainsworth Park Burton Holme YO25 8RT
☎ 01964 542362 Fax 01964 542362
A parkland course with easy walking.
18 holes, 6435yds, Par 71, SSS 71.
Club membership 500.

Visitors	contact in advance.
Societies	telephone initially.
Green Fees	£20 per day; £16 per round (£25/£20 weekends & bank holidays).
Cards	▭ ▭ ▭ ▭
Prof	Paul Binnington
Facilities	⊗ ⅢⓁ 🍴 ♀ ⚐ 🏌
& Leisure	grass tennis courts, fishing.
Location	SW side of village on A165

Hotel	★★ 68% Burton Lodge Hotel, BRANDESBURTON ☎ 01964 542847 7 🛏 Annexe 2 🛏

BRIDLINGTON   Map 08 TA16

Bridlington Belvedere Rd YO15 3NA
☎ 01262 606367 Fax 01262 606367
Clifftop, seaside course, windy at times, with hazards of bunkers, ponds, ditches and trees.
18 holes, 6638yds, Par 72, SSS 72, Course record 66.
Club membership 600.

Visitors	must contact in advance, professional 01262 674721 limited at weekends.
Societies	telephone bookings in advance.
Green Fees	not confirmed.
Prof	Anthony Howarth
Designer	James Braid
Facilities	⊗ ⅢⓁ 🍴 ♀ ⚐ 🏌
Location	1m S off A165

Hotel	★★★ 67% Revelstoke Hotel, 1-3 Flamborough Rd, BRIDLINGTON ☎ 01262 672362 25 🛏

Bridlington Links Flamborough Rd, Marton YO15 1DW
☎ 01262 401584 Fax 01262 401702
Coastal links type course with large greens, numerous water hazards and splendid views towards Flamborough Head. When the wind blows off the sea, the course becomes a challenging test of golf for even the experienced golfer.
Main: 18 holes, 6719yds, Par 72, SSS 72, Course record 70.
Club membership 350.

Visitors	telephone to book tee times.
Societies	telephone for booking.

▶

Green Fees not confirmed.
Cards ⬛⬛⬛⬛
Prof Steve Raybould
Designer Swan
Facilities ⊗ �🎏 ⓛ 💺 ♀ ♨ 📷 ⛳ 🏌 🛒 ♿ ⚐
Location On the B1255 between Bridlington and Flamborough

Hotel ★★★ 66% Expanse Hotel, North Marine Dr, BRIDLINGTON
☎ 01262 675347 48 🛏 📻

BROUGH　　　　　　　　Map 08 SE92

Brough Cave Rd HU15 1HB
☎ 01482 667291 Fax 01482 669873
Parkland course, where accurate positioning of the tee ball is required for good scoring.
18 holes, 6075yds, Par 68, SSS 69, Course record 64.
Club membership 700.
Visitors must have handicap certificate and contact in advance.
Societies apply by letter.
Green Fees £30 per day/round (£40 weekends & bank holidays).
Prof Gordon Townhill
Facilities ⊗ 🎏 ⓛ 💺 ♀ ♨ 📷 ⛳ ⚐
Location 0.5m N

Hotel ★★★ 63% Humber Crown, Ferriby High Rd, NORTH FERRIBY
☎ 0870 400 9044 95 🛏 📻

COTTINGHAM　　　　　　Map 08 TA03

Cottingham Woodhill Way HU16 5RZ
☎ 01482 846030 Fax 01482 845932
Gently undulating parkland course incorporating many natural features, including lateral water hazards, several ponds on the approach to greens, and rolling fairways.
18 holes, 6459yds, Par 72, SSS 71, Course record 69.
Club membership 650.
Visitors may book by telephone in advance, times available weekdays and weekends.
Societies deposit required and confirmation in writing. After 2pm weekends.
Green Fees £14 per round (£20 weekends & bank holidays).
Prof Chris Gray
Designer Terry Litten
Facilities ⊗ 🎏 ⓛ 💺 ♀ ♨ 📷 ⛳ ⚐ ♿
& Leisure equestrian centre.
Location 4m from A63/M62 on A164. Turn off to Cottingham on B1233, in 100yds turn left into Woodhill Way

Hotel ★★ 68% The Rowley Manor Hotel, Rowley Rd, LITTLE WEIGHTON
☎ 01482 848248 16 🛏 📻

DRIFFIELD (GREAT)　　　Map 08 TA05

Driffield Sunderlandwick YO25 9AD
☎ 01377 253116 Fax 01377 240599
An easy walking, mature parkland course set within the beautiful Sunderlandwick Estate.
18 holes, 6215yds, Par 70, SSS 69, Course record 67.
Club membership 693.

Visitors must book in advance and adhere to club dress rule.
Societies apply in writing or telephone.
Green Fees not confirmed.
Prof Dennis Taylor
Facilities ⊗ 🎏 ⓛ 💺 ♀ ♨ 📷 ⚐
& Leisure fishing.
Location 2m S off A164

Hotel ★★★ 70% Bell Hotel, 46 Market Place, DRIFFIELD ☎ 01377 256661 16 🛏 📻

FLAMBOROUGH　　　　　Map 08 TA27

Flamborough Head Lighthouse Rd YO15 1AR
☎ 01262 850333 & 850417 & 850683 Fax 01262 850279
Undulating seaside course.
18 holes, 5976yds, Par 70, SSS 69, Course record 70.
Club membership 500.
Visitors welcome but may not play; before 1pm Sun, Wed between 10.30 & 1.30, Sat between 11.30 & 12.30.
Societies must contact in advance.
Green Fees £17 per day; £15 per round (£20 weekends & bank holidays).
Facilities ⊗ 🎏 ⓛ 💺 ♀ ♨ 📷 🛒 ⚐
Location 2m E off B1259

Hotel ★★ 64% Flaneburg Hotel & Restaurant, North Marine Rd, FLAMBOROUGH
☎ 01262 850284 13 📻

HESSLE　　　　　　　　Map 08 TA02

Hessle Westfield Rd, Raywell HU16 5YL
☎ 01482 650171 & 650190 (Prof) Fax 01482 652679
Well-wooded downland course, easy walking, windy.
18 holes, 6604yds, Par 72, SSS 72, Course record 68.
Visitors not Tue between 9-1 and may not play before 11am on Sat & Sun.
Societies by prior arrangement.
Green Fees £25 per day; £20 per round (£28 weekends).
Prof Grahame Fieldsend
Designer D Thomas/P Allis
Facilities ⊗ 🎏 ⓛ 💺 ♀ ♨ 📷 ⚐
Location 3m SW of Cottingham

Hotel ★★★ 63% Humber Crown, Ferriby High Rd, NORTH FERRIBY ☎ 0870 400 9044 95 🛏 📻

HORNSEA　　　　　　　Map 08 TA14

Hornsea Rolston Rd HU18 1XG
☎ 01964 532020 Fax 01964 532020
Flat, parkland course with good greens.
18 holes, 6685yds, Par 72, SSS 72, Course record 66.
Club membership 600.
Visitors with member only at weekends until 3pm. Must contact in advance.
Societies contact Secretary in advance.
Green Fees £30 per day; £22 per round (£30 per round weekends).
Prof Stretton Wright
Facilities ⊗ 🎏 ⓛ 💺 ♀ ♨ 📷 ⛳ ⚐
& Leisure snooker.
Location 1m S on B1242, follow signs for Hornsea Freeport　▶

Hotel	★★★ 67% Beverley Arms Hotel, North Bar Within, BEVERLEY ☎ 01482 869241 56 ⇄ ♠

HULL   Map 08 TA02

Ganstead Park Longdales Ln, Coniston HU11 4LB
☎ 01482 817754 Fax 01482 817754
Parkland course, easy walking, with water features.
18 holes, 6801yds, Par 72, SSS 73, Course record 67.
Club membership 500.
Visitors	contact in advance.
Societies	telephone in advance.
Green Fees	£24 per day; £18 per round; (£26 weekends & bank holidays).
Prof	Michael J Smee
Designer	P Green
Facilities	⊗ ⅏ ⓛ ⓑ ⚑ ♀ ⚘ 🛆 ↑ ⚲ ∅
Location	6m NE on A165

Hotel	★★★ 65% Quality Hotel Hull, 170 Ferensway, HULL ☎ 01482 325087 155 ⇄ ♠

Hull The Hall, 27 Packman Ln HU10 7TJ
☎ 01482 658919 Fax 01482 658919
Parkland course.
18 holes, 6242yds, Par 70, SSS 70.
Club membership 840.
Visitors	only weekdays. Contact professional 01482 653074.
Societies	only on Tue and Thu by prior arrangement.
Green Fees	not confirmed.
Prof	David Jagger
Designer	James Braid
Facilities	🛆 ⚐ ∅
Location	5m W of city centre off A164

Hotel	★★★ 71% Willerby Manor Hotel, Well Ln, WILLERBY ☎ 01482 652616 51 ⇄ ♠

Springhead Park Willerby Rd HU5 5JE ☎ 01482 656309
Municipal parkland course with tight, tree-lined, undulating fairways.
18 holes, 6402yds, Par 71, SSS 71.
Club membership 667.
Visitors	welcome ex Sun (tee reserved).
Green Fees	not confirmed.
Prof	Barry Herrington
Facilities	⚐ ↑
Location	5m W off A164

Hotel	★★★ 71% Willerby Manor Hotel, Well Ln, WILLERBY ☎ 01482 652616 51 ⇄ ♠

Sutton Park Salthouse Rd HU8 9HF
☎ 01482 374242 Fax 01482 701428
Municipal parkland course.
18 holes, 6251yds, Par 70, SSS 69, Course record 67.
Club membership 300.
Visitors	no restrictions.
Societies	prior arrangement via club, telephone and confirm in writing.
Green Fees	not confirmed.
Prof	To be appointed
Facilities	⊗ by prior arrangement ⅏ by prior arrangement ⓑ ⚑ ♀ 🛆 ⚐ ↑ ⚲ ∅
Location	3m NE on B1237 off A165

Hotel	★★★ 65% Quality Hotel Hull, 170 Ferensway, HULL ☎ 01482 325087 155 ⇄ ♠

SOUTH CAVE   Map 08 SE93

Cave Castle Hotel & Country Club Church Hill, South Cave HU15 2EU
☎ 01430 421286 & 422245 Fax 01430 421118
An undulating meadow and parkland course at the foot of the Wolds, with superb views. Golf breaks are available.
18 holes, 6500yds, Par 73, SSS 72, Course record 71.
Club membership 450.
Visitors	must contact in advance, may not play before 11am weekends/bank holidays.
Societies	by arrangement with Manager.
Green Fees	£12 per round (£18 weekends & bank holidays).
Prof	Stephen MacKinder
Designer	Mrs N Freling
Facilities & Leisure	⊗ ⅏ ⓛ ⓑ ⚑ ♀ 🛆 ⚐ ↑ ⚕ ⚽ ∅ heated indoor swimming pool, fishing, sauna, solarium, gymnasium.
Location	1m from A63

Hotel	★★★ 63% Humber Crown, Ferriby High Rd, NORTH FERRIBY ☎ 0870 400 9044 95 ⇄ ♠

WITHERNSEA   Map 08 TA32

Withernsea Chesnut Av HU19 2PG ☎ 01964 612078
Exposed seaside links with narrow, undulating fairways, bunkers and small greens.
9 holes, 5907yds, Par 72, SSS 69.
Club membership 300.
Visitors	with member only at weekends before 3pm.
Societies	apply in writing/telephone
Green Fees	not confirmed.
Prof	Graham Harrison
Facilities	⊗ ⅏ ⓛ ⓑ ⚑ ♀ 🛆 ⚐
Location	S side of town centre off A1033

Hotel	★★★ 65% Quality Hotel Hull, 170 Ferensway, HULL ☎ 01482 325087 155 ⇄ ♠

YORKSHIRE, NORTH

ALDWARK   Map 08 SE46

Aldwark Manor YO61 1UF
☎ 01347 838353 Fax 01347 830007
An easy walking, scenic 18-hole parkland course with holes both sides of the River Ure. The course surrounds the Victorian Aldwark Manor Golf Hotel. A warm welcome to society and corporate days.
18 holes, 6171yds, Par 71, SSS 70, Course record 69.
Club membership 400.
Visitors	must contact in advance, restricted weekends.
Societies	must telephone in advance.
Green Fees	£30 per day; £25 per round (£35/£30 weekends & bank holidays).
Cards	🟦 🟥 🟦 🟥 🟦 🟥
Prof	Phil Harrison
Facilities & Leisure	⊗ ⅏ ⓛ ⓑ ⚑ ♀ 🛆 ⚐ ↑ ⚕ ∅ fishing.

Location	5m SE of Boroughbridge off A1, 12m NW of York off A19

Hotel ★★★ 69% Aldwark Manor Hotel, Golf & Country Club, ALDWARK
☎ 01347 838146 & 838251 Fax 01347 838867
25 ⇆ ♞ Annexe 3rm (2 ⇆ ♞)

BEDALE   Map 08 SE28

Bedale Leyburn Rd DL8 1EZ
☎ 01677 422451 Fax 01677 422451
Secluded parkland course with many trees and water features. A quiet, testing course ideal for beginners and the more adept golfer.
18 holes, 6610yds, Par 72, SSS 72, Course record 68.
Club membership 600.

Visitors	welcome when course is free, contact Professional or Secretary to book.
Societies	must apply in advance.
Green Fees	£20 per day (£30 weekends).
Prof	Tony Johnson
Facilities	⊗ ⅢⅬ ♥ ♀ ⚘ 🖻 ♞ ♨ ♿
Location	0.25 N of town on A684

Hotel ★ 69% Buck Inn, THORNTON WATLASS
☎ 01677 422461 7rm (5 ⇆ ♞)

BENTHAM   Map 07 SD66

Bentham Robin Ln LA2 7AG ☎ 01524 262455
Moorland course with glorious views.
9 holes, 5760yds, Par 70, SSS 69, Course record 69.
Club membership 480.

Visitors	no restrictions.
Societies	must apply in advance.
Green Fees	£15 per day.
Facilities	⊗ ⅢⅬ ♀ ⚘
Location	N side of High Bentham

Hotel ★★ 66% The Austwick Hotel, AUSTWICK
☎ 015242 51224 12rm

CATTERICK GARRISON   Map 08 SE29

Catterick Leyburn Rd DL9 3QE
☎ 01748 833268 Fax 01748 833268
Scenic parkland/moorland course of Championship standard, with good views of the Pennines and Cleveland hills. Testing 1st and 6th holes.
18 holes, 6329yds, Par 71, SSS 70, Course record 68.
Club membership 700.

Visitors	tee reservation system in operation telephone professional shop 01748 833671, Tuesday is Ladies day, Thursday Senior priority until 10am.
Societies	by arrangement.
Green Fees	£24 per round; £27 per 27 holes (£33 weekends).
Prof	Andy Marshall
Designer	Arthur Day
Facilities	⊗ ⅢⅬ ♥ ♀ ⚘ 🖻 ♞ ♨ ♿
Location	0.5m W of Catterick Garrison Centre

Hotel ★★ 68% King's Head Hotel, Market Place, RICHMOND ☎ 01748 850220
26 ⇆ ♞ Annexe 4 ⇆ ♞

Aldwark Manor Hotel, Golf and Country Club is set within 100 acres of mature parkland and is home to one of the country's most picturesque golf courses.
The Hotel boasts twenty eight individually designed and well appointed bedrooms which offer breathtaking views across the estate.
Our Rendlesham Restaurant and Bunker's Bar & Brasserie are managed by award winning head chef Andrew Burton and offer superb menus with dishes ranging from the traditional to light and contemporary cuisine.
So, whether you visit Aldwark Manor simply for a relaxing evening meal, a game of golf or a holiday break, you will receive a warm welcome and attentive personal service that you will remember long after you leave.

For further information, brochure and bookings, telephone 01347 838146

ALDWARK MANOR
HOTEL, GOLF & COUNTRY CLUB
Aldwark, Near Alne, York, Y061 1UF United Kingdom

Hotel Tel: +44 (0)1347 838146   Hotel Fax: +44 (0)1347 838867
Golf Tel: +44 (0)1347 838353   Golf Fax: +44 (0)1347 830007

COPMANTHORPE   Map 08 SE54

Pike Hills Tadcaster Rd YO23 3UW
☎ 01904 700797 Fax 01904 700797
Parkland course surrounding nature reserve. Level terrain.
18 holes, 6146yds, Par 71, SSS 70, Course record 67.
Club membership 750.

Visitors	welcome weekdays, with member only weekends & bank holidays.
Societies	must apply in advance.
Green Fees	£26 per day; £20 per round.
Prof	Ian Gradwell
Facilities	⊗ ⅢⅬ ♥ ♀ ⚘ 🖻 ♞ ♨ ♿
Location	3m SW of York on A64

Hotel ★★★★ 64% Swallow Hotel, Tadcaster Rd, YORK ☎ 01904 701000 113 ⇆ ♞

EASINGWOLD   Map 08 SE56

Easingwold Stillington Rd YO61 3ET
☎ 01347 821964 (Prof) & 822474 (Sec) Fax 01347 822474
Parkland course with easy walking. Trees are a major feature and on six holes water hazards come into play.
18 holes, 6627yds, Par 72, SSS 72, Course record 67.
Club membership 750.

Visitors	prior enquiry essential.
Societies	prior application in writing essential.
Green Fees	£30 per day; £25 per round (£30 weekends).
Prof	John Hughes
Designer	Hawtree
Facilities	⊗ ⅢⅬ ♥ ♀ ⚘ 🖻 ♨ ♿ ♟
Location	1m S of Easingwold, 12m N of York

▶

Hotel	★★ 67% George Hotel, Market Place, EASINGWOLD ☎ 01347 821698 14 ⇌ ↑

FILEY   Map 08 TA18

Filey West Av YO14 9BQ
☎ 01723 513293 Fax 01723 514952
Parkland course with good views. Stream runs through course. Testing 9th and 13th holes.
18 holes, 6112yds, Par 70, SSS 69, Course record 64.
Club membership 900.

Visitors	must telephone to reserve tee time.
Societies	contact by telephone.
Green Fees	£27 per day (£30 weekends); £21 per round (£28 weekends).
Prof	Gary Hutchinson
Designer	Braid
Facilities	⊗ ⫙ ⓑ ▣ ♀ ⌂ ☆ ↑ ▾ ⇻ ✎
Location	0.5m S of Filey
Hotel	★★ 68% Wrangham House Hotel, 10 Stonegate, HUNMANBY ☎ 01723 891333 8 ⇌ ↑ Annexe 4 ⇌ ↑

GANTON   Map 08 SE97

Ganton YO12 4PA
☎ 01944 710329 Fax 01944 710922
Championship course, heathland, gorse-lined fairways and heavily bunkered; variable winds.
18 holes, 6734yds, Par 73, SSS 74, Course record 65.
Club membership 500.

Visitors	by prior arrangement.
Societies	prior arrangement in writing.
Green Fees	not confirmed.
Prof	Gary Brown
Designer	Dunn/Vardon/Braid/Colt
Facilities	⊗ ⫙ ⓑ ▣ ♀ ⌂ ☆ ↑ ▾ ⇻ ✎
Location	11m SW of Scarborough on A64
Hotel	★★★ 63% East Ayton Lodge Country House, Moor Ln, Forge Valley, EAST AYTON ☎ 01723 864227 11 ⇌ ↑ Annexe 20 ⇌ ↑

HARROGATE   Map 08 SE35

Harrogate Forest Ln Head, Starbeck HG2 7TF
☎ 01423 862999 Fax 01423 860073
One of Yorkshire's oldest and best courses was designed in 1897 by 'Sandy' Herd. A perfect example of golf architecture, its greens and fairways offer an interesting but fair challenge. The undulating parkland course once formed part of the ancient Forest of Knaresborough. Excellent clubhouse.
18 holes, 6241yds, Par 69, SSS 70, Course record 64.
Club membership 650.

Visitors	advisable to contact professional in advance, weekend play limited.
Societies	must contact in writing or intially by telephone.
Green Fees	£35 per day; £30 per round (£40 day/round weekends & bank holidays).
Cards	▭▭ ◻
Prof	Paul Johnson

Designer	Sandy Herd
Facilities & Leisure	⊗ ⫙ ⓑ ▣ ♀ ⌂ ☆ ✎ snooker.
Location	2.25m N on A59
Hotel	★★★ 66% The White House, 10 Park Pde, HARROGATE ☎ 01423 501388 10 ⇌ ↑

Oakdale Oakdale Glen HG1 2LN
☎ 01423 567162 & 567188 Fax 01423 536030
A pleasant, undulating parkland course which provides a good test of golf for the low handicap player without intimidating the less proficient. A special feature is an attractive stream which comes in to play on four holes. Excellent views from the clubhouse which has good facilities.
18 holes, 6456yds, Par 71, SSS 71, Course record 61.
Club membership 1034.

Visitors	no party bookings weekends.
Societies	telephone followed by letter.
Green Fees	£27 per round (£32 weekends & bank holidays).
Prof	Clive Dell
Designer	Dr McKenzie
Facilities	⊗ ⫙ ⓑ ▣ ♀ ⌂ ☆ ↑ ⇻ ✎
Location	N side of town centre off A61
Hotel	★★★ 71% Grants Hotel, 3-13 Swan Rd, HARROGATE ☎ 01423 560666 42 ⇌ ↑

Rudding Park House & Hotel Rudding Park, Follifoot HG3 1DJ ☎ 01423 872100 Fax 01423 873011
The course provides panoramic views over the surrounding countryside and good drainage makes it playable for most of the year. Societies are particularly welcome.
18 holes, 6871yds, Par 72, SSS 73, Course record 72.

Visitors	handicap certificate required, tee reservation available 7 days in advance.
Societies	apply by telephone in advance.
Green Fees	£19 per 18 holes (£22.50 weekends & bank holidays).
Cards	▭▭ ▭▭ ▭ ◻
Prof	Simon Hotham
Designer	Martin Hawtree
Facilities & Leisure	⊗ ⫙ ⓑ ▣ ♀ ⌂ ☆ ↑ ⌂ ▾ ⇻ ✎ ↑ heated outdoor swimming pool.
Location	2m SE of Harrogate town centre, off A658 follow brown tourist signs
Hotel	★★★★ 76% Rudding Park House & Hotel, Rudding Park, Follifoot, HARROGATE ☎ 01423 871350 50 ⇌ ↑

HOWDEN   Map 08 SE72

Boothferry Park Spaldington Ln DN14 7NG
☎ 01430 430364
Pleasant meadowland course in the Vale of York with interesting natural dykes creating extra challenge on some holes. The par3 5th over water will test your nerve.
18 holes, 6651yds, Par 73, SSS 72, Course record 64.
Club membership 500.

▶

Visitors	must contact in advance, tee times bookable.
Societies	must contact for booking form.
Green Fees	not confirmed.
Prof	Nigel Bundy
Designer	Donald Steel
Facilities	⊗ ⁞⁞⁞ ㄴ ♥ ♀ ⚐ 🏌 🏌 ✓ 🦮
Location	2.5m N of Howden off B1228

Hotel ★★ 70% Clifton Hotel, 155 Boothferry Rd, GOOLE ☎ 01405 761336 9rm (8 ⇄ 🦮)

KIRKBYMOORSIDE Map 08 SE68

Kirkbymoorside Manor Vale YO62 6EG
☎ 01751 431525 Fax 01751 433190
Hilly parkland course with narrow fairways, gorse and hawthorn bushes. Beautiful views.
18 holes, 6101yds, Par 69, SSS 69, Course record 65.
Club membership 650.

Visitors	are advised to contact in advance, may not play before 9.30 or between 12.30-1.30.
Societies	must apply in advance.
Green Fees	£20 per day (£27 weekends & bank holidays).
Facilities	⊗ ⁞⁞⁞ ㄴ ♥ ♀ ⚐ 🏌 ✓
Location	N side of village

Hotel ★★ 65% George & Dragon Hotel, 17 Market Place, KIRKBYMOORSIDE ☎ 01751 433334 12 ⇄ 🦮 Annexe 7 ⇄ 🦮

KNARESBOROUGH Map 08 SE35

Knaresborough Boroughbridge Rd HG5 0QQ
☎ 01423 862690 Fax 01423 869345
Undulating parkland course with mature trees and two water features in attractive rural setting.
18 holes, 6433yds, Par 70, SSS 71, Course record 67.
Club membership 802.

Visitors	restricted start times summer weekends.
Societies	apply by telephone or letter, no bookings for Sat, Sun or Tue.
Green Fees	£35 per day; £28 per round (£40/£35 weekends).
Prof	Gary J Vickers
Designer	Hawtree
Facilities	⊗ ⁞⁞⁞ ㄴ ♥ ♀ ⚐ 🏌 ✓
Location	1.25 N on A6055

Hotel ★★★ 70% Dower House Hotel, Bond End, KNARESBOROUGH ☎ 01423 863302 28 ⇄ 🦮 Annexe 3 ⇄ 🦮

MALTON Map 08 SE77

Malton & Norton Welham Park, Norton YO17 9QE
☎ 01653 693882 Fax 01653 697912
Parkland course, consisting of 3 nine hole loops, with panoramic views of the moors. Very testing 1st hole (564 yds dog-leg, left).
Welham Course: 18 holes, 6456yds, Par 72, SSS 71.
Park Course: 18 holes, 6242yds, Par 72, SSS 70.
Derwent Course: 18 holes, 6286yds, Par 72, SSS 70.
Club membership 825.

Visitors	anytime except during competitions.
Societies	telephone and confirm in writing.
Green Fees	not confirmed.
Cards	💳 💳 💳

Prof	S Robinson
Facilities	⊗ ⁞⁞⁞ ㄴ ♥ ♀ ⚐ 🏌 ✓
Location	1m S

Hotel ★★★★♨ 71% Burythorpe House Hotel, Burythorpe, MALTON ☎ 01653 658200 11 ⇄ 🦮 Annexe 5 ⇄ 🦮

MASHAM Map 08 SE28

Masham Burnholme, Swinton Rd HG4 4HT
☎ 01765 688054 Fax 01765 688054
Flat parkland course crossed by River Burn, which comes into play on several holes.
9 holes, 6068yds, Par 70, SSS 69, Course record 73.
Club membership 327.

Visitors	must play with member at weekends & bank holidays.
Societies	write or telephone well in advance.
Green Fees	£20 per day/round.
Facilities	⊗ by prior arrangement ⁞⁞⁞ by prior arrangement ㄴ by prior arrangement ♥ by prior arrangement ♀ ⚐
Location	8m from junction of B6267 off A1 signposted Thirsk/Masham. Then 1m SW off A6108

Hotel ★ 69% Buck Inn, THORNTON WATLASS ☎ 01677 422461 7rm (5 ⇄ 🦮)

MIDDLESBROUGH Map 08 NZ41

Middlesbrough Brass Castle Ln, Marton TS8 9EE
☎ 01642 311515 Fax 01642 319607
Undulating parkland course, prevailing winds. Testing 6th, 12th and 15th holes.
18 holes, 6215yds, Par 70, SSS 70, Course record 63.
Club membership 960.

Visitors	restricted Tue & Sat.
Societies	Wed, Thu & Fri only. Must contact the club in advance.
Green Fees	£31 per day (£36 weekends & bank holidays).
Prof	Don Jones
Facilities	⊗ ⁞⁞⁞ ㄴ ♥ ♀ ⚐ 🏌 🦮 ✓
Location	4m S off A172

Hotel ★★★ 70% Parkmore Hotel, 636 Yarm Rd, Eaglescliffe, STOCKTON-ON-TEES ☎ 01642 786815 55 ⇄ 🦮

Middlesbrough Municipal Ladgate Ln TS5 7YZ
☎ 01642 315533 Fax 01642 300726
Parkland course with good views. The front nine holes have wide fairways and large, often well-guarded greens while the back nine demand shots over tree-lined water hazards and narrow entrances to subtly contoured greens. Driving range.
18 holes, 6333yds, Par 71, SSS 70, Course record 67.
Club membership 630.

Visitors	book on the day weekdays, 7days in advance for weekends & bank holidays.
Societies	apply in writing giving at least 2 weeks in advance.
Green Fees	£10.50 (£13 weekends & bank holidays).
Prof	Alan Hope
Designer	Shuttleworth
Facilities	ㄴ ♥ ♀ ⚐ 🏌 🦮 ✓ 🦮
Location	2m S of Middlesbrough on the A174

▶

Hotel   ★★★ 70% Parkmore Hotel, 636 Yarm Rd,
                   Eaglescliffe, STOCKTON-ON-TEES
                   ☎ 01642 786815   55 ⇔ ♠

NORTHALLERTON   Map 08 SE39

Romanby Yafforth Rd DL7 0PE
☎ 01609 779988 Fax 01609 779084
Set in natural undulating terrain with the River Wiske
meandering through the course it offers a testing round of
golf for all abilities. In addition to the river, two lakes come
into play on the 2nd, 5th and 11th holes. 12-bay floodlit
driving range.
18 holes, 6663yds, Par 72, SSS 72, Course record 72.
Club membership 575.
Visitors   welcome everyday please book tee time in
                    advance.
Societies   contact Grant McDonnell for details, tel 01609
                    778855.
Green Fees not confirmed.
Cards   ▭ ▭ ▭ ▩ 🖭
Prof   Tim Jenkins
Designer   Will Adamson
Facilities   ⊗ �𝍦 ⅃ 🍷 ♀ ⚲ 🏠 ⚑ 🐦 ⚒ ⚓ ⛳ ⛴
Location   On the main Northallerton/Richmond road
                   B6271, 1m W of Northallerton

Hotel   ★★ 68% The Golden Lion, High St,
                   NORTHALLERTON
                   ☎ 01609 777411   25 ⇔ ♠

PANNAL   Map 08 SE35

Pannal Follifoot Rd HG3 1ES
☎ 01423 872628 Fax 01423 870043
Fine championship course. Moorland turf but well-
wooded with trees closely involved with play.
18 holes, 6622yds, Par 72, SSS 72, Course record 62.
Club membership 780.
Visitors   preferable to contact in advance, weekends
                    limited.
Societies   apply in advance.
Green Fees £40 per round; £50 per 36 holes (£50 per
                    round weekends & bank holidays).
Prof   David Padgett
Designer   Sandy Herd
Facilities   ⊗ ⟊ ⅃ 🍷 ♀ ⚲ 🏠 ⚑ ⚒ ⛳
Location   E side of village off A61

Hotel   ★★★ 69% The Imperial, Prospect Place,
                   HARROGATE
                   ☎ 01423 565071   85 ⇔ ♠

RAVENSCAR   Map 08 NZ90

Raven Hall Hotel Golf Course YO13 0ET
☎ 01723 870353 Fax 01723 870072
Opened by the Earl of Cranbrook in 1898, this 9-hole clifftop
course is sloping and with good quality small greens.
Because of its clifftop position it is subject to strong winds
which make it great fun to play, especially the 6th hole.
9 holes, 1894yds, Par 32, SSS 32.
Club membership 120.

Visitors   must contact in advance, busy at weekends,
                    spikes essential, no jeans/T shirts.
Societies   telephone in advance.
Green Fees not confirmed.
Cards   ▭ ▬▬ ▬▬ 🖭
Facilities   ⊗ ⟊ ⅃ 🍷 ♀ ⚑ 🏓
& Leisure   hard tennis courts, heated indoor plus outdoor
                    swimming pool, sauna.
Location   Situated on cliff top

Hotel   ★★★ 64% Raven Hall Country House Hotel &
                   Golf Course, RAVENSCAR
                   ☎ 01723 870353   53 ⇔ ♠

REDCAR   Map 08 NZ62

Cleveland Queen St TS10 1BT
☎ 01642 471798 Fax 01642 471798
The oldest golf club in Yorkshire playing over the only links
championship course in Yorkshire. A true test of traditional
golf, especially when windy. Flat seaside links with easy
walking.
18 holes, 6700yds, Par 72, SSS 72, Course record 67.
Club membership 820.
Visitors   advisable to book in advance.
Societies   initially telephone for details.
Green Fees £22 per day; £20 per round (£26/£22 weekends).
Prof   Stephen Wynn
Facilities   ⊗ ⟊ ⅃ 🍷 ♀ ⚲ 🏠
Location   8m E of Middlesborough, at N end of Redcar

Hotel   ★★★★♨ 71% Grinkle Park Hotel,
                   EASINGTON ☎ 01287 640515   20 ⇔ ♠

Wilton Wilton TS10 4QY
☎ 01642 465265 (Secretary) & 452730 (Prof) Fax 01642 46
5463
Parkland course with some fine views.
18 holes, 6126yds, Par 70, SSS 69, Course record 64.
Club membership 750.
Visitors   telephone professional 01642 452730 to check
                    availability, no visitors Saturday, Ladies
                    competition have priority Tuesday, tee off 10am
                    or later.
Societies   must telephone secretary in advance.
Green Fees £20 per day (£26 Sun & bank holidays).
Prof   P D Smillie
Facilities   ⊗ ⟊ by prior arrangement ⅃ 🍷 ♀ ⚲ 🏠 ⚔
& Leisure   snooker.
Location   3m W of Redcar, on A174

Hotel   ★★★★♨ 71% Grinkle Park Hotel,
                   EASINGTON ☎ 01287 640515   20 ⇔ ♠

RICHMOND   Map 07 NZ10

Richmond Bend Hagg DL10 5EX
☎ 01748 823231(Secretary)
Undulating parkland course. Ideal to play 27 holes, not too
testing but very interesting.
18 holes, 5769yds, Par 70, SSS 68, Course record 63.
Club membership 600.
Visitors   may not play before 3.30am on Sun.
Societies   must contact in writing or telephone 01748
                    822457.
Green Fees £22 per day, £20 per round (£30/25 weekends).
Prof   Paul Jackson

▶

Designer	P Pennink
Facilities	⊗ ℿ ⅃ 🍺 ♀ ⚒ 🏧 🍴 🚡 ⚡
Location	0.75m N
Hotel	★★ 68% King's Head Hotel, Market Place, RICHMOND ☎ 01748 850220 26 ⇆ ⋒ Annexe 4 ⇆ ⋒

RIPON
Map 08 SE37

Ripon City Palace Rd HG4 3HH
☎ 01765 603640 Fax 01765 692880
Moderate walking on undulating parkland course; two testing par 3's at 5th and 16th.
18 holes, 6084yds, Par 70, SSS 69, Course record 66.
Club membership 675.

Visitors	book with professional. Limited play Sat especially Apr-Aug.
Societies	contact in writing or telephone.
Green Fees	£20 (£30 weekends & bank holidays).
Prof	S T Davis
Designer	H Varden
Facilities	⚒ 🍴 🛄 🏧 ⚡
Location	1m NW on A6108
Hotel	★★★ 68% Ripon Spa Hotel, Park St, RIPON ☎ 01765 602172 40 ⇆ ⋒

SALTBURN-BY-THE-SEA
Map 08 NZ62

Hunley Hall Golf Club & Hotel Ings Ln, Brotton
TS12 2QQ ☎ 01287 676216 Fax 01287 678250
A picturesque 27 hole coastal course a providing a good test of golf for all abilities.
Morgans: 18 holes, 6918yds, Par 73, SSS 73, Course record 68.
Millennium: 18 holes, 5948yds, Par 68, SSS 68.
Imperial: 18 holes, 6586yds, Par 72, SSS 71.
Club membership 400.

Visitors	tee off times must be reserved in advance, times available between 9.30-11.30am and after 1pm.
Societies	telephone for information and availability.
Green Fees	£20 per round/day (£30 weekends & Bank holidays).
Cards	🔲🔲🔲🔲🔲
Prof	Andrew Brook
Designer	John Morgan
Facilities	⊗ ℿ ⅃ 🍺 ♀ ⚒ 🏧 🍴 ⛴ 🚡 ⚡ †
Location	From A174 take St Margarets Way 0.5m to club
Hotel	★★★⚓ 71% Grinkle Park Hotel, EASINGTON ☎ 01287 640515 20 ⇆ ⋒

Saltburn by the Sea Hob Hill, Guisborough Rd TS12 1NJ
☎ 01287 622812 Fax 01287 625988
Undulating meadowland course surrounded by woodland. Particularly attractive in autumn. There are fine views of the Cleveland Hills and of Tees Bay.
18 holes, 5846yds, Par 70, SSS 68, Course record 62.
Club membership 900.

Visitors	telephone in advance, no visitors on Saturday.
Societies	apply in writing.
Green Fees	not confirmed.
Prof	Mike Nutter
Designer	J Braid
Facilities	⚒ 🏧 ⚡
Location	0.5m out of Saltburn on Guisborough road
Hotel	★★★★⚓ 71% Grinkle Park Hotel, EASINGTON ☎ 01287 640515 20 ⇆ ⋒

SCARBOROUGH
Map 08 TA08

Scarborough North Cliff North Cliff Av YO12 6PP
☎ 01723 360786 Fax 01723 362134
Seaside parkland course begining on cliff top overlooking bay and castle. Good views.
18 holes, 6425yds, Par 71, SSS 71, Course record 66.
Club membership 895.

Visitors	must be member of a club with handicap certificate. May not play before 10.30am Sun.
Societies	prior booking with secretary for parties of 8-40.
Green Fees	£28 per day; £21 per round (£30/£25 weekends & bank holidays).
Prof	Simon N Deller
Designer	James Braid
Facilities	⊗ ℿ ⅃ 🍺 ♀ ⚒ 🏧 🍴 🚡 ⚡
Location	2m N of town centre off A165
Hotel	★★★ 65% Esplanade Hotel, Belmont Rd, SCARBOROUGH ☎ 01723 360382 73 ⇆ ⋒

Scarborough South Cliff Deepdale Av YO11 2UE
☎ 01723 374737
Parkland/seaside course designed by Dr Mackenzie.
18 holes, 6039yds, Par 70, SSS 69, Course record 66.
Club membership 700.

Visitors	contact in advance may not play before 9.30am Mon-Fri, 10am Sat and 10.30am Sun.
Societies	must contact Secretary in advance.
Green Fees	not confirmed.
Prof	A R Skingle
Designer	McKenzie
Facilities	⊗ ℿ ⅃ 🍺 ♀ ⚒ 🏧 🍴 ⚡
Location	1m S on A165
Hotel	★★ 65% Bradley Court Hotel, Filey Rd, South Cliff, SCARBOROUGH ☎ 01723 360476 40 ⇆ ⋒

SELBY
Map 08 SE63

Selby Brayton Barff YO8 9LD ☎ 01757 228622
Mainly flat, links-type course; prevailing SW wind. Testing holes around the 3rd, 7th and 16th.
18 holes, 6246yds, Par 70, SSS 70, Course record 63.
Club membership 840.

Visitors	contact professional on 01757 228785, members and guests only at weekends.

▶

Societies	welcome Mon-Fri, must apply in advance.
Green Fees	£30 per day; £25 per round.
Cards	▩ ▩ ▩ ▩ 🖥
Prof	Andrew Smith
Designer	J Taylor & Hawtree
Facilities	⊗ �𝄞 ⅃ 💺 ♥ ♀ ♨ 🏠 🖝 ✧
Location	Off A19 at Brayton

Hotel	★★★⚑⚑ 68% Monk Fryston Hall, MONK FRYSTON ☎ 01977 682369 30 ⇄ 🐾

SETTLE   Map 07 SD86

Settle Buckhaw Brow, Giggleswick BD24 0DH
☎ 01729 825288 Fax 01729 825288
Picturesque parkland course with stream affecting play on four holes.
9 holes, 5414yds, Par 68, SSS 66, Course record 59.
Club membership 380.

Visitors	may not play before 4pm on Sun.
Societies	apply in writing or telephone 4 weeks in advance.
Green Fees	£12 per day (£12 per round weekends).
Designer	Tom Vardon
Facilities	⅃
Location	1m N on A65

Hotel	★★ 66% The Austwick Hotel, AUSTWICK ☎ 015242 51224 12rm

SKIPTON   Map 07 SD95

Skipton Off North West By-Pass BD23 1LL
☎ 01756 795657 Fax 01756 796665
Undulating parkland course with some water hazards and panoramic views.
18 holes, 6049yds, Par 70, SSS 69, Course record 67.
Club membership 800.

Visitors	welcome by prior arrangement.
Societies	must apply in writing.
Green Fees	£24 per day (£26 weekends & bank holidays).
Prof	Peter Robinson
Facilities & Leisure	⊗ �𝄞 ⅃ 💺 ♥ ♀ ♨ 🏠 🖝 snooker.
Location	1m N of Skipton on A59

Hotel	★★★ The Devonshire Arms Country House Hotel, BOLTON ABBEY ☎ 01756 710441 41 ⇄ 🐾

TADCASTER   Map 08 SE44

Cocksford Cocksford, Stutton LS24 9NG
☎ 01937 834253
The course is set on undulating meadowland with the famous Cock Beck featuring on 8 of the original 18 holes. Whatever combination you choose the course is relatively short featuring a number of drivable par 4s, but beware danger surrounds many of the greens!
Old Course: 18 holes, 5570yds, Par 71, SSS 69, Course record 65.
Plews Course: 18 holes, 5559yds, Par 70, SSS 68.
Quarry Hills Course: 18 holes, 4951yds, Par 67, SSS 65.
Club membership 450.

Visitors	welcome, contact pro shop.
Societies	telephone the secretary.

Green Fees	Old course: £21 per day; £17 per round (£26/£23 weekends). Plews: £9 per day; £6 per round.
Cards	▩ ▩ ▩ 🖥
Prof	Graham Thompson
Facilities	⊗ �𝄞 ⅃ 💺 ♥ ♀ ♨ 🏠 🖝 ✧
Location	Between York & Leeds, adjacent to the village of Stutton

Hotel	★★★⚑⚑ 75% Wood Hall Hotel, Trip Ln, Linton, WETHERBY ☎ 01937 587271 36 ⇄ 🐾 Annexe 6 ⇄ 🐾

Scathingwell Scarthingwell LS24 9PF
☎ 01937 557864 (pro) 557878 (club) Fax 01937 557909
Testing water hazards and well placed bunkers and trees provide a challenging test of golf for all handicaps at this scenic parkland course, located 4 miles south of Tadcaster.
18 holes, 6771yds, Par 72, SSS 72.
Club membership 500.

Visitors	dress code must be adhered to.
Societies	golf packages available, book one month in advance.
Green Fees	£16 per round (£18 weekends).
Prof	Steve Footman
Facilities	⊗ �𝄞 ⅃ 💺 ♥ ♀ ♨ 🏠 ✧
Location	4m S of Tadcaster on the A162 Tadcaster/Ferrybridge road, approx 2m from the A1

Hotel	★★★ 56% Posthouse Leeds/Selby, SOUTH MILFORD ☎ 0870 400 9050 97 ⇄ 🐾

THIRSK   Map 08 SE48

Thirsk & Northallerton Thornton-le-Street YO7 4AB
☎ 01845 522170 & 525115 Fax 01845 525115
The course has good views of the nearby Hambleton Hills. Testing course, mainly flat land.
18 holes, 6514yds, Par 72, SSS 71.
Club membership 500.

Visitors	must telephone in advance, and have handicap certificate. No play Sun unless with member.
Societies	must apply in writing.
Green Fees	£25 per day; £20 per round (£25 per round Sat & BH).
Cards	▩
Prof	Robert Garner
Designer	ADAS
Facilities	⊗ ⅃ 💺 ♥ ♀ ♨ 🏠 🖝 🛒 ✧
Location	2m N on A168

Hotel	★★ 62% Three Tuns Hotel, Market Place, THIRSK ☎ 01845 523124 11 ⇄ 🐾

WHITBY   Map 08 NZ81

Whitby Low Stragglton, Sandsend Rd YO21 3SR
☎ 01947 600660 Fax 01947 600660
Seaside course with 4 holes along cliff tops and over ravines. Good views and fresh sea breeze.
18 holes, 6134yds, Par 71, Course record 66.
Club membership 800.

Visitors	may not play on competition days, parties must contact in advance.
Societies	must contact in writing.
Green Fees	£20 per day (£25 weekends and bank holidays).

▶

Prof	Richard Wood
Facilities	⊗ ⍫ ⮹ 🛉 ♥ ♀ ⚘ 🖼 ⚑ ✂
Location	1.5m NW on A174

Hotel	★★ 67% White House Hotel, Upgang Ln, West Cliff, WHITBY ☎ 01947 600469 10 ⇋ ₨

YORK   Map 08 SE65

Forest of Galtres Moorlands Rd, Skelton YO32 2RF
☎ 01904 766198 Fax 01904 769400
Level parkland course in the heart of the ancient Forest of Galtres with mature oak trees and interesting water features coming into play on the 6th, 14th and 17th holes. Views towards York Minster.
18 holes, 6312yds, Par 72, SSS 70, Course record 67.
Club membership 450.

Visitors	telephone to book, may play anytime.
Societies	not Sat, booking system, telephone for forms.
Green Fees	£23 per day; £18 per round (£27/£22 weekends & bank holidays).
Prof	Phil Bradley
Designer	Simon Gidman
Facilities	⊗ ⍫ by prior arrangement 🛉 ♥ ♀ ⚘ 🖼 ⚑ ✂
Location	0.5m from the York ring road B1237, just off A19 Thirsk road through the village of Skelton

Hotel	★★ 69% Beechwood Close Hotel, 19 Shipton Rd, Clifton, YORK ☎ 01904 658378 14 ⇋ ₨

Forest Park Stockton-on-the-Forest YO32 9UW
☎ 01904 400425
A parkland/meadowland course with natural features including a stream and mature and new trees.
Old Foss Course: 18 holes, 6600yds, Par 71, SSS 72, Course record 73.
The West Course: 9 holes, 3186yds, Par 70, SSS 70.
Club membership 600.

Visitors	welcome, subject to tee availability. Advisable to contact club in advance.
Societies	by prior arrangement.
Green Fees	£18 per 18 holes; £8 per 9 holes (£23/£10 weekends).
Cards	💳 💳 💳 💳 💳
Facilities	⊗ ⍫ 🛉 ♥ ♀ ⚘ 🖼 ⚑ ✂ ↑
Location	4m NE of York, 1.5m from end of A64, York bypass

Hotel	★★★ 72% York Pavilion Hotel, 45 Main St, Fulford, YORK ☎ 01904 622099 44 ⇋ ₨

Fulford Heslington Ln YO10 5DY
☎ 01904 413579 Fax 01904 416918
A flat, parkland/moorland course well-known for the superb quality of its turf, particularly the greens, and now famous as the venue for some of the best golf tournaments in the British Isles, in past years.
18 holes, 6775yds, Par 72, SSS 72, Course record 62.
Club membership 775.

Visitors	must contact in advance.
Societies	not Tue am, book with the manager.
Green Fees	£45 per day; £35 per round (£45 per round weekends & bank holidays).
Prof	Bryan Hessay
Designer	Dr Mckenzie

Facilities	⚘ 🖼 ⚑ ↘ ✂
Location	2m S of York off A19

Hotel	★★★★ 64% Swallow Hotel, Tadcaster Rd, YORK ☎ 01904 701000 113 ⇋ ₨

Heworth Muncaster House, Muncastergate YO31 9JY
☎ 01904 422389 Fax 01904 426156
12-hole parkland course, easy walking. Holes 3, 7 and 9 played twice from different tees.
12 holes, 6141yds, Par 70, SSS 69, Course record 68.
Club membership 550.

Visitors	advisable to telephone the professional in advance, no catering Mondays
Societies	apply in writing.
Green Fees	£18 per day; £14 per round (£20/£18 weekends).
Prof	Stephen Burdett
Designer	B Cheal
Facilities	⊗ ⍫ 🛉 ♥ ♀ ⚘ 🖼 ⚑ ✂
Location	1.5m NE of city centre on A1036

Hotel	★★★ 67% Monkbar Hotel, St Maurices Rd, YORK ☎ 01904 638086 99 ⇋ ₨

Swallow Hall Crockey Hill YO19 4SG
☎ 01904 448889 Fax 01904 448219
A small 18-hole, Par 3 course with 2 par 4s. Attached to a caravan park and holiday cottages.
18 holes, 3600yds, Par 56, SSS 56, Course record 58.
Club membership 100.

Visitors	no restrictions.
Societies	must telephone in advance.
Green Fees	£8 per 18 holes; £4 per 9 holes (£10/£5 weekends &bank holidays).
Designer	Brian Henry
Facilities	🛉 ♥ ♀ ⚘ 🖼 ⚑ ✂ ↑
& Leisure	hard tennis courts.
Location	Off A19, signposted to Wheldrake

Hotel	★★★ 72% York Pavilion Hotel, 45 Main St, Fulford, YORK ☎ 01904 622099 44 ⇋ ₨

York Lords Moor Ln, Strensall YO32 5XF
☎ 01904 491840 (Sec) 490304 (Pro) Fax 01904 491852
A pleasant, well-designed, heathland course with easy walking. The course is of good length but being flat the going does not tire. The course is well bunkered with excellent greens and there are two testing pond holes.
18 holes, 6301yds, Par 70, SSS 70, Course record 66.
Club membership 700.

Visitors	with member only weekends, must contact in advance.
Societies	more than 16 contact secretary, under 16 contact professional.
Green Fees	£31 per 18 holes.
Prof	A B Mason
Designer	J H Taylor
Facilities	⊗ ⍫ 🛉 ♥ ♀ ⚘ 🖼 ✂
Location	6m NE, E of Strensall village

Hotel	★★★ 75% Dean Court Hotel, Duncombe Place, YORK ☎ 01904 625082 39 ⇋ ₨

> **Looking for a driving range?**
> See the index at the back of the guide

YORKSHIRE, SOUTH

BARNSLEY   Map 08 SE30

Barnsley Wakefield Rd, Staincross S75 6JZ
☎ 01226 382856
Undulating municipal parkland course with easy walking
apart from last 4 holes. Testing 8th and 18th holes.
18 holes, 5951yds, Par 69, SSS 69, Course record 64.
Club membership 450.
Visitors	booking advisable telephone professional on 01226 380358.
Societies	by arrangement.
Green Fees	£9 per round (£10 weekends).
Prof	Shaun Wyke
Facilities	⊗ ⅲ ⅃ ⴹ ♥ ♀ ⌰ 🝙 ❞ ∅
Location	3m N on A61
Hotel	★★★ 71% Ardsley House Hotel & Health Club, Doncaster Rd, Ardsley, BARNSLEY ☎ 01226 309955 74 ⇋ ♠

Sandhill Middlecliffe Ln, Little Houghton S72 0HW
☎ 01226 753444 Fax 01226 753444
The course is reasonably flat with generously wide fairways
laid out between and amongst 25 acres of newly planted
woodlands. Holes of note are the 4th which is a 311 yard Par
4 to a horseshoe green around a 9-foot deep bunker; the 7th
Par 3 to blind reverse Mackenzie Green and the 11th 416
yard Par 4 dogleg where the brave can take on the out of
bounds.
18 holes, 6257yds, Par 71, SSS 70, Course record 69.
Club membership 275.
Visitors	welcome by prior booking.
Societies	telephone for availability, write to confirm.
Green Fees	£9 per round (£12 weekends & bank holidays).
Cards	🖃 💳 🄯
Designer	John Royston
Facilities	⊗ ⅲ ⅃ ⴹ ♥ ♀ ⌰ 🝙 ❛
Location	5m E of Barnsley, off A635
Hotel	★★★ 71% Ardsley House Hotel & Health Club, Doncaster Rd, Ardsley, BARNSLEY ☎ 01226 309955 74 ⇋ ♠

BAWTRY   Map 08 SK69

Austerfield Park Cross Ln, Austerfield DN10 6RF
☎ 01302 710841 Fax 01302 710850
Long moorland course with postage stamp 8th and testing
618-yd 7th. Driving range and Par 3 attached.
18 holes, 6900yds, Par 73, SSS 73, Course record 69.
Club membership 500.
Visitors	welcome weekdays, after 10am weekends.
Societies	must contact in advance.
Green Fees	£18 per day (£24 weekend).
Cards	🖃 💳
Prof	Darran Roberts
Facilities	⊗ ⅲ ⅃ ⴹ ♥ ♀ ⌰ 🝙 ❞ 🝙 ∅ ❛
Location	2m from Bawtry on A614
Hotel	★★★ 61% The Crown Hotel, High St, BAWTRY ☎ 01302 710341 57 ⇋ ♠

CONISBROUGH   Map 08 SK59

Crookhill Park Municipal Carr Ln DN12 2BE
☎ 01709 862979
A naturally sloping parkland course with many holes
featuring tight dog-legs and small, undulating greens. The
signature hole (11th) involves a fearsome tee shot over a
ditch onto a sloping fairway and final shot to an elevated
green surrounded by tall trees and deep bunkers.
18 holes, 5849yds, Par 70, SSS 68, Course record 64.
Club membership 350.
Visitors	booking system for general play.
Societies	bookings taken in advance, deposits taken through booking system.
Green Fees	not confirmed.
Prof	Richard Swaine
Facilities	⅃ ⴹ ♥ ♀ ⌰ 🝙 ∅
Location	1.5m SE on B6094
Hotel	★★★ 62% Danum Hotel, High St, DONCASTER ☎ 01302 342261 66 ⇋ ♠

DONCASTER   Map 08 SE50

Doncaster 278 Bawtry Rd, Bessacarr DN4 7PD
☎ 01302 868316 & 865994 Fax 01302 865994
Pleasant undulating heathland course with wooded
surroundings. Quick drying, ideal all year round course.
18 holes, 6220yds, Par 69, SSS 70, Course record 66.
Club membership 600.
Visitors	must contact in advance for both weekdays and weekends.
Societies	must contact in advance.
Green Fees	£23 per round (£28 weekends).
Prof	Graham Bailey
Designer	Mackenzie/Hawtree
Facilities	⊗ ⅲ ⅃ ⴹ ♥ ♀ ⌰ 🝙 ∅
Location	4m SE on A638
Hotel	★★★ 72% Mount Pleasant Hotel, Great North Rd, ROSSINGTON ☎ 01302 868696 & 868219 Fax 01302 865130 42 ⇋ ♠

Doncaster Town Moor Bawtry Rd, Belle Vue DN4 5HU
☎ 01302 535286 & 533167
Easy walking, but testing, heathland course with good true
greens. Friendly club. Notable hole is 11th (par 4), 464 yds.
Situated in centre of racecourse.
18 holes, 6072yds, Par 69, SSS 69, Course record 66.
Club membership 520.
Societies	must contact in advance.
Green Fees	not confirmed.
Prof	Steven Shaw
Facilities	⊗ ⅲ ⅃ ⴹ ♥ ♀ ⌰ 🝙 ∅
Location	1.5m E,at racecourse,on A638
Hotel	★★★ 62% Danum Hotel, High St, DONCASTER ☎ 01302 342261 66 ⇋ ♠

Owston Park Owston Ln, Owston DN6 8EF
☎ 01302 330821
A flat easy walking course surrounded by woodland. A lot of
mature trees and a few ditches in play. A practice putting
green and chipping area.
9 holes, 2866yds, Par 35, SSS 70.
Visitors	no restrictions.

Societies telephone in advance.
Green Fees £4.25 per 9 holes (£4.50 weekends).
Cards ▭ ▭ ▭ ▭ ▭ 🖸
Prof Mike Parker
Designer M Parker
Facilities ♥ 🏖 🏠 🍴 🏌
Location 5m N of Doncaster off A19

Hotel ★★★ 62% Danum Hotel, High St,
DONCASTER ☎ 01302 342261 66 ⇨ ⋔

Thornhurst Park Holme Ln, Owston DN5 0LR
☎ 01302 337799 Fax 01302 721495
Surrounded by Owston Wood, this scenic parkland course
has numerous strategically placed bunkers, and a lake comes
into play at the 7th and 8th holes.
18 holes, 6490yds, Par 72, SSS 72, Course record 72.
Club membership 160.
Visitors must wear trousers, shirt with collar and golf
shoes, can contact 2 days in advance.
Societies telephone or write in advance.
Green Fees £10 per 18 holes; £5 per 9 holes (£12/£6
weekends & bank holidays).
Cards ▭ ▭ ▭ ▭ 🖸
Prof Kevin Pearce
Facilities ⊗ 🍴 🏖 ♥ 🏖 🏠 🏌
Location On the A19 between Bentley/Askern, easy
access from M62 and A1 (M)

Hotel ★★★ 62% Danum Hotel, High St,
DONCASTER ☎ 01302 342261 66 ⇨ ⋔

Wheatley Armthorpe Rd DN2 5QB
☎ 01302 831655 & 834085 Fax 01302 834085
Fairly flat well-bunkered, lake-holed, parkland course. Well-
drained, in excellent condition all year round.
18 holes, 6405yds, Par 71, SSS 71, Course record 64.
Club membership 600.
Visitors telephone in advance. Must contact in advance.
Societies must contact professional in advance.
Green Fees £26 per round (£38 weekends & bank holidays).
Cards ▭ ▭ ▭ ▭ 🖸
Prof Steven Fox
Designer George Duncan
Facilities ⊗ 🍴 🏖 ♥ 🏖 🏠 🏌
Location NE side of town centre off A18

Hotel ★★★ 67% Regent Hotel, Regent Square,
DONCASTER ☎ 01302 364180 50 ⇨ ⋔

HATFIELD
Map 08 SE60

Kings Wood Thorne Rd DN7 6EP ☎ 01405 741343
A flat course with ditches that come into play on several
holes, especially on the testing back nine. Notable holes are
the 12th par 4, 16th and par 5 18th. Water is a prominent
feature with several large lakes strategically placed.
18 holes, 6002yds, Par 70, SSS 69, Course record 69.
Club membership 100.
Visitors visitors are welcome any time of week.
Societies or telephone in advance.
Green Fees £7 per 18 holes (£8 weekends & bank holidays).
Cards ▭ ▭ ▭ ▭ 🖸
Prof Jonathan Drury
Designer John Hunt
Facilities ♥ 🏠 🍴 🏌
Location 2m SW of junct 1 of M180, take A614 to
Thorne, then Thorne road to Hatfield

Hotel ★★ 70% Belmont Hotel, Horsefair Green,
THORNE ☎ 01405 812320 23 ⇨ ⋔

HICKLETON
Map 08 SE40

Hickleton Lidgett Ln DN5 7BE
☎ 01709 896081 Fax 01709 896081
Undulating, picturesque parkland course designed by Neil
Coles and Brian Huggett offering a good test of golf.
18 holes, 6434yds, Par 71, SSS 71, Course record 68.
Club membership 625.
Visitors restricted weekdays after 9am & weekends after
2.30pm. Must contact in advance.
Societies must contact in advance.
Green Fees £21 per day, £17 per round (£26 per day/round
weekends & bank holidays).
Prof Paul Shepherd
Designer Huggett/Coles
Facilities ⊗ 🍴 🏖 ♥ 🏖 🏠 🏌 🏌
Location 0.5m W on B6411

Hotel ★★★ 62% Danum Hotel, High St,
DONCASTER ☎ 01302 342261 66 ⇨ ⋔

HIGH GREEN
Map 08 SK39

Tankersley Park S35 4LG
☎ 0114 246 8247 Fax 0114 245 5583
Rolling parkland course that demands accuracy rather than
length. Lush fairways. A good test of golf.
18 holes, 6212yds, Par 69, SSS 70, Course record 64.
Club membership 634.
Visitors must contact in advance.
Societies must apply in writing.
Green Fees £32 per day; £25 per round.
Cards 🖸
Prof Ian Kirk
Designer Hawtree
Facilities ⊗ 🍴 🏖 ♥ 🏖 🏠 🏌 🏌
Location Off A61/M1 onto A616, Stocksbridge bypass

Hotel ★★★ 69% Tankersley Manor, Church Ln,
TANKERSLEY ☎ 01226 744700 70 ⇨ ⋔

RAWMARSH
Map 08 SK49

Wath Abdy Ln S62 7SJ
☎ 01709 872149 & 878609 (office) Fax 01709 878609
Parkland course, not easy in spite of its length; 17th hole (par
3) is a difficult 244yds with narrow driving area.
18 holes, 5857yds, Par 68, SSS 68.
Club membership 550.
Visitors must play with member at weekends. Must
contact in advance and have a handicap
certificate.
Societies must contact in writing, may not play at
weekends.
Green Fees not confirmed.
Prof Chris Bassett
Facilities ⊗ 🍴 🏖 ♥ 🏖 🏠 🏌
Location 2.5m N off A633

Hotel ★★★ 61% Carlton Park Hotel, 102/104
Moorgate Rd, ROTHERHAM
☎ 01709 849955 76 ⇨ ⋔

ROTHERHAM   Map 08 SK49

Grange Park Upper Wortley Rd S61 2SJ ☎ 01709 559497
Parkland/meadowland course, with panoramic views
especially from the back nine. The golf is testing, particularly
at the 1st, 4th and 18th holes (par 4), and 8th, 12th and 15th
(par 5).
*18 holes, 6421yds, Par 71, SSS 71, Course record 65.
Club membership 214.*

Visitors	no restrictions.
Societies	apply in writing to professional.
Green Fees	£9.50 per round (£11.50 weekends & bank holidays).
Prof	Eric Clark
Designer	Fred Hawtree
Facilities	⊗ ⪦ ⮬ ♥ ♀ ⚎ 🏠 ⛳ ⫝
Location	3m NW off A629

Hotel   ★★★ 69% Tankersley Manor, Church Ln,
TANKERSLEY ☎ 01226 744700   70 ⇆ 🐾

Phoenix Pavilion Ln, Brinsworth S60 5PA
☎ 01709 363864 & 382624 Fax 01709 363788
Undulating meadowland course with variable wind.
*18 holes, 6182yds, Par 71, SSS 69, Course record 65.
Club membership 1100.*

Visitors	must contact in advance.
Societies	must apply in writing.
Green Fees	not confirmed.
Prof	M Roberts
Designer	C K Cotton
Facilities	⊗ ⪦ ⮬ ♥ ♀ ⚎ 🏠 ⛳ ⫝
& Leisure	hard tennis courts, squash, fishing, gymnasium.
Location	SW side of town centre off A630

Hotel   ★★★ 61% Carlton Park Hotel, 102/104
Moorgate Rd, ROTHERHAM
☎ 01709 849955   76 ⇆ 🐾

Rotherham Golf Club Ltd Thrybergh Park, Doncaster Rd,
Thrybergh S65 4NU
☎ 01709 850812 (Secretary) Fax 01709 855288
Parkland course with easy walking along tree-lined fairways.
*18 holes, 6324yds, Par 70, SSS 70, Course record 65.
Club membership 500.*

Visitors	must contact in advance.
Societies	must contact secretary in advance.
Green Fees	not confirmed.
Prof	Simon Thornhill
Facilities	⚎ 🏠 🐾 ⫝ ⛳
Location	3.5m E on A630

Hotel   ★★★ 67% Elton Hotel, Main St,
Bramley, ROTHERHAM
☎ 01709 545681   13 ⇆ 🐾 Annexe 16 ⇆ 🐾

Sitwell Park Shrogswood Rd S60 4BY
☎ 01709 541046 Fax 01709 703637
Parkland course with easy walking.
*18 holes, 6209yds, Par 71, SSS 70, Course record 61.
Club membership 450.*

Visitors	must contact in advance. May not play on Sat.
Societies	must contact in advance.
Green Fees	£28 per day; £24 per round (£32/£28 weekends & bank holidays).
Prof	Nic Taylor
Designer	A MacKenzie
Facilities	⊗ ⪦ ⮬ ♥ ♀ ⚎ 🏠 ⫝ 🐾 ⛳
& Leisure	snooker.
Hotel	★★★★ 63% Hellaby Hall Hotel, Old Hellaby Ln, Hellaby, ROTHERHAM ☎ 01709 702701 52 ⇆ 🐾

SHEFFIELD   Map 08 SK38

Abbeydale Twentywell Ln, Dore S17 4QA
☎ 0114 236 0763
Parkland course, well-kept and wooded. Testing hole: 12th,
par 3.
*18 holes, 6419yds, Par 72, SSS 72.
Club membership 750.*

Visitors	by arrangement.
Societies	must apply in writing.
Green Fees	not confirmed.
Prof	Nigel Perry
Designer	Herbert Fowler
Facilities	⊗ ⪦ ⮬ ♥ ♀ ⚎ 🏠 ⛏ ⛳
Location	4m SW of city centre off A621

Hotel   ★★★ 65% Sheffield Moat House, Chesterfield
Rd South, SHEFFIELD
☎ 0114 282 9988 95 ⇆ 🐾

Beauchief Public Abbey Ln S8 0DB ☎ 0114 236 7274
Municipal course with natural water hazards. The rolling
land looks west to the Pennines and a 12th-century abbey
adorns the course.
*18 holes, 5452yds, Par 67, SSS 66, Course record 65.
Club membership 450.*

Visitors	are advised to book in advance in summer.
Societies	telephone pro-shop for advice.
Green Fees	not confirmed.
Prof	A Highfield
Facilities	⊗ ⮬ ♥ ♀ ⚎ 🏠 ⫝ ⛳
Location	4m SW of city centre off A621

Hotel   ★★★ 72% Beauchief Hotel, 161 Abbeydale Rd
South, SHEFFIELD
☎ 0114 262 0500 50 ⇆ 🐾

Birley Wood Birley Ln S12 3BP ☎ 0114 264 7262
Undulating meadowland course with well-varied features,
easy walking and good views. Practice range and putting
green.
*18 holes, 5100yds, Par 66, SSS 65, Course record 64.
Club membership 300.*

Visitors	apply in advance.
Societies	apply in advance.
Green Fees	£5.50 per round (£8.50 weekends).
Prof	Peter Ball
Facilities	♀ ⚎ ⫝
Location	4.5m SE of city centre off A616

Hotel   ★★★ 65% Mosborough Hall Hotel, High St,
Mosborough, SHEFFIELD
☎ 0114 248 4353 23 ⇆ 🐾

Concord Park Shiregreen Ln S5 6AE ☎ 0114 257 7378
Hilly municipal parkland course with some fairways wood-
flanked, good views, often windy. Seven par 3 holes.
*18 holes, 4872yds, Par 67, SSS 64, Course record 57.
Club membership 150.*

Visitors	no restrictions.
Societies	pay & play

▶

Green Fees £8-£10.

Prof W Allcroft

Facilities & Leisure hard tennis courts, heated indoor swimming pool, squash, gymnasium.

Location 3.5m N of city centre on B6086 off A6135

Hotel ★★★ 58% Posthouse Sheffield, Mancheater Rd, Broomhill, SHEFFIELD
☎ 0870 400 9071 136 ⇄ 🐾

Dore & Totley Bradway Rd, Bradway S17 4QR
☎ 0114 236 0492
Flat parkland course.
18 holes, 6265yds, Par 70, SSS 70, Course record 65.
Club membership 580.

Visitors must contact in advance a handicap certificate may be requested, may not play weekends.

Societies must apply in writing.

Green Fees not confirmed.

Facilities ⊗ 𝕸 ⅃ 🛢 ♀ ⚘ 🖾 ∂

Location 7m S of city centre on B6054 off A61

Hotel ★★★ 58% Posthouse Sheffield, Mancheater Rd, Broomhill, SHEFFIELD
☎ 0870 400 9071 136 ⇄ 🐾

Hallamshire Golf Club Ltd Sandygate S10 4LA
☎ 0114 230 2153 Fax 0114 230 2153
Situated on a shelf of land at a height of 850 ft. Magnificent views to the west. Moorland turf, long carries over ravine. Good natural drainage.
18 holes, 6359yds, Par 71, SSS 71, Course record 63.
Club membership 600.

Visitors contact professional in advance. Tees reserved for members 8-9.30 and noon-1.30.

Societies parties of 12+ should book in advance with secretary.

Green Fees not confirmed.

Cards ▭▭ ▭▭

Prof G R Tickell

Designer Various

Facilities ⊗ 𝕸 ⅃ 🛢 ♀ ⚘ 🖾 ♀ ∂

Location Off A57 at Crosspool onto Sandygate Rd, clubhouse 0.75m on right

Hotel ★★★ 58% Posthouse Sheffield, Mancheater Rd, Broomhill, SHEFFIELD
☎ 0870 400 9071 136 ⇄ 🐾

Hillsborough Worrall Rd S6 4BE
☎ 0114 234 9151 (Secretary) & 233 2666 (Pro)
Fax 0114 234 9151
Beautiful moorland/woodland course 500 ft above sea-level, reasonable walking. Challenging first four holes into a prevailing wind and a tight, testing 14th hole.
18 holes, 6216yards, Par 71, SSS 70, Course record 64.
Club membership 650.

Visitors contact professional in advance. May not play Tue (Ladies Day), Thu and weekends before 2pm

Societies must apply in writing to secretary.

Green Fees £28 per day (£35 per day weekends & bank holidays).

Prof Lewis Horsman

Facilities ⊗ 𝕸 ⅃ 🛢 ♀ ⚘ 🖾 ∂ 𝄡

Location 3m NW of city centre off A616

Hotel ★★★ 62% Rutland Hotel, 452 Glossop Rd, Broomhill, SHEFFIELD
☎ 0500 636943 (Central Res)
Fax 01773 880321 70 ⇄ 🐾 Annexe 13 ⇄ 🐾

Lees Hall Hemsworth Rd, Norton S8 8LL
☎ 0114 255 4402
Parkland/meadowland course with panoramic view of city.
18 holes, 6171yds, Par 71, SSS 70, Course record 63.
Club membership 695.

Visitors welcome.

Societies must apply in writing.

Green Fees not confirmed.

Prof S Berry

Facilities 𝕸 by prior arrangement ⅃ 🛢 ♀ ⚘ 🖾 ∂

Location 3.5m S of city centre off A6102

Hotel ★★★ 58% Posthouse Sheffield, Mancheater Rd, Broomhill, SHEFFIELD
☎ 0870 400 9071 136 ⇄ 🐾

Rother Valley Golf Centre Mansfield Rd, Wales Bar S26 5PQ ☎ 0114 247 3000 Fax 0114 247 6000
The challenging Blue Monster parkland course features a variety of water hazards. Notable holes include the 7th, with its island green fronted by water and dominated by bunkers to the rear. Lookout for the water on the par 5 18th.
18 holes, 6602yds, Par 72, SSS 72, Course record 70.
Club membership 500.

Visitors 2 days in advance booking format.

Societies apply in writing or telephone in advance.

Green Fees not confirmed.

Cards ▭▭ 📇 ▭▭ 🟧 ▭ 🛢

Prof Jason Ripley

Designer Michael Shattock & Mark Roe

Facilities ⊗ 𝕸 ⅃ 🛢 ♀ ⚘ 🖾 ♀ ⚘ 🔧 ∂ 𝄡

Location Off junct 31 of the M1, follow signs to Rother Valley Country Park

Hotel ★★★ 65% Mosborough Hall Hotel, High St, Mosborough, SHEFFIELD
☎ 0114 248 4353 23 ⇄ 🐾

Tinsley Park Municipal Golf High Hazels Park, Darnall S9 4PE ☎ 0114 2037435
Undulating meadowland course with plenty of trees and rough. A test for all categories of golfer.
18 holes, 6064yds, Par 71, SSS 69.
Club membership 600.

Visitors prior booking essential.

Societies apply in writing to Sheffield City Council, Recreation Dept., Meersbrook Park, Sheffield.

Green Fees £7.50 per round (£8.50 weekends).

Cards ▭▭ ▭ 🛢

Prof A P Highfield

Facilities ⊗ by prior arrangement 𝕸 by prior arrangement ⅃ 🛢 ♀ ⚘ 🖾 ♀ ∂

& Leisure hard tennis courts.

Location 4m E of city centre off A630

Hotel ★★★ 65% Mosborough Hall Hotel, High St, Mosborough, SHEFFIELD
☎ 0114 248 4353 23 ⇄ 🐾

SILKSTONE   Map 08 SE20

Silkstone Field Head, Elmhurst Ln S75 4LD
☎ 01226 790328 Fax 01226 792653
Parkland/downland course, fine views over the Pennines.
Testing golf.
18 holes, 6069yds, Par 70, SSS 70, Course record 64.
Club membership 508.
Visitors   with member only at weekends.
Societies   contact in advance.
Green Fees   £26 per day; £21 per round.
Prof   Kevin Guy
Facilities   ⊗ ⅲ ᴸ ♥ ♀ ♨ 🛍 ⚲ 🚵 ♂
Location   1m E off A628

Hotel   ★★★ 71% Ardsley House Hotel & Health
                  Club, Doncaster Rd, Ardsley, BARNSLEY
                  ☎ 01226 309955   74 ⇆ ☞

STOCKSBRIDGE   Map 08 SK29

Stocksbridge & District 30 Royd Ln, Townend, Deepcar
S36 2RZ ☎ 0114 288 2003 (office) & 288 2779 (pro)
Hilly moorland course.
18 holes, 5200yds, Par 65, SSS 65, Course record 60.
Club membership 470.
Visitors   contact the professional.
Societies   apply to secretary.
Green Fees   not confirmed.
Prof   Timothy Brookes
Designer   Dave Thomas
Facilities   ⊗ ⅲ ᴸ ♥ ♀ ♨ 🛍
Location   S side of town centre

Hotel   ★★★ 58% Posthouse Sheffield, Mancheater
                  Rd, Broomhill, SHEFFIELD
                  ☎ 0870 400 9071 136 ⇆ ☞

THORNE   Map 08 SE61

Thorne Kirton Ln DN8 5RJ
☎ 01405 812084 Fax 01405 741899
Picturesque parkland course with 6000 newly planted trees.
Water hazards on 11th, 14th & 18th holes.
18 holes, 5366yds, Par 68, SSS 66, Course record 62.
Club membership 300.
Visitors   no restrictions.
Societies   telephone in advance.
Green Fees   £9 per round (£10 weekends).
Cards   ▭ ▭ ▭ ▭ ▭ ▭
Prof   Edward Highfield
Designer   R D Highfield
Facilities   ⊗ ⅲ ᴸ ♥ ♀ ♨ 🛍 ⚲ 🚵 ♂
Location   8m E of Doncaster

Hotel   ★★ 70% Belmont Hotel, Horsefair Green,
                  THORNE ☎ 01405 812320   23 ⇆ ☞

WORTLEY   Map 08 SK39

Wortley Hermit Hill Ln S35 7DF
☎ 0114 288 8469 Fax 0114 288 8469
Well-wooded, undulating parkland course sheltered from
prevailing wind.
18 holes, 6028yds, Par 69, SSS 68, Course record 62.
Club membership 510.

Visitors   may not play between 11.30am and 1pm. Must
                  contact professional in advance and hold a
                  handicap certificate.
Societies   telephone in advance and confirm in writing
                  with deposit.
Green Fees   not confirmed.
Cards   ▭ ▭
Prof   Ian Kirk
Facilities   ⊗ ⅲ ᴸ ♥ ♀ ♨ 🛍 ⚲ ♂
Location   0.5m NE of village off A629

Hotel   ★★★ 58% Posthouse Sheffield, Mancheater
                  Rd, Broomhill, SHEFFIELD
                  ☎ 0870 400 9071 136 ⇆ ☞

YORKSHIRE, WEST

ALWOODLEY   Map 08 SE24

Alwoodley Wigton Ln LS17 8SA
☎ 0113 268 1680 Fax 0113 293 9458
A fine heathland course with length, trees and abundant
heather. Many attractive situations - together a severe
test of golf.
18 holes, 6686yds, Par 72, SSS 73, Course record 67.
Club membership 457.
Visitors   must contact in advance,
Societies   must apply in advance.
Green Fees   £50 per day/round (£60 weekends & bank
                  holidays).
Prof   John R Green
Designer   Dr Alistair Mackenzie
Facilities   ⊗ ⅲ ᴸ ♥ ♀ ♨ 🛍 ⚲ ♂
& Leisure   snooker.
Location   5m N off A61

Hotel   ★★★ 69% The Merrion, Merrion Centre,
                  LEEDS ☎ 0113 243 9191 109 ⇆ ☞

BAILDON   Map 07 SE13

Baildon Moorgate BD17 5PP
☎ 01274 595162 Fax 01274 530551
Moorland course set out in links style with outward front
nine looping back to clubhouse. Panoramic views with
testing short holes in prevailing winds.
18 holes, 6225yds, Par 70, SSS 70, Course record 63.
Club membership 500.
Visitors   contact in advance, restricted Tue & weekends.
Societies   large numbers apply in writing, small numbers
                  check with the professional.
Green Fees   £16 per day (£20 weekends).
Prof   Richard Masters
Designer   Tom Morris
Facilities   ⊗ ⅲ ᴸ ♥ ♀ ♨ 🛍 ⚲ ♂
Location   3m N of Bradford, off A6038

Hotel   ★★★★ 70% Marriott Hollins Hall Hotel and
                  Country Club, Hollins Hill, Baildon, SHIPLEY
                  ☎ 01274 530053 122 ⇆ ☞

Bingley Map 07 SE13

Bingley St Ives Golf Club House, St Ives Estate, Harden BD16 1AT ☎ 01274 562436 Fax 01274 511788
Parkland/moorland course.
18 holes, 6485yds, Par 71, SSS 71, Course record 69.
Club membership 450.

Visitors contact professional on 01274 562506, no green fees Sat.
Societies telephone in advance, the professional 01274 562506.
Green Fees not confirmed.
Cards
Prof Ray Firth
Designer Alastair Mackenzie
Facilities
Location 0.75m W off B6429

Hotel ★★ 66% Dalesgate Hotel, 406 Skipton Rd, Utley, KEIGHLEY ☎ 01535 664930 20

Shipley Beckfoot Ln BD16 1LX
☎ 01274 568652 (Secretary) & 563674 (Pro)
Fax 01274 568652
Well established parkland course, founded in 1922, featuring 6 good par 3's
18 holes, 6215yds, Par 71, SSS 70, Course record 65.
Club membership 600.
Visitors may play Mon, Wed-Fri & Sun, but Tue only after 2.30pm & Sat after 4pm.
Societies initial enquiry by phone to secretary 01274 568652 and or by letter.
Green Fees £25 (£20 Mon, £27 weekends).
Cards
Prof J R Parry
Designer Colt, Allison, Mackenzie, Braid
Facilities
Location 6m N of Bradford on A650

Hotel ★★ 66% Dalesgate Hotel, 406 Skipton Rd, Utley, KEIGHLEY ☎ 01535 664930 20

Bradford Map 07 SE13

Bradford Moor Scarr Hall, Pollard Ln BD2 4RW
☎ 01274 771716 & 771693
Moorland course with tricky undulating greens.
9 holes, 5900yds, Par 70, SSS 68, Course record 65.
Club membership 330.
Visitors no visitors at weekends except with member.
Societies can book starting times by application in writing.
Green Fees £8 before 2pm; £12 after 2pm.
Facilities by prior arrangement
Location 2m NE of city centre off A658

Hotel ★★ 68% Park Drive Hotel, 12 Park Dr, BRADFORD ☎ 01274 480194 11

Clayton Thornton View Rd, Clayton BD14 6JX
☎ 01274 880047
Parkland course, difficult in windy conditions.
9 holes, 5407yds, Par 68, SSS 67.
Club membership 300.
Visitors may not play before 4pm on Sun.
Societies apply in writing to the Secretary or Captain.
Green Fees £10 per round (£12 weekends & bank holidays).
Cards
Facilities
Location 2.5m SW of city centre on A647

Hotel ★★★ 62% Novotel, Merrydale Rd, BRADFORD ☎ 01274 683683 127

East Bierley South View Rd, East Bierley BD4 6PP
☎ 01274 681023 Fax 01274 683666
Hilly moorland course with narrow fairways. Two par 3 holes over 200 yds.
9 holes, 4700yds, Par 64, SSS 63, Course record 59.
Club membership 300.
Visitors restricted Sat (am), Sun & Mon evening. Must contact in advance.
Societies must apply in writing.
Green Fees £12 per day (£15 Sat).
Facilities
Location 4m SE of city centre off A650

Hotel ★★★ 62% Novotel, Merrydale Rd, BRADFORD ☎ 01274 683683 127

Headley Headley Ln, Thornton BD13 3LX
☎ 01274 833481 Fax 01274 833481
Hilly moorland course, short but very testing, windy, fine views.
9 holes, 5140yds, Par 65, SSS 65, Course record 57.
Club membership 443.
Visitors must contact in advance.
Societies must contact in advance.
Green Fees £15 per round (£10 winter).
Facilities
Location 4m W of city centre off B6145 at Thornton

Hotel ★★ 68% Park Drive Hotel, 12 Park Dr, BRADFORD ☎ 01274 480194 11

Queensbury Brighouse Rd, Queensbury BD13 1QF
☎ 01274 882155 & 816864
Undulating woodland/parkland course.
9 holes, 5024yds, Par 66, SSS 65, Course record 63.
Club membership 380.
Visitors preferable to telephone in advance, restricted at weekends.
Societies apply in writing.
Green Fees £15 per 18 holes (£30 weekends & bank holidays).
Cards
Prof John Ambler

Designer	Jonathan Gaunt
Facilities	⊗ ⅢⅡ ⅃ ⅃ ⅃ ⅃ ⅃ ⅃
Location	4m from Bradford on A647

Hotel ★★ 68% Park Drive Hotel, 12 Park Dr, BRADFORD ☎ 01274 480194 11 ⇌ ⁛

South Bradford Pearson Rd, Odsal BD6 1BH
☎ 01274 679195
Hilly course with good greens, trees and ditches. Interesting short 2nd hole (par 3) 200 yds, well-bunkered and played from an elevated tee.
9 holes, 6068yds, Par 70, SSS 68, Course record 65.
Club membership 300.

Visitors	must contact professional in advance. Weekends contact for availability. Tuesday Ladies Day.
Societies	must apply in writing to the secretary.
Green Fees	£16 per day (£22 weekends).
Prof	Paul Cooke
Facilities	⊗ ⅢⅡ ⅃ ⅃ ⅃ ⅃ ⅃ ⅃
Location	2m S of city centre off A638

Hotel ★★★ 62% Novotel, Merrydale Rd, BRADFORD ☎ 01274 683683 127 ⇌ ⁛

West Bowling Newall Hall, Rooley Ln BD5 8LB
☎ 01274 393207 (office) & 728036 (pro)
Fax 01274 393207
Undulating, tree-lined parkland course. Testing hole: 'the Coffin' short par 3, very narrow.
18 holes, 5769yds, Par 68, SSS 67, Course record 65.
Club membership 500.

Visitors	must apply in writing, very limited at weekends.
Societies	must apply in writing.
Green Fees	£24 per day; £20 per round (£30 per round weekends & bank holidays).
Prof	Ian A Marshall
Facilities	⊗ ⅢⅡ ⅃ ⅃ ⅃ ⅃ ⅃ ⅃
Location	Corner of M606 & A638 (east)

Hotel ★★★★ 64% Cedar Court Hotel Bradford, Mayo Av, Off Rooley Ln, BRADFORD ☎ 01274 406606 & 406601 Fax 01274 406600 131 ⇌ ⁛

West Bradford Chellow Grange Rd BD9 6NP
☎ 01274 542767 Fax 01274 482079
Parkland course, windy, especially 3rd, 4th, 5th and 6th holes. Hilly but not hard.
18 holes, 5741yds, Par 69, SSS 68.
Club membership 440.

Visitors	restricted Sat & Sun. Tuesday is Ladies day, can play if available, advisable to telephone 01274 542102 to reserve a time.
Societies	must contact in advance.
Green Fees	£20 per day/round.
Prof	Nigel M Barber
Facilities	⊗ by prior arrangement Ⅲ by prior arrangement ⅃ ⅃ ⅃ ⅃ ⅃ ⅃
Location	W side of city centre off B6144

Hotel ★★★★ 70% Marriott Hollins Hall Hotel and Country Club, Hollins Hill, Baildon, SHIPLEY ☎ 01274 530053 122 ⇌ ⁛

BRIGHOUSE — Map 07 SE12

Willow Valley Golf & Country Club Highmoor Ln, Clifton HD6 4JB ☎ 01274 878624 Fax 01274 852805
A championship length 18-hole course offering a unique golfing experience, featuring island greens, shaped fairways and bunkers, and multiple teeing areas. The 9-hole course offers an exciting challenge to less experienced golfers.
South: 18 holes, 6496yds, Par 72, SSS 72, Course record 75.
North: 9 holes, 2039yds, Par 31, SSS 60.
Club membership 320.

Visitors	tee times may be booked by phone on payment of green fee by credit/debit card.
Societies	telephone in advance for availability and booking form.
Green Fees	South: £20 per round (£25 weekends & bank holidays). North: £6 per 9 holes (£7 weekends & bank holidays).
Prof	Julian Haworth
Designer	Jonathan Gaunt
Facilities	⊗ ⅢⅡ ⅃ ⅃ ⅃ ⅃ ⅃ ⅃ ⅃ ⅃ ⅃
Location	Junct 25 of M62 follow A644 towards Brighouse, at small rdbt turn right, A643, course is 2m on righ

Hotel ★★ 70% Healds Hall Hotel, Leeds Rd, Liversedge, DEWSBURY ☎ 01924 409112 24 ⇌ ⁛

CLECKHEATON — Map 08 SE12

Cleckheaton & District Bradford Rd BD19 6BU
☎ 01274 851266 Fax 01274 871382
Parkland course with gentle hills.
18 holes, 5769yds, Par 71, SSS 68.
Club membership 550.

Visitors	parties must arrange in advance, not weekends.
Societies	weekdays only; must contact in advance.
Green Fees	£30 per day; £25 per round.
Prof	Mike Ingham
Facilities	⊗ ⅢⅡ ⅃ ⅃ ⅃ ⅃ ⅃ ⅃
Location	1.5m NW on A638 junc 26 M62

Hotel ★★★ 67% Gomersal Park Hotel, Moor Ln, GOMERSAL ☎ 01274 869386 52 ⇌ ⁛

DEWSBURY — Map 08 SE22

Hanging Heaton White Cross Rd WF12 7DT
☎ 01924 461606 Fax 01924 430100
Arable land course, easy walking, fine views. Testing 4th hole (par 3).
9 holes, 5836yds, Par 69, SSS 67.
Club membership 550.

Visitors	must play with member at weekends & bank holidays. Must contact in advance.
Societies	must telephone in advance.
Green Fees	£15.
Prof	S Hartley
Facilities	⅃ ⅃
Location	0.75m NE off A653

Hotel ★★ 70% Healds Hall Hotel, Leeds Rd, Liversedge, DEWSBURY ☎ 01924 409112 24 ⇌ ⁛

ELLAND
Map 07 SE12

Elland Hammerstones, Leach Ln HX5 0TA
☎ 01422 372505 & 374886 (pro)
Parkland course.
9 holes, 2815yds, Par 66, SSS 66, Course record 64.
Club membership 450.
Visitors welcome.
Societies must contact in writing.
Green Fees not confirmed.
Prof N Krzywicki
Facilities ⊗ ⅷ ⅼ ⅷ ♈ ⅄ ⌂ 🖼 ♂
Location 1m SW

Hotel ★★★ 67% Rock Inn Hotel & Churchills,
Holywell Green, HALIFAX
☎ 01422 379721 30 ⇆ ☞

FENAY BRIDGE
Map 08 SE11

Woodsome Hall HD8 0LQ
☎ 01484 602739 Fax 01484 608260
A parkland course with good views and an historic clubhouse.
18 holes, 6096yds, Par 70, SSS 69, Course record 67.
Club membership 800.
Visitors must contact in advance. Jacket and tie required
in all rooms except casual bar.
Societies must apply in writing.
Green Fees £40 per day, £30 per round (£45 weekends &
bank holidays).
Prof M Higginbottom
Facilities ⊗ ⅷ ⅼ ⅷ ♈ ⅄ ⌂ 🖼 ♂
Location 1.5m SW off A629

Hotel ★★★ 68% Bagden Hall, Wakefield Rd,
Scissett, HUDDERSFIELD
☎ 01484 865330 17 ⇆ ☞

GARFORTH
Map 08 SE43

Garforth Long Ln LS25 2DS
☎ 0113 286 2021 Fax 0113 286 3308
Parkland course with fine views, easy walking.
18 holes, 6005yds, Par 69, SSS 69.
Club membership 500.
Visitors must contact in advance and have handicap
certificate. With member only weekends & bank
holidays.
Societies must apply in advance.
Green Fees £32 per day; £28 per round.
Prof Ken Findlater
Facilities ⊗ ⅷ ⅼ ⅷ ♈ ⅄ ⌂ 🖼 ♂ ⅼ
Location 1m N

Hotel ★★★ 69% Milford Lodge Hotel, A1 Great
North Rd, Peckfield, LEEDS
☎ 01977 681800 47 ⇆ ☞

GUISELEY
Map 08 SE14

Bradford (Hawksworth) Hawksworth Ln LS20 8NP
☎ 01943 875570 & 873719 (Pro) Fax 01943 875570
Moorland course with eight par 4 holes of 360 yds or more.
The course is a venue for county championship events.
18 holes, 6259yds, Par 71, SSS 71, Course record 66.
Club membership 650.

Visitors must have a handicap certificate and contact in
advance. May not play Sat.
Societies make prior arrangements with manager.
Green Fees £30 per day; £25 per round.
Prof Sydney Weldon
Designer W H Fowler
Facilities ⊗ ⅷ ⅼ ⅷ ♈ ⅄ ⌂ 🖼 ♂
Location SW side of town centre off A6038

Hotel ★★★★ 70% Marriott Hollins Hall Hotel and
Country Club, Hollins Hill, Baildon, SHIPLEY
☎ 01274 530053 122 ⇆ ☞

HALIFAX
Map 07 SE02

Halifax Union Ln, Ogden HX2 8XR
☎ 01422 244171 Fax 01422 241459
Hilly moorland course crossed by streams, natural hazards,
and offering fine views. Testing 172-yd 17th (par3).
18 holes, 6037yds, Par 70, SSS 70, Course record 63.
Club membership 700.
Visitors contact professional for tee times, 01422
240047. Limited play weekend.
Societies contact secretary for dates.
Green Fees £15 per round.
Cards 🖃 🖃
Prof Michael Allison
Designer A Herd/J Braid
Facilities ⊗ ⅷ ⅼ ⅷ ♈ ⅄ ⌂ 🖼 ⅼ ♂
Location A629 Halifax/Keighley, 4 miles from Halifax

Hotel ★★★ 74% Holdsworth House Hotel,
Holdsworth, HALIFAX
☎ 01422 240024 40 ⇆ ☞

Lightcliffe Knowle Top Rd, Lightcliffe HX3 8SW
☎ 01422 202459
Heathland course.
9 holes, 5388yds, Par 68, SSS 68.
Club membership 545.
Visitors must be a member of a recognised golf club.
May not play Sun morning/competition days.
Societies must contact 21 days in advance.
Green Fees not confirmed.
Prof Robert Kershaw
Facilities ⅄ ⌂
Location 3.5m E on A58

Hotel ★★★ 74% Holdsworth House Hotel,
Holdsworth, HALIFAX
☎ 01422 240024 40 ⇆ ☞

West End Paddock Ln, Highroad Well HX2 0NT
☎ 01422 341878 Fax 01422 341878
Semi-moorland course. Tree lined. Two ponds.
18 holes, 5951yds, Par 69, SSS 69, Course record 62.
Visitors contact in advance.
Societies must apply in writing to Secretary.
Green Fees £26 per day; £21 per round (£31/£26 weekends
& bank holidays).
Prof David Rishworth
Facilities ⊗ ⅷ ⅼ ⅷ ♈ ⅄ ⌂ 🖼 ♂
Location W side of town centre off A646

Hotel ★★★ 74% Holdsworth House Hotel,
Holdsworth, HALIFAX
☎ 01422 240024 40 ⇆ ☞

HEBDEN BRIDGE   Map 07 SD92

Hebden Bridge Mount Skip, Wadsworth HX7 8PH
☎ 01422 842896 & 842732
Moorland course with splendid views.
9 holes, 5242yds, Par 68, SSS 67, Course record 61.
Club membership 300.
Visitors	weekends after 4pm only.
Societies	contact in advance.
Green Fees	£12 (£15 weekends).
Facilities	⊗ by prior arrangement ▥ by prior arrangement ☖ by prior arrangement ♀ ⌂
Location	1.5m E off A6033

Hotel	★★★ 66% Carlton Hotel, Albert St, HEBDEN BRIDGE ☎ 01422 844400 16 ⇌ ↿

HOLYWELL GREEN   Map 07 SE01

Halifax Bradley Hall HX4 9AN ☎ 01422 374108
Moorland/parkland course, tightened by tree planting, easy walking.
18 holes, 6138yds, Par 70, SSS 70, Course record 65.
Club membership 500.
Visitors	contact in advance.
Societies	must apply in advance.
Green Fees	£18 per round (£28 weekends).
Prof	Peter Wood
Facilities	⊗ ▥ ☖ ☒ ♀ ⌂ ☏ ⌀
Location	S on A6112

Hotel	★★★ 67% Rock Inn Hotel & Churchills, Holywell Green, HALIFAX ☎ 01422 379721 30 ⇌ ↿

HUDDERSFIELD   Map 07 SE11

Bagden Hall Hotel & Golf Course Wakefield Rd, Scissett HD8 9LE ☎ 01484 864839 Fax 01484 861001
Well maintained tree-lined course set in idyllic surroundings and offering a challenging test of golf for all levels of handicap. Lake guarded greens require pin-point accuracy.
9 holes, 3002yds, Par 56, SSS 55, Course record 60.
Club membership 200.
Visitors	anytime.
Societies	company day packages available, telephone Director of golf.
Green Fees	not confirmed.
Prof	Ian Darren
Designer	F O'Donnell/R Brathwaite
Facilities	⊗ ▥ ☖ ☒ ♀ ⌂ ☏ ⌀
Location	A636 Wakefield-Denby Dale

Hotel	★★★ 68% Bagden Hall, Wakefield Rd, Scissett, HUDDERSFIELD ☎ 01484 865330 17 ⇌ ↿

Bradley Park Off Bradley Rd HD2 1PZ
☎ 01484 223772 Fax 01484 451613
Parkland course, challenging with good mix of long and short holes. Also 14-bay floodlit driving range and 9-hole par 3 course, ideal for beginners. Superb views.
18 holes, 6284yds, Par 70, SSS 70, Course record 65.
Club membership 300.
Visitors	may book by phone for weekends and bank holidays from the preceeding Thu. No restrictions on other days.
Societies	welcome midweek, apply in writing to professional.
Green Fees	£13 per round (£15 weekends & bank holidays).
Cards	▦ ▦ ▦ ▨
Prof	Parnell E Reilly
Designer	Cotton/Pennick/Lowire & Ptnrs
Facilities	⊗ ▥ ☖ ☒ ♀ ⌂ ☏ 🛒 ⌀ ↿
Location	2.5m from junct 25 of M62

Hotel	★★★ 66% The George Hotel, St George's Square, HUDDERSFIELD ☎ 01484 515444 60 ⇌ ↿

Crosland Heath Felk Stile Rd, Crosland Heath HD4 7AF
☎ 01484 653216
Moorland course with fine views over valley.
18 holes, 6007yds, Par 70, SSS 70.
Club membership 550.
Visitors	welcome, but advisable to check with professional. May not play Sat.
Societies	must telephone in advance.
Green Fees	on application.
Prof	James Coverley
Facilities	⊗ ▥ ☖ ☒ ♀ ⌂ ☏ ⌀
Location	SW off A62

Hotel	★★★ 66% The George Hotel, St George's Square, HUDDERSFIELD ☎ 01484 515444 60 ⇌ ↿

Huddersfield Fixby Hall, Lightridge Rd, Fixby HD2 2EP
☎ 01484 426203 Fax 01484 424623
A testing heathland course of championship standard laid out in 1891.
18 holes, 6432yds, Par 71, SSS 71, Course record 64.
Club membership 759.
Visitors	must book tee times with professional.
Societies	welcome Mon & Wed-Fri, prior arrangement required.
Green Fees	£33 per 18 holes (£45 weekends & bank holidays).
Prof	Paul Carman
Facilities	⊗ ▥ ☖ ☒ ♀ ⌂ ☏ ⌀
Location	2m N off A641

Hotel	★★★ 66% The George Hotel, St George's Square, HUDDERSFIELD ☎ 01484 515444 60 ⇌ ↿

Longley Park Maple St, Off Somerset Rd HD5 9AX
☎ 01484 422304
Lowland course, surrounded by mature woodland.
9 holes, 5212yds, Par 66, SSS 66, Course record 61.
Club membership 440.
Visitors	by arrangement with professional, must have handicap certificate, restricted Thu & weekends. No catering Mon.
Societies	must apply in writing to secretary.
Green Fees	not confirmed.
Prof	Nick Jones
Facilities	⊗ ▥ ☖ ☒ ♀ ⌂ ☏ 🛒 ⌀
Location	0.5m SE of town centre off A629

Hotel	★★★ 66% The George Hotel, St George's Square, HUDDERSFIELD ☎ 01484 515444 60 ⇌ ↿

ILKLEY   Map 07 SE14

Ben Rhydding High Wood, Ben Rhydding LS29 8SB
☎ 01943 608759
Moorland/parkland course with splendid views over the
Wharfe valley.
9 holes, 4711yds, Par 65, SSS 64, Course record 64.
Club membership 290.

Visitors	contact in advance. May only play at weekend as guest of member.
Societies	advance notice in writing. In view of limited resources requests considered by monthly committee meeting.
Green Fees	£12 per day (£17 weekends & bank holidays).
Designer	William Dell
Facilities	♀ ⌓
Location	SE side of town
Hotel	★★★ 71% Rombalds Hotel & Restaurant, 11 West View, Wells Rd, ILKLEY ☎ 01943 603201 15 ⇌ ⬥

Ilkley Nesfield Rd, Myddleton LS29 0BE
☎ 01943 600214
This beautiful parkland course is situated in Wharfedale
and the Wharfe is a hazard on each of the first seven
holes. In fact, the 3rd is laid out entirely on an island in
the middle of the river.
18 holes, 5953yds, Par 69, SSS 70, Course record 66.
Club membership 450.

Visitors	advisable to contact in advance.
Societies	apply in writing.
Green Fees	not confirmed.
Prof	John L Hammond
Facilities	⊗ by prior arrangement ⫴ by prior arrangement ⌧ ♥ ♀ ⌓ ⌂ ⫪ ⌀
& Leisure	fishing.
Location	W side of town centre off A65
Hotel	★★★ 71% Rombalds Hotel & Restaurant, 11 West View, Wells Rd, ILKLEY ☎ 01943 603201 15 ⇌ ⬥

KEIGHLEY   Map 07 SE04

Branshaw Branshaw Moor, Oakworth BD22 7ES
☎ 01535 643235 (sec) & 647441 (pro) Fax 01535 648011
Picturesque moorland course with fairly narrow fairways and
good greens. Extensive views.
18 holes, 6000yds, Par 69, SSS 69, Course record 64.
Club membership 500.

Visitors	welcome most times, restrictions at weekends advisable to ring.
Societies	apply in writing to Professional.
Green Fees	£20 (£30 weekends & bank holidays).
Prof	Mark Tyler
Designer	James Braid
Facilities	⊗ ⫴ ⌧ ♥ ♀ ⌓ ⌂ ⌀
Location	2m SW on B6149
Hotel	★★ 66% Dalesgate Hotel, 406 Skipton Rd, Utley, KEIGHLEY ☎ 01535 664930 20 ⇌ ⬥

Keighley Howden Park, Utley BD20 6DH
☎ 01535 604778 Fax 01535 604778
Parkland course with good views down the Aire Valley.
18 holes, 6149yds, Par 69, SSS 70, Course record 64.
Club membership 600.

Visitors	restricted Sat & Sun. Must contact in advance. No catering/bar Mondays, Ladies day on Tuesday.
Societies	must apply in advance.
Green Fees	not confirmed.
Cards	▭ ▬ ▨
Prof	Mike Bradley
Facilities	⊗ ⫴ ⌧ ♥ ♀ ⌓ ⌂ ⌀
Location	1m NW of town centre off B6143
Hotel	★★ 66% Dalesgate Hotel, 406 Skipton Rd, Utley, KEIGHLEY ☎ 01535 664930 20 ⇌ ⬥

LEEDS   Map 08 SE33

Brandon Holywell Ln, Shadwell LS17 8EZ
☎ 0113 273 7471
An 18-hole links type course enjoying varying degrees of
rough, water and sand hazards.
18 holes, 4000yds, Par 68.

Visitors	pay & play course booking not usually necessary.
Societies	telephone or write in advance.
Green Fees	not confirmed.
Facilities	⌧ ♥ ⌂ ⫪ ⌀
Location	From Leeds-Wetherby Rd turn left to Shadwell left again up Main St, right at Red Lion Pub
Hotel	★★★ 80% Haley's Hotel & Restaurant, Shire Oak Rd, Headingley, LEEDS ☎ 0113 278 4446 22 ⇌ ⬥ Annexe 7 ⇌ ⬥

Cookridge Hall Golf & Country Club Cookridge Ln LS16
7NL ☎ 0113 2300641 Fax 0113 2857115
American-style course designed by Karl Litten. Expect
plenty of water hazards, tees for all standards. Large bunkers
and fairways between mounds and young trees.
18 holes, 6497yds, Par 72, SSS 72.
Club membership 600.

Visitors	must contact in advance. Strict dress code applies. Soft spikes policy.
Societies	telephone in advance.
Green Fees	£20 per round.
Cards	▭ ▬ ▨ ▨
Prof	Mark Pearson
Designer	Karl Liiten
Facilities	⊗ ⫴ ⌧ ♥ ♀ ⌓ ⌂ ⫪ ⌀ ⫙
& Leisure	heated indoor swimming pool, sauna, solarium, gymnasium.
Location	On Otley Old Road, off A660, 3m N of Leeds
Hotel	★★★ 80% Haley's Hotel & Restaurant, Shire Oak Rd, Headingley, LEEDS ☎ 0113 278 4446 22 ⇌ ⬥ Annexe 7 ⇌ ⬥

Gotts Park Armley Ridge Rd LS12 2QX
☎ 0113 231 1896 & 231 0492
Municipal parkland course; hilly and windy with narrow
fairways. Some very steep hills to some greens. A
challenging course requiring accuracy rather than length
from the tees.   ▶

18 holes, 4960yds, Par 65, SSS 64, Course record 63.
Club membership 200.
Visitors   no restrictions.
Green Fees not confirmed.
Prof   John Marlor
Facilities   ⊗ 🍴 ♟ 🛍 ⛳
Location   3m W of city centre off A647

Hotel   ★★★★ 69% Queen's Hotel, City Square,
                 LEEDS ☎ 0113 243 1323 199 ⇄ ↖

Headingley Back Church Ln, Adel LS16 8DW
☎ 0113 267 9573 Fax 0113 281 7334
An undulating course with a wealth of natural features
offering fine views from higher ground. Its most striking
hazard is the famous ravine at the 18th. Leeds's oldest
course, founded in 1892.
18 holes, 6298yds, Par 69, SSS 70, Course record 64.
Club membership 700.
Visitors   must contact in advance, restricted at weekends.
Societies   must telephone in advance and confirm in
                 writing.
Green Fees £35 per day; £30 per round (£40 per day/round
                 weekends & bank holidays).
Prof   Steven Foster
Designer   Dr Mackenzie
Facilities   ⊗ 🍴 🍺 ♟ 🛍 ⛳ ✓
Location   5.5m N of city centre off A660

Hotel   ★★★ 70% Posthouse Bramhope, Leeds Rd,
                 BRAMHOPE ☎ 0113 284 2911 124 ⇄ ↖

Horsforth Layton Rise, Layton Rd, Horsforth LS18 5EX
☎ 0113 258 6819 Fax 0113 258 6819
Moorland/parkland course overlooking airport.
18 holes, 6243yds, Par 71, SSS 70, Course record 65.
Club membership 750.
Visitors   restricted Sat & with member only Sun.
Societies   must apply in writing.
Green Fees £30 per day; £24 per round.
Prof   Neil Bell
Facilities   ♟ 🛍 🍴 ✓
Location   6.5m NW of city centre off A65

Hotel   ★★★ 70% Posthouse Bramhope, Leeds Rd,
                 BRAMHOPE ☎ 0113 284 2911 124 ⇄ ↖

Leeds Elmete Ln LS8 2LJ ☎ 0113 265 8775
Parkland course with pleasant views.
18 holes, 6097yds, Par 69, SSS 69, Course record 63.
Club membership 600.
Visitors   with member only weekends, yellow tees only.
                 Must contact in advance.
Societies   must apply in writing.
Green Fees not confirmed.
Prof   Simon Longster
Facilities   🛍 🍴 ⛳ ✓
Location   5m NE of city centre on A6120 off A58

Hotel   ★★★ 80% Haley's Hotel & Restaurant, Shire
                 Oak Rd, Headingley, LEEDS
                 ☎ 0113 278 4446 22 ⇄ ↖ Annexe 7 ⇄ ↖

Leeds Golf Centre Wike Ridge Ln, Shadwell LS17 9JW
☎ 0113 288 6000 Fax 0113 288 6185
Two courses - the 18-hole Wike Ridge, a traditional
heathland course designed by Donald Steel. The sand-based
greens are constructed to USGA specification and there are

an excellent variety of holes with some very challenging Par
5's. The 12-hole Oaks is complemented by a floodlit driving
range and other practice facilities. The course is the home of
the Leeds Golf Academy.
Wike Ridge Course: 18 holes, 6482yds, Par 72, SSS 71.
Oaks: 12 holes, 1610yds, Par 36.
Club membership 500.
Visitors   no restrictions, telephone booking advisable.
Societies   tee reservation available in advance.
Green Fees not confirmed.
Cards   ▭ ▭ ▭ ▭ 🖼
Prof   Neil Harvey
Designer   Donald Steel
Facilities   ⊗ 🍴 🍺 🍴 ♟ 🛍 🍴 ⛳ 🏌 🛒 ✓ ⚑
Location   5m N, take A58 course on N side of Shadwell

Hotel   ★★★ 80% Haley's Hotel & Restaurant, Shire
                 Oak Rd, Headingley, LEEDS
                 ☎ 0113 278 4446 22 ⇄ ↖ Annexe 7 ⇄ ↖

Middleton Park Municipal Middleton Park, Middleton LS10
3TN ☎ 0113 270 0449 & 270 9506
Parkland course.
18 holes, 5263yds, Par 68, SSS 66, Course record 63.
Club membership 320.
Visitors   may only use the club 6 times in one year.
Green Fees not confirmed.
Prof   Jim Pape
Facilities   ♟ 🛍 🍴 ⛳
Location   3m S off A653

Hotel   ★★★★ 69% Queen's Hotel, City Square,
                 LEEDS ☎ 0113 243 1323 199 ⇄ ↖

Moor Allerton Coal Rd, Wike LS17 9NH
☎ 0113 266 1154 Fax 0113 237 1124
The Moor Allerton Club, established in 1921, has 27
holes set in 220 acres of undulating parkland, with
testing water hazards and magnificent views extending
across the Vale of York. The Championship Course was
designed by Robert Trent Jones, the famous American
course architect, and provides a challenge to both high
and low handicapped golfers.
Lakes Course: 18 holes, 6470yds, Par 71, SSS 72.
Blackmoor Course: 18 holes, 6673yds, Par 71, SSS 73.
High Course: 18 holes, 6841yds, Par 72, SSS 74.
Club membership 1200.

Visitors   contact professional (0113 266 5209).
Societies   must apply in advance.
Green Fees £46 per day; £42 per round (£76/£67
                 weekends). Reductions in winter.
Prof   Richard Lane   ▶

Designer	Robert Trent Jones
Facilities & Leisure	⊗ ⫯ ⅃ ▮ ♆ ♀ ⚲ 🏠 ⛳ ⤳ 🛒 ⚷ 🏇
	sauna.
Location	5.5m N of city centre on A61
Hotel	★★★ 69% The Merrion, Merrion Centre, LEEDS ☎ 0113 243 9191 109 ⇆ 🐾

Moortown Harrogate Rd, Alwoodley LS17 7DB
☎ 0113 268 6521 Fax 0113 268 0986
Championship course, tough but fair. Springy moorland turf, natural hazards of heather, gorse and streams, cunningly placed bunkers and immaculate greens. Original home of Ryder Cup in 1929.
18 holes, 6782yds, Par 72, SSS 73, Course record 66.
Club membership 566.

Visitors	must contact in advance.
Societies	apply in writing in advance.
Green Fees	£55 per day; £45 per round (£60/£50 weekends & bank holidays).
Prof	Bryon Hutchinson
Designer	A McKenzie
Facilities	⊗ ⫯ ⅃ ▮ ♆ ♀ ⚲ 🏠 🛒 ⚷
Location	6m N of city centre on A61
Hotel	★★★ 69% The Merrion, Merrion Centre, LEEDS ☎ 0113 243 9191 109 ⇆ 🐾

Oulton Park Rothwell LS26 8EX
☎ 0113 282 3152 Fax 0113 282 6290
27-hole championship-length municipal course. Although municipal, a dress rule is applied. 22-bay floodlit driving range. Two tier putting. Host to the City of Leeds Cup (PGA) each July.
Hall Course: 9 holes, 3286yds, Par 36, SSS 36.
Park Course: 9 holes, 3184yds, Par 35, SSS 35.
Royds Course: 9 holes, 3169yds, Par 35, SSS 35.
Club membership 450.

Visitors	must apply up to 5 days in advance. Dress code in operation.
Societies	Mon-Fri. Must contact in advance.
Green Fees	£9.90 per 18 holes; £5.70 per 9 holes (£12.90/£6.70 weekends).
Cards	💳 💳 💳 💳
Prof	Stephen Gromett
Designer	Dave Thomas
Facilities & Leisure	⊗ ⫯ ⅃ ▮ ♆ ♀ ⚲ 🏠 ⛳ 🛒 ⚷ ⚷
	heated indoor swimming pool, squash, fishing, sauna, solarium, gymnasium.
Location	Junc 30 on M62
Hotel	★★★★★ 60% Oulton Hall Hotel, Rothwell Ln, Oulton, LEEDS ☎ 0113 282 1000 152 ⇆ 🐾

Roundhay Park Ln LS8 2EJ ☎ 0113 266 2695
Attractive municipal parkland course, natural hazards, easy walking.
9 holes, 5223yds, Par 70, SSS 65, Course record 61.
Club membership 250.

Visitors	must contact professional at all times.
Societies	telephone or write to the professional.
Green Fees	not confirmed.
Prof	James Pape

Facilities	♀ ⚲ 🏠 ⛳ ⚷
Location	4m NE of city centre off A58
Hotel	★★★ 80% Haley's Hotel & Restaurant, Shire Oak Rd, Headingley, LEEDS ☎ 0113 278 4446 22 ⇆ 🐾 Annexe 7 ⇆ 🐾

Sand Moor Alwoodley Ln LS17 7DJ
☎ 0113 268 5180 Fax 0113 268 5180
A beautiful, undulating course overlooking Lord Harewood's estate and the Eccup Reservoir. The course is wooded with some holes adjacent to water. The 12th is perhaps the most difficult where the fairway falls away towards the reservoir.
18 holes, 6429yds, Par 71, SSS 71, Course record 63.
Club membership 553.

Visitors	restricted weekends & bank holidays.
Societies	must apply in advance.
Green Fees	not confirmed.
Prof	Peter Tupling
Designer	Dr A Mackenzie
Facilities	⊗ ⫯ by prior arrangement ⅃ ▮ ♀ ⚲ 🏠 ⛳ ⚷
Location	5m N of city centre off A61
Hotel	★★★ 70% Posthouse Bramhope, Leeds Rd, BRAMHOPE ☎ 0113 284 2911 124 ⇆ 🐾

South Leeds Gipsy Ln, Beeston LS11 5TU
☎ 0113 277 1676 & 270 2598 (pro)
Parkland course, windy, hard walking, good views.
18 holes, 5769yds, Par 69, SSS 68, Course record 64.
Club membership 500.

Visitors	welcome weekdays except competition time, may not play weekends.
Societies	must apply in advance.
Green Fees	£18.
Prof	Mike Lewis
Facilities	⊗ ⫯ ⅃ ▮ ♀ ⚲ 🏠 ⚷
Location	3m S of city centre off A653
Hotel	★★★★ 69% Queen's Hotel, City Square, LEEDS ☎ 0113 243 1323 199 ⇆ 🐾

Temple Newsam Temple-Newsam Rd LS15 0LN
☎ 0113 264 5624
Two parkland courses. Testing long 13th (563 yds) on second course.
Lord Irwin: 18 holes, 6460yds, Par 68, SSS 71, Course record 66.
Lady Dorothy: 18 holes, 6299yds, Par 70, SSS 70, Course record 67.
Club membership 520.

Visitors	no restrictions.
Societies	must apply in advance in writing.
Green Fees	£6.75 (£8.25 weekends).
Prof	Alan Swaine
Facilities	⊗ ⫯ by prior arrangement ▮ ♀ ⚲ 🏠 ⛳ ⚷
Location	3.5m E of city centre off A63
Hotel	★★★ 80% Haley's Hotel & Restaurant, Shire Oak Rd, Headingley, LEEDS ☎ 0113 278 4446 22 ⇆ 🐾 Annexe 7 ⇆ 🐾

MARSDEN   Map 07 SE01

Marsden Mount Rd, Hemplow HD7 6NN
☎ 01484 844253
Moorland course with good views, natural hazards, windy.
9 holes, 5702yds, Par 68, SSS 68, Course record 63.
Club membership 200.
Visitors	must play with member at weekends but not before 4pm Sat.
Societies	Mon-Fri; must contact in advance.
Green Fees	£10 per round.
Prof	Nick Krzywicki
Designer	Dr McKenzie
Facilities	⊗ ⊤ ⓑ 🍺 🍷 🚶 🏠
& Leisure	hard tennis courts.
Location	S side off A62

Hotel   ★★★ 63% Briar Court Hotel, Halifax Rd, Birchencliffe, HUDDERSFIELD
☎ 01484 519902   48 🛏 🐾

MELTHAM   Map 07 SE01

Meltham Thick Hollins Hall HD7 3DQ
☎ 01484 850227 Fax 01484 850227
Parkland course with good views. Testing 548 yd, 13th hole (par 5).
18 holes, 6379yds, Par 71, SSS 70, Course record 67.
Club membership 550.
Visitors	may not play Sat & Wed (Ladies Day), desirable to contact professional in advance.
Societies	must apply in writing.
Green Fees	£26 per day; £21 per round (£31/£26 weekends & bank holidays).
Prof	Paul Davies
Designer	Alex Herd
Facilities	⊗ ⊤ ⓑ 🍺 🍷 🚶 🏠 🐾
Location	SE side of village off B6107

Hotel   ★★★ 66% The George Hotel, St George's Square, HUDDERSFIELD
☎ 01484 515444   60 🛏 🐾

MIRFIELD   Map 08 SE21

Dewsbury District Sands Ln WF14 8HJ
☎ 01924 492399 & 496030 Fax 01924 492399
Heathland/parkland course with panoramic views and hard walking. Ponds in middle of 3rd fairway, left of 5th green and 17th green.
18 holes, 6360yds, Par 71, SSS 71.
Club membership 650.
Visitors	Sun only after 2.30pm, on non competition days. Telephone in advance.
Societies	telephone bookings.
Green Fees	£22.50 per day; £17.50 per round.
Prof	Nigel P Hirst
Designer	Old Tom Morris/ Peter Alliss
Facilities	⊗ ⊤ ⓑ 🍺 🍷 🚶 🏠 🐾
& Leisure	snooker tables.
Location	Off A644, 6m from junct 25 on M62

Hotel   ★★★ 66% The George Hotel, St George's Square, HUDDERSFIELD
☎ 01484 515444   60 🛏 🐾

MORLEY   Map 08 SE22

Howley Hall Scotchman Ln LS27 0NX
☎ 01924 478417 & 473852 (Prof)
Fax 01924 478417
Parkland course with easy walking and superb views of the Pennines and Calder Valley.
18 holes, 6346yds, Par 71, SSS 71, Course record 66.
Club membership 700.
Visitors	play from yellow markers. May not play Sat.
Societies	contact for details.
Green Fees	£30 per day; £25 per round (£35 day/round Sun & bank holidays).
Prof	Gary Watkinson
Facilities	⊗ ⓑ 🍺 🍷 🚶 🏠 🐾 ➤ 🏹
Location	1.5m S on B6123

Hotel   ★★ 70% Alder House Hotel, Towngate Rd, Healey Ln, BATLEY
☎ 01924 444777   20 🛏 🐾

NORMANTON   Map 08 SE32

Normanton Snydale Rd WF6 1PN
☎ 01924 892943 Fax 01924 220134
A pleasant, flat course with tight fairways in places and an internal out-of-bounds requiring accuracy.
9 holes, 5288yds, Par 66, SSS 66.
Club membership 400.
Visitors	may not play on Sun.
Societies	mid-week only, apply in writing or telephone.
Green Fees	not confirmed.
Prof	Ian Hunt
Facilities	⊗ ⊤ ⓑ 🍺 🍷 🚶 🏠 🏹
Location	0.5m SE on B6133

Hotel   ★★★ 66% Chasley Hotel, Queen St, WAKEFIELD
☎ 01924 372111   64 🛏 🐾

OSSETT   Map 08 SE22

Low Laithes Parkmill Ln, Flushdyke WF5 9AP
☎ 01924 274667 & 266067 Fax 01924 266067
Testing parkland course.
18 holes, 6463yds, Par 72, SSS 71, Course record 65.
Club membership 600.
Visitors	may not play before 9.30am and 12.30-1.30 weekdays and before 10am and 12-2 weekends/bank holidays.
Societies	by prior arrangement.
Green Fees	not confirmed.
Prof	Paul Browning
Designer	Dr Mackenzie
Facilities	⊗ ⊤ ⓑ 🍺 🍷 🚶 🏠 🚜 🐾
Location	Leave M1 at jct 40 then signposted on Dewsbury road 0.5m from M1

Hotel   ★★★ 66% Posthouse Northampton/Rugby, CRICK ☎ 0870 400 9059 88 🛏 🐾

> AA Hotels that have special arrangements with golf courses are listed at the back of the guide

OTLEY
Map 08 SE24

Otley Off West Busk Ln LS21 3NG
☎ 01943 465329 Fax 01943 850387
An expansive course with magnificent views across
Wharfedale. It is well-wooded with streams crossing the
fairway. The 4th is a fine hole which generally needs two
woods to reach the plateau green. The 17th is a good
short hole.
18 holes, 6225yds, Par 70, SSS 70, Course record 66.
Club membership 700.
Visitors	telephone to check tee time. May not play
	Tue morning or Sat.
Societies	telephone enquiries welcome, bookings in
	writing.
Green Fees	£33 per 36 holes, £26 upto 27 holes
	(£39/£33 weekends and bank holidays).
	Reductions in winter.
Prof	Steven Tomkinson
Facilities	⊗ ℳ ⅃ ☕ 🍷 ⚲ 🕮 👜 🛆 ⚑ ✓
Location	1m W of Otley off A6038

Hotel	★★★ 70% Posthouse Bramhope, Leeds
	Rd, BRAMHOPE
	☎ 0113 284 2911 124 🛏 ℉

OUTLANE
Map 07 SE01

Outlane Slack Ln, off New Hey Rd HD3 3YL
☎ 01422 311789 & 374762 Fax 01422 311789
Moorland course.
18 holes, 6015yds, Par 71, SSS 70, Course record 66.
Club membership 600.
Visitors	telephone in advance, must be correctly
	equipped and attired. No play Sat, limited Sun
	morning.
Societies	apply in writing.
Green Fees	not confirmed.
Prof	David Chapman
Facilities	⊗ ℳ ⅃ ☕ 🍷 ⚲ 🕮 ⚑ ✓
Location	S side of village off A640

Hotel	★★★ 69% Old Golf House Hotel, New Hey
	Rd, Outlane, HUDDERSFIELD
	☎ 01422 379311 52 🛏 ℉

PONTEFRACT
Map 08 SE42

Mid Yorkshire Havercroft Ln, Darrington WF8 3BP
☎ 01977 704522 Fax 01977 600823
An 18-hole championship-standard course opened in 1993,
and widely considered to be one of the finest new courses in
Yorkshire.
18 holes, 6500yds, Par 72, SSS 71, Course record 68.
Club membership 500.
Visitors	tee times bookable by telephone, visitors after
	12 noon at weekends.
Societies	apply in writing to the secretary.
Green Fees	variable from £12-£25.
Cards	💳 💳 💳 💳
Prof	Alistair Cobbett
Designer	Steve Marnoch
Facilities	⊗ ℳ ⅃ ☕ 🍷 ⚲ 🕮 👜 ⚑ 🕯 🛆 ✓ ℓ
Location	On the A1, 0.5m south intersection of A1/M62

Hotel	★★★ 70% Wentbridge House Hotel,
	WENTBRIDGE
	☎ 01977 620444 16 🛏 ℉ Annexe 4 🛏 ℉

Pontefract & District Park Ln WF8 4QS
☎ 01977 792241 Fax 01977 792241
Undulating parkland course, some elevated tees.
18 holes, 6227yds, Par 72, SSS 70.
Club membership 800.
Visitors	welcome except Wed & weekends, advisable to
	contact in advance.
Societies	welcome except Wed & weekends.
Green Fees	£25 per day.
Prof	Nick Newman
Facilities	⊗ ℳ ⅃ ☕ 🍷 ⚲ 🕮 👜 ✓
Location	1.5m W on B6134

Hotel	★★★ 70% Wentbridge House Hotel,
	WENTBRIDGE
	☎ 01977 620444 16 🛏 ℉ Annexe 4 🛏 ℉

PUDSEY
Map 08 SE23

Calverley Woodhall Ln LS28 5QY
☎ 0113 256 9244 Fax 0113 256 4362
Parkland course on gently undulating terrain where accurate
approach shots are rewarded to small greens.
18 holes, 5590yds, Par 68, SSS 67, Course record 64.
Club membership 510.
Visitors	advisable to book 18 hole course in advance and
	may not play Sun morning. 9 hole course, pay
	and play at all times.
Societies	contact in writing or telephone.
Green Fees	£21 per day; £15 per round (£20 weekends); £6
	per 9 holes.
Cards	💳 💳 💳 💳
Prof	Derek Johnson
Designer	S Lyle
Facilities	⊗ ℳ ⅃ ☕ 🍷 ⚲ 🕮 👜 ⚑ 🛆 ✓ ℓ
Location	Signposted Calverley from A647
	Leeds/Bradford road

Hotel	★★ 68% Park Drive Hotel,
	12 Park Dr, BRADFORD
	☎ 01274 480194 11 🛏 ℉

Fulneck LS28 8NT ☎ 0113 256 5191
Picturesque parkland course.
9 holes, 5456yds, Par 66, SSS 67, Course record 65.
Club membership 250.
Visitors	with member only weekends & bank holidays.
Societies	must apply in writing.
Green Fees	not confirmed.
Facilities	⊗ by prior arrangement ℳ by prior arrangement
	⅃ ☕ 🍷 ⚲
Location	Pudsey, between Leeds/Bradford

Hotel	★★★ 62% Novotel, Merrydale Rd,
	BRADFORD
	☎ 01274 683683 127 🛏 ℉

Woodhall Hills Calverley LS28 5UN ☎ 0113 255 4594
Meadowland course, prevailing SW winds, fairly hard
walking. Testing holes: 8th, 377 yd (par 4); 14th,
206 yd (par 3).
18 holes, 6001yds, Par 70, SSS 69, Course record 63.
Club membership 570.

▶

Visitors	any day advise secretary/professional in advance.
Societies	telephone in advance.
Green Fees	not confirmed.
Prof	Warren Lockett
Facilities	⊗ Ⅲ ᵇ ᵇ ♥ ♀ ⌂ 🖾 ♂
& Leisure	snooker room.
Location	1m NW off A647

Hotel	★★ 68% Park Drive Hotel, 12 Park Dr, BRADFORD ☎ 01274 480194 11 ⇌ ↾

RAWDON   Map 08 SE23

Rawdon Golf & Lawn Tennis Club
Buckstone Dr LS19 6BD ☎ 0113 250 6040
Undulating parkland course.
9 holes, 5980yds, Par 72, SSS 69.
Club membership 700.

Visitors	must contact in advance & have handicap certificate. With member only at weekends.
Societies	must contact in advance.
Green Fees	not confirmed.
Prof	Simon Toot
Facilities	⊗ Ⅲ ᵇ ᵇ ♥ ♀ ⌂ 🖾 ⍓ ♂
& Leisure	hard and grass tennis courts.
Location	S side of town off A65

Hotel	★★★ 67% Apperley Manor, Apperley Ln, Apperley Bridge, BRADFORD ☎ 0113 250 5626 13 ⇌ ↾

RIDDLESDEN   Map 07 SE04

Riddlesden Howden Rough BD20 5QN
☎ 01535 602148
Undulating moorland course with prevailing west winds, some hard walking and beautiful views. Ten par 3 holes and spectacular 6th and 15th holes played over old quarry sites.
18 holes, 4295yds, Par 63, SSS 61.
Club membership 350.

Visitors	restricted before 2pm weekends.
Societies	apply by telephone or in writing.
Green Fees	not confirmed.
Facilities	⊗ ᵇ ♥ ♀ ⌂
Location	1m NW

Hotel	★★ 66% Dalesgate Hotel, 406 Skipton Rd, Utley, KEIGHLEY ☎ 01535 664930 20 ⇌ ↾

SCARCROFT   Map 08 SE34

Scarcroft Skye Ln LS14 3BQ
☎ 0113 289 2311 Fax 0113 289 3835
Undulating parkland course with prevailing west wind and easy walking.
18 holes, 6426yds, Par 71, SSS 69.
Club membership 667.

Visitors	must contact in advance.
Societies	must contact in advance.
Green Fees	£38 per day; £30 per round (£40 per round weekends & bank holidays).
Prof	Darren Tear
Designer	Charles Mackenzie
Facilities	⊗ Ⅲ ᵇ ᵇ ♥ ♀ ⌂ 🖾 ⍓ ♂
Location	0.5m N of village off A58

Hotel	★★★ 69% The Merrion, Merrion Centre, LEEDS ☎ 0113 243 9191 109 ⇌ ↾

SHIPLEY   Map 07 SE13

Marriott Hollins Hall Hotel & Country Club Hollins Hill, Otley Rd BD17 8QW
☎ 01274 534212 & 534211 Fax 01274 534220
Set in natural heathland amongst the beautiful Yorkshire moors and dales. The course is majestic, challenging and classically designed in the spirit of the game.
18 holes, 6671yds, Par 71, SSS 71, Course record 70.

Visitors	must contact in advance - 10 days max.
Societies	telephone in advance 01274 530053.
Green Fees	£40 per round.
Cards	💳 💳 💳 💳 💳 💳
Designer	Ross McMurray
Facilities	⊗ Ⅲ ᵇ ᵇ ♥ ♀ ⌂ 🖾 ⍓ 🏊 ♀ 🏌 ♂ ↾
& Leisure	heated indoor swimming pool, sauna, solarium, gymnasium, golf academy.
Location	3m N on the A6038 Otley road

Hotel	★★★★ 70% Marriott Hollins Hall Hotel and Country Club, Hollins Hill, Baildon, SHIPLEY ☎ 01274 530053 122 ⇌ ↾

Northcliffe High Bank Ln BD18 4LJ
☎ 01274 596731 Fax 01274 596731
Parkland course with magnificent views of moors. Testing 1st hole (18th green 100 feet below tee).
18 holes, 6104yds, Par 71, SSS 69, Course record 64.
Club membership 700.

Visitors	no restrictions.
Societies	book via secretary in advance, weekdays only.
Green Fees	not confirmed.
Prof	M Hillas
Designer	James Braid
Facilities	⊗ Ⅲ ᵇ ᵇ ♥ ♀ ⌂ 🖾 ⍓ ♂
Location	1.25m SW of Shipley, off A650

Hotel	★★★★ 70% Marriott Hollins Hall Hotel and Country Club, Hollins Hill, Baildon, SHIPLEY ☎ 01274 530053 122 ⇌ ↾

SILSDEN   Map 07 SE04

Silsden High Brunthwaite BD20 0NH ☎ 01535 652998
Tight downland course which can be windy. Good views of the Aire Valley.
14 holes, 4870yds, Par 65, SSS 64, Course record 61.
Club membership 300.

▶

Visitors	may not play before 11am on Sun.
Societies	must apply in advance.
Green Fees	not confirmed.
Facilities	⊗ by prior arrangement ♀ ⌂
Location	1m E

Hotel ★★ 66% Dalesgate Hotel, 406 Skipton Rd, Utley, KEIGHLEY
☎ 01535 664930   20 ⇄ 📻

SOWERBY   Map 07 SE02

Ryburn The Shaw, Norland HX6 3QP ☎ 01422 831355
Moorland course, easy walking.
9 holes, 4984yds, Par 66, SSS 64, Course record 64.
Club membership 200.

Visitors	must contact in advance.
Societies	apply in writing.
Green Fees	not confirmed.
Facilities	⊗ ⅏ ⅂ ♥ ♀ ⌂
Location	1m S of Sowerby Bridge off A58

Hotel ★★ 69% The Hobbit Hotel, Hob Ln, Norland, Sowerby Bridge, HALIFAX
☎ 01422 832202   17 ⇄ 📻 Annexe 5 ⇄ 📻

TODMORDEN   Map 07 SD92

Todmorden Rive Rocks, Cross Stone Rd OL14 8RD
☎ 01706 812986
Pleasant moorland course.
9 holes, 5902yds, Par 68, SSS 68, Course record 67.
Club membership 240.

Visitors	restricted Thu & weekends. Advisable to contact in advance.
Societies	must apply in writing.
Green Fees	not confirmed.
Facilities	⊗ by prior arrangement ⅏ by prior arrangement ⅂ ♥ ♀ ⌂
Location	NE off A646

Hotel ★★★ 66% Carlton Hotel, Albert St, HEBDEN BRIDGE ☎ 01422 844400   16 ⇄ 📻

WAKEFIELD   Map 08 SE32

City of Wakefield Horbury Rd WF2 8QS
☎ 01924 360282
Mature, level parkland course.
18 holes, 6319yds, Par 72, SSS 70, Course record 67.
Club membership 600.

Visitors	restricted weekends.
Societies	must apply in advance to stewardess 01924 367242.
Green Fees	£9 (£11 weekends).
Cards	💳 💳 💳 💳
Prof	Roger Holland
Designer	J S F Morrison
Facilities	⊗ ⅏ ⅂ ♥ ♀ ⌂ 🏠 ⛳ ✎
Location	1.5m W of city centre on A642

Hotel ★★★ 68% Posthouse Wakefield, Queen's Dr, Ossett, WAKEFIELD
☎ 0870 400 9082 99 ⇄ 📻

Painthorpe House Painthorpe Ln, Painthorpe, Crigglestone WF4 3HE ☎ 01924 274527 & 255083 Fax 01924 252022
Undulating meadowland course, easy walking.
9 holes, 4544yds, Par 62, SSS 62, Course record 63.
Club membership 150.

Visitors	pay and play Mon-Sat, after 2.30pm on Sun.
Societies	must telephone in advance.
Green Fees	£5 (£6 weekends).
Cards	💳 💳
Facilities	⊗ ⅏ ⅂ ♥ ♀ ⌂
& Leisure	bowling green.
Location	2m S off A636, 0.5m from jct 39 M1

Hotel ★★★ 68% Posthouse Wakefield, Queen's Dr, Ossett, WAKEFIELD
☎ 0870 400 9082 99 ⇄ 📻

Wakefield Woodthorpe Ln, Sandal WF2 6JH
☎ 01924 258778 (sec) & 255380 (pro) Fax 01924 242752
A well-sheltered meadowland/heath course with easy walking and good views.
18 holes, 6642yds, Par 72, SSS 72, Course record 66.
Club membership 540.

Visitors	contact must be made in advance. Visitors Wed, Thu and Fri only.
Societies	must apply in writing.
Green Fees	on application.
Prof	Ian M Wright
Designer	McKenzie
Facilities	⌂ 🏠 ✎
Location	3m S of Wakefield, off A61

Hotel ★★★ 68% Posthouse Wakefield, Queen's Dr, Ossett, WAKEFIELD
☎ 0870 400 9082 99 ⇄ 📻

WETHERBY   Map 08 SE44

Wetherby Linton Ln LS22 4JF
☎ 01937 580089 Fax 01937 581915
Parkland course with fine views.
18 holes, 6235yds, Par 71, SSS 70, Course record 63.
Club membership 650.

Visitors	may not play Mon & Tues morning.
Societies	apply in writing or telephone in advance.
Green Fees	£35 per day; £28 per round (£40 per round weekends and bank holidays).
Facilities	⊗ ⅏ ⅂ ♥ ♀ ⌂ 🏠 ⛳ 🏌 ✎
Location	1m W off A661

Hotel ★★★🏵 75% Wood Hall Hotel, Trip Ln, Linton, WETHERBY
☎ 01937 587271   36 ⇄ 📻 Annexe 6 ⇄ 📻

CHANNEL ISLANDS

ALDERNEY

ALDERNEY   Map 16

Alderney Route des Carrieres GY9 3YD ☎ 01481 822835
Undulating seaside course with sea on all sides and offering magnificent views from its high tees and greens. Course designed by Frank Pennink.

▶

9 holes, 5006yds, Par 64, SSS 65, Course record 65.
Club membership 400.

Visitors   may not play before 10am at weekends. Advisable to contact in advance.
Societies   must contact in advance.
Green Fees not confirmed.
Facilities   🏌 💪 🍴 ⚐ 👤 🏌 ♦
Location   1m E of St Annes

Inn   ♦♦♦ The Georgian House, Victoria St, St Anne, ALDERNEY ☎ 01481 822471 3 ⇄ ❦

GUERNSEY

L'ANCRESSE VALE   Map 16

Royal Guernsey GY3 5BY
☎ 01481 246523 Fax 01481 243960
Not quite as old as its neighbour Royal Jersey, Royal Guernsey is a sporting course which was re-designed after World War II by Mackenzie Ross, who has many fine courses to his credit. It is a pleasant links, well-maintained, and administered by the States of Guernsey in the form of the States Tourist Committee. The 8th hole, a good par 4, requires an accurate second shot to the green set amongst the gorse and thick rough. The 18th, with lively views, needs a strong shot to reach the green well down below. The course is windy, with hard walking. There is a junior section.
18 holes, 6206yds, Par 70, SSS 70, Course record 64.
Club membership 934.

Visitors   must have a handicap certificate; may not play on Thu, Sat afternoons & Sun.
Green Fees £36 per day.
Cards   🔲
Prof   Norman Wood
Designer   Mackenzie Ross
Facilities   ⊗ �🔥 🏌 💪 🍴 ⚐ 👤 🏠 🏌 ♦ ❧
Location   3m N of St Peter Port

Hotel   ★★★★ 68% St Pierre Park Hotel, Rohais, ST PETER PORT ☎ 01481 728282 132 ⇄ ❦

ST PETER PORT   Map 16

St Pierre Park Golf Club Rohais GY1 1FD
☎ 01481 728282 Fax 01481 712041
Par 3 parkland course with delightful setting, with lakes, streams and many tricky holes.
9 holes, 2610yds, Par 54, SSS 50, Course record 52.
Club membership 200.

Visitors   must book tee times. Strict dress code, contact club in advance for datails.
Societies   must contact in advance.
Green Fees £17 per 18 holes; £12 per 9 holes (£19/£14 weekends & bank holidays).
Cards   🔲 🔲 🔲 🔲 🔲 🔲 🔲
Prof   Roy Corbet
Designer   Jacklin
Facilities   ⊗ 🔥 🏌 💪 🍴 ⚐ 👤 🏠 🏌 🛒 ♦ ❧
& Leisure   hard tennis courts, heated indoor swimming pool, sauna, solarium, gymnasium.

Location   1m W off Rohais Rd

Hotel   ★★★★ 68% St Pierre Park Hotel, Rohais, ST PETER PORT ☎ 01481 728282 132 ⇄ ❦

JERSEY

GROUVILLE   Map 16

Royal Jersey Le Chemin au Greves JE3 9BD ☎ 01534 854416 Fax 01534 854684
A seaside links, historic because of its age: its centenary was celebrated in 1978. It is also famous for the fact that Britain's greatest golfer, Harry Vardon, was born in a little cottage on the edge of the course and learned his golf here.
18 holes, 6059yds, Par 70, SSS 70, Course record 64.
Club membership 1364.

Visitors   restricted to 10am-noon & 2pm-4pm Mon-Fri & 2pm-4pm weekends & bank holidays.
Societies   welcome Mon-Fri. Must apply in writing.
Green Fees £40 per round.
Cards   🔲 🔲 🔲 🔲 🔲 🔲
Prof   David Morgan
Facilities   ⊗ 🔥 🏌 💪 🍴 ⚐ 👤 🏠 🏌 🛒 ♦
Location   4m E of St Helier off coast rd

Hotel   ★★★ 66% Old Court House Hotel, GOREY ☎ 01534 854444 58 ⇄ ❦

LA MOYE   Map 16

La Moye La Route Orange JE3 8GQ
☎ 01534 743401 Fax 01534 747289
Seaside championship links course (venue for the Jersey Seniors Open) situated in an exposed position on the south western corner of the island overlooking St Ouens Bay. Offers spectacular views, two start points, full course all year - no temporary greens.
18 holes, 6664yds, Par 72, SSS 72, Course record 68.
Club membership 1300.

Visitors   must contact course ranger in advance 01534 747166. Visitors may play after 2.30pm weekends and bank holidays.
Societies   apply in writing.
Green Fees £40 per round (£45 weekends & bank holidays).
Cards   🔲 🔲 🔲 🔲 🔲 🔲
Prof   Mike Deeley
Designer   James Braid
Facilities   ⊗ 🔥 🏌 💪 🍴 ⚐ 👤 🏠 🏌 🛒 ♦ ❧
Location   W side of village off A13

Hotel   ★★★★ 73% The Atlantic Hotel, Le Mont de la Pulente, ST BRELADE ☎ 01534 744101 50 ⇄ ❦

> Entries with a green background identify courses considered to be particularly interesting

St Clement
Map 16

St Clement Jersey Recreation Grounds JE2 6PN
☎ 01534 21938
Very tight moorland course. Holes cross over fairways, impossible to play to scratch. Suitable for middle to high handicaps.
9 holes, 2244yds, Par 30.
Club membership 500.
Green Fees not confirmed.
Facilities ⛤
& Leisure hard tennis courts.
Location E side of St Helier on A5

Hotel ★★★★🏨 Longueville Manor Hotel, ST SAVIOUR ☎ 01534 725501 32 ⇆ ❦

St Ouen
Map 16

Les Mielles Golf & Country Club JE3 7FQ
☎ 01534 482787 Fax 01534 485414
Challenging seaside parkland course with bent grass greens, dwarf rye fairways and picturesque ponds situated in the Island's largest conservation area within St Ouen's Bay.
18 holes, 6713yds, Par 70, SSS 68, Course record 59.
Club membership 1500.
Visitors welcome all times, prior booking recommended.
Societies write in advance to avoid disappointment.
Green Fees £21 per 18 holes; £14 per 9 holes (£24/£15.50 weekends).
Cards 🔲 🔲 🔲 🔲 🔲 🔲
Prof Lee Elstone/Wayne Osmand
Designer J Le Brun/R Whitehead
Facilities ⊗ ⌸ 🖥 🍺 ♀ ⛤ 🔺 🏠 ❡ ↘ 🛒 ♐ ⛳
Location Centre of St Ouen's Bay

Hotel ★★★ 69% Mermaid Hotel, ST PETER ☎ 01534 741255 68 ⇆ ❦

ISLE OF MAN

Castletown
Map 06 SC26

Castletown Golf Links Fort Island, Derbyhaven IM9 1UA
☎ 01624 822201 & 822211 (pro shop) Fax 01624 824633
Set on the Langness Peninsula, this superb Championship course is surrounded on three sides by the sea, and holds many surprises from its Championship tees. The hotel offers many leisure facilities.
18 holes, 6750yds, Par 72, SSS 72, Course record 64.
Club membership 600.

Visitors contact in advance. Sat reserved for hotel residents and club members. Ladies only Wed morning
Societies must telephone in advance.
Green Fees £28.50 per day (£35 weekends & bank holidays).
Cards 🔲 🔲 🔲 🔲 🔲 🔲
Prof Murray Crowe
Designer McKenzie Ross
Facilities ⊗ ⌸ 🖥 🍺 ♀ ⛤ 🏠 ❡ 🛒 ↘ 🛒 ♐
& Leisure heated indoor swimming pool, sauna.
Hotel ★★★ 68% Castletown Golf Links Hotel, Fort Island, CASTLETOWN ☎ 01624 822201 58 ⇆ ❦

Douglas
Map 06 SC37

Douglas Pulrose Park IM2 1AE ☎ 01624 661558
Hilly, parkland and moorland course under the control of Douglas Corporation.
18 holes, 5937yds, Par 69, SSS 69, Course record 62.
Club membership 330.
Visitors no restrictions.
Societies telephone to book tee time.
Green Fees £8.50 per day (£10.50 weekends).
Prof Kevin Parry
Facilities ⊗ ⌸ 🖥 🍺 ♀ ⛤ 🏠 ❡ ♐
Location 1m W off A1

Hotel ★★★ 67% The Empress Hotel, Central Promenade, DOUGLAS ☎ 01624 661155 102 ⇆ ❦

Mount Murray Hotel & Country Club Mount Murray, Santon IM4 2HT ☎ 01624 661111 Fax 01624 611116
A challenging course with many natural features, lakes, streams etc. Six Par 5's, five Par 3's and the rest Par 4. Fine views over the whole island.
18 holes, 6664yds, Par 72, SSS 72.
Club membership 378.

Visitors must contact in advance. Visitors may not play before 9.30am weekends
Societies telephone in advance.
Green Fees £18 (£24 weekends).
Cards 🔲 🔲 🔲 🔲 🔲 🔲
Prof Andrew Dyson
Facilities ⊗ ⌸ 🖥 🍺 ♀ ⛤ 🔺 🏠 ❡ ↘ 🛒 ♐ ⛳
& Leisure hard tennis courts, heated indoor swimming pool, squash, sauna, solarium, gymnasium.
Location Located on main road 5m from Douglas towards airport

▶

Hotel   ★★★★ 67% Mount Murray Hotel & Country Club, Santon, DOUGLAS
☎ 01624 661111 90 ⇌ ⟆

ONCHAN   Map 06 SC47

King Edward Bay Golf & Country Club Howstrake, Groudle Rd IM3 2JR ☎ 01624 672709
Club plays over King Edward Bay course. Hilly seaside links course with natural hazards and good views.
18 holes, 5485yds, Par 67, SSS 65, Course record 62.
Club membership 370.
Visitors   must have a handicap certificate.
Societies   must contact in advance.
Green Fees   £12 per day (£14 weekends & bank holidays).
Prof   Donald Jones
Designer   Tom Morris
Facilities   ⊗ ⊪ ㇆ ⬛ ♀ ♨ 🖛 ⤳ ∅
Location   E side of town off A11

Hotel   ★★★★ 67% Sefton Hotel, Harris Promenade, DOUGLAS ☎ 01624 645500 104 ⇌ ⟆

PEEL   Map 06 SC28

Peel Rheast Ln IM5 1BG
☎ 01624 842227 & 843456 Fax 01624 843456
Moorland course, with natural hazards and easy walking. Good views. 11th hole is a par 4, dog-leg.
18 holes, 5850yds, Par 69, SSS 69, Course record 69.
Club membership 856.
Visitors   must contact in advance. Limited availability weekends.
Societies   apply in writing/telephone
Green Fees   £18 per day (£25 weekends & bank holidays).
Cards   ⊟ ⊟
Prof   Murray Crowe
Designer   Robert Braide
Facilities   ⊗ ⊪ by prior arrangement ㇆ ⬛ ♀ ♨ 🖛 ∅
& Leisure   snooker.
Location   SE side of town centre on A1

Hotel   ★★★ 67% The Empress Hotel, Central Promenade, DOUGLAS
☎ 01624 661155 102 ⇌ ⟆

> AA Hotels that have special arrangements with golf courses are listed at the back of the guide

PORT ERIN   Map 06 SC16

Rowany Rowany Dr IM9 6LN
☎ 01624 834108 or 834072 Fax 01624 834108
Undulating seaside course with testing later holes.
18 holes, 5840yds, Par 70, SSS 69, Course record 66.
Club membership 550.
Visitors   must contact in advance.
Societies   telephone in advance.
Green Fees   not confirmed.
Designer   G Lowe
Facilities   ⊗ ㇆ ⬛ ♀ ♨ 🖛 ⤳ ∅
Location   N side of village off A32

Hotel   ★★★ 67% Cherry Orchard Hotel, Bridson St, PORT ERIN ☎ 01624 833811 31 ⇌ ⟆

PORT ST MARY   Map 06 SC26

Port St Mary Kallow Point Rd ☎ 01624 834932
Slightly hilly course with beautiful scenic views over Port St Mary and the Irish Sea.
9 holes, 5418yds, Par 68, SSS 66, Course record 62.
Club membership 432.
Visitors   anytime except between 8-10.30 weekends.
Societies   contact for details.
Green Fees   not confirmed.
Cards   ⊟ ⊟ ⊟ ⊟ ⊟ ⊟ ⊟
Designer   George Duncan
Facilities   ⊗ ⊪ ㇆ ⬛ ♀ ♨ 🖛 ⤳ ∅
& Leisure   hard tennis courts.
Location   Signposted on entering Port St Mary

Hotel   ★★★ 67% Cherry Orchard Hotel, Bridson St, PORT ERIN ☎ 01624 833811 31 ⇌ ⟆

RAMSEY   Map 06 SC49

Ramsey Brookfield IM8 2AH
☎ 01624 812244 Fax 01624 815833
Parkland course, with easy walking. Windy. Good views. Testing holes: 1st, par 5; 18th, par 3.
18 holes, 5960yds, Par 70, SSS 69, Course record 64.
Club membership 1000.
Visitors   contact in advance, visitors may not play before 10am weekdays.
Societies   must apply in advance.
Green Fees   £20 (£22 weekends & bank holidays).
Cards   ⊟ ⊟ ⊟ ⊟
Prof   Calum Wilson
Designer   James Braid
Facilities   ⊗ ⊪ ㇆ ⬛ ♀ ♨ 🖛 ⤳ ∅
Location   SW side of town

Hotel   ★★★ 67% The Empress Hotel, Central Promenade, DOUGLAS
☎ 01624 661155 102 ⇌ ⟆

Scotland

SCOTLAND

The directory which follows has been divided into three geographical regions. Counties have not been shown against individual locations as recent legislation has created a number of smaller counties which will be unfamiliar to the visitor. The postal authorities have confirmed that it is no longer necessary to include a county name in addresses, provided a post code is shown. All locations appear in the atlas section at the end of this guide in their appropriate counties.

HIGHLANDS & ISLANDS

This region includes the counties of Aberdeen City, Aberdeenshire, Highland, Moray, Orkney, Shetland and Western Isles which reflect the national changes.

ABERDEEN   Map 15 NJ90

Auchmill Bonnyview Rd, West Heatheryfold AB16 7FQ
☎ 01224 714577 Fax 01224 648693
This course is definitely not for beginners - the fairways are tree-lined and very tight on most holes. Three holes are quite hilly and although the remainder is flat there are nice views over Aberdeen. The course is not recommended for anyone over 22 handicap unless they have plenty of golf balls!
18 holes, 5123metres, Par 68, SSS 67, Course record 67.
Club membership 300.
Visitors   members have priority Sat & Wed for club competitions.
Societies   apply in writing to Leisure and Recreation Dept, Aberdeen District Council.
Green Fees not confirmed.
Designer   Neil Coles/Brian Hugget
Facilities   ⊗ ⅷ ┗ � ♀ ♨ ┱
Location   Outskirts Aberdeen, A96 Aberdeen/Inverness

Hotel   ★★★ 67% The Craighaar, Waterton Rd, Bankhead, ABERDEEN
                  ☎ 01224 712275   55 ⇔ ⟨

Balnagask St Fitticks Rd AB11 3QT
☎ 01224 876407 Fax 01224 648693
Links course. Used by the Nigg Bay Club.
18 holes, 5986yds, Par 70, SSS 69.
Visitors   book n person on day of play.
Societies   apply to council tel 01224 276276.
Green Fees not confirmed.
Facilities   ⊗ ⅷ ┗ � ♀ ♨ ┱
& Leisure   9 hole pitch & putt course.
Location   2m E of city centre

Hotel   ★★★ 65% Maryculter House Hotel, South Deeside Rd, ABERDEEN
                  ☎ 01224 732124   23 ⇔ ⟨

Deeside Golf Rd, Bieldside AB15 9DL
☎ 01224 869457 Fax 01224 869457
An interesting riverside course with several tree-lined fairways. A stream comes into play at 9 of the 18 holes on the main course.
18 holes, 5971yds, Par 71, SSS 69, Course record 63.
Club membership 900.
Visitors   must contact in advance, may not play competition days.

Societies   apply in writing.
Green Fees £25 per day (£30 weekends & bank holidays).
Prof   Frank J Coutts
Facilities   ⊗ ⅷ ┗ ▼ ♀ ♨ ┱ ♂
Location   3m W of city centre off A93

Hotel   ★★★★ 71% Ardoe House, South Deeside Rd, Blairs, ABERDEEN
                  ☎ 01224 867355   71 ⇔ ⟨

Hazelhead Public Hazlehead AB1 8BD
☎ 01224 321830 Fax 01224 648693
Both No 1 and No 2 courses are tree-lined. The 9 hole course is open but surrounded by trees.
No 1 Course: 18 holes, 6211yds, Par 70, SSS 70.
No 2 Course: 18 holes, 5742yds, Par 67, SSS 67.
Visitors   no restrictions.
Societies   must contact in advance.
Green Fees not confirmed.
Prof   A Smith/G Taylor/C Nelson
Facilities   ⊗ ⅷ ┗ ▼ ♀ ♨ ┱ ♉ ♂
& Leisure   9 hole pitch & putt course.
Location   4m W of city centre off A944

Hotel   ★★★★ 71% Ardoe House, South Deeside Rd, Blairs, ABERDEEN
                  ☎ 01224 867355   71 ⇔ ⟨

Kings Links AB24 1RZ
☎ 01224 632269 Fax 01224 648693
A typical links course with no tree lines and plenty of bunkers.The 14th hole is tricky - a long par 4 with a raised green and not much fairway round the green. The course is playable all year. Nearby there is a 6-hole course. The Bon Accord Club, Caledonian Club and Northern Club play over this course.
18 holes, 6384yds, Par 72, SSS 71.
Visitors   contact starters box on 01224 632269 regarding booking of tee times.
Societies   write to the Arts & Recreation Dept, St Nicholas House, Broad Street, Aberdeen.
Green Fees not confirmed.
Facilities   ⊗ ⅷ ┗ ▼ ♀ ♨
Location   0.75m NE of city centre

Hotel   ★★★ 65% Grampian Hotel, Stirling St, ABERDEEN ☎ 01224 589101 108 ⇔ ⟨

Murcar Bridge of Don AB23 8BD
☎ 01224 704354 Fax 01224 704354
Seaside links course, prevailing SW wind, hard-walking. Testing 4th and 14th holes.
Murcar: 18 holes, 6287yds, Par 71, SSS 71, Course record 65.
Strabathie: 9 holes, 2680yds, Par 35, SSS 35.
Club membership 850.
Visitors   must contact in advance.
Societies   advance booking required.
Green Fees not confirmed.
Cards   ▬▬ ▬▬
Prof   Gary Forbes
Designer   Archie Simpson
Facilities   ⊗ ⅷ ┗ ▼ ♀ ♨ ┱ ♂
Location   5m NE of city centre off A92

Hotel   ★★★ 67% The Craighaar, Waterton Rd, Bankhead, ABERDEEN
                  ☎ 01224 712275   55 ⇔ ⟨

Royal Aberdeen Links Rd, Balgownie, Bridge of Don
AB23 8AT ☎ 01224 702571 Fax 01224 826591
Championship links course with undulating dunes. Windy,
easy walking.
*Balgownie Course: 18 holes, 6372yds, Par 71, SSS 71,
Course record 63.*
Silverburn Course: 18 holes, 4066yds, Par 60, SSS 60.
Club membership 500.

Visitors	times for visitors 10-11.30 and 2-3.30pm weekdays, after 3.30pm weekends. Must contact in advance.
Societies	apply in writing.
Green Fees	not confirmed.
Cards	💳 🏧
Prof	Ronnie MacAskill
Designer	Baird & Simpson
Facilities	⊗ �🏌 🏌 🍺 ♀ ♂ 🏊 🛄 📮 🚜 🏌
Location	2.5m N of city centre off A92

Hotel	★★★ 65% Grampian Hotel, Stirling St, ABERDEEN ☎ 01224 589101 108 ⇄ ↾

Westhill Westhill Heights, Westhill AB32 6RY
☎ 01224 742567 Fax 01224 749124
A highland course.
18 holes, 5921yds, Par 69, SSS 69, Course record 65.
Club membership 930.

Visitors	welcome except Saturdays.
Societies	telephone in advance.
Green Fees	£12 per round.
Cards	💳 🏧 💷
Prof	George Bruce
Designer	Charles Lawrie
Facilities	⊗ �🏌 🏌 🍺 ♀ ♂ 🏊 🛄 📮 🚜 🏌
Location	6m NW of city centre off A944

Hotel	★★★ 68% Westhill Hotel, Westhill, ABERDEEN ☎ 01224 740388 37 ⇄ ↾ Annexe 13 ⇄ ↾

ABOYNE Map 15 NO59

Aboyne Formaston Park AB34 5HP
☎ 013398 86328 Fax 013398 87592
Beautiful parkland with outstanding views. Two lochs on
course.
18 holes, 5975yds, Par 68, SSS 69, Course record 62.
Club membership 930.

Visitors	no restrictions. Advisable to contact in advance.
Societies	prior booking essential.
Green Fees	£25 per day; £19 per round (£30/£23 weekends)..
Cards	💳 🏧 💷
Prof	Innes Wright
Facilities	⊗ �🏌 🏌 🍺 ♀ ♂ 🏊 🛄 📮 🚜 🏌
Location	E side of village, N of A93

Guesthouse	◆◆◆◆◆ Arbor Lodge, Ballater Rd, ABOYNE ☎ 01339 886951 3 ⇄ ↾

ALFORD Map 15 NJ51

Alford Montgarrie Rd AB33 8AE
☎ 019755 62178 Fax 019755 62178
A flat parkland course in scenic countryside. Divided into
sections by a road, a narrow-gauge railway and a burn.

18 holes, 5483yds, Par 69, SSS 65, Course record 64.
Club membership 600.

Visitors	advisable to contact in advance.
Societies	telephone/e-mail in advance.
Green Fees	£19 per day; £13 per round (£26/£20 weekends).
Facilities	⊗ �🏌 🏌 🍺 ♀ ♂ 🏊 🛄 📮 🚜 🏌
Location	In the centre of the village on A944

ALNESS Map 14 NH66

Alness Ardross Rd IV17 0QA ☎ 01349 883877
A testing, parkland course with beautiful views over the
Cromarty Firth and the Black Isle. An additional 9 holes have
been developed, four holes run alongside the Averon river
making the course more scenic and interesting.
18 holes, 4886yds, Par 67, SSS 64, Course record 62.
Club membership 300.

Visitors	telephone in advance for weekend play, parties must telephone for booking
Societies	must contact in advance.
Green Fees	not confirmed.
Facilities & Leisure	⊗ �🏌 by prior arrangement 🛄 📮 ♀ 🏊 🚜 🏌 fishing.
Location	0.5m N off A9

Hotel	★★★ 72% Morangie House Hotel, Morangie Rd, TAIN ☎ 01862 892281 26 ⇄ ↾

ARISAIG Map 13 NM68

Traigh PH39 4NT ☎ 01687 450337 Fax 01678 450293
According to at least one newspaper Traigh is 'probably the
most beautifully sited nine-hole golf course in the world'.
Whether that is true or not, Traigh lies by the sea alongside
sandy beaches with views to Skye and the Inner Hebrides.
The feature of the course is a line of grassy hills, originally
sand dunes, that rise to some 60 feet.
9 holes, 2456yds, Par 68, SSS 65, Course record 67.
Club membership 150.

Visitors	no restrictions.
Societies	contact in advance.
Green Fees	£12 per day.
Designer	John Salvesen 1994
Facilities	🍺 🛄 📮 🏌
Location	2m N of Arisaig on A830

Hotel	★★ 68% Arisaig Hotel, ARISAIG ☎ 01687 450210 13 ⇄ ↾

AUCHENBLAE Map 15 NO77

Auchenblae AB30 1BU ☎ 01561 320002
Picturesque, small, undulating parkland course offering good
views.
9 holes, 2174yds, Par 33, SSS 32, Course record 62.
Club membership 450.

Visitors	restricted Wed & Fri evenings.
Societies	must telephone in advance.
Green Fees	not confirmed.
Facilities	🍺 🏌
Location	0.5m NE

Hotel	★★ 66% County Hotel & Leisure Club, Arduthie Rd, STONEHAVEN ☎ 01569 764386 14 ⇄ ↾

BALLATER   Map 15 NO39

Ballater Victoria Rd AB35 5QX
☎ 013397 55567 Fax 013397 55057
Heather covered course with testing long holes and beautiful scenery.
18 holes, 5638yds, Par 67, SSS 67, Course record 62.
Club membership 750.

Visitors	advisable to contact in advance.
Societies	prior booking recommended.
Green Fees	£27 per day; £18 per round (£31/£21 weekends).
Cards	🔳 💳 💳 💳
Prof	Bill Yule
Facilities	⊗ 𝍢 ᵇ 💻 ♥ ♀ ⚐ ☎ ⛳ ▶ 🚲 ∅
& Leisure	hard tennis courts, fishing, snooker.
Location	W side of town

Hotel ★★★ 74% Darroch Learg Hotel, Braemar Rd, BALLATER
☎ 013397 55443 13 ⇔ ୮ Annexe 5 ⇔ ୮

BANCHORY   Map 15 NO69

Banchory Kinneskie Rd AB31 5TA
☎ 01330 822365 Fax 01330 822491
Sheltered parkland course situated beside the River Dee, with easy walking and woodland scenery. 12th and 13th holes are testing.
18 holes, 5775yds, Par 69, SSS 68, Course record 65.
Club membership 975.

Visitors	must contact in advance, telephone for details on 01330 822447
Societies	must book in advance, no parties Tue & weekends.
Green Fees	£25 per day, £18 per round (£21 per round weekends).
Cards	💳
Prof	David Naylor
Facilities	⊗ 𝍢 ᵇ 💻 ♥ ♀ ⚐ ☎ ⛳ ▶ 🚲 ∅
Location	A93, 300 yds from W end of High St

Hotel ★★★♨ 74% Banchory Lodge Hotel, BANCHORY ☎ 01330 822625   22 ⇔ ୮

BANFF   Map 15 NJ66

Duff House Royal The Barnyards AB45 3SX
☎ 01261 812062 Fax 01261 812224
Well-manicured flat parkland, bounded by woodlands and River Deveron. Well bunkered and renowned for its large, two-tier greens.
18 holes, 6161yds, Par 68, SSS 70, Course record 63.
Club membership 1000.

The Boat Hotel
at Boat of Garten
🄰🄰 ★★★ ◎◎

NOW UNDER NEW OWNERSHIP!
Extensively refurbished
Award-winning cuisine.

Excellent Golfing packages at Boat of Garten or any one of 6 local courses.

Call (01479) 831258,
Fax: (01479) 831414
or email holidays@boathotel.co.uk

Visitors	telephone professional in advance, handicap certificate is preferred. Restrictions at weekends due to members medal play.
Societies	must apply in writing.
Green Fees	£24 per day; £18 per round (£30/£25 weekends).
Cards	💳
Prof	Bob Strachan
Designer	Dr McKenzie
Facilities	⊗ 𝍢 ᵇ 💻 ♥ ♀ ⚐ ☎ ⛳ ▶ ∅
Location	0.5m S on A98

Hotel ★★★ 67% Banff Springs Hotel, Golden Knowes Rd, BANFF
☎ 01261 812881   31 ⇔ ୮

BOAT OF GARTEN   Map 14 NH91

Boat of Garten PH24 3BQ
☎ 01479 831282 Fax 01479 831523
This heathland course was cut out from a silver birch forest though the fairways are adequately wide. There ▶

are natural hazards of broom and heather, good views and walking is easy. A round provides great variety.
18 holes, 5866yds, Par 69, SSS 69, Course record 67.
Club membership 600.

Visitors	must contact in advance. Handicap certificate required. Play restricted to 10am-4pm weekends & 9.20am-7pm weekdays
Societies	must telephone in advance.
Green Fees	£28 per day; £23 per round (£33/£28 weekends).
Cards	⬛ ⬛ ⬛ ⬛ ⬛
Designer	James Braid
Facilities & Leisure	⊗ ⅲ ⮂ ⬛ ⬛ ⏛ ⬛ ⬛ ⬛ ⬛ hard tennis courts.
Location	E side of village
Hotel	★★★ 70% Boat Hotel, BOAT OF GARTEN ☎ 01479 831258 32 ⇌ ⮑

BONAR BRIDGE   Map 14 NH69

Bonar Bridge-Ardgay Migdale Rd IV24 3EJ
☎ 01863 766375 Fax 01863 766738
Wooded moorland course with picturesque views of hills and loch.
9 holes, 5284yds, Par 68, SSS 66.
Club membership 250.

Visitors	no restrictions.
Societies	apply in writing.
Green Fees	£12 per day.
Facilities	⬛ ⏛ ⬛
Location	0.5m E
Hotel	★★ 70% Dornoch Castle Hotel, Castle St, DORNOCH ☎ 01862 810216 4 ⇌ ⮑ Annexe 13 ⇌ ⮑

BRAEMAR   Map 15 NO19

Braemar Cluniebank Rd AB35 5XX ☎ 013397 41618
Flat course, set amid beautiful countryside on Royal Deeside, with River Clunie running through several holes. The 2nd hole is one of the most testing in the area.
18 holes, 5000yds, Par 65, SSS 64, Course record 59.
Club membership 450.

Visitors	are advised to book 24 hours in advance to play at weekends. Tee reserved until 12.30 on Sat for members only.
Societies	must contact secretary in advance 01224 704471.
Green Fees	not confirmed.
Designer	Joe Anderson
Facilities	⊗ ⅲ ⮂ ⬛ ⬛ ⏛ ⬛ ⬛ ⬛
Location	0.5m S
Hotel	★★★ 66% The Invercauld Arms, BRAEMAR ☎ 013397 41605 68 ⇌ ⮑

BRORA   Map 14 NC90

Brora Golf Rd KW9 6QS
☎ 01408 621417 Fax 01408 622157
Typical seaside links with little rough and fine views. Some testing holes.
18 holes, 6110yds, Par 69, SSS 69, Course record 61.
Club membership 704.

Visitors	advisable to book in advance May-Oct.
Societies	advisable to book in advance.
Green Fees	£20 per round (£25 weekends).
Cards	⬛ ⬛ ⬛
Designer	James Braid
Facilities & Leisure	⊗ ⅲ ⮂ ⬛ ⬛ ⏛ ⬛ ⬛ ⬛ snooker.
Location	E side of village. Follow signs to Beach Car Park
Hotel	★★★ 66% The Links Hotel, Golf Rd, BRORA ☎ 01408 621225 23 ⇌ ⮑

BUCKIE   Map 15 NJ46

Buckpool Barhill Rd, Buckpool AB56 1DU
☎ 01542 832236 Fax 01542 832236
Links course with superlative view over Moray Firth, easy walking.
18 holes, 6257yds, Par 70, SSS 70, Course record 64.
Club membership 430.

Visitors	parties please apply in advance.
Societies	apply in advance.
Green Fees	£16 per day; £13 per round (£22/£16 weekends).
Facilities & Leisure	⊗ ⅲ by prior arrangement ⮂ ⬛ ⬛ ⬛ squash.
Location	Off A98
Hotel	★★ 67% Mill House Hotel, Tynet, BUCKIE ☎ 01542 850233 15 ⇌ ⮑

Strathlene Portessie AB56 2DJ
☎ 01542 831798
Raised seaside links course with magnificent view. A special feature of the course is approach shots to raised greens (holes 4,5,6 & 13).
18 holes, 5980yds, Par 69, SSS 69, Course record 65.
Club membership 370.

Visitors	booking essential at weekends.
Societies	telephone for Mon-Fri & apply in writing for weekends.
Green Fees	£20 per day; £14 per round.
Facilities	⊗ ⮂ ⬛ ⬛ ⬛
Location	2m E of Buckie on A942
Hotel	★★ 67% Mill House Hotel, Tynet, BUCKIE ☎ 01542 850233 15 ⇌ ⮑

CARRBRIDGE   Map 14 NH92

Carrbridge Inverness Rd PH23 3AU
☎ 01479 841623
Short but challenging part-parkland, part-moorland course with magnificent views of the Cairngorms.
9 holes, 5402yds, Par 71, SSS 68, Course record 64.
Club membership 650.

Visitors	during May-Sep, course not open to visitors after 5pm Wed & before 4pm most Sun.
Societies	small parties welcome, apply in writing.
Green Fees	£11-£12 per day (£13 weekends). Evening (after 6.30pm) £6-£8.
Facilities	⬛ ⏛ ⬛ ⬛
Location	N side of village
Hotel	★★★ 68% Dalrachney Lodge Hotel, CARRBRIDGE ☎ 01479 841252 11 ⇌ ⮑

CRUDEN BAY
Map 15 NK03

Cruden Bay Aulton Rd AB42 0NN
☎ 01779 812285 Fax 01779 812945
A typical links course which epitomizes the old
fashioned style of rugged links golf. The drives require
accuracy with bunkers and protecting greens, blind holes
and undulating greens. The 10th provides a panoramic
view of half the back nine down at beach level, and to
the east can be seen the outline of the spectacular ruin of
Slains Castle featured in Bram Stoker's Dracula. The
figure eight design of the course is quite unusual.
*Main Course: 18 holes, 6395yds, Par 70, SSS 72, Course
record 65.*
St Olaf Course: 9 holes, 2553yds, Par 64, SSS 65.
Club membership 1100.

Visitors	welcome on weekdays, at weekends only when there are no competitions, advisable to contact for details.
Societies	weekdays only telephone in advance.
Green Fees	not confirmed.
Cards	〓 〓 🔟
Prof	Robbie Stewart
Designer	Thomas Simpson
Facilities	⊗ 🗙 🖺 💻 ♀ 🛆 🛋 🍸 🥢 ℓ
Location	SW side of village on A975

Hotel	★★ 65% Red House Hotel, Aulton Rd, CRUDEN BAY ☎ 01779 812215 6rm (5 ⇆ 🏲)

CULLEN
Map 15 NJ56

Cullen The Links AB56 4UU ☎ 01542 840685
Interesting links on two levels with rocks and ravines
offering some challenging holes. Spectacular scenery.
18 holes, 4610yds, Par 63, SSS 62, Course record 58.
Club membership 600.

Visitors	no restrictions but during summer club medal matches given preference on Mon/Wed/Sat.
Societies	advance applications advisable.
Green Fees	£18 per day; £12 per round (£22/£16 weekends).
Designer	Tom Morris/Charlie Neaves
Facilities	⊗ 🗙 by prior arrangement 🖺 💻 ♀ 🛆 🥢
Location	0.5m W off A98

Hotel	★★ 67% Mill House Hotel, Tynet, BUCKIE ☎ 01542 850233 15 ⇆ 🏲

DORNOCH
Map 14 NH78

The Carnegie Club Skibo Castle IV25 3RQ
☎ 01862 894600 Fax 01862 894601
Set within the grounds of an enchanting castle, with the
sea on three sides and the hills of Sutherland and Ross-
shire all around, this splendid course enjoys a
magnificent position. Although not long by modern
standards, strong and fickle winds will test even the most
experienced golfer. Excellent leisure facilities.
18 holes, 6403yds, Par 71, SSS 71.
Club membership 550.

Visitors	weekdays only by written application to the secretary. Tee times between 11am & 12pm.
Societies	by prior arrangement
Green Fees	£130 per round.

Prof	David Thomson
Designer	J Sutherland/Donald Steel
Facilities	⊗ by prior arrangement 💻 ♀ 🛆 🛋 🍸 🥢 ℓ
& Leisure	hard tennis courts, heated indoor swimming pool, fishing, sauna, solarium, gymnasium.
Location	Off A9 3m before Dornoch

Hotel	★★ 70% Dornoch Castle Hotel, Castle St, DORNOCH ☎ 01862 810216 4 ⇆ 🏲 Annexe 13 ⇆ 🏲

Royal Dornoch Golf Rd IV25 3LW
☎ 01862 810219 Fax 01862 810792
Very challenging seaside championship links, designed
by Tom Morris and John Sutherland.
*Championship: 18 holes, 6514yds, Par 70, SSS 73,
Course record 62.*
Struie Course: 18 holes, 5438yds, Par 69.
Club membership 1550.

Visitors	must have a handicap of 24 for gentlemen (ladies 39) on Championship Course. Must contact in advance.
Societies	must apply in advance.
Green Fees	Championship course: £41-£57 per round (£46-£67 weekends). Struie course: £11-24 per day; £8-17 per round.
Cards	〓 〓 〓 🔟
Prof	A Skinner
Designer	Tom Morris
Facilities	⊗ 🗙 🖺 💻 ♀ 🛆 🛋 🍸 🦃 🏌 ℓ
& Leisure	hard tennis courts.
Location	E side of town

Hotel	★★ 70% Dornoch Castle Hotel, Castle St, DORNOCH ☎ 01862 810216 4 ⇆ 🏲 Annexe 13 ⇆ 🏲

DUFFTOWN   Map 15 NJ33

Dufftown Methercluny, Tomintoul Rd AB55 4BS
☎ 01340 820325 Fax 01340 820325
A short and undulating inland course with spectacular views.
Highest hole over 1200 ft above sea level.
18 holes, 5308yds, Par 67, SSS 67, Course record 64.
Club membership 250.

Visitors	tee reserved Tue & Wed 4.30-6.30 & Sun 7.30-9 & 12.30-2. Prior booking recommended.
Societies	apply in writing or by telephone
Green Fees	£15 per day; £10 per round.
Designer	Members
Facilities	⊗ by prior arrangement ⑂ by prior arrangement ⓑ by prior arrangement ♥ ♀ ⚘ ⚑ ✐
Location	0.75m SW off B9009

Hotel   ★★★ 76% Craigellachie Hotel,
CRAIGELLACHIE ☎ 01340 881204 26 ⇆ ♠

DURNESS   Map 14 NC46

Durness Balnakeil IV27 4PG
☎ 01971 511364 Fax 01971 511205
A 9-hole course set in tremendous scenery overlooking
Balnakeil Bay. Part links and part inland with water hazards.
Off alternative tees for second 9 holes giving surprising
variety. Tremendous last hole played across the sea to the
green over 100 yards away.
9 holes, 5555yds, Par 70, SSS 69, Course record 71.
Club membership 150.

Visitors	restricted 10am-12.30 on Sun during Jun-Sep.
Societies	must telephone in advance 01971 511364 (ex Sun).
Green Fees	£15 per day; £50 per week.
Designer	F Keith
Facilities	⊗ ♥ ⚘ ⚑ ✐
& Leisure	fishing.
Location	1m W of village overlooking Balnakeil Bay

Guesthouse   ♦♦♦♦ Port-Na-Con House, Loch Eribol, by
Sutherland, LAIRG ☎ 01971 511367 3 ⇆ ♠

ELGIN   Map 15 NJ26

Elgin Hardhillock, Birnie Rd, New Elgin IV30 8SX
☎ 01343 542338 Fax 01343 542341
Possibly the finest inland course in the north of Scotland,
with undulating greens and compact holes that demand
the highest accuracy. There are thirteen par 4's and one
par 5 hole on its parkland layout.
18 holes, 6163yds, Par 68, SSS 69, Course record 63.
Club membership 1000.

Visitors	must contact in advance, weekend play only by prior arrangement.
Societies	telephone secretary for details.
Green Fees	£30 per day; £23 per round (£35/£29 weekends).
Prof	Ian P Rodger
Designer	John Macpherson
Facilities	⊗ ⑂ ⓑ ♥ ♀ ⚘ 🖰 ⚑ ⚒ ✐ ⛳
Location	1m S on A941

Hotel   ★★★ 76% Mansion House Hotel, The
Haugh, ELGIN
☎ 01343 548811 23 ⇆ ♠

ELLON   Map 15 NJ93

McDonald Hospital Rd AB41 9AW
☎ 01358 720576 Fax 01358 720001
Tight, parkland course with streams and a pond.
18 holes, 5986yds, Par 70, SSS 69.
Club membership 710.

Visitors	advisable to book in advance
Societies	telephone in advance.
Green Fees	not confirmed.
Prof	Ronnie Urquhart
Facilities	⊗ ⑂ ⓑ ♥ ♀ ⚘ 🖰 ⚑ ✐
Location	0.25m N on A948

Hotel   ★★ 71% Udny Arms Hotel, Main St,
NEWBURGH ☎ 01358 789444 26 ⇆ ♠

FORRES   Map 14 NJ05

Forres Muiryshade IV36 2RD
☎ 01309 672250 Fax 01309 672250
An all-year parkland course laid on light, well-drained
soil in wooded countryside. Walking is easy despite
some hilly holes. A test for the best golfers.
18 holes, 6240yds, Par 70, SSS 70, Course record 64.
Club membership 1000.

Visitors	welcome although club competitions take priority. Weekends may be restricted in summer.
Societies	advised to telephone 2-3 weeks in advance.
Green Fees	not confirmed.
Prof	Sandy Aird
Designer	James Braid/Willie Park
Facilities	⊗ ⑂ ⓑ ♥ ♀ ⚘ ⚑ ✐ 🖰 ⚒ ✐
Location	SE side of town centre off B9010

Hotel   ★★★ 66% Ramnee Hotel, Victoria Rd,
FORRES ☎ 01309 672410 20 ⇆ ♠

FORT AUGUSTUS   Map 14 NH30

Fort Augustus Markethill PH32 4AU ☎ 01320 366660
Moorland course, with narrow fairways and good views.
Bordered by the tree-lined Caledonian Canal to the north and
heather clad hills to the south.
9 holes, 5454yds, Par 67, SSS 67, Course record 67.
Club membership 170.

Visitors	may not play Sat 1.30-4 & occasional Sun.
Societies	telephone in advance.
Green Fees	£10 per day.
Designer	Colt
Facilities	♀ ⚘ ⚑ ✐
Location	1m SW on A82

FORTROSE   Map 14 NH75

Fortrose & Rosemarkie Ness Rd East IV10 8SE
☎ 01381 620529
Seaside links course, set on a peninsula with sea on three
sides. Easy walking, good views. Designed by James Braid;
the club was formed in 1888.
18 holes, 5875yds, Par 71, SSS 69, Course record 64.
Club membership 770.

▶

Visitors restricted 8.45-10.15am & 1-2.15 then 4.45-
6.30pm.
Societies must telephone in advance.
Green Fees £30 per day; £20 per round (£35/£25 weekends
& bank holidays).
Cards
Designer James Braid
Facilities ⊗ ⅲ ♭ 🍺 ♀ ⚐ 👜 🛉 ♂
Location E side of town centre

FORT WILLIAM   Map 14 NN17

Fort William Torlundy PH33 7SN ☎ 01397 704464
Spectacular moorland location looking onto the cliffs of Ben
Nevis. Tees and greens are in excellent condition following
and major drainage improvements to the fairways.
18 holes, 6500yds, Par 72, SSS 71, Course record 67.
Club membership 420.
Visitors no restrictions.
Societies must contact in writing.
Green Fees £18 per day; £15 per round.
Designer Hamilton Stutt
Facilities ♭ 🍺 ♀ ⚐ 🛉 ♂
Location 3m NE on A82

Hotel ★★★ 71% Moorings Hotel, Banavie, FORT
WILLIAM ☎ 01397 772797 21 ⇌ ⋒

FRASERBURGH   Map 15 NJ96

Fraserburgh AB43 8TL
☎ 01346 516616 Fax 01346 516616
Testing seaside course, natural links. An extremely scenic
course, surrounded and protected by substantial sand dunes.
Corbie: 18 holes, 6278yds, Par 70, SSS 70,
Course record 65.
Rosehill: 9 holes, 2400yds, Par 66, SSS 66.
Club membership 650.
Visitors no restrictions but advised to check availability.
Societies must contact in advance.
Green Fees Corbie: £20 per day; £15 per round (£25/£20
weekends). Rosehill: £10 per day (£12
weekends).
Designer James Braid
Facilities ⊗ ⅲ ♭ 🍺 ♀ ⚐ 👜 🛉 ♂
& Leisure Various open competitions throughout the year.
Location 1m SE on B9033

Hotel ★★★★ 68% Waterside Inn,
Fraserburgh Rd, PETERHEAD
☎ 01779 471121 69 ⇌ ⋒ Annexe 40 ⇌ ⋒

GAIRLOCH   Map 14 NG87

Gairloch IV21 2BE ☎ 01445 712407 Fax 01445 712407
Fine seaside links course running along Gairloch Sands with
good views over the sea to Skye. In windy conditions each
hole is affected. The par 5 eighth hole is described by one of
Scotlands teaching professionals as one of the best natural
par 5's in the country.
9 holes, 4514yds, Par 63, SSS 64, Course record 64.
Club membership 275.
Visitors must be competent golfer and member of a
recognised club.
Societies apply in writing to secretary.
Green Fees £15 per day; £49 per week.

Designer Capt Burgess
Facilities ♭ 🍺 ♀ ⚐ 👜 🛉 ♂
Location 1m S on A832

Hotel ★★★ 67% Creag Mor, Charleston,
GAIRLOCH ☎ 01445 712068 17 ⇌ ⋒

GARMOUTH   Map 15 NJ36

Garmouth & Kingston Spey St IV32 7NJ
☎ 01343 870388 Fax 01343 870388
Seaside course with several parkland holes and tidal waters.
Naturally flat and suitable for the elderly.
18 holes, 5905yds, Par 69, SSS 69, Course record 66.
Club membership 560.
Visitors must contact in advance.
Societies advisable to phone in advance.
Green Fees £18 per day; £16 per round (£25/£22 weekends).
Designer George Smith
Facilities ⊗ ⅲ ♭ 🍺 ♀ ⚐ 🛉 ♂
& Leisure fishing.
Location In village on B9015

Hotel ★★★ 76% Mansion House Hotel, The Haugh,
ELGIN ☎ 01343 548811 23 ⇌ ⋒

GOLSPIE   Map 14 NH89

Golspie Ferry Rd KW10 6ST
☎ 01408 633266 Fax 01408 633393
Founded in 1889, Golspie's seaside course offers easy
walking and natural hazards including beach heather and
whins. Spectacular scenery.
18 holes, 5890yds, Par 68, SSS 68, Course record 64.
Club membership 300.
Visitors contact in advance.
Societies contact in advance.
Green Fees £25 per day; £20 per round.
Cards
Designer James Braid
Facilities ⊗ ⅲ ♭ 🍺 ♀ ⚐ 👜 🛉 ♂
Location 0.5m S off A9

Hotel ★★★ 66% The Links Hotel, Golf Rd, BRORA
☎ 01408 621225 23 ⇌ ⋒

GRANTOWN-ON-SPEY   Map 14 NJ02

Grantown-on-Spey Golf Course Rd PH26 3HY
☎ 01479 872079 (Apr-Oct) Fax 01479 873725
Parkland and woodland course. Part easy walking, remainder
hilly. The 7th to 13th really sorts out the golfers.
18 holes, 5710yds, Par 70, SSS 68, Course record 60.
Club membership 750.
Visitors advisable to contact in advance. No visitors
before 10am weekends.
Societies clubhouse open Apr-Oct, apply in advance to
secretary.
Green Fees £20 per day (£25 weekends); £10 evening
round; £10 winter round.
Cards
Designer A Brown/W Park/J Braid
Facilities ⊗ ⅲ by prior arrangement ♭ 🍺 ♀ ⚐ 👜 🛉
⚑ ♂
Location NE side of town centre

▶

Hotel ★★ 77% Culdearn House, Woodlands Ter, GRANTOWN ON SPEY
☎ 01479 872106 9 ⇔ ↟

HELMSDALE Map 14 ND01

Helmsdale Golf Rd KW8 6JA ☎ 01431 821650
Sheltered, undulating course following the line of the Helmsdale River.
9 holes, 1860yds, Par 62, SSS 61.
Club membership 90.
Visitors no restrictions.
Societies apply in writing.
Green Fees not confirmed.
Facilities ⚒
Location NW side of town on A896

Hotel ★★★ 66% The Links Hotel, Golf Rd, BRORA
☎ 01408 621225 23 ⇔ ↟

HOPEMAN Map 15 NJ16

Hopeman Clubhouse IV30 5YA
☎ 01343 830578 Fax 01343 830152
Links-type course with beautiful views over the Moray Firth. The 12th hole, called the Priescach, is a short hole with a drop of 100 feet from tee to green. It can require anything from a wedge to a wood depending on the wind.
18 holes, 5590yds, Par 67, SSS 67.
Club membership 700.
Visitors must contact in advance, restricted tee times at weekend and between 12:45-1:45 weekdays
Societies contact in advance.
Green Fees not confirmed.
Facilities ⊗ ⚑ ♥ ♀ ⚒ 🏠 ✐
Location E side of village off B9040

Hotel ★★★ 76% Mansion House Hotel, The Haugh, ELGIN ☎ 01343 548811 23 ⇔ ↟

HUNTLY Map 15 NJ53

Huntly Cooper Park AB54 4SH ☎ 01466 792643
A parkland course lying between the Rivers Deveron and Bogie.
18 holes, 5399yds, Par 67, SSS 66.
Club membership 850.
Visitors may not play before 8am.
Societies must contact the secretary.
Green Fees not confirmed.
Facilities ⊗ �🍴 ⚑ ♥ ♀ ⚒ 🏠 ✐ ↟
Location N side of Huntly, turn off A96 at bypass roundabout

INSCH Map 15 NJ62

Insch Golf Ter AB52 6JY
☎ 01464 820363 Fax 01464 820363
A challenging 18 hole course, a mixture of flat undulating parkland, with trees, stream and pond.
18 holes, 5500yds, Par 70, SSS 67.
Club membership 400.
Visitors restricted during club competitions and Tee times, ie Mon - Ladies night, Tue - Mens night, Wed - juniors, telephone clubhouse 01464 820363 for information. Pre-booking is advised.

Societies apply in writing or telephone, bookings accepted.
Green Fees £16 per day (£21 weekends).
Designer Greens of Scotland
Facilities ⊗ 🍴 by prior arrangement ⚑ ♥ ♀ ⚒ ✐
Location A96

Hotel ★★ 64% Lodge Hotel, OLD RAYNE
☎ 01464 851205 Annexe 6 ⇔ ↟

INVERALLOCHY Map 15 NK06

Inverallochy Whitelink AB43 8XY ☎ 01346 582000
Seaside links course with natural hazards, tricky par 3s and easy walking.
18 holes, 5351yds, Par 66, SSS 66, Course record 57.
Club membership 600.
Visitors restricted at weekends and competition days, contact for availability.
Societies apply in writing/telephone in advance.
Green Fees not confirmed.
Facilities ⊗ ⚑ ♥ ♀ ⚒
Location E side of village off B9107

Hotel ★★★★ 68% Waterside Inn, Fraserburgh Rd, PETERHEAD
☎ 01779 471121 69 ⇔ ↟ Annexe 40 ⇔ ↟

INVERGORDON Map 14 NH76

Invergordon King George St IV18 0BD ☎ 01349 852715
Fairly easy but windy 18-hole parkland course, with woodland, wide fairways and good views over Cromarty Firth. Very good greens and a fair challenge, especially if the wind is from the west.
18 holes, 6030yds, Par 69, SSS 69, Course record 66.
Club membership 240.
Visitors visitors advised to avoid Tue & Thu 4.30-6, Mon & Wed 5-6 and Sat 8.30-10 & 1-2pm.
Societies must contact in advance, call 01349 852715.
Green Fees £20 per day; £15 per round. ▶

AA Hotels that have special arrangements with golf courses are listed at the back of the guide

Designer	A Rae
Facilities	⚐ 🍽 ♀ ⚘ 🚩 ♂
Location	W side of town centre on B817

Hotel	★★★ 72% Morangie House Hotel, Morangie Rd, TAIN ☎ 01862 892281 26 ⇔ 🅿

INVERNESS
Map 14 NH64

Inverness Culcabock IV2 3XQ
☎ 01463 239882 Fax 01463 239882
Fairly flat parkland course with burn running through it.
Windy in winter. The 14th is one of the most difficult Par 4's
in the north of Scotland.
18 holes, 6226yds, Par 69, SSS 70.
Club membership 1100.

Visitors	restricted at weekends.
Societies	must telephone in advance.
Green Fees	not confirmed.
Prof	Alistair P Thomson
Facilities	⊗ 🍽 ⚐ 🍽 ♀ ⚘ 🚩 ♂
Hotel	★★★★ 71% Swallow Kingsmills Hotel, Culcabock Rd, INVERNESS ☎ 01463 237166 76 ⇔ 🅿 Annexe 6 ⇔ 🅿

Loch Ness Fairways, Castle Heather IV21 6AA
☎ 01463 713335 Fax 01463 712695
Challenging parkland course with superb views over
Inverness, the Beauly Firth and the Black Isle.
18 holes, 6772yds, Par 73, SSS 72, Course record 69.
Club membership 580.

Visitors	please contact in advance, may play at weekends usually after noon.
Societies	telephone for details.
Green Fees	not confirmed.
Cards	🗀 🗀 🗀 🗀
Prof	Martin Piggot
Facilities	⊗ 🍽 ⚐ 🍽 ♀ ⚘ 🚩 🏌 ♂ 〔
Location	SW outskirts of Inverness, along new bypass

Hotel	★★★ 66% Loch Ness House Hotel, Glenurquhart Rd, INVERNESS ☎ 01463 231248 22 ⇔ 🅿

Torvean Glenurquhart Rd IV3 8JN
☎ 01463 711434 (Starter) & 225651 (Secretary)
Fax 01463 225651
Municipal parkland course, easy walking, good views.
18 holes, 5784yds, Par 69, SSS 68, Course record 64.
Club membership 400.

Visitors	must contact in advance.
Societies	advance bookings through The Highland Council, Town House, Inverness.
Green Fees	£16.50 per day; £12.50 per round; £6.30 per 9 holes (£18.70/£14.40 weekends).
Designer	Hamilton
Facilities	⚐ 🍽 ♀ ⚘ 🚩 ♂
Location	1.5m SW on A82

Hotel	★★★ 66% Loch Ness House Hotel, Glenurquhart Rd, INVERNESS ☎ 01463 231248 22 ⇔ 🅿

INVERURIE
Map 15 NJ72

Inverurie Blackhall Rd AB51 5JB
☎ 01467 624080 Fax 01467 621051
Parkland course, part of which is through wooded area.
18 holes, 5711yds, Par 69, SSS 68, Course record 64.
Club membership 750.

Visitors	book tee time through shop up to 24 hrs in advance 01467 620193.
Societies	telephone administrator.
Green Fees	£18 per day; £14 per round (£24/£18 weekends).
Prof	Mark Lees
Facilities	⊗ 🍽 ⚐ 🍽 ♀ ⚘ 🚩 ♂
Location	E side of town off A96

Hotel	★★★ 69% Strathburn Hotel, Burghmuir Dr, INVERURIE ☎ 01467 624422 25 ⇔ 🅿

KEITH
Map 15 NJ45

Keith Fife Park AB55 5DF
☎ 01542 882469 Fax 01542 888176
Parkland course, with natural hazards over first 9 holes.
Testing 7th hole, 232 yds, par 3.
18 holes, 5767yds, Par 69, SSS 68.
Club membership 500.

Visitors	no restrictions except competitions.
Societies	by arrangement with outings secretary (01542 886114)
Green Fees	not confirmed.
Facilities	🍽 ♀ ⚘ ♂
Location	NW side of town centre off A96, onto B9014 and first right

Hotel	★★★ 76% Craigellachie Hotel, CRAIGELLACHIE ☎ 01340 881204 26 ⇔ 🅿

KEMNAY
Map 15 NJ71

Kemnay Monymusk Rd AB51 5RA
☎ 01467 642225 shop & 643746 office Fax 01467 643746
Undulating parkland course with superb views. A stream
crosses four holes.
18 holes, 6342yds, Par 71, SSS 71, Course record 70.
Club membership 800.

Visitors	telephone shop for booking.
Societies	must telephone in advance.
Green Fees	£20 per day (£25 weekends).
Prof	Ronnie McDonald
Designer	Greens of Scotland
Facilities	⊗ 🍽 ⚐ 🍽 ♀ ⚘ 🚩 🏌 ♂
Location	W side of village on B993

Hotel	★★★ 68% Westhill Hotel, Westhill, ABERDEEN ☎ 01224 740388 37 ⇔ 🅿 Annexe 13 ⇔ 🅿

KINGUSSIE
Map 14 NH70

Kingussie Gynack Rd PH21 1LR
☎ 01540 661600 Fax 01540 662066
Hilly upland course with natural hazards and magnificent
views. Stands about 1000ft above sea level at its highest
point, and the River Gynack, which runs through the course,
comes into play on five holes.

▶

18 holes, 5500yds, Par 67, SSS 68, Course record 63.
Club membership 800.
Visitors advisable to book in advance.
Societies must contact in advance.
Green Fees £20 per day; £16 per round (£25/£18 weekends).
Designer Vardon
Facilities ⊗ ⫙ ⯭ ⯰ ♀ ♣ ⌂ ↰ ♬ ♂
Location 0.25m N off A86

Hotel ★★ 74% The Scot House Hotel, Newtonmore Rd, KINGUSSIE ☎ 01540 661351 9 ⇌ ♜

KINTORE   Map 15 NJ71

Kintore Balbithan AB51 0UR
☎ 01467 632631 Fax 01467 632631
The course covers a large area of ground from the Don Basin, near the clubhouse, to mature woodland at the far perimeter. One of the main attractions is the excellent drainage which results in very few days of lost play.
18 holes, 5997yds, Par 70, SSS 69, Course record 62.
Club membership 700.
Visitors during season booking system is in operation & slots for visitors are available. Other times can be booked 24 hours in advance.
Societies apply in writing or telephone.
Green Fees £18 per day; £13 per round (£24/£19 weekends).
Facilities ⊗ ⫙ ⯭ ♀ ♣ ♂
Location 1m from village centre on B977

Hotel ★★ 66% Torryburn Hotel, School Rd, KINTORE ☎ 01467 632269 9rm (8 ♜)

LEWIS, ISLE OF   Map 13 NB43

STORNOWAY   Map 13 NB43

Stornoway Lady Lever Park HS2 0XP ☎ 01851 702240
A short but tricky undulating parkland course set in grounds of Lews Castle with fine views over the Minch to the mainland. The clubhouse has recently been rebuilt and improved.
18 holes, 5252yds, Par 68, SSS 67, Course record 62.
Club membership 440.
Visitors no golf on Sun.
Societies apply in writing.
Green Fees £45 per week; £20 per day; £15 per round.
Facilities ⯭ ♀ ♣ ⌂ ↰ ♂
Location 0.5m from town centre off A857

Hotel ★★★ 66% Cabarfeidh Hotel, STORNOWAY ☎ 01851 702604 46 ⇌ ♜

LOCHCARRON   Map 14 NG83

Lochcarron East End IV54 8YU
Seaside links course with some parkland with an interesting 2nd hole. A short course but great accuracy is required.
9 holes, 1789yds, Par 62, SSS 60.
Club membership 150.
Visitors restricted Mon evening & Sat 2-5pm.
Societies welcome but restricted Mon evening & Sat 2-5pm.
Green Fees not confirmed.
Facilities ↰
Location 1m E

Hotel ★★ 67% Lochcarron Hotel, Main St, LOCHCARRON ☎ 01520 722226 10rm(9 ⇌ ♜)

LOSSIEMOUTH   Map 15 NJ27

Moray IV31 6QS ☎ 01343 812018 Fax 01343 815102
Two fine Scottish Championship links courses, known as Old and New (Moray), and situated on the Moray Firth where the weather is unusually mild.
Old Course: 18 holes, 6643yds, Par 71, SSS 73, Course record 65.
New Course: 18 holes, 6004yds, Par 69, SSS 69, Course record 62.
Club membership 1550.
Visitors must contact in advance 01343 812018 Secretary.
Societies must contact in advance.
Green Fees not confirmed.
Prof Alistair Thomson
Designer Tom Morris
Facilities ⊗ ⫙ ⯭ ♀ ♣ ⌂ ↰ ♂
Location N side of town

Hotel ★★★ 76% Mansion House Hotel, The Haugh, ELGIN ☎ 01343 548811 23 ⇌ ♜

LYBSTER   Map 15 ND23

Lybster Main St KW3 6AE
Picturesque, short heathland course, easy walking.
9 holes, 1896yds, Par 62, SSS 61, Course record 59.
Club membership 140.
Visitors no restrictions.
Societies must contact in advance.
Green Fees not confirmed.
Facilities ♣ ↰
Location E side of village

▶

Hotel   ★★ 63% Mackay's Hotel, Union St, WICK
☎ 01955 602323 27rm (19 ⇌ ↟)

MACDUFF   Map 15 NJ76

Royal Tarlair Buchan St AB44 1TA
☎ 01261 832897 Fax 01261 833455
Seaside clifftop course, can be windy. Testing 13th, 'Clivet'
(par 3).
18 holes, 5866yds, Par 71, SSS 68, Course record 62.
Club membership 520.
Visitors   no restrictions.
Societies   apply in writing.
Green Fees £15 per day; £10 per round (£20/£15 weekends).
Facilities ⊗ ⍫ ᴸ ♟ 🍴 ⛳ ➡ ↟ ⚐
Location   0.75m E off A98

Hotel   ★★★ 67% Banff Springs Hotel,
Golden Knowes Rd, BANFF
☎ 01261 812881   31 ⇌ ↟

MUIR OF ORD   Map 14 NH55

Muir of Ord Great North Rd IV6 7SX
☎ 01463 870825 Fax 01463 870825
Old established (1875), heathland course with tight fairways
and easy walking. Testing 13th, 'Castle Hill' (par 3).
18 holes, 5557yds, Par 68, SSS 68, Course record 63.
Club membership 650.
Visitors   may not play before 11am weekends without
prior agreement and during club competitions.
Societies   telephone followed by letter of confirmation.
Green Fees not confirmed.
Prof   G Leggat
Designer   James Braid
Facilities ⊗ ᴸ ♟ 🍴 ⛳ ➡ ↟ ⚐
& Leisure   snooker & pool tables.
Location   S side of village on A862

Hotel   ★★★ 70% Priory Hotel, The Square,
BEAULY ☎ 01463 782309   36 ⇌ ↟

NAIRN   Map 14 NH85

Nairn Seabank Rd IV12 4HB
☎ 01667 453208 Fax 01667 456328
Championship, seaside links founded in 1887 and
created from a wilderness of heather and whin. Designed
by Archie Simpson, old Tom Morris and James Braid.
Opening holes stretch out along the shoreline with the
turn for home at the 10th. Regularly chosen for national
championships.
18 holes, 6452yds, Par 71, SSS 73, Course record 65.
Newton: 9 holes, 3542yds, Par 58, SSS 57.
Club membership 1150.
Visitors   book in advance through secretary, may not
play between 8-11.00 am & 12-2.30 pm (Fri
& Sat).
Societies   subject to availability bookings through
secretary's office.
Green Fees Nairn: £60 per round (£65 weekends).
Newton: £11.
Cards   ▭ ▭ ▭ ▭
Prof   Robin P Fyfe
Designer   A Simpson/Old Tom Morris/James Braid

Facilities ⊗ ⍫ ᴸ ♟ 🍴 ⛳ ➡ ↟ ⚐
& Leisure   snooker.
Location   16m E of Inverness on A96

Hotel   ★★★★ 67% Golf View Hotel & Leisure
Club, Seabank Rd, NAIRN
☎ 01667 452301   48 ⇌ ↟

Nairn Dunbar Lochloy Rd IV12 5AE
☎ 01667 452741 Fax 01667 456897
Links course with sea views and testing gorse-and whin-lined
fairways. Testing hole: 'Long Peter' (527 yds).
18 holes, 6720yds, Par 72, SSS 73.
Club membership 700.
Visitors   April-Oct only. Weekends restricted, contact in
advance.
Societies   must contact in advance.
Green Fees not confirmed.
Cards   ▭
Prof   David Torrance
Facilities ⊗ ⍫ ᴸ ♟ 🍴 ⛳ ➡ ↟ ▼ ⚐
Location   E side of town off A96

Hotel   ★★ 65% Alton Burn Hotel, Alton Burn Rd,
NAIRN ☎ 01667 452051
19rm (14 ⇌3 ↟) Annexe 7 ⇌ ↟

NETHY BRIDGE   Map 14 NJ02

Abernethy PH25 3ED
☎ 01479 821305
Traditional Highland course featuring a mixture of
undulating parkland and moorland.
9 holes, 2551yds, Par 66, SSS 66.
Club membership 480.
Visitors   contact in advance.
Societies   must contact in advance.
Green Fees £12 per day (£16 weekends).
Facilities ⊗ ᴸ ♟ ➡ ↟ ⚐
Location   N side of village on B970

Hotel   ★★★ 71% Muckrach Lodge Hotel,
DULNAIN BRIDGE
☎ 01479 851257 9 ⇌ ↟ Annexe 4 ⇌ ↟

NEWBURGH ON YTHAN   Map 15 NJ92

Newburgh on Ythan Beach Rd AB41 6BE
☎ 01358 789058 Fax 01358 789956
This seaside course was founded in 1888 and is adjacent to a
bird sanctuary. Testing 550-yd dog leg (par 5).
18 holes, 6162yds, Par 72, SSS 69, Course record 68.
Club membership 700.
Visitors   must contact in advance, may not play Sat am.
Societies   apply in advance.
Green Fees £21 per day; £16 per round (£26/£21 weekends).
Facilities ➡ ⚐
Location   E side of village on A975

Hotel   ★★ 71% Udny Arms Hotel,
Main St, NEWBURGH
☎ 01358 789444   26 ⇌ ↟

NEWMACHAR   Map 15 NJ81

Newmachar Swailend AB21 7UU
☎ 01651 863002 Fax 01651 863055
Hawkshill is a championship-standard parkland course designed by Dave Thomas. Several lakes affect five of the holes and there are well developed birch and Scots pine trees. Swailend is a parkland course designed by Dave Thomas and opened in 1997. It provides a test all of its own with some well positioned bunkering and testing greens.
Hawkshill Course: 18 holes, 6623yds, Par 72, SSS 74, Course record 67.
Swailend Course: 18 holes, 6388yds, Par 72, SSS 71, Course record 67.
Club membership 900.
Visitors contact in advance & must have handicap certificate for Hawkshill course.
Societies apply in writing.
Green Fees Hawkshill: £45 per day; £30 per round (£40 per round weekends). Swailend: £25 per day; £15 per round (£30/£20 weekends).
Cards
Prof Gordon Simpson
Designer Dave Thomas/Peter Allis
Facilities
Location 2m N of Dyce, off A947

Hotel ★★★ 69% Strathburn Hotel, Burghmuir Dr, INVERURIE ☎ 01467 624422 25

NEWTONMORE   Map 14 NN79

Newtonmore Golf Course Rd PH20 1AT
☎ 01540 673328 & 673878 Fax 01540 673878
Inland course beside the River Spey. Beautiful views and easy walking. Testing 17th hole (par 3).
18 holes, 6029yds, Par 70, SSS 69, Course record 68.
Club membership 420.
Visitors contact in advance.
Societies apply in writing to secretary.
Green Fees not confirmed.
Prof Robert Henderson
Facilities
Location E side of town off A9

Hotel ★★ 74% The Scot House Hotel, Newtonmore Rd, KINGUSSIE ☎ 01540 661351 9

OLDMELDRUM   Map 15 NJ82

Old Meldrum Kirk Brae AB51 0DJ
☎ 01651 872648 Fax 01651 873555
Parkland course with tree-lined fairways and superb views. Challenging 196 yard, Par 3, 11th over two ponds to a green surrounded by bunkers.
18 holes, 5988yds, Par 70, SSS 69, Course record 66.
Club membership 700.
Visitors may not play during Club competitions.
Societies apply in writing to secretary
Green Fees £14 per day/round (£24 per day; £20 per round weekends).
Prof Jamie Carver
Facilities
Location E side of village off A947

Hotel ★★★ 69% Strathburn Hotel, Burghmuir Dr, INVERURIE ☎ 01467 624422 25

ORKNEY   Map 16

KIRKWALL   Map 16 HY41

Orkney Grainbank KW15 1RB ☎ 01856 872457
Open parkland course with few hazards and superb views over Kirkwall and Islands.
18 holes, 5411yds, Par 70, SSS 67, Course record 65.
Club membership 402.
Visitors may not play on competition days.
Societies write or telephone if possible.
Green Fees not confirmed.
Facilities
Location 0.5m W off A965

Hotel ★★★ 66% Ayre Hotel, Ayre Rd, KIRKWALL ☎ 01856 873001 33

STROMNESS   Map 16 HY20

Stromness KW16 3DW ☎ 01856 850772
Testing parkland/seaside course with easy walking. Beautiful holiday course with magnificent views of Scapa Flow. New clubhouse opened 1999.
18 holes, 4762yds, Par 65, SSS 63, Course record 61.
Club membership 350.
Visitors no restrictions except during major competitions.
Societies no restrictions.
Green Fees £12 per day.
Facilities
& Leisure hard tennis courts.
Location S side of town centre off A965

Hotel ★★★ 66% Ayre Hotel, Ayre Rd, KIRKWALL ☎ 01856 873001 33

WESTRAY   Map 16 HY44

Westray Rosevale KW17 2DH ☎ 01857 677373
Interesting, picturesque seaside course, easy walking.
9 holes, 2405yds, Par 33.
Club membership 60.
Green Fees not confirmed.
Facilities
Location 1m NW of Pierowall off B9066

Hotel ★★★ 66% Ayre Hotel, Ayre Rd, KIRKWALL ☎ 01856 873001 33

PETERCULTER   Map 15 NJ80

Peterculter Oldtown, Burnside Rd AB14 0LN
☎ 01224 734994 Fax 01224 735580
The course is a tight Par 68 (from Yellow tees) with a beautiful Par 2 2nd and two Par 5 holes in excess of 500 yards. Surrounded by wonderful scenery and bordered by the River Dee, there is a variety of birds, deer and foxes on the course, which also has superb views up the Dee Valley.
18 holes, 5947yds, Par 68, SSS 68, Course record 68.
Club membership 1035.
Visitors contact 3 days in advance, welcome after 2.30pm weekdays & 4pm weekends.
Societies contact up to 7 days in advance.
Green Fees not confirmed.

Prof	Dean Vannet
Designer	Greens of Scotland
Facilities	⊗ 〣 ﯼ 🛒 ♟ 🛎 ⛳
Location	On A93

Hotel ★★★ 68% Westhill Hotel, Westhill, ABERDEEN ☎ 01224 740388
37 ⇆ ☞ Annexe 13 ⇆ ☞

PETERHEAD   Map 15 NK14

Peterhead Craigewan Links, Riverside Dr AB42 1LT
☎ 01779 472149 & 480725 Fax 01779 480725
The Old Course is a natural links course bounded by the sea and the River Ugie. Varying conditions of play depending on wind and weather. The New Course is more of a parkland course.
Old Course: 18 holes, 6173yds, Par 70, SSS 71, Course record 64.
New Course: 9 holes, 2228yds, Par 31.
Club membership 650.

Visitors	welcome any day apart from Saturdays, restricted times on the Old Course. Telephone for details.
Societies	apply in writing, restricted availablility on Saturdays
Green Fees	Old Course: £22 per day; £16 per round (£27/£20 weekends). New Course: £9 per day/round.
Designer	W Park/ L Auchterconie/J Braid
Facilities	⊗ 〣 ﯼ 🛒 ♟ 🛎 ⛳
Location	N side of town centre off A952

Hotel ★★★★ 68% Waterside Inn, Fraserburgh Rd, PETERHEAD ☎ 01779 471121
69 ⇆ ☞ Annexe 40 ⇆ ☞

PORTLETHEN   Map 15 NO99

Portlethen Badentoy Rd AB12 4YA
☎ 01224 782575 & 781090 Fax 01224 781090
Set in pleasant parkland, this new course features mature trees and a stream which affects a number of holes.
18 holes, 6707yds, Par 72, SSS 72, Course record 63.
Club membership 1000.

Visitors	may not play Sat. Contact in advance.
Societies	apply in advance.
Green Fees	not confirmed.
Cards	💳
Prof	Muriel Thomson
Designer	Cameron Sinclair
Facilities	⊗ 〣 ﯼ 🛒 ♟ 🛎 ⛳
Location	Off A90 S of Aberdeen

Hotel ★★ 66% County Hotel & Leisure Club, Arduthie Rd, STONEHAVEN ☎ 01569 764386 14 ⇆ ☞

REAY   Map 14 NC96

Reay KW14 7RE ☎ 01847 811288
Picturesque seaside links with natural hazards, following the contours of Sandside Bay. Tight and testing.
18 holes, 5884yds, Par 69, SSS 68, Course record 64.
Club membership 368.

Visitors	restricted competition days
Societies	apply in writing.

Green Fees	not confirmed.
Facilities	ﯼ 🛒 ♟ 🛎
Location	0.5m E off A836

Guesthouse ◆◆◆◆ Tigh-na-Clash Guest House, Tigh-na-Clash, MELVICH ☎ 01641 531262 8 ☞

ROTHES   Map 15 NJ24

Rothes Blackhall AB38 7AN
☎ 01340 831443 (evenings)
A hilly course on an elevated site overlooking the remains of Rothes castle and the Spey valley. The 2nd fairway and most of the 3rd are sheltered by woodland. The ground alongside the 5th & 6th falls away steeply.
9 holes, 4972yds, Par 68, SSS 64.
Club membership 280.

Visitors	course reserved Mon 5-6.30 & Tue 5-7.30.
Societies	apply in writing to secretary.
Green Fees	£12 per day (£15 weekends).
Designer	John Souter
Facilities	ﯼ 🛎
Location	9m S of Elgin on A941

Hotel ★★★ 76% Craigellachie Hotel, CRAIGELLACHIE ☎ 01340 881204 26 ⇆ ☞

SHETLAND   Map 16

LERWICK   Map 16 HU44

Shetland PO Box 18 ZE1 0YW
☎ 01595 840369
Challenging moorland course, hard walking. A burn runs the full length of the course and provides a natural hazard. Testing holes include the 3rd (par 4), 5th (par 4).
Dale Course: 18 holes, 5800yds, Par 68, SSS 68, Course record 68.
Club membership 450.

Visitors	advisable to contact in advance.
Societies	telephone in advance.
Green Fees	not confirmed.
Facilities	ﯼ 🛒 ♟ 🛎
Location	4m N on A970

Hotel ★★★ 68% Lerwick Hotel, 15 South Rd, LERWICK ☎ 01595 692166 35 ⇆ ☞

WHALSAY, ISLAND OF   Map 16 HU56

Whalsay Skaw Taing ZE2 9AA
☎ 01806 566450 & 566481 & 566705
The most northerly golf course in Britain, with a large part of it running round the coastline, offering spectacular holes in an exposed but highly scenic setting. There are no cut fairways as yet, these are defined by marker posts, with preferred lies in operation all year round.
18 holes, 6009yds, Par 70, SSS 68, Course record 65.
Club membership 205.

Visitors	contact in advance for weekend play.
Societies	telephone in advance.
Green Fees	£10 per day; £40 per week.
Facilities	ﯼ 🛒 ♟ 🛎
Location	Whalsay Island

SKYE, ISLE OF   Map 13 NG53

SCONSER   Map 13 NG53

Isle of Skye IV48 8TD
☎ 01478 613004 Fax 01478 650351
Seaside course with spectacular views. 9 holes with 18 tees. Suitable for golfers of all abilities.
18 holes, 4677yds, Par 66, SSS 64, Course record 62.
Club membership 235.
Visitors no restrictions.
Societies apply in advance.
Green Fees £14 per day.
Facilities ⊗ 🛒 🏌 📮 ⛳ ♂
Location A87 between Broadford and Portree

Hotel ★★ 73% Rosedale Hotel, PORTREE
☎ 01478 613131 20 🛏 🍴 Annexe 3 🛏 🍴

SKEABOST BRIDGE   Map 13 NG44

Skeabost Skeabost House Hotel IV51 9NR
☎ 01470 532202
Short woodland and seaside course featuring some very tight fairways and greens.
9 holes, 3056yds, Par 62, SSS 60, Course record 58.
Club membership 80.
Visitors must contact in advance.
Societies contact in advance.
Green Fees not confirmed.
Designer John Stuart
Facilities ⊗ 🖙 🏌 🛒 📮 🏠 ⛳ 🍴
& Leisure fishing.
Hotel ★★★ 76% Cuillin Hills Hotel, PORTREE
☎ 01478 612003 21 🛏 🍴 Annexe 9 🛏 🍴

SOUTH UIST, ISLE OF   Map 13 NF72

ASKERNISH   Map 13 NF72

Askernish Lochboisdale PA81 5SY ☎ 01878 700298
Golfers play on machair (hard-wearing short grass), close to the Atlantic shore. Excellent views from all tees with constantly changing conditions.
18 holes, 5042yds, Par 68, SSS 67, Course record 64.
Club membership 45.
Visitors no restrictions.
Societies welcome.
Green Fees £10 per day; £6 per round.
Designer Tom Morris
Facilities ⛳
Location 5m NW of Lochboisdale off A865

SPEY BAY   Map 15 NJ36

Spey Bay IV32 7PJ ☎ 01343 820424
Seaside links course over gently undulating banks and well-drained ground. Good views along Moray coast. Driving range.
18 holes, 6092yds, Par 70, SSS 69, Course record 66.
Club membership 350.
Visitors telephone for details (especially for Sun)
Societies book by telephone.
Green Fees not confirmed.

Cards 🔲 🔲 🖃
Prof Hamish MacDonald
Designer Ben Sayers
Facilities ⊗ 🖙 🏌 🛒 📮 🏠 ⛳ 🍴 ♂ 🍸
& Leisure hard tennis courts.
Location 4.5m N of Fochabers on B9104

Hotel ★★ 67% Mill House Hotel, Tynet, BUCKIE
☎ 01542 850233 15 🛏 🍴

STONEHAVEN   Map 15 NO88

Stonehaven Cowie AB39 3RH
☎ 01569 762124 Fax 01569 765973
Challenging meadowland course overlooking sea with three gullies and splendid views.
18 holes, 5103yds, Par 66, SSS 65, Course record 61.
Club membership 850.
Visitors prefer prior booking, may not play before 4pm Sat.
Societies telephone or fax in advance to W A Donald.
Green Fees not confirmed.
Cards 🔲 🔲 🔲 🔲 🖃
Designer C Simpson
Facilities ⊗ 🖙 🏌 🛒 📮 🏠 ⛳ ♂
& Leisure snooker.
Location 1m N off A92

Hotel ★★ 66% County Hotel & Leisure Club, Arduthie Rd, STONEHAVEN
☎ 01569 764386 14 🛏 🍴

STRATHPEFFER   Map 14 NH45

Strathpeffer Spa IV14 9AS
☎ 01997 421219 & 421011 Fax 01997 421011
Upland course with many natural hazards (only 3 sand bunkers), hard walking and fine views. Testing 3rd hole (par 3) across loch.
18 holes, 4792yds, Par 65, SSS 64, Course record 60.
Club membership 500.
Visitors advisable to contact in advance.
Societies apply in writing.
Green Fees £20 per day; £14 per round.
Cards 🔲 🔲 🔲
Designer Willie Park/Tom Morris
Facilities ⊗ 🖙 by prior arrangement 🏌 🛒 📮 🏠 ⛳ ♂
Location 0.25m N of village off A834

Hotel ★★ 69% Achilty Hotel, CONTIN
☎ 01997 421355 12 🛏 🍴

TAIN   Map 14 NH78

Tain Chapel Rd IV19 1JE
☎ 01862 892314 Fax 01862 892099
Heathland/links course with river affecting 3 holes; easy walking, fine views.
18 holes, 6404yds, Par 70, SSS 71, Course record 62.
Club membership 500.
Visitors no restrictions.
Societies must book in advance.
Green Fees £30 per round; £36 per 18 holes (£36/£46 weekends).
Cards 🔲 🔲
Designer Tom Morris

▶

Facilities ⊗ 🍽 by prior arrangement 🖢 💄 ♀ 🏖 🏠 🛦 🐾 🚗 ⚷

Location E side of town centre off B9174

Hotel ★★★ 72% Morangie House Hotel, Morangie Rd, TAIN ☎ 01862 892281 26 ⇌ 🏲

TARLAND   Map 15 NJ40

Tarland Aberdeen Rd AB34 4TB
☎ 013398 81000 Fax 013398 81000
Difficult upland course, but easy walking. Some spectacular holes, mainly 4th (par 4) and 5th (par 3) and fine scenery.
9 holes, 5888yds, Par 63, SSS 68, Course record 65.
Club membership 352.
Visitors must contact in advance.
Societies must telephone in advance.
Green Fees £14 per day (£18 weekends).
Designer Tom Morris
Facilities ⊗ 🖢 💄 ♀ 🏖 ⚷
Location E side of village off B9119

Guesthouse ◆◆◆◆◆Arbor Lodge, Ballater Rd, ABOYNE
☎ 01339 886951 3 ⇌ 🏲

THURSO   Map 15 ND16

Thurso Newlands of Geise KW14 7XF ☎ 01847 893807
Parkland course, windy, but with fine views of Dunnet Head and the Orkney Islands.
18 holes, 5828yds, Par 69, SSS 69, Course record 63.
Club membership 301.
Visitors no restrictions.
Societies contact in advance.
Green Fees not confirmed.
Facilities 🖢 💄 ♀ 🏖 🛦 ⚷
Location 2m SW on B874

Hotel ★★ 70% Park Hotel, THURSO
☎ 01847 893251 11 ⇌ 🏲

TORPHINS   Map 15 NJ60

Torphins Bog Rd AB31 4JU
☎ 013398 82115 & 82402 (Sec) Fax 013398 82402
Heathland/parkland course built on a hill with views of the Cairngorms.
9 holes, 4800yds, Par 64, SSS 64, Course record 63.
Club membership 380.
Visitors must contact in advance. Restricted on competition days (alternate Sat and Sun).
Societies apply in advance.
Green Fees £11 per day/round (£13 weekends).
Facilities 🏖 ⚷
Location 0.25m W of village off A980

Hotel ★★★ 74% Tor-na-Coille Hotel, BANCHORY
☎ 01330 822242 23 ⇌ 🏲

TURRIFF   Map 15 NJ74

Turriff Rosehall AB53 4HD
☎ 01888 562982 Fax 01888 568050
A well-maintained parkland course alongside the River Deveron in picturesque surroundings. 6th and 12th particularly challenging in a testing course.

18 holes, 6107yds, Par 70, SSS 69, Course record 64.
Club membership 894.
Visitors may not play before 10am weekends. Must contact in advance.
Societies apply in writing to the secretary.
Green Fees £20 per day; £16 per round (£27/£21 weekends).
Prof Robin Smith
Facilities ⊗ 🍽 🖢 💄 ♀ 🏖 🏠 ⚷
Location 1m W off B9024

Hotel ★★★ 67% Banff Springs Hotel, Golden Knowes Rd, BANFF
☎ 01261 812881 31 ⇌ 🏲

WICK   Map 15 ND35

Wick Reiss KW1 4RW ☎ 01955 602726
Typical seaside links course, fairly flat, easy walking. 9 holes straight out and straight back. Normally breezy.
18 holes, 5976yds, Par 69, SSS 70, Course record 63.
Club membership 352.
Visitors no restrictions.
Societies apply in writing or telephone in advance.
Green Fees £15 per round.
Designer James Braid
Facilities 🖢 💄 ♀ 🏖 🛦 ⚷
Location 3.5m N off A9

Hotel ★★ 63% Mackay's Hotel, Union St, WICK
☎ 01955 602323 27rm (19 ⇌ 🏲)

CENTRAL SCOTLAND

This region includes the counties of Angus, Argyll & Bute, Clackmannanshire, City of Edinburgh, Dundee City, East Lothian, Falkirk, Fife, Inverclyde, Midlothian, Perth & Kinross, Stirling and West Lothian which reflect the national changes.

ABERDOUR   Map 11 NT18

Aberdour Seaside Place KY3 0TX
☎ 01383 860080 Fax 01383 860050
Parkland course with lovely views over Firth of Forth.
18 holes, 5460yds, Par 67, SSS 66, Course record 63.
Club membership 800.
Visitors must contact in advance, may not play Saturdays.
Societies telephone or write to secretary in advance
Green Fees £28 per day; £17 per round (Sun Nov-Feb £28 per round).
Prof Gordon McCallum
Facilities ⊗ 🍽 🖢 💄 ♀ 🏖 🏠 🛦 🐾 ⚷
Location S side of village

Hotel ★★ 68% Woodside Hotel, High St, ABERDOUR ☎ 01383 860328 20 ⇌ 🏲

ABERFELDY   Map 14 NN84

Aberfeldy Taybridge Rd PH15 2BH
☎ 01887 820535 Fax 01887 820535
Founded in 1895, this flat, parkland course is situated by River Tay near the famous Wade Bridge and Black Watch ▶

Monument and enjoys some splendid scenery. The new layout will test the keen golfer.

18 holes, 5283yds, Par 68, SSS 66, Course record 67.

Club membership 333.

Visitors	are advised to book in advance especially at weekends.
Societies	must contact in advance.
Green Fees	£22 per day; £14 per round (£25/£16 weekends).
Cards	⬛⬛⬛
Designer	Soutars
Facilities	⊗ ⨅ ⭍ ⬛ ♀ ♣ 🏠 ⛶ ⚡ ✐
Location	N side of town centre

Hotel   ★★ 68% The Weem, Weem, ABERFELDY
☎ 01887 820381   12 ⇌ 🏴

ABERFOYLE   Map 11 NN50

Aberfoyle Braeval FK8 3UY ☎ 01877 382493
Scenic heathland course with mountain views.
18 holes, 5210yds, Par 66, SSS 66.
Club membership 665.

Visitors	weekend restrictions.
Societies	must contact in advance.
Green Fees	not confirmed.
Facilities	⊗ ⨅ ⭍ ⬛ ♀ ♣ ✐
Location	1m E on A81

Hotel   ★★★★ 65% Forest Hills Hotel, Kinlochard,
ABERFOYLE ☎ 01877 387277   56 ⇌ 🏴

ABERLADY   Map 12 NT47

Kilspindie EH32 0QD
☎ 01875 870358 Fax 01875 870358
Traditional Scottish seaside course, short but tight and well-bunkered. Situated on the shores of the river Forth. Testing holes: 2nd, 3rd, 4th and 7th. A new 6200 yard par 71 links course opens in mid 2000.
Kilspindie: 18 holes, 5480yds, Par 69, SSS 66, Course record 59.
Club membership 1000.

Visitors	must contact in advance, prefered days for visitors Mon-Fri.
Societies	contact secretary in advance.
Green Fees	£40 per day; £25 per round (£50/£30 weekends).
Prof	Graham J Sked
Facilities	⊗ ⨅ ⭍ ⬛ ♀ ♣ 🏠 ⛶ ✐
Location	N side of village off A198, private road access located at Eastern end of village of Aberlady

Hotel   ★★ 66% Kilspindie House Hotel, Main St,
ABERLADY ☎ 01875 870682   26 ⇌ 🏴

Luffness New EH32 0QA
☎ 01620 843114 & 843336 Fax 01620 842933
Links course, National Final Qualifying Course for Open Championship.
18 holes, 6122yds, Par 69, SSS 70, Course record 62.
Club membership 700.

Visitors	must contact in advance but may not play at weekends & bank holidays.
Societies	telephone for application form.
Green Fees	not confirmed.
Designer	Tom Morris
Facilities	⊗ ⨅ ⬛ ♀ ♣ 🏠 ✐
Location	1m E on A198

Hotel   ★★★⚓ Greywalls Hotel,
Muirfield, GULLANE
☎ 01620 842144   17 ⇌ 🏴 Annexe 5 ⇌ 🏴

ALLOA   Map 11 NS89

Alloa Schawpark, Sauchie FK10 3AX
☎ 01259 722745 & 724476 Fax 01259 724476
Undulating, wooded parkland course, situated under the Ochil hills, scenery and playing conditions are exceptional.
18 holes, 6229yds, Par 69, SSS 71, Course record 63.
Club membership 910.

Visitors	7 day booking system through professional. Advised to book especially at weekends.
Societies	apply in writing/telephone.
Green Fees	not confirmed.
Prof	Bill Bennett
Designer	James Braid
Facilities	⊗ ⨅ ⭍ ⬛ ♀ ♣ 🏠 ⛶ 🛒 ⚡ ✐
Location	1.5m NE on A908

Hotel   ★★ 69% Terraces Hotel, 4 Melville Ter,
STIRLING
☎ 01786 472268   18 ⇌ 🏴

Braehead Cambus FK10 2NT ☎ 01259 725766
Attactive parkland course at the foot of the Ochil Hills, and offering spectacular views.
18 holes, 6086yds, Par 70, SSS 69, Course record 64.
Club membership 800.

Visitors	advisable to telephone in advance.
Societies	must contact the clubhouse manager in advance tel 01259 725766.
Green Fees	£24.50 per day; £18.50 per round (£32.50/£24.50 weekends).
Cards	⬛⬛⬛
Prof	Paul Brookes
Designer	Robert Tait
Facilities	⊗ ⨅ ⭍ ⬛ ♀ ♣ 🏠 ⛶ 🛒 ⚡ ✐
Location	1m W on A907

Hotel   ★★ 69% Terraces Hotel, 4 Melville Ter,
STIRLING
☎ 01786 472268   18 ⇌ 🏴

ALVA   Map 11 NS89

Alva Beauclerc St FK12 5LD ☎ 01259 760431
A 9-hole course at the foot of the Ochil Hills which gives it its characteristic sloping fairways and fast greens.
9 holes, 2423yds, Par 66, SSS 64, Course record 63.
Club membership 318.

Visitors	may not play during medal competitions or Thu evening (Ladies night).
Societies	apply in writing or telephone in advance.
Green Fees	not confirmed.
Facilities	⭍ ⬛ ♀ ♣
Location	7m from Stirling,A91 Stirling/St Andrews rd

ALYTH   Map 15 NO24

Alyth Pitcrocknie PH11 8HF
☎ 01828 632268 Fax 01828 633491
Windy, heathland course with easy walking.
18 holes, 6205yds, Par 71, SSS 71, Course record 65.
Club membership 1000.

▶

Visitors	advance booking advisable, handicap certificate required and dress etiquette must be observed.
Societies	must telephone in advance.
Green Fees	not confirmed.
Prof	Tom Melville
Designer	James Braid
Facilities	⊗ ⅷ ﱠ ﹗ ╄ ﹖ ﹖ ﹖ ﹖ ﹖ ﹖
Location	1m E on B954

Hotel ★★ 64% Angus Hotel, 46 Wellmeadow, BLAIRGOWRIE
☎ 01250 872455   81 ⇔ ﹗

Strathmore Golf Centre Leroch PH11 8NZ
☎ 01828 633322 Fax 01828 633533
The Rannaleroch course is set on rolling parkland and heath with splendid views over Strathmore. The course is laid out in two loops of nine which both start and finish at the clubhouse. Among the challenging holes is the 480yard 5th with a 180yard carry over water from a high tee position (a cop out route available!).
Rannaleroch Course: 18 holes, 6454yds, Par 72, SSS 72, Course record 68.
Leitfie Links: 9 holes, 1666yds, Par 27, SSS 27.
Club membership 400.

Visitors	no restrictions, advised to book in advance.
Societies	phone enquiry recommended.
Green Fees	Rannaleroch: £29 per day; £19 per round; £10 per 9 holes (£36/£24/£13 weekends). Leitfie Links: £8 per day (£10 weekends).
Cards	
Prof	Colin Smith
Designer	John Salvesen
Facilities	⊗ ⅷ ﱠ ﹗ ╄ ﹖ ﹖ ﹖ ﹖ ﹖
Location	2m SE of Alyth, off B954 at Meigle onto A926

Hotel ★★★♨ 75% Old Mansion House Hotel, AUCHTERHOUSE
☎ 01382 320366 5 ⇔ ﹗ Annexe 2 ⇔ ﹗

ANSTRUTHER   Map 12 NO50

Anstruther Marsfield, Shore Rd KY10 3DZ
☎ 01333 310956
Seaside links course with some excellent par 3 holes; always in good condition.
9 holes, 4144mtrs, Par 62, SSS 63, Course record 61.
Club membership 700.

Visitors	advised to phone in advance.
Societies	welcome except Jun-Aug. Must apply in writing.
Green Fees	not confirmed.
Designer	Tom Morris
Facilities	⊗ ﱠ ﹗ ╄ ﹖ ﹖
Location	SW off A917

Hotel ★★ 64% Smugglers Inn, High St East, ANSTRUTHER ☎ 01333 310506 9 ⇔ ﹗

ARBROATH   Map 12 NO64

Arbroath Elliot DD11 2PE
☎ 01241 872069 Fax 01241 875837
Municipal seaside links course, with bunkers guarding greens. Played upon by Arbroath Artisan Club.
18 holes, 6185yds, Par 70, SSS 69, Course record 64.
Club membership 550.

Visitors	contact professional 01241 875837.
Societies	contact professional 01241 875837.
Green Fees	not confirmed.
Cards	
Prof	Lindsay Ewart
Designer	Braid
Facilities	⊗ ﱠ ﹗ ╄ ﹖ ﹖ ﹖
Location	2m SW on A92

Hotel ★★ 64% Hotel Seaforth, Dundee Rd, ARBROATH
☎ 01241 872232 21rm (19 ⇔ ﹗)

Letham Grange Colliston DD11 4RL
☎ 01241 890373 & 809377 Fax 01241 890725
Often referred to as the 'Augusta of Scotland', the Old Course provides championship standards in spectacular surroundings with attractive lochs and burns. The Glens Course is less arduous and shorter using many natural features of the estate.
Old Course: 18 holes, 6632yds, Par 73, SSS 73, Course record 68.
Glens Course: 18 holes, 5528yds, Par 68, SSS 68, Course record 63.
Club membership 850.

Visitors	no visitors weekends before 9.30am, Old Course before 10am Tue & Glens Course before 10am Fri.
Societies	telephone in advance.
Green Fees	Old Course: £35 (£40 weekends). Glens Course: £18 (£22 weekends).
Cards	
Prof	Steven Moir
Designer	G K Smith/Donald Steel
Facilities	⊗ ⅷ ﱠ ﹗ ╄ ﹖ ﹖ ﹖ ﹖ ﹖
Location	4m N on A933

Hotel ★★★★ 64% The Letham Grange Mansion House Hotel, Colliston, ARBROATH
☎ 01241 890373   19 ⇔ ﹗ Annexe 22 ⇔ ﹗

AUCHTERARDER   Map 11 NN91

Auchterarder Orchil Rd PH3 1LS
☎ 01764 662804 (Secretary) Fax 01764 662804
Parkland course with easy walking.
18 holes, 5775yds, Par 69, SSS 68, Course record 61.
Club membership 765.

Visitors	must contact professional in advance.
Societies	must contact in advance.
Green Fees	£30 per day; £20 per round (£38/£25 weekends).
Prof	Gavin Baxter
Designer	Ben Sayers

▶

The Gleneagles Hotel

Auchterarder, *Perthshire & Kinross* ☎ 01764 662231 Fax 01764 694383   Map 11 NN91

e-mail: gleneagles.golf@gleneagles.com

The Monarch's Course, designed by Jack Nicklaus and launched in style in May 1993, boasts an American/Scottish layout with many water hazards, elevated tees and raised contoured greens. Of the Championship courses, The King's Course with its abundance of heather, gorse, raised greens and plateau tees, is set within the valley of Strathearn with the Grampian mountains spectacularly in view to the north. The shorter Queen's course, with its Scots Pine lined fairways and water hazards, is set within a softer landscape and considered an easier test of golf.

You can improve your game at The Golf Academy at Gleneagles, where the philosophy is that golf should be fun and fun in golf comes from playing better. Other pursuits on offer include horse-riding, carriage-driving, shooting, fishing, falconry and purpose-built 4x4 off-road courses. The Club and The Spa provide a relaxing retreat and some well-deserved pampering.

Visitors advance booking essential, 8 weeks notice

Societies contact for details

Green Fees Apr-Oct from £70 per round — 💳 💳 💷 📧 🗨

Facilities ⊗ ⠀ 🝖 🍺 ☕ 🍴 ♟ 📠 🛖 🚗 🛺 ♂ ♞ Professional (Greg Schofield). Golf Academy

Leisure tennis, squash, swimming, sauna, solarium, gymnasium, riding, shooting, fishing

Location Auchterarder PH3 1NF (2m SW of A823)

Holes/Par/Course record 63 holes.
Kings: 18 holes, 6471 yds, Par 70, SSS 73
Queens: 18 holes, 5965 yds, Par 68, SSS 70
Monarch: 18 holes, 6551 yds, Par 72, SSS 73
Wee: 9 holes, 1481 yds, Par 27

WHERE TO STAY NEARBY

Hotels
AUCHTERARDER

★★★★★ 🏵 🏵 The Gleneagles Hotel
☎ 01764 662231. 222 🛏 🐾

★★★ 🏵 🏵 ♨ 77% Auchterarder House ☎ 01764 663646. 15 🛏 🐾

★★ 🏵 🏵 77% Cairn Lodge, Orchil Rd
☎ 01764 662634. 11 (8 🛏 🐾 3 🐾)

Championship Course

Facilities ⊗ 〼 ♥ ♀ ♨ 🏠 ⛳ ✦
Location 0.75m SW on A824

Hotel ★★★★★ The Gleneagles Hotel,
AUCHTERARDER
☎ 01764 662231 229 ⇌ ℞

AUCHTERARDER See page 331.

BANNOCKBURN
Map 11 NS89

Brucefields Family Golfing Centre Pirnhall Rd
FK7 8EH ☎ 01786 818184 Fax 01786 817770
Gently rolling parkland with fine views. Most holes can be
played without too much difficulty with the exception of
the 2nd which is a long and tricky par 4 and the 6th, a par
3 which requires exact club selection and a straight shot.
Main Course: 9 holes, 2513yds, Par 68, SSS 68.
Visitors no restrictions
Societies apply in writing.
Green Fees £14 per 18 holes, £8 per 9 holes (£16/£9
weekends).
Cards 🔲🔲🔲🔲🔲
Prof Kevin Craggs
Designer Souters Sportsturf
Facilities ⊗ 〼 ᕱ ♥ ♀ ♨ 🏠 ⛳ ✦ (
& Leisure par 3 course.
Location Exit at inerchange of M80/M9 (junct 9),
from roundabout take A91, 1st left at sign
for Brucefields

Hotel ★★ 69% Terraces Hotel, 4 Melville Ter,
STIRLING ☎ 01786 472268 18 ⇌ ℞

BARRY
Map 12 NO53

Panmure Burnside Rd DD7 7RT
☎ 01241 855120 Fax 01241 859737
A nerve-testing, adventurous course set amongst
sandhills - its hazards belie the quiet nature of the
opening holes. This tight links has been used as a
qualifying course for the Open Championship, and
features Ben Hogan's favourite hole, the dog-leg 6th,
which heralds the toughest stretch, around the turn.
18 holes, 6317yds, Par 70, SSS 71, Course record 62.
Club membership 700.
Visitors may not play Sat. Parties of 5 or more must
contact in advance.
Societies must contact secretary in advance.
Green Fees £50 per day; £33 per round.
Cards 🔲🔲🔲🔲
Prof Neil Mackintosh
Facilities ⊗ 〼 ᕱ ♥ ♀ ♨ 🏠 ⛳ ✦ (

Location S side of village off A930

Hotel ★★ 68% Hogan House Hotel, Links Pde,
CARNOUSTIE ☎ 01241 853273 7 ⇌ ℞

BATHGATE
Map 11 NS96

Bathgate Edinburgh Rd EH48 1BA
☎ 01506 630553 & 652232 Fax 01506 636775
Moorland course. Easy walking. Testing 11th hole, par 3.
18 holes, 6328yds, Par 71, SSS 70, Course record 58.
Club membership 900.
Visitors casual visitors welcome other than on
competition days. Handicap certificate
advisable.
Societies apply in writing.
Green Fees £21 per day; £16 per round (£32 per day
weekends).
Prof Sandy Strachan
Designer W Park
Facilities ⊗ 〼 ᕱ ♥ ♀ ♨ 🏠 ⛳ 🏌 ⛵ ✦
Location E side of town off A89

Hotel ★★★ 65% The Hilcroft Hotel, East Main St,
WHITBURN ☎ 01501 740818 31 ⇌ ℞

BLAIR ATHOLL
Map 14 NN86

Blair Atholl Invertilt Rd PH18 5TG ☎ 01796 481407
Parkland course, river runs alongside 3 holes, easy walking.
9 holes, 5816yds, Par 70, SSS 68, Course record 65.
Club membership 460.
Visitors apply in advance to avoid competition times.
Societies apply in writing.
Green Fees £13 per day (£16 weekends).
Designer Morriss
Facilities ⊗ ᕱ ♥ ♀ ♨ ⛳ ✦
Location 0.5m S off B8079

Hotel ★★ 68% Atholl Arms Hotel, BLAIR
ATHOLL ☎ 01796 481205 30 ⇌ ℞

BLAIRGOWRIE
Map 15 NO14

Blairgowrie Rosemount PH10 6LG
☎ 01250 872622 Fax 01250 875451
Two 18-hole heathland courses, also a 9-hole course.
*Rosemount Course: 18 holes, 6590yds, Par 72, SSS 73,
Course record 64.*
*Lansdowne Course: 18 holes, 6802yds, Par 73, SSS 74,
Course record 67.*
Wee Course: 9 holes, 2327yds, Par 32.
Club membership 1550. ▶

KINLOCH HOUSE HOTEL
AA ★★★ ☺☺☺
By Blairgowrie, Perthshire, PH10 6SG
Telephone: Blairgowrie (01250) 884 237 Fax: (01250) 884 333
Kinloch House is an award winning, family run, Country house hotel in the heart of
Sporting Perthshire. Located approximately 1½ hours from Glasgow, Edinburgh,
Inverness and Aberdeen, the hotel has 30 golf courses within an hour's drive,
including many Championship ones. Full drying facilities for clothes and equipment
are available, we would be delighted to help plan your golf and book your tee times.
Please write or telephone for a brochure *David and Sarah Shentall*

Visitors must contact in advance & have handicap certificate, restricted Wed, Fri & weekends.
Societies must contact in advance.
Green Fees £60 per day for all courses. Rosemount £50 per round; Lansdowne £40 per round; Wee £20 (£75 per day; £55/£45/£20 per round).
Cards
Prof Charles Dernie
Designer J Braid/P Allis/D Thomas/Old Tom Morris
Facilities
Location (off A93 Rosemount)

Hotel ★★★ Kinloch House Hotel, BLAIRGOWRIE
☎ 01250 884237 21

BONNYRIGG — Map 11 NT36

Broomieknowe 36 Golf Course Rd EH19 2HZ
☎ 0131 663 9317 Fax 0131 663 2152
Easy walking mature parkland course laid out by Ben Sayers and extended by James Braid. Elevated site with excellent views.
18 holes, 6150yds, Par 70, SSS 70, Course record 65.
Visitors must contact in advance.
Societies contact for details.
Green Fees not confirmed.
Prof Mark Patchett
Designer Ben Sayers/Hawtree
Facilities
Location 0.5m NE off B704

BRECHIN — Map 15 NO56

Brechin Trinity DD9 7PD
☎ 01356 622383 Fax 01356 626925
Rolling parkland course, with easy walking and good views of Strathmore Valley and Grampian Mountains.
18 holes, 6092yds, Par 72, SSS 70, Course record 66.
Club membership 850.
Visitors contact Professional on 01356 625270 in advance. Restricted weekends.
Societies must contact club steward in advance.
Green Fees £25 per day; £17 per round (£30/£22 weekends).
Prof Stephen Rennie
Designer James Braid (partly)
Facilities
& Leisure squash.
Location 1m N on B966

Hotel ★★ 63% Northern Hotel, 2/4 Clerk St, BRECHIN ☎ 01356 625505 20rm (5 12)

BRIDGE OF ALLAN — Map 11 NS79

Bridge of Allan Sunnylaw FK9 4LY ☎ 01786 832332
Parkland course, very hilly with good views of Stirling Castle and beyond to the Trossachs. Testing 1st hole, 221 yds (par 3) uphill 6 ft wall 25 yds before green.
9 holes, 4932yds, Par 66, SSS 65, Course record 59.
Club membership 400.
Visitors restricted Sat.
Societies must contact in advance.
Green Fees not confirmed.
Designer Tom Morris
Facilities
Location 0.5m N off A9

Hotel ★★★ 65% Royal Hotel, Henderson St, BRIDGE OF ALLAN
☎ 01786 832284 32

BROXBURN — Map 11 NT07

Niddry Castle Castle Rd, Winchburgh EH52 6RQ
☎ 01506 891097
A 9-hole parkland course. While not very long, it requires accurate golf to score well.
9 holes, 5514yds, Par 70, SSS 67, Course record 65.
Club membership 510.
Visitors advisable to contact at weekends, restricted during competition time.
Societies must contact in advance.
Green Fees not confirmed.
Facilities
Location 9m W of Edinburgh on B9080

Hotel ★★★ 61% Forth Bridges Hotel, 1 Ferrymuir Gait, SOUTH QUEENSFERRY
☎ 0131 469 9955 108

BURNTISLAND — Map 11 NT28

Burntisland Golf House Club Dodhead, Kirkcaldy Rd KY3 9LQ ☎ 01592 874093 (Manager) & 872116 (Pro)
Fax 01592 874093
A lush, testing course offering magnificent views over the Forth Estuary.
18 holes, 5965yds, Par 70, SSS 70, Course record 62.
Club membership 800.

Visitors weekend play may be restricted. Book by telephoning professional.
Societies apply in writing to manager.
Green Fees £25 per day; £17 per round (£37/£25 weekends).
Prof Paul Wytrazek
Designer Willie Park Jnr
Facilities
Location 1m E on B923

Hotel ★★ 64% Inchview Hotel, 69 Kinghorn Rd, BURNTISLAND
☎ 01592 872239 12

Where to stay, where to eat?
Visit the AA internet site
www.theaa.co.uk

Bute, Isle of   Map 10 NS05

Kingarth   Map 10 NS05

Bute Sithean, Academy Rd, Rothesay PA20 0BG
☎ 01700 504369
Flat seaside course with good fenced greens and fine views.
9 holes, 2361mtrs, Par 68, SSS 64, Course record 65.
Club membership 210.
Visitors   restricted Sat until after 11.30am.
Societies   apply in advance.
Green Fees   £8 per day.
Facilities   △
Location   From Rothesay pier 6m on A845

Hotel   ★★★♨ 77% Ardmory House Hotel &
                    Restaurant, Ardmory Rd, ARDBEG
                    ☎ 01700 502346 5 ⇌ ⋔

Port Bannatyne   Map 10 NS06

Port Bannatyne Bannatyne Mains Rd PA20 0PH
☎ 01700 502009
Seaside hill course with panoramic views. Difficult hole: 4th
(par 3).
13 holes, 5085yds, Par 68, SSS 65, Course record 63.
Club membership 200.
Visitors   no restrictions.
Societies   must telephone in advance.
Green Fees   £10 per round (£15 weekends).
Designer   Peter Morrison
Facilities   ⊗ ⓛ ⬛ ♀ △
Location   W side of village off A844

Hotel   ★★★♨ 77% Ardmory House Hotel &
                    Restaurant, Ardmory Rd, ARDBEG
                    ☎ 01700 502346 5 ⇌ ⋔

Rothesay   Map 10 NS06

Rothesay Canada Hill PA20 9HN
☎ 01700 503554 Fax 01700 503554
A scenic island course designed by James Braid and Ben
Sayers. The course is fairly hilly, with views of the Firth of
Clyde, Rothesay Bay or the Kyles of Bute from every hole.
Winds are a regular feature which makes the two par 5 holes
extremely challenging.
18 holes, 5395yds, Par 69, SSS 66, Course record 62.
Club membership 400.
Visitors   pre-booking essential for weekends, telephone
                    professional 01700 503554.
Societies   contact in advance, booking essential at
                    weekends.
Green Fees   £15 per day; £10 per round (£25/£19 weekends).
Prof   James M Dougal
Designer   James Braid & Ben Sayers
Facilities   ⊗ ⓜ ⓛ ⬛ ♀ △ 🛍 ⋔ ❀ ⚷
Location   2 min drive from main ferry terminal

Hotel   ★★★♨ 77% Ardmory House Hotel &
                    Restaurant, Ardmory Rd, ARDBEG
                    ☎ 01700 502346 5 ⇌ ⋔

Callander   Map 11 NN60

Callander Aveland Rd FK17 8EN
☎ 01877 330090 & 330975 Fax 01877 330062
Challenging parkland course with tight fairways and a
number of interesting holes. Designed by Tom Morris Snr
and overlooked by the Trossachs.
18 holes, 5151yds, Par 66, SSS 66, Course record 61.
Club membership 600.
Visitors   prior booking 24-48 hrs is advised in the playing
                    season. Handicap certificate Wed/Sun.
Societies   write or telephone for booking form.
Green Fees   £26 per day; £18 per round (£31/£26 weekends).
Prof   Allan Martin
Designer   Morris/Fernie
Facilities   ⊗ ⓜ ⓛ ⬛ ♀ △ 🛍 ⋔ ⚷
Location   E side of town off A84

Hotel   ★★★♨ 74% Roman Camp Country House
                    Hotel, CALLANDER
                    ☎ 01877 330003 14 ⇌ ⋔

Cardenden   Map 11 NT29

Auchterderran Woodend Rd KY5 0NH ☎ 01592 721579
This is a relatively flat course requiring a lot of thought.
There are two or three holes to test the best.
9 holes, 5250yds, Par 66, SSS 66, Course record 63.
Club membership 120.
Visitors   no visitors between 7-11am & 1-3pm Sat, also
                    some Sun in season.
Societies   apply in writing.
Green Fees   not confirmed.
Facilities   ♀ △
Location   N end Cardendon, Kirkcaldy/Glenrothes road

Hotel   ★★★ 65% Dean Park Hotel, Chapel Level,
                    KIRKCALDY
                    ☎ 01592 261635 29 ⇌ ⋔ Annexe 12 ⇌ ⋔

Cardross   Map 10 NS37

Cardross Main Rd G82 5LB
☎ 01389 841754 Fax 01389 842162
Undulating parkland course, testing with good views.
18 holes, 6469yds, Par 71, SSS 72, Course record 64.
Club membership 800.
Visitors   may not play at weekends unless introduced by
                    member. Contact professional in advance 01359
                    841350.
Societies   must contact in writing.
Green Fees   £35 per day; £25 per round.
Cards   ▭ ▭
Prof   Robert Farrell
Designer   James Braid
Facilities   ⊗ ⓜ by prior arrangement ⓛ ⬛ ♀ △ 🛍 ⋔ ⚷
Location   In centre of village on A814

Hotel   ★★★★★ 72% Cameron House Hotel,
                    BALLOCH ☎ 01389 755565 96 ⇌ ⋔

Carnoustie   Map 12 NO53

Carnoustie See page 335.

Carnoustie Golf Links

Carnoustie, *Angus*   ☎ 01241 853789   Fax 01241 852720   Map 12 NO53

Visitors must contact in advance, Sat after 2pm, Sun after 11.30am. Must have handicap certificate for championship course

Societies must contact in advance

Green Fees £70 per round 〜 ▨ ▨ ▨ ▨ .

Facilities ⛳ 🏠 🍴
Professional (Lee Vannet)

Location Links Parade, Carnoustie DD7 7JE (SW side of town, off A930)

Holes/Par/Course record 54 holes
Championship Course: 18 holes, 6936 yds, Par 72, SSS 74, Course record 68
Burnside Course: 18 holes, 6020 yds, Par 68, SSS 69
Buddon Links: 18 holes, 5420 yds, Par 66, SSS 68

WHERE TO STAY AND EAT NEARBY

Hotels
ARBROATH

★★64% Hotel Seaforth, Dundee Rd.
☎ 01241 872232. 19 (18 ⇆ ◪1 ⇆)

CARNOUSTIE

★★67% Carlogie House, Carlogie Rd.
☎ 01241 853185. 12 (2 ⇆ ◪10 ◪) Annexe 4 ◪

★★68% Hogan House, Links Pde.
☎ 01241 853273. 7 (3 ⇆ ◪4 ◪)

Restaurant
CARNOUSTIE

⚜ 11 Park Avenue. ☎ 01241 853336.

This Championship Course has been voted the top course in Britain by many golfing greats and described as Scotland's ultimate golfing challenge. The course developed from origins in the 1560s; James Braid added new bunkers, greens and tees in the 1920s. The Open Championship first came to the course in 1931 and Carnoustie recently returned to prominence as the host of the Scottish Open in 1995 and 1996 and the venue for the 1999 Open Championship.

The Burnside Course (6020 yards) is enclosed on three sides by the Championship Course and has been used for Open Championship qualifying rounds. The Buddon Course (5400 yards) has been extensively remodelled making it ideal for mid to high handicappers.

LETHAM GRANGE RESORT HOTEL

★★★★

Colliston by
Arbroath
Angus DD11 4RL
Tel: 01241 890373 Fax: 01241 890725
E-mail: lethamgrange@sol.co.uk

Situated in the heart of Angus countryside with
many sporting and leisure pursuits on the estate,
Letham Grange offers a tranquil oasis in which
to recharge.
The main house is a beautifully restored
Victorian mansion and the Golf Estate rooms
set in the grounds offer a good quality. Friendly,
efficient staff serving a mix of Scottish and
French cuisine.

Taste of Scotland Recommended

CARRADALE   Map 10 NR83

Carradale PA28 6SG ☎ 01583 431335
Pleasant seaside course built on a promontory overlooking
the Isle of Arran. Natural terrain and small greens are the
most difficult natural hazards. Described as the most sporting
9-hole course in Scotland. Testing 7th hole (240 yds), par 3.
Beware of wild goats in summer.
9 holes, 2392yds, Par 66, SSS 64, Course record 64.
Club membership 320.
Visitors   no restrictions.
Societies   contact in advance.
Green Fees   £10 per day.
Facilities   ⛵ ✐
Location   S side of village, on B842

Hotel   ★★ 67% Seafield Hotel, Kilkerran Rd,
                 CAMPBELTOWN
                 ☎ 01586 554385 3 ⇄ ➤ Annexe 6 ➤

COLONSAY, ISLE OF   Map 10 NR39

SCALASAIG   Map 10 NR39

Colonsay Machrins Farm PA61 7YP
☎ 01951 200364 Fax 01951 200312
Traditional links course on natural machair (hard wearing
short grass), challenging, primitive. Colonsay Hotel, 2 miles
away, is the headquarters of the club, offering
accommodation and facilities.
18 holes, 4775yds, Par 72, SSS 72.
Club membership 200.

Visitors   no restrictions.
Societies   apply in writing.
Green Fees   not confirmed.
Facilities   ⛵
Location   2m W on A870

Hotel   ★★ 70% Colonsay Hotel, SCALASAIG
                 ☎ 01951 200316 11rm(9 ⇄ ➤)

COMRIE   Map 11 NN72

Comrie Laggan Braes PH6 2LR ☎ 01764 670055
Scenic highland course with two tricky par 3 holes.
9 holes, 6040yds, Par 70, SSS 70, Course record 62.
Club membership 315.
Visitors   apply in advance (for party bookings)
Societies   must contact in advance.
Green Fees   £12 per day; £8 per 9 holes (£16 per day, £12
                  per 18 holes; £8 per 9 holes weekends and bank
                  holidays).
Designer   Col. Williamson
Facilities   ⊗ ⛵ ⚲ ⛵ ✐ ✐
& Leisure   fishing.
Location   E side of village off A85

Guesthouse   ♦♦♦ Mossgiel Guest House, Burrell St,
                 COMRIE ☎ 01764 670567 3 ➤

COWDENBEATH   Map 11 NT19

Cowdenbeath Seco Place KY4 8PD ☎ 01383 511918
A parkland-based 9-hole golf course.
*Dora Course: 9 holes, 6552yds, Par 72, SSS 71, Course
record 68.*
Club membership 400.
Visitors   no restrictions.
Societies   must contact at least 2 weeks in advance.
Green Fees   not confirmed.
Facilities   ⛵ ⛵ ⚲ ✐
Location   6m E of Dunfermline

Hotel   ★★ 68% Woodside Hotel, High St,
                 ABERDOUR ☎ 01383 860328 20 ⇄ ➤

CRAIL   Map 12 NO60

Crail Golfing Society Balcomie Clubhouse, Fifeness
KY10 3XN
☎ 01333 450686 & 450960 Fax 01333 450416
Perched on the edge of the North Sea on the very point
of the golfing county of Fife, the Crail Golfing Society's
course at Balcomie is picturesque and sporting. And here
again golf history has been made for Crail Golfing
Society began its life in 1786. The course is highly
thought of by students of the game both for its testing
holes and the standard of its greens. Craighead Links has
panoramic seascape and country views. With wide
sweeping fairways and large greens it is a testing but fair
challenge, be warned there are hungry bunkers a plenty!
This second links at Fifeness is set to join Balcomie as
one of Scotlands's 'must play' courses.
Balcomie Links: 18 holes, 5922yds, Par 69, SSS 69.
Craighead Links: 18 holes, 6700yds, Par 72, SSS 73.
Club membership 1680.
Visitors   must contact in advance, restricted 10am-
                  noon & 2-4.30pm.

▶

Societies must contact in advance, as much notice as possible for weekend play.

Green Fees £35 per day; £25 per round (£45/£30 weekends).

Cards

Prof Graeme Lennie

Designer Tom Morris

Facilities ⊗ ⅊ ⅃ ⅄ ⅂ ⅏ ⅀ ⅁ ⅂ ⅃

Location 2m NE off A917

Hotel ★★ 68% Balcomie Links Hotel, Balcomie Rd, CRAIL ☎ 01333 450237 11 ⇄ ☙

Additional ♦♦♦♦ The Spindrift, Pittenweem Rd,
Guesthouse ANSTRUTHER
☎ 01333 310573 Fax 01333 310573 8 ⇄ ☙

CRIEFF
Map 11 NN82

Crieff Ferntower, Perth Rd PH7 3LR
☎ 01764 652909 Fax 01764 655096
This course is what you might call 'up and down' but the turf is beautiful and the highland air fresh and invigorating. There are views from the course over Strathearn. Of the two courses the Ferntower is the more challenging. Both parkland, the Dornock has one water hazard.
Ferntower Course: 18 holes, 6427yds, Par 71, SSS 72, Course record 65.
Dornock Course: 9 holes, 2387yds, Par 32, SSS 63.
Club membership 720.
Visitors must contact professional in advance.
Societies must contact professional in advance.
Green Fees £19-£25 weekdays.
Cards
Prof David Murchie

Designer James Braid
Facilities ⊗ ⅊ ⅃ ⅄ ⅂ ⅏ ⅀ ⅁ ⅂ ⅃ ⅄ ⅂
Location 0.5m NE on A85

Hotel ★★ 64% Locke's Acre Hotel, 7 Comrie Rd, CRIEFF ☎ 01764 652526 7rm (4 ☙)

CUPAR
Map 11 NO31

Cupar Hilltarvit KY15 5JT
☎ 01334 653549 Fax 01334 653549
Hilly parkland course with fine views over north east Fife.5th/14th hole is most difficult - uphill and into the prevailing wind.
9 holes, 5074yds, Par 68, SSS 65, Course record 61.
Club membership 400.
Visitors welcome except Sat.
Societies must contact in advance.
Green Fees £12 per day (£15 Sundays)..
Designer Allan Robertson
Facilities ⊗ ⅃ ⅄ ⅂ ⅏ ⅁ ⅂
Location 0.75m S off A92

Hotel ★★ 69% Eden House Hotel, 2 Pitscottie Rd, CUPAR ☎ 01334 652510
9 ⇄ ☙ Annexe 2 ⇄ ☙

DALKEITH
Map 11 NT36

Newbattle Abbey Rd EH22 3AD
☎ 0131 663 2123 & 0131 663 1819 Fax 0131 654 1810
Undulating parkland course on three levels, surrounded by woods.
18 holes, 6005yds, Par 69, SSS 70, Course record 61.
Club membership 700.
Visitors Mon-Fri ex public holidays, before 4pm.
Societies welcome weekdays ex public holidays, before 4pm.
Green Fees £27 per day; £18 per round.
Prof Scott McDonald
Designer S Colt
Facilities ⊗ ⅃ ⅄ ⅂ ⅏ ⅁ ⅂
Location SW side of town off A68

DALMALLY
Map 10 NN12

Dalmally Old Saw Mill PA33 1AE ☎ 01838 200370
A 9-hole flat parkland course bounded by the River Orchy and surrounded by mountains. Many water hazards and bunkers.

▶

9 holes, 2257yds, Par 64, SSS 63, Course record 64.
Club membership 100.

Visitors	no visitors on Sun between 9-10 & 1-2.
Societies	telephone in advance.
Green Fees	£10 per day.
Designer	MacFarlane Barrow Co
Facilities	⊗ ≡ by prior arrangement ⛾ 🛋 by prior arrangement 🏌 by arrangement 🏌 ⛳ ♂
& Leisure	fishing.
Location	On A85, 1.5m W of Dalmally

Hotel ★★ 60% Polfearn Hotel, TAYNUILT
☎ 01866 822251 16rm (3 ⇔11 ⋔)

DOLLAR
Map 11 NS99

Dollar Brewlands House FK14 7EA
☎ 01259 742400 Fax 01259 743497
Compact hillside course with magnificent views along the
Ochil Hills.
18 holes, 5242yds, Par 69, SSS 66, Course record 62.
Club membership 470.

Visitors	weekdays course available but restricted Wed ladies day, weekends advised to contact in advance.
Societies	write or telephone in advance.
Green Fees	£17.50 per day; £13.50 per round (£22 day/round weekends).
Designer	Ben Sayers
Facilities	⊗ ≡ ⛾ 🛋 🏌 🏌 ⛳ ♂
& Leisure	snooker.
Location	0.5m N off A91

Hotel ★★★ 65% Royal Hotel, Henderson St,
BRIDGE OF ALLAN
☎ 01786 832284 32 ⇔ ⋔

DRYMEN
Map 11 NS48

Buchanan Castle G63 0HY
☎ 01360 660307 Fax 01360 870382
Parkland course, with easy walking and good views. Owned
by the Duke of Montrose.
18 holes, 6086yds, Par 70, SSS 69.
Club membership 830.

Visitors	must contact professional on 01360 660330 in advance.
Societies	must contact in advance.
Green Fees	£40 per day; £30 per round.
Cards	🟦 💳 🟦 🟦
Prof	Keith Baxter
Designer	James Braid
Facilities	⊗ ≡ ⛾ 🛋 🏌 🏌 ⛳ ♂
Location	1m W

Hotel ★★★ 67% Buchanan Arms Hotel, DRYMEN
☎ 01360 660588 52 ⇔ ⋔

DUNBAR
Map 12 NT67

Dunbar East Links EH42 1LL
☎ 01368 862317 Fax 01368 865202
Another of Scotland's old links. It is said that it was
some Dunbar members who first took the game of golf
to the North of England. A natural links course on a
narrow strip of land, following the contours of the sea

shore, there is a wall bordering one side and the shore on
the other side making this quite a challenging course for
all levels of player. The wind, if blowing from the sea, is
a problem.
18 holes, 6406yds, Par 71, SSS 71, Course record 64.
Club membership 1000.

Societies	telephone in advance.
Green Fees	£35 per day; £28 per round (£45/£35 weekends).
Cards	🟦 🟦 💳 🟦 🟦
Prof	Jacky Montgomery
Designer	Tom Morris
Facilities	⊗ ≡ ⛾ 🛋 🏌 🏌 ⛳ ♂
Location	0.5m E off A1087

Hotel ★★ 65% Bayswell Hotel, Bayswell Park,
DUNBAR ☎ 01368 862225 13 ⇔ ⋔

Winterfield North Rd EH42 1AY ☎ 01368 863562
Seaside course with superb views.
18 holes, 5155yds, Par 65, SSS 64.
Club membership 300.

Societies	must arrange in advance through professional
Green Fees	not confirmed.
Prof	Kevin Phillips
Facilities	⊗ ≡ ⛾ 🛋 🏌 🏌 ⛳ ♂
Location	W side of town off A1087

Hotel ★★ 65% Bayswell Hotel, Bayswell Park,
DUNBAR ☎ 01368 862225 13 ⇔ ⋔

DUNBLANE
Map 11 NN70

Dunblane New Golf Club Perth Rd FK15 0LJ
☎ 01786 821521 Fax 01786 821522
Well maintained parkland course, with reasonably hard
walking. Testing 6th and 9th holes.
18 holes, 5536yds, Par 69, SSS 67.
Club membership 1000.

Visitors	may play 9.30am-noon & 2.30-4pm Mon-Fri. Must contact in advance.
Societies	welcome Mon, Wed-Fri, contact in advance.
Green Fees	£32 per day; £20 per round (£32 per round weekends).
Prof	Bob Jamieson
Facilities	⊗ ≡ ⛾ 🛋 🏌 🏌 ⛳ ♂
Location	E side of town on A9

Hotel ★★★⚊⚊ Cromlix House Hotel, Kinbuck, Nr
DUNBLANE ☎ 01786 822125 14 ⇔ ⋔

DUNDEE
Map 11 NO43

Caird Park Mains Loan DD4 9BX
☎ 01382 438871 Fax 01382 434601
A pay-as-you-play course situated in extensive parkland in the heart of the Carnoustie countryside. A reasonably easy start belies the difficulty of the middle section (holes 7-13) and the back nine cross the Gelly Burn four times.
18 holes, 6280yds, Par 72, SSS 69, Course record 67.
Club membership 1000.
Visitors   no restrictions.
Societies   must contact in advance 01382 438871.
Green Fees £25 per round day; £15 per round.
Prof   J Black
Facilities   ⊗ ⓑ ♥ ♀ ⚲ ➫ ⓕ ♂
Location   From Kingsway (A90) take Forfar Road, turn left onto Claverhouse Road, 1st left into Caird Park

Hotel   ★★★ 70% Swallow Hotel, Kingsway West, Invergowrie, DUNDEE
☎ 01382 641122 107 ⇆ ⓕ

Camperdown Camperdown House, Camperdown Park DD2 4TF ☎ 01382 432688
A beautiful course located within the Camperdown Country Park with undulating, tree lined fairways. Testing golf for players of all abilities.
18 holes, 6548yds, Par 71, SSS 72.
Club membership 1000.
Visitors   must contact in advance on 01382 432688.
Societies   must contact in advance.
Green Fees £25 per day; £15 per round.
Facilities   ⚲ ⓕ
& Leisure   hard tennis courts.
Location   Kingsway (A90), turn off at Coupar Angus Road (A923) then turn left into Camperdown Park

Hotel   ★★★♨♨ 75% Old Mansion House Hotel, AUCHTERHOUSE
☎ 01382 320366 5 ⇆ ⓕ Annexe 2 ⇆ ⓕ

Downfield Turnberry Av DD2 3QP
☎ 01382 825595 Fax 01382 813111
A 1999 Open Qualifying venue. A course with championship credentials providing an enjoyable test for all golfers.
18 holes, 6803yds, Par 73, SSS 73, Course record 65.
Club membership 750.
Visitors   must contact in advance, no visitors at weekends.
Societies   must contact in advance.
Green Fees Apr & Oct: £35 per day; £25 per round
                      May-Sep £44 per day; £31 per round.
Cards   ▭ ▭ ▬ ◤ ▨
Prof   Kenny Hutton
Designer   C K Cotton
Facilities   ⊗ ⓜ ⓑ ♥ ♀ ⚲ ➫ ⓕ ➤ ⚒ ♂
Location   N of city centre off A923

Hotel   ★★★♨♨ 75% Old Mansion House Hotel, AUCHTERHOUSE
☎ 01382 320366 5 ⇆ ⓕ Annexe 2 ⇆ ⓕ

DUNFERMLINE
Map 11 NT08

Canmore Venturefair Av KY12 0PE ☎ 01383 724969
Parkland course with excellent turf, ideal for 36 hole play, suitable all ages a good test of golf.
18 holes, 5376yds, Par 67, SSS 66, Course record 61.
Club membership 710.
Visitors   Sat not usually available. Limited Sun. Must contact Professional in advance.
Societies   apply in writing to secretary.
Green Fees £20 per day: £15 per round (£30/£20 weekends).
Prof   Jim McKinnon
Designer   Ben Sayers & others
Facilities   ⊗ ⓜ ⓑ ♥ ♀ ⚲ ⓕ ♂
Location   1m N on A823

Hotel   ★★★ 65% King Malcolm, Queensferry Rd, DUNFERMLINE ☎ 01383 722611 48 ⇆ ⓕ

Dunfermline Pitfirrane, Crossford KY12 8QW
☎ 01383 723534 & 729061
Gently undulating parkland course with interesting contours. Five Par 5's, Five Par 3's. No water hazards.
18 holes, 6121yds, Par 72, SSS 70, Course record 65.
Club membership 950.
Visitors   may not play weekends. Contact to check times.
Societies   must contact in advance.
Green Fees £31 per day; £21 per round.
Prof   Steve Craig
Designer   J R Stutt
Facilities   ⊗ ⓜ ⓑ ♥ ♀ ⚲ ⓕ ♂
Location   2m W of Dunfermline on A994

Hotel   ★★★ 65% King Malcolm, Queensferry Rd, DUNFERMLINE ☎ 01383 722611 48 ⇆ ⓕ

Pitreavie Queensferry Rd KY11 8PR
☎ 01383 722591 Fax 01383 722591
Picturesque woodland course with panoramic view of the River Forth Valley. Testing golf.
18 holes, 6086yds, Par 70, SSS 69, Course record 65.
Club membership 700.
Visitors   welcome except for competition days.
Societies   must write or telephone in advance.
Green Fees £26 per day; £19 per round (£38/£24 weekends).
Prof   Colin Mitchell
Designer   Dr Alaistair McKenzie
Facilities   ⊗ ⓜ ⓑ ♥ ♀ ⚲ ➫ ⓕ ♂
Location   SE side of town on A823

Hotel   ★★★ 65% King Malcolm, Queensferry Rd, DUNFERMLINE ☎ 01383 722611 48 ⇆ ⓕ

DUNKELD
Map 11 NO04

Dunkeld & Birnam Fungarth PH8 0HU
☎ 01350 727524 Fax 01350 728660
Interesting heathland course with spectacular views of surrounding countryside.
9 holes, 5322yds, Par 68, SSS 66, Course record 64.
Club membership 450.
Visitors   must contact in advance.
Societies   apply in writing/telephone.
Green Fees £13 per day; £11 per round (£22/£16 weekends & bank holidays).

▶

Designer   D A Tod
Facilities   ⊗ 🎋 🏌 ⛳ ♟ 🏌 🍴 🏠 🍴 ♂
Location   1m N of village on A923

Hotel   ★★★🛥 Kinnaird, Kinnaird Estate,
DUNKELD ☎ 01796 482440 9 ⇆ ☎

DUNNING   Map 11 NO01

Dunning Rollo Park PH2 0RH ☎ 01764 684747
Parkland course with a series of stone built bridges crossing a
burn meandering over a large part of the course.
9 holes, 4836yds, Par 66, SSS 63, Course record 63.
Club membership 580.
Visitors   Gents competitions Saturday, Ladies Tue, other
than that no restrictions.
Societies   must contact in advance in writing.
Green Fees £14 per 18 holes (£16 weekends).
Facilities   🍴 ⛳ ♂
& Leisure   hard tennis courts.
Location   1.5m off A9, 4m N of Auchterarder

Hotel   ★★★ 67% Lovat Hotel, 90 Glasgow Rd,
PERTH ☎ 01738 636555   31 ⇆ ☎

Whitemoss Whitemoss Rd PH2 0QX
☎ 01738 730300 Fax 01738 730300
Undulating parkland course situated in the scenic Strathearn
Valley, ten miles from Perth (off the A9).
18 holes, 5595yds, Par 68, SSS 68, Course record 63.
Club membership 600.

Visitors   advisable to telephone in advance, visitors
welcome all week, may play 9 holes half price.
Societies   please telephone for details.
Green Fees not confirmed.
Designer   Whitemoss Leisure
Facilities   ⊗ 🎋 ⛳ ⛳ 🏠 ♂
& Leisure   practice range, chipping bunkers, practice net.
Location   Turn off A9 at Whitemoss Road junct, 3m N of
Gleneagles

Hotel   ★★ 77% Cairn Lodge, Orchil Rd,
AUCHTERARDER
☎ 01764 662634 & 662431
Fax 01764 664866 7 ⇆ ☎

DUNOON   Map 10 NS17

Cowal Ardenslate Rd PA23 8LT
☎ 01369 705673 Fax 01369 705673
Moorland course. Panoramic views of Clyde Estuary and
surrounding hills.

18 holes, 6063yds, Par 70, SSS 70, Course record 63.
Club membership 900.
Visitors   advisable to book in advance.
Societies   must telephone in advance.
Green Fees not confirmed.
Prof   Russell Weir
Designer   James Braid
Facilities   ⛳ 🏠 🍴 ♂
Location   1m N

Hotel   ★★ 76% Enmore Hotel, Marine Pde, Kirn,
DUNOON ☎ 01369 702230   10 ⇆ ☎

EDINBURGH   Map 11 NT27

Baberton 50 Baberton Av, Juniper Green EH14 5DU
☎ 0131 453 4911 Fax 0131 453 4911
Parkland course.
18 holes, 6129yds, Par 69, SSS 70, Course record 64.
Club membership 900.
Visitors   may not play at weekends or after 3.30pm
weekdays. Contact in advance.
Societies   must contact in advance.
Green Fees not confirmed.
Prof   Ken Kelly
Designer   Willie Park Jnr
Facilities   ⊗ 🎋 🏌 ⛳ ♟ ⛳ 🏠 ♂
Location   5m W of city centre off A70

Hotel   ★★★★ 62% Swallow Royal Scot Hotel,
111 Glasgow Rd, EDINBURGH
☎ 0131 334 9191 259 ⇆ ☎

Braid Hills Braid Hills Approach EH10 6JZ
☎ 0131 447 6666 Fax 0131 557 5170
Municipal heathland course with superb views of Edinburgh
and the Firth of Forth, quite challenging.
Course No 1: 18 holes, 5390yds, Par 70, SSS 68.
Course No 2: 18 holes, 4602yds, Par 65.

Visitors   two courses Braids 1 & Braids 2 operate from
Apr-Sep, one course only during winter. Braids
1 is closed on Sun.
Societies   telephone 0131 557 5457 or apply in writing to
Edinburgh Leisure, 23 Waterloo Place,
Edinburgh EH1 3BH
Green Fees £9.20 per round before 4pm, £11 after 4pm &
weekends.
Designer   Peter McEwan & Bob Ferguson
Facilities   ⛳ 🍴 ♂
Location   2.5m S of city centre off A702

Hotel   ★★★ 70% Braid Hills Hotel, 134 Braid Rd,
EDINBURGH ☎ 0131 447 8888 68 ⇆ ☎

Bruntsfield Links Golfing Society 32 Barnton Av EH4 6JH
☎ 0131 336 1479 Fax 0131 336 5538
Mature parkland course with magnificent views over the
Firth of Forth and to the west. Greens and fairways are
generally immaculate. Challenging for all categories of
handicap.
18 holes, 6407yds, Par 71, SSS 71, Course record 67.
Club membership 1100.

Visitors	must telephone in advance. 0131 336 4050 or 0131 336 1479
Societies	apply in writing.
Green Fees	£50 per day; £38 per round (£42 per round weekends).
Prof	Brian Mackenzie
Designer	Willie Park Jr
Facilities	⊗ �𝄞 ▐ ♥ ⛳ ♠ 𝄢 ⛟ 𝄪 ⛳
Location	4m NW of city centre off A90
Hotel	★★★ 63% The Barnton, Queensferry Rd, Barnton, EDINBURGH ☎ 0131 339 1144 50 ⛟ ⏰

Carrick Knowe Carrick Knowe, Glendevon Park EH12 5UZ
☎ 0131 337 1096 & 557 5457 bookings Fax 0131 557 5170
Flat parkland course. Played over by two clubs, Carrick
Knowe and Carrick Vale.
18 holes, 5697yds, Par 70, SSS 69.

Visitors	may be restricted at weekends.
Societies	telephone 0131 557 5457 or write to Edinburgh Leisure, 23 Waterloo Place EH1 3BH.
Green Fees	£9.20 per round before 4pm; £11 after 4pm & weekends.
Facilities	⛳ 𝄪 ⛳
Location	3m W of city centre, S of A8
Hotel	★★★ 73% Posthouse Edinburgh, Corstorphine Rd, EDINBURGH ☎ 0870 400 9026 303 ⛟ ⏰

Craigentinny Fillyside Rd EH7 6RG
☎ 0131 554 7501 & 557 5457 bookings Fax 0131 557 5170
To the north east of Edinburgh, Craigentinny course is
between Leith and Portobello. It is generally flat although
there are some hillocks with gentle slopes. The famous
Arthur's Seat dominates the southern skyline.
18 holes, 5205yds, Par 67, SSS 65.

Visitors	must contact in advance.
Societies	telephone 0131 557 5457 or apply in writing to: Edinburgh Leisure, 23 Waterloo Place EH1 3BH.
Green Fees	£9.20 per round before 4pm; £11 after 4pm & weekends.
Facilities	⛳ 𝄪 ⛳
Location	NE side of city, between Leith & Portobello
Hotel	★★★ 65% Kings Manor, 100 Milton Rd East, EDINBURGH ☎ 0131 669 0444 69 ⛟ ⏰

Craigmillar Park 1 Observatory Rd EH9 3HG
☎ 0131 667 0047
Parkland course, with good views.
18 holes, 5851yds, Par 70, SSS 69, Course record 63.
Club membership 750.

Visitors	must contact in advance, welcome Monday-Friday and Sunday afternoons
Societies	must contact in writing.
Green Fees	not confirmed.
Prof	B McGhee

Designer	James Braid
Facilities	⊗ �𝄞 ▐ ♥ ⛳ ♠ 𝄢 ⛟ 𝄪 ⛳
Location	2m S of city centre off A7
Hotel	★★ 68% Allison House Hotel, 15/17 Mayfield Gardens, EDINBURGH ☎ 0131 667 8049 23rm (21 ⏰)

Duddingston Duddingston Rd West EH15 3QD
☎ 0131 661 7688 Fax 0131 652 6057
Parkland course with burn as a natural hazard. Testing 11th
hole. Easy walking and windy.
18 holes, 6647yds, Par 71, SSS 71.
Club membership 700.

Visitors	may not play at weekends.
Societies	Tue & Thu only. Must contact in advance.
Green Fees	£48 per day; £31 per round.
Cards	💳
Prof	Alastair McLean
Designer	Willie Park Jnr
Facilities	⊗ ⟒ ▐ ♥ ⛳ ♠ 𝄢 ⛟ 𝄪 ⛳
Location	2.5m SE of city centre off A1
Hotel	★★★ 74% Prestonfield House Hotel, Priestfield Rd, EDINBURGH ☎ 0131 668 3346 31rm (30 ⛟ ⏰)

Kingsknowe 326 Lanark Rd EH14 2JD
☎ 0131 441 1145 (Secretary) & 441 1144 (Club)
Fax 0131 441 2079
Hilly parkland course with prevailing SW winds.
18 holes, 5979yds, Par 69, SSS 69, Course record 63.
Club membership 800.

Visitors	contact in advance and subject to availability of tee times.
Societies	apply in writing or telephone secretary.
Green Fees	£30 per day; £22 per round (£35 per round weekends).
Prof	Andrew Marshall
Designer	A Herd/James Braid
Facilities	⊗ ▐ ♥ ⛳ ♠ 𝄢 ⛟ 𝄪 ⛳
Location	4m SW of city centre on A70
Hotel	★★★ 74% Bruntsfield Hotel, 69/74 Bruntsfield Place, EDINBURGH ☎ 0131 229 1393 75 ⛟ ⏰

Liberton 297 Gilmerton Rd EH16 5UJ
☎ 0131 664 3009 (sec) & 664 1056 (pro)
Fax 0131 666 0853
Undulating, wooded parkland course.
18 holes, 5306yds, Par 67, SSS 67, Course record 61.
Club membership 675.

Visitors	must contact in advance.
Societies	must contact in writing.
Green Fees	not confirmed.
Cards	💳
Prof	Iain Seath
Facilities	⊗ ⟒ ▐ ♥ ⛳ ♠ 𝄢 ⛳
Location	3m SE of city centre on A7

Lothianburn 106A Biggar Rd, Fairmilehead EH10 7DU
☎ 0131 445 2206 & 0131 445 5067
Hillside course with a 'T' shaped wooded-area, situated in
the Pentland foothills. Testing in windy conditions. Fine
views of Edinburgh and the Lothians.
18 holes, 5568yds, Par 71, SSS 68, Course record 66.
Club membership 850.

Visitors   weekends after 3.30pm contact professional, weekdays up to 4pm.
Societies   apply to the secretary or telephone in the first instance.
Green Fees not confirmed.
Prof   Kurt Mungall
Designer   J Braid (re-designed 1928)
Facilities   ⊗ ⅲ ⅼ ♥ ♀ ⚘ 🖢 ⛳ ⌀
Location   4.5m S of city centre on A702

Hotel   ★★★ 70% Braid Hills Hotel, 134 Braid Rd, EDINBURGH ☎ 0131 447 8888 68 ➡ 🐾

MARRIOTT DALMAHOY HOTEL GOLF & COUNTRY CLUB   See page 343.

Merchants of Edinburgh 10 Craighill Gardens EH10 5PY
☎ 0131 447 1219
Testing hill course with fine views over the city and the surrounding countryside.
18 holes, 4889yds, Par 65, SSS 64, Course record 59.
Club membership 900.
Visitors   must contact Secretary or Professional in advance.
Societies   must contact secretary in writing.
Green Fees £15 per round.
Prof   Neil Colquhoun
Designer   R G Ross
Facilities   ⊗ ⅲ ⅼ ♥ ♀ ⚘ 🖢 ⛳ ⌀
Location   2m SW of city centre off A702

Hotel   ★★★ 70% Braid Hills Hotel, 134 Braid Rd, EDINBURGH ☎ 0131 447 8888 68 ➡ 🐾

Mortonhall 231 Braid Rd EH10 6PB
☎ 0131 447 6974 Fax 0131 447 8712
Moorland/parkland course with views over Edinburgh.
18 holes, 6502yds, Par 72, SSS 72, Course record 66.
Club membership 525.
Visitors   advisable to contact by phone.
Societies   may not play at weekends. Must contact in writing.
Green Fees £40 per day; £30 per round.
Cards   VISA
Prof   Douglas Horn
Designer   James Braid/F Hawtree
Facilities   ⊗ ⅼ ♥ ♀ ⚘ 🖢 ⛳ ⌀
Location   3m S of city centre off A702

Hotel   ★★★ 70% Braid Hills Hotel, 134 Braid Rd, EDINBURGH ☎ 0131 447 8888 68 ➡ 🐾

Murrayfield 43 Murrayfield Rd EH12 6EU
☎ 0131 337 3478 Fax 0131 313 0721
Parkland course on the side of Corstorphine Hill, with fine views.
18 holes, 5725yds, Par 70, SSS 69.
Club membership 750.
Visitors   contact in advance, may not play at weekends.
Societies   apply in writing
Green Fees £35 per day; £30 per round.
Prof   J J Fisher
Facilities   ⊗ ⅼ ♥ ♀ ⚘ 🖢 ⛳ ⌀
Location   2m W of city centre off A8

Hotel   ★★★ 73% Posthouse Edinburgh, Corstorphine Rd, EDINBURGH ☎ 0870 400 9026 303 ➡ 🐾

Portobello Stanley St EH15 1JJ
☎ 0131 669 4361 & 557 5457 bookings
Fax 0131 557 5170
Public parkland course, easy walking.
9 holes, 2252yds, Par 32, SSS 32.
Visitors   advanced booking recommended. Contact Edinburgh Leisure.
Societies   contact in advance, telephone 0131 557 5457 or write to Edinburgh Leisure, 23 Waterloo Place EH1 3BH.
Green Fees £4.60 per round before 4pm; £5.10 after 4pm & weekends.
Facilities   ⚘ ⛳ ⌀
Location   3m E of city centre off A1

Hotel   ★★★ 65% Kings Manor, 100 Milton Rd East, EDINBURGH ☎ 0131 669 0444 69 ➡ 🐾

Prestonfield 6 Priestfield Rd North EH16 5HS
☎ 0131 667 9665 Fax 0131 667 9665
Parkland course with beautiful views.
18 holes, 6212yds, Par 70, SSS 70, Course record 62.
Club membership 850.
Visitors   contact secretary in advance. May not play Sat before 10.30am or between 12pm-1.30pm & Sun before 11.30am.
Societies   must contact secretary.
Green Fees £30 per day; £20 per round (£40/£30 weekends & bank holidays).
Prof   John MacFarlane
Designer   James Braid
Facilities   ⊗ ⅲ ⅼ ♥ ♀ ⚘ 🖢 ⛳ 🏌 ⌀
Location   1.5m S of city centre off A68

Hotel   ★★★ 74% Prestonfield House Hotel, Priestfield Rd, EDINBURGH ☎ 0131 668 3346 31rm(30 ➡ 🐾)

Ravelston 24 Ravelston Dykes Rd EH4 5NZ
☎ 0131 315 2486 Fax 0131 315 2486
Parkland course.
9 holes, 5230yds, Par 66, SSS 65, Course record 64.
Club membership 610.
Visitors   must contact in advance but may not play at weekends & bank holidays.
Green Fees £15 per day/round.
Designer   James Braid
Facilities   ⅼ ♥ ⚘
Location   3m W of city centre off A90

Hotel   ★★★ 73% Posthouse Edinburgh, Corstorphine Rd, EDINBURGH ☎ 0870 400 9026 303 ➡ 🐾

Royal Burgess 181 Whitehouse Rd, Barnton EH4 6BY
☎ 0131 339 2075 Fax 0131 339 3712
No mention of golf clubs would be complete without mention of the Royal Burgess, which was instituted in 1735, thus being the oldest golfing society in the world. Its course is a pleasant parkland, and one with very much variety. A club which all those interested in the history of the game should visit.
18 holes, 6111yds, Par 71, SSS 69.
Club membership 620.
Visitors   must contact in advance. Gentlemen only.

Marriott Dalmahoy Hotel

The Championship East Course has hosted many major events including the Solheim Cup, The Scottish Seniors Open Championship and the PGA Championship of Scotland. The greens are large with immaculate putting surfaces and many of the long par 4 holes offer a serious challenge to the golfer. The short holes are well bunkered and the 15th hole in particular, known as the 'Wee Wrecker' will test your nerve and skill.

The shorter West Course offers a different test with small greens requiring accuracy from the player's short game, however, the finishing holes with the Gogar Burn meandering through the fairway creates a tough finale. Training and leisure facilities are extensive with corporate events catered for.

Visitors welcome Mon-Fri, weekend by application. Call in advance to book tee times, subject to availability

Societies telephone or write for details

Green Fees East Course £60 per round (£75 weekends and public holidays); West Course £35 (£45 weekends)

Facilities ⊗ ⋈ ⋤ ⛱ ♀ ♨ 🛍 ⋔ ⋚ ⤵ ⚐ ⚑ Professional (Neal Graham)

Leisure tennis, squash, swimming, sauna, solarium, gymnasium

Location Kirknewton EH27 8EB (7m W of city centre on A71)

Holes/Par/Course record East Course: 18 holes, 6638 yds, Par 72, SSS 72, Course record 62
West Course: 18 holes, 5168 yds, Par 68, SSS 66, Course record 60

WHERE TO STAY AND EAT NEARBY

Hotels
KIRKNEWTON

★★★★ 🌼 🌼 72% Marriott Dalmahoy Hotel & Country Club
☎ 0131 333 1845.
43 ⇆ 🏠 Annexe 172 ⇆ 🏠

EDINBURGH

★★★★ 62% Swallow Royal Scot, 111 Glasgow Rd. ☎ 0131 334 9191.
259 ⇆ 🏠

UPHALL

★★★★ 🌼 67% Houstoun House EH52 6JS. ☎ 01506 853831. 25 ⇆ 🏠

Restaurant
LINLITHGOW
🌼 🌼 Livingston's Restaurant, 52 High St. ☎ 01506 846565

Championship Course

Societies	must contact in advance.
Green Fees	£50 per day; £40 per round Mon-Fri.
Prof	George Yuille
Designer	Tom Morris
Facilities	⊗ ⅙ ⚒ ♀ ⚎ 🖼 🐾 ⬚
Location	5m W of city centre off A90
Hotel	★★★ 63% The Barnton, Queensferry Rd, Barnton, EDINBURGH ☎ 0131 339 1144 50 ⇄ 🐾

Silverknowes Silverknowes, Parkway EH4 5ET
☎ 0131 336 3843 557 5457 adv booking
Fax 0131 557 5170
Public links course on coast overlooking the Firth of Forth
with magnificent views.
18 holes, 6070yds, Par 71, SSS 70.

Visitors	advanced booking recommended in summer, contact Edinburgh Leisure.
Societies	telephone 0131 557 5457 or apply in writing to: Edinburgh Leisure, 23 Waterloo Place, Edinburgh EH1 3BH.
Green Fees	£9.20 before 4pm, £11 after 4pm & weekends.
Facilities	⚐ 🐾 ⬚
Location	4m NW of city centre, easy access from city by-pass
Hotel	★★★ 63% The Barnton, Queensferry Rd, Barnton, EDINBURGH ☎ 0131 339 1144 50 ⇄ 🐾

Swanston 111 Swanston Rd, Fairmilehead EH10 7DS
☎ 0131 445 2239
Hillside course with steep climb at 12th & 13th holes.
18 holes, 5024yds, Par 66, SSS 65, Course record 63.
Club membership 600.

Visitors	contact in advance. Weekends restricted.
Societies	must contact in advance.
Green Fees	not confirmed.
Prof	Ian Taylor
Designer	Herbert More
Facilities	⊗ ⅙ ⚒ ♀ ⚎ 🖼 🐾 🛒 ⬚
Location	4m S of city centre off B701
Hotel	★★★ 70% Braid Hills Hotel, 134 Braid Rd, EDINBURGH ☎ 0131 447 8888 68 ⇄ 🐾

> AA Hotels that have special
> arrangements with golf courses are listed at
> the back of the guide

Torphin Hill Torphin Rd, Colinton EH13 0PG
☎ 0131 441 1100 Fax 0131 441 7166
Beautiful hillside, heathland course, with fine views of
Edinburgh and the Forth Estuary.
18 holes, 4580mtrs, Par 67, SSS 66, Course record 63.
Club membership 550.

Visitors	must contact in advance, limited access Sat & Sun (only after 2pm)
Societies	must contact in advance.
Green Fees	not confirmed.
Prof	Jamie Browne
Facilities	⊗ ⅙ ⚒ ♀ ⚎ 🖼 🐾
Location	5m SW of city centre S of A720
Hotel	★★★ 70% Braid Hills Hotel, 134 Braid Rd, EDINBURGH ☎ 0131 447 8888 68 ⇄ 🐾

Turnhouse 154 Turnhouse Rd EH12 0AD
☎ 0131 339 1014
Hilly, parkland/heathland course, good views over the
Pentland Hills and Forth Valley.
18 holes, 6171yds, Par 69, SSS 70, Course record 62.
Club membership 800.

Visitors	with member only at weekends, and no visitors Wed or Medal days. Must contact professional in advance.
Societies	must contact in writing.
Green Fees	not confirmed.
Prof	John Murray
Designer	J Braid
Facilities	⊗ ⅙ ⚒ ♀ ⚎ 🖼 🐾 ⬚
Location	6m W of city centre N of A8
Hotel	★★★ 63% The Barnton, Queensferry Rd, Barnton, EDINBURGH ☎ 0131 339 1144 50 ⇄ 🐾

EDZELL   Map 15 NO66

Edzell High St DD9 7TF
☎ 01356 647283 (Secretary) Fax 01356 648094
This delightful course is situated in the foothills of the
Scottish Highlands and provides good golf as well as
conveying to everyone who plays there a feeling of
peace and quiet. The village of Edzell is one of the most
picturesque in Scotland.
18 holes, 6348yds, Par 71, SSS 71, Course record 62.
Club membership 750.

Visitors	may not play 4.45-6.15 weekdays & 7.30-10, 12-2 weekends. Not before 2pm on 1st Sat each month. ▶

Societies	must contact secretary at least 14 days in advance.
Green Fees	£32 per day; £22 per round (£42/£28 weekends).
Prof	A J Webster
Designer	Bob Simpson
Facilities	⊗ ⅢⅢ ┗ ♥ ♀ ↄ 🏌 ⌂ ↄ ʳ
Location	S side of village on B966

| **Hotel** | ★★★ 64% Glenesk Hotel, High St, EDZELL ☎ 01356 648319 24 ⇌ ↄ |

ELIE   Map 12 NO40

Golf House Club KY9 1AS
☎ 01333 330301 Fax 01333 330895
One of Scotland's most delightful holiday courses with panoramic views over the Firth of Forth. Some of the holes out towards the rocky coastline are splendid. This is the course which has produced many good professionals, including the immortal James Braid.
18 holes, 6273yds, Par 70, SSS 70, Course record 62.
Club membership 600.

Visitors	advisable to contact in advance, limited availability Sat May-Sep and no visitors Sun May-Sep, ballot in operation for tee times during July and August.
Societies	must contact in advance.
Green Fees	£45 per day; £32 per round (£55/£40 weekends).
Prof	Robin Wilson
Designer	James Braid
Facilities & Leisure	⊗ ⅢⅢ ┗ ♥ ♀ ↄ ⌂ ʳ ↄ ʳ hard tennis courts.
Location	W side of village off A917

| **Hotel** | ★★★ 62% The Golf Hotel, Bank St, ELIE ☎ 01333 330209 22 ⇌ ↄ |

ERISKA   Map 10 NM94

Isle of Eriska PA37 1SD
☎ 01631 720371 Fax 01631 720531
This remote and most beautiful 6-hole course, set around the owners hotel, is gradually being upgraded to a testing 9-hole challenge, complete with stunning views.
6 holes, 1588yds, Par 22.
Club membership 40.

Visitors	contact in advance.
Green Fees	£10 per day.

Cards	💳 💳 🃏
Designer	H Swan
Facilities & Leisure	┗ ♥ ♀ ↄ 🏌 ⌂ ↄ ↄ hard tennis courts, heated indoor swimming pool, sauna, gymnasium.
Location	A828 Connel/Fort William, signposted 4m from North of Benderloch village

| **Hotel** | ★★★★⚑ 78% Isle of Eriska, Eriska, Ledaig, BY OBAN ☎ 01631 720371 17 ⇌ ↄ |

FALKIRK   Map 11 NS88

Falkirk Carmuirs, 136 Stirling Rd, Camelon FK2 7YP
☎ 01324 611061 (club) Fax 01324 639573 (Sec)
Parkland course with trees, gorse and streams.
18 holes, 6230yds, Par 71, SSS 70, Course record 66.
Club membership 800.

Visitors	telephone starter 01324 612219, visiting parties may not play Sat.
Societies	telephone 01324 612219 in advance.
Green Fees	£20 per day; £15 per round (£30/£22.50 Sun).
Cards	💳 💳 🃏 🃏
Designer	James Braid
Facilities	⊗ ⅢⅢ ┗ ♥ ♀ ↄ ⌂ ↄ
Location	1.5m W on A9

| **Hotel** | ★★★★ 70% Inchyra Grange Hotel, Grange Rd, POLMONT ☎ 01324 711911 109 ⇌ ↄ |

FALKLAND   Map 11 NO20

Falkland The Myre KY15 7AA ☎ 01337 857404
A flat, well kept course with excellent greens and views of East Lomond Hill and Falkland Palace.
9 holes, 5216yds, Par 68, SSS 65, Course record 62.
Club membership 300.

Visitors	parties must make prior arrangements, please check availability at weekends.
Societies	must contact in advance.
Green Fees	not confirmed.
Facilities	⊗ ⅢⅢ by prior arrangement ┗ ♥ ♀ ↄ ↄ
Location	N side of town on A912

| **Hotel** | ★★ 67% Lomond Hills Hotel, Parliament Square, FREUCHIE ☎ 01337 857329 & 857498 Fax 01337 858180 25 ⇌ ↄ |

FAULDHOUSE   Map 11 NS96

Greenburn 6 Greenburn Rd EH47 9HG ☎ 01501 770292
Exposed rolling course with sparse tree cover. Water hazards from a pond and a burn.
18 holes, 6045yds, Par 71, SSS 70, Course record 65.
Club membership 900.

Visitors	contact in advance for details.
Societies	by prior arrangement.
Green Fees	not confirmed.
Prof	Malcolm Leighton
Facilities	⊗ ⅢⅢ ┗ ♥ ♀ ↄ ⌂ ↄ
Location	3m SW of Whitburn

| **Hotel** | ★★★ 65% The Hilcroft Hotel, East Main St, WHITBURN ☎ 01501 740818 31 ⇌ ↄ |

FORFAR
Map 15 NO45

Forfar Cunninghill, Arbroath Rd DD8 2RL
☎ 01307 463773 Fax 01307 468495
Moorland course with wooded, undulating fairways and fine views.
18 holes, 6053yds, Par 69, SSS 70, Course record 61.
Club membership 820.

Visitors	may not play before 2.30pm Sat.
Societies	must contact in advance.
Green Fees	£25 per day; £17 per round (£30/£22 weekends & bank holidays).
Prof	Peter McNiven
Designer	James Braid
Facilities	⊗ ℳ ⅃ ⬛ ♀ ⚲ ▥ ⚘
Location	1.5m E of Forfar on A932
Hotel	★★★⚌ 67% Idvies House Hotel, Letham, FORFAR ☎ 01307 818787 11 ⇔ ♞

GIFFORD
Map 12 NT56

Gifford Edinburgh Rd EH41 4JE ☎ 01620 810267
Parkland course, with easy walking.
9 holes, 6243yds, Par 71, SSS 70, Course record 64.
Club membership 600.

Visitors	may not play on the 1st Sun of the month during Apr-Oct. Telephone Starter on 01620 810 591 to book tee times.
Societies	telephone in advance.
Green Fees	£20 per day; £13 per 18 holes; £10 per 9 holes.
Designer	W Wood
Facilities	⬛ ⚲ ⚘
Location	1m SW off B6355
Hotel	★★★ 63% The Johnstounburn House, HUMBIE ☎ 01875 833696 11rm (10 ⇔ ♞) Annexe 9 ⇔ ♞

GIGHA ISLAND
Map 10 NR64

Gigha PA41 7AA
☎ 01583 505287 & 01583 505254 Fax 01583 505244
A 9-hole course with scenic views of the Sound of Gigha and Kintyre. Ideal for the keen or occasional golfer.
9 holes, 5042 yds, Par 66, SSS 65.
Club membership 40.

Visitors	no restrictions.
Societies	telephone for details.
Green Fees	£10 per day/round.
Designer	Members
Facilities	⚲
Location	0.5m N of Druimeonbeg farm shop

GLENROTHES
Map 11 NO20

Glenrothes Golf Course Rd KY6 2LA ☎ 01592 754561
Mature parkland, challenging back nine with burn crossing 4 fairways. Wide fairways offer opportunities for long hitters and birdy chances for those with good short game.
18 holes, 6444yds, Par 71, SSS 71, Course record 67.
Club membership 750.

Visitors	no restrictions except for some times at weekends . Bookings for parties can be made in advance.
Societies	write to secretary.
Green Fees	not confirmed.
Designer	J R Stutt
Facilities	⊗ ℳ ⅃ ⬛ ♀ ⚲
Location	W side of town off B921
Hotel	★★★★⚌ Balbirnie House, Balbirnie Park, MARKINCH ☎ 01592 610066 30 ⇔ ♞

GLENSHEE (SPITTAL OF)
Map 15 NO16

Dalmunzie Dalmunzie Estate PH10 7QG
☎ 01250 885226 Fax 01250 885225
Well maintained Highland course with difficult walking. Testing short course with small but good greens.
9 holes, 2099yds, Par 30, SSS 30.
Club membership 70.

Visitors	restricted Sun 10.30-11.30am.
Societies	advance contact preferred.
Green Fees	not confirmed.
Facilities & Leisure	⊗ ℳ ⅃ ⬛ ♀ ⚲ ▥ ⚷ ⌣ hard tennis courts, fishing.
Location	2m NW of Spittal of Glenshee
Hotel	★★⚌ 69% Dalmunzie House Hotel, SPITTAL OF GLENSHEE ☎ 01250 885224 18rm (16 ⇔ ♞)

GOREBRIDGE
Map 11 NT36

Vogrie Vogrie Estate Country Park EH23 4NU
☎ 01875 821716
A 9-hole municipal course located within a country park. The wide fairways are particularly suited to beginners.
9 holes, 2530yds, Par 33.

Visitors	book by telephone 24 hrs in advance.
Green Fees	not confirmed.
Facilities	⬛ ⚲
Location	Off B6372
Hotel	★★★ 63% The Johnstounburn House, HUMBIE ☎ 01875 833696 11rm (10 ⇔ ♞) Annexe 9 ⇔ ♞

GOUROCK
Map 10 NS27

Gourock Cowal View PA19 1HD
☎ 01475 631001 Fax 01475 631001
Moorland course with hills and dells. Testing 8th hole, par 5. Magnificent views over Firth of Clyde.
18 holes, 6512yds, Par 73, SSS 73, Course record 64.
Club membership 720.

Visitors	must have handicap certificate or letter of introduction. May not play Sat.
Societies	welcome weekdays, must contact in advance.

▶

Muirfield (Honourable Company of Edinburgh Golfers)

Gullane, *East Lothian* ☎ 01620 842123 Fax 01620 842997 Map 12 NT48

e-mail: hceg@btinternet.com

Visitors Tue & Thu only. Must contact in advance and have a handicap certificate.

Societies Tue & Thu with handicap limits (18 gentlemen, 24 ladies). Must be mmbers of recognised golf course. Up to 12 in a group

Green Fees £105 per day, £80 per round

Facilities ⊗ 🍺 ♀ ♨ ☂ ♂

Location Muirfield, Gullane EH31 2EG (NE side of village)

Holes/Par/Course record 18 holes, 6801 yds, Par 70, SSS 73, Course record 63

WHERE TO STAY AND EAT NEARBY

Hotels
ABERLADY

★★66% Kilspindie House, Main St.
☎ 01875 870682. 26 (8 ⌂ 18 ⇆ 🛏)

DIRLETON

★★★68% The Open Arms.
☎ 01620 850241. 10 (6 ⇆ 🛏 1 ⇆ 3 🛏)

GULLANE

★★★ ✿ ✿ ⚏ Greywalls, Muirfield.
☎ 01620 842144. 17 (16 ⇆ 🛏 1 ⇆
Annexe 5 (4 ⇆ 🛏 1 ⇆)

NORTH BERWICK

★★★65% The Marine, Cromwell Rd.
☎ 0870 400 8129. 83 ⇆ 🛏

★59% Nether Abbey, 20 Dirleton Ave.
☎ 01620 892802. 14 (10 ⇆ 🛏 4 🛏)

Restaurant
GULLANE

✿ ✿ ✿ La Potinière, Main St.
☎ 01620 843214.

The course at Muirfield was designed by Old Tom Morris in 1891 and is generally considered to be one of the top ten courses in the world. The club itself has an excellent pedigree, it was founded in 1744, making it just ten years older than the Royal & Ancient but not as old as Royal Blackheath.

Muirfield has staged some outstanding Open Championships, perhaps one of the most memorable was in 1972 when Lee Trevino the defending champion seemed to be losing his grip, until a spectacular shot brought him back to beat Tony Jacklin, who subsequently never won an Open again.

Championship Course

Green Fees not confirmed.
Prof	Gavin Coyle
Designer	J Braid/H Cotton
Facilities	ⓧ ▥ ▙ ♥ ♀ ♨ ⛳ ♂
Location	SW side of town off A770

Hotel ★★★ 58% Manor Park Hotel, LARGS
☎ 01475 520832 10 ⇔ ⋔ Annexe 13 ⇔ ⋔

GREENOCK   Map 10 NS27

Greenock Forsyth St PA16 8RE
☎ 01475 720793 Fax 01475 791912
Testing moorland course with panoramic views of Clyde
Estuary.
18 holes, 5838yds, Par 69, SSS 69.
Club membership 700.
Visitors	may not play Sat. Must contact in advance and have a handicap certificate.
Societies	must telephone in advance.
Green Fees	£28 per day; £25 per 27 holes; £20 per round; £10 per 9 holes (£35/£30/£25/£10 weekends).
Prof	Stewart Russell
Designer	James Braid
Facilities	ⓧ ▥ ▙ ♥ ♀ ♨ ⊞ ♂
Location	SW side of town off A770

Hotel ★★★ 58% Manor Park Hotel, LARGS
☎ 01475 520832 10 ⇔ ⋔ Annexe 13 ⇔ ⋔

Greenock Whinhill Beith Rd PA16 9LN
☎ 01475 724694 evenings & weekends only
Picturesque heathland public course.
18 holes, 5504yds, Par 68, SSS 68, Course record 64.
Club membership 200.
Visitors	may only use club facilities with member.
Green Fees	not confirmed.
Facilities	♀ ♨
Location	1.5m SW off B7054

Hotel ★★★ 58% Manor Park Hotel, LARGS
☎ 01475 520832 10 ⇔ ⋔ Annexe 13 ⇔ ⋔

GULLANE   Map 12 NT48

Gullane West Links Rd EH31 2BB
☎ 01620 842255 Fax 01620 842327
Gullane is a delightful village and one of Scotland's
great golf centres. Gullane club was formed in 1882.
There are three Gullane courses and the No 1 is of
championship standard. It differs from most Scottish
courses in as much as it is of the upland links type and
really quite hilly. The first tee is literally in the village.
The views from the top of the course are magnificent and
stretch far and wide in every direction - in fact, it is said
that 14 counties can be seen from the highest spot.
*Course No 1: 18 holes, 6466yds, Par 71, SSS 72, Course
record 66.*
*Course No 2: 18 holes, 6244yds, Par 71, SSS 70, Course
record 63.*
Course No 3: 18 holes, 5252yds, Par 68, SSS 66.
Club membership 1200.
Visitors	advance booking recommended.
Societies	advance booking advised.

Green Fees	Course no 1: £87 per day; £58 per round (£72 per round weekends). Course no 2: £40 per day; £26 per round (£49/£32 weekends). Course no 3 £25 per day; £16 per round (£32/£21 weekends).
Cards	▬ ▬ ▬ ▬ 🖃
Prof	Jimmy Hume
Designer	Willie Park
Facilities	ⓧ ▥ ▙ ♥ ♀ ♨ ⊞ ⛳ ♙ ♞ ♂ ⏱
Location	At west end of village on A198

Hotel ★★★🏨 Greywalls Hotel, Muirfield,
GULLANE ☎ 01620 842144
17 ⇔ ⋔ Annexe 5 ⇔ ⋔

GULLANE See page 347.

HADDINGTON   Map 12 NT57

Haddington Amisfield Park EH41 4PT
☎ 01620 823627 Fax 01620 826058
Slightly undulating parkland course, within the grounds of a
former country estate.
18 holes, 6317yds, Par 71, SSS 70, Course record 68.
Club membership 650.
Visitors	may not play between 7am-10am & noon-2pm at weekends. Must contact in advance.
Societies	must contact in advance; deposits required.
Green Fees	£26 per day; £18 per round (£32/£23 weekends).
Prof	John Sandilands
Facilities	ⓧ ▥ ▙ ♥ ♀ ♨ ⊞ ♞ ♂
Location	E side off A613

Hotel ★★ 66% Kilspindie House Hotel, Main St,
ABERLADY
☎ 01875 870682 26 ⇔ ⋔

HELENSBURGH   Map 10 NS28

Helensburgh 25 East Abercromby St G84 9HZ
☎ 01436 674173 Fax 01436 671170
Sporting moorland course with superb views of Loch
Lomond and River Clyde.
18 holes, 6104yds, Par 69, SSS 70, Course record 64.
Club membership 880.
Visitors	may not play at weekends.
Societies	weekdays only, must contact in writing.
Green Fees	£35 per day; £25 per round.
Prof	David Fotheringham
Designer	Old Tom Morris
Facilities	ⓧ ▥ by prior arrangement ▙ ♥ ♀ ♨ ⊞ ♂
Location	NE side of town off B832

Hotel ★★★★★ 72% Cameron House Hotel,
BALLOCH ☎ 01389 755565 96 ⇔ ⋔

INNELLAN   Map 10 NS17

Innellan Knockamillie Rd PA23 7SG
☎ 01369 830242 & 702573
Situated above the village of Innellan, this undulating hilltop
course has extensive views of the Firth of Clyde.
9 holes, 4683yds, Par 64, SSS 64, Course record 63.
Club membership 199.

▶

Visitors	welcome but may not play after 5pm on Mondays.
Societies	telephone initially.
Green Fees	not confirmed.
Facilities	🏌 🍴 ♀ 🏌
Location	4m S of Dunoon

Hotel	★★ 68% Royal Marine Hotel, Hunters Quay, DUNOON ☎ 01369 705810 28 ⇔ ♟ Annexe 10 ⇔ ♟

INVERARAY   Map 10 NN00

Inveraray North Cromalt PA32 8XT ☎ 01499 302140
Testing parkland course with beautiful views overlooking Loch Fyne.
9 holes, 5790yds, Par 70, SSS 68, Course record 69.
Club membership 178.

Visitors	no restrictions.
Societies	write or telephone to the secretary.
Green Fees	£10 per day (£15 per day; £10 per round weekends).
Facilities	⛏
Location	1m S of Inveraray

ISLAY, ISLE OF   Map 10 NR34

PORT ELLEN   Map 10 NR34

Machrie Hotel Machrie PA42 7AN
☎ 01496 302310 Fax 01496 302404
Championship links course opened in 1891, where golf's first £100 Open Championship was played in 1901. Fine turf and many holes. Par 4.
18 holes, 6226yds, Par 71, SSS 71, Course record 65.
Club membership 340.

Visitors	no restrictions.
Societies	apply in writing or telephone.
Green Fees	not confirmed.
Cards	▭ ▬ ▭ 🗎
Designer	W Campbell
Facilities	⊗ ⅲ 🏌 🍴 ♀ ⛏ 🍴 🏌 🛒 ♛ 🏌
& Leisure	fishing, snooker, pool tables, carpet bowls.
Location	4m N off A846

Hotel	★★ 60% Lochside Hotel, 19 Shore St, BOWMORE ☎ 01496 810244 8 ⇔ ♟

KENMORE   Map 14 NN74

Kenmore PH15 2HN ☎ 01887 830226 Fax 01887 830211
Testing course in mildly undulating natural terrain. Beautiful views in tranquil setting by Loch Tay.
9 holes, 6052yds, Par 70, SSS 69, Course record 69.
Club membership 200.

Visitors	advance booking advisable.
Societies	telephone in advance.
Green Fees	£12 per 18 holes; £8 per 9 holes (£13/£9 weekends).
Cards	▭ ▭
Designer	Robin Menzies
Facilities	⊗ ⅲ 🏌 🍴 ♀ ⛏ 🍴 🏌 🛒 ♛ 🏌
& Leisure	fishing.
Location	On A827, beside Kenmore Bridge

Taymouth Castle Taymouth Castle Estate PH15 2NT
☎ 01887 830228 Fax 01887 830830
Parkland course set amidst beautiful mountain and loch scenery. Easy walking. Fishing.
18 holes, 6066yds, Par 69, SSS 69, Course record 62.
Club membership 250.

Visitors	parties must book in advance to avoid busy times.
Societies	should contact in advance.
Green Fees	£30 per day; £20 per round (£38/£24 weekends).
Prof	Alex Marshall
Designer	James Braid
Facilities	⊗ ⅲ 🏌 🍴 ♀ ⛏ 🍴 🏌 🛒 ♛ 🏌
& Leisure	hard tennis courts, fishing.
Location	1m E on A827, 5m W of Aberfeldy

KILLIN   Map 11 NN53

Killin FK21 8TX ☎ 01567 820312
Parkland course with good views. Glorious setting.
9 holes, 2600yds, Par 66, SSS 65, Course record 61.
Club membership 250.

Visitors	may not play competition days, parties must book in advance.
Societies	previous record of courses visited required. Apply in writing or telephone in advance.
Green Fees	not confirmed.
Designer	John Duncan
Facilities	⊗ ⅲ 🏌 🍴 ♀ ⛏ 🍴 🏌 🛒 ♛ 🏌
Location	1m N on A827

Hotel	★★★ 65% Dall Lodge Country House Hotel, Main St, KILLIN ☎ 01567 820217 10 ⇔ ♟

KILMACOLM   Map 10 NS36

Kilmacolm Porterfield Rd PA13 4PD
☎ 01505 872139 Fax 01505 874007
Moorland course, easy walking, fine views. Testing 7th, 13th and 14th holes.
18 holes, 5961yds, Par 69, SSS 69, Course record 64.
Club membership 850.

Visitors	must contact in advance, visitors welcome Tuesday, Wednesday & Thursday.
Societies	apply in writing.
Green Fees	not confirmed.
Prof	Iain Nicholson
Designer	Willie Campbell
Facilities	⊗ ⅲ 🏌 🍴 ♀ ⛏ 🍴 🛒 ♛ 🏌
Location	SE side of town off A761

Hotel	★★★★♨ 67% Gleddoch House Hotel, LANGBANK ☎ 01475 540711 39 ⇔ ♟

KINCARDINE   Map 11 NS98

Tulliallan Alloa Rd FK10 4BB
☎ 01259 730798 Fax 01259 730798
Pleasant parkland course with easily negotiable slopes, a meandering burn and scenic views.
18 holes, 5965yds, Par 69, SSS 69, Course record 63.
Club membership 600.

Visitors	restricted at weekends, must contact professional shop.
Societies	may not play on Sat; must contact in advance.

▶

Green Fees £27.50 per day, £15 per round (£35/£20 weekends).
Prof Steven Kelly
Facilities ⊗ ∭ ⅃ ♨ ☕ ☂ ⚐ ☞ ♂
Location 1m NW on A977

Hotel ★★★ 65% Dall Lodge Country House Hotel, Main St, KILLIN ☎ 01567 820217 10 ⇆ ⋔

KINGHORN
Map 11 NT28

Kinghorn Macduff Cres KY3 9RE ☎ 01592 890345
Municipal course, 300 ft above sea level with views over Firth of Forth and North Sea. Undulating and quite testing. Facilities shared by Kinghorn Ladies.
18 holes, 5269yds, Par 65, SSS 67, Course record 62.
Club membership 190.
Visitors may not play between 7.30am-10.30am & 12pm-3pm Sat.
Societies must contact in writing.
Green Fees £12 (£15 weekends).
Facilities ♨
Location S side of town on A921

Hotel ★★★ 65% Dean Park Hotel, Chapel Level, KIRKCALDY ☎ 01592 261635 29 ⇆ ⋔ Annexe 12 ⇆ ⋔

KINROSS
Map 11 N010

Green Hotel 2 The Muirs KY13 8AS
☎ 01577 863407 Fax 01577 863180
Two interesting and picturesque parkland courses, with easy walking.
Red Course: 18 holes, 6256yds, Par 73, SSS 71.
Blue Course: 18 holes, 6438yds, Par 71, SSS 72.
Club membership 600.
Visitors must contact in advance.
Societies must contact in advance.
Green Fees £27 per day, £17 per round (£37/27 weekends).
Prof Stuart Geraghty
Designer Sir David Montgomery
Facilities ⊗ ∭ ⅃ ♨ ☕ ♀ ☂ ⚐ ☞ ⊞ ♂ ✿ ♂
& Leisure hard tennis courts, heated indoor swimming pool, squash, fishing, sauna, solarium, small fitness area in hotel.
Location NE side of town on B996

Hotel ★★★ 73% Green Hotel, 2 The Muirs, KINROSS ☎ 01577 863467 47 ⇆ ⋔

KIRKCALDY
Map 11 NT29

Dunnikier Park Dunnikier Way KY1 3LP
☎ 01592 261599
Parkland, rolling fairways, not heavily bunkered, views of Firth of Forth.
18 holes, 6036metres, Par 72, SSS 72, Course record 65.
Club membership 720.
Visitors visitors must contact course starter in person.
Societies apply in writing.
Green Fees £20 per day; £14 per round (£23/£16 weekends).
Prof Gregor Whyte
Designer R Stutt
Facilities ⊗ ∭ ⅃ ♨ ☕ ♀ ☂ ⚐ ✿ ♂
Location 2m N on B981

Hotel ★★★ 65% Dean Park Hotel, Chapel Level, KIRKCALDY ☎ 01592 261635 29 ⇆ ⋔ Annexe 12 ⇆ ⋔

Kirkcaldy Balwearie Rd KY2 5LT
☎ 01592 205240 & 203258 (Pro Shop) Fax 01592 205240
Challenging parkland course in rural setting, with beautiful views. On-course watering ensures good conditions all season.
18 holes, 6004yds, Par 71, SSS 69, Course record 65.
Club membership 822.
Visitors limited play Sat. Advised to contact pro-shop 01592 203258.
Societies apply in writing/telephone.
Green Fees not confirmed.
Prof Anthony Caira
Designer Tom Morris
Facilities ⊗ ∭ ⅃ ♨ ☕ ♀ ☂ ⚐ ☞ ✿ ⊞ ♂
Location SW side of town off A910

Hotel ★★★ 65% Dean Park Hotel, Chapel Level, KIRKCALDY ☎ 01592 261635 29 ⇆ ⋔ Annexe 12 ⇆ ⋔

KIRRIEMUIR
Map 15 NO35

Kirriemuir Shielhill Rd, Northmuir DD8 4LN
☎ 01575 573317 Fax 01575 573317
Parkland and heathland course set at the foot of the Angus glens, with good view.
18 holes, 5553yds, Par 68, SSS 67, Course record 62.
Club membership 750.

Visitors	must play with member at weekends.
Societies	must apply in advance, may not play weekends.
Green Fees	not confirmed.
Prof	Karyn Dallas
Designer	James Braid
Facilities	⊗ ⫫ 🛄 🏌 ♀ 🛆 🏠 🍴 ⚷
Location	1m N off B955

Hotel ★★★▲▲ 67% Idvies House Hotel, Letham, FORFAR ☎ 01307 818787 11 ⇆ 🐾

LADYBANK   Map 11 NO30

Ladybank Annsmuir KY15 7RA
☎ 01337 830814 Fax 01337 831505
Picturesque parkland/heathland course, popular with visitors.
Qualifying course for the British Open.
18 holes, 6580yds, Par 71, SSS 72, Course record 63.
Club membership 900.

Visitors	advance booking essential.
Societies	must telephone or write in advance.
Green Fees	£40 per day; £30 per round (£35 per round weekends).
Cards	🖃 🖃 🖃 🖃
Prof	Martin Gray
Designer	Tom Morris
Facilities	⊗ ⫫ 🛄 🏌 ♀ 🛆 🍴 🐦 🛒 ⚷
Location	N side of village off B9129

Hotel ★★★ 65% Fernie Castle, Letham, CUPAR ☎ 01337 810381 15 ⇆ 🐾

LARBERT   Map 11 NS88

Falkirk Tryst 86 Burnhead Rd FK5 4BD
☎ 01324 562054 & 562415
Links-type course, fairly level with trees and broom, well-bunkered. Winds can affect play.
18 holes, 6053yds, Par 70, SSS 69, Course record 62.
Club membership 850.

Visitors	must contact in advance no play at weekends.
Societies	visitors welcome Mon-Fri must book or telephone.
Green Fees	not confirmed.
Prof	Steven Dunsmore
Facilities	⊗ ⫫ 🛄 🏌 ♀ 🛆 🏠 🍴 ⚷
Location	On A88 between A9 and A905

Hotel ★★★★ 70% Inchyra Grange Hotel, Grange Rd, POLMONT ☎ 01324 711911 109 ⇆ 🐾

Glenbervie Clubhouse Stirling Rd FK5 4SJ
☎ 01324 562605 Fax 01324 551054
Parkland course with good views.
18 holes, 6423yds, Par 71, SSS 70, Course record 64.
Club membership 600.

Visitors	Mon to Fri till 4pm, parties Tues & Thurs only
Societies	Tue & Thu only. Apply in writing.
Green Fees	not confirmed.
Cards	🖃 🖃
Prof	John Chillas
Designer	James Braid
Facilities	⊗ 🛄 🏌 ♀ 🛆 🏠 ⚷
Location	2m NW on A9

Hotel ★★★★ 70% Inchyra Grange Hotel, Grange Rd, POLMONT ☎ 01324 711911 109 ⇆ 🐾

LESLIE   Map 11 NO20

Leslie Balsillie Laws KY6 3EZ ☎ 01592 620040
Challenging parkland course.
9 holes, 4686yds, Par 63, SSS 64, Course record 63.
Club membership 230.

Visitors	contact secretary in writing.
Societies	letter to the Secretary.
Green Fees	not confirmed.
Designer	Tom Morris
Facilities	🏌 ♀ 🛆
Location	N side of town off A911

Hotel ★★★ 62% Balgeddie House Hotel, Balgeddie Way, GLENROTHES ☎ 01592 742511 18 ⇆ 🐾

LEUCHARS   Map 12 NO42

Drumoig Hotel & Golf Course Drumoig KY16 0BE
☎ 01382 541800 Fax 01382 542211
A developing but challenging young championship course.
Set in a parkland environment, the course is links like in
places. Features include Whinstone Quarries and views over
to St Andrews and Carnoustie. Water features are
demanding, especially on the 9th where the fairway runs
between Drumoigs two mini lochs.
18 holes, 7006yds, Par 72, SSS 73.
Club membership 200.

Visitors	advisable to telephone in advance.
Societies	telephone in advance.
Green Fees	not confirmed.
Cards	🖃 🖃 🖃 🖃 🖃
Facilities	⊗ ⫫ 🛄 🏌 ♀ 🛆 🍴 🐾 🛒 ⚷
& Leisure	Scottish National Golf Centre in grounds.
Location	On the A914 between St Andrews and Dundee

Hotel ★★★ 69% Drumoig Golf Hotel, Drumoig, LEUCHARS ☎ 01382 541800 Annexe 24 ⇆ 🐾

St Michaels KY16 0DX
☎ 01334 839365 & 838666 Fax 01334 838666
Parkland course with open views over Fife and Tayside. The
undulating course weaves its way through tree plantations.
The short Par 4 17th, parallel to the railway and over a pond
to a stepped green, poses an interesting challenge.
18 holes, 5802yds, Par 70, SSS 68, Course record 68.
Club membership 550.

Visitors	may not play on Sun before noon.
Societies	must apply in writing, limited weekends
Green Fees	£25 per day; £18 per round (£27.50/£20 weekends).
Facilities	⊗ ⫫ by prior arrangement 🛄 🏌 ♀ 🛆 ⚷
Location	NW side of village on A919

Hotel ★★ 69% Eden House Hotel, 2 Pitscottie Rd, CUPAR ☎ 01334 652510 9 ⇆ 🐾 Annexe 2 ⇆ 🐾

LEVEN   Map 11 NO30

Leven Links The Promenade KY8 4HS
☎ 01333 428859 & 421390 Fax 01333 428859
Leven has the classic ingredients which make up a golf
links in Scotland; undulating fairways with hills and ▶

hallows, out of bounds and a 'burn' or stream. A top
class championship links course used for British Open
final qualifying stages, it has fine views over Largo Bay.
18 holes, 6436yds, Par 71, SSS 70, Course record 62.
Club membership 1000.

Visitors	contact in advance. Limited availability Fri pm & Sat, contact for these times no more than 5 days in advance.
Societies	apply in advance.
Green Fees	£40 per day; £28 per round (£40/£30 weekends).
Designer	Tom Morris
Facilities	⚑🏠🍴⚑
Hotel	★★★ 58% Caledonian Hotel, 81 High St, LEVEN ☎ 01333 424101 24 ⇌ ⟨⟩

Scoonie North Links KY8 4SP ☎ 01333 423437(Starter) & 307007 (Club)
A pleasant inland links course suitable for all ages.
18 holes, 4979mtrs, Par 67, SSS 65, Course record 63.
Club membership 200.

Visitors	no restrictions.
Societies	apply in writing.
Green Fees	Summer: £17 per day; £11 per round (£21/£15 weekends). Winter: £12 per day; £7 per round (£14/£8 weekends).
Facilities	⊗〣🏠🍴⚑⚑
Hotel	★★★ 58% Caledonian Hotel, 81 High St, LEVEN ☎ 01333 424101 24 ⇌ ⟨⟩

LINLITHGOW   Map 11 NS97

Linlithgow Braehead EH49 6QF
☎ 01506 842585 (Secretary) & 844356 (Pro)
Fax 01506 842764
Slightly hilly parkland course in beautiful setting.
18 holes, 5800yds, Par 70, SSS 68, Course record 65.
Club membership 450.

Visitors	may not play Sat. Must book in advance Sun.
Societies	must contact in writing.
Green Fees	not confirmed.
Prof	Steven Rosie
Designer	R Simpson of Carnoustie
Facilities	⊗〣🏠🍴⚑⚑🏠⚑
Location	1m S off Bathgate Road off A803

Hotel	★★★★ 70% Inchyra Grange Hotel, Grange Rd, POLMONT ☎ 01324 711911 109 ⇌ ⟨⟩

West Lothian Airngath Hill EH49 7RH
☎ 01506 826030 Fax 01506 826030
Hilly parkland course with superb views of River Forth.
18 holes, 6228yds, Par 71, SSS 71.
Club membership 800.

Visitors	weekends by arrangement. Advisable to contact in high season.
Societies	apply in writing.
Green Fees	not confirmed.
Cards	▭▭
Prof	Colin Gillies
Designer	Fraser Middleton
Facilities	⊗🏠🍴⚑⚑🏠⚑
Location	1m S off A706

Hotel	★★★★ 70% Inchyra Grange Hotel, Grange Rd, POLMONT ☎ 01324 711911 109 ⇌ ⟨⟩

LIVINGSTON   Map 11 NT06

Deer Park Golf & Country Club Golfcourse Rd EH54 9EG
☎ 01506 431037 Fax 01506 435608
Long testing course, fairly flat, championship standard.
18 holes, 6688yds, Par 72, SSS 72, Course record 65.
Club membership 650.

Visitors	proper golfing attire to be worn, must book in advance, Sun after 10am.
Societies	telephone or write
Green Fees	£36 per day; £24 per round (£48/£36 weekends).
Cards	▭▭▭▭▭
Prof	Brian Dunbar
Designer	Alliss/Thomas
Facilities	⊗〣🏠🍴⚑⚑🏠⚑⚑⚑
& Leisure	heated indoor swimming pool, squash, sauna, solarium, gymnasium.
Location	N side of town off A809

Hotel	★★★ 67% Cairn Hotel, Blackburn Rd, BATHGATE ☎ 01506 633366 61 ⇌ ⟨⟩

Pumpherston Drumshoreland Rd, Pumpherston EH53 0LH
☎ 01506 432869
Undulating parkland course with testing 6th hole (par 4), and
view of Pentland Hills.
9 holes, 4950yds, Par 66, SSS 64, Course record 64.
Club membership 440.

Visitors	must be accompanied by a member.
Societies	apply in writing to the secretary.
Green Fees	not confirmed.
Facilities	⊗🏠🍴⚑⚑
Location	1m E of Livingston between A71 & A89

Hotel	★★★ 67% Cairn Hotel, Blackburn Rd, BATHGATE ☎ 01506 633366 61 ⇌ ⟨⟩

LOCHGELLY   Map 11 NT19

Lochgelly Cartmore Rd KY5 9PB ☎ 01592 780174
Parkland course with easy walking and often windy.
18 holes, 5491yds, Par 68, SSS 67, Course record 63.
Club membership 650.

Visitors	no restrictions, parties must book in advance.
Societies	must apply in writing.
Green Fees	not confirmed.
Prof	Martin Goldie
Designer	Ian Marchbanks
Facilities	⊗〣🏠⚑⚑🏠
Location	W side of town off A910

Hotel	★★★ 65% Dean Park Hotel, Chapel Level, KIRKCALDY ☎ 01592 261635 29 ⇌ ⟨⟩ Annexe 12 ⇌ ⟨⟩

Lochore Meadows Lochore Meadows Country Park,
Crosshill, Lochore KY5 8BA
☎ 01592 414300 Fax 01592 414345
Lochside course with natural stream running through, and
woodland nearby. Country park offers many leisure facilities.
9 holes, 5554yds, Par 72, SSS 71.
Club membership 160.

Visitors	no restrictions.
Societies	must contact in advance.
Green Fees	not confirmed.

▶

Facilities
& Leisure outdoor swimming pool, fishing, horse riding, water sports centre.
Location 2m N off B920

Hotel ★★★ 73% Green Hotel, 2 The Muirs, KINROSS ☎ 01577 863467 47 ⇄ ♖

LOCHGILPHEAD   Map 10 NR88

Lochgilphead Blarbuie Rd PA31 8LE ☎ 01546 602340
A varied course with short but interesting holes. Some elevated greens and tees and some tight fairways.
9 holes, 2242yds, Par 64, SSS 63, Course record 54.
Club membership 250.
Visitors restricted during weekend club competitions.
Societies apply in advance, restricted wekends.
Green Fees not confirmed.
Designer Dr I McCamond
Facilities ⬛️♿️♨️⛳️♂️
Location Adjacent to the hospital. Signposted from the village.

Hotel ★★ 62% The Stag Hotel, Argyll St, LOCHGILPHEAD ☎ 01546 602496 17 ⇄ ♖

LONGNIDDRY   Map 12 NT47

Longniddry Links Rd EH32 0NL
☎ 01875 852141 & 01875 852228 Fax 01875 853371
Undulating seaside links and partial parkland course. One of the numerous courses which stretch east from Edinburgh right to Dunbar. The inward half is more open than the wooded outward half, but can be difficult in prevailing west wind. No par 5s.
18 holes, 6219yds, Par 68, SSS 70, Course record 63.
Club membership 1140.
Visitors may book tee times up to 7 days in advance, welcome most times except during competitions
Societies Mon-Thu, apply in writing, handicap certificate required.
Green Fees not confirmed.
Cards 🗎🗎🗎
Prof John Gray
Designer H S Colt
Facilities ⊗️♨️♿️⛳️♂️🎾⛳️
Location N side of village off A198

Hotel ★★ 66% Kilspindie House Hotel, Main St, ABERLADY ☎ 01875 870682 26 ⇄ ♖

LUNDIN LINKS   Map 12 NO40

Lundin Golf Rd KY8 6BA
☎ 01333 320202 Fax 01333 329743
The Leven Links and the course of the Lundin Club adjoin each other. The course is part seaside and part inland. The holes are excellent but those which can be described as seaside holes have a very different nature from the inland style ones. The par 3 14th looks seawards across the Firth of Forth towards Edinburgh and the old railway line defines out of bounds at several holes. A number of burns snake across the fairways.
18 holes, 6394yds, Par 71, SSS 71, Course record 63.
Club membership 820.

Visitors visitors welcome weekdays 9-3.30 (3pm Fridays) and Sat after 2.30pm, no vistors Sun. Book well in advance.
Societies book well in advance by telephoning Secretary (mornings).
Green Fees not confirmed.
Cards 🗎🗎
Prof David Webster
Designer James Braid
Facilities ⊗️♨️♿️⛳️♂️🎾⛳️
Location W side of village off A915

Hotel ★★★ 73% Old Manor Hotel, Leven Rd, LUNDIN LINKS ☎ 01333 320368 24 ⇄ ♖

Lundin Ladies Woodielea Rd KY8 6AR ☎ 01333 320832
Short, lowland course with Roman stones on the second fairway, and coastal views.
9 holes, 2365yds, Par 68, SSS 67, Course record 67.
Club membership 350.
Visitors contact in advance. Competition days Wed and some weekends.
Societies telephone secretary.
Green Fees not confirmed.
Designer James Braid
Facilities ⬛️♿️⛳️
Location W side of village off A915

Hotel ★★★ 73% Old Manor Hotel, Leven Rd, LUNDIN LINKS ☎ 01333 320368 24 ⇄ ♖

LUSS   Map 10 NS39

Loch Lomond Rossdhu House G83 8NT
☎ 01436 655555 Fax 01436 655500
This exclusive club is strictly members only and getting to play here is notoriously difficult. Nick Faldo called it the finest new course in Europe and others have given it similar accolades. It was designed by two Americans, Jay Morrish and Tom Weiskopf and was founded in 1993. There is a putting green, practice area and driving range. The clubhouse used to be the home of the chiefs of Clan Colquhoun. We are told that it boasts a Chinese Drawing Room with portraits in oil and beautiful ceilings. There are conference facilities as well as a gym and private fishing.
18 holes, 7060yds, Par 71, Course record 62.
Visitors strictly members only.
no visitors strictly private. ▶

Green Fees	not confirmed.
Prof	Colin Campbell
Designer	Tom Weiskopf
Facilities	⛳ 🏌 ⌘ ♦ ⌜
& Leisure	fishing, gymnasium.
Location	Off A82 at Luss
Hotel	★★★★★ 72% Cameron House Hotel, BALLOCH ☎ 01389 755565 96 ⇌ 🐾

MACHRIHANISH   Map 10 NR62

Machrihanish PA28 6PT ☎ 01586 810213
Magnificent seaside links of championship status. The
1st hole is the famous drive across the Atlantic. Sandy
soil allows for play all year round. Large greens, easy
walking, windy. Fishing.
18 holes, 6228yds, Par 70, SSS 71.
Club membership 1035.

Visitors	no restrictions.
Societies	apply in writing.
Green Fees	not confirmed.
Cards	🟦 🟥 🟩 🟨
Prof	Ken Campbell
Designer	Tom Morris
Facilities	⊗ 🏌 ⌘ 💺 ♀ ⌘ ♦
Location	5m W of Campbeltown on B843
Hotel	★★ 67% Seafield Hotel, Kilkerran Rd, CAMPBELTOWN ☎ 01586 554385 3 ⇌ 🐾 Annexe 6 🐾

MARKINCH   Map 11 NO20

Balbirnie Park Balbirnie Park KY7 6NR
☎ 01592 612095 & 752006 (tee times) Fax 01592 612383
A fine example of the best in traditional parkland design,
with natural contours the inspiration behind the layout.
18 holes, 6214yds, Par 71, SSS 70, Course record 62.
Club membership 900.

Visitors	must contact in advance. Numbers restricted weekends and visitors must play from yellow tees, smart but casual dress code.
Societies	booking forms sent out on request by asst secretary.
Green Fees	£33 per day; £25 per round (£40/£30 weekends).
Cards	🟦 🟥 🟩 🟨
Prof	Craig Donnelly
Facilities	⊗ 🏌 ⌘ 💺 ♀ ⌘ 🏠 ⚑ 🛒 ⚘ ⚒ ♦
Location	2m E of Glenrothes

Hotel	★★★★🏌 Balbirnie House, Balbirnie Park, MARKINCH ☎ 01592 610066 30 ⇌ 🐾

MILNATHORT   Map 11 NO10

Milnathort South St KY13 9XA ☎ 01577 864069
Undulating inland course with lush fairways and excellent
greens for most of the year. Strategically placed copses of
trees require accurate tee shots. Different tees and greens for
some holes will make for more interesting play.
9 holes, 5969yds, Par 71, SSS 69, Course record 65.
Club membership 600.

Visitors	no restrictions.
Societies	advisable to book in advance.
Green Fees	£18 per day; £12 per round (£20/£14 weekends).
Facilities	⊗ 🏌 by prior arrangement 💺 💺 ♀ ⌘
& Leisure	9 hole putting green.
Location	S side of town on A922
Hotel	★★ 65% The Glenfarg Hotel & Restaurant, Main St, GLENFARG ☎ 01577 830241 16rm (15 ⇌ 🐾)

MONIFIETH   Map 12 NO43

Monifieth Princes St DD5 4AW
☎ 01382 532767 (Medal) & 532967 (Ashludie) Fax 01 382 535553
The chief of the two courses at Monifieth is the Medal
Course. It has been one of the qualifying venues for the
Open Championship on more than one occasion. A
seaside links, but divided from the sand dunes by a
railway which provides the principal hazard for the first
few holes. The 10th hole is outstanding, the 17th is
excellent and there is a delightful finishing hole. The
other course here is the Ashludie, and both are played
over by a number of clubs who share the links.
Medal Course: 18 holes, 6655yds, Par 71, SSS 72,
Course record 63.
Ashludie Course: 18 holes, 5123yds, Par 68, SSS 66.
Club membership 1750.

Visitors	must contact in advance. Restricted to after 2pm Sat, 10am Sun & after 9.30pm Mon-Fri.
Societies	must contact in advance by telephone or writing to Medal Starter's Box, Princes St, Monifieth.
Green Fees	Medal: £30 per round; (£36 weekends). Ashludie: £24 per day; £15 per round (£16 per round weekends).
Prof	Ian McLeod
Facilities	⊗ 🏌 by prior arrangement 💺 💺 ♀ ⌘ 🏠 ⚑ ♦
Location	NE side of town on A930
Hotel	★★ 67% Carlogie House Hotel, Carlogie Rd, CARNOUSTIE ☎ 01241 853185 12 ⇌ 🐾 Annexe 4 🐾

AA Hotels that have special
arrangements with golf courses are listed at
the back of the guide

MONTROSE
Map 15 NO75

Montrose Links Trust Traill Dr DD10 8SW
☎ 01674 672932 Fax 01674 671800
The links at Montrose like many others in Scotland are on commonland and are shared by three clubs. The Medal course at Montrose - the fifth oldest in the world - is typical of Scottish seaside links, with narrow, undulating fairways and problems from the first hole to the last. The Broomfield course is flatter and easier.
Medal Course: 18 holes, 6495yds, Par 71, SSS 72, Course record 63.
Broomfield Course: 18 holes, 4800yds, Par 66, SSS 63.
Club membership 1300.

Visitors	may not play on the Medal Course on Sat before 2.30pm & before 10am on Sun. Must have a handicap certificate for Medal Course. Contact in advance. No restrictions on Broomfield Course.
Societies	must contact secretary in advance.
Green Fees	Medal: £38 per day; £28 per round (£48/£32 weekends). Broomfield: £12 per round.
Cards	〰️ 〰️ 〰️ 🉐
Prof	Kevin Stables
Designer	W Park/Tom Morris
Facilities	⊗ ⦀ ⓛ ⛴ ♀ ⏚ 🛄 ⌁
Location	NE side of town off A92

Hotel ★★★ 65% Park Hotel, 61 John St, MONTROSE ☎ 01674 673415 59rm(53 ⇥ ℝ)

Additional hotel ★★★ 67% Links Hotel, Mid Links, MONTROSE ☎ 01674 671000 Fax 01674 672698 25 ⇥ ℝ

Two links courses: MEDAL COURSE (Par 71, SSS72)
BROOMFIELD COURSE (Par 66, SSS 63)
AN INVITATION TO COME AND PLAY OUR HISTORIC LINKS WHICH WAS A FINAL QUALIFYING COURSE FOR THE OPEN IN 1999.
RANKED FIFTH OLDEST IN THE WORLD
VISITORS VERY WELCOME
Individual Round and Day Tickets Available on Both Courses
All Visitors and Parties Very Welcome.
Special packages available including catering and in conjunction with local hotels
Enquiries to: **Mrs M Stewart, Secretary, Montrose Links Trust, Traill Drive, Montrose, Angus DD10 8SW.**
 Tel: 01674 672932
Fax: 01674 671800

MUCKHART
Map 11 NO00

Muckhart FK14 7JH
☎ 01259 781423 Fax 01259 781544
Scenic heathland/downland course.
Muckhart Course: 18 holes, 6034yds, Par 71, SSS 70, Course record 65.
Naemoor Course: 9 holes, 3234yds, Par 35.
Club membership 750.

Visitors	telephone to book - 01259 781423 or professional 01259 781493.
Societies	booking by prior arrangement.
Green Fees	£25 per day; £23 per 27 holes; £17 per round (£35/£32/£25 weekends).
Prof	Keith Salmoni
Facilities	⊗ ⦀ ⓛ ⛴ ♀ ⏚ 🛄 ⌁
Location	SW of village off A91

Hotel ★★★ 66% Gartwhinzean Hotel, POWMILL ☎ 01577 840595 23 ⇥ ℝ

MULL, ISLE OF
Map 10 NM73

CRAIGNURE
Map 10 NM73

Craignure Scallastle PA65 6PB
☎ 01680 812487 & 812416 Fax 01680 300402
A natural links course designed round the estuary of the Scallastle Burn that flows into the Sound of Mull. Completely re designed in 1978/9. Continual improvements such as 5 new tees in 1998 have provided 18 teeing areas for the 9 hole layout.
9 holes, 5233yds, Par 69, SSS 66, Course record 72.
Club membership 100.

Visitors	may not play on competition days, contact for fixture list.
Societies	write to the secretary 10 days in advance.
Green Fees	£11 per day.
Facilities	⏚ ⌁ ⌁
Location	1.5m N of Craignure A849

Hotel ★★★ 73% Western Isles Hotel, TOBERMORY ☎ 01688 302012 26 ⇥ ℝ

TOBERMORY
Map 13 NM55

Tobermory PA75 6PG
☎ 01688 302338 Fax 01688 302140
A beautifully maintained hilltop course with superb views over the Sound of Mull. Testing 7th hole (par 3). Often described as the best 9 hole course in Scotland.
9 holes, 4890yds, Par 64, SSS 64, Course record 65.
Club membership 150.

Visitors	no restrictions except competition days.
Societies	preferable to contact in advance.
Green Fees	£13 per day.
Designer	David Adams
Facilities	⛴ ♀ ⏚ ⌁
Location	0.5m N off A848

Hotel ★★★ 73% Western Isles Hotel, TOBERMORY ☎ 01688 302012 26 ⇥ ℝ

MUSSELBURGH   Map 11 NT37

Musselburgh Monktonhall EH21 6SA ☎ 0131 665 2005
Testing parkland course with natural hazards including trees
and a burn, easy walking.
18 holes, 6614yds, Par 71, SSS 73, Course record 65.
Club membership 1000.
Visitors   must contact in advance.
Societies   must contact in advance.
Green Fees £25 per day; £18 per round (£30/£22 weekends).
Prof   Fraser Mann
Designer   James Braid
Facilities   ⊗ 𝔪 ⅃ 🍴 ♀ 🏌 �ⓣ ⚲ 🛆 ∢
Location   1m S on B6415

Hotel   ★★ 64% Iona Hotel, Strathearn Place,
                    EDINBURGH
                    ☎ 0131 447 6264 & 0131 447 5050
                    Fax 0131 452 8574 17 ⇄ ⌂

Musselburgh Links, The Old Golf Course 10 Balcarres
Rd, Millhill EH21 7SD
☎ 0131 665 5438 (Starter) Fax 0131 665 5438
This course is steeped in the history and tradition of golf.
Mary Queen of Scots reputedly played this 9 hole links
course in 1567, but documentary evidence dates back to
1672.
9 holes, 2808yds, Par 34, SSS 34.
Visitors   must book in advance
Societies   must contact in advance.
Green Fees £16 per 18 holes; £8 per 9 holes.
Facilities   ♀ 🛆 ∢
Location   1m E of town off A1

Hotel   ★★ 64% Iona Hotel, Strathearn Place,
                    EDINBURGH
                    ☎ 0131 447 6264 & 0131 447 5050
                    Fax 0131 452 8574 17 ⇄ ⌂

MUTHILL   Map 11 NN81

Muthill Peat Rd PH5 2DA
☎ 01764 681523 Fax 01764 681557
Parkland course with fine views. Not too hilly, narrow
fairways and small well bunkered greens.
9 holes, 4700yds, Par 66, SSS 63, Course record 61.
Club membership 500.
Visitors   no restrictions.
Societies   book in advance.
Green Fees £15 per day; £13 per 18 holes; £10 per 9 holes
                    (£16 per round weekends).
Designer   Members
Facilities   ⊗ ⅃ ♀ 🛆 🍴 🏌 ∢
Location   W side of village off A822

Hotel   ★★ 64% Locke's Acre Hotel, 7 Comrie Rd,
                    CRIEFF ☎ 01764 652526 7rm (4 ⌂)

NORTH BERWICK   Map 12 NT58

Glen East Links, Tantallon Ter EH39 4LE
☎ 01620 892726 Fax 01620 895447
An interesting course with a good variety of holes. The views
of the town, the Firth of Forth and the Bass Rock are
breathtaking.
18 holes, 6043yds, Par 69, SSS 69, Course record 64.
Club membership 650.

Visitors   booking advisable.
Societies   advance booking recommended.
Green Fees not confirmed.
Designer   Ben Sayers/James Braid
Facilities   ⊗ 𝔪 ⅃ ♀ 🛆 🍴 🏌 ∢
Location   1m E of B198

Hotel   ★ 59% Nether Abbey Hotel, 20 Dirleton Av,
                    NORTH BERWICK
                    ☎ 01620 892802 16rm (6 ⇄5 ⌂)

North Berwick Beach Rd EH39 4BB
☎ 01620 892135 Fax 01620 893274
Another of East Lothian's famous courses, the links at
North Berwick is still popular. A classic championship
links, it has many hazards including the beach, streams,
bunkers, light rough and low walls. The great hole on the
course is the 15th, the famous 'Redan'. Used by both the
Tantallon and Bass Rock Golf Clubs.
West Links: 18 holes, 6420yds, Par 71, SSS 71, Course
record 64.
Club membership 730.
Visitors   must contact in advance 01620 892135
                    (beyond 7 days) or 01620 892666 (within 7
                    days).
Societies   must contact in advance.
Green Fees £54 per day; £36 per round (£72/£54
                    weekends).
Cards   ▭ ▬ 🔳
Prof   D Huish
Facilities   ⊗ 𝔪 by prior arrangement ⅃ ♀ 🛆 🍴
                    🏌 ∢
Location   W side of town on A198

Hotel   ★★★ 65% The Marine, Cromwell Rd,
                    NORTH BERWICK
                    ☎ 0870 400 8129 83 ⇄ ⌂

Whitekirk Whitekirk EH39 5PR
☎ 01620 870300 Fax 01620 870330
Scenic coastal course with lush green fairways, gorse
covered rocky banks and stunning views. Natural water
hazards and strong sea breezes make this well designed
course a good test of golf.
18 holes, 6526yds, Par 72, SSS 72, Course record 64.
Club membership 300.
Visitors   no restrictions.
Societies   apply in writing or telephone.
Green Fees £30 per day, £18 per round (£40/£25 weekends).
Cards   ▭ ▬ 🔳 📇 🔳
Prof   Paul Wardell
Designer   Cameron Sinclair
Facilities   ⊗ 𝔪 ⅃ ♀ 🛆 🏌 ⋈ ⚲ 🛆 ∢ ⓣ
Location   3m off the main A1 Edinburgh/Berwick-upon-
                    Tweed road A198 North Berwick

Hotel   ★ 59% Nether Abbey Hotel, 20 Dirleton Av,
                    NORTH BERWICK
                    ☎ 01620 892802 16rm (6 ⇄5 ⌂)

OBAN   Map 10 NM83

Glencruitten Glencruitten Rd PA34 4PU
☎ 01631 564604
There is plenty of space and considerable variety of hole
on this downland course - popular with holidaymakers. ▶

In a beautiful, isolated situation, the course is hilly and testing, particularly the 1st and 12th, par 4's, and 10th and 15th, par 3's.
18 holes, 4452yds, Par 61, SSS 63, Course record 55.
Club membership 600.

Visitors restricted Thu & weekends.
Societies must contact in writing.
Green Fees not confirmed.
Prof Graham Clark
Designer James Braid
Facilities ⊗ ⋔ ⅃ ♥ ♀ ⅄ ⌂ ⸂ ⋄
& Leisure pool table.
Location NE side of town centre off A816

Hotel ★★ 61% Caledonian Hotel, Station Square, OBAN ☎ 01631 563133 70 ⇔ ⋒

PENICUIK   Map 11 NT25

Glencorse Milton Bridge EH26 0RD
☎ 01968 677189 Fax 01968 674399
Picturesque parkland course with burn affecting ten holes. Testing 5th hole (237 yds) par 3.
18 holes, 5217yds, Par 64, SSS 66, Course record 60.
Club membership 700.

Visitors contact secretary, unable to play during club competitions
Societies contact secretary for details.
Green Fees £24.50 per day; £18.50 per 18 holes.
Prof Cliffe Jones
Designer Willie Park
Facilities ⊗ ⋔ ⅃ ♥ ♀ ⅄ ⌂ ⋄ ⸂
Location 9m S of Edinburgh on A701 Pebbles Road. 1.5m N of Penicuik on A701

Hotel ★★ 63% Roslin Glen Hotel, 2 Penicuik Rd, ROSLIN ☎ 0131 440 2029 7 ⇔ ⋒

PERTH   Map 11 NO12

Craigie Hill Cherrybank PH2 0NE
☎ 01738 620829 & 622644
Slightly hilly, parkland course. Good views over Perth.
18 holes, 5386yds, Par 66, SSS 67, Course record 60.
Club membership 600.
Visitors restricted access Sat. Telephone up to 3 days in advance.
Societies must contact in writing.
Green Fees £20 per day; £15 per round (£25 per day Sun).
Prof Chris Morris

Designer Fernie/Anderson
Facilities ⊗ ⋔ ⅃ ♥ ♀ ⅄ ⌂ ⸂ ⋄
Location 1m SW of city centre off A952

Hotel ★★★ 67% Queens Hotel, Leonard St, PERTH ☎ 01738 442222 51 ⇔ ⋒

King James VI Moncreiffe Island PH2 8NR
☎ 01738 445132 (Secretary) Fax 01738 445132
Parkland course, situated on island in the middle of River Tay. Easy walking.
18 holes, 6038yds, Par 70, SSS 69, Course record 62.
Club membership 650.
Visitors visitors restricted on competition days. Must contact professional in advance for bookings. May not play Sat.
Societies book by telephone.
Green Fees £17 (£20 Sunday).
Prof Andrew Crerar
Designer Tom Morris
Facilities ⊗ ⅃ ♥ ♀ ⅄ ⌂ ⸂ ⋄
Location SE side of city centre

Hotel ★★★ 67% Queens Hotel, Leonard St, PERTH ☎ 01738 442222 51 ⇔ ⋒

Murrayshall Country House Hotel Murrayshall, Scone PH2 7PH ☎ 01738 552784 & 551171 Fax 01738 552595
Murrayshall now offers 36 holes of outstanding golf. The original championship course is set out within the the parkland estate and the Lyndoch is a woodland style course full of natural features.
Murrayshall Course: 18 holes, 6441yds, Par 73, SSS 72.
Lyndoch Course: 18 holes, 5800yds, Par 69.
Club membership 350.
Visitors telephone in advance.
Societies telephone in advance.
Green Fees Murrayshall: £40 per day; £25 per round. Lyndoch: £30 per day; £18 per round.
Cards ▨▨ ▨▨ ▨ ⬛ ▨ ▨ 🔲
Prof Alan Reid
Designer Hamilton Stutt
Facilities ⊗ ⋔ ⅃ ♥ ♀ ⅄ ⌂ ⸂ ⌘ ⊠ 🏌 ⋄ ⸂
& Leisure hard tennis courts, sauna, gymnasium.
Location E side of village off A94

Hotel ★★★⚑ 75% Murrayshall Country House Hotel & Golf Course, New Scone, PERTH ☎ 01738 551171 27 ⇔ ⋒
See advertisement on page 358.

North Inch North Inch, off Hay St PH1 5PH
☎ 01738 636481
An enjoyable short and often testing course incorporating mature trees, open parkland with fine views and attractive riverside.
18 holes, 5178yds, Par 65, Course record 60.
Club membership 476.
Visitors advisable to telephone in advance. Due to a flood prevention wall to be built late 97/98 there may be some disruption.
Green Fees not confirmed.
Designer Tom Morris
Facilities ⊗ ♥ ♀ ⋄
& Leisure squash, gymnasium.
Hotel ★★★ 67% Queens Hotel, Leonard St, PERTH ☎ 01738 442222 51 ⇔ ⋒

MURRAYSHALL HOUSE AND GOLF COURSE
SCONE, BY PERTH
SCOTLAND

Set within 300 acres of parkland golf course, this 3 star, STB highly commended country house hotel has 26 bedrooms and a self-contained lodge house. Leisure facilities include sauna, gymnasium, jacuzzi, tennis courts, driving range and indoor golf school.
Special golf packages available
Society welcome groups
Our clubhouse facilities are available
to non members
Pro Shop 01738 552784

PITLOCHRY   Map 14 NN95

Pitlochry Pitlochry Estate Office PH16 5QY
☎ 01796 472792
A varied and interesting heathland course with fine views and posing many problems. Its SSS permits few errors in its achievement.
18 holes, 5811yds, Par 69, SSS 69, Course record 63.
Club membership 400.
Visitors   Sat & Sun may not play before 9.30am.
Societies   must contact in advance.
Green Fees not confirmed.
Prof   George Hampton
Designer   Willy Fernie
Facilities   ⊗ ⋔ ㄴ ♥ ♀ ㄥ 🏠 🔧 ⛳ ✎
Location   N side of town off A924

Hotel   ★★★ 76% Pine Trees Hotel, Strathview Ter, PITLOCHRY
            ☎ 01796 472121   19 🛏 🐾

POLMONT   Map 11 NS97

Grangemouth Polmont Hill FK2 0YE
☎ 01324 503840 Fax 01324 715818
Windy parkland course. Testing holes: 3rd, 4th (par 4's); 5th (par 5); 7th (par 3) 216 yds over reservoir (elevated green); 8th, 9th, 18th (par 4's).
18 holes, 6314yds, Par 71, SSS 71, Course record 70.
Club membership 700.
Visitors   must contact in advance.
Societies   must contact in writing.

Green Fees not confirmed.
Prof   Stuart Campbell
Facilities   ⊗ ⋔ ㄴ ♥ ♀ ㄥ 🏠 ✎
Location   On unclass rd 0.5m N of M9 junc 4

Hotel   ★★★★ 70% Inchyra Grange Hotel, Grange Rd, POLMONT
            ☎ 01324 711911 109 🛏 🐾

Polmont Manuelrigg, Maddiston FK2 0LS
☎ 01324 711277 Fax 01324 712504
Parkland course, hilly with few bunkers. Views of the River Forth and Ochil Hills.
9 holes, 3073yds, Par 72, SSS 69, Course record 66.
Club membership 300.
Visitors   no visitors on Sat from Apr-Sep, Mon-Fri must tee of before 5pm.
Societies   apply in writing to club secretary.
Green Fees £8 per 18 holes (£14 Sun).
Facilities   ㄥ
Location   A805 from Falkirk, 1st right after fire brigade headquarters

Hotel   ★★★★ 70% Inchyra Grange Hotel, Grange Rd, POLMONT
            ☎ 01324 711911 109 🛏 🐾

PORT GLASGOW   Map 10 NS37

Port Glasgow Devol Rd PA14 5XE
☎ 01475 704181 & 705671 (Sec) Fax 01475 705671
A moorland course set on a hilltop overlooking the Clyde, with magnificent views to the Cowal hills.
18 holes, 5712yds, Par 68, SSS 68.
Club membership 390.
Visitors   may not play on Sat. By prior arrangement or with member Sun.
Societies   apply in writing.
Green Fees £20 per day; £15 per round.
Facilities   ⊗ ⋔ ㄴ ♥ ♀ ㄥ 🏠
Location   1m S

Hotel   ★★★★🏌 67% Gleddoch House Hotel, LANGBANK ☎ 01475 540711   39 🛏 🐾

PRESTONPANS   Map 11 NT37

Royal Musselburgh Prestongrange House EH32 9RP
☎ 01875 810276 Fax 01875 810276
Tree-lined parkland course overlooking Firth of Forth. Well maintained and providing an excellent challenge.
18 holes, 6237yds, Par 70, SSS 70, Course record 64.
Club membership 970.
Visitors   must contact professional in advance, restricted Fri afternoons & weekends.
Societies   must contact in advance,
Green Fees £35 per day; £20 per round.
Prof   John Henderson
Designer   James Braid
Facilities   ⊗ ⋔ ㄴ ♥ ♀ ㄥ 🏠 🔧 🛒 ✎
& Leisure   snooker.
Location   W side of town centre on B1361 Prestonpans to North Berwick rd

Hotel   ★★ 66% Kilspindie House Hotel, Main St, ABERLADY ☎ 01875 870682   26 🛏 🐾

RATHO

Map 11 NT17

Ratho Park EH28 8NX
☎ 0131 333 2566 & 333 1752 Fax 0131 333 1752
Flat parkland course.
18 holes, 5900yds, Par 69, SSS 68, Course record 62.
Club membership 850.

Visitors	must contact in advance.
Societies	must contact in writing. Only able to play Tue-Thu
Green Fees	not confirmed.
Prof	Alan Pate
Designer	James Braid
Facilities	⊗ ⅷ ⅃ ⬛ ⚲ ⚐ ⮐ ⚑
Location	0.75m E, N of A71

Hotel ★★★ 73% Posthouse Edinburgh, Corstorphine Rd, EDINBURGH
☎ 0870 400 9026 303 ⇆ ⌤

ST ANDREWS

Map 12 NO51

British Golf Museum

☎ 01334 478880 (situated opposite Royal & Ancient Golf Club)
The museum which tells the history of golf from its origins to the present day, is of interest to golfers and non-golfers alike. Themed galleries and interactive displays explore the history of the major championships and the lives of the famous players, and trace the development of golfing equipment. An audio-visual theatre shows historic golfing moments. Open: Etr-mid Oct, daily 9.30am-5.30pm (mid Oct-Etr Thu-Mon 11am-3pm, closed Tue & Wed. Admission: There is a charge. Ask for details.

Dukes Course Craigtoun KY16 8NS
☎ 01334 474371 Fax 01334 479456
Blending the characteristics of a links course with an inland course, Dukes offers rolling fairways, undulating greens and a testing woodland section, and magnificent views over St Andrews Bay towards Carnoustie.
18 holes, 6749yds, Par 72, SSS 73, Course record 71.
Club membership 500.

Visitors	booking should be in advance to avoid disappointment through the hotel reservations team.
Societies	apply in writing or fax in advance.
Green Fees	Summer: £50 per round; £30 per 9 holes (£55 per round weekends). Winter: £25 per round.
Cards	▭▭ ▭▭ ⌹ ▭▭ ▭ ⑨
Prof	John Kelly
Designer	Peter Thomson
Facilities & Leisure	⊗ ⅷ ⅃ ⬛ ⚲ ⚐ ⮐ ⚑ ⚐ ⮐ ▨ ⚑ ⚐ ⌇ heated indoor swimming pool, sauna, solarium, gymnasium, tuition available, computer swing analyses.
Location	Follow M90 from Edinburgh onto A91 to Cupar then to St Andrew turning off for Strathkiness

Hotel ★★★★★ 68% The Old Course Hotel Golf Resort & Spa, ST ANDREWS
☎ 01334 474371 125 ⇆ ⌤
Guesthouse ♦♦♦♦ Riverview Guest House, Edenside, St Andrews
☎ 01334 838009 Fax 01334 839944 7 ⌤ ▶

The Glenfarg Hotel & Restaurant

Additional hotel   ★★ 65% The Glenfarg Hotel & Restaurant, Main St, GLENFARG
☎ 01577 830241 Fax 01577 830665
16rm (15 ⇉ ♖)

ST ANDREWS See page 361 & advert on page 359.

ST FILLANS   Map 11 NN62

St Fillans South Loch Earn Rd PH6 2NJ ☎ 01764 685312
Fairly flat, beautiful parkland course. Beside the river Earn and set amongst the Perthshire hills. Wonderfully rich in flora, animal and bird life.
9 holes, 5896yds, Par 68, SSS 67, Course record 73.
Club membership 400.
Visitors	advisable to contact in advance.
Societies	Apr-Oct, apply to starter.
Green Fees	not confirmed.
Designer	W Auchterlonie
Facilities	⊗ ⊪ 🍺 ⚒ ⛳ ✧
Location	E side of village off A85

Hotel   ★★★ 64% The Four Seasons Hotel, Loch Earn, ST FILLANS ☎ 01764 685333
12 ⇉ ♖ Annexe 6 ⇉ ♖

SALINE   Map 11 NT09

Saline Kinneddar Hill KY12 9LT ☎ 01383 852591
Hillside parkland course with excellent turf and panoramic view of the Forth Valley.
9 holes, 5302yds, Par 68, SSS 66, Course record 62.
Club membership 400.
Visitors	advisable to contact in advance and may not play Sat, some restrictions Sun.
Societies	contact in advance.
Green Fees	£9 per day (£12 Sun).
Facilities	🝙 🍺 ♀ ⛳ ✧
Location	Junct 4 of M90, 0.5m E at junc B913/914

Hotel   ★★★ 65% King Malcolm, Queensferry Rd, DUNFERMLINE ☎ 01383 722611   48 ⇉ ♖

SOUTHEND   Map 10 NR60

Dunaverty PA28 6RW
☎ 01586 830677 Fax 01586 830677
Undulating, seaside course with spectacular views of Ireland and the Ayrshire coast.
18 holes, 4799yds, Par 66, SSS 63, Course record 59.
Club membership 400.
Visitors	limited Sat, contact in advance.
Societies	apply in advance.
Green Fees	£14 per round (£16 weekends).
Facilities & Leisure	⊗ ⊪ 🝙 by prior arrangement 🍺 ⛳ 📷 ✧ fishing.
Location	10m S of Campbeltown on B842

Hotel   ★★ 67% Seafield Hotel, Kilkerran Rd, CAMPBELTOWN
☎ 01586 554385 3 ⇉ ♖ Annexe 6 ♖

SOUTH QUEENSFERRY   Map 11 NT17

Dundas Parks Dundas Estate EH30 9PQ
☎ 0131 319 1347 Fax 0131 319 1347
Parkland course situated on the estate of Dundas Castle, with excellent views. For 18 holes, the 9 are played twice.
9 holes, 6024yds, Par 70, SSS 69, Course record 66.
Club membership 500.
Visitors	must contact in advance, only with a member. May not play at weekends.
Societies	must contact in writing.
Green Fees	£10 per round.
Facilities	⛳
Location	0.5m S on A8000

Hotel   ★★★ 61% Forth Bridges Hotel, 1 Ferrymuir Gait, SOUTH QUEENSFERRY
☎ 0131 469 9955 108 ⇉ ♖

STIRLING   Map 11 NS79

Stirling Queens Rd FK8 3AA
☎ 01786 464098 Fax 01786 450748
Undulating parkland course with magnificent views of Stirling Castle and the Grampian Mountains. Testing 15th, 'Cotton's Fancy', 384 yds (par 4).
18 holes, 6438yds, Par 72, SSS 71, Course record 64.
Club membership 1100.
Visitors	may reserve tee off times mid week 9-4.30pm. At weekends tee off times may be reserved on day of play subject to availability.
Societies	must apply in writing or telephone.
Green Fees	£35 per day; £25 per round.
Cards	🗖 📇 🗏
Prof	Ian Collins
Designer	James Braid/Henry Cotton
Facilities	⊗ ⊪ 🝙 🍺 ♀ ⛳ 📷 ✧ ✧ ℓ
Location	W side of town on B8051

Hotel   ★★ 69% Terraces Hotel, 4 Melville Ter, STIRLING ☎ 01786 472268   18 ⇉ ♖

St Andrews Links

e-mail: linkstrust@standrews.org.uk

Visitors must telephone in advance and have handicap certificate. Old Course closed Sun

Societies must book at least a month in advance

Green Fees Old Course £80; New Course £40; Jubilee £35; Eden £25; Strathtyrum £17; Balgove £7 (18 holes)

Facilities ⊗)〔 ⩗ ♭ ☕ ♀ ⚑ 🏠 🍴 🏌 ♂ ℓ

Location Pilmour House, St Andrews KY16 9SF (NW of town, off A91)

Holes/Par/Course record Old Course: 18 holes, 6566 yds, Par 72, SSS 72, Course record 67
New (West Sands Rd): 18 holes, 6604 yds, Par 71, SSS 72
Jubilee (West Sands Rd): 18 holes, 6805 yds, Par 72, SSS 73
Eden (Dundee Rd): 18 holes, 6112 yds, Par 70, SSS 70
Strathtyrum: 18 holes, 5094 yds, Par 69, SSS 64
Balgove: 9 holes, 3060 yds, Par 60

WHERE TO STAY AND EAT NEARBY

Hotels

GLENFARG

★★ 65% Glenfarg, Main St. ☎ 01577 830241. 16 (5 ⇄ ↑ 10 ↑)

ST ANDREWS

★★★★★ ❀ 70% Old Course St Andrews, Old Station Rd. ☎ 01334 474371. 125 ⇄

★★★ ❀ ❀ 77% St Andrews Golf, 40 The Scores. ☎ 01334 472611. 22 (20 ⇄ ↑ 2 ↑)

★★★ 66% Scores, 76 The Scores. ☎ 01334 472451. 30 (28 ⇄ ↑ 2 ↑)

Restaurant

CUPAR

❀ ❀ ❀ Ostlers Close, Bonnygate. ☎ 01334 655574

G olf was first played here around 1400AD and the Old Course is acknowledged world-wide as the Home of Golf. The Old has played host to the greatest golfers in the world and many of golf's most dramatic moments. The course is an average 6566 yards long from the medal tees.

The New Course (6604 yards) opened in 1895, having been laid out by Old Tom Morris. The Jubilee opened in 1897, the championship Jubilee Course is 6805 yards long from the medal tees. A shorter version of the Jubilee Course is also available, known as the Bronze Course, measuring 5674 yards. There is no handicap limit for the shorter course and it is best for lower/middle handicap golfers.

The Eden opened in 1914 and is recommended for middle to high handicap golfers. The Strathtyrum has a shorter, less testing layout best for high handicap golfers. The Balgove nine hole course, upgraded and re-opened in 1993, is best for beginners and children.

Championship Course

STRATHTAY　　　　　　　Map 14 NN95

Strathtay Lyon Cottage PH9 0PG ☎ 01887 840211
A wooded mainly hilly course with pleasing panoramic
views. 5th hole 'Spion Kop' is especially difficult. It is steep,
with heavy rough on both sides of the hilly fairway and an
unsighted green on the back of the hill which is affected by
winds.
9 holes, 4082yds, Par 63, SSS 63, Course record 61.
Club membership 260.

Visitors	restricted May-Sep; Sun 12.30-5pm & Mon 6-8pm. Also some Wed & Thu evenings.
Societies	in writing/telephone Secretary.
Green Fees	£12 per day.
Facilities	🛆
Location	Eastern end of minor rd to Weem, off A827
Hotel	★★ 68% The Weem, Weem, ABERFELDY ☎ 01887 820381　12 ⇌ ↟

TARBERT　　　　　　　Map 10 NR86

Tarbert PA29 6XX ☎ 01546 606896
Beautiful moorland course. Four fairways crossed by
streams.
9 holes, 4460yds, Par 66, SSS 63, Course record 62.

Visitors	may not play Sat pm.
Societies	apply in writing.
Green Fees	£10 per 18 holes.
Location	N1m W on B8024
Hotel	★★★🏖 68% Stonefield Castle Hotel, TARBERT ☎ 01880 820836　33 ⇌ ↟

TAYPORT　　　　　　　Map 12 NO42

Scotscraig Golf Rd DD6 9DZ
☎ 01382 552515 Fax 01382 553130
A rather tight course on downland-type turf with an
abundance of gorse. The sheltered position of this Open
qualifying course ensures good weather throughout the
year.
18 holes, 6550yds, Par 71, SSS 72, Course record 67.
Club membership 850.

Visitors	restricted at weekends. Must contact in advance.
Societies	advance booking.
Green Fees	£40 per day; £30 per round (£45/£35 weekends).
Cards	🔲 🔲 🔳
Prof	S J Campbell
Designer	James Braid
Facilities	⊗ ⅋ 🖪 🖫 🍷 ♀ 🛆 🍴 🥢 🥄 🏌 ♂
Location	S side of village off B945
Hotel	★★★🏖 68% Sandford Hotel, Newport Hill, Wormit, DUNDEE ☎ 01382 541802　16 ⇌ ↟

THORNTON　　　　　　Map 11 NT29

Thornton Station Rd KY1 4DW
☎ 01592 771111 Fax 01592 774955
A relatively flat, lightly tree-lined, parkland course bounded
on three sides by a river which comes into play at holes 14-16.

18 holes, 6155yds, Par 70, SSS 69, Course record 64.
Club membership 700.

Visitors	restricted at weekends before 10am & between 12.30-2pm, also Tue 1-1.30 & Thu 9-10. Booking in advance recommended.
Societies	apply in advance.
Green Fees	£25 per day; £15 per round (£32/£22 weekends).
Cards	🔲 🔳 🔲
Facilities	⊗ ⅋ 🖪 🖫 🍷 ♀ 🛆 ♂
Location	1m E of town off A92
Hotel	★★★★🏖 Balbirnie House, Balbirnie Park, MARKINCH ☎ 01592 610066　30 ⇌ ↟

TIGHNABRUAICH　　　　Map 10 NR97

Kyles of Bute PA21 2EE ☎ 01700 811603
Moorland course which is hilly and exposed to wind. Fine
mountain and sea views.
9 holes, 4778yds, Par 66, SSS 64, Course record 62.
Club membership 150.

Visitors	may not play Wed pm or Sun am.
Societies	telephone in advance.
Green Fees	£8 per day (£10 weekends).
Facilities	🖫 🛆 🍴 ♂
Location	1.25m S off B8000

TILLICOULTRY　　　　　Map 11 NS99

Tillicoultry Alva Rd FK13 6BL
☎ 01259 750124 Fax 01259 752934
Parkland course at foot of the Ochil Hills entailing some hard
walking.
9 holes, 4904metres, Par 68, SSS 66, Course record 61.
Club membership 400.

Visitors	must contact in advance.
Societies	apply to the secretary.
Green Fees	£10.50 & £13 per 18 holes after 4pm (£15 weekends).
Facilities	🖪 🖫 ♀ 🛆
Location	A91, 9m E of Stirling

UPHALL　　　　　　　　Map 11 NT07

Uphall EH52 6JT ☎ 01506 856404 Fax 01506 855358
Windy parkland course, easy walking.
18 holes, 5588yds, Par 69, SSS 67, Course record 62.
Club membership 500.

Visitors	restricted weekends.
Societies	must contact in advance.
Green Fees	not confirmed.
Prof	Gordon Law
Facilities	⊗ ⅋ 🖪 🖫 🍷 ♀ 🛆 🍴 ♂
Location	W side of village on A899
Hotel	★★★★ 67% Houstoun House Hotel and Country Club, UPHALL ☎ 01506 853831　25 ⇌ ↟ Annexe 47 ⇌ ↟

WEST CALDER　　　　　Map 11 NT06

Harburn EH55 8RS
☎ 01506 871131 & 871256 Fax 01506 870286
Moorland, reasonably flat.
18 holes, 5921yds, Par 69, SSS 69, Course record 62.
Club membership 870.

▶

Visitors contact secretary, limited weekends.
Societies contact by telephone.
Green Fees £25 per day; £18 per round (£29/£21 Fri, £34/£23 weekends & bank holidays).
Prof Stephen Mills
Facilities ⊗ ⅏ 🏌 💻 ♀ 👥 🍴 ⛳ 🛒 ♿ ✏
Location 2m S on B7008

Hotel ★★★ 65% The Hilcroft Hotel, East Main St, WHITBURN ☎ 01501 740818 31 ⇔ 🐾

WHITBURN Map 11 NS96

Polkemmet Country Park EH47 0AD ☎ 01501 743905
Public parkland course surrounded by mature woodland and rhododendron bushes. 15-bay floodlit driving range.
9 holes, 2969mtrs, Par 37.
Visitors no restrictions.
Green Fees Summer: £4.50 per round (£5.25 weekends).
Winter £4.
Facilities ⊗ ⅏ 🏌 💻 ♀ ✏ 🍴
Location 2m W on B7066

Hotel ★★★ 65% The Hilcroft Hotel, East Main St, WHITBURN ☎ 01501 740818 31 ⇔ 🐾

SOUTHERN LOWLANDS & BORDERS

This region includes the counties of City of Glasgow, Dumbarton & Clydebank, Dumfries & Galloway, East Ayrshire, East Dunbartonshire, East Renfrewshire, North Ayrshire, North Lanarkshire, Renfrewshire, Scottish Borders, South Ayrshire and South Lanarkshire which reflect the national changes.

AIRDRIE Map 11 NS76

Airdrie Rochsoles ML6 0PQ ☎ 01236 762195
Picturesque parkland course with good views.
18 holes, 6004yds, Par 69, SSS 69, Course record 63.
Club membership 450.
Visitors must contact in advance. With member only weekends & bank holidays.
Societies apply in writing.
Green Fees £25 per day; £15 per round.
Prof G Monks
Designer J Braid

Facilities ⊗ ⅏ 🏌 💻 ♀ 👥 🍴 ⛳ ✏
Location 1m N on B802

Hotel ★★★★ 60% Westerwood Hotel Golf & Country Club, 1 St Andrews Dr, Westerwood, CUMBERNAULD ☎ 01236 457171 49 ⇔ 🐾

Easter Moffat Gordon Miller, Station Rd, Plains ML6 8NP
☎ 01236 842878
Moorland/parkland course.
18 holes, 6221yds, Par 72, SSS 70, Course record 66.
Club membership 500.
Visitors may only play on weekdays.
Societies must contact in advance.
Green Fees £20 per day; £15 per round.
Prof Graham King
Facilities ⊗ ⅏ 🏌 💻 ♀ 👥 🍴 ✏
Location 2m E of Airdrie on A89

Hotel ★★★★ 60% Westerwood Hotel Golf & Country Club, 1 St Andrews Dr, Westerwood, CUMBERNAULD ☎ 01236 457171 49 ⇔ 🐾

ARRAN, ISLE OF Map 10 NR94

BLACKWATERFOOT Map 10 NR82

Shiskine Shore Rd KA27 8HA
☎ 01770 860226 Fax 01770 860205
Unique 12-hole links course with gorgeous outlook to the Mull of Kintyre.
12 holes, 2990yds, Par 42, SSS 42.
Club membership 670.
Visitors must contact in advance.
Societies must contact in writing in advance. Jul and Aug no parties.
Green Fees £18 per day; £13 per round (£22/£16 weekends & bank holidays).
Designer Fernie of Troon
Facilities ⊗ 🏌 💻 ⛳ 🍴 📮 ✏
& Leisure hard tennis courts, bowling green.
Location W side of village off A841

Hotel ★★🔥 Kilmichael Country House Hotel, Glen Cloy, BRODICK ☎ 01770 302219 6 ⇔ 🐾 Annexe 3 ⇔ 🐾

BRODICK Map 10 NS03

Brodick KA27 8DL ☎ 01770 302349 & 302513 (Pro)
Fax 01770 302349
Short seaside course, very flat.
18 holes, 4736yds, Par 65, SSS 64, Course record 60.
Club membership 661.
Visitors must contact in advance but may not play at competition times.
Societies must contact secretary in writing.
Green Fees £25 per day; £18 per round (£30/£22 weekends & bank holidays).
Prof Peter McCalla
Facilities ⊗ ⅏ 🏌 💻 ♀ 👥 🍴 ⛳ ✏
Location N side of village, 0.5m N of Brodick Ferry Terminal

Hotel ★★★ 75% Auchrannie Country House Hotel, BRODICK ☎ 01770 302234 28 ⇔ 🐾

LAMLASH
Map 10 NS03

Lamlash KA27 8JU
☎ 01770 600296 & 600196 (Starter) Fax 01770 600296
Undulating heathland course with magnificent views of the mountains and sea.
18 holes, 4640yds, Par 64, SSS 64, Course record 60.
Club membership 480.

Visitors	book in advance by letter
Societies	must contact in writing.
Green Fees	£16 per day; £12 per round after 4pm (£20 weekends).
Designer	Auchterlonie
Facilities	⊗ ⅷ Ⅼᴮ ■ ♀ ⚑ ⅰ ↑ ⚲ ✓
Location	0.75m N of Lamlash on A841. 3m S of Brodick Ferry Terminal

Hotel ★★★ 75% Auchrannie Country House Hotel, BRODICK ☎ 01770 302234 28 ⇆ ↑

LOCHRANZA
Map 10 NR95

Lochranza KA27 8HL
☎ 01770 830273 Fax 01770 830600
This course is mainly on the level, set amid spectacular scenery where the fairways are grazed by wild red deer, while overhead buzzards and golden eagles may be seen. There are water hazards including the river which is lined by mature trees. The final three holes, nicknamed the Bermuda Triangle, provide an absorbing finish right to the 18th hole - a 530 yard dogleg through trees and over the river. The large greens are played off 18 tees.
9 holes, 5033mtrs, Par 70, SSS 70, Course record 74.

Visitors	no restrictions; course closed Nov-mid Apr.
Societies	advance booking preferred.
Green Fees	not confirmed.
Designer	re laid 1991 I Robertson
Facilities	Ⅼᴮ ■ ⚑ ⅰ ↑ ✓
Location	Main road, Lochranza village.

Hotel ★★♨ Kilmichael Country House Hotel, Glen Cloy, BRODICK ☎ 01770 302219 6 ⇆ ↑ Annexe 3 ⇆ ↑

MACHRIE
Map 10 NR83

Machrie Bay KA27 8DZ
☎ 01770 850232
Fairly flat seaside course. Designed at turn of century by William Fernie.
9 holes, 4400yds, Par 66, SSS 62, Course record 70.
Club membership 315.

Visitors	no restrictions.
Societies	write in advance.
Green Fees	not confirmed.
Designer	W Fernie
Facilities	⊗ Ⅼᴮ ■ ⚑ ⅰ ↑ ✓
& Leisure	hard tennis courts, fishing.
Location	9m W of Brodick via String Rd

Hotel ★★♨ Kilmichael Country House Hotel, Glen Cloy, BRODICK ☎ 01770 302219 6 ⇆ ↑ Annexe 3 ⇆ ↑

SANNOX
Map 10 NS04

Corrie KA27 8JD ☎ 01770 810223 & 810606
A heathland course on the coast with beautiful mountain scenery. An upward climb to 6th hole, then a descent from the 7th. All these holes are subject to strong winds in bad weather.
9 holes, 1948yds, Par 62, SSS 61, Course record 56.
Club membership 300.

Visitors	welcome except Sat pm and first Thu afternoon of the month.
Societies	maximum size of party 16, apply in advance.
Green Fees	£10 per day.
Facilities	⊗ ⅷ Ⅼᴮ ■ ⅰ
Location	6m N of A841

Hotel ★★★ 75% Auchrannie Country House Hotel, BRODICK ☎ 01770 302234 28 ⇆ ↑

WHITING BAY
Map 10 NS02

Whiting Bay KA27 8QT ☎ 01770 700487
Heathland course.
18 holes, 4405yds, Par 63, SSS 63, Course record 59.
Club membership 350.

Visitors	tee reserved 8.45-9.30am, also Sun 11.45-1pm.
Societies	apply by telephone and confirm in writing with deposit.
Green Fees	not confirmed.
Facilities	⊗ ⅷ Ⅼᴮ ■ ♀ ⚑ ⅰ ↑ ⚲ ✓
Location	NW side of village off A841

Hotel ★★♨ Kilmichael Country House Hotel, Glen Cloy, BRODICK ☎ 01770 302219 6 ⇆ ↑ Annexe 3 ⇆ ↑

AYR
Map 10 NS32

Belleisle Belleisle Park KA7 4DU
☎ 01292 441258 Fax 01292 442632
Parkland course with beautiful sea views. First-class conditions.
Belleisle Course: 18 holes, 6431yds, Par 71, SSS 72, Course record 63.
Seafield Course: 18 holes, 5498yds, Par 68, SSS 66.
Club membership 1200.

Visitors	advised to contact in advance, telephone to book.
Societies	advised to contact in advance, telephone 01292 616255.
Green Fees	£28 per day; £19.50 per round (£33/£22 weekends).
Cards	▭ ▭ ▭ ▭
Prof	David Gemmell
Designer	James Braid
Facilities	⊗ ⅷ Ⅼᴮ ■ ♀ ⚑ ⅰ ↑ ⚑ ✓
Location	2m S on A719

Hotel ★★★ 58% Quality Hotel Ayr, Burns Statue Square, AYR ☎ 01292 263268 75 ⇆ ↑

Dalmilling Westwood Av KA8 0QY
☎ 01292 263893 Fax 01292 610543
Meadowland course, with easy walking.
18 holes, 5724yds, Par 69, SSS 68, Course record 61.
Club membership 260.

▶

Visitors	must contact in advance.
Societies	must contact in advance.
Green Fees	£20 per day; £13 per round (£26/£14.50 weekends).
Cards	🖸 🖸
Prof	Philip Cheyney
Facilities	⊗ 🏌 🕎 ♀ 🛆 🏡 ⛳ ⚷
Location	1.5m E of town centre off A719
Hotel	★★★ 58% Quality Hotel Ayr, Burns Statue Square, AYR ☎ 01292 263268 75 ⇄ 🐾

BALMORE   Map 11 NS57

Balmore Golf Course Rd G64 4AW
☎ 01360 620240 Fax 01360 620284
Parkland course with fine views.
18 holes, 5530yds, Par 66, SSS 67, Course record 63.
Club membership 700.

Visitors	must contact in advance and be accompanied by member, may not play at weekends
Societies	apply in writing.
Green Fees	not confirmed.
Designer	James Braid
Facilities	⊗ 🏌 🕎 ♀ 🛆
Location	N off A807
Hotel	★★★ 64% Patio Hotel, 1 South Av, Clydebank Business Park, CLYDEBANK ☎ 0141 951 1133 80 ⇄ 🐾

BARASSIE   Map 10 NS33

Kilmarnock (Barassie) 29 Hillhouse Rd KA10 6SY
☎ 01292 313920 Fax 01292 313920
The club now has a 27 hole layout. Magnificent seaside links, relatively flat with much heather and small, undulating greens.
18 holes, 6817yds, Par 72, SSS 74, Course record 68.
9 hole course: 9 holes, 2888yds, Par 34.
Club membership 600.

Visitors	with member only Wed & weekends. May not play Fri am. Contact secretary in advance.
Societies	must telephone in advance and confirm in writing.
Green Fees	£60 per 36 holes; £50 per 27 holes; £40 per 18 holes;.
Cards	🖸 🖸 🖸 🖸
Prof	Gregor Howie
Designer	Theodore Moone
Facilities	⊗ 🏌 🕎 🛆 ♀ 🛆 🏡 ⛳ ⚷
Location	E side of village on B746, 2m N of Troon
Hotel	★★★★ 66% Marine Hotel, Crosbie Rd, TROON ☎ 01292 314444 74 ⇄ 🐾

BARRHEAD   Map 11 NS45

Fereneze Fereneze Av G78 1HJ
☎ 0141 881 1519 Fax 0141 887 1103
Hilly moorland course, with a good view at the end of a hard climb to the 3rd, then levels out.
18 holes, 5821yds, Par 70, SSS 68, Course record 66.
Club membership 700.

Visitors	must contact in advance but may not play at weekends.
Societies	apply in writing.
Green Fees	£22 per round.
Prof	Stuart Kerr
Facilities	⊗ 🏌 🛆 🕎 ♀ 🛆 🏡 ⛳
Location	NW side of town off B774
Hotel	★★★ 69% Dalmeny Park Country House, Lochlibo Rd, BARRHEAD ☎ 0141 881 9211 20 ⇄ 🐾

BEARSDEN   Map 11 NS57

Bearsden Thorn Rd G61 4BP ☎ 0141 942 2351
Parkland course, with 16 greens and 11 teeing grounds. Easy walking and views over city.
9 holes, 6014yds, Par 68, SSS 69, Course record 67.
Club membership 450.

Visitors	must be accompanied by and play with member.
Societies	apply by writing.
Green Fees	£17 per day; £12 per 18 holes.
Facilities	⊗ 🏌 🛆 🕎 ♀ 🛆
Location	1m W off A809
Hotel	★★★ 64% Patio Hotel, 1 South Av, Clydebank Business Park, CLYDEBANK ☎ 0141 951 1133 80 ⇄ 🐾

Douglas Park Hillfoot G61 2TJ
☎ 0141 942 2220 (Clubhouse) 942 0985 (Secretary) Fax 01 41 942 0985
Parkland course with wide variety of holes.
18 holes, 5962yds, Par 69, SSS 69.
Club membership 900.

Visitors	must be accompanied by member and must contact in advance, Wednesdays and Thursdays for visiting parties only.
Societies	Wed & Thu. Must telephone in advance.
Green Fees	£30 per day; £22 per round.
Prof	David Scott
Designer	Willie Fernie
Facilities	🏌 🕎 ♀ 🛆 🏡 ⛳
Location	E side of town on A81
Hotel	★★★ 64% Patio Hotel, 1 South Av, Clydebank Business Park, CLYDEBANK ☎ 0141 951 1133 80 ⇄

Windyhill Baljaffray Rd G61 4QQ
☎ 0141 942 2349 Fax 0141 942 5874
Interesting parkland/moorland course with panoramic views of Glasgow and beyond; testing 12th hole.
18 holes, 6254yds, Par 71, SSS 70, Course record 64.
Club membership 800.

Visitors	may not play at weekends. Must contact professional in advance. Must have a handicap certificate.
Societies	must apply in writing.
Green Fees	£30 per day; £20 per round.
Prof	G Collinson
Designer	James Braid
Facilities	⊗ 🏌 🛆 🕎 ♀ 🛆 🏡 ⛳ ⚷
Location	2m NW off B8050
Hotel	★★★ 64% Patio Hotel, 1 South Av, Clydebank Business Park, CLYDEBANK ☎ 0141 951 1133 80 ⇄ 🐾

BEITH
Map 10 NS35

Beith Threepwood Rd KA15 2JR
☎ 01505 503166 & 506814 Fax 01505 506814
Hilly course, with panoramic views over 7 counties.
18 holes, 5616yds, Par 68, SSS 68.
Club membership 420.
Visitors contact for details.
Societies apply in writing to secretary at least 1 month in advance.
Green Fees not confirmed.
Facilities ⊗ ♨ ⮂ ⬛ ⛾ ♙ ⛱
Location 1.5m NE off A737

Hotel ★★★ 67% Bowfield Hotel & Country Club, HOWWOOD ☎ 01505 705225 23 ⇌ ↾

BELLSHILL
Map 11 NS76

Bellshill Community Rd, Orbiston ML4 2RZ
☎ 01698 745124
Parkland course.
18 holes, 5900yds, Par 69, SSS 69.
Club membership 500.
Visitors apply in writing in advance, may not play on competition Sat & Sun.
Societies apply in writing in advance.
Green Fees not confirmed.
Facilities ⊗ ♨ ⮂ ⬛ ⛾ ♙ ⛱
Location 1m SE off A721

Hotel ★★ 68% Redstones Hotel, 8-10 Glasgow Rd, UDDINGSTON ☎ 01698 813774 & 814843 Fax 01698 815319 14 ⇌ ↾

BIGGAR
Map 11 NT03

Biggar The Park, Broughton Rd ML12 6AH
☎ 01899 220319
Flat parkland course, easy walking and fine views.
18 holes, 5600yds, Par 68, SSS 67, Course record 61.
Club membership 340.
Visitors Must contact in advance. Smart casual wear required.
Societies must book in advance, observe dress code.
Green Fees £9 per round (£15 weekends & bank holidays).
Designer W Park Jnr
Facilities ⊗ ♨ ⮂ ⬛ ⛾ ♙ ⛱ 🏠 ♝ ⛵ ⛳
& Leisure hard tennis courts.
Location S side of town

Hotel ★★★♨♨ 69% Shieldhill Hotel, Quothquan, BIGGAR ☎ 01899 220035 16 ⇌ ↾

BISHOPBRIGGS
Map 11 NS67

Bishopbriggs Brackenbrae Rd G64 2DX ☎ 0141 772 1810
Parkland course with views to Campsie Hills.
18 holes, 6041yds, Par 69, SSS 69, Course record 63.
Club membership 600.
Visitors must be accompanied by a member and have introduction from own club.
Societies apply in writing to the Committee one month in advance.
Green Fees not confirmed.
Facilities ♙ ⛱ 🏠

Location 0.5m NW off A803

Hotel ★★★ 64% Patio Hotel, 1 South Av, Clydebank Business Park, CLYDEBANK ☎ 0141 951 1133 80 ⇌ ↾

Cawder Cadder Rd G64 3QD
☎ 0141 772 7101 Fax 0141 772 4463
Two parkland courses; Cawder Course is hilly, with 5th, 9th, 10th, 11th-testing holes. Keir Course is flat.
Cawder Course: 18 holes, 6295yds, Par 70, SSS 71.
Keir Course: 18 holes, 5877yds, Par 68, SSS 68.
Club membership 1150.
Visitors must contact in advance & may play on weekdays only.
Societies must contact in writing, not on Bank Holidays
Green Fees not confirmed.
Cards 💳 💳 💳
Prof Ken Stavely
Designer James Braid
Facilities ⊗ ♨ ⮂ ⬛ ⛾ ♙ ⛱ 🏠 ⛳ ⛵
Location 1m NE off A803

Hotel ★★★ 64% Patio Hotel, 1 South Av, Clydebank Business Park, CLYDEBANK ☎ 0141 951 1133 80 ⇌ ↾

Littlehill Auchinairn Rd G64 1UT ☎ 0141 772 1916
Municipal parkland course.
18 holes, 6240yds, Par 70, SSS 70.
Visitors must contact in advance.
Societies advance bookings required in writing
Green Fees not confirmed.
Facilities ⛱
Location 3m NE of Glasgow city centre on A803

BISHOPTON
Map 10 NS47

Erskine PA7 5PH ☎ 01505 862302
Parkland course.
18 holes, 6287yds, Par 71, SSS 70.
Club membership 700.
Visitors introduced by member or by prior arrangement.
Societies apply in writing.
Green Fees £37 per day; £25 per round.
Prof Peter Thomson
Facilities ⊗ ♨ ⮂ ⬛ ⛾ ♙ ⛱ 🏠 ⛳ ⛵
Location 0.75 NE off B815

Hotel ★★★ 65% Posthouse Glasgow, North Barr, ERSKINE ☎ 0870 400 9033 177 ⇌ ↾

BONHILL
Map 10 NS37

Vale of Leven North Field Rd G83 9ET ☎ 01389 752351
Hilly moorland course, tricky with many natural hazards - gorse, burns, trees. Overlooks Loch Lomond.
18 holes, 5162yds, Par 67, SSS 66, Course record 61.
Club membership 640.
Visitors may not play Sat.
Societies apply to the secretary.
Green Fees £28 per day; £18 per round (£32/£24 weekends).
Facilities ⊗ ♨ ⮂ ⬛ ⛾ ♙ ⛱ ⛵
Location E side of town off A813

Hotel ★★ 66% Dumbuck House Hotel, Glasgow Rd, DUMBARTON ☎ 01389 734336 22 ⇌ ↾

BOTHWELL   Map 11 NS75

Bothwell Castle Blantyre Rd G71 8PJ
☎ 01698 853177 Fax 01698 854052
Flattish tree lined parkland course in residential area.
18 holes, 6200yds, Par 71, SSS 70, Course record 63.
Club membership 1000.
Visitors   may only play Mon-Fri 9.30-10.30am & 2-3pm.
Green Fees not confirmed.
Prof   Gordon Niven
Facilities   ⊗ �𝕀𝕀𝕀 ┗ 🖤 ♀ ┻ 🏠 ⊤ 🛒 ⬚
Location   NW of village off B7071

Hotel   ★★★ 67% Bothwell Bridge Hotel, 89 Main St, BOTHWELL ☎ 01698 852246   90 ⇆ ⋒

BRIDGE OF WEIR   Map 10 NS36

Ranfurly Castle The Clubhouse, Golf Rd PA11 3HN
☎ 01505 612609 Fax 01505 610406
A highly challenging, 240 acre, picturesque moorland course.
18 holes, 6284yds, Par 70, SSS 71, Course record 65.
Club membership 825.
Visitors   golf club members on weekdays only.
Societies   Tue only, apply in writing.
Green Fees £30 per day; £20 per round.
Prof   Tom Eckford
Designer   A Kirkcaldy/W Auchterlomie
Facilities   ⊗ ⟩𝕀𝕀𝕀 by prior arrangement ┗ 🖤 ♀ ┻ 🏠 ⊤   ⬚
Location   5m NW of Johnstone

Hotel   ★★★ 67% Bowfield Hotel & Country Club, HOWWOOD ☎ 01505 705225   23 ⇆ ⋒

BURNSIDE   Map 11 NS65

Blairbeth Fernbrae Av, Fernhill G73 4SF
☎ 0141 634 3355
Parkland course.
18 holes, 5518yds, Par 70, SSS 68, Course record 64.
Club membership 600.
Visitors   must contact in advance & may not play weekends.
Societies   apply in advance.
Green Fees £20 per day; £15 per round.
Cards   ▭▭ ▭▭
Facilities   ⊗ ⟩𝕀𝕀𝕀 ┗ 🖤 ♀ ┻
Location   2m S of Rutherglen off Burnside road

Hotel   ★★★ 67% The Macdonald, Eastwood Toll, GIFFNOCK ☎ 0141 638 2225 56 ⇆ ⋒

Cathkin Braes Cathkin Rd G73 4SE
☎ 0141 634 6605 Fax 0141 630 9186
Moorland course, prevailing westerly wind, small loch hazard at 5th hole.
18 holes, 6208yds, Par 71, SSS 71, Course record 64.
Club membership 890.
Visitors   must contact in advance & have handicap certificate but may not play at weekends.
Societies   apply in writing.
Green Fees £35 per day; £25 per round.
Prof   Stephen Bree
Designer   James Braid
Facilities   ⊗ ⟩𝕀𝕀𝕀 ┗ 🖤 ♀ ┻ 🏠 🐎 🛒 ⬚
Location   1m S on B759

Hotel   ★★★ 67% The Macdonald, Eastwood Toll, GIFFNOCK ☎ 0141 638 2225 56 ⇆ ⋒

CARLUKE   Map 11 NS85

Carluke Mauldslie Rd, Hallcraig ML8 5HG
☎ 01555 771070 & 770574
Parkland course with views over the Clyde Valley. Testing 11th hole, par 3.
18 holes, 5853yds, Par 70, SSS 68, Course record 63.
Club membership 750.
Visitors   must contact in advance & may not play weekends and bank holidays.
Societies   prior arrangement required.
Green Fees £25 per day; £20 per round.
Prof   Richard Forrest
Facilities   ⊗ ⟩𝕀𝕀𝕀 ┗ 🖤 ♀ ┻ 🏠 ⬚
Location   1m W off A73

Hotel   ★★★ 71% Popinjay Hotel, Lanark Rd, ROSEBANK ☎ 01555 860441   40 ⇆ ⋒ Annexe 5 ⇆ ⋒

CARNWATH   Map 11 NS94

Carnwath 1 Main St ML11 8JX
☎ 01555 840251 Fax 01555 841070
Picturesque parkland course slightly hilly, with small greens calling for accuracy. Panoramic views.
18 holes, 5953yds, Par 70, SSS 69, Course record 63.
Club membership 550.
Visitors   restricted after 5pm, no visitors Sat.
Societies   apply in writing or telephone.
Green Fees £25 per day; £15 per round (£30/£20 Sun & bank holidays).
Facilities   ⊗ ⟩𝕀𝕀𝕀 ┗ 🖤 ♀ ┻ 🏠 ⬚
Location   W side of village on A70

Hotel   ★★★ 65% Cartland Bridge Hotel, Glasgow Rd, LANARK ☎ 01555 664426   18 ⇆ ⋒

CASTLE DOUGLAS   Map 11 NX76

Castle Douglas Abercromby Rd DG7 1BB
☎ 01556 502801 or 502099
Parkland course, one severe hill.
9 holes, 2704yds, Par 68, SSS 66.
Club membership 500.
Societies   apply by writing to secretary.
Green Fees £12 per day/round.
Facilities   ⊗ ┗ 🖤 ♀ ┻ 🏠 ⊤ ⬚
Location   W side of town

Hotel   ★★ 65% Imperial Hotel, 35 King St, CASTLE DOUGLAS ☎ 01556 502086   12 ⇆ ⋒

CLARKSTON   Map 11 NS55

Cathcart Castle Mearns Rd G76 7YL
☎ 0141 638 9449 Fax 0141 638 1201
Tree-lined parkland course, with undulating terrain.
18 holes, 5832yds, Par 68, SSS 68.
Club membership 995.
Visitors   by prior arrangement with professional, must have a handicap certificate from own club.   ▶

Societies Tue & Thu only; must apply in writing.
Green Fees not confirmed.
Prof Stephen Duncan
Facilities ⊗))| ⛳ ☕ 🍷 ⛰ 🏠 🛒 ✐
Location 0.75m SW off A726

Hotel ★★★ 67% The Macdonald, Eastwood Toll, GIFFNOCK ☎ 0141 638 2225 56 ⇌ ↑

CLYDEBANK Map 11 NS56

Clydebank & District Glasgow Rd, Hardgate G81 5QY
☎ 01389 383831 & 383833 Fax 01389 383831
An undulating parkland course established in 1905 overlooking Clydebank.
18 holes, 5823yds, Par 68, SSS 68, Course record 64.
Club membership 889.
Visitors round only, weekdays only and no bank holidays. Must tee off before 4.30pm. Apply to professional 01389 878686.
Societies must apply in writing.
Green Fees not confirmed.
Designer Members
Facilities ⛰ 🏠
Location 2m E of Erskine Bridge

Hotel ★★★ 64% Patio Hotel, 1 South Av, Clydebank Business Park, CLYDEBANK ☎ 0141 951 1133 80 ⇌ ↑

Dalmuir Municipal Overtoun Rd, Dalmuir G81 3RE
☎ 0141 952 6372
Hilly, compact parkland course with tough finishing holes.
18 holes, 5349yds, Par 67, SSS 66, Course record 63.
Visitors contact in advance.
Societies contact in advance.
Green Fees £7.50 (£9 weekends).
Prof Stewart Savage
Facilities ☕ ⛰ 🏠 ↑ ✐
Location 2m NW of town centre

Hotel ★★★ 64% Patio Hotel, 1 South Av, Clydebank Business Park, CLYDEBANK ☎ 0141 951 1133 80 ⇌ ↑

COATBRIDGE Map 11 NS76

Drumpellier Drumpellier Av ML5 1RX
☎ 01236 424139 Fax 01236 428723
Parkland course.
18 holes, 6227yds, Par 71, SSS 70, Course record 60.
Club membership 827.
Visitors must contact in advance, may not play weekends.
Societies apply in advance.
Green Fees not confirmed.
Prof David Ross
Designer W Fernie
Facilities ⊗))| ⛳ ☕ 🍷 ⛰ 🏠 ↑ ✐
Location 0.75m W off A89

Hotel ★★★ 67% Bothwell Bridge Hotel, 89 Main St, BOTHWELL ☎ 01698 852246 90 ⇌ ↑

COLDSTREAM Map 12 NT83

Hirsel Kelso Rd TD12 4NJ
☎ 01890 882678 & 882233 Fax 01890 882233
A beautifully situated parkland course set in the Hirsel Estate, with panoramic views of the Cheviot Hills. Each hole offers a different challenge especially the 7th, a 170yd par 3 demanding accuracy of flight and length from the tee to ensure achieving a par.
18 holes, 6092yds, Par 70, SSS 70, Course record 65.
Club membership 680.
Visitors contact for details, no restrictions.
Societies write or telephone the secretary in advance.
Green Fees not confirmed.
Facilities ⊗))| ⛳ ☕ 🍷 ⛰ 🏠 ↑ 🛒 ✐
Location At W end of Coldstream on A697

Hotel ★★★ 68% Tillmouth Park Hotel, CORNHILL-ON-TWEED ☎ 01890 882255 12 ⇌ ↑ Annexe 2 ⇌ ↑

COLVEND Map 11 NX85

Colvend Sandyhills DG5 4PY
☎ 01556 630398 & 610878 (Sec) Fax 01556 630495
Picturesque and challenging course on Solway coast. Superb views.
18 holes, 5220yds, Par 68, SSS 67, Course record 64.
Club membership 490.
Visitors restricted Apr-Sep on Tue, 1st tee reserved for weekly Medal 1-1.30 & 4-6pm and some weekends for open competitions.
Societies must telephone in advance.
Green Fees £20 per day.
Designer Allis & Thomas
Facilities ⊗))| ⛳ ☕ 🍷 ⛰ ↑ 🛒 🚗 ✐
Location 6m from Dalbeattie on A710 Solway Coast Rd

Hotel ★★ 64% Clonyard House Hotel, COLVEND ☎ 01556 630372 15 ⇌ ↑

CUMBERNAULD Map 11 NS77

Dullatur 1A Glen Douglas Dr G68 0DW
☎ 01236 723230 Fax 01236 727271
Dullatur Carrickstone is a parkland course, with natural hazards and wind. Dullatur Antonine, designed by Dave Thomas, is a modern course,
Carrickstone: 18 holes, 6204yds, Par 70, SSS 70, Course record 68.
Antonine: 18 holes, 6100yds, Par 70, SSS 69, Course record 67.
Club membership 700.
Visitors telephone for availability.
Societies must apply in writing to secretary.
Green Fees not confirmed.
Cards [card symbols]
Prof Duncan Sinclair
Designer James Braid
Facilities ⊗))| ⛳ ☕ 🍷 ⛰ 🏠 🛒 🚗 ✐
& Leisure hard tennis courts, sauna, solarium, gymnasium, bowls.
Location 1.5m N of A80 at Cumbernauld

Hotel ★★★★ 60% Westerwood Hotel Golf & Country Club, 1 St Andrews Dr, Westerwood, CUMBERNAULD ☎ 01236 457171 49 ⇌ ↑

Palacerigg Palacerigg Country Park G67 3HU
☎ 01236 734969 Fax 01236 721461
Well wooded parkland course.
18 holes, 6444yds, Par 72, SSS 71, Course record 65.
Club membership 350.

Visitors	anytime except club competitions, advance booking advisable.
Societies	apply in writing to the Secretary.
Green Fees	£7.50 per round (£10 weekends).
Designer	Henry Cotton
Facilities	⊗ ⋈ ⮹ ⬛ ♀ ♨ 🏠
Location	2m S of Cumbernauld on Palacerigg road off Lenziemill road B8054

Hotel	★★★★ 60% Westerwood Hotel Golf & Country Club, 1 St Andrews Dr, Westerwood, CUMBERNAULD ☎ 01236 457171 49 ⇆ ↾

Westerwood Hotel Golf & Country Club 1 St Andrews Dr, Westerwood G68 0EW
☎ 01236 457171 Fax 01236 738478
Undulating parkland/woodland course designed by Dave Thomas and Seve Ballesteros. Holes meander through silver birch, firs, heaths and heathers, and the spectacular 15th, 'The Waterfall', has its green set against a 40ft rockface. Buggie track. Hotel facilities.
18 holes, 6616yds, Par 72, SSS 72, Course record 65.
Club membership 1000.

Visitors	advised to book in advance.
Societies	all bookings through golf coordinator on 01236 457171 ext 215.
Green Fees	£22.50 per round (£27.50 weekends).
Cards	💳 💳 💳 💳 💳 💳
Prof	Steven Killin
Designer	Seve Ballesteros/Dave Thomas
Facilities	⊗ ⋈ ⮹ ⬛ ♀ ♨ 🏠 ⛳ ⮕ ⬩ ⚓ ♪ ↾
& Leisure	hard tennis courts, heated indoor swimming pool, solarium, gymnasium.
Location	Adjacent to A80, 14m from Glasgow City Centre

Hotel	★★★★ 60% Westerwood Hotel Golf & Country Club, 1 St Andrews Dr, Westerwood, CUMBERNAULD ☎ 01236 457171 49 ⇆ ↾

CUMMERTREES   Map 11 NY16

Powfoot DG12 5QE
☎ 01461 700276 Fax 01461 700276
This British Championship Course is on the Solway Firth, playing at this delightfully compact semi-links seaside course is a scenic treat. Lovely holes include the

2nd, the 8th and the 11th, also 9th with World War II bomb crater.
18 holes, 6283yds, Par 71, SSS 70, Course record 63.
Club membership 950.

Visitors	contact in advance. May not play before 9am between 11am-1pm and after 3.30pm weekdays, no visitors Sat or before 2pm Sun.
Societies	must book in advance.
Green Fees	£30 per day; £23 per round.
Prof	Gareth Dick
Designer	J Braid
Facilities	⊗ ⋈ ⮹ ⬛ ♀ ♨ 🏠 ⛳
Location	0.5m off B724

Hotel	★★ 70% Powfoot Golf Hotel, Links Av, POWFOOT ☎ 01461 700254 18 ⇆ ↾

DALBEATTIE   Map 11 NX86

Dalbeattie Off Maxwell Park DG5 4JR ☎ 01556 610682
This 9 hole course provides an excellent challenge for golfers of all abilities. There are a few gentle slopes to negotiate but compensated by fine views along the Urr Valley. The 363 yard 4th hole is a memorable par 4. A good straight drive is required to the corner of the course where a right angle dog-leg is taken for a pitch to a smallish green.
9 holes, 5710yds, Par 68, SSS 68.
Club membership 300.

Visitors	club competitions Mon, Wed and Thu, visitors reuqested not to play after 5pm.
Societies	apply in writing to Secretary or telephone 01556 610311/611760.
Green Fees	£15 per day, £12 per 18 holes.
Facilities	⮹ ⬛ ♨
Location	Signposted off B794

Hotel	★★ 64% King's Arms Hotel, St Andrew's St, CASTLE DOUGLAS ☎ 01556 502626 10rm(9 ⇆ ↾)

DUMBARTON   Map 10 NS37

Dumbarton Broadmeadow G82 2BQ
☎ 01389 732830 Fax 01389 765995
Flat parkland course.
18 holes, 5992yds, Par 71, SSS 69, Course record 64.
Club membership 700.

Visitors	may play Mon, Thu & Fri only.
Societies	must apply in writing to Secretary.
Green Fees	£22 per day.
Facilities	⊗ ⋈ ⮹ ⬛ ♀ ♨
Location	0.25m N off A814

Hotel	★★ 66% Dumbuck House Hotel, Glasgow Rd, DUMBARTON ☎ 01389 734336 22 ⇆ ↾

DUMFRIES   Map 11 NX97

Dumfries & County Nunfield, Edinburgh Rd DG1 1JX
☎ 01387 253585 Fax 01387 253585
Parkland course alongside River Nith, with views over the Queensberry Hills.
Nunfield: 18 holes, 5928yds, Par 69, SSS 68,
Course record 63.
Club membership 800.

▶

Visitors	must contact in advance but may not play Saturdays and during competitions on Sundays
Societies	apply in writing.
Green Fees	£26 per day.
Prof	Stuart Syme
Designer	William Fernie
Facilities	⊗ ⫶ ▟ 🍺 ♀ ⚘ 🏠 ⛿ ⚂
Location	1m NE of Dumfries on A701

Hotel	★★★ 68% Station Hotel, 49 Lovers Walk, DUMFRIES ☎ 01387 254316 32 ⇌ ⏚
Additional hotel	★★★ 69% Cairndale Hotel & Leisure Club, English St, DUMFRIES ☎ 01387 254111 Fax 01387 250555 76 ⇌ ⏚

Dumfries & Galloway 2 Laurieston Av DG2 7NY
☎ 01387 263848 Fax 01387 263848
Parkland course.
18 holes, 5803yds, Par 70, SSS 71.
Club membership 800.

Visitors	may not play on competition days.
Societies	apply in writing.
Green Fees	£25 per day/round (£30 weekends).
Prof	Joe Fergusson
Designer	W Fernie
Facilities	⊗ ⫶ ▟ 🍺 ♀ ⚘ 🏠 ⛿ ⚂
Location	W side of town centre on A75

Hotel	★★★ 69% Cairndale Hotel & Leisure Club, English St, DUMFRIES ☎ 01387 254111 76 ⇌ ⏚

DUNS
Map 12 NT75

Duns Longformacus Rd TD11 3NR
☎ 01361 882717 (Sec) & 882194 (Clubhouse)
Interesting upland course, with natural hazards of water and hilly slopes. Views south to the Cheviot Hills. A burn comes into play at 7 of the holes.
18 holes, 6209yds, Par 70, SSS 70.
Club membership 520.

Visitors	welcome except competition days and Mon, Tue and Wed after 4pm. Advisable to contact in advance Apr-Oct.
Societies	write or telephone the secretary in advance for booking details.
Green Fees	£17 per day; £14 per round (£22/£17 weekends).
Designer	A H Scott
Facilities	⊗ ⫶ ▟ 🍺 ♀ ⚘ ⚂
Location	1m W off A6105

Hotel	★★★ 71% Marshall Meadows Country House Hotel, BERWICK-UPON-TWEED ☎ 01289 331133 19 ⇌ ⏚

EAGLESHAM
Map 11 NS55

Bonnyton Kirktonmoor Rd G76 0QA
☎ 01355 302781 Fax 01355 303151
Dramatic moorland course offering spectacular views beautiful countryside as far as snow-capped Ben Lomond. Tree-lined fairways, plateau greens, natural burns and well situated bunkers and a unique variety of holes offer golfers both challenge and reward.
18 holes, 6255yds, Par 72, SSS 71.
Club membership 960.

Visitors	welcome Mon & Thu. Must contact in advance.

Societies	must telephone in advance.
Green Fees	£36 per day.
Prof	Kendal McWade
Facilities	⊗ ⫶ ▟ 🍺 ♀ ⚘ 🏠 ⛿ ⚄ ⚂
Location	0.25m SW off B764

Hotel	★★★ 69% Bruce Hotel, Cornwall St, EAST KILBRIDE ☎ 01355 229771 65 ⇌ ⏚

EAST KILBRIDE
Map 11 NS65

East Kilbride Chapelside Rd, Nerston G74 4PF
☎ 01355 247728
Parkland course of variable topography. Generous fairways and greens but a challenging test of golf.
18 holes, 6419yds, Par 71, SSS 71, Course record 64.
Club membership 850.

Visitors	by appointment.
Societies	must telephone in advance & submit formal application.
Green Fees	£35 per day; £25 per round.
Prof	Willy Walker
Facilities	⚘ 🏠 ⛿ ⚄ ⚂
Location	0.5m N off A749

Hotel	★★★ 69% Bruce Hotel, Cornwall St, EAST KILBRIDE ☎ 01355 229771 65 ⇌ ⏚

Torrance House Calderglen Country Park, Strathaven Rd G75 0QZ ☎ 01355 248638 Fax 01355 570916
A mature parkland course.
18 holes, 6476yds, Par 72, SSS 69, Course record 71.
Club membership 1000.

Visitors	welcome, may book up to six days in advance.
Societies	Mon-Fri. Apply in writing to John Dunlop, South Lanarkshire Council, Civic Centre, East Kilbride.
Green Fees	£8.20 (£9.50 weekends & bank holidays).
Facilities	⊗ ⫶ ▟ 🍺 ♀ ⚘ 🏠 ⛿ ⚂
Location	1.5m SE of Kilbride on A726

Hotel	★★★ 69% Bruce Hotel, Cornwall St, EAST KILBRIDE ☎ 01355 229771 65 ⇌ ⏚

EYEMOUTH
Map 12 NT96

Eyemouth Gunsgreen Hill TD14 5SF
☎ 01890 750551 & 750004 (Starter)
A superb course set on the East Berwickshire coast, containing interesting and challenging holes. The clubhouse overlooks the picturesque fishing village of Eyemouth and provides panoramic views over the course and North Sea.
18 holes, 6472yds, Par 72, SSS 71, Course record 66.
Club membership 400.

Visitors	may not play before 9am Sat or before 10am Sun. Visitors reserve tee times by writing/telephone.
Societies	apply in writing or telephone.
Green Fees	£25 per day; £18 per day (£30/£22 weekends).
Prof	Paul Terras, Tony McLeman
Designer	J R Bain
Facilities	⊗ ▟ 🍺 ♀ ⚘ 🏠 ⛿ ⚄ ⚂
Location	E side of town, 8m N of Berwick and 2m off A1

Hotel	★★★ 71% Marshall Meadows Country House Hotel, BERWICK-UPON-TWEED ☎ 01289 331133 19 ⇌ ⏚

GALSHIELS

Map 12 NT43

Galashiels Ladhope Recreation Ground TD1 2NJ
☎ 01896 753724
Hillside course, superb views from the top; 10th hole very steep.
18 holes, 5185yds, Par 67, SSS 66, Course record 61.
Club membership 311.

Visitors	must contact the secretary in advance especially for weekends.
Societies	arrangements with secretary especially for weekends.
Green Fees	£20 per day; £15 per round (£25/£20 weekends).
Designer	James Braid
Facilities	⊗ ⅏ ᴸ ♥ by prior arrangement ♨ ♂
Location	N side of town centre off A7

Hotel ★★★ 66% Kingsknowes Hotel, Selkirk Rd,
GALASHIELS ☎ 01896 758375 11 ⇥ ♠

Torwoodlee TD1 2NE ☎ 01896 752260
Parkland course with natural hazards designed by Willie Park with a new extension by John Garner, provides a good test for all abilities of play.
18 holes, 6200yds, Par 70, SSS 69, Course record 68.
Club membership 550.

Visitors	restricted Thu - ladies day and Sat - mens competitions.
Societies	letter to secretary.
Green Fees	not confirmed.
Cards	🟦 💳
Prof	R Elliot
Designer	Willie Park
Facilities	⊗ ⅏ ᴸ ♥ ♀ ♨ 🏠 ✝ ☇ ♣ ♂
Location	1.75m NW off A7

Hotel ★★★ 66% Kingsknowes Hotel, Selkirk Rd,
GALASHIELS ☎ 01896 758375 11 ⇥ ♠

GALSTON

Map 11 NS53

Loudoun Edinburgh Rd KA4 8PA
☎ 01563 821993 & 820551 Fax 01563 822229
Pleasant, fairly flat parkland course with many mature trees.
18 holes, 5773yds, Par 68, SSS 68, Course record 61.
Club membership 750.

Visitors	must contact in advance. Weekdays only, must play with member at weekends/public holidays
Societies	telephone in advance.
Green Fees	not confirmed.
Facilities	⊗ ⅏ ᴸ ♥ ♀ ♨ 🏠 ♂
Location	NE side of town on A71

Hotel ★★★ 68% Strathaven Hotel, Hamilton Rd,
STRATHAVEN ☎ 01357 521778 22 ⇥ ♠

GARTCOSH

Map 11 NS66

Mount Ellen Johnston Rd G69 8EY
☎ 01236 872277 Fax 01236 872249
Downland course with 73 bunkers. Testing hole: 10th ('Bedlay'), 156 yds, par 3.
18 holes, 5525yds, Par 68, SSS 67, Course record 67.
Club membership 500.

Visitors	may play Mon-Fri 9am-4pm. Must contact in advance.
Societies	must contact in advance.
Green Fees	not confirmed.
Prof	Iain Bilsborough
Facilities	ᴸ ♥ ♀ ♨ 🏠 ✝ ☇ ♂
Location	0.75m N off A752

Hotel ★★★★ 64% Copthorne Glasgow,
George Square, GLASGOW
☎ 0141 332 6711 141 ⇥ ♠

GATEHOUSE-OF-FLEET

Map 11 NX55

Gatehouse Laurieston Rd DG7 2BE ☎ 01644 450260
Set against a background of rolling hills with scenic views of Fleet Bay and the Solway Firth.
9 holes, 2521yds, Par 66, SSS 66, Course record 60.
Club membership 370.

Visitors	restricted Sun before 11.30am.
Societies	telephone in advance.
Green Fees	not confirmed.
Designer	Tom Fernie
Facilities	♨
Location	0.25m N of town

Hotel ★★★ 64% Murray Arms Hotel,
GATEHOUSE OF FLEET
☎ 01557 814207 12 ⇥ ♠ Annexe 1 ⇥ ♠

Additional hotel ★★★★🏅 67% Cally Palace Hotel,
GATEHOUSE OF FLEET
☎ 01557 814341 Fax 01557 814522 56 ⇥

GIRVAN

Map 10 NX19

Brunston Castle Golf Course Rd, Dailly KA26 9GD
☎ 01465 811471 Fax 01465 811545
Sheltered inland parkland course. A championship design by Donald Steel, the course is bisected by the River Girvan and shaped to incorporate all the natural surroundings. Lined with mature trees and incorporating a number of water features in addition to the river.
▶

Burns: 18 holes, 6792yds, Par 72, SSS 73, Course record 71.
Club membership 400.

Visitors	reserved for members at weekends 8-10 & 12.30-1.30. Must contact in advance.
Societies	telephone 01465 811471 to book.
Green Fees	£40 per day; £26 per round (£45/£30 weekends).
Cards	▭▭ ▬▬ ▬▬ ▭
Prof	Stephen Forbes
Designer	Donald Steel
Facilities	⊗ ⨛ ⅃ ▙ ☕ ♀ ♨ 🍴 🏌 🏍 ✐ ⚓
Location	6m SE of Turnberry, 5m E of Girvan

Hotel	★★★ 77% Malin Court, TURNBERRY ☎ 01655 331457 18 ⇆ ⟰

Girvan Golf Course Rd KA26 9HW ☎ 01465 714346
Municipal seaside and parkland course. Testing 17th hole
(223-yds) uphill, par 3. Good views.
18 holes, 5098yds, Par 64, SSS 65, Course record 61.
Club membership 175.

Visitors	telephone to book.
Societies	welcome.
Green Fees	£20 per day; £13 per round (£26/£14.50 weekends).
Cards	▭▭ ▬▬ ▬▬ ▬▬ ▭
Designer	D Kinnell/J Braid
Facilities	⚘ ✐
Location	N side of town off A77

Hotel	★★★ 77% Malin Court, TURNBERRY ☎ 01655 331457 18 ⇆ ⟰

GLASGOW   Map 11 NS56

Alexandra Alexandra Park, Alexandra Pde G31 8SE
☎ 0141 556 1294
Parkland course, hilly with some woodland. Many bunkers
and a barrier of trees between 1st and 9th fairway. Work
currently in progress to alter greens and improve course.
9 holes, 2800yds, Par 31, Course record 25.
Club membership 85.

Visitors	no restrictions.
Societies	telephone 24 hrs in advance or by writing one week in advance.
Green Fees	not confirmed.
Designer	G McArthur
Facilities	⚘
& Leisure	bowling green.
Location	2m E of city centre off M8/A8

Cowglen Barrhead Rd G43 1AU
☎ 0141 632 0556 Fax 01505 503000
Undulating and challenging parkland course with good views
over the Clyde valley to the Campsie Hills. Club and line
selection is most important on many holes due to the
strategic placing of copses on the course.
18 holes, 6079yds, Par 69, SSS 69, Course record 63.
Club membership 805.

Visitors	play on shorter course. Must contact in advance and have a handicap certificate. No visitors Tue, Fri and weekends.
Societies	must be booked in writing through the secretary.
Green Fees	£32 per day; £25 per round.
Prof	John McTear
Designer	David Adams/James Braid
Facilities	⊗ ⨛ ⅃ ▙ ☕ ♀ ♨ 🏌 ⟰
Location	4.5m SW of city centre on B762

Hotel	★★★ 67% The Macdonald, Eastwood Toll, GIFFNOCK ☎ 0141 638 2225 56 ⇆ ⟰

Haggs Castle 70 Dumbreck Rd, Dumbreck G41 4SN
☎ 0141 427 1157 Fax 0141 427 1157
Wooded, parkland course where Scottish National
Championships and the Glasgow and Scottish Open have
been held. Quite difficult.
18 holes, 6419yds, Par 71, SSS 71, Course record 68.
Club membership 900.

Visitors	may not play at weekends. Must contact in advance.
Societies	apply in writing.
Green Fees	£30 per round.
Cards	▭▭ ▬▬
Prof	Jim McAlister
Designer	James Baird
Facilities	⊗ ⨛ ⅃ ▙ ☕ ♀ ♨ 🍴 🏌 🏍 ✐
Location	2.5m SW of city centre on B768

Hotel	★★★ 67% Swallow Hotel, 517 Paisley Rd West, GLASGOW ☎ 0141 427 3146 117 ⇆ ⟰

Kirkhill Greenless Rd, Cambuslang G72 8YN
☎ 0141 641 8499 Fax 0141 641 8499
Meadowland course designed by James Braid.
18 holes, 6030yds, Par 70, SSS 70, Course record 63.
Club membership 650.

Visitors	must play with member at weekends.
Societies	must contact in advance.
Green Fees	not confirmed.
Prof	Duncan Williamson
Designer	J Braid
Facilities	⊗ ⨛ ⅃ ▙ ☕ ♀ ♨
Location	5m SE of city centre off A749

Hotel	★★★ 63% Stuart Hotel, 2 Cornwall Way, Town Centre, EAST KILBRIDE ☎ 013552 21161 38 ⇆ ⟰

Knightswood Lincoln Av G13 5QZ ☎ 0141 959 6358
Flat parkland course within easy reach of city. Two dog-legs.
9 holes, 5584yds, Par 68, SSS 67.
Club membership 40.

Visitors	reserved tee Wed and Fri am bookings 1 day in advance, no other restrictions.
Societies	welcome, must book 1 day in advance.
Green Fees	£7 per 18 holes; £3.50 per 9 holes.
Facilities	⚘
Location	4m W of city centre off A82

Hotel	★★★ 68% Jurys Glasgow Hotel, Great Western Rd, GLASGOW ☎ 0141 334 8161 136 ⇆ ⟰

Lethamhill 1240 Cumbernauld Rd, Millerston G33 1AH
☎ 0141 770 6220 Fax 1041 770 0520
Municipal parkland course.
18 holes, 5859yds, Par 70, SSS 69.

Visitors	must contact in advance.
Societies	must contact in advance.
Green Fees	not confirmed.
Facilities	⚘
Location	3m NE of city centre on A80

Hotel ★★★★ 64% Copthorne Glasgow, George Square, GLASGOW ☎ 0141 332 6711 141 ⇆ ↾

Linn Park Simshill Rd G44 5EP ☎ 0141 633 0377
Municipal parkland course with six par 3's in outward half.
18 holes, 4952yds, Par 65, SSS 65, Course record 61.
Visitors must contact in advance.
Societies advance booking in writing
Green Fees not confirmed.
Facilities ⬧
Location 4m S of city centre off B766

Hotel ★★★ 69% Bruce Hotel, Cornwall St, EAST KILBRIDE ☎ 01355 229771 65 ⇆ ↾

Pollok 90 Barrhead Rd G43 1BG
☎ 0141 632 4351 & 632 1080 Fax 0141 649 1398
Parkland course with woods and river.
18 holes, 6254yds, Par 71, SSS 70, Course record 62.
Club membership 620.
Visitors Members only until 2pm weekends. Must contact in advance. Ladies only as part of visiting parties
Societies must contact in writing.
Green Fees £42 per day; £32 per round.
Designer James Braid
Facilities ⊗ ℳ by prior arrangement ⬧ ♥ ♀ ⬧
Location 4m SW of city centre on A762

Hotel ★★★ 64% The Tinto Firs, 470 Kilmarnock Rd, GLASGOW ☎ 0141 637 2353 27 ⇆ ↾

Williamwood Clarkston Rd G44 3YR
☎ 0141 637 1783 Fax 0141 571 0166
Undulating parkland course with mature woodlands.
18 holes, 5878yds, Par 68, SSS 69, Course record 61.
Club membership 800.
Visitors apply in writing to secretary, no weekend play.
Societies midweek bookings only, apply in writing to secretary.
Green Fees £35 per day; £25 per round.
Prof Stewart Marshall
Designer James Braid
Facilities ⊗ ℳ ⬧ ♥ ♀ ⬧ ⬧
Location 5m S of city centre on B767

Hotel ★★★ 67% The Macdonald, Eastwood Toll, GIFFNOCK ☎ 0141 638 2225 56 ⇆ ↾

GLENLUCE   Map 10 NX15

Wigtownshire County Mains of Park DG8 0NN
☎ 01581 300420
Seaside links course on the shores of Luce Bay, easy walking but affected by winds. The 12th hole, a dogleg with out of bounds to the right, is named after the course's designer, Gordon Cunningham.
18 holes, 5843yds, Par 70, SSS 68, Course record 67.
Club membership 450.
Visitors may play any day by prior arrangement ex competition days.
Societies must contact in advance.
Green Fees £24 per day; £18.50 per round (£26/£20.50 weekends & bank holidays).
Designer W Gordon Cunningham

Facilities ⊗ ℳ ⬧ ♥ ♀ ⬧ ⬧ ↾ ✈ ⬧
Location 1.5m W off A75, 200 yds off A75 on shores of Luce Bay

Hotel ★★★★ 68% North West Castle Hotel, STRANRAER ☎ 01776 704413 70 ⇆ ↾ Annexe 3 ⇆ ↾

GREAT CUMBRAE ISLAND (MILLPORT)   Map 10 NS15

Millport Golf Rd KA28 0HB
☎ 01475 530305 (Prof) & 530311 (Club)
Fax 01475 530306
Pleasantly situated on the west side of Cumbrae looking over Bute to Arran and the Mull of Kintyre. Exposure means conditions may vary according to wind strength and direction. A typical seaside resort course welcoming visitors.
18 holes, 5828yds, Par 68, SSS 69, Course record 64.
Club membership 525.
Visitors advisable to phone and book tee times especially in summer months.
Societies telephone or write in advance.
Green Fees £24 per day; £19 per round (£29/£24 weekends).
Cards ▭ ⬧
Prof William Haldane Lee
Designer James Braid
Facilities ⊗ ℳ ⬧ ♥ ♀ ⬧ ⬧ ⬧
Location Approx 4m from ferry slip

Hotel ★★★ 73% Brisbane House, 14 Greenock Rd, Esplanade, LARGS ☎ 01475 687200 23 ⇆ ↾

GRETNA   Map 11 NY36

Gretna Kirtle View DG16 5HD ☎ 01461 338464
A nice parkland course on gentle hills. It offers a good test of skill.
9 holes, 3214yds, Par 72, SSS 71, Course record 71.
Club membership 250.
Visitors no restrictions.
Societies telephone in advance.
Green Fees not confirmed.
Designer N Williams
Facilities ⬧ ⬧ ↾
Location 0.5m W of Gretna on B721, signposted

Hotel ★★ 68% Solway Lodge Hotel, Annan Rd, GRETNA ☎ 01461 338266 3 ⇆ ↾ Annexe 7 ⇆ ↾

HAMILTON   Map 11 NS75

Hamilton Carlisle Rd, Ferniegair ML3 7UE
☎ 01698 459537
Beautiful parkland course.
18 holes, 6243yds, Par 70, SSS 71, Course record 62.
Visitors must contact in advance, may not play weekends.
Societies apply in writing.
Green Fees not confirmed.
Prof Maurice Moir
Designer James Braid
Facilities ⬧ ⬧ ⬧
Location 1.5m SE on A72

Hotel L Holiday Inn Express, Strathclyde Country Park, HAMILTON ☎ 01698 858585 120 ↾

Strathclyde Park Mote Hill ML3 6BY ☎ 01698 429350
Municipal wooded parkland course with views into the
Strathclyde Park sailing loch.
9 holes, 3128yds, Par 36, SSS 70, Course record 64.
Club membership 240.

Visitors	telephone, same day booking system in operation. May book up to 1 week in advance in summer months.
Societies	must contact in advance on above telephone number.
Green Fees	£4 per 9 holes.
Prof	William Walker
Facilities	🏌 ⚑ ♀ ⚒ 🏠 ♺
Location	N side of town off B7071
Hotel	L Holiday Inn Express, Strathclyde Country Park, HAMILTON ☎ 01698 858585 120 🏨

HAWICK   Map 12 NT51

Hawick Vertish Hill TD9 0NY ☎ 01450 372293
Hill course with good views.
18 holes, 5929yds, Par 68, SSS 69, Course record 63.
Club membership 600.

Visitors	must contact in advance. Course busy Sat until 3pm. 1st tee off time for visitors on Sun 10.30pm.
Societies	write or telephone for booking arrangement.
Green Fees	£25 per day; £20 per round.
Facilities	⊗ ⑪ 🏌 ⚑ ♀ ⚒ 🏠 ♺
Location	SW side of town
Hotel	★★ 66% Kirklands Hotel, West Stewart Place, HAWICK ☎ 01450 372263 5 ⇨ 🏨 Annexe 4 ⇨ 🏨

INNERLEITHEN   Map 11 NT33

Innerleithen Leithen Water, Leithen Rd EH44 6NL
☎ 01896 830951
Moorland course, with easy walking. Burns and rivers are
natural hazards. Testing 5th hole (100 yds) par 3.
9 holes, 6066yds, Par 70, SSS 69, Course record 65.
Club membership 280.

Visitors	advisable to check for availability for weekends.
Societies	by prior booking.
Green Fees	not confirmed.
Designer	Willie Park
Facilities	🏌 ⚑ ♀ ⚒
Location	1.5m N on B709
Hotel	★★★ 71% Peebles Hydro Hotel, PEEBLES ☎ 01721 720602 133 ⇨ 🏨

IRVINE   Map 10 NS33

Glasgow Gailes KA11 5AE
☎ 0141 942 2011 Fax 0141 942 0770
A lovely seaside links. The turf of the fairways and all
the greens is truly glorious and provides tireless play.
Established in 1882, and is a qualifying course for the
Open Championship.
*Glasgow Gailes: 18 holes, 6539yds, Par 71, SSS 72,
Course record 63.*
Club membership 1200.

Visitors	prior booking through secretary reccomended, no visitors before 2.30pm Sat & Sun.
Societies	initial contact by telephone.
Green Fees	£50 per day; £42 per round (£55 per round weekends).
Cards	💳 💳 💳 💳
Prof	J Steven
Designer	W Park Jnr
Facilities	⊗ ⑪ 🏌 🔔 ⚑ ♀ ⚒ 🏠 ♺ 🛒 ♺
Location	2m S off A737

Irvine Bogside KA12 8SN ☎ 01294 275979
Testing links course; only two short holes.
18 holes, 6400yds, Par 71, SSS 73, Course record 65.
Club membership 450.

Societies	are welcome weekdays and pm weekends, telephone in advance.
Green Fees	not confirmed.
Prof	Keith Erskine
Designer	James Braid
Facilities	⊗ ⑪ 🏌 ⚑ ♀ ⚒ 🏠 🛒 ♺
Location	N side of town off A737
Hotel	★★★ 74% Montgreenan Mansion House Hotel, Montgreenan Estate, KILWINNING ☎ 01294 557733 21 ⇨ 🏨

Irvine Ravenspark 13 Kidsneuk Ln KA12 8SR
☎ 01294 271293
Parkland course.
18 holes, 6702yds, Par 71, SSS 71, Course record 65.
Club membership 600.

Visitors	may not play Sat before 2pm.
Societies	not allowed Sat, contact club steward in advance.
Green Fees	not confirmed.
Prof	Peter Bond
Facilities	⊗ ⑪ 🏌 ⚑ ♀ ⚒ 🏠
Location	N side of town on A737
Hotel	★★★ 74% Montgreenan Mansion House Hotel, Montgreenan Estate, KILWINNING ☎ 01294 557733 21 ⇨ 🏨

Western Gailes Gailes by Irvine KA11 5AE
☎ 01294 311649 Fax 01294 312312
A magnificent seaside links with glorious turf and
wonderful greens. The view is open across the Firth of
Clyde to the neighbouring islands. It is a well-balanced
course crossed by 3 burns. There are 2 par 5's, the 6th
and 14th, and the 11th is a testing 445-yd, par 4, dog-leg.
18 holes, 6639yds, Par 71, SSS 73, Course record 65.

Visitors	welcome Mon, Tue (no ladies) Wed, Fri. Must contact in advance and have a handicap certificate. Time restrictions on Sun.
Societies	Mon/Wed/Fri, must contact in advance.
Green Fees	£95 per day; £70 per round (£80 per round Sun).
Cards	💳 💳 💳 💳
Facilities	⊗ ⑪ by prior arrangement 🏌 ⚑ ♀ ⚒ ♺
Location	2m S off A737
Hotel	★★★ 74% Montgreenan Mansion House Hotel, Montgreenan Estate, KILWINNING ☎ 01294 557733 21 ⇨ 🏨

JEDBURGH

Map 12 NT62

Jedburgh Dunion Rd TD8 6DQ ☎ 01835 863587
Undulating parkland course, windy, with young trees.
9 holes, 5760yds, Par 68, SSS 67, Course record 62.
Club membership 265.
Visitors	weekend restrictions.
Societies	must contact at least one month in advance.
Green Fees	Summer: £15 per day/round. Winter: £8 per day/round.
Designer	William Park
Facilities	⊗ ⓑ ☕ ♀ ♨ ✓
Location	1m W on B6358

Hotel ★★ 66% Kirklands Hotel, West Stewart Place, HAWICK ☎ 01450 372263
5 ⇌ ⋒ Annexe 4 ⇌ ⋒

JOHNSTONE

Map 10 NS46

Cochrane Castle Scott Av, Craigston PA5 0HF
☎ 01505 320146 Fax 01505 325338
Fairly hilly parkland course, wooded with two small streams running through it.
18 holes, 6223yds, Par 71, SSS 71, Course record 65.
Club membership 721.
Visitors	contact in advance, may not play at weekends.
Societies	apply in writing.
Green Fees	£28 per day; £17 per round.
Prof	Jason Boyd
Designer	J Hunter
Facilities	⊗ ⓜ ⓑ ☕ ♀ ♨ ♟ ✓
Location	1m from Johnstone town centre, off Beith Rd

Hotel ★★★ 69% Lynnhurst Hotel, Park Rd, JOHNSTONE ☎ 01505 324331 21 ⇌ ⋒

Elderslie 63 Main Rd, Elderslie PA5 9AZ
☎ 01505 323956 Fax 01505 340346
Parkland course, undulating, with good views.
18 holes, 6175yds, Par 70, SSS 70, Course record 61.
Club membership 940.
Visitors	may not play at weekends & bank holidays. Must contact club in advance and preferably have a handicap certificate.
Societies	must telephone in advance.
Green Fees	£40 per day inc food.
Prof	Richard Bowman
Designer	J Braid
Facilities	⊗ ⓜ ⓑ ☕ ♀ ♨ ♟ ♝ ✓
Location	E side of town on A737

Hotel ★★★ 69% Lynnhurst Hotel, Park Rd, JOHNSTONE ☎ 01505 324331 21 ⇌ ⋒

KELSO

Map 12 NT73

Kelso Racecourse Rd TD5 7SL ☎ 01573 223009
Parkland course. Easy walking.
18 holes, 6046yds, Par 70, SSS 69, Course record 64.
Club membership 500.
Visitors	advisable to telephone in advance.
Societies	apply in writing.
Green Fees	Apr-Oct: £20 per day; £16 per round (£28/£20 weekends). Nov-Mar £8 per day/round (£10 weekends).

Designer	James Braid
Facilities	⊗ ⓜ ⓑ ☕ ♀ ♨ ♟ ✓ ♝ ✓
Location	N side of town centre off B6461

Hotel ★★★ 63% Cross Keys Hotel, 36-37 The Square, KELSO ☎ 01573 223303 28 ⇌ ⋒

Roxburghe TD5 8JZ
☎ 01573 450331 Fax 01573 450611
Opened in 1996 and designed by Dave Thomas, this undulating course is set in 200 acres of mature parkland. Deep challenging bunkers, rolling greens and dramatic water hazards, including the River Teviot, provide a good test for all golfing abilities.
18 holes, 6925yds, Par 72, SSS 74, Course record 67.
Club membership 310.
Visitors	dress code (smart casual, no jeans, no training shoes).
Societies	please telephone in advance, a number of packages available.
Green Fees	£60 per day, £40 per round.
Cards	⊟ ▦ ▦ ▦
Prof	Gordon Niven
Designer	Dave Thomas
Facilities	⊗ ⓜ ⓑ ☕ ♀ ♨ ♟ ✓ ♝ ♞ ✓ ♟
& Leisure	hard tennis courts, fishing.
Location	5m E of Jedburgh on A698, 2m W of Kelso on A698

Hotel ★★★♠ 74% The Roxburghe Hotel & Golf Course, Heiton, KELSO ☎ 01573 450331 16 ⇌ ⋒ Annexe 6 ⇌ ⋒

KILBIRNIE   Map 10 NS35

Kilbirnie Place Largs Rd KA25 7AT ☎ 01505 683398
Easy walking parkland course.
18 holes, 5400yds, Par 69, SSS 67.
Club membership 450.
Visitors   no restrictions weekdays, no parties on Sun.
Societies   must apply in writing in advance.
Green Fees   not confirmed.
Facilities   ♀ ⚲
Location   1m W on A760

Hotel   ★★★ 72% Priory House Hotel, Broomfields,
                  LARGS ☎ 01475 686460   21 ⇌ ♠

KILMARNOCK   Map 10 NS43

Annanhill Irvine Rd KA1 2RT ☎ 01563 521644
Municipal, tree-lined parkland course played over by private
clubs.
18 holes, 6269yds, Par 71, SSS 70, Course record 66.
Club membership 394.
Visitors   must book at starters office.
Societies   apply in writing.
Green Fees   not confirmed.
Designer   Jack McLean
Facilities   ⚲
Location   1m N on A71

Hotel   L Travel Inn, The Moorfield, Moorfield
                  Roundabout, Annandale, KILMARNOCK
                  ☎ 01563 570534   40 ⇌ ♠
Additional   ★★★ 74% Montgreenan Mansion House
hotel   Hotel, Montgreenan Estate, KILWINNING
                  ☎ 01294 557733 Fax 01294 850397   21 ⇌ ♠

Caprington Ayr Rd KA1 4UW
☎ 01563 523702 & 521915 (Gen Enq)
Municipal parkland course.
18 holes, 5810yds, Par 68, SSS 68.
Club membership 400.
Visitors   may not play on Sat.
Societies   must contact in advance.
Green Fees   on application.
Facilities   ⚲ 🏠 ✆
Location   1.5m S on B7038

Hotel   L Travelodge, Kilmarnock By Pass,
                  KILMARNOCK ☎ 01563 573810   40 ⇌ ♠

KILSYTH   Map 11 NS77

Kilsyth Lennox Tak Ma Doon Rd G65 0RS
☎ 01236 824115 Fax 01236 823089
Hilly moorland course, hard walking.
18 holes, 5912yds, Par 70, SSS 70, Course record 66.
Club membership 500.
Visitors   advisable to contact in advance. No restrictions
                  weekdays up to 5pm, may play Sun on
                  application but not Sat.
Societies   must contact in advance.
Green Fees   not confirmed.
Prof   R Abercrombie
Facilities   ⊗ ⫼ ⤵ ⬛ ♀ ⚲ 🏠 ✆
Location   N side of town off A803

Hotel   ★★★★ 60% Westerwood Hotel Golf &
                  Country Club, 1 St Andrews Dr, Westerwood,
                  CUMBERNAULD ☎ 01236 457171   49 ⇌ ♠

KIRKCUDBRIGHT   Map 11 NX65

Brighouse Bay Brighouse Bay, Borgue DG6 4TS
☎ 01557 870409 Fax 01557 870409
A beautifully situated scenic maritime course on free
draining coastal grassland and playable all year. Making use
of many natural features - water, gullies and rocks - it
provides a testing challenge to golfers of all handicaps.
18 holes, 6602yds, Par 74, SSS 73.
Club membership 170.
Visitors   pay as you play - payment at adjacent Golf &
                  Leisure Club. Phoning in advance
                  recommended. Parties over 8 must book in
                  advance.
Societies   prior arrangement necessary.
Green Fees   £18 per day.
Cards   ▭ ▭ ▭ ▭
Designer   D Gray
Facilities   ⊗ ⫼ ⤵ ⬛ ♀ ⚲ 🏠 ⛳ ⤸ ⚓ ✦
& Leisure   heated indoor swimming pool, fishing, solarium,
                  gymnasium.
Location   3m S of Borgue off B727

Hotel   ★★★ 71% Selkirk Arms Hotel, Old High St,
                  KIRKCUDBRIGHT ☎ 01557 330402
                  13 ⇌ ♠ Annexe 3 ⇌ ♠

Kirkcudbright Stirling Crescent DG6 4EZ
☎ 01557 330314
Parkland course. Hilly, with good views over the Harbour
town of Kirkcudbright and the Dee Estuary.
18 holes, 5739yds, Par 69, SSS 69, Course record 63.
Club membership 500.
Visitors   advised to contact in advance.
Societies   contact in advance.
Green Fees   £23 per day; £18 per round.
Facilities   ⊗ ⫼ ⤵ ⬛ ♀ ⚲ ⛳ ⤸ ⚓ ✆
Location   NE side of town off A711

Hotel   ★★★ 71% Selkirk Arms Hotel, Old High St,
                  KIRKCUDBRIGHT ☎ 01557 330402
                  13 ⇌ ♠ Annexe 3 ⇌ ♠

KIRKINTILLOCH   Map 11 NS67

Hayston Campsie Rd G66 1RN
☎ 0141 776 1244 & 775 0723 (Sec)
An undulating, tree-lined course with a sandy subsoil.
18 holes, 6042yds, Par 70, SSS 70, Course record 60.
Club membership 800.
Visitors   must apply in advance, may not play weekends.
Societies   Tue & Thu, apply in writing
Green Fees   £30 per day; £20 per round.
Prof   Steven Barnett
Designer   James Braid
Facilities   ⊗ ⫼ ⤵ ⬛ ♀ ⚲ 🏠 ✆
Location   1m NW off A803

Hotel   ★★★★ 60% Westerwood Hotel Golf &
                  Country Club, 1 St Andrews Dr, Westerwood,
                  CUMBERNAULD ☎ 01236 457171   49 ⇌ ♠

Kirkintilloch Campsie Rd G66 1RN
☎ 0141 776 1256
Parkland course in rural setting.
18 holes, 5860yds, Par 70, SSS 68.
Club membership 650.
Visitors must be introduced by member.
Societies apply in writing.
Green Fees on application.
Designer James Braid
Facilities ⊗ ⓑ ☕ ♀ 🗆 🖱
Location 1m NW off A803

Hotel ★★★★ 60% Westerwood Hotel Golf &
Country Club, 1 St Andrews Dr, Westerwood,
CUMBERNAULD
☎ 01236 457171 49 ⇔ ⎘

LANARK   Map 11 NS84

Lanark The Moor, Whitelees Rd ML11 7RX
☎ 01555 663219 & 661456 Fax 01555 663219
The address of the club, 'The Moor', gives some
indication as to the kind of golf to be found there. Golf
has been played at Lanark for well over a century and the
Club dates from 1851.
*Old Course: 18 holes, 6423yds, Par 70, SSS 71, Course
record 62.*
Wee Course: 9 holes, 1489yds, Par 28.
Club membership 880.
Visitors booking advisable, no visitors weekends.
Societies apply in advance.
Green Fees £38 per day; £25 per round.
Prof Alan White
Designer Tom Morris
Facilities ⊗ ⫚ ⓑ ☕ ♀ 🗆 🖱 🏌 🛺 ⚘
Location E side of town centre off A73

Hotel ★★★ 65% Cartland Bridge Hotel,
Glasgow Rd, LANARK
☎ 01555 664426 18 ⇔ ⎘

LANGBANK   Map 10 NS37

Gleddoch Golf and Country Club PA14 6YE
☎ 01475 540304 Fax 01475 540201
Parkland and heathland course with other sporting facilities
available to temporary members. Good views over Firth of
Clyde.
18 holes, 6330yds, Par 71, SSS 71, Course record 64.
Club membership 500.
Visitors must contact in advance.
Societies must contact in advance.
Green Fees not confirmed.
Cards ▭▭ 🖭 🔳
Prof Keith Campbell
Designer Hamilton Strutt
Facilities ⊗ ⫚ ⓑ ☕ ♀ 🗆 🖱 🏌 🛺 🎱 ⚘ ⚗
& Leisure squash, horse riding.
Location B789-Old Greenock Road

Hotel ★★★★♨ 67% Gleddoch House Hotel,
LANGBANK
☎ 01475 540711 39 ⇔ ⎘

LANGHOLM   Map 11 NY38

Langholm Whitaside DG13 0JR
☎ 013873 80673 & 81247
Hillside course with fine views, easy to medium walking.
9 holes, 6180yds, Par 70, SSS 70.
Club membership 200.
Visitors restricted Sat & Sun.
Societies apply in writing to secretary.
Green Fees £10 per day/round.
Location E side of village off A7

Guesthouse ♦♦♦ The Reivers Rest, 81 High St, LANGHOLM
☎ 01387 381343 4 ⇔ ⎘

LARGS   Map 10 NS25

Largs Irvine Rd KA30 8EU
☎ 01475 673594 Fax 01475 673594
A parkland, tree-lined course with views to the Clyde coast
and Arran Isles.
18 holes, 6115yds, Par 70, SSS 71, Course record 63.
Club membership 850.
Visitors may not play competition days. Other times by
arrangement.
Societies apply in writing.
Green Fees not confirmed.
Prof Kenneth Docherty
Facilities ⊗ ⫚ ⓑ ☕ ♀ 🗆 🖱 🏌 ⚘
Location 1m S of town centre on A78

Hotel ★★★ 72% Priory House Hotel, Broomfields,
LARGS ☎ 01475 686460 21 ⇔ ⎘

Routenburn Routenburn Rd KA30 8QA ☎ 01475 673230
Heathland course with fine views over Firth of Clyde.
18 holes, 5675yds, Par 68, SSS 68.
Club membership 500.
Visitors no restrictions.
Societies apply in writing.
Green Fees not confirmed.
Cards ▭▭▭
Prof J Grieg McQueen
Designer J Braid
Facilities ⊗ ⫚ ⓑ ☕ ♀ 🗆 🖱 ⚘
Location 1m N off A78

Hotel ★★★ 58% Manor Park Hotel, LARGS
☎ 01475 520832 10 ⇔ ⎘ Annexe 13 ⇔ ⎘

LARKHALL   Map 11 NS75

Larkhall Burnhead Rd ML9 3AA ☎ 01698 889597
Small, inland parkland course.
9 holes, 6234yds, Par 70, SSS 70, Course record 69.
Club membership 250.
Visitors restricted Tue & Sat.
Green Fees not confirmed.
Facilities ☕ ♀
Location E side of town on B7019

Hotel ★★★ 71% Popinjay Hotel, Lanark Rd,
ROSEBANK ☎ 01555 860441
40 ⇔ ⎘ Annexe 5 ⇔ ⎘

LAUDER
Map 12 NT54

Lauder Galashiels Rd TD2 6RS ☎ 01578 722240
Inland course and practice area on gently sloping hill with
stunning views of the Lauderdale district.
9 holes, 3001yds, Par 72, SSS 69, Course record 66.
Club membership 350.

Visitors	restricted Wed 4.30-5.30pm and Sun before noon.
Societies	telephone in advance.
Green Fees	£10 per day.
Designer	Willie Park Jnr
Facilities	⌂
Location	On Galashiels Rd, off A68, 0.5m from Lauder

Hotel ★★ 66% Lauderdale Hotel, 1 Edinburgh Rd,
LAUDER ☎ 01578 722231 9 ⇆ ⋒

LEADHILLS
Map 11 NS81

Leadhills ML12 6XR ☎ 01659 74456
A testing, hilly course with high winds. At 1500ft above sea
level it is the highest golf course in Scotland.
9 holes, 4354yds, Par 66, SSS 64.
Club membership 80.

Visitors	groups must contact in advance.
Societies	must contact in advance.
Green Fees	£5 per day.
Location	E side of village off B797

Hotel ★★ 67% Blackaddie House Hotel, Blackaddie
Rd, SANQUHAR ☎ 01659 50270 10 ⇆ ⋒

LENNOXTOWN
Map 11 NS67

Campsie Crow Rd G66 7HX ☎ 01360 310244
Scenic hillside course.
18 holes, 5507yds, Par 70, SSS 68, Course record 69.
Club membership 620.

Visitors	preferred weekdays. Weedends only by prior arrangment, contact professional 01360 310920.
Societies	wrtten application.
Green Fees	£25 per day; £15 per round (£20 per round weekends).
Prof	Mark Brennan
Designer	W Auchterlonie
Facilities	⊗ ⫙ ⮟ ⓑ ♥ ♀ ⚘ 🏠 ⛳
Location	0.5m N on B822

Hotel ★★★★ 60% Westerwood Hotel Golf &
Country Club, 1 St Andrews Dr, Westerwood,
CUMBERNAULD ☎ 01236 457171 49 ⇆ ⋒

LENZIE
Map 11 NS67

Lenzie 19 Crosshill Rd G66 5DA
☎ 0141 776 1535 & 812 3018 Fax 0141 777 7748
Pleasant parkland course.
18 holes, 5984yds, Par 69, SSS 69, Course record 64.
Club membership 890.

Visitors	must contact in advance.
Societies	apply in writing/telephone in advance.
Green Fees	£28 per day; £18 per round.
Prof	Jim McCallum
Facilities	⊗ ⫙ ⮟ ⓑ ♥ ♀ ⚘ 🏠 ♥ ⛳
Location	N of Glasgow, approx 15 mins from Glasgow city centre, Kirkintilloch turn off M80

Hotel ★★★★ 60% Westerwood Hotel Golf &
Country Club, 1 St Andrews Dr, Westerwood,
CUMBERNAULD ☎ 01236 457171 49 ⇆ ⋒

LESMAHAGOW
Map 11 NS83

Holland Bush Acretophead ML11 0JS
☎ 01555 893484 & 893646
Fairly difficult, tree-lined municipal parkland and moorland
course. 1st half is relatively flat, while 2nd half is hilly.
18 holes, 6246yds, Par 71, SSS 70, Course record 63.
Club membership 400.

Visitors	contact shop on 01555 893646 for times etc.
Societies	contact shop on 01555 893646 in advance.
Green Fees	not confirmed.
Designer	J Lawson/K Pate
Facilities	⊗ ⫙ ⮟ ⓑ ♥ ♀ ⚘ 🏠 ⛳ ⚘
Location	2-3m S of Lesmahagow on the Lesmahagow-Coalburn Road

Hotel ★★★ 68% Strathaven Hotel, Hamilton Rd,
STRATHAVEN ☎ 01357 521778 22 ⇆ ⋒

LOCHMABEN
Map 11 NY08

Lochmaben Castlehillgate DG11 1NT ☎ 01387 810552
Attractive parkland course surrounding the Kirk Loch,
excellent views on this well maintained course.
18 holes, 5357yds, Par 67, SSS 66, Course record 61.
Club membership 850.

Visitors	advised to contact in advance.
Societies	must contact in advance.
Green Fees	not confirmed.
Designer	James Braid
Facilities	⊗ ⫙ ⮟ ⓑ ♥ ♀ ⚘ ⛳
& Leisure	fishing, snooker table.
Location	S side of village off A709

Hotel ★★★ 67% Dryfesdale Hotel, LOCKERBIE
☎ 01576 202427 15rm (9 ⇆ ⋒)

LOCHWINNOCH
Map 10 NS35

Lochwinnoch Burnfoot Rd PA12 4AN
☎ 01505 842153 & 01505 843029 Fax 01505 843668
Well maintained parkland course incorporating natural burns.
Throughout the course the majority of fairways are wide with
tricky greens, but always in good condition. Very scenic with
lots of bunkers.
18 holes, 6243yds, Par 71, SSS 71, Course record 63.
Club membership 650.

Visitors	may not play at weekends and bank holidays unless accompanied by member(check with Pro Shop). Restricted during competition days.
Societies	apply in writing to club administrator.
Green Fees	not confirmed.
Cards	🟦 🟦
Prof	Gerry Reilly
Facilities	⊗ ⫙ ⮟ ⓑ ♥ ♀ ⚘ 🏠 ⛳ ♥ ⚘ ⚘
Location	W side of town off A760, between Johnstone & Beith, off A737 on Largs road A760

Hotel ★★★ 67% Bowfield Hotel & Country Club,
HOWWOOD ☎ 01505 705225 23 ⇆ ⋒

LOCKERBIE

Map 11 NY18

Lockerbie Corrie Rd DG11 2ND
☎ 01576 203363 Fax 01576 203363
Parkland course with fine views and featuring the only pond hole in Dumfriesshire. Pond comes into play at 3 holes.
18 holes, 5614yds, Par 68, SSS 67, Course record 64.
Club membership 620.
Visitors restricted Sun. Advisable to book in advance.
Societies must contact secretary in advance.
Green Fees not confirmed.
Designer James Braid
Facilities ⊗ ℳ ⓛ 🍷 ♀ ♨ ✎
Location E side of town centre off B7068

Hotel ★★★ 67% Dryfesdale Hotel, LOCKERBIE
☎ 01576 202427 15rm (9 ⇌ 🐾)

MAUCHLINE

Map 11 NS42

Ballochmyle Catrine Rd KA5 6LE
☎ 01290 550469 Fax 01290 550469
Wooded parkland course.
18 holes, 5972yds, Par 70, SSS 69, Course record 64.
Club membership 730.
Visitors welcome. May not play Sat.
Societies apply in writing.
Green Fees £30 per day; £20 per round (£35/£25 Sun).
Cards ▭ ▭ ▭ ▭
Facilities ⊗ ℳ ⓛ 🍷 ♀ ♨ ✎ ✎
Location 1m SE on B705

Hotel ★★★ 58% Quality Hotel Ayr, Burns Statue
Square, AYR ☎ 01292 263268 75 ⇌ 🐾

MAYBOLE

Map 10 NS20

Maybole Municipal Memorial Park KA19 7DX
☎ 01655 889770
Hilly parkland course.
9 holes, 2635yds, Par 33, SSS 65, Course record 64.
Club membership 100.
Visitors no restrictions, telephone to book.
Societies must contact in advance.
Green Fees £8 per round (£9 weekends).
Leisure heated indoor swimming pool.
Location Off A77 S of town

Hotel ★★ Ladyburn, MAYBOLE
☎ 01655 740585 8rm (4 ⇌ 3 🐾)

MELROSE

Map 12 NT53

Melrose Dingleton TD6 9HS ☎ 01896 822855
Undulating tree-lined fairways with spendid views. Many bunkers.
9 holes, 5579yds, Par 70, SSS 68, Course record 61.
Club membership 380.
Visitors competitions all Sats and many Suns Apr-Oct, ladies priority Tue, junior priority Wed am in holidays.
Societies apply in writing.
Green Fees not confirmed.
Facilities ⊗ by prior arrangement ℳ by prior arrangement ⓛ by prior arrangement 🍷 by prior arrangement ♀ ♨
Location Off A68, S side of town centre on B6359

Hotel ★★ 66% Burt's Hotel, The Square,
MELROSE ☎ 01896 822285 20 ⇌ 🐾

MILNGAVIE

Map 11 NS57

Clober Craigton Rd G62 7HP ☎ 0141 956 1685
Parkland course. Testing 5th hole, par 3.
18 holes, 4824yds, Par 66, SSS 65, Course record 61.
Club membership 600.
Visitors may not play after 4pm Mon-Fri. Must play with member weekends and bank holidays.
Societies must contact in advance.
Green Fees £15 per round.
Prof C Elliott
Facilities ⊗ ℳ ⓛ 🍷 ♀ ♨ ✎
Location NW side of town

Hotel ★★★ 64% Patio Hotel, 1 South Av, Clydebank
Business Park, CLYDEBANK
☎ 0141 951 1133 80 ⇌ 🐾

Esporta, Dougalston Strathblane G62 8HJ
☎ 0141 955 2404 & 955 2434 Fax 0141 955 2406
A golf course of tremendous character set in 400 acres dotted with drumlins, lakes and criss-crossed by streams and ditches. One of the toughest tests of golf in the west of Scotland.
18 holes, 6225yds, Par 71, SSS 72.
Club membership 800.
Visitors contact in advance. May not play on Sat, tee times may be booked 3 days in advance.
Societies weekdays only.
Green Fees Apr-Oct: £20 per round (£25 weekends). Sep-Mar: £15 per round.
Cards ▭ ▭ ▭ ▭ ▭
Prof Craig Everett
Designer Commander Harris
Facilities ⊗ ℳ ⓛ 🍷 ♀ ♨ 🍴 ✎
& Leisure heated indoor swimming pool, sauna, solarium, gymnasium.
Location NE side of town on A81

Hotel ★★★ 64% Patio Hotel, 1 South Av, Clydebank
Business Park, CLYDEBANK
☎ 0141 951 1133 80 ⇌ 🐾

Hilton Park Auldmarroch Estate, Stockiemuir Rd G62 7HB
☎ 0141 956 4657 Fax 0141 956 4657
Moorland courses set amidst magnificent scenery.
Hilton Course: 18 holes, 6054yds, Par 70, SSS 70, Course record 65.
Allander Course: 18 holes, 5374yards, Par 69, SSS 67, Course record 65.
Club membership 1200.
Visitors must contact in advance but may not play at weekends.
Societies apply in advance to secretary.
Green Fees £32 per day; £24 per round.
Prof W McCondichie
Designer James Braid
Facilities ⊗ ℳ ⓛ 🍷 ♀ ♨ 🍴 🍴 ✎
Location 3m NW of Milngavie, on A809

Hotel ★★★ 64% Patio Hotel, 1 South Av, Clydebank
Business Park, CLYDEBANK
☎ 0141 951 1133 80 ⇌ 🐾

Milngavie Laighpark G62 8EP
☎ 0141 956 1619 Fax 0141 956 4252
Very scenic moorland course, which plays its full length,
challenging SSS, testing 1st hole followed by many others.
18 holes, 5818yds, Par 68, SSS 68, Course record 59.
Club membership 700.

Visitors	must contact in advance, may not play weekends.
Societies	apply in writing.
Green Fees	£30 per day; £22 per round.
Designer	The Auchterlonie Brothers
Facilities	⊗ ⊪ ⊾ ⬤ ♀ ⚐
Location	1.25m N

Hotel ★★★ 64% Patio Hotel, 1 South Av, Clydebank
Business Park, CLYDEBANK
☎ 0141 951 1133 80 ⇆ ⌑

MINTO   Map 12 NT52

Minto TD9 8SH ☎ 01450 870220 Fax 01450 870126
Pleasant, undulating parkland course featuring mature trees
and panoramic views of Scottish Border country. Short but
quite testing.
18 holes, 5542yds, Par 69, SSS 67, Course record 63.
Club membership 650.

Visitors	advisable to telephone in advance, and essential for weekends.
Societies	contact in advance.
Green Fees	£23 per day; £18 per round (£28/£23 weekends & bank holidays).
Cards	▭ ▬ ▭ ▨ ▨
Facilities	⊗ ⊪ ⊾ ⬤ ♀ ⬅ ⚐ ✦
Location	5m from Hawick, 1.25m off A698 at Denholm

Hotel ★★ 66% Kirklands Hotel,
West Stewart Place, HAWICK
☎ 01450 372263 5 ⇆ ⌑ Annexe 4 ⇆ ⌑

MOFFAT   Map 11 NT00

Moffat Coatshill DG10 9SB
☎ 01683 220020 Fax 01683 220020
Scenic moorland course overlooking the town, with
panoramic views of southern uplands.
18 holes, 5218yds, Par 69, SSS 67, Course record 60.
Club membership 350.

Visitors	advised to contact in advance, no visitors after 12 noon on Wed.
Societies	apply in writing/telephone the clubmaster.
Green Fees	£22 per day; £18.50 per round (£31/£28.50 weekend).
Cards	▬
Designer	Ben Sayers
Facilities	⊗ ⊾ ⬤ ♀ ⬅ ⬛ ⚐ ✦
& Leisure	snooker, pool table.
Location	From A74 1m on A701 to Moffat, course signposted

Hotel ★★★ 71% Moffat House Hotel, High St,
MOFFAT ☎ 01683 220039 20 ⇆ ⌑

Where to stay, where to eat?
Visit the AA internet site
www.theaa.co.uk

MONREITH   Map 10 NX34

St Medan DG8 8NJ ☎ 01988 700358
Links course with panoramic views of the Solway and Isle of
Man.
9 holes, 4608yds, Par 64, SSS 63, Course record 60.
Club membership 300.

Visitors	no restrictions.
Societies	apply in advance by telephone or writing
Green Fees	£45 per week; £15 per day; £12 per 18 holes; £8 per 9 holes.
Designer	James Braid
Facilities	⊗ ⊪ ⊾ ⬤ ♀ ⬅ ⚐
Location	1m SE off A747

Hotel ★★★♨ 65% Corsemalzie House Hotel,
PORT WILLIAM ☎ 01988 860254 14 ⇆ ⌑

MOTHERWELL   Map 11 NS75

Colville Park New Jerviston House, Jerviston Estate,
Merry St ML1 4UG
☎ 01698 265779 (pro) Fax 01698 230418
Parkland course. First nine, tree-lined, second nine, more
exposed. Testing 10th hole par 3, 16th hole par 4.
18 holes, 6250yds, Par 71, SSS 70, Course record 63.
Club membership 875.

Visitors	must contact in advance in writing. Smart dress code.
Societies	apply in writing.
Green Fees	£20 per round/day.
Prof	Alan Forrest
Designer	James Braid
Facilities	⊗ ⊪ ⊾ ⬤ ♀ ⬅ ⬛
& Leisure	2 outdoor bowling greens.
Location	1.25m NE on A723 from Motherwell town centre

Hotel ★★★ 67% Bothwell Bridge Hotel, 89 Main St,
BOTHWELL ☎ 01698 852246 90 ⇆ ⌑

MUIRHEAD   Map 11 NS66

Crow Wood Garnkirk House, Cumbernauld Rd G69 9JF
☎ 0141 779 4954 Fax 0141 779 9148
Parkland course.
18 holes, 6261yds, Par 71, SSS 71, Course record 62.
Club membership 800.

Visitors	must contact in advance but may not play weekends, bank holidays or competition days.
Societies	apply in advance.
Green Fees	not confirmed.
Prof	Brian Moffat
Designer	James Braid
Facilities	⊗ ⊪ ⊾ ⬤ ♀ ⬅ ⬛ ⚐
Location	0.5m W on A80

Hotel ★★★ 73% Malmaison Hotel, 278 West George
St, GLASGOW ☎ 0141 572 1000 72 ⇆ ⌑

NEWCASTLETON   Map 12 NY48

Newcastleton Holm Hill TD9 0QD ☎ 01387 375257
Hilly course with scenic views over the Liddesdale Valley
and Newcastleton.
9 holes, 5503yds, Par 69, SSS 70, Course record 69.
Club membership 100.

Visitors	contact the Secretary in advance.
Societies	contact by telephone or in writing in advance.
Green Fees	not confirmed.
Designer	J Shade
Facilities	⚒ 🏌
& Leisure	fishing.
Location	W side of village

Hotel   ★★★ 65% Garden House Hotel, Sarkfoot Rd, GRETNA ☎ 01461 337621   21 ⇆ 🏌

NEW CUMNOCK   Map 11 NS61

New Cumnock Lochhill, Cumnock Rd KA18 4PN
☎ 01290 338848
Parkland course.
9 holes, 5176yds, Par 68, SSS 68, Course record 63.
Club membership 280.

Visitors	restricted on Sun competition days. After 4 pm only
Societies	apply in writing.
Green Fees	not confirmed.
Designer	Willie Fernie
Facilities	⊗ ⫟ 🠇 ♥ ♀ ⚒ ⇆
& Leisure	fishing.
Location	0.75m N on A76

Hotel   ★★ 67% Blackaddie House Hotel, Blackaddie Rd, SANQUHAR ☎ 01659 50270 10 ⇆ 🏌

NEW GALLOWAY   Map 11 NX67

New Galloway High St DG7 3RN
☎ 01644 420737 & 450685 Fax 01644 450685
Set on the edge of the Galloway Hills and overlooking Loch Ken, the course has excellent tees and first class greens. The course rises through the first two fairways to a plateau with all round views that many think unsurpassed.
9 holes, 5006yds, Par 68, SSS 67, Course record 63.
Club membership 350.

Visitors	restricted on Sun (competition days). All visitors play off yellow markers. Contact Secretary in advance. Smart/casual dress.
Societies	contact secretary in advance.
Green Fees	£12.50 per day.
Designer	James Braid
Facilities	⊗ by prior arrangement 🠇 ♥ ♀ ⚒
Location	S side of town on A762

Hotel   ★★ 70% Douglas Arms, King St, CASTLE DOUGLAS ☎ 01556 502231   24 ⇆ 🏌

NEWTON MEARNS   Map 11 NS55

East Renfrewshire Pilmuir G77 6RT
☎ 01355 500256 & 500323
Undulating moorland with loch; prevailing SW wind.
18 holes, 6097yds, Par 70, SSS 70, Course record 63.
Club membership 900.

Visitors	must contact Professional in advance
Societies	Tues & Thur only, must contact in advance.
Green Fees	£40 per day; £30 per round.
Prof	Gordon Clarke
Designer	James Braid
Facilities	⊗ ⫟ 🠇 ♥ ♀ ⚒ 🛍 ⚘
Location	3m SW on A77

Hotel   ★★★ 67% The Macdonald, Eastwood Toll, GIFFNOCK ☎ 0141 638 2225 56 ⇆ 🏌

Eastwood Muirshield, Loganswell G77 6RX
☎ 01355 500285
An undulating moorland course situated in a scenic setting.
18 holes, 5864yds, Par 68, SSS 69, Course record 62.
Club membership 900.

Visitors	contact in advance. No visitors at weekends.
Societies	must contact in advance.
Green Fees	£30 per day; £24 per round.
Cards	🃏 🃏 🃏 💳
Prof	Allan McGinness
Designer	Theodore Moone
Facilities	⊗ ⫟ 🠇 ♥ ♀ ⚒ ⚘
Location	2.5m S of Newton Mearns, on A77

Hotel   ★★★ 67% The Macdonald, Eastwood Toll, GIFFNOCK ☎ 0141 638 2225 56 ⇆ 🏌

Whitecraigs 72 Ayr Rd G46 6SW
☎ 0141 639 4530 & 0141 639 2140 pro Fax 0141 639 4530
Beautiful parkland course only twenty minutes from the centre of Glasgow.
18 holes, 6230yds, Par 70, SSS 70, Course record 63.
Club membership 1078.

Visitors	must contact professional in advance and have a handicap certificate.
Societies	apply in advance.
Green Fees	£50 per day inc Tea/coffee, high tea & sandwiches; £37 per round inc tea/coffee & high tea.
Prof	Alistair Forrow
Facilities	⊗ ⫟ 🠇 ♥ ♀ ⚒ 🛍 🏌 ⚘
Location	1.5m NE on A77

Hotel   ★★★ 67% The Macdonald, Eastwood Toll, GIFFNOCK ☎ 0141 638 2225 56 ⇆ 🏌

NEWTON STEWART   Map 10 NX46

Newton Stewart Kirroughtree Av, Minnigaff DG8 6PF
☎ 01671 402172 Fax 01671 402172
Parkland course in picturesque setting. A good test for all standards of golfers with a variety of shots required.
18 holes, 5903yds, Par 69, SSS 70, Course record 66.
Club membership 380.

Visitors	must contact in advance.
Societies	must contact in advance.
Green Fees	£23 per day; £20 per round (£27/£23 weekends & bank holidays).
Facilities	⊗ ⫟ 🠇 ♥ ♀ ⚒ 🛍 🏌 🛒 ⚘
Location	0.5m N of town centre

Hotel   ★★ 72% Creebridge House Hotel, NEWTON STEWART ☎ 01671 402121   19 ⇆ 🏌

PAISLEY   Map 11 NS46

Barshaw Barshaw Park PA1 3TJ ☎ 0141 889 2908
Municipal parkland course.
18 holes, 5703yds, Par 68, SSS 67, Course record 63.
Club membership 100.

Visitors	no restrictions.
Societies	by prior arrangement with Parks Manager, Renfrewshire Council, Enviorment House, Bridge Street, Paisley PA3 2AB.

▶

Green Fees £7.50 per round.
Facilities ♿ ☕
Location 1m E off A737

Hotel ★★★ 69% Glynhill Hotel & Leisure Club, Paisley Rd, RENFREW
☎ 0141 886 5555 & 885 1111
Fax 0141 885 2838 125 ⇄ ♞

Paisley Braehead PA2 8TZ
☎ 0141 884 3903 Fax 0141 884 3903
Moorland course, windy but with good views. The course has been designed in two loops of nine holes.
18 holes, 6215yds, Par 70, SSS 71.
Club membership 800.
Visitors must contact in advance. Visitors may not play weekends or public holidays.
Societies weekdays only, excluding bank holidays. Contact in advance.
Green Fees not confirmed.
Prof Gordon Stewart
Facilities ⊗ ♏ ♐ 🍴 🍷 ♨ 🏠 ♘ ☕
Location S side of town off B774

Hotel ★★★ 69% Glynhill Hotel & Leisure Club, Paisley Rd, RENFREW
☎ 0141 886 5555 & 885 1111
Fax 0141 885 2838 125 ⇄ ♞

Ralston Strathmore Av, Ralston PA1 3DT
☎ 0141 882 1349 Fax 0141 883 9837
Parkland course.
18 holes, 6071yds, Par 71, SSS 69, Course record 62.
Club membership 750.
Visitors Mon-Fri only and must be accompanied by member.
Societies written notice required
Green Fees £28 per day; £18 per round.
Cards 🌐 💳 🆒
Prof Colin Munro
Designer J Braid
Facilities ⊗ ♏ ♐ 🍴 🍷 ♨ 🏠 ☕
Location 2m E off A737

Hotel ★★★ 67% Swallow Hotel, 517 Paisley Rd West, GLASGOW
☎ 0141 427 3146 117 ⇄ ♞

PATNA — Map 10 NS41

Doon Valley Hillside Park KA6 7JT
☎ 01292 531607
Established parkland course located on an undulating hillside.
9 holes, 5886yds, Par 70, SSS 69, Course record 56.
Club membership 100.
Visitors no restrictions mid week, advisable to contact in advance for weekends.
Societies telephone to arrange.
Green Fees £10 per round.
Facilities 🍷 ♨
& Leisure fishing.
Location 10m S of Ayr on the A713

Hotel ★★ Ladyburn, MAYBOLE
☎ 01655 740585 8rm (4 ⇄ 3 ♞)

PEEBLES — Map 11 NT24

Peebles Kirkland St EH45 8EU ☎ 01721 720197
Parkland course with fine views.
18 holes, 6160yds, Par 70, SSS 70, Course record 63.
Club membership 750.
Visitors advisable to ring for information on availability, no visitors on Sat.
Societies apply by telephone or in writing in advance.
Green Fees £27 per day; £20 per round (£34/£25 weekends).
Prof Craig Imlah
Designer H S Colt
Facilities ⊗ ♏ ♐ 🍴 🍷 ♨ 🏠 ♘ ♞ 🚜 ☕
Location W side of town centre off A72

Hotel ★★★ 71% Peebles Hydro Hotel, PEEBLES
☎ 01721 720602 133 ⇄ ♞

PORTPATRICK — Map 10 NX05

Portpatrick Golf Course Rd DG9 8TB
☎ 01776 810273 Fax 01776 810811
Seaside links-type course, set on cliffs overlooking the Irish Sea, with magnificent views.
Dunskey Course: 18 holes, 5908yds, Par 70, SSS 67, Course record 63.
Dinvin Course: 9 holes, 1504yds, Par 27, SSS 27, Course record 23.
Club membership 750.
Visitors must contact in advance. £5 deposite required
Societies must contact in advance.
Green Fees Dunskey: £30 per day; £20 per round (£35/£25 weekends).
Cards 🌐 💳 🆒 🆒
Designer Charles Hunter
Facilities ⊗ ♏ ♐ 🍴 🍷 ♨ 🏠 ♘ ♞ 🚜 ☕
Location On entering village fork right at War Memorial, 300yds signposted

Hotel ★★★ 72% Fernhill Hotel, PORTPATRICK
☎ 01776 810220 14 ⇄ ♞ Annexe 6 ⇄ ♞

PRESTWICK — Map 10 NS32

Prestwick 2 Links Rd KA9 1QG
☎ 01292 477404 Fax 01292 477255
Seaside links with natural hazards, tight fairways and difficult fast undulating greens.
18 holes, 6544yds, Par 71, SSS 73, Course record 67.
Club membership 575.
Visitors restricted Thu; may not play at weekends. Must contact in advance and have a handicap certificate.
Societies must contact in writing.
Green Fees £100 per day; £75 per round.
Cards 🌐 💳 🆒 🆒
Prof F C Rennie
Designer Tom Morris
Facilities ⊗ ♐ 🍴 🍷 ♨ 🏠 ♘ ☕
Location In town centre off A79

Hotel ★★★ 66% Parkstone Hotel, Esplanade, PRESTWICK
☎ 01292 477286 22 ⇄ ♞

Prestwick St Cuthbert East Rd KA9 2SX
☎ 01292 477101 Fax 01292 671730
Parkland course with easy walking, natural hazards and
sometimes windy.
18 holes, 6470yds, Par 71, SSS 71, Course record 64.
Club membership 880.

Visitors	must contact in advance but may not play at weekends & bank holidays.
Societies	Mon-Fri, apply in writing.
Green Fees	£32 per day; £22 per round.
Designer	Stutt & Co
Facilities	⊗ ⫟ ﭢ ♥ ♀ ⚐ ♂
Location	0.5m E of town centre off A77

Hotel ★★★ 66% Parkstone Hotel, Esplanade,
PRESTWICK ☎ 01292 477286 22 ⇌ ⋒

Prestwick St Nicholas Grangemuir Rd KA9 1SN
☎ 01292 477608 Fax 01292 473900
Seaside links course with whins, heather and tight fairways.
It provides easy walking and has an unrestricted view of the
Firth of Clyde.
18 holes, 5952yds, Par 69, SSS 69, Course record 63.
Club membership 750.

Visitors	except Sat, Sun am. Must contact in advance.
Societies	must contact in advance.
Green Fees	£50 per day; £30 per round (£35 per round Sun).
Cards	💳 💳 💳 💳
Designer	Charles Hunter
Facilities	⊗ ⫟ ﭢ ♥ ♀ ⚐ ♂
Location	S side of town off A79

Hotel ★★★ 66% Parkstone Hotel, Esplanade,
PRESTWICK ☎ 01292 477286 22 ⇌ ⋒

RENFREW   Map 11 NS46

Renfrew Blythswood Estate, Inchinnan Rd PA4 9EG
☎ 0141 886 6692 Fax 0141 886 1808
Tree-lined parkland course.
18 holes, 6818yds, Par 72, SSS 73, Course record 65.
Club membership 800.

Visitors	restricted to Mon, Tue & Thu, apply in advance.
Societies	apply in writing in advance.
Green Fees	£35 per day; £25 per round.
Prof	Stephen Dundas
Designer	Commander Harris
Facilities	⊗ ⫟ ﭢ ♥ ♀ ⚐ ♂
Location	0.75m W off A8

Hotel ★★★ 69% Glynhill Hotel & Leisure Club,
Paisley Rd, RENFREW
☎ 0141 886 5555 & 885 1111
Fax 0141 885 2838 125 ⇌ ⋒

RIGSIDE   Map 11 NS83

Douglas Water Ayr Rd ML11 9NP ☎ 01555 880361
A 9-hole course with good variety and some hills and
spectacular views. An interesting course with a challenging
longest hole of 564 yards but, overall, not too testing for
average golfers.
9 holes, 5890yds, Par 72, SSS 69, Course record 64.
Club membership 250.

Visitors	no restrictions weekdays or Sun, competitions on Sat normal restrictions.

Societies	apply in writing/telephone in advance.
Green Fees	£6 per day (£10 Sun & bank holidays).
Facilities	♥ ♀ ⚐
Location	Ayr road A70

Hotel ★★★ 63% Tinto Hotel, Symington, BIGGAR
☎ 01899 308454 29 ⇌ ⋒

ST BOSWELLS   Map 12 NT53

St Boswells Braeheads TD6 0DE
☎ 01835 823527
Attractive parkland course by the banks of the River Tweed;
easy walking.
9 holes, 5250yds, Par 66.
Club membership 320.

Visitors	contact in advance.
Societies	booking by writing to secretary.
Green Fees	not confirmed.
Designer	W Park
Facilities	⚐
& Leisure	fishing.
Location	500yds off A68 east end of village

Hotel ★★★ ♨ 76% Dryburgh Abbey Hotel,
ST BOSWELLS
☎ 01835 822261 37 ⇌ ⋒ Annexe 1 ⇌ ⋒

SANQUHAR   Map 11 NS70

Sanquhar Euchan Golf Course, Blackaddie Rd DG4 6JZ
☎ 01659 50577 & 66095
Parkland course, fine views, easy walking. A good test for all
standards of golfer.
9 holes, 5594yds, Par 70, SSS 68, Course record 66.
Club membership 200.

Visitors	no restrictions.
Societies	must pre-book.
Green Fees	£12 per day (£15 weekends).
Designer	Willie Fernie
Facilities	⚐
Location	0.5m SW off A76

Hotel ★★ 67% Blackaddie House Hotel, Blackaddie
Rd, SANQUHAR
☎ 01659 50270 10 ⇌ ⋒

SELKIRK   Map 12 NT42

Selkirk Selkirk Hill TD7 4NW
☎ 01750 20621
Pleasant moorland course set around Selkirk Hill. Unrivalled
views.
9 holes, 5620yds, Par 68, SSS 67, Course record 61.
Club membership 364.

Visitors	contact in advance, may not play Mon evening, competition/match days.
Societies	must telephone in advance.
Green Fees	£15 per day.
Facilities	ﭢ by prior arrangement ♀ ⚐ ♂ ♂
Location	1m S on A7

Hotel ★★ 66% Burt's Hotel, The Square,
MELROSE
☎ 01896 822285 20 ⇌ ⋒

SHOTTS
Map 11 NS86

Shotts Blairhead ML7 5BJ ☎ 01501 822658
Moorland course with fine panoramic views. A good test for all abilities.
18 holes, 6205yds, Par 70, SSS 70, Course record 63.
Club membership 800.
Visitors visitors by arrangement on Sun.
Societies apply in writing.
Green Fees £22 per day; £14 per round (£28/£16 weekends).
Cards 🖭 📇 🖸
Prof John Strachan
Designer James Braid
Facilities ⊗ ⏸ ⏸ ⏸ ⏸ ⏸ ⏸ ⏸ ⏸
Location 2m from M8 off Benhar Road

Hotel ★★★ 65% The Hilcroft Hotel, East Main St, WHITBURN ☎ 01501 740818   31 ⇌ ⏸

SKELMORLIE
Map 10 NS16

Skelmorlie Beithglass PA17 5ES
☎ 01475 520152
Parkland/moorland course with magnificent views over Firth of Clyde. Designed by James Braid.
18 holes, 5030yds, Par 65, SSS 65.
Club membership 450.
Visitors no visitors before 3pm Sat.
Societies apply by telephone.
Green Fees £20 per day; £16 per round (£22/£18 weekends).
Designer James Braid
Facilities ⏸ ⏸ ⏸ ⏸
& Leisure fishing.
Location E side of village off A78

Hotel ★★★ 58% Manor Park Hotel, LARGS
☎ 01475 520832   10 ⇌ ⏸ Annexe 13 ⇌ ⏸

SOUTHERNESS
Map 11 NX95

Southerness DG2 8AZ
☎ 01387 880677 Fax 01387 880644
Natural links, Championship course with panoramic views. Heather and bracken abound.
18 holes, 6566yds, Par 69, SSS 73, Course record 65.
Club membership 830.
Visitors must have handicap certificate and contact in advance. May only play from yellow markers.
Societies must contact in advance.
Green Fees £32 per day (£45 per day weekends & bank holidays).
Cards 🖭
Designer McKenzie Ross
Facilities ⊗ ⏸ ⏸ ⏸ ⏸ ⏸ ⏸
Location 3.5m S of Kirkbean off A710

Hotel ★★ 64% Clonyard House Hotel, COLVEND
☎ 01556 630372   15 ⇌ ⏸

STEVENSTON
Map 10 NS24

Ardeer Greenhead KA20 4LB ☎ 01294 464542 & 465316
Fax 01294 465316
Parkland course with natural hazards.
18 holes, 6401yds, Par 72, SSS 72, Course record 66.
Club membership 650.

Visitors may not play Sat.
Societies must contact in advance.
Green Fees £30 per day; £18 per round (£40/£25 Sun).
Designer Stutt
Facilities ⊗ ⏸ ⏸ ⏸ ⏸ ⏸ ⏸
Location 0.5m N off A78

Hotel ★★★ 74% Montgreenan Mansion House Hotel, Montgreenan Estate, KILWINNING
☎ 01294 557733   21 ⇌ ⏸

Auchenharvie Moor Park Rd West KA20 3HU
☎ 01294 603103
Long and flat municipal course with narrow greens and a pond affecting the 3rd and 12th holes. Easy walking.
9 holes, 5203yds, Par 65, SSS 64, Course record 67.
Club membership 150.
Visitors municipal course 7 day advance booking system.
Societies apply to professional.
Green Fees not confirmed.
Prof Bob Rodgers
Facilities ⊗ ⏸ ⏸ ⏸ ⏸ ⏸ ⏸ ⏸ ⏸
Location Off A738

Hotel ★★★ 74% Montgreenan Mansion House Hotel, Montgreenan Estate, KILWINNING
☎ 01294 557733   21 ⇌ ⏸

STRANRAER
Map 10 NX06

Stranraer Creachmore by Stranraer DG9 0LF
☎ 01776 870245 Fax 01776 870445
Parkland course with beautiful view of Loch Ryan.
18 holes, 6308yds, Par 70, SSS 72, Course record 66.
Club membership 700.
Visitors must contact in advance. Members times reserved throughout year.
Societies must telephone in advance.
Green Fees £29 per day; £20 per round (£35/£25 weekends).
Designer James Braid
Facilities ⊗ ⏸ ⏸ ⏸ ⏸ ⏸ ⏸ ⏸
Location 2.5m NW on A718

Hotel ★★★★ 68% North West Castle Hotel, STRANRAER
☎ 01776 704413   70 ⇌ ⏸ Annexe 3 ⇌ ⏸

STRATHAVEN
Map 11 NS64

Strathaven Glasgow Rd ML10 6NL
☎ 01357 520421 Fax 01357 520539
Gently undulating, tree-lined, Championship parkland course with panoramic views over town and Avon valley.
18 holes, 6250yds, Par 71, SSS 71, Course record 65.
Club membership 950.
Visitors welcome weekdays up to 4pm only. May not play at weekends. Must contact in advance.
Societies apply in writing to general manager.
Green Fees £35 per day; £25 per round.
Prof Matt McCrorie
Designer Willie Fernie/J Stutt
Facilities ⊗ ⏸ ⏸ ⏸ ⏸ ⏸ ⏸ ⏸ ⏸ ⏸
Location NE side of town on A726

Hotel ★★★ 68% Strathaven Hotel, Hamilton Rd, STRATHAVEN ☎ 01357 521778   22 ⇌ ⏸

Royal Troon

Troon, *South Ayrshire*   ☎ 01292 311555   Fax 01292 318204   Map 10 NS33

e–mail: bookings@royaltroon.com

Visitors must play Mon, Tue and Thu only. Must write in advance and have a letter of introduction from own club and a handicap certificate of under 20. Ladies and under 18s may only play on the Portland

Green Fees £125 per day, 1 round each Old Course and Portland Course plus coffee and lunch. £85 per 2 rounds of Portland — 🍽 🏌 🏳

Facilities ⊗ ⅷ 🍽 🍺 ♀ ☂ 🏠
🏌 ♂ ⚑ Professional (R. B. Anderson)

Location Craigend Rd, Troon KA10 6EP (S side of town on B749)

Holes/Par/Course record 36 holes. Old Course: 18 holes, 6641 yds, Par 71, SSS 73, Course record 64
Portland: 18 holes, 6289 yds, Par 71, SSS 71

WHERE TO STAY NEARBY

Hotels
TROON

★★★★ 🏨 66% Marine, Crosbie Rd.
☎ 01292 314444. 74 🛏 ⚑

★★★ 🏨 🏨 🏨 ♨ Lochgreen House, Monktenhill Rd, Southwood.
☎ 01292 313343. 7 🛏 ⚑

★★★ 🏨 🏨 74% Highgrove House, Old Loans Rd. ☎ 01292 312511.
9 (7 🛏 ⚑2 ⚑)

★★★ 🏨 🏨 74% Piersland House, Craigend Rd. ☎ 01292 314747.
15 (9 🛏 6 ⚑) Annexe 13 🛏 ⚑

Troon was founded in 1878 with just 5 holes on linksland, in its first decade it grew from 5 holes to 6, then 12, and finally 18 holes. It became Royal Troon in 1978 on the occasion of its 100th anniversary.

Royal Troon has been one of the venues of the Open Championship in Western Scotland since 1923. Troon's reputation is based on its combination of rough and sandy hills, bunkers, and a severity of finish that has diminished the championship hopes of many. The most successful players have relied on an equal blend of finesse and power. The British Open Championship has been played at Royal Troon in 1923, 1950, 1962, 1973, 1982, 1989 and 1997. It is recommended that you apply to the course in advance for full visitor information.

Championship Course

THORNHILL   Map 11 NX89

Thornhill Blacknest DG3 5DW
☎ 01848 330546
Moorland/parkland course with fine views over the southern uplands.
18 holes, 6011yds, Par 71, SSS 70, Course record 67.
Club membership 700.
Visitors   apply in advance, restricted competition days.
Societies   apply in writing.
Green Fees £22.50 per day (£29 weekends & bank holidays).
Prof   James Davidson
Facilities ⊗ ⫠ ♭ ⚑ ♔ ♀ ⚐ ⚑ ✓
Location   1m E of town off A76

Hotel   ★★ 73% Trigony House Hotel, Closeburn, THORNHILL
                ☎ 01848 331211 8 ⇋ ⚑

TROON   Map 10 NS33

TROON See page 385.

Troon Municipal Harling Dr KA10 6NE
☎ 01292 312464 Fax 01292 312578
Three links courses, two Championship.
Lochgreen Course: 18 holes, 6820yds, Par 74, SSS 73.
Darley Course: 18 holes, 6360yds, Par 71, SSS 63.
Fullarton Course: 18 holes, 4870yds, Par 72, SSS 72.
Club membership 3000.
Visitors   no restrictions.
Societies   apply in writing.
Green Fees not confirmed.
Prof   Gordon McKinlay
Facilities ♀ ⚐ ⚑ ⚑
Location   100yds from railway station

Hotel   ★★★★ 66% Marine Hotel, Crosbie Rd, TROON ☎ 01292 314444 74 ⇋ ⚑

TURNBERRY   Map 10 NS20

TURNBERRY See page 387.

UDDINGSTON   Map 11 NS66

Calderbraes 57 Roundknowe Rd G71 7TS
☎ 01698 813425
Parkland course with good view of Clyde Valley. Testing 4th hole (par 4), hard uphill.
9 holes, 5046yds, Par 66, SSS 67, Course record 65.
Club membership 230.
Visitors   weekdays before 5pm.
Societies   welcome
Green Fees £18 per day/round.
Facilities ⊗ ⫠ ♭ ⚑ ♀
Location   1.5m NW off A74

Hotel   ★★ 68% Redstones Hotel, 8-10 Glasgow Rd, UDDINGSTON ☎ 01698 813774 & 814843
                Fax 01698 815319 14 ⇋ ⚑

UPLAWMOOR   Map 10 NS45

Caldwell G78 4AU
☎ 01505 850366 (Secretary) & 850616 (Pro)
Fax 01505 850604
Parkland course.
18 holes, 6294yds, Par 71, SSS 70, Course record 63.
Club membership 600.
Visitors   must be with member at weekends & bank holidays. Must contact professional in advance.
Societies   writing to Secretary.
Green Fees £33 per day; £23 per round.
Cards   ▬ ▬ ▬ ▧
Prof   Stephen Forbes
Designer   W. Fernie
Facilities ⊗ ⫠ ♭ ⚑ ♔ ♀ ⚐ ⚑ ✓
Location   0.5m SW A736

Hotel   ★★★ 69% Dalmeny Park Country House, Lochlibo Rd, BARRHEAD
                ☎ 0141 881 9211 20 ⇋ ⚑

WEST KILBRIDE   Map 10 NS24

West Kilbride 33-35 Fullerton Dr, Seamill KA23 9HT
☎ 01294 823911 Fax 01294 823911
Seaside links course on Firth of Clyde, with fine views of Isle of Arran from every hole.
18 holes, 5974yds, Par 70, SSS 70, Course record 63.
Club membership 840.
Visitors   may not play at weekends, must contact in advance.
Societies   Tue & Thu only; must contact in advance.
Green Fees not confirmed.
Prof   Graham Ross
Designer   James Braid
Facilities ⊗ ⫠ ♭ ⚑ ♔ ♀ ⚐ ⚑ ⚑ ✓
Location   W side of town off A78

Hotel   ★★★ 72% Priory House Hotel, Broomfields, LARGS
                ☎ 01475 686460 21 ⇋ ⚑

WEST LINTON   Map 11 NT15

Rutherford Castle Golf Club EH46 7AS
☎ 01968 661 233 Fax 01968 661 233
Undulating parkland set beneath the Pentland hills. With many challenging holes. A good test for the better player whilst offering great enjoyment to the average player.
18 holes, 6525yds, Par 72, SSS 71.
Club membership 360.
Visitors   telephone booking anytime.
Societies   application form forwarded on request.
Green Fees £25 per day; £15 per round (£35/£25 weekends & bank holidays).
Prof   Martin Brown
Designer   Bryan Moore
Facilities ♭ ⚑ ♔ ♀ ⚐ ⚑ ⚐
& Leisure   fishing.
Location   S of Edinburgh city bypass (A720) on A702 towards Carlisle

Hotel   ★★★ 71% Peebles Hydro Hotel, PEEBLES
                ☎ 01721 720602 133 ⇋ ⚑

Turnberry Hotel Golf Courses

Visitors golf courses for residents of hotel only

Societies contact in advance as courses are for residents of the hotel only

Green Fees fees on application —

Facilities ⊗ ∭ ㎘ 💺 ♀ ♨ ♨
🏌 ♂ ☂ Professional (Brian Gunson) Golf Academy

Leisure tennis, squash, swimming, sauna, solarium, gymnasium

Location Turnberry KA26 9LT (15m SW of Ayr on A77)

Holes/Par/Course record 36 holes. Ailsa Course: 18 holes, 6440 yds, Par 69, SSS 72, Course record 63
Arran Course: 18 holes, 6014 yds, Par 68, SSS 69, Course record 65

WHERE TO STAY NEARBY

Hotel
TURNBERRY

★★★★★ Turnberry Hotel, Golf Courses & Spa. ☎ 01655 331000. 132 ⇆ 🐾

The renowned Turnberry Hotel, golf courses and Spa Resort is magnificently situated overlooking its two championship golf courses, with views towards the Mull of Kintyre and the Isle of Arran.

Golf at Turnberry began in 1906. The Ailsa course was developed by the Glasgow and South Western Railway Company and continued to prosper until the outbreak of war in 1914 and again in 1939. Golf course architect Mackenzie Ross was given the task of rebuilding the courses and 1951 the transformation was complete. The Ailsa course is ranked number three in the UK and twenty-one in the world. The Colin Montgomerie Links Golf Academy opened in April 2000, featuring 12 driving bays, 4 short game bays, 2 dedicated teaching rooms and a group teaching room. The Arran course has recently undergone a reconstruction designed by Donald Steel, due to reopen in April 2001.

Championship Course

West Linton EH46 7HN ☎ 01968 660256 & 660970
Moorland course with beautiful views of Pentland Hills.
18 holes, 6132yds, Par 69, SSS 70, Course record 63.
Club membership 800.
Visitors   weekdays anytime, weekends not before 1pm.
     Contact Professional.
Societies   contact the secretary in writing.
Green Fees £30 per day; £20 per round (£30 per round
     weekends).
Prof   Ian Wright
Designer   Millar/Braid/Fraser
Facilities   ⊗ ⅏ ⅃ 🍴 ♀ ♨ 🏠 🍸 🛒 ✓
Location   NW side of village off A702

Hotel   ★★★ 71% Peebles Hydro Hotel, PEEBLES
     ☎ 01721 720602 133 ⇨ ♟

WIGTOWN   Map 10 NX45

Wigtown & Bladnoch Lightlands Ter DG8 9EF
☎ 01988 403354
Slightly hilly parkland course with fine views over Wigtown
Bay to Galloway Hills.
9 holes, 5462yds, Par 68, SSS 67, Course record 62.
Club membership 150.
Visitors   advisable to contact in advance for weekend
     play. Course closed to visitors during open
     competitions.

Societies   contact secretary in advance.
Green Fees not confirmed.
Designer   W Muir
Facilities   ♨
Location   SW on A714

Hotel   ★★ 72% Creebridge House Hotel, NEWTON
     STEWART ☎ 01671 402121 19 ⇨ ♟

WISHAW   Map 11 NS75

Wishaw 55 Cleland Rd ML2 7PH
☎ 01698 372869 (Sec) & 357480 (admin)
Parkland course with many tree-lined areas. Bunkers protect
17 of the 18 greens.
18 holes, 6073yds, Par 69, SSS 69, Course record 64.
Club membership 984.
Visitors   must contact secretary in advance. May not play
     Sat but may play alternate Sun.
Societies   apply in writing.
Green Fees not confirmed.
Prof   Stuart Adair
Designer   James Braid
Facilities   ⊗ ⅏ ⅃ 🍴 ♀ ♨ 🏠 🍸 🛒 ✓
Location   NW side of town off A721

Hotel   ★★★ 71% Popinjay Hotel, Lanark Rd,
     ROSEBANK ☎ 01555 860441
     40 ⇨ ♟ Annexe 5 ⇨ ♟

Wales

WALES

The directory which follows has been divided into three geographical regions. Counties have not been shown against individual locations as legislation has created a number of smaller counties which will be unfamiliar to the visitor. The postal authorities have confirmed that it is no longer necessary to include a county name in addresses, provided a post code is shown. All locations appear in the atlas at the end of this guide in their appropriate counties.

NORTH WALES

& ANGLESEY

This region includes the counties of Conwy, Denbighshire, Flintshire, Gwynedd, Isle of Anglesey and Wrexham which reflect the national changes.

ABERDYFI   Map 06 SN69

Aberdovey LL35 0RT
☎ 01654 767493 Fax 01654 767027
A beautiful championship course at the mouth of the Dovey estuary, Aberdovey has all the true characteristics of a seaside links. It has some fine holes among them the 3rd, the 12th, an especially good short hole, and the 11th. There are some striking views to be had from the course.
18 holes, 6445yds, Par 71, SSS 71, Course record 66.
Club membership 1000.

AA　　　　　　　　　　　　　　　　　　**71%**
★★★
TREFEDDIAN HOTEL

ABERDOVEY

Family owned/managed 3-star country hotel.
Close to sea in Snowdonia National Park.
Views of sand dunes, beaches, Cardigan Bay and
Aberdovey Championship Golf Links.
Bedrooms en-suite, some balcony.
Lift, indoor swimming pool, tennis, snooker.
Children's playroom. A Family Hotel. Ideal
base for touring North/Mid Wales. ½ mile
north of Aberdyfi village.
Telephone for full colour brochure.

ABERDYFI LL35 0SB WALES
Telephone: (01654) 767213
Fax: (01654) 767777

Visitors	handicap certificate required, must contact in advance, restrictions at weekends.
Societies	prior arrangement essential.
Green Fees	£42 per day; £29 per round (£48/£35 weekends).
Cards	〰 📟 💳 💷
Prof	John Davies
Designer	J Braid
Facilities	⊗ ⼺ ⼪ ⼵ ♀ ⽥ 🍴 🛒 🏌
Location	0.5m W on A493
Hotel	★★★ 71% Trefeddian Hotel, ABERDYFI ☎ 01654 767213　46 ⇆ ⼆

ABERGELE   Map 06 SH97

Abergele Tan-y-Gopa Rd LL22 8DS
☎ 01745 824034 Fax 01745 824034
A beautiful parkland course with views of the Irish Sea and Gwyrch Castle. There are splendid finishing holes, a testing par 5, 16th; a 185 yd, 17th to an elevated green, and a superb par 5 18th with out of bounds just behind the green.
18 holes, 6520yds, Par 72, SSS 71, Course record 66.
Club membership 1250.

Visitors	must contact in advance. Limited play weekends.
Societies	must contact in advance.
Green Fees	not confirmed.
Prof	Iain R Runcie
Designer	Hawtree
Facilities	⊗ ⼺ ⼪ ⼵ ♀ ⽥ 🍴 🏌
Location	0.5m W off A547/A55
Hotel	★★★ 65% Kinmel Manor Hotel, St Georges Rd, ABERGELE ☎ 01745 832014　51 ⇆ ⼆

ABERSOCH   Map 06 SH32

Abersoch LL53 7EY ☎ 01758 712622 Fax 01758 712777
Seaside links, with five parkland holes.
18 holes, 5819yds, Par 69, SSS 68, Course record 66.
Club membership 650.

Visitors	must contact in advance. Competition days Sun & Thu.
Societies	must apply in advance.
Green Fees	£25 per day; £18 per round (£20 per round weekends & bank holidays).
Prof	A D Jones
Designer	Harry Vardon
Facilities	⊗ ⼺ ⼪ ⼵ ♀ ⽥ 🍴 🛒 🏌 ⼆
Location	S side of village
Hotel	★★ 76% Neigwl Hotel, Lon Sarn Bach, ABERSOCH ☎ 01758 712363 7 ⇆ ⼆ Annexe 2 ⇆

ANGLESEY, ISLE OF   Map 06

Golf Courses on the island of Anglesey are listed alphabetically by town as follows:

AMLWCH
Map 06 SH49

Bull Bay LL68 9RY
☎ 01407 830960 Fax 01407 832612
Wales's northernmost course, Bull Bay is a pleasant coastal, heathland course with natural rock, gorse and wind hazards. Views from several tees across Irish Sea to Isle of Man, and across Anglesey to Snowdonia.
18 holes, 6217yds, Par 70, SSS 70, Course record 60.
Club membership 700.
Visitors   advisable to contact in advance.
Societies   advance booking essential.
Green Fees £20 (£25 weekends & bank holidays).
Cards
Prof   John Burns
Designer   W H Fowler
Facilities   ⊗ ⅷ ㄴ ♥ ♀ ♨ 🏠 ⛳ ♂
Location   1m W of Amlwch on A5025

Hotel   ★★ 65% Trecastell Hotel, Bull Bay, AMLWCH
☎ 01407 830651 13rm (11 ⇔ 🏠)

BEAUMARIS
Map 06 SH67

Baron Hill LL58 8YW
☎ 01248 810231 Fax 01248 810231
Undulating course with natural hazards of rock and gorse. Testing 3rd and 4th holes (par 4's). Hole 5/14 plays into the prevailing wind with an elevated tee across two streams. The hole is between two gorse covered mounds.
9 holes, 5062mtrs, Par 68, SSS 69, Course record 62.
Club membership 400.
Visitors   ladies have priority on Tue am & club competitions Sun.
Societies   apply in writing to secretary.
Green Fees £13 per 9/18 holes.
Facilities   ⊗ ⅷ ㄴ ♥ ♀ ♨ ♂
Location   Take A545 from Menai Bridge to Beaumaris, course signed on approach to town

Hotel   ★★ 67% Bulkeley Hotel, Castle St, BEAUMARIS
☎ 01248 810415 41rm (40 ⇔ 🏠)

HOLYHEAD
Map 06 SH28

Holyhead Lon Garreg Fawr, Trearddur Bay LL65 2YL
☎ 01407 763279 Fax 01407 763279
Treeless, undulating seaside course which provides a varied and testing game, particularly in a south wind. The fairways are bordered by gorse, heather and rugged outcrops of rock. Accuracy from most tees is paramount as there are 43 fairway and greenside bunkers and lakes. Designed by James Braid. Indoor driving range.
18 holes, 6058yds, Par 70, SSS 70, Course record 64.
Club membership 1200.
Visitors   must contact in advance.
Societies   must contact in advance.
Green Fees £25.90 per day; £19 per round (£29.90/£22 weekends & bank holidays).
Cards
Prof   Stephen Elliot
Designer   James Braid
Facilities   ⊗ ⅷ ㄴ ♥ ♀ ♨ 🏠 ⛳ ⇔ ♂ ⸖
Location   1.25m S on B4545

Hotel   ★★★ 70% Trearddur Bay Hotel, TREARDDUR BAY
☎ 01407 860301 37 ⇔ 🏠

LLANGEFNI
Map 06 SH47

Llangefni (Public) LL77 7LJ
☎ 01248 722193 Fax 01248 750156
Picturesque parkland course designed by Hawtree & Son.
9 holes, 1342yds, Par 28, SSS 28.
Visitors   no restrictions.
Societies
Green Fees not confirmed.
Prof   Paul Lovell
Designer   Hawtree & Sons
Facilities   ⊗ ♥ ♀ ♨ 🏠 ⛳ ♂
Location   1.5m off A5

Hotel   ★★ 66% Anglesey Arms, MENAI BRIDGE
☎ 01248 712305 16 ⇔ 🏠

RHOSNEIGR
Map 06 SH37

Anglesey Station Rd LL64 5QX
☎ 01407 811202 Fax 01407 811202
Links course, low and fairly level with sand dunes and tidal river.
18 holes, 6300yds, Par 68, SSS 68.
Club membership 500.
Visitors   phone in advance, some times are reserved for members. Dress restrictions.
Societies   telephone & confirm in writing.
Green Fees not confirmed.
Prof   Paul Lovell
Designer   H Hilton
Facilities   ⊗ ⅷ ㄴ ♥ ♀ ♨ 🏠 ♂
Location   NE side of village on A4080

Hotel   ★★★ 70% Trearddur Bay Hotel, TREARDDUR BAY
☎ 01407 860301 37 ⇔ 🏠

BALA
Map 06 SH93

Bala Penlan LL23 7YD
☎ 01678 520359 & 521361 Fax 01678 521361
Upland course with natural hazards. All holes except first and last affected by wind. First hole is a most challenging par3. Irrigated greens and good views of surrounding countryside.
10 holes, 4962yds, Par 66, SSS 64, Course record 64.
Club membership 229.
Visitors   book in advance at weekends. Parties of more than 4 people contact the secretary in advance.
Societies   must contact in advance.
Green Fees £12 per day (£15 weekends & bank holidays).
Prof   A R Davies
Facilities   ㄴ by prior arrangement ♀ ♨ 🏠 ⛳ ♂
Location   0.5m SW off A494

Hotel   ★★ 65% Plas Coch Hotel, High St, BALA
☎ 01678 520309 10 ⇔ 🏠

BANGOR — Map 06 SH57

St Deiniol Penybryn LL57 1PX ☎ 01248 353098
Elevated parkland course with panoramic views of
Snowdonia, Menai Straits, and Anglesey.
18 holes, 5068mtrs, Par 68, SSS 67, Course record 61.
Club membership 300.
Visitors must contact in advance.
Societies must contact in advance.
Green Fees £14 per day (£18 weekends).
Cards ⬛
Designer James Braid
Facilities ⊗ �🍽 by prior arrangement 🖫 ⬛ ♀ 🛆 🏠 🏌 ♂
Location E side of town centre off A5122

Hotel ★★ 66% Anglesey Arms, MENAI BRIDGE
☎ 01248 712305 16 ⇆ ♞

BETWS-Y-COED — Map 06 SH75

Betws-y-Coed LL24 0AL ☎ 01690 710556
Attractive flat meadowland course set between two rivers in
Snowdonia National Park.
9 holes, 4996yds, Par 64, SSS 63, Course record 63.
Club membership 350.
Visitors advisable to contact in advance.
Societies must telephone in advance.
Green Fees £15 (£20 weekends).
Facilities ⊗ �🍽 🖫 ⬛ ♀ 🛆 ♂
Location NE side of village off A5

Hotel ★★★ 70% The Royal Oak Hotel, Holyhead
Rd, BETWS-Y-COED
☎ 01690 710219 26 ⇆ ♞

BODELWYDDAN — Map 06 SJ07

Kimnel Park LL18 5SR
☎ 01745 833548 Fax 01745 833544
Flat parkland pay and play course that is suitable for
beginners.
9 holes, 3100, Par 58, SSS 58.
Visitors no restrictions.
Societies telephone for details.
Green Fees £4.50 per 18 holes.
Prof Peter Stebbings
Designer Peter Stebbings
Facilities 🖫 ⬛ 🛆 🏌 ♂ ♞
& Leisure golf academy.
Hotel ★★★ 64% Oriel House Hotel,
Upper Denbigh Rd, ST ASAPH
☎ 01745 582716 19 ⇆ ♞

BRYNFORD — Map 07 SJ17

Holywell Brynford CH8 8LQ
☎ 01352 713937 & 710040 Fax 0707 660453
Links type course on well drained mountain turf, with
bracken and gorse flanking undulating fairways. 720 ft above
sea level.
18 holes, 6100yds, Par 70, SSS 70, Course record 67.
Club membership 505.
Visitors advisable to book in advance particularly for
weekends.

Societies by prior arrangement with the secretary.
Green Fees £16 per day (£21 weekends & bank holidays).
Prof Sean O'Conner
Facilities ⊗ ⍟ 🍽 🖫 ⬛ ♀ 🛆 🏠 🛒 ♂
Location 1.25m SW off B5121

Hotel ★★ 64% Stamford Gate Hotel, Halkyn Rd,
HOLYWELL ☎ 01352 712942 12 ⇆ ♞

CAERNARFON — Map 06 SH46

Caernarfon Llanfaglan LL54 5RP
☎ 01286 673783 & 678359 Fax 01286 672535
Parkland course with gentle gradients.
18 holes, 5891yds, Par 69, SSS 68, Course record 64.
Club membership 730.
Visitors must contact in advance.
Societies must apply in advance, in writing or by
telephone.
Green Fees £18 per day; £15 per round Mon: £15/£10
(£23/£20 weekends & bank holidays).
Cards ⬛
Prof Aled Owen
Facilities ⊗ ⍟ 🖫 ⬛ ♀ 🛆 🏠 🛒 🚲 🛒 ♂
Location 1.75m SW

Hotel ★★★ 65% Celtic Royal Hotel,
Bangor St, CAERNARFON
☎ 01286 674477 110 ⇆ ♞

CAERWYS — Map 06 SJ17

Caerwys Nine Of Clubs CH7 5AQ ☎ 01352 720692
Following the natural contours of the land and with a south-
west aspect, this course could be considered a litle gem. Each
approach to every green is different and there are many
interesting and challenging holes.
9 holes, 3080yds, Par 60, Course record 61.
Club membership 150.
Visitors no restrictions.
Societies telephone then confirm in writing.
Green Fees not confirmed.
Designer Eleanor Barlow
Facilities ⊗ 🖫 🛆 🏠 🏌 ♂ ♞
Location 1.5m SW of A55, midway between St Asaph
and Holywell

Hotel ★★ 64% Bryn Awel Hotel, Denbigh Rd,
MOLD ☎ 01352 758622
8rm (4 ⇆ 3 ♞) Annexe 10 ⇆ ♞

CHIRK — Map 07 SJ23

Chirk Golf Club LL14 5AD
☎ 01691 774407 & 0800 7318598 Fax 01691 773878
Overlooked by the National Trust's Chirk Castle, is a
championship-standard 18-hole course with a 664 yard, par 5
at the 9th - one of the longest in Europe. Also a 9-hole
course, driving range and golf academy.
*Manor Course: 18 holes, 7045yds, Par 72, SSS 73, Course
record 72.*
Club membership 750.
Visitors advisable to contact in advance. May not play in
members preferred tee times 7-10am daily.
Societies must telephone for provisional booking.
Green Fees £18 per round (£25 weekends).

▶

Cards	▓▓ ▓▓ ▓▓ ▓
Prof	Mark Maddison
Facilities	⊗ ⅢⅢ ⅃ ♥ ♀ ⚲ 🛉 🏌 🏌 🏌 🏌
& Leisure	squash, fishing.
Location	5m N of Oswestry

Hotel ★★★ 64% Hand Hotel, Church St, CHIRK
☎ 01691 772479 16 ⇆ ⋔

COLWYN BAY   Map 06 SH87

Old Colwyn Woodland Av, Old Colwyn LL29 9NL
☎ 01492 515581
Hilly, meadowland course with sheep and cattle grazing on it
in parts.
9 holes, 5243yds, Par 68, SSS 66, Course record 63.
Club membership 267.

Visitors	welcome ex Sat. Contact in advance.
Societies	must contact in advance.
Green Fees	£10 per day (£15 weekends & bank holidays).
Designer	James Braid
Facilities	♀ evenings & weekends ⚲
Location	E side of town centre on B5383

Hotel ★★★ 64% Hopeside Hotel, 63-67 Prince's Dr,
West End, COLWYN BAY
☎ 01492 533244 18 ⇆ ⋔

CONWY   Map 06 SH77

Conwy (Caernarvonshire) Beacons Way, Morfa
LL32 8ER ☎ 01492 592423 Fax 01492 593363
Founded in 1890, Conwy has hosted national and
international championships since 1898. Set among
sandhills, possessing true links greens and a profusion of
gorse on the latter holes, especially the 16th, 17th and
18th. This course provides the visitor with real golfing
enjoyment against a background of stunning beauty.
18 holes, 6647yds, Par 72, SSS 72, Course record 69.
Club membership 1050.

Visitors	advisable to contact secretary in advance. Limited play weekends.
Societies	must contact in advance.
Green Fees	£27 per day; £24 per round (£35/£30 weekends & bank holidays).
Prof	Peter Lees
Facilities	⊗ ⅢⅢ ⅃ ♥ ♀ ⚲ 🛉 🏌 🏌
Location	1m W of town centre on A55

Hotel ★★★ 71% The Groes Inn, Tyn-y-Groes,
CONWY ☎ 01492 650545 14 ⇆ ⋔

CRICCIETH   Map 06 SH43

Criccieth Ednyfed Hill LL52 0PH ☎ 01766 522154
Hilly course on Lleyn Peninsula. Good views.
18 holes, 5787yds, Par 69, SSS 68.
Club membership 350.

Visitors	must contact in advance.
Societies	telephone in advance.
Green Fees	not confirmed.
Facilities	⊗ ⅢⅢ ⅃ ♥ ♀ ⚲ 🛉 🏌
Location	1m NE

Hotel ★★★♨ 68% Bron Eifion Country House Hotel,
CRICCIETH ☎ 01766 522385 19 ⇆ ⋔

DENBIGH   Map 06 SJ06

Bryn Morfydd Hotel Llanrhaedr LL16 4NP
☎ 01745 890280 Fax 01745 890488
In a beautiful setting in the Vale of Clwyd, the original 9-
hole Duchess course was designed by Peter Alliss in 1982. In
1992, the 18-hole Dukes course was completed: a parkland
course designed to encourage use of finesse in play.
*Dukes Course: 18 holes, 5650yds, Par 70, SSS 67, Course
record 74.*
Duchess Course: 9 holes, 2098yds, Par 27.
Club membership 450.

Visitors	must book in advance, good standards of dress apply.
Societies	apply in writing.
Green Fees	not confirmed.
Cards	▓▓ ▓▓ VISA ▓▓ ▓▓ ▓
Prof	Ivor Jones
Designer	Peter Allis/Duncan Muirhead
Facilities	⊗ ⅢⅢ ⅃ ♥ ♀ ⚲ 🛉 🏌 🏌 🏌 🏌
& Leisure	heated outdoor swimming pool.
Location	On A525 between Denbigh and Ruthin

Denbigh Henllan Rd LL16 5AA
☎ 01745 814159 Fax 814888
Parkland course, giving a testing and varied game. Good
views.
18 holes, 5712yds, Par 69, SSS 68, Course record 64.
Club membership 725.

Visitors	must contact in advance.
Societies	apply in writing.
Green Fees	£24.50 per round/day (£30.50 weekends & bank holidays).
Prof	Mike Jones
Designer	John Stockton
Facilities	⊗ ⅢⅢ ⅃ ♥ ♀ ⚲ 🛉 🏌
Location	1.5m NW on B5382

Hotel ★★★ 64% Oriel House Hotel, Upper Denbigh
Rd, ST ASAPH ☎ 01745 582716 19 ⇆ ⋔

DOLGELLAU   Map 06 SH71

Dolgellau Hengwrt Estate, Pencefn Rd LL40 2ES
☎ 01341 422603 Fax 01341 422603
Undulating parkland course. Good views of mountains and
Mawddach estuary.
9 holes, 4671yds, Par 66, SSS 63, Course record 62.
Club membership 150.

Visitors	no restrictions
Societies	must contact in advance.
Green Fees	£15 per round (£18 weekends).
Cards	▓▓ VISA ▓▓ ▓▓ ▓
Facilities	⊗ ⅢⅢ by prior arrangement ⅃ ♥ ⚲ 🛉
Location	0.5m N, near to Town Bridge

Hotel ★★★♨ 71% Plas Dolmelynllyn, Ganllwyd,
DOLGELLAU ☎ 01341 440273 10 ⇆ ⋔

EYTON   Map 07 SJ34

Plassey LL13 0SP ☎ 01978 780028
Pleasant 9-hole course set in naturally contoured parkland
with water hazards. It is within Plassey Leisure Park and
Craft Centre and all park facilities are available to golfers.
9 holes, 2379yds, Par 32, SSS 32.
Club membership 166.

▶

Visitors   must contact in advance.
Societies   telephone then confirm in writing.
Green Fees £9 per 18 holes; £6 per 9 holes (£11/£7
                weekends & bank holidays)..
Designer   Welsh Golf Union
Facilities 🏃 ♨ ♇ ♀ ⚒ ⚐ ⚐
Location   2.5m off A483 Chester/Oswestry

Hotel   ★★★ 67% Cross Lanes Hotel & Restaurant,
                Cross Lanes, Bangor Rd, Marchwiel,
                WREXHAM ☎ 01978 780555 16 ⇆ ♜

FLINT   Map 07 SJ27

Flint Cornist Park CH6 5HJ
☎ 01244 812974 Fax 01244 811885
Parkland course incorporating woods and streams. Excellent
views of Dee estuary and the Welsh hills.
9 holes, 6984yds, Par 69, SSS 69, Course record 65.
Club membership 260.
Visitors   must contact in advance, not Sun.
Societies   not weekends.
Green Fees £10 per round.
Designer   H G Griffith
Facilities ⊗ ⋔ 🏃 ♨ ♇ ♀ ⚐
Location   1m W

HARLECH   Map 06 SH53

Royal St Davids LL46 2UB
☎ 01766 780361 Fax 01766 781110
Championship links, with easy walking and natural
hazards.
18 holes, 6571yds, Par 69, SSS 73, Course record 69.
Club membership 800.
Visitors   pre booking essential, must hold current
                handicap certificate.
Societies   telephone secretary in advance. Handicap
                certificates required.
Green Fees Apr-Sep: £35 (£40 weekends). Oct-Mar £25
                (£30 weekends).
Cards   ▭ ▭ ▭ ▨
Prof   John Barnett
Facilities ⊗ ⋔ 🏃 ♨ ♇ ♀ ⚐ 🏠 ⚐ ⚐ ⚐
Location   W side of town on A496

Hotel   ★★ 63% Ty Mawr Hotel, LLANBEDR
                ☎ 01341 241440 10 ⇆ ♜

HAWARDEN   Map 07 SJ36

Hawarden Groomsdale Ln CH5 3EH
☎ 01244 531447 & 520809
Parkland course with comfortable walking and good views.
18 holes, 5842yds, Par 69, SSS 69.
Club membership 550.
Visitors   arrange visit with the professional.
Societies   by prior arrangement.
Green Fees not confirmed.
Prof   Chris Hope
Facilities ⊗ ⋔ 🏃 ♨ ♇ ♀ ⚐ 🏠
Location   W side of town off B5125

Hotel   ★★★ 69% The Gateway To Wales Hotel,
                Welsh Rd, Sealand, Deeside, CHESTER
                ☎ 01244 830332 39 ⇆ ♜

LLANDUDNO   Map 06 SH78

Llandudno (Maesdu) Hospital Rd LL30 1HU
☎ 01492 876450 Fax 01492 871570
Part links, part parkland, this championship course starts
and finishes on one side of the main road, the remaining
holes, more seaside in nature, being played on the other
side. The holes are pleasantly undulating and present a
pretty picture when the gorse is in bloom. Often windy,
this varied and testing course is not for beginners.
18 holes, 6545yds, Par 72, SSS 72, Course record 66.
Club membership 1045.
Visitors   must book in advance.
Societies   must apply in advance to secretary.
Green Fees not confirmed.
Prof   Simon Boulden
Facilities ⊗ ⋔ 🏃 ♨ ♇ ♀ ⚐ 🏠 ⚐ ⚐ ⚐
Location   S side of town centre on A546

Hotel   ★★★ 68% Imperial Hotel, The
                Promenade, LLANDUDNO
                ☎ 01492 877466 100 ⇆ ♜

North Wales 72 Bryniau Rd, West Shore LL30 2DZ
☎ 01492 875325 Fax 01492 875325
Challenging seaside links with superb views of Anglesey
and Snowdonia.
18 holes, 6247yds, Par 71, SSS 71, Course record 65.
Club membership 525.
Visitors   must contact in advance.
Societies   must contact in advance.
Green Fees Summer: £25 per day (£35 weekends &
                bank holidays) Winter: £18 per round (£23
                weekends & bank holidays).
Prof   Richard Bradbury
Designer   Tancred Cummins
Facilities ⊗ ⋔ 🏃 ♨ ♇ ♀ ⚐ 🏠 ⚐ ⚐ ⚐
Location   W side of town on A546

Hotel   ★★ St Tudno Hotel, Promenade,
                LLANDUDNO
                ☎ 01492 874411 19 ⇆ ♜

Rhos-on-Sea Penryhn Bay LL30 3PU
☎ 01492 548115 (Prof) & 549641 (clubhouse)
Fax 01492 549100
Seaside course, with easy walking and panoramic views.
18 holes, 6064yds, Par 69, SSS 69, Course record 68.
Club membership 400.
Visitors   advised to telephone beforehand to guarantee tee
                times.
Societies   booking essential, telephone in advance.
Green Fees not confirmed.
Prof   Mike Macara
Designer   J J Simpson
Facilities ⊗ ⋔ 🏃 ♨ ♇ ♀ ⚐ 🏠 ⚐ ⚐
Location   0.5m W of LLandudno, off the A55

Hotel   ★★★ 64% Hopeside Hotel, 63-67 Prince's Dr,
                West End, COLWYN BAY
                ☎ 01492 533244 18 ⇆ ♜

Entries with a green background
identify courses considered to be
particularly interesting

LLANFAIRFECHAN — Map 06 SH67

Llanfairfechan Llannerch Rd LL33 0ES ☎ 01248 680144
Hillside course with panoramic views of coast.
9 holes, 3119yds, Par 54, SSS 57, Course record 53.
Club membership 197.
Visitors contact in advance, booking necessary at weekends.
Societies apply in writing.
Green Fees not confirmed.
Facilities ♀⚒
Location W side of town on A55

Hotel ★★ 67% Castle Bank Hotel, Mount Pleasant, CONWY ☎ 01492 593888 9 ↸

LLANGOLLEN — Map 07 SJ24

Vale of Llangollen Holyhead Rd LL20 7PR
☎ 01978 860906 Fax 01978 860906
Parkland course, set in superb scenery by the River Dee.
18 holes, 6656yds, Par 72, SSS 73, Course record 66.
Club membership 800.
Visitors must contact in advance. Restricted club competition days. Handicap certificate required.
Societies apply in writing to the secretary.
Green Fees £30 per day; £20 per round (£35/£25 weekends).
Cards
Prof David Vaughan
Facilities ⊗ ⊪⒧⛴♀⚒🏠⚐
Location 1.5m E on A5

Hotel ★★★♨ 66% Bryn Howel Hotel & Restaurant, LLANGOLLEN ☎ 01978 860331 36 ⇆↸

MOLD — Map 07 SJ26

Old Padeswood Station Rd, Padeswood CH7 4JL
☎ 01244 547401 & 550414 Fax 01244 545082
Situated in the beautiful Alyn Valley, half on flat parkland and half undulating. Striking mountain views.
18 holes, 6685yds, Par 72, SSS 72, Course record 66.
Club membership 600.
Visitors welcome, subject to tee availability.
Societies telephone in advance.
Green Fees not confirmed.
Prof Tony Davies
Designer Jeffries
Facilities ⊗ ⊪⒧⛴♀⚒🏠⚐🏌🛒⚒
Location 3m SE off A5118

Hotel ★★ 64% Bryn Awel Hotel, Denbigh Rd, MOLD ☎ 01352 758622 8rm (4 ⇆3 ↸) Annexe 10 ⇆↸

Padeswood & Buckley The Caia, Station Ln, Padeswood CH7 4JD ☎ 01244 550537 Fax 01244 541600
Gently undulating parkland course, with natural hazards and good views of the Welsh Hills.
18 holes, 5982yds, Par 70, SSS 69.
Club membership 700.
Visitors weekdays only, contact secretary in advance.
Societies apply in writing.
Green Fees £20 per round.
Prof David Ashton
Designer Williams Partnership

Facilities ⊗ ⊪⒧⛴♀⚒🏠⚐🏌🛒⚒
Location 3m SE off A5118

Hotel ★★ 64% Bryn Awel Hotel, Denbigh Rd, MOLD ☎ 01352 758622 8rm (4 ⇆3 ↸) Annexe 10 ⇆↸

MORFA NEFYN — Map 06 SH24

Nefyn & District LL53 6DA
☎ 01758 720966 Fax 01758 720476
A 27-hole course played as two separate 18's, Nefyn is a cliff top links where you never lose sight of the sea. A well-maintained course which will be a very tough test for the serious golfer, is still user friendly for the casual visitor. Every hole has a different challenge and the old 13th fairway is approximately 30 yards arcross from sea-to-sea. The course has an added bonus of a pub on the beach roughly halfway round for those whose golf may need some bolstering!
Old Course: 18 holes, 6201yds, Par 71, SSS 71, Course record 67.
New Course: 18 holes, 6548yds, Par 71, SSS 71, Course record 67.
Club membership 800.
Visitors advisable to contact in advance.
Societies apply by telephone.
Green Fees not confirmed.
Prof John Froom
Designer James Braid
Facilities ⊗ ⊪⒧⛴♀⚒🏠⚐🏌🛒⚒
Location 0.75m NW

Hotel ★★ 79% Plas Bodegroes, Nefyn Rd, PWLLHELI ☎ 01758 612363 9 ⇆↸ Annexe 2 ⇆↸

NORTHOP — Map 07 SJ26

Northop Country Park CH7 6WA
☎ 01352 840440 Fax 01352 840445
Designed by former British Ryder Cup captain, John Jacobs, the parkland course gives the impression of having been established for many years. No two holes are the same and designed to allow all year play.
18 holes, 6750yds, Par 72, SSS 73, Course record 64.
Club membership 500.

Visitors must contact in advance.
Societies apply in writing or by telephone in advance.
Green Fees not confirmed.
Prof Matthew Pritchard ▶

Designer John Jacobs
Facilities ⊗ ⑂ ⅃ 🛢 💆 ♀ ⚑ ⛳ ⚐ ⚒ 🚗 ✎ ⌇
& Leisure hard tennis courts, sauna, gymnasium.
Location 150 yds from Connahs Quay turnoff on A55

Hotel ★★★★ 70% St Davids Park Hotel, St Davids
Park, EWLOE
☎ 01244 520800 145 ⇋ ℝ

PANTYMWYN   Map 07 SJ16

Mold Cilcain Rd CH7 5EH
☎ 01352 740318 & 741513 Fax 01352 741517
Meadowland course with some hard walking and natural
hazards. Fine views.
18 holes, 5512yds, Par 67, SSS 67, Course record 63.
Club membership 700.
Visitors contact in advance. Restricted play at weekends
Societies provisional booking by telephone.
Green Fees £18 per round/day (£25 per day, £20 per round
weekends & bank holidays).
Prof Mark Jordan
Designer Hawtree
Facilities ⊗ ⑂ ⅃ 🛢 💆 ♀ ⚑ ⛳ ⚐ 🚗 ✎
Location E side of village

Hotel ★★ 64% Bryn Awel Hotel, Denbigh Rd,
MOLD ☎ 01352 758622
8rm (4 ⇋ 3 ℝ) Annexe 10 ⇋ ℝ

PENMAENMAWR   Map 06 SH77

Penmaenmawr Conway Old Rd LL34 6RD
☎ 01492 623330 Fax 01492 622105
Hilly course with magnificent views across the bay to
Llandudno and Anglesey. Dry-stone wall natural hazards.
9 holes, 5350yds, Par 67, SSS 66, Course record 62.
Club membership 600.
Visitors advisable to contact in advance. May not play
Sat.
Societies must contact in advance.
Green Fees £12 weekdays (£18 Sun and bank holidays)..
Facilities ⊗ ⑂ ⅃ 🛢 💆 ♀ ⚑ ✎
Location 1.5m NE off A55

Hotel ★★★ 64% The Castle, High St, CONWY
☎ 01492 592324 29 ⇋ ℝ

PORTHMADOG   Map 06 SH53

Porthmadog Morfa Bychan LL49 9UU
☎ 01766 514124 Fax 01766 514638
Seaside links, very interesting but with easy walking and
good views.
18 holes, 6363yds, Par 71, SSS 71.
Club membership 900.
Visitors must contact in advance. Handicap certificate
required.
Societies apply by telephone initially.
Green Fees £25 per day (£30 weekends & bank holidays).
Prof Peter L Bright
Designer James Braid
Facilities ⊗ ⑂ ⅃ 🛢 💆 ♀ ⚑ ⛳ 🐾 ✎
& Leisure snooker.
Location 1.5m SW

Hotel ★★★🐾 68% Bron Eifion Country House
Hotel, CRICCIETH
☎ 01766 522385 19 ⇋ ℝ

PRESTATYN   Map 06 SJ08

Prestatyn Marine Rd East LL19 7HS
☎ 01745 854320 Fax 01745 888353
Very flat seaside links exposed to stiff breeze. Testing holes:
9th, par 4, bounded on 3 sides by water; 10th, par 4; 16th, par
4.
18 holes, 6564yds, Par 72, SSS 72, Course record 66.
Club membership 660.
Visitors welcome except Sat & Tue mornings. Must
contact in advance.
Societies prior booking required.
Green Fees £22 per day (£27 Sun & bank holidays).
Prof Malcolm Staton
Designer S Collins
Facilities ⊗ ⑂ ⅃ 🛢 💆 ♀ ⚑ ⛳ ✎
& Leisure snooker.
Location 0.5m N off A548

Hotel ★★ 60% Hotel Marina, Marine Dr, RHYL
☎ 01745 342371 29 ⇋ ℝ

St Melyd The Paddock, Meliden Rd LL19 8NB
☎ 01745 854405
Parkland course with good views of mountains and Irish Sea.
Testing 1st hole (423 yds) par 4. 18 tees.
9 holes, 5829yds, Par 68, SSS 68, Course record 65.
Club membership 400.
Visitors must contact in advance.
Societies must telephone in advance.
Green Fees not confirmed.
Prof Andrew Carr
Facilities ⊗ ⑂ ⅃ 🛢 💆 ♀ ⚑ ⛳
Location 0.5m S on A547

Hotel ★★ 60% Hotel Marina, Marine Dr, RHYL
☎ 01745 342371 29 ⇋ ℝ

PWLLHELI   Map 06 SH33

Pwllheli Golf Rd LL53 5PS ☎ 01758 701644
Easy walking on flat seaside course with outstanding views
of Snowdon, Cader Idris and Cardigan Bay.
18 holes, 6091yds, Par 69, SSS 69, Course record 66.
Club membership 880.
Visitors restricted Tue,Thu & weekends.
Societies must telephone in advance.
Green Fees not confirmed.
Cards 💳 💳 💳 💳 💳 💳
Prof G D Verity
Designer Tom Morris
Facilities ⊗ ⑂ ⅃ 🛢 💆 ♀ ⚑ ⛳ ✎
Location 0.5m SW off A497

Hotel ★★ 79% Plas Bodegroes,
Nefyn Rd, PWLLHELI
☎ 01758 612363 9 ⇋ ℝ Annexe 2 ⇋ ℝ

AA Hotels that have special
arrangements with golf courses are listed at
the back of the guide

RHUDDLAN
Map 06 SJ07

Rhuddlan Meliden Rd LL18 6LB
☎ 01745 590217 (Sec) & 590898(Pro) Fax 01745 590472
Attractive, gently undulating parkland course with good views. Well bunkered with trees and water hazards. The 476 yard 8th and 431 yard 11th require both length and accuracy. The clubhouse has been refurbished.
18 holes, 6482yds, Par 71, SSS 71, Course record 66.
Club membership 1060.

Visitors	must contact in advance. Sun with member only.
Societies	telephone to book reservation.
Green Fees	£24 per day; £18 per round (£30 per round Sat).
Prof	Andrew Carr
Designer	Hawtree & Son
Facilities	⊗ ⫻ ⮢ ⛳ ♀ ⚘ 🗄 ⛾ ↖ 🛒 ⚲
& Leisure	snooker.
Location	E side of town on A547

Hotel ★★★ 65% Kinmel Manor Hotel, St Georges Rd, ABERGELE
☎ 01745 832014 51 ⇌ ☇

RHYL
Map 06 SJ08

Rhyl Coast Rd LL18 3RE
☎ 01745 353171 Fax 01745 353171
Seaside course.
9 holes, 6220yds, Par 70, SSS 70, Course record 65.
Club membership 500.

Visitors	must contact in advance. Limited availability at weekends due to club competitions.
Societies	must contact in advance.
Green Fees	£15 per 18 holes (£20 weekends & bank holidays).
Prof	Tim Leah
Designer	James Braid
Facilities	⊗ ⫻ ⮢ ⛳ ♀ ⚘ 🗄 ⛾ ⚲
Location	1m E on A548

Hotel ★★ 60% Hotel Marina, Marine Dr, RHYL
☎ 01745 342371 29 ⇌ ☇

RUABON
Map 07 SJ34

Penycae Ruabon Rd, Penycae LL14 1TP
☎ 01978 810108
An architecturally designed and built 9-hole parkland course offering a challenge for players of all standards. After a lazy Par 4 start the second Par 3 is wooded on one side and guarded by water on the other. The 6th, a 317yds Par 4 makes a very difficult approach to the green. The 7th is another Par 3 , elevated and wooded to one side. The 8th crosses water twice as the river meanders down the fairway.
9 holes, 2140yds, Par 64, SSS 62, Course record 62.
Club membership 200.

Visitors	advisable to book in advance.
Societies	telephone or write in advance.
Green Fees	not confirmed.
Designer	John Day
Facilities	⊗ ⮢ ⛳ ♀ ⚘ 🗄 ⛾ ⚲
Location	1m off A5

Hotel ★★★ 64% Hand Hotel, Church St, CHIRK
☎ 01691 772479 16 ⇌ ☇

RUTHIN
Map 06 SJ15

Ruthin-Pwllglas Pwllglas LL15 2PE
☎ 01978 790692 Fax 01978 790692
Hilly parkland course in elevated position with panoramic views. Stiff climb to 3rd and 9th holes.
10 holes, 5362yds, Par 66, SSS 66.
Club membership 380.

Visitors	welcome except for competition days.
Societies	apply in writing.
Green Fees	not confirmed.
Facilities	⚘
Location	2.5m S off A494

Hotel ★★★ 66% Ruthin Castle, RUTHIN
☎ 01824 702664 58 ⇌ ☇

ST ASAPH
Map 06 SJ07

Llannerch Park North Wales Golf Range, Llannerch Park LL17 0BD ☎ 01745 730805
9 holes, 1587yds, Par 30.

Visitors	pay & play.
Societies	telephone in advance.
Green Fees	not confirmed.
Designer	B Williams
Facilities	⛳ 🗄 ⛾ ↨
Location	200yds S off A525

WREXHAM
Map 07 SJ35

Clays Farm Golf Centre Bryn Estyn Rd, Llan-y-Pwll LL13 9UB ☎ 01978 661406 Fax 01978 661417
Gently undulating parkland course in a rural setting with views of the Welsh mountains and noted for the difficulty of its par 3s.
18 holes, 5908yds, Par 69, SSS 69, Course record 64.
Club membership 420.

Visitors	must contact in advance.
Societies	prior arrangement in writing.
Green Fees	£13 per round (£17.50 weekends).
Cards	💳 💳 💳 💳 💳 💳
Prof	David Larvin
Designer	R D Jones
Facilities	⚘ 🗄 ⛾ ↖ 🛒 ⚲ ↨
Location	Off A534

Hotel ★★★🏨🏨 66% Llwyn Onn Hall Hotel, Cefn Rd, WREXHAM ☎ 01978 261225 13 ⇌ ☇

Wrexham Holt Rd LL13 9SB
☎ 01978 351476 Fax 01978 364268
Inland, sandy course with easy walking. Testing dog-legged 7th hole (par 4), and short 14th hole (par 3) with full carry to green.
18 holes, 6233yds, Par 70, SSS 70, Course record 64.
Club membership 600.

Visitors	may not play competition days, and are advised to contact in advance. A handicap certificate is required.
Societies	welcome Mon & Wed-Fri. Apply in writing
Green Fees	not confirmed.
Prof	Roy Young
Designer	James Braid
Facilities	⊗ ⫻ ⮢ ⛳ ♀ ⚘ 🗄 ⚲
Location	2m NE on A534

▶

| Hotel | ★★★⚓ 66% Llwyn Onn Hall Hotel, Cefn Rd, WREXHAM ☎ 01978 261225 13 ⇔ 🐾 |

MID & SOUTH WALES

This region includes the counties of Blaenau Gwent, Bridgend, Caerphilly, Cardiff, Carmarthenshire, Ceredigion, Merthyr Tydfil, Monmouthshire, Neath Port Talbot, Newport, Pembrokeshire, Powys, Rhondda Cynon Taff, Swansea, Torfaen and Vale of Glamorgan which reflect the national changes.

ABERDARE   Map 03 SO00

Aberdare Abernant CF44 0RY
☎ 01685 872797 Fax 01685 872797
Mountain course with parkland features overlooking Brecon Beacons.
18 holes, 5875yds, Par 69, SSS 69, Course record 64.
Club membership 550.

Visitors	must have handicap certificate. May play weekends by prior arrangment with secretary.
Societies	apply in writing in advance to the secretary.
Green Fees	£14 per day (£16 weekends & bank holidays).
Prof	A Palmer
Facilities	⊗ �🍴 ⅬⅬ ♥ ♀ ⚄ 🛍 ♂
Location	A470 to Abercynon, take A4059 to Aberdare. Follow sign to hospital, 400 yds on right

| Hotel | ★★★ 69% Tregenna Hotel, Park Ter, MERTHYR TYDFIL ☎ 01685 723627 & 382055 Fax 01685 721951 24 ⇔ 🐾 |

ABERGAVENNY   Map 03 SO21

Monmouthshire Gypsy Ln, LLanfoist NP7 9HE
☎ 01873 852606 Fax 01873 852606
This parkland course is very picturesque, with the beautifully wooded River Usk running alongside. There are a number of par 3 holes and a testing par 4 at the 15th.
18 holes, 5978yds, Par 70, SSS 69, Course record 65.
Club membership 700.

Visitors	must play with member at weekends. Must contact in advance & have handicap certificate.
Societies	must confirm in writing.
Green Fees	£25 per day (£30 weekends & bank holidays).
Prof	B Edwards
Designer	James Braid
Facilities	⊗ ⅢⅢ by prior arrangement ⅬⅬ ♥ ♀ ⚄ 🛍 ♂ ♂
Location	2m S off B4269

| Hotel | ★★ 70% Llanwenarth Arms Hotel, Brecon Rd, ABERGAVENNY ☎ 01873 810550 18 ⇔ 🐾 |

Wernddu Golf Centre Old Ross Rd NP7 8NG
☎ 01873 856223 Fax 01873 852177
A parkland course with magnificent views, wind hazards on several holes in certain conditions and water hazards on four holes. There is a 26 bay floodlit driving range.
18 holes, 5403yds, Par 68, SSS 67, Course record 64.
Club membership 550.

Visitors	advisable to book in advance.
Societies	telephone in advance.
Green Fees	£15 per round.
Cards	🖭 🖭 🖭 🖭
Prof	Alan Ashmead
Designer	G Watkins
Facilities	⊗ ⅬⅬ ♥ ♀ ⚄ 🛍 ♂ ♂
Location	1.5m NE on B4521

| Hotel | ★★★ 66% Llansantffraed Court Hotel, Llanvihangel Gobion, ABERGAVENNY ☎ 01873 840678 21 ⇔ 🐾 |

ABERYSTWYTH   Map 06 SN58

Aberystwyth Brynymor Rd SY23 2HY
☎ 01970 615104 Fax 01970 626622
Undulating meadowland course. Testing holes: 16th (The Loop) par 3; 17th, par 4; 18th, par 3. Good views over Cardigan Bay.
18 holes, 6109yds, Par 70, SSS 70, Course record 67.
Club membership 450.

Visitors	must contact in advance.
Societies	write or telephone in advance.
Green Fees	Apr-Oct £18 (£25 weekends); Nov-Mar £15 (£18 weekends).
Prof	Mark Newson
Designer	Harry Vardon
Facilities	⊗ ⅢⅢ ⅬⅬ ♥ ♀ ⚄ 🛍 ♂ ♂
Location	N side of town

| Hotel | ★★★ 69% Belle Vue Royal Hotel, Marine Ter, ABERYSTWYTH ☎ 01970 617558 34 ⇔ 🐾 |

AMMANFORD   Map 03 SN61

Glynhir Glynhir Rd, Llandybie SA18 2TF
☎ 01269 850472 & 851365 Fax 01269 851365
Parkland course with good views, latter holes close to Upper Loughor River. The 14th is a 394-yd dog leg.
18 holes, 6000yds, Par 69, SSS 70, Course record 66.
Club membership 700.

Visitors	no visitors Sun. Contact professional in advance (01269 851010).
Societies	welcome weekdays only. Contact in advance.
Green Fees	Winter: £10-£17 per round Summer: £16-£22.
Prof	Duncan Prior
Designer	F Hawtree
Facilities	⊗ ⅬⅬ ♥ ♀ ⚄ 🛍 ♂ 🚗 ♂
Location	2m N of Ammanford

| Hotel | ★★ 68% Mill at Glynhir, Glyn-Hir, Llandybie, AMMANFORD ☎ 01269 850672 11 ⇔ 🐾 |

BARGOED

Map 03 ST19

Bargoed Heolddu CF81 9GF
☎ 01443 830143 & 836411 (Prof)
Mountain parkland course, challenging par 70 course with panoramic views.
18 holes, 6049yds, Par 70, SSS 70, Course record 65.
Club membership 600.

Visitors	must contact professional in advance, must play with member at weekends.
Societies	must contact in advance.
Green Fees	not confirmed.
Prof	C Coombs
Facilities	⊗ ⠿ ⌶ ⮊ ♀ ♨ 🍴 🏌 ✓
Location	NW side of town

Hotel ★★★ 67% Maes Manor Hotel, BLACKWOOD ☎ 01495 224551 & 220011 Fax 01495 228217 8 ⇋ Annexe 14 ⇋

BARRY

Map 03 ST16

Brynhill Port Rd CF62 8PN
☎ 01446 720277 Fax 01446 720277
Meadowland course with some hard walking. Prevailing west wind.
18 holes, 6336yds, Par 72, SSS 71.
Club membership 750.

Visitors	must contact in advance. May not play on Sun.
Societies	phone secretary for details.
Green Fees	not confirmed.
Prof	Peter Fountain
Facilities	⮊ 🍴 ✓
Location	1.25m N on B4050

Hotel ★★★ 65% Mount Sorrel Hotel, Porthkerry Rd, BARRY ☎ 01446 740069 43 ⇋ ☏

RAF St Athan St Athan CF62 4WA
☎ 01446 797186 & 751043 Fax 01446 751862
This is a very windy course with wind straight off the sea to make all holes interesting. Further interest is added by this being a very tight course with lots of trees. Beware of low flying RAF jets.
9 holes, 6480yds, Par 72, SSS 72.
Club membership 450.

Visitors	contact in advance, Sun mornings club competitions only.
Societies	apply in advance.
Green Fees	£12 per day (£17 weekends).
Facilities	⊗ ⮊ 🍴 ♀ ⌷ 🍴
Location	Between Barry & Llantwit Major

Hotel ★★ 70% West House Country Hotel & Restaurant, West St, LLANTWIT MAJOR ☎ 01446 792406 & 793726 Fax 01446 796147 21 ⇋ ☏

St Andrews Major Argae Ln, Coldbrook Rd East, Cadoxton CF63 1BL ☎ 01446 722227
A new 9-hole, Pay and Play course with 6 Par 4s, 1 par5 and 2 par3s. Further extensions planned.
9 holes, 3000yds, Par 70, SSS 68.
Club membership 520.

Visitors	must contact in advance.
Societies	telephone in advance.
Green Fees	£8 per 9 holes; £13 per 18 holes.

Designer	Richard Hurd
Facilities	⮊ 🍴 ♀ ⌷ 🍴 🏌 ✓
Location	Off Barry new link road, Coldbrook Road East

Hotel ★★★⭐ 77% Egerton Grey Country House Hotel, Porthkerry, BARRY ☎ 01446 711666 10 ⇋ ☏

BETTWS NEWYDD

Map 03 SO30

Alice Springs NP15 1JY
☎ 01873 880244 & 880708 Fax 01873 880838
Two 18-hole undulating parkland courses set back to back with magnificent views of the Usk Valley. The Queen's course has testing 7th and 15th holes.
Queens Course: 18 holes, 5517yds, Par 67, SSS 67, Course record 65.
Kings Course: 18 holes, 5596yds, Par 70.
Club membership 550.

Visitors	should contact the club in advance for weekend play.
Societies	must telephone in advance.
Green Fees	£18 per day; £13 per round (£20/£15 weekends).
Cards	🃏 ▭ 🃏
Designer	Keith R Morgan
Facilities	⊗ ⠿ ⮊ 🍴 ♀ ⌷ 🍴 🏌 ✓ 🏌 ✓
Location	N of Usk on B4598 towards Abergavenny

Hotel ★★★ 74% Three Salmons Hotel, Porthycarne St, USK ☎ 01291 672133 10 ⇋ ☏ Annexe 14 ⇋ ☏

BLACKWOOD

Map 03 ST19

Blackwood Cwmgelli NP2 1EL
☎ 01495 222121 (Office) & 223152 (Club)
Heathland course with sand bunkers. Undulating, with hard walking. Testing 2nd hole par 4. Good views.
9 holes, 5332yds, Par 67.
Club membership 310.

Visitors	contact club or turn up and pay greens staff, may not play at weekends & bank holidays unless with member.
Societies	by prior arrangement for members of a recognised golf club.
Green Fees	not confirmed.
Facilities	⮊
Location	0.25m N of Blackwood, off A4048

Hotel ★★★ 67% Maes Manor Hotel, BLACKWOOD ☎ 01495 224551 & 220011 Fax 01495 228217 8 ⇋ Annexe 14 ⇋

BORTH

Map 06 SN69

Borth & Ynyslas SY24 5JS
☎ 01970 871202 Fax 01970 871202
Seaside links, over 100 years old, with strong winds at times although part of the course is sheltered amongst the dunes. Some narrow fairways and plenty of natural hazards.
18 holes, 6116yds, Par 70, SSS 70, Course record 65.
Club membership 550.

Visitors	must contact in advance, may play weekends ring to check no competitions in progress.
Societies	telephone in advance.
Green Fees	£25 per day; £20 per round (£32/£27 weekends & bank holidays).

▶

Prof	J G Lewis
Facilities	⊗ ☐ ☐ ♀ ♤ ☐ 〒 🏌 〆
Location	0.5m N on B4353

Hotel ★★★▲▲ Ynyshir Hall, EGLWYSFACH
☎ 01654 781209 8 ⇄ ⋔ Annexe 2 ⇄ ⋔

BRECON   Map 03 SO02

Brecon Newton Park LD3 8PA ☎ 01874 622004
Parkland course, with easy walking. Natural hazards include
two rivers on its boundary. Good river and mountain scenery.
9 holes, 5256yds, Par 66, SSS 66, Course record 61.
Club membership 360.

Visitors	advisable to contact in advance, limited availability at weekends.
Societies	apply in writing.
Green Fees	£10 per day.
Designer	James Braid
Facilities	⊗ ☐ ☐ ♀ ♤
Location	0.75m W of town centre on A40

Hotel ★★ 70% Castle of Brecon Hotel,
Castle Square, BRECON
☎ 01874 624611   30 ⇄ ⋔ Annexe 12 ⋔

Cradoc Penoyre Park, Cradoc LD3 9LP
☎ 01874 623658 Fax 01874 611711
Parkland with wooded areas, ponds and spectacular views
over the Brecon Beacons. Challenging golf.
18 holes, 6331yds, Par 72, SSS 72, Course record 65.
Club membership 700.

Visitors	must contact secretary in advance. Limited availability on Sundays

Societies	apply in writing or telephone in advance to secretary.
Green Fees	£20 per day (£25 weekends & bank holidays).
Cards	▭▭ ▭▭ ▭
Prof	Richard Davies
Designer	C K Cotton
Facilities	⊗ ⫼ ☐ ☐ ♀ ♤ ☐ 〒 〆 ⏇
Location	2m N on B4520

Hotel ★★ 70% Castle of Brecon Hotel,
Castle Square, BRECON
☎ 01874 624611   30 ⇄ ⋔ Annexe 12 ⋔

BRIDGEND   Map 03 SS97

Coed-Y-Mwstwr The Clubhouse, Coychurch CF35 6AF
☎ 01656 862121 & 864 934 Fax 01656 864934
Challenging holes on this 12-hole course include the par 3
3rd (180yds) involving a drive across a lake and the par 4 5th
(448yds) which is subject to strong prevailing winds.
12 holes, 6144yds, Par 70, SSS 70, Course record 71.
Club membership 260.

Visitors	must have handicap certificate, advisable to contact in advance. May only play Sat if with member.
Societies	by prior application.
Green Fees	£15.50 per 18 holes; £10 per 12 holes.
Designer	Chapman/Warren
Facilities & Leisure	⊗ ⫼ by prior arrangement ☐ ☐ ♀ ♤ ☐ 〆 pool table.
Location	1m out of Coychurch, turn at village garage. 2m W of junct 35 on M4

Hotel ★★★ 73% Coed-Y-Mwstwr Hotel, Coychurch,
BRIDGEND ☎ 01656 860621   23 ⇄ ⋔

Southerndown Ewenny CF32 0QP
☎ 01656 880476 Fax 01656 880317
Downland-links championship course with rolling
fairways and fast greens. The par-3 5th is played across a
valley and the 18th, with its split level fairway, is a
demanding finishing hole. Superb views.
18 holes, 6417yds, Par 70, SSS 72, Course record 64.
Club membership 710.

Visitors	must contact in advance & have handicap certificate.
Societies	by arrangement with secretary.
Green Fees	£25 per round; £5 per additional round.
Prof	D G McMonagle
Designer	W Fernie
Facilities	⊗ ℿ ᴸᴸ ▟ ⬛ ♀ ♨ 🏠 ➘ 🚜 ⟋ ⟨
Location	3m SW of Bridgend on B4524
Hotel	★★★ 69% Heronston Hotel, Ewenny Rd, BRIDGEND ☎ 01656 668811 69 ⇉ ▮ Annexe 6 ⇉ ▮

BUILTH WELLS Map 03 SO05

Builth Wells Golf Links Rd LD2 3NF
☎ 01982 553296 Fax 01982 551064
Well guarded greens and a stream running thorough the
centre of the course add interest to this 18-hole undulating
parkland course. The clubhouse is a converted 16th-century
Welsh long house.
18 holes, 5386yds, Par 66, SSS 67, Course record 63.
Club membership 380.

Visitors	contact secretary. Handicap certificate perferred.
Societies	by prior arrangement.
Green Fees	£20 per day; £15 per round (£25/£20 weekends & bank holidays).
Facilities	⊗ ℿ ᴸᴸ ▟ ⬛ ♀ 🏠 ♨ ⟋
Location	N of A483
Hotel	★★ 68% Pencerrig Gardens Hotel, Llandrindod Rd, BUILTH WELLS ☎ 01982 553226 20 ⇉ ▮

BURRY PORT Map 02 SN40

Ashburnham Cliffe Ter SA16 0HN
☎ 01554 832269 & 833846
This course has a lot of variety. In the main it is of the
seaside type although the holes in front of the clubhouse
are of an inland character. They are, however, good holes
which make a very interesting finish. Course record
holder, Sam Torrance.
18 holes, 6916yds, Par 72, SSS 74, Course record 70.
Club membership 730.

Visitors	must be bona fide member of affiliated golf club and produce handicap certificate, very limited weekend times.
Societies	telephone for initial enquiry.
Green Fees	not confirmed.
Prof	Robert Ryder
Designer	J H Taylor
Facilities	⊗ ℿ ᴸᴸ ▟ ⬛ ♀ 🏠 ♨ ⟋
Location	5m W of Llanelli, A484 road
Hotel	★★ 66% Ashburnham Hotel, Ashburnham Rd, Pembrey, LLANELLI ☎ 01554 834343 & 834455

Fax 01554 834483 12 ⇉ ▮

CAERLEON Map 03 ST39

Caerleon NP6 1AY ☎ 01633 420342
Parkland course.
9 holes, 2900yds, Par 34, SSS 34, Course record 29.
Club membership 148.

Visitors	play is allowed on all days, contact for details.
Societies	telephone 01633 420342.
Green Fees	£5.25 per 18 holes; £3.75 per 9 holes (£7/£4.70 weekends).
Prof	Chris Jones
Designer	Steel
Facilities	⊗ ℿ ᴸᴸ ▟ ⬛ ♀ 🏠 ♨ ⟋ ⟨
Location	3m from M4 turn off for Caerleon
Hotel	★★★★ 81% The Celtic Manor Resort, Coldra Woods, NEWPORT ☎ 01633 413000 400 ⇉ ▮

CAERPHILLY Map 03 ST18

Caerphilly Penchapel, Mountain Rd CF83 1HJ
☎ 029 20883481 & 20863441 Fax 029 20863441
Undulating mountain course with woodland affording good
views especially from 10th hole, 700 ft above sea level.
13 holes, 6032yds, Par 73, SSS 71.
Club membership 700.

Visitors	telephone in advance, must produce a current handicap certificate or letter from club secretary, may not play at weekends except with member, no visitors bank holidays.
Societies	apply in writing in advance to the secretary.
Green Fees	£20 per day.
Prof	Richard Barter
Facilities	⊗ ℿ by prior arrangement ᴸᴸ ⬛ ♀ 🏠 ⟋
Location	0.5m S on A469
Hotel	★★★ 73% Manor Parc Country Hotel & Restaurant, Thornhill Rd, Thornhill, CARDIFF ☎ 029 20693723 12 ⇉ ▮

Mountain Lakes & Castell Heights
Blaengwynlais CF83 1NG
☎ 029 20861128 & 20886666 Fax 029 20863243
The 9-hole Castell Heights course within the Mountain Lakes
complex was established in 1982 on a 45-acre site. In 1988 a
further 18-hole course, Mountain Lakes was designed by Bob
Sandow to take advantage of 160-acres of mountain
heathland, combining both mountain top golf and parkland.
Most holes are tree lined and there are 20 'lakes' as hazards.
Host of major PGA tournaments.
*Mountain Lakes Course: 18 holes, 6046mtrs, Par 74, SSS 73,
Course record 69.*
*Castell Heights Course: 9 holes, 2751mtrs, Par 35, SSS 32,
Course record 32.*
Club membership 500.

Societies	written or telephone notice in advance.
Green Fees	not confirmed.
Cards	▭ ▭ ▭ ▱
Prof	Sion Bebb
Designer	Bob Sandow
Facilities	⊗ ᴸᴸ ▟ ⬛ ♀ 🏠 ♨ ➘ 🚜 ⟋ ⟨
Location	Near Black Cock Inn, Caerphilly Mountain
Hotel	★★★ 73% Manor Parc Country Hotel &

Restaurant, Thornhill Rd, Thornhill, CARDIFF
☎ 029 20693723   12 ⇆ 🐾

Virginia Park Golf Club Virginia Park CF83 3SW
☎ 024 20863919 & 20585368
Beside Caerphilly leisure centre, the course is totally flat but
with plenty of trees and bunkers and 2 lakes. It is a tight,
challenging course with 6 par 4 and 3 par 3 holes. Also a 20-
bay flodlit driving range.
9 holes, 2566yds, Par 33.
Club membership 250.
Visitors   telephone in advance.
Societies   telephone then write to confirm.
Green Fees   not confirmed.
Facilities   🏅 💺 ♀ 🍴 🏠 🛈 ✆ ℓ ⟨
Location   Off Pontyewindy Rd

Hotel   ★★★ 73% Manor Parc Country Hotel &
                 Restaurant, Thornhill Rd, Thornhill, CARDIFF
                 ☎ 029 20693723   12 ⇆ 🐾

CAERSWS
Map 06 SO09

Mid-Wales Golf Centre SY17 5SB
☎ 01686 688303 Fax 01686 688303
A 9-hole, Par 3 course with sand bunkers and three ponds.
9 holes, 2554yds, Par 54, SSS 54.
Club membership 95.
Visitors   welcome, restricted during competitions on Sun
                 am.
Societies   telephone in advance.
Green Fees   £6 per 18 holes; £4 per 9 holes (£8/£5 weekends
                 & bank holidays).
Designer   Jim Walters
Facilities   🏅 💺 ♀ 🍴 🏠 🛈 ✆ ℓ ⟨
Location   0.75m off A470 out of Caersws

Hotel   ★★ 64% Elephant & Castle, Broad St,
                 NEWTOWN ☎ 01686 626271
                 23 ⇆ 🐾 Annexe 11 ⇆ 🐾

CAERWENT
Map 03 ST49

Dewstow NP26 5AH ☎ 01291 430444 Fax 01291 425816
Two picturesque parkland courses with easy walking and
spectacular views over the Severn estuary towards Bristol.
Testing holes include the Par three 7th, Valley Course, which
is approached over water, some 50 feet lower than the tee,
and the Par four 15th, Park Course, which has a 50ft totem
pole in the middle of the fairway, a unique feature. There is
also a 26-bay floodlit driving range.
Valley Course: 18 holes, 6141yds, Par 72, SSS 70, Course
record 68.
Park Course: 18 holes, 6226yds, Par 69, SSS 69, Course
record 69.
Club membership 950.
Visitors   may book two days in advance (six days in
                 advance in winter).
Societies   apply in writing or telephone for details.
Green Fees   £23 per day; £14 per 18 holes; £9 per 9 holes
                 (£17 per round; £10.50 per 9 holes weekends &
                 bank holidays).
Cards   💳 💳 💳 🟦
Prof   Jonathan Skuse
Facilities   ⊗ 🍴 🏅 💺 ♀ 🏠 🛈 ✆ 🐾 🛒 ℓ ⟨
& Leisure   golf coaching.
Location   0.5m S of A48 at Caerwent

Hotel   ★★ 67% George Hotel, Moor St,
                 CHEPSTOW ☎ 01291 625363   14 ⇆ 🐾

CARDIFF
Map 03 ST17

Cardiff Sherborne Av, Cyncoed CF2 6SJ
☎ 029 20753320 Fax 029 20680011
Parkland course, where trees form natural hazards.
Interesting variety of holes, mostly bunkered. A stream flows
through course and comes into play on 9 separate holes.
18 holes, 6016yds, Par 70, SSS 70, Course record 66.
Club membership 900.
Visitors   Must contact in advance.
Societies   Thu only, pre-booking essential.
Green Fees   not confirmed.
Prof   Terry Hanson
Facilities   ⊗ 🍴 🏅 💺 ♀ 🏠 🛈 ℓ
& Leisure   snooker.
Location   3m N of city centre

Hotel   ★★★ 70% Posthouse Cardiff, Pentwyn Rd,
                 Pentwyn, CARDIFF
                 ☎ 0870 400 8141 142 ⇆ 🐾

Cottrell Park Cottrell Park, St Nicholas CF5 6JY
☎ 01446 781781 Fax 01446 781707
Two well designed courses, opened in 1996, set in undulating
parkland with mature trees and spectacular views, especially
from the par 35 9-hole course. An enjoyable yet testing game
of golf for players of all abilities.
Mackintosh: 18 holes, 6110yds, Par 72, SSS 71, Course
record 65.
Button: 9 holes, 2660yds, Par 70, SSS 69.
Club membership 1050.
Visitors   must have a valid handicap certificate, advance
                 bookings up to one week.
Societies   welcome on Mon & Tue, apply in writing, min
                 12.
Green Fees   £25 per round; 12.50 per 9 holes (£33.50/£16.75
                 weekends).
Prof   Steve Birch
Designer   MRM Sandow
Facilities   ⊗ 🍴 🏅 💺 ♀ 🏠 🛈 ✆ 🐾 🛒 ℓ ⟨
Location   M4 junct 33 to Culverhouse Cross A48 to
                 Cowbridge, through St Nicholas on right hand
                 side

Hotel   ★★★★ 71% Copthorne Cardiff-Caerdydd,
                 Copthorne Way, Culverhouse Cross, CARDIFF
                 ☎ 029 20599100 135 ⇆ 🐾

Llanishen Cwm Lisvane CF4 5UD
☎ 029 20755078 Fax 029 20755078
Mountain course, with hard walking overlooking the Bristol
Channel.
18 holes, 5296yds, Par 68, SSS 66, Course record 63.
Club membership 600.
Visitors   must play with member at weekends & bank
                 holidays. Must contact in advance.
Societies   contact in advance.
Green Fees   not confirmed.
Prof   Adrian Jones
Facilities   ⊗ 🍴 🏅 💺 ♀ 🏠 🛈 ℓ
Location   5m N of city centre off A469

Hotel   ★★★ 70% Posthouse Cardiff, Pentwyn Rd,
                 Pentwyn, CARDIFF
                 ☎ 0870 400 8141 142 ⇆ 🐾

Peterstone Peterstone, Wentloog CF3 8TN
☎ 01633 680009 Fax 01633 680563
Parkland course with abundant water features and several long drives (15th, 601yds).
18 holes, 6555yds, Par 72, SSS 71, Course record 67.
Club membership 714.

Visitors	contact in advance suggested.
Societies	telephone enquiries welcome.
Green Fees	not confirmed.
Cards	
Prof	Richard Harries
Designer	Bob Sandow
Facilities	
Location	3m from Castleton off A48
Hotel	★★★ 72% St Mellons Hotel & Country Club, Castleton, CARDIFF ☎ 01633 680355 21 Annexe 20

Radyr The Clubhouse, Drysgol Rd, Radyr CF4 8BS
☎ 029 20842408 Fax 029 20843914
Parkland course which can be windy. Good views. Venue for many county and national championships.
18 holes, 6031yds, Par 69, SSS 70, Course record 62.
Club membership 920.

Visitors	must play with member at weekends.
Societies	must contact in advance.
Green Fees	£36 per day.
Cards	
Prof	Robert Butterworth
Facilities	
& Leisure	Table tennis, snooker room.
Location	M4 junct32, 4.5m NW of city centre off A4119
Hotel	★★★ 73% Manor Parc Country Hotel & Restaurant, Thornhill Rd, Thornhill, CARDIFF ☎ 029 20693723 12

St Mellons St Mellons CF3 8XS
☎ 01633 680408 Fax 01633 681219
This parkland course comprises quite a few par-3 holes and provides some testing golf. It is indeed a challenge to the single handicap golfer.
18 holes, 6275yds, Par 70, SSS 70, Course record 63.
Club membership 700.

Visitors	must contact in advance. With member only at weekends.
Societies	must contact in advance.
Green Fees	not confirmed.
Prof	Barry Thomas
Facilities	
Location	5m NE off A48
Hotel	★★★ 72% St Mellons Hotel & Country Club, Castleton, CARDIFF ☎ 01633 680355 21 Annexe 20

Whitchurch Pantmawr Rd, Whitchurch CF14 7TD
☎ 029 20620985 (Sec) Fax 029 20529860
Well manicured parkland course, slightly undulating, with fine views over the city centre and the Bristol Channel beyond.
18 holes, 6321yds, Par 71, SSS 71, Course record 62.
Club membership 750.

Visitors	may not play on competition days, contact secretary/professional in advance.
Societies	Thu only. Must contact in advance.
Green Fees	£35 per day (£40 weekends & bank holidays).
Prof	Eddie Clark
Designer	F Johns
Facilities	
Location	4m N of city centre on A470, near junct 32 off M4
Hotel	★★★ 73% Manor Parc Country Hotel & Restaurant, Thornhill Rd, Thornhill, CARDIFF ☎ 029 20693723 12

CARDIGAN — Map 02 SN14

Cardigan Gwbert-on-Sea SA43 1PR
☎ 01239 621775 & 612035 Fax 01239 621775
A links course, very dry in winter, with wide fairways, light rough and gorse. Every hole overlooks the sea.
18 holes, 6687yds, Par 72, SSS 73.
Club membership 600.

Visitors	may not play between 1-2pm. Handicap certificate preferred. Contact in advance
Societies	must telephone in advance.
Green Fees	£20 per day (£25 weekends & bank holidays).
Cards	
Prof	Colin Parsons
Designer	Hawtree
Facilities	
& Leisure	squash.
Location	3m N off A487
Hotel	★★★ 67% Cliff Hotel, GWBERT-ON-SEA ☎ 01239 613241 70

CARMARTHEN — Map 02 SN42

Carmarthen Blaenycoed Rd SA33 6EH ☎ 01267 281588
Hilltop course with good views.
18 holes, 6245yds, Par 71, SSS 71, Course record 68.
Club membership 700.

Visitors	must have a handicap certificate, telephone for times at weekends.
Societies	apply in writing minimum of ten days in advance.
Green Fees	not confirmed.
Prof	Pat Gillis
Designer	J H Taylor
Facilities	
Location	4m N of town
Hotel	★★ 63% Falcon Hotel, Lammas St, CARMARTHEN ☎ 01267 234959 & 237152 Fax 01267 221277 14

Derllys Court Llysonnen Rd SA33 5DT
☎ 01267 211575 Fax 01267 211575
Gently undulating parkland course with challenging par 3s (5th and 8th) and a testing par 5 involving a shot across a lake.
9 holes, 2859yds, Par 35, SSS 66, Course record 33.
Club membership 60.

Visitors	welcome at all times.
Societies	telephone in advance.
Green Fees	£9.50 per 18 holes; £5.50 per 9 holes (£10.50/£6.50 weekends & bank holidays).

Cards	⬛ ⬛ ⬛ ⬛ ⬛ ⬛ ⬛
Designer	Peter Johnson
Facilities	⊗ 🍴 ⬛ 🍺 ♀ ⚲ 🏧 🛄 ⚐
Location	Just off A40 between Carmarthen/St Clears

Hotel	★★ 63% Falcon Hotel, Lammas St,
	CARMARTHEN ☎ 01267 234959 & 237152
	Fax 01267 221277 14 ⇨ 🎇

CHEPSTOW
Map 03 ST59

CHEPSTOW See page 405.

Shirenewton Shirenewton NP16 6RL ☎ 01291 641642
Parkland course with magnificent views over the Severn
estuary and extending to the Devon coastline.
18 holes, 6605yds, Par 72, SSS 72.
Club membership 300.

Visitors	welcome, advisable to reserve tee times, must
	book at weekends
Societies	apply in writing/telephone.
Green Fees	£12 per round; £8 per 9 holes (£15/£10
	weekends).
Cards	⬛
Prof	Renton Doig
Facilities	⊗ 🍴 ⬛ 🍺 ♀ ⚲ 🏧 🛄 ⚐
Location	Junct 2 of M48 off A48 at Crick

Hotel	★★ 66% Beaufort Hotel, Beaufort Square,
	CHEPSTOW ☎ 01291 622497 18 ⇨ 🎇

CLYDACH
Map 03 SN60

Inco SA6 5PQ ☎ 01792 844216
Flat meadowland course to be extended to 18 holes.
15 holes, 5994yds, Par 70, SSS 69.
Club membership 300.

Visitors	no restrictions.
Societies	must contact in advance.
Green Fees	not confirmed.
Facilities	⬛ ♀ ⚲
Location	0.75m SE on B4291

Hotel	★★ 62% Oak Tree Parc Hotel, Birchgrove Rd,
	BIRCHGROVE ☎ 01792 817781 10 ⇨ 🎇

CREIGIAU (CREIYIAU)
Map 03 ST08

Creigiau Llantwit Rd CF4 8NN ☎ 029 20890263
Downland course, with small greens and many interesting
water hazards.
18 holes, 6015yds, Par 71, SSS 70, Course record 67.
Club membership 1020.

Visitors	must contact in advance. May only play at
	weekends with member.
Societies	Wed only, minimum number 20, must book in
	advance.
Green Fees	not confirmed.
Prof	Iain Luntz
Facilities	⊗ 🍴 ⬛ 🍺 ♀ ⚲ 🏧 🛄 ⚐
Location	6m NW of Cardiff on A4119

Hotel	★★★★ 69% Miskin Manor Hotel,
	Groes Faen, Pontyclun, MISKIN
	☎ 01443 224204 34 ⇨ 🎇 Annexe 8 ⇨ 🎇

CWMBRAN
Map 03 ST29

Green Meadow Golf & Country Club Treherbert Rd,
Croesyceiliog NP44 2BZ
☎ 01633 869321 & 862626 Fax 01633 868430
Undulating parkland course with panoramic views. The 2nd
hole is played partly down hill with the front half of the
green enclosed with water; the 13th is exposed to winds with
large mature trees along righthand side of green.
18 holes, 6029yds, Par 70, SSS 70, Course record 66.
Club membership 400.

Visitors	by prior arrangement advised especially at
	weekends, tel 01633 862626. Correct standard
	of dress compulsory.
Societies	telephone for brochure, Golf Shop 01633
	862626.
Green Fees	Mon: £14 Tues-Fri; £17 (£19 weekends).
Cards	⬛ ⬛ ⬛ ⬛ ⬛
Prof	Peter Stebbings
Designer	Peter Richardson
Facilities	⊗ 🍴 ⬛ 🍺 ♀ ⚲ 🏧 🛄 🐎 ⚐ 🏌
& Leisure	hard tennis courts.
Location	5m N of junct 26 M4, off A4042 from Cardiff

Hotel	★★★★ 65% Parkway Hotel, Cwmbran Dr,
	CWMBRAN
	☎ 01633 871199 70 ⇨ 🎇

Pontnewydd Maesgwyn Farm, West Pontnewydd NP44 1AB
☎ 01633 482170
Mountainside course, with hard walking. Good views across
the Severn Estuary.
10 holes, 5353yds, Par 68, SSS 67, Course record 63.
Club membership 250.

Visitors	must play with member weekends & bank
	holidays.
Green Fees	not confirmed.
Facilities	⬛ ♀ ⚲
Location	N side of town centre

Hotel	★★★★ 65% Parkway Hotel, Cwmbran Dr,
	CWMBRAN
	☎ 01633 871199 70 ⇨ 🎇

DINAS POWIS
Map 03 ST17

Dinas Powis Old High Walls CF64 4AJ
☎ 029 20512727 Fax 029 20512727
Parkland/downland course with views over the Bristol
Channel and the seaside resort of Barry.
18 holes, 5486yds, Par 67, SSS 67, Course record 60.
Club membership 550.

Visitors	must contact in advance (call G Bennett 01222
	513682)
Societies	telephone in advance.
Green Fees	not confirmed.
Prof	Gareth Bennett
Facilities	⊗ 🍴 ⬛ 🍺 ♀ ⚲ 🏧 ⚐
Location	NW side of village

Hotel	★★★ 65% Mount Sorrel Hotel, Porthkerry Rd,
	BARRY
	☎ 01446 740069 43 ⇨ 🎇

Marriott St Pierre

Chepstow, *Monmouthshire*   ☎ 01291 625261   Fax 01291 629975   Map 03 ST59

Beautiful and challenging, the Old Course is one of the finest golf courses in the country and in recent years has played host to many major championships and staged the old Dunlop Masters. Among the many hazards the lake at the short 18th hole is particularly fearsome.

St Pierre is more than just a championship golfing venue. The Mathern presents its own challenges to experienced and weekend players alike, even the novice golfer can enjoy a game here. The hotel has teaching professionals as well as hire of clubs and equipment. A new 13 bay driving range was added in late 1998.

Visitors Mon & Thu (unless guest at Dormy House). Must contact in advance, and have a handicap certificate

Societies must apply to Secretary (large groups Mon & Thu only

Green Fees £82 per round (includes lunch)

Facilities Symbols Symbols Symbols Symbols Symbols Symbols

Leisure snooker

Location Links Gate, Lytham FY8 3LQ (0.5m E of St Annes town

Holes/Par/Course record

WHERE TO STAY AND EAT NEARBY

Hotels
CHEPSTOW

★★★★ ⊛ 69% St Pierre Hotel & Country Club ☎ 01291 626261, 148 ⇆ 🐾

★★★ 61% The Old Course, Newport Road ☎ 01291 626261 31 ⇆ 🐾

★★ 68% Castle View, 16 Bridge St. ☎ 01291 620340 9(8 ⇆ 1 🐾) Annexe 4 ⇆

★★ 67% The George Hotel, Moor St ☎ 01291 625363 14 ⇆ 🐾

TINTERN

★★ ⊛ 72% Parva Farmhouse Hotel ☎ 01291 689411 9(7 ⇆ 2 🐾)

★★ ⊛ 70% Royal George Hotel ☎ 01291 689205 2 ⇆ 🐾 Annexe 14 ⇆ 🐾

WHITEBROOK

★★ ⊛ ⊛ 70% The Crown at Whitebrook ☎ 01600 860254 10 ⇆ 🐾

Restaurant

CHEPSTOW

⊛ ⊛ Wye Knot, The Bank ☎ 01291 622929

GLYNNEATH

Map 03 SN80

Glynneath Pen-y-graig, Pontneathvaughan SA11 5UH
☎ 01639 720452 & 720872 Fax 01639 720452
Attractive hillside golf overlooking the Vale of Neath in the
foothills of the Brecon Beacons National Park. Reasonably
level farmland/wooded course.
18 holes, 5707yds, Par 69, SSS 68, Course record 64.
Club membership 630.
Visitors   restricted starting times at weekend.
Societies   must contact in advance.
Green Fees £15 per day (£20 weekends & bank holidays).
Prof   Huw Thomas
Designer   Cotton/Pennick/Lawri
Facilities   ⊗ ᛩ by prior arrangement 🏌 ⬛ ♀ ♟ 🏡 🍴
                       🛺 ✐
Location   2m NE on B4242

Hotel   ★★ 62% Oak Tree Parc Hotel, Birchgrove Rd,
                       BIRCHGROVE ☎ 01792 817781   10 ⇋ ☏

GWBERT-ON-SEA

Map 02 SN15

Cliff Hotel SA43 1PP ☎ 01239 613241 Fax 01239 615391
This is a short course with 2 Par 4's and the remainder are
challenging Par 3's. Particularly interesting holes are played
across the sea on to a small island.
9 holes, 1545yds, Par 29.

Visitors   telephone to book in advance.
Societies   telephone in advance.
Green Fees not confirmed.
Cards   🈺 🈺 🈺
Facilities   🏌 🏡 🍴 🚐 ✐
& Leisure   heated outdoor swimming pool, squash, fishing,
                       sauna, solarium, gymnasium.
Hotel   ★★★ 67% Cliff Hotel, GWBERT-ON-SEA
                       ☎ 01239 613241   70 ⇋ ☏

HAVERFORDWEST

Map 02 SM91

Haverfordwest Arnolds Down SA61 2XQ
☎ 01437 764523 Fax 01437 764143
Fairly flat parkland course, a good challenge for golfers of all
handicaps. Set in attractive surroundings with fine views over
the Preseli Hills.
18 holes, 6005yds, Par 70, SSS 69, Course record 58.
Club membership 770.
Visitors   restricted at weekends.
Societies   apply in writing or telephone for booking form.
Green Fees not confirmed.
Cards   🈺 🈺

Prof   Alex Pile
Facilities   ⊗ ᛩ 🏌 ⬛ ♀ ♟ 🏡 🍴 🛺 ✐
Location   1m E on A40

Hotel   ★★ 67% Hotel Mariners, Mariners Square,
                       HAVERFORDWEST
                       ☎ 01437 763353   28 ⇋ ☏

HAY-ON-WYE

Map 03 SO24

Summerhill Hereford Rd, Clifford HR3 5EW
☎ 01497 820451
Undulating parkland course set deep in the Wye Valley on
the Welsh Border overlooking the Black Mountains.
9 holes, 2929yds, Par 70, SSS 67.
Visitors   welcome anytime.
Societies   contact for information.
Green Fees not confirmed.
Prof   Graham Priday
Facilities   ♟ 🏡 🍴 ✐
Location   B4350 Whitney toll bridge road

Hotel   ★★★ 66% The Swan-at-Hay Hotel,
                       Church St, HAY-ON-WYE
                       ☎ 01497 821188   16 ⇋ ☏ Annexe 3 ⇋ ☏

HENSOL

Map 03 ST07

Vale of Glamorgan Golf & Country Club Hensol Park
CF72 8JY ☎ 01443 222221 Fax 01443 222220
Two courses set in 200 acres of glorious countryside with
views over Hensol Park lake and castle. The 18-hole par 72
Lake Course features towering trees, bunkers and water on
ten holes. The signature hole, the 12th, has an island green
reached via a stone bridge. The club is also home to the
Welsh Golf Academy.
Lake: 18 holes, 6507yds, Par 72, SSS 71.
Hensol: 9 holes, 3115yds, Par 72, SSS 71.
Club membership 1100.
Visitors   must have a handicap certificate and may only
                       play with member at weekends.
Societies   apply in writing.
Green Fees not confirmed.
Cards   🈺 🈺 🈺 🈺 🈺 🈺
Prof   Peter Johnson
Designer   Peter Johnson
Facilities   ⊗ ᛩ 🏌 ⬛ ♀ ♟ 🏡 🍴 🏐 🛺 ✐ ♟
& Leisure   hard tennis courts, heated indoor swimming
                       pool, squash, fishing, sauna, solarium,
                       gymnasium, many facilities in process of being
                       built.
Location   2 mins from junct 34 of M4

Hotel   ★★★★ 69% Miskin Manor Hotel,
                       Groes Faen, Pontyclun, MISKIN
                       ☎ 01443 224204   34 ⇋ ☏ Annexe 8 ⇋ ☏

KIDWELLY

Map 02 SN40

Glyn Abbey Trimsaran SA17 4LB
☎ 01554 810278 Fax 01554 810889
In the Gwendraeth valley, a 18-hole parkland course with
greens well protected by the planting of 35,000 trees.
18 holes, 6173yds, Par 70, SSS 69, Course record 68.
Visitors   advisable to book for weekends.
Societies   must contact in advance.
Green Fees £12 per round (£15 weekends).   ▶

Prof	Neil Evans
Designer	Hawtrees
Facilities	⊗ ℣ 🏐 ⛳ ♘ 🏌 🏠 ⛳ 🏌 ↝ 🛺 ♂ 🏌
& Leisure	gymnasium.
Location	4.5m W of Llanelli

Hotel ★★ 66% Ashburnham Hotel, Ashburnham Rd, Pembrey, LLANELLI
☎ 01554 834343 & 834455
Fax 01554 834483 12 ⇋ ℟

KNIGHTON Map 07 SO27

Knighton Frydd Wood LD7 1DB ☎ 01547 528646
Upland course with some hard walking. Fine views over the Welsh/English border.
9 holes, 5362yds, Par 68, SSS 66, Course record 65.
Club membership 150.

Visitors	may not play on Sun until after 4.30pm.
Societies	telephone in advance
Green Fees	£10 per day (£12 weekends & bank holidays).
Designer	Harry Vardon
Facilities	⊗ ℣ 🏐 🏌 ♀ 🏌
Location	0.5m S off B4355

Hotel ★★★ 62% The Knighton Hotel, Broad St, KNIGHTON ☎ 01547 520530 15 ⇋ ℟

LETTERSTON Map 02 SM92

Priskilly Forest Castlemorris SA62 5EH
☎ 01348 840276 Fax 01348 840276
Testing parkland course surrounded by rhododendrons. Beautiful panoramic views. Challenging dog-leg 4th with hazards both sides.
9 holes, 5874yds, Par 70, SSS 68, Course record 76.
Club membership 70.

Visitors	advance booking advisable at weekends during summer.
Societies	telephone in advance.
Green Fees	£14 per day; £10 per 18 holes; £8 per 9 holes.
Cards	💳 💳 💳 🖨
Designer	J Walters
Facilities	⊗ 🏐 🏌 ♀ 🏌 🏠 ⛳ 🏌 ↝ 🛺 ♂
& Leisure	fishing.
Location	Off B4331 between Letterston and Mathry

Hotel ★★ 60% Abergwaun Hotel, The Market Square, FISHGUARD
☎ 01348 872077 11rm (7 ⇋ ℟)

LLANDRINDOD WELLS Map 03 SO06

Llandrindod Wells The Clubhouse LD1 5NY
☎ 01597 823873 (sec) & 822247 (shop) Fax 01597 823873
An upland links course, designed by Harry Vardon, with easy walking and panoramic views. One of the highest courses in Wales. (1,100 ft above sea level).
18 holes, 5759yds, Par 69, SSS 69, Course record 65.
Club membership 450.

Visitors	no restrictions.
Societies	must telephone in advance.
Green Fees	not confirmed.
Designer	H Vardon
Facilities	⊗ ℣ 🏐 🏌 ♀ 🏌 🏠 ⛳ 🏌 ↝ 🛺 ♂
& Leisure	Driving tees.
Location	1m SE off A483

Hotel ★★★ 69% Hotel Metropole, Temple St, LLANDRINDOD WELLS
☎ 01597 823700 121 ⇋ ℟

LLANDYSSUL Map 02 SN44

Saron Saron SA44 5EL ☎ 01559 370705
Set in 50 acres of mature parkland with large trees and magnificent Teifi Valley views. Numerous water hazards and bunkers.
9 holes, 2400yds, Par 32, Course record 34.

Visitors	may play at all times no arrangements required.
Societies	telephone for details.
Green Fees	£7 per 18 holes, £5 per 9 holes.
Designer	Adas
Facilities	🏌 ♂
& Leisure	fishing.
Location	Off A484 at Saron

Hotel ★★ 73% Ty Mawr Country Hotel & Restaurant, BRECHFA
☎ 01267 202332 5rm (4 ⇋ ℟)

LLANGATTOCK Map 03 SO21

Old Rectory NP8 1PH
☎ 01873 810373 Fax 018373 810373
Sheltered course with easy walking.
9 holes, 2200yds, Par 54, SSS 59, Course record 53.
Club membership 80.

Visitors	no play Sun mornings, telephone for information.
Societies	telephone for booking.
Green Fees	£7.50 per day.
Cards	💳 💳 💳 🖨 💳
Facilities	⊗ ℣ 🏐 🏌 ♀ 🏌 🏠
& Leisure	outdoor swimming pool.
Location	SW of village

Hotel ★★★ 71% Gliffaes Country House Hotel, CRICKHOWELL
☎ 01874 730371 & 0800 146719 (Freephone)
Fax 01874 730463 19 ⇋ ℟ Annexe 3 ⇋ ℟

LLANGYBI Map 02 SN65

Cilgwyn SA48 8NN
☎ 01570 493286
Picturesque parkland course in secluded valley, with natural hazards of ponds, stream and woodland.
9 holes, 5309yds, Par 68, SSS 66, Course record 66.
Club membership 300.

Visitors	no restrictions, apart from Sun when advisable to telephone.
Societies	apply in advance by letter or telephone.
Green Fees	not confirmed.
Designer	Sandor
Facilities	⊗ by prior arrangement ℣ by prior arrangement 🏐 by prior arrangement 🏌 ♀ 🏌 ⛳ ♂
Location	5m N of Lampeter on A485

Hotel ★★★🏠 70% Falcondale Mansion, LAMPETER
☎ 01570 422910 19 ⇋ ℟

LLANIDLOES   Map 06 SN98

St Idloes Penrallt SY18 6LG ☎ 01686 412559
Hill-course, slightly undulating but walking is easy. Good
views, partly lined with trees. Sand and grass bunkers.
9 holes, 5540yds, Par 66, SSS 66, Course record 61.
Club membership 339.
Visitors   may not play on Sun mornings.
Societies   apply in writing to the secretary at least one
                month in advance.
Green Fees not confirmed.
Facilities ⊗ ⅲ by prior arrangement 🏌 ♨ ♀ ♨ 🏠 🍴 ⚷
Location   1m N off B4569

LLANRHYSTUD   Map 06 SN56

Penrhos Golf & Country Club SY23 5AY
☎ 01974 202999 Fax 01974 202100
Beautifully scenic course incorporating lakes and spectacular
coastal and inland views. Many leisure facilities.
Penrhos: 18 holes, 6641yds, Par 72, SSS 73,
Course record 71.
Academy: 9 holes, 1827yds, Par 31.
Club membership 300.
Visitors   must telephone, no jeans allowed on main
                course.
Societies   must telephone in advance.
Green Fees £25 per day (£32 weekends).
Cards   💳 💳 💳 💳 💳
Prof   Paul Diamond
Designer   Jim Walters
Facilities ⊗ ⅲ 🏌 ♨ ♀ ♨ 🏠 🍴 🚽 🔥 🏌 ⚷ ℩
& Leisure   hard tennis courts, heated indoor swimming
                pool, sauna, solarium, gymnasium, bowling
                green.
Location   Turn off A487 onto B4337 in Llanrhystud.
                Course 0.25m on left

Hotel   ★★★★♨ 73% Conrah Hotel, Ffosrhydygaled,
                Chancery, ABERYSTWYTH
                ☎ 01970 617941   11 ⇨ ℩ Annexe 9 ⇨ ℩

LLANWERN   Map 03 ST38

Llanwern Tennyson Av NP6 2DY
☎ 01633 412029 Fax 01633 412029
Parkland Course.
18 holes, 6115yds, Par 70, SSS 69, Course record 63.
Club membership 650.
Visitors   welcome, but with member only at weekends.
Societies   telephone and confirm in writing.
Green Fees not confirmed.
Cards   💳 💳 💳
Prof   Stephen Price
Facilities ⊗ ⅲ 🏌 ♨ ♀ ♨ 🏠
Location   0.5m S off A455

Hotel   ★★★★ 81% The Celtic Manor Resort, Coldra
                Woods, NEWPORT
                ☎ 01633 413000 400 ⇨ ℩

> Where to stay, where to eat?
> Visit the AA internet site
> www.theaa.co.uk

MACHYNLLETH   Map 06 SH70

Machynlleth Ffordd Drenewydd SY20 8UH
☎ 01654 702000
Lowland course with mostly natural hazards.
9 holes, 5726yds, Par 68, SSS 68, Course record 65.
Club membership 250.
Visitors   Thur ladies day, Sun morning mens competition.
Societies   telephone in advance.
Green Fees not confirmed.
Designer   James Braid
Facilities 🏌 ♨ ♀ ♨ 🏠
Location   0.5m E off A489

Hotel   ★★ 66% Wynnstay Arms Hotel, Maengwyn St,
                MACHYNLLETH ☎ 01654 702941   23 ⇨ ℩

MAESTEG   Map 03 SS89

Maesteg Mount Pleasant, Neath Rd CF34 9PR
☎ 01656 734106 & 732037 Fax 01656 734106
Reasonably flat hill-top course with scenic views.
18 holes, 5929yds, Par 70, SSS 69, Course record 69.
Club membership 789.
Visitors   must be a member of a recognised golf club &
                have a handicap certificate.
Societies   apply in writing.
Green Fees not confirmed.
Prof   Chris Riley
Designer   James Braid
Facilities 🏌 ♨ ♀ ♨ 🏠 🍴 ⚷
Location   0.5m W off B4282

Hotel   ★★★ 67% Aberavon Beach Hotel, PORT
                TALBOT ☎ 01639 884949   52 ⇨

MAESYCWMMER   Map 03 ST19

Bryn Meadows Golf & Country Hotel The Bryn CF82 7FN
☎ 01495 225590 or 224103 Fax 01495 228272
A heavily wooded parkland course with panoramic views of
the Brecon Beacons.
18 holes, 6132yds, Par 72, SSS 69, Course record 68.
Club membership 540.
Visitors   may not play Sun mornings. Must contact in
                advance.
Societies   Tue & Thu only.
Green Fees not confirmed.
Prof   Bruce Hunter
Designer   Mayo/Jeffries
Facilities ♨ 🏠 🍴 🔥 🚽 ⚷ ℩
& Leisure   heated indoor swimming pool, sauna, solarium,
                gymnasium.
Location   On the A4048 Blackwood to Ystrad Mynach rd

Hotel   ★★★ 67% Maes Manor Hotel,
                BLACKWOOD ☎ 01495 224551 & 220011
                Fax 01495 228217 8 ⇨ Annexe 14 ⇨

MARGAM   Map 03 SS78

Lakeside Water St SA13 2PA ☎ 01639 899959
A parkland course with bunkers and natural hazards. Eight
Par 4's and ten Par 3's.
18 holes, 4390yds, Par 62, SSS 63, Course record 65.
Club membership 250.   ▶

Visitors	no restrictions.
Societies	apply in advance by letter or telephone.
Green Fees	not confirmed.
Prof	Mathew Wootton
Designer	Matthew Wootton
Facilities	⊗ � 🏌 💺 ♀ 🏌 🏤 ⚑ ♂ 𝄢 ⌇
Location	Off junct 38 of M4

Hotel   ★★★ 67% Aberavon Beach Hotel, PORT TALBOT ☎ 01639 884949   52 ⇋

MERTHYR TYDFIL   Map 03 SO00

Merthyr Tydfil Cilsanws Mountain, Cefn Coed CF48 2NU
☎ 01685 723308
Mountain-top course with good views. Requires accuracy off the tee.
18 holes, 5625yds, Par 69, SSS 68, Course record 65.
Club membership 210.

Visitors	may not play on Sun.
Societies	by prior arrangement.
Green Fees	£10 per round (£15 weekends).
Designer	V Price/R Mathias
Facilities	⊗ � 🏌 💺 by prior arrangement ⚐
Location	Off A470 at Cefn Coed

Hotel   ★★★ 74% Nant Ddu Lodge Hotel, Cwm Taf, Nant Ddu, MERTHYR TYDFIL
☎ 01685 379111   12 ⇋ ⋒ Annexe 10 ⇋ ⋒

Morlais Castle Pant, Dowlais CF48 2UY
☎ 01685 722822 Fax 01685 722822
Beautiful moorland course overlooking National Park with excellent views of Brecon Beacons and surrounding countryside. The interesting layout of the course makes for a testing game.
18 holes, 6320yds, Par 71, SSS 71.
Club membership 500.

Visitors	must contact in advance for weekends.
Societies	apply in writing.
Green Fees	Summer: £16 per day/round (£20 weekends & bank holidays). Winter: £14 per day/round (£16 weekends & bank holidays).
Prof	H Jarrett
Facilities & Leisure	⊗ � 🏌 💺 ♀ ⚐ 🏤 🏌 ⚐ snooker.
Location	2.5m N off A465. Follow signs for Mountain Railway. Course entrance opposite railway car park

Hotel   ★★★ 74% Nant Ddu Lodge Hotel, Cwm Taf, Nant Ddu, MERTHYR TYDFIL
☎ 01685 379111   12 ⇋ ⋒ Annexe 10 ⇋ ⋒

MILFORD HAVEN   Map 02 SM90

Milford Haven Woodbine House, Hubberston SA73 3RX
☎ 01646 692368 Fax 01646 697762
Parkland course with excellent greens and views of the Milford Haven waterway.
18 holes, 6030yds, Par 71, SSS 70.
Club membership 520.

Visitors	no restrictions, advisable to contact in advance.
Societies	telephone to book.
Green Fees	not confirmed.
Cards	▭▭ ▭▭ ▭▭ ▨
Prof	J Lynch

Facilities	⊗ � 🏌 💺 ♀ ⚐ 🏤 🏌 ⚑ ♂ ⚐
Location	1.5m W

Hotel   ★★★ 64% Cleddau Bridge Hotel, Essex Rd, PEMBROKE DOCK
☎ 01646 685961   24 ⇋ ⋒

MONMOUTH   Map 03 SO51

Monmouth Leasebrook Ln NP25 3SN
☎ 01600 712212 (clubhouse) & 772399 (sec) Fax 01600 77 2399
Parkland course in scenic setting. High, undulating land with good views.
18 holes, 5698yds, Par 69, SSS 69, Course record 68.
Club membership 600.

Visitors	advisable to contact in advance, bank holidays only with member.

advance notice advisable, write or telephone secretary.

Green Fees	£20 per day; £15 per round (£20 per round weekends).
Cards	▭▭ ▭▭
Facilities	⊗ � 🏌 💺 ♀ ⚐ 🏤 🏌 ⚑ ♂ ⚐
Location	1.5m NE off A40

Hotel   ★★ 70% Riverside Hotel, Cinderhill St, MONMOUTH ☎ 01600 715577 & 713236 Fax 01600 712668   17 ⇋ ⋒

Rolls of Monmouth The Hendre NP25 5HG
☎ 01600 715353 Fax 01600 713115
A hilly and challenging parkland course encompassing several lakes and ponds and surrounded by woodland. Set within a beautiful private estate complete with listed mansion and panoramic views towards the Black Mountains. The short 4th has a lake beyond the green and both the 17th and 18th holes are magnificent holes with which to end your round.
18 holes, 6733yds, Par 72, SSS 73.
Club membership 131.

Visitors	must telephone in advance.
Societies	must contact in advance.
Green Fees	£34 per day (£38 weekends).
Cards	▭▭ ▭▭ ▭▭ ▨
Facilities	⊗ � 🏌 💺 ♀ ⚐ 🏤 🏌 ♂ ⚐
Location	4m W on B4233

Hotel   ★★ 70% Riverside Hotel, Cinderhill St, MONMOUTH
☎ 01600 715577 & 713236 Fax 01600 712668   17 ⇋ ⋒

MOUNTAIN ASH   Map 03 ST09

Mountain Ash Cefnpennar CF45 4DT
☎ 01443 479459 Fax 01443 479459
Mountain course on heathland with panoramic views of the Brecon Beacons.
18 holes, 5553yds, Par 69, SSS 67, Course record 63.
Club membership 600.

Visitors	contact in advance for details.
Societies	must contact in writing.
Green Fees	£15.
Prof	Marcus Wills

▶

Facilities 🏌🏠♂
Location 1m NW off A4059

Hotel ★★★ 69% Tregenna Hotel, Park Ter,
MERTHYR TYDFIL
☎ 01685 723627 & 382055
Fax 01685 721951 24 ⇄ ♟

NANTYGLO

Map 03 SO11

West Monmouthshire Golf Rd, Winchestown NP3 4QT
☎ 01495 310233
Established in 1906, this mountain and heathland course was officially designated in 1994 by the Guiness Book of Record as being the highest above sea level, with the 14th tee at a height of 1513ft. The course has plenty of picturesque views, hard walking and natural hazards. Testing 3rd hole, par 5, and 7th hole, par 4.
18 holes, 6013yds, Par 71, SSS 69, Course record 65.
Club membership 350.
Visitors welcome, must be guest of member for play on Sun.
Societies apply in writing or contact golf shop 01495 313052.
Green Fees £15 per day.
Facilities ⊗ ℳ ㄴ ♥ ♀ 🏌 🏠 ♂
Location 0.25m W off A467

Hotel ★★ 70% Llanwenarth Arms Hotel,
Brecon Rd, ABERGAVENNY
☎ 01873 810550 18 ⇄ ♟

NEATH

Map 03 SS79

Earlswood Jersey Marine SA10 6JP
☎ 01792 812198
Earlswood is a hillside course offering spectacular scenic views over Swansea Bay. The terrain is gently undulating downs with natural hazards and is designed to appeal to both the new and the experienced golfer.
18 holes, 5084yds, Par 68, SSS 68.
Visitors no restrictions.
Societies advisable to contact in advance.
Green Fees £8 per round.
Prof Mike Day
Facilities 🏌🏠♂♂
Location Approx 4m E of Swansea, off A483

Hotel ★★ 65% Castle Hotel, The Parade, NEATH
☎ 01639 641119 & 643581
Fax 01639 641624 28 ⇄ ♟

Neath Cadoxton SA10 8AH
☎ 01639 643615 (clubhouse) & 632759 (secretary)
Mountain course, with spectacular views. Testing holes: 10th par 4; 12th par 5; 15th par 4.
18 holes, 6492yds, Par 72, SSS 72, Course record 66.
Club membership 700.
Visitors with member only at weekends & bank holidays.
Societies should either telephone or write in advance.
Green Fees Apr-Sep: £20. Oct-Mar: £11.
Prof   M Bennett
Designer James Braid
Facilities ⊗ ℳ ㄴ ♥ ♀ 🏌 🏠 ♂♂
& Leisure snooker.
Location 2m NE off A4230

Hotel ★★ 65% Castle Hotel, The Parade, NEATH
☎ 01639 641119 & 643581
Fax 01639 641624 28 ⇄ ♟

Swansea Bay Jersey Marine SA10 6JP
☎ 01792 812198 & 814153
Fairly level seaside links with part-sand dunes.
18 holes, 6605yds, Par 72, SSS 72.
Club membership 500.
Visitors welcome.
Societies telephone enquiry or letter stating requirements.
Green Fees £16 per round (£22 weekends & bank holidays).
Prof Mike Day
Facilities ⊗ ℳ ㄴ ♥ ♀ 🏌 🏠 ♂♂
Location 4m E of Swansea off A483

Hotel ★★ 65% Castle Hotel, The Parade, NEATH
☎ 01639 641119 & 643581
Fax 01639 641624 28 ⇄ ♟

NELSON

Map 03 ST19

Whitehall The Pavilion CF46 6ST
☎ 01443 740245
Hilltop course. Testing 4th hole (225 yds) par 3, and 6th hole (402 yds) par 4. Pleasant views.
9 holes, 5666yds, Par 69, SSS 68, Course record 63.
Club membership 300.
Visitors must be a member of a recognised golf club & have a handicap certificate. Must contact in advance to play at weekends.
Societies must contact in writing 4 weeks in advance.
Green Fees £15 per 18 holes.
Facilities ㄴ ♥ ♀ 🏌
Location Turn off A470 to Nelson and take A4054 S

Hotel ★★★ 69% Llechwen Hall Hotel, Llanfabon,
PONTYPRIDD ☎ 01443 742050 & 740305
Fax 01443 742189 12 ⇄ ♟ Annexe 8 ⇄ ♟

NEWPORT

Map 03 ST38

Celtic Manor Resort Coldra Woods NP6 2YA
☎ 01633 410255 & 410260 Fax 01633 410269
Three different courses - Wentwood Hills combines hilly landscapes and links-like features. Roman Road has a long and wide front nine, the back nine weaves its way through ravines, lakes and streams beside the Usk valley. Coldra Woods is a scenic short course and is a challenging test of accuracy.
Roman Road: 18 holes, 6495yds, Par 69, SSS 72, Course record 68.
Coldra Woods: 18 holes, 3807yds, Par 59, SSS 61.
Wentwood Hills: 18 holes, 7097yds, Par 72, SSS 75.
Club membership 400.
Visitors may play subject to availability, must book in advance
Societies telephone with details in advance.
Green Fees Coldra Woods: £15 per round. Roman Road: £35 per round. Wentwood Hills: £45 per round.
Cards 💳 💳 💳 💳
Prof Chris Baron
Designer Robert Trent Jones
Facilities ⊗ ℳ ㄴ ♥ ♀ 🏌 🏠 ♂♂ ⌂ 🍴 ♂ ♀
& Leisure heated indoor swimming pool, sauna, solarium, gymnasium. ▶

Location Off junct 24 on M4, midway between Bristol & Cardiff, take A48 to Newport, turn R after 300 metres

Hotel ★★★★ 81% The Celtic Manor Resort, Coldra Woods, NEWPORT
☎ 01633 413000 400 ⇆ ⌦

Newport Great Oak, Rogerstone NP10 9FX
☎ 01633 892643 Fax 01633 896676
An undulating parkland course, in an ideal situation on an inland plateau 300ft above sea level with fine views over the surrounding wooded countryside. There are no blind holes, but plenty of natural hazards and bunkers.
18 holes, 6460yds, Par 72, SSS 71, Course record 63.
Club membership 800.
Visitors must contact in advance, handicap certificate required. Not on Sat, limited time Sun.
Societies must contact in writing or telephone
Green Fees £30 per day (£40 Sun).
Prof Paul Mayo
Designer W Fernie
Facilities ⊗ ℍ ⅊ ☕ ♀ ⅄ ♙ 🛆 ⚑ ⚙
Location 1m NW of junct 27 on M4 on B4591 just beyond 'Promotive' Garage

Hotel ★★★★ 81% The Celtic Manor Resort, Coldra Woods, NEWPORT
☎ 01633 413000 400 ⇆ ⌦

Parc Church Ln, Coedkernew NP10 8TU
☎ 01633 680933 Fax 01633 681011
A challenging but enjoyable 18-hole course with water hazards and accompanying wildlife. The 38-bay driving range is floodlit until 10pm.
18 holes, 5619yds, Par 70, SSS 68, Course record 71.
Club membership 400.
Visitors must contact in advance 01633 680933.
Societies telephone in advance.
Green Fees £12 per 18 holes (£15 weekends).
Prof B Thomas/D Griffiths
Designer B Thomas/T F Hicks
Facilities ⊗ ℍ ⅊ ☕ ♀ ⅄ 🛆 ⚑ ⚙
Location 3m SW of Newport, off A48

Hotel ★★★ 64% Kings Hotel, High St, NEWPORT
☎ 01633 842020 47 ⇆ ⌦

Tredegar Park Parc-y-Brain Rd, Rogerstone NP10 9TG
☎ 01633 894433 Fax 01633 897152
A new course completed in 1999 with two balanced halves, mostly in view from the clubhouse. A rolling, open course with fine scenic views.
18 holes, 6150yds, Par 72, SSS 72.
Club membership 750.
Visitors must be a member of a golf club affiliated to a national golf union, please contact in advance.
Societies apply to secretary.
Green Fees £28 per day (£35 weekends & bank holidays).

Cards ▭ ▬
Prof M L Morgan
Designer R Sandow
Facilities ⊗ ℍ ⅊ ☕ ♀ ⅄ 🛆 ⚑ ⚙
Location N of M4, Junct 27, B4591, club signposted from here

Hotel ★★★ 64% Kings Hotel, High St, NEWPORT ☎ 01633 842020 47 ⇆ ⌦

NEWPORT (PEMBROKESHIRE) Map 02 SN03

Newport (Pemb) The Golf Club SA42 0NR
☎ 01239 820244 Fax 01239 820244
Seaside links course, with easy walking and good view of the Preselli Hills and Newport Bay.
9 holes, 5815yds, Par 70, SSS 68, Course record 64.
Club membership 350.
Visitors telephone in advance.
Societies must telephone in advance.
Green Fees not confirmed.
Prof Colin Parsons
Designer James Baird
Facilities ⊗ ℍ ⅊ ☕ ♀ ⅄ 🛆 ⚑ ⚙
Location 1.25m N

Hotel ★★ 68% Trewern Arms, NEVERN
☎ 01239 820395 10 ⇆ ⌦

NEWTOWN Map 06 SO19

St Giles Pool Rd SY16 3AJ
☎ 01686 625844 Fax 01686 625844
Inland country course with easy walking. Testing 2nd hole, par 3, and 4th hole, par 4. River Severn skirts four holes.
9 holes, 6012yds, Par 70, SSS 70, Course record 67.
Club membership 350.
Visitors advisable to contact in advance.
Societies must contact in advance.
Green Fees £12.50 per day (£15 weekends & bank holidays).
Prof D P Owen
Facilities & Leisure ⊗ ℍ ⅊ ☕ ♀ ⅄ 🛆 ⚑ ⚙ fishing.
Location 0.5m NE on A483

Hotel ★★ 64% Elephant & Castle, Broad St, NEWTOWN ☎ 01686 626271
23 ⇆ ⌦ Annexe 11 ⇆ ⌦

OAKDALE Map 03 ST19

Oakdale Llwynon Ln NP2 0NF
☎ 01495 220044
9 holes, 1344yds, Par 28, Course record 27.
Visitors no restrictions pay & play.
Societies telephone for further information and arrangements.
Green Fees not confirmed.
Prof Clive Coombs
Designer Ian Goodenough
Facilities ♀ 🛆 ⚙ ⌾
Location B4251 E of Blackwood

PEMBROKE DOCK · · · · · · · · · · · · · Map 02 SM90

South Pembrokeshire Military Rd SA72 6SE
☎ 01646 621453
Parkland course overlooking the Cleddau River.
18 holes, 6100yds, Par 71, SSS 70, Course record 65.
Club membership 350.
Visitors   must contact in advance, especially during
                  season.
Societies   apply in advance.
Green Fees   £12 (£15 weekends).
Designer   Committee
Facilities   ⊗ ⫢ ⌱ ⬛ ♀ ⚐ ☂
Location   SW side of town centre off B4322

Hotel   ★★ 61% Old Kings Arms, Main St,
                  PEMBROKE
                  ☎ 01646 683611   21 ⇌ ⁍

PENARTH · · · · · · · · · · · · · · · · · · Map 03 ST17

Glamorganshire Lavernock Rd CF64 5UP
☎ 029 20701185 Fax 029 20701185
Parkland course, overlooking the Bristol Channel.
18 holes, 6181yds, Par 70, SSS 70, Course record 64.
Club membership 1000.
Visitors   contact professional in advance.
Societies   must contact in advance.
Green Fees   not confirmed.
Prof   Andrew Kerr-Smith
Designer   James Braid
Facilities   ⊗ ⫢ ⌱ ⬛ ♀ ⚐ ⚑ ↘ ⚒ ⚬ ⁋
Location   S side of town centre on B4267

Hotel   ★ 67% Walton House Hotel, 37 Victoria Rd,
                  PENARTH
                  ☎ 029 20707782 13rm (11 ⇌ ⁍)

PENCOED · · · · · · · · · · · · · · · · · · Map 03 SS98

St Mary's Hotel Golf & Country Club St Mary Hill
CF35 5EA ☎ 01656 861100 Fax 01656 863400
A parkland course with many American style features. The
Par 3 10th called 'Alcatraz' has a well deserved reputation.
St Mary's Course: 18 holes, 5291yds, Par 69, SSS 66,
Course record 68.
Sevenoaks Course: 9 holes, 2426yds, Par 35.
Club membership 830.
Visitors   St. Mary's Course: must contact in advance,
                  handicap certificate not required between 9-4
                  Mon-Fri, after 1pm weekends. Seven Oaks: no
                  restrictions
Societies   telephone Kay Brazell.
Green Fees   St Mary's: £15 per round (£17 weekends &
                  bank holidays); Seven Oaks: £5 per round (£6
                  weekends & bank holidays).
Cards   ▭▬ ▬ ▭ ▣ ▨ ◩
Prof   John Peters
Facilities   ⊗ ⫢ ⌱ ⬛ ♀ ⚐ ⚑ ⨝ ⚒ ⚬ ⁋
& Leisure   hard tennis courts.
Location   5m from junct 35 of M4

Hotel   ★★★ 73% St Mary's Hotel & Country Club, St
                  Marys Golf Club, PENCOED
                  ☎ 01656 861100 & 860280
                  Fax 01656 863400   24 ⇌ ⁍
                  See advertisement on page 400

PENRHYS · · · · · · · · · · · · · · · · · · Map 03 ST09

Rhondda Golf Club House CF43 3PW
☎ 01443 441384 Fax 01443 441384
Mountain course with good views.
18 holes, 6205yds, Par 70, SSS 71, Course record 67.
Club membership 600.
Visitors   contact secretary for weekend play.
Societies   contact for details.
Green Fees   £15 (£20 weekends & bank holidays).
Prof   G A Bebb
Facilities   ⊗ ⫢ ⌱ ⬛ ♀ ⚐ ⚑ ↘ ⚒ ⚬ ⁋
Location   0.5m W off B4512

Hotel   ★★★ 67% Heritage Park Hotel, Coed Cae Rd,
                  Trehafod, PONTYPRIDD
                  ☎ 01443 687057   44 ⇌ ⁍

PONTARDAWE · · · · · · · · · · · · · Map 03 SN70

Pontardawe Cefn Llan SA8 4SH
☎ 01792 863118 Fax 01792 830041
Meadowland course situated on plateau 600 ft above sea-
level with good views over Bristol Channel and Brecon
Beacons.
18 holes, 6038yds, Par 70, SSS 70, Course record 64.
Club membership 500.
Visitors   must contact in advance, but may not play on
                  weekends.
Societies   apply in writing.
Green Fees   not confirmed.
Prof   Gary Hopkins
Facilities   ⊗ ⫢ ⌱ ⬛ ♀ ⚐ ⚑ ⚬
Location   N side of town centre M4 junc 45 off A4067

Hotel   ★★ 62% Oak Tree Parc Hotel, Birchgrove Rd,
                  BIRCHGROVE
                  ☎ 01792 817781   10 ⇌ ⁍

PONTLLIW · · · · · · · · · · · · · · · · Map 02 SS69

Allt-y-Graban Allt-y-Grabam Rd SA4 1DT
☎ 01792 885757
A challenging parkland course with fine panoramic views,
opened in 1993.It is a 9-hole course but with plans for 12
holes. There are 6 par-4 holes and 3 par-3 holes. The 6th is a
challenging hole with a blind tee shot into the valley and a
dogleg to the left onto an elevated green.
9 holes, 2210yds, Par 66, SSS 66, Course record 63.
Club membership 158.
Visitors   no restrictions.
Societies   telephone in advance.
Green Fees   £9.50 per 18 holes; £6.50 per 9 holes (£11/£7
                  weekends & bank holidays).
Prof   Steven Rees
Designer   F G Thomas
Facilities   ⌱ ⬛ ♀ ⚐ ⚑ ⨝ ⚬
Location   From junct 47 on M4 take A48 towards
                  Pontardulais. Turn left after Glamorgan Arms

Hotel   ★★★ 65% Posthouse Swansea, The Kingsway
                  Circle, SWANSEA
                  ☎ 0870 400 9078 99 ⇌ ⁍

PONTYPOOL   Map 03 SO20

Pontypool Lasgarn Ln, Trevethin NP4 8TR
☎ 01495 763655
Undulating, mountain course with magnificent views.
18 holes, 6046yds, Par 69, SSS 69, Course record 64.
Club membership 638.
Visitors   must have a handicap certificate, restricted availability at weekends, advisable to call in advance.
Societies   apply in writing or by phone, deposit payable.
Green Fees £20 per day.
Prof   James Howard
Facilities ⊗ ∭ ⅃ ⚑ ♀ ⚒ ➶ ➴ ↘ ⬌ ⌀
Location   1.5m N off A4043

Hotel   ★★ 68% Mill at Glynhir, Glyn-Hir, Llandybie, AMMANFORD
☎ 01269 850672   11 ⇆ ♫

Woodlake Park Golf & Country Club Glascoed NP4 0TE
☎ 01291 673933 Fax 01291 673811
Undulating parkland course with magnificent views over Llandegfedd Reservoir. Superb green constructed to USGA specification. Holes 4, 7 & 16 are Par 3's which are particularly challenging. Holes 6 & 17 are long Par 4's which can be wind affected.
18 holes, 6278yds, Par 71, SSS 72, Course record 67.
Club membership 450.
Visitors   book in advance.
Societies   telephone or write for society package.
Green Fees not confirmed.
Prof   Adrian Pritchard
Facilities ⊗ ∭ ⅃ ⚑ ♀ ⚒ ➶ ➴ ↘ ⬌ ⌀
& Leisure fishing.
Location   Overlooking Llandegfedd Reservoir

Hotel   ★★ 68% Mill at Glynhir, Glyn-Hir, Llandybie, AMMANFORD
☎ 01269 850672   11 ⇆ ♫

PONTYPRIDD   Map 03 ST09

Pontypridd Ty Gwyn Rd CF37 4DJ
☎ 01443 409904 Fax 01443 491622
Well-wooded mountain course with springy turf. Good views of the Rhondda Valleys and coast.
18 holes, 5721yds, Par 69, SSS 68.
Club membership 850.
Visitors   must contact in advance. Must play with member on weekends & bank holidays. Must have a handicap certificate.
Societies   weekdays only. Must contact in advance.
Green Fees not confirmed.
Cards ▭ ▭
Prof   Wade Walters
Facilities ⊗ ∭ ⅃ ⚑ ♀ ⚒ ➶ ↘ ⬌ ⌀
Location   E side of town centre off A470

Hotel   ★★★ 67% Heritage Park Hotel, Coed Cae Rd, Trehafod, PONTYPRIDD
☎ 01443 687057   44 ⇆ ♫

PORT TALBOT   Map 03 SS78

British Steel Port Talbot Sports & Social Club, Margam SA13 2NF ☎ 01639 793194
A 9 hole course with two lakes. All the holes are affected by crosswinds and the 7th, Par 3, is alongside a deep stream, so is very tight.
9 holes, 4726yds, Par 62, SSS 63, Course record 60.
Club membership 250.
Visitors   contact in advance, may not play at weekends.
Societies   by prior arrangement.
Green Fees not confirmed.
Facilities ⚒
& Leisure hard tennis courts, fishing.
Hotel   ★★★ 67% Aberavon Beach Hotel, PORT TALBOT ☎ 01639 884949   52 ⇆

PORTHCAWL   Map 03 SS87

Royal Porthcawl CF36 3UW
☎ 01656 782251 Fax 01656 771687
This championship-standard heathland/downland links course is always in sight of the sea. With holes facing every point of the compass, the golfer is always tested by the wind and the course has hosted many major tournaments.
18 holes, 6406yds, Par 72, SSS 74, Course record 65.
Club membership 800.
Visitors   must contact in advanced & produce handicap certificate limit men 20, ladies 30. Restricted at weekends & bank holidays.
Societies   apply in writing.
Green Fees not confirmed.
Cards ▭ ▭
Prof   Peter Evans
Designer   Charles Gibson
Facilities ⊗ ∭ ⅃ ⚑ ♀ ⚒ ➶ ➴ ↘ ⬌ ⌀
Location   1.5m NW of town centre

Hotel   ★★★ 64% Seabank Hotel, The Promenade, PORTHCAWL
☎ 01656 782261   65 ⇆ ♫

PYLE   Map 03 SS88

Pyle & Kenfig Waun-Y-Mer CF33 4PU
☎ 01656 783093 Fax 01656 772822
Links and downland course, with sand-dunes. Easy walking. Often windy.
18 holes, 6688yds, Par 71, SSS 73, Course record 68.
Club membership 1080.
Visitors   by arrangement midweek, guests of members only at weekends.
Societies   for large numbers apply in writing, small numbers telephone booking accepted.
Green Fees not confirmed.
Cards ▭ ▭ ▭ ▭ ▭
Prof   Robert Evans
Designer   Colt
Facilities ⊗ ∭ ⅃ ⚑ ♀ ⚒ ➶ ↘ ⬌ ⌀ ♫
Location   S side of Pyle off A4229. Access via junct 37 on M4

Hotel   ★★★ 64% Seabank Hotel, The Promenade, PORTHCAWL
☎ 01656 782261   65 ⇆ ♫

RAGLAN
Map 03 SO40

Raglan Parc Parc Lodge, Station Rd NP5 2ER
☎ 01291 690077
New parkland course with well laid greens and a mature back
9 that are already the source of local praise. Several testing
holes where a combination of wind and water make golf
challenging. Easy walking.
18 holes, 6604yds, Par 72, SSS 73, Course record 67.
Club membership 350.
Visitors advisable to contact in advance.
Societies advance arrangement required.
Green Fees not confirmed.
Facilities ⊗ ⊪ ▙ ☱ ♀ ♨ 🏠 🚜
Location Off junct of A449/A40

Hotel ★★★ 66% Llansantffraed Court Hotel,
Llanvihangel Gobion, ABERGAVENNY
☎ 01873 840678 21 ⇄ ♠

ST DAVID'S
Map 02 SM72

St David's City Whitesands Bay SA62 6HR
☎ 01437 720572 & 721751
Links course with alternative tees for 18 holes. Panoramic
views of St David's Head, Ramsey Island and Whitesands
Bay. The course is playable all year.
9 holes, 6117yds, Par 70, SSS 70, Course record 68.
Club membership 200.
Visitors prior booking with secretary is encouraged but
not always necessary, please check for
weekends, Ladies Day Fri pm.
Societies book with the secretary in advance.
Green Fees not confirmed.
Facilities ☱ ♨ ∅
Location 2m W overlooking Whitesands Bay

Hotel ★★★ 77% Warpool Court Hotel, ST
DAVID'S ☎ 01437 720300 25 ⇄ ♠

SOUTHGATE
Map 02 SS58

Pennard 2 Southgate Rd SA3 2BT
☎ 01792 233131 & 233451 Fax 01792 234797
Undulating, cliff-top seaside links with good coastal views.
18 holes, 6265yds, Par 71, SSS 72, Course record 69.
Club membership 1020.
Visitors advisable to contact Professional in advance.
Societies by prior arrangement, telephone in advance.
Green Fees not confirmed.
Cards 💳
Prof M V Bennett
Designer James Braid
Facilities ⊗ ⊪ ▙ ☱ ♀ ♨ 🏠 🚜 ∅
& Leisure squash, snooker.
Location 8m W of Swansea by A4067 and B4436

Hotel ★★♨ Fairyhill, REYNOLDSTON
☎ 01792 390139 8 ⇄ ♠

SWANSEA
Map 03 SS69

Clyne 120 Owls Lodge Ln, The Mayals, Blackpyl SA3 5DP
☎ 01792 401989 Fax 01792 401078
Challenging moorland course with excellent greens and
scenic views of Swansea Bay and The Gower.

18 holes, 6334yds, Par 70, SSS 71, Course record 64.
Club membership 900.
Visitors must be member of a club with handicap
certificate. Groups over 8 advised to book in
advance.
Societies must contact in advance.
Green Fees £25 per 18/27 holes (£30 weekends & bank
holidays).
Prof Jonathan Clenett
Designer H S Colt & Harries
Facilities ⊗ ⊪ ▙ ☱ ♀ ♨ 🏠 🚜 ∅ ⚑
Location 3.5m SW on B4436 off A4067

Hotel ★★★ 69% Langland Court, Langland Court
Rd, LANGLAND
☎ 01792 361545 14 ⇄ ♠ Annexe 5 ⇄ ♠

Langland Bay Langland Bay SA3 4QR
☎ 01792 361721 Fax 01792 361082
Parkland course overlooking Gower coast. The par 4, 6th is
an uphill dog-leg open to the wind, and the par 3, 16th (151
yds) is aptly named 'Death or Glory'.
18 holes, 5857yds, Par 70, SSS 69.
Club membership 850.

Visitors no restrictions. Tue is Ladies Day. No societies
at weekends
Societies must telephone in advance.
Green Fees £28 (£30 weekends).
Prof Mark Evans
Designer Henry Cotton
Facilities ⊗ ⊪ ▙ ☱ ♀ ♨ 🏠 🚜 ∅
Location 6m W on A4067

Hotel ★★★ 69% Langland Court, Langland Court
Rd, LANGLAND
☎ 01792 361545 14 ⇄ ♠ Annexe 5 ⇄ ♠

Morriston 160 Clasemont Rd SA6 6AJ
☎ 01792 796528 Fax 01792 796528
Pleasant parkland course with a very difficult Par 3 15th
hole.
18 holes, 5891yds, Par 68, SSS 68, Course record 61.
Club membership 700.
Visitors may not play Sat. Must contact in advance.
Societies apply in writing.
Green Fees £18 per day/round (£30 weekends).
Prof D A Rees
Facilities ⊗ ⊪ ▙ ☱ ♀ ♨ 🏠 ∅
Location 5m N of Swansea on A48. 1m E of junct 46 of
M4

Hotel ★★ 62% Oak Tree Parc Hotel, Birchgrove Rd,
BIRCHGROVE ☎ 01792 817781 10 ⇄ ♠

TALBOT GREEN   Map 03 ST08

Llantrisant & Pontyclun Off Ely Valley Rd CF72 8HZ
☎ 01443 228169
Parkland course.
12 holes, 5712yds, Par 68, SSS 68, Course record 66.
Club membership 600.
Visitors must have handicap certificate, must contact in advance, not at weekends
Societies apply in writing.
Green Fees not confirmed.
Facilities ⊗ ℍ ⅃ ♥ ♀ ⚐ ☎ ⚒
Location N side of village off A473

Hotel ★★★★ 69% Miskin Manor Hotel, Groes Faen, Pontyclun, MISKIN
☎ 01443 224204   34 ⇌ ⋔ Annexe 8 ⇌ ⋔

TENBY   Map 02 SN10

Tenby The Burrows SA70 7NP
☎ 01834 844447 Fax 01834 844447
The oldest club in Wales, this fine old seaside links, with sea views and natural hazards provides good golf all the year round. Hosts for the Welsh Amateur Championship in 1999.
18 holes, 6224yds, Par 69, SSS 71.
Club membership 800.
Visitors subject to competition & tee reservation. Must produce handicap certificate.
Societies must apply in advance.
Green Fees not confirmed.
Prof Mark Hawkey
Designer James Braid
Facilities ⊗ ℍ ⅃ ♥ ♀ ⚐ ⋔ ⚒
Location Close to railway station in the town

Hotel ★★★ 73% Atlantic Hotel, The Esplanade, TENBY ☎ 01834 842881 & 844176
Fax 01834 842881 ex 256 42 ⇌ ⋔

Trefloyne Trefloyne Park, Penally SA70 7RG
☎ 01834 842165 Fax 01834 842165
Idyllic parkland course with backdrop of mature mixed woodlands and distant views of Tenby, Carmarthen bay and Caldey Island. Opened in 1996, natural features and hazards such as the Old Quarry make for exciting and challenging golf.
18 holes, 6635yds, Par 71, SSS 73.
Club membership 263.
Visitors must contact in advance, must play a reasonable standard of golf and adhere to golf etiquette and dress code of club.
Societies must book in advance by telephone or in writing.
Green Fees £18 per day (£22 weekends and bank holidays).
Cards ⚏ ⚏ ☒ ▧
Prof Steven Laidler
Designer F H Gillman
Facilities ⊗ ♥ ♀ ⚐ ☎ ⋔ ⚒
& Leisure lessons by PGA Professional.
Location Within Trefloyne Park, just west of Tenby

Hotel ★★★ 66% Fourcroft Hotel, North Beach, TENBY ☎ 01834 842886   46 ⇌ ⋔

THREE CROSSES   Map 02 SS59

Gower Cefn Goleu SA4 3HS
☎ 01792 872480 (Off) 879905 (Pro) Fax 01792 872480
Set in attractive rolling countryside, this Donald Steel designed course provides good strategic hazards, including trees, water and bunkers, outstanding views and a challenging game of golf.
18 holes, 6441yds, Par 71, SSS 72, Course record 70.
Club membership 500.
Visitors tee booking upto 7 days in advance, reservations recommended, some weekend vacancies, dress code and course etiquette must be adhered to.
Societies by prior notice for established golfers.
Green Fees £16 per round.
Cards ⚏ ☒ ⚏ ▧ ▨
Prof Alan Williamson
Designer Donald Steel
Facilities ⊗ ℍ ⅃ ♥ ♀ ⚐ ⚒
Location Sign posted from the village of Three Crosses

Hotel ★★ 74% Beaumont Hotel, 72-73 Walter Rd, SWANSEA ☎ 01792 643956   17 ⇌ ⋔

TREDEGAR   Map 03 SO10

Tredegar and Rhymney Cwmtysswg, Rhymney NP2 3BQ
☎ 01685 840743 (club) & 843400 (office)
Fax 01685 843440
Mountain course with lovely views. The course is being developed into an 18 hole course.
9 holes, 5504yds, Par 68, SSS 68, Course record 69.
Club membership 194.
Visitors cannot play Sun.
Societies must contact in advance.
Green Fees £10 per day.
Facilities ℍ by prior arrangement ⅃ by prior arrangement ♥ by prior arrangement ♀ ⚐
Location 1.75m SW on B4256

Hotel ★★★ 69% Tregenna Hotel, Park Ter, MERTHYR TYDFIL
☎ 01685 723627 & 382055
Fax 01685 721951   24 ⇌ ⋔

UPPER KILLAY   Map 02 SS59

Fairwood Park Blackhills Ln SA2 7JN
☎ 01792 203648 Fax 01792 297849
Parkland championship course on the beautiful Gower Peninsula.
18 holes, 6754yds, Par 72, SSS 72, Course record 68.
Club membership 720.
Visitors welcome except when championship or club matches are being held. Must contact in advance.
Societies must contact in advance.
Green Fees £25 per day (£30 weekends & bank holidays).
Cards ⚏
Prof Gary Hughes
Designer Hawtree
Facilities ⊗ ℍ ⅃ ♥ ♀ ⚐ ☎ ⋔ ⚒
Location 1.5m S off A4118

Hotel ★★ 73% Windsor Lodge Hotel, Mount Pleasant, SWANSEA
☎ 01792 642158 & 652744
Fax 01792 648996   18 ⇌ ⋔

WELSHPOOL
Map 07 SJ20

Welshpool Golfa Hill SY21 9AQ ☎ 01938 850249
Undulating, hilly, heathland course with bracing air. Testing
holes are 2nd (par 5), 14th (par 3), 17th (par 3) and a
memorable 18th.
18 holes, 5708yds, Par 70, SSS 68, Course record 68.
Club membership 400.
Visitors must book in advance, restricted at weekends.
Societies must book in advance.
Green Fees £12.50 per day (£20.50 weekend & bank
holiday in summer; £15.50 weekend & bank
holiday in winter).
Designer James Braid
Facilities ⊗ ⅏ ⅃ 🍺 ♀ ⚲ 🖛 🏌
Location 3m W off A458

Hotel ★★★ 68% Royal Oak Hotel, WELSHPOOL
☎ 01938 552217 24 ⇆ 🏌

WENVOE
Map 03 ST17

Wenvoe Castle CF5 6BE ☎ 029 20594371
Parkland course which is hilly for first 9 holes. Pond, situated
280 yds from tee at 10th hole, is a hazard.
18 holes, 6422yds, Par 72, SSS 71, Course record 64.
Club membership 600.
Visitors must be a member of a recognised golf club &
have a handicap certificate. Must play with
member at weekends.
Societies must contact in writing.
Green Fees not confirmed.
Prof Robin Day
Facilities ⊗ ⅏ ⅃ 🍺 ♀ ⚲ 🖛 🏌
Location 1m S off A4050

Hotel ★★★⚓ 77% Egerton Grey Country House
Hotel, Porthkerry, BARRY
☎ 01446 711666 10 ⇆ 🏌

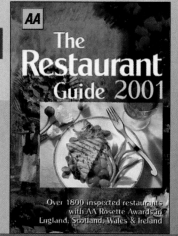

Ireland

NORTHERN IRELAND

CO ANTRIM

ANTRIM — Map 01 D5

Massereene 51 Lough Rd BT41 4DQ
☎ 028 94428096 Fax 028 94487661
The first nine holes are parkland, while the second, adjacent to the shore of Lough Neagh, have more of a links character with sandy ground.
18 holes, 6559yds, Par 72, SSS 71, Course record 66.
Club membership 969.
Visitors must contact in advance.
Societies book in advance.
Green Fees not confirmed.
Prof Jim Smyth
Designer F Hawtree
Facilities
Location 1m SW of town

Hotel ★★★★ 72% Galgorm Manor, BALLYMENA
☎ 028 25881001 24

BALLYCASTLE — Map 01 D6

Ballycastle Cushendall Rd BT54 6QP
☎ 028 20762536 Fax 028 20769909
An unusual mixture of terrain beside the sea, with magnificent views from all parts. The first five holes are inland type; the middle holes on the Warren are links type and the rest, on high ground, are heath type.
18 holes, 5406mtrs, Par 71, SSS 70, Course record 64.
Club membership 920.
Visitors are welcome during the week.
Societies apply in writing.
Green Fees £20 per round (£28 weekends).
Prof Ian McLaughlin
Facilities
Location Between Portrush & Cushendall (A2)

BALLYCLARE — Map 01 D5

Ballyclare 23 Springdale Rd BT39 9JW
☎ 028 93322696 Fax 028 93322696
Parkland course with lots of trees and shrubs and water hazards provided by the river, streams and lakes.
18 holes, 5745mtrs, Par 71, SSS 71, Course record 66.
Club membership 580.
Visitors must contact in advance.
Societies must contact in advance.
Green Fees £16 per round (£22 weekends & bank holidays).
Designer T McCauley
Facilities
Location 1.5m N

Hotel ★★★★ 67% Stormont Hotel, 587 Upper Newtownards Rd, BELFAST
☎ 028 90658621 109

Greenacres 153 Ballyrobert Rd BT39 9RT
☎ 028 93354111 Fax 028 93354166
Designed and built into the rolling Co. Antrim countryside, and with the addition of lakes at five of the holes, provides a challenge for both the seasoned golfer and the higher handicapped player.
18 holes, 5819yds, Par 71, SSS 69.
Club membership 425.
Visitors may not play Sat.
Societies apply in writing.
Green Fees £12 Mon-Fri (£16 weekends and bank holidays).
Cards
Prof Ken Reivie
Facilities
Hotel ★★★ 66% Adair Arms Hotel, 1 Ballymoney Rd, BALLYMENA
☎ 01266 653674 40

BALLYGALLY — Map 01 D5

Cairndhu 192 Coast Rd BT40 2QG
☎ 028 28583324 Fax 028 28583324
Built on a hilly headland, this course is both testing and scenic, with wonderful coastal views. The 3rd hole has a carry of 180 yds over a headland to the fairway.
18 holes, 5611mtrs, Par 70, SSS 69, Course record 64.
Club membership 905.
Visitors may not play on Sat.
Societies must apply in writing.
Green Fees £15 per round Mon-Thu; £20 Fri (£24 Sat & Sun).
Cards
Prof Robert Walker
Designer Mr Morrison
Facilities
Location 4m N of Larne on coast road

Hotel ★★★ 64% Londonderry Arms Hotel, 20 Harbour Rd, CARNLOUGH
☎ 028 28885255 35

BALLYMENA — Map 01 D5

Ballymena 128 Raceview Rd BT42 4HY ☎ 028 25861487
Parkland course of level heathland with plenty of bunkers.
18 holes, 5299mtrs, Par 68, SSS 67, Course record 64.
Club membership 895.
Visitors may not play on Tue or Sat.
Societies must contact in advance.
Green Fees not confirmed.
Prof Ken Revie
Facilities
Location 2m E on A42

Hotel ★★★★ 72% Galgorm Manor, BALLYMENA
☎ 028 25881001 24

Galgorm Castle Golf & Country Club Galgorm Rd BT42 1HL ☎ 028 25646161 Fax 028 25651151
18 hole championship course set in 220 acres of mature parkland in the grounds of a historic castle. The course is bordered by two rivers which come into play and includes five lakes. A course of outstanding beauty offering a challenge to both the novice and low handicapped golfer.
18 holes, 6736yds, Par 72, SSS 72, Course record 68.
Club membership 400.

▶

Visitors	ring to book times.
Societies	apply in writing or telephone in advance.
Green Fees	£30 per day; £20 per round (£38/£25 weekends).
Cards	▭ ▭
Prof	Lesley Callen
Designer	Simon Gidman
Facilities	⊗ ∭ ⬧ 💺 ♀ ⚘ 🏌 🛒 🏌 ♪ ℓ
& Leisure	fishing.
Location	1m S of Ballymena on A42

Hotel   ★★★★ 72% Galgorm Manor, BALLYMENA
☎ 028 25881001   24 ⇄ ♞

CARRICKFERGUS   Map 01 D5

Carrickfergus 25 North Rd BT38 8LP
☎ 028 93363713 Fax 028 93363023
Parkland course, fairly level but nevertheless demanding,
with a notorious water hazard at the 1st. Well maintained,
with an interesting in-course riverway and presenting fine
views across Belfast Lough.
18 holes, 5768yds, Par 68, SSS 68.
Club membership 850.

Visitors	restrictions at weekends.
Societies	must contact in advance.
Green Fees	not confirmed.
Cards	▭ ▭ ▭ ▭
Prof	Mark Johnstonnson
Facilities	⊗ ∭ ⬧ 💺 ♀ ⚘ ℓ
Location	9m NE of Belfast on A2

Hotel   ★ 68% Dobbins Inn, 6-8 High St,
CARRICKFERGUS
☎ 028 93351905   15 ⇄ ♞

Greenisland 156 Upper Rd, Greenisland BT38 8RW
☎ 028 90862236
A parkland course nestling at the foot of Knockagh Hill with
scenic views over Belfast Lough.
9 holes, 5536mtrs, Par 71, SSS 68.
Club membership 740.

Visitors	contact club in advance. Play restricted Sat and Thu.
Societies	by prior arrangement.
Green Fees	£12 per round (£18 weekends & bank holidays).
Facilities	⊗ ∭ ⬧ 💺 ♀ ⚘
Location	N of Belfast, close to Carrickfergus

Hotel   ★ 68% Dobbins Inn, 6-8 High St,
CARRICKFERGUS
☎ 028 93351905   15 ⇄ ♞

CUSHENDALL   Map 01 D6

Cushendall 21 Shore Rd BT44 0NG   ☎ 028 21771318
Scenic course with spectacular views over the Sea of Moyle
and Red Bay to the Mull of Kintyre. The River Dall winds
through the course, coming into play in seven of the nine
holes.
9 holes, 4386mtrs, Par 66, SSS 63, Course record 62.
Club membership 834.

Visitors	Ladies day Thursday, time sheet at weekends.
Societies	must contact in writing.
Green Fees	£13 per day (£18 weekends).
Designer	D Delargy
Facilities	⬧ 💺 ♀ ⚘

Hotel   ★★★ 64% Londonderry Arms Hotel, 20
Harbour Rd, CARNLOUGH
☎ 028 28885255   35 ⇄ ♞

LARNE   Map 01 D5

Larne 54 Ferris Bay Rd, Islandmagee BT40 3RT
☎ 028 93382228 Fax 028 93382088
An exposed part links, part heathland course offering a good
test, particularly on the last three holes along the sea shore.
9 holes, 6686yds, Par 70, SSS 70, Course record 64.
Club membership 430.

Visitors	may not play on Sat.
Societies	apply in writing or telephone in advance.
Green Fees	£8 per day (£15 weekends).
Designer	G L Bailie
Facilities	⊗ ∭ ⬧ 💺 ♀ ⚘
Location	6m N of Whitehead on Browns Bay rd

Hotel   ★★★ 64% Londonderry Arms Hotel, 20
Harbour Rd, CARNLOUGH
☎ 028 28885255   35 ⇄ ♞

LISBURN   Map 01 D5

Aberdelghy Bell's Ln, Lambeg BT27 4QH
☎ 028 92662738 Fax 028 92603432
This parkland course, extended to 18 holes in 1997 has no
bunkers. The hardest hole on the course is the 340metre 3rd,
a dog leg through trees to a green guarded by water. The par-
3 12th high on the hill and the 14th hole over the dam
provide a challenge. The par-4 15th hole is a long dog leg.
18 holes, 4139mtrs, Par 66, SSS 62, Course record 64.
Club membership 150.

Visitors	restricted Sat 7.15am-1pm. Ring in advance for Sun.
Societies	telephone in advance.
Green Fees	£7.20 per 18 holes (£9.20 weekends & bank holidays).
Prof	Ian Murdoch
Designer	Alec Blair
Facilities	💺 ♀ ⚘ 🏌 ℓ
Location	1.5m N of Lisburn off A1

Hotel   ★★★ 66% Posthouse Belfast, Kingsway,
Dunmurry, BELFAST
☎ 0870 400 9005 82 ⇄ ♞

Lisburn Blaris Lodge, 68 Eglantine Rd BT27 5RQ
☎ 028 92677216
Meadowland course, fairly level, with plenty of trees and
shrubs. Challenging last three holes.
18 holes, 6647yds, Par 72, SSS 72, Course record 67.
Club membership 1421.

Visitors	must play with member at weekends. Must tee off before 3pm weekdays.
Societies	must contact in writing.
Green Fees	not confirmed.
Prof	Blake Campbell
Designer	Hawtree
Facilities	⊗ ∭ ♀ ⚘ 🏌 ℓ
Location	2m from town on A1

Hotel   ★★★★ 67% Stormont Hotel, 587 Upper
Newtownards Rd, BELFAST
☎ 028 90658621 109 ⇄ ♞

MAZE   Map 01 D5

Down Royal Park Dunygarton Rd BT27 5RT
☎ 028 92621339 Fax 028 92621339
The 9-hole Valley course and the 18-hole Down Royal Park
are easy walking, undulating heathland courses. Down
Royal's 2nd hole is 628yards and thought to be among the
best par 5 holes in Ireland.
*Down Royal Park Course: 18 holes, 6824yds, Par 72, SSS
72, Course record 69.*
Valley Course: 9 holes, 2500yds, Par 33.
Club membership 80.
Visitors   no restrictions, except dress code.
Societies   reservations in advance.
Green Fees   £15 per round (£17-£20 weekends & bank
                 holidays)..
Facilities   ⊗ by prior arrangement ⫚ by prior arrangement
                 ᴸ by prior arrangement ⬛ by prior
                 arrangement ♀ ⚲ ⛳ ⛴ ⛴ ♂
Location   Inside Down Royal Race Course

Hotel   ★★★ 66% White Gables Hotel, 14 Dromore
                 Rd, HILLSBOROUGH
                 ☎ 028 92682755   31 ⇔ ⋒

NEWTOWNABBEY   Map 01 D5

Ballyearl Golf & Leisure Centre 585 Doagh Rd, Mossley
BT36 8RZ ☎ 028 90848287
9 holes, 2520yds, Par 27.
Visitors   no restrictions.
Societies   telephone in advance.
Green Fees   not confirmed.
Prof   Jim Robinson
Designer   V Lathery
Facilities   ⬛ ⚲ ⛴ ⛳
& Leisure   squash, gymnasium.

Mallusk Antrim Rd BT36 ☎ 028 90843799
Attractive 9-hole parkland course featuring 3 small par 4s
and several water hazards, notably on the tricky, dog-leg 7th
hole.
9 holes, 4444yds, Par 62, SSS 62, Course record 62.
Club membership 150.
Visitors   no restrictions.
Societies   contact for details.
Green Fees   not confirmed.
Designer   David Fitzgerald
Facilities   ⬛ ♀ ⚲ ⛵
& Leisure   hard tennis courts, sauna.

PORTBALLINTRAE   Map 01 C6

Bushfoot 50 Bushfoot Rd, Portballintrae BT57 8RR
☎ 028 20731317 Fax 028 20731852
A seaside links course with superb views in an area of
outstanding beauty. A challenging par-3 7th is ringed by
bunkers with out-of-bounds beyond, while the 3rd has a blind
approach. Also a putting green and pitch & putt course.
9 holes, 5914yds, Par 70, SSS 67, Course record 68.
Club membership 850.
Visitors   must contact in advance.
Societies   must contact in advance.
Green Fees   £15 per round (£20 weekends).
Facilities   ⊗ ⫚ ᴸ ⬛ ♀ ⚲ ⛳ ♂
Location   Off Ballaghmore rd

Hotel   ★★ 68% Beach House Hotel, The Sea Front,
                 61 Beach Rd, Portballintrae, BUSHMILLS
                 ☎ 028 207331214   32 ⇔ ⋒

PORTRUSH   Map 01 C6

PORTRUSH See page 421.

WHITEHEAD   Map 01 D5

Bentra Municipal Slaughterford Rd BT38 9TG
☎ 028 93378996
A well matured course designed with the experienced golfer
and novice in mind with wide fairways and some particularly
long holes.
9 holes, 2885mtrs, Par 37, SSS 35.
Visitors   no restrictions.
Societies   contact in advance.
Green Fees   not confirmed.
Facilities   ⊗ ⫚ ᴸ ⬛ ♀ ⛴ ⛳ ♂ ℓ
Hotel   ★ 68% Dobbins Inn, 6-8 High St,
                 CARRICKFERGUS
                 ☎ 028 93351905   15 ⇔ ⋒

Whitehead McCrae's Brae BT38 9NZ
☎ 028 93370820 & 93370822 Fax 028 93370825
Undulating parkland course with magnificent sea views.
18 holes, 5946yds, Par 69, SSS 68, Course record 67.
Club membership 962.
Visitors   may not play on Sat. Must play with member on
                 Sun.
Societies   must contact in advance.
Green Fees   £14 per round (£20 Sun & bank holidays).
Prof   Colin Farr
Designer   A B Armstrong
Facilities   ⊗ ⫚ ᴸ ⬛ ♀ ⚲ ⛴
Location   1m from town

Hotel   ★ 68% Dobbins Inn, 6-8 High St,
                 CARRICKFERGUS
                 ☎ 028 93351905   15 ⇔ ⋒

CO ARMAGH

ARMAGH   Map 01 C5

County Armagh The Demesne, Newry Rd BT60 1EN
☎ 028 37525861 Fax 028 37525861
Mature parkland course with excellent views of Armagh city
and its surroundings.
18 holes, 6212yds, Par 70, SSS 69, Course record 63.
Club membership 1000.
Visitors   time sheet operates at weekends. Must contact in
                 advance.
Societies   must contact in advance.
Green Fees   £20 per round.
Prof   Alan Rankin
Facilities   ⊗ ⫚ ᴸ ⬛ ♀ ⚲ ⛴ ♂ ℓ
Location   On the Newry road

▶

Royal Portrush

☎ 028 70822311 | Fax 028 70823139 | Map 01 D4

e-mail: rpgc@dnet.co.uk

This course, designed by Harry S Colt, is considered among the six best in the UK. Founded in 1888, it was the venue of the first professional golf event held in Ireland, in 1895, where Sandy Herd beat Harry Vardon in the final.

It is spectacular, breathtaking, but one of the tightest driving tests known to man. On a clear day, you have a fine view of Islay and the Paps of Jura from the 3rd tee and the Giant's Causeway from the 5th. While the greens have to be 'read' from the start, there are fairways up and down valleys, and holes called Calamity Corner and Purgatory for good reason! The second hole - Giant's Grave, is 509 yards, there is an even longer hole at the 17th.

Visitors must contact in advance, have a letter of introduction from their own club and a handicap certificate. Restricted Wed & Fri pm, Sat & Sun am

Societies must apply in writing

Green Fees not confirmed

Facilities ⊗ ⋔ ⓫ ♨ ♥ ♀ ⚐ 🛈
🛈 ⚲ Professional (Gary McNeill)

Location Dunluce Rd, Portrush BT56 8JQ (0.5m from Portrush, on main road to Bushmills)

Holes/Par/Course record 45 holes.
Dunluce Links: 18 holes, 6641 yds, Par 72, SSS 73
Valley Links: 18 holes, 6054 yds, Par 70, SSS 70

WHERE TO STAY AND EAT NEARBY

Hotel
PORTRUSH

★★★ 62% Causeway Coast,
36 Ballyreagh Rd. ☎ 028 70822435.
21 ⇆ 🐾

Restaurant
PORTRUSH

🏵 🏵 Ramore, The Harbour.
☎ 028 70824313

Hotel ★★★★ 67% Stormont Hotel, 587 Upper Newtownards Rd, BELFAST
☎ 028 90658621 109 ⇔ ▮

LURGAN
Map 01 D5

Craigavon Golf & Ski Centre Turmoyra Ln, Silverwood BT66 6NG ☎ 028 38326606 Fax 028 38347272
Parkland course with a lake and stream providing water hazards.
18 holes, 6496yds, Par 72, SSS 72.
Club membership 400.
Visitors restricted Sat am.
Societies telephone in advance.
Green Fees £12 per round (£16 weekends & bank holidays).
Facilities ⊗ ▮ ⚘ ⚐ ♂ ⚘
& Leisure gymnasium, artificial ski slope.
Location 2m N at Silverwood off the M1

Hotel ★★★★ 67% Stormont Hotel, 587 Upper Newtownards Rd, BELFAST
☎ 028 90658621 109 ⇔ ▮

Lurgan The Demesne BT67 9BN
☎ 028 38322087 Fax 028 38325306
Testing parkland course bordering Lurgan Park Lake with a need for accurate shots. Drains well in wet weather and suits a long straight hitter.
18 holes, 6257yds, Par 70, SSS 70, Course record 66.
Club membership 856.
Visitors may not play Sat, contact in advance.
Societies must contact in advance, not Sat.
Green Fees not confirmed.
Prof Des Paul
Designer A Pennink
Facilities ⊗ ⅷ ⚘ ▮ ♀ ⚘ 🏠 ⚘
Location 0.5m from town centre near Lurgan Park

Hotel ★★★★ 67% Stormont Hotel, 587 Upper Newtownards Rd, BELFAST
☎ 028 90658621 109 ⇔ ▮

PORTADOWN
Map 01 D5

Portadown 192 Gilford Rd BT63 5LF
☎ 028 38355356 Fax 028 38355356
Well wooded parkland course on the banks of the River Bann, which features among the water hazards.
18 holes, 5649mtrs, Par 70, SSS 70, Course record 65.
Club membership 981.
Visitors may not play on Tue & Sat.
Societies apply in writing.
Green Fees £17 per round (£22 weekends & bank holidays).
Prof Paul Stevenson
Facilities ⊗ ⅷ ⚘ ▮ ♀ ⚘ 🏠 ♂ ⚘
& Leisure squash.
Location SE via A59

Hotel ★★★★ 67% Stormont Hotel, 587 Upper Newtownards Rd, BELFAST
☎ 028 90658621 109 ⇔ ▮

AA Hotels that have special arrangements with golf courses are listed at the back of the guide

TANDRAGEE
Map 01 D5

Tandragee Markethill Rd BT62 2ER
☎ 028 38841272 Fax 028 38840664
Pleasant parkland course, the signature hole is the demanding par 4 11th known as 'The Wall Hole', the real strength of Tandragee is in the short holes.
18 holes, 5747mtrs, Par 71, SSS 70, Course record 65.
Club membership 1340.
Visitors contact in advance. Ladies day Tues, after 3.30pm Sat & Sun.
Societies must contact in advance.
Green Fees Men: £15 (£20 weekends & bank holidays); Ladies: £11 (£18 weekends & bank holidays).
Prof Paul Stevenson
Designer John Stone
Facilities ⊗ ⅷ ⚘ ▮ ♀ ⚘ 🏠 ♂ ⚘
& Leisure sauna, gymnasium.
Location On B3 out of Tandragee towards Markethill

Farmhouse ◆◆◆◆ Brook Lodge Farmhouse, 79 Old Ballynahinch Rd, Cargacroy, LISBURN
☎ 028 92638454 6rm (4 ▮)

CO BELFAST

BELFAST
Map 01 D5

See also The Royal Belfast, Hollywood, Co Down.

Balmoral 518 Lisburn Rd BT9 6GX
☎ 028 90381514 Fax 028 90666759
Parkland course, mainly level, with tree-lined fairways and a stream providing a water hazard.
18 holes, 6276yds, Par 69, SSS 70, Course record 64.
Club membership 912.
Visitors may not play Sat or Sun before 2.30pm.
Societies Mon & Thu. Must contact in advance.
Green Fees £20 (£24 Wed; £30 weekends & bank holidays).
Prof Geoff Bleakley
Facilities ⊗ ⅷ ⚘ ▮ by prior arrangement ♀ ⚘ 🏠 ♂ ⚘
Location 2m S next to Kings Hall

Hotel ★★★★ 67% Stormont Hotel, 587 Upper Newtownards Rd, BELFAST
☎ 028 90658621 109 ⇔ ▮

Cliftonville 44 Westland Rd BT14 6NH
☎ 028 90744158 & 90746595
Parkland course with rivers bisecting two fairways.
9 holes, 6242yds, Par 70, SSS 70, Course record 65.
Club membership 430.
Visitors may not play: after 5pm unless with member, on Sat or on Sun mornings.
Societies must contact in writing.
Green Fees £16 (£18 weekends & bank holidays).
Prof Robert Hutton
Facilities ⊗ ⚘ ▮ ♀ ⚘ 🏠 ⚘
Location Between Cavehill Rd & Cliftonville Circus

▶

Hotel ★★★★ 67% Stormont Hotel, 587 Upper Newtownards Rd, BELFAST
☎ 028 90658621 109 ⇆ ℝ

Dunmurry 91 Dunmurry Ln, Dunmurry BT17 9JS
☎ 028 90610834 Fax 028 90602540
Maturing very nicely, this tricky parkland course has several memorable holes which call for skilful shots.
18 holes, 5832yds, Par 69, SSS 69, Course record 64.
Club membership 900.
Visitors telephone in advance. May only play Sat after 5pm, restricted Fri (Ladies Day).
Societies must contact in writing.
Green Fees £17 (£26.50 Sunday & bank holidays).
Prof John Dolan
Facilities ⊗ by prior arrangement ▥ by prior arrangement ⬆ by prior arrangement ♥ by prior arrangement ⚲ ⚒ ▦ ☂ ♂
Hotel ★★★★ 67% Stormont Hotel, 587 Upper Newtownards Rd, BELFAST
☎ 028 90658621 109 ⇆ ℝ

Fortwilliam Downview Ave BT15 4EZ
☎ 028 90370770 (Office) & 90770980 (Pro)
Fax 028 90781891
Parkland course in most attractive surroundings. The course is bisected by a lane.
18 holes, 5789yds, Par 70, SSS 68, Course record 65.
Club membership 1000.
Visitors contact professional in advance.
Societies must contact in advance.
Green Fees not confirmed.
Prof Peter Hanna
Facilities ⊗ ▥ ⬆ ♥ ⚲ ⚒ ▦ ☂ ♂
Location Off Antrim road

Hotel ★★★ 64% Lansdowne Court Hotel, 657 Antrim Rd, BELFAST
☎ 028 90773317 25 ⇆ ℝ

Malone 240 Upper Malone Rd, Dunmurry BT17 9LB
☎ 028 90612758 (Office) & 90614917 (Pro)
Fax 028 90431394
Two parkland courses, extremely attractive with a large lake, mature trees and flowering shrubs and bordered by the River Lagan. Very well maintained and offering a challenging round.
Main Course: 18 holes, 6599yds, Par 71, SSS 71.
Edenderry: 9 holes, 6320yds, Par 72, SSS 70.
Club membership 1300.
Visitors advisable to contact pro-shop in advance. Main Course: Unable to play Sat, Sun morning or Tues. Edenberry: no restrictions
Societies apply in writing or fax to club manager. Large group normally Mon & Thu only.
Green Fees not confirmed.
Cards ▭ ▭ ▭
Prof Michael McGee
Designer C K Cotton
Facilities ⊗ ▥ ⬆ ♥ ⚲ ⚒ ▦ ☂ ⚑ ♂
& Leisure squash, fishing, bowls green.
Location 4.5m S opposite Lady Dixon Park

Hotel ★★★★ 67% Stormont Hotel, 587 Upper Newtownards Rd, BELFAST
☎ 028 90658621 109 ⇆ ℝ

Mount Ober Golf & Country Club 24 Ballymaconaghy Rd BT8 4SB ☎ 028 90401811 & 90795666 Fax 028 90705862
Inland parkland course which is a great test of golf for all handicaps.
18 holes, 5419yds, Par 67, SSS 66, Course record 67.
Club membership 400.
Visitors must contact in advance at weekends & bank holidays, may play Sat after 3.30pm and Sun after 10.30am.
Societies book by telephone or fax.
Green Fees not confirmed.
Cards ▭ ▭
Prof Geoff Loughrey/Steve Rourke
Facilities ⊗ ▥ ⬆ ♥ ⚲ ⚒ ▦ ☂ ♂
& Leisure ski slopes, American billiards hall.
Location Off Saintfield Road

Hotel ★★★★ 67% Stormont Hotel, 587 Upper Newtownards Rd, BELFAST
☎ 028 90658621 109 ⇆ ℝ

Ormeau 50 Park Rd BT7 2FX
☎ 028 90640700 Fax 028 90646250
Parkland.
9 holes, 2653mtrs, Par 68, SSS 65.
Club membership 520.
Visitors welcome weekdays except Tue after 2pm. May play Sat after 5.30pm & Sun by arrangement.
Societies contact in advance.
Green Fees £12 (£15 weekends & Bank holidays).
Cards ▭ ▭ ▭
Facilities ⊗ ▥ ⬆ ♥ ⚲ ⚒ ▦ ☂ ♂
& Leisure snooker, bowls.
Location S of city centre between Ravenhill & Ormeau roads

Shandon Park 73 Shandon Park BT5 6NY
☎ 028 90401856
Fairly level parkland offering a pleasant challenge.
18 holes, 6261yds, Par 70, SSS 70.
Club membership 1100.
Visitors may not play on competition days. Must contact in advance and have a handicap certificate.
Societies may play Mon & Fri only, applications to club.
Green Fees not confirmed.
Prof Barry Wilson
Facilities ⊗ ▥ ⬆ ♥ ⚲ ⚒ ▦ ☂ ♂
Location Off Knock road

Hotel ★★★★ 67% Stormont Hotel, 587 Upper Newtownards Rd, BELFAST
☎ 028 90658621 109 ⇆ ℝ

DUNDONALD   Map 01 D5

Knock Summerfield BT16 2QX
☎ 028 90483251 & 90482249 Fax 028 90483251
Parkland course with huge trees, deep bunkers and a river cutting across several fairways. This is a hard but fair course and will test the best of golfers.
18 holes, 6435yds, Par 70, SSS 71, Course record 66.
Club membership 900.
Visitors with member only on Sat, Mon & Thu are Society Days, Tue is Ladies Day, advisable to contact in advance.
Societies must contact in advance.
Green Fees £20 per day (£25 weekends & bank holidays). ▶

Cards	
Prof	Gordon Fairweather
Designer	Colt, Allison & McKenzie
Facilities	⊗ ⁞⁞⁞ 🏌 🛅 💷 ♀ 🏊 🏠 ⛳ 🐕 🛺 ✎
Hotel	★★★★ 75% Culloden Hotel, Bangor Rd, HOLYWOOD ☎ 028 90425223 79 ⇆ ♟

NEWTOWNBREDA   Map 01 D5

The Belvoir Park 73 Church Rd BT8 7AN
☎ 028 90491693 Fax 028 90646113
This undulating parkland course is not strenuous to walk, but is certainly a test of your golf, with tree-lined fairways and a particularly challenging finish at the final four holes.
18 holes, 6516yds, Par 71, SSS 71, Course record 65.
Club membership 1000.

Visitors	must contact in advance, may not play Sat.
Societies	must contact in writing.
Green Fees	Men: £33 per day, excluding Wed (£38 Sun, Wed & Bank holidays) Ladies: £27 per day, excluding Wed (£33 Sun, Wed & bank holidays).
Cards	
Prof	Maurice Kelly
Designer	H Holt
Facilities & Leisure	⊗ ⁞⁞⁞ 🏌 🛅 💷 ♀ 🏊 🏠 ⛳ 🐕 🛺 ✎ snooker.
Location	3m from city centre off Saintfield/Newcastle rd
Hotel	★★★★ 67% Stormont Hotel, 587 Upper Newtownards Rd, BELFAST ☎ 028 90658621 109 ⇆ ♟

CO DOWN

ARDGLASS   Map 01 D5

Ardglass Castle Place BT30 7TP
☎ 028 44841219 Fax 028 44841841
A scenic cliff-top seaside course with spectacular views and some memorable holes.
18 holes, 5498mtrs, Par 70, SSS 69, Course record 65.
Club membership 800.

Visitors	must contact in advance.
Societies	must contact in advance, welcome weekdays & restricted times Sun.
Green Fees	£27 per day; £18 per round (£36/£24 weekends & bank holidays).
Cards	
Prof	Philip Farrell
Designer	David Joans
Facilities	⊗ ⁞⁞⁞ 🏌 🛅 💷 ♀ 🏊 🏠 ⛳ 🐕 🛺 ✎
Location	7m from Downpatrick on the B1
Hotel	★★★★ 64% Slieve Donard Hotel, Downs Rd, NEWCASTLE ☎ 028 43723681 130 ⇆ ♟

Where to stay, where to eat?
Visit the AA internet site
www.theaa.co.uk

ARDMILLAN   Map 01 D5

Mahee Island Mahee Island, Comber BT23 6EP
☎ 028 97541234
An undulating parkland course, almost surrounded by water, with magnificent views of Strangford Lough and its islands, with Scrabo Tower in the background. The first professional here was Fred Daly (1933-4) who became British Open Champion in 1947.
9 holes, 5590yds, Par 68, SSS 67, Course record 68.
Club membership 500.

Visitors	may not play on Wed after 5pm or Sat before 5pm.
Societies	contact in advance.
Green Fees	not confirmed.
Facilities & Leisure	🏠 🏠 🛺 ✎ pool table.
Location	Off Comber/Killyleagh road to the left 0.5m from Comber
Hotel	★★★★ 67% Stormont Hotel, 587 Upper Newtownards Rd, BELFAST ☎ 028 90658621 109 ⇆ ♟

BALLYNAHINCH   Map 01 D5

Spa 20 Grove Rd BT24 8PN
☎ 028 97562365 Fax 028 97564158
Parkland course with tree-lined fairways and scenic views of the Mourne Mountains.
18 holes, 6003mtrs, Par 72, SSS 72, Course record 66.
Club membership 907.

Visitors	must contact in advance. No play on Sat.
Societies	must contact in advance.
Green Fees	£15 per round (£20 weekends & bank holidays).
Designer	F Ainsworth
Facilities	⊗ ⁞⁞⁞ 🏌 🛅 💷 ♀ 🏊 🏠 ⛳ 🛺 ✎
Location	1m S on the Grove Rd
Hotel	★★★★ 64% Slieve Donard Hotel, Downs Rd, NEWCASTLE ☎ 028 43723681 130 ⇆ ♟

BANBRIDGE   Map 01 D5

Banbridge 116 Huntly Rd BT32 3UR
☎ 028 40662211 Fax 028 40669400
A picturesque course with excellent views of the Mourne mountains. The holes are not long, but are tricky.
18 holes, 5003mtrs, Par 69, SSS 67, Course record 61.
Club membership 700.

Visitors may not play Sat or before 11am on Sun. Ladies Day Tue.
Societies must contact in writing.
Green Fees £15 per day (£20 weekends & bank holidays).
Designer F Ainsworth
Facilities ⊗ ⫪ ⬩ ♟ ♀ ♁ ⚐ ✓
Location 0.5m along Huntly road

Hotel ★★★★ 64% Slieve Donard Hotel, Downs Rd, NEWCASTLE ☎ 028 43723681 130 ⇆ ♜

BANGOR   Map 01 D5

Bangor Broadway BT20 4RH
☎ 028 91270922 Fax 028 91453394
Undulating parkland course in the town. It is well maintained and pleasant and offers a challenging round, particularly at the 5th.
18 holes, 6410yds, Par 71, SSS 71, Course record 62.
Club membership 1147.
Visitors may not play Sat & weekdays 1-2.
Societies must contact in advance, Mon/Wed by telephone, Fri by letter.
Green Fees £20 (£25 Sun & bank holidays).
Prof Michael Bannon
Designer James Braid
Facilities ⊗ ⫪ ⬩ ♟ ♀ ♁ ⚐ ✓ ⚑ ✓
Location 1m from town on Donaghadee Road

Hotel ★★★ 62% Royal Hotel, Seafront, BANGOR ☎ 028 91271866 50 ⇆ ♜

Blackwood Golf Centre 150 Crawfordsburn Rd, Clandeboye BT19 1GB
☎ 028 91852706 Fax 028 91853785
The golf centre is a pay and play development with a computerised booking system for the 18-hole championship-standard Hamilton course. The course is built on mature woodland with man-made lakes that come into play on 5 holes. The Temple course is an 18-hole Par 3 course with holes ranging from the 75yd 1st to the 185yd 10th, which has a lake on the right of the green. Banked by gorse with streams crossing throughout, this Par 3 course is no pushover.
Hamilton Course: 18 holes, 6304yds, Par 71, SSS 70.
Temple Course: 18 holes, 2492yds, Par 54.
Visitors pay as you play, computerised booking system for the Hamilton Course, bookable 7 days in advance.
Societies telephone in advance.
Green Fees Hamilton: £15 per round; £8 per 9 holes (£20/£11 weekends). Temple: £8 per round; £4.50 per 9 holes (£10/£6 weekends).
Cards 💳
Prof Roy Skillen/Debbie Hanna
Designer Simon Gidman
Facilities ⊗ ⬩ ♟ ♀ ♁ ⚐ ✓ ⚑
Location 2m from Bangor, off A2 to Belfast

Hotel ★★★ 72% Clandeboye Lodge Hotel, 10 Estate Rd, Clandeboye, BANGOR ☎ 028 91852500 43 ⇆ ♜

Carnalea Station Rd BT19 1EZ
☎ 028 91270368 Fax 028 91273989
A scenic course on the shores of Belfast Lough.
18 holes, 5574yds, Par 69, SSS 67, Course record 63.
Club membership 1354.

Visitors restricted Sat.
Societies must contact in advance.
Green Fees £15.75 per round (£19.75 weekends & bank holidays).
Prof Tom Loughran
Facilities ⊗ ⫪ ⬩ ♟ ♀ ♁ ⚐ ⚑ ✓
Location 2m W adjacent to railway station

Hotel ★★★ 71% Old Inn, 15 Main St, CRAWFORDSBURN ☎ 028 91853255 33 ⇆ ♜

Clandeboye Tower Rd, Conlig, Newtownards BT23 3PN
☎ 028 91271767 Fax 028 91473711
Parkland/heathland courses. The Dufferin is the championship course and offers a tough challenge demanding extreme accuracy, with its mass of gorse, bracken and strategically placed trees that flank every hole. The slightest error will be punished. The Ava compliments the Dufferin perfectly. Accuracy is also the key with a notable 2nd hole.
Dufferin Course: 18 holes, 6469yds, Par 71, SSS 71.
Ava Course: 18 holes, 5755yds, Par 71, SSS 68.
Club membership 1300.

Visitors must contact in advance.
Societies Mon-Wed, Fri & after 3pm Sat & Sun. Must contact in advance.
Green Fees Dufferin: £40 per 36 holes; £27.50 per round (£33 weekends & bank holidays); Ava: £22 per round (£27.50 weekends & bank holidays).
Cards 💳
Prof Peter Gregory
Designer William Robinson
Facilities ⊗ ⫪ ⬩ ♟ ♀ ♁ ⚐ ⚑ ⚐ ✓
Location 2m S on A1 between Bangor & Newtownards

Hotel ★★★ 62% Royal Hotel, Seafront, BANGOR ☎ 028 91271866 50 ⇆ ♜

Helen's Bay Golf Rd, Helen's Bay BT19 1TL
☎ 028 91852815 & 91852601 Fax 028 91852815
A parkland course on the shores of Belfast Lough with panoramic views along the Antrim coast. The 4th hole Par 3 is particularly challenging as the green is screened by high trees.
9 holes, 5181mtrs, Par 68, SSS 67.
Club membership 820.
Visitors welcome Sun, Mon, Wed, Thu (before 1.30pm), Fri (after 11.30am during Jul & Aug) & Sat after 6pm. Book in advance with secretary.
Societies welcome Sun, Mon, Wed, Thu (before 1.30pm), Fri & Sat after 6pm. Telephone secretary in advance. ▶

Green Fees not confirmed.
Facilities ⊗ 🎿 🏌 🍽 ♀ ⚥ ✍
Location A2 from Belfast

Hotel ★★★ 71% Old Inn, 15 Main St,
CRAWFORDSBURN
☎ 028 91853255 33 ⇆ 🐾

CARRYDUFF   Map 01 D5

Rockmount 28 Drumalig Rd, Carryduff BT8 8EQ
☎ 028 90812279 Fax 020 90815851
A demanding 18-hole course set in open parkland with
mature trees, several streams, and a tricky lake at the 11th
hole. Panoramic views.
18 holes, 6373yds, Par 71, SSS 71, Course record 68.
Club membership 700.
Visitors welcome except for Sat or Wed afternoon.
Societies welcome except for Wed & Sat, book by
telephone.
Green Fees £20 (£24 Sun).
Cards 💳 💳 🏧
Designer Robert Patterson
Facilities ⊗ 🎿 🏌 🍽 ♀ ⚥ 🏠 🐾 ✍
Location 10m S of Belfast

Hotel ★★ 58% Balmoral Hotel, Blacks Rd,
Dunmurry, BELFAST
☎ 028 90301234 44 ⇆ 🐾

CLOUGHEY   Map 01 D5

Kirkistown Castle 142 Main Rd, Cloughey BT22 1JA
☎ 028 42771233 Fax 028 42771699
A seaside semi-links popular with visiting golfers because of
its quiet location. The course is exceptionally dry and
remains open when others in the area have to close. The Par
4 10th is particularly distinctive with a long drive and a slight
dogleg to a raised green with a gorse covered motte waiting
for the wayward approach shot.
18 holes, 6167yds, Par 69, SSS 70, Course record 65.
Club membership 948.
Visitors must contact in advance, restricted weekends.
Societies contact in writing or by phone.
Green Fees £15 (£20 weekends & bank holidays).
Prof Jonathan Peden
Designer James Braid
Facilities ⊗ 🎿 🏌 🍽 ♀ ⚥ 🏠 🍴 ✍
& Leisure snooker.
Location 16m from Newtownards on the A2

Hotel ★★★ 71% Old Inn, 15 Main St,
CRAWFORDSBURN
☎ 028 91853255 33 ⇆ 🐾

DONAGHADEE   Map 01 D5

Donaghadee Warren Rd BT21 0PQ
☎ 028 91883624 Fax 028 91888891
Undulating seaside course, part links, part parkland,
requiring a certain amount of concentration. Splendid views.
18 holes, 5570mtrs, Par 71, SSS 69, Course record 65.
Club membership 1160.
Visitors contact in advance.
Societies write in advance.
Green Fees IR£16 per round (IR£22 Sun & bank holidays).
Prof Gordon Drew

Facilities ⊗ 🎿 🏌 🍽 ♀ ⚥ 🏠 🍴 🐾 ✍
Hotel ★★★ 71% Old Inn, 15 Main St,
CRAWFORDSBURN
☎ 028 91853255 33 ⇆ 🐾

DOWNPATRICK   Map 01 D5

Bright Castle 14 Coniamstown Rd, Bright BT30 8LU
☎ 028 44841319
Parkland course in elevated position with views of the
Mountains of Mourne. A good challenge for the energetic
golfer.
18 holes, 7300yds, Par 74, SSS 74, Course record 69.
Club membership 60.
Visitors no restrictions.
Societies must contact in advance.
Green Fees £10 (£12 weekends)..
Designer Mr Ennis
Facilities ⊗ 🏌 🍽 ⚥ 🏍 ✍
Location 5m S

Hotel ★★★★ 64% Slieve Donard Hotel, Downs Rd,
NEWCASTLE ☎ 028 43723681 130 ⇆ 🐾

Downpatrick 43 Saul Rd BT30 6PA
☎ 028 44615947 Fax 028 44617502
This undulating parkland course provides a good challenge.
18 holes, 6100yds, Par 70, SSS 69, Course record 66.
Club membership 960.
Visitors must contact in advance.
Societies must telephone in advance.
Green Fees £15 per day (£20 weekends & bank holidays).
Designer Hawtree & Son
Facilities ⊗ 🎿 🏌 🍽 ♀ ⚥ 🏠 🍴 🐾 🏍 ✍
Location 1.5m from town centre

Hotel ★★ 64% Enniskeen House Hotel, 98
Bryansford Rd, NEWCASTLE
☎ 028 43722392 12 ⇆ 🐾

HOLYWOOD   Map 01 D5

Holywood Nuns Walk, Demesne Rd BT18 9LE
☎ 028 90423135 Fax 028 90425040
Hilly parkland course with some fine views and providing an
interesting game. Several feature holes, including the short
6th "Nuns Walk" and the treacherous 12th "White House".
18 holes, 5480mtrs, Par 69, SSS 68, Course record 64.
Club membership 1100.
Visitors must contact in advance.
Societies must contact in writing.
Green Fees not confirmed.
Prof Michael Bannon
Facilities ⊗ 🎿 🏌 🍽 ♀ ⚥ 🏠 🍴 🏍 ✍ 🍷
Location Just outside Belfast, off the Bangor dual
carriageway, behind the town of Holywood

Hotel ★★★ 71% Old Inn, 15 Main St,
CRAWFORDSBURN
☎ 028 91853255 33 ⇆ 🐾

The Royal Belfast Station Rd, Craigavad BT18 0BP
☎ 028 90428165 Fax 028 90421404
On the shores of Belfast Lough, this attractive course
consists of wooded parkland on undulating terrain which
provides a pleasant, challenging game. ▶

Royal County Down

ewcastle, *Co Down*   ☎ 028 43723314   Fax 028 43726281   Map 01 D5

he Championship Course is consistently rated among the world's top ten courses. Laid out beneath the imperious gaze of the Mountains of Mourne, the course enjoys a magnificent stage. e setting as it stretches out along the shores of Dundrum Bay. As ell as being one of the world's most beautiful courses, it is also one the most challenging, with great swathes of heather and gorse ing fairways that tumble beneath vast sand hills, and wild tussocky ced bunkers defending small subtly contoured greens.

The Second Course offers a less formidable, yet extremely aracterful game played against the same incomparable backcloth. ecently substantially revised under the direction of Donald Steel, the urse begins quite benignly before charging headlong into the nes. Several charming, and one or two teasing holes have been rved out amid the gorse, heather and bracken.

Visitors advisable to contact in advance. May not play Annesley Course on Saturdays. May not play on Championship Course Sat, Sun am or Wed after 9am

Societies telephone for availability and confirm in writing

Green Fees Championship £70 per round (£80 weekends); Annesley £15 per round (£23 weekends) ▬ ▬ ▬ ▬

Facilities ⊗ ♠ ♥ ♀ ♨ ☺ ⚐
♂ Professional (Kevan Whitson)

Location Newcastle BT33 0AN

Holes/Par/Course record 36 holes. Championship Course: 18 holes, 7037 yds, Par 71, SSS 74, Course record 66 Annesley Course: 18 holes, 4681 yds, Par 66, SSS 63

WHERE TO STAY NEARBY

Hotels
NEWCASTLE

★★★★ 64% Slieve Donard Hotel, Downs Rd. ☎ 028 43723681. 130 ⇨ ♣

★★ 64% Enniskeen Hotel, 98 Bryansford Rd. ☎ 028 43722392. 12 (7 ⇨ ♣ 3 ♣ 2 ⇨)

18 holes, 6185yds, Par 70, SSS 69.
Club membership 1200.
Visitors	may not play on Wed or Sat before 4.30pm; must be accompanied by a member or present a letter of introduction from their own golf club. Must contact in advance.
Societies	must contact in writing.
Green Fees	not confirmed.
Prof	Chris Spence
Designer	H C Colt
Facilities	⊗ ⑪ ⓑ ⚑ ⚐ ⚒ ⚖ 🏠 ⚓ ⚙
& Leisure	hard tennis courts, squash.
Location	2m E on A2

Hotel	★★★★ 75% Culloden Hotel, Bangor Rd, HOLYWOOD ☎ 028 90425223 79 ⇆ ⁀

KILKEEL   Map 01 D5

Kilkeel Mourne Park BT34 4LB
☎ 028 41765095 Fax 028 41765095
Picturesquely situated at the foot of the Mourne Mountains. Eleven holes have tree-lined fairways with the remainder in open parkland. The 13th hole is testing and a well positioned tee shot is essential.
18 holes, 6615yds, Par 72, SSS 72, Course record 69.
Club membership 650.
Visitors	contact in advance for weekend play.
Societies	must contact in advance.
Green Fees	£16 per round (£20 weekends).
Designer	Babington/Hackett
Facilities	⊗ ⑪ ⓑ ⚑ ⚐ ⚒ ⚖ 🏠 ⚙ ⚓
& Leisure	fishing.
Location	3m from Kilkeel on Newry road

Hotel	★★★★ 64% Slieve Donard Hotel, Downs Rd, NEWCASTLE ☎ 028 43723681 130 ⇆ ⁀

KILLYLEAGH

Ringdufferin Golf Course 31 Ringdufferin Rd, Toye BT30 9PH ☎ 028 44828812 Fax 028 44828812
The course overlooks Strangford Lough.
18 holes, 4652mtrs, Par 68, SSS 66.
Club membership 300.
Visitors	contact in advance on Saturdays.
Societies	apply in writing/telephone in advance.
Green Fees	£9 per round (£10 weekends).
Prof	Mark Lavery
Designer	Frank Ainsworth
Facilities	⊗ ⓑ ⚑ ⚐ ⚒ ⚖ 🏠 ⚓ ⚙ ⚓
& Leisure	fishing.
Location	2m N of Killyleagh

Hotel	★★★★ 64% Slieve Donard Hotel, Downs Rd, NEWCASTLE ☎ 028 43723681 130 ⇆ ⁀

MAGHERALIN   Map 01 D5

Edenmore Edenmore House, 70 Drumnabreeze Rd BT67 0RH ☎ 028 92611310 Fax 028 92613310
Set in mature parkland with gently rolling slopes. The front nine holes provide an interesting contrast to the back nine with more open play involved. Many new paths and features have been recently added.

18 holes, 6244yds, Par 71, SSS 70, Course record 71.
Club membership 350.
Visitors	telephone in advance, may not play until after 2pm Sat and all day Sun.
Societies	telephone in advance.
Green Fees	Mon-Thur: £12 per round Fri: £13 (£15 weekends).
Cards	▭ ▬ ▰ 🅖
Designer	F Ainsworth
Facilities	⊗ ⑪ ⓑ ⚑ ⚐ ⚒ 🏠 ⚒ ⚓ ⚙
Hotel	★★★ 66% Posthouse Belfast, Kingsway, Dunmurry, BELFAST ☎ 0870 400 9005 82 ⇆ ⁀

NEWCASTLE   Map 01 D5

NEWCASTLE See page 427.

NEWRY   Map 01 D5

Newry 11 Forkhill Rd BT35 8LZ
☎ 028 30263871 Fax 028 30263871
Short 18-hole course enjoying panoramic views of the Mourne Mountains and across Newry.
18 holes, 3000mtrs, Par 53, SSS 52, Course record 51.
Club membership 150.
Visitors	welcome anytime.
Societies	apply in writing or telephone.
Green Fees	not confirmed.
Cards	▭ ▬ 💳 ▰ 🅖
Prof	Larry Heaney
Designer	Michael Heaney
Facilities	⊗ ⑪ ⓑ ⚑ ⚐ ⚒ 🏠 ⚓ ⚓
& Leisure	hard and grass tennis courts, outdoor and indoor heated swimming pools, clay pigeon shooting.
Location	1m from Newry just off the main Dublin road

Hotel	★★ 64% Enniskeen House Hotel, 98 Bryansford Rd, NEWCASTLE ☎ 028 43722392 12 ⇆ ⁀

NEWTOWNARDS   Map 01 D5

Scrabo 233 Scrabo Rd BT23 4SL
☎ 028 91812355 Fax 028 91822919
Hilly and picturesque, this course offers a good test of golf for golfers of all abilities. It benefits from good drainage and remains dry and playable most of the year.
18 holes, 5722mtrs, Par 71, SSS 71, Course record 65.
Club membership 1002.
Visitors	may not play on Saturdays. Contact in advance.
Societies	must contact in advance.
Green Fees	£15 per round.
Prof	Paul McCrystal
Facilities	⊗ ⑪ ⓑ ⚑ ⚐ ⚒ 🏠 ⚙
Location	Borders of Newtownards on the Ards Peninsula, follow signs for Scrabo Country Park

Hotel	★★★★ 67% Stormont Hotel, 587 Upper Newtownards Rd, BELFAST ☎ 028 90658621 109 ⇆ ⁀

> Looking for a driving range?
> See the index at the back of the guide

WARRENPOINT   Map 01 D5

Warrenpoint Lower Dromore Rd BT34 3LN
☎ 028 41753695 Fax 028 41752918
Parkland course with marvellous views and a need for
accurate shots.
18 holes, 6108yds, Par 71, SSS 70, Course record 61.
Club membership 1340.

Visitors	must contact in advance.
Societies	must contact in advance.
Green Fees	£20 per round (£27 weekends & bank holidays).
Cards	〓 ■ 〓 🔟
Prof	Nigel Shaw
Facilities	⊗ ⅲ 🏌 🍴 ♀ ⚷ 🏠 🛒 💈
& Leisure	squash.
Location	1m W

Hotel	★★★★ 64% Slieve Donard Hotel, Downs Rd, NEWCASTLE ☎ 028 43723681 130 🛏 📶

CO FERMANAGH

ENNISKILLEN   Map 01 C5

Ashwoods Golf Centre Sligo Rd BT74 7JY
☎ 028 66325321 & 66322908 Fax 028 66329411
Only 1 mile from Lough Erne, this course is open
meadowland. It has been well planted with many young
trees.
14 holes, 1930yds, Par 42.

Visitors	no restrictions.
Societies	must book in advance.
Green Fees	not confirmed.
Prof	Pat Trainor
Designer	P Loughran
Facilities	🏌 🍴 ⚷ 🏠 🛒 🚜 💈 ⚑
Location	1.5m W

Hotel	★★★ 69% Killyhevlin Hotel, ENNISKILLEN ☎ 028 66323481 43 🛏 📶

Castle Hume Castle Hume BT93 7ED
☎ 028 66327077 Fax 028 66327076
Castle Hulme is a particularly scenic and challenging course.
Set in undulating parkland with large rolling greens, rivers,
lakes and water hazards all in play on a championship
standard course.
18 holes, 5770mtrs, Par 72, SSS 70, Course record 69.
Club membership 350.

Visitors	may play any time subject to advance arrangement.
Societies	telephone in advance.
Green Fees	£15 per day/round (£20 weekends & bank holidays).
Cards	〓 〓
Designer	B Browne
Facilities	⊗ by prior arrangement ⅲ by prior arrangement 🏌 by prior arrangement 🍴 ♀ ⚷ 🏠 🛒 🐾 💈 ⚑ 📶
& Leisure	fishing.
Location	4m from Enniskillen on the Belleek Rd

CO LONDONDERRY

Hotel	★★★ 69% Killyhevlin Hotel, ENNISKILLEN ☎ 028 66323481 43 🛏 📶

Enniskillen Castlecoole BT74 6HZ ☎ 028 66325250
Tree lined parkland course offering panoramic views of
Enniskillen town and the surrounding lakeland area. Situated
beside the National Trust's Castlecoole Estate.
18 holes, 6189mtrs, Par 71, SSS 69, Course record 67.
Club membership 600.

Visitors	restricted Tue and weekends. Contact Hon Secretaryor bar steward.
Societies	must contact club steward in advance.
Green Fees	£15 per day (£18 weekends & bank holidays).
Facilities	⊗ by prior arrangement ⅲ by prior arrangement 🏌 🍴 ♀ ⚷ 🛒 🐾 💈
Location	1m E

Hotel	★★★ 69% Killyhevlin Hotel, ENNISKILLEN ☎ 028 66323481 43 🛏 📶

AGHADOWEY   Map 01 C6

Brown Trout Golf & Country Inn 209 Agivey Rd
BT51 4AD ☎ 028 70868209 Fax 028 70868878
A challenging course with two par 5s. During the course of
the 9 holes, players have to negotiate water 7 times and all
the fairways are lined with densely packed fir trees.
9 holes, 5510yds, Par 70, SSS 68, Course record 66.
Club membership 150.

Visitors	no restrictions.
Societies	must contact by telephone, restricted tee-off times Sun.
Green Fees	£10 per day (£15 weekends & bank holidays).
Cards	〓 ■ 〓 🔟 〓 🔟
Prof	Ken Revie
Designer	Bill O'Hara Snr
Facilities	⊗ ⅲ 🏌 🍴 ♀ ⚷ 🛒 💈
& Leisure	fishing, gymnasium.
Location	Junc of A54 & B66, 7m S of Coleraine

Hotel	★★ 67% Brown Trout Golf & Country Inn, 209 Agivey Rd, AGHADOWEY ☎ 028 70868209 17 🛏 📶

CASTLEDAWSON   Map 01 C5

Moyola Park 15 Curran Rd BT45 8DG
☎ 028 79468468 & 79468830 (Prof) Fax 028 79468626
Parkland course with some difficult shots, calling for length
and accuracy. The Moyola River provides a water hazard at
the 8th. Newly designed par 3, demands good shot placement
to a green on an island in the Moyola river, players
capabilities will be tested by the undulating green.
18 holes, 6522yds, Par 71, SSS 70, Course record 67.
Club membership 1000.

Visitors	contact professional in advance, G.U.I. dress code applies, Ladies day Wednesday, Sat & Sun after 1.30pm, book in advance to avoid disappointment.

▶

Societies	must contact in advance, preferably in writing
Green Fees	£17 per day (£25 weekends & bank holidays).
Prof	Vivian Teague
Designer	Don Patterson
Facilities	⊗ 川 ᴸ ▉ ♀ ⚐ 🏠 ⛾ 🚗 ◊
Location	Take sign for Castledawson. Golf Club signposted
Hotel	★★★★ 72% Galgorm Manor, BALLYMENA ☎ 028 25881001 24 ⇄ ☞

CASTLEROCK   Map 01 C6

Castlerock 65 Circular Rd BT51 4TJ
☎ 028 70848314 Fax 028 70849440
A most exhilarating course with three superb par 4s, four testing short holes and five par 5s. After an uphill start, the hazards are many, including the river and a railway, and both judgement and accuracy are called for. A challenge in calm weather, any trouble from the elements will test your golf to the limits.
Mussenden Course: 18 holes, 6499yds, Par 73, SSS 72, Course record 67.
Bann Course: 9 holes, 2938yds, Par 34, SSS 33.
Club membership 1120.

Visitors	contact in advance, limited number of places at weekends. Must be members of a recognised club.
Societies	must contact in advance.
Green Fees	Mussenden: £30 per round (£40 weekends & bank holidays); Bann: £12 per round (£15 weekends & bank holidays).
Prof	Robert Kelly
Designer	Ben Sayers
Facilities	⊗ 川 ᴸ ▉ ♀ ⚐ 🏠 ⛾ ◊
Location	6m from Coleraine on A2
Hotel	★★★ 62% Causeway Coast Hotel, 36 Ballyreagh Rd, PORTRUSH ☎ 028 70822435 21 ⇄ ☞

KILREA   Map 01 C5

Kilrea Drumagarner Rd BT51 5TB ☎ 028 25821048
A relatively short undulating inland course with tight fairways and small greens. The opening hole is a long par 3, particularly into the wind.
9 holes, 4514yds, Par 62, SSS 62, Course record 61.
Club membership 300.

Visitors	welcome but restricted Tue pm, Wed pm during summer and Sat all year.
Societies	contact D P Clarke (Sec), 37 Townhill Rd, Portglenone, Co Antrim BT44 8AD.
Green Fees	£10 per day (£12.50 weekends).
Facilities	⚐
Location	0.5m outside village of Kilrea on Drumagarner Road
Hotel	★★ 67% Brown Trout Golf & Country Inn, 209 Agivey Rd, AGHADOWEY ☎ 028 70868209 17 ⇄ ☞

> **AA Hotels that have special arrangements with golf courses are listed at the back of the guide**

LIMAVADY   Map 01 C6

Benone 53 Benone Ave BT49 0LQ
☎ 028 77750555 & 77750919
9 holes, 1458yds, Par 27.

Visitors	no reservations.
Societies	telephone in advance.
Green Fees	not confirmed.
Facilities & Leisure	▉ ⚐ ⛾ ☂ hard tennis courts, heated outdoor swimming pool, bowling green.
Location	Between Coleraine/Limavady on A2

Radisson Roe Park Hotel & Golf Resort Roe Park
BT49 9LB ☎ 028 77722222 Fax 028 77722313
A parkland course opened in 1992 on an historic Georgian estate. The course surrounds the original buildings and a driving range has been created in the old walled garden. Final holes 15-18 are particularly memorable with water, trees, out-of-bounds, etc to provide a testing finish.
18 holes, 6318yds, Par 70, SSS 35.
Club membership 500.

Visitors	advance booking recommended. Handicap certificate required. May not play before 10.30am at weekends.
Societies	contact in advance.
Green Fees	£20 (£25 weekends & bank holidays).
Cards	💳
Prof	Seamus Duffy
Designer	Frank Ainsworth
Facilities & Leisure	⊗ 川 ᴸ ▉ ♀ ⚐ 🏠 ⛾ 🛏 ⚓ 🚗 ◊ ☂ heated indoor swimming pool, fishing, sauna, solarium, gymnasium, indoor golf academy.
Location	Just outside Limavady on A2 Ballykelly/Londonderry road
Hotel	★★★★ 67% Radisson Roe Park Hotel & Golf Resort, LIMAVADY ☎ 028 77722222 64 ⇄ ☞

LONDONDERRY   Map 01 C5

City of Derry 49 Victoria Rd BT47 2PU
☎ 028 71346369 Fax 028 71310008
Two parkland courses on undulating parkland with good views and lots of trees. The 9-hole course will particularly suit novices.
Prehen Course: 18 holes, 6406yds, Par 71, SSS 71, Course record 68.
Dunhugh Course: 9 holes, 2354yds, Par 66, SSS 66.
Club membership 823.

Visitors must make a booking to play on Prehen Course at weekends or before 4.30pm on weekdays.
Societies must contact in advance.
Green Fees £20 per day (£25 weekends & bank holidays).
Prof Michael Doherty
Facilities ⊗ ⅷ ┗ ⚑ ♀ ♨ ⌂ ♂
Location 2m S

Hotel ★★★★ 64% Everglades Hotel, Prehen Rd, LONDONDERRY ☎ 028 71346722 64 ⇋ ⋒

Foyle International Golf Centre 12 Alder Rd BT48 8DB
☎ 028 71352222 Fax 028 71353967
Foyle International boasts a championship course, a 9 hole par 3 course and a driving range. It is a fine test of golf with water coming into play on the 3rd, 10th and 11th holes. The 6th green overlooks the Amelia Earhart centre.
18 holes, 6678yds, Par 72, SSS 71, Course record 70.
Club membership 250.
Visitors welcome any time, no retrictions.
Societies booking up to 12 months in advance with deposit.
Green Fees £11 per round (£14 weekends & bank holidays). Par 3 £4/£4.50.
Cards ▭ ▭ ▭ ▭
Prof Kieran McLaughlin
Designer Frank Ainsworth
Facilities ⊗ ⅷ ┗ ⚑ ♀ ♨ ⌂ ⎋ ⌖ ♂ ⌘
& Leisure 9 hole par 3 course, coaching facilities.
Location 1.5m from Foyle Bridge driving torwards Moville

Hotel ★★★ 68% Trinity Hotel, 22-24 Strand Rd, DERRY CITY ☎ 028 71271271 40 ⇋ ⋒

PORTSTEWART
Map 01 C6

Portstewart 117 Strand Rd BT55 7PG
☎ 028 90832015
Three links courses with spectacular views, offering a testing round on the Strand course in particular.
Strand Course: 18 holes, 6784yds, Par 72, SSS 72.
Old Course: 18 holes, 4733yds, Par 64, SSS 62.
3: 9 holes, 2622yds, Par 32.
Club membership 1460.
Visitors preferred on weekdays.
Societies must contact in advance.
Green Fees not confirmed.
Prof Alan Hunter
Facilities ⊗ ⅷ ┗ ⚑ ♀ ♨ ⌂ ⎋ ♂
Hotel ★★★ 62% Causeway Coast Hotel, 36 Ballyreagh Rd, PORTRUSH ☎ 028 70822435 21 ⇋ ⋒

CO TYRONE

COOKSTOWN
Map 01 C5

Killymoon 200 Killymoon Rd BT80 8TW
☎ 028 86763762 & 86762254 Fax 028 867 63762
Parkland course on elevated, well drained land.
18 holes, 5481mtrs, Par 70, SSS 69, Course record 64.
Club membership 950.

Visitors booking essential through proshop on 016487 63460.
Societies must contact in advance.
Green Fees not confirmed.
Cards ▭
Prof Gary Chambers
Facilities ⊗ ⅷ ┗ ⚑ ♀ ♨ ⌂ ♂
Guesthouse ♦♦♦♦♦ Grange Lodge, 7 Grange Rd, DUNGANNON ☎ 028 87784212 5 ⇋ ⋒

DUNGANNON
Map 01 C5

Dungannon 34 Springfield Ln BT70 1QX
☎ 028 87722098 or 87727338 Fax 028 87727338
Parkland course with five par 3s and tree-lined fairways.
18 holes, 5950yds, Par 71, SSS 68, Course record 62.
Club membership 600.
Visitors contact in advance, may not play before 4pm Sat.
Societies apply in writing to secretary.
Green Fees £15 per day (£18 weekends).
Designer Sam Bacon
Facilities ♨ ⌂ ♂
Location 0.5m outside town on Donaghmore road

Hotel L The Cohannon Inn, 212 Ballynakilly Rd, DUNGANNON ☎ 028 87724488 50 ⇋ ⋒

FINTONA
Map 01 C5

Fintona Ecclesville Demesne, 1 Kiln St BT78 2BJ
☎ 028 82841480 & 82840777 (office) Fax 028 82841480
Attractive 9-hole parkland course with a notable water hazard - a trout stream that meanders through the course causing many problems for badly executed shots.
9 holes, 5765mtrs, Par 72, SSS 70.
Club membership 400.
Visitors advised to contact in advance at weekends.
Societies apply in writing well in advance, weekends not advisable as competitions played.
Green Fees £15 per round.
Prof Paul Leonard
Facilities ⊗ ⅷ ┗ by prior arrangement ⚑ ♀ ♨
Location 8m S of Omagh

Hotel ★★ 66% Mahons Hotel, Mill St, IRVINESTOWN ☎ 028 68621656 18 ⇋ ⋒

NEWTOWNSTEWART
Map 01 C5

Newtownstewart 38 Golf Course Rd BT78 4HU
☎ 028 81661466 & 81662242 (pro shop Fax 028 81662506
Parkland course bisected by a stream. Deer and pheasant are present on the course.
18 holes, 5468mtrs, Par 70, SSS 69, Course record 65.
Club membership 700.
Visitors contact club secretary in advance.
Societies must contact secretary in advance.
Green Fees £12 per day (£17 weekends & bank holidays).
Designer Frank Pennick
Facilities ⊗ ⅷ ┗ by prior arrangement ⚑ ♀ ♨ ⌂ ⎋ ⌖ ♂ ⌘
Location 2m SW on B84

Hotel ★★★ 68% Trinity Hotel, 22-24 Strand Rd, DERRY CITY ☎ 028 71271271 40 ⇋ ⋒

OMAGH   Map 01 C5

Omagh 83a Dublin Rd BT78 1HQ
☎ 028 82243160 Fax 028 82241442
Undulating parkland course beside the River Drumnagh, with
the river coming into play on 4 of the holes.
18 holes, 5674mtrs, Par 71, SSS 70.
Club membership 850.
Visitors   play restricted Sat, no need to contact unless
                 large numbers.
Societies   must contact in advance.
Green Fees not confirmed.
Facilities   🛠 ♥ ♀ ☂
Location   On S outskirts of town

Hotel   ★★★ 68% Trinity Hotel, 22-24 Strand Rd,
                 DERRY CITY ☎ 028 71271271 40 ⇄ ♠

STRABANE   Map 01 C5

Strabane Ballycolman Rd ☎ 028 71382271 & 71382007
Testing parkland course with the River Mourne running
alongside and creating a water hazard.
18 holes, 5537mtrs, Par 69, SSS 69, Course record 62.
Club membership 650.
Visitors   by prior arrangement.
Societies   must telephone in advance.
Green Fees not confirmed.
Designer   Eddie Hackett/P Jones
Facilities   ⊗ by prior arrangement ℳ by prior arrangement
                 🛠 ♥ ☂
Hotel   ★★★ 68% Trinity Hotel, 22-24 Strand Rd,
                 DERRY CITY ☎ 028 71271271 40 ⇄ ♠

REPUBLIC OF IRELAND

CO CARLOW

BORRIS   Map 01 C3

Borris Deerpark ☎ 0503 73310 Fax 0503 73750
Testing parkland course with tree-lined fairways situated
within the McMorrough Kavanagh Estate at the foot of
Mount Leinster.
9 holes, 6120mtrs, Par 70, SSS 69, Course record 66.
Club membership 400.
Visitors   advisable to contact in advance, weekends very
                 restricted.
Societies   applications in writing.
Green Fees IR£12 per 18 holes.
Facilities   ⊗ ℳ 🛠 ♥ ♀ ☂ ♂
Hotel   ★★★★♨ Mount Juliet Hotel,
                 THOMASTOWN
                 ☎ 056 73000 32 ⇄ ♠ Annexe 27 ⇄ ♠

CARLOW   Map 01 C3

Carlow Deerpark ☎ 0503 31695 Fax 0503 40065
Created in 1922 to a design by Tom Simpson, this testing
and enjoyable course is set in a wild deer park, with
beautiful dry terrain and a varied character. With sandy

sub-soil, the course is playable all year round. There are
water hazards at the 2nd, 10th and 11th and only two par
5s, both offering genuine birdie opportunities.
18 holes, 5974mtrs, Par 70, SSS 69, Course record 62.
Club membership 1200.
Visitors   are welcome, although play is limited on
                 Tue and difficult on Sat & Sun. Must
                 contact in advance.
Societies   must book in advance.
Green Fees IR£28 (IR£34 weekends & bank holidays).
Cards   💳 💳
Prof   Andrew Gilbert
Designer   Tom Simpson
Facilities   ⊗ ℳ 🛠 ♥ ♀ ☂ 🏠 ☂ 🛒 ♂
Location   2m N of Carlow on N9

Hotel   ★★★ 72% Dolmen Hotel,
                 Kilkenny Rd, CARLOW
                 ☎ 0503 42002 40 ⇄ ♠ Annexe 12 ♠

TULLOW   Map 01 C3

Mount Wolseley Hotel, Golf & Country Club
☎ 0503 51674 Fax 0503 52123
A magnificent setting, a few hundred yards from the banks of
the river Slaney with its mature trees and lakes set against the
backdrop of the East Carlow and Wicklow mountains. There
are no easy holes, with wide landing areas the only
concession to demanding approach shots to almost every
green. There is water in play on eleven holes, with the
eleventh, an all water carry off the tee of 207 yards.
18 holes, 6300yds, Par 72, SSS 70, Course record 68.
Club membership 350.
Visitors   must contact in advance.
Societies   must contact in advance.
Green Fees IR£30 (IR£35 weekends).
Cards   💳 💳
Prof   Jimmy Bolger
Designer   Christy O'Connor
Facilities   ⊗ ℳ 🛠 ♥ ♀ ☂ 🏠 ☂ 🛒 ♥ 🛒 ♂
& Leisure   sauna, solarium, gymnasium.

Hotel   ★★★ 72% Dolmen Hotel,
                 Kilkenny Rd, CARLOW
                 ☎ 0503 42002 40 ⇄ ♠ Annexe 12 ♠

CO CAVAN

BALLYCONNELL   Map 01 C4

Slieve Russell Hotel Golf & Country Club
☎ 049 26444 & 26458 Fax 049 26474
An 18-hole course opened in 1992 and rapidly
establishing itself as one of the finest parkland courses in
the country. A 9-hole course was recently opened to
complement it. On the main course, the 2nd plays across
water while the 16th has water surrounding the green.
The course finishes with a 519 yard, Par 5 18th.
18 holes, 6650yds, Par 72, SSS 72, Course record 67.
Club membership 550.
Visitors   must book in advance for Saturdays.   ▶

Societies write or telephone in advance, not allowed Sat.
Green Fees not confirmed.
Cards ▭▭ ▭▭ ▭▭ ▭▭
Prof Liam McCool
Designer Paddy Merrigan
Facilities ⊗)∭ 🄻 🖳 ♀ ⚲ 🏠 ⛳ 🏌 🛒 ⚘ 🏌
& Leisure hard tennis courts, heated indoor swimming pool, squash, sauna, solarium, gymnasium, snooker and pool room.
Location 1.5m E of Ballyconnell

Hotel ★★★★ 63% Slieve Russell Hotel Golf and Country Club, BALLYCONNELL ☎ 049 9526 444 151 ⇆ 🏳

BELTURBET
Map 01 C4

Belturbet Erne Hill ☎ 049 9522287 & 9524044
Beautifully maintained parkland course with predominantly family membership and popular with summer visitors.
9 holes, 5480yds, Par 68, SSS 65, Course record 64.
Club membership 200.
Visitors must contact in advance.
Societies must contact secretary in advance.
Green Fees IR£10.
Designer Eddie Hackett
Facilities 🄻 🖳 ♀ ⚲ 🏌 ⚘ ⚘

Hotel ★★★★ 63% Slieve Russell Hotel Golf and Country Club, BALLYCONNELL ☎ 049 9526 444 151 ⇆ 🏳

BLACKLION
Map 01 C5

Blacklion Toam ☎ 072 53024
Parkland course established in 1962, with coppices of woodland and mature trees. The lake comes into play on two holes and there are some magnificent views of the lake, islands and surrounding hills. It has been described as one of the best maintained scenic inland courses in Ireland.
9 holes, 5614mtrs, Par 72, SSS 69.
Club membership 250.
Visitors groups of 8 or more must contact in advance on Thu or Sat. No societies Sun.
Societies must contact in advance.
Green Fees not confirmed.
Designer Eddie Hackett
Facilities 🄻 🖳 ♀ ⚲ ⚘
& Leisure fishing, snooker.

Hotel ★★★ 71% Sligo Park Hotel, Pearse Rd, SLIGO ☎ 071 60291 110 ⇆ 🏳

CAVAN
Map 01 C4

County Cavan Drumelis ☎ 049 31541 Fax 049 31541
Parkland course.
18 holes, 5519mtrs, Par 70, SSS 69, Course record 66.
Club membership 830.
Visitors welcome but restricted at weekends.
Societies contact for details.
Green Fees IR£14 (IR£17 weekends).
Prof Ciaran Carroll
Designer Eddie Hackett

Facilities ⊗)∭ 🄻 🖳 ♀ ⚲ 🏠 ⚘ 🏌
Location On Killeshandra rd

Hotel ★★★ 65% Kilmore Hotel, Dublin Rd, CAVAN ☎ 049 32288 39 ⇆ 🏳

VIRGINIA
Map 01 C4

Virginia ☎ 049 47235 & 48066
9 holes, 4139mtrs, Par 64, SSS 62, Course record 57.
Club membership 500.
Visitors may not play Thu & Sun.
Societies must apply in writing to secretary.
Green Fees not confirmed.
Facilities ⚲ 🏌 ⚘
& Leisure fishing.
Location By Lough Ramor

Hotel ★★★ 63% Conyngham Arms Hotel, SLANE ☎ 041 24155 16rm (15 ⇆ 🏳)

CO CLARE

CLONLARA
Map 01 B3

Clonlara Golf & Leisure
☎ 061 354141 Fax 061 354143
A 12-hole parkland course, Par 47, on the banks of the River Shannon with views of Clare Hills. Set in grounds of 63 acres surrounding the 17th century Landscape House, there is also a leisure complex for self-catering holidays.
12 holes, 5187mtrs, Par 71, SSS 69.
Club membership 100.
Visitors players only no accompanying persons.
Societies welcome subject to availability prior notice required.
Green Fees not confirmed.
Designer Noel Cassidy
Facilities 🄻 🖳 ♀ ⚲ 🏌 ⚘ ⚘
& Leisure hard tennis courts, fishing, sauna, games room, childrens play area.
Location 7m NE of Limerick

Hotel ★★★★ 71% Castletroy Park Hotel, Dublin Rd, LIMERICK ☎ 061 335566 107 ⇆ 🏳

ENNIS
Map 01 B3

Ennis Drumbiggle ☎ 065 6824074 Fax 065 6841848
On rolling hills, this immaculately manicured course presents an excellent challenge to both casual visitors and aspiring scratch golfers, with tree-lined fairways and well protected greens.
18 holes, 5338mtrs, Par 70, SSS 69, Course record 65.
Club membership 1000.
Visitors advisable to contact in advance, course available Mon-Sat at most times.
Societies apply in writing/telephone
Green Fees not confirmed.
Prof Martin Ward
Facilities ⊗)∭ 🄻 🖳 ♀ ⚲ 🏠 🏌 🛒 ⚘
Location Close to town, well signposted ▶

Hotel ★★★ 68% Temple Gate Hotel, The Square, ENNIS ☎ 065 6823300 74rm (34)

Woodstock Golf and Country Club Shanaway Rd
☎ 065 6829463 & 6842406 Fax 065 6820304
This parkland course stands on 155 acres of land andincludes 4 hole where water is a major hazard. The course ia playable all year and the sand based greens offer a consistent surface for putting
Woodstock Golf & Country Club: 18 holes, 5864mtrs, Par 71, SSS 71.
Club membership 250.
Visitors booking advisable at weekends.
Societies advisable to telephone in advance.
Green Fees IR£233 per round Mon-Fri (IR£28 weekends and bank holidays).
Cards
Designer Arthur Spring
Facilities
& Leisure heated indoor swimming pool, sauna, gymnasium.
Location Off N85

Hotel ★★★ 66% West County Hotel, Clare Rd, ENNIS ☎ 065 6823000 152

KILKEE Map 01 B3

Kilkee East End
☎ 065 9056209 & 9056977
Well established course on the cliffs of Kilkee Bay, with beautiful views. Spectacular cliff-top holes.
18 holes, 6500yds, Par 72, SSS 71, Course record 68.
Club membership 390.
Visitors must book in advance.
Societies apply in writing.
Green Fees IR£20 per round.
Cards
Designer Eddie Hackett
Facilities
& Leisure squash, sauna.

Hotel ★★ 64% Halpin's Hotel, Erin St, KILKEE ☎ 065 56032 12

Ocean Cove Golf & Leisure Hotel Kilkee Bay
☎ 065 9083111 Fax 065 9083123
A typical coastal course surrounded on two sides by the Atlantic Ocean and the sea can be seen from nearly every hole. A number of greens are situated in a spectacular position along the edge of the Clare Cliffs.
18 holes, 5265metres, Par 69, SSS 69.
Club membership 500.
Visitors must contact in advance, may not play competition days,
Societies apply in writing
Green Fees IR£20.
Cards
Prof Y
Facilities
& Leisure squash, gymnasium.

Hotel ★★★ 61% Ocean Cove Golf & Leisure Hotel, KILKEE ☎ 065 6823000 50

KILRUSH Map 01 B3

Kilrush Parknamoney ☎ 065 51138 Fax 065 52633
Parkland course that was extended to 18 holes in the summer of 1994.
18 holes, 5986yds, Par 70, SSS 70, Course record 68.
Club membership 425.
Visitors welcome, contact in advance.
Societies by prior arrangement.
Green Fees not confirmed.
Designer Arthur Spring
Facilities

Hotel ★★ 64% Halpin's Hotel, Erin St, KILKEE ☎ 065 56032 12

LAHINCH Map 01 B3

Lahinch ☎ 065 81003 Fax 065 81592
Originally designed by Tom Morris and later modified by Dr Alister MacKenzie, Lahinch has hosted every important Irish amateur fixture and the Home Internationals. The par five 5th - The Klondike - is played along a deep valley and over a huge dune; the par three 6th may be short, but calls for a blind shot over the ridge of a hill to a green hemmed in by hills on three sides.
Old Course: 18 holes, 6696yds, Par 72, SSS 73.
Castle Course: 18 holes, 5594yds, Par 70, SSS 70.
Club membership 1840.
Visitors must contact in advance.
Societies apply in writing
Green Fees not confirmed.
Cards
Prof R McCavery
Designer Alister MacKenzie
Facilities
Location 2m W of Ennisstymon on N67

Hotel ★★ 70% Sheedy's Restaurant & Hotel, LISDOONVARNA ☎ 065 74026 11

MILLTOWN MALBAY Map 01 B3

Spanish Point ☎ 065 7084198 & 7084219
A 9-hole links course with 3 elevated greens and 4 elevated tees. Overlooking Spanish Point beach.
9 holes, 4600mtrs, Par 64, SSS 63, Course record 59.
Club membership 250.
Visitors contact in advance. Not before 1pm Sun.
Societies apply in writing to the secretary.
Green Fees IR£12 per day (IR£15 weekends).
Facilities
Location 2m SW of Miltown Malbay, on N67

Hotel ★★★ 66% West County Hotel, Clare Rd, ENNIS ☎ 065 6823000 152

NEWMARKET-ON-FERGUS Map 01 B3

Dromoland Castle Golf & Country Club
☎ 061 368444 & 368144 Fax 061 363355/368498
Set in 200 acres of parkland, the course is enhanced by numerous trees and a lake. Three holes are played around the lake which is in front of the castle. ▶

18 holes, 6098yds, Par 71, SSS 72, Course record 67.
Club membership 500.

Visitors	must contact in advance.
Societies	contact in writing.
Green Fees	not confirmed.
Cards	[card symbols]
Prof	Philip Murphy
Designer	Wigginton
Facilities	[facility symbols]
& Leisure	hard tennis courts, fishing, sauna, solarium, gymnasium.
Location	2m N, on main Limerick/Galway rd

Hotel ★★★ 63% Clare Inn Golf and Leisure Hotel, NEWMARKET-ON-FERGUS
☎ 065 6823000 182 ⇥ 🏌

SCARRIFF
Map 01 B3

East Clare Bodyke ☎ 061 921322
Beside Lough Derg, East Clare was opened in June 1992 as a 9-hole course in 148 acre site with natural trees and water on well-drained land. An 18-hole championship course deigned by Arthur Spring is in preparation.
9 holes, 52yds, Par 70, SSS 70 or 32 holes.
Club membership 130.

Visitors	no restrictions unless there is a club competition or a society playing.
Societies	apply in writing, deposit required.
Green Fees	not confirmed.
Facilities	[facility symbols]

Hotel ★★★ 66% West County Hotel, Clare Rd, ENNIS ☎ 065 6823000 152 ⇥ 🏌

SHANNON AIRPORT
Map 01 B3

Shannon ☎ 061 471849 Fax 061 471507
Superb parkland course with tree-lined fairways, strategically placed bunkers, water hazards and excellent greens, offering a challenge to all levels of players - including the many famous golfers who have played here.
18 holes, 6874yds, Par 72, SSS 74, Course record 65.
Club membership 1000.

Visitors	must contact in advance & have handicap certificate. Restricted play at certain times.
Societies	must contact in writing.
Green Fees	IR£25 (IR£30 weekends & bank holidays).
Cards	[card symbols]
Prof	Artie Pyke
Designer	John Harris
Facilities	[facility symbols]
Location	2m from Shannon Airport

Hotel ★★★ 65% Fitzpatrick Bunratty Hotel, BUNRATTY ☎ 061 361177 115 ⇥ 🏌

AA Hotels that have special
arrangements with golf courses are listed at
the back of the guide

BANDON
Map 01 B2

Bandon Castlebernard ☎ 023 41111 Fax 023 44690
Lovely parkland course in pleasant rural surroundings.
18 holes, 5663mtrs, Par 70, SSS 69, Course record 66.
Club membership 900.

Visitors	welcome but may not play during club competitions. Must contact in advance.
Societies	must apply in writing or telephone well in advance.
Green Fees	IR£20 per day (IR£25 weekends & bank holidays).
Cards	[card symbols]
Prof	Paddy O'Boyle
Facilities	[facility symbols]
& Leisure	hard tennis courts.
Location	2.5km W

Hotel ★★★ 68% Inishannon House Hotel, INISHANNON
☎ 021 775121 12 ⇥ 🏌 Annexe 1 ⇥ 🏌

BANTRY
Map 01 B2

Bantry Bay Bantry Bay
☎ 027 50579 & 50583 Fax 027 50579
Designed by Christy O'Connor Jnr and extended in 1997 to 18 holes, this challenging and rewarding course is idyllically set at the head of Bantry Bay. Testing holes include the par 5 of 487mtrs and the little par 3 of 127mtrs where accuracy is all-important.
18 holes, 5910mtrs, Par 71, SSS 72, Course record 71.
Club membership 600.

Visitors	advance booking recommended. At weekends and bank holidays visitors between 11.30-1.30pm and 3-4.30pm. Catering Mar-Oct only.
Societies	must apply in writing.
Green Fees	not confirmed.
Designer	Christy O'Connor/Eddie Hackett
Facilities	[facility symbols]
Location	3km N of Bantry town on the N71 Glengarrif road

Hotel ★★★ 61% Westlodge Hotel, BANTRY
☎ 027 50360 90 ⇥ 🏌

BLARNEY
Map 01 B2

Muskerry Carrigrohane
☎ 021 385297 Fax 021 385297
An adventurous game is guaranteed at this course, with its wooded hillsides and the meandering Shournagh River coming into play at a number of holes. The 15th is a notable hole - not long, but very deep - and after that all you need to do to get back to the clubhouse is stay out of the water.
18 holes, 6327yds, Par 71, SSS 71.
Club membership 712.

Visitors	may not play Wed afternoon & Thu morning. Some limited opportunities at weekends after 3.30pm & members hour 12.30-1.30pm daily. Must contact in advance. ▶

Societies	must telephone in advance and then confirm in writing.
Green Fees	IR£22 (IR£25 weekends).
Prof	W M Lehane
Designer	Dr A McKenzie
Facilities	⊗ ⅲ 🄻 🕮 ♀ 🄰 🏠 ⫐ ⌀
Location	2.5m W of Blarney

Hotel	★★★ 70% Blarney Park Hotel, BLARNEY ☎ 021 385281 91 ⇌ ◗

CARRIGALINE
Map 01 B2

Fernhill Hotel & Golf Club
☎ 021 372226 Fax 021 371011
Parkland course.
18 holes, 5000mtrs, Par 69, SSS 68.
Club membership 150.

Visitors	available any time.
Societies	telephone in advance.
Green Fees	not confirmed.
Designer	M L Bowes
Facilities	⊗ ⅲ 🄻 🕮 ♀ 🄰 🏠 ⫐ 🛌 🐾 🏌 ⌀
& Leisure	hard tennis courts, heated indoor swimming pool, fishing, sauna, 3 hole academy.
Location	2m from Ringaskiddy

CASTLETOWNBERE
Map 01 A2

Berehaven Millcove ☎ 027 70700
Seaside links founded in 1902. Moderately difficult with four holes over water.
9 holes, 2398mtrs, Par 68, SSS 66, Course record 63.
Club membership 150.

Visitors	welcome. Please check for major events.
Societies	telephone in advance.
Green Fees	IR£12 per day.
Facilities	⊗ ⅲ 🄻 🕮 ♀ 🄰 ⫐ ⌀ 🏌
& Leisure	hard tennis courts, sauna, camping facilities on site.
Location	2m E on Glen Garriff Rd

Hotel	★★★🏊 74% Sea View Hotel, BALLYLICKEY ☎ 027 50073 & 50462 Fax 027 51555 17 ⇌ ◗

CHARLEVILLE
Map 01 B2

Charleville ☎ 063 81257 & 81515 Fax 063 81274
Wooded parkland course offering not too strenuous walking.
West Course: 18 holes, 6212yds, Par 71, SSS 69, Course record 65.
East Course: 9 holes, 6702yds, Par 72, SSS 72.
Club membership 1000.

Visitors	only prebooked at weekends.
Societies	contact in advance.
Green Fees	IR£18 per day (IR£20 weekends & bank holidays).
Cards	▬▬ ▬▬
Prof	David Keating
Designer	Eddie Connaughton
Facilities	⊗ ⅲ 🄻 🕮 ♀ 🄰 🏠 ⫐ 🐾 🏌 ⌀ 🏌
Location	2m W from town centre

Hotel	★★★🏊 Longueville House Hotel, MALLOW ☎ 022 47156 & 47306 Fax 022 47459 20 ⇌ ◗

CLONAKILTY
Map 01 B2

Dunmore Dunmore, Muckross ☎ 023 33352
A hilly, rocky 9-hole course overlooking the Atlantic.
9 holes, 4464yds, Par 64, SSS 61, Course record 57.
Club membership 250.

Visitors	must contact in advance, may not play weekends.
Societies	apply in writing.
Green Fees	not confirmed.
Designer	E Hackett
Facilities	⊗ ⅲ 🄻 🕮 ♀ 🄰 ⫐ 🛌 ⌀
Location	3.5m S of Clonakilty

Hotel	★★ 64% Courtmacsherry, COURTMACSHERRY ☎ 023 46198 12rm (9 ⇌1 ◗)

CORK
Map 01 B2

Cork Little Island ☎ 021 353451 Fax 021 353410
This championship-standard course is always kept in superb condition and is playable all year round. It has many memorable and distinctive features including holes at the water's edge and holes in a disused quarry.
18 holes, 5910mtrs, Par 72, SSS 70, Course record 67.
Club membership 750.

Visitors	may not play 12.30-2pm or on Thu (Ladies Day), and only after 2pm Sat & Sun.
Societies	must contact in advance.
Green Fees	IR£45 per day (IR£50 weekends).
Cards	▬▬ ▬▬ 🔄
Prof	Peter Hickey
Designer	Alister Mackenzie
Facilities	⊗ ⅲ 🄻 🕮 ♀ 🄰 🏠 ⫐ ⌀
Location	5m E, on N25

Hotel	★★★★ 69% Jurys Hotel, Western Rd, CORK ☎ 021 276622 185 ⇌ ◗

Fitzpatrick Silver Springs Tivoli
☎ 021 507533 & 505128
Five Par 4s and 4 Par3s make up this short 9-hole course. The 4th has a 189 metre drive with out of bounds on the righthand side. The 8th is the longest holes, with a 301 metre drive.
9 holes, 1786mtrs, Par 32, Course record 26.
Club membership 84.

▶

Visitors	no restrictions.
Societies	apply by telephone.
Green Fees	IR£6.
Cards	🖩 ▓ ▓
Prof	Freddy Twomey
Designer	Eddie Hackett
Facilities	⊗ ⫴ 🍴 ⭐ ♀ ⚲ ⛳ 🏌 ⚒
& Leisure	hard tennis courts, heated indoor swimming pool, squash, sauna, solarium, gymnasium.
Location	1m E of city centre off Tivoli bypass

Hotel   ★★★★ 65% Fitzpatrick Silver Springs Hotel, Tivoli, CORK ☎ 021 507533 109 ⇄ 🐾

Fota Island Carrigtwohill ☎ 021 883700 Fax 021 883713
Fota Island Golf Club is in the heart of the 780 acre island in Cork Harbour which is recognised as one of Ireland's most outstanding landscapes. The course is gently undulating parkland routed among mature woodlands with occasional views of the harbour. The overall design is very traditional, featuring pot bunkers and undulating putting surfaces. The 10th and 18th holes are narrow Par 5's that require great accuracy and shotmaking skills. Fota has hosted the Irish Club Professional Championship, the Irish PGA Championship and no fewer than three Irish Amateur Opens.
18 holes, 6500yds, Par 71, SSS 71, Course record 67.
Club membership 400.

Visitors	advisable to contact in advance. Metal spikes and blue jeans not permitted.
Societies	contact in advance.
Green Fees	IR£45 (IR£55 Fri & weekends)..
Cards	🖩 ▓ ▓ P
Prof	Kevin Morris
Designer	Jeff Hoves
Facilities	⊗ ⫴ 🍴 ⭐ ♀ ⚲ 🏠 ⛳ ✎ 🏌 ⚒ ⚓ ⛳
Location	Off N25 E of Cork City. Take exit for Cobh, course 500m on right

Hotel   ★★★ 66% Midleton Park, MIDLETON ☎ 021 631767 40 ⇄ 🐾

The Ted McCarthy Municipal Golf Course Blackrock
☎ 021 294280
Municipal course which stretches alongside the river estuary, with some holes across water.
18 holes, 4818mtrs, Par 67, SSS 66.
Club membership 380.

Visitors	please contact in advance, may not play mornings at weekends.
Societies	please telephone in advance.
Green Fees	not confirmed.
Designer	E Hackett
Facilities	⊗ ⫴ 🍴 ⭐ ♀ ⚲ 🏠 🏌 ⚒
Location	2m from city centre

Hotel   ★★★★ 65% Fitzpatrick Silver Springs Hotel, Tivoli, CORK ☎ 021 507533 109 ⇄ 🐾

DONERAILE   Map 01 B2

Doneraile ☎ 022 24137 & 23427 (sec)
Parkland.
9 holes, 5528yds, SSS 66.
Club membership 500.

Visitors	no restrictions
Societies	welcome.
Green Fees	not confirmed.
Facilities	🍴 ⭐ ♀ ⚲ ⚒
Location	Off T11

Hotel   ★★★ 63% Springfort Hall Hotel, MALLOW ☎ 022 21278 50 ⇄ 🐾

DOUGLAS   Map 01 B2

Douglas ☎ 021 895297
Level inland course overlooking the city of Cork. Suitable for golfers of all ages and abilities. The course is under re-development and the measurements/details given below may have changed.
18 holes, 5383mtrs, Par 70, SSS 68.
Club membership 810.

Visitors	advisable to play Mon & Wed-Fri, contact in advance.
Societies	must contact in writing, dates allocated early Feb.
Green Fees	not confirmed.
Prof	Gary Nicholson
Designer	Harry Vardon
Facilities	⚲ 🏠 🏌 ⚒

Hotel   ★★★★ 69% Jurys Hotel, Western Rd, CORK ☎ 021 276622 185 ⇄ 🐾

FERMOY   Map 01 B2

Fermoy Corrin Cross
☎ 025 32694 (office) & 31472 (shop) Fax 025 33072
Rather exposed heathland course, bisected by a road.
18 holes, 5596mtrs, Par 70, SSS 69.
Club membership 950.

Visitors	contact in advance, must telephone in advance for weekends bookings
Societies	advisable to write or telephone in advance.
Green Fees	not confirmed.
Prof	Brian Moriarty
Designer	John Harris

▶

437

Facilities ⊗ 🗦 🖳 ▭ ♀ ⚘ 🏠 ⚐ 🏌 ✐
Location 2m SW

Hotel ★★★⚤ Longueville House Hotel, MALLOW
🕿 022 47156 & 47306 Fax 022 47459 20 ⇆ 🐾

GLENGARRIFF   Map 01 B2

Glengarriff 🕿 027 63150 Fax 027 63575
Founded 1935.
9 holes, 2042mtrs, Par 66, SSS 62.
Club membership 300.
Visitors welcome, details not supplied
Societies apply to club.
Green Fees not confirmed.
Facilities 🖳 ▭ ♀ ⚘ ⚐ ✐
Location On N71

Hotel ★★★ 61% Westlodge Hotel, BANTRY
🕿 027 50360 90 ⇆ 🐾

KANTURK   Map 01 B2

Kanturk Fairhill 🕿 029 50534
Scenic parkland course set in the heart of the Duhallow
region with superb mountain views. It provides a good test of
skill for golfers of all standards, with tight fairways requiring
accurate driving and precise approach shots to small and
tricky greens.
18 holes, 6262yds, Par 72, SSS 70, Course record 70.
Club membership 320.
Visitors Ladies day Wed.
Societies apply in writing or telephone the Secretary.
Green Fees not confirmed.
Designer Richard Barry
Facilities 🖳 ▭ ♀ ⚘ ✐
Location 1m from Kanturk on Fairhill road, 2m off main
Mallow/Killarney road from Ballymacquirke
Cross

Guesthouse ◆◆◆◆◆ Assolas Country House, KANTURK
🕿 029 50015 6 ⇆ 🐾 Annexe 3 ⇆ 🐾

KINSALE   Map 01 B2

Kinsale Farrangalway
🕿 021 774722 Fax 021 773114
In addition to the existing 9-hole (Ringenane) course, a new
18-hole (Farrangalway) course was opened in 1994. Set in
unspoilt farmland and surrounded by peaceful rolling
countryside, it offers a stiff yet fair challenge to be enjoyed
by all standards of golfers. New putting green.
Farrangalway: 18 holes, 6609yds, Par 71, SSS 71, Course
record 70.
Ringenane: 9 holes, 5332yds, Par 70, SSS 68.
Club membership 780.
Visitors welcome but may not be able to play at
weekends. Contact in advance.
Societies apply in writing.
Green Fees IR£22 per 18 holes; IR£12 per 9 holes (IR£27
Fri & weekends).
Cards ▤ ▤
Prof Ger Broderick
Designer Jack Kenneally
Facilities ⊗ 🗦 🖳 ▭ ♀ ⚘ 🏠 ⚐ 🏌 ✐
Location On main Cork/Kinsale rd

Hotel ★★★ 68% Trident Hotel, Worlds End,
KINSALE 🕿 021 772301 58 ⇆ 🐾

Old Head 🕿 021 778444 Fax 021 778022
Opened for play in 1997 and designed by Ron Kirby and Joe
Carr, the Old Head course is spectacularly situated on a
promontory jutting out into the Atlantic. As well as bringing
the sea and cliffs into play, you have to contend with strong
prevailing winds - a fine test for all serious golfers.
18 holes, 6700yds, Par 72, SSS 73.
Club membership 150.

Visitors tee time must be booked in advance.
Societies pre booking necessary, rates for groups over 24.
Green Fees not confirmed.
Cards ▤ ▤ ▤ ▤
Designer R Kirby/J Carr/P Merrigan/E Hackett
Facilities ⊗ 🗦 🖳 ▭ ♀ ⚘ 🏠 ⚐ 🏌 ✐ ▯
Location From Cork city/airport, follow R600 to Kinsale,
then signed to golf course

Hotel ★★★ 73% Actons Hotel, Pier Rd, KINSALE
🕿 021 772135 76 ⇆ 🐾

LITTLE ISLAND   Map 01 B2

Harbour Point Clash Rd 🕿 021 353094 Fax 021 354408
A new championship-standard course in rolling countryside
on the banks of the River Lee at Cork's scenic harbour. A
distinctive and testing course for every standard of golfer.
18 holes, 5883metres, Par 72, SSS 71, Course record 71.
Visitors must contact in advance.
Societies telephone for bookings.
Green Fees not confirmed.
Prof Morgan O'Donovan
Designer Patrick Merrigan
Facilities ⊗ 🗦 🖳 ▭ ♀ ⚘ 🏠 ⚐ 🏌 ✐ ▯
Location 5m E of Cork, take Rosslare road E from Cork
city & exit at Little Island

Hotel ★★★★ 65% Fitzpatrick Silver Springs Hotel,
Tivoli, CORK 🕿 021 507533 109 ⇆ 🐾

MACROOM   Map 01 B2

Macroom Lackaduve 🕿 026 41072 Fax 026 41391
A particularly scenic parkland course located on undulating
ground along the banks of the River Sullane. Bunkers and
mature trees make a variable and testing course and the 12th
has a 50 yards carry over the river to the green.
18 holes, 5574mtrs, Par 72, SSS 70.
Club membership 600.

▶

Visitors	restricted some weekends, contact in advance.
Societies	apply in writing.
Green Fees	not confirmed.
Designer	Jack Kenneally
Facilities	⊗ ⑈ ⅃ ⌗ ♛ ♀ ♨ ↰ ⚐ ♐
Location	Through castle entrance in town square

Hotel ★★ 72% Castle Hotel, Main St, MACROOM ☎ 026 41074 42 ⇄ ⋔

Mallow
Map 01 B2

Mallow Ballyellis ☎ 022 21145 Fax 022 42501
Mallow Golf Club was first established in the late 1800's. A well wooded parkland course overlooking the Blackwater Valley, Mallow is straightforward, but no less a challenge for it. The front nine is by far the longer, but the back nine is demanding in its call for accuracy and the par 3 18th provides a tough finish.
18 holes, 5769metres, Par 72, SSS 71, Course record 67. Club membership 1400.

Visitors	must contact in advance.
Societies	apply in advance.
Green Fees	not confirmed.
Cards	▭▭ ▭▭
Prof	Sean Conway
Designer	D W Wishart
Facilities	⊗ ⑈ ⅃ ⌗ ♛ ♀ ♨ 🏠 ↰ ⚐ ♐
& Leisure	hard tennis courts, squash, sauna.
Location	1m E of Mallow town

Hotel ★★★💥 Longueville House Hotel, MALLOW ☎ 022 47156 & 47306 Fax 022 47459 20 ⇄ ⋔

Midleton
Map 01 C2

East Cork Gortacrue
☎ 021 631687 & 631273 Fax 021 613695
A well wooded course calling for accuracy of shots.
18 holes, 5491yds, Par 69, SSS 67, Course record 64. Club membership 640.

Visitors	may not play Sun mornings.
Societies	must telephone.
Green Fees	IR£15.
Prof	Don MacFarlane
Designer	E Hackett
Facilities	⊗ ⑈ ⅃ ⌗ ♛ ♀ ♨ 🏠 ↰ ⚐ ♐
Location	On the A626

Hotel ★★★ 66% Midleton Park, MIDLETON ☎ 021 631767 40 ⇄ ⋔

Mitchelstown
Map 01 B2

Mitchelstown Limerick Rd ☎ 025 27139
Attractive, gently undulating parkland course set in the Golden Vale, noted for the quality of the greens, the magnificent views of the Galtee Mountains and its friendly atmosphere. Ideal for golfers seeking tranquility and a golfing challenge.
18 holes, 5160mtrs, Par 67, SSS 68, Course record 65. Club membership 400.

Visitors	advisable to check in advance (information line 025 24231)
Societies	apply in writing or telephone.
Green Fees	not confirmed.
Designer	David Jones
Facilities	⅃ ♛ ♀ ♨ ↰ ♐
Location	0.75m on Limerick rd from Mitchelstown

Hotel ★★★💥 Longueville House Hotel, MALLOW ☎ 022 47156 & 47306 Fax 022 47459 20 ⇄ ⋔

Monkstown
Map 01 B2

Monkstown Parkgariffe, Monkstown
☎ 021 841376 Fax 021 841376
Undulating parkland course with five tough finishing holes.
18 holes, 5441mtrs, Par 70, SSS 68, Course record 66. Club membership 960.

Visitors	restricted weekends, must contact in advance.
Societies	apply in writing or telephone. Large groups (24+) should book before Xmas.
Green Fees	Mon-Thur: IR£25 (IR£30 Fri-Sun).
Prof	Batt Murphy
Facilities	⊗ ⑈ ⅃ ⌗ ♛ ♀ ♨ 🏠 ↰ ⚐ ♐ ♐
Location	0.5m SE of Monkstown village

Hotel ★★★★ 69% Jurys Hotel, Western Rd, CORK ☎ 021 276622 185 ⇄ ⋔

Ovens
Map 01 B2

Lee Valley Golf & Country Club Clashanure
☎ 021 7331721 Fax 021 7331695
An undulating test of all golfing abilities designed by Ryder Cup star Christy O'Connor Junior. Seven of the 18 holes have water and the unusual feature of two fairy forts which are over 300 years old - can they be blamed for errors on the testing Par 5 8th and 12th holes?! The 508yard, Par 5 8th is already regarded as one of the best holes in Ireland with its spectacular lake a feature from tee to green.
18 holes, 6434yds, Par 72, SSS 70, Course record 62. Club membership 400.

Visitors	telephone in advance. Avoid Sat/Sun before 11.15am.
Societies	telephone in advance.
Green Fees	Apr-Oct IR£32-IR£25; Nov-Mar IR£29-IR£20.
Cards	▭▭ ▭▭ ▭▭
Prof	John Savage
Designer	Christy O'Connor
Facilities	⊗ ⑈ ⅃ ⌗ ♛ ♀ ♨ 🏠 ↰ ⚐ 🛥 ♐ ♐
Location	8m from Cork on Cork/Killarney road N22

Hotel ★★ 64% Vienna Woods Hotel, Glanmire, CORK ☎ 021 821146 20 ⇄ ⋔

SKIBBEREEN   Map 01 B2

Skibbereen & West Carbery Licknavar
☎ 028 21227 Fax 028 22994
Slightly hilly course in scenic location.
18 holes, 6004yds, Par 71, SSS 69, Course record 67.
Club membership 640.
Visitors   advisable to contact in advance.
Societies   apply in writing or telephone.
Green Fees not confirmed.
Cards
Designer   Jack Kenneally
Facilities   ⊗ ⅃🏌 💺 🍴 ⏖ ⛳ 🛒 ♿ ✎
Location   1m W on Baltimore road

Hotel   ★★★ 61% Baltimore Harbour Resort Hotel &
                  Leisure Cntr, BALTIMORE
                  ☎ 028 20361 64 ⇄ 🛌

YOUGHAL   Map 01 C2

Youghal Knockaverry
☎ 024 92787 & 92861 Fax 024 92641
For many years the host of various Golfing Union
championships, Youghal offers a good test of golf and is
well maintained for year-round play. There are
panoramic views of Youghal Bay and the Blackwater
estuary.
18 holes, 5646mtrs, Par 70, SSS 69, Course record 67.
Club membership 827.
Visitors   may not play Wed (Ladies Day) and should
                  contact in advance for weekends.
Societies   must apply in writing a few months in
                  advance.
Green Fees IR£18 per round (IR£20 weekends).
Cards
Prof   Liam Burns
Designer   Cd. Harris
Facilities   ⊗ ⅏ ⅃🏌 💺 🍴 ⏖ 🏠 ⛳ 🛒 ✎
Location   Located on the N25 main road from
                  Rosslare, between Waterford and Cork City

Hotel   ★★ 66% Devonshire Arms Hotel and
                  Restaurant, Pearse Square, YOUGHAL
                  ☎ 024 92827 & 92018
                  Fax 024 92900 10 ⇄ 🛌

CO DONEGAL

BALLINTRA   Map 01 B5

Donegal Murvagh, Laghy
☎ 073 34054 Fax 073 34377
This massive links course was opened in 1973 and
provides a world-class facility in peaceful surroundings.
It is a very long course with some memorable holes,
including five par 5s, calling for some big hitting.
Donegal is the home club of former Curtis Cup captain,
Maire O'Donnell.
18 holes, 6243mtrs, Par 73, SSS 73, Course record 68.
Club membership 750.
Visitors   must contact in advance, limited availability
                  at weekends.

Societies   must contact in advance.
Green Fees not confirmed.
Prof   Leslie Robinson
Designer   Eddie Hackett
Facilities   ⊗ ⅏ ⅃🏌 💺 🍴 ⏖ 🏠 🛒 ♿ ✎
Location   6m S of Donegal on Ballyshannon road

Hotel   ★★★ 77% Sand House Hotel,
                  ROSSNOWLAGH ☎ 072 51777 46 ⇄ 🛌

BALLYBOFEY   Map 01 C5

Ballybofey & Stranorlar Stranorlar ☎ 074 31093
A most scenic course incorporating pleasant valleys backed
by mountains with three of its holes bordered by a lake.
There are three Par 3s on the first nine and two on the
second. The most difficult hole is the long uphill Par 4 16th.
The only Par 5 is the 7th.
18 holes, 5366mtrs, Par 68, SSS 68, Course record 64.
Club membership 450.
Visitors   may play on weekdays. Advisable to book in
                  advance
Green Fees not confirmed.
Facilities   🍴 ⏖
& Leisure   squash.
Location   0.25m from Stranorlar

Hotel   ★★★ 70% Kee's Hotel, Stranorlar,
                  BALLYBOFEY ☎ 074 31018 53 ⇄ 🛌

BALLYLIFFEN   Map 01 C6

Ballyliffin Clonmany ☎ 077 76119 Fax 077 76672
The Old course is a links course with rolling fairways,
surrounded by rolling hills and bounded on one side by the
ocean. Nick Faldo said 'This is the most natural golf links I
have ever played.' It has an old-fashioned charm with its
uniquely contoured fairways. The new 18-hole course, the
Glashedy (opened summer 1995), offers a modern (and
arguably 'fairer') championship test.
*Old Links: 18 holes, 6612yds, Par 71, SSS 72, Course record
66.*
*Glashedy Links: 18 holes, 6426yds, Par 72, SSS 71, Course
record 68.*
Club membership 1034.
Visitors   telephone in advance.
Societies   telephone in advance.
Green Fees not confirmed.
Cards
Designer   Tom Craddock/Pat Ruddy
Facilities   ⊗ ⅏ ⅃🏌 💺 🍴 ⏖ 🏠 ⛳ 🛒 ♿ ✎

Guesthouse ♦♦♦♦ Mount Royd Country Home,
                  CARRIGANS ☎ 074 40163 4 🛌

BUNCRANA   Map 01 C6

Buncrana Municipal Ballmacarry
☎ 077 62279
A 9-hole course with a very challenging Par-3 3rd with all
carry out of bounds on either side.
9 holes, 2125yds, Par 62, SSS 60, Course record 59.
Club membership 100.
Visitors   during open competitions only visitors with club
                  handicaps.

▶

Societies write in advance.
Green Fees not confirmed.
Facilities ♀ ☂ 📷
Guesthouse ♦♦♦ Mount Royd Country Home,
CARRIGANS ☎ 074 40163 4 ℝ

North West Lisfannon, Fahan
☎ 077 61027 & 61715 Fax 077 63284
A traditional-style links course on gently rolling sandy
terrain with some long par 4s. Good judgement is
required on the approaches and the course offers a
satisfying test coupled with undemanding walking.
18 holes, 5968yds, Par 70, SSS 70, Course record 64.
Club membership 580.
Visitors contact in advance for weekends. Wed -
Ladies Day
Societies telephone in advance.
Green Fees IR£15 (IR£20 weekends).
Prof Seamus McBriarty
Facilities ⊗ �🍴 ᒪ ☂ ♀ ⌱ 📷 ♣ ♂
Location 1m S of Buncanna

Guesthouse ♦♦♦♦ Mount Royd Country Home,
CARRIGANS ☎ 074 40163 4 ℝ

BUNDORAN   Map 01 B5

Bundoran ☎ 072 41302 Fax 072 42014
This popular course, acknowledged as one of the best in
the country, runs along the high cliffs above Bundoran
beach and has a difficult par of 70. Designed by Harry
Vardon, it offers a challenging game of golf in beautiful
surroundings and has been the venue for a number of
Irish golf championships.
18 holes, 5688mtrs, Par 70, SSS 70, Course record 66.
Club membership 700.
Visitors must contact in advance.
Societies must contact in advance.
Green Fees IR£18 per round (IR£22 weekends & bank
holidays).
Prof David T Robinson
Designer Harry Vardon
Facilities ᒪ ☂ ♀ ⌱ 📷 ⌀ ♂
Location Just off Main St, Bundoran on the
Sligo/Derry road, 22m N of Sligo

Hotel ★★★ 77% Sand House Hotel,
ROSSNOWLAGH ☎ 072 51777 46 ⊐ ℝ

CRUIT ISLAND   Map 01 B5

Cruit Island Kincasslagh ☎ 075 43296
A links course on a small island. It is perched along the cliffs
overlooking the Atlantic. The course is short but always
challenging as the wind blows 90% of the time. It is
crowned by a magnificent 6th hole which is played across a
cove to an island green. With the prevailing wind in your
face and the Atlantic waves crashing in front, it is not for the
fainthearted.
9 holes, 4833mtrs, Par 68, SSS 66, Course record 62.
Club membership 350.
Visitors restricted Sun & Thu mornings for Club
competitions.
Societies apply in writing to secretary.
Green Fees not confirmed.
Designer Michael Doherty

Facilities ᒪ ☂ ♀ ⌱
Location 8km N of Dungloe

Hotel ★★★ 65% Arnold's Hotel, DUNFANAGHY
☎ 074 36208 30 ⊐ ℝ

DUNFANAGHY   Map 01 C6

Dunfanaghy Kill ☎ 074 36335 Fax 074 36335
Overlooking Sheephaven Bay, the course has a flat central
area with three difficult streams to negotiate. At the Port-na-
Blagh end there are five marvellous holes, including one
across the beach, while at the Horn Head end, the last five
holes are a test for any golfer.
18 holes, 5066mtrs, Par 68, SSS 66, Course record 63.
Club membership 335.
Visitors must book in advance, time sheet in operation
all year.
Societies must telephone in advance.
Green Fees IR£14 (IR£17 weekends).
Designer Harry Vardon
Facilities ᒪ ☂ ♀ ⌱ 📷 ⍩ ♣ 🛒 ♂
Location On N56

Hotel ★★★ 65% Arnold's Hotel, DUNFANAGHY
☎ 074 36208 30 ⊐ ℝ

GREENCASTLE   Map 01 C6

Greencastle Moville ☎ 077 81013
A typical links course along the shores of Lough Foyle,
surrounded by rocky headlands and sandy beaches. In 1992
to celebrate its centenary, the club increased its size from 9 to
18 holes.
18 holes, 5118mtrs, Par 69, SSS 67.
Club membership 600.
Visitors no restrictions.
Societies telephone in advance.
Green Fees not confirmed.
Facilities ♀ ⌱

Hotel ★★★★ 64% Everglades Hotel, Prehen Rd,
LONDONDERRY ☎ 028 71346722 64 ⊐ ℝ

GWEEDORE   Map 01 B6

Gweedore Derrybeg ☎ 075 31140
This 9-hole links course provides plenty of challenge with
two subtle Par 3s and the Par 5 5th/14th at 556yards into the
prevailing west wind is a monster.
9 holes, 6201yds, Par 71, SSS 69.
Club membership 175.
Visitors golf club must be notified if large numbers wish
to play.
Societies apply in writing.
Green Fees not confirmed.
Cards ▭
Facilities ᒪ ☂ ♀ ⌱ ♂

LETTERKENNY   Map 01 C5

Letterkenny Barnhill ☎ 074 21150 Fax 074 21175
The fairways are wide and generous, but the rough, when
you find it, is short, tough and mean. The flat and untiring
terrain on the shores of Lough Swilly provides good holiday
golf. Many interesting holes include the intimidating 1st with

▶

its high tee through trees and the tricky dog-leg of the 2nd hole. The last 7 holes are on undulating ground, steep climb from 11th green to 12th tee.

18 holes, 6239yds, Par 70, SSS 71, Course record 65.
Club membership 700.

Visitors	preferred Mon-Fri, except Wed evenings after 5pm. Advisable to contact in advance for weekends and bank holidays.
Societies	apply by writing or telephone.
Green Fees	IR£12 (IR£15 weekends & bank holidays).
Designer	Eddie Hacket
Facilities	⊗ ⅢⅡ ⅃ℎ ⬛ 𝔵 ⚲ ➤ 𝑔
Location	2m from town on Rathmelton road

Hotel	★★★ 70% Kee's Hotel, Stranorlar, BALLYBOFEY ☎ 074 31018 53 ⇥ 🖊

MOVILLE   Map 01 C6

Redcastle Redcastle ☎ 077 82073 Fax 077 82214
A testing course enjoying a picturesque setting on the shores of Loch Foyle. The two challenging Par 3 holes should be approached with the necessary respect.

9 holes, 3076yds, Par 36.
Club membership 200.

Visitors	welcome except club times advisable to telephone.
Societies	enquiries welcome by telephone or in writing.
Green Fees	IR£10 per day (IR£14 weekends)..
Cards	💳 📇 📇 🏧
Facilities	⊗ ⅢⅡ ⅃ℎ ⬛ 𝔵 ⚲ ➤ 🚘 𝑔
& Leisure	hard tennis courts, heated indoor swimming pool, fishing, sauna, gymnasium.
Location	Main Londonderry/Moville road

NARIN   Map 01 B5

Narin & Portnoo ☎ 075 45107 Fax 075 45107
Seaside links with every hole presenting its own special feature. The Par 4 5th, for instance, demands a perfectly placed drive to get a narrow sight of the narrow entrance to the elevated green. Cross winds from the sea can make some of the Par 4s difficult to reach with two woods.

18 holes, 5322mtrs, Par 69, SSS 68, Course record 63.
Club membership 550.

Visitors	contact in advance for weekend tee times.
Societies	telephone in advance.
Green Fees	IR£17 per day (IR£20 weekends & bank holidays).
Facilities	⊗ ⅃ℎ ⬛ 𝔵 ⚲ ➤ 𝑔
Location	6m from Ardara

Hotel	★★★ 63% Abbey Hotel, The Diamond, DONEGAL ☎ 073 21014 49 ⇥ 🖊

PORTSALON   Map 01 C6

Portsalon ☎ 074 59459 Fax 074 59459
Another course blessed by nature. The golden beaches of Ballymastocker Bay lie at one end, while the beauty of Lough Swilly and the Inishowen Peninsula beyond is a distracting but pleasant feature to the west. Situated on the Fanad Peninsula, this lovely links course provides untiring holiday golf at its best.

18 holes, 5880yds, Par 69, SSS 68.
Club membership 400.

Visitors	telephone in advance.
Societies	telephone in advance.
Green Fees	IR£17 per round (IR£20 weekends & bank holidays).
Facilities	⊗ ⅃ℎ ⬛ 𝔵 ⚲ ➤ 🚘 𝑔
Location	20m N of Letterkenny

Hotel	★★★ 71% Fort Royal Hotel, Fort Royal, RATHMULLAN ☎ 074 58100 11 ⇥ 🖊 Annexe 4 ⇥

RATHMULLAN   Map 01 C6

Otway Saltpans ☎ 074 58319
9 holes, 4234yds, Par 64, SSS 60, Course record 60.
Club membership 92.

Visitors	welcome.
Societies	contact for details.
Green Fees	not confirmed.
Facilities	𝔵 ⚲
Location	W shore of Loch Swilly

Hotel	★ 59% Pier Hotel, RATHMULLAN ☎ 074 58178 & 58115 Fax 074 58115 10 ⇥ 🖊

ROSAPENNA   Map 01 C6

Rosapenna Downings ☎ 074 55301 Fax 074 55128
Dramatic links course offering a challenging round. Originally designed by Tom Morris and later modified by James Braid and Harry Vardon, it includes such features as bunkers in mid fairway. The best part of the links runs in the low valley along the ocean.

18 holes, 6271yds, Par 70, SSS 71.
Club membership 200.

Visitors	no restrictions.
Societies	must contact in advance.
Green Fees	IR£22 per round (IR£27 weekends).
Cards	💳 📇 📇 🏧
Designer	Old Tom Morris
Facilities	Ⅲ ⅃ℎ 𝔵 ⚲ ➤ 🚘 ➤ 𝑔 ⏏
& Leisure	hard tennis courts, heated indoor swimming pool, gymnasium.
Hotel	★★★ 65% Arnold's Hotel, DUNFANAGHY ☎ 074 36208 30 ⇥ 🖊

CO DUBLIN

BALBRIGGAN   Map 01 D4

Balbriggan Blackhall ☎ 01 8412229 Fax 01 8413927
A parkland course with great variations and good views of the Mourne and Cooley mountains.

18 holes, 5922mtrs, Par 71, SSS 71.
Club membership 650.

Visitors	must contact in advance. With member only at weekends.
Societies	must apply in writing.
Green Fees	IR£10-IR£18.
Cards	💳 📇 📇
Designer	Paramoir
Facilities	⊗ ⅢⅡ ⅃ℎ ⬛ 𝔵 ⚲ ➤ 🚘 𝑔
Location	1km S off Balbriggan on N1

▶

| Hotel | ★★★ 61% Boyne Valley Hotel & Country Club, Stameen, Dublin Rd, DROGHEDA ☎ 041 9837737 35 ⇆ 📞 |

BALLYBOUGHAL   Map 01 D4

Hollywood Lakes
☎ 01 8433406 & 8433407 Fax 01 8433002
A parkland course opened in 1992 with large USGA-type, sand-based greens and tees. There are water features on seven holes. The front nine requires accuracy while the second nine includes a 636yard Par 5.
18 holes, 6246mtrs, Par 72, SSS 72, Course record 67.
Club membership 450.

Visitors	welcome Mon-Fri but may only play weekends from 1pm.
Societies	telephone then write in advance.
Green Fees	IR£19 per round (IR£24 weekends).
Cards	▭ ▬ 🔲
Designer	Mel Flanagan
Facilities	⊗ �🍴 🛏 🍺 ♀ � 🏠 ⚒ 🏌 ✏
Location	3m off main Dublin/Belfast road

| Hotel | ★★★ 70% Marine Hotel, Sutton Cross, DUBLIN 13 ☎ 01 8390000 52 ⇆ 📞 |

BRITTAS   Map 01 D4

Slade Valley Lynch Park
☎ 01 4582183 & 4582739 Fax 01 4582784
This is a course for a relaxing game, being fairly easy and in pleasant surroundings.
18 holes, 5388mtrs, Par 69, SSS 68, Course record 65.
Club membership 800.

Visitors	must contact in advance.
Societies	telephone in advance.
Green Fees	not confirmed.
Prof	John Dignam
Designer	W Sullivan & D O Brien
Facilities	⚒ 🏠 🏌 ✏
Location	9m SW of Dublin on N81

| Hotel | ★★★ 61% Downshire House Hotel, BLESSINGTON ☎ 045 865199 14 ⇆ 📞 Annexe 11 ⇆ 📞 |

CASTLEKNOCK   Map 01 D4

Elm Green ☎ 01 8200797 Fax 01 8226662
Located a short distance from Dublin, beside Phoenix Park, with a fine layout, tricky greens and year round playability.
18 holes, 5796yds, Par 71, SSS 66, Course record 65.
Club membership 400.

Visitors	must book in advance.
Societies	telephone in advance.
Green Fees	£13 per round (£19 weekends and bank holidays).
Cards	▭ ▬ ▭
Prof	Arnold O'Connor/Paul McGavan
Designer	Eddie Hackett
Facilities	⊗ 🛏 🍺 ♀ ⚒ 🏠 🏌 ✏
& Leisure	pitch and putt course.
Location	Off Navan Rd, 15 mins from city centre

| Hotel | ★★★ 70% Finnstown Country House Hotel & Golf Course, Newcastle Rd, LUCAN ☎ 01 6280644 25 ⇆ 📞 Annexe 26 ⇆ 📞 |

Luttrellstown Castle Dublin15
☎ 01 8089988 Fax 01 8089989
Set in the grounds of the magnificent 560-acre Luttrellstown Castle estate, this championship course has retained the integrity of a mature and ancient parkland. It is renowned for the quality of its greens and the log-built Clubhouse which provides excellent facilities.
18 holes, 6032mtrs, Par 72, SSS 73, Course record 66.
Club membership 400.

Visitors	bookings made in advance only, no denims.
Societies	must phone in advance.
Green Fees	not confirmed.
Cards	▭ ▬ ▬ 🔲
Prof	Graham Campbell
Designer	N Bielenberg
Facilities	⊗ �🍴 🛏 🍺 ♀ ⚒ 🏠 🏌 ⚒ ⚒ 🏌 ✏ ⚒
& Leisure	hard tennis courts, heated outdoor swimming pool, fishing, clay shooting.
Location	Porterstown rd

| Hotel | ★★★ 70% Finnstown Country House Hotel & Golf Course, Newcastle Rd, LUCAN ☎ 01 6280644 25 ⇆ 📞 Annexe 26 ⇆ 📞 |

CLOGHRAN   Map 01 D4

Forrest Little ☎ 01 8401183
Testing parkland course.
18 holes, 5865mtrs, Par 70, SSS 70.

Visitors	preferred weekday mornings.
Green Fees	not confirmed.
Prof	Tony Judd
Facilities	♀ 🏠 🏌
Location	6m N of Dublin on N1

| Hotel | ★★★ 70% Marine Hotel, Sutton Cross, DUBLIN 13 ☎ 01 8390000 52 ⇆ 📞 |

DONABATE   Map 01 D4

Balcarrick Corballis
☎ 01 8436228 & 8436957 Fax 01 8436957
Splendid 18-hole parkland course located close to the sea. A strong prevailing wind often plays a big part on every hole. Many challenging holes, notably the 7th - nicknamed 'Amen Corner'.
18 holes, 6273mtrs, Par 73, SSS 71.
Club membership 750.

Visitors	must contact in advance.
Societies	telephone in advance.
Green Fees	not confirmed.
Prof	Stephen Rayfus
Designer	Barry Langan
Facilities	⊗ �🍴 🛏 🍺 ♀ ⚒ 🏠

| Hotel | ★★★ 66% Posthouse Dublin Airport, Dublin Airport, DUBLIN ☎ 01 8080500 249 ⇆ 📞 |

Corballis Public Corballis ☎ 01 8436583
Well maintained coastal course with excellent greens.
18 holes, 4971yds, Par 65, SSS 64.
Visitors   no restrictions.
Societies   apply in writing or telephone.
Green Fees not confirmed.
Facilities   🏖🏌🏡🍴⛳🏌

Hotel   ★★★ 66% Posthouse Dublin Airport, Dublin
                 Airport, DUBLIN
                 ☎ 01 8080500 249 ⇉ 🐾

Donabate Balcarrick ☎ 01 8436346 & 8436001
Level parkland course.
18 holes, 5704yds, Par 70, SSS 69, Course record 67.
Club membership 900.
Visitors   welcome, weekdays & late Sunday afternoon.
Societies   must apply in writing.
Green Fees not confirmed.
Prof   Hugh Jackson
Facilities   ⊗🏌🏖🍴🏌🏡⛳🏌

Hotel   ★★★ 66% Posthouse Dublin Airport, Dublin
                 Airport, DUBLIN
                 ☎ 01 8080500 249 ⇉ 🐾

The Island Corballis
   ☎ 01 8436104 & 8436205 Fax 01 8436860
Links course on a promontory, with sea inlets separating
some of the fairways. Accuracy as well as length of shots
are required on some holes and sand hills provide an
additional challenge.
18 holes, 6078mtrs, Par 71, SSS 72, Course record 67.
Club membership 800.

Visitors   must contact in advance. Preferred on Mon,
                 Tue & Fri limited availability on all other
                 days. Telephone for appointment.
Societies   must apply in advance.
Green Fees May-Oct: IR£60 per round (£70 weekends)
                 Nov-Apr: IR£50 per round (IR£60
                 weekends).
Cards   ⚏ ▦
Prof   Kevin Kelliher
Designer   Hackett/Hawtree
Facilities   ⊗🏌🏖🍴🏌🏡⛳🏌
Location   Take main Dublin/Belfast road N1, pass
                 airport, take turn for Donabate/Portrane,
                 follow signs

Hotel   ★★★ 66% Posthouse Dublin Airport,
                 Dublin Airport, DUBLIN
                 ☎ 01 8080500 249 ⇉ 🐾

DUBLIN   Map 01 D4

Carrickmines Carrickmines ☎ 01 2955972
Meadowland course.
9 holes, 6100yds, Par 71, SSS 69.
Club membership 500.
Visitors   may not play Wed or Sat.
Societies   contact for details.
Green Fees IR£20 per 18 holes; IR£10 per 9 holes
                 (IR£23/IR£11.50 Sun & bank holidays).
Facilities   🏖🍴🏌🏡🏌
Location   7m S of Dublin

Hotel   ★★★ 65% Royal Marine Hotel, Marine Rd,
                 DUN LAOGHAIRE ☎ 01 2801911 103 ⇉ 🐾

Castle Woodside Dr, Rathfarnham
   ☎ 01 4904207 Fax 01 4920264
A tight, tree-lined parkland course which is very highly
regarded by all who play there.
18 holes, 5732mtrs, Par 70, SSS 70, Course record 63.
Club membership 1200.
Visitors   welcome but may not play at weekends & bank
                 holidays.
Societies   must apply in writing 6 months in advance.
Green Fees not confirmed.
Prof   David Kinsella
Designer   Barcroft-Pickman & Hood
Facilities   ⊗🏌🏖🍴🏌🏡⛳🏌
Location   Off Dodder Park Road

Hotel   ★★★★ 72% Jurys Hotel Dublin, Pembroke
                 Rd, Ballsbridge, DUBLIN 4
                 ☎ 01 6605000 294 ⇉ 🐾

Clontarf Donnycarney House, Malahide Rd
   ☎ 01 8331892 Fax 01 8331933
The nearest golf course to Dublin city, with a historic
building as a clubhouse, Clontarf is a parkland type course
bordered on one side by a railway line. There are several
testing and challenging holes including the 12th, which
involves playing over a pond and a quarry.
18 holes, 5317mtrs, Par 69, SSS 68, Course record 64.
Club membership 1100.
Visitors   welcome daily but must contact in advance.
Societies   Tue & Fri. Must contact in advance.
Green Fees IR£26 per round (IR£35 weekends).
Prof   Joe Craddock
Designer   Harry Colt
Facilities   ⊗🏌🏖🍴🏌🏡⛳🏌
Location   2.5m N via Fairview

Hotel   ★★★ 67% Jurys Skylon Hotel, Drumcondra
                 Rd, DUBLIN 9 ☎ 01 8379121 92 ⇉ 🐾

Corrstown Corrstown, Kilsallaghan
   ☎ 01 8640533 & 8640534 Fax 01 8640537
The 18 hole course has a small river meandering through,
coming into play at several holes culminating in a
challenging Island green finish. Orchard course has mature
trees and rolling pastureland offering golfers a relaxing
enjoyable game.
*River Course: 18 holes, 6077mtrs, Par 72, SSS 71, Course
record 69.*
Orchard Course: 9 holes, 5584mtre, Par 70, SSS 69.
Club membership 1050.

▶

Visitors	advisable to contact in advance. May play weekends after 1pm on River Course. Visitors welcome anytime on Orchard Course.
Societies	telephone or write in advance.
Green Fees	River: IR£20 per round; IR£10 per 9 holes (IR£25/IR£13 weekends).
Cards	💳 💳
Prof	Pat Gittens
Designer	Eddie Connaughton
Facilities	⊗ ⊩ ⓛ 🖳 ♀ 📥 🛍 ⛳ 🏌 🚬 ♂
Location	10 minutes W of Dublin Airport via St Margarets

Hotel	★★★ 67% Jurys Skylon Hotel, Drumcondra Rd, DUBLIN 9 ☎ 01 8379121 92 🛏 🎿

Deer Park Hotel & Golf Course Howth D13
☎ 01 8322624 Fax 01 8392405
Claiming to be Irelands largest golf/hotel complex, be warned that its popularity makes it quite busy at times and only hotel residents can book tee-off times.
St Fintans: 9 holes, 3373yds, Par 37.
Deer Park: 18 holes, 6830yds, Par 72.
Grace O'Malley: 9 holes, 3130yds, Par 35.
Short Course: 12 holes, 1810yds, Par 36.
Club membership 350.

Visitors	no restrictions. There may be delays especially Sun mornings.
Societies	must contact by telephone.
Green Fees	IR£11.50 per 18 holes (IR£13.50 weekends).
Cards	💳 💳 💳 💳
Designer	Fred Hawtree
Facilities	⊗ ⊩ ⓛ 🖳 ♀ 📥 🛍 ⛳ 🏌 ♂
& Leisure	hard tennis courts, heated indoor swimming pool, sauna.
Location	On right 0.5m before Howth Harbour

Hotel	★★★ 70% Marine Hotel, Sutton Cross, DUBLIN 13 ☎ 01 8390000 52 🛏 🎿

Edmonstown Edmondstown Rd, Edmondstown
☎ 01 4931082 Fax 01 4933152
A popular and testing parkland course situated at the foot of the Dublin Mountains in the suburbs of the city. An attractive stream flows in front of the 4th and 6th greens calling for an accurate approach shot.
18 holes, 5393mtrs, Par 70, SSS 70.
Club membership 750.

Visitors	must contact in advance as there are daily times reserved for members. Limited times after 3.30pm weekends.
Societies	must contact in advance.

Green Fees	Apr-Sep: IR£30 per round (IR£35 weekends & bank holidays) Oct-Mar: IR£25 (IR£30 weekends & bank holidays).
Cards	💳 💳
Prof	Andrew Crofton
Designer	McAllister
Facilities	⊗ ⊩ ⓛ 🖳 ♀ 📥 🛍 ⛳ 🏌 🚬 ♂

Hotel	★★★ 68% Jurys Montrose Hotel, Stillorgan Rd, DUBLIN ☎ 01 2693311 179 🛏 🎿

Elm Park Golf & Sports Club Nutley House, Nutley Ln, Dennybrook ☎ 01 2693438 Fax 01 2694505
Interesting parkland course requiring a degree of accuracy, particularly as half of the holes involve crossing the stream.
18 holes, 5355mtrs, Par 69, SSS 68, Course record 64.
Club membership 1750.

Visitors	must contact in advance.
Societies	apply in advance.
Green Fees	not confirmed.
Prof	Seamus Green
Facilities	⊗ ⊩ ⓛ 🖳 ♀ 📥 🛍 ⛳ 🏌 ♂
& Leisure	hard and grass tennis courts.
Location	3m from city centre

Hotel	★★★★ 72% Jurys Hotel Dublin, Pembroke Rd, Ballsbridge, DUBLIN 4 ☎ 01 6605000 294 🛏 🎿

Foxrock Torquay Rd, Foxrock ☎ 01 2895668 & 2893992
A well-treed parkland course.
9 holes, 5667mtrs, Par 70, SSS 69.
Club membership 650.

Visitors	welcome but contact in advance, no green fees Tue & weekends.
Societies	apply in writing to William Daly.
Green Fees	not confirmed.
Prof	David Walker
Facilities	♀ 📥 🛍 🏌

Hotel	★★★ 65% Royal Marine Hotel, Marine Rd, DUN LAOGHAIRE ☎ 01 2801911 103 🛏 🎿

Grange Rathfarnham ☎ 01 4932889
Wooded parkland course which provides both interest and challenge.
18 holes, 5517mtrs, Par 68, SSS 69.

Visitors	preferred on weekdays.
Green Fees	not confirmed.
Prof	W Sullivan
Facilities	♀ 📥
Location	6m from city centre

Hotel	★★★ 68% Jurys Montrose Hotel, Stillorgan Rd, DUBLIN ☎ 01 2693311 179 🛏 🎿

Howth St Fintan's, Carrickbrack Rd, Sutton
☎ 01 8323055 Fax 01 8321793
A heathland course with scenic views of Dublin Bay. It is very hilly and presents a good challenge to the novice or expert golfer.
18 holes, 5618mtrs, Par 72, SSS 69.
Club membership 1200.

Visitors	contact in advance. May not play Wed and weekends.
Societies	must contact in advance.

▶

Green Fees not confirmed.
Prof John McGuirk
Designer James Braid
Facilities 🅱 💺 ⌨ ⛳ ♨ ⚐
Location 9m NE of City Centre, 2m from Sutton Cross, on Sutton side of Hill of Howth

Hotel ★★★ 70% Marine Hotel, Sutton Cross, DUBLIN 13 ☎ 01 8390000 52 ⇥ ♞

Milltown Lower Churchtown Rd
☎ 01 4976090 Fax 01 4976008
Level parkland course on the outskirts of the city.
18 holes, 5638mtrs, Par 71, SSS 69, Course record 64.
Club membership 1400.
Visitors must contact in advance but may not play weekends.
Societies apply in writing.
Green Fees IR£35 per round Mon-Fri.
Cards 🃏
Prof John Harnett
Designer Freddie Davis
Facilities ⊗ ⫟ 🅱 💺 ⌨ ⛳ ♨ 🏹 ⚐
Location Lower Churchtown Road, Dublin 14

Hotel ★★★★ 72% Jurys Hotel Dublin, Pembroke Rd, Ballsbridge, DUBLIN 4 ☎ 01 6605000 294 ⇥ ♞

Newlands Clondalkin 22 ☎ 01 4593157 & 4593498
Fax 01 4593498
Mature parkland course offering a testing game.
18 holes, 5714mtrs, Par 71, SSS 70.
Club membership 1000.
Visitors must contact in advance and may play Mon, Thu, Fri and Wed mornings only.
Societies must contact in writing.
Green Fees not confirmed.
Prof Karl O'Donnell
Designer James Braid
Facilities ⊗ ⫟ 🅱 💺 ⌨ ⛳ ♨ 🏹 ⚐

Hotel ★★★ 67% Jurys Green Isle Hotel, Naas Rd, DUBLIN 22 ☎ 01 4593406 90 ⇥ ♞

The Open Golf Centre Newton House, St Margaret's
☎ 01 8640324 Fax 01 8341400
A 27-hole Pay and Play parkland course that is testing for the low handicap golfer but not too intimidating for high handicapper.
Yellow & Red Course: 18 holes, 5973yds, Par 71, SSS 69, Course record 66.
Blue Course: 9 holes, 2479yds, Par 31.
Visitors no restrictions. Booking essential.
Societies telephone for booking form.
Green Fees not confirmed.
Cards 🃏
Prof Roger Yates
Designer M Hawtree
Facilities ⛳ ♨ 🏹 🎣 ⚐ ♟
Location Adjacent to Dublin airport

Hotel ★★★ 70% Marine Hotel, Sutton Cross, DUBLIN 13 ☎ 01 8390000 52 ⇥ ♞

Rathfarnham Newtown
☎ 01 4931201 & 4931561 Fax 01 4931561
Parkland course designed by John Jacobs in 1962.
9 holes, 5815mtrs, Par 71, SSS 70, Course record 69.
Club membership 680.

Visitors must contact in advance, by arrangement only.
Societies restricted to Mon, Wed & Fri.
Green Fees IR£22.50 per round (IR£28 Sun by arrangement)
Prof Brian O'Hara
Designer John Jacobs
Facilities ⊗ ⫟ by prior arrangement 🅱 💺 ⌨ ⛳ ♨ ⚐

Hotel ★★★★ 72% Jurys Hotel Dublin, Pembroke Rd, Ballsbridge, DUBLIN 4 ☎ 01 6605000 294 ⇥ ♞

Royal Dublin North Bull Island, Dollymount
☎ 01 8336346 Fax 01 8336504
A popular course with visitors, for its design subtleties, for the condition of the links and the friendly atmosphere. Founded in 1885, the club moved to its present site in 1889 and received its Royal designation in 1891. A notable former club professional was Christie O'Connor, who was appointed in 1959 and immediately made his name. Along with its many notable holes, Royal Dublin has a fine and testing finish. The 18th is a sharply dog-legged par 4, with out of bounds along the right-hand side. The decision to try the long carry over the 'garden' is one many visitors have regretted.
18 holes, 6030mtrs, Par 72, SSS 71, Course record 63.
Club membership 800.

Visitors must contact in advance & have handicap certificate. May not play Wed, Sat until 4pm summer.
Societies must book one year in advance.
Green Fees not confirmed.
Cards 🃏
Prof Leonard Owens
Designer H S Colt
Facilities ⊗ ⫟ 🅱 💺 ⌨ ⛳ ♨ 🏹 ⚐
Location 3.5m NE of city centre

Hotel ★★★ 69% Longfield's Hotel, Fitzwilliam St, DUBLIN 2 ☎ 01 6761367 24 ⇥ ♞

St Anne's North Bull Island, Dollymount
☎ 01 8336471
Links course, recently extended from 9 holes to 18.
18 holes, 5652mtrs, Par 70, SSS 69.
Club membership 500.
Visitors telephone for restrictions.
Societies must apply in writing.
Green Fees not confirmed.
Facilities 💺 ⛳ ♨ ⚐

Hotel ★★★ 69% Longfield's Hotel, Fitzwilliam St, DUBLIN 2 ☎ 01 6761367 24 🛏 📞

St Margaret's Golf & Country Club St Margaret's
☎ 01 8640400 Fax 01 8640289
A championship standard course which measures nearly 7,000 yards off the back tees, but flexible teeing offers a fairer challenge to the middle and high handicap golfer. The modern design makes wide use of water hazards and mounding. The Par 5 8th hole is set to become notorious - featuring lakes to the left and right of the tee and a third lake in front of the green. Ryder Cup player, Sam Torrance, has described the 18th as 'possibly the strongest and most exciting in the world'.
18 holes, 6917yds, Par 73, SSS 73, Course record 69.
Club membership 200.

Visitors	telephone in advance.
Societies	apply in writing or telephone
Green Fees	IR£45 per round.
Cards	💳 💳 💳 💳
Designer	Craddock/Ruddy
Facilities	⊗ 🍴 🛍 💪 🍵 🏌 🏠 🚗 🛺 ⛳
Location	9m NW of city centre

Hotel ★★★ 70% Marine Hotel, Sutton Cross, DUBLIN 13 ☎ 01 8390000 52 🛏 📞

Stackstown Kellystown Rd, Rathfarnham
☎ 01 4942338 & 4941993 Fax 01 4933934
Pleasant course in scenic surroundings.
18 holes, 5925mtrs, Par 72, SSS 72, Course record 68.
Club membership 1042.

Visitors	preferred Mon-Fri.
Societies	telephone in advance and confirm in writing.
Green Fees	IR£16 per round (IR£20 weekend and bank holidays).
Prof	Michael Kavanach
Facilities & Leisure	⊗ 🛍 💪 🍵 🏠 🛺 ⛳ sauna, snooker.
Location	9m S of city centre

Hotel ★★★ 68% Jurys Montrose Hotel, Stillorgan Rd, DUBLIN ☎ 01 2693311 179 🛏 📞

> Entries with a green background identify courses considered to be particularly interesting

DUN LAOGHAIRE Map 01 D4

Dun Laoghaire Eglinton Park, Tivoli Rd
☎ 01 2803916 Fax 01 2804868
This is a well wooded parkland course, not long, but requiring accurate club selection and placing of shots. The course was designed by Harry Colt in 1918.
18 holes, 5298mtrs, Par 69, SSS 68, Course record 63.
Club membership 1040.

Visitors	may not play Sat until after 5pm. Must contact in advance.
Societies	must apply in writing.
Green Fees	not confirmed.
Prof	Owen Mulhall
Designer	Harry Colt
Facilities	⊗ 🍴 🛍 💪 🍵 🏠 🛺 ⛳
Location	0.75m from town ventre and ferry port

Hotel ★★★ 65% Royal Marine Hotel, Marine Rd, DUN LAOGHAIRE ☎ 01 2801911 103 🛏 📞

KILLINEY Map 01 D4

Killiney Ballinclea Rd
☎ 01 2852823 Fax 01 2852823
The course is on the side of Killiney Hill with picturesque views over south Dublin and the Wicklow Mountains.
9 holes, 5655mtrs, Par 70, SSS 70.
Club membership 450.

Visitors	welcome Mon, Wed, Fri & Sun afternoons.
Green Fees	not confirmed.
Prof	P O'Boyle
Facilities	🛍 💪 🍵 🏠 🛺 🚗 ⛳

Hotel ★★★ 64% Fitzpatrick Castle Hotel, KILLINEY ☎ 01 2840700 113 🛏 📞

KILTERNAN Map 01 D4

Kilternan Golf & Country Club Hotel
☎ 01 2955559 Fax 01 2955670
Interesting and testing course overlooking Dublin Bay.
18 holes, 4952mtrs, Par 68, SSS 66, Course record 66.
Club membership 819.

Visitors	may not play before 1.30pm at weekends. Contact in advance.
Societies	apply in writing/telephone in advance.
Green Fees	IR£18 per round (IR£22 weekends & bank holidays).
Cards	💳 💳 💳 💳

Prof Gary Hendley
Designer Eddie Hackett
Facilities ⊗ ⅏ ⅃ ⅌ ⅍ ⅎ ⅏ ⅌ ⅍ ⅎ ⅏
& Leisure hard tennis courts, heated indoor swimming pool, sauna, gymnasium.

Hotel ★★★ 64% Fitzpatrick Castle Hotel, KILLINEY ☎ 01 2840700 113 ⇌ ⍟

LUCAN   Map 01 D4

Finnstown Fairways Finnstwon Country House Hotel, Newcastle Rd ☎ 01 6280644 Fax 01 6281088
A flat parkland 9-hole course based in grounds originally laid out in the 18th century. Very challenging 6th and 7th holes among many mature trees.
9 holes, 2695yds, Par 66, SSS 66.
Visitors now operates as a pay & play course, all visitors welcome, numeric ticket system.
Societies must reserve in advance.
Green Fees not confirmed.
Cards ⚏ ▦ ▦ ▦ ▦
Prof Barry Power
Designer Robert Browne
Facilities ⊗ ⅏ ⅃ ⅌ ⅍ ⅎ ⅏ ⅌ ⅍ ⅎ ⅏
& Leisure hard and grass tennis courts, heated indoor swimming pool, solarium, gymnasium.
Location Off N4, 8 m W of Dublin

Hotel ★★★ 70% Finnstown Country House Hotel & Golf Course, Newcastle Rd, LUCAN ☎ 01 6280644 25 ⇌ ⍟ Annexe 26 ⇌ ⍟

Hermitage Ballydowd ☎ 01 6265049 & 6268491
Part level, part undulating course bordered by the River Liffey and offering some surprises.
18 holes, 6034mtrs, Par 71, SSS 70.
Club membership 1100.
Visitors contact for details.
Societies must telephone well in advance.
Green Fees not confirmed.
Cards ⚏ ▦
Prof Simon Byrne
Designer Eddie Hackett
Facilities ⅏ ⅃ ⅌ ⅍ ⅎ ⅏ ⅌ ⅍

Hotel ★★★ 70% Finnstown Country House Hotel & Golf Course, Newcastle Rd, LUCAN ☎ 01 6280644 25 ⇌ ⍟ Annexe 26 ⇌ ⍟

Lucan Celbridge Rd ☎ 01 6282106 Fax 01 6282929
Founded in 1897 as a nine hole course and extended to 18 holes in 1988, Lucan involves playing over a lane which bisects the 1st and 7th holes. The first nine is undulating while the back nine is flatter and features water hazards and a 538mtr 5 par 18th hole.
18 holes, 5958mtrs, Par 71, SSS 71.
Club membership 780.
Visitors may play Mon, Tue & Fri.
Societies must apply in writing.
Green Fees not confirmed.
Designer Eddie Hackett
Facilities ⊗ ⅏ ⅃ ⅌ ⅍ ⅎ ⅏ ⅌

Hotel ★★★ 64% Lucan Spa Hotel, LUCAN ☎ 01 6280495 & 6280497 Fax 01 6280841 71rm (61 ⇌ ⍟)

MALAHIDE   Map 01 D4

Malahide Beechwood, The Grange ☎ 01 8461611 Fax 01 8461270
Splendid parkland course with raised greens and water hazards affecting many of the holes, demanding accuracy from tee to green.
Main Course: 18 holes, 5742mtrs, Par 69, SSS 68.
Club membership 1100.

Visitors must contact in advance.
Societies must contact in advance.
Green Fees not confirmed.
Cards ⚏ ▦
Prof David Barton
Designer E Hackett
Facilities ⊗ ⅏ ⅃ ⅌ ⅍ ⅎ ⅏ ⅌ ⅍
Location 1m from coast road at Portmarnock

Hotel ★★★★ 77% Portmarnock Hotel & Golf Links, Strand Rd, PORTMARNOCK ☎ 01 8460611 103 ⇌ ⍟

PORTMARNOCK See page 449.

RATHCOOLE   Map 01 D4

Beech Park Johnstown ☎ 01 4580522 Fax 01 4588365
Relatively flat parkland with heavily wooded fairways. Famous for its 'Amen Corner' (holes 10-13).
18 holes, 5730mtrs, Par 72, SSS 70, Course record 67.
Club membership 955.

▶

Portmarnock

Portmarnock, *Co Dublin* ☎ 01 8462968   Fax 01 8462601   Map 01 D4

Championship Course

Visitors must contact in advance and confirm in writing. Restricted Saturday, Sunday and public holiday. Handicap certificate required

Societies must contact in advance in writing.

Green Fees IR£75 per round Mon-Fri ex weekend & public holidays. —

Facilities ⊗ ⍉ 🏌 ⛳ 🍴 🏌 ⚲ ⛳ 🏠 🏌 🏌 🛺 ◢ Professional (Joey Purcell)

Location 12m from Dublin, 1m from village down Golf Rd.

Holes/Par/Course record 27 holes Old Course: 18 holes, 7182yds, Par 72, SSS73 New Course: 9 holes , 3370yds, Par 37

WHERE TO STAY AND EAT NEARBY

Hotels
PORTMARNOCK

★★★★ ❀ ❀ 77% Portmarnock Hotel & Golf Links. ☎ 01 8460611

61% Halland Forge. ☎ 01825 840456. 103 🛏 🅿

niversally acknowledged as one of the truly great links courses, Portmarnock has hosted many great events from the British Amateur Championship of 1949 and the Canada Cup in 1960, to 12 stagings of the revived Irish Open. Founded in 1894, the championship course offers a classic challenge. Surrounded by water on three sides and laid out in a serpentine fashion, no two successive holes play in the same direction. Unlike many courses which play nine out and nine home, Portmarnock demands a continual discernment of wind direction.

The course has some extraordinary holes including the 14th, which Henry Cotton regarded as the best hole in golf; the 15th which Arnold Palmer regards as the best par-3 in the world, and the 5th regarded as the best on the course by the late Harry Bradshaw, 40 years Portmarnock's golf professional and runner-up to AD Locke in the 1949 British Open after playing his ball from an empty bottle of stout.

Visitors	may not play weekends, telephone in advance.
Societies	apply in writing.
Green Fees	IR£25 per round.
Designer	Eddie Hackett
Facilities	⊗ ⅃ ☕ ♟ ⚐ ♂

Hotel	★★★ 70% Finnstown Country House Hotel & Golf Course, Newcastle Rd, LUCAN ☎ 01 6280644 25 ⇆ ☞ Annexe 26 ⇆ ☞

RUSH
Map 01 D4

Rush ☎ 01 8438177 (Office) 8437548 (Clubhouse)
Fax 01 8438177
Seaside borders three fairways on this links course. There are 28 bunkers and undulating fairways to add to the challenge of the variable and strong winds that blow at all times and change with the tides. There are no easy holes!
9 holes, 5598mtrs, Par 70, SSS 69.
Club membership 350.

Visitors	restricted Wed, Thu, weekends & bank holidays.
Societies	apply in writing.
Green Fees	IR£18.
Facilities	⊗ ⅊ ⅃ ☕ ♟ ⚐ ♂

Hotel	★★★ 66% Posthouse Dublin Airport, Dublin Airport, DUBLIN ☎ 01 8080500 249 ⇆ ☞

SAGGART
Map 01 D4

City West Hotel & Golf Resort
☎ 01 4010500 & 4010900 (shop) Fax 01 4588565
18 holes, 6314yds, Par 70, SSS 70, Course record 65.

Visitors	time sheet in operation, telephone in advance.
Societies	apply in writing/telephone in advance.
Green Fees	IR£25 per 18 holes (IR£30 weekends).
Cards	🖻 🖻 🖻
Prof	Mac Gregor
Designer	Christy O'Connor Jnr
Facilities	⊗ ⅊ ⅃ ☕ ♟ ⚐ ♂ 🏌 ↯ ♂ ♦
& Leisure	heated indoor swimming pool, fishing, sauna, solarium, gymnasium.
Location	Naas road, southbound N7

Hotel	★★★ 65% Bewley's Hotel Newlands Cross, Newlands Cross, Naas Rd, DUBLIN 22 ☎ 01 464 0140 260 ⇆ ☞

SKERRIES
Map 01 D4

Skerries Hacketstown ☎ 01 8491567 Fax 01 8491591
Tree-lined parkland course on gently rolling countryside, with sea views from some holes. The 1st and 18th are particularly challenging. The club can be busy on some days, but is always friendly.
18 holes, 6081mtrs, Par 73, SSS 72.
Club membership 800.

Visitors	must contact in advance but may not play at weekends.
Societies	must contact well in advance in writing.
Green Fees	IR£25 per round.
Cards	🖻 🖻
Prof	Jimmy Kinsella
Facilities	♟ 🏠 ⚐ ♦ ♂
Location	E of Dublin-Belfast road

Hotel	★★★ 61% Boyne Valley Hotel & Country Club, Stameen, Dublin Rd, DROGHEDA ☎ 041 9837737 35 ⇆ ☞

SWORDS
Map 01 D4

Swords Open Golf Course Balheary Av, Swords
☎ 01 8409819 & 8901030 Fax 01 8409819
Parkland course situated beside the River Broadmeadow in unspoilt countryside, 10 miles from Dublin.
18 holes, 5677mtrs, Par 71, SSS 70, Course record 67.
Club membership 395.

Visitors	timesheet bookings available all year, telephone to book, may play at any time
Societies	telephone well in advance.
Green Fees	IR£10 per round (IR£13 weekends & bank holidays).
Designer	R Stillwell/T Halpin
Facilities	♟ ⚐ 🏌 ♂
Location	5 mins from Swords

Hotel	★★★ 67% Jurys Skylon Hotel, Drumcondra Rd, DUBLIN 9 ☎ 01 8379121 92 ⇆ ☞

TALLAGHT
Map 01 D4

Ballinascorney Ballinascorney
☎ 01 4516430 Fax 01 4598445
Set in the valley of Glenasmole, this very scenic course offers a variety of terrain, where every hole is different, many would be considered feature holes.
18 holes, 5466yds, Par 69, SSS 67, Course record 63.
Club membership 500.

Visitors	please contact in advance, welcome weekdays and weekends after 4pm.
Societies	contact for details.
Green Fees	not confirmed.
Cards	🖻
Designer	Eddie Hackett
Facilities	⅃ ☕ ♟ ⚐ 🏌 ♦ 🏹 ♂
& Leisure	hill walking, fishing.
Location	8m SW of Dublin city centre

Hotel	★★★ 67% Jurys Green Isle Hotel, Naas Rd, DUBLIN 22 ☎ 01 4593406 90 ⇆ ☞

> AA Hotels that have special arrangements with golf courses are listed at the back of the guide

CO GALWAY

BALLINASLOE
Map 01 B4

Ballinasloe Rosglos ☎ 0905 42126 Fax 0905 42538
Well maintained parkland course, recently extended from a
par 68 to a par 72.
18 holes, 5865mtrs, Par 72, SSS 70, Course record 69.
Club membership 884.

Visitors	preferably Mon-Sat, contact in advance.
Societies	contact in advance.
Green Fees	IR£15 per day; IR£10 per round.
Prof	Barry Flangan
Designer	E Hackett/E Connaughton
Facilities	♨ 🏠 🚡 🛒 (

Hotel ★★★ 72% Haydens Gateway Hotel,
BALLINASLOE ☎ 0905 42347 48 ⇄ ♠

BALLYCONNEELY
Map 01 A4

Connemara ☎ 095 23502 & 23602 Fax 095 23662
This championship links course is situated on the verge
of the Atlantic Ocean in a most spectacular setting, with
the Twelve Bens Mountains in the background.
Established as recently as 1973, it is a tough challenge,
due in no small part to its exposed location, with the
back 9 the equal of any in the world. The last six holes
are exceptionally long and offer a great challenge to
golfers of all abilities. Also 27 hole championship links.
18 holes, 6611mtrs, Par 72, SSS 75, Course record 67.
Club membership 970.

Visitors	advisable to book in advance.
Societies	telephone in advance.
Green Fees	May-Sep: IR£35; Oct & Apr IR£30; Jan-Mar & Nov-Dec IR£22.
Cards	🖃 🖼
Prof	Hugh O'Neill
Designer	Eddie Hackett
Facilities	⊗ ⥲ 🏚 💺 ♀ ♨ 🏠 ⚐ 🏌 🛢 ⟋ (
Location	9m SW of Clifden

Hotel ★★★ 76% Abbeyglen Castle Hotel, Sky
Rd, CLIFDEN ☎ 095 21201 36 ⇄ ♠

BEARNA
Map 01 B3

Bearna Golf and Country Club Corboley
☎ 091 5926771 Fax 091 592674
Set amid the beautiful landscape of the west of Ireland
and enjoying commanding views of Galway Bay, the
golf course covers more than 100 hectares of unique
countriside. This has resulted in generously proportioned
fairways, many elevated tees and some splendid carries.
Water comes into play at thirteen holes and the final four
holes provide a memorable finish.
18 holes, 5746mtrs, Par 72, SSS 72, Course record 68.
Club membership 500.

Visitors	must telephone in advance.
Societies	contact in advance.
Green Fees	IR£25 per round Mon-Thu (IR£30 Fri-Sun).
Cards	🖃 🖼 🖼
Designer	Robert J Brown
Facilities	⊗ ⥲ 🏚 💺 ♀ ♨ 🏠 ⚐ 🏌 🛢 ⟋

Hotel ★★★ 67% Galway Ryan Hotel,
Dublin Rd, GALWAY
☎ 091 753181 96 ⇄ ♠

GALWAY
Map 01 B4

Galway Blackrock, Salthill
☎ 091 522033 Fax 091 529783
Designed by Dr Alister MacKenzie, this course is inland
by nature, although some of the fairways run close to the
ocean. The terrain is of gently sloping hillocks with
plenty of trees and furze bushes to catch out the unwary.
Although not a long course, it provided a worthy
challenge as the venue of the Celtic International
Tournament in 1984 and continues to delight the visiting
golfer.
18 holes, 6376yds, Par 70, SSS 71, Course record 67.
Club membership 1050.

Visitors	preferred on weekdays, except Tue.
Societies	must apply in writing.
Green Fees	not confirmed.
Prof	Don Wallace
Facilities	⊗ ⥲ 🏚 💺 ♀ ♨ 🏠 ⚐ 🏌 🛢 ⟋
Location	2m W in Salthill

Hotel ★★★ 59% Lochlurgain Hotel, 22
Monksfield, Upper Salthill, GALWAY
☎ 091 529595 13 ⇄ ♠

Glenlo Abbey Bushypark ☎ 091 526666 Fax 091 527800
A parkland course overlooking the magnificent Lough Corrib
but only 10 minutes from the centre of Galway city. Nine
fairways but large double green with two flags and four tee
postions allows 18 diffent holes. The Par 3, 4th hole is on an
island-like green extending into the lough.
9 holes, 6009mtrs, Par 71, SSS 71.

Visitors	advisable to contact in advance at peak times.
Societies	telephone in advance.
Green Fees	not confirmed.
Cards	🖃 🖼 🖼 🄳
Prof	Gary Todd
Designer	Jeff Howes
Facilities	⊗ ⥲ 🏚 💺 ♀ ♨ ⚐ 🏌 🛢 ⟋ (
& Leisure	fishing, clay pigeon, shooting, lake boating.
Location	On N59 Galway/Clifden road 4km from Galway City Centre

Hotel ★★★★ 🏖 Glenlo Abbey Hotel, Bushypark,
GALWAY ☎ 091 526666 45 ⇄ ♠

GORT
Map 01 B3

Gort Kilmacduagh Rd, Castlequarter
☎ 091 632244 Fax 091 632387
Replacing the original 9-hole course, this new 18-hole
course, opened in June 1996, offers golfers a real challenge.
The 564yd 9th and the 516yd 17th are played into a
prevailing wind and the par 4 dog-leg 7th will test the best.
18 holes, 5705mtrs, Par 71, SSS 69.
Club membership 650.

Visitors	advisable to telephone in advance. Sun am reserved for members.
Societies	apply in writing or telephone.
Green Fees	IR£15 per day.

▶

451

Cards	
Designer	Christy O'Connor Jnr
Facilities	⊗ 🏌 📖 🍽 ♀ ⛳ 🏡 🏌 🛒 ⛳

Hotel	★★★ 67% Galway Ryan Hotel, Dublin Rd, GALWAY ☎ 091 753181 96 ⇌ 🐾

LOUGHREA   Map 01 B3

Loughrea Bullaun Rd, Graigue
☎ 091 841049 Fax 091 847472
An excellent parkland course with good greens and extended in 1992 to 18-holes. The course has an unusual feature in that it incorporates a historic souterrain (underground shelter/food store).
18 holes, 5261metres, Par 69, SSS 67, Course record 68.
Club membership 615.

Visitors	contact in advance, may not generally play Sun.
Societies	written application required. Anytime weekdays, 9-11.30 Sat, no play Sun.
Green Fees	not confirmed.
Designer	Eddie Hackett
Facilities	⊗ 🏌 📖 🍽 ♀ ⛳ ⛳

Hotel	★★★ 72% Haydens Gateway Hotel, BALLINASLOE ☎ 0905 42347 48 ⇌ 🐾

MOUNTBELLEW   Map 01 B4

Mountbellew Ballinasloe ☎ 0905 79259
A 9-hole wooded parkland course with 2 quarries and penalty drains to provide hazards.
9 holes, 5143mtrs, Par 69, SSS 66.
Club membership 400.

Visitors	welcome. Contact club if you wish to play at weekends.
Societies	by prior arrangement.
Green Fees	IR£10 per day.
Facilities	📖 🍽 ♀ ⛳ ⛳
Location	Of N63 midway between Roscommon/Galway

Hotel	★★★ 72% Haydens Gateway Hotel, BALLINASLOE ☎ 0905 42347 48 ⇌ 🐾

ORANMORE   Map 01 B3

Athenry Palmerstown ☎ 091 794466 Fax 091 794971
Wooded parkland course.
18 holes, 5552metres, Par 70, SSS 70, Course record 68.
Club membership 1000.

Visitors	advisable to telephone in advance, may not play Sun or Sat am.

Societies	must apply in writing.
Green Fees	IR£15 weekdays (IR£18 weekends except Sun).
Cards	
Prof	Raymond Ryan
Designer	Eddie Hackett
Facilities	⊗ 🏌 📖 🍽 ♀ ⛳ 🏡 🏌 🛒 ⛳
Location	On R582 to Athenry 10km E of Galway City

Hotel	★★★ 67% Galway Ryan Hotel, Dublin Rd, GALWAY ☎ 091 753181 96 ⇌ 🐾

Galway Bay Golf & Country Club Renville
☎ 091 790500 Fax 091 792510
A championship golf course surrounded on three sides by the Atlantic Ocean and featuring water hazards on a number of holes. Each hole has its own characteristics made more obvious by the everchanging seaside winds. The design of the course highlights and preserves the ancient historic features of the Renville Peninsula. A spectacular setting distractingly beautiful and cleverly designed mix of holes presents a real golfing challenge, demanding total concentration.
18 holes, 6091mtrs, Par 72, SSS 71.
Club membership 400.

Visitors	contact in advance.
Societies	contact in advance.
Green Fees	not confirmed.
Cards	
Prof	Eugene O'Connor
Designer	Christy O'Connor Jnr
Facilities & Leisure	⊗ 🏌 📖 🍽 ♀ ⛳ 🏡 🏌 🛒 ⛳ sauna.
Location	N18 S towards Limerick/Shannon, turn right for Oranmore at rdbt, through village, follow signs

Hotel	★★★ 69% Galway Bay Golf & Country Club Hotel, ORANMORE ☎ 091 790500 90 ⇌ 🐾

OUGHTERARD   Map 01 B4

Oughterard ☎ 091 552131 Fax 091 552377
Redesigned in 1998 to USPGA standard, incorporating natural woodland and water features.
18 holes, 6660yds, Par 70, SSS 69, Course record 67.
Club membership 1000.

Visitors	contact secretary or professional in advance.
Societies	must apply in writing.
Green Fees	IR£20 per day.
Cards	
Prof	Michael Ryan
Designer	P Merrigan
Facilities	⊗ 🏌 📖 🍽 ♀ ⛳ 🏡 🏌 🛒 ⛳
Location	1m from Oughterard on N59 from Galway

Hotel	★★★ 66% Ross Lake House Hotel, Rosscahill, OUGHTERARD ☎ 091 550109 & 550154 Fax 091 550184 13 ⇌ 🐾

PORTUMNA   Map 01 B3

Portumna ☎ 0509 41059
Parkland course with mature trees.
18 holes, 5474mtrs, Par 68, SSS 67, Course record 67.
Club membership 650.

Visitors restricted Sun & public holidays.
Societies must contact in writing.
Green Fees IR£15 per day.
Designer E Connaughton
Facilities ⊗ ⵏ ⌷ ⌷ ♌ ⌷ ⌷ ⌷ ⌷ ⌷
Location 2.5m from town on Woodford/Ennis road

Hotel ★★★ 60% County Arms Hotel, BIRR
☎ 0509 20791 24 ⇌ ⌤

RENVYLE   Map 01 A4

Renvyle House Hotel ☎ 095 43511
Pebble Beach course at Renvyle House is an exceptionally
demanding 9 hole course. Exposed to Atlantic winds,
crosswinds are a regular feature. A lake comes into play on 3
holes on one of which is a drive over water. On 4 holes
pebble beach and the sea demand precision.
9 holes, 2000yds, Par 32.
Visitors must contact in advance.
Societies contact in advance.
Green Fees not confirmed.
Prof Gus Murphy
Facilities ⊗ ⵏ ⌷ ⌷ ♌ ⌷ ⌷ ⌷
& Leisure hard tennis courts, heated outdoor swimming
pool, fishing.

Hotel ★★★ 66% Renvyle House Hotel, RENVYLE
☎ 095 4351165 ⇌ ⌤

TUAM   Map 01 B4

Tuam Barnacurragh ☎ 093 28993 Fax 093 26003
Parkland course with plenty of trees and bunkers.
18 holes, 5513mtrs, Par 72, SSS 69.
Club membership 800.
Visitors preferred Mon-Fri, must contact in advance. No
visitors weekends.
Societies telephone/write in advance.
Green Fees IR£15 per round.
Cards 💳 💳
Prof Larry Smyth
Designer Eddie Hackett
Facilities ⊗ ⵏ ⌷ ⌷ ♌ ⌷ ⌷ ⌷ ⌷ ⌷
Location 0.5m from town on Athenry road

Hotel ★★★ 67% Galway Ryan Hotel, Dublin Rd,
GALWAY ☎ 091 753181 96 ⇌ ⌤

CO KERRY

BALLYBUNION   Map 01 A3

BALLYBUNION See page 455.

BALLYFERRITER   Map 01 A2

Ceann Sibeal ☎ 066 9156255 Fax 066 9156409
This most westerly golf course in Europe has a magnificent
scenic location. It is a traditional links course with beautiful
turf, many bunkers, a stream that comes into play on 14 holes
and, usually, a prevailing wind.

18 holes, 6700yds, Par 72, SSS 71, Course record 72.
Club membership 432.
Visitors telephone in advance.
Societies must contact in advance.
Green Fees IR£35 per day; IR£25 per round.
Cards 💳 💳
Prof Dermot O'Connor
Designer Hackett/O'Connor Jnr
Facilities ⊗ ⵏ ⌷ ⌷ ♌ ⌷ ⌷ ⌷
Location 1.5m from Ballyferriter

Hotel ★★★ 72% Dingle Skellig Hotel, DINGLE
☎ 066 51144 115 ⇌ ⌤

CASTLEGREGORY   Map 01 A2

Castlegregory Stradbally ☎ 066 39444
A links course sandwiched between the sea and a freshwater
lake and mountains on two sides. The 3rd hole is visually
superb with a 365yard drive into the wind.
9 holes, 2569mtrs, Par 68, SSS 68, Course record 67.
Club membership 200.
Visitors advisable to contact in advance.
Societies apply in advance.
Green Fees not confirmed.
Cards 💳
Designer Dr Arthur Spring
Facilities ⌷ ⌷ ⌷ ⌷
& Leisure fishing.

Hotel ★★★ 67% The Brandon Hotel, TRALEE
☎ 066 7123333 185 ⇌ ⌤

GLENBEIGH   Map 01 A2

Dooks ☎ 066 9768205 Fax 066 9768476
Old-established course on the sea shore between the
Kerry mountains and Dingle Bay. Sand dunes are a
feature (the name Dooks is a derivation of the Gaelic
word for sand bank) and the course offers a fine
challenge in a superb Ring of Kerry location.
18 holes, 6010yds, Par 70, SSS 68.
Club membership 800.
Visitors must contact in advance. Members time
reserved.
Societies contact in advance.
Green Fees IR£25 per round; IR£35 per 36 holes.
Cards 💳 💳
Facilities ⊗ ⵏ ⌷ ⌷ ♌ ⌷ ⌷ ⌷ ⌷
Location On N70, between Killorglin and Glenbeigh

Hotel ★★★ 68% Gleneagle Hotel,
KILLARNEY ☎ 064 31870 213 ⇌ ⌤

KENMARE   Map 01 B2

Kenmare Kilgarvan Rd ☎ 064 41291 Fax 064 42061
Extended to a championship 18-hole course in 1993 this
challenging parkland course enjoys a magnificent setting
where the cascading waters of the Sheen and Roughty rivers
join the Atlantic. Although it can be exacting on a good
golfer, it is never unfair to the weak or the novice golfer.
18 holes, 5615yds, Par 71.
Club membership 400.
Visitors enquire for weekends.
Societies contact in advance.

▶

Green Fees not confirmed.
Designer Eddie Hackett
Facilities 🏌 🍴 🛒 🏧 🅿 ⛳ ✎

Hotel ★★★★♨ Park Hotel Kenmare, KENMARE
☎ 064 41200 49 ⇔ ♘

KILLARNEY   Map 01 B2

Beaufort Churchtown, Beaufort
☎ 064 44440 Fax 064 44752
A championship standard Par 71 parkland course designed
by Dr Arthur Spring. This relatively new course is in the
centre of south-west Ireland's golfing mecca. Old ruins of an
11th century castle dominate the back nine and the whole
course is overlooked by the MacGillycuddy Reeks. The Par 3
8th and Par 4 11th are two of the most memorable holes.
18 holes, 6587yds, Par 71, SSS 72.
Club membership 260.

Visitors booking advisable for weekends.
Societies advance booking essential.
Green Fees IR£27 per round, IR£10 additional round
(IR£35/IR£15 weekends).
Cards 💳 💳 💳
Prof Hugh Duggan
Designer Arthur Spring
Facilities ⊗ 🏢 🏌 🍴 🛒 🏧 🅿 ⛳ ✎
Location 7m W of Killarney, off N72 w

Hotel ★★★ 67% Castlerosse Hotel, KILLARNEY
☎ 064 31144 110 ⇔ ♘

Killarney Golf & Fishing Club Mahony's Point
☎ 064 31034 Fax 064 33065
The three courses are parkland with tree-lined fairways,
many bunkers and small lakes which provide no mean
challenge. Mahoney's Point Course has a particularly
testing par 5, 4, 3 finish and the courses call for great
skill from the tee. Killarney has been the venue for many
important events, including the 1996 Curtis Cup, and is a
favourite of many famous golfers.
*Mahony's Point: 18 holes, 5826mtrs, Par 72, SSS 72,
Course record 64.*
*Killeen: 18 holes, 6474mtrs, Par 72, SSS 73, Course
record 65.*
Lackabane: 18 holes, 6410mtrs, Par 72, SSS 72.
Club membership 1300.
Visitors must contact in advance & have a handicap
certificate.
Societies must telephone in advance.
Green Fees IR£43 per round.
Cards 💳 💳 💳 💳
Prof Tony Coveney

Designer H Longhurst/Sir Guy Campbell
Facilities ⊗ 🏢 🏌 🍴 🛒 🏧 🅿 ⛳ ✎ ♘
& Leisure sauna, gymnasium.
Location On N 72, Ring of Kerry road

Hotel ★★★★ 78% Aghadoe Heights Hotel,
KILLARNEY ☎ 064 31766 75 ⇔ ♘

KILLORGLIN   Map 01 A2

Killorglin Stealroe ☎ 066 9761979 Fax 066 9761437
A parkland course designed by Eddie Hackett as a challeng-
ing but fair test of golf, surrounded by magnificent views.
18 holes, 6497yds, Par 72, SSS 71, Course record 68.
Club membership 280.
Visitors pre booking of tee time advisable, must be
confirmed in writing. Deposit required.
Societies book by telephone, confirm in writing.
Green Fees IR£15 per round; IR£10 per 9 holes (IR£18
weekends).
Cards 💳 💳 💳 💳
Designer Eddie Hackett
Facilities ⊗ 🏢 🏌 🍴 🛒 🏧 🅿 ⛳ ✎
& Leisure fishing.
Location 3km from Killorglin, on N70 to Tralee

Hotel ★★★ 67% The Brandon Hotel, TRALEE
☎ 066 7123333 185 ⇔ ♘

PARKNASILLA   Map 01 A2

Parknasilla ☎ 064 45122 Fax 064 45323
Recently re-designed course with new tees and greens on
every hole. The view from the eighth tee is breathtaking with
the green on the edge of the sea while the ninth tee is almost
surrounded by water.
9 holes, 5400mtrs, Par 70, SSS 69.
Club membership 150.

Visitors may not play on competition days. Must contact
in advance.
Societies must contact in advance.
Green Fees not confirmed.
Cards 💳
Designer Arthur Spring
Facilities 🏧 🅿 ⛳ ✎
& Leisure hard tennis courts, heated indoor swimming
pool, sauna.
Location 2m E of Sneem village on Ring of Kerry road

Hotel ★★★★ 79% Great Southern Hotel,
PARKNASILLA
☎ 064 45122 26 ⇔ ♘ Annexe 59 ⇔ ♘

Ballybunion

Ballybunion, *Co Kerry* ☎ 068 27146   Fax 068 23787   Map 01 A3

ailed for its excellent links courses, Ballybunion is recognised for its fine development of the natural terrain. Mr Murphy built the Old Course in 1906. With large sand dunes and an Atlantic backdrop, Ballybunion offers the golfer an exciting round of golf in a scenic location but be warned, the Old Course is difficult to play in the wind. President Clinton played Ballybunion on his historic visit to Ireland in 1998.

Although overshadowed by the Old Course, the Cashen Course designed by Robert Trent Jones is also world class. Narrow fairways, small greens and large dunes characterise the course.

Visitors must contact in advance for reservations and details

Societies must contact in advance

Green Fees Old Course IR£60 per round — 🚻

Facilities ⊗ ⋙ 🍴 🥤 🍷 ⛱ 🏠 🚩 ♂

Location Sandhill Rd

Holes/Par/Course record 36 holes. Old Course: 18 holes, 6603 yds, Par 71, SSS 72, Course record 67
Cashen Course: 18 holes, 6216 yds, Par 72, SSS 72

WHERE TO STAY NEARBY

Hotels
BALLYHEIGE

★★★ ✿ 64% The White Sands
☎ 066 7133102. 81 🛏 🐾

TRALEE

★★★ 67% The Brandon
☎ 066 7123333. 185 🛏 🐾

★★★ 64% Abbey Gate, Maine St.
☎ 066 7129888. 100 (95 🛏 5 🐾

Championship Course

455

TRALEE
Map 01 A2

Tralee West Barrow ☎ 066 36379 Fax 066 36008
The first Arnold Palmer designed course in Europe, the
magnificent 18-hole links are set in spectacular scenery
on the Barrow peninsula surrounded on three sides by
the sea. Perhaps the most memorable hole is the par four
17th which plays from a high tee, across a deep gorge to
a green perched high against a backdrop of mountains.
The first 9 holes are relatively easy, but the back 9 are
very difficult and not suitable for beginners.
18 holes, 5939mtrs, Par 71, SSS 71, Course record 66.
Club membership 1182.

Visitors	may play before 4.20pm on weekdays but only between 7.30-10.30am on Wed & 11am-1.30pm on Sat & 11.30-1pm bank holidays. Must have a handicap certificate and contact in advance. May not play Sun.
Societies	weekdays only; must contact in writing.
Green Fees	IR£60 per round.
Cards	🗠 💳 💳
Prof	David Power
Designer	Arnold Palmer
Facilities	⊗ ℿ ⅃ 🍴 💺 ♀ 🏖 🛄 ✐
Location	8m NW of Tralee on Spa-Fenit road
Hotel	★★★ 67% The Brandon Hotel, TRALEE ☎ 066 7123333 185 ⇆ ⌀

WATERVILLE
Map 01 A2

Waterville House & Golf Links
☎ 066 9474102 Fax 066 9474482
On the western tip of the Ring of Kerry, this course is
highly regarded by many top golfers. The feature holes
are the par five 11th, which runs along a rugged valley
between towering dunes, and the par three 17th, which
features an exceptionally elevated tee. Needless to say,
the surroundings are beautiful.
18 holes, 6549yds, Par 72, SSS 72, Course record 71.

Visitors	must contact in advance.
Societies	must contact secretary/manager in advance.
Green Fees	not confirmed.
Prof	Liam Higgins
Designer	Eddie Hackett
Facilities & Leisure	⊗ ℿ ⅃ 🍴 💺 ♀ 🏖 🛄 🏊 🐾 🛄 ✐ heated outdoor swimming pool, fishing, sauna.
Hotel	★★★ 72% Butler Arms Hotel, WATERVILLE ☎ 066 74144 30 ⇆ ⌀

CO KILDARE

ATHY
Map 01 C3

Athy Geraldine ☎ 0507 31729
A meadowland course approaching its centenary year having
been founded in 1906.
18 holes, 6159yds, Par 71, SSS 69, Course record 69.
Club membership 475.

Visitors	time sheet in operation on Sundays
Societies	contact for infromation.
Green Fees	not confirmed.
Facilities	ℿ by prior arrangement 💺 🍴 ♀ 🏖 ✐
Location	2m N of Athy
Guesthouse	◆◆◆◆◆ Coursetown Country House, Stradbally Rd, ATHY ☎ 0507 31101 5 ⌀

CARBURY
Map 01 C4

Highfield Highfield House ☎ 0405 31021 Fax 0405 31021
A relatively flat parkland course but with interesting
undulations, especially by the fast flowing stream which runs
through many holes. The 7th doglegs over the lake, the 10th
is a great Par 5 with a challenging green, the 14th Par 3 is
over rushes onto a plateau green (out of bounds on left) and
the 18th Par 3 green is tucked between bunkers and a huge
chestnut tree.
18 holes, 5707mtrs, Par 72, SSS 69.
Club membership 500.

Visitors	welcome, must contact in advance for weekend play.
Societies	telephone or apply in writing.
Green Fees	IR£10 per day (IR£14 weekends & bank holidays).
Cards	🗠 💳 💳
Prof	Peter O'Hagan
Designer	Alan Duggan
Facilities	💺 🍴 ♀ 🏖 ⚑ 🐾 🛄 ✐ ⌀
Location	9m from Enfield
Hotel	★★★ 73% Keadeen Hotel, NEWBRIDGE ☎ 045 431666 55 ⇆ ⌀

CASTLEDERMOT
Map 01 C3

Kilkea Castle ☎ 0503 45555 Fax 0503 45505
A beautiful course opened in the summer of 1994 in the
grounds of a 12th-century castle - visible from all over the
course. The River Griese and two lakes create numerous
water hazards.
18 holes, 6200mtrs, Par 71, SSS 71.
Club membership 230.

Visitors	must contact in advance for details.
Societies	welcome, contact for details.
Green Fees	IR£25 per 18 holes; IR£15 per 9 holes.
Cards	🗠 💳 💳 💳
Designer	McDaid/Cassidy
Facilities	⊗ ℿ ⅃ 💺 🍴 ♀ 🏖 ⚑ ✐
& Leisure	hard tennis courts, heated indoor swimming pool, fishing, sauna, solarium, gymnasium.

DONADEA
Map 01 C4

Knockanally Golf & Country Club
☎ 045 869322 Fax 045 869322
Home of the Irish International Professional Matchplay
championship, this parkland course is set in a former estate,
with a Palladian-style clubhouse.
18 holes, 6485yds, Par 72, SSS 72, Course record 66.
Club membership 500.

Visitors	may not play on Sun 8.30am-noon.
Societies	must contact in writing or telephone.
Green Fees	IR£20 per round (IR£25 weekends).
Prof	Martin Darcy
Designer	Noel Lyons
Facilities	⚲ 〼 🏌 ☂ ♀ ⚿ 🏠 ⛳ 🎯 ⚷
& Leisure	fishing.
Location	3m off main Dublin-Galway road between Kilcock & Enfield

Hotel ★★★ 64% Lucan Spa Hotel, LUCAN
☎ 01 6280495 & 6280497
Fax 01 6280841 71rm (61 ⇌ ➤)

KILDARE
Map 01 C3

Cill Dara Cill Dara, Little Curragh
☎ 045 521295 & 521433
Only 1 mile from the famous Curragh racecourse, this 9-hole
parkland course is unusual in having links type soil as well as
plenty of trees.
9 holes, 5738mtrs, Par 71, SSS 70, Course record 64.
Club membership 500.

Visitors	welcome, Wed is Ladies Day and may only play after 1.30pm Sun (winter) and 4pm Sun (Summer).
Societies	apply in writing to Mr M O'Boyle, Professional.
Green Fees	not confirmed.
Prof	Mark O'Boyle
Facilities	⚲ 〼 🏌 ☂ ♀ ⚿ 🏠
Location	1m E of Kildare

Hotel ★★★ 73% Keadeen Hotel, NEWBRIDGE
☎ 045 431666 55 ⇌ ➤

The Curragh Curragh
☎ 045 441238 & 441714 Fax 045 441714
A particularly challenging course, well wooded and with
lovely scenery all around.
18 holes, 6035mtrs, Par 72, SSS 71, Course record 63.
Club membership 1040.

Visitors	must contact in advance, preferred on Mon, Wed, Thu & Fri.
Societies	apply in writing.
Green Fees	not confirmed.
Prof	Gerry Burke
Facilities	⚲ 〼 🏌 ☂ ♀ ⚿ 🏠 ⛳ 🎯 ⚷
Location	Off N7 between Newbridge & Kildare

Hotel ★★★ 73% Keadeen Hotel, NEWBRIDGE
☎ 045 431666 55 ⇌ ➤

KILL
Map 01 D4

Killeen ☎ 045 866003 Fax 045 875881
Set in pleasant countryside, the attractive course is
characterised by its many lakes. It provides a challenge to
test the skills of the moderate enthusiast and the more
experienced golfer.
18 holes, 5561mtrs, Par 71, SSS 71, Course record 70.
Club membership 170.

Visitors	please ring for tee-times
Societies	must contact in advance.
Green Fees	IR£17 per round (IR£20 weekends & bank holidays).
Cards	💳 💳 ⊘
Designer	Pat Ruddy/M Kelly
Facilities	⚲ 〼 🏌 ☂ ♀ ⚿ 🏠 🎯 ⚷
Location	Off N7 at Kill signposted

Hotel ★★★ 76% Barberstown Castle, STRAFFAN
☎ 01 6288157 22 ⇌ ➤

NAAS
Map 01 D4

Bodenstown Sallins ☎ 045 897096
The old course in Bodenstown has ample fairways and large
greens, some of which are raised, providing more than a fair
test of golf. The Ladyhill course is a little shorter and tighter,
but still affords a fair challenge.
Bodenstown: 18 holes, 6132mtrs, Par 71, SSS 71.
Ladyhill: 18 holes, 5428mtrs, Par 71, SSS 68.
Club membership 700.

Visitors	may not play on Bodenstown course at weekends.
Societies	must contact by telephone.
Green Fees	not confirmed.
Designer	Richard Mather
Facilities	⚲ 〼 🏌 ☂ ♀ ⚷
Location	4m from town near Bodenstown graveyard

Hotel ★★★ 61% Downshire House Hotel,
BLESSINGTON
☎ 045 865199 14 ⇌ ➤ Annexe 11 ⇌ ➤

Craddockstown Blessington Rd
☎ 045 897610 Fax 045 896968
A gradually maturing parkland course featuring four testing
par 3 holes, all over 140 metres in length, sand-based greens,
and many trees. Easy walking.
*raddockstown Golf Club: 18 holes, 5726mtrs, Par 71, SSS
69, Course record 66.*
Club membership 800.

Visitors	should ring in advance to verify tee times available, limited at weekends.
Societies	apply in writing.
Green Fees	IR£15 per round (IR£20 weekends).
Designer	A Spring
Facilities	⚲ 〼 🏌 ☂ ♀ ⚿ ⚷
Location	Off the main dual carriageway (N7/N97), head towards Naas, turn left on to Blessington Road

Hotel ★★★ 63% Ambassador Hotel, KILL
☎ 045 886700 36 ⇌ ➤

Where to stay, where to eat?
Visit the AA internet site
www.theaa.co.uk

Entries with a green background
identify courses considered to be
particularly interesting

Naas Kerdiffstown
☎ 045 897509 & 874644 Fax 045 896109
Scenic parkland course well bunkered, with a substantial number of trees, greens are both sand based and natural.
18 holes, 5663mtrs, Par 71, SSS 69, Course record 65.
Club membership 1000.

Visitors	may not play on Sun, Tue or Thu.
Societies	must contact in advance.
Green Fees	IR£18 per round (IR£24 weekends & bank holidays).
Cards	〓 〓
Designer	E Hackett/A Spring
Facilities	⊗ ⓑ 🖤 ♀ ⚐ ✧
Location	1m from town on Sallins-Johnstown road
Hotel	★★★ 61% Downshire House Hotel, BLESSINGTON ☎ 045 865199 14 ⇆ ⌂ Annexe 11 ⇆ ⌂

Woodlands Cooleragh, Coill Dubh
☎ 045 860777 Fax 045 860988
Reconstructed 9-hole course opened in March 1997 offering an interesting challenge with completely new greens, tees and an extra 1000 yards coming into play. Extended to 18 hole course which opened in July 1999.
9 holes, 6408yds, Par 72, SSS 71.
Club membership 454.

Visitors	must contact in advance, unable to play most weekends (member competitions).
Societies	telephone in advance for details.
Green Fees	not confirmed.
Designer	Tommy Halpin
Facilities	⊗ ⍦ ⓑ 🖤 ♀ ⚐ 🛒 ✧
Location	Off the Clane/Edenderry road
Hotel	★★★ 73% Keadeen Hotel, NEWBRIDGE ☎ 045 431666 55 ⇆ ⌂

STRAFFAN   Map 01 D4

Castlewarden ☎ 01 4589254 & 4589838 Fax 01 4588992
Founded in 1990, Castlewarden is maturing into a delightful parkland course with water features and excellent greens.
18 holes, 6496yds, Par 72, SSS 70.
Club membership 765.

Visitors	welcome contact for details. Tues Ladies Day.
Societies	by prior application.
Green Fees	Apr-Sep IR£17, IR£23 pm (IR£23 weekends); Oct-Mar IR£17 (IR£23 weekends).
Prof	Gerry Egan
Designer	Tommy Halpin
Facilities	⊗ ⍦ ⓑ 🖤 ♀ ⚐ 🛒 ✧
Location	Between Naas/Rathcoole
Hotel	★★★ 63% Ambassador Hotel, KILL ☎ 045 886700 36 ⇆ ⌂

The K Club ☎ 01 6017300 Fax 01 6017399
Known as The K-Club, this course is growing in reputation. Designed by Arnold Palmer, its 6,456 metre length is a challenge to even the best golfers. Covering 177 acres of prime Kildare woodland there are 14 man-made lakes as well as the River Liffey to create water hazards. There is the promise of a watery grave at the monster 7th (Par 5, 520 metres) and at the 17th the tee shot is to the green on the water's edge. There is also a practise area and driving range.

---

18 holes, 6163mtrs, Par 72, SSS 72, Course record 60.
Club membership 520.

Visitors	contact in advance to book prefered tee times, restricted at members times.
Societies	telephone & write in advance, societies not allowed on weekends & Wed afternoon.
Green Fees	Summer: IR£140 per round; Winter: IR£75 per round.
Cards	〓 〓 〓 📇
Prof	Ernie Jones
Designer	Arnold Palmer
Facilities & Leisure	⊗ ⍦ ⓑ 🖤 ♀ ⚐ 🛒 ✧ 🏇 🚶 ⚐ ✧ ⌇ hard tennis courts, heated indoor swimming pool, squash, fishing, sauna, solarium, gymnasium, clay pigeon shooting, horse riding.
Location	From Dublin take N4 and axit R406, entrance to hotel on right in Straffan
Hotel	★★★★★ ⚓ The Kildare Hotel & Country Club, STRAFFAN ☎ 01 6017200 36 ⇆ ⌂ Annexe 9 ⇆ ⌂

CO KILKENNY

CALLAN   Map 01 C3

Callan Geraldine
☎ 056 25136 & 25949 Fax 056 55155
Meadowland course with well positioned spinneys and water hazards. Not difficult walking and a good test for golfers of all standards.
18 holes, 6374yds, Par 72, SSS 70, Course record 67.
Club membership 700.

Visitors	welcome. Must contact in advance.
Societies	must apply in writing.
Green Fees	IR£15 per round.
Cards	〓
Prof	John O'Dwyer
Facilities & Leisure	⊗ ⍦ ⓑ 🖤 ♀ ⚐ 🛒 ✧ 🚶 ⚐ ✧ fishing.
Location	1m from Callan on the Knocktopher Road
Hotel	★★★ 68% Hotel Kilkenny, College Rd, KILKENNY ☎ 056 62000 103 ⇆ ⌂

Mount Juliet

Mount Juliet, *Co Kilkenny*   ☎ 056 73000   Fax 056 73019   Map 01 C3

e-mail: info@mountjuliet.ie

Mount Juliet's superb 18-hole golf course was designed by Jack Nicklaus, and has been the chosen venue for many prestigious golfing events including the Irish Open on three occasions. The course boasts a cleverly concealed drainage and irrigation system, perfect even when inclement weather would otherwise preclude play, and takes advantage of the estate's mature landscape to provide a world-class 72-par challenge for professionals and high-handicap golfers alike.

A unique three-hole golfing academy has been added to offer both novice and experienced players ample opportunity to improve their games, while a new 18-hole putting course provides an extra dimension of golfing pleasure.

Visitors must contact in advance

Societies book in advance by telephone or writing

Green Fees Jun, Jul, Sep IR£75; Apr, May, Aug, Oct IR£70; Nov-Mar IR£45 (IR£85/£80/£55 weekends) ▬ ▬ ▬ ▣

Facilities ⊗ ⫟ ⫼ ⓛ 🍽 ♀ ⌂ 🏠 ⅌ ✂ ⎰ Professional (Ted Higgins)

Leisure tennis, indoor swimming pool, private fishing, sauna, solarium, gym, horse riding, clay target shooting

Location N9, Dublin/Waterford Rd.

Holes/Par/Course record 18 holes, 6641 yds, Par 72, SSS 72, Course record 65

WHERE TO STAY NEARBY

Hotels
THOMASTOWN

★★★★⭐ ✿ 🌲🌲 Mount Juliet Hotel
☎ 056 73000. 32 ⇆ ⎈ Annexe 7 ⇆ ⎈

KILKENNY

★★★ 68% Hotel Kilkenny, College Rd.
☎ 056 62000. 103 ⇆ ⎈

★★★ 71% Newpark Hotel
☎ 056 22122. 111 (86 ⇆ ⎈ 25 ⎈)

Championship Course

459

KILKENNY   Map 01 C3

Kilkenny Glendine ☎ 056 65400 Fax 056 23593
One of Ireland's most pleasant inland courses, noted for
its tricky finishing holes and its par threes. Features of
the course are its long 11th and 13th holes and the
challenge increases year by year as thousands of trees
planted over the last 30 years or so are maturing. As host
of the Kilkenny Scratch Cup annually, the course is
permanently maintained in championship condition. The
Irish Dunlop Tournament and the Irish Professional
Matchplay Championship have also been held here.
18 holes, 5857mtrs, Par 71, SSS 70, Course record 64.
Club membership 1000.
Visitors   must contact in advance.
Societies   must contact in advance.
Green Fees not confirmed.
Prof   Noel Leahy
Facilities   ⊗ 〗ⵏ ⵏ 🛢 ♀ 🕹 🝙 ⫯ 🏌 🛜 ⫯ ⫯
Location   1m from centre on Castlecomer road

Hotel   ★★★ 68% Hotel Kilkenny, College Rd,
                 KILKENNY ☎ 056 62000 103 ⇌ ⊮

THOMASTOWN   Map 01 C3

THOMASTOWN See page 459

CO LAOIS

ABBEYLEIX   Map 01 C3

Abbeyleix Rathmoyle ☎ 0502 31450 Fax 0502 30108
A pleasant, parkland 9 hole course.
9 holes, 5626mtrs, Par 70, SSS 69.
Club membership 300.
Visitors   welcome weekdays.
Societies   apply in writing.
Green Fees IR£10 per round.
Facilities   ♀ 🕹 ⫯

Hotel   ★★★ 71% Newpark Hotel, KILKENNY
                 ☎ 056 22122 111 ⇌ ⊮

MOUNTRATH   Map 01 C3

Mountrath Knockanina
☎ 0502 32558 & 32643 (office) Fax 0502 32643
A picturesque course at the foot of the Slieve Bloom
Mountains in central Ireland. The 18 hole course has fine
fairways and well bunkered greens, the river Nore flows
through the course.
18 holes, 5493mtrs, Par 71, SSS 69, Course record 68.
Club membership 500.
Visitors   check for availability at weekends, other days no
                 problem but safer to check.
Societies   must contact in advance.
Green Fees not confirmed.
Facilities   ⊗ by prior arrangement ⵏ ⵏ 🛢 ♀ 🕹 ⫯
Location   1.5m from town on Dublin-Limerick road

Hotel   ★★★ 73% Keadeen Hotel, NEWBRIDGE
                 ☎ 045 431666 55 ⇌ ⊮

PORTARLINGTON   Map 01 C3

Portarlington Garryhinch ☎ 0502 23115 Fax 0502 23044
Lovely parkland course designed around a pine forest. It is
bounded on the 16th and 17th by the River Barrow which
makes the back 9 very challenging.
18 holes, 5673mtrs, Par 72, SSS 69, Course record 70.
Club membership 562.
Visitors   welcome but restricted Tue-Ladies Day, Sat &
                 Sun societies and club competitions. Must
                 contact in advance
Societies   must apply in writing.
Green Fees not confirmed.
Designer   Eddie Hackett
Facilities   ⊗ 〗ⵏ ⵏ 🛢 ♀ 🕹 ⫯
Location   4m from town on Mountmellick road

Hotel   ★★★ 73% Keadeen Hotel, NEWBRIDGE
                 ☎ 045 431666 55 ⇌ ⊮

PORTLAOISE   Map 01 C3

The Heath
☎ 0502 46533 & 46622 (Pro shop) Fax 0502 46866
One of the oldest clubs in Ireland. The course is set in pretty
countryside and offers a good challenge.
18 holes, 5736mtrs, Par 71, SSS 69, Course record 69.
Club membership 800.
Visitors   contact in advance, preferred on weekdays.
Societies   apply in writing to Pat Hallinan.
Green Fees IR£10 per round (IR£17 weekends and bank
                 holidays).
Prof   Eddie Doyle
Facilities   ⊗ 〗ⵏ ⵏ 🛢 ♀ 🕹 🝙 ⫯ ⫯ ⫯
Location   3m N on N7

Hotel   ★★★ 73% Keadeen Hotel, NEWBRIDGE
                 ☎ 045 431666 55 ⇌ ⊮

RATHDOWNEY   Map 01 C3

Rathdowney ☎ 0505 46170 Fax 0505 46065
A 18 hole course recently opened. Undulating terrain, 12th &
15th are particularly tough par 4 holes, 6th is a challenging
par 5 (550yds) into the prevailing wind. A good test for
golfers of all abilities. ▶

18 holes, 5894mtrs, Par 71, SSS 70, Course record 67.
Club membership 400.

Visitors	welcome. Ladies have priority on Wed, Sat & Sun mornings are reserved for member & societies.
Societies	must apply in writing and pay deposit to confirm booking.
Green Fees	IR£12 per day.
Designer	Eddie Hackett
Facilities	🛆 ✇
Location	0.5m SE. Follow signs from town square
Hotel	★★★ 68% Hotel Kilkenny, College Rd, KILKENNY ☎ 056 62000 103 ⇌ 🏾

CO LEITRIM

BALLINAMORE
Map 01 C4

Ballinamore ☎ 078 44346
A very dry and very testing 9-hole parkland course along the Ballinamore/Ballyconnell Canal.
9 holes, 5680yds, Par 68, SSS 66, Course record 66.
Club membership 100.

Visitors	restricted occasionally.
Societies	must contact in writing.
Green Fees	not confirmed.
Designer	A Spring
Facilities	⬛ 🍺 🍴 🛆
& Leisure	fishing.
Hotel	★★ 64% Royal Hotel, BOYLE ☎ 079 62016 16 ⇌ 🏾

CO LIMERICK

ADARE
Map 01 B3

Adare Manor ☎ 061 396204 Fax 061 396800
An 18-hole parkland course, Par 69, in an unusual setting.
The course surrounds the ruins of a castle, a friary and an abbey.
18 holes, 5800yds, Par 69, SSS 69.
Club membership 600.

Visitors	welcome weekdays, weekends only by arrangement and subject to availability.
Societies	by prior arrangement, preferably in writing.
Green Fees	IR£15 per round (£IR20 weekends).
Designer	Ben Sayers/Eddie Hacket
Facilities	⊗ ⫙ ⬛ 🍺 🍴 🛆 📠 📺 ✇
Location	10m from Limerick City

AA Hotels that have special
arrangements with golf courses are listed at
the back of the guide

LIMERICK
Map 01 B3

Castletroy Castletroy
☎ 061 335753 & 335261 Fax 061 335373
Parkland course with out of bounds on the left of the first two holes. The long par five 10th features a narrow entrance to a green guarded by a stream. The par three 13th has a panoramic view of the course and surrounding countryside from the tee and the 18th is a daunting finish, with the drive played towards a valley with the ground rising towards the green which is protected on both sides by bunkers. In recent years the club has hosted the finals of the Irish Mixed Foursomes and the Senior Championships.
18 holes, 5802mtrs, Par 71, SSS 71.
Club membership 1062.

Visitors	must contact in advance & have handicap certificate but may not play Sun or 1-2.30pm weekdays.
Societies	apply in writing.
Green Fees	IR£36 per 36 holes; IR£24 per 18 holes (IR£30 per 18 holes weekends).
Cards	▬
Facilities	⊗ ⫙ ⬛ 🍺 🍴 🛆 📠 📺 ✇
Location	3m from city on Dublin road
Hotel	★★★★ 71% Castletroy Park Hotel, Dublin Rd, LIMERICK ☎ 061 335566 107 ⇌ 🏾

Limerick Ballyclough ☎ 061 415146 Fax 061 319219
Tree-lined parkland course which hosted the 1991 Ladies Senior Interprovincial matches. The club are the only Irish winners of the European Cup Winners Team Championship.
18 holes, 5938mtrs, Par 72, SSS 71, Course record 67.
Club membership 1300.

Visitors	may not play after 4pm or on Tue & weekends.
Societies	must contact in writing.
Green Fees	not confirmed.
Cards	▬ ▬
Prof	John Cassidy
Designer	A McKenzie
Facilities	⊗ ⫙ ⬛ 🍺 🍴 🛆 📠 ✇
Location	3m S on Fedamore Road
Hotel	★★★ 72% Jurys Hotel, Ennis Rd, LIMERICK ☎ 061 327777 95 ⇌ 🏾

Limerick County Golf & Country Club Ballyneety
☎ 61 351881 Fax 61 351384
Limerick County was designed by Des Smyth and presents beautifully because of the strategic location of the main features. It stretches over undulating terrain with one elevated section providing views of the surrounding countryside. It features over 70 bunkers with six lakes and several unique design features.
18 holes, 6712yds, Par 72, SSS 74, Course record 70.
Club membership 400.

Visitors	welcome but prebooking essential.
Societies	book by telephone or in writing.
Green Fees	not confirmed.
Prof	Philip Murphy
Designer	Des Smyth
Facilities	⊗ ⫙ ⬛ 🍺 🍴 🛆 📠 📺 🛒 🏐 ✇ ⌇
& Leisure	sauna.
Location	5m SE of Limerick on R512
Hotel	★★★ 62% Greenhills Hotel, Caherdavin, LIMERICK ☎ 061 453033 58 ⇌ 🏾

NEWCASTLE WEST Map 01 B3

Killeline Cork Rd ☎ 069 61600 Fax 069 77428
Set in 160 acres of gently contoured parkland in the heart of the Golden Vale with views to the Galtee Mountains. Because of its design and many mature trees, accuracy in playing is the key to good scoring.
18 holes, 6671yds, Par 72, SSS 68.
Club membership 400.

Visitors welcome weekdays, by arrangement weekends, must contact in advance
Societies telephone in advance.
Green Fees IR£15 per round.
Cards
Prof Kevin Dorrian
Facilities
& Leisure heated indoor swimming pool, sauna, solarium, gymnasium.
Location 0.25m off main Limerick/Killarney route

Hotel ★★★ 78% Dunraven Arms Hotel, ADARE ☎ 061 396633 75

Newcastle West Ardagh ☎ 069 76500 Fax 069 76511
A new course set in 150 acres of unspoilt countryside, built to the highest standards on sandy free draining soil. A practice ground and driving range are included. Hazards on the course include lakes, bunkers, streams and trees. A signature hole is likely to be the Par 3 6th playing 185 yards over a lake.
18 holes, 6317yds, Par 71, SSS 72, Course record 67.
Club membership 730.

Visitors advisable to contact in advance, but available most days.
Societies contact in advance.
Green Fees IR£18 per day.
Cards
Prof Ger Jones
Designer Dr Arthur Spring
Facilities
Location 2m off N21 between Limerick & Killarney

Hotel ★★★ 78% Dunraven Arms Hotel, ADARE ☎ 061 396633 75

Where to stay, where to eat?
Visit the AA internet site
www.theaa.co.uk

CO LONGFORD

LONGFORD Map 01 C4

County Longford Glack, Dublin Rd
☎ 043 46310 Fax 043 47082
A lovely 18-hole parkland course with lots of trees.
18 holes, 6044yds, Par 70, SSS 69, Course record 69.
Club membership 819.

Visitors very welcome, but advisable to telephone in advance for Tue and Sun play.
Societies by prior arrangement.
Green Fees IR£12 per round (IR£15 weekends & bank holidays).
Facilities
Location E of town

Hotel ★★★ 64% Abbey Hotel, Galway Rd, ROSCOMMON ☎ 0903 26240 & 26505 Fax 0903 26021 25

CO LOUTH

ARDEE Map 01 D4

Ardee Townparks ☎ 041 53227
Pleasant parkland course with mature trees and a stream.
18 holes, 6100yds, Par 69, SSS 69.

Visitors may normally play on weekdays (except Wed).
Green Fees not confirmed.
Facilities

Hotel ★★★ 69% Ballymascanlon House Hotel, DUNDALK ☎ 042 9371124 74

BALTRAY Map 01 D4

County Louth ☎ 041 9822329 Fax 041 9822969
Generally held to have the best greens in Ireland, this links course was designed by Tom Simpson to have well guarded and attractive greens without being overly dependant on bunkers. It provides a good test for the modern champion, notably as the annual venue for the East of Ireland Amateur Open.
18 holes, 6613yds, Par 73, SSS 71.
Club membership 1100.

Visitors must contact in advance.
Societies by prior arrangement.
Green Fees not confirmed.
Cards
Prof Paddy McGuirk
Designer Tom Simpson
Facilities
& Leisure hard tennis courts.
Location 5m NE of Drogheda

Hotel ★★★ 63% Conyngham Arms Hotel, SLANE ☎ 041 24155 16rm (15)

DUNDALK   Map 01 D4

Ballymascanlon House Hotel
☎ 042 9371124 Fax 042 9371598
Now a testing 18-hole parkland course with numerous water
hazards and two difficult holes through woodland, this very
scenic course is set at the edge of the Cooley Mountains.
18 holes, 5548yds, Par 68, SSS 66.

Visitors	must telephone in advance to check availability.
Societies	booking by telephone or letter.
Green Fees	not confirmed.
Cards	〰 ▬ 〰
Designer	Craddock/Ruddy
Facilities	⊗ ⊓ ⓛ 🛈 ⚑ ⚲ 🜲 🏠 🛒 ✐
& Leisure	hard and grass tennis courts, heated indoor swimming pool, sauna, gymnasium.
Location	3m N of Dundalk on the Carlingford road
Hotel	★★★ 69% Ballymascanlon House Hotel, DUNDALK ☎ 042 9371124 74 ⇋

Dundalk Blackrock ☎ 042 21731 Fax 042 22022
A tricky course with extensive views.
18 holes, 6115mtrs, Par 72, SSS 72.
Club membership 1000.

Visitors	must contact in advance and may not play Tue or Sun.
Societies	must apply in writing in advance.
Green Fees	not confirmed.
Prof	James Cassidy
Facilities	⚲ 🜲 🏠 ⚑
& Leisure	sauna.
Location	2.5m S on coast road
Hotel	★★★ 69% Ballymascanlon House Hotel, DUNDALK ☎ 042 9371124 74 ⇋

Killinbeg Killin Park ☎ 042 39303
Opened in 1991 and designed by Eddie Hackett, this
undulating 18-hole parkland course has mature woodland and
river features.
18 holes, 5293yds, Par 69, SSS 65, Course record 67.
Club membership 100.

Visitors	no restrictions.
Societies	apply by telephone or in writing in advance.
Green Fees	IR£10 per round (IR£14 weekends & bank holidays).
Designer	Eddie Hackett
Facilities	🛈 ⚑ ⚲ 🜲 ⚑ ✐
Location	Bridge-a-Crinn

Hotel	★★★ 69% Ballymascanlon House Hotel, DUNDALK ☎ 042 9371124 74 ⇋

GREENORE   Map 01 D4

Greenore ☎ 042 9373212 & 9373678 Fax 042 9373678
Situated amidst beautiful scenery on the shores of
Carlingford Lough, with views of the Mourne Mountains.
The pine trees here are an unusual feature on a semi-links
course. There are quite a number of water facilities, tight
fairways and very good greens.
18 holes, 6514yds, Par 71, SSS 71.
Club membership 500.

Visitors	must contact in advance at weekends.
Societies	must contact in advance.
Green Fees	IR£18 per round (IR£25 weekends & bank holidays).
Designer	Eddie Hackett
Facilities	⊗ ⊓ 🛈 ⚑ ⚲ 🜲 🛒 ✐
Hotel	★★★ 69% Ballymascanlon House Hotel, DUNDALK ☎ 042 9371124 74 ⇋

TERMONFECKIN   Map 01 D4

Seapoint ☎ 041 9822333 Fax 041 9822331
A very long championship links course of 7,000 yards with a
particularly interesting 17th hole.
18 holes, 6339mtrs, Par 72, SSS 74.
Club membership 470.

Visitors	phone in advance for restrictions.
Societies	telephone in advance.
Green Fees	Summer: IR£25 (IR£30 weekends & bank holidays); Winter: IR£30 (IR£35 weekends & bank holidays).
Cards	〰 🟦
Prof	David Carroll
Designer	Des Smyth
Facilities	⊗ ⊓ 🛈 ⚑ ⚲ 🜲 🏠 ⚑ 🛒 🛒 🜲 ✐
Location	4m NE of Drogheda
Hotel	★★★ 63% Conyngham Arms Hotel, SLANE ☎ 041 24155 16rm(15 ⇋ ☍)

CO MAYO

BALLINA   Map 01 B4

Ballina Mossgrove, Shanaghy
☎ 096 21050 Fax 096 21050
Undulating but mostly flat inland course.
18 holes, 6103yds, Par 71, SSS 69, Course record 69.
Club membership 478.

Visitors	welcome but may not play Sun before 3.30pm. Restrictions apply depending on competitions/society visits.
Societies	apply in writing or telephone in advance.
Green Fees	IR£16 per day (IR£20 weekends & bank holidays).
Cards	〰 ▬ 🟦
Designer	E Hackett
Facilities	🛈 ⚑ ⚲ 🜲 🛒 🜲 ✐
Location	1m outside town on Bonnocolon Rd

BALLINROBE   Map 01 B4

Ballinrobe Cloonagashel
☎ 092 41118 Fax 092 41889
A championship parkland 18 hole course, set in the mature
woodlands of a historic estate at Cloonacastle. The layout of
the course incorporates seven man made lakes with the river
Robe flowing at the back of the 3rd and 5th greens.
Ballinrobe is full of charm and character typified by the 19th
century period residence now used as the clubhouse.
18 holes, 6043mtrs, Par 73, SSS 72, Course record 69.
Club membership 570.

Visitors	welcome daily, telephone to reserve Tee-time.
Societies	must telephone or write to Secretary in advance.
Green Fees	not confirmed.
Cards	▭▭ ▭▭
Prof	David Kearney
Designer	Eddie Hackett
Facilities	⊗ ఓ ♥ ♀ ஃ ➤ ↖ ⚖ ♂ ↾
Location	Off N84 onto R331 to Claremorris

Hotel   ★★★ 67% Breaffy House Hotel,
CASTLEBAR
☎ 094 22033 62 ⇄ ↾

BALLYHAUNIS   Map 01 B4

Ballyhaunis Coolnaha
☎ 0907 30014 Fax 094 81829
Undulating parkland course with 9 holes, 10 greens and 18
tees.
9 holes, 5413mtrs, Par 70, SSS 68, Course record 68.
Club membership 340.

Visitors	welcome all times but must avoid members competitions on Sun & Thu.
Societies	must apply in writing or telephone.
Green Fees	not confirmed.
Facilities	♥ ♀ ஃ ♂ ↾
Location	3m N on N83

Hotel   ★★★ 67% Breaffy House Hotel,
CASTLEBAR
☎ 094 22033 62 ⇄ ↾

BELMULLET   Map 01 A5

Carne Carne ☎ 097 82292 Fax 097 81477
18 holes, 6119mtrs, Par 72, SSS 72, Course record 72.
Club membership 460.

Visitors	welcome, booking essential to guarantee tee-time.
Societies	booking advisable.
Green Fees	IR£15-IR£25 per day.
Designer	Eddie Hackett
Facilities	⊗ ℿ ఓ ♥ ఓ ♀ ஃ ➤ ↖ ⚖ ♂
Location	2m from Belmullet

CASTLEBAR   Map 01 B4

Castlebar Hawthorn Av, Rocklands
☎ 094 21649 Fax 094 26088
Mature testing treelined parkland course, where an accurate
tee shot is essential. A steady putting stroke is needed if par
is to be achieved on the course's sloping grounds.
18 holes, 5698mtrs, Par 71, SSS 70, Course record 67.
Club membership 950.

Visitors	very welcome weekdays, must contact in advance for weekend play. No vistors on Sun.
Societies	must contact in advance.
Green Fees	IR£20 per day (IR£25 weekends & bank holidays).
Designer	Peter McEvoy
Facilities	⊗ ℿ ఓ ♥ ♀ ஃ ➤ ↖ ⚖ ♂
Location	1m from town on Belcarra road

Hotel   ★★★ 67% Breaffy House Hotel,
CASTLEBAR
☎ 094 22033 62 ⇄ ↾

CLAREMORRIS   Map 01 B4

Claremorris Castlemagarrett
☎ 094 71527
A 9-hole parkland course on hilly terrain. A new 18-hole
course is due to open in 1998 and will feature plenty of
mature trees and numerous water hazards.
18 holes, 6600mtrs, Par 73, SSS 72.
Club membership 300.

Visitors	may play weekdays and weekends on request Contact Willie Feeley 094 71868
Societies	welcome weekdays, contact 094 62554 for details.
Green Fees	not confirmed.
Cards	▭▭ ▭▭ ▭▭ ▭▭ ▭▭ ▭▭ ▭
Designer	Tom Craddock
Facilities	⊗ ℿ ఓ ♥ ♀ ஃ
Location	1.5m from town, on N17 S of Claremorris

Hotel   ★★★ 59% Belmont Hotel, KNOCK
☎ 094 88122 64 ⇄ ↾

KEEL   Map 01 A4

Achill Achill Island, Westport
☎ 098 43456
Seaside links in a scenic location on the edge of the Atlantic
Ocean.
9 holes, 2723yds, Par 70, SSS 66, Course record 69.
Club membership 170.

Visitors	welcome but cannot play on some Sundays
Societies	must write or telephone in advance.
Green Fees	not confirmed.
Facilities	↖ ♂

Hotel   ★★★ 67% Hotel Westport, The Demesne,
Newport Rd, WESTPORT
☎ 098 25122 129 ⇄ ↾

SWINFORD   Map 01 B4

Swinford Brabazon Park ☎ 094 51378
A pleasant parkland course with good views of the beautiful
surrounding countryside.
9 holes, 5542mtrs, Par 70, SSS 68.
Club membership 420.

Visitors	must contact in advance in peak season.
Societies	must apply in writing or telephone in advance.
Green Fees	IR£10 per day.
Facilities	♀ ஃ ♂

Hotel   ★★★ 67% Breaffy House Hotel,
CASTLEBAR ☎ 094 22033 62 ⇄ ↾

WESTPORT   Map 01 B4

Westport Carrowholly
☎ 098 28262 & 27070 Fax 098 27217
This is a beautiful course with wonderful views of Clew
Bay, with its 365 islands, and the holy mountain called
Croagh Patrick, famous for the annual pilgrimage to its
summit. Golfers indulge in a different kind of penance
on this challenging course with many memorable holes.
Perhaps the most exciting is the par five 15th, 580 yards
long and featuring a long carry from the tee over an inlet
of Clew Bay.
18 holes, 6667yds, Par 73, SSS 71, Course record 65.
Club membership 750.

Visitors	must contact in advance. No visitors during members times.
Societies	apply in writing or telephone well in advance.
Green Fees	Summer: IR£20 per round (IR£25 weekends) Winter: IR£15 per round (IR£20 weekends).
Cards	💳 💳
Prof	Alex Mealia
Designer	Fred Hawtree
Facilities	⊗ ⋒ 🏌 🏌 ♥ ♀ 🏌 🏌 🏌 ♥ 🏌 /
Location	2.5m from town
Hotel	★★★ 67% Hotel Westport, The Demesne, Newport Rd, WESTPORT ☎ 098 25122 129 ⇔ 🐾

CO MEATH

BETTYSTOWN   Map 01 D4

Laytown & Bettystown ☎ 041 27170 Fax 041 28506
A very competitive and trying links course, home of famous
golfer, Des Smyth.
18 holes, 5652mtrs, Par 71, SSS 70.
Club membership 950.

Visitors	may not play 1-2pm. Advisable to contact in advance.
Societies	must contact in writing.
Green Fees	IR£25 per round (IR£30 weekends).
Cards	💳 💳
Prof	Robert J Browne
Facilities	⊗ ⋒ 🏌 🏌 ♥ ♀ 🏌 /
& Leisure	hard tennis courts.
Hotel	★★★ 63% Conyngham Arms Hotel, SLANE ☎ 041 24155 16rm (15 ⇔ 🐾)

DUNSHAUGHLIN   Map 01 D4

Black Bush Thomastown ☎ 01 8250021 Fax 01 8250400
Three 9-hole courses, giving three possible 18-hole
combinations, set in lovely parkland, with a lake providing a
hazard at the 1st. Recently added creeks, trees and bunkers
make for challenging and accurate shot-making.
Black Bush: 18 holes, 6930yds, Par 73, SSS 72.
Agore: 18 holes, 6598yds, Par 71, SSS 69.

Thomastown: 18 holes, 6433yds, Par 70, SSS 68.
Club membership 950.

Visitors	must contact in advance but cannot play 1-2pm weekdays.
Societies	advance booking required.
Green Fees	not confirmed.
Cards	💳 💳
Prof	Shane O'Grady
Designer	Bobby Browne
Facilities	⊗ ⋒ 🏌 🏌 ♥ ♀ 🏌 🏌 🏌 ♥ 🏌 / ℓ
Location	1.5m from village on Dunshaughlin-Ratoath road
Hotel	★★★ 70% Finnstown Country House Hotel & Golf Course, Newcastle Rd, LUCAN ☎ 01 6280644 25 ⇔ 🐾 Annexe 26 ⇔ 🐾

KELLS   Map 01 C4

Headfort ☎ 046 40857 40146 Fax 046 49282
A delightful parkland course which is regarded as one of
the best of its kind in Ireland. There are ample
opportunities for birdies, but even if these are not
achieved, Headfort provides for a most pleasant game. A
further 18 hole course has recently opened and promises
to be equally challenging.
36 holes, 6007mtrs, Par 72, SSS 71, Course record 67.
Club membership 1162.

Visitors	restricted Tues Ladies Day. Must contact in advance.
Societies	must apply in writing.
Green Fees	IR£21 (IR£26 weekends & bank holidays).
Cards	💳 💳
Prof	Brendan McGovern
Facilities	⊗ ⋒ 🏌 🏌 ♥ ♀ 🏌 🏌 🏌 /
Hotel	★★★ 62% Ardboyne Hotel, Dublin Rd, NAVAN ☎ 046 23119 27 ⇔ 🐾

KILCOCK   Map 01 C4

Kilcock Gallow ☎ 01 6287592 Fax 01 6287283
A parkland course with gently undulating fairways, flat
greens and light rough only.
18 holes, 5775mtrs, Par 71, SSS 70, Course record 69.
Club membership 450.

Visitors	must contact in advance for weekends, no problem weekdays.
Societies	telephone for dates available.
Green Fees	IR£11 (IR£13 weekends).
Designer	Eddie Hackett
Facilities	🏌 🏌 ♥ ♀ 🏌 🏌 🏌 /
Location	2m from end of M4

▶

Hotel	★★★ 64% Lucan Spa Hotel, LUCAN
	☎ 01 6280495 & 6280497
	Fax 01 6280841 71rm (61 ⇆ 🐾)

NAVAN

Map 01 C4

Royal Tara Bellinter
☎ 046 25508 & 25244 Fax 046 25508
Pleasant parkland course offering plenty of variety. Situated close to the Hill of Tara, the ancient seat of the Kings of Ireland.
New Course: 18 holes, 5757mtrs, Par 71, SSS 70.
Bellinter Nine: 9 holes, 3184yds, Par 35, SSS 35.
Club membership 1000.

Visitors	prior arrangement is advisable. Tue is ladies day.
Societies	apply in writing or telephone.
Green Fees	IR£20 per round; IR£10 per 9 holes (IR£25/IR£13 weekends & bank holidays).
Prof	Adam Whiston
Designer	Des Smyth
Facilities	⊗ ⫘ 🍸⛳🏌
Location	6m from town on N3

| Hotel | ★★★ 62% Ardboyne Hotel, Dublin Rd, NAVAN ☎ 046 23119 27 ⇆ 🐾 |

TRIM

Map 01 C4

County Meath Newtownmoynagh
☎ 046 31463 Fax 046 37554
Originally a 9-hole course opened in 1971, it was extended to 18-holes in 1990. It is maturing into a very challenging and formidable course with four testing Par 5's. Luxurious clubhouse with panoramic views across the course.
18 holes, 6720mtrs, Par 73, SSS 72, Course record 68.
Club membership 900.

Visitors	welcome; some restrictions telephone for details.
Societies	not Sun, enquiries welcome.
Green Fees	not confirmed.
Designer	Eddie Hackett/Tom Craddock
Facilities	⊗ ⫘ 🍸⛳
Location	3m outside Trim on Trim/Longwood rd

| Hotel | ★★★ 63% Conyngham Arms Hotel, SLANE |
| | ☎ 041 24155 16rm (15 ⇆ 🐾) |

CO MONAGHAN

CARRICKMACROSS

Map 01 C4

Mannan Castle Donaghmoyne
☎ 042 9663308 Fax 042 9663195
Parkland and picturesque, the course features the Par 3 2nd to an island green. The short Par 4 12th through the woods and the 14th to 18th, all crossing water at least once. A test of golf for both amateur and professional.
18 holes, 6500yds, Par 70, SSS 69.
Club membership 700.

| Visitors | may play anytime except competition times Sat, Sun & Wed from 2-2.30pm. |

Societies	apply in writing to the secretary.
Green Fees	IR£15.
Designer	F Ainsworth
Facilities	🍸⛳
Location	4m N

| Hotel | ★★★ 69% Ballymascanlon House Hotel, DUNDALK ☎ 042 9371124 74 ⇆ |

Nuremore ☎ 042 9661438 & 9664016 Fax 042 9661853
Picturesque parkland course of championship length incorporating the drumlins and lakes which are a natural feature of the Monaghan countryside. Precision is required on the 10th to drive over a large lake and between a narrow avenue of trees. Signature hole 18th.
18 holes, 6400yds, Par 71, SSS 69, Course record 67.
Club membership 200.

Visitors	welcome all times but must contact Maurice Cassidy in advance.
Societies	must contact in advance.
Green Fees	IR£20 per day (IR£25 weekends & bank holidays).
Cards	💳 💳 💳
Prof	Maurice Cassidy
Designer	Eddie Hackett
Facilities	⊗ ⫘ 🍸⛳🏌
& Leisure	hard tennis courts, heated indoor swimming pool, squash, fishing, sauna, gymnasium.
Location	1m S of Carrickmacross, on main N2

| Hotel | ★★★★ 75% Nuremore Hotel, CARRICKMACROSS ☎ 042 61438 72 ⇆ 🐾 |

CASTLEBLAYNEY

Map 01 C4

Castleblayney Onomy ☎ 042 40451 Fax 042 40451
Scenic course on Muckno Park estate, adjacent to Muckno Lake and Hope Castle.
9 holes, 5378yds, Par 68, SSS 66, Course record 68.
Club membership 275.

Visitors	no visitors allowed during major weekend competitions.
Societies	must contact in advance.
Green Fees	IR£8 (IR£10 weekends).
Designer	Bobby Browne
Facilities	🍸⛳
& Leisure	fishing.
Location	Situated on the Hope Castle Estate, in the town of Castleblayney

| Hotel | ★★★ 69% Ballymascanlon House Hotel, DUNDALK ☎ 042 9371124 74 ⇆ |

CLONES
Map 01 C5

Clones Hilton Park ☎ 047 56017 Fax 042 42333
Parkland course set in Drumlin country. Due to limestone
belt, the course is very dry and playable all year round. There
is a timesheet in operation on Saturday and Sunday.
9 holes, 5206mtrs, Par 68, SSS 67, Course record 62.
Club membership 330.

Visitors	must contact in advance.
Societies	apply in writing.
Green Fees	not confirmed.
Facilities	⊗ ⫵ ⓑ 🍺 ♀ ♨
Location	3m from Clones on Scotshouse rd

Hotel ★★★★ 62% Hillgrove Hotel,
Old Armagh Rd, MONAGHAN
☎ 047 81288 Fax 047 84951 44 ⇆ 📞

MONAGHAN
Map 01 C5

Rossmore Rossmore Park, Cootehill Rd ☎ 047 71222
An undulating 18-hole parkland course amidst beautiful
countryside.
18 holes, 5534mtrs, Par 70, SSS 68, Course record 62.
Club membership 800.

Visitors	must contact in advance, telephone Pro Shop on 047 71222.
Societies	must apply in writing.
Green Fees	IR£20 per day.
Prof	Mark Nicholson
Designer	Des Smyth
Facilities	⊗ ⫵ ⓑ 🍺 ♀ ♨ 🏠 ♈ ♂ ↾
Location	2m S on Cootehill Road

Hotel ★★★★ 62% Hillgrove Hotel,
Old Armagh Rd, MONAGHAN
☎ 047 81288 Fax 047 84951 44 ⇆ 📞

CO OFFALY

BIRR
Map 01 C3

Birr The Glenns ☎ 0509 20082 Fax 0509 22155
The course has been laid out over undulating parkland
utilising the natural contours of the land, which were created
during the ice age. The sandy subsoil means that the course is
playable all year round.
18 holes, 5700mtrs, Par 70, SSS 70, Course record 62.
Club membership 750.

Visitors	contact in advance.
Societies	advance contact to secretary.
Green Fees	IR£12 (IR£14 weekends).
Designer	Eddie Connaughton
Facilities	⊗ ⫵ ⓑ 🍺 ♀ ♨ 🏠 ♈ 🐾 ♂ ↾

Hotel ★★★ 60% County Arms Hotel, BIRR
☎ 0509 20791 24 ⇆ 📞

EDENDERRY
Map 01 C4

Edenderry ☎ 0405 31072
A most friendly club which offers a relaxing game in
pleasant surroundings. In 1992 the course was extended to 18
holes.
18 holes, 6029mtrs, Par 72, SSS 72, Course record 66.
Club membership 700.

Visitors	restricted Thu & weekends, ring for times.
Societies	may not play on Thu & Sun; must contact the secretary in writing.
Green Fees	not confirmed.
Designer	Havers/Hackett
Facilities	ⓑ 🍺 ♀ ♨ ♂

TULLAMORE
Map 01 C4

Tullamore Brookfield ☎ 0506 21439 Fax 0506 41806
Well wooded parkland course.
18 holes, 6500yds, Par 70, SSS 71, Course record 68.
Club membership 975.

Visitors	must contact in advance, restricted on Tue & at weekends.
Societies	must contact in writing.
Green Fees	IR£20 (IR£24 weekends & bank holidays).
Cards	💳 💳
Prof	Donagh McArdle
Designer	James Braid/Paddy Merrigam
Facilities	⊗ ⫵ ⓑ 🍺 ♀ ♨ 🏠 ♈ ♂
Location	2.5m SW on Kinnity road

Hotel ★★★ 64% Prince Of Wales Hotel,
ATHLONE ☎ 0902 72626 73 ⇆ 📞

CO ROSCOMMON

ATHLONE
Map 01 C4

Athlone Hodson Bay ☎ 0902 92073
A picturesque course with a panoramic view of Lough Ree.
Overall, it is a tight, difficult course with some outstanding
holes and is noted for its magnificent greens. Many
championships have taken place here including the 1998 All
Ireland Cups and Shields finals.
18 holes, 5854mtrs, Par 71, SSS 71.
Club membership 1250.

Visitors	must contact in advance.
Societies	apply in writing.
Green Fees	IR£18 per round (IR£20 weekends)..
Cards	💳 💳
Prof	Martin Quinn
Designer	J McAllister
Facilities	⊗ ⫵ ⓑ 🍺 ♀ ♨ 🏠 ♈ 🐾 ♂
Location	4m from town beside Lough Ree

Hotel ★★★ 69% Hodson Bay Hotel, Hodson Bay,
ATHLONE ☎ 0902 92444 97 ⇆ 📞

BALLAGHADERREEN   Map 01 B4

Ballaghaderreen ☎ 0907 60295
Mature 9-hole course with an abundance of trees. Accuracy
off the tee is vital for a good score. Small protected greens
require a good short-iron plan. The Par 3, 5th hole at 178
yards has ruined many a good score.
9 holes, 5727yds, Par 70, SSS 67, Course record 68.
Club membership 250.
Visitors	no restrictions.
Societies	apply in writing or telephone during office hours.
Green Fees	IR£10 per day.
Designer	Paddy Skerritt
Facilities	🏌♨
Location	2m S of town

Hotel ★★ 64% Royal Hotel, BOYLE
☎ 079 62016 16 🛏

BOYLE   Map 01 B4

Boyle Roscommon Rd ☎ 079 62594
Situated on a low hill and surrounded by beautiful scenery,
this is an undemanding course where, due to the generous
fairways and semi-rough, the leisure golfer is likely to finish
the round with the same golf ball.
9 holes, 5324yds, Par 67, SSS 66, Course record 65.
Club membership 288.
Visitors	no restrictions.
Societies	must contact in writing.
Green Fees	IR£10 per day.
Designer	E Hackett
Facilities	🏌♨
& Leisure	practice net.
Location	2m from Boyle on the Roscommon road

Hotel ★★ 64% Royal Hotel, BOYLE
☎ 079 62016 16 🛏

CARRICK-ON-SHANNON   Map 01 C4

Carrick-on-Shannon Woodbrook ☎ 079 67015
A pleasant 9-hole course overlooking the River Shannon. A
fine test of golf for both those with low and high handicaps.
9 holes, 5545mtrs, Par 70, SSS 68.
Club membership 400.
Visitors	welcome, contact in advance to avoid competitions.
Societies	must contact in advance.
Green Fees	IR£10 per day.
Designer	Eddie Hackett
Facilities	🏌♨
Location	4m W beside N4

Hotel ★★ 64% Royal Hotel, BOYLE
☎ 079 62016 16 🛏

CASTLEREA   Map 01 B4

Castlerea Clonalis ☎ 0907 20068 & 20705
The clubhouse is virtually at the centre of Castlerea course
with 7 tees visible. A pleasant parkland course incorporating
part of the River Francis very near the centre of town.
9 holes, 4974mtrs, Par 68, SSS 66, Course record 62.
Club membership 234.

Visitors welcome, but Sunday by arrangement only.
Societies	contact for details.
Green Fees	not confirmed.
Facilities	🏌♨
Location	On Dublin/Castlebar road

Hotel ★★★ 64% Abbey Hotel, Galway Rd,
ROSCOMMON ☎ 0903 26240 & 26505
Fax 0903 26021 25 🛏

ROSCOMMON   Map 01 B4

Roscommon Mote Park
☎ 0903 26382, 26931 & 25281 (catering) Fax 0903 26043
Located on the rolling pastures of the old Mote Park estate,
this recently extended 18-hole course successfully blends the
old established nine holes with an exciting and equally
demanding new 9-hole lay-out. Numerous water hazards,
notably on the tricky 13th, multi-tiered greens and an
excellent irrigation to give an all-weather surface.
18 holes, 6290mtrs, Par 72, SSS 70, Course record 64.
Club membership 650.
Visitors	contact in advance.
Societies	apply in writing.
Green Fees	IR£15 per day; Nov-Mar IR£10.
Facilities	🏌♨
Location	0.5m S of Roscommon town

Hotel ★★★ 64% Abbey Hotel, Galway Rd,
ROSCOMMON ☎ 0903 26240 & 26505
Fax 0903 26021 25 🛏

STROKESTOWN   Map 01 C4

Strokestown Cloonfinlough ☎ 078 33323 & 33084
Picturesque 9-hole course set in parkland with fine views of
Cloonfinlough Lake. The three Par 3's are long and quite
testing.
9 holes, 2615mtrs, Par 68.
Club membership 250.
Visitors	may play any times except during competitions.
Societies	apply in writing or telephone at least 2 weeks in advance.
Green Fees	not confirmed.
Facilities	♨
& Leisure	fishing.
Location	1.5m from Strokestown

Hotel ★★★ 64% Abbey Hotel, Galway Rd,
ROSCOMMON ☎ 0903 26240 & 26505
Fax 0903 26021 25 🛏

CO SLIGO

BALLYMOTE   Map 01 B4

Ballymote Ballinascarrow ☎ 071 83158 & 83089
Although Ballymote was founded in 1940, the course dates
from 1993 and has matured well into a parkland course with
ample fairways and large greens. Wonderful views of
Ballinascarow Lake. Ideal for family groups.
9 holes, 5302mtrs, Par 68, SSS 67.
Club membership 250.

▶

Visitors	must contact in advance.
Societies	telephone in advance.
Green Fees	not confirmed.
Prof	Leslie Robinson
Designer	Eddie Hacket
Facilities	☕ ♨ ♍ ♂
& Leisure	fishing.
Location	1m N

Hotel	★★ 64% Royal Hotel, BOYLE ☎ 079 62016 16 ⇥ ♞

ENNISCRONE

Map 01 B5

Enniscrone ☎ 096 36297 Fax 096 36657
In a magnificent situation with breathtaking views of mountain, sea and rolling countryside, this course offers some unforgettable golf.It was host to the West of Ireland championship and the Ladies Irish Close in 1997. It offers an exciting challenge among its splendid sandhills and a particularly favourite hole is the tenth, with a marvellous view from the elevated tee and the chance of a birdie with an accurate drive.
18 holes, 6620yds, Par 72, SSS 72, Course record 66.
Club membership 750.

Visitors	must contact in advance, may not play before 11am or between 1.00 & 4pm on Sun.
Societies	must telephone in advance.
Green Fees	IR£26 per round (IR£35 weekend & bank holidays).
Cards	💳 💳 💳
Prof	Charlie McGoldrick
Designer	E Hackett
Facilities	⊗ ♍ 🏌 🍴 ♀ ♨ 🏠 ♍ ♈ ♂ ♒
Location	0.5m S on Ballina road

SLIGO

Map 01 B5

County Sligo Rosses Point
☎ 071 77134 or 77186 Fax 071 77460
Now considered to be one of the top links courses in Ireland, County Sligo is host to a number of competitions, including the West of Ireland Championships and Internationals. Set in an elevated position on cliffs above three large beaches, the prevailing winds provide an additional challenge. Tom Watson described it " as a magnificent links, particularly the stretch of holes from the 14th to the 17th."
18 holes, 6037mtrs, Par 71, SSS 72, Course record 66.
Bowmore: 9 holes, 2969mtrs, Par 35, SSS 35.
Club membership 1069.

Visitors	advisable to contact in advance, available most days except Captains or Presidents days.
Societies	must contact in writing & pay a deposit.
Green Fees	IR£35 per round; IR£15 per 9 holes weekdays except Fri (IR£45/IR£15 Fri & weekends).
Cards	💳 💳
Prof	Leslie Robinson
Designer	Harry Colt
Facilities	⊗ ♍ 🏌 🍴 ♀ ♨ 🏠 ♍ ♈ ♂ ♒
Location	Off N15 to Donegal

Hotel	★★★ 65% Tower Hotel, Quay St, SLIGO ☎ 071 44000 58 ⇥ ♞

Strandhill Strandhill ☎ 071 68188 Fax 071 68811
This scenic course is situated between Knocknarea Mountain and the Atlantic, offering golf in its most natural form amid the sand dunes of the West of Ireland. The 1st, 16th and 18th are Par 4 holes over 364 metres in length; the 2nd and 17th are testing Par 3s which vary according to the prevailing wind; the Par 4 13th is a testing dogleg right. This is a course where accuracy will be rewarded.
18 holes, 5516mtrs, Par 69, SSS 68.
Club membership 450.

Visitors	must contact in advance.
Societies	apply in advance.
Green Fees	not confirmed.
Cards	💳 💳
Facilities	⊗ ♍ 🏌 🍴 ♀ ♨ 🏠 ♍ ♈ ♂ ♒
Location	5m from town

Hotel	★★★ 71% Sligo Park Hotel, Pearse Rd, SLIGO ☎ 071 60291 110 ⇥ ♞

TOBERCURRY

Map 01 B4

Tobercurry ☎ 071 85849
A 9-hole parkland course designed by Edward Hackett. The 8th hole, a Par 3, is regarded as being one of the most testing in the west of Ireland.
9 holes, 5490mtrs, Par 70, SSS 69.
Club membership 300.

Visitors	restricted on Sun.
Societies	telephone in advance on 071 85770.
Green Fees	not confirmed.
Designer	Eddie Hackett
Facilities	♨ ♂
Location	0.25m from Tobercurry

CO TIPPERARY

CAHIR

Map 01 C3

Cahir Park Kilcommon ☎ 052 41474 Fax 052 42717
Parkland course dissected by the River Suir which adds a challenge to the par 4 8th and par 3 16th.
18 holes, 5805mtrs, Par 71, SSS 71, Course record 67.
Club membership 550.

Visitors	may play any time except during competitions.
Societies	by prior arrangement, apply in writing.
Green Fees	IR£15 per day.
Designer	Eddie Hackett
Facilities	🏌 🍴 ♀ ♨ 🏠 ♒ ♂
Location	1m from Cahir on the Clogheen road

Hotel	★★★ 67% Cahir House Hotel, The Square, CAHIR ☎ 52 42727 31 ⇥ ♞

CARRICK-ON-SUIR

Map 01 C2

Carrick-on-Suir Garvonne ☎ 051 640047 Fax 051 640558
18 hole parkland course with the backdrop of the Comeragh Mountains on one side and views of the Suir valley on the other.
18 holes, 6061mtrs, Par 73, SSS 71, Course record 69.
Club membership 600.

▶

Visitors	may not play on Sun morning
Societies	contact for details.
Green Fees	not confirmed.
Designer	Eddie Hackett
Facilities	⊗ �𝄡 ⅃ 🛆 ⅃ ♀ ⚐ 🏌 🛒 ♘
Location	2m SW

Hotel	★★★ 73% Minella Hotel, CLONMEL ☎ 052 22388 70 ⇌ ⚑

CLONMEL   Map 01 C2

Clonmel Lyreanearla, Mountain Rd
☎ 052 24050 & 21138 Fax 052 24050
Set in the scenic, wooded slopes of the Comeragh
Mountains, this is a testing course with lots of open
space and plenty of interesting features. It provides an
enjoyable round in exceptionally tranquil surroundings.
18 holes, 5845mtrs, Par 72, SSS 71.
Club membership 850.

Visitors	must contact in advance.
Societies	must contact in advance.
Green Fees	not confirmed.
Prof	Robert Hayes
Designer	Eddie Hackett
Facilities	⊗ ⊪ 🛆 ⅃ ♀ ⅃ 🏠 ⚐ ♘ 🛒 ♘
Location	3m form Clonmel off N24

Hotel	★★★ 73% Minella Hotel, CLONMEL ☎ 052 22388 70 ⇌ ⚑

MONARD   Map 01 B3

Ballykisteen Ballykisteen, Limerick Junction
☎ 062 33333 Fax 062 52457
Ballykisteen is set in emerald green countryside just two
miles from Tipperary. The course, with landscaped
surroundings against a backdrop of mountains, lakes and
streams, offers an excellent challenge for the champion
golfer. The use of forward tees provide a course that is
playable and enjoyable for the average golfer.
18 holes, 6765yds, Par 72, SSS 72.
Club membership 220.

Visitors	no restrictions.
Societies	must contact in advance.
Green Fees	IR£20 (IR£22 weekends & bank holidays).
Cards	⊟
Prof	David Reddan
Designer	Des Smith
Facilities	⊗ ⊪ 🛆 ⅃ ♀ 🛆 🏠 ⚐ ♘ 🛒 ♘ ♙
Location	On N24 2m from Tipperary towards Limerick

NENAGH   Map 01 B3

Nenagh Beechwood ☎ 067 31476 Fax 067 34808
Interesting gradients call for some careful approach shots.
Some magnificent views.
18 holes, 5491mtrs, Par 69, SSS 68, Course record 64.
Club membership 820.

Visitors	must contact in advance.
Societies	must apply in writing.
Green Fees	IR£10 per round.
Prof	Gordon Morrison
Designer	Eddie Hackett
Facilities	⊗ ⊪ 🛆 ⅃ ♀ 🛆 🏠 ⚐ ♘ 🛒 ♘
Location	3m from town on old Birr rd

Hotel	★★★ 68% Nenagh Abbey Court Hotel, Dublin Rd, NENAGH ☎ 067 41111 46 ⇌ ⚑

ROSCREA   Map 01 C3

Roscrea Golf Club Derryvale
☎ 0505 21130 Fax 0505 23410
An 18-hole parkland course.
18 holes, 5750mtrs, Par 71, SSS 70, Course record 69.
Club membership 420.

Visitors	telephone in advance, on Sun by arrangement.
Societies	apply in writing to Hon Secretary.
Green Fees	not confirmed.
Designer	A Spring
Facilities	⊗ ⊪ 🛆 ⅃ ♀ 🛆 🏌 ♘
Location	N7, Dublin side of Roscrea

Hotel	★★★ 67% Grant's Hotel, Castle St, ROSCREA ☎ 0505 23300 25 ⇌ ⚑

TEMPLEMORE   Map 01 C3

Templemore Manna South ☎ 0504 31400 Fax 0504 35450
Parkland course with many mature and some newly planted
trees which offers a pleasant test to visitors without being too
difficult. Ideal for holiday makers.
9 holes, 5443mtrs, Par 70, SSS 69, Course record 68.
Club membership 220.

Visitors	may not play during Special Events.
Societies	must contact in advance.
Green Fees	IR£10 per round (IR£15 weekends & bank holidays).
Facilities & Leisure	⊗ ⊪ 🛆 ⅃ ♀ 🛆 ♘ hard tennis courts.
Location	0.5m S, beside N62

Hotel	★★★ 60% County Arms Hotel, BIRR ☎ 0509 20791 24 ⇌ ⚑

THURLES   Map 01 C3

Thurles Turtulla ☎ 0504 21983 & 22466 Fax 0504 24647
Superb parkland course with a difficult finish at the 18th.
18 holes, 5904mtrs, Par 73, SSS 71, Course record 65.
Club membership 920.

Visitors	welcome, limited availability at weekends, Tuesday is Ladies day.
Societies	apply in writing to Hon Secretary.
Green Fees	not confirmed.
Prof	Sean Hunt
Facilities & Leisure	⊗ ⊪ 🛆 ⅃ ♀ 🛆 🏠 ⚐ ♘ ♙ squash, sauna, gymnasium.
Location	1m from town on Cork road

Guesthouse	♦♦ Ach-na-Sheen Guesthouse, Clonmel Rd, TIPPERARY ☎ 062 51298 10rm (7 ⇌ ⚑)

TIPPERARY   Map 01 C3

County Tipperary Dundrum House Hotel, Dundrum
☎ 062 71116
The course had been built into a mature Georgian estate
using the features of woodland and parkland adorned by the
Multeen River. Designed by Philip Walton. The 4th hole is
one of the most testing Par 5's in Ireland.   ▶

18 holes, 6709yds, Par 72, SSS 72, Course record 70.
Club membership 190.

Visitors	booking is advisable especially at weekends.
Societies	apply in writing.
Green Fees	not confirmed.
Designer	Philip Walton
Facilities	⊗ ⅏ ⅃ ⅃ ♥ ♀ ♨ 🏌 ⚑ 🏋 ✓ ⌂
& Leisure	hard tennis courts, fishing.
Location	7m W of Cashel off N8

Guesthouse ◆◆ Ach-na-Sheen Guesthouse, Clonmel Rd, TIPPERARY ☎ 062 51298 10rm (7 ⇄ ↾)

Tipperary Rathanny ☎ 062 51119
Recently extended to 18-holes, this parkland course has plenty of trees and bunkers and water at three holes to provide additional hazards.
18 holes, 5761mtrs, Par 71, SSS 71, Course record 66.
Club membership 700.

Visitors	advisable to contact by phone, weekend play available but limited on Sun.
Societies	apply in writing.
Green Fees	not confirmed.
Facilities	⊗ ⅏ by prior arrangement
Location	1m S

Guesthouse ◆◆ Ach-na-Sheen Guesthouse, Clonmel Rd, TIPPERARY ☎ 062 51298 10rm (7 ⇄ ↾)

CO WATERFORD

DUNGARVAN   Map 01 C2

Dungarvan Knocknagranagh
☎ 058 41605 & 43310 Fax 058 44113
A championship-standard course beside Dungarvan Bay, with seven lakes and hazards placed to challenge all levels of golfer. The greens are considered to be among the best in Ireland.
18 holes, 6560yds, Par 72, SSS 71, Course record 66.
Club membership 625.

Visitors	welcome weekdays, booking advisable weekends.
Societies	telephone then write to confim booking.
Green Fees	IR£20 per round (IR£25 weekends & bank holidays).
Cards	🖃 ■ 🖾
Prof	David Hayes
Designer	Moss Fives
Facilities	⊗ ⅏ ⅃ ♥ ♀ ♨ 🏌 ⚑ 🏋 ✓
& Leisure	snooker.
Location	Off N25 between Waterford & Youghal

Hotel ★★★ 56% Lawlors Hotel, DUNGARVAN ☎ 058 41122 & 41056 Fax 058 41000 89 ⇄ ↾

Gold Coast Golf & Leisure Ballinacourty
☎ 058 42249 & 44055 Fax 058 43378
A parkland course bordered by the Atlantic Ocean with unrivalled panoramic views of Dungarvan Bay. The mature tree-lined fairways of the old course are tastefully integrated with the long and challenging newer holes to create a superb course.

18 holes, 6171mtrs, Par 72, SSS 72, Course record 72.
Club membership 450.

Visitors	book in advance, times available throughout the week.
Societies	apply by telephone in advance.
Green Fees	IR£20 per round (IR£25 weekends & bank holidays).
Cards	🖃 ■ 🖾 🖾
Designer	Maurice Fives
Facilities	⊗ ⅏ ⅃ ♥ ♀ ♨ 🏌 ⚑ 🏋 ✓ ⌂
& Leisure	hard tennis courts, heated indoor swimming pool, sauna, gymnasium.
Location	Left of N25, 2m bfore Dungarvan

Hotel ★★★ 56% Lawlors Hotel, DUNGARVAN ☎ 058 41122 & 41056 Fax 058 41000 89 ⇄ ↾

West Waterford ☎ 058 43216 & 41475 Fax 058 44343
Designed by Eddie Hackett, the course is on 150 acres of rolling parkland by the Brickey River with a backdrop of the Comeragh Mountains, Knockmealdowns and Drum Hills. The first nine holes are laid out on a large plateau featuring a stream which comes into play at the 3rd and 4th holes. The river at the southern boundary affects several later holes.
18 holes, 6004mtrs, Par 72, SSS 74, Course record 70.
Club membership 185.

Visitors	pre book for tee times.
Societies	telephone or write in advance.
Green Fees	not confirmed.
Cards	🖃 🖾
Designer	Eddie Hackett
Facilities	⊗ ⅏ ⅃ ♥ ♀ ♨ 🏌 ⚑ 🏋 ✓
& Leisure	hard tennis courts.
Location	Approx 3m W of Dungarvan, off N25

Hotel ★★★ 56% Lawlors Hotel, DUNGARVAN ☎ 058 41122 & 41056 Fax 058 41000 89 ⇄ ↾

DUNMORE EAST   Map 01 C2

Dunmore East ☎ 051 383151 Fax 051 383151
Overlooking the village of Dunmore East, with panoramic views of the village, bay and Hook peninsula. This course promises to offer idyllic surroundings and challenging golf for the high or low handicap golfer.
18 holes, 6655yds, Par 72, SSS 70, Course record 69.
Club membership 300.

Visitors	welcome, no restrictions.
Societies	telephone in advance.
Green Fees	IR£10-15.
Prof	Derry Kiely
Designer	W H Jones
Facilities	⊗ ⅏ ⅃ ♥ ♀ ♨ 🏌 ⚑ 🏋 ✓
Location	Follow signs to Dunmore East. After Petrol Stn take left fork. Left at The Strand Inn & 1st right

Hotel ★★★ 63% Majestic Hotel, TRAMORE ☎ 051 381761 57 ⇄ ↾

LISMORE   Map 01 C2

Lismore Ballyin ☎ 058 54026 Fax 058 53338
Picturesque tree-dotted sloping course on the banks of the Blackwater River. Rothwell's is a difficult hole with a sloping green and trees to either side.
9 holes, 5790yds, Par 69, SSS 67, Course record 67.
Club membership 350.

▶

Visitors may not play Sun before noon. Restricted Wed, Thu & weekends.
Societies must apply in writing.
Green Fees not confirmed.
Facilities ⊗ ╠ 💺 ♀ 🛦 ♂

Hotel ★★★ 56% Lawlors Hotel, DUNGARVAN
☎ 058 41122 & 41056 Fax 058 41000 89 ⇥ ♥

TRAMORE
Map 01 C2

Tramore Newtown Hill
☎ 051 386170 Fax 051 390961
This course has matured nicely over the years to become a true championship test and has been chosen as the venue for the Irish Professional Matchplay Championship and the Irish Amateur Championship. Most of the fairways are lined by evergreen trees, calling for accurate placing of shots, and the course is continuing to develop.
18 holes, 5918mtrs, Par 72, SSS 72, Course record 65.
Club membership 1200.
Visitors pre-booking required.
Societies contact in advance.
Green Fees IR£27 per round (IR£33 weekends & bank holidays).
Cards ▬ ▬
Prof Derry Kiely
Designer Capt H C Tippet
Facilities ⊗ ℿ ╠ 💺 ♀ 🛦 🏠 ⛳ 🏌 ⛏ ♂
& Leisure squash.
Location 0.5m from Tramore on Dungaruan coast road

Hotel ★★★ 63% Majestic Hotel, TRAMORE
☎ 051 381761 57 ⇥ ♥

WATERFORD
Map 01 C2

Faithlegg House Dunmore East ☎ 051 382241
Some wicked slopes and borrows on the immaculate greens, a huge 432yard 17th what has a host of problems and a doglegged approach to the two-tier 18th green are just some of the novel features on this course. Set on the banks of the River Suir, the course has been integrated into a landscape textured with mature trees, flowing parkland and five lakes.
18 holes, 6057mtrs, Par 72, SSS 72, Course record 69.
Club membership 65.
Visitors no restrictions.
Societies apply in writing or telephone at least a month in advance.
Green Fees not confirmed.
Prof Ted Higgins
Facilities ♀ 🛦 🏠 ⛳

Hotel ★★★ 61% Jurys Hotel, Ferrybank,
WATERFORD ☎ 051 832111 98 ⇥ ♥

Waterford Newrath ☎ 051 876748 Fax 051 853405
Undulating parkland course in pleasant surroundings.
18 holes, 5722mtrs, Par 71, SSS 70, Course record 64.
Club membership 931.
Visitors must contact in advance.
Societies must apply in writing.
Green Fees IR£22 (IR£25 weekdays & bank holidays).
Prof Joseph Condon
Designer W Park/J Braid
Facilities ⊗ ℿ ╠ 💺 ♀ 🛦 🏠 ⛳ ♂
Location 1m N

Hotel ★★★ 61% Jurys Hotel, Ferrybank,
WATERFORD ☎ 051 832111 98 ⇥ ♥

Waterford Castle The Island, Ballinakill
☎ 051 871633 Fax 051 871634
Parkland course with mature trees, 4 lakes, sandbased tees and greens and good bunkering.
18 holes, 5827mtrs, Par 72, SSS 71, Course record 70.
Club membership 500.
Visitors must contact in advance, pre booking required.
Societies apply in advance.
Green Fees not confirmed.
Designer Den Smyth
Facilities ╠ 💺 ♀ 🛦 🏌 ⛏ ♂ ♪
& Leisure hard tennis courts, heated indoor swimming pool.
Location 2m E of Waterford City, on Island approached by private ferry

Hotel ★★★ 61% Jurys Hotel, Ferrybank,
WATERFORD ☎ 051 832111 98 ⇥ ♥

ATHLONE
Map 01 C4

Glasson Golf & Country Club Glasson
☎ 0902 85120 Fax 0902 85444
Opened for play in 1993 the course has earned a reputation for being one of the most challenging and scenic courses in Ireland. Designed by Christy O'Connor Jnr it is reputedly his best yet! Surrounded on three sides by Lough Ree the views from everywhere on the course are breathtaking.
18 holes, 6664yds, Par 72, SSS 72, Course record 65.
Club membership 220.
Visitors must book in advance.
Societies book in advance.
Green Fees IR£30 (IR£32-£IR35 Fri-Sun).
Cards ▬ ▬ ▬ 💳.
Designer Christy O'Connor Jnr
Facilities ⊗ ℿ ╠ 💺 ♀ 🛦 🏠 ⛳ 🏌 ⛏ ♂
Location 6m N of Athlone on N55

Hotel ★★★ 64% Prince Of Wales Hotel,
ATHLONE ☎ 0902 72626 73 ⇥ ♥

DELVIN
Map 01 C4

Delvin Castle Clonyn
☎ 044 64315 & 64671 Fax 044 64315
Situated in the mature parkland of Clonyn Castle, the course is well known for its unique historic setting with a 16th century ruin in the back nine holes and an imposing Victorian castle in the front nine.
18 holes, 5800mtrs, Par 70, SSS 68.
Club membership 400.
Visitors no restrictions. Advance booking recommemded.
Societies apply in writing in advance.

▶

Green Fees IR£16 per 18 holes; IR£10 per round
(IR£18/IR£12 weekends & bank holidays).
Cards
Prof David Keenaghan
Designer John Day
Facilities
Location On N52, Dundalk to Mullingar road

Hotel ★★★ 62% Ardboyne Hotel, Dublin Rd,
NAVAN ☎ 046 23119 27

MOATE
Map 01 C4

Moate ☎ 0902 81271
Extended in 1994 to 18 holes, the course is parkland with
trees. Although the original 9-holes did not have water
hazards the new section has lakes and many bunkers.
18 holes, 5642mtrs, Par 72, SSS 70, Course record 67.
Club membership 650.

Visitors welcome, advisable to telephone in advance.
Societies must contact in advance.
Green Fees IR£12 per round (IR£15 weekends & bank
holidays).
Designer B Browne
Facilities
Location 1m N

Hotel ★★★ 64% Prince Of Wales Hotel,
ATHLONE ☎ 0902 72626 73

Mount Temple Mount Temple Village
☎ 0902 81841 & 81545 Fax 0902 81957
A traditionally built, highly-rated, all year round course with
parkland and unique links-type greens and natural undulating
fairways. A challenge for all levels of golfers as the wind
plays a major part in the scoring on this course.
18 holes, 5950mtrs, Par 72, SSS 71, Course record 73.
Club membership 150.
Visitors welcome but must book for weekends.
Societies telephone in advance.
Green Fees IR£16 per round (IR£20 weekends & bank
holidays).
Cards
Prof David Keenan
Designer Michael Dolan
Facilities by prior arrangement
Location 4m off N6 to Mount Temple village, 5m from
Athlone

Hotel ★★★ 64% Prince Of Wales Hotel,
ATHLONE ☎ 0902 72626 73

MULLINGAR
Map 01 C4

Mullingar ☎ 044 48366 Fax 044 41499
The wide rolling fairways between mature trees provide
parkland golf at its very best. The course, designed by
the great James Braid, offers a tough challenge and
annually hosts one of the most important amateur events
in the British Isles - the Mullingar Scratch Cup. It has
also been the venue of the Irish Professional
Championship. One advantage of the layout is that the
clubhouse is never far away.
18 holes, 6406yds, Par 72, SSS 71, Course record 63.
Club membership 1000.
Visitors preferred if booked in advance, Sundays are
Medal days, Wednesday Ladies day.
Societies apply in writing.
Green Fees not confirmed.
Prof John Burns
Designer James Braid
Facilities
Location 3m S

Hotel ★★★ 64% Prince Of Wales Hotel,
ATHLONE ☎ 0902 72626 73

CO WEXFORD

ENNISCORTHY
Map 01 D3

Enniscorthy Knockmarshall
☎ 054 33191 Fax 054 37367
A pleasant course suitable for all levels of ability.
18 holes, 6115mtrs, Par 72, SSS 72.
Club membership 900.
Visitors must telephone for booking.
Societies must book in advance.
Green Fees not confirmed.
Prof Martin Sludos
Designer Eddie Hackett
Facilities
Location 1m from town on New Ross road

Hotel ★ 60% Murphy-Flood's Hotel, Market Square,
ENNISCORTHY
☎ 054 33413 21rm (5 13)

GOREY
Map 01 D3

Courtown Kiltennel ☎ 055 25166 Fax 055 25553
A pleasant parkland course which is well wooded and
enjoys views across the Irish Sea near Courtown
Harbour.
18 holes, 5898mtrs, Par 71, SSS 71, Course record 65.
Club membership 1200.
Visitors must contact in advance.
Societies advisable to contact in advance.
Green Fees IR£17/IR£22 per round (IR£22/IR£27
weekends).
Prof John Coone
Designer Harris & Associates
Facilities
Location 3m from town, off Courtown Road ▶

Courtown Golf Club

Hotel ★★★▲▲ Marlfield House Hotel, GOREY
☎ 055 21124 19 ⇄ ⁣🏳

NEW ROSS   Map 01 C3

New Ross Tinneranny ☎ 051 421433 Fax 051 420098
Recently extended to 18-holes, this well kept parkland course
has an attractive backdrop of hills and mountains. Straight
hitting and careful placing of shots is very important,
especially on the 2nd, 6th, 10th and 15th, all of which are
challenging holes.
18 holes, 5751yds, Par 71, SSS 70.
Club membership 700.
Visitors   welcome, booking required for weekend play.
Societies   apply to secretary/manager.
Green Fees IR£14 per round (IR£16 weekends & bank
                holidays).
Designer   Des Smith
Facilities ⊗ 🏌 🏪 ♿ ♀ ⛳ ⁣🏁 ⁣✍
Location   3m from town centre

Hotel ★★ 59% The Old Rectory Hotel, Rosbercon,
NEW ROSS ☎ 051 421719 12 ⇄ ⁣🏳

ROSSLARE   Map 01 D2

Rosslare Rosslare Strand ☎ 053 32203 Fax 053 32263
This traditional links course is within minutes of the
ferry terminal at Rosslare, but its popularity is not
confined to visitors from Fishguard or Le Havre. It is a
great favourite with the Irish too. Many of the greens are
sunken and are always in beautiful condition, but the
semi-blind approaches are among features of this course
which provide a healthy challenge.
*Old Course: 18 holes, 6601yds, Par 72, SSS 72, Course
record 66.*
New Course: 9 holes, 3153yds, Par 35, SSS 70.
Club membership 1000.
Visitors   telephone 053 32203 ext3 in advance.
Societies   apply in writing/telephone.
Green Fees IR£25 (IR£35 weekends & bank holidays).
Cards   💳 💳
Prof   Johnny Young
Designer   Hawtree/Taylor
Facilities ⊗ 🏌 🏪 ♿ ♀ ⛳ ⁣🏁 ⁣✍ 🛒 ⁣✍
& Leisure   sauna.
Location   6m N of Rosslare Ferry Terminal

Hotel ★★★★ 78% Kelly's Resort Hotel,
ROSSLARE ☎ 053 32114 Annexe 99 ⇄ ⁣🏳

St Helen's Bay Golf & Country Club St Helens, Kilrane
☎ 053 33234 & 33669 Fax 053 33803
A championship-standard golf course designed by Philip
Walton. Link and parkland with water hazards, bunkers and
trees incorporated generously. Overlooking the beach with
accommodation on site.
18 holes, 5813mtrs, Par 72, SSS 72, Course record 69.
Club membership 450.
Visitors   contact in advance.
Societies   telephone in advance.
Green Fees IR£28 per 36 holes; IR£22 per round; IR£18 per
                9 holes (IR£29/IR£25/IR£14 weekends & bank
                holidays).
Cards   💳 💳 💳
Designer   Philip Walton
Facilities ⊗ 🏌 🏪 ♿ ♀ ⛳ ⁣🏁 ⁣✍ 🛒 ⁣✍
& Leisure   hard tennis courts, sauna.
Location   5 minutes from the ferryport of Rosslare

Hotel ★★★ 73% Ferrycarrig Hotel, Ferrycarrig,
WEXFORD ☎ 053 20999 90 ⇄ ⁣🏳

WEXFORD   Map 01 D3

Wexford Mulgannon ☎ 053 42238
Parkland course with panoramic view of the Wexford
coastline and mountains.
18 holes, 6100yds, Par 71, SSS 69.
Club membership 800.
Visitors   must contact in advance but may not play Thu &
                weekends.
Societies   must contact in writing.
Green Fees not confirmed.
Prof   G Ronayne
Facilities ♀ ♿ ⁣🏁

Hotel ★★★ 72% Talbot Hotel Conference & Leisure
Centre, Trinity St, WEXFORD
☎ 053 22566 100 ⇄ ⁣🏳

ARKLOW   Map 01 D3

Arklow Abbeylands ☎ 0402 32492 Fax 0402 32492
Scenic links course.
18 holes, 5404mtrs, Par 68, SSS 67, Course record 66.
Club membership 450.
Visitors   may play Mon-Fri and 3hrs Sat 9am-12 noon,
                must book in advance.
Societies   must apply in writing or telephone in advance.
Green Fees not confirmed.
Designer   Hawtree & Taylor
Facilities ⊗ 🏌 🏪 ♿ ♀ ⛳ ⁣🏁 ⁣✍ ⁣✍ 🏳
Location   0.5m from town centre

Hotel ★★★▲▲ Marlfield House Hotel, GOREY
☎ 055 21124 19 ⇄ ⁣🏳

Looking for a driving range?
See the index at the back of the guide

BALTINGLASS
Map 01 D3

Baltinglass Dublin Rd ☎ 0508 81350 Fax 0508 81350
On the banks of the River Slaney, the 9-hole course has 4
Par-4s over 400 yards which have to be played twice.
Reputed to be one of the hardest 9-hole courses in the
Republic.
9 holes, 5554mtrs, Par 68, SSS 69, Course record 68.
Club membership 400.
Visitors advisable to check availability for weekends.
Societies apply in writing.
Green Fees IR£10 per 18 holes (IR£12 weekends).
Facilities 🏌 ♨ 🍴 ♣ ⚙
Location 500 metres N of Baltinglass

Rathsallagh ☎ 045 403316 Fax 045 403295
Designed by Peter McEvoy and Christy O'Connor Jnr, this is
a spectacular course which will test the pro's without
intimidating the club golfer. Set in 252 acres of lush parkland
with thousands of mature trees, natural water hazards and
gently rolling landscape. The greens are of high quality, in
design, construction and condition.
18 holes, 6916yds, Par 72, SSS 74.
Club membership 240.
Visitors must have appropriate attire & book in advance.
Restricted weekends. Soft spikes only.
Societies telephone in advance.
Green Fees Mon-Thu: IR£40 per round (IR£50 per round
Fri, weekends & bank holidays)..
Cards 💳 💳
Prof Brendan McDaid
Designer McEvoy/O'Connor
Facilities ⊗ ⅢⅢ 🏌 ♨ 🍴 ♣ 🏠 ⚓ 🛒 ⚙ 🏌
& Leisure hard tennis courts, heated indoor swimming
pool, sauna.
Location 15m SE of Naas

Hotel ★★★ 61% Downshire House Hotel,
BLESSINGTON
☎ 045 865199 14 🛏 🏌 Annexe 11 🛏 🏌

BLAINROE
Map 01 D3

Blainroe ☎ 0404 68168 Fax 0404 69369
Parkland course overlooking the sea on the east coast,
offering a challenging round to golfers of all abilities.
18 holes, 6070mtrs, Par 72, SSS 72, Course record 71.
Club membership 868.
Visitors must contact in advance.
Societies must telephone in advance.
Green Fees IR£29 (IR£39 weekends).
Cards 💳 💳
Prof John McDonald
Designer C Hawtree
Facilities ⊗ ⅢⅢ 🏌 ♨ 🍴 ♣ 🏠 ⚓ 🛒 ⚙
Location S of Wicklow, on coast road

Hotel ★★★♨♨ Tinakilly Country House &
Restaurant, RATHNEW
☎ 0404 69274 53 🛏 🏌

Where to stay, where to eat?
Visit the AA internet site
www.theaa.co.uk

BLESSINGTON
Map 01 D3

Tulfarris House Hotel & Country Club
☎ 045 867555 Fax 045 867561
Designed by Paddy Merrigan, this course is on the
Blessington lakeshore with the Wicklow Mountains as a
backdrop.
18 holes, 7116yds, Par 72, SSS 74.
Club membership 150.
Visitors tee booking advisable; may not play Sun 8-
11.30pm.
Societies must contact in writing or telephone in advance.
Green Fees IR£40 per round (IR£50 weekends & bank
holidays).
Cards 💳 💳 💳
Prof A Williams
Designer Patrick Merrigan
Facilities ⊗ ⅢⅢ 🏌 ♨ 🍴 ♣ 🏠 ⚓ 🛒 ⚙ 🏌
& Leisure hard tennis courts, heated indoor swimming
pool, fishing, sauna, solarium, gymnasium.
Location Via N81, 2m from Blessington village

Hotel ★★★ 61% Downshire House Hotel,
BLESSINGTON
☎ 045 865199 14 🛏 🏌 Annexe 11 🛏 🏌

BRAY
Map 01 D4

Bray Ravenswell Rd ☎ 01 2862484 Fax 01 2862484
A 9-hole parkland course with plenty of trees and bunkers.
9 holes, 5761mtrs, Par 70, SSS 70, Course record 65.
Club membership 500.
Visitors restricted Mon, Sat & Sun.
Societies contact in advance.
Green Fees not confirmed.
Prof Michael Walby
Facilities 🏌 ♨ 🍴 ♣ 🏠 ⚓ ⚙

Hotel ★★★ 64% Fitzpatrick Castle Hotel,
KILLINEY ☎ 01 2840700 113 🛏 🏌

Old Conna Ferndale Rd
☎ 01 2826055 & 2826766 Fax 01 2825611
Parkland course set in wooded terrain with panoramic views
of Irish Sea and Wicklow mountains.
18 holes, 6550yds, Par 72, SSS 72, Course record 70.
Club membership 900.
Visitors advisable to contact in advance but may not play
weekends. Smart dress essential on course & in
clubhouse.
Societies must telephone well in advance.
Green Fees IR£30 per round (IR£45 weekends).
Cards 💳 💳
Prof Paul McDaid
Designer Eddie Hackett
Facilities ⊗ ⅢⅢ 🏌 ♨ 🍴 ♣ 🏠 ⚓ 🛒 ⚙
Location 2m from Bray

Hotel ★★★ 63% Royal Hotel & Leisure Centre,
Main St, BRAY ☎ 01 2862935 91 🛏 🏌

Woodbrook Dublin Rd ☎ 01 2824799 Fax 01 2821950
Pleasant parkland with magnificent views and bracing sea
breezes which has hosted a number of events, including the
Irish Close and the Irish Open Championships. A testing
finish is provided by an 18th hole with out of bounds on both
sides. ▶

18 holes, 6017mtrs, Par 72, SSS 71, Course record 65.
Club membership 1100.

Visitors	must contact in advance and have a handicap certificate.
Societies	must contact in advance.
Green Fees	IR£40-IR£50 (IR£60 weekends & bank holidays).
Cards	
Prof	Billy Kinsella
Designer	Peter McEvoy
Facilities	⊗))Ⅲ 🏌 🛆 ▼ ♀ 🛆 🎣 ⛳ ✎
Location	11m S of Dublin on N11

Hotel	★★★ 63% Royal Hotel & Leisure Centre, Main St, BRAY
	☎ 01 2862935 91 🛏 ☂

BRITTAS BAY   Map 01 D3

The European Club ☎ 0404 47415 Fax 0404 47449
A links course that runs through a large dunes system.
Since it was opened in 1992 it is rapidly gaining
recognition as one of Irelands Best Courses.
18 holes, 7105yds, Par 71, SSS 71, Course record 69.
Club membership 100.

Visitors	pre-booking advised especially for weekends, no denim.
Societies	must book in advance.
Green Fees	IR£50 per round.
Cards	
Designer	Pat Ruddy
Facilities	⊗))Ⅲ 🏌 🛆 ▼ 🛆 ⛳ ✎
Location	1.5m from Brittas Bay Beach

Hotel	★★★ ♣♣ Tinakilly Country House & Restaurant, RATHNEW
	☎ 0404 69274 53 🛏 ☂

DELGANY   Map 01 D3

Delgany ☎ 01 2874536 Fax 01 2873977
An undulating parkland course amidst beautiful scenery.
18 holes, 5474mtrs, Par 69, SSS 68, Course record 61.
Club membership 967.

Visitors	may play Mon, Wed (until 10am), Thu & Fri. Contact in advance.
Societies	contact in advance.
Green Fees	IR£25 per round (IR£29 weekends & bank holidays).
Cards	
Prof	Gavin Kavanagh
Designer	H Vardon
Facilities	⊗))Ⅲ 🏌 🛆 ▼ ♀ 🛆 🎣 ⛳ ✎
Location	0.75m from village

Hotel	★★★ 63% Royal Hotel & Leisure Centre, Main St, BRAY ☎ 01 2862935 91 🛏 ☂

GREYSTONES   Map 01 D3

Charlesland Golf & Country Club Hotel
☎ 01 2874350 Fax 01 2874360
Championship length, Par 72 course with a double dog-leg at
the 9th and 18th. Water hazards at the 3rd and 11th.
18 holes, 5963mtrs, Par 72, SSS 72.
Club membership 744.

Visitors	must contact in advance.
Societies	must apply in advance.
Green Fees	IR£30 per round; IR£20 before 10am (IR£35 weekends & bank holidays).
Cards	
Prof	Paul Heeney
Designer	Eddie Hackett
Facilities	⊗))Ⅲ 🏌 🛆 ▼ ♀ 🛆 🎣 🐎 ✎
& Leisure	sauna.
Location	1m S of Greystones on the road to Delgany village

Hotel	★★★ ♣♣ Tinakilly Country House & Restaurant, RATHNEW
	☎ 0404 69274 53 🛏 ☂

Greystones ☎ 01 2874136 Fax 01 2873749
A part level and part hilly parkland course.
18 holes, 5322mtrs, Par 69, SSS 68.
Club membership 995.

Visitors	may only play Mon, Tue & Fri morning. Must contact in advance.
Societies	must contact in writing.
Green Fees	IR£25 per round (IR£30 Friday).
Cards	
Designer	P Merrigan
Facilities	⊗))Ⅲ 🏌 🛆 ▼ ♀ 🛆 🎣 🐎 ✎

Hotel	★★★ ♣♣ Tinakilly Country House & Restaurant, RATHNEW
	☎ 0404 69274 53 🛏 ☂

KILCOOLE   Map 01 D3

KILCOOLE See page 477.

Kilcoole ☎ 01 2872066 2872070 Fax 01 2871803
9 holes, 5506mtrs, Par 70, SSS 69.
Club membership 250.

Visitors	restricted Sat & Sun 8-10am.
Societies	apply in writing or telephone.
Green Fees	not confirmed.
Facilities	▼ 🛆 ✎
Location	N11 Kilcoole/Newcastle

Hotel	★★★ ♣♣ Tinakilly Country House & Restaurant, RATHNEW
	☎ 0404 69274 53 🛏 ☂

Druid's Glen

e-mail: druids@indigo.ie

D ruids Glen from the first tee to the eighteenth green (7000 yards in all) creates an exceptional golfing experience that is totally unique with its distinguished surroundings and spectacular views. A masterpiece of inspired planning and golfing architecture, designed by Tom Craddock and Pat Ruddy, it is the culmination of years of preparation, creating a unique inland golf course that challenges and satisfies in equal parts.

Druids Glen hosted the Murphy's Irish Open in 1996, 1997, 1998 and an unprecedented fourth time in 1999. The world's top professionals and club golfers alike continue to enjoy the challenge offered here. A variety of teeing positions are available and there is a practice area, including three full-length 'academy holes'. Individual and corporate members enjoy generous reserved tee times, visitors are very welcome but it is recommended that you book well in advance.

Visitors advance booking essential

Societies advance booking essential

Green Fees IR£85 per round; IR£65 before 9am — 🖩 💳 📠 💻

Facilities ⊗ ⅏ 🏌 💼 ♀ ⛳ 🏠 🍴 🍹 🚌 ♂ ♟

Location 20m S of Dublin, 3m off N11 motorway, immediately S of Glen of Downs

Holes/Par/Course record 18 holes, 6547 yds, Par 71, SSS 73, Course record 62

WHERE TO STAY NEARBY

Hotels
RATHNEW

★★★ 🏵 🏵 ♨ Tinakilly Country House & Restaurant. ☎ 0404 69274. 53 🛏 🎣

★★★ 🏵 67% Hunters Hotel. ☎ 0404 40106. 13 🛏 3 🎣

Championship Course

477

RATHDRUM   Map 01 D3

Glenmalure Greenane ☎ 0404 46679 Fax 0404 46783
A moorland course with elevated tees and greens where
accuracy is required. The 3rd, known as the Helicopter Pad,
is difficult. GUI affiliated.
18 holes, 5300yds, Par 71, SSS 67, Course record 71.
Club membership 250.
Visitors   unable to play Sunday 8-11am
Societies   telephone at least 3 days in advance.
Green Fees not confirmed.
Designer   P Suttle
Facilities   ⊗ ⫟ 🍴 ⬛ ♀ 🏊 ⛳ 🏌 ✈ 🛒 ⚷
Location   2m W

Hotel   ★★★ 64% Woodenbridge Hotel, WOODEN
               BRIDGE ☎ 0402 35146 23 ⇌ 🐾

ROUNDWOOD   Map 01 D3

Roundwood Newtown, Mountkennedy
☎ 01 2818488 & 2802555 Fax 01 2843642
Heathland and parkland course with forest and lakes set in
beautiful countryside with views of the coast and the
Wicklow Mountains.
18 holes, 6685yds, Par 72, SSS 72.
Club membership 120.
Visitors   no restrictions
Societies   pre booking necessary.
Green Fees not confirmed.
Facilities   ⊗ 🍴 ⬛ ♀ 🏊 ⛳ 🏌 🛒 ⚷
Location   2.5m off N11 at Newtown Mountkennedy on
               N765

Hotel   ★★★ 64% The Glendalough Hotel,
               GLENDALOUGH ☎ 0404 45135 44 ⇌ 🐾

SHILLELAGH   Map 01 D3

Coollattin Coollattin ☎ 055 29125 Fax 055 29125
Plenty of trees provide features on this 18-hole parkland
course.
18 holes, 6148yds, Par 70, SSS 68.
Club membership 840.
Visitors   may not play weekends. Must contact in
               advance.
Societies   contact for details.
Green Fees IR£20 per round (IR£25 weekends).
Designer   Peter McEvoy
Facilities   ⊗ ⫟ 🍴 ⬛ ♀ 🏊 🛒 ⚷

Hotel   ★★★ 🏨 Marlfield House Hotel, GOREY
               ☎ 055 21124 19 ⇌ 🐾

WICKLOW   Map 01 D3

Wicklow Dunbur Rd ☎ 0404 67379
Situated on the cliffs overlooking Wicklow Bay this parkland
course does not have many trees. It was extended to 18 holes
in 1994, it provides a challenging test of golf with each hole
having its own individual features.
18 holes, 5126mtrs, Par 71, SSS 70.
Club membership 500.
Visitors   welcome, restrictions on Wed/Thu evening and
               Sun. Recommended to call in advance for times
Societies   contact for details.
Green Fees IR£22 per round.
Prof   David Daly
Designer   Craddock & Ruddy
Facilities   ⊗ ⫟ 🍴 ⬛ ♀ 🏊 🏮 ⚷

Hotel   ★★★ 🏨 Tinakilly Country House &
               Restaurant, RATHNEW
               ☎ 0404 69274 53 ⇌ 🐾

WOODENBRIDGE   Map 01 D3

Woodenbridge Woodenbridge, Arklow
☎ 0402 35202 Fax 0402 35202
A level parkland course with undulating fairways and greens,
traversed by two lovely meandering rivers.
18 holes, 6400yds, Par 71, SSS 70, Course record 71.
Club membership 550.
Visitors   may not play Thu and Sat, prior booking
               strongly recommended.
Societies   Mon, Tue & Fri only, book well in advance.
Green Fees IR£30 per round (IR£35 Sun & bank holidays).
Cards   ⚏ 🔳
Designer   Paddy Merrigan
Facilities   ⊗ 🍴 ⬛ ♀ 🏊 🛒 ⚷
Location   4m NW of Arklow

Hotel   ★★★ 64% Woodenbridge Hotel, WOODEN
               BRIDGE ☎ 0402 35146 23 ⇌ 🐾

AA Hotels that have special
arrangements with golf courses are listed at
the back of the guide

AA Hotels
with special arrangements for golf

AA Hotels with special arrangements for golf are listed below. Arrangements may include reduced green fees, preferential tee times for hotel guests or golfing packages, telephone for details.

ENGLAND

Abberley
The Elms | 01299 896666

Abbot's Salford
Salford Hall Hotel | 01386 871300

Acton Trussell
The Moat House | 01785 712217

Albrighton
Lea Manor Hotel | 01902 373266

Aldeburgh
The Brudenell | 01728 452071

Aldeburgh
Wentworth Hotel | 01728 452312

Aldeburgh
White Lion Hotel Ltd | 01728 452720

Alderminster
Ettington Park Hotel | 01789 450123

Alfriston
Deans Place | 01323 870248

Alnwick
White Swan Hotel | 01665 602109

Alston
Nent Hall Country House Hotel | 01434 381584

Altarnun
Penhallow Manor Hotel | 01566 86206

Altrincham
Cresta Court Hotel | 0161 927 7272

Ambleside
Nanny Brow Country House | 015394 32036

Ambleside
Regent Hotel | 015394 32254

Amesbury
Antrobus Arms Hotel | 01980 623163

Andover
Esseborne Manor | 01264 736444

Andover
Quality Hotel Andover | 01264 369111

Ascot
The Berystede | 0870 400 8111

Ashburton
Dartmoor Lodge | 01364 652232

Ashburton
Holne Chase Hotel | 01364 631471

Ashford
Eastwell Manor | 01233 213000

Aspley Guise
Moore Place Hotel | 01908 282000

Axminster
Fairwater Head Hotel | 01297 678349

Axminster
Lea Hill Hotel | 01404 881881

Aylesbury
Hartwell House | 01296 747444

Balsall Common
Nailcote Hall | 024 76466174

Bamburgh
The Mizen Head Hotel | 01668 214254

Bamburgh
Victoria Hotel | 01668 214431

Bamburgh
Waren House Hotel | 01668 214581

Banbury
Banbury House | 01295 259361

Banbury
Wroxton House Hotel | 01295 730777

Barford
The Glebe at Barford | 01926 624218

Barnstaple
Barnstaple Hotel | 01271 376221

Barnstaple
Park Hotel | 01271 372166

Barnstaple
Royal & Fortescue Hotel | 01271 342289

Barnstaple
The Imperial | 01271 345861

Barton
Barton Grange Hotel | 01772 862551

Basingstoke
Basingstoke Country Hotel | 01256 764161

Bassenthwaite
Castle Inn Hotel | 017687 76401

Bath
The Bath Spa Hotel | 0870 400 8222

Bath
The Francis | 0870 400 8223

Battle
Netherfield Place | 01424 774455

Beaminster
Bridge House Hotel | 01308 862200

Belford
Blue Bell Hotel | 01668 213543

Berwick-upon-Tweed
Marshall Meadows Country House Hotel | 01289 331133

Bideford
Royal Hotel | 01237 472005

Bideford
Yeoldon Country House Hotel | 01237 474400

Birkenhead
Bowler Hat Hotel | 0151 652 4931

Birmingham
Oxford Hotel | 0121 449 3298

Birmingham
Posthouse Birmingham Great Barr | 0870 400 9009

Birmingham Airport
Novotel | 0121 782 7000

Bolton Abbey
The Devonshire Arms Country House Hotel | 01756 710441

Borrowdale
Borrowdale Hotel | 017687 77224

Boscastle
The Wellington Hotel | 01840 250202

Bournemouth
Burley Court Hotel | 01202 552824

Bournemouth
Cumberland Hotel | 01202 290722

Bournemouth
Queens Hotel | 01202 554415

Bournemouth
The Connaught Hotel | 01202 298020

Bournemouth
Winterbourne Hotel | 01202 296366

Bourton-on-the-Water
Chester House Hotel & Motel | 01451 820286

Bourton-on-the-Water
Dial House Hotel | 01451 822244

Bovey Tracey
Coombe Cross Hotel | 01626 832476

Bovey Tracey
Edgemoor Hotel | 01626 832466

Bracknell
Coppid Beech 01344 303333

Bradford
Cedar Court Hotel Bradford
01274 406606

Bradford
Courtyard by Marriott
Leeds/Bradford 0113 285 4646

Bradford
Midland Hotel 01274 735735

Bradford-on-Avon
Leigh Park Hotel 01225 864885

Bradford-on-Avon
Woolley Grange 01225 864705

Bramhall
County Hotel Bramhall
0161 455 9988

Brampton
Farlam Hall Hotel 016977 46234

Brampton
The Tarn End House Hotel
016977 2340

Brandesburton
Burton Lodge Hotel 01964 542847

Branston
Branston Hall Hotel 01522 793305

Bray
Chauntry House Hotel & Restaurant
01628 673991

Bridgnorth
Falcon Hotel 01746 763134

Bridgwater
Walnut Tree Hotel 01278 662255

Bridlington
Expanse Hotel 01262 675347

Bridport
Haddon House Hotel 01308 423626

Bridport
Roundham House Hotel
01308 422753

Brigg
The Exchange Coach House Inn
01652 657633

Bristol
Henbury Lodge Hotel
0117 950 2615

Bristol
Redwood Lodge Hotel
01275 393901

Bristol
Swallow Royal Hotel
0117 925 5100

Brixham
Berryhead Hotel 01803 853225

Brixham
Maypool Park 01803 842442

Brixham
Quayside Hotel 01803 855751

Brockenhurst
Rhinefield House 01590 622922

Brome
Cornwallis Arms 01379 870326

Bromley
Bromley Court Hotel 020 8464 5011

Bromsgrove
Pine Lodge Hotel 01527 576600

Broxton
Broxton Hall Country House Hotel
01829 782321

Buckingham
Villiers Hotel 01280 822444

Bude
Atlantic House Hotel 01288 352451

Bude
Camelot Hotel 01288 352361

Bude
Falcon Hotel 01288 352005

Bude
Hotel Penarvor 01288 352036

Bude
Maer Lodge Hotel 01288 353306

Bude
Stamford Hill Hotel 01288 352709

Burford
The Inn For All Seasons
01451 844324

Burnham
Burnham Beeches 01628 429955

Burnham
Grovefield Hotel 01628 603131

Burrington
Northcote Manor 01769 560501

Buttermere
Bridge Hotel 017687 70252

Buxton
Buckingham Hotel 01298 70481

Buxton
Palace Hotel 01298 22001

Buxton
Portland Hotel & Park Restaurant
01298 71493

Cadnam
Bartley Lodge 023 80812248

Cambridge
Cambridge Garden House Moat
House 01223 259988

Cambridge
Royal Cambridge Hotel
01223 351631

Canterbury
The Chaucer 0870 400 8106

Carlisle
County Hotel 01228 531316

Carlisle
The Crown & Mitre 01228 525491

Castle Donington
The Priest House on the River
01332 810649

Chale
Clarendon Hotel & Wight Mouse Inn
01983 730431

Cheltenham
The Greenway 01242 862352

Cheltenham
The Prestbury House Hotel &
Restaurant 01242 529533

Chelwood
Chelwood House Hotel
01761 490730

Chenies
The Bedford Arms Chenies
01923 283301

Cheshunt
Cheshunt Marriott Hotel
01992 451245

Chideock
Chideock House Hotel
01297 489242

Chipping
The Gibbon Bridge Hotel
01995 61456

Chipping Campden
Cotswold House Hotel & Restaurant
01386 840330

Chollerford
Swallow George Hotel 01434 681611

Chorley
Park Hall Hotel 01257 452090

Churt
Frensham Pond Hotel
01252 795161

Clacton-on-Sea
Esplanade Hotel 01255 220450

Cleator
Ennerdale Country House Hotel
01946 813907

Cleobury Mortimer
Redfern Hotel 01299 270395

Cleobury Mortimer
The Crown Inn 01299 270372

Climping
Bailiffscourt Hotel 01903 723511

Clitheroe
Shireburn Arms Hotel 01254 826518

Colchester
Posthouse Colchester 0870 400 9020

Colerne
Lucknam Park 01225 742777

Constantine Bay
Treglos Hotel 01841 520727

Copthorne
Copthorne Effingham Park
01342 714994

Copthorne
Copthorne London Gatwick
01342 348800

Cornhill-on-Tweed
Tillmouth Park Hotel 01890 882255

Crediton
Coombe House Country Hotel
01363 84487

Croft-on-Tees
Croft Spa Hotel   01325 720319

Croyde
Kittiwell House Hotel & Restaurant
01271 890247

Darlington
Blackwell Grange   01325 509955

Darlington
Devonport Hotel   01325 332255

Dartford
Rowhill Grange Hotel & Spa
01322 615136

Dartmouth
Royal Castle Hotel   01803 833033

Dartmouth
Stoke Lodge Hotel   01803 770523

Dartmouth
The Dart Marina Hotel
0870 400 8134

Dartmouth
Townstal Farmhouse Hotel
01803 832300

Daventry
Fawsley Hall Hotel   01327 892000

Daventry
Hanover International Hotel & Club
Daventry   01327 301777

Dawlish
Langstone Cliff Hotel 01626 868000

Derby
Hotel Ristorante La Gondola
01332 332895

Derby
Mickleover Court Hotel
01332 521234

Dover
The Churchill   01304 203633

Droitwich
The Hadley Bowling Green Inn
01905 620294

Dudley
Copthorne Merry Hill - Dudley
01384 482882

Durham
Bowburn Hall Hotel 0191 377 0311

Durham
Swallow Royal County Hotel
0191 386 6821

East Grinstead
Woodbury House Hotel
01342 313657

Eastbourne
Chatsworth Hotel   01323 411016

Eastbourne
Grand Hotel   01323 412345

Eastbourne
Hydro Hotel   01323 720643

Eastbourne
Langham Hotel   01323 731451

Eastbourne
Lansdowne Hotel   01323 725174

Eastbourne
New Wilmington Hotel
01323 721219

Egham
Runnymede Hotel & Spa
01784 436171

Ely
The Nyton Hotel   01353 662459

Embleton
Dunstanburgh Castle Hotel
01665 576111

Evesham
Northwick Hotel   01386 40322

Evesham
The Evesham Hotel   01386 765566

Evesham
The Mill At Harvington
01386 870688

Evesham
Wood Norton Hall   01386 420007

Exeter
Gipsy Hill Hotel   01392 465252

Exeter
Lord Haldon Hotel   01392 832483

Exeter
Royal Clarence   01392 319955

Exmouth
Royal Beacon Hotel   01395 264886

Fairford
Bull Hotel   01285 712535

Falmouth
Crill Manor Hotel   01326 211880

Falmouth
Falmouth Beach Resort Hotel
01326 318084

Falmouth
Falmouth Hotel   01326 312671

Falmouth
Green Lawns Hotel   01326 312734

Falmouth
Park Grove Hotel   01326 313276

Falmouth
Penmere Manor   01326 211411

Falmouth
Penmorvah Manor   01326 250277

Falmouth
Royal Duchy Hotel   01326 313042

Fareham
Lysses House Hotel   01329 822622

Fareham
Posthouse Fareham 0870 400 9028

Fareham
Solent Hotel   01489 880000

Faringdon
Sudbury House Hotel & Conference
Centre   01367 241272

Farnham
Bishop's Table Hotel   01252 710222

Felixstowe
Orwell Hotel   01394 285511

Ferndown
The Dormy   01202 872121

Fownhope
Green Man Inn   01432 860243

Frinton-on-Sea
Maplin Hotel   01255 673832

Gateshead
Swallow Hotel   0191 477 1105

Gillan
Tregildry Hotel   01326 231378

Gisburn
Stirk House Hotel   01200 445581

Gloucester
Hatton Court   01452 617412

Goodrich
Ye Hostelrie Hotel   01600 890241

Grantham
Kings Hotel   01476 590800

Grantham
Swallow Hotel   01476 593000

Grasmere
Michael's Nook Country House Hotel
015394 35496

Grasmere
Oak Bank Hotel   015394 35217

Grasmere
Rothay Garden Hotel 015394 35334

Grasmere
Wordsworth Hotel   015394 35592

Great Yarmouth
Imperial Hotel   01493 851113

Grimsby
Humber Royal   01472 350311

Guildford
The Manor   01483 222624

Hadley Wood
West Lodge Park Hotel
020 8216 3900

Halifax
Rock Inn Hotel & Churchills
01422 379721

Halifax
The Hobbit Hotel   01422 832202

Halland
Halland Forge Hotel &
Restaurant   01825 840456

Harlow
Harlow Moat House   01279 829988

Harrogate
The Imperial   01423 565071

Harrogate
The White House   01423 501388

Hastings & St Leonards
Royal Victoria Hotel   01424 445544

Hebden Bridge
Carlton Hotel   01422 844400

Helmsley
Feversham Arms Hotel
                       01439 770766

Helmsley
Pheasant Hotel   01439 771241

Helmsley
The Carlton Lodge Hotel
                       01439 770557

Helmsley
The Crown Hotel   01439 770297

Hereford
Ancient Camp Inn   01981 250449

Hereford
Graftonbury Garden
Hotel   01432 268826

Herstmonceux
White Friars Hotel   01323 832355

Hethersett
Park Farm Hotel   01603 810264

Hexham
Beaumont Hotel   01434 602331

Hinckley
Hanover International Hotel & Club
Hinckley   01455 631122

Hinckley
Sketchley Grange Hotel
                       01455 251133

Honiton
Combe House at Gittisham
                       01404 540400

Hope Cove
Cottage Hotel   01548 561555

Horncastle
Admiral Rodney Hotel 01507 523131

Horsham
Random Hall Hotel   01403 790558

Hounslow
The Renaissance London Heathrow
Hotel   020 8897 6363

Huddersfield
Old Golf House Hotel 01422 379311

Huddersfield
The Lodge Hotel   01484 431001

Hunmanby
Wrangham House Hotel
                       01723 891333

Hunstanton
The Lodge Hotel & Restaurant
                       01485 532896

Hunstrete
Hunstrete House Hotel
                       01761 490490

Hythe
Stade Court   01303 268263

Hythe
The Hythe Imperial Hotel
                       01303 267441

Ipplepen
Old Church House Inn
                       01803 812372

Ipswich
County Hotel Ipswich 01473 209988

Ipswich
Novotel   01473 232400

Ivybridge
Glazebrook House Hotel &
Restaurant   01364 73322

Kenilworth
Chesford Grange Hotel
                       01926 859331

Keswick
Keswick Country House Hotel
                       017687 72020

Keswick
Skiddaw Hotel   017687 72071

King's Lynn
Stuart House Hotel   01553 772169

Kingsbridge
Buckland-Tout-Saints 01548 853055

Kington
Burton Hotel   01544 230323

Kirkby Lonsdale
Hipping Hall   015242 71187

Kirkby Lonsdale
Plough Hotel   015395 67227

Kirkby Lonsdale
Whoop Hall Inn   015242 71284

Kirkbymoorside
George & Dragon Hotel
                       01751 433334

Langho
Northcote Manor   01254 240555

Lavenham
The Swan   0870 400 8116

Lea Marston
Lea Marston Hotel & Leisure
Complex   01675 470468

Leicester
Hermitage Hotel   0116 256 9955

Leicester
Leicester Stage Hotel
                       0116 288 6161

Lenham
Chilston Park Hotel   01622 859803

Leominster
Talbot Hotel   01568 616347

Lewes
White Hart Hotel   01273 476694

Lichfield
Little Barrow Hotel   01543 414500

Lifton
Arundell Arms   01566 784666

Lincoln
Washingborough Hall Hotel
                       01522 790340

Little Weighton
The Rowley Manor Hotel
                       01482 848248

London W1
Claridge's   020 7629 8860

London W1
The Westbury Hotel   020 7629 7755

Lostwithiel
Lostwithiel Hotel Golf & Country
Club   01208 873550

Lostwithiel
Restormel Lodge Hotel
                       01208 872223

Lower Beeding
South Lodge Hotel   01403 891711

Lower Slaughter
Lower Slaughter Manor
                       01451 820456

Lower Slaughter
Washbourne Court Hotel
                       01451 822143

Lowestoft
Hotel Hatfield   01502 565337

Lydford
Lydford House   01822 820347

Lyme Regis
Bay Hotel   01297 442059

Lympsham
Batch Country Hotel 01934 750371

Lyndhurst
Crown Hotel   023 80282922

Lyndhurst
Forest Lodge Hotel   023 80283677

Lytham St Annes
Clifton Arms   01253 739898

Maidenhead
Elva Lodge Hotel   01628 622948

Maidenhead
Ye Olde Bell Hotel   01628 825881

Malvern
Foley Arms Hotel   01684 573397

Malvern
The Cottage in the Wood Hotel
                       01684 575859

Manchester
The Waterside Hotel
                       0161 445 0225

March
Olde Griffin Hotel   01354 652517

Market Harborough
Three Swans Hotel   01858 466644

Mawgan Porth
Tredragon Hotel   01637 860213

Mawnan Smith
Budock Vean Golf & Country House
Hotel   01326 252100

Mawnan Smith
Meudon Hotel   01326 250541

Mawnan Smith
Trelawne Hotel 01326 250226

Midhurst
Angel Hotel 01730 812421

Midhurst
Spread Eagle Hotel and Health Spa
01730 816911

Midsomer Norton
Centurion Hotel 01761 417711

Milford on Sea
South Lawn Hotel 01590 643911

Milford on Sea
Westover Hall Hotel 01590 643044

Milton Common
The Oxford Belfry 01844 279381

Milton Keynes
Posthouse Milton Keynes
0870 400 9057

Minehead
Channel House Hotel 01643 703229

Minehead
Periton Park Hotel
01643 706885

Minehead
Wyndcott Hotel 01643 704522

Morecambe
Strathmore Hotel 01524 421234

Moreton-in-Marsh
Manor House Hotel 01608 650501

Mousehole
Old Coastguard Inn 01736 731222

Mullion
Mullion Cove Hotel 01326 240328

Mullion
Polurrian Hotel 01326 240421

Nailsworth
Egypt Mill Hotel 01453 833449

Nantwich
Crown Hotel & Restaurant
01270 625283

Nantwich
Rookery Hall 01270 610016

Newbury
Hollington Country House
01635 255100

Newbury
The Vineyard at Stockcross
01635 528770

Newcastle upon Tyne
Swallow Gosforth Park Hotel
0191 236 4111

Newcastle upon Tyne
Whites Hotel 0191 281 5126

Newick
Newick Park Country Estate
01825 723633

Newquay
Barrowfield Hotel 01637 878878

Newquay
Cedars Hotel 01637 874225

Newquay
Esplanade Hotel 01637 873333

Newquay
Glendorgal Hotel 01637 874937

Newquay
Headland Hotel 01637 872211

Newquay
Hotel Bristol 01637 875181

Newquay
Hotel Riviera 01637 874251

Newquay
Philema Hotel 01637 872571

Newquay
Trebarwith Hotel 01637 872288

Northampton
Courtyard by Marriott Northampton
01604 622777

Northampton
Swallow Hotel 01604 768700

Northwich
Quality Hotel Northwich
01606 44443

Nottingham
Bestwood Lodge 0115 920 3011

Nottingham
Nottingham Gateway
0115 979 4949

Nunney
The George at Nunney
01373 836458

Oakham
Hambleton Hall 01572 756991

Oakham
Whipper-in Hotel 01572 756971

Okehampton
Ashbury Hotel 01837 55453

Okehampton
Manor House Hotel 01837 53053

Okehampton
White Hart Hotel 01837 52730

Onneley
Wheatsheaf Inn at Onneley
01782 751581

Ormskirk
Beaufort Hotel 01704 892655

Oswestry
Pen-y-Dyffryn Country Hotel
01691 653700

Painswick
Painswick Hotel 01452 812160

Parbold
Lindley Hotel 01257 462804

Penzance
The Sea & Horses Hotel
01736 361961

Perranporth
Beach Dunes Hotel 01872 572263

Peterborough
Peterborough Moat House
01733 289988

Petty France
Petty France Hotel 01454 238361

Pickering
White Swan 01751 472288

Pickhill
Nags Head Country Inn
01845 567391

Plymouth
Grand Hotel 01752 661195

Plymouth
Grosvenor Park Hotel 01752 229312

Plymouth
Kitley House Hotel 01752 881555

Plymouth
New Continental Hotel
01752 220782

Poole
Haven Hotel 01202 707333

Poole
Mansion House Hotel
01202 685666

Poole
Salterns Hotel 01202 707321

Poole
Sandbanks Hotel 01202 707377

Porlock
Anchor Hotel & Ship Inn
01643 862753

Port Gaverne
Port Gaverne Hotel 01208 880244

Portsmouth & Southsea
Portsmouth Marriott 023 92383151

Portsmouth & Southsea
Westfield Hall Hotel 023 92826971

Preston
Preston Marriott 01772 864087

Pulborough
Chequers Hotel 01798 872486

Reading
Holiday Inn 0118 925 9988

Reading
Royal County Hotel 0118 958 3455

Renishaw
Sitwell Arms Hotel 01246 435226

Richmond
King's Head Hotel 01748 850220

Ringwood
Tyrrells Ford Country House Hotel
01425 672646

Ripon
Ripon Spa Hotel 01765 602172

Ross-on-Wye
Chasedale Hotel 01989 562423

Ross-on-Wye
King's Head Hotel 01989 763174

Ross-on-Wye
Orles Barn Hotel and Restaurant
01989 562155

Ross-on-Wye
Pencraig Court Hotel 01989 770306

Ross-on-Wye
The Royal   01989 565105

Royal Tunbridge Wells
The Spa Hotel   01892 520331

Rushyford
Swallow Eden Arms Hotel
     01388 720541

Salcombe
Bolt Head Hotel   01548 843751

Salcombe
Soar Mill Cove Hotel   01548 561566

Salcombe
South Sands Hotel   01548 843741

Salcombe
Sunny Cliff Hotel   01548 842207

Salcombe
Tides Reach Hotel   01548 843466

Salisbury
Milford Hall Hotel   01722 417411

Sandiway
Nunsmere Hall Country House Hotel
     01606 889100

Sandwich
The Blazing Donkey Country Hotel
& Inn   01304 617362

Saunton
Saunton Sands Hotel   01271 890212

Scotch Corner
Quality Hotel Scotch Corner
     01748 850900

Seahouses
Bamburgh Castle Hotel
     01665 720283

Seaton
Seaton Heights Hotel   01297 20932

Seaview
Springvale Hotel   01983 612533

Sedgefield
Hardwick Hall Hotel   01740 620253

Sedlescombe
Brickwall Hotel   01424 870253

Sevenoaks
Royal Oak Hotel   01732 451109

Severn Stoke
Old Schoolhouse Hotel &
Restaurant   01905 371368

Shanklin
Brunswick Hotel   01983 863245

Shanklin
Luccombe Hall Hotel   01983 862719

Sherborne
The Grange Hotel & Restaurant
     01935 813463

Shipdham
Pound Green Hotel   01362 820940

Shipley
Marriott Hollins Hall Hotel and
Country Club   01274 530053

Shrewsbury
Radbrook Hall Hotel   01743 236676

Sidmouth
Belmont Hotel   01395 512555

Sidmouth
Devoran Hotel   01395 513151

Sidmouth
Fortfield Hotel   01395 512403

Sidmouth
Hunters Moon Hotel   01395 513380

Sidmouth
Kingswood Hotel   01395 516367

Sidmouth
Mount Pleasant Hotel 01395 514694

Sidmouth
Riviera Hotel   01395 515201

Sidmouth
Royal Glen Hotel   01395 513221

Sidmouth
Salcombe Hill House Hotel
     01395 514697

Sidmouth
Sidmount Hotel   01395 513432

Sidmouth
The Royal York & Faulkner Hotel
     0800 220714

Sidmouth
Victoria Hotel   01395 512651

Sidmouth
Westbourne Hotel   01395 513774

Sidmouth
Westcliff Hotel   01395 513252

Skipton
Coniston Hall Lodge   01756 748080

Skipton
Hanover International Hotel & Club
     01756 700100

South Brent
Brookdale House Restaurant & Hotel
     01548 821661

South Normanton
Swallow Hotel   01773 812000

Southampton
De Vere Grand Harbour
     0023 80633033

Southend-on-Sea
Westcliff Hotel   01702 345247

Southport
Balmoral Lodge Hotel 01704 544298

Spennymoor
Whitworth Hall   01388 811772

St Agnes
Rose in Vale Country House Hotel
     01872 552202

St Albans
Sopwell House Hotel & Country Club
     01727 864477

St Albans
St Michael's Manor   01727 864444

St Austell
Boscundle Manor Hotel
     01726 813557

St Ives
Garrack Hotel & Restaurant
     01736 796199

St Ives
Olivers Lodge Hotel   01480 463252

St Keyne
The Old Rectory   01579 342617

Stevenage
Novotel   01438 742299

Steyning
The Old Tollgate Restaurant &
Hotel   01903 879494

Stockport
Bredbury Hall Hotel & Country Club
     0161 430 7421

Stoke d'Abernon
Woodlands Park Hotel
     01372 843933

Stoke Gabriel
Gabriel Court Hotel   01803 782206

Stokenchurch
The Kings Arms   01494 609090

Ston Easton
Ston Easton Park   01761 241631

Stone
Stone House Hotel   01785 815531

Stonehouse
Stonehouse Court   01453 825155

Stow Cum Quy
Cambridge Quy Mill Hotel
     01223 293383

Stow-on-the-Wold
Fosse Manor   01451 830354

Stow-on-the-Wold
Grapevine Hotel   01451 830344

Stow-on-the-Wold
Old Farmhouse Hotel   01451 830232

Stow-on-the-Wold
Old Stocks Hotel   01451 830666

Stow-on-the-Wold
The Unicorn   01451 830257

Stratford-upon-Avon
Billesley Manor Hotel 01789 279955

Stratford-upon-Avon
Charlecote Pheasant   01789 279954

Stratford-upon-Avon
Stratford Manor   01789 731173

Stratford-upon-Avon
The Alveston Manor 0870 400 8181

Stroud
Burleigh Court   01453 883804

Stroud
The Bell Hotel & Restaurant
     01453 763556

Sunderland
Quality Hotel   0191 519 1999

Sunderland
Swallow Hotel   0191 529 2041

Sutton Coldfield
Quality Hotel Sutton Court
0870 6011160

Swindon
Posthouse Swindon 0870 400 9079

Swindon
Stanton House Hotel 01793 861777

Swindon
Villiers Inn 01793 814744

Talland Bay
Talland Bay Hotel 01503 272667

Tankersley
Tankersley Manor 01226 744700

Tarporley
The Wild Boar 01829 260309

Taunton
Farthings Hotel and Restaurant
01823 480664

Taunton
The Mount Somerset Hotel
01823 442500

Telford
Buckatree Hall Hotel 01952 641821

Telford
Clarion Hotel Madeley Court
01952 680068

Telford
Telford Moat House 01952 429988

Telford
Valley Hotel 01952 432247

Telford
White House Hotel 01952 604276

Tetbury
Calcot Manor 01666 890391

Tetbury
Hare & Hounds Hotel
01666 880233

Thorpe Market
Elderton Lodge Hotel & Restaurant
01263 833547

Thurlestone
Heron House Hotel 01548 561308

Thurlestone
Thurlestone Hotel 01548 560382

Tiverton
The Tiverton Hotel 01884 256120

Torpoint
Whitsand Bay Hotel, Golf & Country
Club 01503 230276

Torquay
Belgrave Hotel 01803 296666

Torquay
Corbyn Head Hotel 01803 213611

Torquay
Grand Hotel 01803 296677

Torquay
Kistor Hotel 01803 212632

Torquay
Livermead Cliff Hotel 01803 299666

Torquay
Norcliffe Hotel 01803 328456

Torquay
Palace Hotel 01803 200200

Torquay
The Imperial 01803 294301

Torquay
The Osborne Hotel 01803 213311

Totland Bay
Sentry Mead Hotel 01983 753212

Tring
Pendley Manor 01442 891891

Tring
Rose & Crown Hotel & Restaurant
01442 824071

Troutbeck
Mortal Man Hotel 015394 33193

Truro
Alverton Manor 01872 276633

Tutbury
Ye Olde Dog & Partridge Hotel
01283 813030

Uckfield
Buxted Park Country House Hotel
01825 732711

Upholland
Quality Hotel Skelmersdale
01695 720401

Uttoxeter
Bank House Hotel 01889 566922

Ventnor
Eversley Hotel 1983 852244

Ventnor
The Royal Hotel 01983 852186

Ventnor
Ventnor Towers Hotel 01983 852277

Veryan
Nare Hotel 01872 501279

Wadebridge
The Molesworth Arms Hotel
01208 812055

Walsall
Abberley Hotel 01922 627413

Walsall
Beverley Hotel 01922 614967

Walterstone
Allt-yr-Ynys Country House Hotel
01873 890307

Waltham Abbey
Swallow Hotel 01992 717170

Wareham
Kemps Country House Hotel
01929 462563

Wareham
Worgret Manor Hotel 01929 552957

Warminster
Bishopstrow House 01985 212312

Warrington
Daresbury Park Hotel 01925 267331

Watergate Bay
Tregurrian Hotel 01637 860540

Watton
Broom Hall Country Hotel
01953 882125

Wells
The Market Place Hotel
01749 672616

Wentbridge
Wentbridge House Hotel
01977 620444

West Bexington
Manor Hotel 01308 897616

Weston-Super-Mare
Beachlands Hotel 01934 621401

Weston-Super-Mare
Commodore Hotel 01934 415778

Weston-Super-Mare
The Grand Atlantic Hotel
01934 626543

Weymouth
Moonfleet Manor 01305 786948

Whickham
Gibside Arms Hotel 0191 488 9292

Whitby
Dunsley Hall 01947 893437

Whitby
Saxonville Hotel 01947 602631

Williton
Curdon Mill 01984 656522

Wilmslow
Stanneylands Hotel 01625 525225

Winchester
Lainston House Hotel 01962 863588

Winchester
Marwell Hotel & Conference Centre
01962 777681

Winchester
Royal Hotel 01962 840840

Windermere
Cedar Manor Hotel & Restaurant
015394 43192

Windermere
Gilpin Lodge Country House Hotel &
Restaurant 015394 88818

Windermere
Langdale Chase Hotel 015394 32201

Windermere
Lindeth Howe Country House
015394 45759

Windermere
Wild Boar Hotel 015394 45225

Windsor
Christopher Hotel 01753 852359

Wolverhampton
Quality Hotel Wolverhampton
01902 429216

Woolacombe
Watersmeet Hotel 01271 870333

48

AA HOTELS WITH SPECIAL ARRANGEMENTS FOR GOLF

Woolacombe
Woolacombe Bay Hotel
01271 870388

Wootton Bassett
Marsh Farm Hotel   01793 848044

Worfield
Old Vicarage Hotel   01746 716497

Yarmouth
George Hotel   01983 760331

York
Dean Court Hotel   01904 625082

York
Heworth Court Hotel   01904 425156

York
Jacobean Lodge Hotel
01904 762749

York
Swallow Hotel   01904 701000

Yoxford
Satis House Hotel   01728 668418

CHANNEL ISLANDS
Perelle
L'Atlantique Hotel   01481 264056

St Brelade
Hotel La Place   01534 744261

St Helier
Pomme D'Or Hotel   01534 880110

St Martin
Green Acres Hotel   01481 235711

St Martin
La Trelade Hotel   01481 235454

St Peter
Mermaid Hotel   01534 741255

St Peter Port
Old Government House Hotel
01481 724921

ISLE OF MAN
Douglas
The Empress Hotel   01624 661155

Port Erin
Cherry Orchard Hotel 01624 833811

SCOTLAND
Aberdeen
Aberdeen Marriott   01224 770011

Aberdeen
Mariner Hotel   01224 588901

Aberdeen
The Marcliffe at Pitfodels
01224 861000

Aberdeen
Westhill Hotel   01224 740388

Aberfeldy
The Weem   01887 820381

Auchterarder
Cairn Lodge   01764 662634

Aviemore
Freedom Inn   01479 810781

Ayr
Grange Hotel   01292 265679

Ballantrae
Glenapp Castle   1465 831212

Balloch
Cameron House Hotel
01389 755565

Banff
Banff Springs Hotel   01261 812881

Beauly
Priory Hotel   01463 782309

Biggar
Tinto Hotel   01899 308454

Birnam
Birnam House Hotel   01350 727462

Brora
Royal Marine Hotel   01408 621252

Brora
The Links Hotel   01408 621225

Buckie
Mill House Hotel   01542 850233

Cairndow
Cairndow Stagecoach Inn
01499 600286

Callander
Roman Camp Country House Hotel
01877 330003

Carnoustie
Hogan House Hotel   01241 853273

Carrutherstown
Hetland Hall Hotel   01387 840201

Castle Douglas
Douglas Arms   01556 502231

Castle Douglas
Imperial Hotel   01556 502086

Castle Douglas
King's Arms Hotel   01556 502626

Castle Douglas
Urr Valley Country House Hotel
01556 502188

Clachan-Seil
Willowburn Hotel   01852 300276

Comrie
Royal Hotel   01764 679200

Contin
Coul House Hotel   01997 421487

Craigellachie
Craigellachie Hotel   01340 881204

Crieff
Crieff Hydro   01764 655555

Crieff
Murraypark Hotel   01764 653731

Cruden Bay
Red House Hotel   01779 812215

Cupar
Eden House Hotel   01334 652510

Dornoch
Burghfield House Hotel
01862 810212

Drymen
Winnock Hotel   01360 660245

Dumfries
Station Hotel   01387 254316

Dunfermline
King Malcolm   01383 722611

Dunoon
Enmore Hotel   01369 702230

Dunoon
Esplanade Hotel   01369 704070

Dunoon
Royal Marine Hotel   01369 705810

East Kilbride
Crutherland Country House Hotel
01355 577000

Edinburgh
Dalhousie Castle Hotel
01875 820153

Edinburgh
Edinburgh Capital Moat House
0131 5359988

Edinburgh
Orwell Lodge Hotel   0131 2291044

Edinburgh
Prestonfield House Hotel
0131 6683346

Edinburgh
Salisbury View Hotel 0131 6671133

Fenwick
Fenwick Hotel   01560 600478

Forfar
Idvies House Hotel   01307 818787

Forres
Ramnee Hotel   01309 672410

Freuchie
Lomond Hills Hotel   01337 857329

Galashiels
Kingsknowes Hotel   01896 758375

Galashiels
Woodlands House Hotel &
Restaurants   01896 754722

Gatehouse Of Fleet
Murray Arms Hotel   01557 814207

Glasgow
Jurys Glasgow Hotel
0141 334 8161

Glasgow
Sherbrooke Castle Hotel
0141 427 4227

Glasgow
The Ewington   0141 423 1152

Glenfarg
The Glenfarg Hotel & Restaurant
01577 830241

Glenluce
Kelvin House Hotel   01581 300303

Glenrothes
Balgeddie House Hotel
01592 742511

Howwood
Bowfield Hotel & Country Club
01505 705225

Humbie
The Johnstounburn House
01875 833696

Inverness
Smithton Hotel   01463 791999

Johnstone
Lynnhurst Hotel   01505 324331

Killiechronan
Killiechronan House   01680 300403

Killin
Dall Lodge Country House Hotel
01567 820217

Kinross
Green Hotel   01577 863467

Kirkcudbright
Royal Hotel   01557 331213

Kirkcudbright
Selkirk Arms Hotel   01557 330402

Kirkwall
Ayre Hotel   01856 873001

Ladybank
Fernie Castle   01337 810381

Largs
Manor Park Hotel   01475 520832

Leven
Caledonian Hotel   01333 424101

Lochcarron
Lochcarron Hotel   01520 722226

Lochearnhead
Lochearnhead Hotel   01567 830229

Lochinver
Inver Lodge Hotel
01571 844496

Lockerbie
Kings Arms Hotel   01576 202410

Lundin Links
Old Manor Hotel   01333 320368

Melrose
George & Abbotsford Hotel
01896 822308

Moffat
Beechwood Country House Hotel
01683 220210

Montrose
Links Hotel   01674 671000

Montrose
Park Hotel   01674 673415

Muir Of Ord
Ord House Hotel   01463 870492

Muir Of Ord
The Dower House   01463 870090

Nairn
Boath House   01667 454896

Nairn
Claymore House Hotel
01667 453731

Newton Stewart
Bruce Hotel   01671 402294

Newton Stewart
Creebridge House Hotel
01671 402121

Newton Stewart
Kirroughtree House   01671 402141

Oban
Argyll Hotel   01631 562353

Peebles
Castle Venlaw Hotel   01721 720384

Peebles
Kingsmuir Hotel   01721 720151

Peebles
Park Hotel   01721 720451

Peebles
Peebles Hydro Hotel   01721 720602

Perth
Kinfauns Castle   01738 620777

Perth
Quality Hotel Perth   01738 624141

Peterhead
Palace Hotel   01779 474821

Pitlochry
Atholl Palace Hotel   01796 472400

Pitlochry
Dundarach Hotel   01796 472862

Port Askaig
Port Askaig Hotel   01496 840245

Port William
Corsemalzie House Hotel
01988 860254

Portmahomack
Caledonian Hotel   01862 871345

Portpatrick
Fernhill Hotel   01776 810220

Portpatrick
Knockinaam Lodge Hotel
01776 810471

Portree
Cuillin Hills Hotel   01478 612003

Portree
Royal Hotel   01478 612525

Powfoot
Powfoot Golf Hotel   01461 700254

Renfrew
Glynhill Hotel & Leisure Club
0141 8865555

Rosebank
Popinjay Hotel   01555 860441

Sanquhar
Blackaddie House Hotel
01659 50270

St Boswells
Dryburgh Abbey Hotel
01835 822261

St Fillans
Achray House Hotel   01764 685231

Strachur
Creggans Inn   01369 860279

Stranraer
North West Castle Hotel
01776 704413

Strontian
Kilcamb Lodge Hotel   01967 402257

Tain
Mansfield House Hotel
01862 892052

Tain
Morangie House Hotel
01862 892281

Tangasdale
Isle of Barra Hotel   01871 810383

Thurso
Park Hotel   01847 893251

Tobermory
Highland Cottage   01688 302030

Tobermory
Western Isles Hotel   01688 302012

Tomintoul
The Gordon Hotel   01807 580206

Tongue
Ben Loyal Hotel   01847 611216

Turnberry
Malin Court   01655 331457

Uphall
Houstoun House Hotel and Country
Club   01506 853831

Uplawmoor
Uplawmoor Hotel   01505 850565

Wick
Mackay's Hotel   01955 602323

WALES
Aberdyfi
Harbour Hotel   01654 767250

Aberdyfi
Maybank Hotel & Restaurant
01654 767500

Aberdyfi
Penhelig Arms Hotel Restaurant
01654 767215

Aberdyfi
Trefeddian Hotel   01654 767213

Abergavenny
Llansantffraed Court Hotel
01873 840678

Abergele
Kinmel Manor Hotel   01745 832014

Aberporth
Hotel Penrallt   01239 810227

Abersoch
Deucoch Hotel   01758 712680

Abersoch
Neigwl Hotel   01758 712363

Abersoch
Riverside Hotel   01758 712419

Abersoch
The White House Hotel
01758 713427

Aberystwyth
Belle Vue Royal Hotel 01970 617558

Aberystwyth
Four Seasons Hotel 01970 612120

Aberystwyth
Groves Hotel 01970 617623

Aberystwyth
Marine Hotel 01970 612444

Aberystwyth
Richmond Hotel 01970 612201

Amlwch
Trecastell Hotel 01407 830651

Ammanford
Mill at Glynhir 01269 850672

Bala
Plas Coch Hotel 01678 520309

Beaumaris
Bulkeley Hotel 01248 810415

Bridgend
Coed-Y-Mwstwr Hotel
01656 860621

Bridgend
Heronston Hotel 01656 668811

Builth Wells
Pencerrig Gardens Hotel
01982 553226

Caernarfon
Seiont Manor Hotel 01286 673366

Caernarfon
Stables Hotel 01286 830711

Cardiff
Cardiff Marriott 029 20399944

Cardiff
New House Country Hotel
029 20520280

Cardiff
St Mellons Hotel & Country Club
01633 680355

Carmarthen
Falcon Hotel 01267 234959

Chepstow
Beaufort Hotel 01291 622497

Chepstow
The Old Course Hotel 01291 626261

Criccieth
Lion Hotel 01766 522460

Criccieth
Parciau Mawr Hotel 01766 522368

Crickhowell
Bear Hotel 01873 810408

Crickhowell
Gliffaes Country House Hotel
01874 730371

Dolgellau
Penmaenuchaf Hall Hotel
01341 422129

Dolgellau
Plas Dolmelynllyn 01341 440273

Eglwysfach
Ynyshir Hall 01654 781209

Ewloe
St Davids Park Hotel 01244 520800

Gwbert-On-Sea
Cliff Hotel 01239 613241

Haverfordwest
Hotel Mariners 01437 763353

Haverfordwest
Wolfscastle Country Hotel
01437 741688

Hay-On-Wye
The Swan-at-Hay Hotel
01497 821188

Knighton
The Knighton Hotel 01547 520530

Langland Bay
Wittemberg Hotel 01792 369696

Llanarmon Dyffryn Ceiriog
West Arms Hotel 01691 600665

Llanbedr
Ty Mawr Hotel 01341 241440

Llanberis
Royal Victoria Hotel 01286 870253

Llandrillo
Tyddyn Llan Country Hotel &
Restaurant 01490 440264

Llandrindod Wells
Hotel Metropole 01597 823700

Llandudno
Bodysgallen Hall Hotel
01492 584466

Llandudno
Esplanade Hotel 0800 318688

Llandudno
Quinton Hotel 01492 876879

Llandudno
Risboro Hotel 01492 876343

Llandudno
St George's Hotel 01492 877544

Llandudno
St Tudno Hotel 01492 874411

Llangammarch Wells
Lake Country House Hotel
01591 620202

Llangollen
Bryn Howel Hotel & Restaurant
01978 860331

Llangybi
Cwrt Bleddyn Hotel & Country Club
01633 450521

Llyswen
Griffin Inn 01874 754241

Llyswen
Llangoed Hall 01874 754525

Machynlleth
Wynnstay Arms Hotel 01654 702941

Merthyr Tydfil
Tregenna Hotel 01685 723627

Miskin
Miskin Manor Hotel 01443 224204

Mold
Beaufort Park Hotel 01352 758646

Monmouth
Riverside Hotel 01600 715577

Newport
Newport Lodge Hotel 01633 821818

Pembroke
Bethwaite's Lamphey Hall Hotel
01646 672394

Pembroke
Court Hotel 01646 672273

Penybont
Severn Arms Hotel 01597 851224

Ponterwyd
The George Borrow Hotel
01970 890230

Pontypridd
Llechwen Hall Hotel 01443 742050

Porthcawl
Glenaub Hotel 01656 788242

Rhossili
Worms Head Hotel 01792 390512

Rhyl
Hotel Marina 01745 342371

Saundersfoot
Jalna Hotel 01834 812282

Saundersfoot
Rhodewood House Hotel
01834 812200

Saundersfoot
St Brides Hotel 01834 812304

St Asaph
Plas Elwy Hotel & Restaurant
01745 582263

St David's
Grove Hotel 01437 720341

St David's
St Non's Hotel 01437 720239

St David's
Warpool Court Hotel 01437 720300

Talsarnau
Tregwylan Hotel 01766 770424

Tal-Y-Bont
Lodge Hotel 01492 660766

Tenby
Atlantic Hotel 01834 842881

Tenby
Fourcroft Hotel 01834 842886

Tenby
Heywood Mount Hotel
01834 842087

Tenby
Penally Abbey Country House
01834 843033

Tenby
Tenby House Hotel 01834 842000

Tintern
Parva Farmhouse Hotel &
Restaurant   01291 689411

Trearddur Bay
Trearddur Bay Hotel   01407 860301

Trefriw
Princes Arms Hotel   01492 640592

Whitebrook
The Crown at Whitebrook
                           01600 860254

NORTHERN IRELAND
Ballymena
Adair Arms Hotel   01266 653674

Ballymena
Galgorm Manor   028 25881001

Bangor
Clandeboye Lodge Hotel
                           028 91852500

Bangor
Marine Court Hotel   028 91451100

Bangor
Royal Hotel   028 91271866

Belfast
Culloden Hotel   028 90425223

Bushmills
Beach House Hotel   028 207331214

Carnlough
Londonderry Arms Hotel
                           028 28885255

Crawfordsburn
Old Inn   028 91853255

Dungannon
The Cohannon Inn   028 87724488

Enniskillen
Killyhevlin Hotel   028 66323481

Irvinestown
Mahons Hotel   028 68621656

Londonderry
Everglades Hotel   028 71346722

Londonderry
Trinity Hotel   028 71271271

Portaferry
Portaferry Hotel   028 42728231

Portrush
Causeway Coast Hotel
                           028 70822435

REPUBLIC OF IRELAND
Adare
Dunraven Arms Hotel   061 396633

Adare
Fitzgeralds Woodlands House Hotel
                           061 605100

Aherlow
Aherlow House   062 56153

Ardmore
Round Tower Hotel   024 94494

Arthurstown
Dunbrody Country House &
Restaurant   051 389600

Ashford
Cullenmore Hotel   0404 40187

Ashford
The Chester Beatty Inn
                           0404 40682

Athlone
Prince Of Wales Hotel 0902 72626

Athlone
Royal Hoey Hotel   0902 72924

Ballinasloe
Haydens Gateway Hotel 0905 42347

Ballybofey
Kee's Hotel   074 31018

Ballyheige
The White Sands Hotel 066 7133102

Ballylickey
Sea View Hotel   027 50073

Baltimore
Baltimore Harbour Resort Hotel &
Leisure Centre   028 20361

Baltimore
Casey's of Baltimore Hotel
                           028 20197

Bettystown
Neptune Beach Hotel & Leisure Club
                           041 9827107

Birr
County Arms Hotel   0509 20791

Birr
Dooley's Hotel   0509 20032

Blarney
Blarney Park Hotel   021 385281

Blarney
Christy's Hotel   021 385011

Bray
Royal Hotel & Leisure Centre
                           001 2862935

Bunbeg
Ostan Gweedore   0075 31177

Bunratty
Fitzpatrick Bunratty Hotel
                           061 361177

Cahir
Cahir House Hotel   52 42727

Carlow
Dolmen Hotel   0503 42002

Carlow
Seven Oaks Hotel   0503 31308

Castlebar
Breaffy House Hotel   094 22033

Castlebar
Welcome Inn Hotel   094 22288

Castleconnell
Castle Oaks House Hotel 061 377666

Cavan
Kilmore Hotel   049 32288

Clonakilty
The Lodge & Spa at Inchydoney
Island   023 33143

Clonmel
Minella Hotel   052 22388

Cork
Ambassador Hotel   021 4551996

Cork
Arbutus Lodge Hotel   021 501237

Cork
Hayfield Manor   021 315600

Cork
Imperial Hotel   021 274040

Cork
Jurys Hotel   021 276622

Cork
Metropole Hotel & Leisure Centre
                           021 508122

Cork
The Kingsley Hotel   021 800500

Courtown Harbour
Courtown Hotel   055 25210

Donegal
Abbey Hotel   073 21014

Dublin
Abberley Court Hotel 01 4596000

Dublin
Radisson SAS St Helen's Hotel
                           01 2186000

Dublin
Red Cow Morans Hotel 01 4593650

Dublin
The Clarence   01 6709000

Dublin
The Herbert Park Hotel
                           01 6672200

Dublin
The Merrion Hotel   01 6030600

Dun Laoghaire
Hotel Pierre   01 2800291

Dundalk
Fairways Hotel & Leisure Centre
                           042 9321500

Dunfanaghy
Arnold's Hotel   074 36208

Dungarvan
Lawlors Hotel   058 41122

Ennis
Magowna House Hotel
                           065 6839009

Ennis
West County Hotel   065 6823000

Enniscorthy
Murphy-Flood's Hotel 054 33413

Enniscorthy
Riverside Park Hotel 054 37800

Fermoy
Castlehyde Hotel   025 31865

Galway
Ardilaun Conference & Leisure
Centre   091 521433

Galway
Galway Bay Hotel Conference &
Leisure Centre   091 520520

Galway
Menlo Park Hotel   091 761122

Garryvoe
Garryvoe Hotel   021 646718

Gorey
Marlfield House Hotel   055 21124

Kenmare
Riversdale House Hotel   064 41299

Kenmare
Sheen Falls Lodge   064 41600

Kilkenny
Hotel Kilkenny   056 62000

Kill
Ambassador Hotel   045 886700

Killarney
Aghadoe Heights Hotel   064 31766

Killarney
Cahernane Hotel   064 31895

Killarney
Castlerosse Hotel   064 31144

Killarney
Gleneagle Hotel   064 31870

Killarney
International Hotel   064 31816

Killarney
Killarney Court Hotel   064 37070

Killarney
Lake Hotel   064 31035

Killiney
Quality Hotel Court   01 2851622

Kingscourt
Cabra Castle   042 9667030

Kinsale
Actons Hotel   021 772135

Kinsale
Trident Hotel   021 772301

Knock
Belmont Hotel   094 88122

Lahinch
Aberdeen Arms Hotel   065 81100

Leixlip
Leixlip House Hotel   01 6242268

Limerick
Castletroy Park Hotel   061 335566

Limerick
Limerick Ryan Hotel   061 453922

Limerick
Royal George Hotel   061 414566

Limerick
South Court Business & Leisure
Hotel   065 6823000

Lismore
Ballyrafter House Hotel   058 54002

Lucan
Finnstown Country House Hotel &
Golf Course   01 6280644

Lucan
Lucan Spa Hotel   01 6280495

Macroom
Castle Hotel   026 41074

Mallow
Longueville House Hotel   022 47156

Mallow
Springfort Hall Hotel   022 21278

Maynooth
Moyglare Manor   01 6286351

Midleton
Midleton Park   021 631767

Newbridge
Keadeen Hotel   045 431666

Newmarket-On-Fergus
Clare Inn Golf and Leisure Hotel
                                065 6823000

Portmarnock
Portmarnock Hotel & Golf Links
                            01 8460611

Rathnew
Tinakilly Country House &
Restaurant   0404 69274

Roscommon
Abbey Hotel   0903 26240

Roscrea
Grant's Hotel   0505 23300

Rosscarbery
Celtic Ross Hotel   023 48722

Rosslare
Kelly's Resort Hotel   053 32114

Rossnowlagh
Sand House Hotel   072 51777

Sligo
Sligo Park Hotel   071 60291

Sligo
Tower Hotel   071 44000

Straffan
Barberstown Castle   01 6288157

Templeglantine
The Devon Inn Hotel   069 84122

Tralee
Meadowlands Hotel   066 7180444

Tramore
Majestic Hotel   051 381761

Waterford
Bridge Hotel   051 877222

Waterford
Dooley's Hotel   051 873531

Waterford
Granville Hotel   051 305555

Waterford
Ivory's Hotel   051 358888

Waterford
Jurys Hotel   051 832111

Waterville
Butler Arms Hotel   066 74144

Westport
Hotel Westport   098 25122

Westport
Knockranny House Hotel   098 28600

Westport
The Olde Railway Hotel   098 25166

Wexford
Ferrycarrig Hotel   053 20999

Wexford
Talbot Hotel Conference & Leisure
Centre   053 22566

Wexford
Whitford House Hotel   053 43444

Woodenbridge
Woodenbridge Hotel   0402 35146

Golf
driving ranges

49

BEDFORDSHIRE
BEDFORD, Mowsbury Golf Club
BEDFORD, The Bedford Golf Club
CHALGRAVE, Chalgrave Manor Golf Club
COLMWORTH, Colmworth & N. Beds. GC
LUTON, Stockwood Park Golf Club
SHEFFORD, Beadlow Manor
TILSWORTH, Tilsworth Golf Centre
WYBOSTON, Wyboston Lakes

BERKSHIRE
ASCOT, Lavender Park Golf Centre
ASCOT, Mill Ride Golf Club
BINFIELD, Blue Mountain Golf Centre
CHADDLEWORTH, West Berkshire Golf Club
COOKHAM, Winter Hill Golf Club
MAIDENHEAD, Bird Hills Golf Course
READING, Hennerton Golf Course
SINDLESHAM, Bearwood Golf Club
WOKINGHAM, Downshire Golf Course
WOKINGHAM, Sand Martins Golf Club

BRISTOL
Bristol and Clifton Golf Club

BUCKINGHAMSHIRE
AYLESBURY, Aylesbury Golf Centre
AYLESBURY, Aylesbury Park Golf Club
BEACONSFIELD, Beaconsfield Golf Club
BLETCHLEY, Windmill Hill Golf Course
BURNHAM, The Lambourne Club
CHALFONT ST GILES, Oakland Park Golf Club
DENHAM, Buckinghamshire Golf Club
IVER, Iver Golf Club
IVER, Richings Park Golf & Country Club
IVER, Thorney Park Golf Club
LOUDWATER, Wycombe Heights Golf Centre
MARLOW, Harleyford Golf
MENTMORE, Mentmore Golf & Country Club
MILTON KEYNES, Abbey Hill Golf Club
STOKE POGES, Stoke Poges Golf Club
WAVENDON, Wavendon Golf Centre
WEXHAM STREET, Wexham Park Golf Club
WING, Aylesbury Vale Golf Club

CAMBRIDGESHIRE
CAMBRIDGE, The Gog Magog Golf Club
HEMINGFORD ABBOTS, Hemingford Abbots GC
LONGSTANTON, Cambridge Golf Club
PETERBOROUGH, Elton Furze Golf Club
PETERBOROUGH, Peterborough Milton Golf Club
PIDLEY, Lakeside Lodge Golf Club
RAMSEY, Old Nene Golf & Country Club
ST NEOTS, Abbotsley Golf Hotel & Country Club
THORNEY, Thorney Golf Centre

CHESHIRE
CHESTER, Carden Park Hotel Golf Resort & Spa
KNUTSFORD, Mere Golf & Country Club
MACCLESFIELD, The Tytherington Club
PRESTBURY, Prestbury Golf Club
TARPORLEY, Portal Golf & Country Club
WILMSLOW, Mottram Hall
WILMSLOW, Styal Golf Club

CO DURHAM
BISHOP AUCKLAND, Bishop Auckland Golf Club
CHESTER-LE-STREET, Roseberry Grange GC
DARLINGTON, Stressholme Golf Club
DURHAM, Ramside Hall Golf Club
NEWTON AYCLIFFE, Oakleaf Golf Club
SEDGEFIELD, Knotty Hill Golf Centre

CORNWALL & ISLES OF SCILLY
BODMIN, Lanhydrock Golf Club
CAMELFORD, Bowood Park Golf Course
FALMOUTH, Falmouth Golf Club
LAUNCESTON, Trethorne Golf Club
LOSTWITHIEL, Lostwithiel Hotel
MAWGAN PORTH, Merlin Golf Course
ROCK, St Enodoc Golf Club
SALTASH, China Fleet Country Club
ST AUSTELL, Porthpean Golf Club
ST AUSTELL, St Austell Golf Club
ST MELLION, St Mellion Hotel
ST MINVER, Roserrow Golf & Country Club
TRURO, Killiow Golf Club
WADEBRIDGE, St Kew Golf Course

CUMBRIA
CROSBY-ON-EDEN, Eden Golf Course
PENRITH, Penrith Golf Club
SEASCALE, Seascale Golf Club

DERBYSHIRE
BREADSALL, Marriott Breadsall Priory
DERBYSHIRE, BUXTON, Buxton & High Peak GC
BUXTON, Cavendish Golf Club
CHESTERFIELD, Grassmoor Golf Centre
HORSLEY, Horsley Lodge Golf Club
LONG EATON, Trent Lock Golf Centre
MORLEY, Morley Hayes Golf Course
NEW MILLS, New Mills Golf Club
STANTON BY DALE, Erewash Valley

DEVON
BLACKAWTON, Dartmouth Golf & Country Club
EXETER, Woodbury Park Golf Club
HIGH BICKINGTON, Libbaton Golf Club
IVYBRIDGE, Dinnaton Sporting & Country Club
NEWTON ABBOT, Dainton Park Golf Club
OKEHAMPTON, Ashbury Golf Course
PLYMOUTH, Elfordleigh Hotel
TEDBURN ST MARY, Fingle Glen Golf Centre

DORSET
BELCHALWELL, Dorset Heights Golf Club
BERE REGIS, East Dorset Golf Club
CHRISTCHURCH, Iford Bridge Golf Course
FERNDOWN, Dudsbury Golf Club
FERNDOWN, Ferndown Forest Golf Club
HALSTOCK, Halstock Golf Enterprises
HURN, Parley Golf Course
POOLE, Parkstone Golf Club
VERWOOD, Crane Valley Golf Club
WIMBORNE, Canford Magna Golf Club

EAST RIDING OF YORKSHIRE
AUGHTON, The Oaks Golf Club
BRIDLINGTON, Bridlington Links
COTTINGHAM, Cottingham Golf Club
HOWDEN, Boothferry Park Golf Club

EAST SUSSEX
DITCHLING, Mid Sussex Golf Club
HAILSHAM, Wellshurst Golf & Country Club
HASTINGS & ST LEONARDS, Hastings Golf Course
HEATHFIELD, Horam Park Golf Course
HOVE, West Hove Golf Club
SEAFORD, Seaford Golf Club
SEDLESCOMBE, Sedlescombe Golf Course
TICEHURST, Dale Hill Hotel & Golf Club
UCKFIELD, East Sussex National Golf Club
UCKFIELD, Piltdown Golf Club

ESSEX
ABRIDGE, Abridge Golf and Country Club
BILLERICAY, Stock Brook Golf & Country Club
BRAINTREE, Towerlands Golf Club
BRENTWOOD, Warley Park Golf Club
BULPHAN, Langdon Hills Golf Centre
CANVEY ISLAND, Castle Point Golf Club
CHELMSFORD, Channels Golf Club
COLCHESTER, Colchester & Lexden Golf Centre
COLCHESTER, Colchester Golf Club
COLCHESTER, Stoke by Nayland Golf Club
EARLS COLNE, The Essex Golf & Country Club
EPPING, Nazeing Golf Club
HARLOW, North Weald Golf Club
MALDON, Forrester Park Golf Club
PURLEIGH, Three Rivers Golf & Country Club
SAFFRON WALDEN, Saffron Walden Golf Club
SOUTH OCKENDON, Belhus Park Golf Course
SOUTH OCKENDON, Top Meadow Golf Course
STANFORD-LE-HOPE, St Clere's Hall Golf Club
STOCK, Crondon Park Golf Club
TOLLESHUNT KNIGHTS, Five Lakes
TOOT HILL, Toot Hill Golf Club
WITHAM, Benton Hall Golf Course
WOODHAM WALTER, Warren Golf Club

DRIVING RANGES

GLOUCESTERSHIRE
CIRENCESTER, Cirencester Golf Club
COLEFORD, Forest Hills Golf Club
GLOUCESTER, Brickhampton Court Golf Club
GLOUCESTER, Jarvis Gloucester
MINCHINHAMPTON, Minchinhampton Golf Club
TEWKESBURY, Tewkesbury Park
THORNBURY, Thornbury Golf Centre
WICK, Tracy Park Golf & Country Club

GREATER LONDON
ADDINGTON, Addington Court
CARSHALTON, Oaks Sports Centre
CHESSINGTON, Chessington Golf Club
CROYDON, Selsdon Park Hotel Golf Course
GREENFORD, Lime Trees Park Golf Club
HADLEY WOOD, Hadley Wood Golf Club
HOUNSLOW, Airlinks Golf Club
NORTHWOOD, Sandy Lodge Golf Club
ORPINGTON, Chelsfield Lakes Golf Centre
ORPINGTON, Cray Valley Golf Club
ORPINGTON, Lullingstone Park Golf Course
ORPINGTON, Ruxley Park Golf Centre
RICHMOND UPON THAMES, The Richmond GC
ROMFORD, Risebridge Golf Centre
RUISLIP, Ruislip Golf Club
TWICKENHAM, Twickenham Golf Centre

GREATER MANCHESTER
ALTRINCHAM, Altrincham Golf Club
MIDDLETON, Manchester Golf Club
PRESTWICH, Heaton Park Golf Centre
ROCHDALE, Castle Hawk Golf Club
STANDISH, Standish Court Golf Club
WHITEFIELD, Whitefield Golf Club

HAMPSHIRE
ALTON, Worldham Park Golf Course
ASHLEY HEATH, Moors Valley Golf Centre
BASINGSTOKE, Dummer Golf Club
BOTLEY, Botley Park Hotel, Golf & Country Club
CRONDALL, Oak Park Golf Club
DIBDEN, Dibden Golf Centre
LEE-ON-THE-SOLENT, Lee-on-Solent Golf Club
LIPHOOK, Old Thorns Hotel, Golf & Country Club
NEW MILTON, Chewton Glen Hotel
OWER, Paultons Golf Centre
PORTSMOUTH, Great Salterns Public Course
PORTSMOUTH, Southsea Golf Club
SHEDFIELD, Marriott Meon Valley
SOUTHAMPTON, Chilworth Golf Club
TADLEY, Bishopswood Golf Course
WINCHESTER, South Winchester Golf Club

HEREFORDSHIRE
KINGTON, Kington Golf Club
ROSS-ON-WYE, Ross-on-Wye Golf Club
ROSS-ON-WYE, South Herefordshire Golf Club
UPPER SAPEY, Sapey Golf Club

HERTFORDSHIRE
BISHOP'S STORTFORD, Great Hadham
BUSHEY, Bushey Golf & Country Club
BUSHEY, Hartsbourne Golf & Country Club
ELSTREE, Elstree Golf Club
GRAVELEY, Chesfield Downs Golf Club
HARPENDEN, Harpenden Golf Club
HEMEL HEMPSTEAD, Little Hay Golf Complex
LETCHWORTH, Letchworth Golf Club
RADLETT, Porters Park Golf Club
REDBOURN, Redbourn Golf Club
RICKMANSWORTH, Moor Park Golf Club
ROYSTON, Heydon Grange Golf & Country Club
ROYSTON, Kingsway Golf Centre
STEVENAGE, Stevenage Golf Centre
WARE, Marriott Hanbury Manor
WARE, Whitehill Golf Course
WELWYN GARDEN CITY, Mill Green Golf Club

KENT
ADDINGTON, West Malling Golf Club
ASH, The London Golf Club
ASHFORD, Homelands Bettergolf Centre
BARHAM, Broome Park Club
BIDDENDEN, Chart Hills Golf Club
BRENCHLEY, Moatlands Golf Club
CHART SUTTON, The Ridge Golf Club
CRANBROOK, Executive Golf Club at Cranbrook
DARTFORD, Birchwood Park Golf Centre
DEAL, Royal Cinque Ports Golf Club
EDENBRIDGE, Edenbridge Golf & Tennis Centre
EDENBRIDGE, Sweetwoods Park
EYNSFORD, Austin Lodge Golf Club
FAVERSHAM, Boughton Golf
FOLKESTONE, Etchinghill Golf Course
GILLINGHAM, Gillingham Golf Club
HEVER, Hever Golf Club
HOO, Deangate Ridge Golf Club
HYTHE, Sene Valley Golf Club
LYDD, Lydd Golf Club
ROCHESTER, Rochester & Cobham Park Golf Club
SANDWICH, Prince's Golf Club
SANDWICH, Royal St George's Golf Club
SITTINGBOURNE, The Oast Golf Centre
SITTINGBOURNE, Upchurch River Valley
SNODLAND, Oastpark Golf Course
WEST KINGSDOWN, Woodlands Manor Golf Club
WESTERHAM, Westerham Golf Club

LANCASHIRE
ACCRINGTON, Accrington & District Golf Club
BLACKPOOL, De Vere Blackpool (Herons Reach)
CLITHEROE, Clitheroe Golf Club
DARWEN, Darwen Golf Club
GARSTANG, Garstang Country Hotel & Golf Club
LEYLAND, Leyland Golf Club
LYTHAM ST ANNES, Royal Lytham & St Annes
ORMSKIRK, Hurlston Hall Golf Club
POULTON-LE-FYLDE, Poulton Le Fylde Golf Club
UPHOLLAND, Beacon Park Public Golf Centre

LEICESTERSHIRE
BOTCHESTON, Forest Hill Golf Club
EAST GOSCOTE, Beedles Lake Golf Centre
HINCKLEY, Hinckley Golf Club
KIBWORTH, Kibworth Golf Club
KIRBY MUXLOE, Kirby Muxloe Golf Club
LEICESTER, Humberstone Heights Golf Club
LEICESTER, Western Golf Course
LUTTERWORTH, Kilworth Springs Golf Course
LUTTERWORTH, Lutterworth Golf Club
WHETSTONE, Whetstone Golf Club
WILSON, Breedon Priory Golf Centre

LINCOLNSHIRE
BELTON, Belton Woods Hotel
BOURNE, Toft Hotel Golf Club
CLEETHORPES, Tetney Golf Club
GAINSBOROUGH, Gainsborough Golf Club
GEDNEY HILL, Gedney Hill Golf Course
HORNCASTLE, Horncastle Golf Club
SCUNTHORPE, Forest Pines Golf Club
TORKSEY, Millfield Golf Course
WOODHALL SPA, Woodhall Spa Golf Club

LONDON POSTAL DISTRICTS
LONDON E4 West Essex Golf Club
LONDON N14 Trent Park Golf Club
LONDON N9 Lee Valley Leisure Golf Course
LONDON NW4 The Metro Golf Centre
LONDON SE28 Riverside Golf Course
LONDON SW15 Richmond Park Golf Course
LONDON SW18 Central London Golf Centre

MERSEYSIDE
HOYLAKE, Royal Liverpool Golf Club
LIVERPOOL, The Childwall Golf Club
RAINHILL, Blundells Hill Golf Club
SOUTHPORT, Hillside Golf Club

NORFOLK
BARNHAM BROOM, Barnham Broom Hotel
BAWBURGH, Bawburgh Golf Club
DEREHAM, The Norfolk Golf & Country Club
GREAT YARMOUTH, Caldecott Hall Golf & Leisure
KING'S LYNN, Eagles Golf Centre
MIDDLETON, Middleton Hall Golf Club
MUNDESLEY, Mundesley Golf Club Ltd
NORWICH, De Vere Dunston Hall Hotel
NORWICH, Sprowston Park Golf Club
NORWICH, Wensum Valley
WATTON, Richmond Park Golf Club

NORTH YORKSHIRE
EASINGWOLD, Easingwold Golf Club
HARROGATE, Rudding Park Hotel & Golf Course
MIDDLESBROUGH, Middlesbro' Municipal GC
NORTHALLERTON, Romanby Golf & Country Club
PANNAL, Pannal Golf Club
SALTBURN-BY-THE-SEA, Hunley Hall
YORK, Forest Park Golf Club
YORK, Swallow Hall Golf Course

NORTHAMPTONSHIRE
CHACOMBE, Cherwell Edge Golf Club
COLLINGTREE, Collingtree Park Golf Course
NORTHAMPTON, Brampton Heath Golf Centre
NORTHAMPTON, Delapre Golf Complex
NORTHAMPTON, Northamptonshire County GC

STAVERTON, Staverton Park Golf Club
WHITTLEBURY, Whittlebury Park

NORTHUMBERLAND
BELFORD, Belford Golf Club
BELLINGHAM, Bellingham Golf Club
BERWICK-UPON-TWEED, Goswick Golf Club
HEXHAM, De Vere Slaley Hall
LONGHORSLEY, Linden Hall Golf Club
MATFEN, Matfen Hall

NOTTINGHAMSHIRE
CALVERTON, Ramsdale Park Golf Centre
CALVERTON, Springwater Golf Club
KIRKBY IN ASHFIELD, Notts Golf Club
OLLERTON, Rufford Park Golf Centre
OXTON, Oakmere Park
RADCLIFFE ON TRENT, Cotgrave Place
WORKSOP, Bondhay Golf & Fishing Club

OXFORDSHIRE
ABINGDON, Drayton Park Golf Course
CHIPPING NORTON, Lyneham Golf Course
DIDCOT, Hadden Hill Golf Club
FARINGDON, Carswell Golf & Country Club
HENLEY-ON-THAMES, Aspect Park Golf Centre
HORTON-CUM-STUDLEY, Studley Wood GC
KIRTLINGTON, Kirtlington Golf Club
MILTON COMMON, The Oxfordshire Golf Club
TADMARTON, Tadmarton Heath Golf Club
WATERSTOCK, Waterstock Golf Course
WITNEY, Witney Lakes Golf Course

RUTLAND
GREAT CASTERTON, Rutland County Golf Club
GREETHAM, Greetham Valley Golf Club

SHROPSHIRE
CLEOBURY MORTIMER, Cleobury Mortimer GC
OSWESTRY, Mile End Golf Course
SHREWSBURY, Shrewsbury Golf Club
TELFORD, Telford Golf & Country Club
WESTON-UNDER-REDCASTLE, Hawkstone Park
WHITCHURCH, Hill Valley Golf & Country Club

SOMERSET
BATH, Lansdown Golf Club
BRIDGWATER, Cannington Golf Course
CONGRESBURY, Mendip Spring Golf Club
FARRINGTON GURNEY, Farrington Golf Club
FROME, Frome Golf Centre
FROME, Orchardleigh Golf Club
KEYNSHAM, Stockwood Vale Golf Club
LANGPORT, Long Sutton Golf Course
LONG ASHTON, Woodspring Golf & Country Club
TAUNTON, Oake Manor Golf Club
TAUNTON, Taunton Vale Golf Club
WELLS, Wells (Somerset) Golf Club

SOUTH YORKSHIRE
BARNSLEY, Sandhill Golf Club
BAWTRY, Austerfield Park Golf Club
HICKLETON, Hickleton Golf Club
ROTHERHAM, Grange Park Golf Club

ROTHERHAM, Phoenix Golf Club
SHEFFIELD, Concord Park Golf Club
SHEFFIELD, Hillsborough Golf Club
SHEFFIELD, Rother Valley Golf Centre

STAFFORDSHIRE
BURTON UPON TRENT, Branston GC
BURTON UPON TRENT, The Craythorne
CANNOCK, Beau Desert Golf Club
LICHFIELD, Seedy Mill Golf Club
NEWCASTLE-UNDER-LYME, Keele Golf Club
PERTON, Perton Park Golf Club
STOKE-ON-TRENT, Trentham Golf Club
STONE, Izaak Walton Golf Club
TAMWORTH, Tamworth Municipal Golf Club
UTTOXETER, Manor Golf Club

SUFFOLK
CRETINGHAM, Cretingham Golf Club
HALESWORTH, Halesworth Golf Club
IPSWICH, Fynn Valley Golf Club
STOWMARKET, Stowmarket Golf Club
WOODBRIDGE, Seckford Golf Course
WOODBRIDGE, Ufford Park Hotel

SURREY
BAGSHOT, Windlesham Golf Course
BRAMLEY, Bramley Golf Club
CAMBERLEY, Camberley Heath Golf Club
CAMBERLEY, Pine Ridge Golf Club
CATERHAM, Happy Valley Golf Club
CHIDDINGFOLD, Chiddingfold Golf Course
CHIPSTEAD, Chipstead Golf Club
COBHAM, Silvermere Golf Club
CRANLEIGH, Fernfell Golf & Country Club
CRANLEIGH, Wildwood Country Club
EAST HORSLEY, Drift Golf Club
EFFINGHAM, Effingham Golf Club
ENTON GREEN, West Surrey Golf Club
EPSOM, Horton Park Country Club
FARLEIGH, Farleigh Court Golf Club
FARNHAM, Blacknest Golf Club
GODALMING, Broadwater Park Golf Club
GUILDFORD, Merrist Wood Golf Club
GUILDFORD, Roker Park Golf Course
HINDHEAD, Hindhead Golf Club
KINGSWOOD, Kingswood Golf Club
LEATHERHEAD, Pachesham Park Golf Centre
LINGFIELD, Lingfield Park Golf Club
NEWDIGATE, Rusper Golf Course
OCKLEY, Gatton Manor Hotel Golf & Country
   Club
OTTERSHAW, Foxhills
REIGATE, Reigate Hill Golf Club
SHEPPERTON, American Golf at Sunbury
VIRGINIA WATER, Wentworth Club
WALTON-ON-THAMES, Burhill Golf Club
WEST CLANDON, Clandon Regis Golf Club
WEST END, Windlemere Golf Club
WOKING, Hoebridge Golf Centre
WOKING, Pyrford Golf Club
WOKING, Woking Golf Club

TYNE & WEAR
BOLDON, Boldon Golf Club
GOSFORTH, Parklands
WALLSEND, Wallsend Golf Club
WASHINGTON, George Washington Hotel

WARWICKSHIRE
BIDFORD-ON-AVON, Bidford Grange Golf Club
BRANDON, City of Coventry-Brandon Wood GC
KENILWORTH, Kenilworth Golf Club
LEA MARSTON, Lea Marston Hotel
LEEK WOOTTON, The Warwickshire
NUNEATON, Purley Chase Golf Club
RUGBY, Whitefields Hotel Golf & Country Club
STRATFORD-UPON-AVON, Stratford Oaks
STRATFORD-UPON-AVON, Welcombe Hotel
WARWICK, Warwick Golf Club

WEST MIDLANDS
COVENTRY, Ansty Golf Centre
DUDLEY, Swindon Golf Club
KNOWLE, Copt Heath Golf Club
MERIDEN, Marriott Forest of Arden
MERIDEN, Stonebridge Golf Centre
SEDGLEY, Sedgley Golf Centre
SOLIHULL, Robin Hood Golf Club
SUTTON COLDFIELD, The Belfry
WALSALL, Calderfields Golf Academy
WOLVERHAMPTON, Three Hammers

WEST SUSSEX
BURGESS HILL, Burgess Hill GC & Academy
CHICHESTER, Chichester Golf Club
CRAWLEY, Tilgate Forest Golf Centre
GOODWOOD, Marriott Goodwood Park
HAYWARDS HEATH, Haywards Heath Golf Club
HAYWARDS HEATH, Paxhill Park Golf Club
HORSHAM, Horsham Golf & Fitness
HURSTPIERPOINT, Singing Hills Golf Course
MANNINGS HEATH, Mannings Heath Golf Club
PULBOROUGH, West Sussex Golf Club
SLINFOLD, Slinfold Park Golf & Country Club
WEST CHILTINGTON, West Chiltington Golf Club
WORTHING, Worthing Golf Club

WEST YORKSHIRE
BRIGHOUSE, Willow Valley Golf & Country Club
GARFORTH, Garforth Golf Club
HUDDERSFIELD, Bradley Park Golf Course
LEEDS, Cookridge Hall Golf & Country Club
LEEDS, Leeds Golf Centre
LEEDS, Moor Allerton Golf Club
LEEDS, Oulton Park Golf Course
PONTEFRACT, Mid Yorkshire Golf Course
PUDSEY, Calverley Golf Course
SHIPLEY, Marriott Hollins Hall

WILTSHIRE
CALNE, Bowood Golf & Country Club
CASTLE COMBE, The Manor House Golf Club
CHAPMANSLADE, Thoulstone Park Golf Course
ERLESTOKE, Erlestoke Sands Golf Course
GREAT DURNFORD, High Post Golf Club

DRIVING RANGES

HIGHWORTH, Wrag Barn Golf & Country Club
OAKSEY, Oaksey Park Golf & Leisure
OGBOURNE ST GEORGE, Ogbourne Downs GC
SWINDON, Broome Manor Golf Complex
TOLLARD ROYAL, Rushmore Park Golf Club,
WOOTTON BASSETT, The Wiltshire Golf Club

WORCESTERSHIRE
BEWDLEY, Wharton Park Golf Club
BISHAMPTON, Vale Golf Club
BRANSFORD, Bank House Hotel
BROMSGROVE, Bromsgrove Golf Centre
DROITWICH, Ombersley Golf Club
FLADBURY, Evesham Golf Club
KIDDERMINSTER, Wyre Forest Golf Club
REDDITCH, Abbey Hotel Golf & Country Club

GUERNSEY
L'ANCRESSE VALE, Royal Guernsey Golf Club
ST PETER PORT, St Pierre Park Golf Club

JERSEY
LA MOYE, La Moye Golf Club
ST OUEN, Les Mielles Golf & Country Club

DOUGLAS, Mount Murray Hotel & Country Club

ANTRIM
BALLYCLARE, Greenacres Golf Course
WHITEHEAD, Bentra Municipal Golf Course

ARMAGH
ARMAGH, County Armagh Golf Club
LURGAN, Craigavon Golf & Ski Centre

BELFAST
BELFAST, Mount Ober Golf & Country Club

CO ANTRIM
BALLYMENA, Galgorm Castle Golf & Country Club

DOWN
BANGOR, Blackwood Golf Centre
HOLYWOOD, Holywood Golf Club
KILKEEL, Kilkeel Golf Club
KILLYLEAGH, Ringdufferin Golf Course

FERMANAGH
ENNISKILLEN, Ashwoods Golf Centre
ENNISKILLEN, Castle Hume Golf Course

LONDONDERRY
LIMAVADY, Benone Golf Course
LIMAVADY, Radisson Roe Park Hotel & Golf Resort
LONDONDERRY, Foyle International Golf Centre

CAVAN
BALLYCONNELL, Slieve Russell Hotel
CAVAN, County Cavan Golf Course

CORK
CASTLETOWNBERE, Berehaven Golf Club
CHARLEVILLE, Charleville Golf Club
CORK, Fota Island Golf Course
KINSALE, Old Head Golf Links
LITTLE ISLAND, Harbour Point Golf Club
MIDLETON, East Cork Golf Club
MONKSTOWN, Monkstown Golf Club
OVENS, Lee Valley Golf & Country Club

DONEGAL
ROSAPENNA, Rosapenna Golf Club

DUBLIN
CASTLEKNOCK, Elm Green Golf Course
CASTLEKNOCK, Luttrellstown Castle
St Margaret's Golf & Country Club
The Open Golf Centre
SAGGART, City West Hotel & Golf Resort

GALWAY
BALLINASLOE, Ballinasloe Golf Club
BALLYCONNEELY, Connemara Golf Club
GALWAY, Glenlo Abbey Golf Course
ORANMORE, Athenry Golf Club
ORANMORE, Galway Bay Golf & Country Club
OUGHTERARD, Oughterard Golf Club

KERRY
KILLARNEY, Killarney Golf & Fishing Club
WATERVILLE, Waterville House & Golf Links

KILDARE
CARBURY, Highfield Golf Course
STRAFFAN, The K Club

KILKENNY
Kilkenny Golf Club
THOMASTOWN, Mount Juliet Hotel & Golf Club

LAOIS
PORTLAOISE, The Heath Golf Club

LIMERICK
Limerick County Golf & Country Club
LNEWCASTLE WEST, Newcastle West Golf Club

MAYO
BALLINROBE, Ballinrobe Golf Club
BALLYHAUNIS, Ballyhaunis Golf Club

MEATH
DUNSHAUGHLIN, Black Bush Golf Club

MONAGHAN
MONAGHAN, Rossmore Golf Club

OFFALY
BIRR, Birr Golf Club

SLIGO
ENNISCRONE, Enniscrone Golf Club

TIPPERARY
MONARD, Ballykisteen Golf & Country Club
THURLES, Thurles Golf Club
TIPPERARY, County Tipperary Golf Course

WATERFORD
DUNGARVAN, Gold Coast Golf Club
WATERFORD, Waterford Castle Golf Club

WESTMEATH
MULLINGAR, Mullingar Golf Club

WEXFORD
ENNISCORTHY, Enniscorthy Golf Club

WICKLOW
ARKLOW, Arklow Golf Club
BALTINGLASS, Rathsallagh Golf & Country Club
BLESSINGTON, Tulfarris House Hotel
GREYSTONES, Charlesland Golf & Country Club
KILCOOLE, Druids Glen Golf Club

ABERDEENSHIRE
CRUDEN BAY, Cruden Bay Golf Club
HUNTLY, Huntly Golf Club
NEWMACHAR, Newmachar Golf Club

ANGUS
ARBROATH, Arbroath Golf Course
BARRY, Panmure Golf Club
EDZELL, Edzell Golf Club

ARGYLL & BUTE
ERISKA, Isle of Eriska
LUSS, Loch Lomond Golf Club
PORT ELLEN, Machrie Hotel & Golf Links

CITY OF EDINBURGH
Bruntsfield Links Golfing Society
EDINBURGH, Marriott Dalmahoy

CITY OF GLASGOW
Cowglen Golf Club

DUMFRIES & GALLOWAY
GRETNA, Gretna Golf Club
KIRKCUDBRIGHT, Brighouse Bay

EAST LOTHIAN
GULLANE, Gullane Golf Club
NORTH BERWICK, Whitekirk Golf Course

FIFE
BURNTISLAND, Burntisland Golf House Club
ELIE, Golf House Club
SALINE, Saline Golf Club
ST ANDREWS, Dukes Course
ST ANDREWS, St Andrews Links Trust

HIGHLAND
DORNOCH, The Carnegie Club
INVERNESS, Loch Ness Golf Course

MIDLOTHIAN
PENICUIK, Glencorse Golf Club

MORAY
ELGIN, Elgin Golf Club
SPEY BAY, Spey Bay Golf Course

NORTH AYRSHIRE
STEVENSTON, Auchenharvie Golf Course

NORTH LANARKSHIRE
CUMBERNAULD, Westerwood Hotel

PERTH & KINROSS
ALYTH, Strathmore Golf Centre
ALYTH, The Alyth Golf Club
AUCHTERARDER, The Gleneagles Hotel
CRIEFF, Crieff Golf Club
PERTH, Murrayshall Country House Hotel

RENFREWSHIRE
LANGBANK, Gleddoch Golf and Country Club

SCOTTISH BORDERS
KELSO, Roxburghe Golf Course

SOUTH AYRSHIRE
GIRVAN, Brunston Castle Golf Course
TROON, Royal Troon Golf Club
TURNBERRY, Turnberry Hotel

SOUTH LANARKSHIRE
HAMILTON, Strathclyde Park Golf Club

STIRLING
BANNOCKBURN, Brucefields Family Golf Centre
STIRLING, Stirling Golf Club

WEST LOTHIAN
WHITBURN, Polkemmet Country Park

WALES

BRIDGEND
BRIDGEND, Southerndown Golf Club
PENCOED, St Mary's Hotel Golf & Country Club
PORTHCAWL, Royal Porthcawl Golf Club
PYLE, Pyle & Kenfig Golf Club

CAERPHILLY
CAERPHILLY, Mountain Lakes & Castell Heights
CAERPHILLY, Virginia Park Golf Club
MAESYCWMMER, Bryn Meadows
OAKDALE, Oakdale Golf Course

CARDIFF
CARDIFF, Cottrell Park Golf CLub

CARMARTHENSHIRE
KIDWELLY, Glyn Abbey Golf Club

CEREDIGION
LLANRHYSTUD, Penrhos Golf & Country Club

DENBIGHSHIRE
BODELWYDDAN, Kimnel Park Golf Course
ST ASAPH, Llannerch Park Golf Course

FLINTSHIRE
MOLD, Padeswood & Buckley Golf Club
NORTHOP, Northop Country Park Golf Club

GWYNEDD
ABERSOCH, Abersoch Golf Club

ISLE OF ANGLESEY
Holyhead Golf Club

MONMOUTHSHIRE
ABERGAVENNY, Wernddu Golf Centre
BETTWS NEWYDD, Alice Springs Golf Club
AERWENT, Dewstow Golf Club
CHEPSTOW, Marriott St Pierre

NEATH PORT TALBOT,
MARGAM, Lakeside Golf Course

NEWPORT
CAERLEON, Caerleon Golf Course
NEWPORT, Parc Golf Course
NEWPORT, NEWPORT, The Celtic Manor Resort

POWYS
BRECON, Cradoc Golf Club
CAERSWS, Mid-Wales Golf Centre

RHONDDA CYNON TAFF,
PENRHYS, Rhondda Golf Club

SWANSEA
SWANSEA, Clyne Golf Club

TORFAEN
CWMBRAN, Green Meadow Golf & Country Club

VALE OF GLAMORGAN
HENSOL, Vale of Glamorgan Golf & Country Club
PENARTH, Glamorganshire Golf Club

WREXHAM
CHIRK, Chirk Golf Club
WREXHAM, Clays Farm Golf Centre

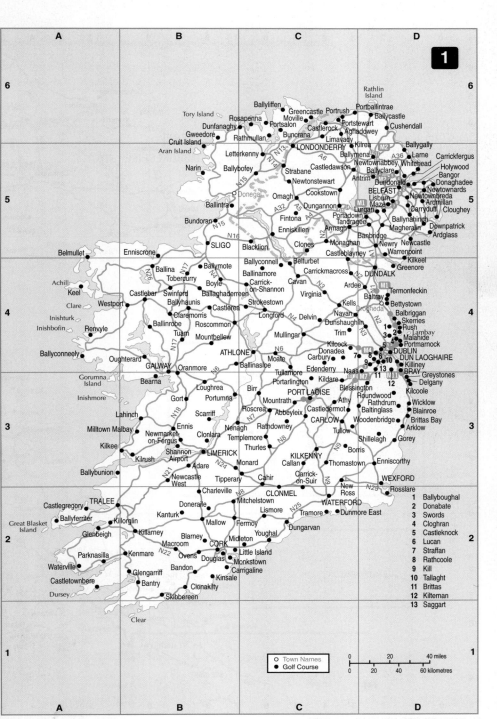

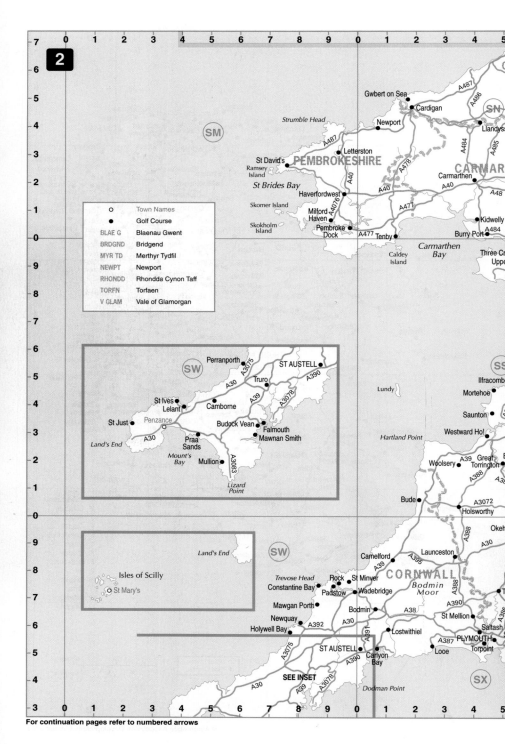

2

	Town Names
○	Golf Course
●	
BLAE G	Blaenau Gwent
BRDGND	Bridgend
MYR TD	Merthyr Tydfil
NEWPT	Newport
RHONDD	Rhondda Cynon Taff
TORFN	Torfaen
V GLAM	Vale of Glamorgan

Gwbert on Sea
Cardigan
SN
A487
A486
Newport
A487
Strumble Head
Llandys
SM
A484
A485
Letterston
St David's PEMBROKESHIRE
Ramsey Island
CARMAR
Carmarthen
A478
St Brides Bay
A40 A40 A40 A48
Skomer Island
Haverfordwest
Skokholm Island
Milford Haven
Pembroke Dock
Tenby
A477
A40
A477
Kidwelly
A484
Burry Port
Caldey Island
Carmarthen Bay
Three Cr
Upper

SW
Perranporth
ST AUSTELL
A3075
Truro
A390
Lundy
SS
Ilfracomb
Mortehoe
St Ives
Lelant
Camborne
A30
A39
A3078
Saunton
St Just
Penzance
Budock Vean
Falmouth
Westward Ho!
Land's End
A30
Praa Sands
Mawnan Smith
Hartland Point
Mount's Bay
Mullion
A3083
Woolsery
A39 Great Torrington
A386
Lizard Point
Bude
A3072
Holsworthy
Okeh
A388
A30

Land's End
SW
Camelford
Launceston
Isles of Scilly
Trevose Head
Rock St Minver
A39
A395
CORNWALL
St Mary's
Constantine Bay
Padstow
Wadebridge
Bodmin Moor
A388
A390
Mawgan Porth
Bodmin
A38
St Mellion
A386
Newquay
A392
A30
Saltash
Holywell Bay
Lostwithiel
PLYMOUTH
A3075
ST AUSTELL
A390
A387
Looe
Torpoint
Carlyon Bay
SX
SEE INSET
A30
A39
A3078
Dodman Point

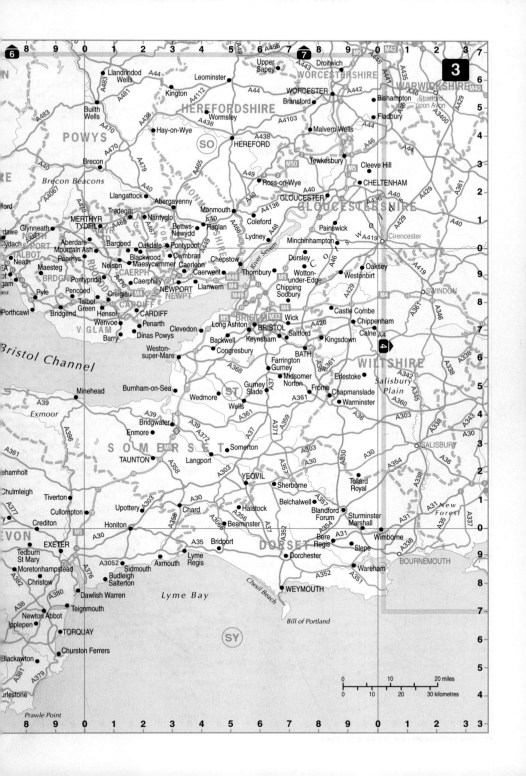

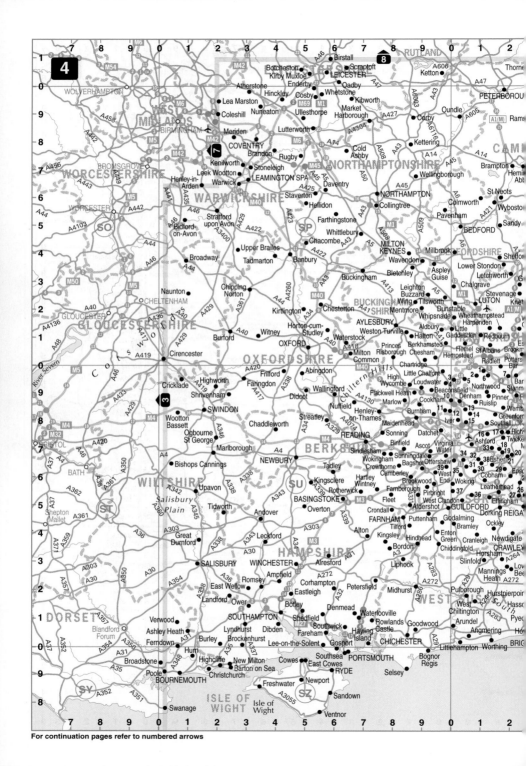

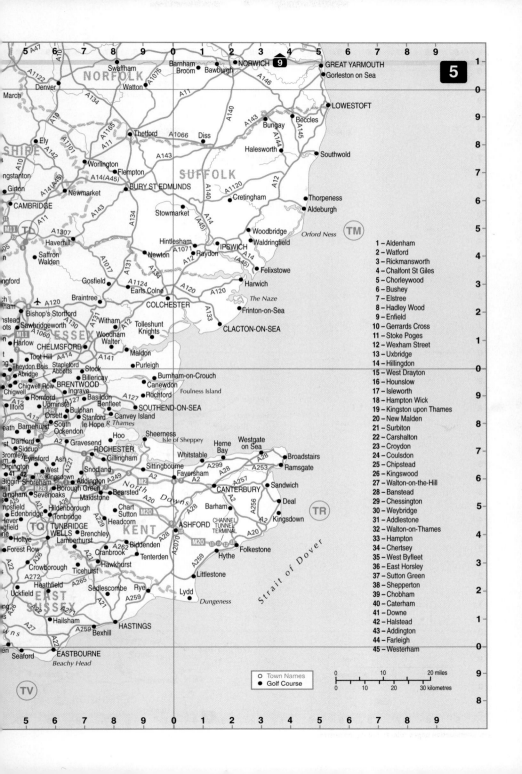

5 A47 6 7 8 9 0 1 2 3 4 5 6 7 8 9

5

NORFOLK

Swaffham
Barnham Broom
Bawburgh
NORWICH **9** GREAT YARMOUTH
Gorleston on Sea
Watton
Denver
March
A1122
A47
A1075
A134
A1066
A11
A146
A140
A143
LOWESTOFT
Bungay
Beccles
BA15
A144
Southwold
Thetford
Diss
Halesworth
Worlington
Flempton
A143
SUFFOLK
Ely
A1101
A1065
A1101
A134
A12
A14 (A45)
BURY ST EDMUNDS
Cretingham
Thorpeness
Aldeburgh
Newmarket
Girton
A14 (A45)
A143
A1120
A140
Stowmarket
CAMBRIDGE
A11
A1307
M11
Haverhill
Hintlesham
Waldringfield
Woodbridge
Orford Ness
TM
Saffron Walden
Newton
Raydon
IPSWICH
A1071
A12
A14 (A45)
Gosfield
Felixstowe
Earls Colne
A1017
A131
A1124
Harwich
Braintree
A120
A120
Bishop's Stortford
A133
COLCHESTER
Frinton-on-Sea
The Naze
Sawbridgeworth
A120
Witham
Tolleshunt Knights
CLACTON-ON-SEA
ESSEX
Woodham Walter
Harlow
CHELMSFORD
Maldon
Toot Hill
A414
A141
Purleigh
Theydon Bois
Stapleford Abbotts
Stock
Abridge
Billericay
Burnham-on-Crouch
Chigwell Row
BRENTWOOD
Ingrave
Canewdon
Chigwell
Romford
Basildon
A127
Rochford
Foulness Island
Ilford
Upminster
Bentfleet
Orsett
Bulphan
Canvey Island
Barnehurst
South Ockendon
Stanford le Hope
R. Thames
SOUTHEND-ON-SEA
Dartford
Gravesend
Hoo
Sheerness
Isle of Sheppey
Sidcup
ROCHESTER
Herne Bay
Westgate on Sea
Eynsford
Ash
Gillingham
Whitstable
Broadstairs
Orpington
West Kingsdown
Snodland
Sittingbourne
Faversham
A299
A253
Ramsgate
Shoreham
Addington
Borough Green
A2
A257
Sandwich
Sevenoaks
Maidstone
Bearsted
CANTERBURY
A256
Deal
Hildenborough
Chart Sutton
Barham
Kingsdown
TR
Edenbridge
Tonbridge
Headcorn
A28
ASHFORD
A20
Hever
TUNBRIDGE WELLS
M20
Brenchley
KENT
CHANNEL TUNNEL TERMINAL
Holtye
Lamberhurst
M20
Forest Row
Biddenden
A2070
Folkestone
Crowborough
Cranbrook
Tenterden
Hythe
Ticehurst
Hawkhurst
A259
Littlestone
Heathfield
Sedlescombe
Rye
Uckfield
A265
A21
Lydd
EAST SUSSEX
Dungeness
Hailsham
A259
Bexhill
HASTINGS
Strait of Dover
A27
Seaford
EASTBOURNE
Beachy Head
TV

| 1 – Aldenham |
| 2 – Watford |
| 3 – Rickmansworth |
| 4 – Chalfont St Giles |
| 5 – Chorleywood |
| 6 – Bushey |
| 7 – Elstree |
| 8 – Hadley Wood |
| 9 – Enfield |
| 10 – Gerrards Cross |
| 11 – Stoke Poges |
| 12 – Wexham Street |
| 13 – Uxbridge |
| 14 – Hillingdon |
| 15 – West Drayton |
| 16 – Hounslow |
| 17 – Isleworth |
| 18 – Hampton Wick |
| 19 – Kingston upon Thames |
| 20 – New Malden |
| 21 – Surbiton |
| 22 – Carshalton |
| 23 – Croydon |
| 24 – Coulsdon |
| 25 – Chipstead |
| 26 – Kingswood |
| 27 – Walton-on-the-Hill |
| 28 – Banstead |
| 29 – Chessington |
| 30 – Weybridge |
| 31 – Addlestone |
| 32 – Walton-on-Thames |
| 33 – Hampton |
| 34 – Chertsey |
| 35 – West Byfleet |
| 36 – East Horsley |
| 37 – Sutton Green |
| 38 – Shepperton |
| 39 – Chobham |
| 40 – Caterham |
| 41 – Downe |
| 42 – Halstead |
| 43 – Addington |
| 44 – Farleigh |
| 45 – Westerham |

○ Town Names
● Golf Course

0   10   20 miles
0   10   20   30 kilometres

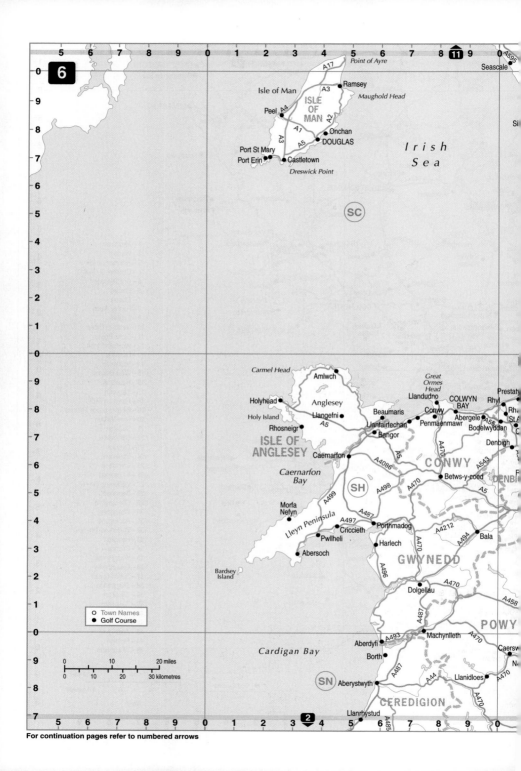

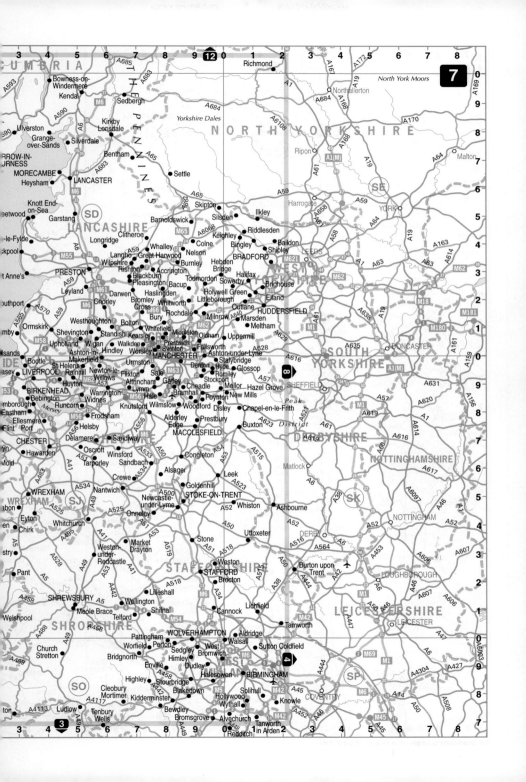

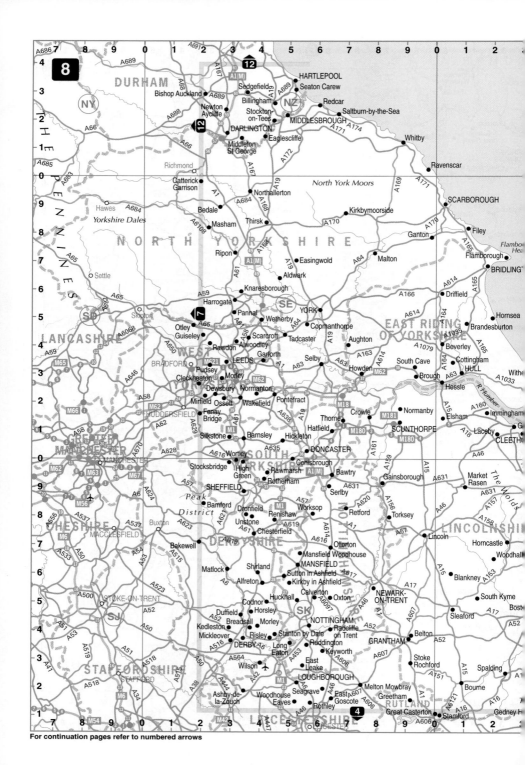

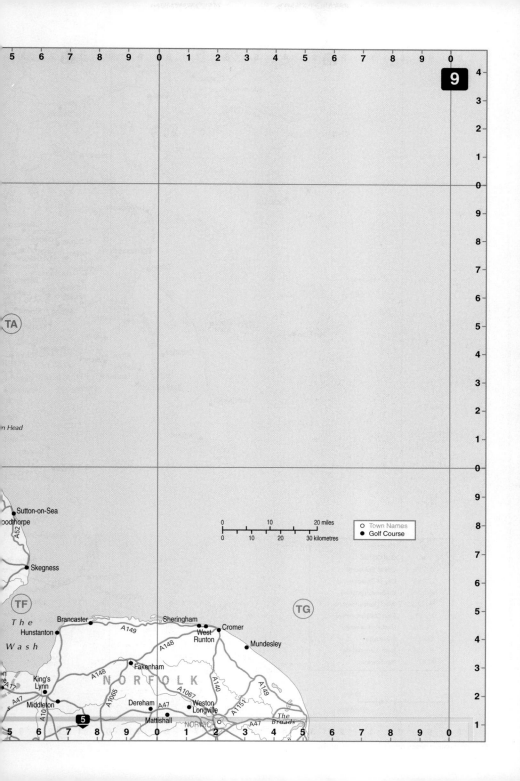

5 6 7 8 9 0 1 2 3 4 5 6 7 8 9 0

9

4
3
2
1
0

9
8
7
6
5
4
3
2
1
0

9
8
7
6
5
4
3
2
1

TA

n Head

Sutton-on-Sea
oodthorpe
A52

Skegness

TF

The
Hunstanton
Brancaster
A149
Sheringham
West Runton
Cromer
Mundesley

Wash

TG

| 0 | 10 | 20 miles |
| 0 | 10 | 20 | 30 kilometres |

○ Town Names
● Golf Course

A148

Fakenham

King's Lynn
A1065
N O R F O L K
A140
A1067
A149

A47

Middleton
A10

Dereham
A47
Weston Longville
A1151
The Broads

5

Mattishall
NORWICH
A47

5 6 7 8 9 0 1 2 3 4 5 6 7 8 9 0

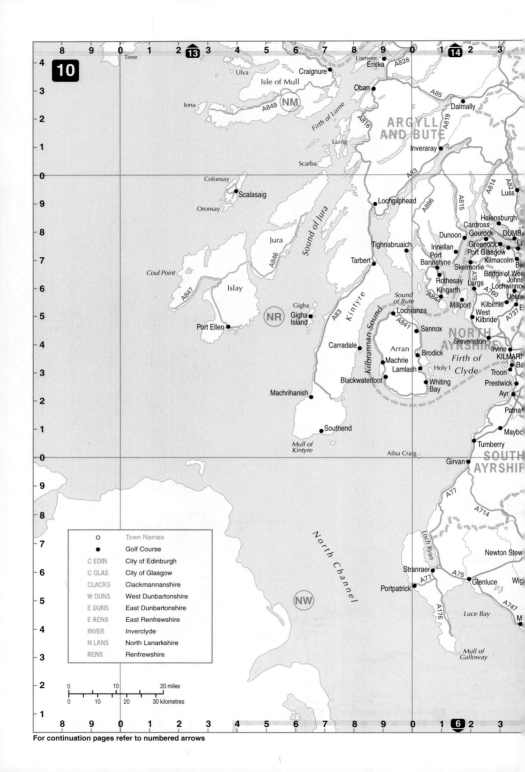

Tiree

Ulva

Craignure

Lismore
Eriska
A828

Isle of Mull

Iona

A849

NM

Oban

Dalmally

A85

Firth of Lorne

A816

A819

ARGYLL
AND BUTE

Luing

Inveraray

Scarba

Colonsay

Scalasaig

Oronsay

Sound of Jura

Lochgilphead

A83

A886

A815

A814

A82

Luss

Jura

A846

Tighnabruaich

Helensburgh
Cardross
Dunoon
Gourock
DUMB
Innellan
Greenock
Li
Port Glasgow
Port
Bannatyne
Kilmacolm
Skelmorlie
Bri
Bridge of Wei
Johns
Largs
Lochwinno
Uplaw

Tarbert

Coul Point

Rothesay
Kingarth

A78

A760
A737

Islay

A847

Gigha
Gigha
Island

NR

Sound
of Bute

Kintyre

Millport

Kilbirnie
West
Kilbride
E

Kilbrannan Sound

Lochranza
A841
Sannox

NORTH
AYRSHIRE

Port Ellen

Carradale

Arran
Machrie
Lamlash

Brodick
Holy I

Stevenston
Irvine
KILMAR

Ba

Machrihanish

Blackwaterfoot

Whiting
Bay

Firth of
Clyde

Troon
Prestwick
Ayr

Patna

Southend

Mull of
Kintyre

Ailsa Craig

Turnberry

Mayb

Girvan

SOUTH
AYRSHIR

North Channel

A77

A714

Newton Stew

Loch Ryan

NW

Stranraer
Portpatrick

A77

A75

Glenluce
Wig

A747

Luce Bay

M

A176

Mull of
Galloway

○	Town Names
●	Golf Course
C EDIN	City of Edinburgh
C GLAS	City of Glasgow
CLACKS	Clackmannanshire
W DUNS	West Dunbartonshire
E DUNS	East Dunbartonshire
E RENS	East Renfrewshire
INVER	Inverclyde
N LANS	North Lanarkshire
RENS	Renfrewshire

0   10   20 miles
0   10   20   30 kilometres

| 8 | 9 | 0 | 1 | 2 | 3 | 4 | 5 | 6 | 7 | 8 | 9 | 0 | 1 | **6** | 2 | 3 |

For continuation pages refer to numbered arrows

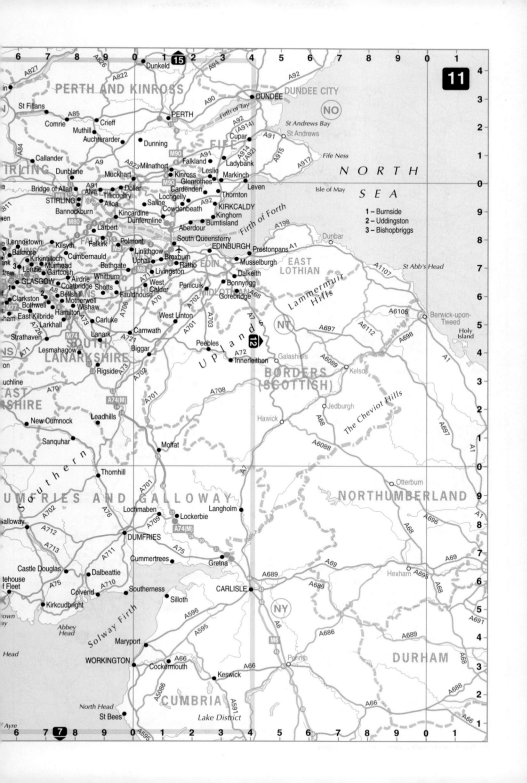

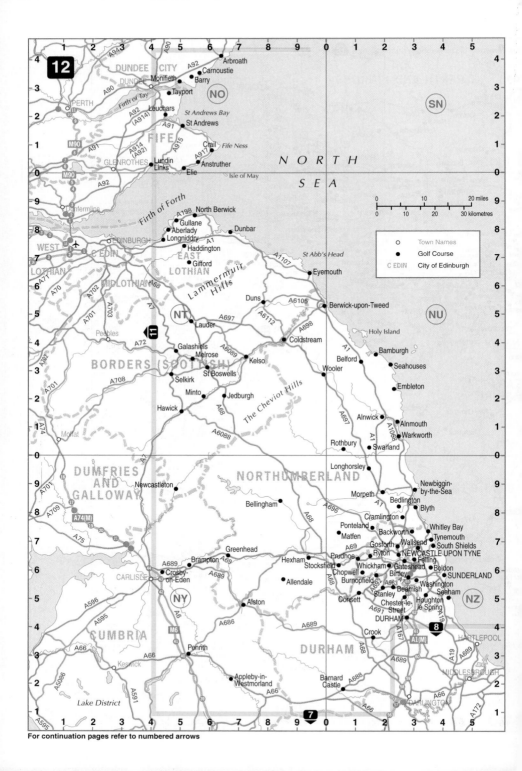

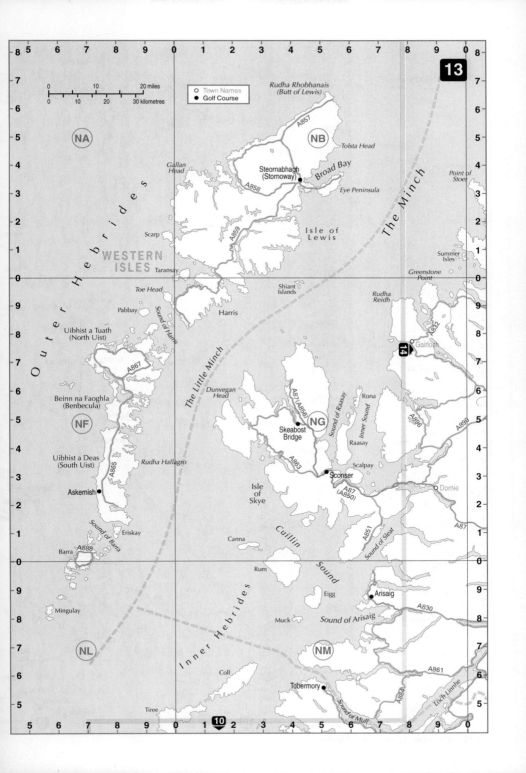

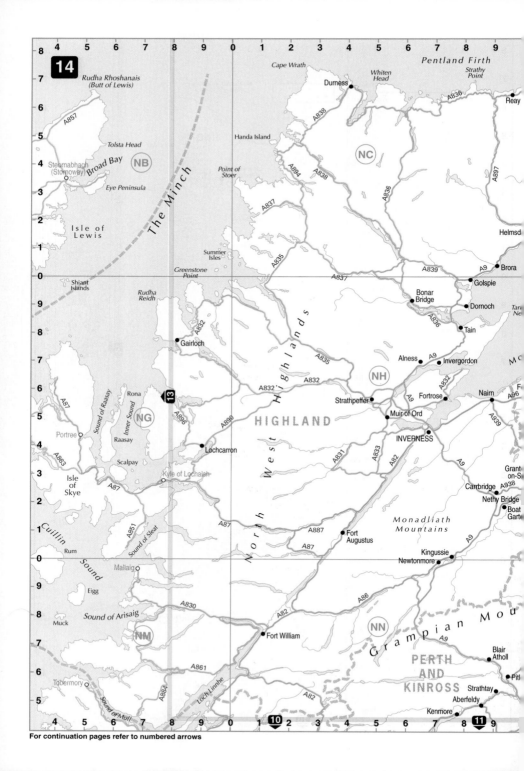

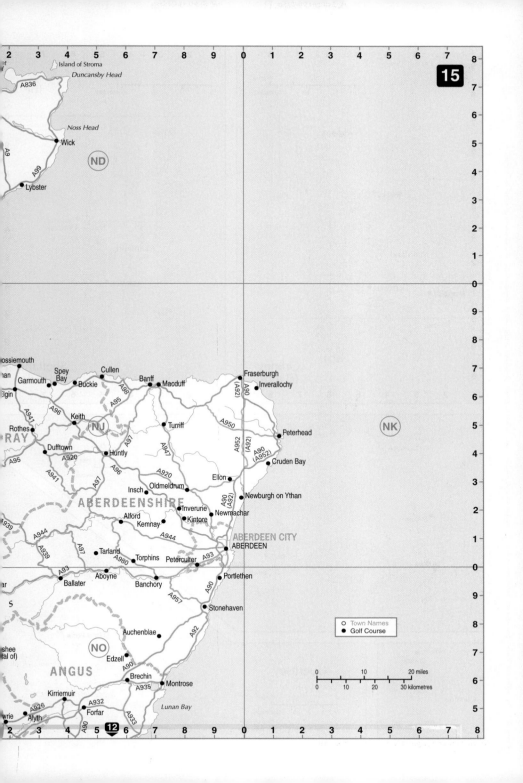

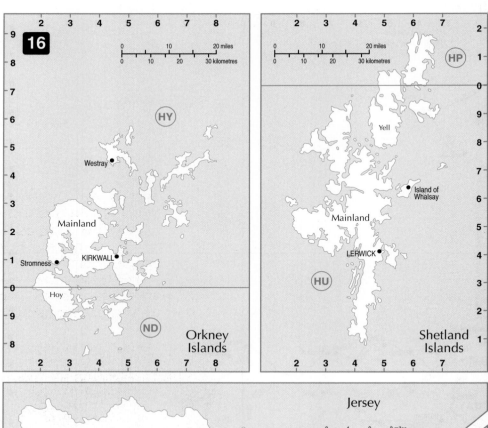

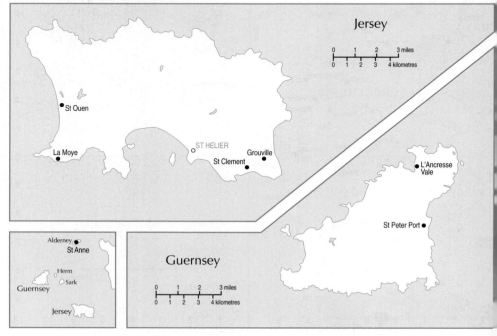

AA Hotel Booking Service

Now you have a free, simple way to book a place to stay for a week, weekend, or a one-night stopover – The AA Hotel Booking Service

From farmhouse charm to five star luxury, we have just the place for you. Whether you wish to stay in a rustic farm cottage, a smart city centre hotel, a family lodge; or if you just want a cosy weekend for two – we can accommodate you.

If you are touring around Britain or Ireland and need accommodation, then just give the AA Hotel Booking Service a call. Provide us with your location and overnight requirements and we'll do the rest!

Why not try booking on-line. Full entries of AA recognised accommodation can be found and booked through the AA Hotel Booking Service via the AA Web Site

Telephone 0870 5050505

Office hours
Monday - Friday 9am - 6pm   Saturday 9am - 1pm
The service is not available Sundays or Bank Holidays

Book on-line: www.theaa.com

INDEX

Y